CW01631163

Crime and Punishment in Islamic Law

A Fresh Interpretation

MOHAMMAD HASHIM KAMALI

بسم الله الرحمن الرحيم

OXFORD
UNIVERSITY PRESS

OXFORD
UNIVERSITY PRESS

Oxford University Press is a department of the University of Oxford. It furthers the University's objective of excellence in research, scholarship, and education by publishing worldwide. Oxford is a registered trade mark of Oxford University Press in the UK and certain other countries.

Published in the United States of America by Oxford University Press
198 Madison Avenue, New York, NY 10016, United States of America.

© Mohammad Hashim Kamali 2019

All rights reserved. No part of this publication may be reproduced, stored in a retrieval system, or transmitted, in any form or by any means, without the prior permission in writing of Oxford University Press, or as expressly permitted by law, by license, or under terms agreed with the appropriate reproduction rights organization. Inquiries concerning reproduction outside the scope of the above should be sent to the Rights Department, Oxford University Press, at the address above.

You must not circulate this work in any other form
and you must impose this same condition on any acquirer.

Library of Congress Cataloging-in-Publication Data
Names: Kamali, Mohammad Hashim, author.
Title: Crime and punishment in Islamic law : a fresh interpretation /
Mohammad Hashim Kamali.
Description: New York, NY : Oxford University Press, [2019] | Includes
bibliographical references and index.
Identifiers: LCCN 2018037058 (print) | LCCN 2018038098 (ebook) |
ISBN9780190910655 (updf) | ISBN 9780190910662 (epub) | ISBN 9780190910679
(online resource) | ISBN 9780190910648 (hardcover : alk. paper)
Subjects: LCSH: Criminal law (Islamic law) | Punishment (Islamic law) |
Criminal law—Islamic countries. | Crime—Islamic countries.
Classification: LCC KBP3791 (ebook) | LCC KBP3791 .K33 2019 (print) |
DDC 345—dc23
LC record available at https://lccn.loc.gov/2018037058

1 3 5 7 9 8 6 4 2

Printed by Sheridan Books, Inc., United States of America

Contents

I

Introduction

THIS BOOK ESSENTIALLY consists of a presentation of issues and reform proposals regarding the prescribed punishments of *ḥudūd* in Islamic criminal law. But the discussion is not confined to *ḥudūd* as such and also delves into other concerns relating to crimes and punishments in shariah. Two main topics are discussed in this book: first, issues that relate to presenting a holistic reading of the Qur'an and hadiths on *ḥudūd* punishments, just retaliation (*qiṣāṣ*), and the discretionary punishments of *taʿzīr*; and second, issues that are encountered in modern-day applications of Islamic criminal law. The first of these subjects, which is addressed in part one of the book, is the main preoccupation and takes up about two-thirds of this volume. Parts two and three examine the applied aspects of Islamic criminal law in a number of Muslim countries.

An overview of *ḥudūd* laws in the Muslim world today reveals many issues relating to perception. The Muslim masses tend to see *ḥudūd* laws and punishments as the core feature of Islam and the Islamic revivalist agenda. *Ḥudūd* laws are generally not enforced, or if they are enforced it is only selectively. Yet there is persistent debate over *ḥudūd* laws and even demand for their enforcement in many parts of the Muslim world. A number of Muslim countries and jurisdictions have consequently attempted to address *ḥudūd*-related issues, and those of Islamic criminal law generally, within their own set of possibilities and conditions. Islamic regimes that come to power as a result of a revolution or coup d'état "need to demonstrate immediately that they are making a start on the construction of a real Islamic state by implementing Islamic criminal law."[1] This book attempts to present a picture of these developments, insofar as the present writer was able to construct this view within limitations on securing accurate information about sensitive religious issues. Obtaining accurate information presents a difficulty due to prevailing uncertainties over ascertaining true positions. *Ḥudūd* laws have become increasingly politicised, and thus politicians often skirt around religious issues just as they also stop short at exploring the jurisprudential dimensions of punishments. The reticence of politicians may also be due to their wish to not heighten concerns of non-Muslim segments of their populations. This has often meant that issues do not find effective responses, which is why it seems there are continuing debates about *ḥudūd* in many Muslim countries, some running over decades, without the emergence of clear responses. Misunderstanding and uncertainties tend to linger on; critics would even say, in Malaysia for instance, that debates on *ḥudūd* laws are kept on the back burner until election time, when they are revived because it is politically convenient. Juristic attitudes toward *ḥudūd* laws are also heavily influenced by the view that *ḥudūd* laws are determined by clear injunctions in the Qur'an and are therefore not amenable to juristic reconstruction and *ijtihād*. All of this has helped *ḥudūd* laws to remain as a mainstay of imitative scholarship (*taqlīd*) such that even leading schools of law have balked at exercising original thinking and *ijtihād* over them. The issues at hand are longstanding and demand a blended approach that is informed by relevant factors, even venturing outside the jurisprudential aspects of a subject if the quest for relevant answers is to be meaningful and to advance out of the prevailing impasse over Islamic criminal laws in the Muslim world.

Muslim countries and jurisdictions have generally shied away from the enforcement of *ḥudūd* punishments due to their apparent severity. Yet because of public sensitivities and politicisation of the subject, parliamentarians, judges, and jurists have also not shown a willingness to depart from hallowed precedents in favour of a fresh and holistic understanding of Qur'anic dispensations on *ḥudūd*. This naturally makes the challenge of adjustment and reform even more difficult to address.

That said, the main thrust of this book is to offer a fresh interpretation of the sources of shariah on the key issues discussed herein and to show how the Qur'an and Sunnah can open a path to possible reform of Islamic criminal law. It hardly needs to be emphasised that a receptive climate of opinion should exist on the part of religious and political leaders to *ijtihād*-based responses over issues. To those who take a position that *ijtihād* does not proceed when there is a textual injunction,[2] it may be said that one would need to understand the textual injunction in the first place before saying that it is definitive (*qaṭʿī*) and close therefore to *ijtihād*. In advancing this argument, the discussion also presents the views and contributions of prominent twentieth-century ulama and scholars on criminal law issues and attempts to integrate these views in the book's conclusions.

A discursive review and appraisal of Islamic criminal law is also called for due to the many changes in modern societies in response to the rampant tides of secularity and materialist culture of the postindustrial revolution. Globalisation and the contemporary human rights discourse have added new dimensions to the existing challenges of innovative interpretation and *ijtihād* in the twenty-first century. How Muslim countries and jurisdictions present their penal laws and procedures to protagonists of human rights is arguably a matter of concern to Islamic civilisation and its claim to universality and inclusiveness, its commitment to justice, its inner resources, and its ability to accommodate changing needs of modern societies and make necessary adjustments along the way.

Islamic criminal law has lagged behind, as already mentioned, due to the stronghold of the imitative tradition of *taqlīd*. Instead of trying to bridge the yawning gap between the law and social reality and to address the challenges, the proponents of *taqlīd* engaged in exaggerations. *Ḥudūd* laws are sometimes seen as paramount indicators of the Islamic identity of states and societies. To measure the Islamicity of a state or a community of believers by reference to a set of punishments is not only a reductionist practice but also tantamount to judging Islam by one of its unwanted elements. A good performance record of a government, Islamic or otherwise, is based on minimising criminality and the recourse to punishment. Islam stands on the Five Pillars (*arkān*),[3] and these principles do not address *ḥudūd* laws, *qiṣāṣ*, or any aspect of criminal law. Punishment of any kind is rather remote from the spiritual core of Islam, yet the general public has maintained a highly exaggerated image of *ḥudūd* punishments as a litmus test of the Islamicity of their governments. This development is largely based on long-held associations and public perceptions that call for reappraisal and adjustment.[4]

The Qur'anic outlook on punishment may be characterised by its emphasis on retribution, deterrence, and reform. This book is based on the premise that the conventional fiqh approach to formulation of the underlying meaning and philosophy of punishments does not adequately reflect the totality of Qur'anic guidance on this subject. Adding rehabilitation and reform to the penal philosophy of *ḥudūd* is not only scripturally justified but tantamount to acknowledging that crime is not a totally isolated phenomenon and that a society increasingly becomes an unwilling partner in the rising tide of criminality and aggression. It is also important for a society to address juridical issues in their proper context to reach well-moderated responses to these concerns. Which should come first, implementing punishments or justice? And what is the higher purpose of shariah and the ultimate goals of the punishments? To ignore this ordering of priorities is one of the challenges of *ḥudūd*.

The remainder of this introductory chapter presents a summary of the various themes and chapters of the book.

The discussion in part one under "Shariah Perspectives" starts with a general characterisation of Islamic criminal law and proceeds to provide a more integrated reading of the *ḥudūd* verses in the Qur'an. This overview covers a number of reform proposals and recommendations on *ḥudūd* laws, along with just retaliation (*qiṣāṣ*) and discretionary punishments. These issues can be appraised and adjusted in line with the broader outlook of the Qur'an on punishment, which has not been duly integrated in juristic doctrines of the various schools and scholars of earlier times. The fiqh-based discussion and analysis that follows reviews the scholastic jurisprudence of *ḥudūd* and identifies positions of the leading schools of Islamic law.

There are only four offences—namely adultery, theft, slanderous accusation, and banditry/terrorism—for which the Qur'an has prescribed punishments, and in none of the relevant passages is there a mention of *ḥadd* or *ḥudūd* as such. The Qur'an has also not used *ḥudūd* specifically in the sense of punishment, let alone fixed and mandatory ones, for which they are typically understood today and throughout the longer history of Islamic juristic thought.

Ḥudūd Allāh (God's limits) in the Qur'an is a much broader concept, which is confined neither to punishments nor to an exclusively legal framework but can provide a comprehensive set of guidelines on moral, legal, and religious themes. Juristic thought has, however, followed a different trajectory whereby this broader view of *ḥudūd* was reduced to mean quantified, mandatory, and invariably fixed punishments. The four offences for which the Qur'an has prescribed punishments were expanded, in the fiqh presentations of *ḥudūd*, to six offences and, according to an alternative version, to seven—and this was done in the face of clear evidence that advised a minimalist rather than a maximalist approach to crimes and punishments.[5] Additionally, whereas the Qur'an has, in all four instances where specified punishments occur, made provisions for repentance, correction, and reform (*tawbah* and *iṣlāḥ*), juristic doctrine has either left this out altogether or reduced it to a mechanical formality that can hardly be said to be reflective of the original teachings of the Qur'an, thus clearly and unequivocally opening *ḥudūd* laws to the prospect of repentance and reform.

In the works of fiqh one also notes a certain linkage between *ḥudūd* and *ḥaqq Allāh* (Right of God), on the one hand, and *ḥaqq al-ādamī* (or *ḥaqq al-ʿabd* –Right of Man) on the other. There is no Qur'anic requirement, nor an expressed justification, for these linkages. Some of the juristic particularities that originate in this scheme not only lead to inconsistencies but also contribute to a degree of regimentation in the development of juristic thought. The fiqh presentation of *ḥudūd* is marked by a tendency to move further away from the original Qur'anic emphasis on repentance/rehabilitation and reform and toward engaging in juristic technicalities.

One would not deny, of course, the reality of differentiation between private rights and public rights nor of differences between civil claims and crimes. Islamic law clearly recognises private rights, such as the right of ownership, the right to inheritance, and a wife's right to financial support, without necessarily labelling these as *ḥaqq al-ādāmī* or *ḥaqq al-ʿabd* as such. A simple distinction between civil claims and crimes is not an issue, but to refer to certain crimes as "Rights of God" is not only odd (as if God Most High wishes to be so punitive!) but also blind to the truism that in Islam all rights and obligations originate, theoretically at least, in the will and command of God. This is clearly acknowledged in the Islamic theory of ownership—which suggests that God is the true owner of all things and that human owners are only the trustees of what they own—without necessarily labelling ownership as either the "Right of God" or the "Right of Man." This is because the two sets of rights under review are almost always an extension of one another and convergent. A substantive revision of the philosophy and jurisprudence of *ḥudūd* is therefore called for, indeed necessary, simply because technicality and regimentation need to be removed or minimised to facilitate a balanced implementation of the original vision of Islamic criminal law and *ḥudūd*.

Part one also looks into issues of evidence, proof, and admissibility, with reference particularly to adultery and theft. The discussion also looks into issues pertaining to apostasy (*riddah*); slanderous accusation (*qadhf*); the punishment of theft, banditry, and terrorism (*ḥirābah*); and consumption of alcohol (*shurb*). The main question raised concerning the latter issue, *shurb*, is whether it should be included among *ḥudūd* offences at all. Other *ḥudūd*-related issues discussed in part one concern the status of non-Muslims and the much-debated yet crucial distinction between rape and *zinā*. This is followed by views on the distinction between a married Muslim (*muḥṣan*) and one who is unmarried (*ghayr muḥṣan*), which has a bearing, in turn, on the application or otherwise of stoning (*rajm*) as a punishment.

The subsequent chapter on *ḥirābah* (terrorism) begins with various definitions that the leading schools of Islamic law, both Sunni and Shia, have given to this crime. The quest to present a more relevant reading of the Islamic law of *ḥirābah* in relation to contemporary terrorism entails a closer look at the existing evidence in fiqh, on one hand, and more recent research on terrorism on the other. Having looked into the jurisprudence of *ḥirābah* and a wider understanding of terrorism, the chapter revisits the Qur'an and attempts a fresh interpretation of its relevant passages that can tackle some of the unprecedented issues of global terrorism today.

The philosophy of *ḥudūd* punishments, which is also the subject of a chapter in part one, provides a brief entry into the three most commonly known theories of punishment in criminal law, namely retribution, deterrence, and reform. The review of the evidence shows that repentance and reform do not find a suitable place in the fiqh expositions of *ḥudūd*. One likely explanation may be that premodern penal systems were ill-equipped to integrate the Qur'anic dispensations on repentance and reform into their working modalities, hence their exclusive focus on fixed penalties and an overly punitive approach to the subject. To apply quantified punishments is a relatively facile task, one might say, for courts and enforcement agencies. Instead they should devise carefully nuanced approaches and procedures of the kind now known and practiced (e.g., probation orders, remand centres, suspended sentences, community service, etc.), in addition, that is, to custodial sentences. These approaches should be contemplated, selectively at least, in a revised theory of punishments in Islamic law.

The enquiry into evidence concerning the punishment of stoning (*rajm*) for adultery highlights differences of opinion among the leading schools of Islamic law. There are two levels of inconsistency in the evidence concerning stoning: one is that the Qur'an is totally silent on this punishment and only the Sunnah seems to have validated it; and the evidence also shows that stoning was practiced during the lifetime of the Prophet. Yet there is uncertainty as to the chronological sequence between the rulings of the Qur'an's "100 lashes of punishment" for adultery and the Sunnah's provision on stoning. Which was revealed earlier and which later? These questions play a crucial role in determining the continued validity or otherwise of stoning as a punishment, and the answers are somewhat less than definitive. To establish a chronological sequence would bring into play the subject, in turn, of abrogation (*naskh*) and the possibility that stoning was actually replaced and abrogated by the standard Qur'anic punishment of 100 lashes for all cases of adultery and fornication for married and unmarried persons alike. Due to these issues and lingering uncertainties over them, the Kharijites and MuÒtazilah overruled the validity of stoning altogether and upheld flogging as the only punishment for *zinā*.

The majority of Islamic schools and scholars (*jumhūr*) have accepted, nevertheless, the ruling of the Sunnah to be conclusive on stoning. Yet the answers that they have given to certain questions were based on presumptions that originated in methodological guidelines pertaining either to abrogation (*naskh*) or specification of general principles (*takhṣīṣ al-ʿām*).

The second level of inconsistency that appears in the hadith reports concerning the punishment of adultery is concerned less with stoning and more on the validity or otherwise of two supplementary punishments, namely of banishment in combination with flogging for an unmarried Muslim (*ghayr muḥṣan*) offender and of flogging in combination with stoning for a married Muslim (*muḥṣan*) offender. During the Prophet's lifetime, these combinations were applied in some cases but not in others. Existing evidence in the hadith thus shows inconsistency, which has, in turn, generated considerable debate among Muslim jurists, who were evidently able to draw different conclusions from the relevant hadiths. In this connection, the majority have validated one year of banishment as a supplementary punishment to the flogging of 100 lashes for an unmarried person, though the Ḥanafīs have not approved of this punishment. This is mainly because the Ḥanafīs considered banishment to be a *taʿzīr* discretionary punishment and not an integral part of the prescribed punishment of flogging; the two cannot be combined, but the majority has held otherwise. An additional consideration is that banishment to another place is not advisable as it would expose the new community to the possibility of repetition, continued debauchery, and mischief.

An analysis of these issues and the lingering uncertainties over the punishment of adultery is then followed by an opinion survey of some of the leading twentieth- century scholars and ulama, including Muḥammad

Abū Zahrah (d. 1974), Muṣṭafā Aḥmad al-Zarqā (d. 1999), Yūsuf al-Qaraḍāwī, Muḥammad Salīm al-ʿAwā, and others who have questioned the veracity of the evidence on stoning as well as the conventional distinction between married and unmarried persons and how it is involved in determining punishment.

The discussion continues with a similar opinion survey of Muslim scholars on the implementation of *ḥudūd* generally in contemporary Muslim societies. Should the *ḥudūd* penalties be enforced as an isolated case in a legal system that originates mainly in Western thought and institutions? Ridding the Muslim world of unwanted colonial legacies was a key objective of the Islamic revivalist movement of the latter part of twentieth century and the rise of so-called political Islam. Many constitutions, civil codes, or criminal codes that are currently in force in many Muslim countries and government institutions are arguably modelled after a Western prototype and tend to be secularist in orientation. This has confronted contemporary Muslim scholars with the question as to which has the greatest priority in legal decisions: an Islamic government, shariah, or *ḥudūd*. The discussion in this part concludes with a brief analysis of a renowned hadith (i.e., legal maxim)— that *ḥudūd* must be suspended when there is doubt. This chapter also advances an argument that rampant secularity and temptations to sin generate a need to be interpreted through deeper readings of hadiths.

Whereas the core aspects of shariah are regulated by textual injunctions of the Qur'an and hadith, rulers and judges have also been granted discretionary powers under shariah principles of judicious policy (*siyāsah sharʿiyyah*) and *taʿzīr*, which allow rulers and judges to determine the best manner in which shariah can be administered. Yet the constitutional principle of legality presents a concern, in cases of both *siyāsah* and *taʿzīr*, that discretion must be carefully tailored to the purpose it is supposed to serve and must not exceed the bounds of government under the rule of law. In light of these remarks, the discussion turns to questions on exploring (1) the existence (or otherwise) of any boundaries and limits that Islamic law itself provides over the operation of *siyāsah* and *taʿzīr*; and (2) how these limits should be understood in a constitutional system of government.

The book's subsequent discussion of scholastic jurisprudence regarding just retaliation (*qiṣāṣ*), blood money, and financial compensation (*diya*) offers an overview of their contemporary applications—each in a separate chapter—that underline the issues they present in various jurisdictions. The discussion offers suggestions as to how *qiṣāṣ* and *diya* may be adjusted and brought into harmony with the given terms of a modern constitution and legal system while maintaining harmony with the higher purposes, or *maqāṣid*, of shariah.

Whereas the prescribed *ḥudūd* punishments generally fall under the rubric of the Right of God, or public rights, *qiṣāṣ* punishments mainly follow the Right of Man (*ḥaqq al-ādamī*), which are each governed by separate rules. This binary classification of rights is clearly a juristic addition that lacks a scriptural origin, therefore it is amenable to further adjustment and *ijtihād*. This book takes the view that the role that *qiṣāṣ* and *diya* played in tribalist societies of earlier times may no longer be significant in the context of a modern legal system where a tribal structure of values is no longer present, thus suggesting parallel adjustments for their application.

More specifically, just retaliation in the Qur'an is explained against the background of pre-Islamic practices of *qiṣāṣ* and how the Qur'an injected equality and objectivity into the rubric of legal institutions. The Prophet and his Companions, especially the second caliph ʿUmar b. al-Khaṭṭāb, continued with the reform of *qiṣāṣ* law. Having reviewed the brief history and jurisprudence of *qiṣāṣ*, the chapter then advances a perspective on how the Qur'an, although recognising *qiṣāṣ* as a right primarily of the next of kin of the deceased, has placed the administration of *qiṣāṣ* entirely in the hands of rulers and judges rather than the next of kin of the deceased. Thus rulers and judges may not take revenge nor retaliate beyond the objective standards of justice.

Blood money (*diya*) features in the succeeding chapter, which highlights two separate aspects of the subject. One of these is a certain departure in the scholastic jurisprudence of fiqh from the principle of equality that finds clear expression in the Qur'an and Sunnah. The schools of law have on occasions introduced views that tend to compromise the egalitarian tenor of the Qur'anic dispensations on *diya* with respect to women and non-Muslims. Another aspect of *diya* presented in the book's treatment of this subject is how it is utilised in the modern laws of some Muslim countries with relation to traffic and work-related accidents, pensions, and life insurance.

The subject of doubts (*shubhat*) features prominently in the fiqh manuals with reference especially to *ḥudūd* punishments. A later chapter ascertains the identification and measurement of doubt and how it impacts the implementation aspects of *ḥudūd* punishments. Highlighted in this connection is the renowned hadith that mandates suspension of *ḥudūd* in the presence of doubt. Then the discussion draws attention to a new dimension of doubt/*shubha* that modern society conditions have brought about in light of the said hadith.

The final chapter on shariah perspectives is titled "Islam as a Total System," which presents a roundup of twentieth-century Islamic scholarship on Islamic criminal law. How should shariah be understood as an integrated system? How does Islamic criminal law operate within the confines of a modern constitution and respond to issues of human rights and concerns of modern critics of *ḥudūd*? Responses to some of these questions are then offered in light of the Qur'anic directives on justice (*ʿadl*) and fair treatment (*iḥsān*) and the concern for accuracy in applying punishments. If human rights discourse and modern constitutional laws advance the cause of justice and better regulation of punishments, ways should be found to contextualise, selectively at least, the contemporary applications of Islamic criminal law. The country-based surveys on the applied aspects of Islamic criminal law that occupy the balance of the book are subdivided into two parts: one looks into developments in Malaysia, and the other provides an overview of developments in about fourteen other Muslim countries.

Part two, "*Ḥudūd* in Malaysia," provides a detailed coverage of the *ḥudūd* debate in Malaysia, focusing mainly on a reading of two *Ḥudūd* Bills introduced, respectively, in the northern states of Kelantan in 1993 and then in Terengganu in 2002 under the Islamic Party of Malaysia (known as PAS) that ruled those two states.[6] The two bills were duly passed by state legislatures in the two states and received assent from their respective sultans at the time, but both bills have remained in abeyance ever since due mainly to constitutional issues and resistance on the part of the federal government, then under the leadership of Prime Minister Dr. Mahathir Mohamad. Ever since its ratification in 1993 by the State Legislative Assembly of Kelantan, the Hudud Bill of Kelantan,[7] and Islamic criminal law generally, have been the focus of public debate and media coverage in Malaysia. The book's discussion revolves around the six *ḥudūd* offences the two bills have introduced. This is a narrative mainly of the actual problems encountered and how they have been raised, discussed, and debated in public media and the multireligious context of Malaysia. Issues have been raised concerning the actual implementation of the two bills and how they are likely to impact the non-Muslims of Kelantan and Terengganu. Then the discussion presents representative views and responses of non-Muslim spokespersons of Chinese and Indian political parties. The Muslim protagonists of *ḥudūd*, especially the PAS, have persistently challenged their Chinese and Indian counterparts and critics on how the *ḥudūd* bills should be seen and understood and, in some cases, how they can be amended and improved. The chapter also examines provisions of the Hudud Bill of Kelantan that stand in conflict with Malaysia's Federal Constitution of 1957 and the Penal Code of 1936 (amended on numerous occasions and last revised on 7 August 1997).

Malaysia has in many ways been singled out as a showcase as it presents an interesting scenario of the applied aspects of Islamic criminal law and its problematics. Malaysia is a multireligious society, a federal state, and a self-acclaimed democracy,[8] where the present author also resides and where a lively *ḥudūd* debate has been ongoing for the last three decades. The Muslims of Malaysia that constitute about 60 percent of its population take Islam, the Malay language, and customs as the three major criteria of their identity. Islam is in many ways a living tradition and way of life of the Malay Muslims and constitutes a major theme and context, such that almost all important socioeconomic and political developments in this country must negotiate and find accommodation with Islam. In Malaysia, Islam as a religion and, increasingly, as an emerging legal system—after the colonial suppression and marginalisation of shariah—can be seen as a case study as to the ways and means by which it has engaged with contemporary issues generally and those of concern to the present study. The case of Malaysia shows how a reasonably successful country—with a market economy, high exposure levels to the outside world, and a credible claim to inclusivity—deals with Islamic and shariah-related issues. Unlike Indonesia, Pakistan, and some other Muslim countries where Islam is the religion of the vast majority of the population, Muslims in Malaysia are challenged by the presence of much larger and economically powerful non-Muslim minorities.

Issues have also arisen over shariah courts' jurisdiction and the extent of their powers to adjudicate *ḥudūd* offences in Malaysia.[9] References have been made to policy statements by both state and federal government representatives on possible amendments to the Hudud Bill of Kelantan 1993 that have featured in the media over the years. This is followed by similar, although less detailed, coverage of the Hudud Bill of Terengganu 2002, which was also tabled before the Terengganu Legislative Assembly by the PAS. The Terengganu Hudud Bill is a near-replica of its Kelantan antecedent, albeit with minor amendments with reference particularly to non-Muslims. The book's presentation of these issues highlights the likely implications of applying this bill to a dual system of law and justice that obtains in Malaysia.

Even after twenty-four years since the introduction of the Hudud Bill of Kelantan (HBK), it appears that one can hardly claim meaningful progress on the *ḥudūd* issue in Malaysia. Why this is so becomes a compelling question. The HBK has come under criticism on specific points as well as generally and thus indicates an eagerness to inflict punishment and pain. This approach may need to be moderated by other influences that are also important in the formulation of a comprehensive philosophy of punishment.

It seems ironical that Kelantan has gone so far as to celebrate Hudud Day as an annual event, as if to prove its credentials as the one, true authority on the religion among the thirteen states of Malaysia by being the most punitive. It also seems odd somehow to choose punishments as deserving of celebration and calling on people to publicly observe the occasion. It is easy to forget, however, that *ḥudūd* laws are not even implemented in Kelantan—yet the people are still asked to observe Hudud Day!

An update of more recent developments in the *ḥudūd* debate from 2012 to 2017 is presented in a separate section of the chapter. Here one may see the arrival, for the first time, of a different political scenario that tends to be more receptive to approval of HBK by the federal government.

Part three on "*Ḥudūd* in Other Muslim Countries" provides brief comparative reviews of *ḥudūd*-related legislation and developments in a select number of Muslim countries in Asia, Africa, and Southeast Asia. This part consists mainly of bird's-eye views on the legal system in each of the countries under review, including their particular circumstances and concerns. The book's comparative coverage of Islamic criminal law issues in these countries also touches on common features of *ḥudūd* as well as the gap between theory and practice of *ḥudūd* in these countries. In almost every country discussed in the book, issues arise over the religious sensitivity of shariah punishments that negatively affect, in turn, the prospects of advancing open rational discourse about *ḥudūd*. The climate of understanding concerning *ḥudūd* has been increasingly restricted in the post-Islamic revivalist environment of these countries.

Notwithstanding the difficulty of disentangling the politics of *ḥudūd* from jurisprudence, the book's main concern is to advance an understanding of the jurisprudence of *ḥudūd* through a reading of the sources of shariah, especially the Qur'an and Sunnah, in a way that a modern student of law can understand. The discussion also aims to open the space for advancing fresh interpretations and perspectives on scriptural sources relating to shariah and *ḥudūd* along with fiqh-related developments.

Governments in Muslim societies have generally not encouraged *ijtihād*-oriented discourse over Islamic issues. This epiphenomenon to some extent involves rampant secularism and marginalisation of the role of religion and ulama in the nation-states of Western origins, which have dominated postcolonial polities in much of the Muslim world. The increasingly assertive tone of Islamic revivalist discourse in many multireligious societies has been espoused by similar developments among other religious communities. Muslim governments are consequently faced with fresh demands to accommodate different voices and be more inclusive in their quest to find answers to religious and shariah issues. These concerns are thus no longer treated as if they were exclusively the realm of ulama and jurisconsults; leaders are asked to be more receptive to other voices that may express the needs and aspirations of non-Muslim constituencies.

History has shown that Islam is no stranger to inclusivity and that it has the resources to accommodate different voices—amply demonstrated by the Prophet Muḥammad's own example and precedent on how he dealt with the Arab pagans of Quraysh and Jews and Christians. That early precedent has also in many ways reverberated throughout the longer history of Islam, which was severely disrupted by the colonialist onslaught and the problematic legacies left in its wake.

The argument of this book is thus mainly over the approach that is taken towards understanding shariah and Islamic criminal law. In the history of Qur'an interpretation (*tafsīr*) and hadith, as well as the main body of Islamic juristic thought, the literalist approach has had the upper hand over a rationalist and pragmatic understanding of Islam and shariah. Although the schools of law (*madhhabs*) did to some extent open the scope for rationality and pragmatism in the formulation of fiqh rules, their attempts were on the whole timebound and reflective of the concerns of the respective societies and cultures in which they occurred.

The historical controversy between Rationalists and Traditionists (*ahl al-ra'y* and *ahl al-ḥadīth*, respectively) was essentially over restricting the scope of *ijtihād* to a degree that Imam al-Shāfiʿī (d. 205/820) confined *ijtihād* to analogical reasoning (*qiyās*) alone when he wrote in his renowned *Risālah* that *ijtihād* and *qiyās* were two words that had the same meaning. With reference to Qur'an hermeneutics, it is common knowledge that *tafsīr* based on opinion (*tafsīr bi'l-ra'y*) was given little weight vis-a-vis *tafsīr* on the basis of precedent (*tafsīr bi'l-ma'thūr*). The *uṣūlī* methodological thought of earlier centuries ignored the broader approach to the understanding of shariah taken by advocates of the *maqāṣid al-Sharīʿah* (goals and purposes of shariah), which laid greater emphasis on the ends and purposes of the law. It was not until the eighth century Hijrah that the Andalusian scholar, Ibrāhīm al-Shāṭibī (d. 790/1388), developed his theory of the *maqāṣid* and opened a new chapter in the history of Islamic jurisprudential thought. Yet it was already too late for al-Shāṭibī to make much of an impact on scholastic jurisprudence and the works of the leading schools of law (*madhāhib*), which had by then developed to an advanced stage. Scholastic studies also showed limited acceptance of the *maqāṣid al-Sharīʿah* theory due to its somewhat philosophical overtones. Twentieth-century Islamic scholarship showed renewed interest in the revival of the *maqāṣid* and original *ijtihād* that may well mean departing from some of the hallowed positions of conventional jurisprudence on a number of issues including *ḥudūd*.

The present generation of Muslims would need to continue the tenor of those endeavours and offer relevant responses to the issues they face in light of their own needs and experiences. Considerations of piety and devotion in the interpretation of Qur'an and hadith were strong enough perhaps to keep jurists and interpreters close to the texts of sacred scripture. Even in the sphere of juristic thought (fiqh and *ijtihād*), attention was focused on formulas and methods that ensured conformity to the text and restrictive forms of analogy—at the expense sometimes of the higher purposes (*maqāṣid*) of shariah such as justice and public welfare (*maṣlaḥah*). The divine words of the Qur'an were in many ways taken as value points in themselves rather than as a vehicle and carrier of values. A great deal of that legacy remains with us to this day and has even found fresh impetus through the radicalisation of Islam in recent decades. This also relates to the challenges involved in Islamic criminal law and *ḥudūd*.

In sum, this book offers a modest contribution towards a better understanding of an evidently difficult subject that continues to generate controversy and misunderstanding about shariah and Islam. The avenues of originality and self-renewal have been exceedingly restricted concerning Islamic criminal law, especially regarding *ḥudūd* punishments. There is clearly a need for better answers and for opening the avenues of discursive enquiry to facilitate an understanding of these issues. This book raises many questions and answers some, but there is scope for further enquiry, and it is hoped that other researchers will continue the quest to address issues and help bridge the gap between shariah and social reality.

PART ONE

Shariah Perspectives

II

Islamic Criminal Justice

AN OVERVIEW

DIFFERENCES HAVE EXISTED among various criminal justice systems throughout history. They have all shared certain basic components, such as normative provisions, procedural rules, evidential requirements, and applicable sanctions. The Islamic criminal justice system contains all of these components and shares a number of similarities with other systems. Yet the Islamic system also has peculiarities that are largely derived from its use of scriptural sources as well as the juristic doctrines that were developed by scholars in tandem with the cultures and customs of their communities.

Islamic criminal law is composed of three main categories of crimes and punishments: *ḥudūd* (prescribed crimes and punishments), *qiṣāṣ* (just retaliation) crimes and punishments, and *taʿzīr* (crimes that call for deterrent but discretionary punishments that fall outside the *ḥudūd* and *qiṣāṣ* categories). Each category has its own substantive norms, evidentiary standards, and procedures. For instance, *ḥudūd* crimes are prescribed in the Qur'an and the Sunnah, whereas *qiṣāṣ* crimes appear in these sources only as statements of principles. *Taʿzīr* offences are found in the Qur'an or Sunnah only by indication, and they are then elaborated through juristic construction, analogy, and custom. In the conventional theory of *ḥudūd* laws, human legislatures do not have the authority to change them by adding to or reducing them, and there is theoretically no room for the application of pardon by rulers and judges. *Qiṣāṣ* crimes consist of aggression on life and limb through homicide and bodily injuries. These crimes are also based on scripture, yet they are amenable to adjustment and pardoning by relevant parties and authorities. *Taʿzīr* crimes and punishments encompass all offence types and transgressions—sometimes even within the rubrics of *ḥudūd* and *qiṣāṣ* (e.g., when a *ḥudūd* crime does not fulfil all or some of its stipulated conditions, it may fall under *taʿzīr*). Yet they are not quantified and remain open to judicial discretion by rulers and judges.[1]

Crimes and punishments in the traditional fiqh sources are established through shariah evidence and are not based on personal choices of jurists and judges. A punishment is shariah-compliant when it is based on valid sources and issued by lawful authorities. The sources are the Qur'an, the Sunnah, and general consensus (*ijmāʿ*), as well as statutory law (*qānūn*)—the last two of which are duly validated by learned scholars and those in charge of community affairs (i.e., the *ūli al-amr*). The latter must also not contravene the textual injunctions of Qur'an and Sunnah. Analogy (*qiyās*), although a recognised proof in shariah, is generally not relied upon in crimes and punishments due to elements of doubt that inhere in *qiyās*, although this is also subject to juristic disagreement. The legality (*mashrūʿiyyah*) of punishment also means that "the judge does not order a punishment based on his own thinking, even if he thinks it to be the most suitable and shariah-compliant punishment."[2] For this would amount to an "arbitrary exercise of power" (*sulṭah taḥakkumiyyah*) in the imposition of punishment, which has no basis in shariah.

The first two of the three categories of punishment, namely of *ḥudūd* and just retaliation (*qiṣāṣ*), are regulated and quantified by the text, leaving little scope for the judge to alter, substitute, or omit. Whenever a crime is duly proven, the judge applies the specified punishment for it. Should there be no specified punishment for a crime in the text or the general consensus, it would likely fall under *taʿzīr*. But even here, although the judge has wider discretionary powers, "this is not arbitrary power—*taḥakkumiyyah*,"[3] as the scriptural sources of shariah and consensus provide the basis of the wrongful conduct in question. In the meantime, the judge is authorised to specify a suitable punishment in light of the principles and guidelines found in the fiqh expositions of the offences.

Another aspect of the legality of punishments in shariah is that they are determined by reference to objective principles that apply to all people equally, regardless of their personal attributes and social standing, such that everyone—from the head of state to the man in the street, rich and poor, learned or otherwise—stand equal before the law and court of justice without discrimination and privilege of any kind. This degree of objectivity is a prerequisite especially of *ḥudūd* and *qiṣāṣ*, but in *taʿzīr* the judge pays some attention to the personal attributes of the offender and his social standing in the determination of a suitable punishment. That still does not derogate from the shariah principle of equivalence between the crime and its punishment in that no one must suffer punishment in excess to the pain the offender has inflicted on another and the wrongful conduct he or she may have committed. Some exceptions to this principle may exist on grounds of religion (e.g., non-Muslims are not liable to punishment for drinking or apostasy).

All punishments are personal in the sense that no one else but the offender is to be punished for wrongdoing, and no one else must be made to suffer due to the conduct of another person. This too is one of the fundamental premises of the legality of punishments in shariah. It was due to the commitment to this principle that Islam overruled the tribalist practices of pre-Islamic Arabia, especially those customs that were deemed oppressive and failed to qualify under the Islamic standards of objectivity. Equality before the law and before the court of justice, a substantive line of equivalence between the crime and its punishment, and the principle of non-retroactivity in crimes and penalties underline the Islamic law of crimes and punishments. These were among the reform measures that marked a departure from the tribalist system of justice in pre-Islamic Arabia.[4]

One may add to this analysis an emerging trend that views *ḥudūd* laws from a different angle, namely the unprecedented increase of terrorism and violence, suicide bombing, drone attacks, and state terrorism. In conflict-ridden communities and postconflict justice scenarios, suspicious situations are sometimes encountered wherein warlords and criminals themselves take high positions and become influential in government. Even the state is sometimes seen as complicit to crime—hence a fresh demand is made for the restoration of *ḥudūd* laws that are known to be more resolute and less dependent on the vicissitudes of politics and the divergent demands of questionable interest groups.

Furthermore, the era of constitutionalism and its articulations—more specifically, the principle of legality in crimes and punishments—have brought about the reality and demand that Islamic criminal law must be codified and articulated in a definitive text that is approved by elected bodies and parliaments. This is because historically and even now Islamic law and jurisprudence is contained in the fiqh juristic manuals authored by private jurists, not by state institutions or functionaries. Although the statutory law codes in Muslim countries provide a comprehensive articulation of the substantive and procedural aspects of crimes and penalties and are largely taken from shariah manuals, they are not a total replica of those juristic manuals. Twentieth-century codification of laws in the Muslim world has also espoused extraneous elements and served as a medium, to some extent, of transformation. This has been prompted, in turn, by the ubiquitous drive toward secularity and Westernisation of laws, especially under colonial rule. But since then, many Muslim countries and law-making bodies of the postcolonial era have sought to take mixed and intermediate approaches in retaining some Western ideas and principles and combining them, as and when deemed appropriate, with substantive shariah law doctrines. This and the historical background developments just reviewed have been more noticeable in the spheres of public law, including commercial law, criminal law and procedure, and constitutional law, but not as much in the private and personal law aspects of shariah.

III

Ḥudūd *in the Qur'an, Sunnah, and Fiqh*

THIS PART EXPLORES the hypothesis that the juristic concept of *ḥadd* and *ḥudūd* in the fiqh expositions differ from what they mean in the Qur'an. Some contend that the rigidities attendant in the juristic doctrines are not Qur'anic. The discussion begins with a brief review of the concept and meaning of *ḥadd* and *ḥudūd* and then examines the manner of their exposition in the Qur'an and Sunnah. The fiqh formulations of *ḥudūd* will be looked at in a separate section that follows.

Ḥudūd *in the Qur'an*

The literal and technical meanings of *ḥudūd* (the plural form of *ḥadd*) are closely interrelated and often interchangeable. In Arabic, *ḥadd* literally means a boundary or limit that separates and prevents one thing from intruding another. The door keeper (*bawwāb*) and prison guard (*sajjān*) in Arabic are also referred to as *ḥaddād* as they both prevent the public from entering into the place that they try to keep separate and protect from outside intrusion. Technically, *ḥudūd* refer to fixed punishments as divinely ordained limits and punishments God Most High has specified for certain varieties of conduct. They are understood as God's Rights that seek to prevent transgression of His limits and also signify the limits of what is tolerable in shariah and what is not. *Ḥudūd* as such preclude the deterrent punishment of *taʿzīr* as this is not specified, just as they also preclude just retaliation (*qiṣāṣ*) in the sense that *qiṣāṣ*, according to fiqh jurists, consists largely of private rights or the Rights of Man in contradistinction with *ḥudūd*, which all fall under the Right of God. The juristic usage of *ḥadd* also carries two other related meanings, one of which refers to the crime itself, such as by saying that so and so committed a *ḥadd*, by which is meant the offence itself rather than the punishment it carries. This would be roughly equivalent to the Arabic word *jināyah* except that the latter is more general and includes all kinds of crimes. And then *ḥadd* is also used to refer to the punishment, as in the expression "the *ḥadd* was applied to so and so," meaning that the prescribed punishment was applied to him. This usage would be a rough equivalent of the Arabic word *ʿuqūbah*, which is also a general term for all types of punishments, whereas *ḥudūd* refer to a certain category of specified or quantified punishments.[1]

Ḥudūd Allāh (lit., God's limits) is a familiar Qur'anic expression that occurs fourteen times in the Holy Book in the typical sense of signifying the "limits," whether moral or legal, of acceptable behaviour from that which is unacceptable—for example, in the sense of separating the halal and *ḥarām* (lawful and unlawful) from one another. On no occasion has the Qur'an, however, used *ḥadd* or *ḥudūd* in the sense specifically of punishment, fixed or otherwise. The fact that *ḥadd* and *ḥudūd* later began to signify punishments is derived from juristic terminology and expression, although it may arguably have some origins in the Sunnah. Punishment also signifies a limit and as such can be subsumed within the meaning of *ḥadd* and *ḥudūd*. The idea of "limit" is thus basic both to the literal and the Qur'anic usage of *ḥadd*, which is in one way or another reflected in all of the other usages of this term.

When the Qur'anic usage of *ḥadd* (in the sense of limit) is compared with its usage in fiqh manuals, one notices that a basic development has taken place, which is that *ḥadd* has been used to signify a fixed and unchangeable punishment that has been laid down in the Qur'an or Sunnah. The concept of *ḥadd* in the Qur'an in the sense generally of a "separating or preventing limit was thereby replaced by the very specific idea of a fixed and mandatory punishment.[2]

Ḥadd, according to its fiqh definition, is "a quantitatively fixed punishment which is imposed for violation of the Right of God." This juristic characterisation of *ḥadd* as the Right of God signifies that it is meant to be a mandatory punishment, a demand from God that requires fulfillment, and that no one, including the victim, judge, or head of state, has the authority to pardon, change, or suspend it.[3]

The basic philosophy of *ḥudūd*, as one of the three classes of punishments in Islamic criminal law, is to inflict pain on the perpetrator as an expression of the society's rejection of his conduct, to deter the perpetrator and others from such acts, and to protect the essential interests (*al-maṣāliḥ al-ḍarūriyyah*) of the people. Deterrence is the overriding objective of *ḥudūd*, so much so that the renowned Shāfiʿī jurist and judge al-Māwardī (d. 450/1058) makes a point of it in his definition of *ḥudūd* as "deterrent punishments which God Most High has enacted in order to prevent man from committing what He forbade and from neglecting what He commanded."[4] There is a certain degree of objectivity in the fiqh concept of *ḥudud* as mandatory punishments in that they must be enforced, in exact quantity and specification, on everyone regardless of the place or circumstance in which they are committed. Factors such as the personality, status, even previous record of the offender, or of the victim, are of little consequence in the enforcement of *ḥudūd*. This position is different in *taʿzīr* (lit., deterrence, i.e., a deterrent but unprescribed sanction or punishment) and *qiṣāṣ* (retaliation), both of which take into account the personality of the offender and also the victim's right and desire to retaliate. The victim in the case of *qiṣāṣ*, and the judge or the head of state in the case of *taʿzīr*, are entitled, under certain conditions, to pardon the offender, to effect a compromise solution, or to choose a punishment that might seem suitable under the circumstances. There is also room in theory for juristic construction or *ijtihād* by the judge and the head of state in both *taʿzīr* and *qiṣāṣ*, but not in *ḥudūd*. The prescribed punishment, for example, of eighty lashes for slanderous accusation (*qadhf*) may not be increased or decreased regardless of such factors as the social status and public image of the victim or the motive, personality, and character of the offender.[5]

Of the fourteen instances where *ḥudūd* is referred to in the Qur'an, no less than six occur in just one passage on the subject of divorce, which is as follows:

> Divorce [may be given] twice. Thereafter either retain [the wife] according to good custom, or a decent manner [*bi'l-maʿrūf*] or let [her] go with kindness. And it is impermissible for you to take back anything you have given her unless the couple fear that they may transgress God's limits [*ḥudūd Allāh*]. If there is fear that they may transgress *ḥudūd Allāh*, they commit no sin if the wife willingly gives anything back [of the dower she may have received]. These are the *ḥudūd Allāh*, do not transgress them. Those who transgress *ḥudūd Allāh*, they are unjust. But if he [the husband] divorces her,

> she will not be lawful to him thereafter until she marries another man. If he [the second husband] divorces her, there is no harm if the two return to each other, if they think they can observe the *ḥudūd Allāh*. And these are the *ḥudūd Allāh*, which He makes clear for a people who know. (al-Baqarah, 2:229–230)
>
> الطَّلَاقُ مَرَّتَانِ ۖ فَإِمْسَاكٌ بِمَعْرُوفٍ أَوْ تَسْرِيحٌ بِإِحْسَانٍ ۗ وَلَا يَحِلُّ لَكُمْ أَن تَأْخُذُوا مِمَّا آتَيْتُمُوهُنَّ شَيْئًا إِلَّا أَن يَخَافَا أَلَّا يُقِيمَا حُدُودَ اللَّهِ ۖ فَإِنْ خِفْتُمْ أَلَّا يُقِيمَا حُدُودَ اللَّهِ فَلَا جُنَاحَ عَلَيْهِمَا فِيمَا افْتَدَتْ بِهِ ۗ تِلْكَ حُدُودُ اللَّهِ فَلَا تَعْتَدُوهَا ۚ وَمَن يَتَعَدَّ حُدُودَ اللَّهِ فَأُولَٰئِكَ هُمُ الظَّالِمُونَ ۝ فَإِن طَلَّقَهَا فَلَا تَحِلُّ لَهُ مِن بَعْدُ حَتَّىٰ تَنكِحَ زَوْجًا غَيْرَهُ ۗ فَإِن طَلَّقَهَا فَلَا جُنَاحَ عَلَيْهِمَا أَن يَتَرَاجَعَا إِن ظَنَّا أَن يُقِيمَا حُدُودَ اللَّهِ ۗ وَتِلْكَ حُدُودُ اللَّهِ يُبَيِّنُهَا لِقَوْمٍ يَعْلَمُونَ ۝

Ḥudūd Allāh carries slightly different meanings in its various applications even in this passage. While the idea of limits is common to all six incidents above, in its uses of 2, 3, and 6 it refers to the specific injunctions contained in the body of the text. Uses of 1, 4, and 5 do not refer to anything specifically stated, let alone enjoined, either here or indeed elsewhere in the Qur'an. In other words, when the Qur'an speaks of observing *ḥudūd Allāh* it states neither here nor elsewhere specifically what these "limits" actually are.

With reference to marital relations, the Qur'an demands that the spouses treat one another decently and in accord with the approved custom of society (*bi'l-maʿrūf*). This is not to say that there are no other injunctions concerning marital relations in the Qur'an, but for the purposes of this text, *ḥudūd Allāh* is a general reference to the total conduct of marital life that is conveyed by *bi'l-maʿrūf*. The content of good or approved custom in this context is thus integrated into the general meaning of *ḥudūd Allāh*.

There are two more points of note in this passage. Firstly, *ḥudūd Allāh* has no reference to punishment but is concerned mainly with a moral situation that may or may not have legal or punitive implications. Secondly, the content of "good or approved custom" is evidently liable to change and is not in tune with the idea of a fixed and invariable position. This must also imply that the content of *ḥudūd Allāh* is variable to that extent and also that it is conceptually amenable to comprising changeable conditions or provisions.[6]

The basic concern of *ḥudūd Allāh* in the Qur'an is clearly with the moral limits of conduct in the sense of identifying what is generally good and righteous. This can be even more vividly seen in the following verse, which promises great reward:

> Those who repent, worship and praise God, those who fast and bow down and prostrate, and those who enjoin good and forbid evil and preserve the limits of God [*ḥudūd Allāh*] and give good news to the believers. (al-Tawbah, 9:112)
>
> التَّائِبُونَ الْعَابِدُونَ الْحَامِدُونَ السَّائِحُونَ الرَّاكِعُونَ السَّاجِدُونَ الْآمِرُونَ بِالْمَعْرُوفِ وَالنَّاهُونَ عَنِ الْمُنكَرِ وَالْحَافِظُونَ لِحُدُودِ اللَّهِ ۗ وَبَشِّرِ الْمُؤْمِنِينَ

In a preceding passage of the same sura, the Qur'an censures the perfidy of certain Bedouin tribes who had violated their defence pact with the Muslims:

> The Bedouins are most intense in disbelief and hypocrisy and most disposed not to know the limits that God has revealed [*ḥudūda mā anzal Allāh*] to His Messenger. And God is Most Knowing, Wise. (al-Tawbah, 9:97)
>
> الْأَعْرَابُ أَشَدُّ كُفْرًا وَنِفَاقًا وَأَجْدَرُ أَلَّا يَعْلَمُوا حُدُودَ مَا أَنزَلَ اللَّهُ عَلَىٰ رَسُولِهِ ۗ وَاللَّهُ عَلِيمٌ حَكِيمٌ

Although "the limits that God has revealed to His Messenger" must still have a general meaning as a reference to the totality of Qur'anic teachings, the verse here nevertheless alludes, according to reports, to the Bedouin tribes' nonparticipation in jihad, despite the definite agreements that were made to that effect—which are however nowhere stated in the Qur'an but only indirectly indicated in the succeeding portion of the text.

In two other places (al-Baqarah, 2:187 and al-Ṭalāq, 65:1) *ḥudūd Allāh* is concerned with marital relations: the first with conjugal relations during the fasting month of Ramadan, and the second with the waiting period (i.e., *ʿiddah*) that the wife must observe following a divorce. The text in both places warns against violating *ḥudūd Allāh*. But an interesting example of this expression occurs in the following passage where the text recommends kindness to orphans and the needy and specifies fixed shares in inheritance for legal heirs, and then declares:

> These are the limits of God [*ḥudūd Allāh*]; whosoever obeys God and His Messenger, He will grant him entry into Paradise underneath which rivers flow—and this is a great success. But whosoever disobeys God and His Messenger and violates His limits [*ḥudūdahu*],

> He will make him enter fire wherein he shall reside, and this is for him a humiliating torment. (al-Nisā', 4:13–14)
>
> تِلْكَ حُدُودُ اللَّهِ ۚ وَمَن يُطِعِ اللَّهَ وَرَسُولَهُ يُدْخِلْهُ جَنَّاتٍ تَجْرِي مِن تَحْتِهَا الْأَنْهَارُ خَالِدِينَ فِيهَا ۚ وَذَٰلِكَ الْفَوْزُ الْعَظِيمُ ۝ وَمَن يَعْصِ اللَّهَ وَرَسُولَهُ وَيَتَعَدَّ حُدُودَهُ يُدْخِلْهُ نَارًا خَالِدًا فِيهَا وَلَهُ عَذَابٌ مُّهِينٌ ۝

Notwithstanding the fact that the text in the three verses referred to contains specific injunctions of a legal nature, yet the consequences of conformity and disobedience to them are postponed to the Hereafter. This might indicate "how little concerned the Qur'an is with the purely legal side and how much more with the setting of the moral tone of the community."[7] The Qur'an shows little inclination to enforce its instruction through the modality of fixed punishment.

Ḥudūd Allāh also occurs in the Qur'an in reference to atonement or self-imposed punishment (i.e., *kaffārah*) in conjunction with *ẓihār*. This is a form of divorce, originally a pre-Islamic practice, where the husband declares his wife to be unlawful to him "like the back of his mother." The atonement or *kaffārah* that the husband needs to observe in the event of resuming marital relations here consists of one of the following three: to release a slave, to fast for sixty consecutive days, or to feed sixty poor persons. The text then proceeds to declare that "these are God's limits [*ḥudūd Allāh*] and [appointed] for disbelievers is painful torture" (al-Mujādalah, 58:3–5). It is of interest to note here the use of *ḥudūd Allāh* in reference to a specific but self-imposed punishment that does not involve either the court or other enforcement authorities but only the individual himself. Moreover, by suggesting three alternative atonements for *ẓihār*, the Qur'an seems to admit the idea of alternative/variable punishment for *ḥudūd Allāh* in line with the ability and condition of the persons who observe the *kaffārah* in question.

Our analysis here is confirmed by Maududi's characterisation of *ḥudūd Allāh*, or "Divine Limits," as he phrases it, a broad Qur'anic concept that reaches far beyond the limitations of fixed or invariable punishments:

> Limitations on human freedom, provided they are appropriate...are absolutely necessary....That is why God has laid down those limits, which in Islamic phraseology are termed "Divine Limits" [*ḥudūd Allāh*]. These limits consist of certain principles, checks and balances, and specific injunctions in different spheres of life and activity—and they have been prescribed in order that man may be trained to lead a

> balanced and moderate life. They are intended to lay down the basic framework within which man is free to legislate, decide his own affairs and frame subsidiary laws and regulations for his conduct.[8]

It is thus evident that the Qur'anic concepts of *ḥudūd* and *ḥudūd Allāh* are not necessarily meant to consist of punishments nor of purely mandatory ones. They are used in the Qur'an to imply a set of broad moral and legal guidelines that must be observed and upheld. But nowhere has the text specified the manner in which they should be observed other than the emphasis, perhaps, that compassion should not impede one's determination in combatting crime. This must surely be observed, but in the meantime it should be merged and reconciled with the Qur'anic directives on repentance and reform, and it is to this that we now turn.

Repentance (Tawbah) *and Reform* (Iṣlāḥ) *in the Qur'an*

In all the four instances where the Qur'an specifies a punishment for an offence, there is also a provision on repentance, forgiveness, and reform. This is a consistent feature of the penal philosophy of the Qur'an, which has, however, not been adequately reflected in the juristic blueprint of *ḥudūd* nor indeed in *ḥudūd*-related enactments, laws, and acts of parliament that various Muslim countries, including Malaysia, have introduced in recent decades. Notwithstanding the dual emphasis that the Qur'an lays on punishment and repentance, juristic doctrine pays undivided attention to punishment to such a degree as to maintain persistently that once the offender has been convicted of a *ḥudūd* offence, repentance has no value and no one has the authority to pardon him. But then one reads a different message in the Qur'an. Let us begin by looking at the passage on the punishment of theft:

> As to the thief, male or female, cut off their hands as retribution for their deeds and exemplary punishment from God. And God is exalted in power, Most Wise. But if he repents after his crime and amends his conduct, God redeems him. God is Forgiving, Most Merciful. (al-Mā'idah, 5:38–39)
>
> وَالسَّارِقُ وَالسَّارِقَةُ فَاقْطَعُوا أَيْدِيَهُمَا جَزَاءً بِمَا كَسَبَا نَكَالًا مِّنَ اللَّهِ ۗ وَاللَّهُ عَزِيزٌ حَكِيمٌ
>
> فَمَن تَابَ مِن بَعْدِ ظُلْمِهِ وَأَصْلَحَ فَإِنَّ اللَّهَ يَتُوبُ عَلَيْهِ ۗ إِنَّ اللَّهَ غَفُورٌ رَّحِيمٌ

While the first part of this verse prescribes the crime and its punishment, the second part balances that approach immediately by opening the door to repentance, self-emendation, and reform. The Qur'an here establishes a certain perspective, which is that punishment should not be hastily carried out because repentance and correction naturally come as a result of enlightenment, advice, and education. The reference to repentance in the text is followed by *aṣlaḥa* (rectifies or reforms himself), and the two together would seem to require that the convict should not only be given time in which repentance and reformation can occur but also that this should be facilitated, on a selective basis at least, by positive incentives. The Qur'anic perspective here is hardly compatible with the rigid approach that has characterised *ḥudūd* in the established juristic doctrine of the leading schools of Islamic law.

Commenting on this verse, the renowned Egyptian scholar Abū Zahrah (d. 1974) wrote, with regard to the Qur'anic words '*al-sāriq wa'l-sāriqah*' (thief—male or female), that these are adjectives, not verbs, and adjectives do not materialise in a person without a measure of repetition. A person is not, for example, described as "generous," "honest," or "liar" merely by a single act of generosity, honesty, or lying that does not show consistency or establish a pattern. These adjectives carry their full meanings when there is recurrence and repetition. The verse did not begin by saying, for instance, that theft is punishable with such and such a punishment; it refers instead to '*sāriq*' and '*sāriqah*'. When we read the verse from this perspective, then the punishment that it conveys should apply to repeat offenders and recidivists, and if it is applied to first-time offenders it should only be in aggravating circumstances. This analysis also finds support in the Sunnah of the Prophet and also precedent of the caliph ʿUmar b. al-Khaṭṭāb. In the reports concerning the well-known case of al-Makhzumiyyah, a woman whose hand was mutilated for theft, it is noted that she was a recidivist and known for the fact that she did not return goods that were deposited with her or things that she borrowed from others. Many Ḥanbalī scholars have gone on record to say that this was, in fact, the nature of her offence; but the majority maintains that it was a specific case of theft. Be that as it may, what is certain is that she was known for having committed similar offences, which is why she had acquired a reputation for it. When the Prophet determined al-Makhzumiyyah's predicament, this was notwithstanding the fact that she was an important figure among the Quraysh tribe, hence the leaders of Quraysh interceded on her behalf and asked the Prophet if she could be pardoned—and it was on this occasion when the Prophet uttered his renowned statement that "if Fāṭimah, Muḥammad's daughter, committed theft, Muḥammad would cut her hand." According to another report, when the caliph ʿUmar b. al-Khaṭṭāb decided to mutilate the hand of a young offender, his mother said: "Pardon him O Commander of the Faithful, because it was his first time." To this the caliph responded, "God is too merciful to reveal the nakedness of His servant for his first failure." The culprit was not punished.

Abū Zahrah has also discussed, in this connection, the issue of repentance and observed that the wording of the text before us is such that repentance can only find a logical place in it if there is an opportunity before the imposition of punishment. This, he adds, is not the view of the majority of jurists but a view that is sustainable by the text itself. Some jurists have in fact arrived at this conclusion. It is then added that the Qur'an opens the door to repentance, as the verse that will be quoted next indicates, not to recidivists and confirmed criminals, who are not likely to be sincere repenters anyway, but to first-time offenders who may well be ready to repent: "Repentance with God is only for those who do evil in ignorance, then turn [to God] soon. It is to these that God turns with mercy. God is indeed all-knowing and most wise" (al-Nisāʾ, 4:17).

إِنَّمَا التَّوْبَةُ عَلَى اللَّهِ لِلَّذِينَ يَعْمَلُونَ السُّوءَ بِجَهَالَةٍ ثُمَّ يَتُوبُونَ مِن قَرِيبٍ فَأُولَٰئِكَ يَتُوبُ اللَّهُ عَلَيْهِمْ ۗ وَكَانَ اللَّهُ عَلِيمًا حَكِيمًا.

A Qur'an commentator, al-Ṭabarī (d. 310/923), records the view that "ignorance" in this verse applies to anyone who indulges in sinful conduct until he withdraws from it and returns to the right path.[9] According to al-Māwardī, "ignorance" in this context has two meanings, one of which is ignorance of the evil nature of conduct and the other when one succumbs to one's desire and does something knowing that what one does is wrong. While quoting both these meanings, Fatḥī al-Khammāsī considers the latter the more likely of the two.[10] In yet another view attributed to al-Zuzanī, it is noted that when "it is said that so and so is ignorant" it often refers to a youth who does not think of the consequences of his conduct and gives way to his whims and desires.[11] Understanding the implications of "ignorance" in the verse is thus likely to widen the scope of its application in the context of repentance: the first-time offender and a remorseful youth; or one with no criminal record, who may have fallen into sin, committed adultery or theft, and then repented. Then he or she should be entitled to relief.

The broader perspective of the Qur'an on repentance and the general encouragement towards it can hardly be overestimated when it is openly stated elsewhere that "God loves those who turn to Him in repentance and He loves those who purify themselves" (al-Baqarah, 2:222).

إنّ اللّه يُحِبُّ التّوّابِينَ وَيُحِبُّ الْمُتَطَهِّرِين.

The conclusion is thus drawn not only that repentance purifies one from guilt but also that mutilation of the hand for the capital crime of theft is not for the first-time offender who acts out of ignorance but for confirmed criminals with a criminal record. This would also tally well with our understanding and analysis that the idea of limit or *ḥadd* should signify the uppermost limit, or the end of the road, so to speak, and not be applied to an inconclusive situation.[12]

Another Qur'anic verse that needs to be looked at, however briefly, is the one on the punishments both of adultery (*zinā*) and slander (*qadhf*), which occur in a sequence that relate the one to the other.

> The woman and the man guilty *of zinā,* flog each of them a hundred lashes. Let not compassion move you in their case from carrying out God's law (*dīn Allāh*) if you believe in God and the Last Day. And let their punishment be witnessed by a group of the believers....And those who accuse chaste women and produce not four witnesses, flog them eighty lashes and reject their testimony ever after. For they are transgressors. Except for those who repent thereafter and reform themselves, then God is Forgiving, Most Merciful. (al-Nūr, 24:2–5)
>
> الزّانِيَةُ وَالزّاني فَاجلِدوا كُلّ واحِدٍ مِنهُما مِائَةَ جَلدَةٍ ۖ وَلا تَأخُذكُم بِهِما رَأفَةٌ في دينِ اللّهِ إن كُنتُم تُؤمِنونَ بِاللّهِ وَاليَومِ الآخِرِ ۖ وَليَشهَد عَذابَهُما طائِفَةٌ مِنَ المُؤمِنينَ ... وَالّذينَ يَرمونَ المُحصَناتِ ثُمّ لَم يَأتوا بِأَربَعَةِ شُهَداءَ فَاجلِدوهُم ثَمانينَ جَلدَةً وَلا تَقبَلوا لَهُم شَهادَةً أَبَدًا ۚ وَأُولئِكَ هُمُ الفاسِقونَ. إِلّا الّذينَ تابوا مِن بَعدِ ذٰلِكَ وَأَصلَحوا فَإِنّ اللّهَ غَفورٌ رَحيمٌ.

Some commentators have raised questions about the precise implications of the pronoun *illā'l-ladhīna* ("except for those") whether the reference is to slanderous accusers or to transgressors (*fāsiqūn*) in general, and whether the adulterer can also be included among those who may be allowed to repent. Be that as it may, based on the principle that criminal legislation should be interpreted in favour of the accused and on the side of leniency, it is submitted that all of the preceding categories of offenders are included in the meaning of the last passage and should all be given the opportunity, on a selective basis at least, to repent and to reform themselves.

For otherwise the repeated Qur'anic emphasis on this theme would have been relegated to the realm of moral teaching. The juristic doctrine of *ḥudūd* is, on the other hand, formulated such that leaves little room for a blended approach that might reconcile the notion of certainty and decisiveness in the enforcement of punishment with the prospects of repentance and reform. It is submitted that court procedures and adjudication of *ḥudūd* should be suitably amended and changed so as to reflect the Qur'an's repeated directives on repentance.

We have already discussed the verses concerning three of the four instances where a specific punishment is provided. The only other instance where a punishment is specified is concerned with highway robbery and terrorism (*ḥirābah*). *Ḥirābah* is a separate topic that will be discussed in some detail in the following sections. It may briefly be mentioned here that the text (al-Māʾidah, 5:33) on *ḥirābah* provides for a fourfold punishment of execution, with or without crucifixion and cutting of limbs, depending on whether the robber/terrorist has killed, terrorised, and robbed or only committed one of these crimes without the others. Having spelled out these eventualities, the text then provides, "Except for those who repent before they fall into your power. In that case know that God is Forgiving, Most Merciful" (al-Māʾidah, 5:34).

إِلَّا الَّذِينَ تَابُوا مِن قَبْلِ أَن تَقْدِرُوا عَلَيْهِمْ ۖ فَاعْلَمُوا أَنَّ اللَّهَ غَفُورٌ رَّحِيمٌ

It is thus evident that the Qur'an leaves the door of repentance and reform open in all of the *ḥudūd* offences without any exception, although in the case of *ḥirābah*, it is contingent on the criminal's surrender to the authorities.

The subject of repentance is almost totally absent in the general run of *ḥudūd* debate in Malaysia or in any other Muslim jurisdiction. One commentator who was a committee member that drafted the Hudud Bill of Kelantan, and who was also state executive councillor of Terengganu in Malaysia, Wan Abdul Muttalib, referred to repentance when he said in an interview: "In Islam, God says it is better for you, if you commit an offence against God, that you don't surrender yourself to be punished, but pray for forgiveness."[13] But with a prayer for forgiveness, it was added, "One must be sure to turn over a new leaf. You can't pray for forgiveness for robbing a person and when you see someone else in the afternoon, you rob him too." Further added was the point that redemption is important in Islam. You don't seek redemption in jest nor for a joke, but so as to purify yourself. It is not easy as one would always need to take a firm resolve to surrender oneself. This is like the woman (probably meaning al-Ghamidiyyah) who came to the Prophet to confess that she had committed adultery/*zinā*. The Prophet turned to her askance: "Are you mad? Go back." But the woman came back saying, "I have done this—the proof is in my womb." Once again she was asked to go back in case she had made a mistake. The woman came back after she had delivered and said, "This is the illicit child I have given birth to." Then she was told, "Go back and nurse him until he can eat on his own. The child is not a criminal." The sentence was then carried out two years later after the baby had been weaned.[14] The question one may pertinently ask: Has the spirit of this exchange, and other incidents like this on record, been integrated into the juristic doctrine of *ḥudūd*?

Juristic Views on Repentance

Scholars of the leading schools of Islamic law, including the Shia Imamiyyah, are in agreement that in banditry and apostasy repentance prior to arrest absolves the offender from punishment insofar as it relates to the Right of God content of that offence, but not if there is a violation of the Right of Man or private right. The bandit who repents prior to arrest is consequently exempted from the prescribed punishment, but he must return the private property he might have taken. If he is guilty of armed robbery, killing, and terrorising and then repents prior to arrest, the punishment for killing, insofar as the Right of God content of the crime of killing is concerned, is suspended, but he must return the property. Even if the bandit repents and the *ḥadd* punishment is suspended because of it, he will still be liable to retaliation (*qiṣāṣ*), and this latter punishment can only be suspended if the legal heirs of the deceased grant a pardon and make such a request. This is partly because repentance prior to subjugation is presumed to be indicative of sincerity on the part of the offender and it therefore merits consideration and encouragement. But repentance after subjugation, or arrest, is regarded to be out of fear of the expected punishment, which is why it is not admissible.[15]

The majority of jurists have taken the position with regard to all the rest of the *ḥudūd* offences (except for *ḥirābah*) that repentance does not suspend the punishment after the offence has been reported to the authorities. Yet according to a minority view (*muqabil al-aẓhar*—contrary to the manifest position) of the Ḥanafī and Shāfiʿī schools, and "an opinion also of the Ḥanbalī school," repentance suspends the *ḥudūd* punishments generally.[16] The mainstream position of the Mālikī and Shāfiʿī schools, and also an alternative view of that of the Ḥanbalī school, maintain that *ḥudūd* penalties are not suspended by repentance, even if it occurs before the matter is reported to the authorities. For otherwise, it is asserted, repentance will come in the way of due enforcement of *ḥudūd*.[17] These views are further explained in the following discussion.

As for the effect of repentance with regard to the rest of the *ḥudūd* crimes, Muslim jurists have held three different views, which may be summarised as follows:

1. The first view maintains that repentance suspends the prescribed punishments, if it is offered, as already noted, prior to the completion of the crime and that the crime in question belongs to the Right of God category of *ḥudūd*. The jurists of the Shāfiʿī and Ḥanbalī schools who subscribe to this view have done so by way of analogy to banditry (*ḥirābah*). It is thus argued that *ḥirābah* is the most serious of all crimes, and if repentance in this is admissible, as is stipulated in the clear text of the Qur'an, then the argument for its admissibility is even stronger in lesser crimes, namely of *zinā*, drinking/*shurb*, and theft. Imam al-Shāfiʿī has added that when the adulterer repents, his repentance resembles retraction of a confession, which suspends the *ḥudūd* punishment. Punishment is also suspended if he runs away at the time of the execution thereof. This being the case, a sincere repentance by the offender provides a stronger basis by which to suspend the *ḥudūd* punishment—even after arrest and prosecution and any time prior to enforcement. Al-Shāfiʿī also wrote that "one who repents prior to arrest and prosecution, the *ḥudūd* punishment, but not any private right claim, concerning him is suspended; it is probable that all Rights of God are suspendable by virtue of repentance."[18] The proponents of this view have further stated, with reference to *zinā*, that the initial ruling of the Qur'an on the punishment of *zinā* contained an equally explicit provision on repentance. The relevant text thus provides:

> If any of your women are guilty of lewdness, take the evidence of four witnesses from amongst you against them, and if they testify, confine them to their houses until death claims them or God ordains

> for them some (other) way. If the two of them are guilty of lewdness, punish them both. If they repent and amend, leave them alone; for God is Oft-Returning, Most Merciful. (al-Nisāʾ, 4:15–16)
>
> وَٱلَّتِى يَأۡتِينَ ٱلۡفَٰحِشَةَ مِن نِّسَآئِكُمۡ فَٱسۡتَشۡهِدُواْ عَلَيۡهِنَّ أَرۡبَعَةً مِّنكُمۡۖ فَإِن شَهِدُواْ فَأَمۡسِكُوهُنَّ فِى ٱلۡبُيُوتِ حَتَّىٰ يَتَوَفَّىٰهُنَّ ٱلۡمَوۡتُ أَوۡ يَجۡعَلَ ٱللَّهُ لَهُنَّ سَبِيلاً. وَٱلَّذَانِ يَأۡتِيَٰنِهَا مِنكُمۡ فَـَٔاذُوهُمَاۖ فَإِن تَابَا وَأَصۡلَحَا فَأَعۡرِضُواْ عَنۡهُمَآۗ إِنَّ ٱللَّهَ كَانَ تَوَّابًا رَّحِيمًا.

Unlike the rather obscure view of some jurists that this verse has been abrogated, Abū Zahrah and al-Khammāsī, and before them Ibn Taymiyyah, have refuted the claim of abrogation saying that the text before us is perspicuous (*muḥkam*) and, as such, it is not amenable to abrogation in the first place. It is then stated that the wording of this verse makes the suspension of punishment obligatory upon repentance, for the text here contains a command to "leave them alone—*faʿriḍu*" once they have sincerely repented. There is no conflict, and therefore no abrogation, between this verse and the one that specifies the punishment at 100 lashes for the same offence. The command concerning repentance in this verse is therefore still operative.[19]

The proponents of repentance have also referred to the Qur'anic text on the punishment of theft, which clearly leaves the door open to it:

> But he who repents after his crime and amends his conduct, God turns to him in forgiveness; for God is Oft-Forgiving, Most Merciful. (al-Māʾidah, 5:39)
>
> فَمَن تَابَ مِن بَعۡدِ ظُلۡمِهِ وَأَصۡلَحَ فَإِنَّ ٱللَّهَ يَتُوبُ عَلَيۡهِۗ إِنَّ ٱللَّهَ غَفُورٌ رَّحِيمٌ.

The fact that the provision on repentance here immediately follows the reference to punishment indicates that an exception has been made to the general application of the punishment of theft by way of specification (*takhṣīṣ*) in favour of those who repent.[20] The Prophet has, moreover, said in a hadith: "One who repents from a sin is like one who has committed no sin [التائب من الذنب كمن لاذنب له]". It follows therefore that one who is not guilty of a sin is not liable to its punishment either. The Prophet is also on record to have said concerning the renowned case of Māʿiz b. Mālik, when he was informed that Māʿiz ran away (while being stoned for *zinā*): "Did you not leave him alone to repent so that God would have granted him pardon." The *ḥadd* offence in this case consisted of violation of the Right of God proper, like that of banditry/terrorism, and repentance in both cases leads to the suspension of punishment.[21] Among the proponents of this view some have further elaborated that repentance, in order to be admissible and convincing, should be accompanied by correction in conduct and this would require time (some suggest a period of six months whereas others only say a long time) in which the sincerity of repentance can be ascertained. There are still others who have not stipulated a probation period of this kind and have merely spoken of repentance itself. Imam Abū Ḥanīfah and his disciples have held that expiry of a long period of time prior to adjudication is by itself enough to suspend the *ḥudūd* punishments, even without repentance, as it would introduce an element of doubt and doubt suspends the *ḥudūd* punishments. But the majority view here maintains that if the offender repents prior to completing the crime and turns away from it, and that if the crime in question is also one that involves a violation of the Right of God, but not if it involves a violation of the Right of Man or a private right, his repentance should be accepted.[22]

2. The second view which is held by the Imams Mālik and Abū Ḥanīfah as well as some Shāfiᶜī and Ḥanbalī jurists maintains that repentance has no bearing on the *ḥudūd,* except in the case of banditry, which is based on a clear text of the Qur'an. This view is premised on the argument that the wording of the Qur'anic verse concerning the punishments of adultery and theft (in al-Nūr, 24:2, and al-Māʾidah, 5:38, respectively) are general (*ᶜām*), which must apply to repenters and nonrepenters alike. When we read the text, for example, "as for the thief, male or female, cut off their hands," the text consists of a general provision and should be enforced in the same manner regardless of repentance. The proponents of this view maintain somehow that the references to repentance in the Qur'anic verses on theft and adultery are concerned with repentance after the imposition of punishment and not before. To this rather weak assertion, it is further added that when the Prophet ordered stoning in the cases of Māᶜiz and al-Ghamidiyyah, or when he adjudicated in certain cases of theft, on the basis of confession, the offenders in these cases had all shown signs of remorse as many of them told the Prophet that they wished to be purified of their sins, but the Prophet nevertheless enforced the *ḥudūd* punishment on them. Thus it is concluded that although repentance is likely to lighten the offender's guilt in spiritual terms, it does not relieve him of the punishment. The proponents of this view have argued further that it is not reasonable to extend the logic of the Qur'anic text on repentance in *ḥirābah* by

> analogy to other offences. For *ḥirābah,* it is said again, somewhat unconvincingly, is sui generis in that prior to arrest the offender is out of the reach of law enforcement authorities and the incentive for him to repent and be exempted serve a good purpose, which is not the case in these other offences. For "the ordinary criminal is a person who can be subjugated anytime and there is no special incentive in his case to warrant suspension of the *ḥudūd* punishment on the ground of repentance."[23] Besides, to open the door of repentance in this way might lead to uncertainty and abeyance in the enforcement of *ḥudūd.* For any offender could be said to be capable of offering repentance in anticipation of suspension and delay in the execution of punishment.[24]

As already noted, some of the points in this view are less than convincing although not entirely without merit. The point to note, for instance, that banditry and terrorism are deemed to be totally different to other *ḥudūd* crimes is presumptive because, unlike other ordinary criminals who can be arrested anytime, the bandit/terrorist is out of reach of enforcement authorities and is, in any case, not likely to be as valid now as it might have been in earlier times. One might say the same about all other offenders in that the authorities have no effective control over criminals as such. The critique here is particularly relevant to repentance in inchoate crimes. No one, it may broadly be said, would know or have power over the criminal at that stage of his or her activity. We also have some reservations over the practical value of the proposed stipulation, which makes repentance admissible only prior to the completion of a crime. How does this sort of stipulation fit into the process and provide a realistic basis or a meaningful role for repentance? These are, it would seem, mostly unanswered questions. Abū Zahrah tells us that he has investigated many of these issues, and save for *ḥirābah,* he found no authority to confine the admissibility of repentance to a particular time frame, whether before or after the matter is brought to the attention of the court. Abū Zahrah concluded that it can indeed be after that event, despite the fact that jurists like Abū al-Ḥasan al-Māwardī (d. 450/1058) and Abū Yaʿlā al-Farrā' (d. 458/1066) have stated that it should be before. What Abū Zahrah is saying is that repentance may be during adjudication or before it, and this seems to be a balanced view to take. For otherwise the court would not have been given a meaningful role in the matter, and granting or rejecting repentance would be left to the prosecutor and police.[25]

And lastly, one notes in this argument the somewhat disjointed logic that the wording of the text in the relevant passages of the Qur'an is conveyed in general terms and should therefore be closed to the whole idea of reformation and repentance. Yes, of course, these texts are general, but we also know that a general (*ʿām*) text may be specified and qualified in various ways by the preceding or succeeding portions of the text and that necessary exceptions may be made when it is suggested in the text itself. As it is, each one of the Qur'anic passages under review makes a provision for repentance mainly by way of exception (*istithnāʾ*), which means that its general application is qualified and specified in cases where taking a different course, that is, other than an undiluted emphasis on punishment, warrants consideration. This is perhaps one of the instances of taking a literalist approach to the understanding of scripture where the different segments of an otherwise logical whole are taken separately without there being a convincing argument to recommend such a course.

3. The third view, which is mainly attributed to Ibn Taymiyyah (d. 728/1328) and his disciple Ibn Qayyim al-Jawziyyah (d. 751/1350) of the Ḥanbalī school, maintains that punishment purifies one from criminality and sin, and so does repentance. That punishment should be suspended when the perpetrator of a Right of God offence repents and, in the meantime, does not himself insist that only the punishment can purify him of his guilt. But if he does so insist, then he or she may be punished even after repentance. Hence when the perpetrator of a *ḥudūd* crime repents prior to completing the crime, he or she will not be punished if the offence in question is a public right or Right of God offence, provided also that the offender does not demand to be punished. The proponents of this view have also stated, like the other two groups discussed above, that repentance does not have the same effect with reference to Right of Man offences, that is, crime that involves violation of private rights. In offences of this kind, such as slander (*qadhf*), it is not repentance but pardon that may be granted by the victim or his heirs that absolves the offender from punishment.[26]

Fatḥī al-Khammāsī has discussed the scholastic views in some detail and drawn the conclusion that one should look into the evidential basis of each opinion but also base one's preference on that which may be more suitable to one's own time and conditions. One may select a view that is more appropriate to the prevailing conditions of our society, even if it be a weak opinion, provided that it is founded on a valid evidential basis. Al-Khammāsī thus wrote, "Our choice is the position upheld by the Ḥanbalī school and Imam al-Shāfiʿī, in one of his views at least," which is that repentance suspends the Right of God-based *ḥudūd* punishments, be it before or after arrest and prosecution. This would in effect include all the *ḥudūd* punishments except perhaps that of slanderous accusation, in which the Right of Man or private right is arguably more predominant. The Ḥanbalī position is clear on this, but al-Khammāsī adds that the Shāfiʿī position on this is not devoid of some ambiguity.[27]

When one looks at the evidence in the Sunnah, one finds that the Prophet has on many occasions tried to persuade persons who had confessed to a *ḥudūd* offence to retract their confession and find for them a way out of their punitive predicament, presumably because confession is often indicative of repentance and the Prophet has positively encouraged it. Yet there is no reference to repentance in the reported hadith of Māʿiz or al-Ghamidiyyah that says, for instance, that he or she had explicitly repented before the Prophet. Then to say that a confession is always tantamount to repentance is not a certainty, as there can be a different motive or story to a confession.

Only in the case of apostasy can it be said that repentance has found a place in the juristic doctrine of fiqh, but only just so, because imposing a strict time limit of three days prior to execution of punishment (see also Clause 23.3 of the Hudud Bill of Kelantan) within which the offender must repent is really reducing the concept of repentance to a mechanical formality that is almost meaningless. With reference to *ḥirābah*, the Qur'an has stipulated that repentance should take place before the criminal has been arrested, a stipulation that is reflective of the nature of this offence. For one who challenges the authority of a lawful government must willingly surrender, and that is when an opportunity can be granted for repentance. Surrender itself, one might say, can in most cases be equivalent to actual repentance. Clearly the logic of the Qur'an stands beyond dispute. The challenger to the constitutional authority of government may be so powerful as to put the government in a helpless situation, and surrender may play a crucial role in restoring normal order in that situation.

As for the rest of the *ḥudūd* offences, the Sunnah has proscribed intercession (*shafāʿah*), that is, intervention by others asking the authorities for a grant of forgiveness after the offence has been brought to the attention of the authorities. That said, intercession is, of course, different from repentance, and the Sunnah has not taken the same attitude concerning repentance. The Sunnah is, however, explicit on the point that, once a *ḥudūd* crime is reported to the authorities, it must be diligently pursued, which must mean that the offender should neither be released nor pardoned because of intercession, considerations of social status, or an easy attitude to outside intervention. The Prophet was concerned with establishing the rule of law in a strongly tribalist environment and not necessarily with enforcing punishments in every case. This discussion contends that opening the door to repentance does not necessarily suggest a compromise on firmness nor on the deterrent attributes of the penal policy of *ḥudūd*, because all of these influences can play a role provided that one does not insist on reducing *ḥudūd* to a mechanical process—one that is made absolutely mandatory and precludes the opportunity of repentance in all cases.

Furthermore, in pre-Islamic times, Arab society was dominated by tribal influences, and tribal practices remained strong particularly in respect to crime and punishment. The Prophet/head of state tried to establish a new order wherein this area was no longer to be dominated by tribal law and practice. Hence his repeated emphasis, in regard to both intercession and repentance, that once the matter has been brought to his attention, tribal spokesmen must stop interfering. From that point onwards, the matter falls within the ambit of government authority and due process must be allowed to take its course. He did not totally overrule tribal authority; instead he conveyed the message that they could practice their own methods at the initial stages but must stop when the matter was brought to his attention. He was, in other words, drawing the line between the authority of the Medinan government under his leadership and the ever so pervasive tribalism that had historically dominated crimes and penalties. To read the hadith without contextualising the politics of the nascent state of Medina versus the tribal power of that time is likely to amount to unwarranted literalism, which still appears to dominate the jurisprudence of *ḥudūd*.

Juristic thinking over *ḥudūd* may not have taken into account these considerations, and it was probably caught, as from early times, in a web of technicality, partly because of linking *ḥudūd* with the binary division of rights into the Right of God and the Right of Man in a manner that created more problems rather than solving them. These juristic developments made it difficult to integrate the Qur'anic outlook on repentance and reform with the underlying philosophy of *ḥudūd*. One also notes discrepancy in the juristic doctrine regarding the two classes of rights. On one hand it is said that the Right of God is open to repentance and pardoning, as God Most High is forgiving and merciful, but not the Right of Man, where repentance carries little weight and only the right-bearer can grant forgiveness. But then the opposite of this is asserted in regard to the *ḥudūd* —nearly all of which are Rights of God, and are as such not amenable to pardon or repentance!.

The repeated Qur'anic emphasis on repentance caught the attention of the key scholar of the Ẓāhirī school, Ibn Hazm (d. 456/1064), who wrote in a distinctly different tone of language to that of the majority of jurists:

> Since repentance is ordained by God and it is highly recommended, it is obligatory on all Muslims (*fariḍah ʿala kull-i muslim*) to invoke it in accordance with the injunctions (*al-nuṣuṣ*) that were discussed. Hence inviting the offender to repent prior to the enforcement of *ḥudūd* is an obligation and diligence in it is a duty. If the Imam [head of state] failed to invite the offender to repent prior to enforcement, an invitation to repentance should still be extended after the enforcement of *ḥudūd*.[28]

It is not certain as to what would be the benefit of repentance after the enforcement of *ḥudūd,* insofar as the punishment itself is concerned, except perhaps when it is seen as an act of merit that might earn spiritual reward, but it can also serve as a means of restoring social respect and public confidence in the sincerity of the repentant. In any case, Ibn Hazm's emphatic tone here clearly indicates that he saw an invitation to repentance as a Qur'anic obligation and an integral part of the penal policy of *ḥudūd*.

Tawfiq al-Shāwī, author of a four-volume encyclopedia on Islamic criminal law, has even more forcefully spoken on repentance to say that, by ignoring this aspect of Islamic criminal law, the fiqh scholars have turned a blind eye to the religious character of this discipline and to God's illustrious revelation that "made repentance obligatory and promised its acceptance out of His unbounded mercy." He intimates that there is a limit to the positivist thrust of fiqh, even though positivism has become even more pervasive, but "this is an impermissible aberration nevertheless [*hadha al-inḥirāf lā-yajūz*]."[29]

If one were to open the juristic concept of *ḥudūd* to the broader Qur'anic philosophy of repentance, rehabilitation, and reform, one would have to depart from the notion of the fixed and mandatory punishments of *ḥudūd* to a concept that is open to considerations of the offender's personality and past record as well as circumstantial evidence and other relevant factors the court might consider important. It would be possible perhaps to combine the Qur'anic directives on repentance with the notion of fixed penalties, or a range of quantified penalties, while considering *ḥudūd* as the uppermost limits. It would be difficult, however, to integrate into this approach the notion of both fixed and mandatory sentences that are totally closed to the attendant conditions and circumstances of individual offenders and the society at large.

Ḥudūd *in the Sunnah*

This section explores several aspects of the hadith on *ḥudūd*, one of which is the occurrence or otherwise of the expressions *ḥadd* and *ḥudūd* therein. Here one notes in many hadith statements that the Prophet has used *ḥadd* and *ḥudūd* in reference to both specific crimes as well as punishments. But it seems that they have been used in reference to all punishments and not just a particular number or type of punishment. Whereas our foregoing review of the Qur'an verses has shown that the technical usage of *ḥudūd* in the sense of punishable crimes does not originate in the Qur'an, the information in the hadith is mixed, thus signifying both the technical and generic usages of *ḥadd* and *ḥudūd* in the sense of violation of the limits of acceptable behavior as well as crimes and punishments. The evidence reviewed in the following paragraphs occurs on five separate yet interrelated themes: (1) The Prophet himself has spoken about *ḥadd* and *ḥudūd* in a generic sense of transgressing the limits as well as its two other senses—crime and punishment, respectively. It remains uncertain, however, whether he has used these terms in the technical sense of fixed and unchangeable punishments that the fiqh scholars have used later. (2) The Prophet has stressed strict and impartial observance of the rule of law in relationship to penalties. (3) The Prophet has proscribed intercession *(shafāʿah)* concerning penalties. (4) The Prophet has also advised concealment of the nakedness of others *(satr al-ʿawrat)* including instances of *ḥudūd*. And (5) the Prophet has denounced broadcasting of evil conduct *(jahr bi'l-maʿāṣī)* including the *ḥudūd*.

Exploring these various aspects of the hadith literature relating to *ḥudūd* will serve to show that a degree of diversity is present in the language of hadith on *ḥudūd*. One does not, in other words, see the kind of predominantly punitive stress and lack of flexibility in the language of the hadith, as one later finds developing in the juristic doctrine of the leading schools on *ḥudūd*. The hadith speaks of stricture as well as forgiveness, of combining moral advice with legal concerns, and of giving credit to the good deeds of people suspected of *ḥudūd*—with tangible results in the way they should expect to be treated. The Prophet has tried, whenever he noted signs of remorse on the part of the culprit, to turn a blind eye to instances of *ḥudūd* and even persuaded guilty persons to retract their confessions in a quest to exonerate them.

In a hadith recorded by al-Bukhārī, *ḥadd* has been used in the sense of a punishable offence. Abī Talhah has reported from the Companion, Anas b. Mālik:

> While I was with the Prophet, a man came and said, "O God's Messenger! I have committed a legally punishable act (*aṣabtu ḥaddan*), please apply the punishment on me." The Prophet did not ask him what he had done. Then the time for prayer fell due and the man offered prayer alongside the Prophet. When the Prophet finished the prayer, the man got up and said, "O God's Messenger! I have committed a punishable act; please inflict [the punishment] on me according to the Book of God." The Prophet said, "Have you not prayed with us?" He said, "Yes." The Prophet then said, "God has forgiven your sin" or said "your *ḥadd*—[reporter unsure]."[30]
>
> عن أنس بن مالك رضي الله عنه قال : كنت عند النبي (ص) فجاءه رجل فقال :يا رسول الله إني أصبت حدأ فأقمه على قال ولم يسأل عنه قال وحضرت الصلاة فصلى مع النبي (ص) فلما قضى النبي (ص) قام إليه الرجل فقال يا رسول الله إني أصبت حدأ فأقم في كتاب الله قال اليس صليت معنا ؟ قال نعم قال إن الله قد غفر لك ذنبك, أو قال حدك.

The Prophet's response in this case was in typical conformity with the Qur'an, which advised, for instance, with reference to admitting repentance even from unbelievers: "But if they repent and keep up prayer and pay the zakah, leave their way free. Surely God is Forgiving, Merciful" (al-Tawbah, 9:5).

And a few passages later in the same chapter of the Qur'an, one reads on a broader note.

> But if they repent and keep up prayer and pay the zakah, they are your brethren in faith. Thus do We explain the signs in detail for those who understand. (al-Tawbah, 9:11)
>
> فَإِن تَابُوا وَأَقَامُوا الصَّلَاةَ وَآتَوُا الزَّكَاةَ فَإِخْوَانُكُمْ فِي الدِّينِ ۗ وَنُفَصِّلُ الْآيَاتِ لِقَوْمٍ يَعْلَمُونَ.

When the man said twice, "I have fallen into an *ḥadd-aṣabtu ḥaddan*," it is likely that by *ḥadd* he meant a Qur'anic offence, which was, however, not specified. But in the succeeding phrase, "then apply it (i.e., the *ḥadd*) on me (*fa-aqīmhu ʿalayya*)," it seems that the reference is to the punishment. This is further confirmed in the repeated plea when the man said to "apply on me [the punishment] according to the Book of God." All that this hadith tells us regarding the usage of *ḥadd* is that it was used on this occasion in both senses of an offence and a punishment. The man probably knew what it was but neither he nor the Prophet spelled it out, apparently due to the Prophet's desire not to expose the conduct in question. This leaves an element of ambiguity in the hadith in that it remained unclear as to what the guilty man had actually done. Al-Nawawī has said in his commentary of *Ṣaḥīḥ Muslim*, who recorded this hadith, that the transgression involved was a minor one that called for an unspecified *taʿzīr*, which is why it was exonerated by the prayer (*ṣalāh*) that followed. Had it been an *ḥadd* crime, it would not be omittable by *ṣalāh*. Qāḍī ʿIyāḍ has commented that the meaning of the *ḥadd* in question remained unclear, and the Prophet did not enquire into it as he practiced "concealment" (*satr*) and did not want to expose it.[31]

In a similar hadith reported on the authority of Wāthilah b. al-Asqaʿ, Wāthilah said:

> I saw the Messenger of God, pbuh, and was with him one day when a man came to him saying, "O God's Messenger! I have committed an *ḥadd* of God's prohibited *ḥudūd*. The Prophet turned away from him. Then he turned to him again, and the Prophet turned away from him, then he said the same to the Prophet a third time, and again he turned away from him. Then it was time for prayer. When the prayer ended, the man told the Prophet a fourth time that he had committed a *ḥadd* of the *ḥudūd* God had prohibited, so apply to me God's (ordained) punishment. The Prophet then said to him: "Did you not do your ablution (*wuḍūʾ*) well—for you prayed with us just now! Go away, that is your expiation (*kaffārah*)."[32]

شهدت رسول الله صلى الله عليه وسلم ذات يوم وأتاه رجل فقال : يا رسول الله ، إني أصبت حدا من حدود الله تعالى ، فأعرض عنه ، ثم أتاه الثانية فأعرض عنه ثم قالها الثالثة فأعرض عنه ، ثم أقيمت الصلاة ، فلما قضى الصلاة أتى الرابعة ، فقال : أصبت حدا من حدود الله فأقم في حد الله قال : ألم تحسن الطهور - أو الوضوء - ثم شهدت الصلاة معنا آنفا ؟ اذهب فهي كفارتك.

What is of interest here is that the Prophet did not pursue the matter and declared that God had forgiven "the *ḥadd*" in question—on at least two reported occasions. Here the word *ḥaddak* (your punishment) is probably used interchangeably with *dhanbak* (your sin). As it is, this hadith does not support the idea that, as a Right of God, *ḥadd* is unpardonable nor that it is absolutely mandatory.

In another hadith, which is recorded in *Ṣaḥīḥ Muslim, ḥadd* occurs in the sense only of crime rather than punishment. Abī Burdah al-Anṣārī reported, in an agreed-upon hadith, that he heard the Prophet saying:

> No one shall be flogged above ten lashes unless it be for a *ḥadd* among the *ḥudūd Allāh.*[33]

عَنْ أبي بُرْدَةَ ٱلْأ نصَاريّ - رضى الله عنه - أنَّهُ سَمِعَ رَسُولَ ٱللهِ - صلى الله عليه وسلم -يَقُولُ " لَا يُجْلَدُ فَوقَ
عَشَرَةِ أسوَاطٍ, إلَّا فِي حَدّ مِنْ حُدُودِ ٱللهِ" مُتَّفَقٌ عَلَيهِ

Ḥadd in this hadith is most likely used in the sense of a crime, which is also likely to be inclusive of *ḥudūd* crimes that are expounded in the Qur'an.

In yet another hadith, which Abū Yūsuf (d. 182/798) has recorded in his *Kitāb al-Kharāj*, the Prophet has authorised suspension of the *ḥudūd* in cases of uncertainty and doubt. Abū Yūsuf has discussed the hadith in some detail and said that a number of Companions have reported it. Al-Tirmidhī, al-Bayhaqī, al-Suyūṭī, and al-Tabrīzī have also recorded the same hadith, which is as follows:

> ʿĀʾishah reported that the Prophet, pbuh, said: "Avoid condemning the Muslims to *ḥudūd* whenever you can, in all instances of doubt, and when you can find a way out for a Muslim, then clear his way. If the Imam errs, it is better that he errs on the side of forgiveness than on the side of punishment."[34]

عن عائشة رضي الله عنها عن النبي (ص) إدر أوا الحدود بالشبهات من المسلمين ما استطعتم فإن كان له
مخرجاً فخلوا سبيله فإن الإمام أن يخطئ في العفو خير من أن يخطئ في العقوبة .

Abū Yūsuf has also recorded, on the same page, a slightly shorter version of the same hadith where he stated that a number of Companions and Followers have reported it. The shorter version reads:

> Drop the *ḥudūd* in cases of doubt as far as you can. For it is better to err in forgiveness then making an error in punishment.
>
> إدرأوا ا لحدو د بالشبهات ما استطعتم والخطأ في العفو خير من الخطأ في العقوبة .

This shorter version is broader in scope as it omits the reference to Muslims, thereby making it clear that the message contained in it is meant to be for all people. Abū Yūsuf has also stated that the Prophet consistently discouraged people from accusing each other of conduct that carried a prescribed punishment. *Ḥudūd* in this text can be a reference to prescribed punishments by that name or indeed to any punishment. It is common knowledge that on numerous occasions and whenever a person confessed to an *ḥudūd* offence the Prophet tried to persuade him or her to retract his or her confession and has in this way shown a consistent disinclination toward the imposition of penalties. While elaborating on this, Abū Yūsuf has recorded a statement of the second caliph ʿUmar b. al-Khaṭṭāb: "I prefer to suspend rather than implement the *ḥudūd* in cases of doubt."[35] A separate section in the following discussion advances a perspective on the subject of doubt in the context of *ḥudūd,* but first a few words may be said on intercession.

The most renowned case of intercession (*shafāʿah*) that hadith scholars have recorded is that of Fāṭimah bt. al-Aswad b. ʿAbd al-Asad, better known as al-Makhzumiyyah, as earlier mentioned, of Quraysh nobility, who had committed theft. Quraysh tribal leaders were dubious as to who could intercede on her behalf knowing that the Prophet did not encourage intercession in religious offences. They decided to ask Usāmah b. Zayd, who was very close to the Prophet; they thought he might be able to persuade the Prophet to pardon al-Makhzumiyyah. However, Usāmah's intercession angered the Prophet, who told him, "O Usāmah, are you interceding regarding a punishment ordained by God?" It also turned out that Usāmah, who was a teenager at the time, had actually acted on something he did not know much about, especially with reference to the limits of intercession. The Prophet did not stop there but convened a congregation to address them with his famous statement as follows:

> Abū 'l-Walīd reported to us from al-Layth, from Ibn Shihāb, from ʿUrwah, from ʿĀʾishah, that Usāmah spoke to the Prophet concerning a woman, the Prophet, pbuh, said: "People before you perished because they would inflict the legal punishment (*ḥadd*) on the

> poor and let the rich go free. By Him in whose hand my soul rests! If Fāṭimah, Muḥammad's daughter, committed theft, I would cut off her hand."[36]
>
> حَدَّثَنَا أَبُو الْوَلِيدِ، حَدَّثَنَا اللَّيْثُ، عَنِ ابْنِ شِهَابٍ، عَنْ عُرْوَةَ، عَنْ عَائِشَةَ، أَنَّ أُسَامَةَ، كَلَّمَ النَّبِيَّ صلى الله عليه وسلم إِنَّمَا هَلَكَ مَنْ كَانَ قَبْلَكُمْ أَنَّهُمْ كَانُوا يُقِيمُونَ الْحَدَّ عَلَى الْوَضِيعِ، وَيَتْرُكُونَ الشَّرِيفَ، فَقَالَ وَالَّذِي نَفْسِي بِيَدِهِ لَوْ فَاطِمَةُ فَعَلَتْ ذَلِكَ لَقَطَعْتُ يَدَهَا.

Al-Bukhārī, who recorded this hadith, elaborated: when Usamah saw the Prophet's anger over his intercession, he apologised profusely, saying that he was mistaken. The woman was duly punished, and she used to come to the Prophet for guidance. The reference to "people before you" in the hadith is to Jews who used to punish the weak but were lenient on the rich and powerful. This incident, it is further added, occurred on the day of the conquest of Mecca (in the eighth year of the Hijrah). It then became firmly established that intercession was not permitted in crimes after they had been reported to the authorities, nor were authorities themselves permitted to accept intercession or to grant a pardon on its basis. But intercession to government authorities was allowed in private/civil litigation outside the sphere of crimes and penalties. This is known as "benevolent intercession" (*shafāʿah ḥasanah*), which was approved of in the Qur'an as in the following verse: "Whoever recommends/intercedes and helps a good cause becomes a partner therein. And whoever recommends and helps an evil cause, shares in its burden. And God has power over all things" (al-Nisāʾ, 4:85).

> مَّن يَشْفَعْ شَفَٰعَةً حَسَنَةً يَكُن لَّهُۥ نَصِيبٌ مِّنْهَا ۖ وَمَن يَشْفَعْ شَفَٰعَةً سَيِّئَةً يَكُن لَّهُۥ كِفْلٌ مِّنْهَا ۗ وَكَانَ ٱللَّهُ عَلَىٰ كُلِّ شَىْءٍ مُّقِيتًا.

Other hadith reports recorded in the main collections also confirm that the Prophet encouraged intercession in good causes, and those who did so were commended for it. Intercession in crimes and punishments was also allowed, but only prior to reporting to the authorities.[37]

It seems that by referring to "people before you" and how they handled crimes, the Prophet did not refer to the Qur'anic punishments or any particular type of Islamic punishment for that matter—as the reference was to the Jewish people. The text of this hadith is definite on the point that *ḥadd* in the hadith quoted above was used interchangeably with punishment in reference to people to whom the Qur'an did not apply. What the hadith tells us is that there must be no discrimination in the enforcement of legal punishments, and the Prophet spoke emphatically that the law will apply with a total sense of objectivity, thereby marking a complete departure from the discriminatory practices of the past.

Another aspect of the hadith on intercession is the recurrent advice therein that people should not show eagerness in the reporting of offences to authorities but try to gracefully conceal and turn a blind eye to them. But even when an offence is reported, the judge may not impose any punishment unless there is clear proof by way of confession or impartial witnesses. According to a hadith on the authority of ʿAbd Allāh b. ʿAbbās, the Prophet had said the following concerning a woman of ill-repute: "If I were to stone anyone without proof, I would have stoned so and so (*fulānah*), for doubts surrounded her and her condition, and those who visited her."

لَوْ كُنْتُ رَاجِمًا أَحَدًا بِغَيْرِ بَيِّنَةٍ لَرَجَمْتُ فُلَانَةً فَقَدْ ظَهَرَ فِيهَا الرِّيبَةُ فِي مَنْطِقِهَا وَهَيْئَتِهَا وَمَنْ يَدْخُلُ عَلَيْهَا.

This hadith is recorded by Ibn Majah, where it is clarified that "doubt surrounded her" meant her reputation for lewdness, and the person referred to was the wife of Hilal b. Umayyah. The latter is known to have cursed his wife. The advice of restraint in this hadith (that one must have proof before one acts) is not only addressed to the general public but also to law enforcement authorities and judges who should themselves observe the rule of law and shariah, just as the Prophet did himself, concerning the enforcement of penalties.

According to yet another hadith on the subject of concealment (*satr*), "One who conceals the nakedness of a believer, God will conceal his nakedness in this world and the hereafter."[38]

من ستر مسلما ستره الله في الدنيا والآخرة.

Several other hadith reports are found on "concealment of the nakedness of others" (*satr al-ʿawrat*), and their collective message concurs on the point of making *satr al-ʿawrat* an entrenched aspect of the ethos of Islam firmly grounded in the Qur'an and Sunnah.[39] To quote the Qur'an:

> Those who love to see scandal broadcast among the believers, will have a grievous penalty in this life and in the hereafter. God knows and you know not. (al-Nūr, 24:19)

إِنَّ ٱلَّذِينَ يُحِبُّونَ أَن تَشِيعَ ٱلْفَـٰحِشَةُ فِى ٱلَّذِينَ ءَامَنُوا۟ لَهُمْ عَذَابٌ أَلِيمٌ فِى ٱلدُّنْيَا وَٱلْـَٔاخِرَةِ ۚ وَٱللَّهُ يَعْلَمُ وَأَنتُمْ لَا تَعْلَمُونَ

The substance of this message extends to all sins and crimes, including *ḥudūd*, which is that they should neither be broadcast nor eagerly and hurriedly reported to the authorities. The Muslim community is thus expected to exercise restraint in exposing the weaknesses of those who have fallen into error. The offender himself is similarly advised to avoid broadcasting his evildoing. This is the subject of "broadcaster of evil" (*mujāhir bi'l-maʿāṣī*), an allied theme of *satr al-ʿawrat*, which also features prominently in the sources. The Qur'an thus denounces those who speak openly about their sinful conduct (al-Nisāʾ, 148). Those who broadcast something they might have done away from the public eye, in conditions of privacy, but then publicise it and speak openly about it clearly do something that should be avoided. People are similarly instructed in the explicit language of a hadith to be assiduous in making concealment (*satr*) a part of their ethical outlook and conduct in social relations:

> O People! You must now end violating God's limits (*ḥudūd Allāh*), and forsake these detestable acts (*al-qādhūrāt*). But one who commits them, let him be shielded by God's protective cover. For otherwise, when the matter becomes known to us, we shall implement the Book of God on its perpetrator.
>
> يأيها الناس قد آن لكم أن تنتهوا عن حدود الله، من أصاب شيئاً من هذه القاذورات فليستتر بستر الله، فإنه من يبد لنا صفحته نقم عليه كتاب الله تعالى.

Al-Jazīrī, who quoted this hadith, follows it with this observation: The more openly that criminality and evil are talked about in a society, the more it is likely to mar the moral fabric of that society. For the perpetrator has evidently lost the sense of modesty and restraint that would otherwise deter him from talking openly about it. He does so before God's illustrious presence showing little regard for His limits as well as belittling the moral vision of the society. By doing so the evildoer is effectively inciting others to do what he has done. In another hadith, the Prophet has reportedly said: "All of my Ummah is exonerated except the broadcasters of evil [كل أمتي معافى إلا المجاهرين]". *Mujāharah* (broadcasting) is when a person does something evil at night, then wakes up the next day and announces openly that which God had shielded in His protective grace. People of moral probity who are modest would be inclined, on the contrary, to be remorseful and try to abandon the evil they might have fallen into and conceal it.[40]

A question arose with regard to a witness who sees a crime happening before his eyes—whether he should report it or keep quiet about it. In a conversation between two leading Companions, Abū Ayyūb al-Anṣarī and ʿUqbah b. Amīr, the governor of Egypt, it transpired that the witness had the option as to whether to exercise the recommended concealment (*satr*) or to expose and report the incident.[41] It seems that concealment is advised unless the witness is called upon to testify, but the matter would much depend on the nature of the conduct in question. If it is something that is particularly damaging to the general public or committed in an outrageously indecent or oppressive manner, it may be no longer be optional for the witness to conceal. The moral advice of recommended silence is also extended to a physician who knows for a fact that a man is infertile and yet his wife has become pregnant. It is not advisable for him to declare that the wife had become pregnant due to adultery. He may even run the risk of being charged with slander if he declares the matter and fails to prove his claim by four witnesses. Similarly, if the physician knows of a woman who disposes of her illicit infant in a certain way, he is not under obligation to declare it, lest it become a means of greater harm to the woman and her family. However, if the physician knows that his patient is afflicted with a contagious disease, he is duty-bound to declare this in order to prevent harm to others before it happens.[42]

Ḥadd *(Limit) and* Ḥaqq *(Right)* in *the Juristic Expositions of Fiqh*

Juristic developments concerning Islamic criminal law and the *ḥudūd* punishments of concern to us can be seen in two areas: one is a move away from the Qur'anic references to repentance and reform; and the other is development of a discourse on the binary division of rights into the Right of God and Right of Man (*ḥaqq Allāh* and *ḥaqq al-ādamī*), respectively. The first of these has already been expounded in the discussion of repentance in the previous sections. That analysis will be kept in mind, but the focus here is on the second theme and how it has impacted and narrowed down the concept of *ḥudūd*. An attempt is then made to recapture the original Qur'anic conception of *ḥudūd* as God's limits in the Qur'an.

Muslim jurists have defined *ḥadd* as a fixed/quantified punishment (*ʿuqūbah muqaddarah*) imposed for violation of the Rights of God.[43] By defining *ḥadd* as a fixed punishment, it is meant that the punishment is invariably specified and fixed but also not fixed in the sense of fixing minimum and maximum limits for it. The main purpose of laying down a fixed punishment of this kind is to ensure that no one—whether the victim, the judge, or head of state—has any authority to increase or decrease the punishment.

The designation of *ḥadd* in the juristic doctrine of fiqh as the Right of God, in contradistinction with the Right of Man, also meant that the victim or his family may not pardon, reduce, or adjust the punishment. This is unlike *qiṣāṣ* (retaliation) and *diya* (blood money), which are classified as Rights of Man and allow the victim or his legal heirs to reduce, adjust, and even grant a pardon concerning them. The Right of God here signifies a right that belongs to the community and has a bearing on its vital interests, security, and welfare. If anyone grants a pardon or concession over *ḥudūd* they are ultra vires.

This is in contradistinction with the *taʿzīr* punishment in which state authorities and judges are entitled to exercise discretion in determining the quantum of punishment. Protecting the vital interests of the community, one may add, is the basic objective of all punishment, including *ḥudūd, qiṣāṣ, diya,* and *taʿzīr*. Yet while this is generally acknowledged, it is implied that, compared to *ḥudūd,* punishing offences in these other categories are not seen as crucial for protecting the basic fabric of society. Yet they relate more closely to the rights and interests of individuals than that of the community as a whole, even though it is acknowledged that the two categories of rights and interests can hardly be totally separate from one another.[44]

It is of interest to recount here how ʿAbd al-Qādir ʿAwdah (d. 1373/1954), author of a renowned two-volume textbook on Islamic criminal law, reiterates the conventional fiqh doctrine and some of the questionable premises on which it is based. ʿAwdah thus wrote that theft, drinking (*shurb*), highway robbery, rebellion, *zinā,* and apostasy pose a greater threat to society than the pain and grief they might inflict on their victims. A victim of theft may lose his property but his grief is relatively light compared with the terror and insecurity inflicted on his neighbours and fellow citizens. As for crimes such as "murder and injury, they affect the individuals more than the society and these are to some extent personal crimes in the sense that their perpetrators do not face everyone they meet with violence but confine their aggression to a particular individual." ʿAwdah continues: "If the criminal cannot reach his victim, he does not go on attacking others. Even when the aggression does take place, it does not shake the community nor does it have a serious impact on its security." To quote ʿAwdah:

> When the thief, for example, strikes in pursuit of material gain, he may steal from anyone; if he does not get what he wants from one victim, he goes after another, without necessarily aiming at a particular individual. For what the thief is after is property in the hands of all individuals. This is also true of *zinā*, for the perpetrator of *zinā* is not after a particular woman as such but any woman, and if he cannot reach one woman he will search for others.[45]

The passage quoted here is part of the basic argument often seen in the fiqh manuals advanced for the purpose of distinguishing the *ḥudūd* crimes as a separate category and labelling them as exclusive manifestations of the Right of God. The rationale cited here does not really bear out and would, in any case, seem to have lost much of its force in contemporary times. For it is grounded in the questionable assertion that killing and bodily injury represent a lesser threat to society than such other crimes as theft, adultery, and slander.

Ḥadd in the fiqh manuals is described as a crime that violates the Right of God, the limits He has laid down, and the punishment He has specified. Abū Zahrah (d. 1974) explains this by giving examples of *zinā* and *qadhf*: These are offences that violate the vital interests of the community, that is, protecting the family and the purity of lineage within it, in the case of *zinā*, and the good name and reputation of its law-abiding citizens—in the case of *qadhf*. Both of these offences, on the other hand, have aspects that also involve the personal rights and interests of individuals, or the Right of Man, but these are relatively less significant compared to the threat they pose to law and order in the community. One might even be persuaded to think, Abū Zahrah continues, that *zinā* does not necessarily involve violation of personal rights of individuals, especially when it occurs between two unmarried persons. This line of analysis is extended, mutatis mutandis, to other *ḥudūd* crimes in support of the argument that they all consist, first and foremost, of violation of the community's rights.[46]

If there is a force in this argument, then it is submitted that it is not unique to *zinā* nor to *ḥudūd* as such but that it relates, in varying degrees of course, to all crimes within or outside *ḥudūd*. Any crime, it may be said, is likely to threaten the rights and interests of both the community and its members. Then to put them under two separate categories as such is a speculative exercise.

When one looks at the *ḥudūd* punishments as a separate category of punishments in contradistinction with *qiṣāṣ*, one is reminded of the conditions that prevailed in the tribalist environment of Arabia at the advent of Islam. The manner in which *qiṣāṣ* was practiced and implemented often meant that personal vendettas and a tribalist urge for revenge transgressed the essence of just retaliation. The Qur'anic reform of *qiṣāṣ* laid emphasis on the objectivity of justice and maintenance of law and order independently of tribalist and sectarian interests. The *ḥudūd* punishments would appear to have also served this purpose in that, in regards to a certain number of crimes, they took the law out of the scope of tribal justice to clearly convey a message that these crimes were not open to negotiation. But when one considers that the course of history has altered the picture—and massive changes have taken place as a result of such developments as urbanisation, communications, and modern methods of government—one finds that the basic rationale of the early distinctions has been substantially eroded.

While criminality poses a serious threat to the fabric of society and civilisation, there is no compelling argument to confine this only to a handful of specified or unspecified crimes. The changing conditions of society have never ceased to generate new problems, new opportunities for crime, and unprecedented varieties of criminal behaviour, which are often no less of a threat to the basic fabric of society and its values than *ḥudūd* crimes. Would it not be right, one might ask, to classify irresponsible dumping of industrial waste and radioactive pollutants, international drug trafficking, and human trafficking as violations of the Right of God and the vital interests of the community! These may even be seen as far more serious than perhaps some of the *ḥudūd* offences such as drinking and slander.

The basic distinction between the Right of God and the Right of Man is often determined based on a preponderance of the respective interests of the individual and those of the community. Assigning a particular interest or right to one or the other of these is often a matter of juristic opinion, and it is open to subsequent revision and adjustment, perhaps in line with the realities of social change. Even the specific definitions of *ḥudūd* and its varieties, it may be said, are based on juristic opinion. It is known, of course, that the Qur'an has determined specific punishments for certain offences. But thus defining *ḥudūd* crimes and relating them to the Right of God and Right of Man has consequences that ensue from these formulations are instances of juristic construction. They might have served a good purpose at one time, but the Muslim community and its scholars should be free to make further adjustments in line with the prevailing needs and conditions of their own society and generation—as they are not determined by the scripture.

In an essentialist sense, all rights in Islam, as the Mālikī jurist al-Qarāfī (d. 684/1285) has rightly pointed out, consist primarily of the Rights of God, which are in turn exercised and represented by the community of believers and their lawful government.[47] One may conclude therefore that all crimes consist of violations of the limits of God, the *ḥudūd Allah,* and that the community and its leadership are within their rights to take all necessary measures to defend their common interests against criminality and violence without the need to draw hard and fast divisions between God's rights and man's rights as such. One may also add that there remains no urgent need for distinguishing the Rights of God from the Right of Man, nor of *ḥudūd* crimes on this basis alone from other offences that are equally if not more threatening to public security and interest. It would seem difficult also to extend this binary distinction with a degree of accuracy to new crimes such as human trafficking, hijacking of passenger airlines, and Mafia-like crime syndicates that kidnap people and terrorise communities.

A certain degree of confusion in the juristic understanding of *ḥudūd* has thus been caused by linking this concept with that of *ḥaqq Allāh.* From very early times, probably the mid- or late second century Hijrah/eighth century CE, juristic doctrine had clearly identified *ḥadd* as a Right of God in contradistinction with *qiṣāṣ,* which was a Right of Man.[48] It seems that juristic thought along these lines was influenced by the attempt to draw a parallel between the two notably similar ideas of *ḥudūd Allāh* and *ḥuqūq Allāh.*The former was present in the text and the latter is a juristic rejoinder. It then seemed just another step along that path, even more questionable perhaps, to identify *qiṣāṣ* as the Right of Man in contradistinction with *ḥudūd.* To say that *ḥudūd* are God's limits is accurate, but to say that they are God's rights is not. *Ḥadd* and *ḥaqq* are two different concepts and it is proposed here that they be retained as such. Although the claim of the victim or his legal heirs to seek just retaliation (*qiṣāṣ*) was confirmed in the Qur'an, it seemed doubtful whether this could be taken to justify the bipolarity of rights that marked the juristic approach to the classification of crimes on that basis.

One can naturally understand the difference between a civil or a private claim and a crime, which is a public rights issue and is not open to the same influences as a civil claim. But the division between God's Right and Man's Right is not as clear-cut as that, simply because rights and obligations in Islam, whether public or private, are rooted in the structure of values determined in the textual specifications of the Qur'an and hadith. The bipolarity of rights in juristic thought seemed decidedly at odds with the all-embracing, unitarian, and integrationist influence of *tawḥīd,* the idea that all rights take their origin from the same source. Hence any duality that is depicted in the basic scheme of rights could not have been devoid of a measure of speculation. Once the fiqh scholars had placed the *ḥudūd* and *qiṣāṣ* respectively under the Right of God and Right of Man categories, the need was evident for an intermediate category that could subsume the offences that were not covered by either. The new category of *ta'zīr* was introduced to cover every other offence that did not fall under either *ḥudūd* or *qiṣāṣ*.

Although juristic doctrine had initially little difficulty in classifying *ḥudūd* under the *ḥaqq Allāh* and *qiṣāṣ* under *ḥaqq al-ādamī,* the relationship of *ta'zīr* with one or the other of these was not immediately clear. To identify *qiṣāṣ* as a violation purely of the latter was evidently controversial. For it made little sense to classify murder as a violation only or even predominantly of the Right of Man and theft as a violation only of the Right of God—as if property carried greater value than human life! Furthermore, to classify murder as the Right of Man seemed totally oblivious of the clear text of the Qur'an, which declared killing another human being a crime against the whole of humanity:

> Whoever slew a person, unless it be for murder or for spreading mischief in the land, it would be as if he slew the whole of humankind, and if any one saved a life, it would as if he saved the life of the whole of humankind. (al-Mā'idah, 5:35)
>
> مَن قَتَلَ نَفْسًا بِغَيْرِ نَفْسٍ أَوْ فَسَادٍ فِي الْأَرْضِ فَكَأَنَّمَا قَتَلَ النَّاسَ جَمِيعًا وَمَنْ أَحْيَاهَا فَكَأَنَّمَا أَحْيَا النَّاسَ جَمِيعًا.

Fiqh manual writers somehow thought it always important to identify the Rights of God and Rights of Man content of all crimes, because it was on this basis, as they thought, that the sentencing policy of the judges must be determined. Questions as to whether or not an offence was pardonable and whether the judge or head of state could exercise discretion in the determination of punishment—and whether the wishes of the victim and his personal conditions carried any weight in determining the fate of the accused and so on—were determined by ascertaining the relationship of the offence type or category with the Right of God and Right of Man respectively.

A basic confusion had already set in regarding the understanding of the Qur'anic concept of *ḥudūd Allāh* as a reference exclusively to fixed punishments. Yes, the Qur'an did provide quantified punishments for a small number of offences, but it was most likely not the Qur'an's intention to confine the *ḥudūd Allāh* to these offences nor to suggest *ḥudūd* as an offence category in contradistinction with *qiṣāṣ* nor indeed with offences that were later labelled as *taʿzīr*. There was no reason why the limits of God (*ḥudūd Allāh*) should not have retained its general meaning as a basic philosophy of punishment that was reflective of the broader understanding of the Qur'anic outlook. To say that *ḥadd* is an offence that is not open to adjustment, repentance, or pardon after it is reported to the authorities, thereby closing the door on the whole idea of repentance, rehabilitation, and reform in the face of clear Qur'anic references to these, marked the beginning of a basic imbalance. Yet juristic thought hardly looked back to amend and rectify these in line with subsequent developments. If the Prophet had issued certain instructions that specified a number of crimes to be prosecuted once brought to his attention, this too was most likely intended to emphasise the rule of law vis-a-vis the all-too-pervasive tribal power than to establish rigidities of the kind that juristic thought stipulated over the course of time.

Another instance of inconsistency in the juristic formulation of *ḥudūd* was that *ḥadd*, by definition, referred to an offence for which the Qur'an or Sunnah prescribed a quantified punishment, yet in the face of this definition liquor drinking (*shurb*) and, according to some, even mutiny (*bagha* or *bugha*) were still classified as *ḥudūd* offences despite the fact that neither the Qur'an nor the Sunnah had prescribed or quantified a punishment for them.

It is a questionable approach to also see that the three-tiered division of crimes into *ḥudūd, qiṣāṣ,* and *taʿzīr* originated in the assumption that if crimes were defined by the punishment they carried it would really be putting the cart before the horse. Crime should naturally be defined by reference to the nature of the conduct, its moral enormity, and the suffering or harm it inflicts on its victim and society, and only then should a punishment be determined for it and not vice versa. For the punishment-based approach puts one at a loss with regard to a new crime that may have no known punishment. The fiqh manual writers seem to have started from a position of distinguishing *ḥudūd* and *qiṣāṣ* by reference to such criteria as to whether or not the punishment was fixed or variable, who had the right to grant a pardon and forgive, and what sort of violation did they represent, of the Right of God or the Right of Man—all refer more to consequences and classifications rather than the nature of conduct. The punishment-based approach also fails to respond to findings such as that punishment severity is not necessarily linked to reduction in crime rates. One also notes that a heavily punitive approach would not offer the best option to accommodate the balance of influences that one detects in the Qur'an. There is admittedly no comprehensive data available about the effectiveness of *ḥudūd* in combating crime as most of the Muslim countries surveyed here do not apply *ḥudūd* consistently enough to provide a reliable basis for analysis. Criminality in the modern urban/industrial environment relates to a variety of new factors that may not have existed in traditional societies. Issues need to be seen in their proper settings, and suitable philosophical approaches to punishment should be taken to meet the more complex set of conditions associated with criminality in changing times.

The Qur'an offers a set of guidelines for a more comprehensive theory of punishment, which is inclusive of retribution, rehabilitation, and reform, and also that punishment must be commensurate to the suffering inflicted. Crime is strictly seen as an individual matter (e.g., al-Anʿām, 6:164), yet patience and forgiveness are recommended on the part of both the victim and the judge. Punishment severity and firmness in its application is always to be moderated by the demand for justice and fairness (*al-ʿadl wa'l-iḥsān*—Q. al-Naḥl, 16:90). The basic policy on punishment is thus stated in such terms as the following; "And if you decide to punish, then punish with the like of that with which you were afflicted. But if you show patience, that is indeed the best [course] for those who remain patient" (al-Naḥl, 16:126; al-Baqarah, 2:194).

وَإِنْ عَاقَبْتُمْ فَعَاقِبُوا بِمِثْلِ مَا عُوقِبْتُم بِهِ ۖ وَلَئِن صَبَرْتُمْ لَهُوَ خَيْرٌ لِّلصَّابِرِينَ.

The basic message of this text is general and need not be confined to the context only of *qiṣāṣ*. The verse evidently discourages eagerness in the application of all punishment. Patience (*ṣabr*) can either mean a reflective pause that delays hasty conclusions or abstaining from rash decisions so as to allow time for reflection and the possibility of repentance and pardoning as the case may be. But then when it is said that repentance has no place in *ḥudūd*, one risks going against the clear text of the Qur'an. The substance of the message before us is even more vividly conveyed in another verse, where one reads "and the recompense for an injury is an injury equal to it. But one who forgives and reconciles, his reward is with God, for God loves not the transgressors" (al-Shūrā, 42:40).

وَجَزَاءُ سَيِّئَةٍ سَيِّئَةٌ مِّثْلُهَا ۖ فَمَنْ عَفَا وَأَصْلَحَ فَأَجْرُهُ عَلَى اللَّهِ ۚ إِنَّهُ لَا يُحِبُّ الظَّالِمِينَ.

In contrast with the exclusive emphasis on retribution and deterrence that characterises the juristic doctrine on *ḥudūd*, the Qur'an takes a blended approach to punishment, one that is open to a variety of other influences, such as forgiveness, restraint, mending, and reform, all of which may be necessary for the formulation of a comprehensive penal policy. This is, we believe, a dynamic philosophy and outlook that can relate more meaningfully to contemporary realities than the juristic doctrines of fiqh that have moved in questionable directions.

It may be concluded from the foregoing analysis that this division of rights does not offer a sound basis for distinguishing the *ḥudūd* punishments from other punishments, if only because there is no satisfactory formula as to what are the Rights of Humans and what are the Rights of God and what precisely constitutes the violation of one separately from the other or, indeed, if they can be meaningfully separated as such.

From his own enquiry into the theory of *ḥudūd* punishments, Fazlur Rahman has drawn the conclusion that if one were to apply the basic concepts of deterrence, rehabilitation, and reform in the interest of striking a balanced and adequately diversified approach to punishment, one would not only observe the original outlook of the Qur'an on *ḥudūd* but also avoid in the meantime a great deal of inconsistency and confusion that should not have arisen in the first place.[49]

This chapter concludes with a selection of fiqh legal maxims (*qawāʿid kulliyyah fiqhiyyah*) relating to punishments and some of the fiqh specifications on *ḥudūd* that underline the basic contours of juristic thought on the subject. Legal maxims are characteristically concise and confined to a declaration of principles. They are often extracted from the more detailed formulations of fiqh on a variety of topics, some general and others more specific. Yet the fiqh maxims are on the whole instructive and educational. They do not bind the judge, yet they play an exceedingly important role in juridical decision-making and *ijtihād*.

Legal Maxims on Ḥudūd

- “When the *ḥudūd* are brought to the attention of ruler or judge, punishment falls due and no intercession is accepted.”[50]
  - إذا رفعت الحدود للإ مام و القاضي فلا شفاعة ووجب الحد.
- “*Ḥudūd* [punishments] are not enforced without the order of the head of state [or his representative].”
  - لا تقام الحدود إلا بأمر الأمام.
- “The Rights of God are predicated in easiness unlike the Rights of Man [which are not].”
  - حقوق الله مبنية على المسامحة بخلاف حقوق الأدميين.
- “The Right of Man is not omitted except by means of pardon or waiver.”
  - حق العبد لايسقط إلا بالعفو والإبراء.
- “A person may exercise indulgence [waive or forgive] in his own rights but not with regard to the rights of others.”
  - يسمح الإنسان في حقوق نفسه وليس له المسامحه في حق غيره.
- “*Ḥudūd* [punishments] are amalgamated prior to enforcement but not thereafter.”
  - يتدخل الحد قبل إقامته لا بعد.
- “Retaliation is indivisible.”
  - القصاص لا يتجزأ.
- “Retaliation is not omitted by way of expiry but there is disagreement concerning the *ḥudūd*.”
  - القصاص لا يسقط بالتقادم وفي الحدود خلاف.
- “When the victim of killing has no heir, the head of state retaliates on his behalf.”
  - من قتل ولا وارث له إقتص له الإمام.
- “When the direct perpetrator and proximate causer are both present, the ruling falls on the direct perpetrator.”
  - إذا اجتمع المباشر و المتسبب يضاف الحكم للمباشر.
- “The norm [of shariah] is freedom from liability.”
  - الأصل براءة الذمة
- “*Ḥudūd* [punishments] are suspended when there is doubt.”
  - الحدود تسقط بالشبهات.
- “One who unknowingly drinks alcohol is not liable either to the *ḥadd* [punishment] or *taʿzīr*.”
  - من شرب خمرا جاهلا به فلا حد ولا تعزير.

- "One who doubts whether he did something or did not, the norm is that he has not done it."
  - من شك هل فعل شيئا أو لا؟ فالأصل أنه لم يفعل.
- "Doubt does not suspend *taʿzīr* punishment, but it does suspend expiation."
  - الشبهة لا تسقط التعزير وتسقط الكفارة.
- "A purpose of the *ḥudūd* is to inflict pain."
  - الحدود المقصود بها الزجر.
- "In what is not amenable to substitution [and divisibility], choosing a part is tantamount to choosing the whole, and omitting a part is also tantamount to omitting the whole."[51]
  - ما لا يقبل التعويض يكون اختيار بعضه كإختيار كله و إسقاط بعضه كإسقاط كله.
- "Prevention is stronger than remedy."[52]
  - الدفع أقوى من الرفع.
- "When two things from one genus coexist and their purpose is not different, the one is amalgamated into the other."[53]
  - إذا إجتمع أمران من جنس واحد, ولم يختلف مقصودهما, دخل احد هما في الأخر.
- "Settlement of litigations and disputes is an obligation."
  - قطع الخصومة والمنازعة واجب.
- "The norm is to prefer the version of one who supports the apparent, and evidence is on the shoulder of one who claims the opposite of that."
  - الأصل أن من ساعده الظاهر فالقول قوله والبينة على من يدعي خلاف الظاهر.
- "The norm is to hear the word of the one who defends his property."
  - الأصل أن يسمع بقول دافع ماله.
- "Enforcement of the prescribed *ḥudūd* is authorised by the head of state."
  - إ قامة الحد للإمام.

IV

Prescribed Ḥudūd *Crimes*

Preliminary Remarks

This brief chapter presents an overview of prescribed *ḥudūd* crimes and punishments as specified in the Qur'an and the issues that will be discussed in subsequent chapters.

The succeeding chapters draw attention to issues many Muslim jurisdictions face in the implementation of *ḥudūd*, especially regarding the manner in which flogging and other prescribed punishments are administered. Another aspect discussed refers to procedural issues over the enforcement of *ḥudūd* and the uncertainty that exists over determining the precise number of *ḥudūd* offences when applying punishments.

The chapter on adultery addresses some of the unresolved issues regarding the distinction of rape from *zinā* that many Muslim countries are experiencing. Other issues to be discussed relate to the juridical distinction between married and unmarried persons (*muḥṣan* and *ghayr muḥṣan*, respectively) and problems that originate in admitting pregnancy as the sole proof of *zinā*.

Muslim jurists have also engaged in lengthy debates over the validity of stoning to death (*rajm*) as the punishment of *zinā*, on which the Qur'an is silent. The chapter presents a review of the scriptural evidence and contributions of twentieth-century Muslim scholars on these issues. The discussion proceeds to examine, in a series of chapters, issues that arise with regard to theft, wine drinking, slanderous accusation, apostasy, and banditry/terrorism.

The discussion in this part of the volume generally takes an issue-oriented approach. Issues are identified and then addressed in light of the data in the sources that are examined. An analysis of the scriptural data is then espoused with reviews of contemporary opinion on the pertinent issues.

The chapter on theft, for example, begins with a review of the Qur'an and hadith, and proceeds with the definition of theft and how the two components of this offence, namely of the Right of God and Right of Man, play out in a modern legal system. Questions also arise over the meaning of "guarded property" (*māl muḥraz*), the actual concept of safeguarding (*ḥirz*), and whether amputation of the left foot for the second offence of theft has convincing shariah validity.

A similar stock-taking applies to the discussion of slanderous accusation (*qadhf*), one of which is whether slander consists of the violation of private rights or public rights, and the chapter provides an overview of the scholastic positions on this issue. Questions are also encountered in determining the position of a non-Muslim in regards to slander/*qadhf* that may in some ways differ from the viewpoint of a Muslim.

Subsequent chapters review issues relating to apostasy (*riddah*) and consumption of liquor (*shurb*). One aspect of the discussion is concerned with the question whether these matters should be considered *ḥudūd* crimes at all and why they were included in the first place. Both of these offences also raise issues over the position of non-Muslims and the basic and wider issue in apostasy over the freedom of religion.

With regard to banditry and terrorism (*ḥirābah*), which is a capital offence, questions arise over the admissibility or otherwise of repentance, whether or not *ḥirābah* can only be committed outside main cities, whether its perpetrators must be armed and able to carry out their crimes, and whether a legitimate government must also exist. Questions have also arisen over the type and sequence of the fourfold punishment the Qur'an has stipulated for *ḥirābah* and conditions that should be present for each of these to apply. The responses to these questions are based on the scriptural evidence, juristic views of the leading schools of law, both Sunni and Shia, and contemporary opinion. Whether the Qur'anic conception of *ḥirābah* can provide effective responses to issues of global terrorism and atrocities committed by groups such as Boko Haram, al-Shabab, al-Qaeda, the Taliban, and ISIS! The chapter concludes with a reminder that the menace of terrorism the world is facing today is not a question entirely of legality. Legal questions need to be considered, of course, but the larger challenges humanity faces arise from the lawless world of adventurist individuals and states, irresponsible drone attacks, and other acts of aggression. The result has been massive loss of life and vast numbers of displaced people and refugees who suffer within their own countries and abroad and who desperately quest for an abode of peace. The scale and intensity of human tragedy witnessed due to these acts of aggression is simply disillusioning.

V

Zinā *(Adultery and Fornication)*

Meaning and Attributes of Zinā

Zinā in shariah is inclusive of fornication (consensual sexual intercourse between unmarried adults) whereas adultery is extramarital sex. *Zinā* is defined as illicit sexual intercourse outside of marriage that involves actual penetration of a man's sexual organ into that of a woman with both knowing that they are prohibited to one another. Initially the Qur'an penalised adultery with imprisonment and detention of the accused women in their houses "until death came to them, or God ordained for them some other way" (al-Nisā', 4:15), provided that the charge was proven by the testimony of four upright witnesses. This was taken to mean a temporary measure awaiting a more definite pronouncement, which subsequently came in sura al-Nūr (24:2), and determined 100 lashes of the whip for both parties as standard Qur'anic punishment for the offence. In both of these two separate verses, the emphasis on repentance and reform is clearly articulated. Later it was claimed that the second of these punishments (of 100 lashes) was abrogated with respect to married persons by the Sunnah of the Prophet, who ordered stoning to death (*rajm*) for a married adulterer. This meant that the Qur'anic 100 lashes remained applicable only to unmarried adulterers. A general consensus (*ijmā'*) was also claimed, although disputed by many, for this instance of abrogation.[1] These issues will presently be examined side by side with such other questions that have also arisen concerning married persons, admissibility or otherwise of pregnancy as proof of adultery, issues over rape, and whether banishment (*tab'īd*) can still be upheld as a supplementary punishment for a convicted adulterer.

In addition to its clear prohibition in the Qur'an and hadith, adultery is labelled as the gravest of Major Sins (*akbar al-kabā'ir*), only lesser than the association of other deities with God (*shirk*) and murder (*qatl*). The Qur'an praises "those who invoke not, with God, any other deity, nor slay life that God has made sacrosanct, except for a just cause, nor commit adultery" (al-Furqān, 25:68).

وَٱلَّذِينَ لَا يَدْعُونَ مَعَ ٱللَّهِ إِلَٰهًا ءَاخَرَ وَلَا يَقْتُلُونَ ٱلنَّفْسَ ٱلَّتِى حَرَّمَ ٱللَّهُ إِلَّا بِٱلْحَقِّ وَلَا يَزْنُونَ ۚ

The verse continues to accentuate the enormity of the three crimes it mentions by painful punishment in the hereafter. But then it is added in the succeeding passage: "Unless the perpetrator repents, believes, and works righteous deeds. Then God will change the evil of such persons into good, and God is forgiving, most merciful" (25:70).

إِلَّا مَن تَابَ وَءَامَنَ وَعَمِلَ عَمَلًا صَٰلِحًا فَأُوْلَٰٓئِكَ يُبَدِّلُ ٱللَّهُ سَيِّـَٔاتِهِمْ حَسَنَٰتٍ ۗ وَكَانَ ٱللَّهُ غَفُورًا رَّحِيمًا.

This combination of repentance and its actual return to a changed life of devotion and righteous work is further emphasised in the same passage: "And whoever repents and does good has truly turned to God with an [acceptable] conversion [or self-emendation]" (25:71).

وَمَن تَابَ وَعَمِلَ صَٰلِحًا فَإِنَّهُۥ يَتُوبُ إِلَى ٱللَّهِ مَتَابًا.

Every step that leads to adultery and brings one closer to it must also be avoided: "Nor come close to adultery; for it is a lascivious deed, and an evil opening the road [to other evils]" (al-Isrā', 17:32).

وَلَا تَقْرَبُوا۟ ٱلزِّنَىٰٓ ۖ إِنَّهُۥ كَانَ فَٰحِشَةً وَسَآءَ سَبِيلًا

In a Bukhārī hadith, it is reported from the prominent Companion, ʿAbd Allāh b. Masʿūd: "I asked the Messenger of God, pbuh: which sin is the gravest in the eyes of God? And he said 'when you associate another deity with God your Creator.' I asked further 'Then what else?' And he said 'to kill your offspring for fear of feeding on your food'; and I said: Then what else? And he said: 'to commit adultery with your neighbour's woman.' "[2]

Based on these and similar other indications in the sources, Muslim jurists have identified certain degrees of gravity for adultery. Thus it is held that adultery committed with a married woman is a heavier transgression than that with an unmarried woman. If the woman happens to be a neighbour, the enormity of adultery intensifies as it also combines disgrace and ill-treatment of one's neighbour, which is a transgression in its own right. Should the neighbour also happen to be a relative, adultery combines both the latter and also incest, thus further intensifying the enormity of the crime. The Prophet has stressed in a hadith: "One whose neighbour is not safe from his evil-doing shall not enter Paradise."[3]

لايدخل الجنة من لا يأمن جاره بوائقه.

The act becomes even more ugly in the event where the neighbour is away for devotional purposes such as the hajj, pursuit of knowledge, and jihad. This is the subject, in particular, of a hadith wherein the Prophet has been quoted to have spoken on the predicament of those who commit the prohibited act.[4] The enormity of adultery is further intensified if it takes place in certain special times and places, such as during the month of Ramadan, in a sacred place like the mosque, or at Friday prayer times.

Proof of Adultery by Witnesses and Confession

Adultery is provable by witnesses and confession and, notwithstanding some reservations, also by pregnancy. As for proof by witnesses, Muslim jurists are in agreement that there must be four male eyewitnesses of probity who have not undergone a *ḥudūd* punishment themselves. The number must be no less than four as per Qur'anic stipulation (al-Nisā', 4:15). This textual specification at four is also the basis of the conclusion that women's testimony is not admitted—and if it were, the number would have to change, which would also mean a departure from the text, although the Shia Imamiyyah accepts testimony of three male and two female witnesses. They must all testify seeing actual penetration of the male organ into the woman's vagina in explicit words clear of all ambiguity and allusive language. Their testimony must also concur on the precise timing and place where and when the intercourse took place (city, town, locality, house, etc.; if in a room, exactly where, such as a corner, middle, direction; also the day of the week, date and time, etc.). Any discrepancy with respect to these details would, according to both the Sunni and Shii laws, vitiate the testimony altogether. The number of four witnesses is peculiar to adultery, as there is no such requirement for any other crime including murder and theft, and the fact that its conditions are also made extremely difficult to obtain is expressive of the Lawgiver's desire for requital and concealment. If all four witnesses testify that they saw the act of adultery but then the woman is found to be a virgin, testimony is vitiated. All four witnesses must testify in one and the same court session before the judge, and in identical terms. In the event of a material discrepancy, they would themselves be liable to the punishment of slander (*qadhf*). Should any of the four witnesses testify in one session and the rest in another, their testimony will not be admissible according to the Ḥanafīs, Mālikīs, and the Shia Imamiyyah. They must all come together to the same court session, although the Shāfiʿī and Ḥanbalī schools do not stipulate this and admit the possibility of them either coming individually to the court session or all together. The Mālikīs have further added that, after their collective testimony before the court, when the witnesses have departed and then each one is asked to recount what they said and they differ from one another, their testimony is nullified and they will themselves become liable to the punishment of slander. Testimony should preferably be fresh without involving a lapse of time that would weaken its reliability. In the event where one (or more) of the witnesses retracts his testimony after having given it, the testimony collapses altogether and no punishment can be imposed. The Ḥanafīs also maintain that testimony in *zinā* collapses with the death or disappearance of one of the witnesses even after it is given any time before sentencing.[5]

Muslim jurists are also in agreement over confession as a proof of adultery based on the Sunnah of the Prophet, who implemented the prescribed punishment on Māʿiz b. Mālik and al-Ghamidiyyah on the basis of their confession. But then by virtue of the same precedent, it is held that confession must be repeated four times, and the Ḥanafīs have further stipulated that the four instances are not at once but in four separate court sessions. The Mālikī and Shāfiʿī schools do not insist on separate sessions. Confession must in all cases be explicit and detailed such that it eliminates all doubt and suspicion of falsehood. For the Prophet is known to have asked Māʿiz in such terms, "Maybe you only kissed, looked at or touched her!" And in another report he has said, "Until your organ penetrated hers completely! And did you know what adultery was [i.e., if it was unlawful]!"[6]

Confession can be retracted at any stage, and once retracted or denied, it cannot be proven by the testimony even of four witnesses of verification. Thus if someone denies he made a confession, and then witnesses come forth and assert that he did make a valid confession and even repeated it four times, this kind of testimony is inadmissible. For denial in this case creates a doubt (*shubha*) and the prescribed punishment is suspended because of it. Personal knowledge of the judge or of the Imam (head of state) does not prove claims of adultery and there is general agreement on this. The most one can say would be that he (the Imam or judge) is counted as one witness and three others will be needed to create the basis of an admissible proof.[7]

Issues over Rape, Its Evidence, and Proof

Muslim jurists are in agreement to the effect that a woman who has been raped and subjected to irresistible force is not liable to any punishment. This is based on the authority of the following hadith:

> God will not take to task my community for their mistake, forgetfulness and what they have been compelled into.[8]
>
> إن الله تجاوز عن أمتي الخطأ والنسيان وما استكرهوا عليه.

Also quoted in support is a hadith on the authority of ʿAbd al-Jabbar b. Wāʾil from his father who said: "A woman was compelled [into *zinā*] during the time of the Prophet, pbuh, and he dropped the *ḥadd* in her case."[9]

Another version of this hadith gives the following details:

> When a woman went out for prayer at dawn, a man attacked her on the way and raped her. She shouted but the rapist escaped. When another man came by, she complained: "That man did such and such to me."
>
> And when a company of the Emigrants came by, she said: "That man did such and such to me." They went and seized the man whom they thought had raped her and brought him to her.
>
> She said: "Yes, this is the man." Then they brought him to the Messenger of God.
>
> When he (the Prophet) was about to pass sentence, the man who (actually) had raped her stood up and said: "Messenger of God, I am the man who did it to her."
>
> He (the Prophet) said to her: "Go away, for God has forgiven you." But he told the man some good words [Abū Dāwūd said: meaning the man who was seized], and of the man who had had intercourse with her, he said: "Stone him to death."

> The Prophet then said (concerning the man who confessed): "He has repented such a repentance that if [it were divided among] the people of Medina, it would have been accepted from them."
>
> Abū Dāwūd said: "Asbat b. Naṣr has also transmitted it from Simak."[10]
>
> حَدَّثَنَا مُحَمَّدُ بْنُ يَحْيَى بْنِ فَارِسٍ، حَدَّثَنَا الْفِرْيَابِيُّ، حَدَّثَنَا إِسْرَائِيلُ، حَدَّثَنَا سِمَاكُ بْنُ حَرْبٍ، عَنْ عَلْقَمَةَ بْنِ وَائِلٍ، عَنْ أَبِيهِ، أَنَّ امْرَأَةً، خَرَجَتْ عَلَى عَهْدِ النَّبِيِّ صلى الله عليه وسلم تُرِيدُ الصَّلاَةَ فَتَلَقَّاهَا رَجُلٌ فَتَجَلَّلَهَا فَقَضَى حَاجَتَهُ مِنْهَا فَصَاحَتْ وَانْطَلَقَ فَمَرَّ عَلَيْهَا رَجُلٌ فَقَالَتْ إِنَّ ذَاكَ فَعَلَ بِي كَذَا وَكَذَا وَمَرَّتْ عِصَابَةٌ مِنَ الْمُهَاجِرِينَ فَقَالَتْ إِنَّ ذَلِكَ الرَّجُلَ فَعَلَ بِي كَذَا وَكَذَا . فَانْطَلَقُوا فَأَخَذُوا الرَّجُلَ الَّذِي ظَنَّتْ أَنَّهُ وَقَعَ عَلَيْهَا فَأَتَوْهَا بِهِ فَقَالَتْ نَعَمْ هُوَ هَذَا . فَأَتَوْا بِهِ النَّبِيَّ صلى الله عليه وسلم فَلَمَّا أَمَرَ بِهِ قَامَ صَاحِبُهَا الَّذِي وَقَعَ عَلَيْهَا فَقَالَ يَا رَسُولَ اللَّهِ أَنَا صَاحِبُهَا . فَقَالَ " اذْهَبِي فَقَدْ غَفَرَ اللَّهُ لَكِ " . وَقَالَ لِلرَّجُلِ قَوْلاً حَسَنًا . قَالَ أَبُو دَاوُدَ يَعْنِي الرَّجُلَ الْمَأْخُوذَ وَقَالَ لِلرَّجُلِ الَّذِي وَقَعَ عَلَيْهَا " ارْجُمُوهُ " . فَقَالَ " لَقَدْ تَابَ تَوْبَةً لَوْ تَابَهَا أَهْلُ الْمَدِينَةِ لَقُبِلَ مِنْهُمْ " . قَالَ أَبُو دَاوُدَ رَوَاهُ أَسْبَاطُ بْنُ نَصْرٍ أَيْضًا عَنْ سِمَاكٍ

The Prophet thus accepted the solitary statement of the raped woman and did not ask her for further proof of witnesses to support her claim. She was also not charged of making a false accusation of adultery against another person, nor was there any mention of *qadhf*. The accused person was charged with rape because of the victim's claim, but he was convicted through his own confession to the charge.

It is also reported that a case was brought to the second caliph ʿUmar b. al-Khaṭṭāb of a woman who claimed that she was a heavy sleeper, that a man had forced himself on her while asleep and had intercourse with her, and she did not know it until she woke up and also had no clear memory of her attacker. The caliph did not enforce the *ḥadd* of adultery on her and accepted her explanation. This was seen as an instance of doubt (*shubha*) and the *ḥadd* punishment was suspended because of it. The argument is then extended to a scenario if she also got pregnant as a result—would that be used as a proof against her? In response it is said that pregnancy under the said conditions would also be deemed as doubtful and that it would not be enough to invoke the punishment unless it was reinforced by confession or other objective evidence. This is the majority (*jumhūr*) position upheld by the Ḥanafī, Shāfiʿī, and Ḥanbalī schools, simply because of the possibility of *shubha*. The Mālikīs have held, on the contrary, that pregnancy in an unmarried woman is by itself a proof of *zinā* and that the punishment would be due on its basis unless there be evidence to prove that the woman was subjected to irresistible force. When there is such evidence, then the *ḥadd* of adultery is suspended.[11]

The view, however, that pregnancy is a conclusive proof of *zinā* has aroused controversy as it can lead to miscarriage of justice. Instances have thus arisen when the victim of rape was unable to prove the charge of rape against her attacker and was herself subjected to punishment. This is because her charge of rape is often taken as an implied confession of adultery and made the basis of invoking the punishment on her. Then again, if the rape victim fails to prove her charge against the rapist by four witnesses, which is the most likely scenario, she is charged with slander (*qadhf*). An often-cited case in point is that of Safia Bibi of Pakistan. In 1985, Safia Bibi, a sixteen-year-old, nearly blind domestic servant, reported that she was repeatedly raped by her employer and his son and became pregnant as a result. When she charged the man with rape, the case was dismissed for lack of evidence, as she was the only witness against them. Safia, however, being unmarried and pregnant, was charged with *zinā* for not having conclusive evidence to show that the pregnancy was because of rape. The session court at Shahiwal district convicted her for *zinā* and sentenced her to three years' rigorous imprisonment, fifteen lashes, and a fine of Rs.1000.[12] Is this not miscarriage of justice?

A question arose whether duress in the case of a man also absolves him from the standard punishment. A basic answer to this question is in the affirmative on the assumption that duress applies to both. This response refers to the authority of the foregoing hadith, which does not draw an exception in the case of men, and also because the claim of duress would in any case give rise to a doubt (*shubha*) and suspend the punishment. This is the position taken by the two disciples of Imam Abū Ḥanīfah, a minority view of the Mālikī and preferred view of the Shāfiʿī school. The majority view of the Mālikī and Ḥanbalī schools and some Shāfiʿīs maintain that the case of a man is different as erection cannot materialise without an element of volition and consent—hence he is liable to punishment.[13]

Imam Abū Ḥanīfah has made an exception for compulsion by the Sultan "under pain of the sword," a position that does not apply to other government officials. The Imam's disciples and other leading scholars of the Ḥanafī school have thought differently, however, and held that times have changed, adding that perhaps what the Imam wrote was good for his time but that compulsion can originate from the sultan or any other person in effective power. The Shāfiʿīs, Mālikīs, and Ḥanbalīs also maintain that duress may be from the sultan or from any other person, government official or otherwise.[14]

According to another report, a woman who was struck with severe thirst in the desert asked a shepherd for a drink, but he refused to serve her any milk unless she had intercourse with him. The woman gave in to his demand and had intercourse with the shepherd. When the case was brought before the caliph ʿUmar b. al-Khaṭṭāb, he did not enforce the punishment on either of them, on the assumption that the milk would be her dower and, since there was an element of consent, a temporary but voidable (*fāsid*) marriage could be assumed in their case, which provided the basis of a doubt and the suspension of punishment.[15] The assumption here worked to the benefit of the shepherd, as the woman who had acted due to necessity would have also had a separate ground for a defence.

It is further stated in this connection that when a man hires a woman to have intercourse with him and she agrees and they have intercourse, the prescribed punishment of adultery would not apply, but they may be punished by way of a deterrent *taʿzīr* punishment.[16] This is again a case of doubt created by the existence of a quasi-contract (*shibh al-ʿaqd*), similar perhaps to the previous case.

Notwithstanding the well-established position of scholastic jurisprudence that refuses to admit circumstantial evidence in the proof of *ḥudūd*, an exception has been made in the case of pregnancy and rape. Rape can be proven by the fact of pregnancy if there is no other explanation, but the victim is allowed to rebut the charge and bring forth supportive evidence. Imam Mālik has actually held that the victim's claim of rape is not proven unless it is buttressed by evidence such as bleeding or screaming or other reasonable indicators to show that the victim was raped against her will.[17] For the majority of juristic schools, it is unlikely in any case that she will be punished with the fixed punishment, since her statement that she was raped, even if unsupported, gives rise to a doubt (*shubha*). Another ground for doubt, at least under the Ḥanafī and Shāfiʿī laws, could be if the woman has confessed only once but not four times, as a single confession is not enough for a conviction.[18]

Zinā can also be proven through the process of imprecation (*liʿān*), that is, when a man accuses his wife of adultery and disowns her child and then takes four solemn oaths in support of his accusation. The prescribed punishment may be applied to her if she does not refute the claim, but the punishment is suspended if she refutes the claim and takes four solemn oaths in support of her refutation.[19] This is incidentally cited by some scholars as a case where a woman's testimony overrules that of a man.

Yet by excluding circumstantial evidence in the proof of *ḥudūd*, mainstream fiqh would also stand to preclude important scientific evidence like semen stains, vaginal swabs, blood samples, scratch marks, genetic fingerprinting, and so on, which would presumably fall under circumstantial evidence and therefore be inadmissible as proof in *zinā*. Modern opinion is critical of this, side by side with the inadmissibility of female witnesses in the proof of *ḥudūd* crimes.

One commentator noted, on both of these issues, namely precluding female witnesses and material circumstantial evidence, that the mainstream fiqh position (as also in the case of the Hudud Bill of Kelantan 1993), go against not only scientific knowledge but also the Qur'anic position, which clearly records the presence of a single female witness plus material circumstantial evidence to solve an accusation of rape.[20] A reference is made here to sura Yūsuf (12:23–29), the story in particular of Prophet Yūsuf, who was accused by a woman of seducing her after she herself had failed to seduce him. This issue was solved by just one female witness and circumstantial evidence when it was pointed out that, since Prophet Yūsuf's shirt was torn from behind, it must have been the woman who attempted to seduce him.[21] This is ironically the basic Qur'anic authority that Muslim jurists have generally quoted in support of circumstantial evidence (*qarāʾin*) as a method of proof for crimes outside the *ḥudūd* category.[22]

A Malaysian researcher, Nik Noriani, has scrutinised the position of female witnesses in the Qur'an (al-Nūr, 24:4) and drawn the conclusion that the requirement of four witnesses in this verse was specially meant to protect women against slander and casual accusation of *zinā* "and not to protect men from charges of rape."[23] The fact that mainstream fiqh disqualifies women as witnesses in all *ḥudūd* cases and just retaliation (*qiṣāṣ*), it was added, also had no precedent in the Prophet's practice. There were cases in which the Prophet accepted women's evidence, such as the case of a girl who had been robbed and brutally assaulted and the case of a woman who was raped by an unknown man on her way to the mosque for the dawn prayer.[24]

Another Malaysian observer, Norani Othman, raised a question over the objectivity of justice and whether the fiqh exclusions of female testimony and acceptance of pregnancy as a proof of *zinā*, which are both followed without change in the Malaysian draft laws, fail to be equitable and just. "The purpose of all laws, God's law as well as man-made law, is to dispense justice." These positions need to be carefully scrutinised, not just by "a selected number" of religious scholars but through wider participation of the ummah.[25] While sharing the same sentiment, Nakhaie Ahmad referred to the ubiquitous emphasis on the objectivity of justice in the Qur'an and then tersely stated, "If a Muslim is exhorted to be just towards an enemy, he should surely be just also to women."[26]

To explore the scholastic position on the evidential value of pregnancy a little further, it will be noted that the majority (*jumhūr*) have classified pregnancy as circumstantial evidence of the occurrence of *zinā* on the part of an unmarried woman, in the case of one who is married but whose husband is incapable of being a fertile partner; or when there is a child born within the first six months of marriage. Pregnancy is not decisive circumstantial evidence (*qarīnah qāṭiʿah*) in that it cannot on its own be the basis of adjudication, but it is circumstantial evidence (*qarīnah)* that can be rebutted by other evidence. The law thus leaves open the possibility of its rebuttal. The court may hear evidence to prove that pregnancy has occurred without *zinā,* or that sexual intercourse has occurred under duress, by mistake, or even without the knowledge of the defendant. When this is proven, the prescribed punishment of *zinā* must be suspended, and there may well be no case for any punishment. Should there be a possibility that pregnancy occurred without penetration, the *ḥadd* punishment must again be suspended. This may happen, for instance, when semen is planted in a woman by artificial methods, either by herself or by another person, or through sex without penetration. The case will be all the more credible if the woman is still found to be a virgin. The Imams Abū Ḥanīfah, al-Shāfiʿī, and Ibn Ḥanbal have held that when all of these possibilities are eliminated, the woman should be asked if she has any explanation; and if she herself claims that she was either mistaken or compelled, the fixed punishment will be suspended. There will be no *ḥadd* punishment even if she did not make such a claim so long as she has not made a full confession.[27]

If a woman accused of *zinā* is asked whether she was compelled and she says, "I was forced into *zinā*" or "I acted under a mistake," her words are to be admitted and no *ḥadd* is to be applied on her. This is because shariah prefers concealment (*satr*) in the *ḥudūd.* Al-Jazīrī who wrote this also added that this should be the position even if she had initially made a confession. For the fiqh rules clearly allow the accused who makes a confession to retract it, especially if the latter claims duress as a reason for doing so.[28]

The majority position—to admit pregnancy as circumstantial evidence—is based on a saying of the Companion (*qawl al-ṣaḥābi*), a statement in particular of caliph ʿUmar b. al Khattab, who is reported to have said that "stoning is obligatory on anyone who commits *zinā,* man or woman, provided that they are *muḥṣan* [lit., guarded, i.e., married] and that it is proven by witnesses, pregnancy or confession." It is similarly reported that it came to the attention of the third caliph ʿUthmān that a married woman had given birth to a child upon expiry of only six months from the date of her marriage. ʿUthmān was of the view to convict the woman to punishment by stoning, but ʿAlī b. Abū Ṭalib advised him against it and cited the Qur'anic verse (al-Aḥqāf, 46:15) that declared that the carrying of the child to his weaning takes thirty months. Elsewhere in the Qur'an it is also stated that mothers shall breastfeed their offspring for two whole years (al-Baqarah, 2:233). Reading these two verses together, ʿAlī b. Abū Ṭalib concluded that a period of six months was the minimum duration of pregnancy, and the woman who had given birth upon completion of six months was not to be convicted of *zinā.*

Imam Mālik has, as already noted, considered pregnancy as a conclusive proof of *zinā* above the category of circumstantial evidence. The defendant's claim as to compulsion and mistake will not be enough to suspend the punishment unless it is confirmed by supportive evidence. Thus her claim of compulsion and rape will be upheld if it is supported by circumstantial evidence such as screaming and calling for help, signs of violence, and bleeding from loss of virginity or otherwise.[29]

Muhammad Sidahmad is supportive of acceptance of women's testimony generally, including in *ḥudūd* offences. He argues that it would be irrational if an Islamic judicial system today were to reject the testimonies of women living in a hostel strictly prohibited for men. These women may witness a rapist or a male stalker in the full act of *zinā* in circumstances where no one else can act as witness. It is a matter of serious concern, Sidahmad adds, that this gender limitation in the proof of *ḥudūd* crimes is likely to help criminals who may even use it to avoid the *ḥudūd* punishment altogether.[30]

Furthermore, the possibilities of accident, error, and abuse are in many ways greater today than in premodern times. There is general availability, for instance, of artificial insemination, test tube pregnancy, and semen banks that keep alive and preserve semen for very long periods; thus there are increased possibilities for falsification and fabrication. Although signs of virginity cannot survive actual childbirth, it is possible, according to expert opinion, for sexual intercourse, and also pregnancy, to take place and the hymen to remain intact. Modern medicine has also made it possible to repair, through surgery, the hymen after perforation.

The availability of modern medical facilities pertaining to pregnancy, prenatal care, and childbirth has meant that women tend to spend more time in hospital beds, maternity care units, and outside the home environment. They are often put under anaesthetics, pain-relieving drugs, and so on. Under these circumstances, the possibility is even greater for accidents and abuse to take place without a woman's knowledge or even with her knowledge but under compromised circumstances. It would therefore seem rather presumptuous to regard pregnancy as a conclusive proof of *zinā*.

In response to a question on whether the DNA (*basmah warathiyyah*) can provide decisive answers to some of the queries raised over pregnancy as the proof of *zinā*, Wahbah al-Zuḥaylī noted that DNA analysis may identify the other party to *zinā* but it cannot eliminate doubt about the presence of mistake, fabrication, and duress. The reliability or otherwise of the DNA and other scientific means of establishing facts, next to traditional methods of witnessing and confession in the *ḥudūd* and *qiṣāṣ* prosecutions, enrich and equip the legal process with new and reliable means. These matters are not entirely juridical issues but also related to scientific knowledge and need to be recognised.

Wahbah al-Zuḥaylī admits the impressive contribution of DNA analysis in crime detection and identification of criminals, but he holds that for purposes of court decisions, unless the law takes a decisive position otherwise, "the DNA does not provide independent evidence in the sense of the court issuing a sentence solely on its basis, but it does provide supportive and persuasive evidence for a court decision."[31] This is a sound response, as DNA evidence can be tampered with, and its reliability is also diminished with the lapse of time between collection of evidence and the actual incident.

*Definition of a Guarded Person (*Muḥṣan*)*

Muḥṣan as a derivative of *iḥṣān* refers to a person who is "immune," or protected against the temptations of *zinā*, because of Islam and marriage. Muslim jurists have premised the distinction between *muḥṣan* and non-*muḥṣan* on the (somewhat exacting) rationale that once a person has experienced the joy of marriage he is bound to be eager to safeguard and protect the sanctity of that precious relationship, regardless as to whether there was an effective or functioning marriage at the material time the offence was committed.[32] The Ḥanafī and Ḥanbalī schools require that, for the punishment of stoning to be applicable, both partners must have this status. The Shii law is significantly different in its definition of a *muḥṣan*, who is defined to be an adult, free Muslim who is in a position to have lawful sexual intercourse and whose partner is actually available and not absent on a journey, imprisoned, or similar other circumstances.[33]

Sexual intercourse under Islamic law is permitted in a valid marriage only, such that any sexual intercourse outside this context is most likely to fall under *zinā*. The Qur'an penalises *zinā* and slanderous accusation of *zinā* as in the following verse:

> The adulterer and adulteress, flog each of them a hundred lashes. Let not compassion move you in their case from carrying out God's law, if you believe in God and the Last Day. And let a party of the believers witness their punishment. . . .And those who lay a charge against a chaste woman, and produce not four witnesses [to prove it] flog them with eighty lashes, and do not admit them to be witnesses ever again, for they are evil-doers. Except for those who repent thereafter and reform, for indeed, Allah is Forgiving and Merciful.
>
> (al-Nūr, 24:2–5)
>
> ٱلزَّانِيَةُ وَٱلزَّانِى فَٱجْلِدُوا۟ كُلَّ وَٰحِدٍ مِّنْهُمَا مِا۟ئَةَ جَلْدَةٍ ۖ وَلَا تَأْخُذْكُم بِهِمَا رَأْفَةٌ فِى دِينِ ٱللَّهِ إِن كُنتُمْ تُؤْمِنُونَ بِٱللَّهِ وَٱلْيَوْمِ ٱلْءَاخِرِ ۖ وَلْيَشْهَدْ عَذَابَهُمَا طَآئِفَةٌ مِّنَ ٱلْمُؤْمِنِينَ ... وَٱلَّذِينَ يَرْمُونَ ٱلْمُحْصَنَٰتِ ثُمَّ لَمْ يَأْتُوا۟ بِأَرْبَعَةِ شُهَدَآءَ فَٱجْلِدُوهُمْ ثَمَٰنِينَ جَلْدَةً وَلَا تَقْبَلُوا۟ لَهُمْ شَهَٰدَةً أَبَدًا ۚ وَأُو۟لَٰٓئِكَ هُمُ ٱلْفَٰسِقُونَ

The Qur'an makes no reference to stoning for *zinā*, which originates in the hadith with respect only to married adulterers. Case records also indicate that the Prophet implemented stoning for *zinā* in a few instances during the ten years of his rule in Medina. The majority of Sunni and Shii scholars maintain that the available hadiths on stoning specify the general of the Qur'an: the 100 lashes are thus applied generally, which has then been specified with regard to married persons.[34] Qur'an commentators understand the phrase "let not compassion move you in their case" to mean that the punishment in their case should neither be postponed nor reduced in severity on grounds of compassion. This interpretation is attributed to three Successors (*tābiʿīn*), namely Mujāhid, ʿIkrimah, and Saʿīd b. Jubayr. According to another interpretation, since the verse makes no reference to married or unmarried persons as such, the 100 lashes therein apply to all without any distinction.[35]

For the majority (*jumhūr*), it matters little if a person has separated or divorced and had no access to his/her spouse for a long time—he/she is still a *muḥṣan.*[36] Muḥammad ʿAbdūh and his disciple Muḥammad Rashīd Riḍā have held, however, that the punishment of *zinā* is only applicable to offenders who were parties to a valid marriage at the time of committing the offence. As for the offender who has been married once but is no longer so, he or she should be punished lightly or equally to that of the unmarried offender.[37]

Abū Zahrah has similarly observed that there is no clear text to determine that a woman who has been divorced, or a man whose wife has died, should be classified as *muḥṣan.* He also refers to the views of ʿAbdūh and Riḍā and then concurs with them that "a *muḥṣan* is a person who is protected (physically and morally), in the case of a woman, by her husband, and when there is a separation, or divorce, she no longer qualifies as a *muḥṣanah* in the same way as she is no longer a *mutazawwijah,* or a married woman." Somewhat like the *musāfir* (traveller) who is no longer a *musāfir* after returning from his journey; or indeed like a sick person (*marīḍ*) who enjoys certain concessions under the law, but not if he has already recovered and no longer an ill person (*marīḍ*), so is the case with the *muḥṣan* who is no longer a *muḥṣan* after the termination of his marriage. There is even a view that the word *muḥṣanat* in the Qur'an means "virgin women" and not, as is commonly said, "married women." This is because virginity is a great disincentive and preventer from *zinā,* just as it also means that a woman who has kept her virginity has not been intimately involved with men. How is it then justified to subject a woman who might have lost two great protections against *zinā,* namely virginity and marriage, to heavier punishment? Is it because her previous marriage is still regarded to be her protector, and if so, where is the logic in this? Reason would surely tell us that a woman who was once married but is married no longer should not be treated more harshly than a virgin, to say the least. If anything, the former should be given a lighter punishment, not harsher, or preferably perhaps the two are treated equally and there is nothing in the Qur'an and Sunnah to say otherwise.[38]

The offspring of *zinā* is alien to the biological father and has no legal tie of paternity with him, nor do the rules of inheritance flow between them. The biological father has no power of guardianship (*wilāyah*) over the offspring, be it male or female. It is also not permissible for one to be in close proximity with one's illegitimate daughter nor to marry her or her ascendants and descendants. It is permissible for the parties to *zinā* though to marry one another based on a new contract. Thus it is reported that during the time of the first caliph Abū Bakr, a man and a woman were convicted of *zinā* and were punished with 100 lashes and also banished for a year. Then they married one another, and cases of a similar kind are also reported during the time of the second caliph ʿUmar.[39]

Issues over Stoning, Banishment, Doubtful hadiths, and Abrogation

The main question over the punishment of *zinā* is concerned with the validity or otherwise of stoning (*rajm*) side by side with the standard Qur'anic punishment of flogging. Questions have also arisen over the combination of different punishments, namely of stoning, flogging, and banishment. The majority (*jumhūr*) have held that the punishment of *zinā* in the case of a married Muslim is death by stoning as laid down in the hadith, and it is 100 lashes for an unmarried person. The variant opinion on this subject, as elaborated below, maintains that the Qur'anic punishment of 100 lashes applies to everyone, married and unmarried alike.

The first view maintains that the Prophet applied stoning in the widely reported cases of Māʿiz b. Mālik al-Aslamī and that of al-Ghamidiyyah and a person (not named) as reported by the Companion Abū Hurayrah. Then it is added that the Pious Caliphs have also applied stoning, and their precedent is generally seen as conclusive evidence on the continued validity of this punishment.

Māʿiz belonged to the Aslam tribe and was an orphan. He was brought up by Hizal b. Naim, and it was in Hizal's house that Māʿiz committed adultery with a freed slave girl. Upon learning this, Hizal, who did not know about the punishment of stoning, as the report says, sent Māʿiz to the Prophet. He instructed Māʿiz to admit to his guilt before the Prophet and requested that he pray for the atonement of his sin. Māʿiz came to the Prophet and said: "Purify me for I have committed adultery." The Prophet turned his face away from Māʿiz and told him to go away and repent. Māʿiz repeated what he had said twice, but the Prophet avoided answering him on both occasions. Abū Bakr, who was also present, reminded Māʿiz that if he repeated it for the fourth time, the Prophet would have to order him stoned. But Māʿiz repeated the same for the fourth time. The Prophet then inquired about minute factual details. He inquired whether he was drunk, which he denied. Then the Prophet inquired from the people of his tribe over the sanity of Māʿiz. The Prophet then addressed Hizal with this remark: "I wish you had pulled a curtain over it." Then he ordered the stoning punishment for Māʿiz.[40]

The variant view that questions the validity of stoning is based on the analysis that the Qur'an is totally silent on stoning. Had God Most High intended to validate stoning as a punishment, the Qur'an would have made a reference to it. The proponents of this view have questioned the evidence in the Sunnah by saying that the reported instances of stoning actually took place prior to the revelation of sura al-Nūr (24:2) which prescribed 100 lashes. If this is accepted, it would mean that the Qur'an had overruled and abrogated stoning (*rajm*). It is further argued that the evidence in the Sunnah is all in the form of solitary (*aḥad*) hadiths, and the fact that there is inconsistency in the contents of these hadith reports only aggravates the situation further.

It is further stated that some of the hadiths reported on al-Ghamidiyyah's case contain a reference to banishment (*taghrīb*) as a supplementary punishment to stoning but that this element is absent in other hadiths concerning the same case. There is a similar discrepancy in hadiths on the question of combining stoning with flogging and banishment. In some reports flogging is held to be supplementary to stoning whereas other hadith reports mention stoning as the only punishment without any reference to flogging. The Mālikī and Shii schools have also upheld banishment for a year as a supplementary punishment but they apply it only to men, as banishment for women could expose them to corruption. The other schools require that women be accompanied by a male relative (*maḥram*).

In a chapter titled "Stoning for *Zinā* by a *Muḥṣan*, and Flogging for a *Non-Muḥṣan*," al-Shawkānī has recorded six hadiths in *Nayl al-Awṭār* in which the following is observed:[41]

1. In the hadith of al-ʿAsīf (lit., employee or servant), an unmarried young man committed *zinā* with a married woman who had employed him. The hadith provides further details to the effect that the Prophet sentenced al-ʿAsīf to 100 lashes and banishment of one year, and the woman was convicted of stoning only. The case has been reported in all the Six Collections of hadith. The substance of this hadith, in so far as it concerns the woman, has also been confirmed by the hadith of Māʿiz and the conclusion is drawn that the Prophet did not combine lashing and stoning together.

2. According to a hadith al-Bukhārī has recorded on the authority of Abū Hurayrah, the Prophet determined the punishment of *zinā* by an unmarried person at 100 lashes and banishment for one year.

وعن أبي هريرة (رضى) أن النبي (ص) قضى في من زنا ولم يحصن بنفي عام وإقامة الحد عليه.

3. The hadith of ʿUbadah b. al-Ṣamit in which the Prophet declared: "Take it from me, take it from me: Allah has opened a way for them. The unmarried and virgin are liable to 100 lashes and banishment for a year. For a married person the punishment is 100 lashes and stoning."

خذوا عني خذوا عني قد جعل الله لهن سبيلا : البكر جلد مائة ونفي سنة , والثيب بالثيب ,جلد مائة والرجم.

Except for al-Bukhārī and al-Nasāʾī, this hadith has been recorded in the rest of the Six hadith collections. Al-Zaylāʿī has recorded the information that this is probably one of the earliest hadiths on the subject.[42] This hadith is apparently in conflict with the hadith of al-ʿAsīf and also the hadith of Māʿiz in which the punishment of a married person was confined to stoning only without flogging. Al-Sarakhsī has stated the Ḥanafī position, which is also that of the majority, that stoning and flogging may not be combined because flogging a person who is sentenced to stoning seems superfluous and does not serve any good purpose.[43] The leading schools of law have maintained that the Prophet has never combined the two punishments of stoning and flogging together.[44] But unlike the majority who combine flogging with banishment, the Ḥanafīs do not accept this combination either.

4. The hadith of Jābir b. Samurah to the effect that "the Prophet ordered that Māʿiz b. Mālik be stoned to death but did not mention flogging."

   Al-Shawkānī wrote concerning this hadith: notwithstanding the fact that only Imam Ibn Ḥanbal and al-Nasāʾī have reported it, "its transmitters are reliable."

5. There is a report from al-Shaʿbī recorded by al-Bukhārī and Aḥmad b. Ḥanbal, to the effect that the fourth caliph ʿAlī b. Abū Ṭalib applied the prescribed punishment of *zinā* on a married woman by the name of Sharāḥah al-Hamadāniyyah and it consisted of both stoning and flogging. She was flogged on a Thursday and stoned on the following Friday, and the caliph is reported to have said, "I flogged her in accordance with the Book of God and stoned her in accordance with the Sunnah of the Prophet." This is once again inconsistent with the hadith

of both al-ʿAsīf and Māʾiz in which flogging was not applied in combination with stoning. A further inconsistency here is that al-Bukhārī (Kitab al-Muḥāribīn, Bāb Rajm al-Muḥṣan) has recorded only a shorter version of this hadith in which there is no mention of flogging. Caliph ʿAlī, according to this version, only said, "I stoned her in accordance with the Sunnah of the Prophet."[45]

6. The hadith of Jābir b. ʿAbd Allāh reported by Abū Dāwūd that "a man committed *zinā* with a woman and the Prophet applied the prescribed punishment to him. Then he was informed that the man was a *muḥṣan,* upon receiving this information the Prophet sentenced him to stoning and he was stoned."

Al-Shawkānī has also recorded the hadith of Sahl b. Saʿd to the effect that a man from the tribe of Bakar who was unmarried confessed to have committed *zinā* and the Prophet flogged him but did not issue any order about banishment.[46]

The Ḥanafī jurist al-Zaylāʿī wrote that the hadith of ʿUbādah b. al-Ṣāmit (no. 3 above) has been abrogated and explains this by saying that initially the punishment for *zinā* was unspecified but could be any painful act (*īdhā*ʾ), followed by incarceration as prescribed in the two verses in sura al-Nisāʾ *"fa-ādhūhuma*—punish/annoy them both" and *"famsikūhunnna fi'l buyūt*—detain the women in their houses" respectively (al-Nisāʾ, 4:15–16). These portions of the Qur'an were subsequently abrogated by the hadith of ʿUbadah b. al-Ṣāmit, which fixed the punishment of an unmarried person at 100 lashes and banishment for one year, and that of the married person at flogging and stoning. But all this happened, al-Zaylāʿī adds, before the revelation of the sura al-Nūr and that this has been indicated in the hadith of ʿUbadah b. al-Ṣāmit, which began with the words *khudhū ʿanni* (take it from me). Had the Prophet uttered this hadith after the sura al-Nūr, he would most likely have said *khudhū ʿan Allāh* (take it from God). The hadith of ʿUbādah was thus abrogated by the verse revealed in the sura al-Nūr, and flogging 100 lashes became the only punishment for all cases of *zinā*. But then al-Zaylāʿī further adds that this verse was also partially abrogated, that is, in regards to a married person, by the application of stoning to Māʿiz and al-Ghamidiyyah.[47]

There is further information, however, which casts doubt as to the timing of Māʿiz and al-Ghamidiyyah. The relevant report recorded by al-Bukhārī has it that a Companion, Ibn Abī Awfa, was asked this question by one al-Shaybānī who was a Follower (*tābiʿi*): "Did the Prophet apply the punishment of stoning?" Abī Awfa said, "Yes." He was then asked whether this was before the revelation of sura al-Nūr or after? And he said, "I do not know" (see text of hadith below). This raises doubt as to whether the hadiths, which validated stoning, and actual cases in which stoning was implemented had all preceded the revelation of the sura al-Nūr and that they were consequently abrogated by it. Prior to this event, the Prophet might have simply applied stoning by reference to the ruling of the Torah.[48]

Even al-Zaylāʿī, who considered the hadith of al-Ghamidiyyah to have partially abrogated the Qur'anic verse in sura al-Nūr, recorded two variant versions of that hadith, one of which is explicit to the effect that the Prophet postponed the stoning of al-Ghamidiyyah until the weaning of her child, and the other that omits this part and suggests that she was stoned to death as soon as a man from the Anṣār undertook the custody of her child. To this al-Zaylāʿī commented, "It is possible that there were two women from the tribe of Ghāmid, one whose punishment of stoning was delayed until the weaning of her child and the other who was stoned without such a delay. It is also possible that one of them was from the tribe of Ghāmid and the other from another tribe but that the narrator made a mistake in reporting, and God Knows Best."[49]

We have also seen, in the various reports before us, references to abrogation (*naskh*), itself an issue that raises methodological questions and warrants a brief discussion as follows:

A basic question arises as to whether abrogation is of any relevance to the issue before us. In answer it may be noted that only the Ḥanafīs consider it relevant but not the majority. The majority, including Imam al-Shāfiʿī, have viewed the provisions of the Qur'an and Sunnah on the punishment of *zinā* within the context of specification of the general (*takhṣīṣ al-ʿām*), saying that the general provision of the Qur'an has in this instance been specified by the Sunnah. The Qur'an laid down a certain punishment and the Sunnah adjusted it with respect to married persons. The Ḥanafis have, however, seen this as a case not of specification but of partial abrogation of the Qur'an by the Sunnah, based on the analysis that death by stoning is a capital punishment on which the Qur'an is silent, and if the Sunnah validates it over and above the Qur'anic provision on flogging, then the issue involved here is one of abrogation rather than a mere specification. This seems a sound argument as flogging cannot be specified by death, as the latter far exceeds the former and also exceeds the logical boundaries of "specification." Another question is whether the Sunnah can actually abrogate the Qur'an.

Although the majority admits in principle the validity of abrogation of the Qur'an by the Sunnah, many prominent scholars, including Imam al-Shāfiʿī, held otherwise to say that it was the proper role of the Sunnah to explain and supplement the Qur'an but not to abrogate it. This is again a sound statement of principle, which Imam al-Shāfiʿī has explicitly adopted in his exposition of the theory of abrogation.[50] This would naturally imply that abrogation should not be too readily brought in and it must be seen as the last resort. The fiqh scholars have consequently shown reluctance to invoke abrogation in order to resolve the discrepancy between the Qur'an and Sunnah on the punishment of *zinā*.

The Ḥanafīs have further added that all the hadiths on the subject of stoning are solitary (*aḥad*) reports that are not totally devoid of doubt, and it would be incorrect to validate death by stoning on the basis of doubtful evidence. The Qur'anic text on the punishment of flogging for *zinā* is perspicuous (*muḥkam*), definitive, and conclusive, which leaves no room for speculative interpretation, whereas the hadiths of Māʾiz and al-Ghamidiyyah are both *aḥad*. Imam Abū Ḥanīfah has considered the hadith of al-Ghamidiyyah to be doubtful and should not be given credibility vis-a-vis the definitive text of the Qur'an.[51] Imam al-Shāfiʿī's understanding of abrogation is distinguished from that of the majority in that only the Qur'an can abrogate the Qur'an and that the Sunnah cannot be the abrogator of the Qur'an. Since the Qur'an is the first source of shariah, it is superior in respect of both authority and authenticity to the Sunnah. Hence any incidence of conflict between the definitive of the Qur'an and the *aḥad* hadith should naturally be determined in favour of the Qur'an. But al-Shāfiʿī, along with the majority, maintains that the general of the Qur'an has been specified by the Sunnah in respect of a married person.

There is also the report, attributed to the second caliph ʿUmar, stating that the Qur'anic text on flogging for *zinā* was abrogated by the Qur'an itself. It is thus stated that a verse was revealed as a part of the sura al-Aḥzāb (i.e., sura 33), which declared that "when a married man or woman commits adultery, stone them to death as a deterrence from God, and God is Most Powerful, Most Wise."

الشيخ والشيخة إذا زنيا فارجموهما البتة نكالا من الله والله عزيز حكيم.

It is stated that although the wording of this report did not become a part of the Qur'anic text, its ruling has become a part of shariah. It is then stated that the reported addition was not incorporated into the standard text simply because it did not amount to continuously proven, or *mutawātir*, and anything less than *mutawātir* cannot, as a rule, become a part of the Qur'an. ʿUmar b. al-Khaṭṭāb has widely been quoted as having said, "Had it not been for people saying that ʿUmar made an addition to the Qur'an, I would have added this to the Qur'an." The renowned Qur'an commentator, Shihāb al-Dīn al-Alūsī (d. 1854), has related this in his *Rūḥ al-Maʿanī*. The conclusion he has reached is that the evidence in support of this episode is doubtful, adding that the prominent Ḥanafī jurist, Kamal al-Din Ibn al-Humam (d. 861/1457), has arrived at the same conclusion. Both scholars have also held that the actual wording of the alleged verse falls short of the eloquent style of the Qur'an and then said that there was an addition on stoning but that God Most High ordered the Prophet to eliminate it from the text while retaining its ruling, which all sounds rather imaginary. This is also the position taken by the Kharijites and the Muʿtazīlah. Had God, May He be Glorified, willed to prescribe stoning for *zinā*, He would have made a clear provision in the Qur'an for it. The conclusion is thus drawn that ʿUmar's report of the added verse remains doubtful and cannot be taken to overrule the clear text on flogging.

The claim that the Companions have reached a consensus on ʿUmar b. al-Khaṭṭāb's version of events has also been questioned by both Ibn al-Humam and al- Alūsī when they stated that it was debatable whether a tacit consensus (*al-ijmāʿ al-sukūtī*) of this kind could present credible evidence in the face of the clear text of the Qur'an. The fact is that by the time of caliph ʿUmar most of the leading Companions had either lost their lives (e.g., in the wars of apostasy) or they were away from Medina, and this weakens the claim of general consensus (*ijmāʿ*) in support of ʿUmar's version of events, on which there is only ʿUmar's report, but other Companions have remained silent concerning it.[52]

Further on banishment as a supplementary punishment, the Ḥanafīs and the Shia have held that the punishment of an unmarried person is only 100 lashes. If the head of state decides to banish the fornicator, he may do so by way of shariah-oriented policy (*siyāsah sharʿiyyah*), but they maintain that this is not a requirement. Imam al-Shāfiʿī maintained on the other hand that banishment for one year is a requirement and an integral part of the prescribed punishment for an unmarried person, whether male or female. They are to be flogged 100 lashes and banished from their place of residence to another place, which takes a journey of at least twenty-four hours. This is also the position of the Ḥanbalīs and the Ẓāhiriyyah. But Imam Mālik (d. 179/795) and al-Awzāʿī (d. 157/774) have exempted women from the general ruling of the hadith on banishment based on considerations of public interest (*maṣlaḥah*), which is meant to prevent further indulgence in corruption. It is also stated that the requirement that a woman may only be banished with the company of a close relative means that an innocent person is also condemned to banishment with her. The Ḥanafīs have also added that the Pious Caliphs, including ʿUmar b. al-Khaṭṭāb, are on record to have punished *zinā* by unmarried persons with flogging only without banishment.[53]

Modern Opinion on Stoning (Rajm)

This section examines the views of Muḥammad Abū Zahrah, Muṣṭafā Aḥmad al-Zarqā, Yūsuf al-Qaraḍāwī, Sheikh Ali Gomma, and others on death by stoning as a punishment for adultery.

As already noted, the majority of the leading schools of Islamic law have upheld the validity of stoning for adultery, except for some of the Muʿtazīlah and the Kharijites, who maintain that stoning was the punishment at an early stage but was abrogated with the revelation of the Qur'anic verse (al-Nūr, 24:2) that declared 100 lashes for both men and women adulterers.[54] As already noted, there are differences of opinion as to how the ruling of the Sunnah on stoning relates to the Qur'an: Is it a case of specification (*takhṣīṣ*) or of abrogation (*naskh*)? Then there is the ruling of the second caliph ʿUmar, also mentioned before, that it is not a case of the Sunnah abrogating the Qur'an but one of abrogation of the Qur'an by the Qur'an itself. This is a kind of hidden abrogation, which means that the abrogating text is not in the Qur'an, yet the Qur'an has retained the actual ruling thereof. Current practice in many Muslim countries is dominated by the ruling of the Sunnah on stoning for married adulterers. Twentieth-century scholars have reflected further on this and offered additional clarifications and insights as discussed below.

ʿAlī Manṣūr, author of *Niẓām al-Tajrīm wa'l-ʿIqāb fi'l-Islām* (1976), former president of the Constitutional Court of Egypt and chairman of the Committee on the Harmonisation of Shariah and Law, wrote that "Muḥammad Abū Zahrah, who is one of the leading scholars of shariah of this century, sent to me in writing his opinion on the subject of stoning where he concluded that the evidence for this punishment was doubtful and it was therefore preferable not to apply it."[55] Manṣūr added that Abū Zahrah expressed his views at a conference in the Moroccan city of Casablanca on 22nd Rabī'al-Awwal 1392H, which corresponds to 6 May 1972. Abū Zahrah's views on this have also to a large extent appeared in his own book, *al-Jarīmah wa' l-ʿUqūbah fī 'l- Fiqh al-Islāmī: al-ʿUqūbah,* published in several editions (initially published ca. 1959), which may be summarised as follows:

1. There is no disagreement among the jurists and ulama of the four leading schools of Islamic law that the punishment of flogging for *zinā,* prescribed in the Qur'an, applies to unmarried men and women. The majority (*jumhūr*) have added that a male fornicator is also liable to banishment, that is, removal from society or imprisonment, for a year so that he is not ostracised for what he has done and that in course of time the people may forget about it. Imam Mālik has held that banishment should not apply to women convicted of *zinā* for fear of immorality and corruption.[56]
2. As for the punishment of stoning for a married person, Abū Zahrah refers to the relevant hadiths especially the hadith of al-ʿAsīf, the report from ʿUmar b. al-Khaṭṭāb concerning the verse according to him of stoning, and then the stoning of Māʿiz and al-Ghamidiyyah. But then he notes that all of these hadiths are solitary or *aḥad* and the mere fact that there are several of them does not elevate them to the rank of continuously proven or *mutawātir.* Only the *mutawātir* inspires conviction and precludes the possibility of lying and doubt in the transmission of hadith.
3. Abū Zahrah draws attention to the hadith recorded in *Ṣaḥīḥ al-Bukhārī* that one of the Followers (*tābiʿūn*) asked a leading scholar (*mujtahid*) among the Companions whether the sura al-Nūr, which prescribed the punishment of flogging, was revealed before the hadiths on stoning or thereafter. The Companion answered that he did not know. The person who asked the question was al-Shaybānī and the Companion was ʿAbd Allāh Ibn Abī Awfa. The text of this hadith is as follows:

> Narrated from Iṣḥāq—from Khālid—from al-Shaybānī: I asked ʿAbd Allāh Ibn Abī Awfa. Did God's Messenger carry out the stoning punishment? He said yes. I then asked: Before the revelation of sura al-Nūr or after it? He replied "I do not know."[57]

حدثني اسحاق كما حدثني خالد عن الشيباني قال : سألت عبد الله ابن أوفى : هل رجم رسول الله (ص)
؟ قال نعم قلت قبل سورة النور أم بعدها؟ قال : لا أدري .

Hadith scholars have, however, attempted to resolve the doubt raised in this report by saying that the hadiths of stoning came after the revelation of sura al-Nūr and therefore abrogated the latter, which is why ʿUmar b. al-Khaṭṭāb acted on the rulings of these hadiths. The sura al-Nūr was revealed in the year four Hijrah and, according to some reports, five or six Hijrah, and that the transmitters of the hadiths on stoning included persons like Abū Hurayrah and Ibn ʿAbbās who came to Medina in the years seven and nine respectively. But then it is said that they might have reported the hadiths from other Companions without actually saying so—hence the question still remains unanswered as to the timing of the hadith reports. The issue is then addressed on methodological grounds, as the majority maintains that the general (*ʿām*) does not abrogate the specific (*khāṣṣ*) but is itself specified by it even if the specific is later in time. The general terms of the verse of *zinā* in sura al-Nūr have thus been specified by the hadith. But the Ḥanafīs, as already noted, do not allow this by means only of *aḥad* hadith, saying that the hadith in question must be either continuously proven or widely known, *mutawātir* or *mashhūr,* and the hadiths on stoning do not qualify as either.

Furthermore, the Ḥanafīs do not follow the hadith of al-ʿAsīf despite the fact that it has been recorded by four of the Six Compilations of hadiths, because the provision of banishment therein is an addition to the Qur'an, and this cannot be done by means only of an *aḥad* hadith. The Qur'an has made no reference to banishment and that must prevail over the doubtful addition of the *aḥad* hadith. Although the Ḥanafīs do not consider banishment to be obligatory, they still maintain that the head of state is within his rights to combine it with flogging if he deems this would serve a good purpose. Banishment, in other words, is not a part of the *ḥadd* punishment but may be added to it by way of *taʿzīr.* This is also the view of the Imami and Zaydī Shia. The Imams Mālik, al-Shāfiʿī, Ibn Ḥanbal, and the Ẓāhirī school have, on the other hand, held that banishment is an integral part of the prescribed punishment, and this they have ruled on the authority of the hadith of al-ʿAsīf.[58]

4. At this point Abū Zahrah relates the views of the Kharijites, some Shia, and Muʿtazīlah to the effect that there is no other punishment for *zinā* other than flogging. Had God Most High intended to validate stoning, the Qur'an would have been explicit on it. They have further argued

> that stoning is the most severe of all punishments, it should therefore be proven by decisive evidence of either the Qur'an or hadith *mutawātir*, and all the available hadiths on stoning fall short of *mutawātir*. Although the solitary or *aḥad* hadith can create obligation and a shariah ruling, it cannot override what is proven by decisive evidence. Added to this is the unresolved doubt expressed by a Companion as to whether the stoning of Māʿiz and al-Ghamidiyyah preceded or succeeded the Qur'anic text. Stoning as a punishment thus collapses on the basis of the rule that doubt suspends the implementation of *ḥudūd*.

ʿAlī Manṣūr then observes that "based on these reasons and the attending doubts concerning the proof of stoning and its severity, the learned author (Abū Zahrah) was not inclined to recommend its enforcement."[59] This is also intimated in Abū Zahrah's own writing (some fifteen years previously), which stopped short, however, of making a categorical statement (i.e., on whether enforcement should be suspended).[60] Abū Zahrah's own analysis, however, contains additional information to the effect that stoning was initially introduced in the Torah, which was applied by the Jews and the Bible did not overrule it, and since the Old Testament was also proof that the Christians too applied it. There is in fact clear confirmation in the Qur'an that the Jews of Medina were governed by their own scripture:

> And how do they make you a judge and they have the Torah wherein is God's judgement! Yet they turn away after that! And these are not [true] believers."[61]
>
> وَكَيْفَ يُحَكِّمُونَكَ وَعِندَهُمُ ٱلتَّوْرَىٰةُ فِيهَا حُكْمُ ٱللَّهِ ثُمَّ يَتَوَلَّوْنَ مِنۢ بَعْدِ ذَٰلِكَ ۚ وَمَآ أُو۟لَـٰٓئِكَ بِٱلْمُؤْمِنِينَ

Qur'an commentators have stated the occasion of the revelation of this verse as follows: One of the leading Jewish figures who was residing in Medina had committed *zinā*, and the Jewish community was distressed with the predicament of their leader being stoned in accordance with the Torah. So they came to the Prophet in the hope of securing a lighter punishment for the accused. The Prophet mentioned the ruling of Torah to them. So the story goes, but perhaps we need not go into the details of it here. Abū Zahrah has said concerning this case that it happened at a time when the Jews lived peacefully in Medina under the Prophet's leadership but that relations turned hostile soon thereafter.[62]

Mohammad Suleman Siddiqi's research leads him to the conclusion that the verse above was revealed to the Prophet as late as in the year 7th Hijrah, whereas al-Nisā' (sura 4) was revealed in 3rd Hijrah and al-Nūr (sura 24) in the year 5th Hijrah, all of which deal with the punishment of unmarried offenders. With reference to married offenders, the Prophet referred to the rulings of previous revelations, especially the Torah, which provided stoning for married offenders. Siddiqi also mentions that the case of adultery committed by a man and woman from the Jewish tribe of Khaybar occurred in the 1st year Hijrah immediately after the Prophet's migration to Medina.[63]

It was probably during the closing months of the 5th year Hijrah and the beginning of the 6th Hijrah that the verse in sura al-Nūr (24:2–3) was revealed. The events between the 1st year Hijrah until the revelation of this verse leave little doubt that the Prophet had implemented the punishment of stoning by reference to Torah.[64]

ʿAlī Manṣūr, who quoted Abū Zahrah's view on this issue, adds that another prominent jurist, Muṣṭafā Aḥmad al-Zarqā, was present at the same conference and heard Abū Zahrah's views on the subject of stoning: "He too sent his opinion in writing to me in my capacity as Chairman of the then United Arab Republic's Committee for Harmonisation of Shariah and Law, wherein he had reached the conclusion that stoning as a punishment for *zinā* should not be enforced, not because of the doubt in the authenticity of hadith but because it is quite possible that the Prophet imposed stoning as a *taʿzīr* punishment." Al-Zarqā then added that this was also the opinion of Shaykh Maḥmūd Shaltūt. The text of al-Zarqā's letter contained the following:

> In my view there is a distinct possibility that the Prophet ordered stoning, in the related incidents by way, not of *ḥadd*, but of *taʿzīr* punishment. For he saw under the circumstances that only a strong and decisive stand on this issue could curb the rampant immorality and corruption of the Time of Ignorance (*jāhiliyyah*). Since the lawful government and the *ūli al-amr* are within their rights to introduce *taʿzīr* punishment in their effort to combat criminality and to secure benefit for the community, it is likely that the Prophet also exercised his authority in this way and introduced stoning as a *taʿzīr* punishment.[65]

Al-Zarqā refers to the current climate of modern opinion among the ulama to the effect that stoning "is a *taʿzīr* punishment, not one of the *ḥudūd*, and it is as such, a matter for the head of state to apply it in aggravated circumstances. This view also finds support in the Sunnah of the Prophet and the manner he actually applied stoning as a punishment for *zinā*."[66] Al-Zarqā continues that the textually prescribed and standard punishment for *zinā* is 100 lashes of the whip. He adds further that the shariah has made the application of *ḥudūd*, including that of *zinā*, contingent on strict conditions that must be observed in the material aspects of the offence, its evidence and proof. If all these conditions are properly observed, *ḥudūd* can only be expected to be rarely applied as they will, for the most part, be converted to *taʿzīr* penalties that the *qāḍī* determines by reference to the attending conditions of the crime. The presence of any doubt, even a slight one, will suspend the *ḥadd* in question. For this is the clear directive of the hadith: "Suspend the *ḥudūd* whenever there is doubt."[67]

With reference to the proof of *zinā*, al-Zarqā is of the view that "it is impossible to prove *zinā* except by the confession of its perpetrator," simply because proof by witnesses would require eye witnessing by four upright persons, which is almost impossible to obtain. Confession by the perpetrator "must also be four times in four different sessions, and when these strict conditions are not met in the proof of *zinā*, the punishment in question, be it lashing or stoning, would be abandoned and recourse had to be made to *taʿzīr* punishment, the type and quantity of which is determined by the ruler in accordance with its attending circumstances."[68] In the event of retraction of a confession, the prescribed punishment is also abandoned and substituted with a *taʿzīr* punishment.

Cheriff Bassiouni also wrote concerning the punishment of *zinā* that the Qur'an provides flogging as the punishment for this offence and not stoning as is often assumed. Death by stoning "was first imposed by the Prophet during his days in Madinah (620–632 CE), when he applied Jewish law to the Jewish tribes in and around Madinah, and whose laws required such a penalty. In other words, Islam itself does not require stoning, and its use was mistakenly transposed onto Islam."[69]

Yūsuf al-Qaraḍāwī has forcefully spoken on another aspect of the *ḥudūd* enforcement, which is that it is a matter for the ruling authorities, not for individual Muslims, to attempt the implementation of *ḥudūd*. Even if they know the perpetrator and are able to enforce the punishment, their role would be to report the matter to the authorities but not to take the law into their own hands. For that would lead to chaos and confusion. It is not for individuals to cut the hand of the thief, lash the adulterer or stone him, lash the wine drinker, retaliate against the murderer, and so forth. Some people may think that this is expected of them and thus "appoint themselves as police, judge and enforcement officers."[70] This would be patently erroneous. It is not their role, and they should not take it on themselves.

Al-Qaraḍāwī further adds that, in the event where the government and the *ūli al-amr* fall short of enforcing the rules of shariah, or when they breach the trust and order of duty entrusted to them, then it is for the community to advise the leaders by way of constructive advice (*naṣiḥah*). Otherwise the people should resort to all lawful means until they succeed to impress their message on their leaders, but they should also bear in mind the shariah guideline that one should not try to repel an evil with a bigger evil. It is an obligation under such circumstances to take the lesser of the two evils. Hence the role of the individual in regard to law enforcement is to assist honest employees and enforcement officers and work with them to apply the law but not to take their place and become the law enforcers themselves.[71]

In a fatwa issued with regard to the applicability in modern times of Islamic corporal punishments, the former Grand Mufti of Egypt, Sheikh Ali Gomaa, stated the following:

> *Ḥudūd* have not been implemented in countries such as Egypt for a very long time. This is because the legal conditions for their implementation, which describe specific means for establishing guilt and stipulate the possibility of retracting a confession, are not met . . . Most of the penal codes of the remainder of the Islamic countries...remain silent on the issue of corporal punishment (*ḥudūd*). This is because our age is one of general uncertainty (*shubha*), and the Prophet, may the peace and blessings of God be upon him said, "Stay the enforcement of corporal punishments when there is doubt."[72]

*Homosexuality, Incest, and Lesbianism (*Liwāṭ, Zinā bi'l-maḥārim, Siḥāq*)*

Homosexuality and adultery have an aspect in common, which is that both involve prohibited sexual intercourse, except that the former consists of penetration of the male organ into the anus of a man or woman, whereas *zinā* consists of penetration of the male organ into a woman's vagina.[73] *Zinā* according to the majority thus requires actual penetration by the man into the vagina of a woman, whereas the Ḥanbalī and the Shii schools also include anal intercourse in the definition of *zinā*. For the Shia, in addition, sexual acts without penetration, as well as homosexuality and pimping, are regarded as *ḥudūd* offences, whereas the Sunni schools regard such acts not as *ḥudūd* crimes can nonetheless be punished by the judge under *taʿzīr* deterrent punishment.[74] For homosexuality to be punishable under *ḥudūd* in Shii law, the perpetrator must confess four times, or by four witnesses, failing which it is punishable only under *taʿzīr*, regardless as to whether the person is in the active or passive position. There is also a choice, under Shii law, for the authorities to kill the perpetrator by the sword, stoning, throwing from a great height, or burning. Homosexuality and lesbianism even without actual penetration are punishable with 100 lashes of the whip.[75]

Muslim jurists quote the following Qur'anic passages, addressed to the people of Lot, on the prohibition of homosexuality:

> You practice your lusts on men in preference to women: you are indeed a people transgressing beyond bounds. (al-Aʿrāf, 7:81)
>
> إِنَّكُمْ لَتَأْتُونَ ٱلرِّجَالَ شَهْوَةً مِّن دُونِ ٱلنِّسَآءِ ۚ بَلْ أَنتُمْ قَوْمٌ مُّسْرِفُونَ
>
> Of all the creatures in the world, will you approach males, and leave those whom God has created for you to be your mates! Nay, you are a people transgressing (all limits). (al-Shuʿarāʾ, 26:165–166)
>
> أَتَأْتُونَ ٱلذُّكْرَانَ مِنَ ٱلْعَٰلَمِينَ. وَتَذَرُونَ مَا خَلَقَ لَكُمْ رَبُّكُم مِّنْ أَزْوَٰجِكُم ۚ بَلْ أَنتُمْ قَوْمٌ عَادُونَ

Muslim jurists have also quoted the hadith in which the Prophet is reported to have said: "God has cursed those who practice what the people of Lot did (and the Prophet repeated it three times [لعن الله من عمل قوم لوط]"[76]; and: "Kill the active and passive partners both [اقتلوا الفاعل والمفعول]"; and "Stone the upper and the lower partners both" [ارجموا الأعلى والأسفل].[77] A longer version of this last hadith has additional information from the Companion Ibn ʿAbbās, who was asked whether the notion of virginity was relevant in homosexuality; he replied and quoted a longer version: "Kill the active and the passive partners, be they married or unmarried."[78]

> اقتلوا الفاعل والمفعول به احصن او لم يحصن .

Whereas the majority apply the rules of *zinā* also to homosexuality, Imam Abū Ḥanīfah has differed over the analogy of *liwāṭ* with *zinā* and the analogical application also of the prescribed punishment of *zinā* to that of *liwāṭ*. Yet the two disciples of Abū Ḥanīfah, Abū Yūsuf and al-Shaybānī, have sided with the majority and held that *liwāṭ* is like *zinā* and subject to the same punishment. Homosexuality is thus punished with 100 lashes if committed by an unmarried person and punished with stoning if the perpetrator is married.[79] But if the validity of stoning as a valid punishment collapses in the case of adultery, that position will also apply to homosexuality.

There is a difference of opinion, however, about the punishment of *liwāṭ*. The Mālikīs, some Shāfiʿīs, Ḥanbalīs, and the Shia are of the opinion that this punishment should be death by stoning (Mālikīs), the sword (some Shāfiʿīs and Ḥanbalīs), throwing from a high wall or burning, or death by the sword or at the discretion of the court (Shia). Some scholars of the Shāfiʿī and Ḥanbalī schools maintain that the concept of a married person (*muḥṣan*) only applies to the active partner and is not relevant to the passive partner. This also means that only the former, if a married person, can be stoned to death (assuming the validity stoning) and that the punishment for the latter is always flogging.[80]

As for the proof of homosexuality, it is like that of adultery: four male eyewitnesses who have observed the actual penetration with the same specifications as are required in the proof of *zinā*. This is the position of the Mālikī, Shāfiʿī, Ḥanbalī, and Shii schools. The Shii school also maintains that homosexuality (*liwāṭ*) is similarly proven by a confession that is repeated four times. The death penalty for the active partner is maintained even if the passive party is a child or insane, in which case the child may be subjected to a disciplinary sanction. If a non-Muslim (i.e., a *dhimmī*) commits the act with a Muslim, the *dhimmī* is to be killed, but if both parties are *dhimmī*, the ruler/imam may decide on the manner and quantum of punishment.[81]

The Ḥanafī school maintains that homosexuality is proven by the testimony of two male witnesses since there is no clear text in the Qur'an or hadith to equate it with adultery and also that the harm of *liwāṭ* is less than that of *zinā* as it does not involve interference in the family line of descent. *Liwāṭ* is also not punished as a *ḥudūd* crime but as a *taʿzīr* offence, and the quantum of punishment is determined by the ruler and judge. If there is repetition and the offender is not deterred by that punishment, he is to be executed by the sword, again by way of *taʿzīr*, but not as a *ḥudūd* offence.

The renowned Zaydī Shii scholar from Yemen, Muḥammad b. ʿAlī al-Shawkānī, has criticised Abū Ḥanīfah's comment in saying that there is no clear text on the subject of *liwāṭ*—for there is sufficient evidence in the hadith to make this a textually prescribed offence.[82] Abū Zahrah, himself a Ḥanafī, takes up the point and effectively concurs with al-Shawkānī's assessment and also adds that there is no need for an analogy between homosexuality and adultery, as the majority has drawn, simply because the death punishment for the former is based on the text (of hadith) and not any analogy. Analogy is in principle not valid in *ḥudūd* and that position still prevails. It is further added that the reason Abū Ḥanīfah took a different view of homosexuality and considered it a *taʿzīr* offence is that he thought the hadiths on the punishment of homosexuality were all solitary and generally weak of authenticity.[83]

As for a man who has anal sex with his wife, there is general agreement that the perpetrator is not liable to the prescribed punishment of *liwāṭ* but that he has committed an act of lewdness that is greatly sinful and liable to punishment in the hereafter. According to a hadith on the authority of Khuzaymah b. Thabit, Abū Hurayrah, and ʿAlī b. Talq, the Prophet has said, "Do not approach your women from their backs *(la-ta'tu al-nisā' fī-adbārihinna)*." It is also reported by ʿUmar b. Shuʿayb—from his father/ from his grandfather—in a hadith from the Prophet, who said that "it is a minor *liwāṭ* (*hiya al-liwāṭah al-ṣughra*)." According to another hadith, also from Abū Hurayrah, the Prophet has said, "One who approaches his wife from behind, be she in her menstrual cycle or otherwise . . . has given a lie to what has been revealed to Muḥammad."[84]

Musāḥaqah literally means rubbing fiercely without penetration, typically the act of two women rubbing their private parts against one another, which can also occur between two males. As for the juridical basis of *musāḥaqah*, fiqh textbooks refer to the Qur'anic passage that speaks in praise of believing women who "guard their private parts (*li-furūjihim ḥāfiẓun*) except with those who joined to them in the marriage bond." The text continues to declare "those whose desire exceed these limits," to be transgressors (23:5–7). The fiqh scholars also subsume lesbianism under the Qur'anic term *fāḥishah* (al-Aʿrāf, 7:80) and hold that it as impermissible. Hence all sex outside marriage, including *musāḥaqah*, is transgressive of the shariah limits. Also quoted is the hadith that provides: "A woman may not look at the private parts of another woman nor may she sleep under the same cover with her." In yet another hadith, it is declared: "When a woman [sexually] approaches another woman, both of them are adulterers (*zāniyatān*)." [86]

إذا أتت المرأة المرأة ، فهما زانيتان.

No punishment is, however, mentioned for *musāḥaqah*, hence the conclusion that it is a transgression (*maʿṣiyah*) that may be punished under *taʿzīr*. This is also the position under Shii law. The equation of *musāḥaqah* to *zinā* in the second hadith is in its literal sense, as *zinā* in Arabic means transgression and sin. But *zinā* and lesbianism are different in that the latter does not involve penetration nor does it threaten purity of the family lineage.[85]

Incest (*zinā bi'l-maḥārim*) is *zinā* with someone within the prohibited degrees of relationship, whether by blood or marriage, such as one's mother and daughter or one's step-mother, be it by consent or without. All are punishable by death, it is said, by the sword, regardless of whether the perpetrator is married or unmarried, Muslim or non-Muslim. The Qur'an does not specifically mention incest as a separate category nor as a separate offence, hence it is subsumed by its rulings on *zinā*. Much of the information on incest comes from the evidence in hadith. In a hadith narrated by al-Bara b. Azib, he said: "I met my maternal uncle—in some reports it is paternal uncle—and he was carrying a sword. I asked him: where are you going? And he said "The Prophet, pbuh, sent me for a man who married his step-mother—to strike his neck and take away his property."[87]

حديث البراء بن عازب – رضي الله عنه – في قتل من نكح امرأة أبيه ، وقد جاء بعدة ألفاظ منها : لقيت خالي – وفي بعض الروايات : عمي– ومعه راية ، فقلت له ؟ . فقال : بعثني رسول الله – صلى الله عليه وسلم – إلى رجل تزوج امرأة أبيه أن أقتله أو أضرب عنقه

Another hadith refers to the authority of Muawiyah b. Qurrah from his father, to the effect that the Prophet sent his grandfather [Mu'awiyah] for a man who had married the wife of his son to "strike his neck and take away his property." The reason for expropriation was that, by committing incest, the perpetrator had renounced Islam in the meantime, for he committed a sexual act with a woman who he knows is *ḥarām* to him. Hence applying the prescribed punishment in his case is strictly obligatory.[88]

Another Companion, Jābir b. ʿAbd Allāh, has been quoted to have said concerning one guilty of incest that his head should be struck and his assets to be handed over to the public treasury as punishment for himself and deterrence to others. Imam Ibn Ḥanbal has held that killing the perpetrator of incest is obligatory, whether the perpetrator is married (*muḥṣan*) or otherwise, especially one who commits it with his step-mother. In another hadith recorded by Ibn Majah, it is reported on the authority of Ibn

ʿAbbās, who quoted the Prophet, pbuh, as saying, "One who has intercourse with a close relative [prohibited to him] should be killed."[89] For he has violated what God has made *ḥarām*; he is a renegade and renouncer of Islam who may be slain and his property given to the public treasury. This is also the conventional fiqh position with one who renounces Islam and becomes an infidel (*kāfir*). This hadith is inclusive of all instances of incest regardless as to whether they involve marriage with a close relative or intercourse without marriage; all of it is considered as *zinā*. Muslim jurists are in agreement on the enormity of incest in all of its varieties as an act that is beyond sound human nature and that the perpetrator stoops so low as to become an ugly beast who calls upon himself the wrath of God and mandatory enforcement of the death punishment.[90]

In a book entitled *al-Ḍarūrah al-Marḥaliyyah fī Taṭbīq al-Qānūn al-Jināʾī al-Islāmī* (The Necessity of Gradualism in the Implementation of Islamic Criminal Law), Fatḥī al-Khammāsī argues that, following the Islamic revivalist discourse of recent decades, the Muslim world has been witnessing a revival of certain aspects of the shariah. This came as a new phase in the experience of the ummah following aggressive colonial policies to suppress shariah in the sphere especially of public law. What many countries are experiencing is nothing less than a new beginning, fraught with new challenges, especially concerning the hard-core aspects of Islamic criminal law.

With regards to homosexuality (*liwāṭ*), the author proposes a two-phased approach, the first of which should opt for the view of Imam Abū Ḥanīfah that *liwāṭ* should be punishable as a *taʿzīr* offence, as there is, unlike with *zinā*, no mixing of genealogy and family descent in *liwāṭ*. The second phase of implementation should bring in the position of the majority (*jumhūr*), which treats homosexuality as a *ḥudūd* crime and subjects it to the same punishment as that of adultery (*zinā*).[91]

VI

*Theft (*Sariqah*)*

THEFT IS THE subject of a great deal of writings in both traditional and contemporary scholarship. The discussion that follows focuses on a select number of issues, beginning with a review of the Qur'anic verse on theft and then discussing issues pertaining to theft from one's relatives, issues over the quorum (*nisāb*) (i.e., the minimum quantitative value that invokes the prescribed punishment), and issues about safekeeping and ownership (*ḥirz, milkiyyah*), respectively. Other aspects of theft explored in this chapter are the proof of theft, the punishment and consequences of theft, and repentance by the accused. References to contemporary opinion, contributions of leading Muslim scholars, and reform proposals are also featured.

Theft is the subject of the following Qur'anic verse:

> As for the thief, both male and female, cut off his or her hands: a retribution for their deeds and exemplary punishment from God. And God is exalted in power, most wise. But if the thief repents after his crime and amends his conduct, God redeems him, God is forgiving, most merciful. (al-Mā'idah, 5:38–39)

وَٱلسَّارِقُ وَٱلسَّارِقَةُ فَٱقْطَعُوٓا۟ أَيْدِيَهُمَا جَزَآءًۢ بِمَا كَسَبَا نَكَـٰلًا مِّنَ ٱللَّهِ ۗ وَٱللَّهُ عَزِيزٌ حَكِيمٌ (٣٨) فَمَن تَابَ مِنۢ بَعْدِ
ظُلْمِهِۦ وَأَصْلَحَ فَإِنَّ ٱللَّهَ يَتُوبُ عَلَيْهِ ۗ إِنَّ ٱللَّهَ غَفُورٌ رَّحِيمٌ (٣٩)

Due to the severity of its punishment, Muslim jurists have defined theft narrowly and stipulated a large number of conditions it must fulfill before the prescribed punishments can be implemented. Every act of theft must fulfil the following requirements. First, the act must involve surreptitiously taking away the (movable) property of another with a minimum value (*nisāb*). The act is not surreptitious if someone steals goods from a market stall in broad daylight, hence the fixed penalty for theft cannot be imposed. The stolen property must not be partially owned by the perpetrator nor entrusted to him; and it is taken by a legally competent person (*ʿaqil, bāligh*) from a place that is locked or under guard (*ḥirz*). Theft thus differs from usurpation (*ghasb*) wherein the property of another person is taken openly, often by force. These elements are also present in banditry or *ḥirābah*, also known as the "great theft" (*al-sariqat al-kubrā*) where life and property are often both attacked through acts of terror openly involving a display of power and subjugation of the victim(s).[1] The leading schools of Islamic law have recorded different opinions on the types of safeguarding and the details, which will not be discussed here beyond saying that all the leading schools, including the Shia Imamiyyah, have held that recourse should be *ḥadd*—in a due understanding of *ḥirz*—to general customs that prevail at time of the theft.[2] This is also the position many contemporary scholars have taken on the subject.

One of the tests of valuability and quorum fulfillment of the stolen good is that, if someone destroys it, he or she is held liable for compensation or replacement. The property taken must also have market value (*māl mutaqawwim*) and fulfils the required quorum (*nisāb*).

Theft from Relatives

Theft from a close relative is not punishable, according to Imam Abū Ḥanīfah, as close relatives often enter each other's quarters. There is an implicit permission, which means that it does not meet the requirement of a guarded place (*ḥirz*). But this is not necessarily so in the case of theft from relatives further removed, such that assuming an implicit permission would seem out of place. However, theft in this case would amount to severing the ties of kinship, which is also prohibited (*ḥarām*) under shariah. The Imams al-Shāfiʿī, Mālik, and Ibn Ḥanbal, as well as the Shia Imamiyyah, maintain that theft is not punishable for a father regarding the property of his son and grandson and that this exemption also applies to a mother and her descendants. Imam Mālik has differed slightly on this to say that the forebears are not punished by the prescribed punishment, but that if the descendants steal from their forebears, they are liable to punishment. Imam Mālik has in this case followed more closely the hadith to the effect that "you and your property belongs to your father"—(انت ومالك لابيك). The Shia also follow the ruling of this hadith.[3] Differences of opinion have been recorded as to whether spouses are liable to the prescribed punishment for stealing from one another. Whereas the Ẓāhirī school makes them both liable for stealing from one another, Imam Abū Ḥanīfah absolves them both. Imam Mālik and al-Shāfiʿī hold that they are only liable for theft of property they have segregated or locked away from each other's access. An alternative Shāfiʿī view is that the wife is not liable if she steals from her husband, as the latter is responsible for her maintenance, but that the husband is liable if he steals from his wife.[4] The Shia Imamiyyah maintain that neither the husband nor the wife are liable to mutilation if the one steals from the other, and that the same applies also if a person steals from his brother.[5] Theft is generally punishable if committed by one's collateral relatives such as brothers and sisters and their descendants. That said, theft from a relative in all these categories may be subjected to a lighter *taʿzīr* punishment if deemed appropriate by a competent judge.

*Issues over the Quorum (*Nisāb*)*

Differences of opinion have arisen over the quorum, or minimum quantitative value, of stolen goods. According to the jurists of the Hijaz (Mecca and Medina), as well as the Mālikīs, Shāfiʿīs, and Shia Imamiyyah, the value of the stolen goods must be equivalent to at least three silver dirhams or one-quarter of a gold dinar. The jurists of Iraq, including the Ḥanafīs, maintain that the quorum is ten silver dirhams, or one dinar, and that no mutilation is permissible for anything less. This is based on the authority of a hadith narrated by ʿAbd Allāh b. Masʿūd: "Hand is not mutilated except [for the theft of] one dinar or ten dirhams [لا قطع إلا في دينار].[6]

In yet another hadith reported by Abū Hurayrah, it is stated: "God curses a thief whose hand is cut for stealing [merely] of an egg and one who steals a rope."

لعن الله السارق يسرق البيضة تقطع يده ويسرق الحبل فتقطع يده.

There are two other hadith reports on this, one narrated by Imam Mālik from Nafiʿ– from Ibn ʿUmar that "the [hand of] thief is not mutilated except for the price of *al-mijn* [shield], which was estimated at ten dirhams at the time of the Prophet." Al-Qurṭubī, who quoted this hadith, adds that the jurists of Iraq who have relied on this hadith also record the information attributed to Ibn ʿAbbās, who said that the price of a shield during the

Prophet's time was ten dirhams and that no mutilation should be ordered for anything below this. Al-Qurṭubī, who considers this a good position, also adds that the recommendation would have prevailed had it not been for the hadith of ʿĀʾishah on which al-Shāfiʿī relied (i.e., that the quorum is a quarter of a dinar).[7]

Notwithstanding the Ḥanafī claim of a general consensus (*ijmāʿ*) in favour of ten dirhams as the minimum quorum, there is considerable variation in the sources over this, which makes the claim of general consensus difficult to sustain. Thus, according to an alternative opinion, mutilation is not required for the theft of anything less than ten dinars or forty dirhams. The fifth Shii Imam, Muḥammad al-Bāqir, has on the other hand given the quorum at five dirhams.

Differences of opinion also obtain in regards to the question as to which of the these two, the dirham or the dinar, or both, are the unit of value for the purpose of determination of the prescribed punishment. This is because the two precious metals are not always in precise correlation with one another, and factors of time and place often move their prices differently according to local preferences. Imam Mālik maintains that both are units of value, each in their own right, and has in this connection added that the people of Baghdad look at the dominant practice and the people's preference, which may be either for the dirham or the dinar. Imam al-Shāfiʿī has held that the standard is the gold dinar, which is the base (*al-aṣl*) in the evaluation of other goods and commodities. In part these differences are due to variations that are also observed in several hadith reports available on the subject and the way these reports have been interpreted by reporters and commentators.[8] The key Ḥanbalī scholar Ibn Qayyim al-Jawziyyah understood the purpose of identification in the Sunnah of the Prophet of one-quarter of a gold dinar as the quorum, suggesting that this is sufficient to provide a person and his family with sustenance for a day and a night of an average kind of food without prodigality or stinginess.[9]

Whereas the majority of scholastic jurists have considered a quantitative quorum for stolen goods, it is of interest to note that Ḥasan al-Baṣrī (d. 110/728), Dāwūd al-Ẓāhirī (d. 270/885), and the Kharijites maintained that amputation applies to any amount, small or large. They took this position on the analysis apparently based on how the Qur'an simply orders the punishment of mutilation for a thief and makes no reference to any quantity of stolen goods as such. The majority position on this is that the Qur'anic verse in this regard has been specified by way of specification of the general (*takhṣīṣ al-ʿām*) by the Sunnah of the Prophet.[10] Yet as our review of the

Sunnah has shown, there is wide variation on what precisely the Sunnah has specified and how the various schools of law understood it.

Muḥammad Salīm al-ʿAwā, a prominent Egyptian jurist and author of important works on Islamic criminal law, draws the conclusion that one should depart from a fixed amount. But one should also revisit, from time to time, the quorum value in line with the prevailing prices of food commodities, fluctuation in the prices of gold and silver, and the socioeconomic realities of the country and people. He has also cited, in this connection, two different positions taken—one by the Azharite scholars and the other by an Egyptian member of Parliament—on the subject of quorum values for imposing prescribed punishments.[11] Having examined these positions, al-ʿAwā wrote that the correct understanding of Sunnah on this subject is that the Prophet disallowed mutilation for small amounts of goods below a certain limit. This decision also represents the juristic opinions of all the schools to the effect that pilferage and theft of negligible amounts do not invoke the prescribed punishment. What is considered a "small amount" in people's eyes is also liable to change in the light of prevailing socioeconomic conditions and general customs at the time the offence was committed. The best course to take for those who seek to ascertain the shariah position is therefore to consider the effective cause and purpose of the shariah ruling and not necessarily to recite the views and quantitative specifications of fiqh jurists on the quorum issue. For the fiqh scholars may have arrived at certain conclusions, which reflected their *ijtihād* at the time but that may not be suitable for our time: "It is not advisable therefore always to stand by scholastic positions of the fiqh scholars of the past regardless of their suitability or otherwise with the people's living standards" because they work under a totally different set of conditions.[12]

This is a sound analysis. It may also be in order for us to take it a step further and relate it perhaps to the changing socioeconomic conditions of a country and its customs. These conditions tend to be changeable. Taxpayers are usually allowed to claim a minimum amount for personal needs as tax-exempt, and any income above that level is subjected to income tax. This may arguably provide an indicator of the poverty line in a particular country and may be considered relevant to the purposes of the present discussion. One need not perhaps have a fixed quantity of *nisāb* for imposing a *taʿzīr* punishment on theft; but for the capital punishment to apply, relevant factors such as the availability of social support for the poor, per-capita income of the country or locality, and personal needs should be considered. The subject would admittedly call for further scrutiny by scholars and researchers, but it would be a worthwhile step to take if one were to bring the theory of *ḥudūd* in regards to theft closer to the prevailing socioeconomic conditions of our time.

Differences of opinion also obtain regarding the question as to whether the thief should know the value of an object at the material time, for if he was unsure of the quorum value and knew it was above that level he might have hesitated. Some Ḥanafī and Mālikī jurists have disregarded the question and found it sufficient to ascertain the element of intention. If the thief intended to steal, his knowledge of the value, it is said, is immaterial. But custom, circumstantial factors, and experience do play a role.[13] One would have thought that personal knowledge of the thief, important as it is, is rather too subjective to be reliably ascertained; it may play some role but not a highly significant one.

Disagreement has also arisen among the leading schools of law over the quorum value of theft by a group of persons in collusion. Should each one of them fulfill the quorum requirements, or is the quorum value calculated as one for the whole group? A similar question has arisen over the application of safekeeping (*ḥirz*) as to whether only the person who took the goods out of the safe place is punished with mutilation or whether the whole group may be so punished. The majority, including Imams Mālik, al-Shāfiʿī, and Ibn Ḥanbal, have held that one quorum is enough and all of them are liable to mutilation, whereas Abū Ḥanīfah has held that the quorum requirement must be individually fulfilled. The Shia school has recorded two different views, one of which is that if two people steal, one quorum is enough for both to be punished. The second view maintains that only if the share of each of the two thieves reach the quorum are they both liable to the punishment. An illustration is given: if one person makes a hole in the wall and the other takes the goods away, neither is liable for capital punishment. Detailed views and replies are given with regard to the question as to who actually takes away the goods from the safe place. The views offered incline toward saying that shariah requires one hand mutilated for one offence and not expanding this to a larger number, but they go on to say that this is not accurate. The answer depends on a more accurate study of the circumstances. It would vary, for instance, with regard to a house that has four walls, a main entrance, and many rooms that are likely to raise detailed questions on how they are used.[14] Questions have also arisen with regard to kidnapping and stealing from a child. In our view in the case of capital punishment for theft, the quorum should be individually fulfilled, although this question may be more flexibly decided in the case of *taʿzīr* punishment. This may also be stated regarding the issue as to who removed goods from safe custody. Only the person who played the principal role should be liable for the higher punishment, and others involved may perhaps be only subject to *taʿzīr*.[15]

Furthermore, the goods must be capable of being owned and must also have market value. There are goods, on the other hand, that may have market value but no juridical (*sharʿī*) value as such. Items such as pigmeat, idols, gambling tools, and liquor are forbidden for Muslims and can only be owned by non-Muslims. As a consequence, theft of these items can only be penalised if they are stolen from a non-Muslim. A further requirement for the enforcement of capital punishment is that the thief does not have the goods legally at his disposal nor is he a co-owner. For example, a person who steals from state property or the public treasury, a soldier who steals from the spoils of war, or even a guest who stays in one's place by invitation cannot be punished with amputation as they have a share, however small or insignificant, in these assets or a kind of implied permission to be there.[16]

Issues over Safekeeping (Hirz) and Ownership (Milkiyyah)

Amputation does not apply if the stolen goods are not properly guarded or are kept in an inadequate or unlikely place. Locked houses, shops, safety boxes, and coffers count as guarded places, taking also into account the nature of the object. Stealing fruit hanging on trees in public places does not invoke the prescribed punishment; and a stable is a suitable place for keeping horses but not for keeping jewellery. Similarly, an item found in a public bath or mosque does not qualify under the requirement of safekeeping (*ḥirz*). Imam Abū Ḥanīfah also precludes from the prescribed punishment the taking of fruits hanging from trees in guarded places, even when not accessible to the public, based on the analysis that such fruit is usually perishable and thus not subject to the prescribed punishment. However, if such fruit is picked and then placed in containers that preserve them, or if they are dried for future use, they may be excluded from the perishable category.[17] Furthermore, the judge must ask the witnesses for details of the manner, place, and modality of the theft. Details may reveal factors that could well suspend the prescribed punishment. Thus if a thief has taken something away from a house or room without actually entering the place, this may fail to qualify the requirements of taking something away from a guarded place. Safekeeping in this case is signified by the house or room, which, technically speaking, the thief has not violated.

The leading schools of Islamic law also preclude from capital punishment the stealing of fresh and perishable foodstuffs and goods that are not storable for future use. Similarly, goods that are originally permissible (*mubāḥ*) for everyone to take, such as game and firewood, are precluded from the application of prescribed punishment. The latter is further restricted by the presence of doubt (*shubha*) as already mentioned. The Ḥanafī and Shia schools have included in *shubha* uncertainty that may arise from the existence of a contract or an understanding over the existence of a right on the part of the thief for the stolen goods. Furthermore, the capital punishment cannot be applied if someone steals copies of the Qur'an.[18]

The correct understanding of safekeeping (*ḥirz*), it is observed, should be in line with the general custom, which may well be changeable from time to time. Any place that is considered safe for the stolen goods, according to the prevailing customary understanding of people, should be considered as *ḥirz* and not necessarily the *taqlīdī* (imitationist) views recorded by earlier jurists.[19] The views have also been criticised of fiqh scholars who held that punishment is not applied to a thief who steals from the assets of a public treasury or from other public places, especially when the thief happens to be working there or is allowed to enter. The correct view recorded by some jurists, in al-ʿAwā's assessment, is that one who steals from public places should not be treated differently from one who steals from a private place. The first should even be prioritised in the matter of punishment. This is because those who are employed and allowed to enter the public treasury and other government offices are trustees and custodians of the state as well as guardians of state or public property. Theft from such places can involve large amounts that signify a serious breach of trust for government employees and officials. This should even be considered an aggravating factor, rather than a mitigating one, which has been the case in much of the scholastic writings on the subject.[20]

Disagreement has also arisen over the validity of imposing the capital punishment of theft for stealing goods that are subject to litigation and disputed ownership. The majority maintain that the punishment of theft is not enforced in the case of goods whose owner is not known unless he comes forth and establishes his ownership. The owner must in all cases be known and also initiate a claim.[21] In the event where witnesses voluntarily come forth and give testimony regarding theft of goods belonging to someone who is absent, the witnesses may be granted a hearing, as there may be an issue over protection of the Right of God, or of public right, but the capital punishment of theft cannot be enforced unless the owner or his representative is present and presses a claim against the thief.[22]

Questions have arisen, moreover, as to who is authorised to initiate litigation (*khuṣūmah*) in the case of theft. In response to this the Imam Abū Ḥanīfah has held that anyone who validly possessed the goods at the time they were stolen—which includes, in addition to the owner, one who may be holding them in trust (i.e., the *amīn*) or surety, such as a trading manager (*muḍarīb*) or mortgagor—all of whom are qualified to claim return of the stolen goods and initiate litigation, although Imams al-Shāfiʿī, Ibn Ḥanbal, and Zufar b. Huzayl (the latter a disciple of Imam Abū Ḥanīfah) maintain that only the owner may initiate litigation. Unlawful possession does not entitle one to litigation. Thus if someone steals the goods from the thief, the latter will have no *locus standi* to litigate for their return. Since he has no valid title on the goods, stealing from him would be tantamount to picking it up from a public path. This would also mean that the capital punishment cannot be enforced on the second thief as this second theft would not qualify the condition of stealing from a lawful owner.[23]

Theft has two aspects, as already noted: one is the Right of God (*ḥaqq Allāh*) aspect, which is predominant; and the other is the Right of Man (*ḥaqq al-ādamī*), which is deemed to be the lesser part and consists of a private claim for the return of the stolen goods or compensation to their owner. Whenever a claim of theft is proven, two main consequences follow, one of which is liability for the return of goods or compensation regarding the private right; and the other is applying the punishment for violation of the public right. There is some disagreement, however, on the first of these. The Ḥanafī school maintains that the two aspects are not separate in that, once the thief is duly punished, he is not liable for anything else. The reason given is that the Qur'an only imposes mutilation and makes no reference to compensation. They have also referred to a hadith on the authority of ʿAbd al-Raḥmān b. Awf, who states that the Prophet said, "When the thief's hand is mutilated he is not liable for compensation" [اذا قطع السارق فلا غرم عليه]. Some Ḥanafī scholars have added that he must return the stolen goods if they still exist but is not liable to compensation if they are not.[24]

Imams al-Shāfiʿī and Ibn Ḥanbal have held on the contrary that liability for compensation and punishment always go together and the thief remains liable even after punishment. For theft involves transgression of both the Right of God and the Right of Man; the former is satisfied by punishment and the latter by compensation. They say that one of the narrators of the hadith of ʿAbd al-Raḥmān b. ʿAwf is unknown (*majhūl*), and they have instead referred to another hadith that "the taking hand is liable for what it has taken until repayment [على اليد ما اخذ ت حتى تؤده]." Hence the thief must return the goods if they exist, but he has to pay the price or its equivalent independently of whether or not his hand is mutilated. Regardless of his own financial status—solvent or insolvent—he must return the goods or pay compensation. Should there be more than one victim of the theft, the thief remains answerable to each one of them, even regardless of whether or not they all initiate litigation. Imam Mālik also concurs with these positions except for adding that, after mutilation of the hand, the thief is only liable to compensation if he is solvent and can afford to pay. The Shii position on this corresponds with that of the Ḥanafī school to the effect that liability for compensation does not combine with mutilation.[25]

Proof and Punishment of Theft

There is general agreement among the leading schools, both Sunni and Shia, that the capital offence of theft is proven by the testimony of two upright male witnesses, or one male and two female witnesses, or even one male witness and a solemn oath by the defendant and also by confession of the thief. The preferred position is, however, that the solemn oath is not admissible in the proof of theft. Should the proof of theft fall below these, the judge may not order the prescribed punishment but may still penalise the accused with a discretionary *taʿzīr* punishment. The confession need not be repeated four times, as was the case in the proof of *zinā*; hence a valid confession by a legally competent person is sufficient if made only once. This is the position of the Ḥanafī, Shāfiʿī, and Ẓāhirī schools, which represents the standard position with regard to testimony in most litigations, although even here the Ḥanbalī school, Abū Yūsuf the disciple of Imam Abū Ḥanīfah, and the Shia Imamiyyah have maintained that confession should be made twice, not just once, in order to eliminate all doubt, and that the prescribed punishment of theft is not implemented by only one instance of confession. Quoted in authority for this is a hadith narrated by the Companion Abī Umayyah al-Makhzumī who reported that a thief (not named) was brought before the Prophet and confessed that he had committed theft. Then the Prophet asked him questions that made the man repeat his confession two or three times before he was ordered to be punished. Hence it is concluded that the judge must meet the thief and ask for confirmation and repetition of the confession so as to remove doubt before sentencing him. Quoted in authority for this is the precedent of the fourth caliph ʿAlī b. Abū Ṭālib, who apparently drew a parallel between witnesses and confession. Two witnesses are thus matched by two instances of confession, and it is further added that the confession is repeated in two different settings. One instance of confession is thus not enough for imposing the capital punishment, but the judge may consider punishing the accused by way of *taʿzīr* and also order him to return the goods if still available or repay their price to the owner.[26]

Confession is considered as a weak method of proof and may be retracted any time prior to punishment or when the *ḥadd* of theft is suspended as a result—but then it is added that this retraction is effective in respect only to the Right of God aspect of the offence. Retraction does not, in other words, affect the private right aspect of the theft. The owner of the stolen goods may still proceed to claim compensation, and the judge is also within his rights to order a lesser *taʿzīr* punishment based on his original confession even if subsequently retracted. The Ẓāhirī school maintains, however, that retraction of a confession, once validly made, is of no effect, as they also do not suspend *ḥudūd* on the basis of doubt/*shubha*.[27]

The judge must also ask the thief and witnesses about the time of the incident as there may be a significant lapse of time that may well bring the rule of expiration (*taqādum*) of testimony into the picture. Should there be a lapse of time involved, the thief is held liable for the private right aspect of the claim but not the *ḥadd* punishment, which represents the public right (*ḥaqq Allāh*). The other three Imams do not recognise expiration and do not agree to it, saying that valid testimony may be admitted regardless of expiry of time provided that the judge is satisfied with it. Yet a variant report from Imam Aḥmad b. Ḥanbal has it that he considered expiration applicable to the *ḥudūd*.[28]

The judge must also ask about the place where theft took place, for if it happened to be in a country at war (*dār al-ḥarb*) the punishment is likely to be suspended. Some of these details are also required to be made known in the case of confession except for lapse of time, which does not affect the validity of a confession, nor is the confessor asked to specify the place where he committed the act. But other details pertaining to the safeguarding (*ḥirz*), quorum value, and other specifications of the stolen goods, as well as his own condition, may be included in the confession and the judge may ascertain and enquire about them.[29]

Whereas the majority have understood mutilation by severing the right hand from the wrist, according to the Shia, based on the precedent of the fourth caliph ʿAlī, mutilation is required only of the four fingers of the right hand such that the palm and thumb are left intact.[30]

Repentance and Its Impact on the Punishment of Theft

The leading schools, including the Shia Imamiyyah, have validated amputation of the left foot for the second offence except that in Shii law it means the foot from the middle joint such that leaves the heel and the person's ability to walk intact. This is based on the authority of the fourth caliph, ʿAlī b Abi Ṭālib, whose precedent on this is followed by Shii jurisprudence. The Sunni law position on this is mutilation of the left foot from the ankle.[31] With regard to repentance, the Shiis hold that the prescribed punishment of theft is suspended by virtue of repentance before prosecution and judgment but not thereafter, yet they add that, based on a weak opinion, the Imam may drop the prescribed punishment on account of repentance even after confession. Furthermore, mutilation is contingent on the demand for it by the victim of theft, which must be made prior to adjudication and arrest, failing which the judge may not order mutilation. The victim's demand is of no account, however, if it is after prosecution and judgment.[32]

The second amputation has been disputed, however, and there is a minority opinion against it, for the simple reason that the Qur'an is silent on it (cf. al-Māʾidah, 5:38). The majority (*jumhūr*) position that approves of the second amputation is based on rather a questionable interpretation of the Qur'anic verse—saying that *aydihima* (their hands) therein also include feet, drawing the drastic conclusion that the foot is mutilated from the ankle. Two prominent Companions, Ibn ʿAbbās and ʿAṭa, are reported to have held that no further amputation is valid for the second (and subsequent) theft, and they supported this by citing the Qur'anic text, "And your Lord is never forgetful" [وما كان ربك نسيا] (Maryam, 19:64). Ibn Ḥazm of the

Ẓāhirī school has strongly criticised the majority ruling here and found it to be quite remarkable that such drastic positions were taken (mainly by the Ḥanafīs and Mālikīs) without there being any evidence in the sources to support them.[32] Al-ʿAwā's enquiry into this has also led him to the conclusion that the minority opinion here is "nearest to the spirit of Islamic law."[33] Our guideline on this issue should surely be the hadith of the Prophet, discussed in the following section, which states that if there is a choice between leniency and severity one should, in the context of punishments especially, adopt the course that leads to leniency and not otherwise.

The Hudud Bill of Kelantan, Malaysia, also follows the mainstream fiqh position and penalises the first offence of theft with amputation of the right hand from the wrist. The second offence of theft is punishable, however, with amputation of a part of the left foot "in the middle of the foot in such a way that the heel may still be usable for walking and standing" (Clauses 6 and 52). This is in accord with the precedent of the fourth caliph ʿAlī, who has ordered mutilation of the foot from the middle joint—as is the position also taken by the Shia Imamiyyah.[34]

As for the admissibility of repentance and its bearing, if any, on the *ḥadd* of theft, it is generally held that the *ḥadd* punishment of mutilation is not pardonable by anyone, including the victim or the head of state, nor may it be substituted, once it is proven, by any other punishment.

In support of this is quoted the Prophet's well-known instruction that *ḥudūd* may be exonerated prior to being reported to the authorities, but once reported they must be implemented. No one, it is said, has disagreed with this position except for the Zaydiyyah Shia, who maintain that mutilation is suspended as a result of repentance as this is the clear purport of the Qur'an. Even if there are a number of persons involved in the theft, they all stand a chance to be exonerated if they all repent. They have further added that it is the obligation generally for the Imam to enforce *ḥudūd*, and to suspend its enforcement based on the public interest (*maṣlaḥah*), on a carefully selective basis at least, or to delay enforcement to another time if the public interest would so require. However some in their ranks have denied this power to the Imam in two cases, namely the *ḥadd* of slander (*qadhf*) and that of theft.[35]

Al-Jazīrī elaborates, "the leading Imams of jurisprudence have agreed that when the thief repents and renounces sincerely his act, and regrets it while there are also indications of his sincerity and remorse, and he resolves not to repeat his offence a second time, God Most High admits his repentance as is clearly declared in the Qur'an [al-Mā'idah, 5:39, quoted in full]. For God has [promised] to forgive the blunder of His repentant servant and exonerate him."[36] This line of discourse is continued with a degree of emphasis when al-Jazīrī further quotes two hadiths that "repentance wipes out what has preceded it [التوبة تجب ما كان قبله] and that "one who repents his sin is like the one who has not incurred a sin."

(التائب من الذنب كمن لا ذنب له)

It is further added that when the culprit undergoes the *ḥadd* punishment, it become an expiation (*kaffārah*) for him, and he will not be punished for the same in the hereafter. For the Prophet, pbuh, has said:

> One who has committed a sin in this world and has been punished for it, God's justice does not admit of the prospect of doubling the punishment in the hereafter.
>
> (من أصاب في الدنيا ذنبا فعوقب به فاالله أعدل من أن يثني عقوبته على عبده).

Yet all of this seems to have been subsumed under moral advice. The *ḥadd* of mutilation for theft is consequently not suspended by repentance, nor even by the offender's purposeful change for the better and whether or not he stays clear of criminality for a long time. Once the crime of theft is proven, it must be punished. The main reason given for this is that suspending the *ḥadd* due to repentance will encourage criminality and diminish the deterrent effect of *ḥudūd*. Some evidence in the hadith has also been quoted to support this position [37] It is hardly an overstatement to say that the Prophet has tried to strike a balance between the concerns for the rule of law and enforcement of *ḥudūd*, on the one hand, and consideration of concealment (*satr*) and intercession (*shafāʿah*) on the other. This was at a time when Islam was faced with the larger challenge of establishing law and order in a hostile tribal environment. The Prophet has exercised both leniency and stricture in the application of *ḥudūd* in light of his insight and knowledge of the personality and character of individuals and the prevailing conditions of those times.

What al-Jazīrī and others have stated on the need for consistency and firmness in the application of *ḥudūd* penalties is, of course, a valid argument and hard to turn away from, nor is it our purpose to dispute the soundness of that position. But this also does not justify total exclusion of self-correction, rehabilitation, and reform from the purview of Islamic criminal justice in respect to *ḥudūd,* especially of the *ḥadd* of theft. The scriptural basis of what is presented here is clearly in the Qur'an, not just in the verse that specifies the *ḥadd* of theft (al-Mā'idah, 5:39) but as a consistent feature of the Qur'anic outlook on repentance and reform that is present in all of the *ḥudūd* verses. What is proposed here is that both of these positions are valid and that repentance should not be excluded altogether but treated as an integral part of the penal philosophy of *ḥudūd.* No one would say that repentance and reform should be featured so forcefully that it would erode the deterrent effect of punishment, but no one can deny that including them is an integral part of both the Qur'an and Sunnah. An integrated approach is therefore important if one were to take a fresh look at *ḥudūd* in our time. Finding a correct balance of these two admittedly somewhat conflicting interests is the crux of the challenge of the *ḥudūd* sentencing policy, and if successfully attempted, it may well usher the way toward a more nuanced and also realistic approach to the enforcement of *ḥudūd.*

Amputation of the hand for theft is still used today in countries like Iran, Saudi Arabia, and Northern Nigeria. In Iran, amputation as punishment was described as "uncommon" in 2010, but in 2014 there were three sentences of amputation of fingers, but not the complete hand; and amputation was carried out as punishment four times in 2012–2013.[38]

VII

Banditry and Terrorism (Ḥirābah, *also* Qaṭʿ al-Tarīq)

Ḥɪʀāʙᴀʜ ɪs ᴛʜᴇ nearest shariah concept to contemporary terrorism. But modern technological changes have altered the nature of this crime so much that corresponding adjustments in the law of *ḥirābah* are inevitable. Remote control devices, precision timing of devices, vastly destructive weapons, and even suicide bombings were not addressed by early Muslim jurists in their scholastic articulations of *ḥirābah*. The Qur'anic conception of this crime, on the other hand, is broad enough to accommodate the needed adjustments. This chapter attempts to reconnect the fiqh of *ḥirābah* to its Qur'anic origins. The discussion is necessary, because the global reach of the scourge of contemporary terrorism has caused great pain and anguish not only to Muslims but also to humanity at large. To facilitate this analysis, an attempt has been made to comprehend contemporary terrorism in its own terms. The discussion therefore begins by defining terrorism and *ḥirābah*. A review of the principal Qur'anic verse on *ḥirābah* is presented at the outset and then followed by a review and analysis of the fiqh of *ḥirābah* in the works of leading schools of Islamic law. Since *ḥirābah* is one of the prescribed *ḥudūd* crimes, the Qur'an provides a fourfold punishment for *ḥirābah*, which Muslim scholars have elaborated in considerable details. The present discussion seeks to bridge the gap between the fiqh conception of *ḥirābah* and its contemporary manifestations, while taking into consideration the salient new features of contemporary terrorism, such as suicide bombing, which have not been addressed in the traditional fiqh. Also presented is a roundup of Muslim responses to global terrorism and a conclusion.

Definition and Meaning of Ḥirābah

Ḥirābah literally means "to fight or wage war." It denotes terrorism and highway robbery (*qaṭʿ al-ṭarīq*) as well as any act that involves the use or threat of using force to terrorise and intimidate people passing through streets on their way to places of business, homes, shops, and so forth. *Ḥirābah* also covers all instances of mass destruction and sabotage, such as poisoning drinking water, food, or air, as well as gross criminal damage to the peace, security, and economic livelihood of communities and states. According to the general consensus of Muslim jurists of all the leading schools of jurisprudence, both Sunni and Shia, *ḥirābah* is a major sin and a capital *ḥudūd* crime.[1] *Ḥirābah* is the nearest shariah legal concept to terrorism, notwithstanding some differences between them, which will be explored in the following discussion. This presentation refers mainly to the Qur'anic conception of *ḥirābah* more than the fiqh elaborations thereof; the latter tend to specify the broader Qur'anic positions in line with prevailing conditions of earlier times. This too will be explained. It is hoped that the interpretation and analysis offered here will help bridge the gap between the fiqh conception of *ḥirābah* and contemporary terrorism. The Qur'anic conception of *ḥirābah*, the fiqh framework of the same, and contemporary terrorism thus constitute the three major components of this presentation.

Concerning terrorism, it has proven difficult to find a comprehensive definition for it, as many years of fruitless attempts in the United Nations have proven that it cannot be defined to the satisfaction of everyone: "There is no all-encompassing definition of terrorism, there are only common elements that are used to determine actions as such, and actions that promote fear."[2] The very inadequacy of this description of terrorism is problematic as one cannot clearly draw the lines of distinction between violence, terrorism, freedom fighters, and separatist movements. The one factor that connects all forms of terrorism, however, also underlies *ḥirābah*: the desire to cause fear, terror, and insecurity in society through the indiscriminate use of violence, often for political ends. This characterisation of both terrorism and *ḥirābah* covers acts of terror perpetrated by individuals, groups, and even states (as exercised by Israel against the Palestinian people).

Sherman Jackson has compared *ḥirābah* with "domestic terrorism" in the United States and finds similarities between them. According to a definition attributed to the Federal Bureau of Investigation (FBI), terrorism is "the unlawful use of force or violence against persons or property to intimidate or coerce a government, the civilian population, or any segment thereof, in furtherance of political goals."[3] Jackson adds that a principal ingredient of this definition is clearly its focus on the inducement or spread of fear, which is also how Muslim jurists have described *ḥirābah*. Another aspect in common between *ḥirābah* and "domestic terrorism" is a certain lack of personal relationship between the parties in the sense that the victim and terrorist may not even know one another. A fresh interpretation of the Qur'an on *ḥirābah* is offered in the following discussion to attempt to relate the Qur'an's guidelines to contemporary terrorism.

Terrorism in the oft-cited phrase "the war on terror" refers to violent, fear-inducing attacks by individuals, groups, or the state against civilians. There is thus a distinct exclusion of attacks against the military and other state agents.[4] Other definitions include "the use or threat of action" that endangers life, or poses a serious risk to health or to property, and is "designed to influence the government or to intimidate the public, or a section of the public"; and where "the use or threat of violence is made for the purpose of advancing a political, religious, or ideological cause" (Section 1 of the Terrorism Act 2000 of the United Kingdom).

The discussion that follows begins with a review of the scriptural evidence on *ḥirābah* and proceeds to examine the fiqh writings on the subject and the punishment of *ḥirābah*.

Ḥirābah *in the Qur'an and Sunnah*

It is due to the extreme gravity of *ḥirābah* that the Qur'an refers to its perpetrators and those who spread terror and insecurity as the ones who "wage war on God and His Messenger." *Ḥirābah* in the Qur'an is envisaged as a composite crime that can subsume banditry, highway robbery, terrorism, theft, and murder. It is a *ḥudūd* crime consisting usually, but not necessarily, of collective activity committed by more than one person. In addition, it is seen as a crime where everyone acts on behalf of the group; if the crime is committed by one of them, all of them are liable for the consequences. The principal Qur'anic verse on *ḥirābah* thus reads:

> The only punishment of those who wage war on God and His Messenger and strive with might and main for mischief-making through the land (*fasād fi'l-arḍ*) is execution or crucifixion, or mutilation of their hands and feet on alternate sides, or banishment

> from the land. Such will be their disgrace in this world, and in the Hereafter theirs will be a heavy punishment. Save those who repent before you overpower them. For know that God is Forgiving, Most Merciful. (al-Māʾidah, 5:33–34)
>
> إِنَّمَا جَزَٰٓؤُاْ ٱلَّذِينَ يُحَارِبُونَ ٱللَّهَ وَرَسُولَهُۥ وَيَسۡعَوۡنَ فِى ٱلۡأَرۡضِ فَسَادًا أَن يُقَتَّلُوٓاْ أَوۡ يُصَلَّبُوٓاْ أَوۡ تُقَطَّعَ أَيۡدِيهِمۡ وَأَرۡجُلُهُم مِّنۡ خِلَٰفٍ أَوۡ يُنفَوۡاْ مِنَ ٱلۡأَرۡضِۚ ذَٰلِكَ لَهُمۡ خِزۡىٞ فِى ٱلدُّنۡيَاۖ وَلَهُمۡ فِى ٱلۡأٓخِرَةِ عَذَابٌ عَظِيمٌ. إِلَّا ٱلَّذِينَ تَابُواْ مِن قَبۡلِ أَن تَقۡدِرُواْ عَلَيۡهِمۡۖ فَٱعۡلَمُوٓاْ أَنَّ ٱللَّهَ غَفُورٞ رَّحِيمٞ.

On the authority of the Companion Anas b. Mālik, Qur'an commentators have identified the incident of ʿUraniyyin (from the tribe of ʿUraynah) as the occasion of revelation of this verse:

> A group of people came to Medina but found its climate unsuitable and they became unwell. They came to the Prophet and informed him of their condition. The Prophet advised them to go where the camels of Ṣadaqah were, drink their milk and urine and rest. They did so and recovered well. But then they renounced Islam, killed the shepherd and drove off with the camels. Upon hearing this, the Prophet ordered that they be caught. They were chased, caught and brought to the Prophet who ordered that their hands and feet be mutilated and their eyes gouged and were left in the heat to die.[5]
>
> أن ناسا من عرينة قدموا على رسول الله صلى الله عليه وسلم المدينة فاجتووها فقال لهم رسول الله صلى الله عليه وسلم إن شئتم أن تخرجوا إلى إبل الصدقة فتشربوا من ألبانها وأبوالها ففعلوا فصحوا ثم مالوا على الرعاة فقتلوهم وارتدوا عن الإسلام وساقوا ذود رسول الله صلى الله عليه وسلم فبلغ ذلك النبي صلى الله عليه وسلم فبعث في أثرهم فأتي بهم فقطع أيديهم وأرجلهم وسمل أعينهم وتركهم في الحرة حتى ماتوا.

In a renowned hadith all the major collections of hadith have reported, the Prophet has also said: "One who carries arms against us is not one of us [من حمل علينا السلاح فليس منا].[6] This is further endorsed in another similar hadith that says, "One who unleashes his sword on us is not one of us [من سل علينا السيف فليس منا].[7]

In yet another hadith, the Prophet said, "All that belongs to a Muslim is forbidden to other Muslims: his blood, his property and his honour."[8]

> كل المسلم على المسلم حرام : دمه وماله وعرضه.

Next we review the fiqh scholastic positions on *ḥirābah*.

A Fiqh *Discourse on* Ḥirābah

Fiqh scholars have been assiduous in their efforts to protect the community from those within its midst who sought to bring it harm through violence and terror. They did so through developing legal constructs that served this interest, and in doing so took their lead mainly from the Qur'anic dispensations on *ḥirābah*. The law of *ḥirābah* has also not remained static due partly to a degree of flexibility in its Qur'anic expositions that allowed space for interpretation, which the jurists have attempted from time to time. Yet the creative endeavours of jurists and interpreters were negatively affected by the so-called closure of the door of *ijtihād* around the fifth/eleventh century. This is partly why a contemporary observer of terrorism will notice a certain gap in the fiqh discourse of *ḥirābah*, which is of medieval origin for the most part. The narrative developing in this chapter is self-evident on the need for further reconstruction and renewal toward a more relevant understanding of *ḥirābah*.

The fiqh discourse on *ḥirābah* is focused on highlighting the main features and characteristics of this offence rather than advancing a comprehensive theoretical framework for it. It also revolves mainly around the meaning and implications of the principal Qur'anic verse on *ḥirābah* and application of the fourfold punishment therein—depending on the presence or otherwise of killing, taking of money and property, and obstructing free movement of people in a public space.

Ḥirābah resembles mutiny/rebellion (*baghy*) but differs from the latter in that mutiny opposes a legitimate authority or government on the basis of a plausible interpretation (*ta'wīl*), while the agent of *ḥirābah* does so without any such pretence.[9] *Ḥirābah* also differs from theft in that theft means taking another's property surreptitiously, whereas in *ḥirābah* if property is taken it is done openly by force.

The Ḥanafī jurist, al-Kāsānī (d. 587/1189), defined *ḥirābah*, or *qaṭ' al-ṭarīq*, as "attacks upon pedestrians for the purpose of taking their property by force in such a way that people are rendered unable to pass freely through the streets. The attacker/s may be a group or a single person that possess overwhelming power to obstruct the public passage, and may be using weapons or weapon-substitutes such as sticks and stones."[10]

The Mālikī school described the agent of *ḥirābah* as "anyone who brandishes weapons in order to obstruct free passage in the streets and renders it unsafe to travel by killing people, taking their money, and spreading corruption in the land. The agent of *ḥirābah* (*muḥārib*) may be a Muslim or a non-Muslim, free or slave, and it may be committed in a city or countryside, by an individual or group—[all this] simply because the Qur'an has not specified the perpetrator in any such ways."[11]

The Shāfiʿī school identifies the agents of *ḥirābah* in similar terms but stresses that the perpetrator must be a competent person (*mukallaf*), Muslim, *dhimmī*, or apostate who is bound by the injunctions of Islam and has overwhelming power to subjugate others and take their money and property, with such actions occurring away from a main city.[12]

The Shia Imamiyyah identifies the agent of *ḥirābah* as "anyone who brandishes weapons in order to terrorise passengers during night or day, on land or sea, even if the perpetrator is not a known criminal."[13] The crime is proven either by a valid confession, even if it is not repeated, or by the testimony of two just witnesses; the latter may include some of the suspects themselves giving testimony against the others. This is a *ḥudūd* crime and carries a fourfold punishment as the Qur'an has specified, but the Imam is entitled to select which will be applied.[14]

The Ẓāhirī school defines a *muḥārib* (terrorist) as one who insolently terrorises street passengers and spreads corruption through acts of terror in the city or countryside, individually or collectively, exhibiting overwhelming power with or without the use of weapons.[15] This may be said to be broad enough to encapsulate many of the points of the preceding definitions.

Muslim jurists have held the two material elements of *ḥirābah* to be (1) a show of weapons by assailants ready to terrorise people and block their normal movements on public passages and (2) killing, looting and taking people's property forcefully, especially in areas outside the main cities. Hence if one or two persons commit raids on a large caravan, plunder its property, and run, they would not be committing *ḥirābah*, but if they so act against a small caravan manned by a few persons, they would be considered guilty of *ḥirābah*. There is some disagreement on whether *ḥirābah* can also be committed in urban areas. For Imam Mālik, it can be committed within the city or outside, and it matters little whether it is by one person or a group of persons, males or females, Muslims or non-Muslims. This is because the Qur'anic verse on *ḥirābah* is conveyed in general terms without any specification or exception—hence it remains in its originally general and inclusive form. The Mālikī school also includes under *ḥirābah* attacks on the honour of people, their women, and their families with a show of superior force. Thus if an armed attacker enters another's private dwelling to dishonor the victim and his family, be it within or outside the city, he commits the crime of *ḥirābah*. The Ḥanafī school maintains that *ḥirābah* can only be committed in secluded places away from main cities, as within the city surroundings the public and the authorities are likely come to the aid of the victim. Imam al-Shāfiᶜī has held that an attack in the city can constitute *ḥirābah* if the government/sultan is weak and lacks effective power, and if the attacker is also capable of striking fear on the part of the victim. The Ḥanbalī understanding of *ḥirābah* resembles that of the Shāfiᶜī school in that it may be committed in cities or outside the cities and the perpetrator may be armed with any kind of weapon, or that which may resemble a weapon, provided it can create fear and can terrorise. The Shia also regard possession of weapons of any description as a requirement of *ḥirābah*, and the offence may take place anywhere provided that the perpetrator possesses the capacity to terrorise their victim. The majority (*jumhūr*) view on this is that committing *ḥirābah* in cities and urban centres is an aggravating factor that renders the crime even more dangerous.[16]

It is essential that the assailants are superior in strength and carry arms such that their victims cannot overpower them nor can they escape. *Ḥirābah* is also committed openly (*bi'l-mujāharah*) and it differs in this respect from theft. Hence if a group of people act surreptitiously and commit theft or kidnapping, they would fail to fulfil the requirement of *mujāharah*. Aggravating circumstances consist of taking the property of the victim and/or killing them. As is clearly stipulated in the verse of *ḥirābah*, repentance by the terrorists before capture and arrest exonerates them from capital punishment but does not necessarily exempt them from criminal responsibility for other crimes committed during the attack, such as homicide, injury, and armed robbery, which combine both public and private rights (*ḥaqq Allāh* and *ḥaqq al-ādamī*).[17]

The Ḥanafīs are in the minority to stipulate that the bandits must be men and that women are not punished by the prescribed punishment if they perpetrate the crime, as they argue that the show of power and vanquishing is a condition that is only suited to men. If women join hands with men in banditry, according to Imam Abū Ḥanīfah and his disciple Muḥammad al-Shaybānī, they are not subject to the *ḥudūd* punishment. Abū Yūsuf, the Imam's other disciple, has held that if women directly commit killing and plunder, they are liable to the punishment of *ḥirābah* together with the men. The Mālikī, Shāfiᶜī, Ḥanbalī, and Shii schools do not regard male gender as a prerequisite of *ḥirābah* in the first place. Thus if women commit banditry in groups that terrorise people and obstruct the highway, they are liable to the capital punishment in the same way as men.[18]

Many fiqh scholars have highlighted in their discussion of *ḥirābah* the concept of obstructing free movement of people in the streets, attacking pedestrians, and taking their money,[19] But there are questions as to whether these actions play the same role in contemporary terrorism, as will be further elaborated later in the chapter. Furthermore, Imams Mālik (d. 179/795) and Abū Ḥanīfah's (d. 150/767) stipulation that *ḥirābah* is only committed in unpopulated areas would seem to be tangential to contemporary terrorism.[20] For instance, a misguided Muslim youth who under heavy indoctrination of ISIS/Daesh or the Taliban blows himself up in order to kill and destroy is most likely not after taking money but to "gain direct passage to Paradise." Nor are such nefarious acts of terror confined to unpopulated places: quite the opposite, one might say, as terrorists now deliberately choose densely populated areas and crowds as their principal targets. Even the fiqh provision that *ḥirābah* is typically committed openly with defiance of the authorities, and where culprits exhibit overwhelming power to subjugate their victims, may no longer be as relevant to contemporary terrorism. For the latter is often committed through hit-and-run tactics wherein the terrorists usually do not declare themselves openly, especially in the case of suicide bombing. Thus it becomes manifest that many of the fiqh underpinnings of *ḥirābah* reviewed here call for fresh examination and reconstruction in ways that would make the law of *ḥirābah* more relevant to contemporary terrorism.

What remains most relevant of the fiqh specifications of *ḥirābah* and its contemporary manifestations is perhaps the spreading of fear (*ikhāfah, irhāb*) and the victims' helplessness (*ʿadam al-ghawth*) against it. The helplessness aspect is described so as to mean that no effective security measures can be taken to prevent it (*taʾadhdhur al-ihtirāz*). These are often seen as the constituent elements and *sine qua non* of *ḥirābah*, as can also be said of contemporary terrorism. Rashīd Riḍā (d. 1354/1935) confirmed this when he wrote that, unlike the other *ḥudūd* crimes in which the victim may be able to defend himself, in *ḥirābah* he is helpless since he is overwhelmed by a superior force. Furthermore, whereas in other common crimes the criminal can be subjugated by the authorities, this is also not certain in the case of *ḥirābah* as it often involves challenging the authority of the government itself.[21]

Punishment of Ḥirābah

For the prescribed punishment to be carried out, the perpetrator of *ḥirābah* must be adult and competent. There is disagreement, however, when a child or an insane person participates in the crime together with a group. The majority (*jumhūr*) have held that capital punishment applies to them all, for doubt attaches to one member of the group and that should not get in the way of enforcing the punishment. In addition, the case here may resemble a situation where a group of persons commit adultery with one woman; all of them are punished. The Ḥanafī school differs and regards the participation of a child in *ḥirābah* as an element of doubt (*shubha*) that suspends the prescribed punishment on all of them, although they may be punished otherwise under *taʿzīr*. Abū Ḥanīfah's disciple, Abū Yūsuf, has held, however, that only competent persons among the group who carried out the actual crime of *ḥirābah* are liable to capital punishment, and the child is not.[22]

The fourfold punishment that the Qur'an has prescribed for *ḥirābah* envisages death, crucifixion, cross-amputation of the hand and foot from opposite sides, and banishment. There is disagreement over the order and choice of these punishments. While the majority of Sunni schools and the Shia authorise the ruler to select one or more of these punishments in proportion to the severity of the crime, Imam Mālik has held that if the assailants have killed their victim, the Imam/judge has no choice but to order the capital punishment. The only choice he would have is whether or not to combine crucifixion with the capital punishment of death. If property of whatever value has also been taken, the offender must be punished with cross-amputation, and if there has been a holdup and looting, the offender must be sentenced to mutilation and or banishment. The other Sunni schools, and one view of the Shia Imamiyyah attributed to Shaykh Naṣr al-Dīn al-Ṭūsī (d. 672/1274), maintain that the Qur'an has provided a sequence that is indicative of a certain correlation between the crime and its punishment, which the authorities must observe: the offender is not killed if he has not committed homicide, and he is not mutilated or banished unless property is taken. Finally, if the assailant has both plundered and killed, his punishment is both death and crucifixion. A group of Muslim jurists including the Shia Imamiyyah have held, on the other hand, that the Imam has the discretion absolutely to select and determine the appropriate punishment or combination thereof regardless of whether or not homicide, holdup, and/or robbery are present. There is some disagreement on whether crucifixion should take place before or after execution, based on the analysis that crucifixion can be regarded a punishment, as per Imams Abū Ḥanīfah, Mālik, and the Shia Imamiyyah, only when the criminal is still alive, not after he has died. Imams al-Shāfiʿī and Ibn

Ḥanbal have held that the Qur'an mentions killing first, then crucifixion, and that should be the order. This is perhaps a preferable view on the assumption that crucifixion is for public display and not necessarily to make the execution more painful. It is generally held, and this is also the Shii position, that crucifixion is for three days only. There is general consensus that if the offender has neither killed nor looted, he shall be imprisoned for such a period as the court deems necessary in the circumstances of a particular case. The Ḥanafis and some other jurists have, furthermore, equated banishment with imprisonment on the analysis that banishment to another place will place the safety of those other people at risk and that the purpose of banishment is best served by imprisonment.[23] If the bandits have taken property, the property in question must qualify according to the attributes of stolen goods, namely that it has market value, reaches the minimum quorum, and is also guarded property in which the owner has no share or claim of ownership, although, unlike in cases of theft, it may have been taken openly even with the knowledge of its owner.[24]

A question has arisen as to whether the capital punishment of *ḥirābah* combines with liability for financial compensation and bodily injuries even after the bandits have been punished. Muslim jurists have differed in their responses. The basic principle that comes into the picture here, according to the Ḥanafis at least, is that capital punishment does not combine with liability for loss. But in their responses, most Sunni and Shii jurists have tended to separate the capital punishment of *ḥirābah* from these additional inflictions. The majority across the board is of the view that if the bandits have plundered property, they are liable to return it, if it exists, or to compensate for it if it does not. Many have held that only those who have actually taken the property are individually liable for compensation, as liability for compensation is not a part of the prescribed penalty per se and does not therefore affect one who is not directly involved. The Mālikīs have held that each one of the bandits acts on behalf of the group and thus they are all liable for compensation. As for bodily injuries, if the injured person has recovered, there is no retaliation (*qiṣāṣ*), otherwise he or she may either retaliate, if that is possible, or grant forgiveness in exchange for financial compensation. However, if the injury has worsened and leads to death, then retaliation becomes due. The Ẓāhirī school has held, on the other hand, that the crime of *ḥirābah* is committed by causing bodily injury only, even if there is no killing or plunder involved, and the bandits are therefore liable to the capital punishment of execution.[25]

The majority of Sunni schools and the Shia maintain that killing by the bandits needs no proof of intention and that the act of killing itself makes them liable to the prescribed punishment. It makes no difference whether the homicide so committed is intentional, quasi-intentional, or erroneous. It is also immaterial as to what kind of weapons the bandits have used to commit the crime. The Shāfiʿī school maintains, however, that proof of intention to kill is required for imposition of the prescribed punishment but that the terroristic features of the crime of *ḥirābah* need no proof of intention as this is revealed by the show of force and striking of fear among people.[26]

Fresh reflection on the conditions and component elements that Muslim jurists have stipulated in their expositions of *ḥirābah* suggests that these are undoubtedly instructive, yet some changes may be required if one were to legislate on terrorism today. The view that allows the ruling authorities to determine the component elements of the crime merits attention as it not only bears harmony with the Qur'anic dispensations on the subject but can also accommodate the change of conditions in recent times. As already mentioned, terrorists nowadays often use remote control devices that may or may not involve the actual presence of the perpetrators at the crime scene. The terrorists may also use minor persons, as they often do, as suicide bombers. Certain other aspects of *ḥirābah* may also call for further reflection and review. It is of interest to note that the Qur'an determines the crime of *ḥirābah* by its consequences—terror, killing, injury, and plunder, without specifying further details. The Qur'an lays down the essential elements of the crime, which is perhaps sufficient for rulers and legislative authorities today to determine the component elements of *ḥirābah* (terrorism) in light of prevailing conditions.

Repentance in Ḥirābah

As for the attributes of repentance that suspend the capital punishment and its consequences, Muslim jurists have differed over details and held different views. Repentance in this crime means expression of regret and remorse for its commission and expressed determination not to commit it in the future. The Qur'an allows repentance only if it precedes subjugation of the offender by the authorities and not afterwards. It is suggested that even if the assailants surrender, they must still show that they have actually mended their ways, disarmed, and abandoned what they were doing, and only then can the prescribed *ḥadd* punishment be suspended. Fiqh scholars have also differed as to the consequence of repentance: Does it suspend both God's Rights and the Right of Man, and if so, which takes precedence? In response, it is stated, in the Mālikī opinion, that repentance before arrest only suspends the capital punishment of *ḥirābah* and nothing else. All other claims in both categories remain unaffected. This means that the authorities may impose alternative punishments and the individuals affected also remain entitled to claim their rights in whatever way they may have been harmed, unless they grant forgiveness. The Shāfiʿī school maintains that the Right of Man takes priority: if homicide or bodily injury has been committed during a holdup, it must be tried first according to the relevant rules. This view has the support of other schools too in that the assailant is not exonerated for homicide and bodily injury due to repentance or surrender. If, however, the victims' relatives grant forgiveness or accept blood money, and the authorities also grant pardon, action may be suspended against the terrorist. An alternative view has it that repentance suspends both of the said categories of rights except for any property that may still exist, which must be returned. It would appear that the Imam and/or judicial authorities have residual jurisdiction in regard to determining the precise consequences of a genuine repentance and surrender.[27]

Suicide and Suicide Bombing

Historically, the first organised suicide attack in Islam was carried out by the Nizārī Ismāʿīlīs, a Shii community who tried to establish an independent state. They initiated an open revolt against the Seljuq emirs and assassinated the prominent Saljūq vizier, Niẓām al-Mulk, in 485/1092.[28] Terrorism has largely been inconclusive and failed to achieve its desired purposes. The nineteenth and twentieth centuries saw large-scale terrorism practices by Russian anarchists and Bolshevik state terrorists. Later nationalist movements like the IRA, the Zionist Stern Gang, and Armenian Nationalists also indulged in terrorist practices. They all considered terrorism as the most cost-efficient and effective form of warfare for the poor, putting public pressure on governments to change their policies. In most cases, their terrorism was, however, counterproductive. "Virtually nowhere has terrorism produced the desired result. Rather in most cases, it has stiffened resistance and caused untold suffering to friends and foes alike."[29]

Contemporary suicide bombing that does not distinguish among political, military, and civilian targets has no precedent in Islamic law and history. Suicide bombing has become a highly disturbing aspect of contemporary terrorism such that a decisive ruling and consensus on it would be necessary to curb it. Suicide (*intihār*) does occur in Islamic law, but not in the way twenty-first-century Muslims are experiencing it.

Suicide falls under the Qur'anic provision of "killing without just cause [*illā bi'l-ḥaqq*]" (al-Isrāʾ, 17:33), simply because a person does not have the right to take his own life. Under conventional fiqh, suicide is not subsumed by *ḥirābah* or terrorism—rather it is part of the general discussion of the right of life. That is the main context, but here it is treated next to *ḥirābah* as it has clearly become an aspect of contemporary terrorism.

Since life is a God-given gift, it may not be subjected to destruction and abuse even by oneself. This is why shariah forbids suicide without any exception. It is a heinous sin for which the perpetrator is liable, in the event of an unsuccessful attempt, to a deterrent penalty of *taʿzīr*. If the attempt succeeds, the person is still liable to an expiation (*kaffārah*), which may be taken from his property, according to the Shāfiʿīs and some Ḥanbalī jurists, whereas the Imams Abū Ḥanīfah and Mālik do not make expiation a requirement.[30] The Qur'anic authority on this is: "Kill yourselves not, for God is truly Merciful unto you" (al-Nisāʾ, 4:29).

وَلَا تَقْتُلُوٓاْ أَنفُسَكُمْۚ إِنَّ ٱللَّهَ كَانَ بِكُمْ رَحِيمًا.

Life is a trust (*amānah*) in the hands of its bearer, who is expected to safeguard and cherish it with responsibility and care. People who are driven to despair are advised to have faith in God's mercy as in the following verse:

> Say: O my servants who have transgressed their souls not to despair from God's mercy. For God forgives all sins. (al-Zumar, 39:53)
>
> قُلْ يَٰعِبَادِىَ ٱلَّذِينَ أَسْرَفُواْ عَلَىٰٓ أَنفُسِهِمْ لَا تَقْنَطُواْ مِن رَّحْمَةِ ٱللَّهِۚ إِنَّ ٱللَّهَ يَغْفِرُ ٱلذُّنُوبَ جَمِيعًاۚ إِنَّهُۥ هُوَ ٱلْغَفُورُ ٱلرَّحِيمُ

The prohibition of suicide by the clear text also means that anyone who facilitates or collaborates in the act of suicide is also liable to a deterrent punishment.[31]

Qur'an commentators and jurists have drawn the following conclusions from this verse (4:29):

- The obvious meaning is that suicide is forbidden. It is *ḥarām* for a person to kill himself. This is the obvious meaning of the text.

- It also means that "you may not kill one another." This is the interpretation of Ibn ʿAbbās, Saʿīd b. Jubayr, ʿIkrimah, Qatādah, and others.
- No one may do something nor take an assignment if it may cause his own death—even if it is in pursuit of a religious duty. This is the understanding of ʿAmr b. al-ʿĀṣ, who expressed it in the battle of Dhat al-Salasil— he prayed together with other Companions while he was impure (*junūb*) on a bitterly cold night. When he mentioned it to the Prophet, the Prophet said: You and your companions prayed while you were *junūb*! To this he replied, O Messenger of God, I had a wet dream in the night and feared I might be struck with perdition if I took a bath and I recited this verse. The Prophet, pbuh, laughed but did not say anything.
- No one should deprive himself of the essentials of life that may lead to his death.
- One may not indulge in self-destructive crimes and consumption of lethal substances.[32]

> According to a hadith report, a person [engaged in battle] killed himself with a broad-headed arrow. The Messenger of God said: As for me, I will not pray [funeral prayer] over him.[33]
>
> أخبرنا اسحق بن منصور قال أنبأنا أبو الوليد قال حدثنا أبو خيثمة زهير قال
> أن رجلا قتل نفسه بمشاقص فقال رسول الله صلى الله عليه وسلم أما أنا فلا أصلي عليه

The Prophet has strongly condemned suicide, as in the following hadith:

> The one who throws himself off a mountain cliff and kills himself will be doing the same to himself perpetually in Hell. The one who takes poison and kills himself shall be holding the same in his hand and permanently taking it in Hell, and the one who kills himself with a weapon will be piercing his body with it perpetually in Hell.[34]

A similar hadith proclaims that the "one who kills himself with something in this life will also be tortured by it in the fire of Hell."[35]

مَنْ قَتَلَ نَفْسَهُ بِشَيْءٍ عُذِّبَ بِهِ فِي نَارِ جَهَنَّمَ

Al-Bukhārī has recorded a long hadith to the effect that the Prophet looked at a man, in a battle against the pagans, and he was by all accounts one of the most capable of Muslim warriors. But the Prophet said concerning him:

> He is from the people of the Hell. A man amongst the audience said: "I will accompany him." So he went along with him, and whenever he stopped he stopped with him, and whenever he hastened, he hastened with him. The [brave] man then got wounded severely, and seeking to die at once, he planted his sword into the ground and put its point against his chest in between his breasts, and then threw himself on it and committed suicide."[36]
>
> فَقَالَ رَسُولُ اللَّهِ صلى الله عليه وسلم أَمَا إِنَّهُ مِنْ أَهْلِ النَّارِ. فَقَالَ رَجُلٌ مِنَ الْقَوْمِ أَنَا صَاحِبُهُ. قَالَ فَخَرَجَ مَعَهُ كُلَّمَا وَقَفَ وَقَفَ مَعَهُ، وَإِذَا أَسْرَعَ أَسْرَعَ مَعَهُ ـ قَالَ ـ فَجُرِحَ الرَّجُلُ جُرْحًا شَدِيدًا، فَاسْتَعْجَلَ الْمَوْتَ، فَوَضَعَ سَيْفَهُ بِالأَرْضِ وَذُبَابَهُ بَيْنَ ثَدْيَيْهِ، ثُمَّ تَحَامَلَ عَلَى سَيْفِهِ، فَقَتَلَ نَفْسَهُ.

Suicide bombing in our time is not addressed in the scholastic discourse, but it can find some historical connection with martyrdom, especially in the Shii tradition—in particular, the Shii narrative that developed following the death of the Prophet's grandson Ḥusayn in 680 CE. Ḥusayn and his followers did not choose martyrdom at the Battle of Karbala in the manner that is familiar of most other Islamic martyrs in that martyrs usually fought for a cause but did not choose to be martyrs as such. Nevertheless, Shii tradition embellishes his death with prophetic foreknowledge of the outcome. It also embodies the model of a woefully small force of believers arrayed against an overwhelming Umayyad army of "evildoers." As a result of his death, the role of martyrdom would forever serve as a basis for the distinction of Shiism, which also gave it the power to affect ideological change from within.

Furthermore, by couching their opposition to the ruling of the Umayyad caliphate as a protest against a false understanding of the faith, the nascent Shii community cast their martyrs as the "opposition" par excellence. As Farhad Khosrokhavar states in his study of suicide bombers: "The martyrdom of [Ḥusayn] provided an opportunity to denounce the usurpers so as to reestablish the true religion of [Muḥammad]."[37]

The Ismāʿīlī Assassins, a Shii offshoot of the eleventh and twelfth centuries, also represent an example of Muslims who identified themselves so differently from the ruling sect that violence and death became a desirable option for pursuing their collective goals. Responding to their oppression at the hands of Sunni caliphs, the Assassins refocused their allegiance on their sect rather than the more encompassing Islamic faith.

Fiqh manuals in mainstream Islam are silent on suicide bombing, which has a short history and drew public attention when Israel unleashed a new wave of aggression on street processions of Palestinian youth (2000–2001). The upsurge ever since in suicide bombing by those claiming to be Islamic warriors has brought mixed responses from Muslim scholars. Most scholars of standing have not hesitated to condemn this and also the September 11, 2001 attacks as being contrary to Islamic principles.[38]

It is simplistic to lump together the Palestinian suicide bombings with al-Qaeda and ISIS terrorist activities, as few would deny the genuine suffering of the Palestinian people nor the legitimacy of their demand for a homeland and state. It is also simplistic to equate suicide bombing with martyrdom as many have claimed. This is because suicide bombing challenges two fundamental principles of Islam: the prohibition against suicide and the deliberate killing of noncombatants.

The Muslim warrior enters a battle, not with the intention of dying, but with the conviction that if he should die it would be for reasons beyond his control. Martyrdom does not begin with a suicidal intention, let alone the linkage of that intention with the killing of noncombatants, such as women and children. Suicide bombers intentionally set out to kill themselves and their victims, thus violating the norms of Islamic law and ethics.

Those who have raised the issue of "collateral damage" in this context are mistaken, because noncombatants are chosen as the direct target of suicide bombing. They are neither collateral nor incidental. Even if the cause of fighting the Israeli aggression is a valid one, that still does not justify killing noncombatants. What drives the bombers—often impressionable teenagers—on their suicidal missions are promises of a martyr's reward by the so-called religious scholars, who fuel the frustration and volatility of tender emotions with their misguided instructions.

Suicide bombing is a wider phenomenon, not always related to religion. Robert Pape, a political scientist who studied suicide terrorism from 1980 to 2001, points out that "religion is not the force behind suicide terrorism." He says, "The data shows that there is little connection between suicide terrorism and Islamic fundamentalism, or any religion for that matter," adding that the group responsible for the highest percentage (40 percent) of all suicide attacks has been the Tamil Tigers in Sri Lanka, who are adamantly opposed to religion. Rather, he suggests, nearly all suicide terrorist campaigns are "coherent political or military campaigns" whose common objectives are strategic, either to compel military forces to withdraw from their homeland or to bring down a regime they are opposed to—as in the case of Taliban suicidal missions in Afghanistan. Suicide bombing in the name of Islam is thus for the most part a "socio-political phenomenon, not a theological one."[39] Since 2001 the motivation aspects of suicide have become even more diversified, as explained in the next section.

Terrorism Then and Now: A Survey of Contemporary Opinion and Research

Terrorism has been distinguished from an ordinary crime not only by reference to the nature of the harm caused but by terrorists' ideology. This partly explains why some criminal activities, such as a school shooting, were not labelled as terrorist attacks in the media, while others like the 2013 Boston marathon bombing were quickly reported as acts of terrorism.[40] Comparing contemporary terrorism with *ḥirābah*, there is a certain shift of context and motivation from the political to the religious: whereas *ḥirābah* was mainly politically motivated, the practitioners of contemporary terrorism have added a religious dimension as they are also motivated either in whole or in part by a religious imperative and consider violence as a divine duty or a sacramental act. Bruce Hoffman (1998) noted that religious terrorists differ from secular terrorists in motivation: whereas secular terrorists attempt to appeal to actual and potential sympathisers, religious terrorists appeal to no constituency other than themselves. For Audrey Cronin (2002), religious terrorists act "directly or indirectly to please the perceived commands of a deity." This is why, for Hoffman and Cronin, such distinguishing factors make religious terrorism more destructive in nature.[41]

It needs to be mentioned that ordinary criminal law functioned under the traditional principle that motive was not the defining element of a crime in that a political or religious motive could not excuse the commission of a crime. To maintain otherwise would be tantamount to undermining the integrity of the judicial process. If one were to accept the motive element, particularly a religious one, it could also provide the accused with a platform to influence the trial process by offering extensive evidence on his own interpretations and beliefs.[42]

In a book chapter titled "The Revolt of Islam 1700 to 1993," Nikkie Keddie, an American professor of Middle Eastern history, explains the rise of militancy among Muslims. She notes that with the curious exception of Wahhabism, militant jihad movements in the modern era began and grew mostly as a response to Western colonialism. The earliest ones in the eighteenth century in Sumatra and West Africa emerged in the face of "disruptive economic change influenced by the West." In the nineteenth century, broader waves of jihad movements cropped up in Algeria, Sudan, the Caucasus, and Libya as "a direct response to French, British, Russian and Italian colonial conquest."[43]

At a press interview bearing the title "There Is Nothing in Islam That Is More Violent Than Christianity,"[44] Karen Armstrong replied to a question on the causes of Muslim terrorism by referring to "a more violent way" the West has taken toward Muslims. The West imposed their own concepts of modernity, democracy, and secularism on the Muslim world through colonial subjugation. "There was no self-determination. In Egypt there were 17 general elections between 1922 and 1952—all won by the Wafd Party, which was only allowed by the British to rule five times. Democracy was a bad joke." Secularism was introduced by these army officers with great violence. The Muslim clergy had their stipends confiscated, they were shot down, and they were tortured to death. The shah shot a hundred unarmed demonstrators in a holy shrine because they didn't want to wear Western clothes. And those in the West have consistently supported rulers like Saddam Hussein who denied their people any freedom of expression. All this has helped to push Muslims into violence. "When people are attacked, they invariably become extreme." But only a tiny proportion of Muslims actually agree with terrorism: 93 percent answered "no" to the question in the Gallup poll whether the 9/11 attacks were justified. And the reasons they gave were entirely religious. Of the 7 percent who said "yes," the reasons they gave were entirely political. Paul Hedges, a Singapore-based scholar of interreligious studies, commented that groups such as ISIS have grown, simply due to a power vacuum "created by the havoc caused by military interventions in the Middle East which have not been properly thought through nor followed up."[45]

In response to another question whether the terrorists are traumatised, Armstrong said that "some of them are, and some of them are plain wicked. Osama bin Laden was a plain criminal. But there is also great fear and despair among them. There have been surveys done by forensic psychiatrists who interviewed people convicted of terrorism since 9/11. They interviewed hundreds of people in Guantanamo and other prisons. And one forensic psychiatrist, who was also an officer of the Central Intelligence Agency (CIA), concluded that Islam had nothing to do with it. The problem was rather ignorance of Islam. Had they had a proper Muslim education, he said, they wouldn't be doing this. Only 20 percent of the prisoners had a regular Muslim upbringing. The rest were either new converts—like the gunmen who attacked the Canadian Parliament—or nonobservant, which means they don't go to the mosque (like the bombers of the Boston marathon). Similarly, there is the case of two young men, both twenty-two, who before leaving Britain to join the jihad in Syria ordered from Amazon copies of *Islam for Dummies* and *The Koran for Dummies.* That explains their ignorance of Islam. Furthermore, tedium in societies must be taken seriously. There are some who are ridden with misery and a sense of no hope: "Misery, oppression and injustice—great injustice and we are still unjust." Look at the founding fathers of the United States who said that all men are created equal: they had no problem owning African slaves! "Liberty was only for Europeans. And it still is like that, because of the greed for oil. We give huge support to the Saudis, who give their people no human rights."

American political scientist Steven Fish in his book titled *Are Muslims Distinctive?* finds no evidence that countries with a larger share of Muslims experience disproportionate acts of mass political violence. He notes, in fact, as Saleena Saleem mentions in her review of his book, that when it comes to violent crimes such as murder, Muslim-majority countries have consistently low rates compared with Christian-majority countries. Such facts get lost when the focus is on the Muslim extremists who commit the majority of violent political and terrorist acts on a global scale. As for the role of religion, it is further noted that violent upheavals in the Middle East are driven by regional political interests rather than religion.[46]

Regarding the young French jihadists, Fareed Zakaria observed that most of the young jihadists in Europe have no background in political activism (say, Palestine), fundamentalist Islam, or social conservatism. Quoting the French Islamic scholar Olivier Roy in support, Zakaria states that radicalisation in France arises around the fantasy of heroism, violence, and death, not of *shahādah* and utopia. Abdelhamid Abaaoud, the ringleader of the Paris attacks, regularly used drugs and drank alcohol, as did many of his comrades-in-arms. Today the decision to join Daesh is usually sudden and impulsive. Daesh is the ultimate gang, celebrating violence for its own sake. These young men—and some women—are usually second-generation Europeans. They are often revolting against their more traditional, devout immigrant parents.[47] These people are unsure of their identity, rooted in neither the old country nor the new, and often face discrimination and exclusion. And in this context they choose a life of rebellion, crime, and then the ultimate adventure, jihad.

These circumstances also explain why Belgian Muslims make up a disproportionate share of Daesh volunteers. Fifteen percent of native-born Belgians live below the poverty line, compared with the staggering half of Belgians with a Moroccan background. In addition, Belgium has a particularly poor record of assimilation because it has its own crisis of identity, torn between two cultures, Flemish and Walloon. All of this tends to paint a picture of a new kind of terrorist, one who is less drawn into terrorism through religion but has chosen the path of terror as the ultimate act of rebellion. Radical Islam holds an appeal and is easily available through the internet and social media. This still does not absolve Muslims from the challenge to eradicate the cancer of radical Islam in their midst. As for Western law enforcement, it also suggests that bugging mosques and patrolling Muslim community centres might be focusing attention in the wrong direction. The real terrorists might instead be in bars, drug alleys, unemployment lines, and prisons getting radicalised before they get Islamised.[48]

Terrorism has evidently become more diverse and has developed in new directions. Looking at the regional and geographical manifestations of terrorism, Azhari Karim, a former Malaysian diplomat explains: "Whereas al-Qaeda, and more recently the IS group, are seen to be accountable for much of the terrorist attacks in Europe (Paris, Nice and Brussels) and the United States (San Bernardino and Orlando), the majority of incidents seem to have been by individuals who acted alone."[49] However, in the crescent states of the Middle East stretching from Libya, Tunisia, Egypt, Sudan, and Somalia, and on to Afghanistan, Pakistan, Yemen, Iraq, Turkey, Syria, and Saudi Arabia, groups such as al-Qaeda, the Taliban, Houthis, and Nusrah al-Qudra have fought wars with the local authorities. They have been supported in part by ISIS as a means of settling old scores with corrupt government officials and states that are seen as overly dependent on the West for their survival. Elsewhere there are different clones of such radicalised and irredentist movements in the Ukraine (pro-Russians), China (Uighurs), Nigeria (Boko Haram), and also in parts of South America (e.g., Colombia, Peru, and Brazil). Their aims have centred on the need for change and transformation of the economy with development and social progress being at the top of the agenda. Things are not the same in Israeli-occupied Palestine and in the countries of South and Southeast Asia. Some have resorted to violence to draw attention to their local "nationalist" problems. Others, mainly in Southern Thailand (Patani United Liberation Organisation [PULO]) and the Philippines (Abu

Sayyaf), are involved in struggles that are mainly motivated by autonomy and self-rule.

Only in the triangle of countries such as Malaysia, the Philippines, and Indonesia do we note groups akin to ISIS or al-Qaeda, whose sole purpose is to bring in a new "Islamic Order" or the "New Caliphate." Groups, such as the Jemaah Islamiyyah, al-Mauunah, and Abu Sayyaf have not only resorted to kidnapping and ransom-taking but also to inflicting gross violence in their acts and reprisals against local governments and populations.[50]

Muslims certainly need to create a positive image and an inspiring narrative that show how Islam is compatible with life in pluralistic societies. They should help combat the militant interpretations of Islam that endorse violent terrorism as jihad, which violates centuries of tradition.

At a speech in Sharjah in the United Arab Emirates, the young Nobel Prize winner, Malala Yusafzai, urged the world's Muslims to "come together...and join hands in the struggle for peace." She added: "we cannot talk about investing in our future without calling for an end to these bombings and these attacks." One must not forget that the majority of those suffering because of these conflicts and wars are Muslims, she added.[51]

Radicalisation by external forces has been identified as a principal means of recruitment of the region's youth and Islamic faithful. These influences could stem from "returnees" from the battlefronts in Iraq and Syria or from various ISIS-based social media postings. Another new development and source may be the 2016 U.S. presidential election campaign, especially that of the Republican nominee and now president, Donald Trump. He made immigration, especially of Muslims from the Middle East, a campaign topic emblematic of a policy to disallow Muslims completely from entering the United States. Democratic presidential nominee, Hillary Clinton, also discussed setting in place extensive screening methods on Muslims entering the United States. Events such as these were seen as providing terrorist groups with additional armour to intensify their nefarious methods to win over new, impressionable Muslim youth and others to their side. Trump's rhetoric about Muslims being a threat to the United States "play into the fears of citizens in the US and many Western nations, stoked by mainly right-wing media outlets spreading accusations and scare-mongering about Islam, immigration and jihad. It also plays into the perception of Muslims around the world who see themselves as abused and on the defensive against Western aggression."[52]

One more addition to an already confused scenario were the waves of mass migration of Muslims to Germany, Scandinavian countries, the United Kingdom, and other European destinations in 2015 and 2016. As large numbers of young migrants from wartorn Syria, Iraq, and Afghanistan entered Europe, there was a rise in crime and terrorist attacks, such as the July 14, 2016 Nice truck attack in France that killed eighty-six people, as well as lesser incidents in Germany and Belgium that alarmed the host countries about the possibility of even worse occurrences. Peter Apps thus commented that "it became increasingly less relevant whether an attack—such as the gun attack in Munich which killed nine, or the stabbing of an orthodox Jew in France, or a machete attack on a bus in Brussels is directly related to a militant group like ISIS or not "provided a migrant or someone of migrant descent is involved, it all falls into the same divisive narrative."[53] In many ways, what happened on the beach at Nice is exactly what groups like ISIS want: to deepen divisions within society.

Dealing with terrorists also pose legal challenges. Practices differ in different countries. In France, one could not detain a terrorist suspect unless one was caught in the act or had strong evidence. In the United States a suspect could be detained on the basis of evidence received from other countries. The problem revolves around security and human rights issues. Admittedly, countries can devise their own approaches, and many countries have, in fact, proposed or passed new antiterrorism laws according to their own needs and realities.

Muslim Responses to Global Terrorism

The upsurge in suicide bombing by those claiming to be "Islamic warriors" has brought mixed responses from Muslim scholars. Most scholars of standing have not hesitated to condemn this and also the September 11, 2001 attacks as being contrary to Islamic principles.

In its sixteenth session (5–10 January 2002), the Jeddah-based Islamic Fiqh Academy, affiliated with the Organisation of Islamic Conference (OIC; now known as the Cooperation), condemned all forms of terrorism as follows:

> Terrorism is an outrageous attack carried out either by individuals, groups, or states against human beings. It includes all forms of intimidation, harm, threats, killing without a just cause, all forms of armed robbery, banditry, every act of violence or threat intended to

> fulfil a criminal scheme individually or collectively, terrify and horrify people by hurting them or by exposing their lives, liberty and security, to danger. It can also take the form of inflicting damage on the environment, a public or private utility—all of which are resolutely forbidden in Islam.[54]

Muslim religious and political notables expressed unqualified condemnation of the ISIS and Charlie Hebdo atrocities. International organisations and fatwa councils, including the Majlis Ulama Indonesia, the National Fatwa Committee of Malaysia, and the Mufti of Saudi Arabia, denounced the brutality and violence of the ISIS group as violating the core principles of Islam.

In September 2003 the then former (and now incumbent) Malaysian prime minister, Dr. Mahathir, denounced Palestinian suicide bombing and said that suicide bombing was unacceptable in Islam. He added that they resorted to suicide bombing because they did not have proper weapons in their fight for an independent homeland. He stated, "Nevertheless, it is wrong to commit suicide bombing because it causes loss of innocent lives. Fighting is one thing, but if you go on board a school bus and kill all the school children, I don't think it is a brave move."[55]

In November 2003, the Arab states condemned the suicide car bombing in Riyadh that killed seventeen and wounded more than a hundred, mainly Arabs. The twenty-two-member Arab League denounced the attack as "terrorist and criminal," while Saudi Arabia and its five neighbours in the Gulf Cooperation Council condemned it as "cowardly and terrorist." The Arab League secretary-general, Amar Musa, also said such acts "only aim to destabilise . . . terrify and kill" innocent people.[56]

Abusive interpretations of jihad notwithstanding, jihad is also an instrument of peaceful self-education and improvement. The pathways to peace in Islam are also enriched by its teachings on human fraternity, compassion, honouring one's neighbour, avoidance of harm to others, and the rich tradition of Sufism. Islam also advocates peace through nonviolence, universalism, and a generally positive view of human nature and potential.

Maḥmūd Shaltūt, the Shaykh of al-Azhar University (1958–1963), lent considerable weight to the argument that the Qur'an only allows warfare to be waged in self-defence. He quotes verses from the Qur'an, including al-Anfāl (8:61) and Mumtaḥanah (60:8–9), which together with al-Baqarah (2:190) and al-Ḥajj (22:39–40) uphold and substantiate that principle.[57]

The mufti of Saudi Arabia, ʿAbd al-Azīz al-Shaykh, declared that suicide bombings have never been an accepted method of fighting in Islam. "To my knowledge so-called 'suicide missions' do not have any legal basis in Islam and do not constitute a form of Jihad. I fear that they are nothing but a form of suicide, and suicide is also prohibited in Islam." This echoes an earlier fatwa by his predecessor, the late Saudi mufti Shaykh ʿAbd al-Azīz b. Bāz.

Shaykh Yūsuf al-Qaraḍāwī issued a fatwa condemning the tragic suicide attacks of 9-11, stating:

> "Even in times of war, Muslims are not allowed to kill anybody save the one who is engaged in face-to-face confrontation with them." He added that they are not allowed to kill women, old persons, or children, and that haphazard killing is totally forbidden in Islam. Shaykh al-Qaraḍāwī on another occasion defined terrorism as "the killing of innocent people...with no differentiation between the innocent and the foe."

Al-Azhar's Research Academy, shortly after September 11, declared that a "Muslim should only fight those who fight him; children, women and the elderly must be spared." Therefore, terrorism and its crimes against civilians are impermissible under any interpretation of Islamic law. This ruling does not change based on geographical locality.[58]

Another Shaykh of al-Azhar, Muḥammad Sayyid Ṭanṭāwī, issued a fatwa in 2001 to condemn the hostage-taking in the Philippines: "Islam rejects all forms violence. These acts of violence have nothing to do with Islam."[59] He also condemned the terrorist act of September 11, 2001, in America.[60] The Chief Mufti of Saudi Arabia, ʿAbd al-Azīz b. ʿAbd Allāh al-Shaykh, also declared in 2004:

> You must know Islam's firm position against all these terrible crimes. The world must know that Islam is a religion of peace, justice and guidance....Islam forbids the highjacking of airplanes, ships and other means of transport, and it forbids all acts that undermine the security of the innocent.[61]

The Washington-based Fiqh Council of North America (FCNA) issued the following fatwa and press release on July 29, 2005:

> Islam strictly condemns religious extremism and the use of violence against innocent lives. There is no justification in Islam for extremism or terrorism. Targeting civilians' life and property through suicide bombings or any other method of attack is *ḥarām* —forbidden—and those who commit these barbaric acts are criminals, not "martyrs."...We clearly and strongly state: 1) All acts of terrorism targeting civilians are *ḥarām*. 2) It is *ḥarām* for a Muslim to cooperate with any individual or group that is involved in any act of terrorism or violence. 3) It is the civic and religious duty of Muslims to cooperate with law enforcement authorities to protect the lives of all civilians.[62]

On 18 April 1983, the Lebanese Shii organisation Islamic Jihad (the precursor of Hezbollah) carried out suicide attacks on the US embassy in West Beirut, killing sixty-three staff members.[63] On 23 October the same year, the headquarters of the US and French forces in Beirut were attacked by suicide bombers, resulting in the death of 298 military men and women. According to Saad Ghorayeb, these suicide attacks took place because Khomeini, the supreme Shii leader, authorised them. The "martyrs," as he termed them, at the US Marines compound "saw nothing before them but God, and they defeated Israel and America for God. It was the Imam of the Nation [Khomeini] who showed them this path and instilled this spirit in them."[64]

The leading figure among the Lebanese Shii community, Sayyid Muḥammad Ḥusayn Faḍlallāh, initially denied that he supported these attacks, but eventually he offered his endorsement. He argued that, in the absence of any other alternative, unconventional methods became admissible and perhaps even necessary. On the other hand, Faḍlallāh was one of the first high-ranking Shii scholars publicly to condemn the September 11 attacks, probably the most horrific example of suicide attacks.

On 25 February 1994, Baruch Goldstein, a Jewish settler, massacred twenty-nine Muslim worshippers during *fajr* (dawn) congregational prayer in a Hebron mosque. In response, the Islamic resistance movement Hamas introduced suicide attacks into its conflict with Israel and started to strike at Israel's heartland. The suicide attack on 13 April 1994 at the central bus station in Hadera was probably the first such attack by Hamas. Ramadhan Shellah, a leader of Islamic Jihad in the Occupied Territories, acknowledged that the tactic had been taken over from the

Lebanese Hezbollah. In an interview given to *al-Hayat* newspaper on 7 January 2003, he was asked whether the organisation had borrowed the idea of "martyrdom operations" from Hezbollah. "Of course," he said.[65] Muhammad Munir, who has discussed Faḍlallāh's views, says that he does not distinguish between suicide attacks by combatants (not pretending to be civilians) of either side during an ongoing war and those against military objectives or civilians and civilian objects. Munir then draws his main conclusion as follows: When a suicide bomber targets civilians, he might be committing at least five crimes, according to Islamic law, namely killing civilians, mutilating them by blowing them up, killing enemy civilians, committing suicide, and, finally, destroying civilian objects or property. In his opinion, Munir said, because of the crimes committed, he—or she—is not a *shahīd* (martyr). Those who call such a person *shahīd* are simply ignoring the teachings of the Qur'an and the Sunnah with regard to the Islamic jus in bello and are making a mockery of God's law.[66]

Unless the root causes of radical extremism are addressed, many have warned that incidents of violent extremism is likely to increase. Once a radical group falls by the wayside, is discredited, or is made irrelevant, another group emerges, which is often even more radical and violent. This is how ISIS is a successor to al-Qaeda—upping the stake in the radicalisation contest and becoming even more destructive and violent than its predecessor.[67] Unless the legitimate claims of those who suffer from oppression and injustice are heard, angry and disillusioned men and women—whether Sunni, Shia, Kurds, Palestinians, or others— often feel that the path of violence is the only one left for them to take.[68]

In 2012 Mark Winer wrote, in an article titled "Fundamentalists versus Moderates," that the future of humanity may well depend on the ability of religious moderates to overcome their extremist coreligionists. Extremism, he argued, only spawns interfaith bigotry while sanctioning violence, war, and terrorism. A great deal therefore depends on our understanding of the eternal conflict between extremism and moderation and on the strategies devised by religious moderates to combat this common scourge. [69]

It is indicative of the wisdom of the early Muslims that they labelled a group that behaved similarly to modern-day terrorists the "Kharijites" (from *Khawārij*, lit., outsiders). By this name they made it known that the group had exited from the mainstream community, thereby giving them the choice of either changing their behaviour and rejoining the community or else staying as outsiders. The same can be said of *ghulāt* (lit., exaggerators), the name so unmistakably expressive of its purpose, which was given to a small group of Shia who exaggerated their interpretation of the doctrine of imamate so as to elevate the first Shii Imam, ʿAlī b. Abī Ṭālib, to a deity.

One can hardly think that anyone could soil Islam's name as badly as the likes of ISIS, Boko Haram, and al-Shabab have done. If the militants should even realise this—that they are doing more harm than good in the cause of their religion, as Islamic leaders all over the world are already pointing out—their numbers will eventually diminish.[70]

Ḥirābah *in the Qur'an Revisited*

The Qur'anic phrase "waging war on God and His Messenger" put the Muslim jurists in a certain quandary as to its precise import and implications. For it is a generic expression evidently not meant to be taken for its literal meaning, but since it is immediately followed by "making mischief in the land [*fasād fi'l-arḍ*]," the two phrases were read together in order to provide a clearer understanding of the verse. Yet this latter phrase too is less than specific, for *fasād fi'l-arḍ* can also include a variety of criminal activities and transgressions. It is even suggested that the latter phrase is wider than the former in that spreading "corruption in the earth" can include criminal activities that may not even qualify as *ḥirābah* or "waging war" as such. Hence the relationship between the two phrases is seen as one of the specific (*khāṣṣ*) to the general (*ʿām*). *Ḥirābah* is thus seen as only one of the many manifestations of *fasād fi'l-arḍ*. Al-Shawkānī (d. ca. 1255/1839) wrote that the manifest meaning of *fasād fi'l-arḍ* is broad enough to subsume not only highway robbery but also propagation of false deities (*shirk*); destruction of peoples' lives; looting their properties; attacking their dignity; destruction of trees, waterways, and livestock; and aggressive dictatorships that humiliate people.[71] Some commentators also included under *ḥirābah* recidivist thieves, notorious rapists, and homosexuals whose evil and mischief-making cannot be stopped in any way other than execution. Most however understood the verse under review to be referring to bandits and those who stage armed rebellions with a show of force that threaten peace and order in society. Ibn Ḥazm al-Ẓāhirī (d. 456/1064) observed that, since many other crimes such as adultery and theft were specifically mentioned in the Qur'an and that the text had also assigned quantified penalties for them, what was left unspecified was the crime of banditry (*qaṭʿ al-ṭarīq*). The verse of *ḥirābah* was thus understood to have contemplated it. Yet to read that particular theme into the meaning of *ḥirābah* and "spreading of corruption in the earth" was evidently by way of interpretation that in due course found common acceptance. In sum, unlike the other *ḥudūd* crimes that are mentioned specifically by name, *ḥirābah* (banditry) is arrived at through juristic construction and general consensus (*ijmāʿ*).[72]

It is not only natural but necessary for Muslim scholars and jurists of all persuasions to continue this interpretative endeavour by subsuming the global menace of contemporary terrorism under the umbrella of the Qur'anic concept of "waging war against God and His Messenger" and indeed as one of the greatest instances of spreading corruption in the earth humanity has known. This understanding of *ḥirābah* is clear from reading the text without recourse even to any methodology or formula of reasoning, such as analogy (*qiyās*) or *ijtihād*. Muslim jurists have commonly understood "waging war against God and His Messenger" as to mean waging war on the people, including, of course, the Muslim community. This is clear enough. Juristic thought in the fiqh sources has focused on a variety of related themes, raising such questions, as already reviewed, as to whether *ḥirābah* can be committed by an individual or if it is a collective crime that only a group can commit; whether it can be committed within or only outside city areas; whether or not it must involve the use of weapons; and whether or not it is politically motivated. Most of these questions, or perhaps some of them, are also relevant to contemporary terrorism, but the availability of remote-control devices and a host of other modern methods of destruction that the terrorists have utilised, as well as the ever-expanding scope of contemporary terrorism, have made some aspects of the fiqh specifications of *ḥirābah* almost totally redundant. Certain manifestations of contemporary terrorism, such as suicide bombing, were also not familiar to the earlier schools and scholars and tend to fall outside of the scope of their writings. That said, one also finds that the fiqh literature on *ḥirābah* is internally diverse; much of it is not supported by general consensus (*ijmāʿ*) and thus remains open to further development and *ijtihād* in light of the pressing needs and common good (*maṣlaḥah*) of the people.

According to some early commentators, the verse of *ḥirābah* contemplated Muslim rebels and mutineers only since repentance is normally not accepted from unbelievers until they embrace Islam. But the majority of jurists have disputed this and maintain that *ḥirābah* as addressed by the Qur'an is not confined to Muslims and may be committed by anyone,

Muslim or non-Muslim, provided that the crime is committed in a territory that is ruled by a Muslim government.[73]

Furthermore, it is worth mentioning that "spreading of mischief/corruption in the earth" is a major theme of the Qur'an and occurs in a variety of other contexts. Included under *fasād fi'l-arḍ* are thus the spreading of heresies (al-Baqarah, 2:11–12); destruction of the living environment (al-Rum, 30:41); destruction of farmland, gardens, and waterways (al-Shu'arā', 26:141); persistent criminality (al-Mā'idah, 5:32); inciting enmity and hatred among people (5:64); the practice and spreading of sorcery (Yūnus, 10:79); humiliating people through pharaonic absolutism (al-Qaṣaṣ, 28:4); practice and incitement to sodomy and homosexuality (al-'Ankabūt, 29:28); killing and brutalising innocent people (2:30); and persistent hypocrisy (2:204). The Qur'anic conception of "spreading corruption in the earth" is indeed comprehensive and clearly strikes a note with almost all the various manifestations of contemporary terrorism.

Having reviewed the Qur'anic passages on *fasād fi'l-arḍ*, al-Khaṭṭāf observes, and rightly so, that the concept is broad enough to subsume such other criminal activities experienced in our time such as drug trafficking, human trafficking, Mafia-like crime syndicates, and loan sharks. These criminals kidnap people and destroy and brutalise them and their families, as well as those who stage armed rebellions and military coups that topple lawfully elected governments. To quote al-Khaṭṭāf:

> This is why *ḥirābah* acquires enormous significance in our lives today, especially after what we witnessed in the Arab region through the so-called Arab Spring; the inciters to violence and war that invaded peoples' lives and properties, wreaked havoc on them and the lives of entire communities and their homelands. . . .The Qur'anic concept of "spreading mischief in the earth" also includes the agents of corruption who shake the constitutional order, play with people's lives and collude with enemies to carry out their sinister designs.[74]

The strong textual grounding of *ḥirābah* and its wide-ranging implications can hardly be underestimated in view especially of the global reaches of terrorism and emergence of terrorist organisations and networks. People need to be protected and laws need to be revised to equip law enforcement agencies and governments against them. The world has witnessed horrendous atrocities in so many places, including crimes committed by warlords, drug barons, and mischief-makers in places such as wartorn Syria, Iraq, Afghanistan, Nigeria, and Somalia. Included in these are, of course, those who terrorise innocent people, committing genocide and crimes against humanity in the name of a caliphate or any other name. These are the enemies of Islam and peace, the destroyers of people's lives, who are not entitled to use Islam's name in association with their heinous crimes. There is absolutely no room for atrocity and the shedding of innocent blood in shariah by anyone, including ISIS, al-Qaeda, the Taliban, al-Shabab, Boko Haram, and the like. Both the means and the ends must be lawful, for shariah proscribes a pursuit of lawful ends through unlawful means. Justice must be served, and truth uncovered and told, through approved processes and means, as far as possible, or amnesty granted in the hope for a peaceful end to hostilities except for the criminals who have committed atrocities. Only then can one nurture a realistic prospect of a peaceful future for the affected individuals and communities.

VIII

Issues over Apostasy (Riddah)

THERE ARE BASICALLY three issues that Muslim commentators have highlighted concerning the treatment of apostasy in scholastic jurisprudence and also the manner of its occurrence in contemporary legal instruments, such as that of the Hudud Bills of Kelantan and Terengganu in Malaysia. One of these is over the definition of apostasy, which is so general as to be lacking in focus. Unless apostasy is given a clear definition, it is likely to conflict with both the Qur'anic position as well as many of the applied constitutions of Muslim countries on freedom of religion. The Hudud Bill of Kelantan 1993 defines apostasy very much in line with how it is done in the fiqh manuals:

> Apostasy (*irtidād*) is any act done or any word uttered by a Muslim who is *mukallaf* (legally competent), being an act or word which according to Shariah law affects or which is against the *ʿaqīdah* (belief) in Islamic religion. (Sec. 23.1)

The bill goes on to specify that the act or word in question must be voluntary and that there must be no compulsion. It is further provided that the act or word affecting the belief (*ʿaqīdah*) must be such that they concern "the fundamental aspects of Islamic religion which are deemed to have been known and believed by every Muslim...pertaining to the Rukun (pillar or fundamental of) Islam, Rukun Iman (fundamentals of dogma), and matters of halal (the allowable or the lawful) or *ḥarām* (the prohibited or the unlawful)" (Sec. 23.2). These expressions are still too broad and have come under scrutiny because they often fall short of offering a clear and exclusive definition. There is also nothing in these provisions, or anywhere else in the Hudud Bill of Kelantan, to draw a distinction between apostasy and blasphemy. This definition is also broad enough to lump together a variety of different concepts: blasphemy, apostasy, disbelief (*kufr*), and heresy (*bidʿah*). The sum total of this approach would be that there will be no difference, for the purposes of enforcing the death punishment under this bill, between a simple conversion that is neither contemptuous nor hostile and one that inflames the masses of Muslims and is capable of causing bloodshed and civil strife. The Hudud Bill of Kelantan provides that anyone found guilty of committing the offence shall be given three days in which to repent, failing which "the court shall pronounce the death sentence on him and order the forfeiture of his property . . . for the Baitul-Mal" (Sec. 23.4).

What is striking about the Hudud Bill of Kelantan is an unmediated rendering of the traditional fiqh text materials on apostasy. What follows next is a review of the source evidence in the Qur'an and hadith as well as some of the early and more recent scholarly contributions on the subject, concluding with our own assessment.

Review of the Source Evidence on Apostasy

The leading schools of Islamic law, both Sunni and Shia, have adopted as standard law the ruling of the hadith that provides that one "who changes his religion shall be killed" [من بدل دينه فاقتلوه]). But the issue of death as a punishment for apostasy is controversial as the Qur'an is totally silent on the subject,[1] and on the contrary provides that "there shall be no compulsion in religion" (al-Baqarah, 2:256). This basic Qur'anic position is further endorsed in a number of other verses, such as the following:

> Those who accept the faith and then disbelieve, then accept the faith again and disbelieve again, and go on increasing in disbelief, God will not forgive them nor guide them on the [right] path. (al-Nisāʾ, 4:137)
>
> إِنَّ ٱلَّذِينَ ءَامَنُوا۟ ثُمَّ كَفَرُوا۟ ثُمَّ ءَامَنُوا۟ ثُمَّ كَفَرُوا۟ ثُمَّ ٱزْدَادُوا۟ كُفْرًا لَّمْ يَكُنِ ٱللَّهُ لِيَغْفِرَ لَهُمْ وَلَا لِيَهْدِيَهُمْ سَبِيلًۢا
>
> If God had willed, everyone on the face of the earth would have been believers. Are you then [O Muḥammad] compelling the people to become believers? (Yūnus, 10:99)
>
> وَلَوْ شَآءَ رَبُّكَ لَءَامَنَ مَن فِى ٱلْأَرْضِ كُلُّهُمْ جَمِيعًا ۚ أَفَأَنتَ تُكْرِهُ ٱلنَّاسَ حَتَّىٰ يَكُونُوا۟ مُؤْمِنِينَ .

> Say, the Truth [has come] from your Lord. Let him who will, believe, and let him who will, disbelieve. (al-Kahf, 18:29)
>
> وَقُلِ ٱلْحَقُّ مِن رَّبِّكُمْۖ فَمَن شَآءَ فَلْيُؤْمِن وَمَن شَآءَ فَلْيَكْفُرْۚ
>
> Unto you your religion, and unto me my religion. (al-Kāfirūn, 109:6)
>
> لَكُمْ دِينُكُمْ وَلِىَ دِينِ

The Qur'an evidently maintains that faith must be sustained through conviction and that religion induced by compulsion is meaningless.

The second issue to raise, and one that many jurists have also discussed, is over reducing the element of repentance (*tawbah*) in apostasy to little more than a technical formality. Scholastic jurisprudence is affirmative on offering the apostate an option to repent and return to Islam but he must do so in three days; failing that, he will be liable to the death punishment.

The third issue is concerned with the total neglect in mainstream fiqh scholarship, and also more recent laws, of a body of opinion among the ulama that has been known to exist ever since the early days of Islam: The view that apostasy is not a *ḥudūd* but a *taʿzīr* offence. This view is based on the fact that the death punishment for apostasy is not mentioned in the Qur'an. Similarly, the hadith that provided the sole authority for the death punishment for the apostate is open to interpretation. The main hadith on this states that "whoever changes his religion shall be killed," a text that needs to be interpreted as it would otherwise cause confusion. For instance, would it be right to say that a Jew who converts to Islam or a Hindu who becomes Christian should be liable to the death punishment? This would evidently distort the message of the hadith—hence the need for its interpretation.

According to the rules of interpretation, as are expounded in *uṣūl al-fiqh*, once the general meaning of a decisive (*qaṭʿī*) text has been specified in some respect, the part that remains unspecified becomes speculative (*ẓannī*) and, as such, is open to further interpretation.[2]

This analysis is sustained by another hadith, which is often quoted in support of the death punishment for apostasy:

> The blood of a Muslim who professes that there is no god but God and that I am His Messenger is sacrosanct except in three cases: a married adulterer, a person who has killed another human being,

> and a person who has abandoned his religion, while splitting himself off from the community .[3]
>
> قَالَ رَسُولُ اللَّهِ صلى الله عليه و سلم "لَا يَحِلُّ دَمُ امْرِئٍ مُسْلِمٍ يشهد أن لا إله إلا الله، وأني رسول الله إلَّا بِإِحْدَى ثَلَاثٍ: الثَّيِّبُ الزَّانِي، وَالنَّفْسُ بِالنَّفْسِ، وَالتَّارِكُ لِدِينِهِ الْمُفَارِقُ لِلْجَمَاعَةِ

The apostate is thus one who boycotts the community (*mufāriq li'l-jamāʿah*) and challenges its legitimate leadership. This is where the death punishment may be invoked.[4]

There were cases during the time of the Prophet when certain individuals apostatised after professing Islam, yet the Prophet did not penalise them let alone condemn them to death. Affirmative evidence on this point is found in the following hadith, which is recorded in both al-Bukhārī and Muslim texts:

> A Bedouin came to the Prophet, peace be on him, and pledged his allegiance to him. The next day he came back, ill with fever and said repeatedly: "Return my pledge to me," but the Prophet refused—thrice. Then the Prophet said: Medina is like the bellows which rejects its dross and retains that which is pure.[5]
>
> فَجَاءَ الأَعْرَابِيُّ إِلَى رَسُولِ اللَّهِ صلى الله عليه وسلم فَقَالَ يَا رَسُولَ اللَّهِ أَقِلْنِي بَيْعَتِي . فَأَبَى ثُمَّ جَاءَهُ فَقَالَ أَقِلْنِي بَيْعَتِي. فَأَبَى فَخَرَجَ الأَعْرَابِيُّ فَقَالَ رَسُولُ اللَّهِ صلى الله عليه وسلم " إِنَّمَا الْمَدِينَةُ كَالْكِيرِ تَنْفِي خَبَثَهَا وَتَنْصَعُ طَيِّبَهَا.

This was a clear case of apostasy, in which the Prophet made no reference to any punishment at all, and the Bedouin, despite his persistent renunciation of Islam, was let go unharmed. The Prophet even intimated that the person was like those in Medina who would have been thrown out—not quite an expression of resistance but still taking stock of the relevant situation. The purport of this hadith also harmonizes with the Qur'anic text (4:137—the first of the four passages previously quoted), which clearly provides a strong argument against the death penalty for apostasy.

The implication (of the verse 4:137) is unmistakable in that the initial reference to belief and then disbelief is followed by further confirmation of disbelief and then an "increase in disbelief." One might be inclined to think that if the first instance of apostasy did not qualify for capital punishment, the repeated apostasy might have provoked it—had such a punishment ever been intended in the Qur'an.

As for the hadith on the death punishment for apostasy (quoted in the preceding section), it is conveyed in the form of a general provision (*ʿām*), which is in need of specification (*takhṣīṣ*). The general purport of this hadith, as al-Shawkānī stated, has even been specified, at least in one respect, in the Qur'an itself (al-Naḥl, 16:106) with regards particularly to a person who changes his religion outwardly under duress but remains faithful otherwise. Such a person is exonerated and may not be subjected to any punishment. The Ḥanafīs and Shia Imamiyyah have also specified the general purport of this hadith with respect of a woman apostate who is not punished by death but by imprisonment only. This is because the masculine pronominal suffix that occurs in the wording of the hadith gives rise to an element of doubt concerning its application to women. They also quote in this connection the hadith concerning jihad in which the Prophet has said, "Do not kill a woman—*lā taqtulu al-marʾata*." Since a woman is not killed for original unbelief, she is not killed for apostasy either.[6]

Having been subjected to one level of interpretation, the hadith in question becomes open to other levels of interpretation. The death punishment therein may consequently be reserved for apostasy, which is accompanied by active hostility to the Muslim community and its leadership and would effectively be tantamount to high treason.[7]

As for the issue over repentance, two different positions have been taken, one of which is attributed to Imams Mālik (d. 179/795), Sufyān al-Thawrī (d. 161/778), and Abū ʿAmr al-Awzāʿī (d. 157/774) and upheld also by the majority to the effect that the apostate should be asked to repent over a period of three days and should not be killed before then. This position is roughly similar to those of the enemies at war (*muḥaribīn*) who must be offered the choice to embrace Islam before war is waged on them. The second view is attributed to Imams al-Shāfiʿī and Ibn Ḥanbal, which is the view also of Ḥasan al-Baṣrī (d. 110/728) and maintains that asking the apostate to repent is not necessary, even though recommended, and may be dispensed with altogether. The proponents of this view refer to the hadith just reviewed, which states that "one who changes his religion shall be killed", saying that the wording of the hadith is general and makes no provision for repentance.[8]

Juristic Opinion on Apostasy

A number of prominent ulama across the centuries and down to our own times have taken the view that apostasy is not a *ḥudūd* offence. Ibrāhīm al-Nakhaʿī (d. ca. 96/717), the teacher of Imam Abū Ḥanīfah (a leading jurist and traditionist of the generation succeeding the Companions), and Sufyān al-Thawrī (d. 161/778), who is known as "the prince of the believers in hadith" (*amīr al-muʾminīn fīʾl-ḥadīth*) and who authored two important compilations on hadith,[9] both held that the apostate should be reinvited to Islam and should not be condemned to death. They maintained that the invitation should continue for as long as there is hope that the apostate might change his mind and repent.[10] Al-Nakhaʿī elaborated that asking the apostate to repent is not limited to once or three times, nor to one or three days, but that he should be continually asked to return to Islam. Abū Zahrah, who quotes al-Nakhaʿī, also agrees with him.[11] The Mālikī jurist Abū al-Walīd al-Bājī (d. 474/1081) and the Ḥanbalī jurist Ibn Taymiyyah (d. 728/1328) have held that apostasy is a sin that carries no prescribed punishment and that a sin of this kind may be punished by one year of imprisonment under the discretionary punishment of *taʿzīr*.[12] ʿAbd al-Wahhāb al-Shaʿrānī (d. 973/1565), author of the comparative fiqh work, *Kitāb al-Mizān*, has cited the views of al-Nakhaʿī and al-Thawrī and added that "the apostate is thus permanently to be invited to repent."[13] Further endorsement of this comes from the renowned Ḥanafī jurist, al-Sarakhsī (d. 490/1096, also known as Shams al-Aʾimmah), the author of the thirty-two-volume fiqh work *al-Mabsūṭ*, who held that apostasy does not qualify for temporal punishment and that there is no prescribed punishment (*ḥadd*) for it either. To quote al-Sarakhsī:

> Renunciation of the faith and conversion to disbelief is admittedly the greatest of transgressions, yet it is a matter between man and his Creator, and its punishment is postponed to the Day of Judgment [فالجزاء عليها مؤخر الى دار الجزاء].[14]

Three twentieth-century scholars and authors of works in contemporary fiqh, ʿAbd al-Ḥakīm Ḥasan al-ʿIlī, Ismāʿīl al-Badawī, and Abū Zahrah, have commented that by al-Nakhaʿī's time Islam was secure from the hostility of disbelievers and apostates. This, they maintain, indicates that al-Nakhaʿī understood the hadith quoted in the preceding discussion, which made apostasy punishable by death, to be political in character and aimed at the inveterate enemies of Islam.[15]

The late Shaykh of al-Azhar, Maḥmūd Shaltūt (d. 1383/1963), analysed the relevant evidence in the sources and drew the conclusion that apostasy carried no temporal punishment because in reference to apostasy the Qur'an only speaks of punishment in the Hereafter. To quote Shaltūt:

> The hadith "one who changes his religion shall be killed" has evoked various responses from the ulama many of whom are in agreement that the *ḥudūd* cannot be established by solitary (*aḥad*) hadith, and that unbelief by itself does not call for the death punishment.[16]

Shaltūt also concurred with the analysis that the key factor underlining the prohibition of apostasy was to curb "aggression and hostility against the believers and the prevention of *fitnah* (sedition, civil strife) against the religion and state."[17] Issues of public security and defence of the community against hostility and sedition were, in other words, behind the prohibition of apostasy.

Ṣubḥī Muḥmaṣṣānī (d. 1407/1986) of Lebanon and Salīm al-ʿAwā of Egypt, both highly respected scholars, have observed that the death punishment was meant to apply not to simple acts and pronouncements of apostasy from Islam but to cases when apostasy was linked to an act of political betrayal of the community and high treason. The Prophet never killed anyone solely for apostasy. This being the case, the death penalty was not meant to apply to a simple change of faith but to punish acts of treason that consisted of joining forces with the enemy and sedition.[18]

The late Murtaza Mutahhari (d. 1399/1979) of Iran highlighted the incompatibility of coercion with the spirit of Islam as well as the basic redundancy of punitive measures in the propagation of its message. He wrote that it is impossible to force anyone to acquire the kind of faith that is required by Islam, just as "it is not possible to spank a child into solving an arithmetical problem. His mind and thought must be left free in order that he may solve it. The Islamic faith is something of this kind."[19]

Apostasy in Malaysia: An Overview

Notwithstanding some attention that apostasy has received in a few court decisions, it remains basically unregulated in Malaysia. Incidental references of the kind that are seen in these cases are not enough to overcome the basic constitutional question of whether or not penalising apostasy will be *ultra vires* the constitutional clause on freedom of religion. There is also the question of jurisdiction as to whether the civil courts or the shariah courts have the jurisdiction to adjudicate over cases of apostasy and conversion. This is because as soon as a person renounces Islam, he or she is no longer a Muslim, and the shariah court jurisdiction in Malaysia only covers disputes by or among the Muslim parties. Even if one reaches the conclusion that the shariah court ought to have jurisdiction to determine issues pertaining to religious offences, the absence of particular laws to determine matters of personal freedom, the absence of undue influence and coercion, and the nature of any sanctions to be applied may prove problematic.

The Hudud Bill of Kelantan in Malaysia 1993 has offered a definition, as previously reviewed in this chapter, and the discussion concludes with a reiteration of the fiqh conception of this offence without any attempt to reconstruct it or bring it up to date. Apostasy is a highly contested concept and should be reviewed in line with the realities of contemporary Malaysian society, its multireligious makeup, the constitution and other laws, or a leading court decision with relevance to it. It has also made no attempt even to integrate the views of many prominent scholars discussed here who distinguish between apostasy and blasphemy and a carefully constructed educational approach to the issue of repentance. The sum total of this approach would be that there will be no difference, for the purposes of enforcing the death punishment under this bill, between a simple conversion that is neither contemptuous nor hostile and one that inflames the masses of Muslims and capable of causing civil strife beyond control.

The substance of this problem became the focus of attention in a Kuala Lumpur seminar where one of the speakers, then professor of Islamic law at the University of Malaya, Mahmud Zuhdi Abdul Majid, was quoted to have said in reference to the Hudud Bill of Kelantan that "there is no room for inquiry. This results in a blind acceptance of everything....The prevailing intellectual hollowness among the ulama [is such] that they cling to *kitāb fiqh* [books on jurisprudence] of jurists such as Shāfiʿī, Ḥanafī, or Mālikī, but these are law books, equivalent to that of Blackstone and Solomon, and they are not mandatory provisions. There must be an exertion of the intellect based on the Qur'an." The speaker then highlighted the "clergymen's inability" to differentiate the essence of the law and the jurists' opinion and said that "this poses a problem to the administration of Islamic laws in this country."[20]

Apostasy was a punishable offence in the early years of the advent of Islam due to its subversive effects on the nascent Muslim community and state. Non-Muslims and hypocrites, as per Qur'anic affirmation, acted in collusion to embrace Islam in large numbers in the morning only to renounce it by the end of day so as to weaken the hearts of nascent Muslims. The present writer has elsewhere enquired into the early history of apostasy and the hadith that makes it punishable with death. There were about half-a-dozen such cases during the Prophet's time in Medina in which he had ordered the death punishment, although not all were carried out as some fled to Mecca before they were caught. It merits attention that the ten years or so of the Prophet's life in Medina witnessed at least twenty-six military engagements wherein the Prophet himself participated, and a much larger number of skirmishes (totalling over eighty), all in a relatively short space of time. It was wartime, in other words, and people who renounced Islam were actually individuals who would renounce Islam in Medina, immediately flee to Mecca, join the enemy forces, and fight back against Muslims. It was in this order and context that the hadith "whoever changes his religion shall be killed" was pronounced. For otherwise there is no case on record where the Prophet has actually ordered the killing of anyone for mere renunciation of Islam without the elements of active hostility and treason.[21] Evidence in the Qur'an that have been examined here and elsewhere is also supportive of the freedom of belief, attested by the fact that the Qur'an has discussed apostasy in no less than twenty-one places but has nowhere provided a punishment for it. Freedom of religion thus remains to represent the normative position of shariah on nonsubversive apostasy that is due purely to personal conviction and belief. Only when it is committed under aggravating circumstances, or when the lawful authorities consider that it is committed under conditions that represent a threat to the sensibilities of believers, may it then be subject to a deterrent punishment of *taʿzīr*.

Lastly, in the detailed discussion of repentance (*tawbah*) earlier, it was proposed that repentance should become an integral part of the penal philosophy of *ḥudūd*. We extend that proposal also to apostasy and concur with the view that repentance should not be confined to any particular time or number of days and should be continually sought and repeated as part of an educational approach that allows for a meaningful role for repentance.

IX

*Slanderous Accusation (*Qadhf*)*

THIS CHAPTER BEGINS with a definition of *qadhf* and proceeds with a review of the textual authority on it, along with a review of the typical words and expressions that convey the meaning of *qadhf* either directly or by implication. The chapter continues with an exposition on the scholastic views and issues that have arisen concerning the Right of God and Right of Man components of this offence—the status of the slandered person (*maqdhūf*) and the punishment of *qadhf*—followed by a conclusion.

Slander is defined, under both Sunni and Shii laws, as making an accusation of *zinā* against a Muslim of upright character or denying a person's legitimate descent, and the charge so made is not proven by four witnesses.[1] Textual authority on *qadhf* is provided in the Qur'anic verse as follows:

> And those who accuse chaste women but bring not four witnesses [to prove it], flog them with eighty stripes, and never accept their testimony [thereafter]. They indeed are evildoers. Unless they repent thereafter and mend [their conduct]; For God is forgiving, most merciful. (al-Nūr, 24:4–5)

> وَٱلَّذِينَ يَرْمُونَ ٱلْمُحْصَنَٰتِ ثُمَّ لَمْ يَأْتُوا۟ بِأَرْبَعَةِ شُهَدَآءَ فَٱجْلِدُوهُمْ ثَمَٰنِينَ جَلْدَةً وَلَا تَقْبَلُوا۟ لَهُمْ شَهَٰدَةً أَبَدًا ۚ وَأُو۟لَٰٓئِكَ هُمُ ٱلْفَٰسِقُونَ. إِلَّا ٱلَّذِينَ تَابُوا۟ مِنۢ بَعْدِ ذَٰلِكَ وَأَصْلَحُوا۟ فَإِنَّ ٱللَّهَ غَفُورٌ رَّحِيمٌ.

The offence thus carries a fixed punishment of eighty lashes and a supplementary punishment that disqualifies the offender from acting as a witness until he repents and amends his acts. Muslim jurists have, by way of analogy, extended the prohibition of slander to include men in the same way as women. Anyone who accuses an upright person, woman or man, of *zinā* and fails to prove the veracity of his or her charge is thus liable to the punishment of eighty lashes of the whip. The accuser stands as one who has lied and is permanently discredited as the result of becoming an upright witness. For the offence of *qadhf* to stand, the slandered individual (*maqdhūf*) must fulfil five conditions: being an adult who has reached the age of majority, being of sound mind, being a Muslim, having purity of character (*ʿiffah*), and being a freeman (this condition may now seem redundant).[2] If the slandered person is a minor, an unbeliever, or one who has a record of past prosecution of adultery or other crimes, his or her accuser will not be subject to the prescribed penalty. The charge of slander against such a person may fail to qualify, but it may still be considered as a malicious expression partaking in obscene language and subjected to a lesser punishment under *taʿzīr*.[3]

The occasion of revelation of this verse is reported to be connected with the famed episode over the loss of a necklace belonging to ʿĀʾishah, the Prophet's wife, when she accompanied the Prophet on the occasion of the Battle of the Ditch. Upon leaving for a three-day journey out of Medina, the Prophet took two of his wives with him, Umm Salmah and ʿĀʾishah. The latter lost her onyx necklace on the return journey while travelling on a howdah. The clasp of this necklace, which ʿĀʾishah's late mother had given her, was insecure and she lost it on the move. At the next stop, ʿĀʾishah "realised her loss and slipping away from under the curtain she went back to look for it. The men who had saddled and were leading the camel . . . failed to notice that one of the two howdahs was without its occupant. ʿĀʾishah found her necklace and when she returned, the army had left. Thinking that they would miss her and come back for her, ʿĀʾishah sat and waited until she noticed another traveler, Safwan the son of Mu'attal, one of the emigrants who had also fallen behind the army for some reason. When he saw ʿĀʾishah he stopped and recognised her saying 'Verily we are for God, and verily unto Him we return. This is the wife of the Messenger of God.' "[4] Safwan offered his camel and escorted her himself on foot to the next halt.

This episode became the talk of the town and eventually became known as "The lie—*al-ifk*" due to a Qur'anic revelation that ascertained ʿĀʾishah's innocence, but only after a great deal of anguish, in a long Qur'anic passage calling the rumour mere calumny and vindicating the truth of the matter (al-Nūr, 24:15–17). In the same sura the Qur'an also specified the punishment of adultery, and then also the penalty for those who slander honourable women—that the slanderer who charges such women be punished with eighty lashes of the whip. The reports add that this sentence of slander (*qadhf*) was subsequently carried out on three of ʿĀʾishah's accusers, Misṭaḥ, Ḥassan, and Ḥamnah, from among the Hypocrites, who had spread the calumny and had also confessed to their guilt and thus were punished.[5]

It is a requirement of slander that the accusation of *zinā* is made in clear and unequivocal words that are in no need of interpretation. Slander that carries the prescribed punishment consists specifically of the attribution of adultery to a chaste and upright person, attesting that he or she has committed adultery or that he or she is the offspring of adultery; in the latter case the act of adultery is attributed to his or her father or mother. All of these factors constitute slander. It is a requirement also that the victim is a known person without any ambiguity as to his or her identity. Thus if someone addresses two or three persons by such terms that "one of you is an adulterer (*zānī*)," the prescribed punishment will not apply. Other insulting words that offend and humiliate a victim are also likely to fall below capital punishment but may be punishable under the principle of *taʿzīr*. Slander differs from other terms of insult in that its subject (i.e., adultery) is amenable to proof as to its truth or falsehood. Other terms of insult (such as calling someone a "son of a bitch," "dog," "ass," etc.) are mostly not amenable to that process and do not align with the idea of being proven or even refuted.[6]

Terms such as "O thief," "drunkard," "idiot," and so on, even though possible to prove or truthful, still do not constitute *qadhf* proper but are punishable under the discretionary principle of *taʿzīr*. Disagreement has arisen as to whether the charge of slander would hold if the accuser attributes adultery to someone who is incapacitated, such as being impotent or ill. Imam Ibn Ḥanbal considers that this charge can indeed invoke the punishment of slander, as the purpose of the shariah punishment for this offence is to protect the honour and good name of upright individuals regardless of the veracity of the charge, so long as the offence is degrading and humiliating. The majority position on this charge, however, is that the prescribed punishment will not apply. Thus according to the Imams Mālik, Abū Ḥanīfah, and al-Shāfiʿī, this is not a case of *ḥudūd* but one of *taʿzīr* because the proof of its veracity would "fall to the ground," but the accuser may be punished for hurting the feelings of the victim.[7] There is also disagreement as to whether accusing a chaste person of homosexuality and sodomy (*liwāṭ*) falls under slander proper. Whereas the Imams Mālik, al-Shāfiʿī, and Ibn Ḥanbal include this charge under slander, Imam

Abū Ḥanīfah maintains that adultery and homosexual intercourse are different and have different consequences. Charging someone with homosexuality is not a prescribed offence but it is punishable otherwise, and he recommends severe punishment for it.[8] Abū Ḥanīfah's view is justified, partly due to the guidelines of hadith that one should try to find a way out of the *ḥudūd* as far as possible, and the Ḥanafī view seems to offer a way out of that predicament.

The offence of slander is proven, under both Sunni and Shii laws, by the normal standards of proof, which is two witnesses of upright character who are impartial and have no background of hostility or close ties of kinship with any of the parties to the charge. If the victim of the charge denies the charge and says it is a lie, this may also be testified by any method of proof or documentation. However, if the accuser presses the truth of his claim, he has to prove the charge of adultery by the method of proof for that offence, which consists of testimony from four witnesses, excluding himself. Otherwise he would himself be liable to the punishment of slander.[9] However, if the accuser admits to the charge of slander, a valid confession before the court is sufficient without repetition.[10]

The offence of slander is premised, as already noted, in the concern for the protection of honour and the good name of upright individuals as well as to protect the integrity of the family unit against unjustified charges of adultery. Yet slander can also be abused and, especially in the context of rape, be used as an instrument to protect the rapist rather than the victim of rape.

The three Imams, Abū Ḥanīfah, al-Shāfiʿī, and Ibn Ḥanbal (and also the Shia Imamiyyah), have held that a father and grandfather are not liable to the prescribed punishment of slander if he/they accuse his/their son or grandson of adultery. This exemption also applies to the mother in the same way as to the father. The exemption here is due primarily to the special position of honour the parents are granted in the Qur'an and hadith; this position is not peculiar to slander but extends to all the other *ḥudūd* crimes. Yet the son is liable to the prescribed punishment, under both Sunni and Shii laws, if he accuses his father. The fixed *ḥudūd* penalties are thus not enforceable on the parents, but the parent may nevertheless be subjected to discretionary sanctions under *taʿzīr*. Only Imam Mālik has held that parents are also liable to the prescribed punishment of slander, based on an analysis that the Qur'anic verse on slander does not make an exception in this regard and so applies also to the father (but this is believed to be a weak opinion).[11]

For a perpetrator to be subject to the prescribed punishment of slander, under both Sunni and Shii laws, he or she must be a free and adult person (whether the perpetrator is a man or woman, Muslim or non-Muslim). The victim of slander must, in addition, be a Muslim and an upright person who is capable of sexual intercourse. An upright person here means one with a clean record who has never been convicted of unlawful sexual intercourse nor subjected to the imprecation (*liʿān*) procedure. Under Mālikī law, a woman need not be an adult but must be capable of intercourse, free, and Muslim. Unlike the other schools, the Mālikīs also penalise one who uses an indirect or metaphorical expression. For the other schools this would constitute uncertainty (*shubha*), which would suspend the standard punishment but may still be penalised under *taʿzīr*. The perpetrator is absolved of the charge if he or she actually proves the charge of adultery. If a charge is laid against a group of persons, the perpetrator is punished only once unless each person in the group has been individually addressed with the charge, in which case the punishment will multiply accordingly.[12]

The leading schools of law are in agreement that the punishment of slander is not enforceable unless it is requested by the victim; if the latter forgives the offender, there will be no punishment. This is so because, unlike most of the other *ḥudūd* offences, slander is a violation predominantly of the Right of Man/private right. Imams al-Shāfiʿī and Ibn Ḥanbal have thus held that, since slander consists mainly of the violation of the Right of Man, it resembles just retaliation, or *qiṣāṣ,* both of which are amenable to pardoning by the victim, and this is upheld by the majority. Those who differ—maintaining that all the *ḥudūd* crimes, including that of slander, consist primarily of the claims or Rights of God—also disregard any request made by the victim of the offence and entitle the ruler and judge to enforce it as soon as it is proven. Whereas the majority opinion entitles the victim of slander to grant forgiveness to the offender—whether before or even after it is reported to the authorities—the Ḥanafī school holds that the victim of slander is not entitled to grant forgiveness at any stage (i.e., before or after it is reported to the authorities). The Mālikī school holds that the victim of slander may not grant forgiveness after reporting it to the authorities but may do so before that eventuality. These positions relate to the differential views taken on whether slander belongs to the Right of God or to the Right of Man category of rights.[13]

The victim of slander must not only qualify the conditions of moral probity (or *muḥṣan*) at the time of the offence, according to the Ḥanafīs, Mālikīs, Shāfiʿīs, and Shia, but also continue to possess them until the time of implementation of the prescribed punishment. If he or she loses that status and commits adultery, for instance, or becomes insane during the interval, the offender is not punished by the prescribed punishment. The Ḥanbalīs maintain, on the other hand, that punishment is enforceable once the offence is proven even if the condition of the victim changes afterward.[14]

The punishment of slander is also amenable to amalgamation (*tadākhul*) in the event of repetition. Thus if A charges B with adultery and repeats that charge again, even if several times, A is punished only once, regardless as to whether the charge is for the same offence of adultery or new offences after that. This can be said also of a situation where A is punished for the offence and then again charges B of the same or another offence of adultery. The prescribed punishment is not repeated, but A may be punished for repetition by way of *ta*ʿ*zīr*.[15]

Notwithstanding some differences of opinion, the majority also apply the prescribed punishment of slander if the victim is a deceased person, whether male or female, provided that the legal heirs of the deceased demand it. This is so because the good name and reputation, as well as the state of probity (i.e., *muḥṣan*) of a person, are not terminated by his or her death. It is further added that attribution of adultery to a deceased person is also likely to soil the good reputation of his or her surviving relatives.[16]

There is general agreement also that the offender is permanently disqualified from being a witness before the courts of justice unless he repents. The repentance is acceptable, but whether that will qualify him to be a witness again is a subject of disagreement. While Imam Abū Ḥanīfah maintains that the offender is permanently disqualified, Imams Mālik and al-Shāfiʿī maintain that he may be admitted as a witness again, apparently based on an analogy (*qiyās*) with other *ḥudūd* offences. Since the perpetrators of theft and adultery are not disqualified from being a witness once they have been duly punished, that same position applies to the accuser in slander.[17] Slander in this sense is no graver, in other words, than other *ḥudūd* offences, all of which consist of violation of the Right of God, the only difference being that in slander the victim's right is stronger and also entails the right to decide whether or not to prosecute. But according to Imams Abū Ḥanīfah and Mālik, slander belongs to the Right of God category of offences, and it is not amenable to pardon after the matter has been brought to the attention of the court. Once that process has begun, enforcing the punishment of slander, it is said, is a matter of defending the Right of God, or the community's right, in the sense of demanding punishment for those who attack the good name and honour of one of its members. Al-Qurṭubī, who has discussed the scholastic views, concludes that the mainstream position maintains slander to be a violation primarily of the Right of Man. Hence the victim is entitled to grant pardon or to prosecute, whether before or after the violation is reported to the authorities.[18]

It would undoubtedly bear greater harmony with the letter and spirit of shariah on the subject of *ḥudūd* to open the avenues of redemption and the possibilities whereby a prescribed punishment could be mitigated or reduced to *taʿzīr*. One such avenue would have been to make a provision for the victim of slander to determine whether he or she wishes that the punishment should be carried out. Failure to do so, which is the case, for instance, in the Hudud Bills of Kelantan and Terengganu in Malaysia, is tantamount to turning a blind eye to the Qur'anic provisions on repentance and forgiveness as well as the hadith to the effect that making an error on the side of leniency is preferable than making an error on the side of severity.

X

*Issues over Wine Drinking (*Shurb*)*

THIS CHAPTER RAISES the question at the outset as to whether or not *shurb* is one of the *ḥudūd* offences and then proceeds to review the textual authority on *shurb*. Questions have also arisen over the precise punishment of this offence, how is it proven, how and when it can be enforced, whether the punishment can be extended to other intoxicants and narcotics, and certain exemptions that the law grants on grounds of necessity. Responses to these questions will be reviewed alongside scholastic differences over the juridical descriptions of a drunken person, the actual duration of that condition, and its impact on punishment.

One of the basic issues over wine drinking is that it does not belong in the category of *ḥudūd* and that the evidence for classifying it under *ḥudūd* offences is less than decisive. Yet the majority (*jumhūr*) have held that *shurb* is one of the *ḥudūd* offences, but they have differed on the quantum of its punishment.

The Qur'an forbids wine drinking along with other activities and enjoins the faithful to avoid them:

> O you who believe, wine and games of chance and idols [worshipping] and divination with arrows are only an infamy of Satan's handiwork. Avoid it in order that you may succeed. (al-Mā'idah, 5:90)
>
> يَـٰٓأَيُّهَا ٱلَّذِينَ ءَامَنُوٓاْ إِنَّمَا ٱلْخَمْرُ وَٱلْمَيْسِرُ وَٱلْأَنصَابُ وَٱلْأَزْلَـٰمُ رِجْسٌ مِّنْ عَمَلِ ٱلشَّيْطَـٰنِ فَٱجْتَنِبُوهُ لَعَلَّكُمْ تُفْلِحُونَ.

The prohibition here is conveyed in a command form to "avoid," which the jurists have understood to mean not only drinking but also the sale and purchase of wine and liquor, taking a price for these items, carrying them from place to place, or making a gift of them.[1] Although wine drinking and activities relating to liquor have been clearly declared forbidden in the Qur'an, the text has not specified any punishment for them. The evidence in the Sunnah also indicates that the Prophet has not treated them as strictly *ḥudūd* offences. Wine drinking was very widespread at the time of pre-Islamic Arabs and was undoubtedly an entrenched aspect of their lifestyle, which is why the Qur'an took a gradual approach toward its prohibition. The practice was the subject of three separate verses revealed over a period of time in Medina. Initially the text spoke in a persuasive language advising people of the ill effects of wine drinking, and subsequently discouraged it near prayer times; it was only in the third of the three verses that it was declared totally forbidden. The Prophet is also known to have imposed different types of punishments for wine-drinking. According to reports, on occasion he ordered his Companions to reprimand the offender, in most cases it seems by beating him with hands, shoes, lashes with palm shoots and rolled-up clothes, and so on. There were also occasions where the Prophet only imposed a verbal rebuke of the wine drinker, just as instances are also known of him ordering dust to be splashed on the face of the drinker after punishment. This wide variety of sanctions is not known for any other *ḥudūd* offence, and it provides an indication that the Prophet did not treat wine drinking as a *ḥudūd* crime but as a *taʿzīr* offence, for which the punishment characteristically varies from person to person and takes into account the surrounding circumstances. *Ḥudūd* punishments are typically uniform and not variable according to persons and circumstances.

Several hadith reports have been recorded by al-Bukhārī and others, indicating that the Prophet has not determined a fixed punishment for drinking. Note for example:

> Al-Saib b. Yazid reported: During the Prophet's time, and also that of Abū Bakr and the early period of the caliphate of ʿUmar we used to strike the drunken with our hands, shirts and clothes (twisted into the shape of lashes) and it was toward the end of the caliphate of ʿUmar that he ordered forty lashes, and raised it to eighty when the accused was mischievous and disobedient.[2]

حدثنا السائب بن يزيد : كنا نؤتي بالشارب على عهد رسول الله (ص) وإمرة أبي بكر وصدرا من خلافة عمر فنقوم بأيدينا ونعالنا وأرديتنا حتى كان أخر إمرة عمر فجلد أربعين حتى إذا عتوا وفسقوا فجلد ثمانين.

Reports further indicate that when the first caliph, Abū Bakr, was faced with the issue over punishment of liquor drinking, he asked the Companions about it but they did not know of any precise punishment for it. The Shāfiʿīs seem to have followed the early precedent of ʿUmar b. al-Khaṭṭāb that also finds support in the Prophet's own Sunnah, which made drinking wine punishable with forty lashes. When ʿUmar further consulted the Companions, Abū Saʿīd al-Khudrī informed him that "the Prophet, pbuh, punished drinking with forty blows of the shoes," so ʿUmar converted the shoe strikes to lashes.[3] Then it is also reported that ʿUmar later followed ʿAlī b. Abū Ṭālib's response in which the latter drew an analogy between drinking and slander (*qadhf*): "When a person drinks, he is intoxicated, and when intoxicated, he raves and he hurls accusations." So the caliph ʿUmar determined the punishment at eighty lashes, evidently by analogy to slander, which carried eighty lashes of the whip by the clear ruling of the Qur'an. Both the Sunni and Shii schools maintain that the punishment applies only when the offender has recovered and is not in a state of intoxication.[4]

Those who maintain the punishment for drinking is eighty lashes follow the precedent of the caliphs ʿUmar and ʿAlī. The former is known to have increased the punishment to eighty lashes as already explained. Al-Qurṭubī, who wrote on this also, added that the majority have followed ʿAlī's (and ʿUmar's) version, whereas the Shāfiʿīs and the Ẓāhirīs and the Zaydī Shia have followed Abū Saʿīd al-Khudrī's version and held the punishment to be forty lashes only. Others have seen this variation between forty and eighty lashes as the range in which the punishment can vary, depending on the severity of the offence and the social mischief it might be representing. This is also perhaps an indication for the authorities to determine the punishment in light of the prevailing conditions of their societies.[5]

Muslim jurists are in agreement, in the meantime, that consumption of liquor is permissible for non-Muslims who may be living in a Muslim country, provided that their own religion has not prohibited the practice. This is based on the clear authority of a hadith that states, "We have been commanded to leave them alone in regards to their own religious beliefs."

أمرنا بتركهم وما يدينون.

Non-Muslims may, however, be punished for drinking, either by way of a prescribed (*ḥadd*) or of a discretionary *taʿzīr* punishment, if this is done in a manner that causes corruption and social mischief or in a way that promotes debauchery and drinking among the Muslims.[6]

Imam Muslim has recorded a hadith from Anas Ibn Mālik that the Prophet used to punish wine drinking with lashes from palm twigs and shoes forty times, and that this was deemed sufficient even if the offender had repeated the offence. As for the increased amount of punishment during the time of ʿUmar, it was because liquor consumption had increased significantly and had given rise to adverse consequences, which is why he increased the punishment. But this increase, it is added, is not a part of the *ḥudūd*; rather it is done by way of a discretionary deterrent punishment of *taʿzīr*—as the leader/Imam has the authority to do so.[7] According to a minority opinion, the Prophet's own precedent creates an obligation and must be followed. The variations that are reported are ad hoc additions, and the normative position remains that which the Prophet himself has authorised.[8]

Some scholars have reached the conclusion that the instrument used to implement the punishment of drinking should be confined to those that were employed during the Prophet's time: palm twigs, shoes, twisted clothes, and hands. The majority has held, however, that these as well as a whip may be employed. Some have even viewed that the whip should be reserved for the hardened offender who is unlikely to be deterred by the use of these other lighter instruments, thus suggesting variation in the pain inflicted for different categories and types of offenders.[9]

It is generally held by both the Sunni and Shii laws that the element of intent must be present for the prescribed punishment of drinking to be administered. The drinker must, in other words, have prior knowledge that what he was drinking was liquor and caused intoxication. If someone drank an intoxicating drink while thinking that it did not intoxicate, he is not liable to the prescribed punishment. The liquor drinker must also know that drinking wine and other intoxicants are prohibited. This being the basic position, it is added that ignorance of this kind is sustainable in a non-Muslim locality but not so in the Muslim land.[10] It is also necessary that intoxication materialises as a result of the drink. Many scholars have maintained that there are two aspects to the offense at issue: drinking as an intoxicant itself and actually getting intoxicated, both of which must be present. If someone drinks while knowing it is an intoxicant but does not actually become intoxicated, the prescribed punishment is not applied if the drink is something other than *khamr* (*khamr* is wine obtained specifically from grapes). The Ḥanafīs are alone in this last position, but their ruling is based on how they understand the hadith that "*Khamr* is *ḥarām*, be it a large amount or small"; that it mentions *khamr* and its ruling does not therefore apply to other intoxicants in the same way. The majority of schools, namely the Mālikī, Shāfiʿī, Ḥanbalī, and Shia, do not consider actual intoxication as a separate element. So long as a person knowingly drinks an intoxicating drink, regardless of the name, quantity, or substance from which it is obtained, he commits the offence.[11]

Although a minority view stipulates that the intoxicating substance should be a drink in liquid form and taken in a quantity, however small, that reaches the digestive system, this view is superseded by the obvious meaning of another hadith saying that "every intoxicant is *khamr* and all *khamr* is forbidden [كل مسكر خمر وكل خمر حرام]." Hence all intoxicants, whether liquid, solid, or gas, are equated with *khamr* and equally made *ḥarām*. This would include opium, heroin, cocaine, hashish, and all other narcotics that intoxicate and overwhelm the faculties of reason and discernment. There is disagreement on the point as to whether the substance must be taken by mouth, a condition that the Ḥanafīs and Mālikīs have stipulated. Thus if a substance is taken in some other way, it may invoke a *taʿzīr* punishment but not the prescribed punishment of drinking.[12] Others have disagreed. It seems that subsequent developments have made the Ḥanafī and Mālikī positions obsolete—as many drugs are taken by injection, sniffing, and other methods that reach the system even faster. It further appears that the uncertainty about drinking alcoholic beverages other than *khamr* also relates to different views and locality specifications. Most of the ulama of Hijaz (Mecca and Medina) and the majority of schools of that region put other alcoholic beverages on par with *khamr* and hold that their consumption in whatever quantity is punishable on the same basis. The jurists of 'Iraq including the Ḥanafīs have held that if a person drinks these other beverages, he would only be punished if he actually gets intoxicated.[13]

The majority view proscribes the use of liquor and liquor derivatives in medicine based on the authority of the hadith that "God does not make cure for [the ailments of] my ummah what He has made *ḥarām* to them [إن الله لم يجعل شفاء امتي ما حرم عليها]." Imam Abū Ḥanīfah has held otherwise, however, on the condition that no other alternative is available and the case falls under necessity.[14] The basis for this view is the renowned legal maxim that derives from the Qur'an, also supported in the Sunnah, which says,

"Necessities make the unlawful lawful [الضرورات تبيح المحظورات]." It would appear then that pure wine or liquor should be excluded from the purview of this maxim. Yet it may be difficult to say the same about all alcohol derivatives. If they are present in a medication that saves life and no easy alternative is available, the physician may prescribe it, and the position would be subsumed under the rules of necessity.

As for the actual condition of intoxication that constitute the offence of drinking, Imam Abū Ḥanīfah has held that it means "the person loses his rational capacity (*ʿaql*) altogether; he cannot tell the difference between a small and a large amount, cannot distinguish the earth from the sky, nor a man from a woman."[15] Abū Ḥanīfah's two disciples, Abū Yūsuf and al-Shaybānī, have held, however, that intoxication means that the person speaks nonsense and does not know what he says. They derive this understanding from the Qur'an (al-Nisāʾ, 4:34) and their understanding is in conformity with the majority of other leading Imams.

The leading scholars of hadith, al-Bukhārī, Muslim, Abū Dāwūd, and Ibn Mājah, have also recorded a report from the fourth caliph ʿAlī in which it is said that he used to implement the *ḥudūd* on people and did not have any regrets even if the person died as a result of the punishment. An exception applied to the wine drinker, for if he died then ʿAlī was concerned about the payment of blood money (*diya*) for him as this was what the Prophet himself had done. What this meant was that the public treasury was not responsible for the consequences of *ḥudūd* proper, except for the wine drinker, because *ḥudūd* proper were determined by the texts of the Qur'an or Sunnah but the punishment of drinking was determined through *ijtihād*. Abū Dāwūd and Imam Aḥmad b. Ḥanbal have also recorded a hadith from Ibn ʿAbbās, who said that "the Prophet, pbuh, did not fix any punishment for wine drinking—*inna rasul Allāh lam yaqit fi'l-khamri ḥaddan*," which evidently means that it is a flexible *taʿzīr* punishment.[16]

General consensus has materialised to the effect that only the lawful authorities are within their rights to enforce *ḥudūd*, including the punishment for drinking. Notwithstanding this there has been confirmation by a majority of jurists, including the key Ḥanbalī scholar Ibn Qayyim al-Jawziyyah (d. 751/1350), the Shii Zaydī scholar al-Shawkānī (d. ca. 1255/1839), and the Mālikī jurist Ibn Farḥūn (d. 799/1397), who have not only classified drinking as a *ḥudūd* offence but also claimed a general consensus (*ijmāʿ*) on its punishment to have been fixed at eighty lashes—which is evidently not the case. Twentieth-century Muslim scholars including Muṣṭafā

Shalabī, Fatḥī Bahnasī, Muḥammad Salīm al-ʿAwā, and others have stated that the alleged *ijmāʿ* on drinking being a *ḥudūd* offence is incorrect and have held that it is a *taʿzīr* offence. The basic argument for this is based on the view that *ḥudūd* are by definition offences for which a fixed punishment is prescribed in the Qur'an or Sunnah. When this is not the case, the whole concept of *ḥudūd* collapses.[17]

The punishment is enforced, according to general consensus, by the confession of the accused or testimony of two upright witnesses. Only one instance of confession is enough, according to all the leading schools, although the Ḥanafī scholar Abū Yūsuf has held that all confessions should be twice, by analogy apparently to two witnesses being the standard requirement. Imam Abū Ḥanīfah and his disciple Abū Yūsuf have confined admissibility of confession in drinking to the time until the smell of alcohol on the breath still obtains and no longer after it has disappeared. So if someone confesses to drinking after the breath smell has perished, his confession is inadmissible. There is disagreement over the question as to whether the prescribed punishment of drinking can be enforced based on the smell of the drinker's breath alone. The majority considers breath smell as to be no more than circumstantial evidence, which is not free of an element of doubt, and that the punishment is not enforced on this basis alone. Thus it is said that the breath smell can be caused by merely tasting wine or gargling it or even by some natural resemblance of one's breath to the smell of alcohol.[18]

Imam Abū Ḥanīfah and Abū Yūsuf have, on the other hand, considered the duration of breath smell as the criterion of admissibility both for confession and witnesses in drinking, saying that testimony is also admissible only during this fragment of time. As soon as the breath smell ceases, testimony also ceases to be admissible. The majority have not agreed on this point with Abū Ḥanīfah and do not confine witnessing to that particular time segment.[19]

The question as to whether the judge may impose the prescribed punishment for drinking, based on his personal knowledge in the event that he has himself seen the incident or that the offender has confessed to him outside the courtroom environment, has invoked a negative response. The basic rule here is that the judge must rely on objective evidence presented in the courtroom. Muslim jurists have also held that the punishment for drinking is suspended: (a) when the offender retracts his confession and there is no other evidence; (b) when one or both of the witnesses retract their testimony and there is no other evidence; and (c) when one or more of the witnesses loses their competence at any stage after adjudication and prior to enforcement.[20]

Al-Jazīrī has discussed the key Ḥanbalī scholar Ibn Taymiyyah's views in the latter's book, *al-Siyāsah al-Sharʿiyyah*, where he declared cannabis and hashish as *ḥarām* and subject to the prescribed punishment of liquor drinking, for these substances also overwhelm the faculty of reason and become an agent of corruption like liquor and even worse. Al-Jazīrī then concurs with Ibn Taymiyyah and his disciple Ibn Qayyim al-Jawziyyah, who declared cannabis and opium to be forbidden (*ḥarām*).[21] In advancing these views and speaking forcefully for them, al-Jazīrī goes on to quote a number of hadith reports that equate all intoxicants to *khamr* (wine) and declare them all as *ḥarām* (most of the relevant hadiths have been reviewed in the preceding discussion in this chapter). Al-Jazīrī's review of the relevant hadith literature also includes the hadith that Ibn Abī Shaybah has narrated from Ibn ʿAbbās as follows: "When God makes something *ḥarām* He also makes earning through it *ḥarām* [إن الله إذا حرم شيئا حرم ثمنه]." The Prophet has declared every intoxicant *ḥarām*, which subsumes not only the consumption and smoking of opium, hashish, and all hard-core narcotics but also buying, selling, and promoting them. For hard-core drugs such as cocaine and heroin far exceed liquor in their damaging and dangerous effects on individuals and societies. Al-Jazīrī thus wrote: "Anyone who declares any of these permissible is attributing a lie to God Most High."

Also recounted in this connection are the views of some Ḥanafī scholars to the effect that "one who permits [smoking] hashish is a heretic [*zindīq*] and a pernicious innovator [*mubtadiʿ*]."[22] Muslims who occupy themselves in activities that involve trading in liquor, narcotics, hashish, opium, and cocaine and procure huge profits through them are engaging in *ḥarām* and live their lives through *ḥarām* earnings.[23] The majority (*jumhūr*) have held by consensus that, regarding one who knowingly sells grapes to a wine maker, "the price earned through it is *ḥarām* for him, contrary to selling grapes to those who buy them for their own consumption or lawful trades. Similarly one who knowingly sells arms to one who fights Muslims, the price earned through it is *ḥarām*."[24]

The leading Imams are in agreement on the prohibition (*ittifāq al-aʾimmah ʿalā taḥrīm*) of the cultivation of hashish and poppy seeds in order to obtain the prohibited substances from them for trading and other uses.

This is because by growing these substances, the farmers aid and abet others in the perpetration and spread of corruption.[25] Engaging oneself in growing these substances is surely indicative of consent for people to use them and trade and transact in them. For farmers who sell what they grow is tantamount to aiding and abetting in the spread of this evil. It is a moral and religious duty of every Muslim therefore to refrain from all activities that help the spread of drug addiction, such as farming and trading in them and promoting them in any way they know would harm society and spread corruption in the land, especially among the youth.[26]

XI

Enforcement of Ḥudūd *Punishments*

PROCEDURAL CONSTRAINTS

THIS CHAPTER DISCUSSES the fiqh provisions on how *ḥudūd* punishments, especially those that consist of flogging, are actually carried out with a degree of procedural accuracy and restraint. It also looks into the amalgamation and overlap of *ḥudūd* punishments and the effects, if any, of repentance in their enforcement. The discussion also considers two other issues: delay (*ta'khīr*) and the expiration of time (*taqādum*) in the proof, adjudication, and enforcement of *ḥudūd* punishments. The chapter begins with a note on the relative gravity and weighting of *ḥudūd* crimes in relationship to one another.

Muslim jurists have attributed a certain order and level of gravity in considering various *ḥudūd* offences. Thus it is held that the offence of liquor drinking is of lesser gravity than that of adultery, for the latter is proven by clear text in the Qur'an, whereas drinking is established in the authority of Sunnah. An additional factor is that adultery involves violation of the rights of others, whereas drinking is primarily an aggression upon one's own self. Adultery is also said to pose a greater threat to society compared to drinking. Then the commentary adds that the gravity of liquor drinking outweighs that of slander (*qadhf*), for drinking can be easily detected and prosecuted, whereas slander can involve a degree of uncertainty and interpretation as to its veracity or otherwise.

This manner of relative weighting and comparison is also reflected in how the punishment of flogging is carried out for each of these offences. The majority (*jumhūr*) and the Shia Imamiyyah have held that flogging in the case of drinking is applied on bare skin. The offender's clothes are removed except for his trousers (*shalwar*) that cover his private parts

(*ʿawrah*), as is also the case with regard to other *ḥudūd* offences that involve flogging. But in the case of slander, it is held that the offender may keep one layer of his clothing and remove the rest, such as woolen clothing and furs. An exception is recorded by Imam Muḥammad b. Ḥasan al-Shaybānī, the disciple of Imam Abū Ḥanīfah, who is of the view that the punishment of drinking and slander should both be executed in the same manner. In both cases, the convict is allowed to keep one layer of clothing and remove additional clothes. Then Imam Muḥammad b. Ḥasan al-Shaybānī quotes as an authority the fourth caliph ʿAlī's famed analogy, which equates drinking with slander: One who is drunk raves, and one who raves is also likely to utter slander—hence the two are about equal with respect to punishment. There is also a requirement of restraint in the enforcement of punishments, including *ḥudūd* and *qiṣāṣ*, so that in cases where there is fear of adverse effects they should be carried out under medical supervision, and enforcement may be delayed if expert opinion recommends such until the patient/convict recovers.[1]

Further on the manner of implementation of flogging in *ḥudūd* offences, it is stated that flogging should neither be too light nor too severe but rather shall be moderate. One who strikes the whip should not exaggerate either way. Flogging should not be concentrated on one spot or organ of the body but be evenly distributed. Flogging should in no case inflict injury, break the skin, or cause intolerable pain or death. The manner of application should also be tempered with the age and health conditions of the convict. Flogging should not be applied in sickness and the convict should be given time to recover. Additionally, flogging is not administered in excessively hot or exceedingly cold weather and must be put on hold until a milder climate or season arrives. If the person is elderly or ill with an incurable disease such as cancer, the instrument may be changed and a lighter tool, such as a palm shoot or light sandals, may be used. It is thus implied that any suitable instrument may be employed. The Shāfiʿīs and Ḥanbalīs have held that palm leaves, twined clothes, or shoes may be used for flogging an elderly drinking offender.

The whip that is used for flogging is usually made of a strip of leather about half a meter in length with a short wooden handle; and it is said that the instrument in question should be neither brand-new nor too old but in-between. If the person is drunk, flogging is delayed until he becomes sober. It is administered such that the striker does not raise his arm up to his head but only raises his arm up to his elbow. Flogging is to be administered by a man. The offender is not to be humiliated nor subjected to undignified handling or treatment.

The Companion Abū Hurayrah has in this connection reported, as recorded in al-Bukhārī, that a man who had drunk intoxicating drinks was brought before the Prophet and then was ordered to be punished. So those present started striking the man with their shoes, others with their hands, and some also with rolled-up clothes. When the man was going away, some of those present scolded him with the words "may God humiliate you—*akhzak* Allah," to which the Prophet responded by saying to them, "Do not say this; and do not be an advocate of the Satan upon him."[2]

وعنه قال أتى النبي صلى الله عليه وسلم برجل قد شرب خمرا قال اضربوه قال أبو هريرة: فمنا الضارب بيده والضارب بنعله والضارب بثوبه فلما انصرف قال بعض القوم أخزاك الله قال لا تقولوا هكذا لا تعينوا عليه الشيطان.

On the authority of the Qur'an (al-Nūr, 24:2), it is recommended that flogging shall be carried out in public and witnessed by a number of Muslims.

If the number of lashes is one hundred, they may be divided in two parts and administered separately; but if the lashes are below that number, they shall be administered all at once and during the same session. Flogging is also not applied, under both Sunni and Shii laws, on a pregnant woman, nor shall they be applied to a breast-feeding woman until she weans the child. The woman is allowed to keep on all the clothing she wears. The genital area, head, and face (and, according to the Ḥanbalīs, also the chest and stomach) are to be excluded in all cases. There is a difference of opinion, however, on excluding the head. The Shāfiʿīs generally have held that the head is not excluded, and this view is shared by Abū Yūsuf, a disciple of Imam Abū Ḥanīfah. Whereas men are flogged in the standing position, women are allowed to sit. Exposure of *ʿawrah* (private parts) is forbidden in all cases of flogging.[3]

These limits and guidelines are also observed in flogging by way of a deterrent (*taʿzīr*) punishment, although opinions differ on whether or not the *taʿzīr* flogging should be more severe than that of the *ḥudūd* punishment. The best advice would seem to be that of moderation in the administration of flogging generally. The number of lashes are fixed in all three *ḥudūd* crimes, namely adultery, wine drinking, and slander, which may neither be increased or decreased. However, a fixed and predetermined number is not a strict requirement in flogging for *taʿzīr* offences.

According to the Shāfiʿīs and Imam Abū Ḥanīfah, as well as a minority opinion in the Ḥanbalī school, the maximum number of *taʿzīr*-related floggings should not reach that of the lowest number of lashes in the *ḥudūd* category, which would be thirty-nine lashes—assuming that forty lashes are prescribed for consumption of liquor. Imam Ibn Ḥanbal himself is reported to have held that flogging under *taʿzīr* should not exceed ten lashes of the whip, whereas the Mālikīs have not specified any limit and said they may, if necessary, even exceed 100 lashes in the *taʿzīr* category. The majority position on this is that no particular number is specified and it is for the Imam or his deputy and the judge to specify the number of lashes based on the principles of considerations of public interest (*maṣlaḥah*) and judicious policy (*siyāsah sharʿiyyah*).[4]

Some of the *ḥudūd* penalties amalgamate with one another, especially if they belong to the same binary categories of public and private rights, *ḥaqq Allāh* and *ḥaqq al-ādamī* respectively. Thus if someone commits both drinking and homicide, they both belong to the Right of God category and may amalgamate, in which case only the punishment for homicide is carried out. Similarly, if an unmarried person is convicted of drinking and adultery, and the latter carries 100 lashes, only the latter is carried out. This is the majority opinion except for Imam al-Shāfiʿī, who maintains that the *ḥudūd* punishments are separately carried out and none amalgamate with others. Thus if someone is convicted of liquor drinking, theft, and *zinā* and he is a married person (*muḥṣan*), each of the three punishments are separately enforced. Imam Abū Ḥanīfah has also held that the punishment of drinking does not amalgamate with any other *ḥudūd* penalties except for execution for murder. Imam Mālik has held that the punishment for drinking amalgamates with the one for slander as they share similar characteristics, and even motives (*mawjib*), reminiscent perhaps of the caliph ʿAlī's famed parallel between them.[5]

Ḥudūd punishments are also amenable to amalgamation if repeated. Thus if someone commits theft, adultery, or any of the other *ḥudūd* crimes two or three times before he is punished for the offence in question, he is punished only once, but if he repeats his crime after punishment for the first instance, he is liable to punishment again. Usually a lesser punishment also merges into a larger or more severe one. For instance, if a person causes death to one person and causes injury to another, he is liable to the death punishment only. But if the offences are numerous and are different in nature, all the punishments would amalgamate and only one is applied, provided that the purpose of all the prescribed punishments for the offences committed is one and the same. For instance, if a person slanders a government officer, confronts him, and commits an act of injustice against him, he would be liable to a single punishment for all three offences for the purpose of the punishments is about the same, namely to protect abuse against government employees.[6]

A salient feature of *ḥudūd* crimes is that the doctrine has made it very difficult to obtain a conviction as the law avails numerous opportunities for the judge and the defendant to avoid conviction. This is achieved by (1) the strict rules of evidence for the proof of these crimes; (2) extensive opportunities to use the notion of uncertainty and doubt (*shubha*) in the defence; and (3) defining the crime very strictly, so that it becomes difficult to fulfill all the requirements. By the same token, many similar crimes fall outside the definition and cannot be punished nor subsumed under a prescribed *ḥudūd* crime. This often means that a lesser punishment is meted out by the judge under the principle of *taʿzīr.* "In the Hanafite doctrine in particular," as Peters wrote, "it is nearly impossible for a thief or fornicator to be sentenced, unless he wishes to do so and confess."[7] But even the rules of confession have made it possible for the accused to retract his confession at any stage prior to enforcement, even after he has been sentenced based on that confession. The *ḥudūd* offences, according to Muslim jurists, represent the claims or Rights of God, and God is sublime and without need, which may well make it unnecessary that all of His Rights are satisfied. In this regard, the claims or Rights of God differ from the Rights of Men, which must always be fulfilled if they are not waived by the right-bearer or claimant. It is further argued that the laws of *ḥudūd,* and especially the rules pertaining to theft and unlawful intercourse, are meant as rhetorical devices that set the standards of conduct very high. The severity of the punishments, namely of 100 lashes or stoning, if stoning is deemed valid, and amputation, serve in the first place as warnings to the public, but in reality they are made very difficult to implement.[8]

There is general agreement, under both the Sunni and Shii laws, that *ḥudūd* punishments are not implemented during military engagements nor in the *Dār al-ḥarb* (abode of war), that is, a country at war with the Muslims. The Prophet is reported to have said: "*Ḥadd* is not enforced on a Muslim in enemy territory."[9]

لا يقام الحد على مسلم في أرض العدو.

That said, it is added that army commanders and soldiers are advised to observe religious duties in the battlefield and refrain from sinful conduct—if they were to merit Divine help—and "there is no succour except from God, the Exalted, the Wise" (Q 3:126).

وَمَا ٱلنَّصْرُ إِلَّا مِنْ عِندِ ٱللَّهِ ٱلْعَزِيزِ ٱلْحَكِيمِ

This was also the advice the second caliph ʿUmar b. al-Khaṭṭāb gave to Saʿd b. Abī Waqqāṣ, an army commander in the battle of Qadisiyyah with the Persians. It is further reported that Saʿd b. Abī Waqqāṣ did not penalise a valiant warrior, Abū Mahjan al-Thaqafī, who fought the Persians with him. He was alcoholic and was even punished and banished for it by the caliph and later imprisoned; yet he was a fine man and a poet, and was not punished for repeated drinking offences during the Qadisiyyah expedition.[10]

> Saʿīd [from] Saʿd b. ʿUbādah, may God be pleased with them, narrated, "A small and frail man was staying in our tribe, and he committed adultery with one of their slave-women." Saʿd mentioned this to the Messenger of God Most High, and thereupon he said, "Flog him (according to) the prescribed penalty." The people then said, "O Messenger of God! He is too weak to bear it." The Messenger of God then said, "Get a stalk of the raceme of a palm tree with a hundred twigs and strike him just once." So, they did. Related by Aḥmad, al-Nasāʾī and Ibn Mājah with a good chain of narrators—but they differ on whether it is connected [all the way] or broken.[11]
>
> وَعَنْ سَعِيدِ بنِ سَعْدِ بنِ عِبَادَةَ رَضِيَ اَللَّهُ عَنهُمَا قَالَ: كَانَ بَينَ أَبيَاتِنَا رُوَيجِلٌ ضَعِيفٌ, فَخَبَثَ بِأَمَةٍ مِنْ إِمَائِهِمْ, فَذَكَرَ ذَلِكَ سَعْدٌ لِرَسُولِ اَللَّهِ - صلى الله عليه وسلم -فَقَالَ: "اِضْرِبُوهُ حَدَّهُ". فَقَالُوا: يَا رَسُولَ اَللَّهِ! إِنَّهُ أَضْعَفُ مِنْ ذَلِكَ, فَقَالَ: "خُذُوا عِثْكَالًا فِيهِ مِائَةُ شِمْرَاخٍ, ثُمَّ اِضْرِبُوهُ بِهِ ضَرْبَةً وَاحِدَةً". فَفَعَلُوا رَوَاهُ أَحْمَدُ, وَالنَّسَائِيُّ, وَابنُ مَاجَه, وَإِسْنَادُهُ حَسَنٌ . لَكِنِ اخْتُلِفَ فِي وَصْلِهِ وَإِرْسَالِهِ

As already discussed, repentance plays a special role in the context of *ḥirābah* and highway robbery, a role that is, however, determined by the clear text of the Qur'an. Repentance as such exonerates the bandit/terrorist if it is offered prior to subjugation and arrest by the authorities, but only in respect to a violation of the Right of God aspect thereof, but it does not affect liability for theft and homicide. Repentance is also given a legal role in the context of apostasy. The apostate is given an opportunity to repent and return to Islam and thus obtain impunity. Yet in actual practice, the role of repentance even in apostasy has been confined to a relatively short segment of time, about three days prior to the enforcement of the death punishment, based on the precedent of the second caliph ʿUmar b. al-Khaṭṭāb.[12] The Ḥanafīs have accordingly maintained that it is recommended to ask the apostate to repent (*istitābah*) and return to Islam, which Imam Mālik has considered to be unnecessary. The Shāfiʿīs and Ḥanbalīs have recorded two different views, one of which corresponds with that of the Ḥanafīs and the other with that of Imam Mālik. The majority opinion thus stipulates *istitābah* as a requirement prior to the enforcement of punishment. This chapter has already discussed the view attributed to the fourth caliph ʿAlī, also supported by Ibrāhīm al-Nakhaʿī and Sufyān al-Thawrī (d. 161/778), that the door of repentance always remains open to an apostate for as long as he lives.[13]

Ḥudūd punishments may be suspended due to doubt caused by delay (*taʾkhīr*) in their claims, prosecution, adjudication, and enforcement proceedings. Delays caused by late claims may in turn become a ground for suspension, especially if the delay is due to the existence of doubt. This would need to be ascertained. If the delay is due to long-distance travel by witnesses who will give testimony, or due to illness that prevents prompt attendance, neither would be a reason for suspending the *ḥudūd* punishments, and the judge is expected to allow time until testimony can be duly obtained. Should the delay in testimony be due to intervention by influential people or intimidation of witnesses, the judge should again evaluate and decide whether to admit or decline the witnesses.[14]

As for the question whether doubt and delay in enforcement even after adjudication and sentencing can suspend the *ḥudūd* punishments, Imam Abū Ḥanīfah and his two disciples, Abū Yūsuf and al-Shaybānī, are of the view that it does, a view that is, however, not accepted by Imams Mālik, al-Shāfiʿī, and Ibn Ḥanbal. The Ḥanafī view is based on the rationale that, just as the expiry of a certain period of time (*taqādum*) is a ground for the suspension of *ḥudūd* prior to sentencing, it also works the same way after sentencing. The doubt may be due to retraction of testimony in the event where the witnesses retract what they have testified even after adjudication and sentencing. The retraction may be true or false, but in either case a doubt (*shubha*) is created and, based on the authority of a renowned hadith, doubt suspends *ḥudūd*.[15] Abū Zahrah has discussed this and found it to be a weak opinion, and he has also quoted the Ḥanafī jurist Kamāl Ibn al-Humām (d. 861/1457), the author of *Fatḥ al-Qadīr*, who is critical of giving any weight to retraction or delay after sentencing. A delay in the claim or enforcement may, however, be due to remorse and repentance on the part of the perpetrator, which is given some consideration, especially by jurists who allow the suspension of *ḥudūd* offences that are proven based on confession of the accused person only. In the event where the latter runs away, even during the course of enforcement, and does not return for some time—this too can cause suspension of the prescribed punishment.[16]

Criminal sentences should ideally be carried out without unnecessary delay as justice delayed can compromise the integrity of justice, or even be tantamount to justice denied, as is commonly said. While immediate execution of punishment should never be at the expense of accuracy and due process, it is also desirable that the society is not burdened by protracted delays and the expenditure of excessive fees and resources on hired lawyers and court proceedings. However, should there be circumstances that endanger the life and safety of the convict, such as illness, pregnancy, and extremes of climatic conditions, the execution of corporal punishment is postponed, as already discussed, until circumstances permit safer application. Abū Zahrah adds that taking an attitude of care and compassion in the implementation of *ḥudūd* that the fiqh scholars have advised is taken from clear textual injunctions of the Qur'an and Sunnah and not merely a juristic opinion.[17]

Imam Abū Ḥanīfah has not specified the time lag that causes suspension of the *ḥudūd* punishments. Abū Zahrah takes this up and quotes Abū Yūsuf, Abū Ḥanīfah's disciple, to the effect that he urged the Imam Abū Ḥanīfah to specify the time lag but that he refused, saying that this should be for the judge to determine in light of the customs and prevailing conditions. But there is a second view, as is recorded by Kamal b. al-Humam, which has determined the expiry time for testimony at six months, and two other Ḥanafī scholars, al-Ṭaḥāwī as well as al-Zaylāʿī, have also concurred.[18]

According to yet another view attributed to Abū Yūsuf, al-Shaybānī, and even one view of Abū Ḥanīfah, doubt (*shubha*) is created by delay in testimony by even one month if no reason can be found to explain the delay. For one month marks the difference between promptness and lateness (*al-taʾjīl wa'l-taʾkhīr*). For instance, if someone swears to pay a debt promptly, he is expected to pay it within a month. Abū Ḥanīfah has also been reported to have said: "If the judge asks the witness 'when did so and so commit *zinā*?' and the witness replies: 'less than a month ago' the punishment for it is enforceable, but if he says 'a month ago,' it is to be suspended."[19]

Then it is added that the whole of this discussion over the expiry of time and whether or not a doubt is created by it relates to adultery and theft. As for wine drinking, there are two views, one of which maintains that, like the two *ḥudūd* just mentioned, expiration (*taqādum*) in wine-drinking is also one month. Imam Abū Ḥanīfah and his other disciple al-Shaybānī have held, as already mentioned, that the time lag in drinking is disappearance of the breath smell, and expiry takes place as soon as the smell has gone. For drinking is a weak *ḥadd*, which is not based on a clear text of the Qur'an or hadith, and it collapses when there is a slight doubt in its proof.[20]

Delay in the claim or enforcement of prescribed punishment for slanderous accusation is generally inconsequential. This is because slander according to the majority (*jumhūr*) of jurists belongs to the private rights category of *ḥudūd*, and delay in their enforcement or adjudication does not suspend any of the private rights. These are suspended, waived, or terminated only by the right-bearer and no one else. This is also the case, at least partially, with regard to theft, which consists of both Right of God and Right of Man components, the former of which is held to be the more dominant. The prescribed punishment of theft (i.e., the Right of God aspect) must be carried out when the offence is duly proven. Yet if the punishment of theft is suspended for reasons of doubt as explained above, the private right aspect of theft still remains and can only be satisfied by return of the stolen goods to the owner. Testimony and evidence with respect to this portion of theft may also be presented on a delayed basis, and the question of expiry of time is therefore not relevant to this aspect of theft or to slanderous accusation (*qadhf*).[21]

On a historical note, it may be said that Muslim judges who applied the rules of fiqh also took the Prophet's directive to ward off the *ḥudūd* by ambiguities as a divine command. All indications are that the *ḥudūd* punishments were very rarely carried out historically. A Scottish doctor working in Aleppo in the mid 1700s observed that there were only six public executions in twenty years. Theft was rare, he observed, and when it occurred it was punished by bastinado. A famous British scholar of Arabic in Egypt in the mid 1800s reported that the *ḥudūd* punishment for theft had not been inflicted in recent memory. In the roughly five hundred years that the Ottoman Empire ruled Constantinople, records show that only one instance of stoning for adultery took place.[22] In Europe from the Middle Ages through the 1700s, horrendous types of mutilation were standard punishment, such as amputating hands, fingers, ears, and tongues; burning with hot tongs; and drawing and quartering. The shariah would thus appear to have historically been a restraining influence and also provided the people with a set of criteria on which to judge the conduct of their rulers.[23]

The Ottoman Penal Code of 1858 is an unquestionably shariah-compliant criminal law. Yet the code never mentions *ḥudūd* punishments, not because it eliminated them but rather because the whole code explicitly limited itself to reforming the *taʿzīr* level of punishments. Since the *ḥudūd* had not been an effective presence in legal applications, replacing all the shariah punishments with *taʿzīr* was tantamount to overhauling the whole of Ottoman criminal law.[24] *Taʿzīr* crimes were classified under three categories as *jināyah, janḥah,* and *qabaḥah,* each carrying a specified range of punishments (Arts. 1–47). While *jināyah* included the more serious crimes, including most of the *ḥudūd* crimes, *janḥah* subsumed crimes that were punishable for up to three years of imprisonment, and *qabaḥah* applied to minor violations.[25] The code recognised, in the meantime, people's rights to the *qiṣāṣ* in the case of homicide should they choose it.[26]

XII

The Philosophy of Ḥudūd

THE PHILOSOPHY OF punishment refers mainly to the objectives of punishment, such as deterrence, retribution, rehabilitation, and reform, which are discussed here in conjunction mainly with *ḥudūd*. It is generally recognised that the aims of punishment in all legal traditions, as also in the shariah, are mainly temporal and manifold: deterrence, retribution, rehabilitation, protecting the general public by incapacitating the offender, and ultimately justice. The shariah also adds to this the religious concept of expiation or atonement, which will be elaborated in the following discussion. Punishment also relates closely to the notion of redress by means of damages and compensation for the loss incurred. Broadly, it is stated that punishment has two principal objectives—one immediate and the other more remote. The immediate purpose of punishment is to inflict pain on the criminal for what he or she did and also to prevent him or her from repeating the act. The broader and more remote purpose of punishment is to protect the society against mischief and uphold its basic interests (*maṣāliḥ*) and standards of justice.[1]

The philosophy of punishment (*ḥikmat al-ʿuqūbah*) in *ḥudūd*, as well as in punishments generally, according to Ibn Taymiyyah, is to inflict pain on the evildoer and deter him from further indulgence in criminal behaviour. It is also to reform the criminal and rid him of the consequences of crime. Additionally, it is intended to protect the community from corruption and violence.[2] Wahbah al-Zuḥaylī has quoted both Ibn Taymiyyah and his disciple, Ibn Qayyim al-Jawziyyah, who maintained that penalising criminal behaviour partakes in the mercy and wisdom of God Most High to protect innocent people against the menace of crime by those who attack and destroy the lives and properties of people and damage their honour. The shariah thus enacted penalties for purposes mainly of deterrence and retribution (*al-radʿ waʾl-zajr*) and devised for every crime just and proportionate punishment. The punishments so validated fall under the six headings of execution, mutilation, lashing, banishment, fines, and *taʿzīr*.[3]

The Arabic word *ʿuqūbah*, which is commonly used for the term "punishment," derives from the root word *ʿaqiba*, literally meaning that which follows or chases something else. Here the infliction of pain follows the crime, and it is in this sense that *ʿuqūbah* also occurs in the Qur'an (al-Naḥl, 16:126). *ʿUqūbah* is differentiated, in turn, from *ʿiqāb* (also *ʿadhāb*),[4] in the sense that *ʿuqūbah* refers to temporal punishment, whereas *ʿiqāb* is inflicted in the hereafter.

Jazāʾ is also synonymous with *ʿuqūbah* but again with a minor difference, which is that *jazāʾ* (recompense) carries both positive and negative connotations. The term is used in the Qur'an in both these capacities: as recompense for a good deed (al-Kahf, 18:88); and as recompense for an evil deed (al-Shūrā, 42:40).

It thus appears that the affirmative purposes of punishment are a familiar dimension of punishment in both the scriptural sources and the juristic doctrines of Islamic law. Yet the affirmative purposes of punishment in the scriptures have in many ways been diminished in the juristic doctrines of various schools and scholars of Islamic law.

Deterrence and Expiation in Ḥudūd

Deterrence underlines the notion that punishment will deter the offender from repeating the same course of conduct, which will also protect the society against his harm. Deterrence is the primary purpose of all punishment. One of the chief purposes of criminal law is to make the evildoer an example and a warning to all who may be similarly inclined. The society's typical response is that, through the rigour of penal sanctions, the offender's fate should be a terror and a warning to himself and to others.[5]

The idea of a fixed punishment, or an "exemplary punishment," also reinforces deterrence, as it integrates certainty and predictability that the offender will suffer the stated punishment. This is typical of the juristic concept of *ḥudūd*: fixed and predictable. Another feature of the deterrence theory is that punishment is carried out in public so that enforcement is seen by the society as a certain consequence of a particular crime. This aspect of deterrence is well illustrated in the Qur'anic punishment of 100 lashes for adulterers. The verse reinforces the deterrent effect of this punishment by prescribing, immediately after pronouncing the punishment, to "let a party of the believers witness their punishment" (al-Nūr, 24:2). The prescribed measure for banditry or highway robbery in the Qur'an (al-Māʾidah, 5:36) is expounded in a fourfold punishment that culminates in death and crucifixion. In this case the executed body of the offender, according to the fiqh provisions, is placed on public display for a period of three days, evidently to serve as a warning and deterrence to potential offenders. The element of predictability and assurance is further endorsed by the fact that *ḥudūd* punishments are scripturally determined and command a degree of objectivity that is not amenable to adjustment and alteration by human lawmakers. Deterrence in all these cases is premised on giving a stiff lesson to the offender and protecting the society against his mischief in the future.[6]

As already stated, the primary objective of *ḥudūd* punishments is deterrence. This has two aspects: namely, special deterrence, which is to deter the criminal from further criminality; and general deterrence, which is achieved by publicising the enforcement of punishment. Individual deterrence has a restraining effect on the offender himself, and this has an aspect in common with rehabilitation and reform. These deterrents may also have a moral signification in that the offender renounces crime on moral grounds, whereas punitive deterrence merely frightens him off. It would seem, in the final analysis, that the various theories of punishment have aspects in common with one another, and a clear distinction between them may therefore be difficult to sustain. Muslim jurists have generally highlighted the deterrent effect of *ḥudūd* punishments more than any other such penalties. The main objective of *ḥudūd* penalties is thus to inflict suffering on the criminal so he does not repeat the crime, to make the penalty a lesson for others, and to protect the society against the criminal's menace.

Whereas the principal purpose of the institution of *ḥudūd* crimes and penalties is deterrence from acts that are harmful to humanity and that spread corruption among people, expiation (*kaffārah*) or purification from sin (*taṭhīr*) is also mentioned as an aspect of *ḥudūd* punishments. But this is only a secondary purpose and does not, in any case, extend to all their possible applications—as most of these punishments also apply to non-Muslims to whom the notions of repentance, expiation, and purification may not be applicable.[7] Repentance, however sincere, does not suspend *ḥudūd* punishments according to scholastic jurisprudence. It is generally agreed, nevertheless, that *ḥudūd* penalties act as a "concealer of sin" (*kaffārah*) for the offender and absolves him of the torment of the hereafter. According to Shii law and some minority opinions among the Shafiʿī and Ḥanbalī schools, repentance expressed before the crime that has been proven in court prevents the enforcement of all the prescribed *ḥudūd* penalties, except for the prescribed punishment of slander (*qadhf*), which consists predominantly of a private right (the Right of Man).[8]

Kaffārah, which is the Qur'anic term for expiation, signifies the attempt on the part of a perpetrator of a sin/crime to hide his sin and to make up for his failing in a dominantly moral and religious sense. This is amply manifested in the aftermath of the renowned cases of adultery of Māʿiz b. Mālik al-Aslamī and that of al-Ghamidiyyah, both of whom confessed to adultery, repeated their confessions to the Prophet, and consequently were punished by stoning. The Prophet then said, concerning al-Ghamidiyyah, that she repented sincerely and was remorseful and "repented such that if it were to be distributed among seventy [sinners] of the people of Medina, it would have been more than enough to exonerate them all."

لقد تابت توبةً لو قسمت على سبعين من أهل المدينة لوسعتهم.

The Prophet also said, concerning Māʿiz, that he confessed to his act of adultery, expressed sincere remorse, and was punished. "God Most High forgave him and admitted him to Paradise. ...By God in whose hand my life reposes, he is now by the streams of Paradise immersing [with enjoyment] [والذي نفسي بيده إنه الآن لفي أنهار الجنة ينغمس فيها]." In a hadith that ʿUbādah b. Ṣāmit narrated, which features in all the major collections of hadith except for Abū Dāwūd, the Prophet has said the same about all of the *ḥudūd* punishments to the effect that one who commits these offences and is "then punished in this world, that would act as an expiation (*kaffārah*) for him in the hereafter [فعوقب به فهو كفارة له]." In a longer hadith recorded by al-Tirmidhī, the Prophet similarly said: "One who commits these ugly offences and is then punished in this world, God is too noble to double the punishment of His servant in the hereafter [من اصاب من ذلك القاذورات شيئا فعوقب به فى الدنيا فالله أكرم من أن يثنى العقوبة على عبده]." Al-Jazīrī, who quoted this, follows with a comment that this statement is the unequivocal authority on the point that *ḥudūd* punishments act as "concealers of sins." He also adds that this is the preferred position of the majority (*jumhūr*) and it prevails over the minority view of some that regard *ḥudūd* as crimes that also beget punishment in the hereafter.[9]

Expiation is the principal shariah requirement for the neglect of one's religious and moral duties—such as taking a false oath, failing to observe obligatory fasting, disrespect to one's parents, and neglect of certain religious rituals during the performance of hajj and so forth—except perhaps for expiation in accidental homicide, which is a legal requirement. Expiation or atonement is primarily concerned with the relationship of man with his Creator; even in cases where it is mentioned in the context of *ḥudūd* punishments, it deals with the relationship of the wrongdoer with God Most High, and not with one's fellow citizens or the society as such.[10] Expiation may also signify a point of difference between the Western and Islamic legal theories on punishments.

According to a longer hadith that all the major hadith collections have recorded, except for Abū Dāwūd, ʿUbadah b. Ṣāmit narrated the following:

> We were present at a meeting with the Prophet, pbuh, when he said: pledge me your allegiance that you do not associate any other deity with God; that you do not commit adultery and theft. Any of you who abide by this, his reward will be with God. . . . If any of you commit these acts, and God conceals his conduct, his affair rests with God; if God so wills He will forgive the offender or punish him.[11]

عَنْ عُبَادَةَ بْنِ الصَّامِتِ، قَالَ كُنَّا عِنْدَ النَّبِيِّ صلى الله عليه وسلم فِي مَجْلِسٍ فَقَالَ " تُبَايِعُونِي عَلَى أَنْ لاَ تُشْرِكُوا بِاللَّهِ شَيْئًا وَلاَ تَسْرِقُوا وَلاَ تَزْنُوا " . قَرَأَ عَلَيْهِمُ الآيَةَ " فَمَنْ وَفَّى مِنْكُمْ فَأَجْرُهُ عَلَى اللَّهِ وَمَنْ أَصَابَ مِنْ ذَلِكَ شَيْئًا فَسَتَرَهُ اللَّهُ عَزَّ وَجَلَّ فَهُوَ إِلَى اللَّهِ إِنْ شَاءَ عَذَّبَهُ وَإِنْ شَاءَ غَفَرَ لَهُ "

While quoting this hadith, Bahnasī adds that some jurists (namely al-Samarqandī, the commentator of *al-Kanz*) have held that punishments are inflictions on the offender in this life and protectors of him against torture in the hereafter, which is to say that they are concealers (*mukaffirāt*) in the hereafter.[12]

Muslim jurists have differed over the question as to whether just retaliation (*qiṣāṣ*) can also function as an expiation for the murderer and whether it can cleanse the murderer of his great sin. Some have responded that it does, and they quote to that effect the hadith that "*ḥudūd* (punishments) are expiators to their perpetrators [الحدود كفارات لأهلها]," saying that the hadith is generally worded and is as such inclusive of all punishments without making homicide an exception. Other jurists have disagreed, however, saying that punishment does not expiate the killer nor does it conceal his sin. For retaliation (*qiṣāṣ*) does not benefit the deceased person but may be of some benefit to his family and those who are living.[13]

The juristic debate over this revolves around two verses in the Qur'an, one of which is affirmative on repentance generally and another that closes this avenue to murderers. The former passage is general in saying that God Most High will accept sincere repentance from anyone, even those guilty of associating other deities with Him or those who have committed adultery and murder, provided they repent, rectify, and then do good deeds (see also al-Furqān, 25:68–69). The passage even goes further to say that God will "change the evil of such persons into good, and God is oft-forgiving, most merciful." The other verse quoted is decisive on the enormity of murder and declares that, if anyone slays an innocent person deliberately, "his recompense is Hell to abide therein forever, and the wrath and curse of God will be upon him" (al-Nisā', 4:93).

وَمَن يَقْتُلْ مُؤْمِنًا مُّتَعَمِّدًا فَجَزَآؤُهُ ۥ جَهَنَّمُ خَـٰلِدًا فِيهَا وَغَضِبَ ٱللَّهُ عَلَيْهِ وَلَعَنَهُ ۥ وَأَعَدَّ لَهُ ۥ عَذَابًا عَظِيمًا.

The leading Companion Ibn ʿAbbās was asked a question as to whether the door to repentance remains open to the murderer. His response was in the negative and he quoted the latter verse in support, adding also that the previous verse was revealed in Mecca but that the latter was a Medinan verse and thus prevailed over the former. Murder is therefore not amenable to repentance even after the just retaliation (*qiṣāṣ*) is duly carried out.[14]

Retribution and Retaliation

Retribution and retaliation are both primarily meant to take vengeance against the wrongdoer and allay the victim's feelings and his or her yearning for justice. Such is the case in the "tooth for tooth, eye for eye and nose for nose" concept, which effectively translates into retaliation. The theory of retribution is based in ethical considerations: if someone commits wrong intentionally, it must be avenged; the evildoer is morally culpable and his case merits a stiff response from society. In ancient laws, retribution was the primary purpose of criminal jurisprudence and penal policy. With the progress of society, crimes began to be considered as wrong against humanity, society, and the state, and not only the individual victim, which is why the state initiates proceedings against the offender. This is also the reason that society is keen to punish the wrongdoer. Retribution has a pivotal place in the Islamic criminal justice system, including *ḥudūd, qiṣāṣ,* and *taʿzīr*. Punishment is meant to inflict pain and secure justice for the victim, his family, and his relatives.[15]

The Islamic law of homicide is generally based on both retaliation and retribution, although deterrence also plays an important role. This is understood from the majority view of the Muslim jurists who hold that the way the death penalty for homicide is executed must be similar to the way the victim was killed and that, under supervision of the authorities, the heirs of the victim may carry out the death penalty themselves. This is the view of the Māliki and Shāfiʿī schools, whereas the majority maintain that the death penalty for murder must be carried out by an executioner under government supervision. The Ḥanafīs and Shia Imamiyyah allow execution only by the sword, whereas the other schools, on the basis of their readings of the relevant Qur'anic verses, hold that death shall be inflicted in the same way as the victim was killed. Only in cases when this would result in torture and delay, the death penalty may be carried out by the sword.[16]

The discretionary *taʿzīr* punishment is aimed mainly at deterrence and rehabilitation of the offender, that is, to deter him from repeating his wrongdoing and also to help in bringing him back to normal life. To achieve this, *taʿzīr* is meted out in accordance with the special conditions of the accused and the attending circumstances of the offence.

Punishment delineates the community's disapproval of crime, which it must, as the theory of retribution maintains, emphatically express. A community that is too ready to forgive the criminal may indulge in condoning crime. Muslim jurists have commonly acknowledged the retributive emphasis in *ḥudūd* punishments, and there is also ample evidence in the Qur'an to prove it.[17] God Most High expresses His disapproval in unmistakable terms by assigning a punishment for certain forms of conduct, and when this is the case there remains no question that the Muslim community should stand for it and enforce it. Retribution as a feature of *ḥudūd* punishments is manifested in the severity of these punishments as well as in foreclosing the possibilities of their suspension and adjustment by means of intercession, mediation, substitution, repentance, and pardoning. The *ḥudūd* are, in other words, all deemed to be mandatory. This rigour and the mandatory feature of these punishments have, on the other hand, been softened somewhat through the operation of such rules as "doubts suspend the *ḥudūd*." The fiqh position, for example—that a confession can be retracted at almost any point in the process, and once retracted the *ḥudūd* punishments are suspended because of it—is also a case in point. There are a variety of other situations whereby the *ḥudūd* punishments are suspended, and when taken together they represent a significant reservation on the mandatory aspect of *ḥudūd* as well as their severity to some extent. But outside of these situations, the leading schools and scholars of fiqh have unequivocally emphasised the mandatory and invariable application of *ḥudūd*.[18]

Retribution also strikes a note with expiation but the two are different in some respects. By "expiation" it is meant that the offender has suffered his punishment, has purged his conscience, and his account with society is therefore clear. This attitude is seen, for example, behind the commonly expressed reluctance to hold a man's record against him after he has been punished.

Punishment can also be a means of protecting society by incapacitating the offender and removing him from society through a term of imprisonment, banishment, or execution. This is also the main rationale given by the proponents of punishment by way of judicious policy (*siyāsah*), imposed by the head of state or his representative, for the maintenance and protection of public order and security. Recidivists and habitual criminals who are not deterred by prescribed punishments may be kept in prison, based on judicious policy, and if necessary for long periods, so as to protect society against their harm.[19]

Rehabilitation and Reform

In recent decades, developments in criminology and penology tend to place an increased emphasis on the reform theory, which seems to bring this concept closer to the idea of treatment and cure. The criminal is accordingly regarded as a sick person—not necessarily an evil person—who is in need of treatment. The earlier emphasis on deterrent/retributive punishment has thus given way to some extent to methods of treatment in the direction of rehabilitation. Society acknowledges, in other words, that something has gone wrong for which the offender may or may not have been entirely or solely accountable. However, from the Islamic perspective, the culprit is primarily responsible for his actions. That said, it will be noted that society's role is recognised in some ways in Islamic law theories as the binary division of rights into the Right of God and Right of Man—the former is entrenched in society's claims and rights. Another concept of relevance is *ʿaqīlah,* which is inclusive even of one's colleagues in the workplace, who bear responsibility for some of the adverse consequences of the criminal's conduct by the group to which he belongs. Additionally, *qasamah* (from *qasam*, putting on oath) is a near parallel to *ʿaqīlah*, as both refer to group responsibility.[20] Yet there is a tendency in the theory of *ḥudūd* to minimise the role that rulers and judges may play in the determination of punishment and its enforcement—although the theory of *taʿzīr* is clearly affirmative of that role. Fiqh sources generally recognise, nevertheless, that punishing the criminal means both retaliation and correction. Thus all punishments, including *ḥudūd*, consist of this dual purpose, yet the degree of emphasis varies in accordance with the nature of the transgression.[21] It is further stated that punishments emanate in the mercy of God Most High on His servants and the realisation of their welfare, like the father punishing his son or the physician treating his patient.[22] While quoting these, Tawfīq al-Shāwī is even persuaded to saying that "we prefer to use the word *al-jazāʾ* [recompense, sanction] rather than *'al-ʿuqūbah'* [punishment], for the latter stresses severity and revenge while the objectives of Shariah sanctions are not all confined to retribution and revenge but include ones that are not meant to inflict pain but to reform and correct the transgressor. That this can also be said of most of the sanctions visualized under *taʿzīr*."[23]

Al-Shāwī acknowledges that combining the two aspects of reformation and retribution is a fundamental aspect of Islamic criminal law, yet reforming the offender's personality has not received adequate attention in the conventional fiqh and he therefore calls for fresh *ijtihād*. Then it is added that, in the absence of a well-moderated theory of punishment, judges can hardly be expected to rectify this historical imbalance of paying scant attention to the personality and character of the offender in *ḥudūd*.[24] Clearly this presents a mixed scenario. Earlier in the chapter there is a discussion of *ʿaqīlah* and *qasamah*, both of which occur in the context mainly of *qiṣāṣ* and are clearly cognisant of society's responsibility and role for the conduct of their individual members. Yet they are also closely associated with tribes and clans and thus call for adjustment and transition to modern society conditions and modalities of government. There is scope for further research to ascertain the Islamic philosophy of punishment and the place and role of society/government therein with reference particularly to the reform and rehabilitation aspects of that philosophy.

This shift of emphasis towards rehabilitation and reform in modern penology has brought with it visible changes in the penal system and has led to the development of methods of treatment such as probation services, rehabilitation centres, and psychiatric services operating side by side with prisons. There have even been adjustments in the methods of prison administration and the availability of books, television, and other services in prisons. Rehabilitation and reform would also require that the offender is given an opportunity in which he can be exposed to corrective and educational influences over a period of time. The idea of the prompt execution of punishment, especially in the case of heavy corporal punishments, does not afford the kind of opportunity that a reformative outlook on punishment might demand. Corporal punishments are usually meant to teach a sharp-and-shock lesson, which is in the nature of peremptory retribution and emphasises deterrence.[25]

Repentance, which is a recurrent theme in the Qur'an, has also not found a proportionate role in the juristic writings of fiqh nor even in the exposition of a theory of punishment. Insisting on automatic and mandatory enforcement of *ḥudūd* punishments, the fiqh scholars were consequently unable to make much of the Qur'anic references to repentance. For repentance is a state of mind that is not expected to come about through insistence on retribution and deterrence alone and thus necessitates a certain shift of attitude toward such other corrective and educational efforts as may seem appropriate. This shift should take place without lessening firmness or dropping vigilance in combating crime, but rather it should be done as part of a comprehensive approach that is richer, more resourceful, and capable of adaptation to the changing conditions of a contemporary Muslim society.

For a variety of reasons, including perhaps Muslim jurists' general aversion to philosophy and their textualist orientations, a comprehensive theory of punishment in Islamic criminal law has yet to be articulated. It would appear that a great deal of the ingredients are already there, and it may be a question to a large extent of consolidation and restatement of much of what is known in the source data of shariah. This shift should pay attention to modern scholarly contributions and experience and include a clear articulation of the role and place of repentance as well as the personal conditions of offenders in the determination and imposition of punishment.

XIII

Discretionary Punishment of Taʿzīr

TAʿZĪR (LIT., DETERRENCE) is a derivative of the root word *ʿazzara*, which means to avert, to deter, and to discipline and even to honour, help, and dignify, such as in saying that A aids B (against his enemy) (*ʿazzarahu fīʿaduwwihi*). It is a homonym that carries contrarious meanings. Punishment is called *taʿzīr* as it deters the offender from repeating the offence and reverting back to criminality. Juridically, *taʿzīr* signifies unquantified punishment for wrongdoing that is not included in *ḥudūd*, retaliation (*qiṣāṣ*), or expiation (*kaffārah*) offences, and it is imposed for violation of the Right of God, the Right of Man, or a combination of both. For the renowned Shāfiʿī jurist al-Māwardī (d. 450/1058), *taʿzīr* meant "punishment inflicted in cases of crimes for which the shariah has not prescribed any penalty. The rules relating to it differ depending on the circumstances in which it is imposed and the conditions of the offender."[1] *Taʿzīr* also differs from *ḥudūd* and *qiṣāṣ* in that the latter two do not afford the ruler and judge discretion or choice but require them to impose the prescribed penalty as soon as the offence is proven by admissible evidence, without increase or decrease. There is also no room for intercession and pardon in *ḥudūd*, although in *qiṣāṣ* the next of kin may grant forgiveness, in which case *qiṣāṣ* is likely to be suspended. Yet the authorities may consider imposing a *taʿzīr* penalty as public interest may so require.[2]

There is no minimum for *taʿzīr*; it may consist of any measure that inflicts suffering, whether a verbal reprimand; measures that entail social degradation, such as dismissal from public office; financial loss; flogging; or imprisonment.[3] Muslim jurists have differed as to the maximum limits of *taʿzīr*. Ibn Taymiyyah's account on this subject is generally considered to be representative of the majority, which is as follows: *taʿzīr* must not exceed ten lashes, and a vast number of ulama have held that it must not reach the extent of the *ḥudud* penalty in any case.[4] Then there are two other views. One view is that *taʿzīr* must not reach the minimum of the *ḥudūd* or the lowest penalty in the range of the *ḥudud*. The other view holds that, in ascertaining the maximum limit of *taʿzīr*, one must refer to the offence type in the *ḥudūd* categories. In this way *taʿzīr* in property offenses (theft of unprotected property, for example) must not reach the prescribed punishment for theft even if it exceeds another *ḥadd*. Similarly, *taʿzīr* for sexual offences must not reach the capital punishment of *zinā* even if it exceeds another *ḥudūd*. This view refers to the precedent of ʿUmar Ibn Khattab, who punished the forger of his official seal with 300 lashes applied during three consecutive days. The Rightly Guided Caliphs are also reported to have ordered 200 lashes for an unmarried couple who were found under the same blanket.[5] Ibn Taymiyyah and his disciple Ibn Qayyim al-Jawziyyah hold that the number of lashes in *taʿzīr* should be limited to such categories but be left to the discretion and *ijtihād* of the Imam and judge to determine the punishment, based on considerations of public interest in what they may deem most appropriate, be it less or even more than the scholastic specifications listed in the doctrines of the various schools. This is considered to be the most preferable view, which also finds support in the valid Sunnah and early precedent.[6]

Qur'anic authority for *taʿzīr* is found in many of its verses, including:

> Whoever commits evil, he/she will be punished accordingly.
>
> مَن يَعۡمَلۡ سُوٓءٗا يُجۡزَ بِهِۦ.

The type and severity of punishment are to be determined with reference to the nature of the offence, the pain it has inflicted on the victim, and its implications for the community. Just punishment is neither too severe nor too light, as in the Qur'anic address to the believers (al-Shūrā, 42:40):

> And the recompense of an injury is an injury like it, but if a person forgives and amends, his reward is with God, and God loves not the oppressors.
>
> وَجَزَٰٓؤُاْ سَيِّئَةٖ سَيِّئَةٞ مِّثۡلُهَاۖ فَمَنۡ عَفَا وَأَصۡلَحَ فَأَجۡرُهُۥ عَلَى ٱللَّهِۚ إِنَّهُۥ لَا يُحِبُّ ٱلظَّٰلِمِينَ

Commenting on this, Abdullah Yusuf Ali wrote: "When you stand up for your rights, you may do so through processes of law and you must not seek a compensation greater than the injury suffered. The most you can do is to demand equal redress, that is, a harm equivalent to the harm done to you. The ideal mode is, however, not to pursue vengeance but to follow better ways leading to the reform of the offender and reconciliation."[7] Further affirmation for this is found in another Qur'anic verse (al-Naḥl, 126) addressing the believers:

> And if you take your turn, then punish with the like of that with which you were afflicted. But if you show patience, it is surely better for those who exercise patience.
>
> وَإِنْ عَاقَبْتُمْ فَعَاقِبُوا۟ بِمِثْلِ مَا عُوقِبْتُم بِهِۦ ۖ وَلَئِن صَبَرْتُمْ لَهُوَ خَيْرٌ لِّلصَّـٰبِرِينَ

It thus appears that the Qur'an discourages impulsive revenge and haste in any form of punishment. Patience (*ṣabr*), one of the virtues that is emphasised in numerous places in the Qur'an, including the verses just reviewed, can either mean pardon or abstaining from rash decisions so as to allow time for investigation, reflection, and the possibility of forgiveness. It is also significant that most of the references to punishment and just retaliation in the Qur'an are accompanied by an allusion to the virtues of tolerance and forgiveness. The lesson here must be that even in combating criminality, a society cannot resolve its problems by means only of coercive measures, but must try to find better ways to educate its people, promote moral virtues, and reform wrongdoers. But the main purpose of the foregoing passages is also that in the enactment of laws or issuance of judicial decisions, the ruler and judge must mete out punishments that are just and proportionate to the enormity of the crime. If there is a margin of error, as would often be expected, then an error committed on the side of leniency and forgiveness is preferable, on the authority of hadith, to the one on the side of severity and harshness.

All acts of transgression and sinful conduct that the text has not specifically regulated but that partake in mischief and corruption are, in principle, punishable under *taʿzīr*. The head of state and judge may, at their discretion, impose deterrent and corrective punishments on the perpetrators of such acts. *Taʿzīr* has often been used as a residual category, and it has as such been more widely practiced than both the *ḥudūd* and *qiṣāṣ* penalties. Yet *taʿzīr* has also been extensively applied with regard to both *ḥudūd* crimes and retaliation (*qiṣāṣ*) in bodily injuries in which the offender could not be punished with the *ḥudūd* or *qiṣāṣ* proper for procedural reasons, lack of legally required proof, or presence of an element of doubt (*shubha*). In bodily injuries and *qiṣāṣ* offences, when a pardon is granted by the victim or his next of kin, a reduced but suitable punishment under *taʿzīr* could be imposed in the public interest. Instances of such acts are illicit sexual acts not amounting to *zinā* or homosexual intercourse, misappropriation of the property of others not amounting to theft, embezzlement and forgery, as well as defamation and libel cases that do not fulfil the requirements of theft and slander respectively.

Taʿzīr is thus an open-ended category wherein the head of state and judge may decide to punish or even grant amnesty if this is deemed to be the best course of action. There is general consensus on this, but disagreement has arisen as to whether such discretionary powers exist with regard to all *taʿzīr* offences. Thus it is said that when a *ḥudūd* punishment is reduced to *taʿzīr*—due to some deficiency in proof or other material aspects of the offence—it would be a reduced case of a *ḥudūd* in which the authorities are not at liberty to grant amnesty.[8]

Muslim jurists have listed numerous acts and transgressions that can be punished by way of *taʿzīr*. Transgression in this range can consist of acting on what is prohibited (*ḥarām*) and abandoning what the shariah has made obligatory. The latter subsumes persistent refusal, for instance, to pay the obligatory alms of zakah, persistent neglect of ritual prayer (*ṣalāh*), refusal to repay a debt by a solvent debtor, concealment by the seller of what he must declare of the hidden defects of the goods he offers for sale, refusal to return usurped property to its lawful owner, and so forth. Betrayal of trust, or refusal to fulfill one, is also a *taʿzīr* offence, which may include disciplinary action against a witness, a jurisconsult, or even a judge for abandonment of an obligation (*wājib*) and manifest miscarriage of justice. Instances of forbidden acts and conduct also include theft of what may not be liable to the prescribed punishment; flirting, kissing, and illicit proximity (*khalwah*) with a woman that fall short of *zinā*; practice of usury (*ribā*); fraudulent sales; and all cases of perjury. All of these may be punished by way of *taʿzīr*. Juristic manuals tend to identify a scriptural basis for all of these in the Qur'an and Sunnah and have quoted most of the relevant passages to support why certain acts are deemed as transgression and may be accordingly penalised under *taʿzīr*. Yet when compared to the Qur'anic verses on *ḥudūd* crimes, the verses and expressions that support *taʿzīr* are less categorical. They mention an objectionable act or form of conduct without specifying any punishment for it, or even when a punishment is vaguely mentioned, it is not clear enough to offer a firm scriptural basis for an offence, and subsuming it under *taʿzīr* is therefore often based on interpretation and *ijtihād*.[9]

A permissible act may also be made liable to a *taʿzīr* punishment if it is used as a means to mischief and procurement of an unlawful end, such as the double sale of *ʿīnah*, or some of the worst forms of it at least, according to the majority, which are used as means to procure the prohibited *ribā*. The Mālikī school would often apply the principle of blocking the (lawful) means to an unlawful end (i.e., *sadd al-dharāʾiʿ*).[10] This principle is often regarded as "one of the most important tools where judicious policy (*siyāsah sharʿiyyah*) can be utilised in order to improve the conditions of the community."[11] Since shariah is concerned with the ends and consequences of conduct (*maʾālat al-afʿāl*), it empowers the ruler to obstruct the means that lead to illegality and corruption. In other words, the ruler can authorise "forbidding the permissible (*mubāḥāt*) which are being used by the people as means to criminality and evil."[12] When the ruler or *walī al-amr* observes, for example, that the transaction of a sale (which is otherwise lawful) is being used solely as a means to procuring usury, or that marriage is contracted for the sole purpose of *taḥlīl*,[13] he is authorised to obstruct the means that open the ways to abuse and ensure that the permissible or *mubāḥ* act in question is only practiced for its legitimate purposes. It makes no difference whether the evil is obtained through deliberate abuse or through common practice in which the element of intention is not prominent. If, for example, due to the change of time and circumstance, something that was once lawful is subsequently turned into a mischief or *mafsādah*, the ruler may exercise discretion and ban and penalise it in order to safeguard the public interest.[14]

The foregoing has been mainly concerned with the lawful and the unlawful, the *wājib* and *ḥarām*, and ways in which they are manipulated in order to avoid a *wājib* or procure a *ḥarām*. Disagreement has also arisen with regard to the application of *taʿzīr* to someone who abandons what might be only recommendable (*mandūb*) or a person who acts on a reprehensible (*makrūh*) course of conduct. Many have considered these not relevant to *taʿzīr* as shariah designated them to be unrestricted and optional, and they do not therefore provide a suitable basis for punishment. Some jurists have referred in this connection to the precedent of the second caliph, ʿUmar b. al-Khaṭṭāb, who has, for instance, punished by way of *taʿzīr* someone for cruelty to animals. The incident in question involved a man who was whipped by way of *taʿzīr* for dragging a goat to the slaughter place. What the man did was reprehensible (*makrūh*), but the caliph punished him for it nonetheless. This is also said with regard to disciplining one's child beyond what is reasonable; a nonbeliever who may be violating the mores of a Muslim community in an unacceptable way; or one who may be playing certain games or operating corrupt lines of trading, gambling, and so on. Another well-known precedent set by caliph ʿUmar in this connection is the renowned case of Naṣr b. Ḥajjāj. On one of his usual nighttime reconnaissance tours of Medina, the caliph heard a woman singing and wistfully mentioning the name of Naṣr b. Ḥajjāj. This man had evidently become well known for his good looks. The caliph summoned him and ordered his head to be shaved but this even increased his good looks! He then banished him to Basrah. It is said that this order was based on public interest, which was to curb a source of temptation for the women of Medina (operating somewhat like preventive detention, which is also permissible on the basis of public interest). Ḥajjāj had committed no offence but was convicted of banishment nonetheless, to which he objected but to no avail. Muslim jurists have recorded the concern, however, that *taʿzīr* for public interest should not be arbitrary but carefully verified by the ruler and judge.[15]

Taʿzīr is a subtheme basically of *siyāsah* and subsumed by considerations of public interest and justice. However, the judge does not create the offence, which is determined, for the most part, by the Qur'an or Sunnah, albeit less categorically than *ḥudūd* and *qiṣāṣ*. There is, in other words, basic authority in the scriptural sources, or the general consensus, on an offensive conduct or transgression in the first place. The judge is then granted flexibility to determine a suitable punishment for it.[16]

The principal purpose of *taʿzīr* is to deter the perpetrator from repeating the offence. Retribution as well as rehabilitation and reform all play a role in the selection of the punishment quantum and type. The main purpose of *taʿzīr* is not to inflict pain nor to humiliate persons or destroy their property or reputation. Jamāl al-Dīn al-Zaylāʿī (d. 762/1361), the commentator of the Ḥanafī text *al-Hidāyah*, wrote that the main purpose of *taʿzīr* is discipline (*taʾdib*), and it is contingent on safety (*salāmah*) such that destruction and loss is not the result. The renowned Mālikī jurist Ibn Farḥūn (d. 799/1397) also wrote that what is permitted in *taʿzīr* is that which ends with safety, otherwise it would not be permissible. No mutilation or infliction of injury can therefore be included in *taʿzīr*, for the simple reason that shariah has not validated it as such. The majority (*jumhūr*) have also proscribed degrading punishments such as slapping on the face, shaving of a beard, and blackening of the face, although this last is mentioned to have been practiced for perjury (on the assumption that the convict blackened the face of truth!), but that is still regarded as a departure from the norm.[17]

Taʿzīr punishment is likely to be harsher for the hardened criminal and also when the offence committed is feared to spread fast if not curbed with exemplary sternness by the authorities. The offender's status also plays a role, for it is assumed that persons of distinction who may have fallen into error and are unlikely also to repeat the offence can be constrained by a mere rebuke or lighter punishment than the hardened criminal types.[18]

The most common type of punishment historically applied under *taʿzīr*, which may no longer be seen as the best option now, was flogging, but other punishments included public rebuke and publicity (*tashhir*), corporal punishment, and imprisonment. The authority for flogging as *taʿzīr* is also found in the hadith that states, "No one may flog above ten lashes of the whip except for a *ḥadd* of the God-ordained *ḥudūd*."[19]

لا يجلد فوق عشرة اسواط الا في حد من حدود الله.

Taʿzīr punishment in some cases may also include fines (*taʿzīr bi'l-māl*) although with the reservation that the state might use them to increase its revenue. Yet in principle *taʿzīr* is not confined to any particular type of punishment, financial or otherwise, and may consist of any appropriate sanctions, or a combination thereof, that the judge considers adequate based on his discretion and *ijtihād* in selecting the most appropriate sanctions (*al-ijtihād fī ikhtiyār al-aṣlāḥ*).[20] It may include, in our time, for instance, community work, police attendance, house arrest, and rehabilitation measures.

The schools of law have differed over the maximum punishment under *taʿzīr* and whether or not it can include the death penalty. The Mālikī school, which does not fix a maximum limit for *taʿzīr*, holds that the Imam has the authority to specify the number of lashes even if it be in excess of 100 lashes, provided that it does not lead to death. The majority maintain that *taʿzīr* should be below the *ḥudūd* punishments, and the authority quoted for this is the hadith that "one who punishes the equivalent of a *ḥadd* in what is not a *ḥadd* is a transgressor."

من بلغ حدا في غير حد فهو من المعتدين.

The schools of law have integrated the substance of this hadith to say that *taʿzīr* against a person may not reach the level of *ḥudūd* punishments in each category of the offences they may fall into, including defamation and sexual offences, property crimes, and so forth.[21]

As for the question as to whether capital punishment is a lawful *taʿzīr* penalty, Muslim jurists have debated this and agreed to allow it for specific crimes with certain conditions. Mention is thus made of a Muslim spying on Muslims for the enemy, spreading heresies, and some varieties of homicide that cannot be punished under retaliation (*qiṣāṣ*) proper. Imam Mālik and some jurists of the Ḥanbalī school have allowed the death penalty under *taʿzīr*, but the Imams Abū Hanīfah, al-Shāfiʿī, and also some followers of the Ḥanbalī school have disallowed it in principle, although Abū Ḥanīfah makes an exception to say that the ruler may punish recidivists and hardened criminals to death under *taʿzīr*. Ibn Taymiyyah has held that a persistent agent of corruption, whose spread of evil cannot be curbed except by killing him, may be killed.[22]

In support of this Ibn Taymiyyah quotes the hadith wherein the Prophet has permitted killing one who had staged an uprising against a legitimate leader duly elected by the people. "When you have all come to an agreement on one man to be your leader and then someone splits asunder this unity and rises against the leader, kill him."[23]

من أتاكم وأمركم جميع على رجل واحد يريد أن يفرق جماعتكم فاقتلوه.

There is a valid concern that open-ended *taʿzīr* can be abused and made an instrument of arbitrariness within the courtroom and beyond by judges, political leaders, and others. This is the concern also of the constitutional law principle of legality in crimes and punishments: there should be no crime and no punishment without a legal text that validates it. This principle has been widely adopted in the constitutions of the present-day Muslim countries, which would arguably make it a part of the *aḥkām ūli al-amr* (commands of the lawful rulers) that also command obedience in shariah. It is proposed therefore that parliamentary legislation may duly stipulate and limit the use of *taʿzīr* powers—as has already been the case to a large extent. It is our belief also that open-ended *taʿzīr* is not in harmony either with the constitutional principle of legality or even of shariah itself. The ugly realities of official corruption present a pressing concern that justifies the idea of a carefully regulated *taʿzīr*. The discussion here does not propose total elimination of *taʿzīr* discretionary powers but advocates for a carefully regulated *taʿzīr* within the larger rubric of government under the rule of law that meets the requirements of both shariah and contemporary constitutional law principles in crimes and penalties.

XIV

Judicious Policy (Siyāsah Sharʿiyyah)

SIYĀSAH SHARʿIYYAH IS a broad doctrine of Islamic public law that authorises the ruler to determine the best manner in which shariah can be administered. The ruler may accordingly take discretionary measures, enact rules, and initiate policies that he deems are in the interest of good government, provided that no substantive principle of shariah is violated. The discretionary powers of the ruler under *siyāsah sharʿiyyah* (henceforth *siyāsah*) are particularly extensive in the field of criminal law outside *ḥudūd* and *qiṣāṣ*. The head of state and those who are in charge of public affairs, the *ʿūli al amr*, may thus decide on appropriate rules and procedures in order to discover truth and determine guilt. With regard to the substantive law of crimes, the authorities have powers to determine what behavior constitutes an offence and what punishment is to be applied in each case.[1] For example, in a case of legislation in 1897 in Egypt, which remains valid to this day, the law denied admission to witnesses in some cases and confined the means of legal proof to documentary evidence in others.[2] The purpose of this legislation was, as ʿAbd al-Wahhāb Khallāf (d. 1375/1956) put it, "to prevent corruption and to facilitate benefit which were in accord with the principles of shariah even if it disagreed with the views of the *mujtahidūn* of the past."[3] The learned author went on to quote the Mālikī jurist Shihāb al-Dīn al-Qarāfī (d. 684/1285) at length to the effect that nothing could be found in shariah against taking measures, in any area of government, that would eliminate corruption and facilitate benefit to the community.[4]

The jurists of the later ages (*al-mutaʾakhkhirūn*) have, however, used *siyāsah* in a more restricted sense, that is, the administration of penalties meted out by rulers and judges in order to combat criminality and evil. This is especially applicable under emergency situations when normal rules seem difficult to apply, thereby confining *siyāsah* to criminal justice alone.[5] Rulers have thus ordered the killing of criminals who robbed people's houses at times when calamities, such as fire, earthquake, and war, caused the occupants to escape danger, or when kidnappers terrorised people and inflicted suffering on the parents and relatives of their victim. But to confine *siyāsah* to the administration of penalties is not totally justified, for *siyāsah* has a much wider scope, which can equally apply in other areas of government such as taxation, economic development, foreign policy, and so forth where the ruling authorities can take initiatives in the interest of good governance and justice.

Islamic criminal justice is only partially regulated by the clear text, which obtains mainly with regard to *ḥudūd* crimes and *qiṣāṣ*, but throughout the greater part of Islamic history a much larger realm of crimes and penalties has been regulated by state laws and ordinances that broadly fell under the rubric of judicious policy, or *siyāsah*, which subsumed, in turn, the deterrent yet unquantified punishment of *taʿzīr*. Measures introduced by way of *siyāsah* must address issues as they arise in a manner that also observes the higher purposes of shariah (*maqāṣid al-sharīʿah*).[6] This is, indeed, the overriding theme of all *siyāsah*, as ʿAbd al-Raḥmān Tāj rightly noted: "*Siyāsah*, in its widest sense, has five purposes: the protection of life, religion, mind, lineage, and property."[7] Muslim jurists are unanimous that protection of these values constitutes the ultimate objective of shariah, even if no specific reference can be found to that effect in the Qur'an or the Sunnah. The general consensus of Muslim scholars on these values is based not on a particular provision of the Qur'an or the Sunnah but on the overall content of these texts and the numerous commands and prohibitions therein that seek to protect these values. [8]

Bringing ease to the people and removing hardships from them are among the general objectives (*maqāṣid*) of shariah, which is grounded, in turn, in the textual authority of the Qur'an—as in the following verse:

> God intends every facility for you and He does not intend to put you in hardship. (al-Baqarah, 2:185; see also al-Ḥajj, 22:78)
>
> يُرِيدُ ٱللَّهُ بِكُمُ ٱلْيُسْرَ وَلَا يُرِيدُ بِكُمُ ٱلْعُسْرَ.

Ibn Taymiyyah, who wrote a book on *siyāsah*, has quoted a pertinent hadith: "Gentleness does not fail to create beauty whereas harshness is most likely to lead to ugliness."[9]

> إِنَّ الرِّفْقَ لَا يَكُونُ فِي شَيْءٍ إِلَّا زَانَهُ وَلَا يُنْزَعُ مِنْ شَيْءٍ إِلَّا شَانَهُ

And he quotes another hadith that states: "God is Gentle and loves gentleness (*rifq*) and gives through gentleness what He gives not through oppression (*ʿunf*)."[10]

إنّ اللّه رَفِيقٌ يُحِبُّ الرِّفْقَ وَيُعطِي عَلَى الرِّفقِ مَا لَا يُعطِي عَلَى العُنفِ.

The Companion Abū Burdah al-Anṣarī has reported that when the Prophet sent Muʿādh b. Jabal and Abū Mūsā al-ʿAsharī to Yemen (they were each appointed to govern a part of Yemen), he instructed them: "Be gentle to the people and not hard on them, bring them good tidings [of mercy] and scare them not, and do not incite them to aversion."[11]

يَسِّرَا وَلَا تُعَسِّرَا ، وَبَشِّرَا وَلَا تُنَفِّرَا

Another important aspect of just and judicious sentencing based on *siyāsah* is the fulfilment of trusts (*al-amānāt*) and giving to everyone their due, as the Qur'an has enjoined in the following verse: "God commands you to hand over the trusts to whom they are due, and when you judge among people you judge with justice" (al-Nisāʾ, 4:58). Commenting on this passage, Ibn Taymiyyah noted that the ruler and the ruled both are enjoined to pay their dues to one another.[12] The citizens must not expect from the government more than what they deserve, nor must they withhold any payment to which the government may be entitled. The Prophet has ordered the Muslims to "pay the ruling authorities what they are entitled to, for in their capacity as custodians, they [both ruler and ruled] are answerable to God in respect of what has been placed in their custody."[13]

Questions also arise at the policy level over philosophical viewpoints and attitudes taken toward punishment, including deterrence, retaliation, and reform, as well as the possibility of amnesty to individuals and groups, especially in the context of postconflict justice situations where strict rules of law may be difficult to apply. Similarly, whether a legal punishment is to be carried out against a repentant, first-time offender or a nonrepentant recidivist, one should not be bound by issues of legality while facing larger concerns of peace and normal order in a fragile environment such as now obtains in many Muslim countries, including Afghanistan, Iraq, Libya, and Syria. This viewpoint underscores the importance of the Islamic public law principle of *siyāsah*, for it empowers the authorities to act in accordance with the spirit and objectives of shariah at the expense even of a departure from scholastic interpretations and *ijtihād*.[14]

Ibn Qayyim al-Jawziyyah, Ibn Taymiyyah's disciple who also authored a book on *siyāsah*, noted that the Prophet occasionally ordered flogging, or doubled the amount of compensation in mitigated cases of theft, and gave orders to smash the container in which wine was found. Ibn Qayyim maintains that in cases where a judge sets free the accused, after taking an oath for instance, and insists there should be no punishment without the testimony of upright witnesses, even though the accused has a reputation for corruption and robberies, verily acts contrarily to *siyāsah sharʿiyyah*.[15] It is not just *siyāsah* to always reject claims that are not accompanied by upright witnesses.

The judge is authorised to admit witnesses of lesser qualification (*ghayr ʿudūl*) if this would prove to be the only way to protect the lives and properties of people.[16] In their efforts to protect people against aggression, the most capable of rulers have exercised intuitive judgment (*farāsah*) and took decisions on the basis of circumstantial evidence (*amārāt*).[17]

Qur'anic authority for *siyāsah* is found in a number of its injunctions, especially those enjoining the believers to promote the good and prevent the evil.[18] *Siyāsah* is thus an instrument in the hands of lawful authorities and the *ulū al amr* with which to discharge this duty. But more specifically, the Qur'anic command, addressing the believers to "obey God, obey the Messenger and those who are in charge of authority from among you" (al-Nisā', 4:58), provides the necessary authority for *siyāsah*. Obedience to legitimate leaders is thus a Qur'anic duty of Muslims, provided that the latter themselves are obedient to God and to His Messenger. Every Muslim must, therefore, comply with the dictates of a just policy when it consists of measures that protect and advance the ideals of justice and *maṣlaḥah*.[19] In numerous places, then, the Qur'an has enjoined Muslims to focus on the pursuit of good and prevent corruption and evil. The forms of good and evil are not listed in the Qur'an or the Sunnah, but they can be known through a general investigation of these sources. The renowned Mālikī jurist from Andalus, Ibrāhīm al-Shāṭibī, also drew attention to the point that rights and wrongs cannot all be known in detail in advance without referring to particular acts and their surrounding circumstances as and when they occur.[20] Hence, the authorities must have powers to uphold and protect the objectives of shariah and be able to order punishment for conduct that violates the sanctity of these values.[21]

Taʿzīr is a subcategory of *siyāsah* as both validate discretionary punishment in pursuit of justice, with the main difference being that *taʿzīr* involves a judicial process whereas *siyāsah* may not. Another difference of note is that *ta'zīr* can on the whole be imposed only for acts of transgression already committed where those acts are also forbidden, explicitly or through interpretation, by shariah, whereas punishment under *siyāsah* may be imposed for acts that may not amount to an offence per se. *Siyāsah shar'iyyah*, as Khallaf has observed, is tantamount to acting on *maṣlaḥah*, or public interest, which the Lawgiver has neither upheld nor overruled.[22] Judicious policy, as such, "denotes administration of public affairs in an Islamic polity with the aim of realising the interests of, and preventing harm to, the community in harmony with the general principles of shariah even if it disagrees with the particular rulings of *mujtahidūn*"[23] An example of this is the often-cited case of Naṣr b. Ḥajjāj of Medina at the time of the second caliph 'Umar b. al-Khaṭṭāb. Naṣr's good looks had become a temptation for women. The caliph banished him from Medina, and in response Naṣr protested and asked what he had done to deserve this banishment. 'Umar is reported to have replied: "You have not committed a sin, but I would have committed one if I had not cleansed this town from your mischief." Whereas *ta'zīr* mainly aims at deterrence and reform of the offender, *siyāsah*-based punishment is for protection of the public interest and protection of society from anticipated mischief, sedition (*fitnah*), and danger to public order. In the Ottoman Empire, *siyāsah* punishment very often consisted of the death penalty, or severe corporal punishment, for habitual criminals.[24]

Many observers have expressed concern over the wide discretionary powers that rulers and judges enjoy under *siyāsah* and *ta'zīr*. Thus it is said that *siyāsah* defies effective control and is open to abuse, which may ultimately undermine the ideals of justice under the rule of law. One observer has thus considered *siyāsah* as "direct negation of what may be regarded as the second essential implication of the idea of the rule of law in a secular system—namely, the principle that the sovereign must not possess any arbitrary power over the subject."[25]

According to Ibn Qayyim, *siyāsah shar'iyyah* does not necessarily mean conforming to the explicit rules of shariah. In his widely quoted words on this subject, "any measure which actually brings the people closest to beneficence (*ṣalāḥ*) and takes them furthest away from corruption (*fasād*) partakes in just *siyāsah* even if it has not been approved by the Prophet, pbuh, nor regulated by divine revelation. Anyone who says that there is no *siyāsah shar'iyyah* where the shariah itself is silent is wrong and has misunderstood the Companions."[26] Ibn Qayyim also divides *siyāsah* into two types: unjust *siyāsah* (*siyāsah ẓālimah*), which shariah forbids; and just *siyāsah* (*siyāsah ʿādilah*), which seeks to serve the cause of justice. Since justice is the principal goal of *siyāsah ʿādilah*, it is an integral part of shariah and always in harmony with it. "We merely call it *siyāsah* because of the linguistic usage, but it is nothing other than the justice ordained by God and His Messenger."[27] God Almighty sent messengers and scriptures to mankind in order to establish justice among people. When there are signs that indicate the path to justice, it is in accord with the Law of God to aim toward it.[28]

XV

*Just Retaliation (*Qiṣāṣ*)*

MUSLIM JURISTS, BOTH Sunni and Shia, have classified homicide into three main types: (1) murder (*qatl al-ʿamd*), which is punishable by just retaliation (*qiṣāṣ*); (2) killing that is a result of error (*qatl al-khaṭāʾ*), such as when a hunter shoots and kills a human being whom he mistook for game (this is punishable by payment of blood money (*diya*) to the heirs of the deceased plus an expiation (*kaffārah*) that consists of charity to the poor or of atonement by fasting; and (3) culpable homicide (*qatl shibh al-ʿamd*), such as when A strikes B with a stick without intending to kill him but his hostile act actually kills B (this too is punishable by payment of blood money (*diya*)).

Qiṣāṣ (lit., equivalence) juridically requires that the perpetrator of a given crime is punished in the same way, in the same proportion, and if possible by the same means that he used in killing or hurting his victim. The punishment should, in other words, be equal to the crime as far as possible. *Qiṣāṣ* under Islamic law applies to a murderer who kills with the intention to kill or with the intention to cause bodily injury that is likely to cause death. The use of a weapon or lethal instrument in homicide is often indicative of the intention to cause death on the part of its user.

Retaliation, or *lex talionis*, is the principal punishment for murder, whereas payment of blood money is the principal punishment in unintentional homicide. Blood money is also paid in murder cases in which the victim's relatives waive their right to retaliation and choose to receive compensation. As a general rule, blood money is payable by the killer himself or his agnatic relatives and legal heirs (*ʿāqilah*).

The Qur'an provides the basic authority for just retaliation, as in the following passage:

> We prescribed to them [the Jews in the Torah] that life is for life, and eye for eye, and nose for nose, and ear for ear, and tooth for tooth,

> and retaliation for wounds. But he who grants a pardon, it shall be an expiation for him. If any fail to judge by [the light of] what God has revealed, they are the transgressors. (al-Māʾidah, 5:47)
>
> وَكَتَبْنَا عَلَيْهِمْ فِيهَآ أَنَّ ٱلنَّفْسَ بِٱلنَّفْسِ وَٱلْعَيْنَ بِٱلْعَيْنِ وَٱلْأَنفَ بِٱلْأَنفِ وَٱلْأُذُنَ بِٱلْأُذُنِ وَٱلسِّنَّ بِٱلسِّنِّ وَٱلْجُرُوحَ قِصَاصٌ ۚ فَمَن تَصَدَّقَ بِهِۦ فَهُوَ كَفَّارَةٌ لَّهُۥ ۚ وَمَن لَّمْ يَحْكُم بِمَآ أَنزَلَ ٱللَّهُ فَأُو۟لَٰٓئِكَ هُمُ ٱلظَّٰلِمُونَ

The Qur'an has thus upheld the rulings of the previous revelations on this subject. Jewish law provided for retaliation but not for blood money, whereas Christianity emphasised the latter and Islam validated both. The purpose in all of these has been to limit the punishment and also to curb vindictive violence, which was rife in pre-Islamic Arabia.[1] Retaliation in pre-Islamic times often exceeded the limits of equivalence, and it was also not personal but a collective revenge exacted on the group or tribe of the offender.

Discriminatory practices in homicide were also encountered among the Jews. The renowned Companion Ibn ʿAbbās has thus reported concerning the two Jewish tribes of Medina, Banū al-Naḍīr and Banū Qurayẓah, that the former discriminated against the latter. When a man of Banū Qurayẓah killed one of Banū al-Naḍīr, the latter would retaliate by killing a member of Banū Qurayẓah, but if a member of Banū al-Naḍīr killed one of Banū Qurayẓah, the former gave in compensation one hundred *wasaqs* (camel load) of dates. On one such occasion when a man of Banū al-Naḍīr had killed someone of the Banū Qurayẓah, the latter brought the case for adjudication to the Prophet. It was concerning this case that the Qur'anic verse was revealed addressing the Prophet:

> And if they [non-Muslims] ask you to adjudicate, then judge among them with justice (*bi'l-qisṭ*). For God loves those who do justice. (al-Māʾidah, 5:42)
>
> .وإن حكمت فاحكم بينهم بالقسط، إن الله يحب المقسطين.

It is stated in a hadith that *bi'l-qisṭ* in this context means life for life, that is, just retaliation without any discrimination.[2]

> والقسط النفس بالنفس.

Ibn Taymiyyah has explained that, driven by revenge, the family or tribe of the deceased would kill not only the killer but also one or more of his family members and often went on to kill many persons, such as the tribal chief or group leader. Just as the killer acted out of aggression in killing his victim, the latter's family would go to excess in taking revenge. This would lead to continued hostility and a thirst for revenge killings on both sides.[3] Blood money, or *diya*, was also practiced in pre-Islamic times. Like retaliation, it too was not limited by the rules of equivalence and represented the least preferred option. People in those times considered it a compromise of personal and tribal honour to settle murder disputes by way of reconciliation (*ṣulḥ*) or payment of blood money. They would rather "wash blood with blood"; women would often taunt persons who attempted peaceful methods, and even pre-Islamic poetry recorded these practices in such terms.[4]

The Qur'anic reform on retaliation was marked by making it exclusively of concern to the person of the offender and could no longer involve anyone else, including his family, clan, or tribe. The rules of equivalence that characterised the Qur'anic *qiṣāṣ* also disregard the status and personal standing of the killer or the victim. Then there was a fresh emphasis on the element of intention, which was not always the case previously. Retaliation became due only for intentional killing or bodily injury. Blood money, which was basically optional in pre-Islamic times, also became an integral part of the Islamic law of homicide, with reference especially to unintentional killing and bodily injuries.[5] "Life for life" thus became the essence of equivalence in retaliation regardless of any factors of discrimination, and it makes no difference whether the victim is an adult or a child, insane, elderly or ill, man or woman, Muslim or non-Muslim.[6] Scholastic jurisprudence has, however, added details not always in tune with the Qur'anic spirit of this principle. Thus we read that according to Imams Mālik and al-Shāfiʿī, a Muslim may not be executed for killing a non-Muslim, based apparently on a hadith, which says just that: "A Muslim is not killed for killing a non-Muslim." The Ḥanafīs have disagreed and upheld instead the Qur'anic mandate of equivalence in the verse under review. They have understood the hadith just quoted to be applicable to a belligerent non-Muslim (*ḥarbī*) who is at war with the Muslims.[7] Muḥammad al-Ghazālī (d. 1416/1996) and his commentator, Yūsuf al-Qaraḍāwī (b. 1344/1926), have held that the hadith is a solitary (*aḥad*) hadith and cannot, therefore, override the Qur'anic textual ruling on the subject. Equality in the right of life also bears harmony with the rest of shariah. Al-Ghazālī further wrote that earlier scholars preceding Imam Abū Ḥanīfah, including al-Shaʿbī and al-Nakhaʿī, held the same view as that of Imam Abū Ḥanīfah.[8]

An exception to the rule of retaliation is made, under both the Sunni and Shii laws, when the father kills his own son, intentionally or otherwise. In this case there would be no retaliation but instead there may be a deterrent punishment (*taʿzīr*). If there are several culprits and one of them is exempted from retaliation, the rest are also exonerated from it, although they may still be punished and given deterrent sentences under *taʿzīr*.

Furthermore, the Qur'an permits retaliation in certain types of bodily injuries. If a person wilfully cuts off the hand of another, his hand is to be cut off in retaliation, and if a person strikes out the tooth of another, he is also liable to retaliation. But *qiṣāṣ* may not be inflicted in the case of breaking any other bone except for the teeth, for it is sometimes next to impossible to observe equality in other fractures. *Qiṣāṣ* for parts of the body also holds between a Muslim and a non-Muslim, both being equal as human beings with respect to the consequences of their offences. There is a degree of emphasis in both the Qur'an and the hadith on how the parties to retaliation and blood money should consider forgiveness at every opportunity that arises. Thus according to a hadith on the authority of Anas b. Mālik, "As far as I have observed, no case of retaliation came before the Prophet wherein he did not direct grant of forgiveness."[9]

ما رأيت النبي صلى الله عليه وسلم رفع إليه شيئ فيه قصاص إلا أمر فيه العفو.

In another hadith on the authority of Abū Hurayrah:

> When a man grants pardon (to an act of injustice he suffered) God Most High increases him in honour.[10]

ما زاد الله عبدا بعفو إلا عزا.

In yet another hadith, the Prophet has given the following instruction:

> The slain (or his family) has a choice of two things, either to take blood money or to retaliate.[11]

ومن قتل له قتيل فهو بخير النظرين إما أن يودي وإما أن يقاد.

Thus, it is either retaliation or blood money in the sense of one or the other, but the two do not combine in the same case, especially when the family of the deceased has granted a pardon or waived their right to retaliation and opted for blood money.

"Life for life," although occurring in the singular, also subsumes the killing of one person by a group of persons. A certain debate arose over the correct understanding of this Qur'anic phrase during the time of ʿUmar b. al-Khaṭṭāb concerning brutal murder of a person by a group in Yemen. Having investigated the matter, the caliph declared that people's lives could not be protected unless all the perpetrators were duly executed, and this became a standard ruling that is also upheld by the leading schools of law, both Sunni and Shia. The fourth caliph, ʿAlī b. Abū Ṭalib, is also reported to have executed three persons who had colluded in the murder of a man, and the position has consequently been upheld by general consensus.

As for the situation where one person kills two people, and each one presents a case for retaliation—if the relatives on both sides also demand retaliation—this will be carried out. But if both sides grant forgiveness, each will be entitled to blood money if they demand it. This is the position also in Shii law. However, if one forgives and the other demands retaliation, according to the Imams al-Shāfiʿī and Ibn Ḥanbal, blood money is payable for one who forgave and retaliation for the other, whereas Abū Ḥanīfah and Mālik maintain that the stronger of the two punishments will prevail, which means retaliation only and no entitlement to blood money. Shii law maintains that grant of forgiveness by some suspends retaliation, and others who do not grant forgiveness can only have a share in the blood money.[12] The Qur'an underscores the rationale of the law of retaliation in the verse: "And there is life for you in retaliation, O people of understanding" (al-Baqarah, 2:179).

وَلَكُمْ فِى ٱلْقِصَاصِ حَيَوٰةٌ يَـٰٓأُو۟لِى ٱلْأَلْبَـٰبِ لَعَلَّكُمْ تَتَّقُونَ

Retaliation saves lives in that it is a deterrent for others and also curbs vendettas and unwarranted continuation of hostilities. There is further instruction in the Qur'an (2:178–179) and the hadith that, once the law of *qiṣāṣ* is applied, the victim's family must cease hostility. They are strongly advised also in the same sources to grant pardon, or if they wish they may take blood money instead. The relatives of the deceased may, on the other hand, choose to forgo the blood money altogether, as it is their right, not an obligation; they are in fact encouraged not to punish but to forgive.

In another hadith on the subject, it is provided that the victim of bodily injury himself, or in the event of his death his legal heirs, may take one of the following three options:

> One who is victim of death or injury has one of the three options, and if he opts for a fourth, he must be grabbed by the hand [and stopped]: To retaliate, or forgive, or take blood money. One who does other than these indulges into excess and will suffer the torment of Hell forever.[13]
>
> من أصيب بدم أو خيل فهو بالخيار بين إحدى ثلاث: فإن أراد الرابعة فخذوا على يديه: بين أن يقتض أو أم يعفو، فإن أخذ من ذلك شيئا ثم عدا بعد ذلك فله النار خالدا فيها مخلدا أبداً".

Ibn Taymiyyah has quoted this and commented that the warning of this hadith is particularly concerned with pursuit of revenge after grant of pardon or acceptance of blood money. As soon as one of the available options is exercised, all hostility must cease as of that moment.[14]

As a general rule, the death of the offender himself extinguishes all claims. The rules of retaliation also provide that it must be carried out in the least painful manner. If the offender is a minor or insane there shall be no retaliation, but only blood money, which, according to the majority of Sunni jurists, as well as the Shia Imamiyyah, would be payable by the family or agnatic relative (*ʿaqīlah*) of the offender. Others maintain that a minor or or insane person is not liable to blood money either.[15]

The personalised features of *qiṣāṣ* law in the Qur'an and the fact that the next of kin (*walī al-dam*) of the deceased has been given a say in the execution of *qiṣāṣ* is a function partly of the phenomenon of graduality (*tanjīm*) in the Qur'anic legislation, a phenomenon that has also been seen in all the other *ḥudūd* punishments.[16] For these were mostly introduced gradually, and each of the *ḥudūd* crimes with respect, for instance, to drinking, adultery, and slander were also prohibited through gradual and successive instances of legislation over a period of time. The gradualist approach in the *ḥudūd* legislation was meant to avoid inflicting hardship on people through sudden changes in some of the most entrenched aspects of pre-Islamic practices. Retaliation was definitely one of them.

In pre-Islamic Arabia, the next of kin would retaliate against anyone from the family or tribe of the offender. Islam also empowered the next of kin of the murder victim with a say in the matter of *qiṣāṣ*, but it stipulated it in several other ways, which effectively meant that *qiṣāṣ* was henceforth to be administered by the state and under its close supervision. Thus the Qur'an passage that gives the next of kin a say in retaliation is immediately followed by an address to the Muslim community and the Prophet to "let him not exceed the bounds in the matter of taking life. For he is helped [by the law]" (al-Isrāʾ, 17:33).

فَلَا يُسْرِف فِّى ٱلْقَتْلِ ۖ إِنَّهُۥ كَانَ مَنصُورًا

This clearly means that only the killer is executed and no one else, but also that it is done under the Prophet's own supervision. For leaving the execution aspect also to the next of kin to control the process would corrupt the meaning of the text. The renowned Qur'an commentators—Ibn Jarīr al-Ṭabarī, Abū Bakr al-Qurṭubī, and Jalāl al-Dīn al-Suyūṭī, authors of *Tafsīr al-Ṭabarī, Tafsīr al-Qurṭubī,* and *Tafsīr al-Jalalayn,* respectively, as well as the latter's commentator in *Ḥāshiyat al-Ṣāwī*—have all held that whenever hostile intentional killing is proven, the lawful ruler (*al-hakīm al-sharʿī*) enables the next of kin of the deceased by offering him the option of whether to carry out retaliation, grant forgiveness, or take blood money. "But the next of kin is not allowed to deal directly with the killer, for that will cause corruption and distortion to proliferate." The state control over the process of retaliation is further endorsed by the fact that even when the next of kin of the deceased grants forgiveness to the killer, the state is still entitled to punish the latter in order to protect the public interest as is elaborated in the following section.[17]

In al-Ṣāwī's view, today's conditions necessitate that the next of kin (or the crime victim) are prohibited from executing *qiṣāṣ* in the old way. Rather, this should be the task of state enforcement agencies and those who are knowledgeable. The next of kin should only be asked for permission whether they allow and wish *qiṣāṣ* to be carried out or if they choose to grant forgiveness. If the latter, there will be no *qiṣāṣ* punishment. This is a privilege that shariah has granted to the next of kin of the victim, but it is confined to killing and does not apply to bodily injuries, and then only to asking for permission. The next of kin is, in other words, not asked for permission in bodily injuries.[18]

The state also plays a similar role regarding the person who is convicted of intentional bodily injury. If not subjected to retaliation for some reason, or even when he pays monetary compensation (*diya*) of limbs, he may still be punished with a suitable punishment by the state in order to protect the society against criminality and violence. In sum, a grant of forgiveness by the next of kin of the deceased does not affect the public right aspect and the authority of the state to impose additional punishments of flogging and imprisonment. This is the position, it is further added, of

Imam Mālik, representing also the practice of the Medinans (*ʿamāl ahl al-Madīnah*) and also the precedent of the second caliph ʿUmar b. al-Khaṭṭāb on this matter.[19]

Bahnasī quotes Imam Mālik's *al-Muwaṭṭa'* and the Mālikī jurist al-Dusūqī (in *Ḥāshiyat al-Dusūqī ʿalā l-Sharḥ al-Kabīr*), regarding the person who is convicted of deliberate killing but exonerated by the next of kin of the deceased, the state may still punish him with 100 lashes of the whip and banishment for one year.[20] This was seen as a suitable punishment at the time, as Abū Zahrah has pointed out, but the basic idea is that the government is within its rights to punish the culprit under the principle of *taʿzīr*, which is not limited to the Mālikī specifications but may take into consideration the prevailing conditions of the time and gravity of the offence. The punishment may be imprisonment for a limited period or a long time, even life imprisonment.[21]

Giving the next of kin of the deceased the right to forgive is a Qur'anic dispensation, as in the verse: "An alleviation from your Lord and a mercy from Him, but anyone who becomes aggressive after that shall bring upon himself a painful chastisement" (al-Baqarah, 2:178).

ذَٰلِكَ تَخۡفِيفٞ مِّن رَّبِّكُمۡ وَرَحۡمَةٞۗ فَمَنِ ٱعۡتَدَىٰ بَعۡدَ ذَٰلِكَ فَلَهُۥ عَذَابٌ أَلِيمٞ

This is an alleviation and relief in particularly stressful situations that would otherwise inflict severity and hardship. Imagine when someone kills his own brother, and the next of kin in this case is the father, who has no other son. He would be in an unfortunate situation of having to lose both his sons, and the possibility of forgiveness may offer a much preferable option. Having given this illustration, Abū Zahrah goes on to make the point that the Prophet encouraged forgiveness only when it seemed preferable and appropriate, but he was firm not to offer it in brutal murder cases where forgiveness would have no place. This is illustrated by the well-known case of a Jewish man who had killed his female slave by placing her head between two rocks and crushing her to death, showing extreme callousness.[22] The case was brought to the Prophet, who ordered retaliation in the like manner and it was carried out. This, it is added, was also the occasion of revelation of the Qur'anic verse, as already quoted, "And there is life for you in [the law of] *qiṣāṣ*, O people of understanding" (2:179).

The Qur'an leaves little doubt, Bahnasī continues, on the public rights aspect of intentional homicide due to the extreme gravity of this crime.

This is reflected in many places in the text, including the verse: "One who kills another human being without the latter being guilty of murder and corruption in the land, it would be as if he has killed the whole of mankind" (al-Mā'idah, 5:32).

مَن قَتَلَ نَفْسًا بِغَيْرِ نَفْسٍ أَوْ فَسَادٍ فِى ٱلْأَرْضِ فَكَأَنَّمَا قَتَلَ ٱلنَّاسَ جَمِيعًا.

The verse continues immediately to provide further that "one who gives life to one person, it would be as if he gives life to the whole of mankind."[23] Quoting this verse, Fazlur Rahman wrote that it "explicitly makes the crime of murder a crime against humanity. Now a legal solution could have been derived from this general statement, but this was never done."[24] Based on his overall reading of the Qur'anic evidence on *qiṣāṣ*, Bahnasī wrote: "It is a common misconception then and evidently erroneous to say that *qiṣāṣ* is a private punishment in Islam." Yet the misconception has taken hold, he adds on the same page, and has persisted notwithstanding the repeated Qur'anic designation of murder and slaying of innocent blood as the greatest of all *ḥarām* known to the Islamic scriptural sources. *Ḥarām* is not a private concept in shariah, especially in this particular context—hence the assertion that *qiṣāṣ* is a private crime/punishment is hardly justified.

Questions have arisen as to who is the rightful next of kin, or the legal prosecutor, to grant forgiveness or demand retaliation. In the event where there is only one person who is next of kin, he or she would have the right either to choose retaliation or to forgive, but issues arise when there are many members in the family. The Ẓāhirī school maintains that the right of prosecution belongs to all the relatives, be they male, female, agnates, or nonagnates and whether or not they are entitled to inheritance from the deceased. This is the widest view of all the schools on record with the underlying concern evidently that the blood of a slain person should never go unclaimed, even if it concerns a remote relative. Any relative that decides to prosecute for *qiṣāṣ* is therefore entitled to do so. The majority of schools (*jumhūr*), except for the Mālikīs, hold that the prosecutors are the victim's legal heirs at the time of his death, regardless of their sex and the grounds of their entitlement to inheritance, whether through blood tie, agnatic tie, or marriage. Only the Shāfiʿīs and Shia exclude the spouse relict from the right to prosecute for retaliation. Mālikī law is different from the other schools in that it gives priority to male agnatic relatives who must demand retaliation or grant forgiveness.[25] Having compared the views of the leading schools of fiqh, Abū Zahrah prefers, and rightly so, the Ẓāhirī position that entitles all the relatives who are hurt by the killing of the deceased to initiate the retaliation claim. This view, he says, is not all that different from the position of Imam Aḥmad Ibn Ḥanbal and even the Ḥanafī school, who virtually include all the legal heirs in all categories of relationships to the deceased person.[26]

Disagreement has arisen, however, when some of the relatives choose retaliation and others decide to forgive, and also when the relatives include minor persons, when some of the relatives happen to be absent, or when the killer has died. The Ḥanafī, Mālikī, and Shii schools entitle the next of kin either to demand retaliation or to forfeit this right, thereby pardoning the killer. They cannot claim blood money or any other financial consideration without the agreement of the killer. The other schools are of the opinion that the prosecutors may demand retaliation, decide to pardon the culprit, or demand blood money. The implications of the difference become clear if the murderer dies before his execution. In Shāfiʿī, Ḥanbalī, and Shii law, the victim's next of kin can still demand the blood money from the murderer's legal heirs, whereas according to the other schools, the victim's next of kin have lost their rights as a result of the killer's death.[27]

Imams Abū Ḥanīfah, al-Shāfiʿī, and Ibn Ḥanbal, and also the Shia Imamiyyah, have held that forgiveness by only some of the relatives overrules retaliation altogether, as one of the conditions of retaliation is that it is demanded by all the relatives. If some grant forgiveness and others do not, this creates an element of doubt and doubt suspends *qiṣāṣ*, as is also the case with regard to other *ḥudūd* penalties. In a real scenario that arose during the time of the second caliph ʿUmar b. al-Khaṭṭāb, the relatives of a murder victim demanded retaliation, and it was at this time when the sister of the deceased, who was also the wife of the murderer, turned up and said that, as far as she was concerned, she forgave her husband. Upon hearing this, the caliph decided to suspend the retaliation. This case also serves to illustrate the value of forgiveness: the woman lost her brother and was now about to lose her husband, were it not for the possibility of forgiveness to prevent that from happening. In the event where the relatives of the deceased include a minor person, many have held that his or her legal guardian should make a decision that is to the minor's advantage. For instance, they may decide to grant forgiveness in consideration of blood money should the minor be in need of financial support. In Mālikī law, the issue does not arise in the first place, as this law only entitles adult relatives to have a say in the matter.[28]

There is some disagreement on the manner in which retaliation is enforced. Whereas many have suggested a reciprocal method of executing the murderer in the way he killed his victim, the preferred view is that it should be done by decapitation with a sword that is supervised by the authorities. Most jurists, including the Shia Imamiyyah, have concurred on the use of the sword as this was deemed to be swift in view of the fact that shariah did not validate maiming and torture. Since the purpose is to apply a swift and clean method, there should, in principle, be no objection from the viewpoint of shariah to other methods that are now available, such as lethal injection, shooting, the electric chair, and the like that may be even faster and more efficient. With regard to retaliation in bodily injuries, most jurists, both Sunni and Shia, stipulate that it should not be carried out in extremely hot or cold weather and rather should take place in moderate conditions.

For *qiṣāṣ* to be implemented, legal capacity and intent to kill on the part of the killer and innocence (*ʿiṣmah*) of the victim must be proven. The victim is not, in other words, one whose life is not legally protected, such as an enemy warrior or a rebel. Attention is also paid to the motive of the crime, the whereabouts of the deceased's body, and the kind of instrument used: whether it was a lethal weapon or not. Uncertainty in the proof of these requirements is likely to reduce the charge of murder (*qatl al-ʿamd*) to quasi-intentional homicide (*qatl shibh al-ʿamd*).[29] Furthermore, retaliation proper applies to murder only, and it is not applicable to mitigated cases or manslaughter, which may involve mistakes or accidents, as the presence of these would preclude *qiṣāṣ*.

According to the majority opinion, excepting the Ḥanafīs, the offender in the cases both of retaliation and blood money is also liable to an expiation (*kaffārah*). Expiation in this case consists of the release of a slave (when this was possible—a suitable alternative may nowadays be to donate towards saving the life of a needy patient who requires a transplant or expensive operation), feeding sixty poor persons, or two months of fasting. The Ḥanafīs have held that expiation is only applicable to erroneous killings but not to cases where the murderer has been sentenced to retaliation (*qiṣāṣ*). Lastly, in the event of bodily injury and loss of limbs, Muslim jurists, including the Shia Imamiyyah, are in agreement that only the victim has the prerogative to grant forgiveness and no one else.[30]

Based on the foregoing analysis, this chapter proposes that the right of the legal heirs/next of kin to prosecute in murder cases should now be confined to asking for permission only. From that point onwards, the law enforcement agencies take responsibility to ensure due process. Granting permission by the next of kin to prosecute is tantamount to their asking for *qiṣāṣ* prosecution to proceed. If the next of kin grant a pardon, or ask for blood money, the prosecution will make a record of these, and it will be for the court to evaluate these positions side by side with the prosecution claims over the public rights aspect of the case.

XVI

*Blood Money and Financial Compensation (*Diya*)*

DIYA IS A quantity of a valuable asset (*māl*) the shariah has assigned to be paid to the crime victim or his heirs by the perpetrator of a crime even if the latter has died. It is a part of the criminal law that resembles civil damages or compensation. Compensation (*taʿwīḍ*) is purely civil in nature, which is why the judge may determine its amount, but not so in *diya*, which is objectively determined. *Diya* also differs from *gharāmah*, which is a punishment pure and simple and is payable to the public treasury. *Diya* combines elements both of punishment and compensation. *Diya* is quantified at a standard amount by shariah that does not vary by reference to the offender's personality and status but does vary by reference to the type of crime and injury inflicted. That is why the *diya* of a child, an adult, the rich, or the poor are all the same, and so is the *diya* of man and woman, or Muslim and non-Muslim, according to contemporary *ijtihād*. This discussion takes a position that differs, as also does Tawfīq al-Shāwī, from the scholastic positions that differentiate between man and woman or Muslim and non-Muslim in this regard. For the normative position of shariah is the equality of all human beings with respect to their right to life. The level of objectivity in the essence of this right and also of essential human dignity are firm commitments that are not open to derogation and compromise.[1]

Whereas retaliation is the principal punishment for murder, payment of blood money (*diya*) is the principal punishment for unintentional killing and culpable homicide; the latter resembles murder and represents an intermediate category between intentional and unintentional killing. Blood money can also be paid in murder cases in which the relatives of the victim waive their right to retaliation and choose to receive blood money. An intensified *diya* (*diya mughāllaẓah*) is payable to the heirs of the deceased in culpable homicide not amounting to murder. As a general rule, blood money is payable by the criminal himself or his legal heirs in the category of agnates (*ʿāqilah*).[2] Originally the *ʿāqilah* consisted of adult able-bodied tribesmen of the killer who had the duty to protect all members of their tribe. This is roughly the basis of the Mālikī, Ḥanbalī, and Shii definitions of *ʿāqilah*, in which it consists of all the agnatic male relatives of the killer.[3] The Ḥanafī concept of *ʿāqilah* widens its scope and holds that other groups may be included, like traders in the same market or colleagues in a workplace who could offer assistance and can be counted as a solidarity group. Al-Qaradawi makes this the basis of a fatwa to say that *ʿāqilah* today may be transferred to professional associations and unions, such as those of medical doctors, architects, and so forth. When a medical doctor kills someone by mistake, for example, his association may be considered as his *ʿāqilah* and pay the *diya* on his behalf.[4] If a person has no *ʿāqilah*, the public treasury bears the responsibility for payment of blood money.[5]

Grant of a pardon by the relatives exonerates the offender from *qiṣāṣ* even if the relatives accept blood money. This is the view of Imams al-Shāfiʿī and Ibn Ḥanbal, whereas Imam Abū Ḥanīfah has held that pardoning in *qiṣāṣ* means that the relatives do not take anything as this would be an act of goodwill and *iḥsān* on the part of the relatives within the meaning of the Qur'anic terms "*maʿrūf* and *iḥsān*" (2:178).[6]

Blood money is also applicable as a substitute for retaliation in cases where the requirements of the latter cannot be fulfilled. Furthermore, reconciliation between the parties is generally recommended before adjudication, although the community and state retain the right to impose a deterrent (*taʿzīr*) punishment even after reconciliation. The Imams Mālik and Abū Ḥanīfah have held that the state must impose a *taʿzīr* punishment in every case of intentional killing wherein neither retaliation nor blood money is imposed. Imams al-Shāfiʿī and Ibn Ḥanbal have held, however, that once the victim's relatives grant a pardon to a *qiṣāṣ* convict, he is exempt from all punishment. The other two Imams mention that although *taʿzīr* punishment is not compulsory in every case, it should be given when public interest demands it. However, *taʿzīr* in such cases must as a general rule be less than the death penalty.[7] *Diya* does not combine with a pardon in unintentional homicide in that a grant of pardon disallows the next of kin from demanding a *diya*.

Blood money for loss of life is determined at one hundred camels of roughly equal combinations of one, two, three, and four years of age. The monetary equivalent of this is cited, according to some reports, at eight hundred (gold) dinars or eight thousand (silver) dirhams. Later it is reported that, due to price rises, the caliph ʿUmar b. al-Khaṭṭāb raised these monetary equivalents to one thousand dinars and twelve thousand dirhams respectively. There arose some differences of opinion over the question as to which is the basic unit of value in determining the quantitative aspect of *diya*: is it camels or gold? Abū Zahrah's response to this question is that times have changed and camels are not found in all places, nor is their price commonly known as much as the prices for gold and silver. Hence gold has been made the unit of value for the evaluation of *diya*. To this it is added that, whenever feasible, one must maintain a comparative parity between the gold value of *diya* and its equivalent in camels.[8]

The details of blood money are determined mostly by the Sunnah, which, like the Qur'an, does not draw any distinction on the basis of gender and religion, yet juristic opinion of the fiqh scholars, in both the Sunni and Shii schools, has held the blood money of a woman at half that of a man, a distinction that has remained somewhat controversial. This is because the source evidence does not recognise any gender-based distinction; the Qur'an has in fact provided an egalitarian formula on the inherent value of human life. We may refer here to the combined account of Muḥammad al-Ghazālī and his commentator, Yūsuf al-Qaraḍāwī, on this issue. The latter has endorsed the former's position to the effect that "the *diya* of a woman is equal to that of a man, the reason being that the Qur'an has not differentiated between them. The assumption then that a woman's life is cheaper (*arkhās*) than that of man, or that her right is of a lesser value is a false assumption (*zaʿm kādhib*) and it is contrary to the noble Qur'an. A man who kills a woman is executed, just as is a woman who kills a man. Their blood is equal. Then what is the reason for inequality in their blood money (*diya*)?"[9] This is a clear example perhaps of how a medieval society's values have found their way into the fabric of scholastic jurisprudence and gained recognition over the course of time.

Qaradawi continues: "The Shaykh (al- Ghazālī) could have perhaps added the hadith that the blood money for loss of life is one hundred camels [في النفس مائة من الأبل] ", which shows that the Prophet did not differentiate the blood money of a man from that of a woman.[10] The claim that the *diya* of a woman is half that of a man refers to a hadith to that effect, but that hadith is unsound. It has a broken chain of transmitters (*isnad*) attributed to (and may be a statement of) the Companion Muʿādh b. Jabal.

Al-Bayhaqī wrote that its *isnad* is certainly unreliable and there is nothing to that effect in either al-Bukhārī or Muslim or their commentators. The claim over general consensus (*ijmāʿ*) in support of the alleged distinction is also weak. Al-Shawkānī has gone on record to say that at least two early scholars, Abū Bakr al-Asamm and Ibn ʿUlayyah, have opposed it. More recently, Muṣṭafā al-Zarqā and Muḥammad Abū Zahrah have also opposed the discriminatory position over blood money. The hadith does not differentiate in this regard between the blood money of "a man and that of a woman, nor between the blood money of Muslim and non-Muslim, nor even of a slave and a freeman."[11] Abū Zahrah has also looked into the details of the relevant juristic views and concluded by saying that they are weak and depart from the guidelines of the Qur'an and hadith. "We prefer therefore the position taken by Abū Bakr al-Asamm," which was taken at a time before these additional accretions were added on.[12] The Qur'an draws no distinction between one life and another, even if one is that of an infant and the other an adult in his prime, a great scholar (*ʿālim*) and a commoner, a man and a woman—all are equally subject to the laws of *qiṣāṣ* and *diya*.[13]

When the slain body of a person is found in a locality without any trace of the killer and all efforts fail to identify the killer, the state is responsible to pay blood money to the victim's family in lieu of its basic commitment and responsibility to protect the lives of its citizens.[14] The principle of blood money (*diya*) finds analogous expression in contemporary criminology, which often recommends decriminalisation of certain acts and recourse to victim compensation as an alternative to imprisonment. *Diya* is, however, not totally analogous to civil damages. This is because *diya* has a punitive component that gives it certain characteristics of its own. It is akin to the imposition of a fine for a particular crime with the proviso perhaps that, in the case of *diya*, the fine goes to the victim's family rather than to the state. The rules of *diya* also permit the state to stand as a substitute, if need be, for the victim's family in order to secure the *diya* from the perpetrator and provide the victim or his family with appropriate compensation. Thus it is not necessary for *diya* always to be paid directly to the victim or his family. It can be paid to the state in the form of a fine provided that the state assumes responsibility for being able to satisfy the needs of the victim's family.[15]

If the offender himself can pay the *diya*, he is responsible to pay it in the first place as the agnatic group (*ʿāqilah*) comes in only to help with the payment when the offender is unable to pay. This is also implied in the

Qur'anic text on the subject of *diya* (i.e., al-Nisā', 4:92). Since this verse does not make any reference to *ʿāqilah*, it is understood that *diya* is payable by the offender himself. The *ʿāqilah* provision in Islamic law represented a departure from the basic principle of personal responsibility of the offender on grounds of introducing a level of cooperation in unintentional crime. The purpose was also to make security and crime prevention a concern directly of the family and tribe. During the time of the second caliph, ʿUmar b. al-Khaṭṭāb, the colleagues at the workplace of the offender (*ahl al-dīwān*) were included in his *ʿāqilah*, and this marked an early shift in the composition of *ʿāqilah*, a provision that was altogether characteristic of the tribal society and its particular set of conditions.[16]

In response to a question whether the rules of the agnatic group (*ʿāqilah*) can be meaningfully applied at the present time, it may be difficult to apply them now, not only because of the weaker tribal ties but also because of a certain tension that exists between the rules of *ʿāqilah* and the constitutional principle of legality in crimes and punishments. In this connection, the former Rector of al-Azhar, Maḥmūd Shaltūt, has rightly observed, and has quoted Ibn ʿĀbidīn al-Shāmī in support of his own view, that the *ʿāqilah* provision in the Sunnah represented temporary legislation (*tashrīʿ zamānī*) that was meaningful within the tribal setting of earlier times but that no longer obtains.[17] One may also add that even though the *ʿāqilah* provision is no longer applicable, the basic idea of payment of some kind of financial compensation to the family of the victim in traffic accidents and certain crimes of violence still holds good. The offender himself should be required to pay the whole of the *diya*, and failing that, it should wholly or partially be the responsibility of the state. In the event where the offender can pay a part of the *diya*, the state may bear responsibility for the rest. Pension regulations, especially relating to the state pension and the question of the deceased person's entitlement to a state pension, Islamic insurance (*takāful*), or life and disability insurance, are some of the additional new factors that are likely to be taken into consideration by the court in the determination of *diya* or its equivalent in compensation for crime.

There is another provision in the Sunnah, as already mentioned, concerning homicide in obscure circumstances, or when a dead body is found in a locality and the case cannot be solved even after strenuous efforts to find the killer. Recourse may be had in that situation to the principle of *qasamah* (oath-taking) applied to all the people who might be suspected in the incident or who live in the vicinity. Fifty men of the nearest locality, town, or village, which may be identified by the family of the deceased, must take solemn oaths that they have neither killed nor have any knowledge of the killer. When they all take such oaths, they are all absolved of *qiṣāṣ* but they are still collectively liable to pay a *diya* to the family of the deceased for their negligence to ensure safety within the area under their supervision and control.[18]

Qasamah (oath-taking) is premised on the rationale that shariah does not accept the notion of human bloodshed in vain (*hadr al-dam*) nor of a killing for which no one is held accountable. Basic authority for *qasamah* is provided in a long hadith, narrated by Ziyad b. Abi Maryam, that may be summarised as follows:

> A man came to the Prophet, pbuh, and informed him that he found the dead body of his brother amidst such and such a tribe. The Prophet told him to bring together fifty persons from among them who must swear by God that they have neither killed nor known the killer. The man then asked if this was all that was to be done, to which the Prophet replied that he was also entitled to one hundred camels [as *diya*].[19]

Even when the parties reach an agreement to convert *qiṣāṣ* into the payment of blood money, the authorities remain entitled to impose a punishment on the offender. For payment of blood money only settles the Right of Man aspect of the crime, whereas crimes of violence are also crimes against the society, which is represented by the state, and may as such grant pardon or impose a punishment if it deems this to be in the public interest (*maṣlaḥah*).[20]

Retaliation and Blood Money in Modern Law: An Overview

With reference to its contemporary applications, it may be noted that the right to blood money has been utilised in Saudi Arabia where the state plays an increasingly prominent role in cases of murder, assault, and damage to property. In the interest of public order and internal security, "the state is not content with private settlement of disputes through the payment of blood money. Although in shariah payment of blood money is preferable to retaliation as a way of settling disputes, as it is inclined toward clemency, it is no longer sufficient to terminate a dispute (through payment of *diya*) and the assailant is therefore held liable to a state-imposed sanction."[21] It is also prescribed by the traffic regulations of Saudi Arabia that someone who knocks down and kills a person in a traffic accident shall be liable to pay *diya* to his legal heirs and, in addition, be liable to imprisonment. The blood money payable for a woman's accidental death is half as much as that of a man.[22]

One or two points of general interest may briefly be made here, one of which is that *diya*, whether for loss of life or loss of a limb, should not be seen as putting a price tag on human life and limbs. It is concerned mainly with the plight of the family that has suffered, including their potential loss of income and other factors. The purpose of *diya* in the Qur'an is after all alleviation of suffering and a show of compassion, not a rigid imposition that is unrelated to the surrounding conditions of the offence and its victim. Another point that may have a bearing on the assessment of a suitable *diya* in our times would be to refer to the prevailing general customs and conditions of employment, the cost of living, insurance indicators and so on.

The shariah provisions on *diya* that are applied in Saudi Arabia raise questions over certain factors that play a role in the implementation aspect of the law, such as the value of money in cases of involvement of people from other countries, changes in the exchange rate of currency, and the desire to curb excessive demand for blood money. Blood money for non-Muslims in Saudi Arabia has been equated with that for Muslims. A combination of statutory legislation and Islamic criminal law is also applied with regard to labour relations and motor vehicles. The rates of compensation for work accidents are fixed by a special committee, which on the whole relies on Islamic law guidelines. In motor vehicle accidents, the police determine the guilty parties, while the shariah court fixes the amount of the blood money.[23]

As explained earlier, for reasons of utility and pressing circumstances, classical fiqh doctrines grant the ruler extensive powers to exercise judicious policy or *siyāsah*. In Saudi Arabia, the king still uses this power. He pronounces *siyāsah*-based sentences in cases of urgent public necessity if the proof of guilt is overwhelming and if normal processes of justice seem too gradual to meet the urgency of a situation. A formal trial will not be required, but prior to issuing a policy-based sentence, the king will instruct a shariah court to establish the facts of the case or consult senior ulama. A typical case for a *siyāsah*-based judgment may be where a man kills his child, since a parent may not experience retaliation for killing his or her child. A sentence of this kind utilises the combined resources of both deterrent punishment and judicious policy (*taʿzīr* and *siyāsah*). The king's approval is also required prior to execution of all death sentences in Saudi Arabia.[24]

In 2001 the Saudi government enacted a code of criminal procedure in 225 articles. An important principle of this law is that no punishment can be inflicted except for crimes prohibited by shariah and Saudi regulations, based on a final judgment issued after due process. This code prohibits torture during criminal investigations and gives the accused the right to a lawyer. The Saudi justice system has thus been undergoing reform that integrates the requirements of due process and pays attention also to the constitutional law principles of legality in crimes and punishments.[25]

An instance of the application of *qiṣāṣ* law in Saudi Arabia was the Gilford case, which gained international publicity at the time. Frank Gilford from South Australia had to decide whether to insist on death by *qiṣāṣ* or to accept blood money (*diya*) in connection with the death of his sister, Yvonne Gilford. The case was tried in Riyadh, where two nurses were charged with killing the deceased. In the end, the brother of the deceased chose to accept *diya*, which he in turn donated to a hospital in the memory of his sister.

Another case of conversion of *qiṣāṣ* to *diya* was that of Sarah Balabagan in 1995. A fifteen-year-old Muslim from the Philippines was sentenced to death by *qiṣāṣ* in the United Arab Emirates. She was found guilty of killing her employer, Almas Mohammed al-Baloushi, by stabbing him thirty-four times. She pleaded self-defence as the employer had tried to rape her. The trial court had earlier confirmed that Balabagan was the victim of rape, but she was also found guilty of manslaughter. She was sentenced to seven years of imprisonment and was ordered to pay 150,000 dirhams to the victim's relatives. The sentence was contested and appealed, and the appeal court imposed the death sentence by firing squad. The Philippines authorities intervened, and later the victim's family was persuaded to grant a pardon from *qiṣāṣ* and instead accepted the 150,000 dirhams as *diya*. Balabagan's sentence was also reduced to one year of imprisonment and 100 lashes.[26]

Iran and Pakistan have also adopted the shariah provisions on *qiṣāṣ* and *diya* in their respective laws. The Iranian Law of *Ḥudūd* and *Qiṣāṣ* 1982 (sections 62–68) and also the Law of Taʿzīr 1983 regulated *ḥudūd, taʿzīr, qiṣāṣ, diya*, and *kaffārah* in accordance with the Shia Imamiyyah School and thus almost codified the law with respect of the offences of murder, homicide, bodily injury, sexual offences, and offences against property such as theft and robbery. These laws were later revised and partially amended in 1996. The amended laws, which were approved by Parliament, tend to emphasise accuracy in the enforcement of *qiṣāṣ* so that the victim is not exposed to pain in excess of what is proportionate and equivalent to his or her offence. Retaliation (*qiṣāṣ*) under Iranian law may not be implemented in conditions where inflicting injury is likely to become infectious.[27]

It is of interest to note that *qiṣāṣ* gained considerable attention and coverage in the Western media in 2009 when Ameneh Bahrami, an Iranian woman, was blinded in an acid attack. Since Islamic law enables the victim to demand retaliation or grant pardon, Bahrami demanded that her attacker be blinded as well. Thus it appeared that the victim had the ability, under Iranian law, to pardon the perpetrator and withhold punishment even in cases of both murder and bodily injury. Bahrami pardoned her attacker and stopped his punishment (drops of acid in his eyes) just before it was to be administered in 2011.[28]

With regard to the law of homicide, a judge who pronounces a sentence of retaliation may allow one of the prosecutors to carry out the execution. Somewhat like Saudi Arabia, the Iranian law had also retained, however, the disputed fiqh provision that specified the woman's blood money at an amount that was half of the blood money of a Muslim man. This half of a *diya* has been determined at 75 million riyals (equivalent to 7,750 Euros). However, when in 2003 such a case arose, the state offered to pay part of this sum. A few months before then, at the instigation of some of the female members of Parliament, a draft law was passed to abolish this difference in blood money. However, the Council of Guardians was reported to have declined its approval. The campaign for eliminating the difference in the blood money of women as well as non-Muslims continued for some time.[29]

In Pakistan, the Criminal Laws (Amendment) Ordinance 1991 amended the Penal Code and the Criminal Procedure Code to enable *qiṣāṣ* and *diya* to be applied. The punishments of *qiṣāṣ, diya,* and *arṣh* (compensation for injury) are added to the scale of punishments provided in the codes. The offences of murder and bodily injuries can be compounded with *ṣulḥ* or mutual agreement and can be settled by payment of *diya* or *arṣh*. Because of this, even intentional murder is not liable to the mandatory sentence of death. Homicide that is caused by negligence or accident is liable only to the payment of *diya, arṣh,* or *taʿzīr* punishment. Offences of bodily injury are also dealt with by these methods. Some offences are thus treated both as crimes and as torts. But the position here differs with civil law in that *diya* and *arṣh* are mainly determined by law and not by the assessment of the court.[30]

These amendments were the result of a decision made by the Shariat Bench of the Supreme Court which determined that the law of homicide under the Pakistan Penal Code 1860 was not in accordance with the Islamic law and therefore was null and void.[31] A bill to remedy this, based on the Ḥanafī doctrine, was published in 1981, which generated much public debate especially on account of provisions that barred female testimony in *qiṣāṣ* cases and took the position that the blood money of a woman was half that of a man. Issues remained unresolved and clear positions remained difficult to ascertain due partly to political changes and indecision. Civil societies and women's groups later resumed their egalitarian campaign during General Musharraf's rule, and the federal shariah court also tended to exercise a moderating influence in the application of *ḥudūd* laws.[32]

In the Sudan a number of laws were enacted in the late 1980s with a view to bringing the country's laws in conformity with shariah and amending or enhancing some of the existing laws. Included in these were the Penal Code 1983 and Criminal Procedure Code 1983. The Penal Code went into force on 8 September 1983 and introduced the *ḥudūd* and *qiṣāṣ* laws. The Criminal Procedure Code regulated criminal investigations, prosecution, and trials in conformity with shariah.[33] Further details on Sudan and some other countries can be found in part three of this book.

Shariah penal codes in Northern Nigeria, including Zamfara and Kano, follow the classical Mālikī doctrine on homicide and bodily injuries. Some codes specify that the killer can be sentenced to be executed in the same way as he killed his victim. As in Mālikī law, heinous murder (*qatl al-ghīlah*), defined as "the act of luring a person to a secluded place and killing him" (Art. 50, Zamfara Shariah Penal Code), is a capital offence for which the position of the prosecutors is also irrelevant. The reintroduction of Islamic criminal law in Northern Nigeria is burdened, however, by political and legal complications, and it is likely to remain a bone of contention between the Muslim North and the rest of Nigeria. One of the major legal problems is that the shariah penal codes are on several points at variance with the federal constitution of Nigeria.[34] A somewhat similar scenario also obtains in Malaysia as explained in the following section.

In Malaysia, two of its northern provinces, Kelantan and Terengganu, have proposed to enforce the *ḥudūd, qiṣāṣ*, and *diya* laws in their respective Enactments. The Shariah Criminal Code (II) 1993 of Kelantan deals with *qiṣāṣ* offences in part II (sections 24–38) and makes wilful killing (*qatl al-ʿamd*) punishable with death by *qiṣāṣ* if the next of kin does not grant a pardon; but if a pardon is granted, and the heir/prosecutor opts for *diya*, it will be payable to the victim's relative or in some cases the offence may be punished by *taʿzīr*. The bill also makes provisions on bodily injuries and specifies circumstances where *qiṣāṣ* may or may not be enforced. It also addresses issues of proof and evidence in part II (see Appendix at end of this book). The attached schedules II and III to this bill specify the types of injuries and the amounts of blood money (*diya*) or compensation for bodily injury (*arṣh*) that they carry.

Section 28 of the Hudud Bill of Kelantan thus provides:

> The *wali* (guardian, next of kin) may at any time before the punishment of death as the *qiṣāṣ* punishment is executed, pardon the offender either with or without a *diya*; and if the pardon is with a *diya*, this shall be paid either in a lump sum or by installments, within a period of three years from the date of final judgment, and if in the meantime the offender dies, the *diya* shall be recoverable from his estate.

Section 35 provides:

> Whoever causes bodily injury to a person shall be punished with *qiṣāṣ* punishment, that is, with similar bodily injury as that which he has inflicted upon his victim, and where *qiṣāṣ* punishment cannot be imposed or executed because the conditions required by the shariah law are not fulfilled, the offender shall pay *irsh* to his victim and may be liable to a *taʿzīr* punishment by imprisonment.

Terengganu introduced its Shariah Criminal Enactment on *Hudud* and *Qisas* 2002 in seventy-four sections, which has closely followed the provisions of the Hudud Bill of Kelantan. Its sections on *qiṣāṣ* and *diya* are identical to those of the Kelantan Bill.

As of this writing (November 2018), neither of these Enactments are being enforced and both remain as proposed bills due mainly to their conflict with the federal constitution of Malaysia. A detailed discussion of this appears in part two of this volume.

What follows next is a juridical review of doubt (*shubha*) and its application to crimes and punishments in light particularly of a leading hadith on this subject.

XVII

*Doubt (*Shubha*) and Its Impact on Punishment*

THE DISCUSSION IN this volume has frequently referred to doubt (*shubha*) and its impact on the enforcement of punishments. This chapter presents a juristic analysis of *shubha* in relationship to *ḥudūd*. A question has arisen as to whether the prevailing conditions of modern society would amount to juridical doubt, which suspends *ḥudūd* according to the directive of the hadith that will be discussed here. The hadith in question is a general and unqualified address to all Muslims, but perhaps primarily to rulers and judges, with the statemet to "suspend the *ḥudūd* in all cases of doubt" [إدرؤ الحدود بالشبهات]. Since this is a general (*ʿām*) ruling, it can be applied not only to courtroom situations but also to matters outside the courtroom environment and in society at large. Although the hadith would appear to be primarily concerned with the evidential process and trial proceedings, its wording does not qualify it as such. It would seem a fair assumption that in issuing this directive, the Prophet addressed his people and society and not necessarily court proceedings in particular.

The basic message of this hadith has also been conveyed in a legal maxim of fiqh (*qāʿidah kulliyyah fiqhiyyah*), which is a rehash of the hadith itself, simply providing that "*ḥudūd* are suspended/omitted in doubtful situations" [الحدود تسقط بالشبهات]. In a commentary on this maxim, the Mālikī jurist al-Jarḥazī (d. 1201/1787) discussed the authenticity of its underlying hadith and explained that it was reported by al-Tirmidhī, al-Ḥākim, al-Bayhaqī, al-Ṭabarānī, and Ibn Mājah, among others, and that "in view of the numerous chains of its transmission, many scholars, including Ibn Ḥajar al-ʿAsqalanī [the commentator of al-Bukhārī], have concluded that it is sound (*ṣaḥiḥ*)."[1] According to another report, three prominent

Companions, ʿAbd Allāh b. Masʿūd, Muʿādh b. Jabal, and ʿUqbah b. ʿAmīr, are quoted to have said: "When doubt befalls [you] concerning a *ḥadd,* suspend it" إذا اشتبه الحد فادرأه. This tends to underline the subjective aspect of doubt assessment: when a learned person, judge, or ruler is personally convinced as to the existence of doubt, he should suspend the punishment. In the context of punishments, it is not necessarily an overwhelming doubt but even a small amount that is at issue.

The renowned scholar of hadith, Ibn Shihāb al-Zuhrī (d. 124/724), conducted an investigation that led him to state in principle that "*ḥudūd* should be dropped in all cases of doubt" [الحدود تسقط بالشبهات].[2]

'Shubhāt' (s., *shubha*) as the key element in both the hadith and its related legal maxims is synonymous with *iltibās, ikhtilāt,* and *shakk* (confusion, ambiguity, and doubt). The doubt here also comprises probability (*iḥtimāl*), all of which stand in contradistinction with certainty (*yaqīn*).[3] *Shubha* is defined as a mere resemblance to certainty of that which is not certain. The juristic interpretations of *shubha* in conjunction with *ḥudūd* relate this concept to situations where the perpetrator of a *ḥudūd* offence acts under a mistaken perception. Typical examples of *al-shubhāt* in fiqh manuals include, in relationship to drinking (*shurb*), for example, cases where liquor is taken mistakenly for vinegar or medicine or when adultery is committed between a finally divorced couple who might have thought they were still in a lawful marriage. Similarly, theft from the public treasury (*bayt al-māl*), according to fiqh scholars, does not invoke the prescribed punishment because the thief is deemed to have a share, however slight, in its assets, which would introduce an element of doubt. By the same token when a poor person steals from assets earmarked for charity, there will be no prescribed punishment.[4] These are some of the obvious applications of doubts (*shubhāt*) in the enforcement of *ḥudūd.* The proof of the offence must also be clear of doubt, which refers to any doubt, however slight, that compromises the reliability of a proof such that it fails to establish certainty in ascertaining the relevant facts. Another instance of doubt that suspends the *ḥudūd* punishments is when the accused person retracts his confession. For when this happens, it casts doubt on the veracity of that confession, and the prescribed punishment is consequently suspended.

The majority of jurists (*jumhūr*) have adopted the substance of the hadith under review and ruled that doubt suspends the implementation of *ḥudūd.* Only the Ẓāhirīs have held otherwise on the analysis that this would interfere with the implementation of clear shariah injunctions; they have also questioned the authenticity of this hadith. The majority have, on the other hand, differed among themselves as to what exactly amounts to doubt (*shubha*) and what does not. Whereas the Mālikīs, Ḥanbalīs, and the Shia do not classify *shubha* in any manner of classification and tend to look at each *shubha* individually, the Ḥanafīs, Shāfiʿīs, and Mālikīs have divided *shubha* into the following three types. The first is doubt pertaining to acts (*shubha al-fiʿl*) whereby a person is in doubt over the permissibility or prohibition of an act owing to ignorance, such as sexual intercourse with one's estranged wife during her waiting period (*ʿiddah)* following a final divorce, on the wrong assumption that it is lawful. It is also a requirement that the perpetrator of a *ḥudūd* crime knows that his act was unlawful. If the person convicted of adultery, for instance, says at the time of enforcement of punishment that he did not know that adultery was unlawful and takes an oath to that effect, what he says would create a *shubha* and suspend the prescribed punishment.[5] (2) The second is doubt pertaining to ownership or existence of a right (*shubha al-milk*), such as stealing from one's debtor or one's son, in which case the prescribed punishment is not enforced. This is based on the hadith that states, "you and your property belongs to your father." Yet it is also doubtful whether the father's ownership of his son's belongings also extends to illegal acts, such as theft and *zinā*! The third variety of doubt is known as contractual doubt (*shubha al-ʿaqd*), which Imam Abū Ḥanīfah himself, along with his disciple, Zufar, and Sufyān al-Thawrī (d. 161/778), have added to the foregoing two types. It means that the existence of an agreement or contract, even an unlawful one—such as marriage with a close relative that was only discovered at a later date—would introduce an element of doubt in the enforcement of the prescribed punishment of adultery. There will be no prescribed punishment due to a contractual doubt. If he knew of the prohibited degree of relationship in advance, he would be liable to the prescribed punishment. The majority of jurists, including the Shia, however, do not agree with this variety of *shubha*. They say that the person should investigate first and establish the legality of the marriage before he or she actually proceeds with it.[6] The Ḥanbalī school does not divide *shubha* into the said three varieties but gives relevant examples that tend to cover most of its manifestations, based on the analysis that doubt cannot be encapsulated into typologies and that this was how the Companions of the Prophet have also dealt with the subject.[7]

The Ḥanafīs also maintain, as already mentioned, that delay in confession and testimony without a valid excuse amounts to doubt that suspends the *ḥudūd* punishments in the Right of God type of crimes, such as theft, adultery, and consumption of intoxicants, but not in slander (*qadhf*). The other three schools do not agree and maintain that a mere delay does not invalidate a confession or testimony that is sound in all other respects. According to the renowned jurist Ibn Abī Layla (d. 83/702), delay (*ta'khīr*) invalidates all types of proofs and causes suspension of *ḥudūd* penalties. This is because delay has an adverse effect on deterrence, just as it also raises the possibility that the offender might have regretted his conduct and repented or that the witnesses might have had certain reservations.[8] The Ḥanafīs and Shia Zaydiyyah maintain that the inability of the defendant to reveal a doubt (*shubha*) is also a *shubha* that invalidates *ḥudūd*, such as in the case of a dumb person who might have spoken about a possible doubt if he or she had the ability to speak. The majority have disagreed and maintain that a dumb person may express him- or herself by writing or even gestures.[9]

The consequences of applying the principle that doubt suspends *ḥudūd* tend to vary in that it may either completely absolve the accused of all charges or it may exempt him from the prescribed punishment and leave open the possibility of a lesser punishment under *ta'zīr*. The accused is thus cleared of all charges in the following three situations. The first is when doubt affects the essence of the accusation in question, such as when a person steals his own property while believing that it belongs to someone else, he or she cannot be punished for theft by way either of *ḥadd* or *ta'zīr*. The act here does not qualify as theft in the first place, which by definition is stealing the property of another person. The second is if there is doubt in the legal text or rules and their relevance to the conduct in question. For example, sexual relations in a marriage that is concluded without witnesses, or without the consent of the guardian (*walī*), cannot be punished by way either of *ḥadd* or *ta'zīr* since jurists have disagreed on the validity of such a marriage (some saying it is basically valid but voidable), and their disagreement introduces doubt. And the third situation is when doubt pertains to proof of a crime, where, for instance, witnesses retract their testimony or when it is not certain whether the offender suffered from insanity at the material time of committing the offence. In this case the accused will also be cleared of all charges.

In certain other situations, doubt (*shubha*) may suspend the principal punishment of *ḥudūd*, but a lesser punishment may still be imposed. Thus when a person steals from the public treasury, or when a father steals from his son, the prescribed punishment of theft is suspended but the judge may consider imposing a lesser punishment of *taʿzīr*. Similarly a person who retracts his or her confession is acquitted of the prescribed punishment but may still be punished under *taʿzīr*.[10]

It is further suggested that doubts also extend to the personality and character of the perpetrator of *ḥudūd*. The conventional position is thus disputed that the judge enforces *ḥudūd* crimes as soon as they are duly proven regardless of the personal conditions of the perpetrator. How can the judge ignore the personal factors and circumstances of perpetrators if they introduce elements of doubt? They must surely be considered in the adjudication of *ḥudūd*. It is further suggested that the hadith under review is not confined to *ḥudūd* but includes all punishments: *ḥudūd, qiṣāṣ*, and *taʿzīr*.[11]

The basic position in Islamic law that doubt overrules the enforcement of *ḥudūd* is also upheld in contemporary legal systems, especially with reference to its two well-known positions—one on the presumption of innocence and the other on giving the benefit of doubt to the accused. The main difference between the Islamic and contemporary penal systems, however, lies in the scope of the application of the principle. The predominant view among Muslim jurists seems to be that the principle of suspending *ḥudūd* because of doubt applies only to prescribed *ḥudūd* and *qiṣāṣ* crimes but not to *taʿzīr*. But the discussion here proposes that the word *ḥudūd* in the hadith under review includes all punishments, whether they fall under categories of *ḥudūd, qiṣāṣ*, or *taʿzīr*. They should all be suspendable when there is doubt. This is, in fact, the position in many other legal systems that embrace and apply the presumption of innocence and the principle of favouring the accused in the case of doubt in all classes of crimes.[12]

It thus appears that the fiqh interpretations of doubt in the hadith under review has included a wide range of circumstances that were perceived as doubt in light of the prevailing conditions of earlier times. It is a mere extension of the same logic to extend the application of the hadith/legal maxim to contemporary conditions. Bearing in mind the general language of the hadith, it is arguably not confined to the evidential process but encapsulates all doubt, within or outside the judicial process, all of which would fall within the range of cautionary advice of the hadith.

Modern society, with its temptations to sin, rampant secularity, and absence in most present-day Muslim countries of an appropriate context and environment for the enforcement of *ḥudūd*, do, we believe, present us with doubtful situations that can be subsumed under the purview of the hadith under review. This may still leave open, however, the prospects of some disciplinary or deterrent action. The doubt we propose is not a total eliminator of a charge but one that would most likely reduce the *ḥudūd* and *qiṣāṣ* to *taʿzīr*, which may in turn warrant some disciplinary or punitive sanctions the court may consider appropriate.

XVIII

Islam as a Total System

THE IMPLEMENTATION OF Islamic criminal law is generally seen as a component of Islamic revivalism. As such, it is not confined to any particular Muslim country but represents a wider development. A number of prominent Muslim scholars have spoken on the subject, and this chapter reviews the salient points of what they have said. There are those, of course, who maintain that the implementation of Islamic criminal law offers a good answer to the problem of rising criminality and that, in any case, Muslims have little choice in the matter of implementing God's law. There has also been a general expression of concern that implementing shariah penalties under contemporary conditions, where the individual is surrounded by modern society's temptations and the disabilities they entail, could amount, in some cases at least, to a miscarriage of justice. It is widely accepted that Islam is a way of life and that if implemented in its entirety in itself can operate as a major deterrent against crime. But there are challenges in achieving the objectives of Islamic criminal justice in an environment strongly influenced by the currents of secularist modernity, liberalism, and globalisation, which have impacted culture and religion in many different ways. These challenges frustrate, rather than satisfy, the Islamic vision of justice and fair play.

"A remarkable fact about the Shariah," according to Abūl Āʿla Maududi of Pakistan (d. 1399/1979), is that it is "an organic whole" and any arbitrary and selective division of the general scheme of shariah is therefore "bound to harm the spirit as well as the structure of the Shariah." There were people, Maududi added, who selected a few provisions of the Islamic penal code for implementation without realising that those provisions need to be viewed against the background of the whole Islamic system of life. "To enforce those provisions in isolation would in fact be against the intention of the Lawgiver," he said.[1]

With reference to the amputation of the hand for theft, Maududi added that this was meant to be promulgated in an Islamic society wherein the wealthy paid zakah to the state and the state provided for the basic necessities of the needy—a society wherein all citizens enjoyed equal opportunities to seek an economic livelihood, monopolistic tendencies were discouraged, and people were God-fearing and helped each other for the sake of gaining God's pleasure. The prescribed punishment of theft is "not meant for the present-day society where you cannot get a single penny without having to pay interest; where in place of Baitul Māl [the public treasury], there are implacable money-lenders and banks," which treat the poor with brutal contempt. In a world where everyone is out for himself, where the economic system leads to the enrichment of the few at the cost of crushing poverty of the many, then "enforcing the *ḥadd* of theft would amount to protecting the ill-gotten wealth of the exploiters."[2]

As for the prescribed punishment of adultery, it is meant for a society where marriage is made easy; where traces of suggestiveness are minimised; and where virtue, piety, and remembrance of God are kept ever-fresh in the minds and hearts of people. It is not meant for a society where "sexual excitement is rampant, wherein nude pictures, obscene books and vulgar songs have become common recreation" and economic conditions and social customs have made marriage difficult generally and extremely difficult for the very poor.[3]

In his book *Punishment in Islamic Law,* the prominent Egyptian scholar and jurist, Salīm al-ʿAwā, has quoted Maududi and confirmed his analysis to the effect that Islam envisages a comprehensive scheme of values for society. What has happened is that many Muslim countries have borrowed the penal philosophy of an alien system. Under such circumstances, it is totally wrong, al-ʿAwā adds, to attempt to enforce *ḥudūd* as an isolated case. The contemporary Muslim society could hardly be said to have adopted, or even to have understood thoroughly, the Islamic way of life, and there is "no exception to this statement even in the widely-cited examples of some Muslim societies" (presumably Saudi Arabia). It does not make sense under the present circumstances to amputate a thief's hand when he might have no means of livelihood or to "punish in any way *zinā* (let alone by stoning to death) in a community where everything invites and encourages unlawful sexual relations."[4] Al-ʿAwā then concludes: "One can say that the application of the Islamic penal system under the present circumstances would not lead to the achievement of the ends recommended by this system."[5]

It is further added on a historical note that the change of circumstances is not a peculiarity of twentieth-century Muslim societies but that significant changes had begun to occur from as early as the late second century Hijrah. Al-ʿAwā thus wrote that, from a perusal of Abū Yūsuf's (d. 182/798) *Kitāb al-Kharāj*, one obtains a "clear understanding that by his time the Islamic penal system was far from being enforced."[6] In his discussion of punishments, Abū Yūsuf, who later became chief justice of the ʿAbbāsid empire under Hārūn al-Rashīd, wrote, for example, an address to the caliph, stating that "if you would order that the *ḥudūd* should be implemented, it would help reducing the prison population, frighten the transgressors and prevent crime."[7]

لو أمرت بإقامة الحدود لقل أهل الحبس واخاف الفساق وأهل الدعارة.

Abū Yūsuf obviously made a point suggesting that *ḥudūd* were being neglected, and he said so to the head of state himself.

Cheriff Bassiouni has observed that Islamic criminal justice is essentially what in contemporary terms would be called a "policy," or *siyāsah*-oriented system, in that a great deal of it is open to the input and influence of judicious policy (*siyāsah sharʿiyyah*). Bassiouni adds that Islamic law is not a rigid and repressive system as has sometimes been represented or, for that matter, even practised by some states. It is rather the opposite of that, he says. A good example, in the area of penalties, a subject that is often "misunderstood and misapplied," is the penalty of theft, for which the punishment is the cutting of the hand. But the Islamic *ḥudūd* penalties contemplate a thief who steals in a "just society, which eliminates needs," where the punishment may be appropriately deterring. The punishment is "not necessarily applied in a society which does not have the characteristics of being just."[8] In support of this view, Bassiouni refers to the following evidence in the precedent of the caliph ʿUmar b. al-Khaṭṭāb:

> It was reported to ʿUmar b. al-Khaṭṭāb that some boys in the service of Ḥāṭib Ibn Abī Baltaʿah had stolen the she-camel of a man from the tribe of Muznah. When the caliph "ʿUmar questioned the boys, they admitted the theft, so he ordered their hands to be cut. But on second thoughts he said addressing Abī Baltaʿah: "By God I would cut their hands if I did not know that you employ these boys and

> starve them so that they would be permitted to eat that which is prohibited unto them." Then he addressed their employer saying "Since I decided not to cut their hands, I am going to penalise you with a fine that shall pain you," and he ordered him to pay double the price of the she camel.[9]

The social policy orientation of Islamic criminal law can clearly be seen in the precedent and Sunnah of the Prophet himself and that of the Pious Caliphs that came after him in that they took into account the prevailing economic and political conditions of the community in the enforcement of *ḥudūd*. These were not to be enforced, the Prophet had so instructed, in times of military engagement with the enemy forces, as there would otherwise be the danger of defection, disunity, and military weakness. Concern for preventing these dangers from occurring commanded a higher priority than enforcing *ḥudūd*. We also note that the caliph ʿUmar b. al-Khaṭṭāb suspended, once again on grounds of judicious policy, the prescribed penalty of theft during the year of the famine (*ʿām al-majāʿah*) for the obvious reason that enforcing the punishment under such circumstances would be unjust and would violate the basic objective and philosophy for which the punishment of theft was validated in the first place.[10]

Fazlur Rahman was critical of the rigidity that Islamic juristic thought had webbed into *ḥudūd*. The juristic concept of *ḥudūd* deems these punishments as mandatory, a demand from God Most High that required fulfillment in an absolute manner. It is a matter of attention, Fazlur Rahman observed, and a potent issue of deep authentic research that the Qur'anic concept of *ḥudūd*, which stands for "separating or preventing," by virtue of later developments, "has been reserved to signify fixed and unchangeable punishment that is laid down in the Qur'an and Sunnah. The concept of separating or preventing limit of the Qur'an is thereby replaced by the idea of fixed punishment."[11]

The all-embracing character of Islam and its shariah were also underlined in an article by Abdullah al-Khalifah, who stated that Islam provided comprehensive instructions not only on devotional matters but also on social relations within and outside the family. It laid emphasis on enjoining good and preventing evil; kindness to parents and relatives; treating neighbours, orphans, the poor, and wayfarers properly; and taking care of one's possessions.[12] Most forms of worship in Islam are performed in public, which tends to encourage social awareness and discipline. Al-Khalifah adds that religious observances help to act as disincentives to crime, so much so that a pious Muslim person would consider criminality a violation of God's law and contrary to his/her religious beliefs. This was the case in earlier times, but it is uncertain whether a social environment of that kind still obtains in contemporary Muslim societies in the borderless age of secularity and globalisation.[13]

With reference particularly to Malaysia and whether its people were ready to implement *ḥudūd*, Mahmud Zuhdi Abdul Majid, a university professor and scholar of shariah, spoke at an international conference in Kuala Lumpur and made the observation that "Malaysia in the 20th century is not the same as the Arab lands were in the 12th century." He stressed the need for "ijtihad or innovative thinking based on the philosophy of Islam," adding that it was simplistic to think that one can implement the same Islamic laws here and now. For this will "invite failure as we will be doing something that precedes something that should have been done first."[14]

Commenting on the prescribed punishment of adultery, the learned Shaykh Yūsuf al-Qaraḍāwī has also underscored the change of environment and the temptations that modern society has created. This discussion has, on one hand, examined the high and, in some places, exorbitant costs that are incurred in marriage, dower, and wedding ceremonies and what follows these events (i.e., providing a house, furniture etc.); on the other hand, there are 101 temptations that do not fail to tax the limits of individual self-restraint. In al-Qaraḍāwī's phrase, "When there is a dramatic change of circumstances, when the door to halal (lawful) is closed and one thousand doors to *ḥarām* (unlawful) are opened...the individual is surrounded by temptations to sin. Is it then certain that justice will be served by insisting on the *ḥadd* of adultery?" Al-Qaraḍāwī made a similar comment on the prescribed punishment of theft in discussing the prevailing conditions of modern society when he wrote:

> The justice of Islam does not admit the logic that the command of God is executed on the thief as punishment for what he or she might have stolen and yet we neglect the command of God on the payment of zakah (legal alms) and the social support system (*al-takāful al-ijtimāʿī*) of Islam. There is only one verse in the Qur'an on the *ḥadd* of theft but literally dozens of verses on zakah and helping the poor.[15]

Shaykh Muḥammad al-Ghazālī has advanced a similar argument and finds certain aspects of the debate insisting on the enforcement of *ḥudūd* to be less than acceptable and convincing. "We do not dispute" wrote al-Ghazālī, "that *ḥudūd* are a part of Islam, but we find it strange that they are considered to be the whole of it."[16] To enforce *ḥudūd*, one needs to establish an Islamic political order first. Al-Ghazālī went on to write, "We wish to see these punishments enforced...but not so that the hand of a petty thief be cut while those punishments are waived in cases of embezzlement of stupendous funds from the public treasury."[17]

These and similar other considerations have led the prominent Syrian scholar, Muṣṭafā Aḥmad al-Zarqā (d. 1999), to the conclusion that the prevailing environment is unsuitable for the enforcement of *ḥudūd*. He then invokes the legal maxim of shariah that "necessity makes the unlawful permissible—*al-ḍarūrāt tubīḥ al-maḥzurāt*" (the origin of this legal maxim is Qur'anic; al-Baqarah, 2:173). Al-Zarqā further wrote: "When emergency or unavoidable situations hinder the enforcement of an obligatory command [i.e., *wājib*] then the latter may be temporarily postponed." Based on this argument, al-Zarqā concluded that *ḥudūd* may be substituted with alternative punishments until such a time when conditions are right for their proper enforcement. To quote al-Zarqā:

> When it is observed that enforcing the four *ḥudūd* offences has become unfeasible at a certain time or place, until then, it should be possible to apply an alternative punishment, and doing so does not necessarily mean abandonment of the shariah.[18]

Al-Zarqā wrote this in the 1960s, but he revisited the issue again in the revised edition of his highly acclaimed book in the 1990s. It is instructive to note that he maintained his earlier views and has even further elaborated on some of them. His views appear under the heading, "The Difficulty over the Implementation of Hudud," where he discusses the various *ḥudūd* punishments and explores their implementation prospects.[19] Al-Zarqā refers to contemporary conditions and contextualises at least three of the five *ḥudūd* punishments therein as follows:

(1) Implementation of the prescribed punishment for theft, for instance, is connected to the amount of effort the society is making to take care of the poor and the deprived in their midst and see to their needs through fair redistribution of wealth and realisation of the social support system of Islam.[20]

(2) Implementation of the prescribed punishment for adultery is also related to the care and attention given to the cleansing of society from the temptations of enticement (*fitnah*) and promiscuity. It also relates to awareness-raising among people of their religious obligations that would inculcate piety and facilitate easy access to marriage.
(3) The prescribed punishment for wine drinking similarly relates to the question of access and the restrictions imposed on its manufacture, advertisement, and trading as well as awareness-raising among people that would discourage its use.[21]

These interconnections between the vices at issue and their related punishments should be seen as prerequisites for effective implementation of *ḥudūd* under shariah.

Al-Zarqā added: "When the mass media is preoccupied by publicity and advertisements on consumption of liquor, actually informing the public on how to compare and choose the best in the available range of liquor varieties, then implementation of the proposed punishment becomes a far cry from actual reality. Similarly, when women expose their bodily beauty in the name of progress and civilisation, and when the prevailing economic system is protective of exorbitant differentials in income levels and wealth—such that the vast majority is deprived and the minute minority is privileged beyond measure, then "how can one consider implementation of *ḥudūd* under such conditions to be tantamount to correct application of the shariah? Or is this application only in name, but in reality nothing more than indulgence in doubtful exercises, even contradictions?"[22]

In a section of his 2014 book, Shaykh Bin Bayyah advances a more detailed argument for postponing the implementation of *ḥudūd*—basically under three points as follow:

(1) Shariah and religion are two distinct but separate aspects of Islam. Whereas religion is primarily dogma and faith, shariah consists of practical rules. The former is founded on decisive proof (*thubūt qaṭʿī*) of the Qur'an and *mutawātir* hadith independently of interpretation, and the practical rules stand on effective causes and conditions. Neglect of practical rules does not amount to renunciation of Islam provided it is not espoused with rejection or denial in principle. *Ḥudūd* punishments fall under practical rules, and they depend on effective causes (*asbāb*) and are enforced when causes and conditions are present and no juridical hindrance (*māniʿ*) gets in the way of their enforcement.[23]

(2) *Ḥudūd* are enforced by command of the leader, which means the head of state and Parliament. For they take responsibility based on their election and pledge of allegiance. Past leaders, including the Prophet himself and his Companions, have taken charge of the enforcement of *ḥudūd* punishments and suspended them when public interest or *maṣlaḥah* so dictated. The Prophet suspended *ḥudūd* during military engagements for fear of the soldiers defecting and joining the enemy forces. The caliph ʿUmar b. al-Khaṭṭāb suspended *ḥudūd* in the year of the famine to avoid oppression and manifest injustice. ʿUmar also did the same in the case of theft of the slaves of Hatib b. Abi Balta'ah. Saʿd b. Abī Waqqāṣ did not enforce the *ḥadd* of drinking on Abī Mahjan al-Thaqafī as he was such a fine general and successful warrior. The Caliph ʿUmar b. ʿAbd al-ʿAzīz ordered his governors to refer to him all cases of death and mutilation sentences and obtain his approval—quoting the hadith that *ḥudūd* should be suspended as far as possible in all cases of doubt (*adraʾū al-ḥudūd ʿan mā istataʿtum biʾl-shubhat*). Thus we find that in each case leaders have suspended *ḥudūd* for a specific reason or cause. When a leader is convinced that enforcing *ḥudūd* or *qiṣāṣ* would bring about greater harm than the benefit that accrues with their enforcement, then he suspends enforcement. Here Bin Bayyah mentions both Imam Abū Ḥanīfah, who spoke of *taʿṭīl*, and Imam Aḥmad Ibn Ḥanbal, who used *taʾkhīr* (postponement, suspension).[24]

(3) *Ḥudūd* punishments are suspended in the face of doubt, as per the ruling of hadith. The question Bin Bayyah raises is on what grounds/causes. Should the doubts (*al-shabbāt*), which are the effective causes of suspension, be specific? Or can the effective cause be something general? In response, Bin Bayyah mentions that some of the instances of postponement in the past were based on "Islam's interests" (*maṣlaḥat al-Islām*), which Ibn Qayyim al-Jawziyyah has also spoken about, and it is not a specific cause but a general one (resembling *ḥikmah* as opposed to *ʿillah*). We do not really have a good reason to think that our soldiers will join the enemy forces as not all Muslims are now engaged in warfare with enemies. *Ḥudūd* punishments are in principle suspended in "enemy territory" (*fī arḍ al-ʿaduww*), but then who are the enemies? And if there are enemies, how are they affecting the Muslim homeland and in what way? Here Bin Bayyah says that the Muslim world is not a monolithic entity. Some countries may be engaged in war, others may be suffering from hunger, and still others are faced with different

> levels of doubt. If a Muslim country can enforce *ḥudūd* and there is no impediment or fear of greater harm or of foreign aggression, it should enforce *ḥudūd*. If all the *ḥudūd* punishments cannot be enforced but some can be, the latter should be enforced based on the fiqh legal maxim: "What is feasible is not omitted by the omission of that which is unfeasible' (*lā yusqat al-maysūr bi-suqūt al-maʿsūr*). That said, Bin Bayyah regards the overall situation prevailing in the Muslim world as imbued with doubts of different kinds. If a country does enforce the *ḥudūd* punishments, it should make sure: (a) to assign teachers and propagators of Islam constantly to instill moral values and purity of character among people; (b) to strengthen the foundations of shariah and its comprehensive enforcement away from negative influences of secular modernity; and (c) to conduct sustained dialogue and communication with groups and parties that poison the minds of the general populace.[25]

Bin Bayyah has thus held that the enforcement of *ḥudūd* should be approved by the head of state and Parliament; that *ḥudūd* may be suspended if enforcement means that greater harm will definitely materialise; and that one size does not fit all (i.e., some countries may be able to enforce the *ḥudūd* punishments either wholly or partly, and their judgments should be based on prevailing realities).

PART TWO

Islamic Criminal Law in Malaysia

Introductory Remarks

Islamic criminal law in Malaysia that is expounded in the following pages is based mainly on developments in its two northern states of Kelantan and Terengganu and, in particular, on the State Enactments they have introduced for the purpose of introducing Islamic criminal law, including *ḥudūd* punishments, in their respective states. (For purposes of this discussion, other states of Malaysia and the federal government are referred to for context.) As of this writing, no other state of Malaysia has introduced Islamic criminal law, an Islamic state, or *ḥudūd*. Even in the two states mentioned, *ḥudūd* punishments still remain at the level of discussion and debate as relevant Enactments; though both have been duly passed by their respective state authorities, they are yet to be implemented. What follows is a review of the two Enactments and the public debate and media coverage of events concerning them.

XIX

Hudud Bill of Kelantan 1993

ISSUES IN RAPE AND *Zinā*, WITNESSES, AND CONFESSION

THE SHARIAH CRIMINAL Code (II) Bill 1993 of Kelantan (henceforth referred to as HBK) consists of seventy-two clauses and five supplementary schedules, divided into six parts—namely *ḥudūd* offences, *qiṣāṣ* (just retaliation), evidence, implementation of punishments, general provisions, and shariah court proceedings. The *ḥudūd* offences in part one appear, in turn, under the six headings of theft, highway robbery (*ḥirābah*), unlawful carnal intercourse (*zinā*), slanderous accusation (*qadhf*) of adultery (which is not proved by four reliable witnesses), wine drinking (*shurb*), and apostasy (*irtidād*).[1] This chapter reviews the provisions of HBK pertaining to *ḥudūd,* which have become the focus of public attention and debate ever since 1991, when the State Government of Kelantan announced its plans for the implementation of Islamic criminal law in that state. In November 1993 the state legislature unanimously passed HBK and the then chief minister, Nik Aziz Mat, announced that HBK "could not be implemented until the Federal Government of Malaysia made changes to the Federal Constitution."[2] This was evidently an acknowledgement that, in passing HBK, the state legislature had exceeded its jurisdiction under the federal constitution and had, as such, set the scene for a possible confrontation with the federal government, which is what actually happened.

The state government also announced that HBK "was prepared by a committee and reviewed and approved by the Jumaah Ulama [group of ulama] of the State Islamic Religion and Malay Council [MAIK] and the state Mufti after considering it from all aspects of the Islamic Shariah."[3]

The chief minister added that, by enacting HBK, the state government was "performing a duty required by Islam" and that failure to act in this regard "would be a great sin."[4] As for the question as to whether the people had accepted the state government's plan to implement *ḥudūd* laws, the then deputy chief minister, Abdul Halim, made the remarkable announcement that "the question did not arise as Muslims in the State who rejected the laws would be considered *murtad* (apostate)."[5]

The punishments that the bill has introduced read like a reproduction of the all too familiar fiqh manuals on the subject. It was even said that HBK had adopted the renowned Shāfiʿī jurist Abū l-Ḥasan al-Māwardī's (d. 450/1058) *Kitāb al-Aḥkām al-Sulṭāniyah* and merely changed it into a statute book format. The punishments so adopted range from mutilation of the hand for theft, flogging and stoning for a proven offence of adultery (*zinā*), the death punishment for terrorism (*ḥirābah*), and flogging for both wine drinking and slander (*qadhf*).

In its section on theft, HBK penalises the first offence when it fulfills all the prescribed conditions (fifteen such conditions provided under clause 7)—with amputation of the right hand from the wrist—and the second offence with amputation of the left foot (in the middle in such a way that the heel may still be usable for walking and standing). The third and subsequent offences of theft are punishable with imprisonment for such terms as in the opinion of the court are "likely to lead to repentance" (clauses 6 and 52). The punishment for banditry (*ḥirābah*) is death and crucifixion if robbery is accompanied by killing; and it is death only if the victim is killed but no property is taken away. But if the robber only takes the property without killing or injuring his victim, the punishment is amputation of the right hand and the left foot (clause 9).

Adultery is punishable by stoning to death (with stones of medium size) for a married person (*muḥṣan*) and flogging of 100 lashes, plus one-year imprisonment for the unmarried offender. Four eyewitnesses are required to prove the act. Each witness must be an adult male Muslim of just character, and witnesses are presumed to be just until the contrary is proven. The HBK also states that pregnancy on the part of an unmarried woman, or when she delivers a child, shall be evidence of adultery, which would make her liable to the prescribed punishment (clauses 1, 41, and 46). There is no further elaboration on the predicament of the male partner in adultery, especially in situations where he might have escaped arrest and cannot be interrogated or the accuracy of information about him cannot be verified.

Slanderous accusation of adultery (*qadhf*), which the accuser is unable to prove by four witnesses, carries eighty lashes of the whip, and punishment for drinking liquor based on oral testimony of two persons is whipping of not more than eighty lashes but not less than forty (clauses 13 and 22).

A Muslim (adult and sane) who is accused of apostasy is required to repent within three days, and failure to do so makes him or her liable to the punishment of death as well as forfeiture of his or her property. The offender will be free of the death sentence, even if it has been passed, if he or she duly repents, in which case his or her property will be returned but the defendant would still be liable to imprisonment "not exceeding five years" (clause 23).

The HBK provides for the establishment of a Special Shariah Trial Court consisting of three judges, two of whom shall be ulama, and a Special Shariah Court of Appeal, consisting of five judges, including three ulama. These courts are to be in addition to the shariah courts that normally operate in Kelantan. Any person who held the office of judge at the High Court or the Supreme Court may be appointed as judge of the Special Shariah Court. Similarly, ulama who hold or have held office as a chief judge (*qāḍī besar*) or mufti, or who possess equivalent qualifications, may be appointed as judges (clauses 63–68). All sentences can be appealed. And sentences are enforceable, in the case of prescribed *ḥudūd* offences, only when confirmed by the Special Appeal Court (clause 49). Finally, the *ḥudūd* punishments are all mandatory and inflexible as HBK provides that "the *ḥudūd* punishments imposed under this Enactment shall not be suspended, substituted for any other punishment, reduced or pardoned or otherwise varied or altered" (clause 48).

In March 2015 the State Legislature of Kelantan passed amendments to some of the sections of HBK 1993 that excluded non-Muslims from the purview of its implementation. These amendments have been reviewed in a separate section below. The substance of these amendments also applies to the Hudud Bill of Terengganu 2002 (HBT) as also discussed in the following section.

Differentiating rape from *zinā,* and their proofs—whether by witnesses, pregnancy, or confession—are the most widely debated issues concerning HBK and HBT and similar prevailing practices in other Muslim countries.

Ḥudūd legislation in Malaysia and elsewhere, such as in Pakistan, Nigeria, and Iran, came under criticism for their total silence over the problem of rape, the preclusion of women from being witnesses in *ḥudūd*, and the preclusion also of circumstantial evidence in the proof of *ḥudūd* crimes. While HBK has a section on adultery (*zinā*), it makes no mention of rape, presumably because rape is covered in the national Penal Code. However, HBK has not stated this explicitly and has left the subject vague. Adultery has been broadly defined as "sexual intercourse between a man and a woman who are not married to each other and such intercourse did not come within the meaning of intercourse by mistake (*waṭi shubhah*)" (clause 10, HBK). Intercourse in doubtful circumstances is when the man mistook the woman for his wife or acted in the belief that there was a valid marriage (clause 10, HBK). In the absence of a provision to separate rape from *zinā*, rape is likely to be subsumed by *zinā* and the same rules will apply to both. Thus reads clause 46(2) of HBK: "In the case of *zinā*, pregnancy or delivery of a baby by an unmarried woman shall constitute evidence on which to find her guilty of *zinā* and therefore the *ḥudūd* punishment shall be passed on her unless she can prove to the contrary." This potentially equates rape with *zinā*. While *zinā* is consensual, rape is intercourse under duress. To apply the rules of *zinā* to rape would mean that the rape victim must bring four male witnesses of just character to prove the charge against her attacker, and if she fails to produce these witnesses or proof by other means, she would herself be liable to the punishment of slander (*qadhf*). The burden of proof is thus placed on the defendant to prove that she was the victim of coercive force. "To shift the burden of proof to the woman in the case of pregnancy or delivery of a child," as one commentator noted, "is ludicrous" as she will not find the required proof. Notwithstanding the fact that this clause has been the focus of public criticism "There appears to be a doggedness on the part of the State Government to retain the Clause as it has been drafted."[6]

Another problematic aspect of the *ḥudūd* proceedings in Malaysia and many other Muslim jurisdictions is the exclusion of female witnesses in the proof of these crimes. This is an aspect of the fiqh provisions that has proven difficult to change. Yet a third issue to consider is the acceptance of pregnancy as proof of *zinā*, despite the fact that pregnancy is circumstantial evidence, which is, in principle, not admissible in *ḥudūd*. With regard to the witnesses of *zinā*, HBK provides that "each witness shall be an adult male Muslim who is *akil baligh* (adult and competent) and shall be a person who is just" (clause 41). Women have thus been disqualified to be witnesses not only in *zinā* but in all the *ḥudūd* offences. Confession, which is the only other means of proof in *ḥudūd* crimes, binds only the confessor and not any other party charged with the same offence—and it can, in any case, be retracted by the accused any time "even while he is undergoing the punishment" (clause 44). The textually prescribed proof of *zinā* by four eyewitnesses is next to impossible to produce. Then confession by the accused, whether in adultery or rape, is also retractable. Thus it becomes obvious that a woman who has either been lured into sin or raped, and who may only be able to present female witnesses, or a combination of males and females, has no prospects of proving her case.

A pregnant woman is put in a position, in the cases both of *zinā* and rape, to prove the crime against her or face prosecution for slander. Unless the man makes a confession that he can in any case retract later, the woman is doomed to be punished either for *zinā* or for *qadhf*.[7] The dilemma of the rape victim is made worse due to the fact that it is common among rape survivors not to seek medical aid immediately out of fear and shame. And it is not uncommon that the rape survivor did not struggle for fear of her own safety or the safety of others who might have been threatened along with her.[8]

Women activists and critics of HBK drew attention to the plight of rape victims in Pakistan and stated that the Pakistani experience since the passing of the Shariah Ordinance in May 1991 has shown that *ḥudūd* offences account for 60 to 70 percent of women in detention. According to 1991 figures compiled by the Karachi-based committee for the repeal of the Hudud Ordinance, more than 2,000 women were at that time in jail awaiting trial under this law. Most of them were accused of *zinā* by their relatives who were intent on keeping them in forced marriages or simply because they left home with a man of their choice. Rich landlords abused peasant women and servants, and when the latter complained of rape to the authorities, they were themselves punished because they could not find four male eyewitnesses of good character to testify for them.[9]

A charge of *zinā* against a man is provable by four male eyewitnesses or his own confession, there being no other way of proof other than these two. But the charge of *zinā* against a woman is provable by four male eyewitnesses, her confession, or (being unmarried) by pregnancy or delivery of a child. In the case of a married woman who is accused of *zinā* by her husband, HBK allows her husband, through the procedure of imprecation (*liʿān*), to disown the child, in which case the marriage will be dissolved even if the wife exercises a counteroath to rebut the accusation of *zinā* (clauses 14 and 15).[10] What follows next is an overview of the Hudud Bill of Terengganu.

XX

Hudud and Qisas Bill of Terengganu 2002

THE TERENGGANU SHARIAH Criminal Offences (Hudud and Qisas) Bill 2002 (henceforth HBT) was introduced after the 1999 general election in which the Islamic Party (PAS) won the state of Terengganu in addition to Kelantan. The HBT is a near-replica of its Kelantan antecedent. Hence this chapter's appraisal and comments on HBK 1993 also apply, mutatis mutandis, to HBT. One of the few differences of note between the two documents under review is that HBT omitted, though at a later stage, the offence of *bugha* (armed rebellion), which was included as a *ḥudūd* crime in section 4 of its original draft. This was deleted in mid-2002 at a time when Abdul Hadi Awang, then chief minister of Terengganu, tabled HBT before the Legislative Assembly of Terengganu.[1]

The state legislature passed HBT in July 2002, followed by Hadi Awang's announcement the same month that the sultan of Terengganu, Sultan Mizan Zainal Abidin, "gave his consent last week after a briefing by the state government." The chief minister said that the "enactment would be effective 30 days after it was passed even if it had not received the Sultan's consent."[2] The HBT could still not be enforced, however, due to conflicts of jurisdiction and constitutional issues.

The HBT consists of seventy-four sections and a similar chapter division and wording as that of HBK, presenting its readers with the same set of unresolved issues. The HBT goes a step further in fact to articulate some of the most controversial aspects of HBK. Sections 9(2) and 48(2) of HBT state, for instance, that a woman who reports she has been raped but does not provide clear or circumstantial evidence will be charged with *qazaf* (slanderous accusation) and liable to be flogged eighty lashes. As a proof, the victim must provide four Muslim male witnesses to the crime or, alternatively, get the rapist to make a confession. Then it is further provided that women and non-Muslims, whether male or female, cannot act as witnesses. An unmarried woman who becomes pregnant is thus assumed to have committed *zinā* even if she has been raped! Some of these rulings are also found in HBK, albeit indirectly and by implication, but HBT boldly articulated them with the inevitable consequence that the burden of proving rape is placed squarely on the victim's shoulders instead of the prosecutor. Why should a crime victim need to prove her innocence?

The HBT provisions pertaining to rape became media topics even before the bill was passed by the state legislature. The then minister of women and family development, Shahrizat Abdul Jalil, commented with reference to rape that it placed a cruel and unfair burden on the victim to be raped and then forced to bear the responsibility of proving that she was raped. "The implications will be disastrous as rape victims will avoid making reports for fear of being punished," she said. Shahrizat also stated that under the Penal Code and the Criminal Procedure Code, the burden of proving a crime lay with the public prosecutor and not the victim, as stipulated in the proposed enactment.[3] She added, "It is impossible to provide witnesses because rape usually happens in quiet and secluded places." The Malaysian Muslim Youth Movement (ABIM) did not oppose HBT in principle but proposed that the government amend its discriminatory provisions.[4] In the event that a public prosecutor fails to prove the charge beyond a reasonable doubt, the court would free the accused, but that does not necessarily mean that the plaintiff was lying and should be punished instead. Minister Shahrizat then said that approving HBT would be equivalent to giving criminals the "license to rape without providing the victims a fair and adequate defence." Shahrizat appealed to "all Terengganu women, including members of PAS women's wings" to join her ministry in protesting against the enactment. She criticised PAS for "frequently using minority and negative interpretations in handling women's issues"; it should advocate instead for interpretations that do not discriminate against anyone.[5] Ali Rustam, the then chief minister of Melaka, commented that HBT was "definitely unfair to rape victims because it is impossible for a victim to identify four witnesses who can prove that she was violated....The rape victims have already been through a lot and the Terengganu state is trying to aggravate their situation."[6]

Women's Aid Organisation director Ivy Josiah, along with another women's advocacy organisation, Sisters in Islam, also spoke in support of

Minister Shahrizat's call. The Federal Territory Wanita Malaysian Chinese Association (MCA) representative, Tai Sim Yew, and the Democratic Action Party (DAP) representative, Ng Siew Lai, all registered their criticism of HBT as being "retrogressive and contradictory to the Evidence Act 1950," saying that the Terengganu government should call for a public hearing in addition to holding seminars and forums to better inform the public.[7] Whereas Minister Shahrizat, representing the government's view and presumably that of the United Malays National Organisation (UMNO, the ruling party), suggested that HBT should be withdrawn altogether, Fauziah Salleh, chief of the Wanita (Women's) Wing of Keadilan (the Justice Party), commented that "Parti Keadilan National does not oppose the implementation of the *ḥudūd* law ... but has reservations on certain sections of the law." She called for a review of sections 9(2) and 48(2) of HBT to ensure that rape victims are treated fairly and that the burden of proof should not be on the rape victim as the bill stipulates. Fauziah Salleh added that the section on the witnesses should include DNA sampling and blood or semen samples apart from the four witnesses. She also suggested that separate sections should be added to the existing draft to deal with rape and incest.[8] Other aspects of HBT that needed to be studied, Fauziah went on to add, were the addition of a subsection to define rape under the chapter on adultery and the creation of a special section to deal with incest and rape.[9]

Dr. Lo' Lo' Ghazali, PAS's only elected woman MP and head of the *muslimat* wing, responded that only certain clauses of HBT needed to be reviewed. The state government "should amend the draft to ensure that the Bill would not discriminate against women. The issue is not to oppose the *ḥudūd* laws but to modify the wordings and legal interpretations related to rape so as not to victimise women."[10]

The then chief minister of Terengganu and PAS deputy president, Hadi Awang, responded, oddly enough, that parties opposing the *ḥudūd* laws "have no strong ground" to criticise as "they have little understanding of them." He added, however, that if necessary the state government was willing to meet with critics to clear the air: "It seems like they need some guidance on this matter," he said. With reference to the specific aspects of the public criticism of HBT, Hadi Awang responded that "the state government was already rectifying flaws on rape cases by making amendments on the final draft" before it was tabled to the next state Legislative Assembly meeting in July 2002.[11] With reference to Minister Shahrizat's critique of HBT, Hadi Awang reiterated that the Qur'an assured that women will get justice. "Under *qazaf,* the one who makes false accusations against women will be flogged 80 times. And this provision protects only women."[12]

Khalid Samad, a PAS member of Parliament, commented that "PAS cannot change at random or even at the will of members. It has a fixed basis and that's the ideology of the party, the role of the ulama, the central placing of the religion. That remains irrespective of who comes or goes."[13] The PAS's vice president, Mustafa Ali, elaborated that "the respect for *ulama* is genuine. We will continue to turn to them for guidance."[14]

Prime Minister Dr. Mahathir said that Terengganu should submit the draft to the attorney general's chamber before enforcing it: "the Attorney General would have to examine whether the proposed law is consistent with the federal laws and the concept of justice."[15] In response, Chief Minister Hadi Awang said that this was done when Kelantan wanted to implement shariah laws: "the only problem was that it never came back to the state for implementation."

On 17 June 2002, Chief Minister Hadi Awang held an open session in Kuala Lumpur to which he invited the nongovernmental organisations (NGOs), women's organisations' representatives, and others to address their queries so that he could explain HBT to them. Just before this meeting, Hadi Awang announced that the HBT provision concerning rape had been revised such that the proposed law would not be unfair to women. He also surprisingly announced that "the amendments were now classified under the Official Secrets Act and would not be made public until they are tabled."[16]

A Kuala Lumpur law firm had challenged the constitutionality of HBT before the federal court, and the chief minister's response to this was that they could take their case anywhere they want but that he was going to table HBT before the Legislative Assembly of Terengganu that was due to meet in July 2002. Then followed Dr. Mahathir's announcement that the federal government would block any attempt by the Terengganu government to implement "its so-called *ḥudūd* law."[17] Dr. Mahathir added that HBT was unjust and therefore not Islamic: "Islamic laws are fair and just," he said.

The then deputy prime minister Abdullah Badawi and the minister in the Prime Minister's Department Rais Yatim both separately commented that Terengganu also lacked the expertise to administer the proposed law. There were no competent shariah judges nor even a well-equipped police force to implement it.[18]

The then inspector general of police, Norian Mai, also followed to say that the police would not get involved with implementation of the *ḥudūd* and *qiṣāṣ* laws passed by the Terengganu state assembly, adding that the police force was governed by federal laws and, as such, could not get involved with state-approved criminal legislation.[19]

In Professor Ahmad Ibrahim's assessment, "the citizens of Malaysia, including the Muslims, are not yet convinced of the justice of the Islamic criminal law, and it may be difficult to enact the laws on the Islamic punishments."[20] He then suggested that "the [*ḥudūd*] laws should not be brought into force until all preparations needed for their implementation have been completed."[21] The preparations he referred to primarily related to the necessary amendment of the federal constitution and repeal of the Shariah Courts (Criminal Jurisdiction) Act 1965. He then suggested a voluntary approach to the issue whereby the federal government would enact "the *Ḥudūd, Qiṣāṣ, Diyat* and *Taʿzīr* laws for the purpose of promoting uniformity of laws between the states under Article 76(1)(b) of the Federal Constitution." Such a compilation would help to clarify the *ḥudūd* laws and could be adopted by the Council of Islamic Religion in the federal territories and the states.[22] It was not elaborated, however, how that model should be worked out, a challenge that remained largely unmet.

It is important, of course, that the *ḥudūd* debate is conducted in a spirit of consultation that may generate consensus, supported also by a credible jurisprudential substance and not politicised.

XXI

Problematics of the Hudud Bills

THE POLITICAL LANDSCAPE of Malaysia moved further away from the prospects of developing consensus-based solutions to *ḥudūd* issues when, in the first quarter of 2015, *ḥudūd* became a main issue that led to disintegration of the opposition coalition Pakatan into two separate parties. The splinter party, Parti Amanah Rakyat (National Trust Party), was formed under the leadership of the former deputy president of PAS, Mat Sabu, who did not attach a high priority to *ḥudūd*. The latter part of 2016 and early 2017 saw a certain rapproachement between PAS and then the ruling party UMNO over the introduction in Parliament of a Private Member's Bill (PMB) that sought to empower the State of Kelantan to implement *ḥudūd* punishments in that state. This opened a new context for the *ḥudūd* debate that is discussed below. Here we draw attention to three basic issues over the two *ḥudūd* bills. One of these is over a conflict of jurisdiction and a potential violation of the federal constitution. Then there is the issue whether Malaysia should be governed by two sets of laws, one for Muslims and the other for non-Muslims! Tension is also generated by the fact that only one (i.e., Kelantan as Terengganu is no longer ruled by PAS) of the thirteen states has charted a different path for itself in confronting the national government with difficult choices, which also raises questions over the position of non-Mulims. And lastly, the two bills under review raise questions over the wisdom of a literalist approach to the understanding of *ḥudūd* laws.

Constitutional Issues

The administration of criminal justice and the powers to enact criminal laws in Malaysia is under the purview of the Federal Government, as per

List I, 9th Schedule of the Federal Constitution, much of which is covered under the Penal Code.

Some offences under Hudud Bill of Kelantan (HBK) are also federal law offences, which raises the issue of double jeopardy. Offences such as theft, robbery, homicide, rape, causing bodily harm, and unnatural sex offences have been dealt with by the Penal Code, just as there are provisions in this code that also relate to false accusation, consumption of liquor, and contempt of religion.

In an attempt to overcome this, HBK barred any proceedings or trial under the Penal Code of a person who has been tried for the same offence under HBK (Clause 61). But then it is questionable whether this formula can resolve the conflict that HBK has given rise to in the first place. It is quite unprecedented for the laws of one jurisdiction to prohibit trial under the laws of another jurisdiction, particularly when it is the former that is exceeding the limits of its jurisdiction under the constitution.[1]

In addition, HBK creates a problematic situation when it is made applicable not only to the Muslims of Kelantan but also to non-Muslims. A non-Muslim might elect, according to HBK, "that this Enactment applies to him in respect of any offence committed by him within the state of Kelantan" (Clause 56). Notwithstanding the optional nature of this provision, it is in conflict with the state list of the constitution, which provides that the state can make laws only for "offences by persons professing the religion of Islam." Similarly, the shariah courts can have "jurisdiction only over persons professing the religion of Islam" and with respect only to matters included in the constitution (item 1 of the state list). Moreover, the option given to non-Muslims should preferably be with respect to the entire HBK and not only regarding particular offences. For it is possible that some provisions of HBK, such as those relating to retaliation (*qiṣāṣ*) or even adultery (*zinā*), are advantageous to a non-Muslim (since the proof of *zinā* is exceedingly strict under HBK). The latter should not therefore enable the non-Muslims to pick and choose only such provisions as may be favorable to them.[2]

This was acknowledged by Chief Minister Hadi Awang, who said in December 2002 that the state would not enforce Hudud Bill of Terengganu (HBT) despite having obtained Royal Assent.[3] He said that this was because Terengganu wanted to observe first how such laws were being practiced in other Islamic countries, adding that the state government would send a delegation to Saudi Arabia, Iran, and Sudan for this purpose. The

Federal Territory Mufti, Abdul Kadir Talip, also commented that PAS was ill-prepared to enforce HBT despite its ratification by the state assembly.[4]

In addition, HBK and HBT provided for a range of punishments that are in excess of the limitations Parliament has imposed on the shariah courts. The Shariah Courts (Criminal Jurisdiction) Act 1965 (Act 355), as amended in 1984, restricted the jurisdiction of these courts only to Muslims who may be tried for offences punishable with imprisonment of up to three years, fines of up to RM 5,000, whipping not exceeding six strokes, or any combination of these. The *ḥudūd* punishments are generally above these limits. It is doubtful also whether the Special Shariah Court that is envisaged in HBK could lawfully exercise its functions unless Parliament amends the provisions of the 1965 Act on jurisdictional limits.

To resolve HBK and HBT's conflict with the federal constitution, it was suggested that Parliament should pass an act using article 76A of the constitution specifically to authorize the Kelantan government to enforce the (proposed) laws.[5] In a media article entitled "Resolving the Hudud Law Dilemma," a civil society commentator noted:

> In the event the federal government declares the Hudud Bill unconstitutional, PAS will fault the federal government for obstructing Islamic law. But if the federal government gives its approval, then it stands accused of not carrying out Islamic law in the other states under its control.[6] The then Chief Minister of Kelantan, Nik Aziz, made it clear that "the Bill will not be enforced without prior approval from the federal government."[7] A government spokesman announced in the meantime that "several renowned Muslim experts who were shown a copy of the *ḥudūd* laws passed by the PAS-led Kelantan state government did not agree with the bill saying it was done in haste."[8]

Prime Minister Dr. Mahathir went on to say that the PAS version of the Hudud Bill "punishes victims while actual criminals were often let off with minimum punishment." For instance, if two people, a Muslim and a non-Muslim, committed a crime, the Muslim offender will be punished severely (e.g., having his hands chopped off) while the non-Muslim offender will escape with a light sentence (e.g., a fine or a month's imprisonment).

Mahathir declared, however, that the ruling party "UMNO did not reject *ḥudūd* laws but we (i.e., the federal Government) are rejecting the laws created by PAS to gain political mileage," thus suggesting that the ruling party and the government were not on the same page over the issue.[9]

The Shariah and Hudud Laws Committee of the Malaysian Bar Council announced in early October 1994 its finding that it had studied HBK and concluded that it was consistent with Islamic law. The committee chairman, Sulaiman Abdullah, said that the inconsistency in certain provisions between *ḥudūd* laws and the federal constitution could be overcome by amending the constitution.[10] The Kelantan chief minister, Nik Aziz, then said that "there was no reason for the Kelantan government to withdraw the *ḥudūd* law unless UMNO was willing to come up with its own version of the law." He offered the observation that "when UMNO has its own *ḥudūd* law, we can compare the two and come to an amicable agreement to choose one of the two and enforce it."[11]

The then law minister, Syed Hamid Albar, stated in a seminar paper presented in Kuala Lumpur that the federal government may introduce a new law "to check inconsistencies" in the legislation of shariah law by state governments. He added that shariah law should be legislated at the federal level and no longer treated as a state matter. The federal government would consult state governments and shariah experts, the minister added, before introducing new legislation, which he referred to as the "Hukum Syarak Act."[12] No further action was taken.

It is instructive also to note a statement by Karpal Singh (d. 2014), then an MP and chairman of the Democratic Action Party (DAP), to the effect that the prosecution must produce four witnesses to prove cases like adultery. This is sometimes impossible for the prosecution, hence "criminals will definitely opt for *ḥudūd*. *Ḥudūd* will only serve to set criminals free and lead to an increase in crime."[13] On another, evidently contrasting note, the president of Malaysia's Bar Council, Lim Chee Wee, commented that bringing *ḥudūd* into the legal system of Malaysia will mean the "importation of Islamic penal laws into laws which ought to be secular." This could give rise to discrimination in criminal justice, as it would mean that the Muslim offender "faces the possibility of stricter punishment under *ḥudūd* for the same offence compared to a non-Muslim offender."[14]

Critics have also commented concerning incest that there are more prosecutions of incest under the Penal Code than under shariah laws of various states because of the differential penalties. Plaintiffs prefer to lodge reports with the police for action under federal law. The maximum penalties for incest in shariah courts is three years in jail, a fine of RM5,000, or six strokes of the rotan.[15] Under the Penal Code, however, "anyone convicted of incest faces a mandatory minimum of six years jail and not more than 20 years and shall also be liable to whipping." The following figures were reported on incest cases in the federal courts: 1995 (173), 1996 (200), 1997 (223), 1998 (271), and 1999 (260). The number of cases in shariah courts as reported, however, was one each in 1995, 1996, 1997, 2000, and 2002. In 2003 there was also one case and one pending.[16]

Position of Non-Muslims

As already noted, the attempt in HBK and HBT to make the proposed law applicable to Muslims only, and the eclectic method proposed for it, has come under criticism. Some citizens (non-Muslims in this case) are afforded a choice that is denied to the Muslims of Kelantan and Terengganu.

Questions have also arisen over the state of the law when both Muslims and non-Muslims are involved in a case of adultery or theft. The choice of law that is envisaged in Clause 56 of HBK, for instance, gives rise to uncertainties as to which law applies in cases where the victim is of a faith different from that of a criminal or if witnesses to a crime or accomplices therein are non-Muslim.[17]

What if the other party to the offence, whether Muslim or non-Muslim, is a native of another state of Malaysia where *ḥudūd* punishments are not applied? Clearly HBK applies to every Muslim "in respect of any offence committed by him in the state of Kelantan" (Clause 56). Imagine a situation where a resident of Kelantan commits theft just outside the borders of Kelantan or if he chooses to go there for the very purpose of committing adultery, theft, and drinking liquor. Then HBK could be manipulated, and there is little that the government of Kelantan could do to prevent that.

Shariah itself does not provide for such choices, because in most of the *ḥudūd* crimes a difference of religion does not affect the unified application of the law. The only exemptions found in shariah are with regard to the consumption of liquor, which is not an offence with respect to a non-Muslim, and there is no inconsistency in this case as drinking alcohol does not necessarily involve a victim. The same notion applies to apostasy, which cannot be committed by a non-Muslim.

Furthermore, HBK provides that "every person who abets or assists or conspires or plots for the commission of such offence shall be guilty of that offence and shall be liable to be punished with imprisonment as *taʿzīr* punishment for a term not exceeding ten years" (Clause 57). The terms "abets," "assists," "conspires," and "plots" are broad enough to comprise every possible case in which a non-Muslim might be involved in the perpetration of a *ḥudūd* offence. So in reality HBK is applicable to both Muslims and non-Muslims, especially in cases of abetment and conspiracy, only that with respect to the non-Muslim party and with regards to *ḥudūd,* such as cases of adultery and slander (*zinā* and *qadhf*), the punishment is reduced to *taʿzīr* punishment of up to ten years' imprisonment. But then ten years is off limits according to the stipulated three years of the shariah courts' jurisdiction.

In a Kuala Lumpur seminar held prior to the publication of HBK, of which the present writer was a participant, a non-Muslim speaker stated that "Malaysian non-Muslims fear the imposition of the Shariah," adding that "if less than enlightened and principled understandings of Islam are used to justify attitudes toward, or the treatment of, non-Muslims that fall far short of the Qur'anic ideals...how much worse—we are entitled to wonder—may things become once Shariah law, or rather a certain limited version or understanding of it, is enforced in this country."[18] In voicing their concerns, the non-Muslim community leaders have on the whole spoken positively of the Qur'anic ideals of justice and equality, as well as "the impressive cultural openness, inclusiveness and cosmopolitanism of Islam," but they have warned against restrictive and legalistic approaches towards the implementation of those ideals.[19]

Wan Abdul Muttalib Embong, the State Executive Council member of Terengganu who was on the committee that drafted HBT, was presented with a question: "Is there an Islamic model that allows people of other religions to set up their own legal systems?" Wan Muttalib replied, "You can't come under different systems. One system must provide for all, otherwise you have a state within a state. If the Buddhists start saying they want their own law and their own courts and the Christians say the same, then we will have war."[20]

It may be said, in conclusion, that notwithstanding its Clause 56, which confines the application of HBK to the Muslim residents of Kelantan, Clause 57 tends to cast doubt on on that position. Since every person who abets, assists, conspires, or plots in the perpetration of a *ḥudūd* offence stands guilty of that offence, much would seem to depend on the attitude of judges and law enforcement agencies of Kelantan and Terengganu toward interpretation. Lastly, although the established fiqh across the leading schools of Islamic law precludes the applications of the prescribed punishment of drinking on non-Muslims, Clause 22 of HBK does not stipulate so, and when this clause is read together with Clause 57, an anomaly might emerge in that drinking (*shurb*) may not be an offence for a non-Muslim; yet abetment, plot, conspiracy, or assistance by a non-Muslim in the perpetration of *shrub* may well be held to be a punishable offence.

XXII

The Ḥudūd *Debate Continued*

UPDATE 2012–2017

TO ENABLE SHARIAH courts to deal with cases of *ḥudūd, qiṣāṣ,* and *diya,* it will be necessary to amend the constitution and to repeal or amend the Shariah Courts (Criminal Jurisdiction) Act 1965.[1] The constitution can only be amended according to certain procedures, but the federal government has not given a clear indication of its willingness to initiate them.

Politicisation of juridical issues has thus become an obstacle in the way of *ijtihād*-oriented efforts. The then Prime Minister Najib Razak was right to say that consensus-based solutions are wanting: "That is why we need ulama to conduct an in-depth study on the viability of implementing *ḥudūd* in the country and to come up with ijtihad and consensus on the matter. We need to make sure that justice, which is the ultimate goal of Islamic law, can be delivered through *ḥudūd.*"[2]

In October 2013 the minister responsible for religious affairs in the prime minister's department, Jamil Khir Baharom, announced that a technical committee would be formed at the federal level to study the implementation of *ḥudūd* in Kelantan.

On 18 March 2015, it was announced that the state legislature had passed the *ḥudūd* law amendments. The Kelantan chief minister, Ahmad Yakob, said that these amendments meant that Hudud Bill of Kelantan (HBK) applies to normal (*mukallaf*) Muslims of eighteen years of age and above committing offences in Kelantan. The initial provision that accorded non-Muslims the option to be tried under the 1993 Enactment was abolished. Consequently, the Islamic criminal law cannot be applied to non-Muslims. Also amended was Section 15(2) of HBK by adding the provision for the *taʿzīr* penalty for sodomy offences on the wife. The amendments also involved section 46 by removing section 46(2) on *qarīnah* or proof of adultery for pregnant women without husbands. The fourth amendment was on the changing of names of courts due to certain new developments in the judiciary.[3] The 2015 amendments also provided, regarding theft, that if the thief became owner of the property before the judgment he would be exempted from the prescribed punishment of theft, although he could still be made liable to *taʿzīr*. Similarly, a thief with only one hand was exempted from losing his other hand. In the case of adultery and sodomy, the new amendments provided for admissibility of testimony (*shahādah*) and evidence (*bayyinah*) in the proof of these offences. Section 46(2) of HBK 1993, which admitted pregnancy and childbirth as proof of *zinā*, was repealed due to the pressure of public opinion on the issue. The 2015 amendments also abolished the provisions of HBK 1993 concerning lesbianism, necrophilia, and bestiality (*musāḥaqah, ityān al-mayyitah,* and *ityān al-bahimah,* respectively). These offences were previously punishable under *taʿzīr* but were now abolished as they were covered by the Penal Code.

It will be noted that the four *ḥudūd* offences mentioned (adultery, drinking, slander, and apostasy) were already present in the shariah criminal codes of most other states, but what set HBK apart is the stiffer punishments for them. For instance, those guilty of drinking (*shurb*) can be punished with forty to eighty lashes, while other states can only punish the same offence with up to six lashes.[4]

A 2014 Gallup Survey (25–31 May) by a state agency in Kelantan revealed that 91.7 percent of the 8,940 Kelantan residents surveyed wanted the *ḥudūd* to be implemented. The survey was conducted after the minister, Jamil Baharom, had announced that "the federal government would support the state's efforts to enforce *ḥudūd*."[5]

Azhar Abdullah, a member of the joint *ḥudūd* technical committee, explained at a forum on *ḥudūd* at Universiti Malaya (1 April 2015) that of all the *ḥudūd* offences, only four—namely adultery, liquor drinking, slander, and apostasy, which are not in the Penal Code—could be implemented. As for theft, murder, and assault, since these are covered in the Penal Code, they will be left out.

The de facto law minister and MP from Sarawak, Nancy Shukri, announced, however, that there was hardly a realistic chance for the proposed Private Member's Bill (PMB) to be adopted, for it was "impossible to implement the Islamic penal code" when provisions for criminal offences were already available in the Penal Code. Besides, "it will never get a single vote from Sarawak lawmakers in Parliament."[6] Another cabinet minister,

Nazri Aziz, said that *ḥudūd* could only be implemented by amending the federal constitution, and this would require a two-thirds majority in Parliament: "No need to dismiss something that will not happen," he said.[7]

Tun Abdul Hamid, the former chief justice, commented that the Kelantan "State Government's strategy is set to make the law first. Then it will try to get the approval of the Parliament under Article 76A(1)." The key question is whether the state legislative assembly can make the law without the prior approval of Parliament. "In my opinion, no, because at the date the State Assembly had no jurisdiction to do so. . . .To me, this law is null and void."[8] Even if subsequent permission is given, it will not make the law a valid law. Supposing that Parliament gives permission, the offences involved will fall under the jurisdiction of the civil courts and will not be included in offences under the State List, because the Ninth Schedule of the Federal Constitution has not been amended to transfer such offences from the Federal List to the State List. Hence the law cannot be made applicable to Muslims only, as is often said by its advocates in Kelantan, simply because it violates article 8 of the federal constitution.[9]

Tun Hamid added that, while in other states criminal law is under federal jurisdiction, applicable to both Muslims and non-Muslims and administered by the civil courts, in Kelantan part of it would be under jurisdiction of the state. Thus it would be applicable only to Muslims and administered by the shariah court, while another part would remain under federal jurisdiction, applicable to both Muslims and non-Muslims and administered by the civil courts. "Is that what the State and federal Governments wish?" Hamid asked.[10]

The then former prime minister, Tun Mahathir, also commented that the PAS ambition to enact *ḥudūd* laws is "used as a ploy to win votes." To create two sets of laws, one for Muslims and the other for non-Muslims was fundamentally unjust "and against the principles of Islam."[11]

On a broader note, the sultan of Perak, Dr. Nazrin Muizzuddin Shah, called for the country's laws to be infused with justice and fairness. Any law without this commitment would fail to fulfil its objectives. Furthermore, the failure to ensure that the law adapts to the times would result in the law becoming either irrelevant or a hindrance to development potentially leading to inequality within the society.[12]

Ḥudūd made headlines again in May 2016 when the PAS president, Abdul Hadi Awang, tabled a Private Member's Bill (PMB) in Parliament proposing to enhance the powers of shariah courts. Hadi Awang added, however, that the PMB was not meant to introduce *ḥudūd* but to expand the range of punishments that the shariah courts would be able to impose. A PMB only needs the support of a simple majority—112 MPs (of a total of 222 MPs) —or else the majority of MPs sitting at the time the bill comes up for a vote. Additionally, for this bill to become law in Kelantan, the federal constitution (item 1 of List II of the Ninth Schedule) and its Article 76A would need to be amended to extend the legislative powers of the state to enable the handling of criminal cases in shariah courts. And then Article 8 on "Equality" may also call for amendment so as to allow differential treatment of citizens on grounds of religion.[13]

A motion was consequently placed, as a result of Hadi Awang's initiative, on Parliament's working agenda to amend the relevant provisions of Act 355 of 1965. The PAS was in the meantime split into two parties, and the splinter party named Parti Amanah Negara (National Trust Party or PAN, founded 16 September 2015) toned down demand for the implementation of *ḥudūd*. The PAN president Mat Sabu said that "PAN wants to see other issues resolved first and when conditions are conducive to implement the *ḥudūd*, they will do it. To them, there are many considerations [to be taken care of] before implementing *ḥudūd*."[14]

Due to a new rapprochement between PAS and UMNO, the latter did not object to the PMB to expand the powers of shariah courts to impose penalties "to an amount and time period deemed acceptable."[15] Tun Abdul Hamid, former chief justice, commented in the meantime that no bill as such had been made for the purpose: "All we know is the motion which is very brief. So all the discussions are based on the motion," he said.[16] The motion in question seeks to replace section 2 of Act 355 with a new section, which reads:

> The Shariah court shall have jurisdiction over persons professing the religion of Islam in respect of offences regarding matters listed in item 1 of the State List of the Ninth schedule of the Federal Constitution.

A new section (2A) is also proposed to be added, and it provides:

> In dealing with the criminal law under Section (2), the Shariah court is entitled to impose penalties allowed by the Shariah in relation to offences listed under the section mentioned above, other than the death penalty.

All that is needed then is for the state legislature to make a law that empowers the shariah courts to impose punishments permitted by Islamic law. The allegation many have made, Tun Hamid added—that the proposed amendment has nothing to do with *ḥudūd* punishments and is only concerned with court jurisdiction matters—is therefore no more than an empty assertion. Yet even if Hadi Awang's motion succeeds, it remains doubtful, according to another observer, whether the Kelantan government can actually implement the 1993 Enactment and its 2015 amendments.[17]

Then almost unexpectedly came a government announcement on 30 March 2017 that it will not table in Parliament the proposed amendments to Act 355. This was a decision of Barisan Nasional (BN) (the coalition government), which was arrived at in the BN supreme council meeting. The then Prime Minister Najib Razak, who chaired that meeting, said that this was in line "with our policy that BN makes decisions based on consensus," adding that "the bill would consequently remain as a PMB which PAS President and MP Abdul Hadi Awang had moved in Parliament on May 26 last year."[18] It was earlier reported that the government would take over Hadi's PMB and make it a government bill to be tabled in Parliament. Several BN leaders from Sabah and Sarawak (mainly Christian) had voiced objections to the bill, while the presidents of MCA and Gerakan (Chinese) parties had threatened to quit their position in the cabinet if the bill was passed in Parliament. It was further explained by the UMNO information chief, Annuar Musa, that there were still procedural steps and other matters that needed to be done to amend the act.[19] The coalition government was evidently faced with the threat of a split from within and decided therefore to abandon its planned action. The *ḥudūd* debate in Malaysia remained inconclusive as a result.

Then came the somewhat unexpected announcement in July 2017 to say that the State Legislative Assembly of Kelantan passed an amendment to its Shariah Criminal Procedure Enactment 2002 to allow public caning for four shariah offences of *zinā*, false accusation of *zinā*, sodomy, and alcohol consumption—to be applicable to Muslims only. Nassuruddin Daud, State Da'wah, Information and Liaison committee chairman, stated that the amendments have yet to be assented to by the sultan of Kelantan and duly gazetted. Previously the offenders were caned in the prison, but now this will be done in a public place and it will be the first time for Kelantan to practice public caning. Daud added that a total of thirty-three amendments were passed mostly on technical matters: how caning is to be carried out by a prison warden, that it must be witnessed by a Muslim doctor and at least four Muslim witnesses, what parts of the body that can be caned, the position of men and women when they are caned, how the caning is carried out, and when it can be stopped. "If the doctor sees that the offender is lifeless or in pain after receiving one or two strokes of the rotan, he can order the warden to stop the caning."[20]

It was further announced that public caning will start in two months at which time the gazetting procedure is expected to be completed. The main purpose of public caning was to educate the public, especially the offenders, "as we do not want them to repeat the crime."[21]

Early reactions to these changes were supportive from the state Muftis and government leaders, whereas the Chinese voiced criticism. The Malaysian Chinese Association Religious Harmony Bureau chairman, Ti Lian Ker, commented that PAS was trying to gain political mileage in the runup to the next general election by trying to appease the Muslim electorate, adding also that such punishment fell under the purview of the federal law.[22]

The then deputy prime minister, Ahmad Zahid Hamidi, said that Kelantan had the right to pass the amendment on public caning as they have the majority (in the Kelantan government). He added that public caning would apply only to Muslims and that Parliamentary approval was not required because they are not adding to the number of strokes in caning. Hence Kelantan did not have to wait for the RUU 355 (Shariah Courts Criminal Jurisdiction Act 1965) to be passed in Parliament first.[23]

A minister in the prime minister's department, Jamil Khir [Baharom], said that the Kelantan government's plan for public caning should not be turned into polemics as it merely shifts the venue of punishment from inside the prison to outside it, and it is only applicable to Muslims.[24]

The mufti of Perak, Harussani Zakaria, said that the purpose of public caning was to serve as a reminder to other people. The cane used under shariah law is not the same as in civil cases (canes made of rotan). Under shariah law, a thin cane is used and the person executing the punishment will raise only his forearm when performing the punishment. Zakaria added that public caning had already been implemented in Aceh Indonesia and Saudi Arabia.[25]

PART THREE

Islamic Criminal Law in Other Muslim Countries

Part three provides an overview of developments on Islamic criminal law in fourteen Muslim majority countries. Unlike Malaysia that was covered in greater details and as a showcase in part two, part three provides a general picture of developments on *ḥudūd* and other aspects of Islamic criminal law. But before entering a country-by-country survey, the introduction that immediately follows gives an outline of developments in the colonial and then postcolonial periods pertaining to Islamic criminal law. The colonial legacy presented issues and also influences that provided a backdrop to subsequent developments.

XXIII

Introductory Remarks

THIS INTRODUCTION IS presented in four sections that begin with an overview of Islamic criminal law reform in the nineteenth and twentieth centuries with reference to early developments in Ottoman Turkey, India, and Egypt. Section two is about the Indian Penal Code 1860 that has remained influential in a number of Muslim countries ever since. Section three reviews Islam and Islamic law in the post–Soviet Central Asian republics, and the last section follows on with the emergence of Islamic revivalism in the neighbouring Iran and Afghanistan. These four sections provide a backdrop to the rest of part three that consists of a survey of developments in Islamic criminal law in fourteen Muslim majority countries.

Early Reforms in Ottoman Turkey, India, and Egypt

In the Islamic world, reform of criminal law during the nineteenth century took three forms: complete abolition of Islamic criminal law; reform of Islamic criminal law; and reform of *siyāsah* justice. The first was followed in most colonial states. Here Islamic criminal law was simply abolished and replaced by Western statute law. This was, for instance, done by the French in North Africa. The French penal code, with some changes to adapt it to the colonial situation, was introduced in the Muslim territories over which the French had acquired control.

The second type of reform is the one followed by the British in India and, a century later, in Northern Nigeria. Here, Islamic criminal law continued to be applied but was subjected to a gradual process of change until, in the end, it was abolished and replaced by statute law. This was part of British colonial policy, which emphasised ruling through the existing power structures. As a result, a type of criminal law emerged that was Islamic only in name. In both countries it was in the end replaced by Western-inspired penal codes.

In India, between 1790 and 1807, the British transformed Islamic criminal law totally. Private prosecution was replaced with prosecution by the state. Anyone who had committed an act of willful homicide could be sentenced to death, regardless of the circumstances. The heirs of the victim in cases of homicide, and the victim himself in cases of wounding, could no longer claim blood money. Culpable homicide and wounding would be punished with imprisonment, whereas in those cases where, under Islamic law, there was liability for the blood money, there would be neither compensation nor imprisonment. The criminal law that was thus created was only formally abolished when, in 1861, the new Indian Penal Code (IPC) was promulgated.[1] The IPC remained influential and was adopted with some modifications by countries such as Pakistan, Malaysia, Nigeria, and Singapore.

The third method is the one chosen by independent Muslim countries with modernising elites, notably the Ottoman Empire and Egypt. Here, the states focused on the reform of *siyāsah* justice and subjected it to some form of the rule of law by codifying it and by creating specialised courts to apply it, whereas Islamic criminal law, without modifications, continued to be implemented through the shariah courts. This dual system of criminal law enforcement came to an end in Egypt in 1883, with the wholesale introduction of French law and creation of a new national court system, and in the Ottoman Empire in 1917, when the new Code of Shariah Procedure of 1917 removed the jurisdiction over homicide and wounding from shariah courts.

Reform of criminal law in the Ottoman Empire was heralded by the 1839 Gulhane Decree, which led to the promulgation of a Penal Code in 1840. The most important feature of this law was the principle of legality: Art. 12(2) stipulated that punishment shall be inflicted only according to the law and that persons against whom nothing has been proven during a trial shall not be punished. Torture during investigation and general confiscation of the property of offenders were outlawed. The aim of the law was to restrict the arbitrariness of *siyāsah* justice that was to be generally regulated by statutory law.[2]

In some independent Muslim states that fell outside the Western sphere of influence, or where the central government was very weak, a traditional system of Islamic justice continued to function for a long time—as in Saudi Arabia and Yemen—and to a large extent also in Iran and Afghanistan.[3]

Notwithstanding how Islamic criminal law took a different path to modernisation in British India, the Ottoman Empire, and Egypt, the results of the reforms introduced were, in the end, quite similar: the emergence of a body of authoritative and clearly articulated criminal law. In Egypt and the Ottoman Empire, the severe fixed punishments of amputation and stoning to death became obsolete without any express government decree. This happened during the first half of the nineteenth century. Documentary evidence with regard to Egypt shows that, even if lower *qāḍīs* sentenced a defendant to such penalties, higher courts would find grounds to reverse such sentences. They were never officially abolished due to the sensitivity of the subject and likelihood of strong religious opposition. Apparently these considerations did not exist with regard to doing away with flogging and caning, which were abolished by decree in the Ottoman Empire in 1858 and in Egypt in 1861.[4] Egyptian law was based on Islamic law and civil law (particularly French codes). After attaining independence from the Ottoman Empire in matters of legal and judicial administration in 1874, judicial reform began in 1875 and led to the establishment of mixed national courts. Subsequent attempts in Egypt to adopt Islamic criminal law remained inconclusive. Between 1976 and 1982 various parliamentary committees were set up to draft Islamic laws, including an Islamic criminal code. This was partly to demonstrate the Islamic credentials of the state and to repel the ideological attacks of the Islamic opposition. But with the assassination of President Anwar Sadat in 1981, the political climate changed and legislative projects were also shelved.

The Indian Penal Code 1860

The draft of the Indian Penal Code (IPC) was prepared by the First Law Commission, chaired by Thomas Babington Macaulay. Its basis is the law of England, but elements were also derived from the Napoleonic Code and from Edward Livingston's Louisiana Civil Code of 1825. The IPC was passed into law on 6 October 1860 and came into operation on 1 January 1862.

After independence, the IPC was inherited by Pakistan (known as the Pakistan Penal Code) and (now) Bangladesh, formerly part of British India. It was also adopted wholesale by the British colonial authorities in Burma, Sri Lanka, Malaysia, Singapore, and Brunei, and it remains the basis of the criminal codes in those countries. David Moussa Pidcock, who wrote the book *Napoleon and Islam*, interestingly said that 96 percent of the Napoleonic Code came from the rulings of Imam Mālik. If there is merit in this claim, it must have something to do with Napoleon's Egyptian campaign.[5] The adoption of the IPC thus transcended religion: Pakistan, Bangladesh, Brunei, and Malaysia are not only Muslim-majority countries but also Islamic countries. Sri Lanka and Myanmar (formerly Burma) have Buddhism as their state religion, while Singapore is a modern cosmopolitan nation-state.

Among the Islamic countries that inherited the IPC from the British rule, Malaysia is "happy to keep it as it was introduced except for the unavoidable amendments necessitated by time and place." Bangladesh too seems to have made little changes to the IPC. Brunei, in its quest to be shariah-compliant, had been struggling for the past thirty years to Islamize its penal code, and it introduced some changes in 2015. On the other hand, Pakistan, where politics play a more powerful role than in Brunei, has gone further. It has Islamized its Penal Code.[6]

One would have thought that penal codes would have been replaced totally with new Islamic criminal law. Yet without going into details, in Pakistan, the IPC remains intact. The name, the language, the structure, and the style, even the contents, remain unchanged. They were retained presumably because they were not contrary to shariah.

New sections were added, however, to provide for the introduction of shariah punishments in Pakistan like *qiṣāṣ*, *diya*, *arṣh*, *ḍaman*, and *taʿzīr* (Section 53). There are major amendments in Chapter XVI, "Of Offences Affecting the Human Body." And there are also lengthy additions on causing hurt and the various punishments they invoked.[7]

Islam in Central Asia

Islam reached Central Asia during the mid-seventh century, and within some fifty years, Transoxiana was co-opted into the Islamic Caliphate. The roots of Islamic faith were further strengthened during the Karakhanid and Seljuk empires. Central Asian Islamic scholarship during the medieval period was strong and distinctive and left an indelible mark on the Muslim world. In the eighteenth century, Tsarist penetration started in the region, and the conquest of the Khanates began with the fall of Tashkent in 1865. Bukhara and Khiva became protectorates in 1868 and 1873, respectively; Kokand was integrated into the Russian Empire in 1876, and Turkmenistan in the 1880s.

The Soviet Union was a federation of fifteen communist republics, which lasted from 1922 until its dissolution in 1991. Six of the fifteen republics had a Muslim majority: Azerbaijan SSR, Kazakh SSR, Kirghiz SSR, Tajik SSR, Turkman SSR, and Uzbek SSR. A large number of Tatar Muslims also lived in Siberia and other regions. The majority of the Muslims within the USSR were Sunnis, and about 10 percent were Shii Muslims who mostly lived in Azerbaijan. An estimated fifty million people identified themselves as Muslims. After 1991, Central Asian Muslims who had been forced to renounce or hide their religion for seventy-four years were able to reconnect themselves with their Islamic past. Yet Soviet law forbade Islamic religious activity outside of the mosques and Islamic schools.[8]

There is an Islamic revival in Central Asia, which is, however, almost exclusively concerned with matters of ritual knowledge, religious beliefs, and practices and not with legal or political mobilisation. The general public is somewhat isolated from the world outside the former Soviet orbit. The former Communist and now nationalist ruling elites remained hostile toward Islamic political ideals and movements.[9] As Nazif Shahrani commented, the most significant achievement of Soviet colonial rule in Central Asia may well have been the extent of its success in "colonising the minds and consciousness of the people of Central Asia." The predicament of Central Asians under Soviet rule was succinctly described by Islam Karimov, the then president Uzbekistan in 1991, who said, "endowed properties belonging to Muslim religious institutions [*awqaf*] were confiscated, Muslim shariah laws abrogated, and mosques, madrasah-maktabs (mosque schools) and shrines were destroyed or desecrated."[10]

Broadly, Islamic law was in force in these republics until 1920 but ceased to be applied under Soviet rule. At the present time, officially Islamic law has no influence on civil or criminal laws in almost all the Muslim republics. In these republics, civil law and criminal law rely largely on Soviet law with minor changes since independence. There is also no evidence of informal shariah courts or Qur'anic punishments (*ḥudūd*).[11]

Iran and Afghanistan

Two momentous events occurred in 1979, one of which was the Soviet invasion of Afghanistan and the other the Islamic revolution of Iran. Both events provided fresh impetus for Islamic revivalism and gave rise, in turn, to demands for an Islamic state and *ḥudūd* in many Muslim countries.

The renewed Islamic consciousness of the early 1980s was mostly at the expense, or partial replacement, of ideologies espousing Arab nationalism and socialism in one form or another. Resistance to the Soviet occupation gained momentum in Afghanistan mainly from an Islamic platform. The Islamic revolution in Iran was similarly launched in the name of Islam, which, like most revolutions, gave rise to political uncertainty and upheaval, as was also true in the case of Afghanistan. The events in Iran and elsewhere in the Muslim world were not merely a reaction against the domination and culture of the West but also part of a broader movement that was driven by a multitude of factors.[12]

These factors included disenchantment with secular models of development in many postindependence Muslim nations, in particular socialist models. The calls to implement Islamic criminal law (ICL) in the Muslim world were part of a broader quest for dignity and identity and rejection of the colonial legacy. In what follows, we look at some Muslim countries that tried in one way or another to implement shariah punishments. An examination of the details shows that almost each one of these cases have faced challenges that came in the way of effective implementation of the punishments. The number of countries reviewed here is fairly limited. An overview is thus provided of related developments in the Indonesian province of Aceh, the Islamic Sultanate of Brunei Darussalam, the Kingdom of Saudi Arabia, and the Islamic Republics of Afghanistan, Pakistan, Iran, Mauritania, Yemen, and Maldives. We also look at *ḥudūd*-related developments in the Republics of Sudan, Nigeria Libya, the United Arab Emirates (UAE), and Qatar.

This comparative review attempts, in each case, to ascertain milestones of development and significant positions taken on the ICL, in particular *ḥudūd*, with coverage, as far as possible, of actual or suggested measures and plans. As has been mentioned, *ḥudūd* punishments tend to touch on religious sensitivities in most Muslim countries and are mostly politicised, and thus they pose difficulties as to the accuracy of available information one can secure on them. Another factor is opposition from the international community and human rights activists. In places where shariah courts and jurisdictions exist to adjudicate *ḥudūd*, judges and lawyers exhibit reservations on discussing issues openly. Judges are also reluctant to pass *ḥudūd* sentences due to their severity and in some cases, as in Malaysia, due to constitutional issues and insufficiency or lack of jurisdiction. The picture one gets is thus uneven in that each country presents a set of dynamics often peculiar to its own sociopolitical environment.

Many of the countries reviewed also tend to have a two-track system of courts consisting of shariah courts and civil courts, the latter of which are courts of general jurisdiction in such countries as Brunei, Malaysia, Nigeria, the Sudan, and Pakistan. They mostly tend to have two sets of laws as a result: a penal code that is meant for the whole populace, Muslims and non-Muslims alike; and a separate set of shariah laws, inclusive sometimes but not always of *ḥudūd*. Complications tend to arise over conflicts of jurisdiction as well as legacy issues due to the domination of the common law system that still characterises the judicial systems in these countries. Unresolved issues are thus encountered in regard to the methods of proof that differ, at least partially, in shariah and civil courts. These are also among the issues that also lead to excessive delays in the settlement of disputes before the courts.

On a broader note, the three models of nineteenth-century developments concerning Islamic criminal law in the Muslim world, discussed above (i.e., total exclusion of shariah, selective reform, and *siyāsah* justice) also influenced subsequent developments in the postcolonial period. Only after the so-called Islamic revivalism of the latter part of twentieth century, total exclusion of shariah was effectively abandoned, and a mixed pattern of selective reform of shariah and modern law side by side became the principal approach. Constitutionalism, codification and rule of law were continued with renewed emphasis, but new reforms also exhibited greater harmony with shariah. A blend of Islamic and British law came about in India that was known as Anglo-Muhammadan law. Basic tenets of Western law that influenced developments also included the principle of legality: there can be no crime or punishment except by law (*nullum crimen sine lege, nulla poena sine lege*), nonretroactivity of laws, and the principle of territoriality of jurisdiction.[13]

An overview of developments in Islamic criminal law, especially *ḥudūd* crimes, that follows begins with Aceh and proceeds with Brunei Darussalam, Saudi Arabia, Afghanistan, and a number of other Muslim-majority countries.

XXIV

Qanun Jinayat *of Aceh, Indonesia*

THIS RELATIVELY DETAILED account of the introduction of *Qanun Jinayat* (Islamic criminal law) in Aceh reveals many similarities with the experience of HBK 1993 of Malaysia. Yet unlike Malaysia, which is a federal state with various states that have their own legislative assemblies, Indonesia is a centralised administration, and only Aceh has been granted a special autonomous status under the Aceh Special Autonomy Law of 1999. This was further elaborated later in the 2006 Law No. 11 on Aceh Government, explicitly stating that the government of Aceh has the authority to organise religious life in accordance with the Islamic religion for Muslims without disrupting interreligious harmony. A dual system of civil courts with general jurisdiction, and shariah courts with specialised jurisdiction obtains in both countries, and they both have criminal or penal codes that apply generally to the whole of their respective countries and also cover some *ḥudūd* crimes—hence there is a degree of duplication of laws in both scenarios.

Indonesian law on shariah is generally vague, however, and has developed in different directions. The constitution of Indonesia 1945 states that the Muslim-majority nation is secular, but the national parliament in Jakarta in 2003 passed legislation that allowed shariah to be implemented for Aceh's five million populace. Since then several local district governments in Indonesia have in one way or another followed suit. Although Indonesia has 190 million Muslims, the country has historically been liberal in many ways, allowing bars, nightclubs, and the sale of alcohol in the country.[1] Reports in 2015 indicate, however, that Indonesia has also introduced restrictions on the sale of alcohol in retail shops around the country on health and moral grounds, due to concerns that underage drinking is being fueled by the wide availability of alcohol in local neighbourhoods. Fahira Idris, a lawmaker and founder of the National Anti-Alcohol Movement, likened alcohol to a "machine killing our youth."[2]

Reports further added, however, that the Trade Minister Rachmat Gobel "was shouted at" during a meeting with community leaders in the mainly Hindu-populated island of Bali and "has now pledged to ease the restrictions on the island to ensure street vendors can still sell beer at the beach."[3]

Aceh is in many ways an exception as it is said to be Indonesia's most devout Islamic province, having first received Islam through Arab and Indian traders sometime around 800 CE. It was from here that Islam spread to the rest of the archipelago from about the thirteenth century onwards. That may explain why Aceh was nicknamed *Serambi Mekkah* ("Veranda of Mecca") by Arab traders. Islam has consequently become deeply entrenched in Aceh society, which is described as locally defined, externally focused, and open to external influences of a more tolerant type.

Like most of Southeast Asia, Islamic Aceh is predominantly Sunni and follows the Shāfiʿī school or *madhhab*, except for a minority of about 15 percent Shia; yet there are differences of interpretation among the Sunni Shāfiʿīs within Aceh. Residents of the somewhat remote west Aceh tend to be more conservative, whereas liberal currents of opinion are found within the densely populated eastern and northern parts of the province.[4]

One of the key characteristics of the Aceh province is that the moral basis of social codes of behaviour derives from Islam. Islamic values and laws, spread and formulated by the ulama, have been a way of life of the Aceh people since the times of Aceh Sultanates.[5] Yet the status of Islam in Aceh is somewhat confused by what some observers have called "the externally driven introduction of shariah," which included Islamic legal codes, primarily referring to moral issues, along with the existing civil laws.[6]

On 14 September 2009, two weeks before its tenure was due to expire, the outgoing legislature of Banda Aceh passed the *Qanun jinayat* (Islamic criminal law). By doing so, the outgoing state legislature "breached fundamental democratic principles,"[7] in that it passed legislation just before the swearing in of a newly elected legislature. The commonly expressed view was that shariah was imposed as a "divide and conquer" tactic by the Indonesian military at the peak of the Aceh war. The idea was to create a division between the Free Aceh Movement (Gerakan Aceh Merdeka or GAM), which saw its war as one of national liberation and not over Islam, and the province's otherwise supportive religious leaders and Imams, who would be obliged to accept shariah. The *Qanun jinayat* consequently became moot among the Acehnese since it was not reflective of the expressed choice of the people of Aceh. The failure to sign *Qanun jinayat* into law or the possibility of its ultimately being rejected by the new provincial legislature raised almost no public concern in Aceh. It was not an issue in the February 2012 gubernatorial election campaign either, indicating that no one seeking election for public office would risk his reputation with such a sensitive issue.

However, *Qanun jinayat* was approved by the Aceh House of Representatives, known as DPRA, in September 2014, in order to implement shariah.[8] This *Qanun jinayat* is a revised version of the 2009 *qanun*, which became controversial due to the introduction of stoning to death as a punishment for adultery. Under the *Qanun jinayat* 2014 (Art. 129), non-Muslims in Aceh can choose to submit themselves to *Qanun jinayat* voluntarily when committing *jinayat* crimes with Muslims, but when committing crimes not regulated under the 1981 Law of Criminal Procedure (KUPH), they must submit to *Qanun jinayat*. Aceh residents who commit *Qanun jinayat* crimes outside Aceh must submit to KUPH.[9]

The head of Wilayatul Hisbah, Samsuddin, told Benar News: "We printed 8,000 brochures containing a summary of penalties in the *qanun jinayat* so it would be easy for the public to understand. In early May 2015, we're going to distribute them so people won't be surprised when it's implemented." Al Yasa' Abubakar, head of the Islamic Shariah Agency and head also of Muhammadiyah Aceh, who participated in the DPRA deliberations, said that implementation was set to be in one year in order to provide enough time to inform the public and prepare enforcement officials: "When it is implemented, the hope is that Acehnese people will no longer violate Shariah of Islam."[10] The *Qanun jinayat* was expected to go into effect one year after its passage by the DPRA.[11]

However, Teungku Faisal Ali, the chairman of Nahdlatul Ulama (lit., "Awakening of Religious Scholars," one of the two largest popular movements) of Indonesia believes that the bylaws had failed to have a substantial effect on Acehnese society because they were not strong enough and also because there is lack of political will by local governments. He said that conditions today and five years ago are about the same. Shariah has been going nowhere in terms of regulations and enforcement, and he is of the opinion that the bylaws on crimes cannot be implemented to this day because there are punishment clauses considered controversial.[12]

The *Qanun jinayat* that was passed by the outgoing provincial legislature 2009 included the following:

- Adultery: "Any person who deliberately commits adultery is punished with 100 cane lashes for the unmarried and stoning to death for those who are married."

- Homosexuality: "Any person who deliberately performs homosexuality or lesbianism is punished with up to one hundred cane lashes and a maximum of 1,000 grams of fine gold or imprisonment of up to 100 months."
- Paedophilia: "Any person who deliberately commits a sexual crime against children is punished with a variable sentence of up to 200 cane lashes and a fine of up to 2,000 grams of fine gold, or maximum imprisonment of 200 months."
- Rape: "Any person who deliberately commits rape is punished with at least 100 cane lashes and a maximum of 300 cane lashes or imprisonment of at least one hundred months and a maximum of 200 months."

It was not clear at any point what Islamic sources were consulted in the drafting of this legislation, or why the various penalties imposed were not consistent with shariah law as understood in the neighbouring countries. The structure of punishments, especially the number of lashes in *Qanun jinayat*, are far in excess of those found in the scriptural sources of shariah. "Although some legislators expressed concern over the legislation, when it was put to the vote, all legislators voted in its favour."[13] The view was expressed by "two senior Acehnese politicians" that dissenting legislators could not openly oppose the bill because their opposition would then be used to challenge their commitment to Islam. *Qanun jinayat* 2009 was opposed by Aceh civil society groups as well as senior provincial government officials. Many of its provisions on penalties were in conflict with the Penal Code of Indonesia by either exceeding the Penal Code specifications or making parallel provisions to the same offences.

It is noteworthy that, in practice, the implementation of *ḥudūd* penalties is quite different in Aceh. The shariah court of Aceh ordered a uniform punishment of eight lashes of the whip for *ḥudūd* offences, excluding theft and *zinā*. Most of the other *ḥudūd* offences are thus penalised with reduced penalties to what is listed for them in the fiqh sources. Part of the explanation is that *ḥudūd* penalties are seen as the upper limits of punishment for the offences concerned, and the upper levels of punishments are reserved for the most severe cases. But they are otherwise understood to carry moral opprobrium, and that purpose is achieved through a uniform punishment of eight lashes and publicity that brings shame to the offender.[14]

Aceh is thus caught in a similar predicament to that of Kelantan in Malaysia, both taking an exception to the rest of their respective mother countries. Even though the people of Aceh are considered among the most devout Muslims in Indonesia, the province had not officially implemented shariah or *ḥudūd* punishments before. That is why both foreign and Acehnese activists were somewhat surprised with the introduction of *Qanun jinayat* and shariah police activities. There were instances in the past when hundreds of Acehnese women marched through the capital, demanding nondiscriminatory implementation of shariah and an end to heavy-handed tactics by enforcement officers.[15] A point of complaint has also been recorded on the "formalisation" of Islamic law as a new and in some ways unwanted development in Aceh. Marcen Naga observed in this connection that Islamic values had historically become a part of life and were observed by the people of Aceh since the times of Aceh sultanates in the thirteenth century CE. Instead of strengthening these features, their formalisation in codified laws by the state could weaken the degree to which Islam is practised by the Acehnese, who might regard these Islamic aspects as being forced upon them without choice, ignoring their individual agency in adhering to Islam.[16] In a similar vein, Moch Ichwan pointed at what is termed as "shariatism" by "progressive Muslim intellectuals, feminists, and queer residents of Aceh." They have developed "non-shariah spaces" and "alternative politics" in Aceh, essential for the future of Islamic democracy, under the rubric of "plural democracies" in Aceh.[17]

As already indicated, during the five years' interval between ratification of the *Qanun jinayat* 2009 by the Aceh House of Representatives (DPRA) and issuance of the revised *Qanun jinayat* in 2014, with its final ratification by both the DPRA and the governor, the *qanun* was stopped at the executive level due to tensions in the general public with regard to its punishments, especially regarding its provision on stoning to death for married adulterers. During extended discussions between all the concerned parties in that period, the governor of Aceh at the time, Irwandi Yusuf, stated that this punishment was disruptive of Aceh's peace and was upsetting the international investment community. Scholarly opinion of the ulama of earlier times was also cited to the effect that this punishment was not to be taken lightly. Irwandi's vice governor, Muhammad Nazar, added that even the *ḥudūd* punishments of flogging should be reduced and preferably replaced with *taʿzīr* to consist of imprisonment and fines, reasoning that this was more suited to the current Aceh society. Two Islamic Shariah Agency heads, Al Yasa' Abubakar and Shahrizal Abbas, mentioned that the stoning (*rajm*) punishment was included unilaterally by the DPRA based only on general opinion or public input and without government consultation or sufficient scholarly study. After much deliberation, the stoning (*rajm*) clause was finally removed, but the *ḥudūd* clauses on flogging were retained in the ratified version of the *qanun*. It was mentioned in this connection that flogging was still practised as a punishment in the United Kingdom and the United States.[18] Even after the ratification of *Qanun jinayat* in 2014, it is common to hear differences of opinion and the rhetoric that foreign hands and the enemies of Islam are hard at work to revoke the *qānūn*.

Qanun jinayat Aceh (2014) consists of ten chapters and seventy-five articles (in twenty-three pages). The introductory and opening sections provide an overview of sociological and juridical considerations and the steps taken that led to its final ratification. Of the ten chapters, the longest is chapter IV on criminal offence and punishment (fifty articles), whereas the remaining nine chapters all occupy twenty-five articles.[19]

The fifty articles in chapter IV specify in detail the offences and punishments that fall under the purview of the *qanun* in ten separate segments, with three articles on drinking (*khamar*), five articles on gambling (*maisir*), two articles on illicit privacy (*khalwat*), eight articles on sexual promiscuity (*ikhtilāt*), thirteen articles on adultery and fornication (*zinā*), two articles on sexual harassment (*pelecehan seksual*), seven articles on rape (*pemerkosaan*), six articles on slander (*qazaf*), two articles on homosexuality (*liwāṭ*), and one article on lesbianism (*musāḥaqah*).

Qanun Jinayat *Goes to the Supreme Court*

After a year of the *Qanun*'s obligatory period of "socialisation," it became enforceable in 2015, but it was soon followed by a landmark case in which two civil society organisations, the Institute for Criminal Justice Reform (ICJR) and United Women Solidarity (UWS), filed a petition at the Indonesian Supreme Court. The plaintiffs demanded that *Qanun jinayat Aceh* be revoked on grounds of unconstitutionality, and they provided details in a sixty-page statement as well as a long list of arguments for their demands. Included in these was the *qanun*'s opposition to ten other Indonesian laws of superior status to that of the *Qanun jinayat,* which was a bylaw passed by the provincial legislature, not an Act of Parliament. The discussion here need not elaborate much on the details of that sixty-page petition for reasons that will presently become obvious. What may be said at this juncture, however, is that the plaintiffs critiqued the *qanun* provisions that required the rape victim to provide proof to support her charge.

This, they asserted, was a violation of Article 52(1) of Indonesia's Criminal Procedural Law 1981 and the 1999 Law (No. 39) on Human Rights. It was further stated that a phrase in the *qanun*, "guilt admission by the perpetrator," infringed the principle of "non-self-incrimination" stipulated in the 2005 Law (No. 12) on ICCPR (International Covenant of Civil and Political Rights), the Civil Code of Indonesia, and the 2009 Law (No. 12) on Judicial Power. The plaintiffs further argued that taking an oath is admissible evidence under Articles 52 and 56 of the *Qanun jinayat*, which is, however, not recognised as proof in Indonesia's criminal justice system—although it is so recognised in the context of civil litigation. Logic dictates, it was added, that "every criminal will take the oath if given the option to exonerate himself." Further adding to the list of critiques, the plaintiffs stated that the provisions of the *qanun* in its sections on sexual offences (e.g., Art. 36) created scenarios in which pregnancy of an unmarried woman is taken as proof of *zinā* against her.

The Aceh government in its capacity as the defendant used the Autonomy Law No. 11 of 2006 on Aceh Government, stating that it had amended the provisions of the *qanun* so as to afford non-Muslims a certain choice as to whether or not to be adjudicated under the *qanun*.[20] The Aceh government further stated that the *qanun* had undergone the required legal procedures that were necessary for a law to be passed in Aceh. Included among these were several steps toward its preparation. The steps so taken were preparation of an Academic Draft, along with the Aceh Qanun Draft, the Aceh Legislation Programme procedure, the Aceh Government Team Discussion with Aceh House of Representatives (DPRA), an Interior Ministry Consultation, a General Hearing Meeting attended by all Aceh stakeholders, and DPRA approval. Following this, it was added that the *qanun* had also been submitted to the Interior Ministry of Indonesia, which did not provide any comment or critique after sixty days of submission. The *qanun* became official Aceh law.[21] Thus it was asserted that it was a valid law in every respect.

The Supreme Court finally issued a ten-page decision and rejected the application on what was basically a technical ground, holding that the *qanun* review at the Supreme Court at the given time was "premature." The main reason for this was that one of the ten regulations the plaintiffs had mentioned and relied upon, namely the 2011 Law No. 12 on Law Formation, was still under review by the Indonesian Constitutional Court with the registration number 59/PUU-XIII/2015. The Supreme Court panel of judges further added that the 2003 Law No. 24 (Art. 55) on the Constitutional Court stipulated that the review of regulations under the level of law in the Supreme Court must be halted when the laws that are being used as the basis of the review are themselves under review in the Constitutional Court—until the latter had decided on its review. The Supreme Court thus decided that the application cannot yet be considered and the plaintiffs were ordered to pay the application fee of one million rupiah. There was little public response. Although one or two members of the DPRA were quoted to have welcomed the Supreme Court decision, there has generally been little coverage in the media of the Supreme Court's rejection. Notably, only the ICJR uploaded the Supreme Court decision on its website.[22]

Subsequent information on the enforcement aspect of *ḥudūd* in Aceh indicates that instances of arbitrary enforcement occur now and then. An example of this may be an occurrence on 14 April 2016 when a Christian woman was whipped thirty lashes for selling alcohol in Banda Aceh. This is considered to be the first instance where a non-Muslim was punished under Islamic criminal law. Reports also indicate that a Muslim couple was whipped 100 lashes for committing adultery at around the same time.[23] There are complaints also that the law enforcement agencies should go after more substantive public crimes, such as corruption, nepotism, collusion, and complicity, instead of only perceived private and sex-related crimes.

XXV

Shariah Penal Code in the Islamic Sultanate of Brunei Darussalam

THE SULTAN OF Brunei, Hassanal Bolkiah, made a widely publicised announcement on 22 October 2013 that immediately became a worldwide media event. The sultan announced on that occasion that a new shariah penal code, which was in the works for years, had been gazetted and would come into force in phases over the next six months. He added that, based on the details of particular cases, punishments could include amputation for theft, stoning for adultery, and flogging for violations ranging from abortion to consumption of alcohol.[1] The sultan, who has reigned since 1967, is Brunei's head of state and prime minister with full executive powers. Public criticism of his policies is extremely rare in Brunei.

The sultan said in his initial speech on the subject that the shariah penal code in Brunei would be applied to Muslims only, and that Brunei's initiative in this regard should be seen as a form of "special guidance from Allah." To quote the sultan: "By the grace of Allah, with the coming into effect of this legislation, our duty to Allah is therefore being fulfilled." The sultan said this at a legal conference in Brunei's capital Darussalam. Brunei was a British protectorate until 1984, and it had as such ceased to apply Islamic criminal law, including *ḥudūd*. Although the shariah, or Islamic, courts had previously existed in Brunei even under the British, they handled mainly family-related disputes. Even to this day, and somewhat similar to Malaysia, Brunei has a dual-track judicial system combining civil courts based on British law.

Two years preceding the sultan's 2013 announcement, a top official in the attorney general's office stated that Brunei would apply an extremely high standard of proof for shariah criminal infractions under the code and that judges would have wide discretion in applying Islamic punishments.[2] This last point—that is, giving judges wide discretion in the implementation of *ḥudūd*—is a new development that marks a departure from the theoretical blueprint of *ḥudūd* that was discussed in part one.

The longstanding awareness and concern in the Islamic State of Brunei over the implementation of *ḥudūd* is also shown by the fact that, back in 1996, the sultan had first called for the introduction of shariah criminal punishments in Brunei, where Muslims comprise about two-thirds of the population of nearly 420,000 people. The minorities are mainly Buddhist, Christians, and people of local indigenous beliefs.

Following the sultan's announcement on *ḥudūd*, Brunei's mufti, Awang Abdul Aziz (also the country's top Islamic scholar), made a statement at a press conference to the effect that the shariah law "guarantees justice for everyone and safeguards their well-being." The mufti then added:

> Let us not just look at the hand-cutting or the stoning or the caning per se, but let us also look at the conditions governing them. ... It is not indiscriminate cutting or stoning or caning. There are conditions and there are methods that are just and fair.[3]

Mufti Awang also offered assurance that foreign travellers and tourists should not be concerned about shariah law or avoid Brunei after the law was implemented:

> Please listen to our answer: do all potential tourists to Brunei plan to steal? If they do not, then what do they need to fear. ... Believe me when I say that with our shariah criminal law, everyone, including tourists, will receive proper protection.

The implementation of shariah criminal law was not expected to face vocal opposition in Brunei, which has long been known for conservative policies such as banning the public sale of liquor. Under secular laws, Brunei had also prescribed caning as a penalty for crimes including immigration offences, for which convicts could be flogged with a rattan cane (*rotan* in the Malay language).

On 22 April 2014, it was announced that Brunei had postponed the proposed implementation of Islamic criminal punishments that were due to begin on that day. The delay was due partly to widespread negative media coverage abroad, international pressure, and the occurrence of criticism at home. No confirmed new date was given for the start of the shariah penalties, but an official told the Brunei media that they would begin "in the very near future." Jauyah Zaini, assistant director of the sultanate's Islamic Legal Unit, was quoted by the *Brunei Times* as saying that implementation had been delayed "due to unavoidable circumstances." He did not elaborate nor provide a new date.[4]

Then on 30 April 2014 the sultan of Brunei announced that the new Islamic criminal punishments would be phased in starting on the following day.[5] "Today I place my faith in and am grateful to Allah the Almighty to announce that tomorrow, Thursday, 1 May 2014, will see the enforcement of shariah law phase one, to be followed by the other phases." The sultan added that shariah law penalties would be introduced over time, and eventually the penalties would include flogging, severing of limbs, and death by stoning for various crimes. In response to foreign criticism, the sultan said: "Critics state that Allah's law is harsh and unfair, but Allah Himself has said that His law is indeed fair."[6]

On 1 April 2015 (i.e., one year after the sultan's announcement), Tun Hamid, the former chief justice of Malaysia, presented a lecture in Kuala Lumpur on Islamic criminal law in Malaysia. He made the following remarks on developments in Brunei:

> First of all, I would like to correct a common mistake. Many people thought that Brunei has implemented *ḥudūd* laws. That is not correct. In fact, to this day, Brunei has yet to enforce that part of the Shariah Penal Code Order 2013 which contains *ḥudūd* offences. Brunei has gazetted the law. The effective date has not been fixed yet. The most recent information I received from the Assistant Solicitor General of Brunei on 15 December 2014 confirmed that the *ḥudūd* law had not been enforced. In fact, the provisions of the Criminal Procedure Code necessary for the implementation are still under discussion.[7]

Matters became more complex than were initially thought. Pressure from international opinion and internal factors were behind the repeated delays in the implementation of *ḥudūd* in Brunei.

Subsequent information that came to light indicates, however, that the core *ḥudūd* penalties have been postponed to a later stage but that some of the lighter aspects thereof, which are strictly not included in *ḥudūd*, have been introduced and labelled as "the first phase" of Islamic criminal law. Reports thus indicate that this phase of the enforcement had started:

> The first phase, introduced on 1 May 2014, includes fines, imprisonment or both for eating, drinking or smoking during fasting hours, skipping Friday prayers for men and giving birth out of wedlock. According to some reports fewer than 20 people have been convicted for smoking during Ramadan and for *Khalwat* (intimate proximity offence). All of these offenders were fined.

However, the second phase, which includes whipping and the amputation of limbs, has yet to be implemented. It will be followed by the third and final phase, which allows for the stoning of those found guilty of homosexuality and adultery.

XXVI

Islamic Criminal Law in Saudi Arabia

ON 1 MARCH 1992, King Fahad announced the following three fundamental laws, established by Royal Orders, which changed the domestic legal and political environment of Saudi Arabia:

- The Basic System of Governance (hereafter referred to as the Basic Law);
- The Consultative Council Law; and
- The Regional Law.

The Basic Law (BL) is the most important. Article 7 of the law states that the Qur'an and the Sunnah govern all administrative regulations of the state as well the nature, the objectives, and the responsibilities of the state organs. Thus the relationship between the ruler and the ruled will be based on consultation, friendship, and cooperation.

The BL also confirms the monarchy side by side with the state's commitment to the principles of justice and the equality of citizens under Islamic shariah. The law then defines the authority of the three organs of state—the judiciary, the executive, and the legislative—along with their interrelationships. However, there is no expressed commitment to the separation of powers as such, especially between the legislative and the executive branches. The legislative authority is shared by the king, the council of ministers, and the Consultative Council (Majlis al-Shūrā). The BL also declares that Islamic shariah will be the basis of legislation, and there are numerous statutory laws governing criminal, administrative, and commercial affairs in the country. In his capacity as the enforcer of divine law, the king enjoys extensive powers over government affairs relating especially to Islamic public policy (*al-siyāsah al-sharʿiyyah*) and public interest (*al-maṣlaḥah al-mursalah*).

Introduced in 1993, the Consultative Council (Majlis al-Shūrā) had 61 appointed members and the number increased to 90 in 1996. Although the Majlis has no legislative powers, it can examine government policies and propose laws or amendments to existing laws. Decisions or suggestions from the Majlis are first sent to the council of ministers for review and then to the king for his approval.[1]

The BL also declares that the king must comply with shariah. Criminal law comprises three categories of crimes and penalties: *ḥudūd* (fixed Qur'anic punishments for specific crimes), *qiṣāṣ* (retaliatory punishments), and *taʿzīr* (a general category). *Ḥudūd* crimes are the most serious and include theft, robbery, blasphemy, apostasy, adultery, sodomy, and fornication. *Qiṣāṣ* crimes include murder and bodily injuries.

Since the Qur'an and Sunnah require interpretation, it is usually provided by the ulama. The Board of Senior Ulama (BSU), an official body of thirty to forty of the kingdom's most senior scholars, heads the religious authority in the Kingdom of Saudi Arabia (KSA). Created in 1971, it provides fatwas on issues submitted to it by the government or that require the establishment of general rules. The BL recognises the existence of this board. It states that "the sources for fatwa (religious legal opinion) in the Kingdom of Saudi Arabia shall be the Book of God and the Sunnah of His Messenger. The Law shall set forth the hierarchy and jurisdiction of BSU and the Department of Religious Research and Fatwa." The BSU has been a participant in the legislative process, which has in many cases been crucial in gaining public support for the statutory laws. Similar bodies exist at the regional level, though they are characterised by a more academic composition and functions. They include the Islamic Fiqh Academy at the Muslim World League, sponsored by Saudi Arabia and located in Mecca, and the Jeddah-based International Islamic Fiqh Academy of the Organization of Islamic Cooperation.

The public prosecutor's office was instituted in 1989 in order to modernise the Saudi judicial system. A code of criminal procedure of 225 articles was introduced in 2001 and contains provisions taken from Egyptian and French law.

A central principle of this law was a requirement that the accused could only be convicted of a crime that was identified in shariah or government regulations and that due process needed to be followed before a conviction could be handed down. The law also prohibits torture and gives the accused the right to a lawyer.

Currently, Saudi Arabia has a dual judicial system composed of shariah courts and an independent administrative judiciary introduced in 2008 and operating under the Board of Grievances (Diwan al-Mazalim).[2] In addition there are several administrative committees that have jurisdiction to hear certain specified cases. Moreover, the Law of the Judiciary 1975 permits the establishment of specialised courts by Royal Decree on the recommendation of the Supreme Judicial Council. The Commercial Court (al-Mahkamah al-Tijariyyah) and the Mazalim are not required to decide in accordance with shariah; their procedure is simple and their composition of judges (mostly lawyers with modern backgrounds) ensures greater flexibility in the conduct of cases.

The competence of the Saudi courts system is expounded by the Law of the Judiciary 1975. Shariah courts have jurisdiction over all disputes and crimes except those excluded from their jurisdiction by law. Shariah courts hear cases related to personal status, family and civil disputes, and most criminal cases. However, statutory laws and regulations have granted jurisdiction over different claims and crimes to either the Board of Grievances or administrative committees. Cases involving claims against the government and the enforcement of foreign judgments are heard by specialised tribunals and the Board of Grievances.[3]

The Law of the Judiciary 1975 (LJ) organises the Courts System in the following descending order:

- Supreme Judicial Council;
- Courts of Appeal; and,
- First-Instance Courts (General Courts and Summary Courts).

Article 5 of the LJ identifies the Supreme Judicial Council (SJC) as the highest judicial authority in the current system. It is composed of eleven members. Five full-time members constitute the Permanent Panel of the Council.

The SJC plays a key role in establishing general principles and procedures that lower courts are bound to follow. The Council also looks into shariah questions that require a statement of general shariah principles when these questions are referred to the Council by the Minister of Justice.

A three-judge panel always renders the Court of Appeal's judgment. However, for cases that involve capital punishments of death and amputations, a five-judge panel renders the decision.

Cases involving abduction or burglary and death sentences are automatically considered by the Court of Appeal. The latter does not reverse lower court decisions. Instead, it either affirms them or sends them back to the lower trial judge(s) for modification. If the latter maintained its judgement, the Court of Appeal can overrule the original decision and have another judge or panel of the lower court review the case.

There are two types of first-instance courts: Summary Courts and General Courts. The composition and jurisdiction of the Summary Courts are determined by the Minister of Justice on the recommendation of the SJC. A single judge hands down the judgments. Summary Courts have jurisdiction over certain *ḥudūd* offences, *taʿzīr* cases, and fines up to 20,000 Saudi Riyals. They also have jurisdiction over civil claims for sums less than 8,000 Saudi Riyals.

The General Courts are presided over by one or more judges. Composition and jurisdiction of these courts are also determined by the Minister of Justice on the recommendations of the SJC. General Courts have jurisdiction over crimes that carry the death penalty and *qiṣāṣ* in bodily injuries and also civil claims of up to 20,000 Saudi Riyals. A single judge renders judgments in a General Court, except in death punishments or retaliation, which require a three-judge panel.

Saudi judges mete out the death penalty even for *taʿzīr* offenses, a position that is upheld in classical Ḥanbalī and, in some cases, Mālikī jurisprudence. General Courts are not empowered, however, to issue a death sentence by *taʿzīr* , unless a unanimous vote has been reached by the panel of judges. *Taʿzīr* represents the bulk of General Court decisions, many of which are issued under national regulations and include bribery, traffic violations, and drug abuse. The most common punishment for a *taʿzīr* offence is flogging.

There are more than twenty-two General Courts in Saudi Arabia. There are also two courts for the Shii minority of the Jaʿfarī school in the Eastern Province dealing with family, civil, and religious disputes. Appellate courts sit in Mecca and Riyadh and review decisions for compliance with shariah.

A conviction requires proof in one of three ways. The first is an uncoerced confession. Alternatively, the testimony of two male witnesses can convict (four in the case of adultery), unless it concerns a *ḥudūd* crime, in which case a confession is also required. Women's evidence normally carries half the weight of men in shariah courts. However, in criminal trials women's testimony is generally not admitted. Testimony from non-Muslims or Muslims whose doctrines are considered unacceptable may come under scrutiny and are discounted. A solemn oath or a denial to take it can be also used as evidence. Oath taking is taken particularly seriously in a religious society such as Saudi Arabia, and refusal to take an oath will be taken as an admission of guilt that could result in conviction.

As in the classical view, which differentiates the evidential standards of *ḥudūd* from other crimes, the standard of proof in *taʿzīr* offences is usually lower than the standard of proof required in *ḥudūd* offences. For example, if a person retracts his or her confession during the trial, alleging coercion, punishment is suspended. If additional circumstantial evidence exists, the person may be tried under *taʿzīr*. However, circumstantial evidence is not admitted in *ḥudūd* or retaliation offences.[4]

In 2009, the king made a number of significant changes to the judiciary's personnel at the most senior level by bringing in a younger generation. This included a new Minister of Justice and a new chairman of the SJC. The outgoing chairman was known to oppose the codification of shariah. The king also appointed a new head of the Board of Grievances, and Abdulrahman b. Abdulaziz al-Kelya was appointed as the first Chief Justice of the new Supreme Court. As of a January 2013 Royal Decree, the SJC will be headed by the Minister of Justice. The Chief Justice of the Supreme Court will also be a member.

Statutory law in KSA is often known as *niẓām* (regulations), which is subordinate to shariah and in theory may not conflict with it. Saudi Arabian judges adjudicate on the basis of the Ḥanbalī interpretations of shariah in *ḥudūd* and *qiṣāṣ* crimes as well as in *taʿzīr* offenses. They cross-reference the opinions found in the works of renowned scholars, and on occasion in unprecedented cases, through novel interpretation of the sources and *ijtihād*. Saudi judges enjoy a degree of independence from the king, in line with the shariah principle of impartiality of justice, understood to mean that the state should not interfere in the judicial process.[5] Traditional areas of law continue to be governed by shariah while certain other areas relating to corporation, tax, oil and gas, immigration, and so forth have been regulated under Royal Decrees and Nizam.

The application of Islamic criminal law in KSA is often said to be a success story. Thus it is noted that, in the early years of the establishment of the Saudi Kingdom under King ʿAbd al-Azīz b. Saʿūd, the country suffered from rampant crime and insecurity, especially in view of the vast numbers of hajj pilgrims that came to the country from all places. After the introduction of Islamic criminal law and its regular enforcement, crime rates fell consistently, so much so that Saudi Arabia became one of the world's safest countries.[6]

Ḥudūd sentences are pronounced infrequently. For example, in 1982–1983, there were 4,925 *taʿzīr* convictions for theft but only two amputations for theft. All *ḥudūd* offences are first tried in courts consisting of three judges, and the king reviews death judgments before any execution takes place. Stoning to death and amputation are relatively rare: between 1981 and 1992, there were forty-five judicial amputations and four death sentences by stoning.[7]

Death punishment for capital offences is carried out in Saudi Arabia through decapitation or beheading. Other countries that use beheading include Yemen, Iran, and Qatar. In 2007 there were a total of 151 beheadings in Saudi Arabia, exceeding the previous record of 113 in 2000.[8] According to Amnesty International reports, there were approximately 26 beheading cases in 2011, which is the year of the Arab Spring, and 90 cases in 2014. However, the number of cases rapidly increased in 2015. In the first half of 2015, the Saudi government beheaded more than 100 people, most of them foreign nationals.[9]

Amnesty International says that in 2015 the kingdom carried out at least 158 death sentences, making it the third most prolific executioner after Iran and Pakistan. As of mid-October 2016, according to an Agence France Presse (AFP) tally of ministry statements, the number of locals or foreigners put to death in Saudi Arabia had reached 134.[10] The last of this execution was reported to be that of a member of Saudi royalty, Prince Turkī b. Saʿūd al-Kabīr, who was put to death in Riyadh for shooting to death Adel al-Mahemid, a Saudi, during a brawl, the interior ministry said in a statement. *Arab News* quoted the victim's uncle, Abdul Rahman al-Falaj, as saying that the sentence reflected the kingdom's "fair judicial system."[11] Beheadings are normally carried out in major cities on Fridays, after prayers, in the vicinity or in front of mosques.[12]

In recent years, there have been a number of robbery and theft cases. On 29 March 2011, Riyadh's General Court sentenced Amir 'Iyada and five other defendants to have their right hands and left legs amputated for committing armed (highway) robbery or *ḥirābah*. The court found that on the morning of 9 October 2010, the defendants cornered three employees of the Tamimi supermarket on Riyadh's King Fahd Road as they were transporting the week's proceeds of SAR 4 million (about USD$1.07 million) in the boot of their car. They threatened the employees with a gun and took the money from them. No one was physically harmed. The court of appeal was said to have upheld the verdict in October of that year.[13] In a separate case of theft, the hand of Amr Nasr, an Egyptian man, was amputated in 2007. In December 2011, the right hand of a Nigerian man, Abdulsamad Ismail Abdullah Hawsawe, was amputated after he was found guilty of stealing gold, a pistol, and a mobile phone.

An informed observer commented that "punishments in Saudi Arabia are now generally much less draconian. Since the Middle Ages, when these doctrines were formulated, the trend has been towards more lenient punishments."[14] He further added that "the doctrines formulated by Muslim jurists in the Middle Ages made it very difficult to convict, either because they defined the crimes extremely narrowly or because the requirement for evidence was extremely high. . . .It wouldn't be sensible to go around maiming the population. There was a realistic view of the punishments, and the jurists were generally humane. The jurisprudence is generally favourable to the defendant."[15]

XXVII

Shariah Punishments in the Islamic Republic of Afghanistan

HISTORICALLY AFGHANISTAN, A landlocked country with a population of about 30 million, has applied shariah as the general law of the land and the country has subscribed to the Ḥanafī school of jurisprudence. Shariah courts were courts of general jurisdiction that were adjudicated mainly on the basis of Ḥanafī law manuals that were mostly available in Arabic. The country is also mostly tribal; reports indicate that an estimated 80 percent of disputes are determined under tribal customary rules and the jirga council methods. Tribalism and its internal authority structures tend to be inherently opposed to the rule of law and concentration of power in a centralised government and, by the same token, also opposed to constitutionalism and the institutionalisation of power in outside bodies. Tribal customary laws are often applied side by side with shariah, mostly by tribal jirga decisions. The Pashtuns, who are the largest of the five major ethnic groups of Afghanistan (the other four being Tajik, Hazarah, Uzbek, and Turkmen), are the main bastion of tribalism in the country. Their traditional code of conduct, known as Pashtunwali, sets the standards of acceptable behaviour both within and between the tribes and continues to dominate social relations as well as matrimonial disputes, property and water disputes, and crimes. The institution of the jirga tribal council ensures the observance of Pashtunwali and functions as an informal tribunal for dispute settlement. Customary rules, such as Badal (revenge) and Beramtah (seizure of the opponent's property in pursuit of a claim), impede the enforcement of state laws and are entrenched enough to take priority even over shariah. Tribal customary laws usually do not apply *ḥudūd* due presumably to their stricter evidential standards.[1]

The fact that about 80 percent of disputes in Afghanistan are handled by local jirgas (in some places called *shūrā*) is due mainly to the lack of popular trust in the regular judiciary, which is infested with widespread corruption. It is also known that official corruption reached unprecedented levels during the Karzai period (2001–2014) and ever since. Lack of effective government, insecurity, and terrorism tend to strengthen tribalism, most noticeably since the American military invasion of October 2001. President Ghani has made several attempts to curb official corruption, mostly under international pressure from aid donors and also based on his own earnestness, but the results are limited due to the daunting size of the problem and the fact that the country's vitality and resources are constantly consumed by the ongoing war with the Taliban and the spread of the ISIS insurgency in recent years. This is not helped by internal disunity and Ghani's differences of opinion with his chief executive Dr. Abdullah.

Jirgas are convened on a case-by-case basis to decide on specific disputes, usually meeting in an open space or local mosque. They hear the disputing parties and then discuss the matter and reach a decision. There is no appeal mechanism, but the disputing parties may take the case to the regular judiciary if they are dissatisfied with the jirga resolution. Jirgas are traditionally male-dominated and may or may not include local religious leaders, but they do usually include representatives, often family members, of both disputing parties. Jirga practices are, however, vehemently opposed by Afghan women activists, the Afghan Independent Human Rights Commission, and the regular judiciary for reasons that they condone violence against women and privilege the rights of male parties and those with power and influence.[2]

Ḥudūd punishments were traditionally applied in the courts of justice and that is still, at least theoretically, the case. But the introduction of formal laws and constitutions tended to introduce uncertainties over the application of *ḥudūd* due partly to the prevalence of statutory laws that are often taken from Egyptian sources and French legal tradition via Egypt. The *ḥudūd* punishments were, in any case, not frequently applied in Afghanistan and were usually converted to *taʿzīr* penalties often consisting of imprisonment, especially when an element of doubt was deemed to exist in the proof or other material elements of the offence.

A General Penal Code (*Nizamnama-e 'omumi-e jaza*) and a series of other statutes were introduced under the reformist king Amanullah (1919–1929) between 1919 and 1923, which paved the way for the introduction of the first constitution in 1923. Known as *Nizamnama-e Tashkilat-e Asasi*, this constitution adopted, for the first time, the modern principle of legality in criminal law by enacting that "no punishment may be imposed on any person except as provided in the General Penal Code, and the Military Penal Code (*Nizamnama-e jaza-e 'askari*)" (Art. 24).

Islamic revivalism, foreign invasion, and civil war, as well as continuing conflict that has engulfed the country ever since the Russian military invasion of 1979, have weakened the authority of the central government, strengthened tribalism, and reasserted adherence to Islam in the laws and constitutions of Afghanistan. The 2004 constitution thus declared the country as an Islamic Republic for the first time and also provided that "in Afghanistan no law may be contrary to the beliefs and provisions of the sacred religion of Islam" (Art. 3). Article 130 provides further: when adjudicating cases before them, the courts shall apply the constitution and other laws. But when no provision exists in these sources, the courts shall apply the principles of "the Ḥanafī school of law, within the limits set in the constitution and render a decision that secures justice in the best possible way." Ḥanafī jurisprudence is often used in the courts of justice side by side with statutory laws and often provides ready recourse for judges in the event of ambiguity or a gap in the applied statutes. Yet Article 130 also subjects Ḥanafī law to the application of the principle of legality.

The Penal Code (*qanun-e jaza* 1355) 1976 (in 523 Articles) does not legislate on *ḥudūd*, due presumably to the sensitivity of the subject and the pro-status quo attitude of government of then President Mohammad Daud. Thus it is proclaimed at the very outset that "this law regulates crimes and punishments in the *taʿzīr* category. The perpetrators of crimes of *ḥudūd, qiṣāṣ* [retaliation] and *diya* [blood money] offences are punished in accordance with the provisions of the Ḥanafī jurisprudence of the Shariah of Islam" (Art. 1).[3] Then it is provided in the succeeding two articles that "no act shall be considered a crime unless the law says so" (Art. 2); and "no one may be punished except under a law that has been put into effect prior to the perpetration of such crime" (Art. 3) The succeeding two articles further proclaim that everyone is presumed innocent unless proven guilty; and that no punishment may violate basic human dignity (Arts. 4 and 5).

Chapter eight of the Afghan Penal Code 1976 on adultery (*zinā*) and homosexuality begins, however, with the following provision: "When the crime of *zinā* falls short of fulfilling the prerequisites for implementation of the prescribed punishment [*ḥadd*] of *zinā* due to the presence of doubt or any other ground, the perpetrator shall be punished in accordance with the provisions of this chapter" (Art. 426). The succeeding article then stipulates "long-term imprisonment" for *zinā* but then goes on to articulate in a seven-itemed list the aggravating circumstances of *zinā* that would invoke more severe punishments. This is when the victim of *zinā* is an underage person; the perpetrator is the teacher or employer of his victim or someone in a position of authority; when the victim is a married woman; when a girl loses her virginity as a result of the act of *zinā*; or when the victim has been afflicted with venereal disease as a result. If the act of *zinā* leads to the death of the victim, the punishment will be life imprisonment or death by execution (Arts. 427–428). All of these will be dealt with under the rubric of *taʿzīr*.

Slanderous accusation (*qadhf*) is defined somewhat more widely in Article 436 in that it is not confined to a false accusation of *zinā* but includes also libel and other attributions that humiliate its victim in the public. As for its punishment, the next article merely provides that "if the [shariah] prerequisites of *qadhf* are not fulfilled due to doubt [*shubha*] or other factors, the perpetrator will be liable to imprisonment that does not exceed two years, or fines between ten thousand and twenty thousand Afghanis, or both (Art. 436).

A similar approach is taken with regard to the prescribed crime of theft. Thus it is provided in the Penal Code: "In the event where the required conditions of the crime of theft are not fulfilled due to the presence of doubt [*shubha*] or other factors that come in the way of enforcement of the *ḥadd* punishment, the thief shall be punished in accordance with the provisions stipulated in this chapter" (Art. 454). The next article provides a short list of aggravating circumstances, which, if present, will make the offender liable to life imprisonment. These are as follows: (1) when theft occurs between sunset and sunrise; (2) when two or more persons collude in committing the theft; (3) when theft is accompanied by firearms carried by one or more of the offenders, be it openly or hidden; when the premises are broken into, forged keys are used, or when military or police uniforms are used; or when any other state authority is falsely represented.

Consumption of alcohol appears in a chapter titled "Use of Narcotics and Intoxicants," and it consists of four articles (349–353) detailing instances of punishable uses of these substances and the punishment provided for them, which ranges between three to six months of imprisonment or fines of 3,000 to 6,000 Afghanis or both. When an intoxicated person is seen in a public place or recreation ground and has evidently lost his faculty of intellect or annoys or harms others, the offender is liable to a short-term imprisonment that may not be less than three months or to fines between 3,000 to 12,000 Afghanis (Art. 352).

The Penal Code 1976 also contemplates the provisions of the Law of Criminal Procedure (*qānūn-e ijra'āt-jazā'i* 1344/1961) (Art. 11), an extensive piece of legislation of 500 articles that was influenced by Egyptian law and has followed a parallel classification of all crimes under the three classes of *jināyah* (felony), *janḥah* (misdemeanour), and *qabahah* (violations). This classification of crimes is also a *taʿzīr*-based arrangement and tends to override the traditional fiqh classifications. The Penal Code 1976 merely mentions the fiqh classification but in essence upholds the classification of crimes under the Law of Criminal Procedure 1961.

The Penal Code also bypasses the shariah rules on just retaliation (*qiṣāṣ*) and also opts for the application of *taʿzīr* punishments when any of the prerequisites of *qiṣāṣ* are not fulfilled. This is partly because all cases of murder and manslaughter would be subsumed under felonies (*jināyat*) and the structure of punishments that the law has provided for them. The Penal Code makes provisions for murder, manslaughter, and unintentional killing (Arts. 394–407), which are then followed by additional provisions on bodily injuries (Arts. 407–417). Thus it is provided with reference to murder: "If in a case of murder, *qiṣāṣ* cannot be implemented due to the absence of one or more of the required conditions, the perpetrator shall be liable to *taʿzīr* punishments in accordance with the provisions of this chapter" (Art. 394). The succeeding article provides a nine-item list of aggravating circumstances, which, if present, make the act of killing liable to death by execution. Included in these are premeditated murder, killing by the use of explosives or poisoning, killing a police officer or other public service employee during the conduct of duty, when the victim is a blood relative in the ascendant line (father, grandfather, mother, grandmother) of the offender, or when the victim's body has been maimed.

The constitution and other laws of Afghanistan stipulate that judges must rely on statutory codes as a matter of priority. Even though recourse to the provisions of the Ḥanafī fiqh is validated in the same sources for *ḥudūd* and *qiṣāṣ*, the Afghan judges tend to take a ready recourse to the resources of Ḥanafī fiqh generally but perhaps relatively less so in the case of *ḥudūd* and *qiṣāṣ* due mainly to the severity of these punishments. This often means that *ḥudūd* and *qiṣāṣ* are rarely implemented. An exception of note here may be the offence of blasphemy and apostasy for which the death penalty has been passed in a handful of cases in the last few decades. Yet the offender seems to have in most cases managed to escape and taken asylum in a foreign country. In sum, *ḥudūd* and *qiṣāṣ* remain valid law in Afghanistan, but they are not codified in sufficient detail, and direct recourse to Ḥanafī sources on these laws is also not without uncertainties.

XXVIII

Shariah Punishments in the Islamic Republic of Pakistan

PAKISTAN IS THE second-largest Muslim-majority nation next to Indonesia. Supported by the *Jamaat-e-Islami* of Pakistan, General Zia ul Haq seized power in Pakistan in a 1977 military coup; deposed (and eventually executed) the then elected prime minister, Zulfikar Ali Bhutto; and declared martial law. In February 1979, the year of the Iranian revolution, the general announced a comprehensive Islamisation programme. The constitution was amended to ban banking interest, implement the collection of the religious tax of zakah, and strengthened the Federal Shariat Court of Pakistan. The latter was to determine, inter alia, "whether or not any law or provision of a law is repugnant to the injunctions of Islam, as laid down in the Holy Quran and the Sunna."[1]

Article 203D of the amended Constitution 1973 had specified that the Federal Shariat Court (FSC) must, at the request of a citizen or the government, examine any law and rescind it if there is a finding that the law contravenes any injunction of Islam. General Zia's Islamisation programme also included the implementation of criminal legislation. On 9 February 1979, Zia issued five presidential decrees on *ḥudūd*, known as the Enforcement of Hudood Ordinances.

One of the features of these Hudood Ordinances was to make rape one of the *ḥudūd* offences that was to be subsumed under *zinā* as the ordinances did not distinguish the one from the other. Subsequently there were cases of injustice to victims of rape who became pregnant, but they could not produce the required number of witnesses and thus were convicted themselves for adultery. In 2006 the offence of rape was removed from the Hudood Ordinances and placed under the Penal Code of Pakistan

1860 again. Subsequently it began to be tried by the civil courts and has remained so ever since.

Three amendments were added in 1980, 1982, and 1986, respectively, to the Pakistan Penal Code 1860 criminalising—by words or acts—defiling of the Prophet, his wives, or relatives and desecrating the Qur'an. These amendments made the defiling of the Prophet into the capital offence of apostasy. In 1990, the passing of the Qisas and Diyat Ordinances also brought the Pakistan Penal Code into conformity with shariah on homicide and wounding.[2]

In addition to the *ḥudūd* crimes, the ordinances contain provisions on the application of *taʿzīr* discretionary punishments. These provisions impose punishments for acts that fall under the definition of a *ḥudūd* crime but which can be proven according to the normal rules of evidence and not according to the strict standards of *ḥudūd* offences. *Taʿzīr* was applicable to acts resembling *ḥudūd* but that did not fall under its strict definition.[3] The punishment for such crimes is almost always flogging, sometimes accompanied by imprisonment.

For example, the law concerning illicit sexual intercourse states that if a person accused of adultery/fornication cannot be convicted according to the requirements of shariah (confession or four eye witnesses), the accused can still be punished with a *taʿzīr* punishment of up to ten years of imprisonment and thirty lashes of the whip (Art. 10, Offences of *Zinā* [Enforcement of *Hudood*] Ordinance).[4]

Rape is identified as a separate crime, but the same punishment applies to it as in the case of *zinā*. However, the court can still mete out, in addition to one hundred lashes, any "other punishment, including the sentence of death, as the court may deem fit, having regard to the circumstances of the case" (Art. 6, Offences of *Zina* [Enforcement of *Hudood*] Ordinance).

The punishment for an unfounded accusation of *zinā* contains a novel rule: The punishment for a slanderous accusation "lapses" if the accusation is made "in the public interest" or by a person who has authority over the accused (Art. 3, Offences of *Qazf* [Enforcement of *Hudood*] Ordinance, 1979). This means that an accusation of sexual misconduct may be reported by the father or husband of a woman accused in this way without any fear on the part of the accuser of being punished for slander. Under this rule, the accuser will not be punished if he or she made the accusation "in the public interest."[5]

The FSC ruled in the case of Hazoor Bakhsh vs. Federation of Pakistan PLD (1981), FSC 145, by a majority of four to one that the provision of *rajam* (stoning), as had been stipulated in sections five and six of the Offence of *Zina* of the 1979 Ordinance, was repugnant to Islam. In a departure from the classical doctrine, the court mentioned that the Qur'an only specifies 100 lashes as punishment for *zinā*. The court found that the Qur'an prescribes 100 lashes for both the man and the woman when found guilty of *zinā*. The court also examined some hadiths and found that the stoning was not mandatory but only discretionary (*taʿzīr*). The court did not raise the question on what grounds a judge could mete out a greater penalty (death by stoning) under *taʿzīr*, which will supersede the prescribed Qur'anic 100 lashes for the offence of *zinā*.[6] General Zia did not like this decision, and as a consequence he had the court judges replaced by other judges. He also amended the constitution to enable the court to hear the case again. The newly reconstituted court ruled in Federation of Pakistan vs. Hazoor Bakhsh[7] that stoning to death is not repugnant to Islam. It was also stated that no legislature is authorised to change this punishment because there is nothing therein contrary to the Qur'an or Sunnah. Thus, the judgment of 21 March 1981 was withdrawn.[8] Nevertheless, this punishment has not been officially carried out in recent decades. In a similar vein, notwithstanding the new composition of the FSC, convictions for *ḥudūd* offenses appear to be rare.[9]

Before 1998, lower courts would routinely convict women of illicit sexual intercourse on the evidence of a mere accusation by their husbands, and then they would mete out punishment on the basis of *taʿzīr*. In 1998, however, the Supreme Court ruled that the imprecation, or *līʿān*, procedure (Art. 14, Offences of *Qazf* [Enforcement of *Hudood*] Ordinance, 1979) must be followed. This meant that if a husband wished to accuse his wife of adultery, he would have to take a solemn oath to that effect four times, with a fifth oath calling the curse of God on himself if she was telling the truth. The wife could avert punishment by taking four solemn oaths and say in rebuttal that she did not commit adultery, with a fifth oath calling the curse of God on herself if the husband was telling the truth. After this, the marriage is dissolved and both go unpunished.[10]

Following the international publicity of the gang rape of Mukhtaran Mai in 2002, the then president of Pakistan, General Parviz Musharraf, called for "possible amendments to the *Hudood* Ordinances 1979 that might include amending the requirement for a rape victim to produce 'four pious male witnesses' to support her accusation." It was further proposed that sex with a girl under the age of sixteen, with or without her consent, should be declared as rape. Provisions were also envisaged to cover cases such as kidnapping and "forced elopement"—neither of which were adequately addressed under the *ḥudūd* laws. Trafficking of women for prostitution and gang rape were also not covered. It was further suggested that the death penalty should be imposed for proven cases of gang rape.[11]

In November 2005, the National Commission on the Status of Women (NCSW) recommended that the *zinā ḥudūd* laws are altogether flawed and needed to be thoroughly revised in order to make them nondiscriminatory and fair. The NCSW also stated that "currently, the recommendations are under review by the government and legal experts."[12]

In August 2006, Shaheen Sardar Ali presented a paper at the International Judicial Conference on *Hudood* Laws. She wrote that, in response to the consistent challenge, the Government of Pakistan was considering an amendment to the *Hudood* Ordinances comprising both substantive and procedural modifications. She then added: "Since no official draft has been circulated to date," it was not possible to discuss it only from sketchy excerpts appearing in the newspapers.[13]

In another report on the status of *ḥudūd* laws in Pakistan, Zahirjan Mohamed wrote that the Protection of Women (Criminal Laws Amendment) Act (PWA), 2006, also informally known as the Women's Protection Bill, was passed by the National Assembly and the Senate in November 2006, and the president assented to it on 1 December 2006. This act introduced a number of significant amendments (elaborated in the following section) to the *ḥudūd* laws and other criminal statutes.[14]

In December 2010, the FSC, declared that it had exclusive jurisdiction over all matters relating to *hudood*, including *zinā*, which it defined as "adultery, fornication and rape," and *qazaf* (imputation of *zinā*). The declaration asserts that four sections of the PWA dealing with adultery and slander are unconstitutional because they contravene the *Hudood* Ordinances, and it ordered the federal government to repeal those sections by 22 June 2011. Shirkat Gah, a Pakistani women's rights organisation, stated that the judgement was an attempt by the FSC to "expand its jurisdiction and oust the jurisdiction of the superior courts" and to "undermine the legislative powers of the parliament" (Shirkat Gah, 29 December 2010).

Several sources indicated that the implementation of the PWA had reduced the number of women accused of or charged with adultery. Another study on the effect of the PWA similarly reported that a "radical drop in charges of *zinā* against women" was observed among all survey respondents, which included session judges, police officials, prison authorities, and lawyers. A decrease in the number of female prisoners was also noted. It was further stated that more women had been reporting rape to the police.[15]

The *ḥudūd* narrative in Pakistan thus remained unfinished. The various initiatives taken by different agencies, regimes, and political leaders, not all of them consistently or in tune with one another, have brought about a mixed picture of developments concerning Islamic criminal law, especially *ḥudūd*. A degree of variance is also observed in the roles respectively of the two juridical authorities of the land—the Supreme Court of Pakistan, which is the epic court, and the FSC, also possessing exclusive jurisdiction in shariah matters—and that they sometimes issued divergent rulings.

There were other cases where tribal courts (Panchayat) issued judgements and implemented the *ḥudūd* punishments, even though it had no legal basis for such rulings. One example is the case of Arifa Bibi, a young mother of two, who was sentenced to death by stoning by a Pakistani tribal court and was executed on 11 July 2013 at the hands of her family. Her uncle, cousins, and other family members threw stones at the woman until she died, all because, as reports indicated, she had a mobile phone and was accused of committing adultery. Since the stoning of Arifa Bibi, women's rights groups have launched an even stronger campaign to put a ban on stoning.[16] Further developments of a more decisive nature would seem to be in order to clarify the remaining unresolved issues of concern to Islamic criminal law and *ḥudūd* punishments in Pakistan.

XXIX

Shariah Punishments in the Islamic Republic of Iran

IN MARCH 1975 the shah of Iran, Mohammed Reza Pahlavi, dissolved all political parties and announced the formation of a one-party state under the newly formed Iran People's Resurgence Party. He required all Iranians to become members of this party. The shah had ruled Iran with an iron fist and was seen as a close ally of the West and a supporter of Western ways of life and culture. Ayatollah Khomeini was in the meantime conducting his antiregime activities from abroad. The Iranian Islamic Revolution of February 1979 put an end to the shah's regime and introduced a new constitution in the same year. Article 1 of the Islamic Republic of Iran (IRI) Constitution 1979, which has undergone several amendments since, stated that "the form of government of Iran is that of an Islamic Republic." Article 4 provides that all civil, penal, financial, economic, administrative, cultural, military, political, and any other laws must be based on Islamic criteria. Article 12 provides that the official state religion is Islam and the Twelver Jaʿfarī school; other schools of law are to be accorded full respect and freedom of religious practice, including matters of personal status.

Revolutionary courts were established after the Islamic revolution, and a law was introduced in June 1979 to declare these courts to be competent to adjudicate cases of oppression and homicide committed in support of the Pahlavi regime.

As time went by, the courts expanded their jurisdiction. After the 1979 revolution and as early as 1981 they began to try sexual offenses and impose *ḥudūd* punishments, including amputations and stoning to death. Frequently the charge on which the accused persons were convicted was based on sura 5, verse 33 of the Qur'an: "waging war against God and His

Messenger" and "spreading corruption in the earth," for which the courts imposed amputation or the death penalty.[1]

In 1982 and 1983, four laws were introduced: (1) The Law Concerning *Ḥudūd* and *Qisas* and Other Relevant Provisions, (2) The Law Concerning *Diyat*, (3) The Law Concerning Islamic Punishments, and (4) The Law Concerning Provisions on *Taʿzīr*. All of these were later replaced and incorporated initially into the Penal Code 1991, subsequently revised in 1996, and finally passed into a new Islamic Penal Code (IPC) containing 428 articles, which was, in turn, ratified by the Council of Guardians in January 2012.[2] It was subsequently sent to the president for his signature as required by article 123 of the constitution. However, the Guardian Council recalled it in October 2012 before it received the president's signature on the basis of "incompatibility with shariah in 52 cases."[3] The code was last amended by Parliament in February 2013 and was approved for the second time by the Guardian Council. The president signed the code, and it came into force in June 2013.[4]

A certain commitment to the rule of law was shown in article 289 of the Code of Criminal Procedure, which stipulated that sentences in criminal cases must identify the specific article on which a conviction is based. Yet the initial rigour of this ruling was diluted by a subsequent provision to the effect that, in cases where no specific legal provision existed, the court was obliged to apply shariah. It is on this basis that the death sentence for apostasy can be imposed. However, in cases of doubt, *ḥudūd* penalties were to be suspended.[5]

The IPC 2013 provides that "the *ḥadd* punishment for *zinā* committed by an unmarried person (*zinā-ye gheyre-mohsaneh*) is one hundred lashes." But when it comes to adultery of a married man or woman (*zinā-ye mohsaneh*), the code is silent and makes no provision in this regard.[6] Article 36 of the constitution and article 2 of the IPC 2013 only consider acts to be crimes if the law provides a punishment. Therefore, stoning to death for adultery is no longer legally prescribed.[7] Yet according to Amnesty International reports in 2014 and 2015, at least one stoning-to-death sentence was reported in Ghaemshahr, Mazandaran province, but no execution is reported to have been carried out.[8]

The international media in December 2002 reported that Iran's judiciary had suspended the enforcement of death by stoning. Jamileh Kadivar, an MP, reportedly said that "the head of the judiciary has sent a ruling to judges telling them not to order stoning." She added that the decision would be upheld pending a permanent change in the law.[9] Kadivar also stated that execution by stoning for adultery could be imposed but that such verdicts were seldom issued in practice. The alternative punishments were expected to be most likely imprisonment.

The offence of "armed disturbance of the peace (*muharābah*)" has been broadly defined so as to include acts of a political nature, such as supporting rebellion (Art. 198, IPC 2013) and making preparations to overthrow the Islamic regime (Art. 199). These offences were punishable by death, crucifixion, or alternate amputations.[10]

According to article 260 of the IPC 2013, any person who insults the Prophet of Islam or other Great Prophets shall be considered as one who reviles the Prophet (*sābb al-nabī*) and thus may be punished by death. The note attached to this article extends the same punishment to those insulting the twelve Shii Imams and the daughter of the Prophet Muḥammad (i.e., Fāṭimah, who was married to ʿAlī, the fourth caliph and first Shii Imam). This article has, however, omitted the ambiguous notion of "insulting the sacred values of Islam," a phrase that appeared in article 513 of the old Penal Code, which was open to broad interpretation and possible abuse.

Article 544 of the IPC provides that "the *diyat* [blood money] for murdering a woman is half that of a man." However, and in order to soften the discriminatory component of this article, the IPC, even though insisting on inherent gender inequality, prescribed a new solution in its succeeding article 545, which reads:

> In all the cases of homicide that the victim is not a man, the difference between her *diyat* and the *diyat* of a man shall be paid from the Fund for Compensation of Bodily Harms.[11]

Furthermore, pursuant to article 225 of the IPC, the following sexual offenses are punishable by death:

(a) Adultery with one's consanguine relative, that is, sister, mother, maternal and paternal aunt, maternal and paternal grandparent, niece and nephew or their children;
(b) Adultery with one's stepmother, in which case the adulterer shall receive the death penalty;
(c) Adultery between a non-Muslim man and a Muslim woman, in which case the adulterer shall receive the death penalty;
(d) Forcible rape, in which case the rapist shall be liable to the death penalty.

A commentator (Shadi Sadr) observed, however, that even though there was no reference to *zinā-yi muḥṣaneh* in the IPC 2013 it did not mean that death by stoning was abolished. Indeed, *zinā-yi muḥṣaneh* remains a crime, albeit one for which no punishment is specified. In such instances, judges have the authority under the constitution to exercise discretion in delivering verdicts of death by stoning by referencing shariah sources in the absence of codified laws.

Further clarification is thus needed on the subject of stoning, as silence on this issue can be given different interpretations. The Shii law position on blood money (*diya*) of a woman, as being half that of a man, has received different responses in other schools of Islamic law. The Ḥanafī school and a substantive body of modern opinion, earlier reviewed, both maintain that the inherent value of life is the same regardless of gender. They refer in this connection to the Qur'anic text on the subject of *qiṣāṣ* (just retaliation), especially the phrase "life for life" (*al-nafsu bi'l-nafs*—Q 5:32) without any further qualification. There is no Qur'anic basis for this differentiation, and the evidence in hadith on it is also inconclusive.

Shaykh Muḥammad al-Ghazālī and his commentator, Yūsuf al-Qaraḍāwī, both Ḥanafī scholars, maintain the principle of equality and refute the assumption that a woman's life is cheaper (*arkhās*) than that of a man as a false assumption (*zaʿm kādhib*). A man who kills a woman is executed, and the same punishment applies to a woman who kills a man. Their blood is equal, and this is the standard shariah position. There is no reason therefore for inequality in their *diya*.[12]

XXX

Islamic Criminal Law in Republic of Nigeria

ISLAM CAME TO Northern Nigeria in the seventh century CE through the jihad of Uthman Dan Fodio who was a Fulani clergy from Mali. However, it peacefully spread in south-western Nigeria through the activities of Arab traders from North Africa and Turkish merchants. The spread of Islam in Nigeria is somewhat similar to how it spread in Malaysia and Southeast Asia, where Islam arrived through traders and Sufis. Nigeria gained independence from Great Britain in 1960. A civilian government ruled first but the military took over in 1966. The civil war broke out the following year and lasted until 1970. The nation returned to civilian rule in 1979, but the military ruled again until another civilian government was formed in 1999.

Nigeria is the most populous country in Africa and the seventh-largest in the world. It is an oil-rich state and the world's twenty-first-largest economy. It comprises two regional/religious zones: north and south. Muslims mainly live in the north and Christians in the south. Unlike Sudan, where the non-Muslim south became a separate country in 2011, Nigeria is a federal republic that is governed by the same government and constitution. The legal system of Nigeria is based on English common law, Islamic law, and customary law. The current constitution of 1999 provides for the establishment of an Appeal Court that hears appeals from the Federal High and State High Courts, shariah courts, and Customary Courts of Appeal. The Federal Court of Appeal is to have at least fifteen judges, no less than three of whom will be well versed in Islamic law and no less than three in customary law (Art. 236.1). Jurisdiction of the shariah appeal courts relates mainly to personal law and religious matters.[1] The constitution further provides, however, that "the Government of the

Federation or of a State shall not adopt any religion as the State religion" (Art. 10).[2]

A Criminal Code based on English law was introduced in 1904. The code allowed courts to try and convict people even of acts not identified as crimes in the code as long as such acts were identified as crimes under customary law and shariah. Thus, a person could be convicted of illegal sexual intercourse even though adultery was not identified as a crime in the Criminal Code.

The Criminal Code 1904 was amended in 1933 to ensure that convictions took place on the basis of written law. Yet the amended code continued to be interpreted in ways that enabled the application of shariah, albeit with some restrictions on sentencing, which precluded punishments repugnant to human dignity and natural justice.[3] This meant that the penalty of stoning to death for adultery or of amputation could not be applied.

British residents maintained extensive overall powers in supervising local courts. Punishments that were seen as excessive by the British, such as crucifixion, stoning to death, or amputation, were commuted to imprisonment. Caning and flogging were permitted, subject to approval of the emir or the district officer. Flogging sentences of women were commuted to prison terms or fines.

A new Penal Code was introduced in Northern Nigeria in 1959. Some *ḥudūd* offences remained punishable. These included drinking alcohol (section 403), illegal sexual intercourse (sections 387–388), and defamation. The 1959 Penal Code, administered by Magistrate Courts, also applies to non-Muslims in the north. The south was governed by the Criminal Code Act of 1961. Beginning in 2000, the 1959 Penal Code in Northern Nigeria was supplanted by Shariah Penal Codes. The reintroduction of shariah penalties was driven by popular demand.

Islamic punishments were thus reintroduced in Northern Nigeria from 2000 onwards. In some states existing laws were merely amended. In other states entirely new codes were passed, The state of Zamfara in the Muslim north enacted the nation's first Shariah Penal Code in 2000, and it was followed by Niger State. By 2002 twelve out of thirty-six Nigerian states and one territory had introduced shariah criminal laws and set up courts for the purpose. Each state has its own governor and legislative assembly.

Shariah courts in Nigeria follow the Mālikī rules of evidence, which allow circumstantial evidence for the conviction of certain crimes. For example, pregnancy of an unmarried woman is considered as sufficient proof to convict a person of adultery, unless the accused could prove that she was raped.

In 2002, two divorced women were convicted of adultery and sentenced to death by stoning. Safiyyatu Hussaini and Amina Lawal were convicted by lower courts for unlawful sexual intercourse because they were pregnant while unmarried. The court of appeal quashed both convictions on technical grounds. Penal law was not yet duly promulgated when the convictions were passed. The appeal court ruled that pregnancy of an unmarried woman is not sufficient to prove that the accused committed illegal sexual intercourse. The reason was that, according to Mālikī doctrine, the maximum period of gestation is five years. Since both the accused were divorcees, they could theoretically have been pregnant from their previous unions.

Several amputations under just retaliation (*qiṣāṣ*) were reported. In one case, Ahmad Tijani was sentenced in Malunfashi, Katsina in 2001 to be blinded in his right eye after he was convicted of blinding another man in an assault. He was convicted on the basis of the testimony of seven witnesses. There were no reports about whether the sentence was actually executed.

In another case, the upper shariah court in Bauchi ordered in 2003 an amputation of the leg from the knee of a man who cut off the leg of his wife after accusing her of overexposing herself to a doctor during a medical examination. The amputation was to take place without the use of anaesthetics or painkillers, as directed by the court. It is not known whether this sentence had been carried out either.

The Nigerian legal system is characterised by a number of oddities. Some provisions in the federal constitution appear to be at odds with other provisions, just as some of its clauses are also at odds with some provisions of the state Shariah Penal Codes.

For example, while Article 10 of the constitution precludes adoption of any state religion, it also permits, in Article 259.1, establishment of shariah courts of appeal "for any state that requires it." Moreover, jurisdiction of the shariah courts may extend as far "as may be conferred upon it by the law of the State."[4] Questions tend to arise as to the feasibility of these combinations.

The federal constitution allows the northern Muslim states to establish shariah courts and enact Shariah Penal Codes. Oddly, however, the constitution does not permit them to pass legislation governing the rules of evidence. Legislation pertaining to laws of evidence remains a federal matter according to the constitution. In the interest of consistency, a state that enacts and enforces legislation on certain offence types should also be able to determine what constitutes the evidence of that offence. The application of shariah punishments in any state of the federation is also inconsistent with the Nigerian constitution, as the constitution limits the scope of the application of shariah mainly to the Islamic personal law.

Inconsistencies are also apparent between some provisions in the federal constitution and state shariah penal codes. For example, article 36 (12) of the Nigerian constitution states that "a person shall not be convicted of a criminal offence unless that offence is defined and the penalty for it is prescribed in a written law."[5]

Yet all state shariah penal codes (except the Kano penal code) stipulate that even acts not identified as offences in written law, such as apostasy, may still be punishable as long as they are identified as punishable offences in the Qur'an, the Sunnah, or classical fiqh doctrine. Thus, a person can be convicted of apostasy despite the fact that apostasy is not identified as a crime in any written law, including, in particular, the shariah penal codes.

Moreover, article 38 of the Nigerian constitution safeguards the right to change one's religion: "Every person shall be entitled to freedom of thought, conscience and religion, including freedom to change his religion or belief, and freedom (either alone or in community with others, and in public or in private) to manifest and propagate his religion or belief in worship, teaching, practice and observance."[6] This might once again seem inconsistent with allowing the states to punish people for apostasy.

Inconsistencies are also encountered in law enforcement matters. The Nigerian police force is under federal jurisdiction and comprises both Muslim and non-Muslim officers. As a result of the laxity—perceived or real—in the enforcement of *ḥudūd* by non-Muslim police officers, Muslim vigilante groups sometimes take the law into their own hands, justifying their activities as a form of *ḥisbah* (the Qur'anic principle, that is, of promotion of good and prevention of evil).

The Federal Court of Nigeria has to this day not ruled on the constitutionality of enactment of the shariah penal codes. There are fears that if the court rules on this issue, and finds the shariah penal codes unconstitutional, the existence of the federation might be placed in jeopardy.

An uneasy coexistence between the constitution and the state shariah penal codes and practices is becoming increasingly evident. The anomalies within the Nigerian legal system are thus reflective of the dual legal heritage (Islamic and colonial) of Nigeria. The fact that Nigeria is made up of two distinct communities (Muslim and Christian) certainly played a role. While lawmakers attempted to accommodate both of the faith communities, their efforts were met with limited success and compromises were made along the way to accommodate diverging interests.

The challenge remains as to how to harmonise the two systems in a way that can safeguard the interests of each community without infringing on the aspirations and legitimate claims of the others.

XXXI

Shariah Punishments in Republic of Sudan

AS AFRICA'S THIRD-LARGEST country, Sudan includes many religious, ethnic, and socioeconomic groups. Prevailing issues of access to resources, economic opportunity, and power relations against the background of such diversity has unfortunately resulted in some of Africa's longest-running conflicts since the country became independent in 1956. These conflicts have occurred between Muslims and Christians, Arabs and Africans, nomads and farmers, and other groups. The rule of law is but one of many casualties resulting from the permanent presence of conflict (or threat thereof) in the south, west, and eastern regions. The Mālikī school was the predominant madhhab in Sudan although the dominant school is now the Ḥanafī, due mainly to Ottoman and Egyptian influences.[1]

The administration of justice traditionally was regarded by Arabised Sudanese and a number of southern ethnic groups as the most important function of government. In precolonial times supervision of justice was solely in the hands of the ruler. In the north, most cases were tried by an Islamic judge (*qāḍī*) who was trained in one of the Sunni Islamic legal schools. Crimes against the government, however, were heard by the ruler and decided by him with the advice of the Grand Mufti, who served as his legal adviser.

Although the Muslim influence on Sudanese law remained important, the long years of British colonial rule left the country with a legal system derived from a variety of sources. The primary legal influence remained British because of the weight given to British legal precedent and also due to the fact that most of the lawyers and judges were British-trained. After independence, much discussion took place on the need to reform or abrogate the system inherited from the British. A commission was preparing a revision of the legal system when Gafaar Mohamed el-Nimeiri and the Free Officers' Movement carried out a military coup against the elected civilian government in 1969. The Nimeiri regime dissolved this commission and formed a new one dominated by twelve Egyptian jurists. In the ensuing years, many Egyptian laws and Egyptian civil, commercial, and penal codes became important sources of legislation in Sudan.[2]

Following a 1971 abortive coup attempt against Nimeiri and a negative turn in Sudan-Egypt relations, a committee of Sudanese lawyers was formed to reexamine the Egyptian-based codes. In 1973 the government repealed these codes, returning the country's legal system to its pre-1970 common law basis. The 1973 constitution of Sudan, article 9, proclaims shariah as the principal source of legislation.

A Committee for the Revision of Laws was again established in 1977. Ḥasan al-Turābī (d. 1437/2016), the then leader of the National Islamic Front, was selected as a member of this committee. However, proposals to ban alcohol and banking interests and to implement legal alms (*zakāh*) were shelved, and so were the plans to implement shariah generally. In 1983, Nimeiri announced that the government would introduce Islamic law by means of a presidential decree.[3]

Nimeiri issued several decrees, known as the September Laws, that made shariah the law of the land, with an emphasis on the enforcement of *ḥudūd* punishments, retaliation, and *qiṣāṣ* laws, followed by introduction of the Penal Code 1983.

This code did not, however, explicitly identify all punishable offenses. But it stated in Article 458.3 that if a defendant could not be punished with a fixed punishment due to uncertainty (*shubha*), he could still be punished in any way the court saw fit, even if the offense was not identified as such in the code. Widespread criticism of the code followed, especially based on its departure from many of the classical fiqh positions. Article 3 of the Law Concerning the Bases of Judicial Sentences (*qānūn uṣūl aḥkām al-qaḍāʾiyyah*) 1983 required that, in the absence of applicable rules in the Penal Code, the judge must uphold and apply Islamic law. It was on this basis that Mahmoud Mohammed Taha, a scholar and political opponent of Nimeiri, was convicted of apostasy and executed in 1985 at the age of seventy-six. Taha was sentenced to death even though the 1983 Penal Code did not identify apostasy as a crime.[4]

The 1983 Penal Code broadened the scope of *ḥudūd* punishments to acts that were not designated as *ḥudūd* crimes in classical fiqh. For instance, the definition of theft became wider than under classical Islamic law. It was no longer a requirement that the theft originated in a secure place or area and was carried out surreptitiously. This meant that the scope for the application of punishment by amputation was greatly expanded.[5]

In a similar vein, Article 457 of the Penal Code made membership in a criminal organisation punishable with the prescribed punishment for armed robbery, *ḥirābah,* which could be carried out in one or more of the following methods: execution, execution with crucifixion, alternate amputation, imprisonment, or banishment.[6] The scope of *taʿzīr* punishments was also expanded.

Thus, if an unmarried couple was seen together in public, they could be charged with the new punishable offence of "attempted unlawful intercourse."[7] The fiqh manuals record *khalwah* (illicit privacy) as an offense, but that is most likely not committed in a public place.

Convictions for *ḥudūd* crimes showed a marked increase as a result of relaxing the rules of evidence (Evidence Act of 1983). If the required two (or, in the case of adultery, four) male witnesses of good character were not available, the accused may still be convicted by the testimony of other witnesses at the discretion of the court (Arts. 77 and 78, Evidence Act 1983).[8]

Amputations also increased greatly. In 1985, 65 judicial amputations were reported to have taken place, including 20 alternate amputations. The total number of amputations between September 1983 and April 1985, when Nimeiri was overthrown, is given as between 96 and 120.[9] After April 1985, the government suspended all amputations and other harsh punishments.

Both the transitional military government of General Siwar Adh-Dhahab and the democratic government of Ṣādiq al-Mahdī expressed support for shariah but criticised its method of implementation under Nimeiri.

In April 1986, the Law Concerning the Bases of Judicial Sentences was amended to the effect that the propagation of a new interpretation of Islam does not amount to apostasy. On 18 November 1986, the Constitutional Court declared that Taha's death sentence, carried out the year before, was unconstitutional. Other Sudanese have been convicted of apostasy in subsequent years but escaped the death penalty for various reasons, including renunciation of their new faith.

In August 1986, a resolution by the National Islamic Front (NIF) demanded that all amputation sentences be carried out, but this resolution was defeated in Parliament. In 1989, the NIF, becoming apprehensive that its project of restoring shariah law would fail, organised a coup d'état and overthrew the multiparty system. In 1998, Sudan adopted a new constitution, which called for restoration of the multiparty system to which it was so vehemently opposed before.[10]

The military coup of June 1989 by General Omar al-Bashīr occurred only twenty-four hours before Ṣādiq al-Mahdī's government was scheduled to vote on rescinding the September Laws. Although al-Bashīr's government initially retained the official freeze on implementation of those laws, unofficially judges were advised to apply shariah in preference to secular codes. Later he promised to implement Islamic law more strictly.[11] Hasan al-Turabi, who had played an influential role in drafting the September Laws, was enlisted to help prepare new laws based on Islamic principles. In January 1991, al-Bashīr decreed that Islamic law would be applied in courts throughout the north but not in the three southern provinces.

Ḥudūd punishments were once again carried out. Al-Bashīr's government adopted, in the meantime, the Criminal Act 1991 (Law 8/1991),[12] which made provisions for *ḥudūd* punishments and extended their scope to cases of homicide and bodily injuries. Other offences were to be punished by flogging, fines, or imprisonment. The 1991 Act (Art. 126) also included the crime of apostasy, which is punishable by death, unless the accused person repents and returns to Islam.[13]

Among the many weaknesses of the *ḥudūd* legislation in Sudan were the extensive powers given to courts to punish people at their discretion, which was based apparently on the principle of *taʿzīr* even if a given act was not identified as an offence in the statute.

On 1 July 1998 a new constitution was introduced following a referendum the previous month. Article 1 of this constitution states that Islam is the religion of the majority of the population but does not proclaim it to be the state religion. Article 65 identified the sources of law as shariah, consensus of the people, the constitution, and custom.

The courts in Sudan have convicted persons for robbery, apostasy, adultery, and other *ḥudūd* crimes, yet their sentences were frequently reduced or quashed, or charges were dropped altogether, in almost all reported cases. In 2007, Sadia Idriss Fadul and Amouna Abdallah Daldoum were sentenced to death by stoning for adultery in the state of al-Gezira. However, their sentences were quashed on the ground of a lack of legal representation at the trial court. In the same year the criminal court of Nyala in south Darfur sentenced two males aged sixteen, Abdelrahman Zakaria Mohamed and Ahmed Abdullah Suleiman, to death by hanging for murder, causing injury intentionally, and robbery. In April 2012, Intisar Sharif Abdallah was sentenced to death by stoning for adultery in the city of Omdurman near Khartoum. However, the Sudanese authorities dropped all the charges after receiving thousands of protest letters from Amnesty International and other sources.[14] In another case, Laila Ibrahim Issa Jamool was sentenced to death by stoning for adultery in Hay Alnasir, Khartoum.[15] In May 2014, Mariam Yahia Ibrahim Ishag was sentenced to death and 100 lashes for apostasy and adultery respectively. She was born to a Muslim father and a Christian mother, but she was raised in her mother's faith and married to a Christian man. She was given three days to revert back to Islam. However, she refused and was eventually convicted. On appeal her sentence was quashed due to international protests.[16]

Extensive debate continued about stoning and the attempt to reform all *ḥudūd* laws under al-Bashīr's administration, but to no avail. The congress of the Sudan's People's Liberation Movement proposed an initiative to abolish the stoning punishment on the premise that it was not part of the Qur'an, but the proposal was rejected by government ministers. The dispute over the possession and allocation of natural resources increased in the meantime in the south culminating in its secession in 2011 to become South Sudan.[17]

The Transitional Constitution of the Republic of South Sudan was ratified in July 2011 by the South Sudan Legislative Assembly, coming into force on the independence day of South Sudan on 9 July 2011. The constitution established a presidential system headed by a president who is head of state, head of government, and commander-in-chief of the armed forces.

On 22 February 2015, two months before a controversial election took place, al-Bashīr approved new amendments to the country's criminal laws, tackling three major areas: bribery and counterfeit money, apostasy and insulting religion, sexual harassment and rape.

These amendments invoked negative responses from civil society and international quarters. The case of Mariam Yahia, as already mentioned, became a big media issue. Campaigns were launched in Sudan and abroad calling for legal reform, specifically the abolishment of Article 126 of the Criminal Act 1991. This article was amended, yet the amended version of both this (on apostasy) and Article 125 (on insulting religions) is more punitive. The new law redefined apostasy to include anyone who questions the credibility of the Qur'an, the wives of the Prophet, the four caliphs, or other Companions of the Prophet. Moreover, even apostates who "repent" can face up to five years of imprisonment. The punishment for insulting religions was increased from six months to five years of imprisonment.[18]

With regard to rape and sexual harassment, the problematic Article 149, which confused rape and adultery, was amended. Under the earlier version, if a rape victim failed to prove her case she could be punished with 100 lashes for adultery (*zinā*) if she was unmarried, or with death by stoning if she was married. The new amendment expands the definition of rape but separates it from *zinā,* which was seen as an improvement, yet the new amendments raise doubts with regard to achieving justice for survivors of rape. In an interview, Hikma Yagoub, a human rights lawyer who runs a legal aid organisation in Khartoum, said: "The new definition will give victims and their lawyers the opportunity to achieve justice. However, it's rather meaningless without amending the evidence law of 1994, which is still in line with the old definition of rape." Yagoub and other human rights activists have consequently demanded wider changes in the entire legal system beyond amendment of a few articles in a particular law, calling for "dignity and equality for Sudanese men and women."[19]

In conclusion, the case of Islamic criminal law and *ḥudūd* in Sudan is not untypical of the status of *ḥudūd* issues in other Muslim countries. Unresolved issues remain over important aspects of Islamic criminal law, including *ḥudūd.* The talk of reform to some or all of *ḥudūd* seem to have been initiated on many occasions and under different regimes; however, reaching consensus-based solutions over them and the modalities of their reform have proven difficult to obtain.

XXXII

Shariah Punishments in the Islamic Republics of Mauritania and Maldives, and Islamic State of Yemen

THE ISLAMIC REPUBLIC of Mauritania (IRM) is an Arab country with a population of 3.89 million (2013). Almost 90 percent of IRM is land surface in the African Sahara region. Mauritania proclaimed its independence in 1960 after agreement with France earlier in the same year. It has a mixed legal system of French civil law and shariah. Articles 2 and 5 of the IRM Constitutions of 1961 and 1991, respectively, declared Islam to be "the religion of the people and of the State" but provided that shariah is a compelling source only for the legislators and must be translated into legislation before it is made applicable in courts.[1]

The Mauritanian legal system inherited its French legal and judicial components from its declaration of independence, an influence that is most visible in its civil, commercial, and penal codes.[2] This was affirmed by the 1961 Constitution of IRM, which provides for the continuation of the French laws until it is specifically amended or repealed.[3] However, the continued application of French laws was challenged in the 1980s by the introduction of shariah civil and criminal codes. An Islamic court system was also established beside the existing courts of the Republic. *Ḥudūd* punishments such as flogging, amputation of the hand, and capital punishments became part of applied criminal law, and were implemented in a number of cases. In September 1980, the Islamic courts handed down their first verdict, which resulted in the execution of one man for homicide and the amputation of the hands of three others. Nine people were subsequently whipped in public for stealing. By February

1982, three persons were executed for murder, and dozens of petty thieves either had their hands amputated or were subjected to public flogging.[4]

The Mauritanian Criminal Code (*qanun jinayi*), which was introduced in 1983, identified a number of *ḥudūd* crimes, including adultery, theft, and drinking liquor. In 1984, the code was amended to include the death penalty for apostates. *Ḥudūd* crimes feature in this code as follows:

1. *Apostasy*: Article 306 of the Mauritanian Criminal Code (MCC) deals with apostasy by providing that "any Muslim guilty of the crime of apostasy" is to be given the opportunity to repent within three days. If the accused does not repent within that period, he/she is to be sentenced to death, and the government shall confiscate all of his/her property. The MCC also provides under the same article that if a person who has been sentenced to death for apostasy repents before his/her execution, the Mauritanian Supreme Court can commute his/her death sentence to a jail sentence of between three months and two years plus a fine of 5,000 to 60,000 MRO (360 Mauritanian Ouguiya = 1US$).[5] The only reported case whereby a person was convicted is that of Mohamed Cheikh Ould Mkhaitir in 2012. He was sentenced to death for apostasy for "speaking lightly of the Prophet Mohammed" in an article that was published on his blog. He also challenged some of the Prophet's actions in that article. The only information as of this writing is that the defendant has appealed to the Supreme Court.
2. *Adultery*: Article 307 of the MCC states: any adult Muslim who is guilty of the crime of *zinā* that is proven either through confession or the testimony of four adult witnesses shall be punished by 100 lashes and a year's imprisonment, if the offender is single. For male offenders, the sentence will be carried out where the crime was committed. If the offender is married or divorced, he/she will face the death penalty by public stoning. With regard to pregnant female offenders, the execution of the death penalty will be postponed until after delivery. Article 308 of the code extends the punishment of married persons to those convicted of homosexuality, stating that any adult Muslim man who commits an indecent act or a homosexual act against another will be punished to death by public stoning. Female offenders will be punished for practice of lesbianism by imprisonment between three months and two years and a fine of 5,000 to 60,000 MRO.

3. *Drinking alcohol:* Under Article 341 drinking is liable to eighty lashes of the whip. The offence could be proved through confession, testimony of two witnesses, vomiting, or the smell of alcohol.
4. *Theft*: Article 351 of the MCC penalises theft with amputation of the hand after the fulfillment of all the conditions as provided in this article.

However, these punishments were only applied for a short period after the reforms of the 1980s and have not been enforced since then.

Islamic Republic of Maldives

Maldives is an Islamic republican state, and unlike so many other Muslim countries that have mixed populations, it is almost 100 percent Muslim. It is a follower also of the Shāfiʿī school or madhhab with considerable presence of influential Sufi orders. At the 2006 census, the population of Maldives had reached 298,968 and was projected to reach 317,280 in 2010. Accurate information about its practice of shariah law and *ḥudūd* is scanty. It may be useful to learn, however, that a package of judicial reforms was introduced and passed by the Peoples Majlis (parliament) as early as 1950 following a proposal submitted by the then Minister of Home Affairs and the interim head of the government, Mohamed Amin. Under the authority vested in him by the Majlis, he introduced several changes in the judiciary of Maldives, including the appointment of a separate head of Mahkamatul Sharuiyya (the shariah court). The main functions of this court were divided among several desks, with each desk specialising in specific types of cases.[6] On 25 August 1950 a separate attorney general's office was established for the first time. Until then, its functions were carried out by his desk at the Mahkamatul Sharuiyya. As part of these reforms, a legal profession was formally established. Mohamed Amin devised a set examination for those seeking to become qualified lawyers, and he also commenced implementation "of the *ḥudūd* punishments as prescribed in the Islamic Shariah."[7]

Article 29 of the 1953 Republican Constitution stated that the judicial power of the state is to be vested in the Mahkamatul Sharuiyya (also known as Fandiayaruge), which was to be headed by the chief justice. The latter had a number of Naibs (deputies) whose number was determined by law. The chief justice and his Naibs were to be appointed by the president. On 7 April 1953, two years after the decision was made to implement *ḥudūd* laws, capital punishment was enforced and the first execution was carried out. On 1 July 1953, sentences passed by the court ordered amputations of the hands of two persons for theft, which were implemented.[8] The Makamtul Sharuiyya were courts of general jurisdiction in the Maldives, and its powers extended to all the *ḥudūd* offences. This was the subject, in fact, of the 1955 regulations that established separate divisions under the supervision of the chief justice and his deputies. These regulations placed all the *ḥudūd* offences, including *zinā*, *qazf*, "serious offences of theft," murder, homosexuality (*liwāṭ*), and cases of assault and battery involving just retaliation (*qiṣāṣ*) under the division of the chief justice.[9]

Legal and judicial reforms introduced by President Amin came to an abrupt end, however, when he was toppled by a coup led by his vice president on 31 August 1953. It was rumoured that the implementation of *ḥudūd* laws had immensely contributed to Amin's downfall.[10]

In 2008, Maldives adopted a new constitution that proclaims in article 10(a): "The religion of Islam shall be one of the bases of all the laws of the Maldives." Article 10(b) provides that "no law contrary to any of the tenets of Islam can be enacted in the Maldives." Article 2 of the constitution says that the republic "is founded on the principles of Islam." Article 9 says, somewhat surprisingly, that "a non-Muslim may not become a citizen"; article 19 states that "citizens are free to participate in or carry out any activity that is not expressly prohibited by Shariah Islamic law or by the law"; and article 61(b) of the constitution states: "No person may be subjected to any punishment except pursuant to a statute or pursuant to a regulation made under authority of a statute, which has been made available to the public and which defines the criminal offence and the punishment for commission of that offence." Some of these articles clearly stand in disharmony with the Universal Declaration of Human Rights, especially on freedom of religion, even though this constitution clearly adopted the principle of legality in crimes and punishments.[11]

A new penal code was adopted by the Majlis in 2014, which came into effect on 15 July 2015. Consisting of 1,205 sections. This law codifies the whole range of offences and punishments and also clearly subscribes to the principle of legality in criminal law and punishments.[12]

The penal code 2014 has separate sections on "sexual assault offences" (s. 130–135), "unlawful sexual intercourse" (411ff), theft and other property offences, and the like. The law is generally couched in the language and style of a modern statute without articulating an explicit affinity with the terminology or definitions of Islamic criminal law and *ḥudūd*. With regard to the latter, the penal code has only one section, the very last in fact, which reads as follows:

> Offences for which punishments are prescribed in the Holy Quran: If the offender is found guilty of committing an offence for which punishments are predetermined in the Holy Quran, that person shall be punished according to Islamic Shariah and as prescribed by this Act and the Holy Quran. (Sec. 1205)

Thus it would seem that *ḥudūd* are enforceable under the applied laws of Maldives, including under the penal code, which takes a clear yet sweeping position on the subject. The three sources the code has referred to, namely the Quran, Islamic shariah, and "this act," may not always provide for an easy combination and may well require clarification with reference to particular issues. It has yet to be seen how the courts of Maldives synthesise these and various other sections of the penal code with its article 1205 on *ḥudūd*.

It is worth mentioning perhaps that past practice is indicative of a much lighter approach to *ḥudūd* penalties, as they have been reduced, somewhat like in the Indonesian province of Aceh, and in many states also of Malaysia, to a smaller number of strokes of the whip or the rotan. Applying the punishment of whipping was not severe nor incapacitating in the previous Maldivian practices.

Islamic State of Yemen

The fall of the Soviet Union in 1989, along with the deportation of Yemeni workers from the Kingdom of Saudi Arabia and other Gulf countries after Iraq's invasion of Kuwait in 1990, accelerated the unification of the Yemen Arabic Republic and the People's Democratic Republic of Yemen. The merger of North and South Yemen took place on 22 May 1990. This resulted in the fusion of all institutions of both states, including their distinct legal systems, by declaring the codes of the Yemen Arabic Republic as the official legislation of the new Republic of Yemen.

The nascent republic's leaders used presidential decrees to introduce new laws and regulations that reflected a process of democratisation and economic liberalisation. This was also reflected in the 1990 Constitution of the Republic of Yemen. However, the traditional religious elite resisted these changes, challenged the constitution and other presidential decrees, and proposed Islamic amendments.[13] The constitution was consequently amended in September 1994 to declare in article 1 that Yemen was an "Arab Islamic State." Article 2 declares Islam to be the official state religion, and Article 3 states that Islamic shariah is "the basis of all laws."

This amendment paved the way for the introduction of a penal code that contained provisions on *ḥudūd* and *taʿzīr* laws. The Law of Crimes and Punishments (12/1994) was introduced as the first penal code in the history of Yemen. Article 11 of this code divided crimes into two types: crimes punished with *ḥudūd* or *qiṣāṣ*; and crimes punished by the judge's discretion (*taʿzīr*). Article 48 provided that only the president of the republic can delay or annul the implementation of these punishments. Further on *ḥudūd*, Article 12 declares that "there are seven crimes for which punishment is prescribed by the religious sources: they are crimes for which a specific religious jurisdictional stipulation exists and is a pure or mixed Right of God, which religious jurisdiction expresses as the limits." The following seven *ḥudūd* crimes are as follows:

1. Mutiny (*baghy*): article 125, Law of Crimes and Punishments 1994 (henceforth LCP) provides that "anyone who undertakes an act with the intention of violating the independence, unity or territorial integrity of the Republic shall be punished by the death penalty." Article 127 further provides that the "death penalty shall be meted out to any of the following: (i) Yemenis who, in any way, enlist with the armed forces of a state that is at war with the Republic; (ii) whoever surrenders any personnel of the armed forces to the enemy, or whoever assists any prisoners to return to the enemy ranks; (iii) whoever supports the enemy with troops, personnel, and funds and whoever acts as a guide to the enemies.
2. Apostasy (*riddah*): Apostasy is subject to the death penalty under article 12 of LCP 1994, which identifies crimes, including apostasy, that are punished according to the provisions of Islamic shariah. Article 259 provides "anyone who turns back from or renounces the religion of Islam, is punished by the death penalty after being questioned for repentance three times and after giving him a respite of thirty days. The apostasy in public by speech or acts is considered a violation of the principles of Islam and its pillars when espoused with intention and determination. If the intention or determination is not established and the guilty shows repentance, there will be no punishment. In November 2012, Ali Qasim Al-Saeedi was arrested by the authorities

and charged with apostasy for posting articles and research on his personal Facebook account that questioned the teachings of the Qur'an. However, it has been reported that Yemen does not enforce the death penalty for apostasy.[14]

3. Banditry and terrorism (*ḥirābah*): Article 306 of LCP provides: "Whoever subjects people to any form of force whatsoever, for any illegal purpose on a public road, desert or structure, at sea or on an airplane; thereby terrorises them and frightens them for their lives or property or honour, whether the victim is an individual or a group and whether by compulsion or by declaration shall be construed and considered as being a *muḥārib* at war." Based on article 307, bandits shall be punished:
   a. By imprisonment up to a maximum of five years if his felony was confined to just threatening on a roadway.
   b. By amputation of the right hand from the wrist and the left foot from the ankle, if he took movable property owned by someone else, whereas his partners who do not take any property shall be punished by imprisonment up to a maximum of ten years.
   c. By execution, as a religiously ordained punishment if such crime leads to killing a human being; any accomplices who do not take part in the killing shall be punished by imprisonment up to a *maximum* of fifteen years.
   d. By execution and crucifixion, if the criminal took property and killed an individual; the accomplices, who do not take part in the theft or the killing, shall be punished by a maximum of up to fifteen years imprisonment.

At least three people were reported to have been sentenced to amputation of limbs. In January 1997 a Court of First Instance in Hadramaut province was reported to have sentenced three men to cross-amputation (of the right hand and left foot) on charges of highway robbery. It was not clear whether these sentences or those passed in previous years were carried out or commuted upon appeal.[15]

4. Theft: Articles 294–304 of Law of Crimes and Punishments 1994 deal with the definition, evidential requirements of proving theft, and its punishment. Article 298 provides that anyone who steals what equals the legal minimum for a theft and complies to the conditions for meting out the religiously ordained punishment shall be punished by amputation of the right hand at the wrist. Repeated theft by the same person, is

punishable with amputation of the left foot at the heel; if the latter again repeats the same crime, imprisonment shall replace amputation for a maximum of up to 15 years. In cases involving more than one thief, the punishment shall be meted out to all of them, regardless of their respective contribution in the theft. In a reported case, Abdulrahman al-Juri, received the cross-amputation sentence for armed robbery on 15th September 2013 at the Sana'a's Specialised Criminal Court. However, due to the paucity of reliable information to the Yemeni judicial process, it remained unverified whether or not the sentence was carried out, due to protest and criticism by Amnesty International.[16]

5. Adultery: Article 263 provides: "Sexual intercourse which is considered adultery is the intercourse that does not involve elements of doubt as from the outset; the adulterer and adulteress without suspicion or coercion are punished with whipping by one hundred strokes as a penalty if not married. It is also lawful for the court to reprimand the perpetrator with imprisonment for a period not exceeding one year. If the adulterer or the adulteress is married, he or she is punished by stoning to death." In December 2002, Layla Radman A'esh was sentenced to execution by stoning and Naji Hizam Abdullah was convicted to flogging after they were found guilty and convicted of adultery by the Court of First Instance in Aden.[17] The defendants appealed the sentence—no further information is made available.
6. Slander: Articles 289–293 of LCP 1994 deal with the slander or defamation of an upright person. "Anyone who defames an upright person by accusing the latter of adultery or refutes the lineage of a person, and fails to prove such claims shall be punished by 80 lashes of the whip as ordained by religious law" (Art. 289).
7. Drinking alcohol: Chapter 5 of LCP deals with gambling, drugs, and alcoholic beverages. Article 283 states that "every adult sane Muslim who drank an alcoholic beverage shall be punished by fifty lashes of the whip in a public area in due fulfillment of religious ordinances, which may be augmented thereafter by imprisonment for a maximum term of one year."

In conclusion, it may be said that the Yemeni law has increased the number of *ḥudūd* crimes to the maximum of seven. The law has turned a blind eye to the growing body of learned opinion on the various aspects of *ḥudūd*, which were discussed in part one of this volume.

XXXIII

Shariah Punishments in Libya, the United Arab Emirates, and Qatar

Libya

Soon after his takeover of power in a military coup in 1969, Muammar Gaddafi banned alcoholic beverages and the giving and taking of banking interest in Libya. A committee was set up in 1971 to prepare for the Islamisation of the Libyan legal system. While the committee was still in deliberation, the Revolutionary Command Council issued a decree identifying shariah as the principal source of all legislation. Legal principles for the purpose of bringing legislation into accord with shariah were to be based on *takhayyur, maṣlaḥah,* and custom. After the revolution, the dual court system was abolished, and civil and shariah courts were merged in 1973. The committee's work resulted in the introduction of four laws, enacted between 1972 and 1974, on *ḥudūd* crimes and other related offences. They dealt with theft and highway robbery (Law 148 of October 1972); illegal sexual intercourse (Law 70, October 1973); unfounded accusation of fornication (Law 52 of October 1974); and lastly on the drinking of alcoholic beverages (Law 89 of November 1974). In 1994 another statute (Law 6 of 1994 consisting of only eight sections) was introduced and ordered the courts to follow the classical rules of retaliation and blood money in homicide cases.[1]

These laws were generally based on the Mālikī school of jurisprudence, which is the prevailing *madhhab* of Libya. The laws so introduced also made provisions based on *taʿzīr* for offences resembling *ḥudūd* crimes, such as punishing minor persons for committing *ḥudūd* offences and offences pertaining to the production and sale of alcoholic beverages that did not fulfil the fiqh requirements of this offence. In some respects, these laws also adjusted certain aspects of the Mālikī doctrine: first, criminal responsibility begins at age eighteen, not at puberty or fifteen years of age as specified in Mālikī law; and second, a highway robber who has not killed another person nor taken property is to be punished with imprisonment instead of banishment, and one who has both killed and plundered is punished with the death penalty only without public exposure and crucifixion of his body.[2] Third, if a person who has already been punished with amputation and commits another theft offence or banditry, he will not be punished with further amputation. He will suffer a minimum of three years imprisonment until he repents .[3] Fourth, illicit sexual intercourse is only punished with flogging and not by stoning to death, but the court may, in addition, impose imprisonment at its discretion.[4] Whereas until 1998 adultery under the Code of Criminal Procedure could be proven by normal evidence and did not have to fulfill the strict shariah rules of evidence for its proof, in that year the law was amended such that sexual intercourse had, from then onwards, to be proven on the basis of shariah rules or by other scientific methods of proof. Regarding the other *ḥudūd* crimes, the laws also stipulate that the shariah rules of evidence have to be followed.

Furthermore, the new laws were to be applied by the existing courts, and no special tribunals were created for the purpose. In addition, the death penalty and amputation could only be carried out after the case had been reviewed on appeal.[5] Judicial amputations were to be carried out under anaesthesia by a qualified surgeon. There were no reports of amputations for many years even after the introduction of these laws until July 2003, when Amnesty International reported judicial amputations that were carried out on four robbers who were convicted of cross-amputations and were accordingly punished.[6]

United Arab Emirates

Islam is the largest and the official state religion of the United Arab Emirates (UAE), where Muslims constitute 76 percent of its population of 9.4 million. Based on the Ministry of Economy's 2005 census, of the remainder of 76 percent percent were Christian, and 15 percent other (mainly Hindu). Census figures do not take into account the many "temporary" visitors and workers but they also count Baha'is and Druze as Muslim. Among Emirati citizens, 85 percent are Sunni Muslim while 15 percent are

Shia, mostly concentrated in the emirates of Sharjah and Dubai. Omani immigrants are mostly Ibadi. Sufi movements and influences are also active up and down the country.

The government subscribes to a policy of tolerance toward other religions and rarely interferes in the activities of non-Muslims. By the same token, non-Muslims are expected to avoid interfering in Islamic religious matters or the Islamic upbringing of Muslims.

The government has imposed restrictions on proselytising and spreading of other religions among Muslims through any form of media activities and programmes. There are approximately thirty-one churches throughout the country and one each of Hindu, Sikh Gurudwara, and Buddhist temples.

The core principles of the UAE laws are drawn from shariah but, unlike some other jurisdictions that specify a particular school of jurisprudence, the UAE does not mention any one in particular for purposes of legislation. For judicial practice too, the UAE allows the consideration of all schools of law according to the discretion of the presiding judge.[7] Most of the UAE laws are of mixed origins, comprising Islamic and civil laws and usually bearing influences of Egyptian laws.[8] The UAE Constitution 1971 states that "Islam is the official religion of the Union and . . . Islamic Shariah is the main source of its legislation." This last phrase is understood to mean that, in addition to shariah, other sources may also be utilised for purposes of legislation and, it seems, for purposes of court practice as well.

The UAE judiciary consists of three types of courts: civil, criminal, and shariah. The judicial system is derived mainly from the civil law system and shariah. Another line of division is that the UAE has a federal court system, consisting of civil courts and shariah courts. Article 1 of the Federal Penal Code makes the provisions of the Islamic law applicable to the prescribed religious crimes, retaliation, and blood money. The Federal Penal Code has declared as repealed only those provisions of the penal codes of individual emirates that are contradictory to the Federal Penal Code. Otherwise they are enforceable simultaneously.[9]

Shariah courts have exclusive jurisdiction over family law matters and crimes, including adultery, premarital sex, robbery, alcohol consumption, and related crimes. Apostasy is also a crime punishable by death in the UAE (Article 1 and Article 66 of the UAE's Penal Code). Blasphemy is illegal; expatriates involved in insulting Islam are liable to deportation.

Amputation is also a legal punishment in the UAE and shariah courts are empowered to impose it. Flogging is a punishment for criminal offences such as adultery, premarital sex, and alcohol consumption. Flogging sentences issued by shariah courts range from 80 to 200 lashes. Verbal abuse pertaining to a person's honour is punishable by 80 lashes of the whip. Between 2007 and 2014, many people in the UAE were sentenced to 100 lashes. In 2015 an expatriate in Abu Dhabi was sentenced to ten years in prison and 80 lashes after alcohol consumption and raping a toddler. Alcohol consumption for Muslims is illegal and punishable by 80 lashes; many Muslims have been sentenced to 80 lashes of the whip for the offence. Sometimes 40 lashes are also given. Sex outside marriage is punishable by 100 lashes.

In October 2013, a Filipino housemaid was sentenced to 100 lashes for illegitimate pregnancy. Drunk driving is strictly illegal and punishable by 80 lashes.

Stoning is a legal punishment in the UAE for married persons that commit adultery. In May 2014, an Asian housemaid was sentenced to death by stoning in Abu Dhabi. Reports indicate that between 2009 and 2013, several people were sentenced to death by stoning. Yet there are also reports that, in recent years, several people have retracted their guilty plea in illicit sex cases after being sentenced to stoning or 100 lashes. Article 80 of the Abu Dhabi Penal Code makes sodomy punishable with imprisonment of up to fourteen years, while article 177 of the Penal Code of Dubai imposes imprisonment of up to ten years on consensual sodomy.[10]

Qatar

Following Ottoman rule, Qatar became a British protectorate in the early twentieth century until gaining independence in 1971. Qatar has been ruled by the House of Al-Thani since the early nineteenth century. Sheikh Jassim b. Mohammed Al Thani was the founder of the State of Qatar and established a hereditary monarchy. Whether Qatar should be regarded as a constitutional or an absolute monarchy is a matter of opinion. In 2003, the constitution was overwhelmingly approved in a referendum, with almost 98 percent in favour. In 2013, Qatar's total population was 1.8 million: 278,000 Qatari citizens and 1.5 million expatriates.[11]

Qatar's Penal Code (Law No. 11 of 2004) incorporates the shariah *ḥudūd* punishments for various offenses. Article 1 of this law states that the provisions of Islamic law for the following offenses are applied if the defendant or victim is a Muslim:

1. The *ḥudūd* offenses related to theft, banditry, adultery, defamation, alcohol consumption, and apostasy.
2. Just retaliation (*qiṣāṣ*) offences and blood money (*diya*).

Flogging is used in Qatar as a punishment for alcohol consumption or illicit sexual relations. Article 88 of Qatar's Penal Code 2004 declares the punishment for adultery at 100 lashes. Adultery is punishable by death, however, when a Muslim woman and a non-Muslim man are involved. Muslims are not allowed to consume alcohol in Qatar and if caught consuming alcohol they may be liable to flogging or deportation. Non-Muslim expatriates can obtain a permit to purchase alcohol for personal consumption.[12]

In 2010, at least eighteen people (mostly foreign nationals) were sentenced to floggings of between 40 and 100 lashes for offences related to "illicit sexual relations" or alcohol consumption. In 2011, at least twenty-one people (mostly foreign nationals also) were sentenced to floggings of between 30 and 100 lashes for offences related to illicit sexual relations or alcohol consumption. In 2012, six expatriates were sentenced to floggings of either 40 or 100 lashes. Only Muslims considered medically fit were liable to have such sentences carried out.

While apostasy is subject to the death penalty under Qatar law, Qatar has not imposed any penalty for this offence since its independence in 1971. Blasphemy is punishable by up to seven years, and proselytising can be punished by up to ten years of imprisonment.

XXXIV

Conclusion and Recommendations

THIS BOOK'S REVIEW of developments concerning Islamic criminal laws in Muslim countries is indicative of considerable diversity in the ways in which these laws are understood and implemented. The *ḥudūd* debate in the countries surveyed is also marked by strong currents of opinion both for and against these punishments. This seems to be the case even in countries that do not apply them or apply them selectively, with or without amendments. Muslim opinion is clearly divided on the various aspects of *ḥudūd* laws. Some countries tend to exhibit a certain lack of political will, and there is also a paucity of credible jurisprudential input over Islamic criminal law issues.

Most of the *ḥudūd*-related debates underline the wider question of justice in that a literal application of these punishments, which is usually the case, may actually not secure justice. Then there is the parallel concern as to whether enforcing the *ḥudūd* as an isolated case in an otherwise predominantly secular legal system and state can actually serve its desired purposes. In multireligious societies, including Malaysia, Nigeria, Sudan, and Pakistan, questions are asked over the status of non-Muslims with regard to shariah punishments. Even if the political leaders emphasise in their public statements and speeches that Islamic criminal law will not be applied to non-Muslims, the latter tend to remain circumspect. Their reservations may not be altogether unjustified, as in terms of actual practice, it is difficult to draw clear demarcation lines among citizens based on religion. Suppose a Muslim and a non-Muslim are involved in a case of adultery. It would be difficult to maintain that the two parties will be treated differently under two separate laws and two separate courts! To do this would likely contravene the constitutional principle of equality before the law, and it would also raise case management problems in two separate court systems.

Our survey has also shown that the Muslim world is internally diverse with varying customary practices and cultural, economic, and political characteristics of their own. Saudi Arabia is evidently different from Indonesia, Iran from Afghanistan and Somalia, and so forth. Whereas some are afflicted with endemic conflict, massive refugee problems, and poverty, others have heterogeneous populations and have to adjust their policies accordingly, not to mention the official corruption that plagues many Muslim societies and jurisdictions. The conservative and modernist strata of populations in Muslim countries tend to differ widely on Islamic criminal law (ICL) issues. The picture is made more complex by the presence or otherwise of non-Muslim minorities, internal dualities in the legal system, legacy issues, and so forth. Thus it is evident that one measure does not fit all and that any reform proposals one may advance should also allow flexibility and contemplate different options. Reform proposals for Malaysia may, for instance, be relevant for Southeast Asian Muslim-majority countries but not for all Muslim countries and cultural zones. Whereas interest in Islam and shariah has generally been on the uptrend, critical voices and negative profiling of shariah have also been getting louder, and even more so, regarding shariah punishments. The proponents of human rights and democracy have also recorded negative views of ICL. Notwithstanding the fact that *ḥudūd* laws have hitherto resisted the prospects of internal reform, a reformist *ijtihād*-oriented approach to some aspects of ICL and *ḥudūd* would seem inevitable.

Some Muslim countries, including Saudi Arabia, Afghanistan, Pakistan, and Iran, have in principle applied and upheld classical doctrines on shariah offences and *ḥudūd*. Others, like the Sudan, have veered from classical fiqh in some respects. Southeast Asian countries, including Malaysia, Brunei, and Aceh Indonesia have yet to embark on the implementation of ICL and *ḥudūd* punishments—and the laws they have either passed or proposed to pass on the introduction of ICL have invoked critical voices within their own countries and populations. There are also countries that have regulated aspects of ICL but that have not been able to consistently enforce them.

Countries and jurisdictions that have not codified shariah punishments, but commit themselves to the application simultaneously of *ḥudūd* and the constitutional principle of legality in crimes and punishments, place their judges in difficult situations when they adjudicate cases under shariah law. For they would not only be faced with procedural uncertainties but also find themselves in the realm of interpretative jurisprudence rather than clearly written statutes.

It is a cause for concern also to note that *ḥudūd* punishments are sometimes applied by laymen and the mob who take the law unto their own hands and act beyond the pale of due process of law and shariah. One is often shocked by gruesome images of "desert courts" caning of women, and "hanging from trees" of defenceless girls by angry mobs, the Taliban, Daesh and their own relatives in the tribal belts, especially those of Pakistan and Afghanistan. The ardent agents of "honour killing" have also carried out acts in remarkably crude and oppressive ways, and usually only on women, in total disdain for due process and standards of evidence the shariah itself has envisaged for *ḥudūd* punishments.

Another aspect of concern in this discussion relates to the implementation of whipping, even by regular law enforcement agencies. The relevant procedural guidelines and advice of restraint for the actual administration of whipping are often neglected. Proper shariah guidelines would ensure that whipping is neither too severe nor too light. Our investigation shows wide-ranging inconsistency and variation on both sides in the countries and regions of the Middle East, Southeast Asia, and elsewhere.

Our review of substantive ICL in part one has shown that shariah law often provides lenient options and the prospects of selection among diverging interpretations. When that is the case, one ought to be guided by the general guidelines of shariah and the higher purposes of justice, people's benefit, and *maṣlaḥah* without compromising on basic principles. It is instructive in this connection to read in the Qur'an: "So announce the good news to those of My Servants who listen to the word [of God] and follow the best [sense] of it. Those are the ones whom God has guided; and those are the ones endowed with understanding" (al-Zumar, 39:18).

The Prophet Muḥammad also went on record to say in a hadith that "the best part of your religion is that which [offers] easier/lighter [options [*khayru dinikum aysaruhu*]." These aspects of the scriptural guidelines are known and recognised, yet they are often neglected and ignored with respect particularly to *ḥudūd*. Our opinion survey of leading twentieth-century shariah scholars record a resolute call on their part for the postponement of *ḥudūd* punishments, especially of mutilation for theft and of stoning for *zinā*, and their replacement with other suitable alternatives.

Their advice has yet to find a suitable place in Muslim public opinion on ICL and *ḥudūd*.

Following aggressive colonialist suppression of shariah, the twentieth century saw the Islamic revivalist call for the return of shariah and an enlightened *ijtihād*-based approach in its understanding, which has been continuously taking place ever since. Progress has been made as a result not only on reviving parts of shariah but also on introducing legal and constitutional reforms within and outside shariah. Malaysia in the second decade of the twenty-first century is not the same as that of thirty years ago, and this can also be said for many other Muslim-majority countries in Southeast Asia and beyond. There is definitely a greater awareness of making Islam a living reality for more Muslims than was the case in colonial times. This can also be generally said of Muslim minorities in the West. So when leading Muslim scholars offer an opinion and suggest that more time is needed for proper understanding and implementation of shariah punishments, one may see it as a fair assessment rather than an escapist opinion. There has to be, in addition, an effective government to be able not only to ensure an orderly enforcement of *ḥudūd* but also to ensure due process and prevent brutality and lawlessness. It is better to suspend *ḥudūd* rather than to see terrorism and lawlessness proliferating in the name of Islam—such as when so-called desert courts passing summary *ḥudūd* judgments or when a punitive approach to shariah is taken in conflict-ridden countries such as Afghanistan, Somalia, and Iraq. Therefore, one does not see ICL and *ḥudūd* as absolute issues in themselves but instead may recommend gradual steps toward more refined, *ijtihād*-oriented measures for their enforcement.

For Muslim countries that do have an effective government and are able to take a comprehensive approach to the enforcement of *ḥudūd*, wholly or partially, the recommendation is that they should do so in a holistic and compassionate manner as the Qur'an has envisaged, even if it means a departure from some scholastic and conventional positions. They should also place ICL within the larger rubric of government under the rule of law and due process. This may, in turn, require parliamentary approval for ICL or any part thereof to become the applied law of the land. Countries that are not in that position may take a gradual and selective approach and do what they consider to be within their capabilities. Some countries may be able to enforce and reform only certain aspects of ICL, and these actions are in accordance with the Islamic gradualist vision and advice. It is important in every case to obtain the required public support and parliamentary approval for the new initiative. What follows next are theme-specific conclusions and recommendations regarding the main headings of *ḥudūd*: adultery, theft, banditry/terrorism, slander, and consumption of alcohol. The discussion offers a number of juridical proposals that would hopefully contribute to carefully considered steps toward Islamic criminal law reform.

Pertaining to Zinaā *and Rape*

- The evidence we have reviewed shows that *zinā* under duress is not liable to punishment. Scholastic jurisprudence has recorded this but has fallen short of providing a separate definition and procedure for rape. Judges and muftis have consequently subsumed rape under *zinā*, which has often amounted to blatant miscarriage of justice. A clear and unequivocal separation between *zinā* and rape is therefore necessary. Many Muslim-majority countries have already done so and it is proposed that this becomes the standard position, not only in substantive terms and definitions but also in terms of separate procedures that govern their respective evidential processes and trials. The victim of rape should never be charged with slander in the event of her inability to prove her charge against the rapist, nor should she be asked to prove her innocence. The rape victim should, of course, be free to give evidence, failing which she only reports the matter to the police, and it is for them and the prosecution agencies to bring the criminal to justice.
- As for the punishment of *zinā*, we have examined a cross-section of opinion of the leading twentieth-century ulama and concluded that the maximum punishment of *zinā* is 100 lashes of the whip for married and unmarried persons alike. All claims and prosecutions of *zinā* that fail to present the textually stipulated proof by four eyewitnesses will most likely fall under *taʿzīr*, which would then enable the trial court to order a lesser punishment. The court should take into consideration all relevant factors, including the nature of the relationship, if any, between the parties, use or otherwise of oppressive behaviour, the age factor, indications of repentance and remorse, whether they are a first-time offender or recidivist, their personal reputation, and so forth.
- Pregnancy and confession should both be treated as circumstantial evidence that needs corroboration and endorsement. In the case of confession, it is offered four times and may still be retractable any time prior to the actual enforcement of punishment. If a pregnant woman

also makes a confession, the one will corroborate the other. Yet it is for the court of justice to determine the extent of reliability of that confession.

- A detailed enquiry further reveals that the Prophet, pbuh, most likely applied stoning (*rajm*) for *zinā* as a *taʿzīr* punishment. It has also been found that the existing evidence has fallen short of clarifying the question as to whether stoning was applied before or after the revelation of sura al-Nūr and its stipulated punishment of 100 lashes. The lingering doubt over this would invoke, in turn, the hadith directive that *ḥudūd* should be suspended when there is doubt. Most of the leading twentieth-century shariah scholars have actually taken the view that stoning for *zinā* is no longer an available option, and the present author concurs with that conclusion.
- As for reviving the Qur'anic provisions on repentance and reform, it is proposed that repentance should be made an integral part of the shariah court proceedings in all criminal trials, including *ḥudūd*. This should be mandated by an act of parliament that would hopefully also provide suitable procedural guidelines for verification of the merit of repentance before the court.
- It is patently unjust to single out the female party for punishment in *zinā* prosecutions, especially in the event of pregnancy and cases where the male party has escaped or denied the charges laid against him. The male party to the offence must be present and only then should court proceedings take their due course. Otherwise one is bound to be operating in a doubtful situation.
- On the punishment of homosexuality (*liwāṭ*), the recommendation is to adopt Imam Abū Ḥanīfah's view that *liwāṭ* should be punishable as a *taʿzīr* offence as, unlike *zinā*, there is no mixing of genealogy and family descent in *liwāṭ*. For hardened criminals who openly advocate and practice this offence, and repeat the same after the first conviction, the majority position treats it as a *ḥudūd* crime and subjects it to the same punishment as that of *zinā*.

*Theft (*Sariqah*)*

- With regard to theft, it is proposed to integrate the Qur'anic provisions on repentance and reform and authorise the trial judge to grant a suitable opportunity for it in the trial proceedings. This should also be done through an act of parliament that sets in place clear guidelines, both substantive and procedural, for judges and law enforcement agencies to ascertain the credibility of repentance.

- It is further proposed, on grounds of perennial doubt (*shubha*) that characterise the liberal capitalist economy and culture, that the capital punishment of mutilation for theft be substituted with alternative modes of punishment. A survey of expert opinion earlier presented on this included that of al-ʿAwā, who observed that "the application of the Islamic penal system under the present circumstances would not lead to the achievement of the ends visualised by this system." Abūl Āʿla Maududi had earlier recorded the view that "enforcing the *ḥadd* of theft would amount to protecting the ill-gotten wealth of the exploiters." Al-Qaraḍāwī found it unacceptable to neglect zakah and the social support system of Islam before enforcing the prescribed punishment of theft. Shaykh Muḥammad al-Ghazālī similarly thought it unacceptable to cut the hand of a petty thief while not applying the same to an embezzler of a stupendous amount of funds from the public treasury. In Muṣṭafā Aḥmad al-Zarqā's assessment, *ḥudūd* may generally be substituted with alternative punishments until such a time when conditions are right for their proper enforcement. And lastly, Shaykh ʿAbd Allāh Bin Bayyah's review of the early Islamic precedent led him to this conclusion: In the event when the Imam/leader is convinced that enforcing *ḥudūd* or *qiṣāṣ* would bring about a greater harm than benefit, he may suspend enforcement.
- Some of the fiqh textbook stipulations concerning theft should also be revised. For instance, theft and robbery from the public treasury, banks, and places where people deposit their assets, as well as embezzlement of large sums by corrupt officials, should not be regarded as mitigating factors on the assumption that the culprit as taxpayer had a share in the stolen assets but should, on the contrary, be regarded as aggravating factors that call for stiffer penalties.

Ḥiraābah, *Banditry, and Terrorism*

- All acts of terror by individuals and groups as well as state terrorism and suicide bombing, along with its organisers and unsuccessful perpetrators; those who destroy people's livelihood through contaminating water, air, and food; and hijackers of airplanes should be subsumed under *ḥirābah*.
- It is further proposed that the shariah concept of *ḥirābah* should apply to human trafficking, ransom-taking, and kidnapping of persons, be

they children or adults and regardless of gender and status. The perpetrators of *ḥirābah* should be liable, upon conviction, to one or more of the prescribed Qur'anic punishments for this crime. Relevant details should be articulated in an act of parliament.

- Terrorism has become exceedingly diversified and multidimensional. It has unfortunately also become a universal scourge that no country or community has the capacity to exterminate altogether or by acting alone. It requires effective international cooperation to address it.
- Terrorism cannot be effectively addressed without identifying its perpetrators and causes. These should be at the forefront of attention in each case and addressed collectively by all the concerned parties. This is an urgent task as terrorism has brutalised and traumatised individuals, communities, and nations, and any neglect in finding effective ways to address it is likely to condone it and lead to its proliferation.
- Violence breeds violence, and despite the claims of some to the contrary, military means have not only failed but increased the scope and scale of terrorism further.
- Among the various scholastic positions on *ḥirābah* reviewed here is a proposal to adopt the one that authorises the head of state and parliament to determine and select from the fourfold Qur'anic punishments for *ḥirābah* that which is deemed to be most suitable and effective.
- In the event where terrorists surrender to the authorities prior to subjugation and arrest, the authorities may grant a pardon absolutely or contingent upon conditions. Judicial proceedings should be involved to determine the credibility of terrorists' repentance.
- Pardon by the authorities does not absolve the culprit of any loss or damage inflicted on the person or property of the victim, whether public or private. The actual property must be returned when it exists, failing which any loss/damage caused should, subject to a court decision, be compensated by the perpetrators or by the state—unless of course the right-bearer decides to waive it.

Consumption of Liquor

- With regard to the punishment for consumption of liquor and other intoxicants, based on a review of the evidence, it is proposed that the lower of the two recorded punishments for this offence should be applied, that is, the maximum of forty lashes of the whip for cases, including those of drunken driving, that are proven by admissible evidence. This last may involve additional sanctions depending on the severity of violation and its actual consequences.

- The lighter of the two penalties advocated does not, however, extend to drug trafficking, which is a more serious crime and may be determined separately by statutory law that is duly informed by the gravity of the offence and the input, if any, of a judicious policy (*siyāsah*).
- As for the proof of this offence, one may mention the use of breathalyser test as an admissible means of proof even though it is not mentioned in the fiqh manuals. This would actually overcome the much-debated fiqh questions that have been reviewed over the reliability and duration of time of the breath smell and the actual condition of the drunken person. This analysis may also be extended, *mutatis mutandis,* to substance abuse, which may or may not involve the use of a breathalyser but that can be proven by alternative yet reliable scientific tests that establish beyond a doubt the offence in question.
- Our review and examination of the fiqh discourse on the subject also leads us to the conclusion that liquor consumption is not strictly a *ḥudūd* offence in the first place, and the proposed punishment for it also belongs to the category of *taʿzīr*. This would mean, in turn, that penal sanctions for the offence may consist of any number of lashes below the maximum of forty or indeed other alternative sanctions deemed appropriate by the competent authority.
- The open availability of alcohol in many Muslim countries, supermarkets, shops, restaurants, and means of transport by air and land also introduces an element of doubt, which is not helped, in turn, by the prevalence of a secularist culture and environment that should be taken into consideration by the judges and law enforcement authorities.

*Slanderous Accusation (*Qadhf*)*

- Slander (*qadhf*) is one of the *ḥudūd* offences that carries a punishment of eighty lashes upon proof. Our review of the juristic debate on the public and private (Right of God/Right of Man) components of this offence indicates the private claim aspect of *qadhf* to be the more predominant. Thus it would follow that prosecution of this offence should be made contingent on the request of its victim, and only then should necessary action by law enforcement agencies be taken.

- The victim of slander can also grant a pardon with or without compensation and thus put an end to the dispute. One can imagine the possibility that the victim of slander may want to bring the matter to an early close so as to avoid further publicity. This should be possible for, after all, the Qur'an is supportive of reconciliation (*ṣulḥ*) in disputes, to which *qadhf* should also be open, although the rest of the *ḥudūd* offences are, in theory, not open to pardoning or reconciliation.
- From a perusal of the Qur'anic verse on slander, it is also clear that this offence is closely tied to an unproven charge of *zinā* against a chaste woman. The relevant Qur'anic passage (al-Nūr, 24:2–4) underlines the seriousness of this charge and imposes a supplementary punishment of disqualifying the slanderer from becoming a witness. Slander is thus theme-specific and closely tied to *zinā*; it should not therefore be treated as a generic offence, nor analogically extended to similar offences, such as libel, insult, negative media publicity, and the like, which should be separately regulated and not subsumed under *qadhf*.

*Retaliation and Blood Money (*Qiṣaāṣ and Diya*)*

- The basic objectives of shariah in punishing murder and intentional injury by way of *qiṣāṣ* is realisation of measure-for-measure justice and avoidance of excess in the infliction of punishment. Yet the modalities of realising these objectives and the means or procedures by which they are best achieved may be adjusted in accordance with the prevailing conditions of each society and generation. They may also be duly adjusted in line with the higher purposes, or *maqāṣid*, of shariah and that of a judicious policy (*siyāsah*).
- Just retaliation may be demanded by the attorney general, representing the community, with prior permission of the next of kin of the deceased. It may also be demanded by the victim himself in the case of bodily injuries and approval of public authorities. The next of kin may demand *qiṣāṣ* or grant forgiveness for their part of the claim, or do so in combination with financial compensation (*diya*) to facilitate peaceful

settlement, although forgiveness according to a minority opinion does not combine with compensation.

- *Qiṣāṣ* law that assigns a role to the next of kin is an entrenched aspect of shariah—provided that it is not made into an instrument of abuse—in which case it is for the authorities to ban and prevent abusive practice. Many of the juristic formulations of *qiṣāṣ* and how the balance of the private and public right components thereof are adjusted and maintained are amenable to the rulers' judicious policy and pursuit of the *maqāṣid* of shariah.
- The purpose of *qiṣāṣ* is protection of innocent life and putting an end to vendettas and continued violence. These are the expressed objectives of the law of *qiṣāṣ*, which must remain valid. Yet the society's transition from tribalism to nation-states and then on to the still unfolding borderless world of globalisation would need to be duly reflected in the adjustment of private claim and public claim components of the *qiṣāṣ* law—and in any review/reform thereof.

*Judicious Policy (*Siyaāsah*) and Deterrent Punishment (*Taʿzīr*)*

- As already mentioned, *siyāsah* is a broad principle of Islamic public law of concern to good governance and administration of justice within or outside the sphere of criminal law. In introducing policy initiative and procedural regulation of court affairs, and to some extent also of substantive criminal law, *siyāsah* is the concern mainly of government leaders, the head of state, the judiciary, and parliament.
- *Siyāsah* relates to *ḥudūd* in a regulatory sense of ensuring the best methods of court procedures and case management in the judiciary. It also relates to regulating the role of law enforcement agencies with regard to Islamic criminal law and *ḥudūd*. That said, many of the reformist measures of ICL proposed here would also entail a greater role for *siyāsah* not only in introducing the suggested reforms but also with respect to their orderly implementation and enforcement.
- Early juristic opinion holds that the application of *siyāsah* in the sphere of criminal justice is of concern mainly, or even exclusively, to *taʿzīr*. But to reduce *siyāsah* entirely to *taʿzīr* is less than justified. Be that as it may, both *siyāsah* and *taʿzīr* are now subsumed by the constitutional

principle of legality in that all organs of state, including the head of state, are to comply with the principle of government under the rule of law. Discretionary powers are, in other words, subject to more limitations than before. Whereas the availability of some discretionary powers cannot be overruled altogether, it should nevertheless be defined and regulated in harmony with the guidelines of constitutional law and shariah.

- It is within the realm of *siyāsah* to note that the *ḥudūd* penalties may be frozen under certain conditions when it would cause greater harm than benefit, in which case the rulers' authority comes into the picture. As earlier mentioned, the Prophet, pbuh, suspended *ḥudūd* during warfare for fear of Muslim warriors defecting to the enemy ranks. In the year of famine (*ʿām al-majāʿah*—638–639 CE), the second caliph ʿUmar b. al-Khaṭṭāb exempted people from the payment of *jizyah* and froze the corporal punishment for theft. Muslim jurists have further maintained that there are no capital punishments in the following situations: (a) in non-Muslim territories; (b) in travels during war; (c) when people do not have prior knowledge of the existence of a crime or its rulings; (d) when there is no legitimate ruler; (e) when there are doubts that overwhelm the surrounding circumstances; and (f) when they cause far more damage than actual benefit. In short, shariah punishments and *ḥudūd* are not meant to be tyrannical but to deter crime and secure justice.

As for the conflict of jurisdiction between the civil and shariah courts, which occurs frequently in many Muslim-majority countries with dual court systems, the two courts systems should be combined or else there should be an attempt to establish mixed benches of shariah and civil law judges in order to solve the perennial conflict of jurisdiction between them. This is because justice is essentially monolithic and would differ little whether it is served in civil or shariah courts. To facilitate case management involving Muslim and non-Muslim parties in shariah litigations, there should be mixed benches of shariah and civil law judges sitting together. The discussion in this book has consistently maintained the unitarian character of justice and mentioned that the concept of specification of courts (*takhṣīṣ al-qaḍāʾ*) and setting up of specialised jurisdictions does not interfere with the essentially unitarian conception of justice in shariah. This is also the view of Tun Hamid, the former chief justice of Malaysia, who spoke from experience when he wrote that he had faced problems since the 1990s and cited cases he had adjudicated in support of his views.[1] Should there be different options over a matter, the ruler, judge, and mufti are advised to opt for the most appropriate yet lighter options that may be available, especially in the imposition of penalties. For as we read in the Qur'an, God Most High desires for us ease, not hardship (al-Baqarah, 2:185), and He does not desire to make religion a burden on people (al-Ḥaj, 22:79). The Prophet has similarly instructed his Companions to facilitate people's affairs, give them good news, and not repel them with doom and gloom (and talk of pain and punishment).[2]

Muslim scholars and judges tend to neglect these instructions and the well-known position that the ultimate goal of shariah is to secure people's welfare, mercy, and justice. This aspect of shariah does not receive due attention within and outside the courts of justice. It is not surprising therefore why shariah is often associated with punitiveness. Punishment in itself has never been a shariah priority and purpose. Yet common perceptions persist that the most intricate and difficult is the most pious—as it takes more effort and self-sacrifice! Legal pedantry thus manages to repress the softer voices of Islam. It then becomes a calling of Muslim religious and political leaders to change this negative profiling through capturing the bigger picture of shariah. This can best be done through affirmative action and the setting of good examples in the true spirit of *iḥsān*.

Acknowledgments

THIS BOOK HAS been developed over many years of piecemeal writing and research on issues of concern to Islamic criminal law, which has entailed numerous contacts, informative encounters and correspondence with individual researchers, libraries and colleagues in many countries. I take this opportunity to thank them all even if I am unable to recount their names and the context of our encounter. In what follows next, I begin by mentioning those who have actively helped me in the completion of the manuscript and were still assisting me even at the publication stage.

Siti Mar'iyah Chu Abdullah, my Personal Assistant at this Institute, has been instrumental in the completion of this book, especially with the computer work, website searches and outside correspondence. I take this opportunity to thank her warmly for all her good work. I also wish to thank most warmly Mohd Fariz Zainal Abdullah, head of the administration and human resource unit of the Institute, and Norliza Saleh, head of the Institute publication unit, for their assistance, whenever I have asked, with data checking and bibliographic information in the Arabic sources. I also thank my colleague Dr Muhammad Adha Shaleh, research fellow at the Institute, for his help with the keying in of Arabic segments into the running text.

Dr Mohamed Azam Mohamed Adil, Deputy CEO of this Institute, has been generous in advising me on queries I raised with him regarding the law and legal practice of Malaysia over matters of mutual interest.

I have known Tun Abdul Hamid Mohamad, the former Chief Justice of Malaysia, over many years and we have on occasions communicated and exchanged views on matters of mutual interest. I have benefited by his insights and would like to thank him for his valuable advice. I have similarly communicated on many occasions, and had in-depth discussions, with Tan Sri Syed Hamid Albar, former Foreign Minister of Malaysia and an Islamic scholar, who has generously shared his valuable insight and experience, but also criticism, regarding aspects of my work I had occasion to discuss with him, and I take this opportunity to thank him warmly. I also record my appreciation to Dr Chandra Muzaffar, a public personality and valuable resource I have consulted on issues of concern to Malaysia. He is a friend and supportive of my work and that of the Institute. I thank him warmly for his and valuable advice and counsel. Tan Sri Mohamed Jawhar Hassan, also a prominent public personality and a personal friend, has been generous in availing me of his insight and advice, and also criticism, over issues of mutual interest.

I take this opportunity also to acknowledge with profound appreciation the works of prominent Islamic scholars I have frequently cited throughout the text. I want to mention, in particular, the erudite works and contributions to Islamic law and shariah, of Yūsuf al-Qaraḍāwī, Muḥammad Abū Zahrah, Muḥammad Salīm al-ʿAwā, Muṣṭafā Aḥmad al-Zarqā, and ʿAbd Allāh Bin Bayyah. I have found their contributions to a better understanding of the shariah inspirational and reassuring in the stage-by-stage progress of this research.

Cynthia Read of Oxford University Press, New York, and my main contact with the OUP, has been most helpful with the communication of reviewer feedback and follow-up on research and publication. The outstandingly supportive reviewer comments and feedback also generated a degree of enthusiasm that she has generously shared with me.

Last but not least, I thank most warmly my wife, Susannah Abdullah, who has been generously supportive of my work and has patiently helped me to concentrate and devote so much time to this work.

A work of this size, with many fresh inroads for that matter, into some of uncharted territories of the shariah, and my inquisitive approach to research, can hardly be free of imperfection. I have not spared any effort to overcome weaknesses, but if there are any remaining, only I am responsible. Should there be any reader/reviewer input, and occasion for me to respond, I remain open to the prospects of further refinement.

Mohammad Hashim Kamali
International Institute of Advanced Islamic Studies (IAIS) Malaysia
November 2018

APPENDIX

Syariah Criminal Code (II) Bill 1993 of Kelantan, Malaysia

IT IS HEREBY ENACTED by the Legislature of the State of Kelantan as follows:

PRELIMINARY

1. This Enactment may be cited as the Syariah Criminal Code (II) Enactment 1993 and shall come into force on such date as His Royal Highness the Sultan may by notification in the *Gazette*, appoint.

2. (I) In this Enactment unless the context otherwise requires –

"Court" means the Special Syariah Trial Court and the Special Syariah Court of Appeal established under Part VI of this Enactment;

"diyat" means a sum of money or property payable as a compensation for death or loss of intelligence or injury to any organ which is complete or injury to any organ which is in pairs or the loss of function of any such organ caused to the victim of an offence. A diyat is equivalent to the prevailing price of 4,450 grams of gold or such sum as may be fixed by His Royal Highness the Sultan from time to time in accordance with Syariah Law;

"imprisonment" includes an order restricting an offender to reside within a particular area or district in the State;

"irsy" means a sum of money or property or a part of a diyat payable as compensation for injury (jurh) caused to the victim of an offence as specified in Schedule II, III and IV of this Enactment;

"judge" means a judge appointed under Part VI of this Enactment;

"Jumaah Ulama" means the Jumaah Ulama established under section 12 of the Kelantan Council of Islamic Religion and Malay Custom Enactment 1966;

"mohsan" and "ghairu mohsan" have the same meaning as defined in section 10(2);

"mukallaf" means a person who has attained the age of eighteen years and of sound mind;

"nisab" means a sum of money equivalent to the prevailing price of 4.45 grams of gold; or such sum as may from time to time be fixed by His Royal Highness the Sultan according to Syariah law;

"qisos" means the law of retaliation and equality governing offences of causing death of, and causing bodily injuries to persons;

"son" includes a grandchild and any person in descending order;

"State Service Commission" means the State Service Commission established under Article LXI of the Laws of the Constitution of Kelantan (First Part);

"wali" means a relative of the victim of crime who is entitled to remit the offence committed by an offender on the victim of the offence;

(II) To avoid doubts with regard to identity of the words or expressions used in this Enactment which are listed in Schedule 1, reference may be made to the Arabic Script of the said words and expressions shown against them in the said Schedule.

(III) All words, expressions, definitions and terms used in this Enactment which are not expressly defined in this Enactment shall be deemed to have the meaning given to them in the Interpretation Act 1948 and 1967, if not contrary to Syariah law.

(IV) Save where the context otherwise requires, any reference in this Enactment to a specific Part or section or subsection or Schedule shall be construed as a reference to the specific Part or section or subsection or Schedule in this Enactment.

3. All offences under this Enactment shall be divided into three categories, namely—

(a) offences the punishments of which are ordained by the Holy Quran and the Sunnah. Such offences are referred to as ḥudūd offences and their punishments as ḥudūd punishments;

(b) offences to which qisos applies and such offences also are ordained by the Holy Quran and the Sunnah and are referred to as qisos offences, and their punishments as qisos punishments; and

(c) offences which are neither ḥudūd nor qisos but left to the discretion of the legislature or, according to this Enactment left to the discretion of the Court. Such offences are referred to as ta'zir offences and their punishments as ta'zir punishments:

Provided that where a ḥudūd or a qisos offence cannot be punished with the ḥudūd or qisos punishment respectively because it cannot fulfill the conditions required to attract such punishment, the offence shall become a ta'zir offence and be punished accordingly.

PART I

Ḥudūd Offences

4. Ḥudūd offences are as follows:
   (a) sariqah (theft);
   (b) hirabah
   (c) zina (unlawful carnal intercourse)
   (d) qazaf (accusation of zina which cannot be proved by four witnesses)
   (e) syurb (drinking liquor or intoxicating drink); and
   (f) irtidad or riddah (apostasy)

5. Sariqah consists of an act of removing by stealth a movable property from the custody or possession of its owner without his consent and with the intention to deprive him.

6. Whoever commits sariqah, except in the circumstances enumerated in section 7, shall be punished with ḥudūd punishment as follows:
   (a) for the first offence with amputation of his right hand;
   (b) for the second offence with amputation of part of his left foot; and
   (c) for the third and subsequent offences with imprisonment for such term as in the opinion of the Court, may likely to lead him to repentance.

7. The ḥudūd punishment for sariqah shall not apply in any of the following circumstances:
   (a) where the value of the stolen property is less than the nisab;
   (b) where the offence is not proved by evidences required under the provisions of Part III;
   (c) where the offender is not a mukallaf;
   (d) where the owner of the stolen property has not taken sufficient precaution to guard it against theft, having regards to the nature of the property and place where the property is kept or left;
   (e) where the offender has not obtained full possession of the stolen property, although its owner has already been deprived of its custody and possession;
   (f) where the stolen property is of trifling nature and can be found in abundance in the land or is of perishable nature;
   (g) where the property is of no value according to Syariah law, such as intoxicating drink or instruments used for amusement;
   (h) where the offence is committed by a creditor in respect of the property of his debtor, who refuses to pay the debt:
   Provided that the value of the stolen property shall not exceed the amount of the debt or the value of the stolen property exceeds the amount of the debt but does not exceed the nisab;
   (i) where the offence is committed in circumstances of extreme difficulties, such as war, famine, pestilence and natural disaster;

(j) where the offence is committed within the family, such as a wife stealing from her husband and vice versa or son from his father and vice versa;
(k) where in the case of an offence being committed by a group of persons, the share of each offender after dividing the stolen property or the proceeds thereof is less than the nisab;
(l) where the offender returns the stolen property before the execution of the ḥudūd punishment;
(m) where the owner of the stolen property denies the theft notwithstanding the confession by the offender;
(n) where the offender makes objection accepted by Syariah law against the witnesses; and
(o) where the stolen property is or the circumstances in which the offence is committed are such that according to Syariah law there is no ḥudūd punishment.

8. Hirabah is an act of taking another person's property by force or threat of the use of force done by a person or a group of persons armed with weapon or any instrument capable of being used as weapon.

9. Whoever commits hirabah shall be punished with the "ḥudūd punishments as follows:
(a) death and thereafter crucified, if the victim is killed and his or other person's property is taken away;
(b) death only, if the victim is killed without any property being taken away;
(c) amputation of right hand and left foot; if only the property is taken away without killing the victim or injuring him, but where the property is taken away and bodily injury is caused, diyat or irsy shall be payable in addition to the punishment of amputation of hand and foot; such diyat or irsy being an appropriate amount consistent with the type and nature of injuries caused as specified in Schedules II, III and IV; and
(d) imprisonment for such term as in the opinion of the Court would lead the offender to repentance, if only threats are uttered without any property being taken away or bodily injury caused

10. (1) Zina is an offence which consists of sexual intercourse between a man and a woman who are not married to each other and such intercourse does not come within the meaning of "wati syubhah" as defined in subsection (3).
(2) where an offender is validly married and has experienced sexual intercourse in such marriage, such offender is called "mohsan", but where an offender is not married, or is already married but has not experienced sexual intercourse in such marriage, such offender is called "ghairu mohsan".
(3) Wati syubhah is a sexual intercourse performed by a man with a woman who is not his wife and such intercourse took place
(a) in doubtful circumstances in which he thought that the woman with whom he had sexual intercourse was his wife, when in fact she was not; or
(b) in doubtful circumstances in which he believed his marriage to the woman with whom he had sexual intercourse was valid according to Syariah law, when in fact his marriage to her was invalid.

11. (1) Where the offender who commits the offence of zina is a mohsan, such offender shall be punished with the punishment of rejam, being the punishment of stoning the offender with stones of medium size to death.

(2) Where the offender who commits the offences of zina is a ghairu mohsan such offender shall be punished with the punishment of whipping of one hundred lashes and in addition thereto to one year imprisonment.

12. (1) Qazaf is an offence of making an accusation of zina, being an accusation incapable of being proved by four witnesses, against a Muslim who is akil baligh and known to be chaste.

(2) It is also an offence of qazaf for any person to make a statement by expressly saying that a particular individual has committed zina or by impliedly saying that a particular individual is not the parent or not the offspring of another particular individual.

(3) The statement under subsection (2) shall be deemed to be qazaf unless proved by four male witnesses; and if unproved the person who makes the statement shall be guilty of an offence of qazaf; but where such statement is proved, the person against whom the statement is made shall be guilty of an offence of zina.

(4) The statement under subsection (2) shall be deemed to be unproved, if one or more of the four witnesses called to give evidence to support the statement decline to testify or do testify but their testimonies are against such statement; and in that event each of the witnesses who give evidence in support of the statement shall be deemed to have committed an offence of qazaf.

13. Whoever commits qazaf shall be punished with eighty lashes of whipping and his testimony shall no longer be accepted until he repents.

14. (1) Al-li'an is an accusation of zina on oath made by a husband against his wife, whilst the wife on oath rejects such accusation; and bothe accusation and rejection are made before a judge by uttering words which according to Syariah law are sufficient to prove al-li'an; and such words shall be as contained in subsection (2).

(2) The husband who makes the accusation shall repeat four times consecutively the following utterance:

"Allah is my witness that I speak the truth that my wife . . . . has committed zina."

(3) When he has completed repeating those words as contained in subsection (2) four times, he shall make the fifth utterance by saying:

"The curse of Allah shall fall on me if I have lied."

(4) To reject the accusation, the wife shall also repeat four times consecutively the following utterance:

"Allah s my witness that my husband . . . . had lied in making this accusation against me."

(5) when she has completed repeating those words as contained in subsection (4) four times, she shall make the fifth utterance by saying:

"Allah's anger shall fall on me if my husband has spoken the truth."

(6) If the wife has given birth to a child or if she is pregnant both the birth and the pregnancy being considered as the consequence of the zina alleged by the husband, he shall deny fathering the child by adding to the words in subsection (2) which shall be repeated four times, the following utterance:

"The child/what is being carried by my wife is not from me."

15. Where a married couple resorts to al-li'an to settle an accusation of zina between them neither the husband shall be quilty of qazaf, nor the wife of zina, and both shall be free from punishment for such offence; but the marriage shall automatically be dissolved forthwith; and the judge shall make an order accordingly; and the couple shall forever not be capable of marrying each other again; and if they thereafter have sexual intercourse between them such act is zina.

16. Liwat is an offence consisting of carnal intercourse between a male and another male or between a male and a female other than his wife, performed against the order of nature, that is through the anus.

17. Whoever commits liwat shall be punished with the same punishment prescribed for zina.

18. The offence of liwat shall be proved by the same mode as that required to prove zina.

19. (1) Musahaqah is a ta'zir offence consisting of an act of sexual gratification between females by subbing the vagina of one against that of the other and the punishment thereof shall be at the discretion of the Court.

(2) The offence shall be proved by the same mode as that required to prove a ta'zir offence.

20. Ittiyan almaitah is an offence of performing carnal intercourse on a dead body, irrespective of whether such dead body is male or female, and if it is a female dead body whether it is that of the wife of the offender or that of any other person; and whoever commits this offence shall be punished with ta'zir punishment of imprisonment not exceeding five years.

21. Ittiyan albahimah is an offence of performing carnal intercourse with an animal; and whoever commits this offence shall be punishment with ta'zir punishment of imprisonment not exceeding five years.

22. (1) Syurb is an offence of drinking liquor or any other intoxicating drinks and any person who commits this offence, whether intoxicated or not, and irrespective of the quantity consumed, shall be punished with whipping of not more than eighty lashes but not less than forty lashes.

(2) The offence may be proved by oral testimonies of two witnesses or the accused's own confession as provided for in Part III.

23. (1) Irtidad is any act done or any word uttered by a Muslim who is mukallaf, being act or word which according to Syariah law, affects or which is against the 'aqidah (belief) in Islamic religion:

Provided that such act is done or such word is uttered intentionally, voluntarily and knowingly without any compulsion by anyone or by circumstances.

(2) The acts or the words which affect the 'aqidah (belief) are those which concern or deal with the fundamental aspects of Islamic religion which are deemed to have been known and believed by every Muslim as part of his general knowledge for being a Muslim, such as matters pertaining of Rukun Islam, Rukun Imam and matters of halal (the allowable or the lawful) or haram (the prohibited or the unlawful).

(3) Whoever is found guilty of committing the offence of irtidad shall, before a sentence is passed on him, be required by the Court to repent within a period of not less than three days after he has been so found.

(4) where he is reluctant to repent and still continues with his attitude as regards the act he has done or the word he has uttered, the Court shall pronounce the death sentence on him and order the forfeiture of his property irrespective of whether such property was required before or after the commission of the offence to be held for the Baitul-Mal:

Provided that when he repents, whether the repentance is done before the death sentence is pronounced or after such pronouncement but before the sentence is carried out, he shall be free from the death sentence and his property ordered to be forfeited shall be returned to him:

Provided further that he shall be imprisoned for a term not exceeding five years.

PART II

Qisos

24. Both qisos and diyat shall apply to offences of homicide and causing bodily injuries.

25. Homicide shall be divided into three categories –

(a) Qatl-al-'amd (wilful killing);

(b) Qatl-syibhi-al-'amd (quasi-wilful killing); and

(c) Qatl-al-khata' (killing without intention).

26. (1) Whoever causes the death of a person by doing an act with the intention of causing death or bodily injury which in the ordinary course of nature is likely or sufficient to cause death; or by doing an act with the knowledge that his act is so imminently dangerous that it must in all probability cause death, is said to commit qatl-al-'amd.

(2) Whoever by doing an act with the intention or knowledge that the aforesaid act is likely to cause death, causes the death of any person whose death he neither intends nor knows himself to be likely to cause, is also said to commit qatl-al-'amd.

(3) Whoever by doing an act with the intention or knowledge that the aforesaid act is likely to cause death, causes the death of any person who death he neither intends nor knows himself to be likely to cause, is also said to commit qatl-al-'amd.

27. (1) Except as provided in subsection (2), whoever commits qatl-al-'amd shall be punished with death as qisos punishment.

(2) The punishment of death in subsection (1) shall not be imposed where –

(a) the offence is not proved by the evidence required under Part III; or

(b) notwithstanding such proof, the wali remits the qisos.

28. The wali may at any time before the punishment of death as the qisos punishment is executed, pardon the offender either with or without a diyat; and if the pardon is with a diyat, this shall be paid either in a lump sum or by instalments within a period of three years form the date of the final judgement, and if in the meantime the offender dies, the diyat shall be recoverable from his estate.

29. Where the punishment of death as qisos punishment is not imposed the offender shall be liable to the ta'zir punishment of imprisonment for life or having regards to the circumstances of the case to such term of imprisonment as in the opinion of the Court would lead the offender to repentance.

30. Whoever with the intention of causing injury to the body or mind of any person causes the death of that person or any other person by doing an act with or without a weapon which in the ordinary course of nature is not likely to cause death is said to commit qatl-al-syibhi-al-'amd.

31. Whoever commits qatl-al-syibhi-al-'amd shall pay diyat to the victim's wali and in addition thereto shall be punished with the ta'zir punishment of imprisonment for a term not exceeding fourteen years.

32. Whoever without an intention of causing death or injury causes the death of a person by doing an act which is not anticipated to cause the death of such person or any person or by doing an unlawful act which later becomes the cause for the death of such person is said to commit Qatl-al-khata'.

33. Whoever commits qatl-al-khata' shall pay diyat to the victim's wali and in addition thereto may be liable to the ta'zir punishment of imprisonment for a term not exceeding ten years.

34. Whoever causes pain, harm, disease, infirmity or injury to any person, or impairs or destroys or causes the loss of function of any organ of the body of any person or part thereof without causing his death is said to cause bodily injury.

35. (1) Whoever causes bodily injury to a person shall be punished with the qisos punishment, that is with similar bodily injury as that which he has inflicted upon his victim and where qisos punishment cannot be imposed or executed because the conditions required by the Syariah law are not fulfilled, the offender shall pay irsy to his victim and may be liable to ta'zir punishment of imprisonment.

(2) The amount of irsy payable and the term of imprisonment to be imposed shall be fixed by the Syariah law and shall vary according to the nature and gravity of the injuries caused to the victim, and the circumstances in which the offence is committed.

36. For the purpose of awarding punishments, bodily injuries shall be classified as follows:

(a) Itlaf-al-udhw (causing dismemberment of any organ of the body or injury to a part of or organ of the body);

(b) Itlaf-solahiyyatu-al-udhw (causing destruction or permanent impairment of the function, of use of an organ of the body or permanently disfiguring such organ;

(c) Syajjah (causing injury on the head or face which injury does not amount to itlaf-al-udhw or itlaf-solahiyyatu-al-udhw);

(d) Jurh (causing injury on any part of the body save the head and the face which injury leaves a mark or wound whether temporary or permanent); and

(e) All other bodily injuries.

37. Qisos punishment shall not be imposed in the following cases:
   (a) Where the offender who has committed the qisos offence is dead;
   (b) Where the limb or the organ for which qisos punishment is to be applied is already non-functional or otherwise incapacitated;
   (c) Where pardon is given by the victim or his wali; or
   (d) Where a settlement (solh) and agreement between the victim and the offender has been made.

38. Where qisos punishment is not imposed –
   (a) The term of imprisonment as ta'zir punishment for causing itlaf-al-udhw and itlaf-solahiyyatu-al-udhw is ten years; and the irsy payable for causing the injury shall be as specified in Schedule II;
   (b) The term of imprisonment as ta'zir punishment and the irsy payable for causing syajjah shall be as specified in Schedule III; and
   (c) The term of imprisonment as ta'zir punishment and the irsy payable for causing jurh shall be as specified in Schedule IV.

PART III

Evidence

39. (1) Save where it is in conflict with the provisions of this Enactment, the Evidence Enactment of the Syariah Court 1991 shall apply for the purpose of proving offences under this Enactment.
   (2) All offences under this Enactment, whether ḥudūd offences or qisos offences or ta'zir offences shall be proved by oral testimonies or by confession made by the accused.

40. (1) The number of witnesses required to prove all offences under this Enactment except zina shall be at least two.
   (2) The number of witnesses required to prove zina shall not be less than be less than four.

41. (1) Each witness shall be an adult male Muslim who is akil baligh, and shall be a person who is just.
   (2) A person shall be considered just if he does what is required of him by Islam and avoids committing great sins and does not continuously commit lesser sins and further has isti'mal al-muru ah, (a sense of honour).
   (3) A person shall be deemed to be just, until the contrary is proved.

42. (1) To prove the charge against the accused and render him liable to ḥudūd or qisos punishment the evidence given shall be one of absolute certainty and free from any ambiguity or doubt.
   (2) Each witness shall state clearly that he has actually seen the act complained of and in the case of zine the four witnesses shall state that they have actually seen the act of penetration of the sex organ of the male partner into that of the female partner of the copulating pair and further there shall neither be contradiction nor inconsistency among the witnesses in such testimony.

43. (1) To make the accused liable to a ḥudūd punishment each witness shall maintain his testimony against the accused not only during the trial and thereafter but also during the execution of the punishment because if such testimony is withdrawn before the execution of the punishment the accused shall cease to be liable to the ḥudūd punishment, and if it is withdrawn at the time when the accused is undergoing the punishment, the punishment shall forthwith cease.

(2) In the case of zina, where one witness declines to give evidence, or gives evidence in support of the charge but later withdraws such evidence so that the number of witnesses in support of the charge becomes less than four, the charge of zine against the accused shall remain unproved and he shall cease to be liable to the ḥudūd punishment; but the remaining witnesses who have testified in support of the charge shall be guilty of an offence of qazaf.

44. (1) The best evidence to convict the accused and make him liable to ḥudūd punishment is his own confession.

(2) The confession must be made voluntarily and without any force before a judicial officer and shall afterwards be repeated before the trial judge during the course of the trial, and if the trial is one of zina the confession shall be repeated four time before the judge during the course of the trial:

Provided that both the making and the repetition of the confession must be without any threat, promise or inducement and must clearly prove in detail that the accused has actually committed the offence with which he is charged and that he understands that he will be punished for making such confession.

(3) The confession shall be admissible only against the accused who makes it, and cannot be used against any other person; and to be valid the confession must not be a retracted confession.

45. (1) A confession may be retracted by the accused who makes it at any time even while he is undergoing the punishment.

(2) If the confession is retracted before the execution of the punishment on him, the accused shall no longer be liable to punishment and if he retracts the confession at the time when he is undergoing the punishment such execution shall forthwith cease.

(3) If at any time before or at the time when the punishment is being executed the accused manages to escape from the authorities, he shall be deemed to have retracted the confession and as such the provision of subsection (2) shall apply.

46. (1) Save as provided in subsection (2) and (3) circumstantial evidence, though relevant, shall not be a valid method of proving a ḥudūd offence.

(2) In the case of zina, pregnancy or delivery of a baby by an unmarried woman shall constitute evidence on which to find her guilty of zina and therefore the ḥudūd punishment shall be passed on her unless she can prove to the contrary.

(3) In the case of drinking liquor or any other intoxicating drinks, the smell of liquor in the breath of the accused, or the fact of his vomiting liquor or any other intoxicating drinks or traces thereof, or the observation by the Court of the accused being in a state of intoxication shall be admissible as evidence to prove that he has committed the offence of syurb unless he can prove to the contrary.

47. Where the accused cannot be made liable to a ḥudūd punishment because the witnesses have withdrawn their testimonies as provided for in section 43 or because the accused has retracted his confession as provided for in section 45 or the evidence available does not fulfil; the conditions required to prove a ḥudūd offence, the accused may be liable to a ta'zir punishment; and the Court shall proceed to pass such punishment if there is sufficient evidence for that purpose.

PART IV

How Punishment is Carried Out

48. The ḥudūd punishment imposed under this Enactment shall not be suspended, substituted for any other punishment, reduced or pardoned or otherwise varied or altered.

49. Every sentence imposing a ḥudūd punishment and every death sentence imposed as qisos or ta'zir punishment under this Enactment shall be referred by the Special Syariah Trial Court which has passed the sentence to the Special Syariah Court of Appeal for confirmation and the punishment imposed shall not be carried out before such confirmation is obtained.

50. A ḥudūd punishment imposed, other than the punishment of death and rejam shall not be executed unless the offender is medically examined by a Muslim medical officer and certified to be fit by that officer.

51. If an offender is guilty of several offences, the punishment which shall be carried out on him shall be as follows:

(a) If the punishments are of the same kind and graveness, only one punishment shall be carried out;

(b) If the punishments are of the same kind, but of different graveness, only the severest punishment shall be carried out;

(c) If the punishments are of different kinds, all shall be carried out; and

(d) If one of the punishments is death all other punishments shall be set aside.

52. (1) The punishment of amputation of a hand shall mean an amputation of the hand at the wrist; that is the joint between the palm and the forearm.

(2) The punishment of amputation of a foot shall mean an amputation of the foot in the middle of the foot in such a way that the heel may still be usable for walking and standing.

53. The punishment of whipping shall be carried out in accordance with the Rules specified in Schedule V.

54. The punishment of rejam shall not be carried out on a pregnant female offender until after she has delivered her child, and thereafter become clean of blood and is fit again to undergo the punishment; and in the event of the child being suckled by her, the rejam shall not be executed until after the completion of full two years of suckling unless there is a wet nurse who is willing to undertake to suckle the child during the said period.

55. The punishment of whipping shall not be executed on a pregnant female offender until after she has delivered her child, and thereafter become clean of blood and is fit again to undergo the punishment without hazard.

PART V

General Provisions

56. (1) Subject to subsection (2), this Enactment shall apply to every Muslim who is a mukallaf in respect of any offence committed by him in the State of Kelantan.

(2) Nothing in this Enactment shall preclude a non-Muslim from electing that this Enactment apply to him in respect of any offence committed by him within the State of Kelantan, and in the event of such non-Muslim electing as aforesaid, the provisions of this Enactment shall, mutatis mutandis, apply to him as they apply to a Muslim.

57. Where an offence is committed as a result of, or in furtherance of an abetment, assistance, conspiracy or plot, every person who abets or assists or conspires or plots for the commission of such offence shall be guilty of that offence and shall be liable to be punished with imprisonment as ta'zir punishment for a term not exceeding ten years.

58. When an offence is committed by several persons in furtherance of a common intention of all, each of such persons is liable for that offence in the same manner as if the offence were done by him alone and shall be liable to be punished with the ta'zir punishment of imprisonment not exceeding ten years.

59. Where several offenders commit sariqah, each of them shall be punished with the ḥudūd punishment as if each offender has committed it all alone:

Provided that the share obtained from the stolen property bye ach of them when divided equally amongst them, is equal to or exceeds the amount of nisab.

60. Whoever attempts to commit an offence under this Enactment shall be punished with the ta'zir punishment of imprisonment for a term not exceeding ten years.

61. Where a person has been tried or faced any proceeding for an offence under this Enactment, he shall not be tried and no proceeding shall be taken against him under the Penal Code in respect of the same or similar offence provided in the Code.

62. (1) All offences under this Enactment and the provisions relating thereto shall be interpreted according to the Syariah law and the precedents found therein; and reference to such law shall be made in respect of any matter not provided for in this Enactment.

(2) If any doubt or difficulty arises in the interpretation of any word, expression or term relating to Syariah law, the Court trying the case shall have jurisdiction to give meaning to such word, expression or term.

PART VI

Court

63. (1) There shall be established the Special Syariah Trial Court and the Special Syariah Court of Appeal.

(2) The Special Syariah Trial Court shall have jurisdiction to try offences under this Enactment.

(3) The Special Syariah Court of Appeal shall have jurisdiction to hear appeals from the decisions of the Special Syariah Trial Court.

64. The Courts established under section 63 shall be an addition to the Syariah courts established under the Administration of the Syariah Court Enactment 1982, and the provisions of that Enactment shall be appropriate matters apply to the Courts, unless they are in conflict with the provisions of this Enactment or are not intended by the provision of this Enactment.

65. The Syariah Criminal Procedure Enactment 1983 shall apply to all proceedings of the Courts with or without such modifications as the Courts think fit in the interest of justice.

66. When it is sitting to try an offence under this Enactment the Special Syariah Trial Court shall consist of three judges, two of who shall be ulamak; and the session shall be presided over by any one of the said judges.

67. When it is sitting to hear an appeal from the decision or order of the Special Syariah Trial Court, the Special Syariah Court of Appeal shall consist of five judges, three of who shall be ulamak and the session shall be presided over by any one of the said judge.

68. A person who hold or had held office as a judge of the High Court of Malaya or Borneo or the Supreme Court of Malaysia or any person who has the qualification to be appointed as a judge of any of those Courts may be appointed to be a judge; whilst an ulamak who may be appointed a judge shall be a person who holds or has held office as a Qadhi Besar or Mufti Kerajaan or any one who has the qualification to hold any of those offices and is known to have deep knowledge of Syariah Law.

69. (1) These judges shall be appointed by the His Royal Highness the Sultan by an Instrument of Appointment under His Sign Manual and Seal after consulting the State Service Commission and the Jumaah Ulama and in addition High Highness may also consult any other authority or body or individual who is ighHighness Opinion is considered fit and proper and such appointment shall be published in the Gazette.

(2) In making of the appointment under subsection (1), His Royal Highness the Sultan shall signify whether the appointee is the President of the Special Syariah Court of Appeal or the Chief Judge of the Special Syariah Trial Court or a judge of the Special Syariah Court of Appeal or a judge of the Special System Trial Court.

70. The principle of independence of the judiciary shall apply to the Courts and every judgement appointed this Enactment shall be free from interference from any authority or individual.

71. (1) Every judge is entitled to hold office until he voluntarily resigns from his office, unless in the meantime he is required to leave the service because of unsound mind or ill-health which has to be certified by not less than three medical experts or because he is found by an independent Judicial Commission to have committed an offence which renders him unfit to be a judge.

(2) Both the medical experts and the independent Judicial Commission shall be appointed by His Royal Highness the Sultan after consulting such authority, body or individual whom His Highness thinks fit and proper.

(3) The offence referred to in subsection (1) shall be an offence known to the secular law or the Syariah law and the evidence in support thereof must be clear.

72. (1) The salaries, allowances and other privileges of the judges shall be a charge on the Consolidated Fund of the State and shall not be less than those enjoyed by a judge of the High Court of Malaya or Borneo or of the Supreme Court of Malaysia.

(2) The Legislative Assembly of the Sate may make law to fix the salaries, allowances and other privileges of the judges of the Courts established by this Enactment.

SYARIAH CRIMINAL CODE (II) 29

SCHEDULE I

SYARIAH CRIMINAL CODE (II) 29

SCHEDULE I

Schedule I (attached to Section 53)

The Whipping Rules

1. The Rules in this Schedule shall apply to the execution of whipping punishment under section 53 of this Enactment.
2. A whipping punishment to be executed on an offender shall be carried out by an officer specifically authorised by the prison authority at a place and time directed by the Court and shall be in the presence of and witnessed by a Muslim medical officer and at least four adult male Muslims as witnesses; provided that before the punishment is carried out the offender shall first be examined by the medical officer and certified by him to be fit to receive such punishment.
3. No whipping punishment shall be carried out on an offender unless a period of fourteen days have lapsed after the date of the judgement; provided that in the event of an appeal, the punishment shall be carried out as soon as possible after the punishment is confirmed by the Special Syariah Court of Appeal.
4. The whipping punishment shall be carried out by the aforesaid officer hitting the offender with a rattan, the size of which (save in the case mentioned in Rule 8(2)(ii)) shall be one meter long and one centimeter in diameter.
5. The whipping shall be administered in such a way that the strokes shall be well distributed on all parts of the body except the face, head, chest and private parts.
6. The whipping shall be carried out with a moderate force in that the officer administering the punishment shall not raise the rattan whip high up to the level of his head; and such whipping shall be given consecutively and shall not exceed the number of strokes ordered by the Court.
7. When receiving the whipping, the offender shall be in standing position and clothed in thin clothing which covers the ‘aurat according to Syariah law.
8. (1) If during the course of the whipping being administered to him the offender is found to be incapable of receiving further whipping, on the certification by the medical officer, the whipping shall forthwith stop and postponed until

the Court shall give a new direction as to the resumption of the punishment; and in the meantime the offender shall be detained in prison or set free on bail.

(2) Such direction shall be made on the basis of a report made by the aforesaid medical officer and shall be as follows:

(i) if according to the report the offender is likely to recover from his present incapacity, the punishment shall be resumed as soon he recovers from his ailments; and (ii) if according to the report the offender is not likely to recover from his present incapacity, notwithstanding the ailments, the punishment shall also be resumed at a suitable time but the rattan to be used to continue the whipping shall be lighter and of smaller size than that specified in Rule 4 of these Rules.

Notes

CHAPTER I

1. Rudolph Peters, *Crime and Punishment in Islam: Theory and Practice from the Sixteenth to the Twentieth Century*, Cambridge, UK: Cambridge University Press, 2005, 144–145.
2. This is also conveyed in a legal maxim of fiqh: "there shall be no ijtihad when there is a textual injuction—*lā ijtihāda fī'l-naṣṣ*." It may be added, however, that legal maxims (*qawā'id kulliyyah fiqhiyyah*) are advisory and instructive in principle, not binding. Further advances in knowledge and science, or in people's life conditions and experiences, may provide cause for fresh reflection and a basis therefore to revise a legal maxim. For an extended selection of these maxims, see Mohammad Hashim Kamali, *Shariah Law: Questions and Answers*, Oxford: Oneworld Publications, 2017, 216–249.
3. The five pillars of Islam are faith in God, the daily prayers (*ṣalāh*), paying the poor due (*zakāh*), fasting during Ramadan, and the hajj (pilgrimage).
4. Cf. Mohammad Hashim Kamali, "Strictly from the Qur'anic Perspective," *New Straits Times* (Kuala Lumpur), 25 April 2009, 14.
5. ʿAbd al-Raḥmān b. Muḥammad Awaḍ al-Jazīrī, *al-Fiqh ʿalā'l-Madhāhib al-Arbaʿah*, new rev. ed., Cairo: Dār al-Ghad al-Jadīd, 2005, 1148, discusses the scholastic differences on the number of *ḥudūd* and then records the minimalist account of *ḥudūd* to three, namely the *ḥudūd* of adultery, slander, and theft, on which there is no disagreement, whereas disagreement abounds on almost every other addition to this minimum.
6. Kelantan has remained under PAS ever since, whereas Terengganu changed hands in the 2004 election and is currently also ruled by the Islamic Party of Malaysia (PAS).
7. Official title: Shariah Criminal Code (II) Bill 1993. Appended at the end of this volume, the reader will find a copy of the standard English translation of the Hudud Bill of Kelantan 1993 that was circulated in Malaysia at the time.

8. The only country of the Muslim world perhaps with an impressive record of having held fourteen successive elections without major problems since its independence in 1957.
9. Referring to this aspect of the *ḥudūd*, the then PAS assistant secretary general, Takiyuddin Hassan, confirmed that "offences under *ḥudūd* would only be tried in the shariah court as it is clearly stated in our Enactment." See article by Nik Imran Abdullah et al., "Confusion over DAP's Stand: PAS Leaders at Odds over whether Partner Agreeable on *Hudud*," *New Straits Times* (Kuala Lumpur), 13 October 2011, 11.

CHAPTER II

1. Cf. M. Cheriff Bassiouni, *The Shari'a and Islamic Criminal Justice in Time of War and Peace*, New York: Cambridge University Press, 2014, 120; Muḥammad Sālim al-ʿAwā, *al-Fiqh al-Islāmī fī Ṭarīq al-Tajdīd*, 3rd enhanced ed., Beirut: al-Maktab al-Islāmī, 1419/1998, 169. See also generally Rudolph Peters, *Crime and Punishment in Islam: Theory and Practice from the Sixteenth to the Twentieth Centuries*, Cambridge, UK: Cambridge University Press, 2005.
2. Abd al-Qādir ʿAwdah, *al-Tashrīʿ al-Jināʾī al-Islāmī Muqārinah bi'l-Qānūn al-Waḍʿi*, 13th ed., 2 vols., Beirut: Muʾassasah al-Risālah, 1415/1994, 1:629.
3. Ibid., 1:630.
4. Ibid.

CHAPTER III

1. Cf. Burhān al-Dīn al-Marghīnānī, *al-Hidāyah*, Cairo: Muṣṭafā al-Bābī al-Ḥalabī, n.d., vol. 2, 94; Shams al-Dīn al-Sarakhsī, *al-Mabsūṭ*, Beirut: Dār al-Maʿrifah, 1406/1986, vol. 11, 36; al-Jazīrī, *al-Fiqh ʿalā'l-Madhāhib*, 1168; Wizārat al-Awqāf wa'l-Shuʾūn al-Islāmiyyah, *al-Mawsūʿah al-Fiqhiyyah*, Kuwait: Dār al-Salāsil, 1434/2003, vol. 7, 130; Aḥmad Fatḥī Bahnasī, *al-ʿUqūbah fī l-Fiqh al-Islāmī*, 6th ed., Cairo: Dār al-Shurūq, 1409/1989, 123.
2. Cf. Fazlur Rahman, "The Concept of Hadd in Islamic Law," *Islamic Studies* 4 (1965), 237; Kassim Ahmad, "Resolving the 'Ḥudūd' Law Dilemma," *New Straits Times* (Kuala Lumpur), 4 December 1993, 13.
3. al-Marghīnānī, *al-Hidāyah*, 2:94; al-Sarakhsī, *al-Mabsūṭ*, 9:36.
4. Abū al-Ḥasan al-Māwardī, *Kitāb al-Aḥkām al-Sulṭāniyyah*, 3rd ed., Cairo: Muṣṭafā al-Bābī al-Ḥalabī, 1393/1973, 221; see also, al-Marghīnānī, *al-Hidāyah*, 2:94.
5. Bahnasī, *al-ʿUqūbah*, 124; Mohamed S. el-Awa, *Punishment in Islamic Law*, Indianapolis: American Trust Publications, 1982, 30.
6. Cf. Fazlur Rahman, "The Concept of Hadd," 238.
7. Ibid., 240.

8. Sayyid Abūl Āʿla Maududi, *The Islamic Law and Constitution*, Lahore: Islamic Publication Ltd., reprint 1979, 142.
9. Abū Jaʿfar Yaʿqūb Ibn Jarīr al-Ṭabarī, *Tafsīr al-Ṭabarī, Tafsīr al-Qurʾān al-ʿAẓīm* (also known as *Tafsīr al-Ṭabarī*), Beirut: Dār al-Maʿrifah, 1400/1980, 8:89.
10. Fatḥī b. al-Ṭayyib al-Khammāsī, *al-Ḍarūrah al-Murḥaliyyah fī-Taṭbīq al-Qānūn al-Jināʾī al-Islāmī*, Damascus and Beirut: Dār Qutaybah, 1421/2001, 202.
11. As quoted in al-Khammāsī, *al-Ḍarūrah*, 198.
12. Muḥammad Abū Zahrah, *al-Jarīmah wa'l ʿUqūbah fī'l-Fiqh al-Islāmī: al-ʿUqūbah*, 10th ed., ed. Muḥyī al-Dīn Fatḥī al-Shaludī, Cairo: Dār al-Fikr al-ʿArabī, 2006, 134–136.
13. Shaila Khoshy, "PAS: Our Right to Pass Shariah Law," *The Star* (Kuala Lumpur), 19 August 2003, 23.
14. Ibid.
15. Muwaffaq al-Dīn Ibn Qudāmah, *al-Mughnī*, Beirut: Dār al-Kitāb al-ʿArabī, 1403/1983, 1:315; ʿAwdah, *al-Tashrīʿ al-Jināʾī*, 1:353.
16. Cf. *al-Mawsūʿah al-Fiqhiyyah* (Kuwait), 7:133–134.
17. Ibid., 7:134.
18. Muḥammad b. Idrīs al-Shāfiʿī, *Kitāb al-Umm*, Beirut 1413/1993, 6:229. Also quoted in al-Khammāsī, *al-Ḍarūrah*, 192.
19. Aḥmad Taqī al-Dīn Ibn Taymiyyah, *Majmūʿ al-Fatāwā Shaykh al-Islām Ibn Taymiyyah*, Riyadh, n.d., 29 vols., 15:202; Abū Zahrah, *al-ʿUqūbah*, 244; al-Khammāsī, *al-Ḍarūrah*, 193.
20. Ibid. [[Clarify—ibid. to which ref. above?]]
21. Cf. Ibn Qudāmah, *al-Mughnī*, 1:316; ʿAwdah, *al-Tashrīʿ al-Jināʾī*, 1:353.
22. Shihāb al-Dīn al-Ramlī, *Nihāyah al-Muḥtāj*, Cairo: Muṣṭafā al-Bābī al-Ḥalabī, 1386/1967, 7:8; Abū Zahrah, *al-ʿUqūbah*, 250; ʿAwdah, *al-Tashrīʿ al-Jināʾī*, 1:354.
23. ʿAwdah, *al-Tashrīʿ al-Jināʾī*, 1:354; Abū Zahrah, *al-ʿUqūbah*, 246.
24. ʿAlāʾ al-Dīn al-Kāsānī, al-Kāsānī, *Badāʾiʿ al-Ṣanāʾiʿ fī Tartīb al-Sharāʾiʿ*, Cairo: Maṭbaʿah al-Jamaliyyah 1328/1910, 2nd ed., Beirut: Dār al-Kitāb al-ʿArabī, 1982; Ibu Qudāmah, *al-Mughnī*, 10:316; ʿAwdah, *al-Tashrīʿ al-Jināʾī*, 1:354.
25. Abū Zahrah, *al-ʿUqūbah*, 247.
26. Ibn Qayyim al-Jawziyyah, *Iʿlām al-Muwaqqiʿīn*, ed. Muḥammad Munīr al-Dimashqī, Cairo: Idārah al-Ṭabāʿah al-Munīriyyah, n.d., 2:97–98; ʿAwdah, *al-Tashrīʿ al-Jināʾī*, 1:355.
27. al-Khammāsī, *al-Ḍarūrah*, 191 and 193.
28. Abū Muḥammad ʿAlī b. Aḥmad Ibn Ḥazm al-Ẓāhirī, *al-Muḥallā*, ed. A. G. Sulāyman al-Bandarī, Beirut: Dār al-Kutub al-ʿIlmiyyah, 1468/1988, 12:36.
29. Tawfīq Muḥammad al-Shāwī, *al-Mawsūʿah al-ʿAṣriyyah fī'l-Fiqh al-Jināʾī al-Islāmī*, Cairo: Dār al-Shuruq, 1422/2001, 4:296.
30. *Ṣaḥīḥ al-Bukhārī*, Eng. trans. Muhammad Muhsin Khan, 6th ed., Lahore: Kazi Publications, 1983, 8:533–534, hadith no. 812. See also *Ṣaḥīḥ al-Bukhāri, Kitāb al-Ḥudūd, Bāb Idha Aqarra bi'l-Ḥudūd wa-lam Yubayyin*, hadith no. 6823.

31. See for details ʿAbd al-Raḥmān b. Muḥammad ʿAwaḍ al-Jazīrī, *al-Fiqh ʿalā'l-Madhāhib al-Arbaʿah*, new rev. ed., al-Mansurah, Egypt: Dār al-Ghad al-Jadīd, 2005, 1211. Al-Jazīrī recounts yet another hadith on the same page on the authority of Saʿīd b. al-Mussayib, who said: "It has reached me that a person who had embraced Islam by the name Hizāl complained to the Prophet concerning an incident of *zinā* by another man, to which the Prophet responded: 'O Hizal, if you had covered this with your wrapper, it would have been better for you (*Ya Hizāl! law satartahu bi-ridā'ika, kāna khayran laka*).'"
32. Aḥmad b. Ḥanbal, *Musnad Ibn Ḥanbal: Musnad al-Makkiyīn*, hadith Wāthilah b. al-Asqaʿ min al-Shamiyyīn, Cairo: Dār al- Ḥadīth, 2005. See also al-Khammāsī, *al-Ḍarūrah*, 195.
33. Muslim b. Ḥājjāj al-Nishāpūrī, *Mukhtaṣar Ṣaḥīḥ Muslim*, ed. M. Nāṣir al-Dīn al-Albānī, 2nd ed., Beirut: Dār-Maktab al-Islāmī, 1404/1984, 279, Hadith no. 1049.
34. Abū Yūsuf Yaʿqūb b. Ibrāhīm, *Kitāb al-Kharāj*, 5th ed. Cairo: al-Maṭbaʿah al-Salafiyyah, 1396/1976, 164; Abū ʿĪsā Muḥammad al-Tirmidhī, *Sunan al-Tirmidhī*, Beirut: Dār al-Fikr, 1400/1980, 2:439, hadith no. 1447; ʿAbd Allāh al-Khaṭīb al-Tabrīzī, *Mishkāt al-Masābiḥ*, ed. Muḥammad Nāṣir al-Dīn al-Albānī, 2nd ed., Beirut: al-Maktab al-Islāmī, 1399/1979, 2:1061, hadith no. 3570. For a discussion, see also Muṣṭafā Shalabī, *al-Fiqh al-Islāmī Bayn al-Mithāliyyah wa'l-wāqiʿiyyah*, Beirut: al-Dār al-Jamiʿiyyah, 1982, 232–233.
35. Abū Yūsuf Yaʿqūb b. Ibrāhīm, *Kitāb al-Kharāj*, 5th ed. Cairo: al-Maṭbaʿah al-Salafiyyah, 1396/1976, 165.
36. *Ṣaḥīḥ al-Bukhārī*, Eng. trans., Muhsin Khan, 8:512, hadith no. 778.
37. Cf. al-Jazīrī, *al-Fiqh ʿalā'l-Madhāhib*, 1144.
38. al-Nawawī, *Riyāḍ al-Ṣāliḥīn*, 488, hadith 1530. See also for a discussion al-Jazīrī, *al-Fiqh ʿalā'l-Madhāhib*, 1212.
39. For details on *satr al-ʿawrat*, see Mohammad Hashim Kamali, *Freedom of Expression in Islam*, 123–127.
40. al-Jazīrī, *al-Fiqh ʿalā'l-Madhāhib*, 1212.
41. Ibid.
42. Cf. Wahbah al-Zuḥaylī, *Qaḍāyā al-Fiqh*, 333–334. This hadith is recorded in *Ṣaḥīḥ al-Bukhārī, Kitāb al-muhāribīn min ahl al-kufr wa'l-riddah, bāb idhā uqirra bi'l-ḥadd wa-lam yubayyin*, hadith 6437.
43. The meaning of "fixed punishment" has been most clearly articulated perhaps in the Hudud Bill of Kelantan Malaysia 1993, so as to say that "the *hudud* punishments shall not be suspended, substituted for any other punishment, reduced or pardoned or otherwise varied or altered" (clause 48).
44. Cf. ʿAwdah, *al-Tashrīʿ al-Jinā'ī*, 1:76 and 620.
45. Ibid., 621.
46. Abū Zahrah, *al-ʿUqūbah*, 65.
47. Shihāb al-Dīn al-Qarāfī, *Kitāb al-Furūq*, Cairo: Maṭbaʿah Dār al-Iḥyā' al-Kutub al-ʿArabiyyah, 1346/1928, 141.

48. Fazlur Rahman, "The Concept of Hadd," 242.
49. Ibid., 248–250.
50. For this and other legal maxims that immediately follow, see, in alphabetical order, Mu'assasah Zayid b. Sultan al-Nahyan and Majmaʿ al-Fiqh al-Islāmī al-Duwalī, *Muʿallimah Zayid li'l-Qawāʿid ul-Fiqhiyyah wa'l-Uṣūliyyah*, 41 vols., Abu Dhabi, 1434/2013.
51. Thus, if in retaliation (*qiṣāṣ*) a relative exonerates his/her part, or some relatives do, but not others, the whole of retaliation collapses.
52. Prevention is thus preferable to compensation, retaliation, and punishment.
53. Thus, if someone is convicted of adultery twice, or of slander more than once, he will most likely be punished only once.

CHAPTER V

1. Cf. *al-Mawsūʿah al-Fiqhiyyah* (Kuwait), 14:21. Shii law records similar positions and a roughly parallel discourse over the issues involved. See, for details, Muḥaqqiq al-Ḥillī, *Mokhtasar-e Nafi'*, Persian translation (from Arabic) by Muḥammad Taqī Danish-pazhoh, Tehran: Bongah-e Tarjomah wa Nashr-e Kitab, 1343/1964, 351f.
2. Quoted in *al-Mawsūʿah al-Fiqhiyyah* (Kuwait), 24:19–20, from *Ṣaḥīḥ al-Bukhārī*, hadith bearing the title "Ayy al-Dhanb Aʿẓam."
3. Muslim, *Mukhtaṣar Ṣaḥīḥ Muslim* (hadith no. 33), *Kitāb al-Ômān, bāb lā yadkhulu al-jannah*, quoted also in *al-Mawsūʿah al-Fiqhiyyah* (Kuwait), vol. 14:20.
4. Hadith "*ḥurmatu nisā' al-mujāhidin*," in *al-Mawsūʿah al-Fiqhiyyah*, vol. 24:20. The hadith is as follows: "The prohibition (or sanctity) of the women of *mujāhidin* (those engaged in jihad) to those who have stayed behind (i.e., the home-dwellers *al-qāʿidīn*) is like the prohibition of their own mothers to them. If a man of the latter betrays the former by attempting to commit *zinā* with their women, he shall be at risk on the day of resurection of the *mujāhid* standing up and taking any of his good deeds as he may choose."
5. al-Jazīrī, *al-Fiqh ʿalā'l-Madhāhib*, 1180; *al-Mawsūʿah al-Fiqhiyyah* (Kuwait), 24:38–47; al-Ḥillī, *Mokhtasar-e Nafi'*, 353.
6. *al-Mawsūʿah al-Fiqhiyyah* (Kuwait), 24:41, records these details quoting the hadith "Istijwāb Māʿiz" (Māʿiz's interrogation) from al-Bukhārī and Abū Dāwūd.
7. *al-Mawsūʿah al-Fiqhiyyah* (Kuwait), 24:42.
8. Quoted in *al-Mawsūʿah al-Fiqhiyyah* (Kuwait), 24:31, hadith narrated by Ibn ʿAbbās. See also http://articles.islamweb.net/media/index.php?id=78251&lang=A&page=article.
9. Ibid. Hadith recorded in al-Bayhaqī, Dā'iratul Maʿarif al-ʿUthmaniyyah edition, 8:235.
10. Imam Ḥāfiẓ Abū ʿĪsā Muḥammad b. ʿĪsā al-Tirmidhī, *Jāmiʿ al-Tirmidhī*, English trans. by Abū Khalīl, 3:239, Riyadh: Maktaba Dār al-Salam, 2007, hadith 1454.

11. Cf. *al-Mawsūʿah al-Fiqhiyyah* (Kuwait), 24:43; al-Jazīrī, *al-Fiqh ʿalā'l-Madhāhib*, 1193.
12. Bibi v. State, 1985 PLD Fed. Shariat Ct. 120. See also Asma Jahangir and Hina Jilani, *The Hudud Ordinances, a Divine Sanction?* Lahore: Rhotas Books, 1990, 88.
13. Bibi v. State, 1985 PLD Fed. Shariat Ct. 120. See also *al-Mawsūʿah al-Fiqhiyyah* (Kuwait), 24:32.
14. *al-Mawsūʿah al-Fiqhiyyah* (Kuwait), 24:32; al-Jazīrī, *al-Fiqh ʿalā'l-Madhāhib*, 1193.
15. al-Jazīrī, *al-Fiqh ʿalā'l-Madhāhib*, 1194.
16. Ibid., 1193–1194.
17. Sulaymān b. Khalaf Abū 'l-Walīd al-Bājī, al-*Muntaqā Sharḥ al-Muwaṭṭa'*, ed. ʿAbd al-Qādir ʿAṭa, Beirut: Dār al-Kutub al-ʿIlmiyyah, 1999, 7:146.
18. Cf. al-Jazīrī, *al-Fiqh ʿalā'l-Madhāhib*, 1193; also Peters, *Crime and Punishment*, 62.
19. *al-Mawsūʿah al-Fiqhiyyah* (Kuwait), 24:43.
20. Syed Akbar Ali, "Syariah Criminal Code Not without Loopholes," *New Straits Times* (Kuala Lumpur), 29 November 1993.
21. Ibid.
22. Cf. Abd al-Karīm Zaydān, *Niẓām al-Qaḍa' fi'l-Sharīʿah al-Islāmiyyah*, Baghdad: Maṭbaʿah al-ʿĀnī, 1404/1984, 220.
23. Brenda Benedict, "Islamic View," including an interview with Nik Noriani Nik Badli Shah, *The Star* (Kuala Lumpur), 2 February 2004, 3.
24. Ibid.
25. Norani Othman, "Implementation of Sharī'ah Criminal Law in Modern Society: Some Sociological Questions," paper presented at the ISIS forum, Kuala Lumpur, 19 November 1993, 1–3.
26. Ustaz Nakhaie Ahmad, quoted in Mazian Nordin, "Many Questions on Ḥudūd Laws Still Unanswered," *New Straits Times* (Kuala Lumpur), 19 November 1993.
27. Ibn Qudāmah, *al-Mughnī*, 192; ʿAwdah, *al-Tashrīʿ al-Jinā'ī*, 2:441.
28. al-Jazīrī, *al-Fiqh ʿalā'l-Madhāhib*, 1193.
29. Shams al-Dīn al-Shaykh Muḥammad b. ʿArafah al-Dusūqī, *Ḥāshiyah al-Dusūqī ʿalā al-Sharḥ al-Kabīr*, Cairo: ʿĪsā al-Ḥalabī, n.d., 4:319. See also *al-Mawsūʿah al-Fiqhiyyah* (Kuwait), 14:43.
30. Muhammad Ata Sidahmad, *The Ḥudūd*, Kuala Lumpur: Perpustakaan Negara, 1995, 174.
31. Wahbah al-Zuḥaylī, *Qaḍāyā al-Fiqh wa'l-Fikr al-Muʿāṣir*, Damascus: Dār al-Fikr, 2007, 444.
32. Cf. ʿAlī Aḥmad al-Marʿī, *al-Qiṣāṣ wa'l-Ḥudūd fi'l-Fiqh al-Islāmī*, 2nd ed. Beirut: Dār Iqrā', 1402/1982, 64.
33. al-Ḥillī, *Mokhtasar-e Nafi'*, 353; Peters, *Crime and Punishment*, 34 and 61.
34. Abū 'l-Walīd Muḥammad Ibn Rushd al-Qurṭubī (known as Ibn Rushd al-Ḥafīd), *Bidāyat al-Mujtahid wa-Nihāyat al-Muqtaṣid*, Lahore: Faran Academy, n.d., 2:325.
35. al-Jazīrī, *al-Fiqh ʿalā'l-Madhāhib*, 1211.
36. Cf. el-Awa, *Punishment*, 19.

37. Muḥammad Rashīd Riḍā, *Tafsīr al-Manār,* 4th ed., vol. 5, Cairo: Maṭbaʿah al-Manar, 1373/1953, 5:25.
38. Abū Zahrah, *al-Uqūbah,* 103–104.
39. al-Jazīrī, *al-Fiqh ʿalā'l-Madhāhib,* 1214–1215.
40. Sayyid Abūl Āʿla Maududi, *Tafhīm al-Qurʾān,* vol. 3, Delhi: n.p., 1963, 3:321–323; Mohammad Suleman Siddiqi, "The Concept of Hudud and Its Significance," *Islamic Culture* 55 (1981), 198.
41. Muḥammad b. ʿAlī al-Shawkānī, *Nayl al-Awṭār Sharḥ Muntaqā al-Akhbār,* Cairo: Muṣṭafā al-Bābī al-Ḥalabī, n.d., 7:97–100; see also for these and other hadiths Jamāl al-Dīn al-Zaylāʿī, *Naṣb al-Rāyah li-Aḥādith al-Hidāyah,* 2nd ed., Beirut: al-Maktab al-Islāmī, 1393 H, 3:328–383; al Sarakhsī, *al-Mabsūṭ,* 9:36ff.
42. al-Zaylāʿī, *Naṣb al-Rāyah,* 3:329.
43. al-Sarakhsī, *al-Mabsūṭ,* 9:43–44.
44. Shihāb al-Dīn Maḥmūd al-Alūsī, *Rūḥ al-Maʿānī fī Tafsīr al-Qurʾān al-ʿAẓīm,* 4th ed., Cairo: Idārah al-Ṭabāʿah al-Munīriyyah, 1405/1985, 18:79.
45. *The Translation of the Meaning of Ṣaḥīḥ al-Bukhārī by Muhammad Muhsin Khan,* 6th ed., Lahore: Kazi Publications, 1983, 8:526, hadith no. 803.
46. al-Shawkānī, *Nayl al-Awṭār,* 7:100.
47. Jamāl al-Dīn al-Zaylāʿī, *Tabyīn al-Ḥaqāʾiq fī Sharḥ Kanz al-Daqāʾiq,* Egypt, Bulaq: al-Maṭbaʿah al-Amiriyyah, 1313 AH, 3:174.
48. Cf. ʿAli Manṣūr, *Niẓām al-Tajrīm wa'l-ʿIqāb fī l-Islām,* Medina: Muʾassasah al-Zahrā, 1396/1976, 175ff.
49. See for details al-Zaylāʿī, *Tabyīn,* 3:175; Manṣūr, *Niẓām al-Tajrīm,* 176.
50. For further detail on *naskh* and the differences of *madhāhib* therein see Mohammad H. Kamali, *Principles of Islamic Jurisprudence,* Cambridge: Islamic Texts Society, 2003, 202–228.
51. Cf. Manṣūr, *Niẓām al-Tajrīm,* 172.
52. al-Alūsī, *Rūḥ al-Maʿānī,* 8:79.
53. al-Sarakhsī, *al-Mabsūṭ,* 9:44–45; Manṣūr, *Niẓām al-Tajrīm,* at 181–182.
54. Cf. al-Jazīrī, *al-Fiqh ʿalā'l-Madhāhib,* 1179.
55. Manṣūr, *Niẓām al-Tajrīm,* 181–182.
56. Ibid., 182–183; Abū Zahrah, *al-ʿUqūbah,* 100ff.
57. *Ṣaḥīḥ al Bukhārī,* trans. Muhsin Khan, 7:527, hadith 804; Abū Zahrah, *al-ʿUqūbah,* 101; Manṣūr, *Niẓām al-Tajrīm,* 182–183.
58. Abū Zahrah, *al-ʿUqūbah,* 101 Manṣūr, *Niẓām al-Tajrīm,* 101–102; ʿAwdah, *al-Tashrīʿ al-Jināʾī,* 2:380. See also al-Sarakhsī, *al-Mabsūṭ,* 9:45.
59. Manṣūr, *Niẓām al-Tajrīm,* 182.
60. Abū Zahrah, *al-ʿUqūbah,* 98–105.
61. Q. al-Māʾidah, 5:43.
62. Abū Zahrah, *al-ʿUqūbah,* 104.
63. Suleman Siddiqi, "The Concept of Hudud," 191–207 at 195.
64. Ibid., 197.

65. Manṣūr, *Niẓām al-Tajrīm*, 182–183.
66. Muṣṭafā Aḥmad al-Zarqā, *al-Madkhal al-Fiqhī al-ʿĀm: Ikhrāj Jadīd fi'l-Tartīb wa'l-Tabwīb wa'l Ziyādat*, Damascus: Dār al-Qalam, 1st ed., 1418/1991, 1:290.
67. al-Zarqā, *al-Madkhal*, 1:283.
68. al-Zarqā, *al-Madkhal*, 1:291.
69. Bassiouni, *The Shari'a and Islamic Criminal Justice*, 136.
70. Yūsuf al-Qaraḍāwī, *Ḥawla Qaḍāya al-Islām wa'l-ʿAṣr*, 3rd ed., Cairo: Maktabah Wahbah, 1427/2006, 96.
71. Ibid., 96–97.
72. http://www.virtualmosque.com/islam-studies/faqs-and-fatwas/review-of-gomaas-responding-from-the-tradition/ (accessed 2 October 2015). See also Sheikh Ali Gomaa, *Responding from the Tradition: One Hundred Contemporary Fatwas by the Grand Mufti of Egypt*, Louisville, KY: Fons Vitae, 2011.
73. "Liwāṭ," *al-Mawsūʿah al-Fiqhiyyah* (Kuwait), 35:339–340.
74. al-Ḥillī, *Mokhtasar-e Nafi'*, 356; Peters, *Crime and Punishment*, 61.
75. al-Ḥillī, *Mokhtasar-e Nafi'*, 356–357.
76. As quoted in *al-Mawsūʿah al-Fiqhiyyah*, 35:340. The hadith is recorded by Aḥmad b. Ḥanbal in his *Musnad* (1:309) and al-Ḥākim in his *al-Mustadrak* (4:356).
77. Abū Dāwūd, *Sunan Abī Dāwūd, Kitāb al-ḥudūd*, hadith no. 4462; *Sunan al-Tirmidhī, Kitāb al-ḥudūd*, hadith no. 1456.
78. All three reports are quoted in al-Jazīrī, *al-Fiqh ʿalā'l-Madhāhib*, 1216. Abū Zahrah, *al-ʿUqūbah*, 180–181, also quotes the same hadith reports.
79. "Liwāṭ," *al-Mawsūʿah al-Fiqhiyyah* (Kuwait), 35:340.
80. Cf. al-Jazīrī, *al-Fiqh ʿalā'l-Madhāhib*, 1216; Peters, *Crime and Punishment*, 61.
81. al-Ḥillī, *Mokhtasar-e Nafi'*, 356–357.
82. al-Jazīrī, *al-Fiqh ʿalā'l-Madhāhib*, 1217.
83. See for details Abū Zahrah, *al-ʿUqūbah*, 180–181.
84. al-Jazīrī, *al-Fiqh ʿalā'l-Madhāhib*, quotes other hadith reports on the subject at 1220–1221, all of which concur that anal sex with one's wife is sinful and emphatically denounced.
85. Abū Zahrah, *al-ʿUqūbah*, 181, adds the somewhat questionable comment that *siḥāq* is common in countries and places that do not practice female genital mutilation (FMG), like Syria, but that it is rarely practiced in Egypt where FMG is widely practiced.
86. This hadith has been reported in slightly different versions. Al-Muttāqī al-Hindī, *Kanz al-ʿUmmāl*'s section on *zinā*, hadith no. 13103, adds a sentence, "When a man sexually approaches another man they are like adulterers (*idha ja'a al-rajulu al-rajula fa-huma zaniyan*)." Jalāl al-Dīn al-Suyūṭī (*al-Jāmiʿ al-Ṣaghīr*) has a similar hadith (no. 12699) on the authority of Abī Mūsā with the following words: "*la-tubāshir al-marʾatu al-marʾata illā wa-huma zāniyatan, wa-lā yubāshir al-rajulu al-rajula illā wa-huma zāniyān.*" Abū Zahrah, *al-ʿUqūbah*, 181, also quotes the shorter versions. See also al-Ḥillī, *Mokhtasar-e Nafi'*, 356, who discusses *siḥāq* but does not quote any hadith.

87. This is considered as a fair (*ḥasan*) hadith. Abū Dāwūd and al-Tirmidhī have reported it, see al-Jazīrī, *al-Fiqh ʿalā'l-Madhāhib*, 1195. See also http://majles.alukah.net/t9073/.
88. al-Jazīrī, *al-Fiqh ʿalā'l-Madhāhib*, 1195.
89. Ibn Mājah, *Sunan Ibn Mājah*, Lahore, Pakistan: Kazi Publications, 1993.
90. al-Jazīrī, *al-Fiqh ʿalā'l-Madhāhib*, 1195.
91. al-Khammāsī, *al-Ḍarūrah*, 222. This was, in fact, the practice of the Ottoman caliphate—but this subject will be revisited in our conclusion at the end of this volume.

CHAPTER VI

1. *al-Mawsūʿah al-Fiqhiyyah* (Kuwait), 24:292–294; al-Ḥillī, *Mokhtasar-e Nafi'*, 362.
2. Cf. ʿAwdah, *al-Tashrīʿ al-Jinā'ī*, 2:579.
3. The Ẓāhirīs have held, however, the somewhat exaggerated position that both the ascendants and descendants are liable to the prescribed punishment of theft if they steal, saying that the hadith that maintains otherwise has been abrogated by the Qur'anic verses on inheritance (*ayāt al-mawārith*). See for details ʿAwdah, *al-Tashrīʿ al-Jinā'ī*, 2:577. See also https://sunnah.com/urn/1323800 (accessed 17 January 2017)
4. al-Kāsānī, *Badā'iʿ al-Ṣanā'īʿ*, 7:75; Ibn Qudāmah, *al-Mughnī*, 10:287; ʿAwdah, *al-Tashrīʿ al-Jinā'ī*, 2:578; al-Ḥillī, *Mokhtasar-e Nafi'*, 362.
5. al-Ṭabarsī, *Mustadrak al-Wasā'il*, 13:135.
6. Ibn Qudāmah, *al-Mughnī*, 10:242; ʿAwdah, *al-Tashrīʿ al-Jinā'ī*, 2:582.
7. Both hadiths are quoted in al-Qurṭubī, *Bidāyat al-Mujtahid*, 2:334–335.
8. Ibid., 2:335.
9. Ibn Qayyim al-Jawziyyah, *Iʿlām al-Muwaqqiʿīn*, 2:64.
10. Cf. al-Qurṭubī, *Bidāyat al-Mujtahid*, 2:373; ʿAwdah, *al-Tashrīʿ al-Jinā'ī*, 2:581.
11. al-ʿAwā, *al-Fiqh al-Islāmī*, 163–164. Al-ʿAwā recounts the two differential assessments on the subject of quorum, one by Azhar university scholars, and the other by the late Dr. Ismāʿīl Maʿtūq, a member of the Egyptian Parliament. They worked on two separate projects relating to the preparation of a draft penal law for Egypt, one of which was being prepared by Azhar University and the other by Dr. Maʿtūq. One of them assessed the quorum of theft at two grams of pure gold and the other at 4.457 grams of pure gold. Each thought that this would be equivalent to the ten dirhams recorded by the Ḥanafī school. Al-ʿAwā is critical of both positions, which he considered to be based on a *taqlīdī* (imitationist) approach.
12. al-ʿAwā, *al-Fiqh al-Islāmī*, 163.
13. *al-Mawsūʿah al-Fiqhiyyah* (Kuwait), 24:305
14. Cf. al-Qurṭubī, *Bidāyat al-Mujtahid*, 2:336; *al-Mawsūʿah al-Fiqhiyyah* (Kuwait), 24:307–308; al-Ḥillī, *Mokhtasar-e Nafi'*, 362.
15. The kidnapping of a free person is a different crime and does not invoke the prescribed penalty for theft, since a free person cannot be owned and has no market value. This is also the case with the Qur'an, which was, initially at least,

not sellable, but later the fatwa of the leading schools changed over this. Stealing from a child is also not punished with mutilation, as there would be doubt over his ability at safekeeping.

16. *al-Mawsūʿah al-Fiqhiyyah*, 24:308; al-Ḥillī, *Mokhtasar-e Nafi'*, 362.
17. Cf. al-Qurṭubī, *Bidāyat al-Mujtahid*, 2:335–338; ʿAwdah, *al-Tashrīʿ al-Jināʾī*, 1:652–653; *al-Mawsūʿah al-Fiqhiyyah* (Kuwait), 24:308.
18. Ibid., al-Ḥillī, *Mokhtasar-e Nafi'*, 362 n.
19. al-ʿAwā, *al-Fiqh al-Islāmī*, 161.
20. al-ʿAwā, *al-Fiqh al-Islāmī*, 162.
21. ʿAwdah, *al-Tashrīʿ al-Jināʾī*, 2:616.
22. ʿAwdah, *al-Tashrīʿ al-Jināʾī*, 2:613.
23. ʿAwdah, *al-Tashrīʿ al-Jināʾī*, 2:615.
24. al-Kāsānī, *Badāʾiʿ al-Ṣanāʾīʿ*, 7:84; ʿAwdah, *al-Tashrīʿ al-Jināʾī*, 2:618.
25. ʿAwdah, *al-Tashrīʿ al-Jināʾī*, 2:620–621.
26. al-Jazīrī, *al-Fiqh ʿalāʾl-Madhāhib*, 1229–1230. Al-Jazīrī further adds that the narrators of this hadith are reliable (*thiqāt*) and that it is recorded in Sunan Abū Dāwūd, *Sunan al-Nasāʾī*, and the *Musnad* of Imam Aḥmad b. Ḥanbal.
27. al-Jazīrī, *al-Fiqh ʿalāʾl-Madhāhib*, 1230; ʿAwdah, *al-Tashrīʿ al-Jināʾī*, 2:615–617.
28. ʿAwdah, *al-Tashrīʿ al-Jināʾī*, 2:612.
29. al-Jazīrī, *al-Fiqh ʿalāʾl-Madhāhib*, 1230.
30. Cf. ʿAwdah, *al-Tashrīʿ al-Jināʾī*, 1:652; ʿAwdah also cites the precedent of caliph ʿAlī on the point. See also al-Ḥillī, *Mokhtasar-e Nafi'*, 363.
31. al-Ḥillī, *Mokhtasar-e Nafi'*, 364.
32. Ibn Ḥazm al-Andalūsī, *al-Muḥallā*, ed. A. G. Sulaymān al-Bandarī, Beirut: Dār al-Kutub alʿIlmiyyah, 1468/1988, 9:62: ʿAlī A. Manṣūr, *Niẓām al-Tajrīm waʾl ʿIqāb fī ʾl-Islām*, Medina Munawwarah, Muʾassasah al-Zahrā, 1396/1976, 331.
33. el-Awa, *Punishment in Islamic Law*, 6.
34. al-Shāwī, *al-Mawsūʿah al-ʿAṣriyyah*, 4:99.
35. Cf. ʿAwdah, *al-Tashrīʿ al-Jināʾī*, 2:621–622; al-Kāsānī, *Badāʾiʿ al-Ṣanāʾīʿ*, 7:55.
36. al-Jazīrī, *al-Fiqh ʿalāʾl-Madhāhib*, 1252.
37. al-Jazīrī, *al-Fiqh ʿalāʾl-Madhāhib*, 1252.
38. https://en.wikipedia.org/wiki/Islamic_criminal_jurisprudence (accessed 28 October 2016).

CHAPTER VII

1. Muhammad Ata al-Sid Sidahmad, *Islamic Criminal Law: The Hudud*, Petaling Jaya: Eagle Trading, 1995, 62; See also Mohammad Shabbir, *Outlines of Criminal Law and Justice in Islam*, Kuala Lumpur: International Law Book Services, 2003, 173.
2. Nadirsyah Hosen, "Law, Religion and Security," in Silvio Ferrari, ed., *Routledge Handbook of Law and Religion*, Abingdon, UK and New York: Routledge, 2015, 338.

3. Sherman A. Jackson, "Domestic Terrorism in the Islamic Legal Tradition," *Muslim World* 91, nos. 3–4 (2001), 293–310 at 295.
4. When considering illegitimate state action marked as self-defence, such as the bombings of Nagasaki and Hiroshima, and US military attacks on Afghanistan and Iraq, it quickly becomes clear that the existing definitions of terrorism are on the whole unsatisfactory.
5. Abū al-Ḥusayn Muslim b. al-Ḥajjāj al-Nishapūrī, *Ṣaḥīḥ Muslim, Kitāb al-Qasamah wa'l-Muḥāribīn wa'l-Qiṣāṣ wa'l-Diyah, Bāb Ḥukm al-muḥāribin wa'l-murtaddīn*, hadith 1671, Beirut: Dār al-Kutub al-ʿIlmiyyah, 2006, 659.
6. Muslim, *Mukhtaṣar Ṣaḥīḥ Muslim, Kitāb al-Imārah, bāb man ḥamala ʿalaynā al-silāḥa*, ed. al-Albānī, hadith 1235.
7. This is a slight variation of the previous hadith on the authority of Salamah b. al-Akwaʿ, whereas the first is on the authority of ʿAbd Allāh b. ʿUmar. Both are deemed as reliable.
8. al-Nawawī, *Riyāḍ al-Ṣāliḥīn*, ed. al-Albānī, 2nd ed., Beirut: Dār al-Maktab al-Islāmī, 1418/1998, hadith 1527.
9. Wahbah al-Zuḥaylī, *al-Fiqh al-Islāmī wa-Adillatuh*, Beirut: Dār al-Fikr, 1417/1996, 6:128.
10. al-Kāsānī, *Badāʾiʿ al-Ṣanāʾīʿ*, 7:7.
11. Sayyid al-Sābiq, *Fiqh al-Sunnah*, 21st printing, Dār al-Fatḥ li'l-Aʿlām al-ʿArabī, 1420/1999, 2:298; Ibn ʿAbd al-Barr (d. 463/1070), *al-Kāfī fī Fiqh al-Madīnah al-Mālikī*, Beirut: Dār al-Kutub al-ʿIlmiyyah, 1418/1997, 582–583.
12. Muḥammad al-Sharbīnī al-Khaṭīb, *Mughnī al-Muḥtāj ilā Maʿrifat Maʿānī al-Minhāj*, Cairo: Muṣṭafā al-Bābī al-Ḥalabī, 1414/1933, 4:180.
13. al-Ḥillī, *Mokhtasar-e Nafi'*, 365.
14. Ibid. Other details over the enforcement of punishment, including crucifixion, repentance, and so on under Shii law, do not differ significantly from the Sunni expositions of the same.
15. Ibn Ḥazm, *al-Muḥallā*, 11:306.
16. *al-Mawsūʿah al-Fiqhiyyah* (Kuwait), "Ḥirābah," 17:157; Ibn Qudāmah, *al-Mughnī*, 8:287; Muntaṣir Saʿīd Ḥamudah, *al-Irhāb: Dirāsah Fiqhiyyah fī'l-Tashrīʿ al-Jināʾī al-Islāmī*, Alexandria, Egypt: Dār al-Jamīʿah al-Jadīdah li'l-Nashr, 2008, 74; al-Ḥillī, *Mokhtasar-e Nafi'*, 365.
17. al-Qurṭubī, *Bidāyat al-Mujtahid*, 2:340–341; *al-Mawsūʿah al-Fiqhiyyah* (Kuwait), "Ḥirābah," 17:153, 158; ʿAwdah, *al-Tashrīʿ al-Jināʾī*, 2:657; al-Ḥillī, *Mokhtasar-e Nafi'*, 365.
18. al-Kāsānī, *Badāʾiʿ al-Ṣanāʾīʿ*, 7:91; *al-Mawsūʿah al-Fiqhiyyah* (Kuwait), 17:156–157.
19. Ibn Qudāmah (d. 620/1223) defined *ḥirābah* as "the act of openly holding people up in the desert with weapons in order to take their money" (*al-Mughnī*, Beirut: Dār al-Kutub al-ʿIlmiyyah, n.d., 10:315).
20. Ibn Qudāmah, *al-Mughnī*, 10:303.
21. Riḍā, *Tafsīr al-Manār*, 6:94.

22. *al-Mawsūʿah al-Fiqhiyyah* (Kuwait), "Ḥirābah," 17:156.
23. al-Qurṭubī, *Bidāyah*, 2:341; ʿAwdah, *al-Tashrīʿ al-Jināʾī*, 2:658–659.
24. ʿAwdah, *al-Tashrīʿ al-Jināʾī*, 2:645; al-Ḥillī, *Mokhtasar-e Nafi'*, 365. Al-Ḥillī further mentions that a normal burial ceremony should be accorded to the deceased person after three days of crucifixion.
25. al-Kāsānī, *Badāʾiʿ al-Ṣanāʾīʿ*, 7:95; *al-Mawsūʿah al-Fiqhiyyah*, 17:162; ʿAwdah, *al-Tashrīʿ al-Jināʾī*, 2:658–659.
26. Ibn Qudāmah, *al-Mughnī*, 10:309; ʿAwdah, *al-Tashrīʿ al-Jināʾī*, 2:657.
27. al-Qurṭubī, *Bidāyat*, 2:342–343; Peters, *Crime and Punishment*, 59. See also ʿAwdah, *al-Tashrīʿ al-Jināʾī*, 2:658–661.
28. Known as حشاشين, *Ḥashāshīn* (from *Assasiyyun*: "those faithful to the foundation"), is the name used to refer to the medieval Nizari Ismailis. Often characterised as a secret order led by a mysterious "Old Man of the Mountain," the Nizārī Ismāʿīlīs were an Islamic sect that was formed in the late eleventh century due to a split within Ismailism. The Nizārīs posed a military threat to Sunni Saljūq authority within their territories by capturing and inhabiting many unconnected mountain fortresses throughout Persia (and later also Syria) under the leadership of Ḥassan Ṣabbāh (who is typically regarded as the founder of the Assassins), therefore founding the so-called Nizārī Ismāʿīlī state with Alamut Castle as its headquarters. See, for details, https:// enc.wikipedia.org/ wiki/ Assassins. See also Asaf A. Fyzee, *Outlines of Muhammadan Law*, 2nd imp., New Delhi: Oxford University Press, 1999, 39–43.
29. Murad Wilfred Hofmann, "Fanaticism, Extremism and Terrorism and Islam's Position towards these Phenomena," conference paper presented at the international conference in Amman on "True Islam and Its Role in Modern Society," organised by the Aal al-Bayt Institute for Islamic Thought, 4–6 July 2005, 2.
30. Maḥmūd Shaltūt, *al-Islām: ʿAqīdah wa-Sharīʿah*, 328; ʿAwdah, *al-Tashrīʿ al-Jināʾī*, 1:446; Zuḥaylī, *Ḥuqūq al-Insān*, 144.
31. ʿAwdah, *al-Tashrīʿ al-Jināʾī*, 1:447.
32. Cf. Jamāl al-Dīn Abū 'l-Faraj ʿAbd al-Raḥmān Ibn al-Jawzī, *Zād al-Masīr fī ʿIlm al-Tafsīr*, Damascus: Dār Ibn Ḥazm li'l-Ṭabaʿah wa'l-Nashr wa'l-Tawzīʿ, 202, 2:61–62; see also al-ʿIbadī, *Min al-Adab wa'l-Akhlāq*, 164–165.
33. http://www.islamicsupremecouncil.org/understanding-islam/legal-rulings/21-jihad-classical-islamic-perspective.html?start=15 (accessed 21 May 2017).
34. al-Tabrīzī, *Mishkāt al-Maṣābīḥ*, vol. 2, hadith no. 3453.
35. al-Bukhārī, *Ṣaḥīḥ al-Bukhārī*, *Kitāb al-Adab*, *bāb mā yunha ʿanhu min al-sibāb*, hadith no. 6105.
36. https://sunnah.com/bukhari/64/242.
37. As quoted by Benjamin T. Acosta, "The Suicide Bomber as Sunni-Shīʿi Hybrid," *Middle East Quarterly* (Summer 2010), 13–20. See also www.meforum.org/1003/ the-religious-foundations-of-suicide-bombings) (accessed 4 August 2017).

38. For details on suicide bombing, see Mohammad Hashim Kamali, *The Right to Life, Security, Privacy and Ownership in Islam*, Cambridge: Islamic Texts Society, 2008, 29–35.
39. Robert A. Pape, *New York Times*, 22 September 2003, as quoted in Imam Feisal Abdul Rauf, *What Is Right with Islam Is What Is Right with America*, New York: Harper Collins, 2005, 146.
40. Nadirsyah Hosen, "Law, Religion and Security," in Silvio Ferrari, ed., *Routledge Handbook of Law and Religion*, Abingdon, UK and New York, 2015, 337.
41. Hoffman and Cronin are both quoted in Hosen, "Law, Religion and Security," 337–338.
42. Cf. Kent Roach, "The Case for Defining Terrorism with Restraint and without Reference to Political and Religious Motives," in A. Lynch et al., eds., *Law and Liberty in the War on Terror*, Sydney: Federation Press, 2007, 39–48 at 41.
43. Nikkie R. Keddie, "The Revolt of Islam from 1700 to 1993," in Bryan S. Turner, ed., *Islam: Critical Concepts in Sociology*, Oxford: Routledge, 2003, 2:89.
44. http://www.nieuwwij.nl/english/karen-armstrong-islam-violent-christianity/ (accessed 18 March 2015). Armstrong was interviewed by Lisette Thooft.
45. Paul Hedges, "Need for Global Solidarity with Muslims," *New Straits Times* (Kuala Lumpur), 29 April 2016, 17.
46. Saleena Saleem, "It's More Politics Than Religion," *New Straits Times* (Kuala Lumpur), 24 March 2016, 17.
47. Fareed Zakaria, "Radicals before They Were Religious," *New Straits Times* (Kuala Lumpur), 2 April 2016, 17.
48. Ibid.
49. Azhari Karim, "Dealing with Different Types of 'Terrorists,'" *New Straits Times* (Kuala Lumpur), 19 July 2016, 15.
50. Ibid.
51. "Malala urges Muslim unity," *New Straits Times* (Kuala Lumpur), 20 October 2016, 25.
52. Paul Hedges, "Need for Global Solidarity with Muslims," *New Straits Times* (Kuala Lumpur), 29 April 2016, 17.
53. Peter Apps, "Is Europe Overreacting to Terror?" *New Straits Times* (Kuala Lumpur), 3 September 2016, 15.
54. For details, see Ghazi b. Muhammad, Ibrahim Kalin, and Mohammad Hashim Kamali, eds., *War and Peace in Islam: The Uses and Abuses of Jihad*, Cambridge: Islamic Texts Society, 2013, Introduction by Kamali at xv.
55. As quoted in Kamali, *The Right to Life*, 34.
56. www.utusan.com.my/utusan/content.asp?y=2003&dt=1111&pub=utusan_Express.
57. Shaykh Maḥmūd Shaltūt, *Warfare in the Qur'an*, trans. Joel Howard, in Ghazi et al., eds., *War and Peace in Islam*, 43ff.

58. http://www.islamicsupremecouncil.org/understanding-islam/legal-rulings/21-jihad-classical-islamic-perspective.html?start=15 (accessed 21 May 2017).
59. Shaykh Muḥammad Sayyid Ṭanṭāwī as quoted by Anicee Van Engeland Nourai, "The Challenge of Fragmentation of International Humanitarian Law," in M. Cheriff Bassiouni, ed., *Jihad and Its Challenges*, The Hague: Hague Academic Press, 2010, 147.
60. As quoted in Seyyed Hossein Nasr, *The Heart of Islam: Enduring Values for Humanity*, New York: HarperCollins, 2004, 263.
61. Quoted in Nourai, "The Challenge of Fragmentation," 148.
62. http://www.npr.org/s.php?sId=4775588&m=1 (accessed 24 May 2017). See also "US Muslim Scholars to Forbid Terrorism" http://www.washingtonpost.com/wp-dyn/content/article/2005/07/27/AR2005072702082. html.
63. It has rightly been pointed out by Donald Neff that, without anticipating it, and certainly without wanting it, the policy of Israel in Lebanon "created...its own worst enemies"—the Hezbollah and (later and only indirectly) Hamas movements. See www.wrmea.com/archives/november02/0211020.html (accessed 21 May 2017).
64. Amal Saad Ghorayeb, *Hizbu'llah: Politics and Religion*, London: Pluto Press, 2002, 67. Casualty levels fluctuate wildly, but average around twelve deaths per suicide attack. The majority of suicide attacks originate from al-Qaeda and are carried out by zealous recruits from all over the Muslim world who have been flooding into Iraq. Other organisations that have also carried out suicide attacks are the Salafi-jihadi umbrella group Jaysh Ansar al-Sunnah (JAS) and the Shii cleric Muqtadā al-Ṣadr's Mahdī Army. See also A. B. Atwan, *The Secret History of al-Qa'ida*, London: Saqi Books, 2006, 100.
65. See Saad Ghorayeb, *Hizbu'llah*; Judith Palmer Harik, *Hezbollah: The Changing Force of Terrorism*, London and New York: I. B. Tauris, 2004, 65, 70.
66. Muhammad Munir, "Suicide Attacks and Islamic Law," *International Review of the Red Cross* 2008, 90 (899): 71–89 at 73. See Munir's article also at https://www.icrc.org/eng/assets/files/other/irrc-869_ munir.pdf (accessed 21 May 2017).
67. Cf. Farish Noor, "Radicalism's Pool of Support," *New Straits Times* (Kuala Lumpur), 25 August 2014, 12.
68. Amnesty International, *Escape from Hell: Torture and Sexual Slavery in Islamic State Captivity in Iraq*, London: Amnesty International, 2014.
69. Mark L. Winer, "Fundamentalists vs. Moderates: The War within Judaism," *Arches Quarterly* (2012) 5(9): 117.
70. Scott Thompson, "Liberty's 9/11," *New Straits Times* (Kuala Lumpur), 14 January 2015, 17.
71. Muḥammad b. ʿAlī al-Shawkānī, *Fatḥ al-Qadīr*, Damascus: Dār al-Kalam al-Ṭayyib, n.d., 2:39.
72. See for details Ḥasan al-Khaṭṭāf, "Mafhum al-ḥirābah wa-ḍawābiṭuha: Dirāsah bayn al-nāṣṣ al-Qurʾānī wa'l-turāth al-fiqhī," in *Islāmiyyat al-Maʿrifah: Majallat al-Fikr al-Islāmī al-Muʿāṣir*, Herndon, VA (1436/2015), 21:11 and 42.

73. Riḍā, *Tafsīr al-Manar*, 6:93.
74. Ḥasan al-Khaṭṭāf, "Mafhum al-ḥirābah wa-ḍawābiṭuha," 12.

CHAPTER VIII

1. This is so notwithstanding the fact that apostasy appears in a large number (about twenty-one) verses of the Qur'an.
2. Cf. Kamali, *Freedom of Expression in Islam*, 96.
3. Muslim, *Mukhtaṣar Ṣaḥīḥ Muslim*, 271, hadith no. 1023.
4. Cf. el-Awa, *Punishment*, 52.
5. al-Bukhārī, *Jawāhir Ṣaḥīḥ al-Bukhārī*, 150, hadith no. 229; and al-Nasā'ī, *Sunan, Kitāb al-Bayʿah, Bāb Istiqalāt al-Bayʿah*, hadith no. 4185. See also https://sunnah.com/nasai/39/37.
6. Abū Zahrah, *al-ʿUqūbah*, 165, discusses this hadith and also the Ḥanafī views concerning it in some detail.
7. Muḥammad b. ʿAlī al-Shawkānī, *Nayl al-Awṭār Sharḥ Muntaqā al-Akhbār*, Cairo: Muṣṭafā al-Bābī al-Ḥalabī, n.d., 7:218–219.
8. See for details Abū Zahrah, *al-ʿUqūbah*, 166.
9. Sufyān al-Thawrī's two works on hadith are *al-Jāmiʿ al-Ṣaghīr*, and *al-Jāmiʿ al-Kabīr*.
10. Ibn Taymiyyah, *al-Ṣārim al-Maslūl ʿalā Shatīm al-Rasūl*, ed. Muḥyī al-Dīn ʿAbd al-Ḥamīd, Beirut: Dār al-Kitāb, 1398/1978, 321; al-Shawkānī, *Nayl al-Awṭār*, 7:230.
11. See Abū Zahrah, *al-ʿUqūbah*, 167.
12. Ibn Taymiyyah, *al-Ṣārim al-Maslūl*, 318; ʿAbd al-Wahhāb al-Shaʿrānī, *Kitāb al-Mizān*, Cairo: Maṭbaʿah al-Ḥusayniyyah, 1329/1911, 2:134.
13. al-Shaʿrānī, *Kitāb al-Mizān*, 2:152.
14. al-Sarakhsī, *al-Mabsūṭ*, 10:110.
15. al-ʿIlī, *al-Ḥurriyyat al-ʿĀmmah*, 426; Badawī, *Daʿā'im al-Ḥukm*, 166.
16. Shaltūt, *al-Islām, ʿAqīdah wa-Sharīʿah*, 292–293.
17. Ibid.
18. Ṣubḥī Muḥmaṣṣānī, *Arkān Ḥuqūq al-Insān*, Beirut: Dār al-ʿIlm li-l'Malayīn, 1979, 123–124; el-Awa, *Punishment*, 55.
19. Mutahhari, "Islam and the Freedom of Thought," *al-Tawḥīd*, 154.
20. Mahmud Zuhdi Abdul Majid, "Rational Approach to Pursuit of Islamic Order," *New Straits Times* (Kuala Lumpur), 20 July 1994, 12.
21. Cf. Mohammad Hashim Kamali, *Freedom of Expression in Islam*, Cambridge: Islamic Texts Society, 1997, chapter on Blasphemy, 212–250.

CHAPTER IX

1. al-Jazīrī, *al-Fiqh ʿalā'l-Madhāhib*, 1256; al-Ḥillī, *Mokhtasar-e Nafi'*, 358. This is also how *qadhf* is defined in the Hudud Bill of Kelantan (clause 12).

2. al-Māwardī, *The Ordinances of Government: A Translation of al-Ahkām al-Sultāniyyah wa'l-Wilāyāt al-Dīniyyah,* trans. Wafaa H. Wahba, Reading, UK: Center for Muslim Contribution to Civilization, 1996, 251; al-Ḥillī, *Mokhtasar-e Nafi',* 359.
3. al-Jazīrī, *al-Fiqh ʿalā'l-Madhāhib,* 1256; al-Ḥillī, *Mokhtasar-e Nafi',* 359.
4. See for details Martin Lings, *Muhammad: His Life Based on the Earliest Sources,* Cambridge: Islamic Texts Society, reprint 2007, 241.
5. Ibid., 246.
6. ʿAwdah, *al-Tashrīʿ al-Jināʾī,* 2:455, 462.
7. al-Kāsānī, *Badāʾiʿ al-Ṣanāʾīʿ,* 7:44; ʿAwdah, *al-Tashrīʿ al-Jināʾī,* 2:471.
8. al-Kāsānī, *Badāʾiʿ al-Ṣanāʾīʿ,* 463 [[what volume? or this should be ʿAwdah, *al-Tashrīʿ al-Jināʾī,* 2:463?]]; al-Ḥillī, *Mokhtasar-e Nafi',* 259.
9. ʿAwdah, *al-Tashrīʿ al-Jināʾī,* 2:488; al-Ḥillī, *Mokhtasar-e Nafi',* 359.
10. ʿAwdah, *al-Tashrīʿ al-Jināʾī,* 2:489.
11. ʿAwdah, *al-Tashrīʿ al-Jināʾī,* 2:465; al-Ḥillī, *Mokhtasar-e Nafi',* 359.
12. al-Qurṭubī, *Bidāyat al-Mujtahid,* 2:330; *al-Mawsūʿah al-Fiqhiyyah,* "Qadhf," 33:20–21; al-Ḥillī, *Mokhtasar-e Nafi',* 358.
13. Cf. *al-Mawsūʿah al-Fiqhiyyah,* vol. 33 under "Qadhf" at 14; ʿAwdah, *al-Tashrīʿ al-Jināʾī,* 2:480.
14. *al-Mawsūʿah al-Fiqhiyyah,* "Qadhf," vol. 33, 15; ʿAwdah, *al-Tashrīʿ al-Jināʾī,* 2:476–477; al-Ḥillī, *Mokhtasar-e Nafi',* 359.
15. *al-Mawsūʿah al-Fiqhiyyah,* 33:16; ʿAwdah, *al-Tashrīʿ al-Jināʾī,* 2:473.
16. *al-Mawsūʿah al-Fiqhiyyah,* 33:20; ʿAwdah, *al-Tashrīʿ al-Jināʾī,* 2:482.
17. al-Kāsānī, *Badāʾiʿ al-Ṣanāʾīʿ,* 1328/1910, 12:62; Ibn Qudāmah al-Maqdisī, *al-Mughnī,* Riyadh: Maktabah al-Riyadh al-Ḥadīthah, 1401/1981, 8:217; el-Awa, *Punishment,* 22; al-Ḥillī, *Mokhtasar-e Nafi',* 359–360; Peters, *Crime and Punishment,* 54.
18. al-Qurṭubī, *Bidāyat al-Mujtahid,* 2:331; Abū Zahrah, *al-ʿUqūbah,* 319–320.

CHAPTER X

1. Cf. al-ʿAwā, *al-Fiqh al-Islāmī,* 150.
2. *Ṣaḥīḥ al-Bukhārī,* 8:507, hadith no. 770; el-Awa, *Punishment,* 48.
3. Abū 'l-Walīd Muḥammad Ibn Rushd al-Qurṭubī (known as Ibn Rushd al-Ḥafīd), *Bidāyat al-Mujtahid wa-Nihāyat al-Muqtaṣid,* Lahore: Faran Academy, n.d., 2:333.
4. Ibid., 2:332; al-Ḥillī, *Mokhtasar-e Nafi',* 361; al-Jazīrī, *al-Fiqh ʿalā'l-Madhāhib,* 1157–1158. The third, or preferably fourth, instance of drinking under both Shii and Sunni laws is punishable by death.
5. The Hudud Bill of Kelantan in Malaysia 1993 identified *shurb* as a *ḥadd* offence, which is punishable with "whipping of not more than eighty lashes but not less than forty lashes" (clause 22). What is of interest to note here is that the Kelantan Bill adopted a variable punishment of forty to eighty lashes for *shurb,* which is a

(accessed 30 June 2017). See also Fariba Zarinebaf-Shahr, "Women in the Public Eye in Eighteenth-Century Istanbul," 302–304.

23. Anne-Marie Cusac, *Cruel and Unusual: The Culture of Punishment in America*, New Haven: Yale University Press, 2009, 21–22; John Langbein, "The Historical Origins of the Sanction of Imprisonment for Serious Crimes," *Journal of Legal Studies* 5, no. 1 (1976): 36.
24. The Ottoman experience in this regard seems to have been replicated in Afghanistan's current Penal Code (1976), which is also entirely based on *taʿzīr* (see for details on this the discussion on Afghanistan in part three).
25. See for details Ahmed Akgunduz, *Introduction to Islamic Law*, Rotterdam: IUR Press, 2010, 432.
26. Jonathan Brown, "Stoning and Handcutting," https://yaqeeninstitute.org/en/jonathan-brown/stoning-and-hand-cutting-understanding-the-ḥudūd-and-the-shariah-in-islam/ (accessed 30 June 2017). This manner of classification has been retained in the criminal codes of Egypt and Afghanistan. The triple classification (*jināyah, janḥah,* and *qabāḥah*) thus subsumes basically all crimes, all of which have also been subsumed under *taʿzīr*.

CHAPTER XII

1. See Fatḥī Bahnasī, *al-ʿUqūbah*, 18.
2. Aḥmad Taqī al-Dīn b. Taymiyyah, *al-Siyāsah al-Sharʿiyyah fī Iṣlāḥ al-Raʿy wa'l-Raʿiyyah*, Beirut: Dār al-Kutub al-ʿArabiyyah, 1966, 98; also quoted in Wahbah al-Zuḥaylī, *al-Fiqh al-Islāmī*, 4:285.
3. Wahbah al-Zuḥaylī, *al-Fiqh al-Islāmī*, 4:285.
4. A subtle difference is also recognised between *ʿiqāb* and *ʿadhāb* in that *ʿiqāb* refers to a punishment justly deserved, whereas *ʿadhāb* is torture that may be disproportionate to the conduct for which it is inflicted. See for details *al-Mawsūʿah al-Fiqhiyyah*, entry on "*ʿUqūbah*," 4:269.
5. J. W. Salmond, *Salmond on Jurisprudence*, 11th ed., London: Sweet & Maxwell, 1957, 115.
6. Cf. Muhammad Iqbal Siddiqi, *The Penal Law of Islam*, 2nd ed., Lahore: Sh Muhammad Ashraf, 1985, 9.
7. Cf. Peters, *Crime and Punishment*, 53.
8. Ibid., 27–28.
9. See for details al-Jazīrī, *al-Fiqh ʿalā'l-Madhāhib*, 1212–1213.
10. Hadith quoted al-Khaṭīb by al-Tabrīzī, *Mishkāt*, vol. 2, hadith 3626, *Kitāb al-Ḥudūd, Bāb mā lā yad'a ʿalā al-ḥudūd*, Egypt: al-Maktabah al-Tawfīqiyyah, n.d., 293: من اصاب ذنبا أقيم عليه حد ذلك الذنب فهو كفارته "Whoever commits a crime and is punished for it, this will be its expiation."
11. See https://sunnah.com/nasai/47/18 (accessed 18 March 2017).
12. Bahnasī, *al-ʿUqūbah*, 14–15.

13. Ibid., 16.
14. See for details Bahnasī, *al-ʿUqūbah*, 15–16.
15. Cf. Mohammad Shabbir, *Outlines of Criminal Law and Justice in Islam*, Petaling Jaya, Malaysia: International Law Book Services, 2003, 24f.
16. Qur'an, al-Nahl, 16:126: "If you punish, then punish with the like of that with which you were afflicted"; and Qur'an, al-Baqarah, 2:194: "And one who transgresses against you, then transgress against him in the like manner as he transgressed you."
17. Cf. al-Mā'idah, 5:33, 38; Yūnus, 10:27; al-Shūrā, 42:40.
18. Cf. ʿAwdah, *al-Tashrīʿ al-Jinā'ī*, 1:636; el-Awa, *Punishment*, 26.
19. al-Māwardī, *al-Aḥkām al-Sulṭāniayyah*, 220.
20. *ʿAqīlah* refers to group responsibility, usually of male agnatic relatives or the clan of the offender, for the payment of *diya* when the offender himself is unable to pay. *Qasamah* refers to cases of homicide, especially when a dead body is found in a locality without any traces of the killer. The rules of *qasamah* hold up to fifty persons of the nearest residential groups responsible for the consequences.
21. al-Māwardī, *al-Aḥkām al-Sulṭāniyyah*, 205.
22. ʿĀlā' al-Dīn ʿAlī b. Muḥammad al-Dimashqī al-Ḥanbalī, *al-Ikhtiyārat al-Fiqhiyyah li-Shaykh al-Islām Ibn Taymiyyah*, ed. Shaykh al-ʿUthaymīn, [[Place?]] Dār al-ʿAsīmah lī'l-Nashr wa'l-Tawzīʿ, 171, also quoted by Tawfīq al-Shāwī, *al-Mawsūʿah al-ʿAṣriyyah*, 4:12.
23. Ibid. [[to al-Ḥanbalī or al-Shāwī? Write out this source.]]
24. al-Shāwī, *al-Mawsūʿah al-ʿAṣriyyah*, 4:192.
25. al-Shāwī, *al-Mawsūʿah al-ʿAṣriyyah*, 4:30; see also ʿAlī Manṣūr, *Niẓām al-Tajrīm*, 314.

CHAPTER XIII

1. al-Māwardī, *al-Aḥkām al-Sulṭāniyyah*, 236.
2. *al-Mawsūʿah al-Fiqhiyyah* (Kuwait), "*Taʿzīr*," 12:254–255.
3. The Prophet, pbuh, is reported to have imposed seclusion (*iʿtizāl*) as a punishment on three of his companions who did not participate in the battle of Tābūk. They were denied the courtesy of *salām* (greeting), and a social boycott was imposed on them until a revelation came with respect to the acceptance of their penance. For details see lbn Taymiyyah, *al Siyāsah*, 121.
4. This would be 40 lashes, or 80 for a free man, depending on which one of these constitutes the *ḥadd* of *shurb*, as there is some disagreement on this. Cf. Mohamed S. el-Awa, "Taʿzīr in the Islamic Penal System," *Journal of Islamic and Comparative Law* 6 (1976), 51.
5. Ibid.
6. *al-Mawsūʿah al-Fiqhiyyah*, 12:267; see also al-Jazīrī, *al-Fiqh ʿalā'l-Madhāhib*, 1355.
7. Abdullah Yusuf Ali, *The Holy Qur'an, Text Translation and Commentary*, n4581.
8. Cf. ʿAwdah, *al-Tashrīʿ al-Jinā'ī*, 1:777, 559–560.

9. For full citations of the Qur'an verses and hadith in support of *taʿzīr* offences, see Anwarullah, *Criminal Law*, 211–229.
10. *al-Mawsūʿah al-Fiqhiyyah* (Kuwait), "*Taʿzīr*," 12:257–259.
11. Tāj, *al-Siyāsah*, 76; al Qarāfī, *al Furūq*, 3:266.
12. Ibid., 71.
13. *Taḥlīl* is an intervening marriage that legalises the marriage of a woman who has been divorced by triple *ṭalāq* to her former husband again.
14. Tāj, *al-Siyāsah*, 71–72.
15. Cf. ʿAwdah, *al-Tashrīʿ al-Jinā'ī*, 2:510–511; Anwarullah, *The Criminal Law of Islam*, 3rd printing, Kuala Lumpur: A. S. Nordeen, 238.
16. See for further details on the limitations of *taʿzīr*: Mohammad Hashim Kamali, *The Right to Life, Security, Privacy and Ownership in Islam*, Cambridge: Islamic Texts Society, 2008, 96–97. See for details on *Siyāsah Sharʿiyyah*, Mohammad Hashim Kamali, *Freedom, Equality and Justice in Islam*, Cambridge: Islamic Text Society, 2000, 143–149.
17. Both al-Zaylāʿī and Ibn Farḥūn are quoted in *al-Mawsūʿah al-Fiqhiyyah*, "*Taʿzīr*," 12:256–257.
18. Cf. Peters, *Crime and Punishment*, 66.
19. Hadith recorded by both al-Bukhārī and Muslim; also quoted in *al-Mawsūʿah al-Fiqhiyyah*, "*Taʿzīr*," 12:264.
20. *al-Mawsūʿah al-Fiqhiyyah* (Kuwait), "*Taʿzīr*," 12:254–255; al-Jazīrī, *al-Fiqh ʿalā'l-Madhāhib*, 1354–1355.
21. See for details of the scholastic positions on the maximum lashes for *taʿzīr* in these various categories, *al-Mawsūʿah al-Fiqhiyyah*, "*Taʿzīr*," 12:265–268.
22. *al-Mawsūʿah al-Fiqhiyyah* (Kuwait), "*Taʿzīr*," 12;264.
23. This hadith appears in *Ṣaḥīḥ* Muslim, *Kitāb al-Imārah, Bāb Ḥukmī Man Farraqa Amr al-Muslimīn*, hadith no. 1852; as also quoted in *al-Mawsūʿah al-Fiqhiyyah*, 12:264.

CHAPTER XIV

1. See for details Mohammad Hashim Kamali, "Siyasah Shar'iyyah or the Policies of Islamic Government," *American Journal of Islamic Social Sciences* (*AJISS*) 6 (1989), 59–81.
2. The Egyptian Code of Organization and Procedure for Shariah Courts 1897 (Art. 31) provided that no claim of marriage, divorce, or acknowledgement thereof may be heard after the death of either party unless it is supported by valid documents.
3. Khallāf, *al-Siyāsah*, 14.
4. Ibid., 15–16.
5. Ibid., 3.
6. The *maqāṣid al-sharīʿah* includes the safety and protection of human life and intellect; a normal order in society; and protection of religion, private property, and family. For details on *maqāṣid* see Kamali, *Shari'ah Law*, chap. 6, 123–141 in the next note.

7. Tāj, *al-Siyāsah*, 28.
8. Cf. Mohamed S. el-Awa, "Taʿzīr in the Islamic Penal System," *Journal of Islamic and Comparative Law* 6 (1976), 56–57.
9. Hadith recorded in *Ṣaḥīḥ Muslim, Kitāb al-Birr wa'l-Ṣillah wa'l-Adab, Bāb Faḍl al-Rifq*, hadith no. 2594, on the authority of ʿĀ'ishah.
10. Both of these hadith appear in Ibn Taymiyyah, *al-Siyāsah*, 145.
11. Hadith recorded in *Ṣaḥīḥ Muslim*, book 32, hadith 7. See also Ibn Taymiyyah, *al-Siyāsah*, 145.
12. Ibn Taymiyyah, *al-Siyāsah*, 27.
13. Ibid., 28.
14. For details on *siyāsah* see also Mohammad Hashim Kamali, "Beyond the Shari'ah: An Analysis of Shari'ah-Oriented Policy (*Siyasah Shar'iyyah*)," in *Shari'ah Law: An Introduction*, Oxford: Oneworld Publications, 2008, 225–246.
15. Ibn Qayyim al-Jawziyyah, *al-Ṭurūq al-ḥukmiyyah fī 'l Siyāsah al-Sharʿiyyah* (Cairo: al Muʾassissah al-ʿArabiyyah li'l-Ṭibāʿah, 1380/1961), 28.
16. Tāj, *al-Siyāsah*, 43.
17. Ibn Qayyim al-Jawziyyah, *al-Ṭurūq*, 28.
18. E.g., the Qur'an (Óli ʿImrān, 3:104 and 100; al-Tawbah, 12:71 and 124).
19. Cf. el-Awa, *Punishment*, 116.
20. Abū Isḥāq Ibrāhīm al-Shāṭibī, *al Muwāfaqāt fī Uṣūl al-Sharīʿah* (Cairo: Maktabah al-Tijāriyyah al-Kubrā), 2:7.
21. Ibrāhīm b. ʿAlī Ibn Farḥūn, *Tabṣirah al-Ḥukkām fī Uṣūl al-ʿAqīdah* (Cairo: al-Maṭbaʿah al-Bahiyyah, 1302), 2:106.
22. ʿAbd al-Wahhāb Khallāf, *al-Siyāsah al-Sharʿiyyah*, Cairo: al-Maktabah al-Salafiyyah, 1350/1931, 3.
23. Ibid., 4.
24. Cf. ʿAwdah, *al-Tashrīʿ al-Jināʾī*, 2:510; Peters, *Crime and Punishment*, 68.
25. Noel J. Coulson, "The State and Individual in Islamic Law," *International and Comparative Law Quarterly*, 6, 1956: 52.
26. Ibn Qayyim al-Jawziyyah, *al-Ṭurūq*, 16.
27. Ibn Qayyim al-Jawziyyah, *al-Ṭurūq*, 5.
28. Ibid., 17.

CHAPTER XV

1. See for details on *qiṣāṣ* Mohammad Hashim Kamali, *The Right to Life, Security, Prinvacuy and Ownership in Islam*, Cambridge: Islamic Texts Society, 2008, 12ff.
2. Abū Dāwūd, ed., *Sunan Abū Dāwūd, Kitāb al-Diyyāt, bāb al-nafs bi'l-nafs*, hadith 4494. See also Ibn Taymiyyah, *al-Siyāsah al-Sharʿiyyah*, 142.
3. Ibn Taymiyyah, *al-Siyāsah*, 156.
4. Cf. Aḥmad Fatḥī Bahnasī, *al-ʿUqūbah fī'l-Fiqh al-Islām*, 5th rev. ed., Beirut and Cairo: Dār al-Shuruq, 1403/1983, 66.

5. Ibid., 72–74.
6. Ibid., 15–16; see also al-Ḥillī, *Mokhtsar-e Nafi'*, 371.
7. Cf. ᶜAwdah, *al-Tashrīᶜ al-Jināʾī*, 1:122.
8. Yūsuf al-Qaraḍāwī, *al-Shaykh al-Ghazālī kama ᶜAraftuhu Riḥlata Nisf Qarn*, Cairo: Dār al-Wafā liʾl-Ṭibāᶜah waʾl-Nashr waʾl-Tawzīᶜ, 1997, 167.
9. Abū Dāwūd, *Muktaṣar Sunan Abī Dāwūd*, ed. Muṣṭafā al-Bughā, 643, hadith 4497.
10. Muslim, *Mukhtaṣar Ṣaḥīḥ Muslim*, 475, hadith no. 1790.
11. al-Bukhārī, *Ṣaḥīḥ al-Bukhārī, Kitāb al-Diyyāt, bāb man qutila lahu qatilun*, hadith 6880.
12. Abū Zahrah, *al-ᶜUqūbah*, 475; al-Ḥillī, *Mokhtasar-e Nafi'*, 379.
13. Tabrīzī, *Mishkāt*, vol. 2, hadith 3477.
14. Ibn Taymiyyah, *al-Siyāsah al-Sharᶜiyyah*, 141.
15. Cf. Bassiouni, *Islamic Criminal Justice*, 209; al-Ḥillī, *Mokhtasar-e Nafi'*, 379.
16. Bahnasī, *al-ᶜUqūbah*, 75–78.
17. Ibid., 76.
18. al-Shāwī, *al-Mawsūᶜah al-ᶜAṣriyyah*, 4:251.
19. Bahnasī, *al-ᶜUqūbah*, 78.
20. Ibid., 77.
21. Abū Zahrah, *al-ᶜUqūbah*, 484.
22. Ibid., 483.
23. Bahnasī, *al-ᶜUqūbah*, 77.
24. Fazlur Rahman, "Law and Ethics in Islam," in Richard G. Hovannisan, ed., *Ethics in Islam*, Malibu, CA: Undena Publications, 1983, 10.
25. See for details Abū Zahrah, *al-ᶜUqūbah*, 455; see also Peters, *Crime and Punishment*, 45.
26. Abū Zahrah, *al-ᶜUqūbah*, 457.
27. al-Ḥillī, *Mokhtasar-e Nafi'*, 378; Peters, *Crime and Punishment*, 46.
28. Abū Zahrah, *al-ᶜUqūbah*, 487; al-Ḥillī, *Mokhtasar-e Nafi'*, 379.
29. See for details al-Zuḥaylī, *al-Fiqh al-Islāmī*, 4:2; 60f; Mohammad Ibn Ibrahim al-Hewesh, "Murder and Homicide in Islamic Criminal Law: Textual Foundations," in Tahir Mahmood, *Criminal Law in Islam and the Muslim World: A Comparative Perspective*, New Delhi: Institute of Objective Studies, 2012, 158; al-Ḥillī, *Mokhtasar-e Nafi'*, 371ff.
30. Abū Zahrah, *al-ᶜUqūbah*, 485; al-Ḥillī, *Mokhtasar-e Nafi'*, 380.

CHAPTER XVI

1. Cf. al-Shāwī, *al-Mawsūᶜah al-ᶜAṣriyyah*, 4:135.
2. Cf. al-Kāsānī, *Badāʾiᶜ al-Ṣanāʾīᶜ*, 7:237; ᶜAlī ᶜAbd al-Wāḥid Wafī, *Ḥimāyat al-Islām*, Cairo: Dār Nahdah, 1979, 8. The intensified *diya*, like the normal *diya* for life, is 100 camels, which consists, however, of different types and age groups of camels;

Cf. Bassiouni, *Criminal Justice*, 203. Some Shii jurists, including Naṣr al-Dīn al-Ṭūsī and Shaykh Mufīd, also stipulate intensified blood money (*diya mughāllaẓah*) for killing in the vicinity of the Ḥarām (Bayt al-Ḥarām, in Mecca). Cf. al-Ḥillī, *Mokhtasar-e Nafi'*, 384.

3. ʿ*Aqīlah* has tribal origins: when the Prophet migrated to Medina, Medinan life was strongly tribal. Each tribe, whether Arab or Jewish, constituted an independent unit, had tribal chiefs, a meeting place for the deliberation of tribal affairs and entertainment, etc. Judging by the Abū Naḍīr Jews, each tribe possessed a treasury (*kanz*) containing contributions of the members of the tribe to be expended on all group expenditures, such as wars: "A sort of social insurance existed among the Arabs: if one of them committed some offence or other bringing about pecuniary compensation, especially that of a blood-money, it was the tribal group as a whole, and not the guilty individual, that was responsible for the payment." This also reinforced the members' responsibility to adhere to the tribal rules. Cf. Muhammad Hamidullah, *The Life and Work of the Prophet of Islam*, English trans. and ed. Mahmood Ahmad Ghazi, Islamabad: Islamic Research Institute, 1998, 1:142–143. See also al-Ḥillī, *Mokhtasar-e Nafi'*, 383–384.
4. Yūsuf al-Qaraḍāwī, *Dirāsah fī Fiqh Maqāṣid al-Sharīʿah: Bayn al-Maqāṣid al-Kulliyyah wa'l-Nuṣūṣ al-Juzʾiyyah*, 4th ed., Cairo: Dār al-Shurūq, 2012, 82.
5. al-Shāwī, *al-Mawsūʿah al-ʿAṣriyyah*, 4:135; Peters, *Crime and Punishment*, 50.
6. al-Qurṭubī, *Tafsīr al-Qurṭubī*, 1:255.
7. Ibn Qudāmah, *al-Mughnī*, 7:745; ʿAwdah, *al-Tashrīʿ al-Jināʾī*, 1:245 (S. 198); al-Shāwī, *al-Mawsūʿah al-ʿAṣriyyah*, 1:308.
8. Abū Dāwūd, *Sunan*, ed. al-Bugha (hadith reported by ʿAbd Allāh b. ʿUmar), 652, hadith 4542. For quantitative details of *diya* under Shii law, which are about the same as under Sunni law, namely 100 camels or their equivalent in gold and silver, see Abū Zahrah, *al-ʿUqūbah*, 514; al-Ḥillī, *Mokhtasar-e Nafi'*, 383f.
9. Yūsuf al-Qaraḍāwī, *al-Shaykh al-Ghazālī*, 166. For Shii law, which holds that the woman's *diya* is half that of the man, see al-Ḥillī, *Mokhtasar-e Nafi'*, 384.
10. al-Qaraḍāwī, *Shaykh al-Ghazālī*, 384.
11. Abū Zahrah, *al-ʿUqūbah*, 515.
12. Ibid., 516.
13. The *diya* provision appears in a long verse of the Qur'an in reference to unintentional killing that shall be compensated by freeing of a slave and payment of blood money to the family of the deceased. If the killer is unable to pay, his expiation shall be fasting for two consecutive months (al-Nisāʾ, 4:92). There is no distinction anywhere in this passage, which is the principal verse on *diya*, between man or woman, Muslim or non-Mulim.
14. A long hadith text and the episode of a slain body that was found in Khaybar appears in al-Kāsānī, *Badāʾiʿ al-Ṣanāʾīʿ*, 7:286; see also Wafī, *Ḥuqūq al-Insān*, 264.
15. Cf. Bassiouni, *Criminal Justice*, 205–207.

16. al-Kāsānī, *Badā'iᶜ al-Ṣanā'ī*ᶜ, 7:256; al-Khaṭīb, *Mughnī al-Muḥtāj*, 4:95; Maḥmūd Shaltūt, *al-Islām, ᶜAqīdah wa-Sharīᶜah*, Kuwait: Dār al-Qalam, 1963, 315; ᶜAwdah, *al-Tashrīᶜ al-Jinā'ī*, 1:673ff.
17. Shaltūt, *al-Islām*, 316. Shaltūt refers to Ibn ᶜĀbidīn's view in his *Ḥashiyah*, vol. 5, in *Kitāb al-Maᶜāqill*.
18. Should the deceased's body be found between two or more villages, *qasamah* is applicable to the one that is physically closer to where the body is found. See for details Abū Dāwūd, *Mukhtaṣar Sunan Abī Dāwūd*, 647–649.
19. al-Kāsānī, *Badā'iᶜ al-Ṣanā'ī*ᶜ, 7:286; Wafī, *Ḥuqūq al-Insān*, 263. Al-Tirmidhī recorded another long hadith, that one Muhayyisah found ᶜAbd Allāh b. Sahl's dead body and buried him. Then he went to the Prophet together with an elder companion and informed him of it. The Prophet ordered *qasamah*, which could not for some reason be carried out, and the Prophet in his capacity as head of state eventually paid the *diya* to ᶜAbd al-Raḥmān b. Sahl, the deceased person's brother. See the hadith at https://sunnah.com/tirmidhi/16/39.
20. ᶜAwdah, *al-Tashrīᶜ al-Jinā'ī*, 1:777.
21. Cf. Aharon Layish, "Saudi Arabia Legal Reform as a Mechanism to Moderate Wahhabi Doctrine," *Journal of the American Oriental Society*, 1987, 282; see also Al-Ṣādiq al-Mahdī, *al-ᶜUqubāt al-Shariᶜyyah wa-Mawāqifah min al-Niẓām al-Ijtimaᶜī al-Islāmī* [Islamic Punishment and Its Place in an Islamic Social Order], Cairo: Zahrā' li'l-ᶜAlām al-ᶜArabī, 1986, 92.
22. Akgunduz, *Introduction*, 291; Layish, "Saudi Arabia Legal Reform," 282.
23. Akgunduz, *Introduction to Islamic Law*, 291.
24. Peters, *Crime and Punishment*, 151.
25. Cf. Eugene Coran and Chibli Mallat, eds., *Yearbook of Islamic and Middle Eastern Law*, vol. 4, London: Kluwers Law International, 2000–2001, 276.
26. Both these cases appeared in 2001, 1 L.M. (*Law Majalla*), International Islamic University Malaysia, 215.
27. Ibid.
28. https://en.wikipedia.org/wiki/Islamic_criminal_jurisprudence (accessed 28 October 2016).
29. Cf. Peters, *Crime and Punishment*, 162.
30. Cf. Ahmad Ibrahim, *The Administration of Islamic Law in Malaysia*, Kuala Lumpur: Institute of Islamic Understanding Malaysia (IKIM), 2000, 637; Tanzilur Rahman, *Islamization of Pakisan Law: Surveying from Islamic Point of View*, Karachi: Hamdard Academy, 1978, 16.
31. Gul Hassan Khan vs. the Government of Pakistan, PLD 180 Peshawar 154.
32. Cf. Peters, *Crime and Punishment*, 159.
33. See for details Tahir Mahmood, "Criminal Procedure at the Sharīᶜah Law," in Tahir Mahmood, ed., *Criminal Law in Islam and the Muslim World: A Comparative Perspective*, Delhi: Institute of Objective Studies, 1996, 320f.
34. See for details Peters, *Crime and Punishment*, 172–173.

XVII

1. ʿAbd Allāh Ibn Sulaymān al-Jarḥazī, *Kitāb al-Mawāhib al-Sunniyyah ʿalā Sharḥ al-Fawāʾid al-Bahiyyah,* on the margin of *Jalāl al-Dīn al-Suyūṭī, al-Ashbāh wa'l-Naẓāʾir,* Beirut: Dār al-Fikr, n.d., 189–190.
2. al-Zaylāʿī, *Naṣb al-Rāyah,* 2:333.
3. Cf. al-Majlis al-Aʿla li'l-Shuʾūn al-Islāmiyyah, "al-Ishtibāh fi'l-Ḥudūd," *Mawsūʿah Jamāl ʿAbd al-Nāsir,* Cairo: Maṭābīʿ al-Ihrām al-Tijāriyyah, 1973/1393, 10:74.
4. Cf. al-Kāsānī, *Badāʾiʿ al-Ṣanāʾīʿ,* 7:42: *Mawsūʿah Jamāl,* 10:382ff; ʿAwdah, *al-Tashrīʿ al-Jināʾī,* 2:209.
5. al-Jazīrī, *al-Fiqh ʿalā'l-Madhāhib,* 1196. This also represents the Shii position. They give the same example, but add to it and extend it as follows: if a woman deliberately resembles herself to the wife of another, say in the dark of the night, in order to seduce the latter and *zinā* occurs as a result, she will be liable to the prescribed *ḥadd* but the man will not be (note: this example and the reverse of it, that a man mistook another woman for his wife, occur frequently in the early fiqh writings that precede the invention of electricity and other means of lighting). See also al-Ḥillī, *Mokhtasar-e Nafi',* 351.
6. See for a fuller exposition of *shubha, al-Mawsūʿah al-Fiqhiyyah* (Kuwait), 1:26–32; see also al-Ḥillī, *Mokhtasar-e Nafi',* 351.
7. Ibid., 30. [[Ibid. to *al-Mawsūʿah al-Fiqhiyyah* ? write this out.]]
8. See for details, al-Sarakhsī, *al-Mabsūṭ,* 9:58ff; Manṣūr, *Niẓām al-Tajrīm,* 184.
9. ʿAwdah, *al-Tashrīʿ al-Jināʾī,* 1:370.
10. Ibid., 2:214; Abū Zahrah, *al-ʿUqūbah,* 219–228.
11. al-Shāwī, *al-Mawsūʿah al-ʿAṣriyyah,* 4:27.
12. Mohamed S. el-Awa, "The Basics of Islamic Penal Legislation," in C. Bassiouni, ed., *The Islamic Criminal Justice System,* London: Oceana Publications, 1982, 146.

CHAPTER XVIII

1. Sayyid Abūl Aʿla Maududi, *The Islamic State and Constitution,* 8th printing, Lahore: Islamic Publication Ltd., 1983, 52.
2. Ibid., 54.
3. Ibid., 55.
4. el-Awa, *Punishment,* 136.
5. Ibid.
6. Ibid., 137.
7. Abū Yūsuf, *Kitāb al-Kharāj,* 163.
8. Bassiouni, *The Islamic Criminal Justice System,* 5.
9. Ibid., 5. This report and the saying of caliph ʿUmar also appear in Bahnasī, *al-ʿUqūbah,* 26.
10. al-Sarakhsī, *al-Mabsūṭ,* 9:141: Yūsuf al-Qaraḍāwī, *Sharīʿah al-Islāmiyyah Ṣāliḥah li'l-Taṭbīq fī Kull Zamān wa-Makān,* Cairo: Dār al-Ṣaḥwah, 1393/1973, 35.

11. Fazlur Rahman, "The Concept of *Hadd*," 237.
12. Abdullah H. H. al-Khalifah, "Religiosity in Islam as a Protective Mechanism against Criminal Temptation," *American Journal of Islamic Social Sciences*, 11, no. 1 (1194): 5.
13. Ibid., 8.
14. Mahmud Zuhdi Abdul Majid's remarks appeared in the *New Straits Times* report by Rozi Ali of the seminar entitled, "Rational Approach to Pursuit of Islamic Order," 20 July 1994, 12.
15. al-Qaraḍāwī, *Sharīʿah al-Islām*, 162.
16. Muḥammad al-Ghazālī, *Min Hunā Naʿlam*, Cairo: n.p., 1948, 5. Also discussed by Hamid Enayat, *Modern Islamic Political Thought*, London: Macmillan Press, 1989, 90.
17. Ibid., 30–31; Enayat, *Modern Islamic Political Thought*, 90.
18. Muṣṭafā Aḥmad al-Zarqā, *al-Madkhal al-Fiqhī al-ʿĀm*, Damascus: Dār al-Fikr, 1387/1968, 1:51.
19. Muṣṭafā Aḥmad al-Zarqā, *al-Madkhal al-Fiqhī al-ʿĀm: Ikhrāj Jadīd fi'l-Tartīb wa'l-Tabwīb wa'l Ziyādat*, 1st ed., Damascus: Dār al-Qalam, 1418/1991, 1:282.
20. Ibid., 1:284.
21. Ibid.
22. Ibid.
23. ʿAbd Allāh b. al-Mafuz Bin Bayyah, *Tanbih al-Waqīʿ ʿalā Ta'sīl Fiqh al-Waqīʿ* [Reading the Jurisprudence of Pragmatism into the Sources of Shariah], UAE: al-Majlis al-Waṭanī al-ʿĀm, 2014, 82–83. [[check title of highlighted book]]
24. Ibid., 85–86.
25. Ibid., 88–89.

CHAPTER XIX

1. The full text of the Kelantan Bill in its official English translation appears under Appendix A at the end of this volume.
2. *New Straits Times*, 25 November 1993, 8.
3. Ibid.
4. Ibid.
5. "Hudud Laws for Muslims Only," *News Straits Times* (Kuala Lumpur), 19 November 1993.
6. Rose Ismail, "Hudud Laws," *New Straits Times* (Kuala Lumpur), 10 July 1994, 12.
7. Linna Yong, "The Burden of Proof in Hudud," *The Star* (Kuala Lumpur), 22 November 1993, 18.
8. Salbiah Ahmad, "An Issue Paper of Zina and Rape under the Syariah Criminal Code (II) Bill 1993 (Kelantan)," presented to a forum at the Institute of Strategic and International Studies, 19 January 1993, 8. A summary of this paper was also reported in Mazian Nordin, *New Straits Times* (Kuala Lumpur), 19 October 1993.

9. Rose Ismail, "Hudud Law in Other Countries," paper presented to an ISIS (Institute of Strategic and International Studies) forum in Kuala Lumpur on 19 November 1993, 2. A summary of this paper also appeared in Yong, "The Burden of Proof in Hudud," 18.
10. Salbiah Ahmad, "An Issue Paper," 7.

CHAPTER XX

1. Shaila Khoshy and Mustafa Kamal Basri, "PAS: Hudud Good for Muslims," *The Star* (Kuala Lumpur), 9 July 2002, 4.
2. Mustafa Kamal, "Sultan Mizan Gives Consent to Hudud Law," *The Star* (Kuala Lumpur), 1 August 2002, Nation, 10.
3. "Women Unite: Oppose Hudud Laws, Says Shahrizat," *The Star* (Kuala Lumpur), 29 May 2002, Front page and 3.
4. Ibid., 3.
5. Ibid.
6. *The Star* (Kuala Lumpur), 30 May 2002, Nation, 2; *New Straits Times* (Kuala Lumpur), 31 May 2002, National, 4.
7. *New Straits Times* (Kuala Lumpur), 31 May 2002, National, 4.
8. *New Straits Times*, "PAS Hudud Laws: Keadilan Wants Rape Victims Treated Fairly," 31 May 2002, National, 4.
9. Ibid.
10. "Lo' Lo' Ghazali: Review, [but] Don't Oppose Hudud Bill," *The Star* (Kuala Lumpur), 30 May 2002, Nation, 2.
11. "Hadi: Many Do Not Understand the Bill," *New Straits Times* (Kuala Lumpur), National, 31 May 2002, 4.
12. "Women Leaders to Meet on Bill," *The Star* (Kuala Lumpur), 31 May 2002, 2.
13. Joceline Tan, "New Hands That May Reshape PAS," *The Star* (Kuala Lumpur), Focus, 16 June 2002, 23.
14. Ibid.
15. "Attorney General Will Get Draft Bill," *The Star* (Kuala Lumpur), 2 June 2002, Nation, 5.
16. "Hadi: Hudud Bill Will be Tabled," *The Star* (Kuala Lumpur), 17 June 2002, Nation, 2.
17. *The Star* (Kuala Lumpur), 19 June 2002, Nation, 2. See also *New Straits Times*, 19 June 2002, Front page.
18. *The Star* (Kuala Lumpur), July 10, 2002, Nation, 2, quoting both Rais Yatim and Abdullah Ahmad Badawi.
19. Lourdes Charles and Mustafa Kamal Basri, "Cops Won't Help Enforce Hudud Laws in Terengganu," *The Star* (Kuala Lumpur), 11 July 2002, Front Page.
20. Ahmad Ibrahim, *The Administration*, 639.
21. Ibid., 640.
22. Ibid., 639–640.

XXI

1. Cf. Mohammed Imam, "Islamic Criminal Law in Malaysia: Federal State Jurisdictional Conflict," [1004] *Current Law Journal* (March 1994), xxix.
2. Ibid., xxiv.
3. "Ex-FT Mufti: PAS Shows It Was Not Ready to Enforce Hudud," *New Straits Times* (Kuala Lumpur), 14 December 2002, Nation, 24.
4. Ibid.
5. According to Art. 76A of the Federal Constitution, Parliament may authorise the state legislature to make laws pertaining to matters that appear under the Federal List.
6. Kassim Ahmad, "Resolving the 'Hudud' Law Dilemma," *New Straits Times* (Kuala Lumpur), 4 December 1993, 13.
7. "MB: Federal Consent Needed to Enforce Hudud Law," *New Straits Times* (Kuala Lumpur), 11 July 1994, 9.
8. *The Star* (Kuala Lumpur), 26 July 1994, 2.
9. *New Straits Times* (Kuala Lumpur), 10 September 1994, 1–2.
10. *New Straits Times* (Kuala Lumpur), 2 October 1994, 6.
11. Ibid.
12. *New Straits Times* (Kuala Lumpur), 15 October 1994, 2.
13. "Karpal: Hudud Will Lead to Lawlessness," *New Straits Times* (Kuala Lumpur), 31 October 2011, 10.
14. Masami Mustaza, "Law Doesn't Allow for Hudud in States," *New Straits Times* (Kuala Lumpur), 30 October 2011, 29.
15. Shaila Khoshy, "Incest Victims Prefer Federal Law to Shariah," *Sunday Star* (Kuala Lumpur), 30 November 2003, Nation, 15.
16. Ibid. Zakaria, who is also Senior Federal Counsel, added that there was a technical committee under the Religious Affairs Department that was studying whether offences such as incest, which already exist in the penal code, should be excluded from the state shariah criminal offences laws.
17. Rose Ismail, "Hudud Laws," *New Straits Times* (Kuala Lumpur), 10 July 1994, 12.
18. K. Haridas, "Islamization of State and Society," in Norani Othman, ed., *Shariah Law and the Modern Nation State: A Malaysian Symposium*, Kuala Lumpur: Sisters in Islam, 1994, 99.
19. Ibid.
20. Koshy's interview with Wan Muttalib Embong, "PAS: Hudud Law Will Run Its Course," *The Star* (Kuala Lumpur), 18 August 2002, 26.

CHAPTER XXII

1. The 9th schedule of the federal constitution provides three lists: list 1 sets out matters within the exclusive jurisdiction of the federal parliament; list 2 states matters for which only the state legislature can make laws; and the third list (the

concurrent list) covers matters where both the state and federal legislatures can make laws. Only the federal parliament (list 2) can legislate on matters relating to criminal law and procedure.

2. Adie Suri Zulkefli and Jasmine Kaur, "PM: Hudud Not Rejected by Government," *New Straits Times* (Kuala Lumpur), 15 April 2014, 2.
3. "Kelantan Tables Hudud Amendments," *The Sun*, 19 March 2015, 2.
4. Sheridan Mahavera, "State Government Survey Finds 90% in Kelantan Want Hudud," 2 April 2015, htpp://www.themalaysiainsider.com/Malaysia/article/state-government-survey-finds-90-in-kelantan-want-ḥudūd (accessed 15 April 2015).
5. Ibid. The survey was conducted via text messages to more than 156,000 residents in 24 out of 45 state constituencies and the survey received only 9,654 replies, of which 8,940 were validated.
6. Elizabeth Zakariah, "Impossible to Enforce Hudud in Malaysia, says Law Minister," *The Malaysian Insider*, 24 March 2015, http://www.the malaysianinsider.com/malaysia/article/impossible-to-enforce-ḥudūd-in-malaysia-says-law-minister (accessed 15 April 2015).
7. Ibid.
8. Tun Abdul Hamid Mohamad, "Implementation of the Islamic Criminal Law (*hudud, qisas, ta'zir*) in Malaysia—Prospects and Challenges," keynote address delivered at a seminar on implementation of *ḥudūd* in Malaysia—history and the future, Putrajaya, 1 April 2015, 8 (Eng. trans. of original address in Bahasa Malaysia), complement of Tun Hamid to the present writer.
9. Tun Hamid's Speech, ibid., 10.
10. Ibid., 11.
11. Rozannea Latiff, "Dr. M: Pas 'Hudud Un-Islamic," *New Straits Times* (Kuala Lumpur), 5 April 2015, 16.
12. "Laws Must Be Fair, Infused with Justice," *New Straits Times* (Kuala Lumpur), 27 March 2015, 12. The Sultan of Perak made these remarks at the 20th Certificate in Legal Practice Convocation by Legal Profession Qualifying Board Malaysia in Kuala Lumpur.
13. Khairul Azwan Harun, "Why Act 355 Needs Amending?" *New Straits Times* (Kuala Lumpur), 21 September 2016, 15.
14. Ibid.
15. Ibid.
16. Abdul Hamid Mohamad, "Amendment of Act 355: The Real Effect," *New Straits Times* (Kuala Lumpur), 29 September 2016, 12. See also Fernando Fong, "Tun Abdul Hamid Mohammad: Combine Courts to Solve Conflict of Jurisdiction," *New Straits Times* (Kuala Lumpur), 9 December 2016.
17. Mohamed Azam Mohamed Adil, "Shariah Criminal Code (II) Enactment 1993 Amendment 2015: Can Kelantan Enforce Hudud?" *Islam and Civilisational Renewal*, Vol. 7, No. 4, 548–551.

18. Adrian Ali and Esther Landau, "Govt Won't Table Bill," *New Straits Times* (Kuala Lumpur), 30 March 2017, 6.
19. Annuar Musa, "Rejection of Tabling Done in Consensus," *New Straits Times* (Kuala Lumpur), 30 March 2017, 11.
20. "Public Caning in Kelantan for 4 Shariah Offences," *New Straits Times* (Kuala Lumpur), 13 July 2017 (Front page), quoting Daud Nassuruddin.
21. Sharifah Mahsinah Abdullah, "Public Caning to Start in Two Months," Kuala Lumpur: *New Straits Times*, 14 July 2017, 8.
22. Ibid.
23. Go Pei Pei and Zafira Anwar, "Zahid: Kelantan Has Right to Amend Law," Kuala Lumpur, *New Straits Times* (Kuala Lumpur), 14 July 2017, 8.
24. "Amendments Involve Only Venue of Punishment, Says Jamil Khir," *New Straits Times* (Kuala Lumpur), 16 July 2017, 7.
25. "Mufti: Public Caning a Reminder to the People," *New Straits Times* (Kuala Lumpur), 13 July 2017, 4.

CHAPTER XXIII

1. Peters, *Crime and Punishment*, 119.
2. Ibid., 189.
3. Ibid., 104–105.
4. Ibid., 107–109.
5. See, for details, Tun Abdul Hamid Mohamad (former Chief Justice of Malaysia), "In Search of a Suitable Model of Penal Code for Afghanistan," *Islam and Civilisational Renewal* 4, no. 2 (2013): 298.
6. Ibid., 299.
7. Ibid.
8. Mosques operated in most large cities within these territories, though the number decreased dramatically from 25,000 in 1917 to 500 in the 1970s. See "Islam in the Soviet Union," https://en.wikipedia.org/wiki/Islam_in_the_Soviet_Union (accessed 27 October 2017).
9. Cf. Nazif Shahrani, "Islam and Scientific Atheism in Post-Soviet Central Asia: Future Predicament," *Islamic Studies* (Special Issue on Central Asia), Islamabad: Islamic Research Institute, 1994, 146–147.
10. Islam Karimove as quoted in Shahrani, ibid., 144.
11. https://en.wikipedia.org/wiki/application_of_Islamic_law_by_country (accessed 15 October 2017). See also Riyaz Ahmad Sheikh, "Soviet and Post-Soviet Discourses on Islam: A Comparative Study of Uzbekistan," *Social Science Review* 2, no. 1 (June 2016): 36. See also Enayatollah Yazdani, "Globalization and the Role of Islam in the Post-Soviet Central Asia," *Alternatives: Turkish Journal of International Relations* 8, no. 2 (Summer 2009): 53.

12. Cf. Butti Sultan Butti Ali Al-Muhairi, "Islamisation and Modernisation within the UAE Penal Law: Shari'ah in the Modern Era," *Arab Law Quarterly* 11, no. 1 (1996): 34–49, 35, and 43.
13. Cf. Akgunduz, *Introduction*, 294; Peters, *Crime and Punishment*, 145.

CHAPTER XXIV

1. Bars and nightclubs are generally permitted businesses under the Regulation of the President of the Republic of Indonesia, Number 36 of 2010, 46, 70–71.
2. AFP Report, "Indonesia Cracks Down on Alcohol Sales," *The Sun* (Kuala Lumpur), 17 April 2015, 9.
3. Ibid.
4. Cf. Joseph Camilleri and Sven Schottmann, "Culture, Religion and the Southeast Asian State," in *Culture, Religion and Conflict in Muslim Southeast Asia: Negotiating Tense Pluralisms*, London: Routledge, 2013, 1–16.
5. There are questions on whether Islamic law could be considered "native" or "foreign" in Indonesia. Even in the times of Aceh sultanates, there are reports of gambling and alcohol drinking in Acehnese courts. See Tim Lindsey, "When Words Fail: Syariah Law in Indonesia: Revival, Reform or Transformation," in Penelope Nicholson and Sarah Bidulph, eds., *Examining Practice, Interrogating Theory: Comparative Legal Studies in Asia*, Leiden: Brill-Nijhoff, 2008, 212.
6. It has not been clarified but it seems that the external factor in the picture might be a reference to the Indonesian military.
7. Tim Lindsey et al., *Examining Practice*, 212.
8. The official title in Indonesian is Qanun Aceh Nombor 6 Tahun 2014 tentang Huokum Jinayat (Aceh Regional Regulation No. 6, 2014 on Islamic criminal law).
9. See also http://themonsoonproject.org/2014/05/30/justified-injustice-sharia-law-in-aceh-indonesia/ (accessed 14 July 2015).
10. Retrieved from: http://www.benarnews.org/english/news/indonesian/Aceh-sharia-04292015183548.html (accessed 9 March 2017).
11. Retrieved from: http://www.ucanews.com/news/sharia-law-draws-rave-reviews-in-indonesias-aceh/73112 (accessed 9 March 2017).
12. N. Hasan, "A Look at Shariah in Aceh, 10 Years On," *Jakarta Globe*, 28 November 2011.
13. Ibid.
14. The present writer wishes to thank Dr. Hafas Furqani of Banda Aceh for this information. He is a scholar of shariah himself. Interestingly, his father, Dr. Soufyan Mohd Soleh, was the chief judge of the Shariah Court of Aceh (Personal conversation with the author, Banda Aceh, 29 April 2015).
15. Topo Santoso, "Implementation of Islamic Criminal Law in Indonesia: Ta'zir Punishment as a Solution?," *IIUMLJ*, vol. 19 (2011), 123–149. [[write out the journal name]]

16. Marsen S. Naga, "Logical Flaws in Aceh's 'Qanun Jinayat,'" *Jakarta Post*, 6 October 2014, http://www.thejakartapost.com/news/2014/10/06/logical-flaws-aceh-s-qanun-jinayat.html (accessed 1 October 2016).
17. Moch Nor Ichwan, "Alternative to Shariatism: Progressive Muslim Intellectuals, Feminists, Queers and Sufis in Contemporary Aceh," in *Regime Change, Democracy and Islam: The Case of Indonesia*, Final Report Islam Research Programme Jakarta, Leiden: Leiden University Institute for Area Studies, 2013. Most papers in the report are quite critical of shariah in Aceh.
18. See Husni Mubarak A. Latief, "Hukuman Rajam dalam Rancangan Qanun Jinayay Aceh," *Socio-Religio*, vol. 9, issue 3 (May 2010), 829f.
19. The nine chapters include such themes as general provisions, exemptions and excuses, compensation and rehabilitation, offences by children, transitional provisions, and concluding provisions.
20. Article 125 of the 2006 Law further elaborated the provisions for Muslims and stated that the Islamic religion, which consists of faith (*ʿaqīdah*), law (shariah), and morality (*akhlāq*), covers matters of worship (*ʿibādah*), family law (*aḥwal shakhṣiyyah*), civil law (*muʿāmalah*), criminal law (*jināyah*), adjudication (*qaḍā*), education (*tarbiyah*), propagation (*daʿwah*), dissemination (*shiʿār*), and the defence of Islam.
21. See aceh.tribunnews.com (accessed 10 October 2016).
22. See icjr.or.id; see also hukumonline.com (accessed 27 September 2016). In its rebuttal, the S/C also mentioned that the defendant had organised a Public Hearing, which involved all components of Aceh society. However, in the list of proofs supplied by the defendant, which include letters from DPRA and the Aceh governor, state attorney, police, the shariah court, and the interior minister, this Public Hearing is not mentioned at all. In the previous DPRA ratification of the *qanun jinayat* in 2009, the head of the DPRA committee responsible for the *qanun* formulation stated that the public, such as the ulama, civil society representatives, universities, and youth organizations were invited for a public hearing. However, no one attended. One wonders whether a similar situation took place in 2014. See Putusan nomor 60P/HUM/2015 [putusan.mahkamahagung.go.id] (accessed 5 October 2016).
23. Indonesia: Elderly Christian Woman Whipped under Sharia Law for Selling Alcohol, https://asiancorrespondent.com/2016/04/indonesia-elderly-christian-woman-whipped-in-public-for-selling-alcohol/ (accessed 24 April 2016).

CHAPTER XXV

1. AFP report, "Brunei to Introduce Shariah Penal Code," *News Straits Times* (Kuala Lumpur), 23 October 2013, 29.
2. Ibid.
3. https://www.facebook.com/BukanZombie/posts/207798052733306 (accessed 8 January 2015).

4. http://www.straitstimes.com/asia/se-asia/brunei-delays-introduction-of-tough-islamic-law (accessed 8 January 2015).
5. https://www.theguardian.com/world/2014/apr/30/sultan-brunei-sharia-penal-code-flogging-death-stoning (accessed 8 January 2015).
6. Ibid.
7. Abdul Hamid Mohamad, "Implementation of the Islamic Criminal Law (*hudud, qisas, ta'zir*) in Malaysia—Prospects and Challenges," Kuala Lumpur, 1 April 2015, 1. The present writer wishes to thank the learned author for a personal copy he sent me of the English translation of his original lecture in the Malay language.

CHAPTER XXVI

1. Akgunduz, *Introduction*, 290.
2. This court was originally created to deal with complaints against the government, but as of 2010 its jurisdiction had expanded over commercial and some criminal cases, such as bribery and forgery, and it acts as a court of appeal for a number of non-shariah government tribunals.
3. Akgunduz, *Introduction*, 291; Aharon Layish, "Saudi Arabia Legal Reform as a Mechanism to Moderate Wahhabi Doctrine," *Journal of the American Oriental Society*, vol. 107, issue 2 (1987), 280; "A Brief Overview of Saudi Arabian Legal System," http://www.nyulawglobal.org/globalex/Saudi_Arabia.html (accessed 13 April 2017).
4. Akgunduz, *Introduction*, 291–292.
5. Peters, *Crime and Punishment*, 148–149.
6. al-Shāwī, *al-Mawsūʿah al-ʿAṣriyyah*, 4:184.
7. Ibid., 4:150.
8. Jon Weinberg, "Sword of Justice? Beheadings Rise in Saudi Arabia," *Harvard International Review*, vol. 29, issue 4 (Winter 2008), http://www.freepatentsonline.com/article/Harvard-International-Review/177028385.html (accessed 29 May 2017).
9. "100 Beheadings, 6 Months: Why the Saudi Kingdom Is on an Execution Spree," http://www.thedailybeast.com/articles/2015/06/18/100-beheadings-6-months-why-the-saudi-kingdom-is-on-an-execution-spree.html (accessed 3 September 2015).
10. "Saudi Prince Executed for Murder," AFP report carried in *The Sun* (Kuala Lumpur), 20 October 2016, 11.
11. Ibid.
12. Weinberg, "Sword of Justice?.
13. Letter to Saudi Rights Body on Amputation Case, https://www.hrw.org/news/2011/12/16/letter-saudi-rights-body-amputation-case (accessed 3 September 2015).
14. See comment by Joseph E. Lowry, Associate Professor of Arabic and Islamic Studies at the University of Pennsylvania, at http://www.middleeasteye.net/

news/crime-and-punishment-islamic-state-vs-saudi-arabia-1588245666 (accessed 27 January 2017).

15. Ibid.

CHAPTER XXVII

1. See for details Mohammad Hashim Kamali, *Law in Afghanistan: A Study of the Constitution, Matrimonial Law and the Judiciary*, Leiden: E. J Brill, 1985, 4-7 and passim.
2. See for details Mohammad Hashim Kamali, *Afghanistan's Constitution Ten Years On: What Are the Issues?* Kabul: Afghanistan's Research and Evaluation Unit (AREU), 2014, 20f.
3. The substance of these provisions is also upheld in the Civil Code 1976 (Art. 2), however, with an added element, which provides that when no ruling is found in Ḥanafī fiqh pertaining to a case under adjudication, the court shall issue judgment in accordance with the general custom, provided that such custom does not contravene the fundamental principles of law and justice.

CHAPTER XXVIII

1. Rudolph Peters, "The Islamization of Criminal Law: A Comparative Analysis," *Die Welt des Islams, New Series*, vol. 34, issue 2 (Nov. 1994), 246–274, 256, http://www.jstor.org/stable/1570932 (accessed 20 May 2014).
2. See also Peters, *Crime and Punishment*, 166.
3. Peters, "The Islamization of Criminal Law," 257.
4. Ibid.
5. Peters, *Crime and Punishment*, 157.
6. Qur'an, al-Nūr, 24:2. See also Jones-Pauly, "Use of the Qur'an in Key Pakistani Court Decisions on Zina and Qadhf," *Arabica*, T. 47 (3), July 2000," 540.
7. PLD [1983], 255.
8. http://www.dawn.com/news/1110944 (accessed 29 May 2017).
9. Peters, "The Islamization of Criminal Law," 259.
10. Cf. Peters, *Crime and Punishment*, 159.
11. "*Hudood* Ordinances: Changes in Pakistan's Rape Laws (Slowly) Make Progress," http://www.patheos.com/blogs/altmuslim/2006/08/changes_in_pakistans_rape_laws_slowly_make_progress/ (accessed 4 August 2014).
12. "Legal Injustices—The *Zina Hudood* Ordinance," *Journal of International Women's Studies*, vol. 7, issue 2 (November 2005), 20.
13. Shaheen Sardar Ali, "Applying Islamic Criminal Justice in Plural Legal Systems Exploring Gender-Sensitive Judicial Responses to Hudood Laws in Pakistan," Paper for International Judicial Conference, Islamabad, Pakistan, 11–14 August 2006, 18 (accessed 4 August 2014).

14. http://www.pakistani.org/pakistan/legislation/hudood.html 8th August 2006 by Zahirjan Mohamed (accessed 4 August 2014).
15. Ibid.
16. Report by Dominic Kelly, http://www.independent.co.uk/news/world/politics/special-report-the-punishment-was-death-by-stoning-the-crime-having-a-mobile-phone-8846585.html (accessed 29 May 2017).

CHAPTER XXIX

1. Peters, "The Islamization of Criminal Law," 246–274, 260.
2. Peters, *Crime and Punishment*, 161. See also Maryam Hosseinkhah of Iran Human Rights Documentation Center, "The Execution of Women in Iranian Criminal Law: An Examination of the Impact of Gender on Laws Concerning Capital Punishment in the New Islamic Penal Code."
3. Report of the spokesman of the Judicial and Legal Commission of the Parliament (in Persian), http://dadazmoon.ir/?p=20 (accessed 27 December 2013).
4. Electronic Journal of Islamic and Middle Eastern Law (EJIMEL), vol. 2 (2014), 24–38, http://www.ejimel.uzh.ch (accessed 20 January 2015).
5. Mohammad Ghaffari and Habibollah Najafi, "Inflation of Criminal Laws in Iran, Causes, and Consequences," *International Research Journal of Applied and Basic Sciences*, vol. 3, issue 7, 1360–1368 (2012), 1361, http://www.irjabs.com/files_site/paperlist/r_458_121110155810.pdf (accessed 24 May 2014).
6. Mohammad Hossein Nayyeri, *Research Paper Series:* New Islamic Panel Code of the Islamic Republic of Iran: An Overview, 2012, 16.
7. http://www.iranhrdc.org/english/publications/legal-commentary/1000000059-the-question-of-stoning-to-death-in-the-new-penal-code-of-the-iri.html (accessed 20 January 2015).
8. https://www.amnesty.org/en/countries/middle-east-and-north-africa/iran/report-iran/ (accessed 21 April 2017).
9. AFP report published in *The Star* (Kuala Lumpur), 30 December 2002, 36.
10. Peters, *Crime and Punishment*, 162.
11. See also Nayyeri, New Islamic Panel Code, 2012, 18.
12. al-Qaraḍāwī, *al-Shaykh al-Ghazālī*. See also Mohammad Hashim Kamali, *The Right to Life, Security, Privacy and Ownership in Islam*, Cambridge: The Islamic Texts Society, 2008, 20–21.

CHAPTER XXX

1. Article 262 of the federal constitution of Nigeria elaborates as follows: (1) The Shariah Court of Appeal shall, in addition to such other jurisdiction as may be conferred upon it by an Act of the National Assembly, exercise appellate and supervisory jurisdiction in civil proceedings involving questions of Islamic

personal law, such as marriage, divorce, family relationships, guardianship of infants or of the mentally ill and infirm, *waqf*, and gifts.

2. Cf. Akgunduz, *Introduction*, 300.
3. Elizabeth Peiffer, "The Death Penalty in Traditional Islamic Law and as Interpreted in Saudi Arabia and Nigeria," *William & Mary Journal of Women and the Law*, vol. 11, issue 3 (2005), 526; http://scholarship.law.wm.edu/cgi/viewcontent.cgi?article=1132&context=wmjowl (accessed 27 October 2014).
4. Peiffer, "The Death Penalty," 529.
5. Rudolph Peters, "The Re-introduction of Shariah Criminal Law in Nigeria: New Challenges for the Muslims of the North," *Amsterdam School for Cultural Analysis (ASCA)*, 2004, 15, downloaded from UvA-DARE, the institutional repository of the University of Amsterdam (UvA); http://hdl.handle.net/11245/2.80489 (accessed 28 October 2014).
6. Peiffer, "The Death Penalty," 534.

CHAPTER XXXI

1. http://www.nyulawglobal.org/globalex/Sudan.html (accessed 27 January 2017); see also Akgunduz, *Introduction*, 307.
2. Einas Ahmed, "Political Islam in Sudan: Islamists and the Challenge of State Power (1989–2004)," in Benjamin F. Soares and Rene Otayek, eds., *Islam and Muslim Politics in Africa*, New York: Palgrave Macmillan, 2007, 189–204, 191.
3. Ibid.
4. Mohammed Saeed and Hamza Hendawi, "Pregnant Sudanese woman Sentenced to Death for Marriage to Christian," *The Globe and Mail*, 16 May 2014. See also https://www.thestar.com/news/world/2014/05/15/woman_doctor_sentenced_to_death_for_marrying_christian.html (accessed 26 May 2014); Peters, "The Islamization of Criminal Law," 46–274, 265.
5. Peters, *Crime and Punishment*, 165–166.
6. Qur'an, al-Mā'idah, 5:33.
7. Peters, *Crime and Punishment*, 165–167.
8. Ibid., 166.
9. Peters, "The Islamization of Criminal Law," 265.
10. Ahmed, "Political Islam in Sudan," 189–204, 189.
11. Saeed and Hendawi, "Pregnant Sudanese Woman."
12. Peters, The Islamization of Criminal Law, 254.
13. Peters, *Crime and Punishment*, 168.
14. Sudan: Ban Death by Stoning, https://www.hrw.org/news/2012/05/31/sudan-ban-death-stoning (accessed 3 September 2015).
15. "Yet Another Case of Stoning: Sudan Women Continue to be Caught up in the Chaos," http://www.sudantribune.com/spip.php?article43703 (accessed 3 September 2015).

16. "Pregnant Woman to be Flogged, Hanged for Marrying Christian," http://nypost.com/2014/05/15/pregnant-woman-to-be-flogged-hanged-for-marrying-christian/ (accessed 3 September 2015).
17. http://www.wluml.org/media/stoning-interview-sudanese-human-rights-lawyer-hikma-ahmed (accessed 4 August 2014). See also Saeed and Hendawi, "Pregnant Sudanese Woman."
18. https://www.opendemocracy.net/arab-awakening/walaa-salah/new-amendments-to-sudanese-criminal-law (accessed 25 January 2017).
19. Ibid.

CHAPTER XXXII

1. Mo Salah, *Quelques aspects de la reception du droit français en Mauritanie* (1989), 5 *Revue mauritanienne de droit et d'économie* 25, quoted from *Researching the Legal System and Laws of the Islamic Republic of Mauritania*, http://www.nyulawglobal.org/globalex/Mauritania.html (accessed 10 September 2015).
2. *Legal System of Mauritania*, http://www.country-data.com/cgi-bin/query/r-8563.html (accessed 10 September 2015)
3. Article 60 of the 1961 Constitution of Mauritania states, "Legislation and regulations in force in the Islamic Republic of Mauritania shall remain applicable insofar as they have not been modified by this Constitution."
4. Anthony G. Pazzanita, *Historical Dictionary of Mauritania*, https://books.google.com.my/books?id=-KU_9MfXKKYC&pg=PA201&lpg=PA201&dq=penal+code+of+mauritania&source=bl&ots=nUg_YLPbaS&sig=4W2hhsFMhNibRnNlxvFedQfZ4ic&hl=en&sa=X&redir_esc=y#v=onepage&q=penal%20code%20of%20mauritania&f=false (accessed 14 September 2015).
5. Law Criminalizing Apostasy, http://www.loc.gov/law/help/apostasy/#_ftnref47 (accessed 14 September 2105).
6. Husnu al-Suood, *The Maldivian Legal System*, Maldives: Maldives Law Institute, 2014, 47.
7. Ibid., 49. See also https://en.wikipedia.org/wiki/Maldives (accessed 28 October 2016).
8. Al-Suood, *The Maldivian Legal System*, 49.
9. Ibid., 50–51.
10. See Dhivehi Raajjeyge Ekieki Kankan, *Hingigoiy*, vol. 10 (Records of the Government of Maldives), 2013 (Male, Maldives: Reprinted by Novelty Printers and Publishers), 923–925. See also https://books.google.com.my/books?id=FUHnAgAAQBAJ&pg=PA49&lpg=PA49&dq=legal+and+judicial+reforms+%2B+President+Amin+%2B+Maldives&source=bl&ots=1wIZ6BzGXe&sig=1Q2HPax_r0BlLR_ix-Wh1CaWxXw&hl=en&sa=X&redir_esc=y#v=snippet&q=President%20Amin&f=false.

11. Ibid.
12. https://minivannewsarchive.com/politics/comment-new-penal-code-comes-into-effect-a-truly-historic-moment-101000 (article by Hussein Shameem, accessed 30 May 2017).
13. ʿAbd Allāh al-Miṣrī, *Maʿrakat al-Dustūr fī'l-Yaman: Risālat al-ʿulamāʾ bi-khuṣūṣ mashrūʿ dustūr dawlat al-waḥdah* [The Constitutional Movement in Yemen: Letter from the Ulama regarding the Draft Constitution of the Unitary State], Sanaa, n.d.
14. Law Criminalizing Apostasy, http://www.loc.gov/law/help/apostasy/#_ftn82 (accessed 7 September 2015).
15. Amnesty International Report 1998: Yemen, http://www.refworld.org/docid/3ae6aa014c.html (accessed 2 September 2015).
16. Yemeni Man Sentenced to Hand and Foot Amputation for Armed Robbery; <https://www.amnesty.org/en/press-releases/2013/09/yemeni-man-sentenced-hand-and-foot-amputation-armed-robbery/> (accessed 2 September 2015).
17. Death by stoning and flogging, http://www2.amnesty.se/uaonnet.nsf/dfab8d-7f58eec102c12570110064 66e1/f45a9ac5cf75908ac1256c95002cda22?OpenDocu ment (accessed 7 September 2015).

CHAPTER XXXIII

1. Eugene Cotran and Chibli Mallat, eds., *Yearbook of Islamic and Middle Eastern Law*, London: Kluwers Law International, 1994, 1:543. See also Akgunduz, *Introduction*, 296–297.
2. Law No. 148 of 1972 (Art. 5).
3. Ibid., Article 13.
4. Law No. 70 of 1973 (Art. 2).
5. Law No. 148 of 1972 (Art. 19).
6. Cf. Peters, *Crime and Punishment*, 155.
7. Markus D. Dubber, *The Oxford Handbook of Criminal Law*, https://books.google.com.my/books?id=DE5VBQAAQBAJ&pg=PA264&lpg=PA264&dq=Islamic+criminal+law+in+united+arab+emirates&source=bl&ots=WuBwo6r7ex&sig=xd7uUrYFZu4T4FwadZZ6MXS24Fc&hl=en&sa=X&redir_esc=y#v=onepage&q=Islamic%20criminal%20law%20in%20united%20arab%20emirates&f=false (accessed 15 September 2015).
8. Aly Kheder Ahmed, *A Guide to United Arab Emirates Legal System*; <http://www.nyulawglobal.org/globalex/United_Arab_Emirates.htm> (accessed 15 September 2015).
9. https://en.wikipedia.org/wiki/United Arab Emirates (accessed 27 October 2016).
10. https://en.wikipedia.org/wiki/UnitedArabEmirates (accessed 27 October 2016).
11. https://en.wikipedia.org/wiki/Qatar.
12. Ibid.

CHAPTER XXXIV

1. The cases cited involved Muslim and non-Muslim parties in conversion and property disputes. In one case, the son converted to Islam and then he died, and the mother filed the case stating that the son had reverted to his previous religion before he died, but whether a person is a Muslim or not is a shariah issue. She could not bring the case to a shariah court as she was non-Muslim and shariah courts had no jurisdiction over her. As such she had nowhere to go. In another court case over a land dispute, the case involved a non-Muslim and *waqf* charitable endowment, which fell under the shariah court's jurisdiction. The shariah judge would be able to look into the *waqf* issue, but not the land laws, such as adverse possession, estoppels, and indefeasibility of title, as those were beyond the shariah court's jurisdiction. Even if both parties were Muslim, Tun Hamid added, they could resolve only the *waqf* issue but not the land law part—for this is "a matter for Parliament to resolve, not the court, as it involves amending the constitution." See Tun Hamid's views in *New Straits Times* (Kuala Lumpur), 9 December 2016, 20.
2. Muslim, *Mukhtaṣar Ṣaḥīḥ Muslim*, hadith no. 1784, 474.

Glossary

ʿadam al-ghawth: an expression that signifies the victim's helplessness.
adbār (pl. of *dubur*): back, posterior.
ʿām: general, especially words in a legal text that are unspecified as to the scope of their application.
ʿāqil, bāligh: legally an adult and competent person.
aḥādith (pl.of hadith): sayings of Prophet Muḥammad.
aḥkām ūli al-amr: commands of the lawful rulers.
akbar al-kabāʾir: gravest of the major sins.
amānah: trust.
amārāt: circumstantial evidence.
amīn: trustee.
arkān (pl. of *rukun*): pillars.
aṣl: origin, basis, root.
aṣlaḥa: to rectify or reform.
ʿawrah: private parts.
āyah (pl. *āyāt*): lit., sign, usually a verse of the Qur'an.
baghy (or *bugha*) : mutiny, rebellion.
basmah warāthiyyah: DNA (deoxyribonucleic acid).
bawwāb: door keeper.
bidʿah: Pernicious innovation signifying the opposite of Sunnah, against the established precedent.
bi'ı-maʿrūf: according to custom or in a decent manner.
dār al-ḥarb: abode of war.
dhanb: sin.
dhimmī: non-Muslim citizen (now *mawatin*).
dīn Allāh: God's religion.
diya: blood-money.
fāḥishah (or *faḥshāʾ*): immorality, lewdness.

fasād: corruption.
fāsid: legally voidable.
fiqh: lit., understanding, usually Islamic law and jurisprudence.
fitnah: sedition, incitement to crime and rebellion against lawful government.
ghaṣb: usurpation.
ghayr muḥṣan: an unmarried Muslim.
ghayr ʿudūl: of lesser qualification in reference usually to witnesses.
ghulāt: exaggerators, also a group of the Shia.
ḥadd (pl. *ḥudūd*): lit., limit, prescribed punishment in Islamic law for a specified number of offences; it also refers to the offence itself.
hadith: saying of Prophet Muḥammad.
hadr al-dam: bloodshed for no valid cause.
halal: lawful, permissible.
ḥaqq: right, truth, justly deserved.
ḥaqq al-ādamī / ḥaqq al-ʿabd: Right of Man or private right.
ḥaqq Allāh: Right of God, often signifying a public or community right.
ḥarām: forbidden.
ḥikmah : wisdom, balanced judgement.
ḥirābah: highway robbery, terrorism, waging war against the community.
ḥirz: safeguarding or safekeeping.
ʿiddah: probation period a woman must observe following dissolution of her marriage.
īdhāʾ : hurt, any painful act.
ʿiffah: purity of character.
al-ifk: the lie.
iḥṣān: lit., protection, a legal status achieved when a Muslim is lawfully married.
ijmāʿ: general consensus.
ikhtilāf: reasoned disagreement, differential interpretation.
iktilāṭ : ambiguity.
ijmāʿ sukūtī : tacit consensus, as opposed to *ijmaʿ qawlī* (verbal consensus).
ijtihād: lit., striving, intellectual exertion by a qualified scholar, in order to derive the ruling of an issue from the source evidence of shariah.
iḥtimāl : probability.
ikhāfah, irhāb : spreading of fear.
iltibās : confusion.
intiḥār : suicide.
irtidād : apostasy, deliberate renunciation of Islam.
iṣlāḥ : reform, change for the better.
jāhiliyyah : time of ignorance.
jihad : lit., struggle — for a righteous cause, also known as holy war.
jumhūr: dominant majority.

kaffārah : lit. a concealer, expiation, self-imposed punishment.
kāfir : infidel.
khamr : wine obtained specifically from grapes.
Khārijites : lit., outsiders, a sectarian movement that staged an uprising against the caliph ʿAlī in the early days of Islam.
khāṣṣ : specific **(as opposed to a general, *ʿām*) text** or statement that conveys a specific meaning.
khuṣumah : litigation.
liʿān : imprecation, a form of divorce in Islamic law.
liwāṭ : homosexuality/sodomy.
madhhab (pl. *madhāhib*): legal school.
mafsadah : mischief.
maḥram : a close relative.
majhūl : unknown.
makrūh : reprehensible, abominable – as opposed to *mandūb*.
māl mutaqawwim: property with a market value.
maqāṣid al-sharīʿah: the overriding objectives of shariah.
maqdhuf: slandered person/individual.
marīḍ: ill , sick.
maʿsiyah : transgression.
maṣāliḥ ḍarūriyyah : essential interests.
mashhūr : lit., famous, also a well-known variety of hadith.
mashrūʿiyyah : legality.
maṣlaḥah : lawful benefit.
mijn : shield.
milkiyyah : ownership.
mubāḥ : permissible.
mubtadiʿ : pernicious innovator.
mudārib : trade manager.
mufāriq li'l-jamāʿah: one who boycotts the community
muftī jurisconsult, one who is qualified to give a legal opinion or *fatwa*.
muḥarib (pl. *muḥaribīn*): terrorist.
muḥkam : firm, perspicuous, a text usually of the Qur'an that conveys a firm and indisputable meaning.
muḥṣan : a married Muslim.
mujāharah : declaring openly.
mujtahid : one who is qualified to conduct *ijtihād*.
mukallaf: a legally competent person.
muqābil al-azhar : contrary to the manifest position.
murtad : apostate.
musāfir : traveller.

musāḥaqah, also *siḥāq*: lesbianism.

Muʿtazilah : a sectarian movement of early Islam well-known for its rationalist tendencies.

mutawātir : proven by continuous testimony (a variety of hadith).

mutazawwijah : a married woman.

nafs : living soul, self.

naṣhah : sincere advice.

naskh : abrogation of one ruling by another.

nisāb : quorum.

qadhf : slanderous accusation.

qāḍī : judge.

qānūn : statutory law.

Qānūn Jināyat: Islamic Criminal Law.

qarīnah (pl. *qarā'in*): clue, circumstantial evidence.

qarīnah qāṭiʿah : decisive circumstantial evidence.

qasamah : oath-taking.

qatl: murder.

qaṭʿī : definitive.

qaṭʿ al-ṭarīq: highway robbery/banditry.

qawl al-ṣaḥābi : saying of the companion.

qiṣāṣ : just retaliation.

qiyas : analogy.

rajm : stoning.

ribā : usury, banking interest.

riddah: apostasy.

ṣaḥīḥ : sound, usually of a sound hadith.

saḥq / suḥq : hard contagion, rubbing fiercely without penetration, lesbianism.

sajjān / ḥaddād: prison guard.

ṣabr: patience.

ṣalāh: ritual prayers.

sāriq: thief.

sariqah: theft.

al-sariqat al-kubrā: great robbery.

satr : concealment.

satr al-ʿawrāt: concealing the nakedness of others.

shafāʿah : intercession.

shafāʿah ḥasanah : benevolent intercession.

shak : doubt.

shibh al-ʿaqd : quasi contract.

shirk : association of other deities with God.

shubhāt (pl. *shubha*): doubt, uncertainty.

shurb : (offence of) wine drinking.

siyāsah sharʿiyyah : judicious policy, shariah-oriented policy.
sulṭah taḥakkumiyyah : arbitrary exercise of power.
sunnah : normative conduct and teachings of Prophet Muḥammad.
taʿadhdhur al-iḥtirāz : inability to avoid.
tabʿīd : banishment.
tābiʿi (pl. *tabiʿīn*): successor, the generation immediately after Companions.
tadākhul : amalgamation.
tafsīr : explanation, interpretation usually of Qur'an.
tafsīr bi'l-maʾthūr : *tafsir* based on precedent.
tafsīr bi'l- raʾy : *tafsir* based on opinion.
taghrīb : banishment.
taḥakkumiyyah: arbitrary ruling.
taḥrīm : prohibition.
taʾkhīr : delay.
takhṣīṣ al-ʿām: specification of the general.
taqādum : expiry, expiration due to lapse of time.
taqlīd : indiscriminate imitation.
taqlīdī: imitationist.
taʾwīl : plausible interpretation.
tawbah : repentance.
tawḥīd : monotheism, belief in the Oneness of God.
taʿzīr : deterrent punishment.
taʿzīrāt (plural of *taʿzīr*): deterrent penalties.
ʿulamāʾ (sing. *ʿālim*): Eng. ulama: scholars, learned persons.
ūli al-amr: persons charged with authority.
ummah: Muslim community, fraternity of believers.
ʿuqūbah : punishments.
uṣūl al-fiqh : science of the sources and proofs of Islamic Law.
wājib : obligatory.
wilāyah: guardianship.
walī (pl. *awliyāʾ*): guardian, supporter.
walī al-dam: next of kin.
wuḍūʾ: ablution.
zakat: poor due.
zānī : adulterer.
ẓannī : speculative.
ẓihār : a form of divorce in Islamic Law.
zinā: adultery and fornication.
zinā bi'l-maḥārim : incest.
zindīq : heretic.

References

Abdul Jalil, Shahrizat. Women, unite: oppose Hudud laws. *The Star*. 29 May 2002:Front page, 3.

Abdul Majid, Mahmud Zuhdi. Rational approach to pursuit of Islamic Order. *New Straits Times*. 20 July 1994:12.

Abdullah, Nik Imran, et al. Confusion over DAP's Stand: PAS Leaders at Odds over whether Partner Agreeable on *Hudud*. *New Straits Times*. 13 October 2011:11.

Abdullah, Nik Imran, et al. PAS' weapon of convenience. *New Straits Times*. 11 November 2013: 16.

Abdullah, Nik Imran, et al. Can Parliament settle hudud issue? *New Straits Times*. 9 February 2015: 16.

Abu Dhabi Court of Cassation Judgment No. 9/19 dated 18 October 1997. https://books.google.com.my. Accessed 20 September 2015.

AFP report. Indonesia cracks down on alcohol sales. *The Sun*. 17 April 2015: 9.

AFP report. Brunei to introduce shariah penal code. *New Straits Times*. 23 October 2013: 29.

AFP report. Saudi prince executed for murder. *The Sun*. 20 October 2016:11

Ahmad, Kassim. Resolving the 'Ḥudūd' Law Dilemma. *New Straits Times*. 14 December 1993:13.

Ahmad, Salbiah. An issue paper of zina and rape under the Syariah Criminal Code (II) Bill 1993 (Kelantan). Unpublished paper presented at the Kuala Lumpur forum of the Institute of Strategic and International Studies, 19 January 1993.

Ahmad, Wan Farid. The challenges ahead for hudud technical committee. *New Straits Times*. 7 May 2014: 17.

Ahmed, Einas. Political Islam in Sudan: Islamists and the challenge of state power (1989–2004). In Benjamin F. Soares and Rene Otayek (Eds.), *Islam and Muslim Politics in Africa*. New York: Palgrave Macmillan, 2007.

Akgunduz, Ahmed. *Introduction to Islamic Law*. Rotterdam: IUR Press, 2010.

Akmar, Shamsul. Wielding hudud as a weapon. *New Straits Times*. 22 November 1993.

Ali, Adrian, and Esther Landau. Govt won't table bill. *New Straits Times*. 30 March 2017:6.

Ali, Shaheen Sardar. Applying Islamic Criminal Justice in Plural Legal Systems Exploring Gender-Sensitive Judicial Responses to Hudood Laws in Pakistan. Paper for International Judicial Conference, Islamabad, Pakistan, 11–14 August 2006: 18.

Ali, Syed AkbarSA. Syariah Criminal Code not without loopholes. *New Straits Times*, 29 November 1993.

Alias, Aswadi. Don't jump the gun, defiant Hadi tells critics. *New Straits Times*. 27 March 2015: 6.

Al-Alūsī, Shihāb al-Dīn Maḥmūd. *Rūḥ al-Maʿānī fī Tafsīr al-Qurʾān al-ʿAẓīm*. 4th ed. Vol. 18. Cairo: Idārah al-Ṭabāʿah al-Munīriyyah, 1405/1985.

Al-ʿAwā, Muḥammad Sālim. *Al-Fiqh al-Islāmī fī Ṭarīq al-Tajdīd*. 3rd enhanced ed. Beirut: al-Maktab al-Islāmī, 1998/1419.

Aly Khedr, Ahmed. A Guide to United Arab Emirates Legal System. http://www.nyulawglobal.org/globalex/United_Arab_Emirates.htm. Accessed 15 September 2015.

Anwarullah. *The Criminal Law of Islam*. Kuala Lumpur: A. S. Nordeen, 1997.

El-Awa, Mohamed Salim. *Punishment in Islamic Law*. Indianapolis: American Trust Publications, 1982.

El-Awa, Mohamed Salim. Taʿzīr in the Islamic penal system. *Journal of Islamic and Comparative Law* 1976;6:56–57.

El-Awa, Mohamed Salim. The basics of Islamic penal legislation. In Cherif Bassiouni (Ed.), *The Islamic Criminal Justice System*. London: Oceana Publications, 1982.

ʿAwdah, ʿAbd al-Qādir. *Al-Tashrīʿ al-Jināʾī al-Islāmī Muqārinah bi'l-Qānūn al-Waḍʿi*. 13th ed. 2 vols. Beirut: Muʾassasah al-Risālah, 1994/1415.

ʿAwdah, Abd al-QÉdir. *Al Tashrīʿ al-Jināʾī al-Islami Muqārinah bi'l-Qānūn al-Waḍʿi*. Vol. 2. Beirut: Muʾassasah al-Risālah, n.d.

Badawī, Isma'il. *Daʿāʾim al-Ḥukm fi'l-Shari'ah al-Islamiyyah wa'l-Nuzum al-Dusturiyyah al-Mu'asirah*. Cairo: Dār al-Fikr al-ʿArabī, 1980/1400.

Bahnasī, Aḥmad Fatḥī. *Al-ʿUqūbah fī l-Fiqh al-Islāmī*. 5th rev. ed., Beirut and Cairo: Dār al-Shurūq, 1983/1403.

Bahnasī, Aḥmad Fatḥī. *Al-ʿUqūbah fī l-Fiqh al-Islāmī*. 6th ed. Cairo: Dār al-Shurūq, 1989/1409.

Al-Bājī, Sulaymān b. Khalaf Abū 'l-Walīd. *Al-Muntaqā Sharḥ al-Muwaṭṭaʾ*. Ed. ʿAbd al-Qādir ʿAṭa. Vol. 7. Beirut: Dār al-Kutub al-ʿIlmiyyah, 1999.

Bassiouni, Cheriff. *The Islamic Criminal Justice System*. London: Oceana Publications, 1982.

Bassiouni, Cheriff. *The Shari'a and Islamic Criminal Justice in Time of War and Peace*. New York: Cambridge University Press, 2014.

Al-Bayhaqī, Aḥmad b. al-Ḥusayn. *Al-Sunan al-Kubrā*. Hyderabad: Dāʾiratul Maʿārif al-ʿUthmāniyyah, 1355/1934.

Bayyah, ʿAbd Allāh b. al-Mafuz Bin. *Tanbih al-Waqīʿ ʿalā Taʾsīl Fiqh al-Waqīʿ* [Reading the Jurisprudence of Pragmatism into the Sources of Shariah]. UAE: al-Majlis al-Waṭanī al-ʿĀm, 2014, 82–83.

Begum, Faridah. Up to people to reject Hudud Bill, says Rais. *The Star*. 10 July 2002: 2.

Benedict, Brenda. "Islamic View," including an interview with Nik Noriani Nik Badli Shah. *The Star*. 2 February 2004: 3.

Brown, Jonathan. Stoning and Handcutting: Understanding Hudud and the Shariah in Islam. https://yaqeeninstitute.org/en/jonathan-brown/stoning-and-hand-cutting-understanding-the-hudud-and-the-shariah-in-islam/. Accessed 30 June 2017.

Al-Bukhārī, Muḥammad b. Ismāʿīl. *Ṣaḥīḥ al-Bukhārī*. Eng. trans. Muhammad Muhsin Khan. 6th ed. Lahore: Kazi Publications, 1983.

Camilleri, Joseph and Steven Schottmann. *Culture, Religion and Conflict in Muslim Southeat Asia: Negotiating Tense Pluralisms*. Routledge Contemporary Southeast Asia Series (eBook). http://book.google.com.my/books?isbn=1136163433 Accessed 9 January 2015.

Chanen, Jill Schachner. Beheading and blood money. *ABA Journal*, 1998; 84:34–35. http://search.proquest.com.myaccess.library.utoronto.ca/saveasdownloadprogress/48A1F3AF8814D46PQ/false?accountid=14771. Accessed 22 May 2014.

Charles, Lourdes, and Basri, Mustafa Kamali. Cops won't help enforce hudud laws in Terengganu. *The Star*. 11 July 2002: Front page.

Cotran, Eugene, and Chibli Mallat. Eds. *Yearbook of Islamic and Middle Eastern Law*. Vol. 1. London: Kluwers Law International 1994, 543.

Cotran, Eugene, and Chibli Mallat. Eds. *Yearbook of Islamic and Middle Eastern Law*. Vol. 7. London: Kluwers Law International, 2001.

Coulson, Noel J. The state and individual in Islamic law. *International and Comparative Law Quarterly* 1956: 6.

Cusac, Anne-Marie. *Cruel and Unusual: The Culture of Punishment in America*. New Haven: Yale University Press, 2009.

Abū Dāʾūd. *Sunan Abu Dawud*. Eng. trans. Ahmad Hasan. Lahore: Sh. M. Ashraf, 1984.

Dubber, Markus. *The Oxford Handbook of Criminal Law*. https://books.google.com.my/. Accessed 15 September 2015.

Al-Dusūqī, Shams al-Dīn al-Shaykh Muḥammad b. ʿArafah. *Ḥāshiyah al-Dusūqī ʿalā al-Sharḥ al-Kabīr*. Cairo: ʿĪsā al-Ḥalabī, n.d.

Ibn Farḥūn, Ibrāhīm b. ʿAlī. *Tabṣirah al-Ḥukkām fī Uṣūl al-ʿAqīdah*. Cairo: al-Maṭbaʿah al-Bahiyyah, 1302.

Fong, Fernando. Combine courts to solve conflict of jurisdiction. *New Straits Times*. 9 December 2016.

Ghaffari, Mohammad, and Habibollah Najafi. Inflation of criminal laws in Iran, causes, and consequences. *International Research Journal of Applied and Basic*

Sciences 2012;3(7): 1360–1368. http://www.irjabs.com/files_site/paperlist/r_458_121110155810.pdf. Accessed 24 May 2014.

Ghazali, Lo'Lo', Dr. Review: don't oppose Hudud Bill. *The Star*. 30 May 2002: 2.

Al-Ghazālī, Muḥammad. *Min Hunā Naʿlam*. Cairo: n.p., 1948.

Gomaa, Sheikh Ali. *Responding from the Tradition: One Hundred Contemporary Fatwas by the Grand Mufti of Egypt*. Louisville, KY: Fons Vitae, 2011.

Gomez, Lydia. Hudud is not for Malaysia. *New Straits Times*. 21 August 2010, 14.

Gul Hassan Khan vs. Government of Pakistan. PLD 1980 Peshawar-1, Section 54.

Enayat, Hamid. *Modern Islamic Political Thought*. London: Macmillan Press, 1982.

Hamidullah, Muhammad, Mahmood A. Ghazi, and Mehboob Ahmad. *The Life and Work of the Prophet of Islam*. Islamabad: Islamic Research Institute, 1998.

Ḥamudah, Muntaṣir Saʿīd. *Al-Irhāb: Dirāsah Fiqhiyyah fi'l-Tashrīʿ al-Jināʾī al-Islāmī*. Alexandria, Egypt: Dār al-Jamīʿah al-Jadīdah li'l-Nashr, 2008.

Haridas, K. Islamization of state and society. In Norani Othman (Ed.), *Shariah Law and the Modern Nation State: A Malaysian Symposium*. Kuala Lumpur: Sisters in Islam, 1994, 89–105.

Hasan N. A look at Shariah in Aceh, 10 years on. *Jakarta Globe*, 28 November 2011.

Ibn Ḥazm al-Ẓāhirī, Abū Muḥammad ʿAlī b. Aḥmad. *Al-Muḥallā*. Ed. A. G. Sulāyman al-Bandarī. Beirut: Dār al-Kutub al-ʿIlmiyyah, 1468/1988.

Al-Hewesh, Mohammad Ibn Ibrahim. Murder and homicide in Islamic criminal law: textual foundations. In Tahir Mahmood (Ed.), *Criminal Law in Islam and the Muslim World: A Comparative Perspective*. New Delhi: Institute of Objective Studies, 2012, 158.

Al-Ḥillī, Muḥaqqiq. *Mokhtasar-e Nafi'*. Persian trans. Muḥammad Taqī Danish-pazhoh. Tehran: Bongah-e Tarjomah wa Nashr-e Kitab, 1964/1343.

Al-Hindī, al-Muttāqī. *Kanz al-ʿUmmāl: Fī sanan al-Aqwāl wa-al-afʿāl*. Hyderabad: Dāʾirat al-Maʿārif al-ʿUthmāniyyah, 1945.

Hosseinkhah, Maryam. The execution of women in Iranian criminal law: an examination of the impact of gender on laws concerning capital punishment in the new Islamic penal code. http://www.iranhrdc.org/english/publications/legal-commentary/1000000102-the-execution-of-women-in-iranian-criminal-law.html. Accessed 19 September 2016.

Ibn Ḥanbal, Aḥmad. *Musnad Ibn Ḥanbal: Musnad al-Makkiyīn, hadith Wāthilah b. al-Asqaʿ min al-Shamiyyīn*. Cairo: Dār al- Ḥadīth, 2005.

Ibrahim, Ahmad. Suitability of Islamic punishments in Malaysia. *IIUM Law Journal* 1993;2(1): 14–15.

Ibrahim, Ahmad. *The Administration of Islamic Law in Malaysia*. Kuala Lumpur: Institute of Islamic Understanding Malaysia (IKIM), 2000.

Ichwan, Moch Nor. Alternative to shariatism: progressive Muslim intellectuals, feminists, queers and Sufis in contemporary Aceh. In *Regime Change, Democracy and Islam: The Case of Indonesia, Final Report Islam Research Programme Jakarta*. Leiden: Leiden University Institute for Area Studies, 2013.

Al-ʿIlī, ʿAbd al-Ḥakīm Ḥasan. *Al-Ḥurriyyat al-ʿĀmmah.* Kuwait: n.p., 1983.

Imam, Mohammed. Islamic law in Malaysia: federal-state jurisdictional conflict. 1004 *Current Law Journal* 1994;29:n.p.

Imran, Rahat. Legal injustices: The Zina Hudood Ordinance of Pakistan and its implications for women. *Journal of International Women's Studies* 2005; 7(2): 96.

Ismail, Rose. Hudud laws. *New Straits Times.* 10 July 1994:12.

Ismail, Rose. Hudud laws in other countries. Paper presented to ISIS Forum, Kuala Lumpur, 19 November 1993.

Jaafar, Sulaiman. No let up in Kelantan on hudud. *New Straits Times,* 28 October 2013:Front Page.

Jahangir, Asma, and Hina Jillani. *The Hudud Ordinances: A Divine Sanction?* Lahore: Rhotas Books, 1990.

Jamin, Satiman. DPM: UMNO has never been against hudud. *New Straits Times,* 23 December 2012: 2.

Al-Jarḥazī, ʿAbd Allāh Ibn Sulaymān. *Kitāb al-Mawāhib al-Sunniyyah ʿalā Sharḥ al-Fawāʾid al-Bahiyyah, on the margin of Jalāl al-Dīn al-Suyūṭī, al-Ashbāh waʾl-Nazāʾir.* Beirut: Dār al-Fikr, n.d.

Al-Jazīrī, ʿAbd al-Raḥmān b. Muḥammad ʿAwaḍ . *al-Fiqh ʿalāʾl-Madhāhib al-Arbaʿah.* New revised ed. al-Mansurah, Egypt: Dār al-Ghad al-Jadīd, 2005.

Al-Jawziyyah, Ibn Qayyim. *Iʿlām al-Muwaqqiʿīn.* Ed. Muḥammad Munīr al-Dimashqī. Vol. 2. Cairo: Idārah al-Ṭabāʿah al-Munīriyyah, n.d.

Al-Jawziyyah, Ibn Qayyim. *Al-Ṭurūq al-ḥukmiyyah fī ʾl Siyāsah al-Sharʿiyyah.* Cairo: al-Mu'assissah al-ʿArabiyyah liʾl-Ṭibāʿah, 1961/1380.

Jones-Pauly, Chris. Use of the Qur'an in Key Pakistani Court Decisions on *Zina* and *Qadhf. Arabica,* T. 47, Fasc. 3, Les usages du Coran. Présupposés et Méthodes: Formgebrauch des Korans.

Kahar, Shamsul. Hudud Laws for Muslims only. *New Straits Times.* 19 November 1994.

Kamal, Mustafa. Sultan Mizan gives consent to Hudud law. *The Star.* 1 August 2002: 10.

Kamali, Mohammad Hashim. *Principles of Islamic Jurisprudence.* Cambridge, UK: The Islamic Texts Society, 1991; 3rd enhanced ed. by the same publisher, 2003.

Kamali, Mohammad Hashim. *Freedom of Expression in Islam.* Cambridge: Islamic Text Society, 1997.

Kamali, Mohammad Hashim. *The Right to Life, Security, Privacy and Ownership in Islam.* Cambridge: Islamic Texts Society, 2008.

Kamali, Mohammad Hashim. *Freedom, Equality and Justice in Islam.* Cambridge: Islamic Text Society, 2000.

Kamali, Mohammad Hashim. *Shari'ah Law: An Introduction.* Oxford: Oneworld Publications, 2008.

Kamali, Mohammad Hashim. *Law in Afghanistan: A Study of the Constitution, Matrimonial Law and the Judiciary.* Leiden: E. J. Brill, 1985.

Kamali, Mohammad Hashim. Siyasah Shar'iyyah or the Policies of Islamic Governments. *American J. of Islamic Social Sciences* 1989;6: 59–81.

Kamali, Mohammad Hashim. Strictly from the Qur'anic perspective. *New Straits Times*, 25 April 2009: 14.

Kamali, Mohammad Hashim. Afghanistan's Constitution ten years on: what are the issues? Kabul: Afghanistan Research and Evaluation Unit, 2014.

Kamali, Mohammad Hashim. *The Middle Path of Moderation in Islam: The Qur'anic Principle of Wasatiyyah*. New York and London; Oxford University Press, 2015.

Kamali, Mohammad Hashim. *Shariah Law: Questions and Answers*. Oxford: Oneworld Publications, 2017.

Al-Kāsānī, ʿAlāʾ al-Dīn al-Kāsānī. *Badāʾiʿ al-Ṣanāʾīʿ fī Tartīb al-Sharāʾiʿ*. Cairo: Maṭbaʿah al-Jamaliyyah 1328/1910. 2nd ed. Beirut: Dār al-Kitāb al-ʿArabī, 1982.

Khallāf, ʿAbd al-Wahhāb. *Al-Siyāsah al-Sharʿiyyah*. Cairo: al-Maktabah al-Salafiyyah, 1931/1350.

Al-Khalifah, Abdullah H. H. Religiosity in Islam as a protective mechanism against criminal temptation. *American Journal of Islamic Social Sciences* 1994;11: 1–13.

Al-Khammāsī, Fatḥī b. al-Ṭayyib. *Al-Ḍarūrah al-Marḥaliyyah fī-Taṭbīq al-Qānūn al-Jināʾī al-Islāmī*. Damascus and Beirut: Dār Qutaybah, 2001/1421.

Al-Khaṭṭāf, Ḥasan. Mafhum al-ḥirābah wa-ḍawābiṭuha: Dirāsah bayn al-nāṣṣ al-Qurʾānī wa'l-turāth al-fiqhī. In: *Islāmiyyat al-Maʿrifah: Majallat al-Fikr al-Islāmī al-Muʿāṣir*. Vol. 21. Herndon, VA: 1436/2015.

Koshy, Shaila. PAS: Our Right to Pass Shariah Law. *The Star*. 19 August 2003: 23.

Koshy, Shaila, and Mustafa Kamal Basri. PAS: Hudud good for Muslims. *The Star*. 9 July 2002: 4.

Koshy, Shaila, and Mustafa Kamal Basri. PAS: Hudud law will run its course (interview with Wan Abdul Muttalib Embong). *The Star*. 18 August 2002: 26.

Koshy, Shaila, and Mustafa Kamal Basri. Incest victims prefer federal law to Shariah. *Sunday Star*. 30 November 2003: 15.

Lacroix, Stéphane. Between Islamists and Liberals: Saudi Arabia's new "Islamo-Liberal" reformists. *Middle East Journal* 2004; 58(3): 355.

Langbein, John. The historical origins of the sanction of imprisonment for serious crimes. *Journal of Legal Studies* 1976; 5(1): 36.

Latief, Husni Mubarak A. Hukuman Rajam dalam Rancangan Qanun Jinayay Aceh. *Socio-Religio* 2010; 9(3): 829f.

Latiff, Rozanna. Dr M: Pas hudud un-Islamic. *New Straits Times*, 5 April 2015: 16.

Layish, Aharon. Saudi Arabia legal reform as a mechanism to moderate Wahhabi doctrine. *Journal of the American Oriental Society* 1987; 107(2).

Legal System. http://www.country-data.com/cgi-bin/query/r-8563.html. Accessed 10 September 2015.

Letter to Saudi Rights Body on Amputation Case. *Human Rights Watch*. xhttps://www.hrw.org/news/2011/12/16/letter-saudi-rights-body-amputation-case. Accessed 3 September 2015.

Lindsey, Tim. *Islam, Law and the State in Southeast Asia*. London: I. B. Tauris, 2012.

Lindsey, Tim. When words fail: Syariah law in Indonesia: revival, reform or transformation. In: Nicholson P, Biddulph S, eds., *Examining Practice, Interrogating Theory: Comparative Legal Studies in Asia*. Leiden: Brill-Nijhoff, 2008, 212.

Lynch, Andrew et al., eds. *Law and Liberty in the War on Terror*. Sdyney: Federation Press, 2007, 39–48 at 41.

Mahavera, Sheridan. State government survey finds 90% in Kelantan want hudud. 2 April 2015. http://www.themalaysiainsider.com/Malaysia/article/state-government-survey-finds-90-in-kelantan-want-hudud. Accessed 15 April 2015.

Al-Mahdī, Al-Ṣādiq. *Al-ʿUqubāt al-Shariʿyyah wa-Mawāqifah min al-Niẓām al-Ijtimaʿī al-Islāmī* [Islamic Punishment and Its Place in an Islamic Social Order]. Cairo: Zahrāʾ lil-ʿAlām al-ʿArabī, 1986.

Muḥmaṣṣānī, Ṣubḥī. *Arkān Ḥuqūq al-Insān*. Beirut: Dār al-ʿIlm li-l'Malayīn, 1979.

Mahmood, Tahir. Criminal procedure at the Sharīʿah law. In: Tahir Mahmood, ed., *Criminal Law in Islam and the Muslim World: A Comparative Perspective*. Delhi: Institute of Objective Studies, 1996.

Ibn Mājah. *Sunan Ibn Mājah*. Lahore, Pakistan: Kazi Publications, 1993.

Al-Majlis al-Aʿla lil-Shuʾūn al-Islāmiyyah. Al-Ishtibāh fīl-Ḥudūd. In: *Mawsūʿah Jamāl ʿAbd al-Nāsir* . Vol. 10. Cairo: Maṭābiʿ al-Ihrām al-Tijāriyyah, 1393/1973, 74ff.

Manṣūr, ʿAli. *Niẓām al-Tajrīm wa'l-ʿIqāb fī l-Islām*. Madinah Munawwarah: Muʾassasah al-Zahrā, 1396/1976.

Al-Marghīnānī, Burhān al-Dīn. *Al*-Hidāyah. Vol. 2. Cairo: Muṣṭafā al-Bābī al-Ḥalabī, n.d., 94.

Al-Marʿī, ʿAlī Aḥmad. *al-Qiṣāṣ wa'l-Ḥudūd fīl-Fiqh al-Islāmī*. 2nd ed. Beirut: Dār Iqrāʾ, 1402/1982.

Maududi, Sayyid Abūl Āʿla. *The Islamic Law and Constitution*, Lahore: Islamic Publications, 1979.

Maududi, Sayyid Abūl Aʿla. *The Islamic State and Constitution*. 8th printing. Lahore: Islamic Publications, 1983.

Maududi, Sayyid Abūl Āʿla. *Toward Understanding the Qur'an*. English version of *Tafhīm al-Qur'ān*. Ed. Zafar Ishaq Ansari. Leicester: Islamic Foundation, 1408/1988.

Al-Māwardī, Abū al-Ḥasan. *Kitāb al-Aḥkām al-Sulṭāniyyah*. 3rd ed. Cairo: Muṣṭafā al-Bābī al-Ḥalabī, 1393/1973.

Māwardī, 'Alī M, and Wafaa H. Wahba. *The Ordinances of Government: A Translation of Al-Ahkām Al-Sultāniyya Wa'l-Wilāyāt Al-Dīniyya*. Reading, UK: Center for Muslim Contribution to Civilization, 1996.

Ministry of Legal Reform, Information and Arts, the Republic of Maldives. *Constitution of the Republic of Maldives 2008*.

Al-Miṣrī, ʿAbd Allāh. *Maʿrakat al-Dustūr fīl-Yaman: Risālat al-ʿulamāʾ bi-khuṣūṣ mashrūʿ dustūr dawlat al-waḥdah* [The Constitutional Movement in Yemen: Letter from the ulama regarding the draft constitution of the unitary state]. San'a: n.p., n.d.

Mohamad, Abdul Hamid, Tun. Implementation of the Islamic Criminal Law (hudud, qisas, ta'zir) Malaysia—Prospects and Challenges. Keynote address delivered at a seminar on implementation of hudud in Malaysia—history and the future, Putrajaya, 1 April 2015. (Eng. tr. of original address in Bahasa Malaysia).

Mohamed Adil, Mohamed Azam. Shariah Criminal Code (II) Enactment 1993 Amendment 2015: Can Kelantan enforce Hudud? *Islam and Civilisational Renewal* 7(4): 548–551.

Mu'assasah Zayid b. Sultan al-Nahyan, and Majmaʿ al-Fiqh al-Islāmī al-Duwalī. *Muʿallimah Zayid li'l-Qawāʿid al-Fiqhiyyah wa'l-Uṣūliyyah*. 41 vols. Abu Dhabi: n.p., 2013/1434.

Al-Mubarakfūrī, Muḥammad ʿAbd al-Raḥmān. *Tuḥfat al-Aḥwadhī bi-sharḥ Jāmiʿ al-Tirmidhī*. Vol. 5. Beirut: Dār al-Kutub al-ʿIlmiyyah, 1990.

Al-Muhairi, Butti. The Federal Penal Code and the aim of unification. *Arab Law Quarterly* 1997;12(2): 197–210.

Al-Muhairi, Butti. Islamisation and modernisation within the UAE Penal Law: Sharī'ah in the modern era. *Arab Law Quarterly* 1996;11(1): 34–49.

Mutahhari, Murtaza. Islam and the Freedom of Thought and Belief. *Al-Tawhid*. Vol. XI, No. 2, pp. 143-63, 1412/1991.

Mustaza, Masami. Law doesn't allow for hudud in states. *New Straits Times*. 30 October 2011: 29.

Naga Marsen S. Logical flaws in Aceh's "Qanun Jinayat." *Jakarta Post*. 6 October 2014.

Al-Nawawī, Muḥyī al-Dīn. *Riyāḍ al-Ṣāliḥīn*. 2nd ed. Ed. Muḥammad Nāṣir al-Albānī. Beirut: Dār al-Maktab al-Islāmī, 1404/1984.

Nayyeri, Mohammad Hossein. New Islamic Penal Code of the Islamic Republic of Iran. *Research Paper Series: An Overview*. 31 March 2012: 18–19.

New Straits Times. Hudud laws for Muslims only. 19 November 1993.

New Straits Times. Hudud laws may not be enforced. 22 November 1993.

New Straits Times. MB: federal consent needed to enforce Hudud law. 11 July 1994:9F.

New Straits Times. Rational approach to pursuit of Islamic order. 20 July 1994:20.

New Straits Times. Hadi: many do not understand the Bill. 31 May 2002: 4.

New Straits Times. PAS hudud laws: Keadilan wants rape victims treated fairly. 31 May 2002: 4.

New Straits Times. DAP will leave Pakatan if PAS goes for hudud. 15 January 2009: 4.

New Straits Times. Laws must be fair, infused with justice. 27 March 2015: 12.

New Straits Times. Karpal: Hudud will lead to lawlessness. 31 October 2011:10.

Al-Nishāpūrī, Muslim b. Ḥājjāj. *Mukhtaṣar Ṣaḥīḥ Muslim*. Ed. M. Nāṣir al-Dīn al-Albānī. 2nd ed. Beirut: Dār-Maktab al-Islāmī, 1404/1984.

Nordin, Mazlan. Many questions on Hudud laws still unanswered. *New Straits Times*. 19 October 1993.

Othman, Norani. Implementation of Sharī'ah Criminal Law in Modem Society, Some Sociological Questions. Paper presented at the Institute of Strategic and International Studies Forum, Kuala Lumpur, 19 November 1993.

Pazzanita, Anthony G. *Historical Dictionary of Mauritania*. xhttps://books.google.com.my. Accessed 14 September 2015.

Peiffer, Elizabeth. The death penalty in traditional Islamic law and as interpreted in Saudi Arabia and Nigeria. *William & Mary Journal of Women and the Law* 2005;11(3) 526. http://scholarship.law.wm.edu/wmjowl/ vol11/iss3/9. Accessed 27 October 2014.

Peters, Rudolph. *Crime and Punishment in Islam: Theory and Practice from the 16th to the 20th Centuries*. Cambridge, UK: Cambridge University Press, 2005.

Peters, Rudolph. The Re-introduction of Shariah Criminal Law in Nigeria: New Challenges for the Muslims of the North. Amsterdam School for Cultural Analysis (ASCA), 2004 (accessed from UvA-DARE, the institutional repository of the University of Amsterdam (UvA), 28 October 2014. http://hdl.handle.net/11245/2.80489.

Peters, Rudolph. The Islamization of criminal law. *Die Welt des Islams, New Series* 1994;34(2): 246–274. http://www.jstor.org/stable/1570932. Accessed 20 May 2014.

Al-Qaraḍāwī, Yūsuf. *Sharīʿah al-Islāmiyyah Ṣāliḥah li'l-Taṭbīq fī Kull Zamān wa-Makān*. Cairo: Dār al-Ṣaḥwah, 1973/1393.

Al-Qaraḍāwī, Yūsuf. *Ḥawla Qaḍāya al-Islām wa'l-ʿAṣr*. 3rd ed. Cairo: Maktabah Wahbah, 2006/1427.

Al-Qaraḍāwī, Yūsuf. *Al-Shaykh al-Ghazālī kama ʿAraftuhu Riḥlata Nisf Qarn*. Cairo: Dār al-Wafā li'l-Ṭibāʿah wa'l-Nashr wa'l-Tawzīʿ, 1997.

Al-Qaraḍāwī, Yūsuf. *Dirāsah fī Fiqh Maqāṣid al-Sharīʿah: Bayn al-Maqāṣid al-Kulliyyah wa'l-Nuṣūṣ al-Juzʾiyyah*. 4th ed. Cairo: Dār al-Shurūq, 2012.

Al-*Qarāfī*, Shihāb al-Dīn. *Kitāb al-Furūq*. Cairo: Maṭbaʿah Dār al-Iḥyāʾ al-Kutub al-ʿArabiyyah, 1346.

Ibn Qudāmah, Muwaffaq al-Dīn. Vol. 1. *Al-Mughnī*. Beirut: Dār al-Kitāb al-ʿArabī, 1403/1983/1403.

Al-Qurṭubī, Abū 'l-Walīd Muḥammad Ibn Rushd (known as Ibn Rushd al-Ḥafīd). *Bidāyat al-Mujtahid wa-Nihāyat al-Muqtaṣid*. 2 vols. Lahore: Faran Academy, n.d.

Rahman, Fazlur. The Concept of Hadd in Islamic Law. *Islamic Studies* 1965;4:237–253.

Rahman, Fazlur. Law and ethics in Islam. In Richard G. Hovannisan (Ed.), *Ethics in Islam*. Undena Publications, Malibu, CA 1983.

Rahman, Tanzil-ur. *Islamization of Pakisan Law: Surveying from Islamic Point of View*. Karachi: Hamdard Academy, 1978.

Al-Ramlī, Shihāb al-Dīn. *Nihāyah al-Muḥtāj*. Vol. 7. Cairo: Muṣṭafā al-Bābī al-Ḥalabī, 1967/1386.

Riḍā, Muḥammad Rashīd. *Tafsīr al-Manār*. 4th ed. Cairo: Maṭbaʿah al-Manar, 1373.

Saeed, Mohammed and Hamza Hendawi. Pregnant Sudanese woman sentenced to death for marriage to Christian. *The Globe and Mail*, 16 May 2014. https://www.thestar.com/news/world/2014/05/15/woman_doctor_sentenced_to_death_for_marrying_christian.html Accessed online 26 May 2014.

Salmond, John William, and Glanville L. Williams. *Salmond on Jurisprudence*. 11th ed. London: Sweet & Maxwell, 1957.

Santoso, Topo. Implementation of Islamic criminal law in Indonesia: Ta'zir punishment as a solution? *IIUMLJ* 2011;19:123–149.

Al-Sarakhsī, Shams al-Dīn. *Al-Mabsūṭ*. Vols. 9, 10, and 11. Beirut: Dār al-Maʿrifah, 1986/1406.

Al-Shāfiʿī, Muḥammad b. Idrīs. *Kitāb al-Umm*. Beirut. 1993/1413.

Shalabī, Muṣṭafā. *al-Fiqh al-Islāmī Bayn al-Mithāliyyah wa'l-wāqiʿiyyah*. Beirut: al-Dār al-Jamiʿiyyah, 1982.

Shaltūt, Maḥmūd. *Al-Islām, ʿAqīdah wa-Sharīʿah*. Kuwait: Dār al-Qalam, 1963.

Al-Shāṭibī, Abū Isḥāq Ibrāhīm. *Al-Muwāfaqāt fī Uṣūl al-Sharīʿah*. Cairo: Maktabah al-Tijāriyyah al-Kubrā.

Al-Shaʿrānī, ʿAbd al-Wahhāb. *Kitāb al-Mizān*. Cairo: Maṭbaʿah al-Ḥusayniyyah, 1329.

Al-Shāwī, Tawfīq Muḥammad. *Al-Mawsūʿah al-ʿAṣriyyah fī'l-Fiqh al-Jināʾī al-Islāmī*. Vol. 4. Cairo: Dār al-Shuruq, 2001/1422, 4:296.

Al-Shāwī, Tawfīq Muḥammad. *Al-Mawsūʿah al-ʿAṣriyyah fī'l-Fiqh al-Jināʾī al-Islāmī*. Vol. 4. Cairo: Dār al-Shuruq, 2001/1422.

Al-Shawkānī, Muḥammad b. ʿAlī. *Nayl al-Awṭār Sharḥ Muntaqā al-Akhbār*. Vol. 7. Cairo: Muṣṭafā al-Bābī al-Ḥalabī, n.d.

Al-Shawkānī, Muḥammad b. ʿAlī. *Fatḥ al-Qadīr*. Damascus: Dār al-Kalam al-Ṭayyib, n.d.

Sidahmad, Muhammad 'Ata Alsid. *The Hudud*. Kuala Lumpur: A. S. Nordeen, 1997.

Siddiqi, Muhammad Iqbal. *The Penal Law of Islam*. 2nd ed. Lahore: n.p., 1985.

Siddiqi, Muhammad Iqbal. The concept of Hudud and its significance. *Islamic Culture*. 1981;55:191–207.

Al-Suood, Husnu. *The Maldivian Legal System*. Maldives: Maldives Law institute, 2014.

Al-Ṭabarī, Abū Jaʿfar Yaʿqūb Ibn Jarīr. *Tafsīr al-Ṭabarī, Tafsīr al-Qurʾān al-ʿAẓīm* (also known as *Tafsīr al-Ṭabarī*). Beirut: Dār al-Maʿrifah, 1980/1400.

Al-Tabrīzī, ʿAbd Allāh al-Khaṭīb. *Mishkāt al-Masābiḥ*. Ed. Muḥammad Nāṣir al-Dīn al-Albānī. 2nd ed. Beirut: Al-Maktab al-Islāmī, 1979/1399.

Tāj, ʿAbd al-Raḥmān. *al-Siyāsah al-Sharʿiyyah wa-al-Fiqh al-Islāmī*. Cairo: Maṭbaʿah Dār al-Taʾlīf, 1373/1953.

Tan, Joceline. New hands that may reshape PAS. *The Star*. 16 June 2002:23.

Ibn Taymiyyah, Aḥmad Taqī al-Dīn. *al-Ṣārim al-Maslūl ʿalā Shatīm al-Rasūl*. Ed. Muḥyī al-Dīn ʿAbd al-Ḥamīd. Beirut: Dār al-Kitāb, 1978/1398.

Ibn Taymiyyah, Aḥmad Taqī al-Dīn. *Al-Siyāsah al-Sharʿiyyah fī Iṣlāḥ al-Raʿy wa'l-Raʿiyyah*. Beirut: Dār al-Kutub al-ʿArabiyyah, 1966.

Ibn Taymiyyah, Aḥmad Taqī al-Dīn. *Majmūʿ al-Fatāwā Shaykh al-Islām Ibn Taymiyyah*. 29 vols. Riyadh: n.p., n.d.

The Star. Women leaders to meet on Bill. 31 May 2002:2.

The Star. Attorney General will get draft Bill. 2 June 2002:5.

The Star. Hadi: Hudud Bill will be tabled. 17 June 2002:2.

The Star. Ex-FT mufti: PAS shows it was not ready to enforce hudud. 14 December 2002:24.

The Star. MCA slams PAS on hudud goals. 12 April 2008:N6.

The Sun. Kelantan Tables hudud amendments. 19 March 2015:2.

The Sun. Hudud law passed. 20 March 2015:Front page.

Al-Tirmidhī, Abū ʿĪsā Muḥammad. *Sunan al-Tirmidhī*. Beirut: Dār al-Fikr, 1980/1400.

Weinberg, Jon. Sword of justice? Beheadings rise in Saudi Arabia. *Harvard International Review*. 2008;29(4).

Wizārat al-Awqāf wa'l-Shu'ūn al-Islāmiyyah. *Al-Mawsūʿah al-Fiqhiyyah*. 45 vols. Kuwait: Dār al-Salāsil, 2003/1424.

Yong, Linna. The burden of proof in Hudud. *The Star*. 22 November 1994:18.

Abū Yūsuf, Yaʿqūb b. Ibrāhīm. *Kitāb al-Kharāj*. 5th ed. Cairo: Al-Maṭbaʿah al-Salafiyyah, 1396.

Yusuf Ali, Abdullah. *The Holy Qur'an, Text Translation and Commentary*.

Abū Zahrah, Muḥammad. *Al-Jarīmah wa'l ʿUqūbah fī'l-Fiqh al-Islāmī: al-ʿUqūbah*. 10th ed. Ed. Muḥyī al-Dīn Fatḥī al-Shaludī. Cairo: Dār al-Fikr al-ʿArabī, 2006.

Zakariah, Elizabeth. Impossible to enforce hudud in Malaysia, says law minister. *The Malaysian Insider*, 24 March 2015. htttp://www.the malaysianinsider.com/malaysia/article/impossible-to-enforce-hudud-in-malaysia-says-law-minister. Accessed 15 April 2015.

Al-Zarqā, Muṣṭafā Aḥmad. *Al-Madkhal al-Fiqhī al-ʿĀm*. Damascus: Dār al-Fikr, 1387/1968.

Al-Zarqā, Muṣṭafā Aḥmad. *Al-Madkhal al-Fiqhī al-ʿĀm: Ikhrāj Jadīd fī'l-Tartīb wa'l-Tabwīb wa'l Ziyādat*. 1st ed. Damascus: Dār al-Qalam, 1991/1418.

Zaydān, ʿAbd al-Karīm. *Niẓām al-Qaḍa' fī'l-Sharīʿah al-Islāmiyyah*. Baghdad: Maṭbaʿah al-ʿĀnī, 1404/1984.

Al-Zaylāʿī, Jamāl al-Dīn. *Naṣb al-Rāyah li-Aḥādith al-Hidāyah*. 2nd ed. Beirut: Al-Maktab al-Islāmī, 1393 H.

Al-Zaylāʿī, Jamāl al-Dīn. *Tabyīn al-Ḥaqā'iq fī Sharḥ Kanz al-Daqā'iq*. Bulaq: Al-Maṭbaʿah al-Amiriyyah, 1313 H.

Al-Zuḥaylī, Wahbah. Al-Fiqh al-Islāmī wa-Adillatuhu. 8 vols. Damascus: Dār al-Fikr, 1985.

Al-Zuḥaylī, Wahbah. 11 vols. Damascus: Dār al-Fikr, 1997.

Al-Zuḥaylī, Wahbah. *Qaḍāyā al-Fiqh wa'l-Fikr al-Muʿāṣir*. Damascus: Dār al-Fikr, 2007.

Zulkefli, Adie Suri, and Jasmine Kaur. PM: Hudud not rejected by government. *New Straits Times*. 15 April 2014: 2.

Index

CW01626716

HOPSCOTCH

"Cortázar's masterpiece. This is the first great novel of Spanish America . . . The astonishing moment when all the figures seem to have fallen into their right positions in the hopscotch court . . . [is] not only among the constituent scenes of a powerful anti-novel but, like deeply understood moments in life itself, rich with many kinds of potential meanings and intimations"

Times Literary Supplement

"Hopscotch, a . . . superb work, should establish Cortázar as an outstanding writer of our day . . . The dialogue is brilliant, whether the subject is literature, love, Mondrian, jazz or the fallibility of science. Individual scenes are superbly alive . . . the rapid-fire invention of the language makes every page sparkle, thanks to the translation by Gregory Rabassa, which gives a dazzling parallel . . . to Cortázar's stylistic magic"

DONALD KEENE, ***New York Times***

"The most brilliant novel in years . . . It is a spiralling, convulsive, exploding universe of a novel. It is the most powerful encyclopedia of emotions and visions to emerge from the postwar generation of international writers" **C. D. B. BRYAN,** ***Books and the Arts***

"Hopscotch . . . marks the true possibility of encounter between the Latin-American imagination and the contemporary world"

CARLOS FUENTES

"Everything that we take for granted . . . is subtly but ruthlessly brought to a crisis, and Cortázar does so in the midst of everyday life" ***Boston Globe***

"Here is literary cunning and accomplishment of a high order"

ROBERT NYE, ***Guardian***

"Julio Cortázar is one of the most distinctive voices in Latin American literature" ***Newsday***

JULIO CORTÁZAR lived in Buenos Aires for the first thirty years of his life, and after that in Paris. His stories, written under the dual influence of the English masters of the uncanny and of French surrealism, are extraordinary inventions, just this side of nightmare. In later life Cortázar became a passionate advocate for human rights and a persistent critic of the military dictatorships in Latin America. He died in 1984.

GREGORY RABASSA has translated some of the classics of modern Spanish and Portuguese literature, including *One Hundred Years of Solitude*, by Gabriel García Márquez. His most recent translation is *The Posthumous Memoirs of Brás Cubas*, by Machado de Assis. His translation of *Hopscotch* received the National Book Award for Translation.

"Cortázar is an original writer, circuitous and powerful . . . His method is to keep tight control over a world in which, just below the surface of charming, sophisticated social life, lies the unfaceable and unmentionable. At the centre of it, the narrator's voice is civilised, the main characters are eminently knowable and even nice, but the ice they walk on is thin"

ISABEL QUIGLY, *Financial Times*

"One gets to know a milieu, an atmosphere and a group of people with a closeness that is characteristic of only serious and lasting works of fiction . . . the reader is left with the conviction that Mr Cortázar has marked off a corner of the world singularly his own"

THOMAS LASK, *New York Times*

Also by Julio Cortázar in a Harvill edition

BESTIARY: SELECTED STORIES

Julio Cortázar

HOPSCOTCH

Translated from the Spanish
by Gregory Rabassa

THE HARVILL PRESS
LONDON

First published with the title *Rayuela*, by Editoral Sudamericana Sociedad Anonima, in 1963
First published by The Harvill Press in 1967

This paperback edition published in 1998 by
The Harvill Press, 84 Thornhill Road, London N1 1RD

www.harvill-press.com

1 3 5 7 9 8 6 4 2

Copyright © Julio Cortázar, 1963 and the heirs of Julio Cortázar
English translation copyright © Random House and The Harvill Press, 1966

A CIP catalogue record for this book is available from the British Library

ISBN 1 86046 428 9

Designed and typeset in Minion at Libanus Press, Marlborough, Wiltshire

Printed and bound in Great Britain by Clays Ltd, St Ives plc

Half title illustration by Ronald Gunn

CONDITIONS OF SALE
All rights reserved. No part of this publication may be reproduced, stored in a retrieval system, or transmitted in any form or by any means, electronic, mechanical, photocopying, recording or otherwise, without the prior permission of the publisher

This book is sold subject to the condition that it shall not, by way of trade or otherwise, be lent, re-sold, hired out or otherwise circulated without the publisher's prior consent in any form of binding or cover other than that in which it is published and without a similar condition including this condition being imposed on the subsequent purchaser

The Random House Group Limited supports The Forest Stewardship Council® (FSC®), the leading international forest-certification organisation. Our books carrying the FSC label are printed on FSC®-certified paper. FSC is the only forest-certification scheme supported by the leading environmental organisations, including Greenpeace. Our paper procurement policy can be found at www.randomhouse.co.uk/environment

MIX
Paper from responsible sources
FSC® C018072

AUTHOR'S NOTE

In its own way, this book consists of many books, but two books above all. The reader is invited to choose between these two possibilities:

The first can be read in a normal fashion and it ends with chapter 56, at the close of which there are three garish little stars which stand for the words *The End.* Consequently, the reader may ignore what follows with a clean conscience.

The second can be read by beginning with chapter 73 and then following the sequence indicated at the end of each chapter. In case of confusion or forgetfulness, one need only consult the following list:

73 – 1 – 2 – 116 – 3 – 84 – 4 – 71 – 5 – 81 – 74 – 6 – 7 – 8 – 93 – 68 – 9 – 104 – 10 – 65 – 11 – 136 – 12 – 106 – 13 – 115 – 14 – 114 – 117 – 15 – 120 – 16 – 137 – 17 – 97 – 18 – 153 – 19 – 90 – 20 – 126 – 21 – 79 – 22 – 62 – 23 – 124 – 128 – 24 – 134 – 25 – 141 – 60 – 26 – 109 – 27 – 28 – 130 – 151 – 152 – 143 – 100 – 76 – 101 – 144 – 92 – 103 – 108 – 64 – 155 – 123 – 145 – 122 – 112 – 154 – 85 – 150 – 95 – 146 – 29 – 107 – 113 – 30 – 57 – 70 – 147 – 31 – 32 – 132 – 61 – 33 – 67 – 83 – 142 – 34 – 87 – 105 – 96 – 94 – 91 – 82 – 99 – 35 – 121 – 36 – 37 – 98 – 38 – 39 – 86 – 78 – 40 – 59 – 41 – 148 – 42 – 75 – 43 – 125 – 44 – 102 – 45 – 80 – 46 –47 – 110 – 48 – 111 – 49 – 118 – 50 – 119 – 51 – 69 – 52 – 89 – 53 – 66 – 149 – 54 – 129 – 139 – 133 – 140 – 138 – 127 – 56 – 135 – 63 – 88 – 72 – 77 – 131 – 58 – 131 –

Each chapter has its number at the top of every right-hand page to facilitate the search.

And moved by the hope of being of particular help to youth, and of contributing to the reform of manners in general, I have put together this collection of maxims, counsels and precepts which are the basis of those universal morals that are so much a part of the spiritual and temporal happiness of men of all ages, states and conditions, and of the prosperity and orderliness not only of the civil and Christian republic in which we live, but of any other republic or government that the most thoughtful and serious philosophers of the world might wish to contrive.

> *Spirit of the Bible and Universal Morals,*
> *drawn from the Old and New Testaments*
> Put down in Tuscan by the Abbot Martini
> with footnotes
> Rendered into Castilian
> by a member of the Regular Clergy of the
> Congregation of San Cayetano of this Court
> With permission
> Madrid: Aznar, 1797

Everytime it starts to get cool, I mean in the middle of autim, I start gettin nutty ideas like I was thinkin about what was forein and diffrent, like for exsample how I'd like to turn into a swallow and get away and fly to countrys where it gets hot, or be an ant so's I could get deep into a cave and eat the stuff I stored away durin the summer or be a snake like what they got in the zoO, the ones they keep lockt up in glass cages thats heated so's they don't get stiff from the cold, which is what happens to poor human beans who cant buy no close cause the price is to high, and cant keep warm cause theys no keroseen, no coal, no wood, no fule oil and besides theys no loot, cause when you go around with bread you can go into any bar and get some booze that can be real warmin, even tho it aint good to overdo it cause if you overdos it it gets to be a bad habbit and bad habbits is bad for your body just like they is for youre selfrespeck, and when you start goin downhill cause your actin bad in everythin, they aint nobody or nothin can stop you from endin up a stinkin piece of human garbidge and they never gone give you a hand to haul you up outen the dirty muck you rollin around in, not even if you was a eaglE when you was young and could fly up and over the highest hills, but when you get old you like a highflyin bomber thats lost its moral engines and fall down outen the sky. I jes hope what I been writin down hear do somebody some good so he take a good look at how he livin and he dont be sorry when it too late and everythin is gone down the drain cause it his own fault.

CÉSAR BRUTO, *What I Would Like to Be If I Wasn't What I Am* (Chapter: "A St Bernard Dog")

From the Other Side

Rien ne vous tue un homme comme d'être obligé de représenter un pays.

JACQUES VACHÉ, letter to André Breton

1

Would I find La Maga? Most of the time it was just a case of my putting in an appearance, going along the Rue de Seine to the arch leading into the Quai de Conti, and I would see her slender form against the olive-ashen light which floats along the river as she crossed back and forth on the Pont des Arts, or leaned over the iron rail looking at the water. It was quite natural for me to climb the steps to the bridge, go into its narrowness and over to where La Maga stood. She would smile and show no surprise, convinced as she was, the same as I, that casual meetings are apt to be just the opposite, and that people who make dates are the same kind who need lines on their writing paper, or who always squeeze their toothpaste up from the bottom of the tube.

But now she would not be on the bridge. The thin glow of her face was probably peeking into the old doorways in the Marais ghetto, or maybe she was talking to a woman who sells fried potatoes, or she might be eating a hot sausage on the Boulevard de Sébastopol. In any case, I went out onto the bridge and there was no Maga. I did not run into her along the way either. We each knew where the other lived, every cranny we holed up in in our pseudo-student existence in Paris, every window by Braque, Ghirlandaio, or Max Ernst set into cheap postcard frames and ringed with gaudy posters, but we never visited each other at home. We preferred meeting on the bridge, at a pavement café, at an art movie, or crouched over a cat in some Latin Quarter courtyard. We did not go around looking for each other, but we knew that we would meet just the same. Oh, Maga, whenever I saw a woman who looked like you a clear, sharp pause would close in like a deafening silence, collapsing like a wet umbrella being closed. An umbrella, precisely. Maybe you remember, Maga, that old umbrella we sacrificed in a gully in Montsouris Park one sunset on a cold March day. We threw it away because you had found it half-broken in the Place de la Concorde and you had got a lot of use from it, especially for digging into people's ribs on the Métro or on a bus as you lethargically thought about the design the flies on the ceiling made. There was a cloudburst that afternoon and you tried to open your umbrella in the park in a proud sort of way, but your hand got all wrapped up in a catastrophe of cold lightning bolts and black clouds, strips of torn cloth falling from the ruins of unfrocked spokes, and we both laughed like madmen as we got soaked, thinking that an umbrella found in a public square ought to die a noble death in a park and not get involved in the mean cycle of dustbin or gutter. Then I rolled it up as best I could and we took it to the top of the park near the little bridge over the railway tracks, and from there I threw it with all my might to the bottom of the gully where it landed on the wet grass as you gave out a shout in which I thought I vaguely recognized the curse of a Valkyrie. It sank into the gully like a ship into green water, stormy green water, into *la mer qui est plus félonesse en été qu'en hiver*, into the treacherous wave, Maga, as we counted for a long time, in love with Joinville or with the park, embracing like wet trees or like actors in some second-rate Hungarian movie. And it stayed down there in the grass, small and black, like some trampled insect. And it did not move, none of its springs popped out as once before. Ended. Over. Oh Maga, and still we were not satisfied.

Why was I coming to the Pont des Arts? It seems to me that on that Thursday in December I had intended to cross over to the Right Bank to have some wine in the little café on the Rue des Lombards where Madame Léonie reads my palm and tells me of trips and surprises. I never took you to have your palm read by Madame Léonie, probably because I was afraid that she would read some truth about me in your hand, because you have always been a frightful mirror, a monstrous instrument of repetitions, and what we had called loving was perhaps my standing in front of you holding a yellow flower while you held two green candles and a slow rain of renunciations and farewells and Métro tickets blew into our faces. So I never took you to Madame Léonie's, Maga. You told me so and that is how I know that you did not like my watching you go into that little bookshop on the Rue de Verneuil, where a burdened old man fills out thousands of reference cards and knows everything there is to know about the study of history. You used to go there to play with a cat, and the old man let you in and didn't ask questions, content for you to get him a book from time to time from the upper shelves. You used to get warm at that stove of his with its big black chimney, and you didn't like me to know that you were going to sit next to that stove. But all of this should have been said in its proper time, except that it was difficult to know what the proper time for things was, and even now, with my elbows on the railing of the bridge, as I watched a small, must-coloured *péniche*, sparkling clean like a great big beautiful cockroach, with a woman in a white apron hanging washing on a wire strung along the prow, as I looked at its windows, painted green, with Hansel and Gretel curtains, even now, Maga, I wondered if this roundabout route made any sense, since it would have been easier to reach the Rue des Lombards by the Pont Saint-Michel and the Pont au Change. But if you had been there that night, as so many other times, then I would have known that the roundabout made sense, while now, on the other hand, I debase my failure by calling it a roundabout. I raised the collar of my lumber-jacket, and it was a matter of going along by the docks until I came to where the large shops finish at the Châtelet, passing underneath the violet shadow of the Tour Saint-Jacques, and turning into my street, thinking about the fact that I had not bumped into you and about Madame Léonie.

I know that one day I came to Paris. I know that I was living in hock for a while, doing what the others did and seeing what they saw. I know that you were coming out of a café on the Rue du Cherche-Midi and that we spoke. Everything had been going badly that afternoon because the clothes I had brought from Argentina would not permit me to cross from one pavement to the other to look at trivial items in the dimly lit shop windows on streets I don't remember any more. I followed you grudgingly then, finding you petulant and rude, until you got tired of not being tired and we went into a café on the Boul' Mich' and all of a sudden in between two croissants you told me a whole chunk of your life.

How could I have suspected that what seemed to be a pack of lies was all true, a Figari with sunset violets, with livid faces, with hunger and blows in the corners. I came to believe you later on, later on there was reason to, there was Madame Léonie, who looked at my hand which had gone to bed with your breasts, and she practically repeated your exact words: "She is suffering somewhere. She has always suffered. She is very cheerful, she adores yellow, her bird is the blackbird, her time is night, her bridge is the Pont des Arts." (A must-coloured *péniche*, Maga, and I wonder why we didn't sail off on it while there was still time.)

We had barely got to know each other when life began to contrive everything necessary for us to stop meeting little by little. Since you didn't know how to dissemble I realized at once that in order to see you as I wanted to I would have to begin by shutting my eyes, and then at first some things like yellow stars (moving around in a velvet jelly), then red jumps of humour and time, a gradual entry into a Maga world, awkward and confused, but also with ferns signed by a Klee spider, a Miró circus, Vieira da Silva ash-mirrors, a chess world where you moved about like a knight trying to move like a rook trying to move like a bishop. In those days we used to go to art movies to see silent pictures, because I had my culture, maybe not, but you, poor thing, didn't understand anything at all about that yellow and convulsed shrieking which had all taken place before you were born, that grooved emulsion in which dead people ran about. But suddenly Harold Lloyd would go by and then you would shake off the water of your dream and would finally be convinced that all was well, and that Pabst, and that Fritz Lang. You wore me out a little with your mania for perfection, with your rundown shoes, with your refusal to accept the acceptable. We used to eat hamburgers in the Carrefour de l'Odéon and we went cycling to Montparnasse, to any hotel, any pillow. Then other times we would go all the way to the Porte d'Orléans and we became more and more familiar with the vacant lots beyond the Boulevard Jourdan, where sometimes at midnight the members of the Serpent Club used to get together to talk to a blind seer, a stimulating paradox. We used to leave the bicycles on the street and go in a little way, stopping to look at the sky because it is one of the few places in Paris where sky is worth more than ground. Sitting on a pile of rubbish we would smoke for a while, and La Maga would stroke my hair or hum songs which hadn't been invented yet, absurd tunes broken with sighs or memories. I took advantage of such moments to think about useless things, a practice I had begun some years before in a hospital and which seemed increasingly richer and more necessary. With great effort, marshalling auxiliary images, thinking about smells and faces, I managed to extract from the void a pair of chestnut-coloured shoes

I had owned in Olavarría in 1940. They had rubber heels and very thin soles, and when it rained the water used to seep in up to my very soul. With that pair of shoes in the hand of my memory the rest came along by itself: the face of Doña Manuela, for example, or the poet Ernesto Morroni. But I rejected them because the game consisted in bringing back only the insignificant, the unnoticed, the forgotten. Trembling at not being able to remember, attacked by those moths suggested by postponement, an imbecile for having kissed time, I finally saw beyond the shoes a can of Sol tea that my mother had given me in Buenos Aires. And the little double teaspoon, a mousetrap spoon, where little black mice were scalded alive in the cup of water as they gave off hissing bubbles. Convinced that memory keeps everything, not just the Albertines and the great journals of the heart and kidneys, I persisted in reconstructing the contents of my desk in Floresta, the face of a girl impossible to remember named Gekrepten, the quantity of drawing pens in my pencil box in junior school, and I ended up trembling and desperate (because I had never been able to remember those pens; I know that they were in the pencil box, in a special compartment, but I cannot remember how many they were, nor the precise moment when there were two or six), until La Maga, kissing me and blowing smoke and her hot breath into my face, brought me back and we laughed, and began to walk around again among the piles of rubbish, looking for the members of the Club. It was about that time I realized that searching was my symbol, the emblem of those who go out at night with nothing in mind, the motives of a destroyer of compasses. I spoke about pataphysics with La Maga until we were both tired, because the same thing used to happen to her (and our meeting had been like that, and so many things, dark as a match), always falling into exceptions, seeing herself stuck in huts not meant for people and all this without despising anyone, without thinking we were Maldorors at the end of the trail or Melmoths privileged to wander about. I do not believe the firefly gets any great satisfaction from the incontrovertible fact that he is one of the most amazing wonders of this circus, and yet one can imagine a consciousness alert enough to understand that every time he lights his belly this light-bearing bug must feel some inkling of privilege. In just this way La Maga was fascinated with the strange mixups she had become involved in because of the breakdown of the laws governing her life. She was one of those people who could make a bridge collapse simply by walking on it, or who could sobbingly remember having seen in a shop window the lottery ticket which had just won five million. As for me, I'm already used to the fact that modestly exceptional things happen to me, and I don't find it too horrible when I go into a dark room looking for a record album and feel in my hand the wriggling body of a centipede who has chosen to sleep in the binding. That sort of thing. Or finding great grey or green tufts in a pack of cigarettes, or hearing the whistle of a locomotive coincide *ex officio* in time and pitch with a passage from a symphony by Ludwig van, or going into a *pissotière* on the Rue de Médicis and seeing a man studiously urinating then step back from the urinal and towards me as he holds in the palm of his hand as if it were a precious and liturgical object a member of incredible colours and dimensions, and my realizing at that moment that this man is the replica of another (although they are not the same) who twenty-four hours before in the Salle de Géographie had been lecturing on totems and taboos and had held up carefully in the palm of his hand ivory sticks, lyrebird feathers, ritual coins, magic fossils, starfish, dried fish, photographs of royal concubines, offerings of hunters, enormous embalmed beetles which made the inevitable ladies present quiver with startled delight.

All things considered, it's not easy to talk about La Maga, who right now must certainly be walking around Belleville or Pantin, carefully looking at the ground until she finds a piece of red cloth. If she doesn't find it she'll go on like that all night. She'll rummage in dustbins, her eyes glassy, convinced that something horrible will happen to her if she doesn't find that piece of ransom, that sign of forgiveness or postponement. I know what it's all about because I too obey these signs, and there are times when I must find a red rag. Ever since childhood, whenever I drop something I must pick it up, no matter what, because if I don't a disaster will happen, not to me, but to someone I love whose name begins with the same letter as the thing I dropped. The worst of it is that nothing can stop me when I drop something, and it doesn't work if somebody else picks it up because the curse will still be effective. People usually think I'm crazy and I really am crazy when I do it, when I pounce on a pencil or a piece of paper that I have dropped, like the night I dropped a lump of sugar in that restaurant on the Rue Scribe, a posh place overloaded with salesmen, whores with silver foxes, and well-established married couples. We were there with Ronald and Étienne, and I dropped a lump of sugar. It landed underneath a table some distance from ours. The first thing that had drawn my attention was how it had rolled so far away, because usually a lump of sugar will stay where it lands, obeying obvious geometrical principles. But this one took off like a mothball, heightening my worry, and I began to feel that it had actually been snatched out of my hand. Ronald knows me, and when he saw where it had landed he began to laugh. That caused me further anxiety, along with a touch of rage. A waiter came by and thought I had lost something of value, a Parker pen, a false tooth, and all he did was upset me even more. I didn't even excuse myself but fell to the floor to look for the lump among the shoes of people who were curious and thought (quite rightly) that something important was involved. I went under a table where there was a fat redhead and another woman, not so fat but just as whorey, and two businessmen, or so they seemed. The first thing I managed to find out was that the lump was nowhere in sight, even though I had seen it leap among the shoes which now were moving about restlessly like a flock of chickens. A carpet on the floor made things worse, and despite the fact that it was dirty from so much use, the lump had hidden itself in the pile and could not be found. The waiter was crawling around on the other side of the table and there we were, two quadrupeds making our way about among those chicken-shoes which all the while were cackling madly up above. The waiter was still looking for a Parker or a louis d'or, and when we were well under the table, with a feeling of great intimacy in the shadows, he asked me what it was and I told him the truth. His face was ready to fly off its hinges, but I was not in any mood to laugh. Fear had doubled the knot in my stomach, and I had become by then quite desperate and began to grab at the women's shoes to see if the lump might not be hiding under the arch of one, while the chickens cackled and the business-cocks pecked me on the back. I could hear Ronald and Étienne breaking up with laughter as I moved from one table to another until I found the lump ensconced behind an Empire foot. Everybody was furious and so was I, as I held the sugar tightly in my palm and felt it dissolve in the sweat of my hand, as if it were some sort of mean and sticky vengeance meant to terminate another one of those episodes that I was always getting involved in.

(–2)

2

At first it had been like a bloodletting, being here, a flogging to be taken internally, the need to feel a stupid blue-covered passport in my coat pocket, the hotel key hung securely on its rack. Fear, ignorance, bewilderment. This is the name of this thing, that's how you ask for that thing, now that woman is going to smile, the Jardin des Plantes starts at the end of that street. Paris, a postcard with a drawing by Klee next to a dirty mirror. La Maga had appeared one afternoon on the Rue du Cherche-Midi. When she came to my room on the Rue de la Tombe Issoire she would always bring a flower, a Klee or Miró postcard, and if she didn't have any money she would pick up the leaf of a plane tree in the park. At that time I used to pick up pieces of wire and empty boxes on the street early in the morning and I made them into mobiles, silhouettes which swung around the fireplace, useless gadgets which La Maga would help me paint. We didn't love each other, so we would make love with an objective and critical virtuosity, but then we would fall into terrible silences and the foam on the beer glasses would start to look like burlap, getting warm and shrivelling up while we looked at each other and figured that this was Time. La Maga would finally get up and walk uselessly around the room. More than once I saw her admire her body in the mirror, cup her breasts in her hands like a small Syrian statue, moving her eyes slowly over her body in a sort of caress. I could never resist the urge to call her over to me, to have her fall on top of me, unfold again after having been so alone and so in love for a moment, face to face with the eternity of her body.

We didn't talk much about Rocamadour those days; our pleasure was selfish and it used to come moaning over us with its narrow brow, tying us up with its salty hands. I had come to accept La Maga's disorder as the natural condition of every moment, and we would go from memories of Rocamadour to a plate of heated-up noodles, mixing wine and beer and lemonade, going to the corner to buy two dozen oysters from the old woman there, playing Schubert songs on Madame Noguet's shell of a piano, or Bach preludes, or putting up with *Porgy and Bess* along with steak and pickles. The disorder in which we lived, or the order, rather, which saw a bidet gradually and naturally changed into a storage place for records and unanswered letters, seemed to me like some sort of necessary discipline, although I didn't care to tell my feelings to La Maga. It didn't take me long to understand that you didn't discuss reality in methodical terms with La Maga. Praise of disorder would have horrified her as much as criticism of it. Disorder did not exist for her, as I discovered while I was finding out simultaneously what her purse contained (it was in a café on the rue Réaumur, it was raining and we were beginning to want each other). But I accepted it and even approved of it once I had identified it. My relations with practically all the rest of the world were based on these disadvantages, and how many times had I lain on a bed left unmade for several days listening to La Maga cry because a little girl on the Métro had reminded her of Rocamadour, or watched her comb her hair after she had spent all afternoon before a portrait of Eleanor of Aquitaine and was killing herself trying to look like the painting, and it occurred to me like a sort of mental belch that this whole alphabet of my life was painful stupidity, because it was based solely on a dialectical pattern, on the choice of what could be called non-conduct rather than conduct, on faddish indecency instead of social decency. La Maga was putting up her hair, taking it down, putting it up again. She was thinking about Rocamadour. She sang something from Hugo Wolf (badly), she kissed me, she asked me about her hairdo, she began to sketch on a scrap of yellow paper. That was all she, no doubt about it, and there was I on a deliberately dirty bed, drinking a glass of deliberately flat beer, always being myself and my life; there was I with my life face to face with other people's lives. But I was proud nonetheless to be a conscious layabout and to have lived under all sorts of moons, in all kinds of scrapes with La Maga and Ronald and Rocamadour and the Club and the streets and my moral sickness and other worse ones, and Berthe Trépat and sometimes hunger and old man Trouille, who used to get me out of trouble, under the eaves of vomity nights of music and tobacco and little meannesses and all kinds of exchanges, because underneath and on top of it all I had refused to pretend like normal bohemians that the chaos of my affairs and finances was some sort of higher spiritual order or something else with an equally disgusting label, nor had I accepted the notion that all one needed was just one split second of decency (decency, young fellow!) to crawl out from the midst of so much filthy cotton. And that's how I had met La Maga, who was my witness and my spy without being aware of it; and the irritation of thinking about all this and knowing that, since it was always easier to think than to be, that in my case the ergo of the expression was no ergo nor anything at all like it, so that we used to go along the Left Bank and La Maga, without knowing she was my spy and my witness, would be amazed at how much I knew about things like literature and cool jazz, which were great mysteries for her. And I felt antagonism for all these things when I was with La Maga, for we loved each other in a sort of dialectic of magnet and iron filings, attack and defence, ball and wall. I suppose La Maga had her notions about me and she must have thought I had been healed of my prejudices or that I was coming over to hers, more lighthearted and poetic. In the midst of this precarious happiness, this false truce, I held out my hand and touched the tangled ball of yarn which is Paris, its infinite material all wrapped up around itself, the precipitate of its atmosphere falling on its windows and forming images of clouds and garrets. There was no disorder then. The world was still something petrified and established, swinging on its hinges, a skein of streets and trees and names and months. There was no disorder to open escape-hatches, there was only filth and misery, glasses with stale beer, stockings in a corner, a bed which smelled of sex and hair, a woman who ran her small, thin hand along my thighs, holding off the stroke that would have plucked me out of this vigilance in the depths of emptiness for just a moment. Too late, always too late, because even though we made love so many times, happiness must have been something else, something sadder perhaps than this peace, this pleasure, a mood of unicorn or island, an endless fall in immobility. La Maga did not know that my kisses were like eyes that began to open up beyond her, and that I went along outside as if I saw a different concept of the world, the dizzy pilot of a black prow which cut the water of time and negated it.

During those days in the fifties I began to feel myself penned in between La Maga and a different notion of what really should have happened. It was idiotic to revolt against the Maga world and the Rocamadour world, when everything told me that as soon as I got my freedom back I would stop feeling free. A hypocrite like few others, it bothered me to spy on my own skin, my legs, my way to get pleasure from La Maga, my attempts at being a parrot in a cage reading Kierkegaard through the bars, and I think that what bothered me most was that La Maga had no idea at all that she was my witness and, on the contrary, was convinced that I was eminently master of my fate. But no, what really exasperated me was knowing that I would never again be so close to my freedom as in those days when I felt myself hemmed in by the Maga world, and that my anxiety to escape was an admission of defeat. It grieved me to recognize that with artificial blows, with Manichaean beams of light, or desiccated, stupid dichotomies I could not make my way up the steps of the Gare de Montparnasse where La Maga had dragged me to visit Rocamadour. Why couldn't I accept what was happening without trying to explain it, without bringing up ideas of order and disorder, of freedom and Rocamadour, as one sets out geranium pots in a courtyard on the Calle Cochabamba? Maybe one had to fall into the depths of stupidity in order to make the key fit the lock to the latrine or to the Garden of Olives. For the moment it surprised me that La Maga had let fantasy carry her to the point of calling her son Rocamadour. In the Club we had given up looking for reasons. La Maga had only said that her son had been named after his father, but when his father had disappeared it had seemed better to call him Rocamadour and send him to the country to be brought up *en nourrice.* Sometimes La Maga would go for weeks without mentioning Rocamadour and those would always be the same times that she was hoping to become a singer of *Lieder.* Then Ronald would sit down at the piano with his cowboy-red hair and La Maga would bellow something from Hugo Wolf with a ferocity that made Madame Noguet tremble as she sat next door stringing plastic beads to sell at a stand on the Boulevard de Sébastopol. La Maga's singing of Schumann was rather pleasant, but it all depended on the moon and what we were going to do that night, and also on Rocamadour, because no sooner did La Maga think of Rocamadour than her singing went to pot and Ronald was left alone at the piano, with all the time in the world to try out some of his bop ideas or to kill us softly with some blues.

I don't want to write about Rocamadour, at least not right now, because I would have to get so much closer to myself, to let everything that separates me from the centre drop away. I always end up talking about the centre without the slightest guarantee that I know what I'm saying, and I slip into the trap of geometry, that method we Occidentals use to try to regulate our lives: axis, centre, *raison d'être*, Omphalos, nostalgic Indo-European names. Even this existence I sometimes try to describe, this Paris where I move about like a dry leaf, would not be visible if behind it there did not beat an anxiety for an axis, a coming together with the central shaft. All these words, all these terms for the same disorder. Sometimes I am convinced that triangle is another name for stupidity, that eight times eight is madness or a dog. Holding La Maga, that materialized nebula, I begin to think that it makes just as much sense to model a doll out of crumbled bread as to write the novel I will never write or to give my life in the defence of ideas that could redeem whole peoples. The pendulum immediately changes direction and there I am again among calming notions: a worthless doll, a great novel, a heroic death. I line them up, from least to greatest: doll, novel, heroism. I think about the orders of values so well explored by Ortega, by Scheler: aesthetics, ethics, religion. Religion, aesthetics, ethics. Ethics, religion, aesthetics. Doll, novel. Death, doll. La Maga's tongue tickles me. Rocamadour, ethics, doll, Maga. Tongue, tickle, ethics.

(–116)

3

Horacio Oliveira was sitting on the bed smoking his third insomniac cigarette. Once or twice he softly stroked the skin of La Maga, who was next to him, asleep. It was just before dawn on Monday and they had already let Sunday afternoon and evening slip by reading, listening to records, getting up alternately to warm up some coffee or prepare some *mate*. La Maga had fallen asleep during the last movement of a Haydn quartet and since he did not want to listen any more, Oliveira had unplugged the record-player as he lay there on the bed. The record kept on spinning a little more, but there was no more sound from the speaker. He didn't know why, but this stupid inertia had made him think about the apparently useless movements of some insects, of some children. He couldn't sleep and he looked out of the open window towards the garret where a hunchbacked violinist was practising very late. It was not a warm night, but La Maga's body warmed up his leg and his right side; he moved away little by little and thought that it was going to be a long night.

He felt very well, as he always did when La Maga and he could get to the end of a date without quarrelling or annoying each other. He wasn't worried too much by the letter from his brother, a solid-citizen lawyer from Rosario, who had filled up four onion-skin pages with an account of the filial and civic duties that Oliveira had ignored. The letter was a real delight and he had hung it on the wall with Scotch tape so that his friends could enjoy its full flavour. The only important item was the confirmation of some money sent through the black market, which his brother delicately referred to as his "agent". Oliveira planned to buy some books he had been wanting to read and he would give La Maga three thousand francs which she could do with as she pleased, probably buy a near-life-size felt elephant to surprise Rocamadour with. In the morning he would have to go to old man Trouille's and bring the correspondence with Latin America up to date. Going out, doing things, bringing up to date were not ideas calculated to help him get to sleep. To bring up to date: what an expression. To do. To do something, to do good, to make water, to make time, action in all of its possibilities. But behind all action there was a protest, because all doing meant leaving from in order to arrive at, or moving something so that it would be here and not there, or going into a house instead of not going in or instead of going into the one next door; in other words, every act entailed the admission of a lack, of something not yet done and which could have been done, the tacit protest in the face of continuous evidence of a lack, of a reduction, of the inadequacy of the present moment. To believe that action could crown something, or that the sum total of actions could really be a life worthy of the name was the illusion of a moralist. It was better to withdraw, because withdrawal from action was the protest itself and not its mask. Oliveira lit another cigarette and this little action made him smile ironically and tease himself about the act itself. He was not too worried about superficial analyses, almost always perverted by distraction and linguistic traps. The only thing certain was the weight in the pit of his stomach, the physical suspicion that something was not going well and that perhaps it never had gone well. It was not even a problem, but rather the early denial of both collective lies and that grumpy solitude of one who sets out to study radioactive isotopes or the presidency of Bartolomé Mitre. If he had made any choice when he was young it was that he would not defend himself with the rapid and anxious accumulation of "culture", the favourite dodge of the Argentine middle class to avoid facing national reality, or any other reality for that matter, and to think of themselves as safe from the emptiness surrounding them. Thanks, perhaps, to this systematic mopiness, as his buddy Traveler had defined it, he had managed to steer clear of that order of Pharisees (many of his friends did belong to it and generally in good faith, because it was just possible and there were examples), those who plumbed the depths of problems with some sort of specialization, and who, ironically, were awarded the highest pedigrees of Argentinity for doing just that. Furthermore, it seemed slippery and facile to mix up historical problems, such as one's being Argentinian or Eskimo, with problems like the ones that deal with action or withdrawal. He had lived long enough to be suspicious of anything stuck to someone's nose that keeps falling off: the weight of the subject in the notion of the object. La Maga was one of the few people who never forgot that someone's face would always have something to do with his interpretation of communism or of Creto-Mycenaean civilization, and that the shape of someone's hands had something to do with what he felt about Ghirlandaio or Dostoevsky. That's why Oliveira tended to admit that his blood-type, the fact that he had spent his childhood surrounded by majestic uncles, a broken love affair in adolescence, and a tendency towards asthenia might be factors of first importance in his vision of the cosmos. He was middle class, from Buenos Aires, had been to an Argentinian school, and those things are not dismissed lightly. The worst of it was that by dint of avoiding excessively local points of view he had ended up weighing and accepting too readily the yes and no of everything, becoming a sort of inspector of scales. In Paris everything was Buenos Aires, and vice versa; in the most eager moments of love he would suffer loss and loneliness and relish it. A perniciously comfortable attitude which even becomes easy as it grows into a reflex or technique; the frightful lucidity of the paralytic, the blindness of the perfectly stupid athlete. One begins to go about with the sluggish step of a philosopher or a *clochard*, as more and more vital gestures become reduced to mere instincts of preservation, to a conscience more alert not to be deceived than to grasp truth. Lay quietism, moderate ataraxia, attentive lack of attention. What was important for Oliveira was to experience this Tupac Amarú quartering and not faint, not fall into that pitiful egocentrism which he heard all about him every day in every possible shape. When he had been ten years old, during an afternoon spent under some *paraíso* trees and surrounded by uncles and historico-political homilies, he had shown his first timid reaction against that so very Hispano-Italo-Argentine *¡Se lo digo yo!* punctuated with a pound on the table. *Glielo dico io! I* say so, God damn it! That *I*, Oliveira had begun to think, does it have any value as proof? What omniscience was contained in the *I* of grownups? At the age of fifteen he discovered the business of "all I know is that I know nothing"; the hemlock that went with it seemed inevitable. One doesn't challenge people that way, I say so. Later on he was amused to see how more refined forms of culture produced their own versions of "I say so!" delicately disguised even for the person using them. Now he heard, "I've always thought so," "if I'm sure of anything . . . ," "it's obvious that . . . ," almost never softened by a disinterested appreciation of the other person's point of view. As if the species in every individual were on guard against letting him go too far along the road of tolerance, intelligent doubt, sentimental vacillation. At some given point the callus, the sclerosis, the definition is born: black or white, radical or conservative, homo- or heterosexual, the San Lorenzo team or the Boca Juniors, meat or vegetables, business or poetry. And it was all right, because the species should not trust people like Oliveira; his brother's letter was the precise form of that rejection.

"The worst part of all this," he thought, "is that it always ends up in the *Animula vagula blandula*. What is there to do? With that question I'll never get to sleep. Oblomov, *cosa facciamo*? The great voices of History stir us to action: revenge, Hamlet! Shall we avenge ourselves, Hamlet, or settle for Chippendale, slippers and a good fire? The Syrian, after all, made the scandalous choice of Martha, as is well known. Will you give battle, Arjuna? You cannot deny values, reluctant king. Fight for fight's sake, live dangerously, think about Marius the Epicurean, Richard Hillary, Kyo, T. E. Lawrence . . . Happy are those who choose, those who accept being chosen, the handsome heroes, the handsome saints, the perfect escapists."

Perhaps. Why not? But it's also possible that your point of view is the same as that of the fox as he looks at the grapes. And it also might be that reason is on your side, but a lamentable and mean little reason, the reason the ant uses against the grasshopper. If lucidity ends up in inaction, doesn't it become suspect? Wouldn't it be covering up a particularly diabolical type of blindness? The stupidity of a military hero who runs forward carrying a keg of powder, Cabral, the heroic soldier covering himself with glory, is hinted to be a revelation, the instantaneous melding with something absolute, beyond all consciousness (that's a lot to ask for in a sergeant), in face of which ordinary vision, bedroom insight at three o'clock in the morning and with a half-smoked cigarette, is about as good as a mole's.

He spoke to La Maga about all this. She had woken and was snuggling up against him, mewing sleepily. La Maga opened her eyes and remained thoughtful.

"You couldn't do it," she said. "You think too much before you do anything."

"I believe in the principle that thought must precede action, silly."

"You believe in the principle," said La Maga. "How complicated. You're like a witness. You're the one who goes to the museum and looks at the paintings. I mean the paintings are there and you're in the museum too, near and far away at the same time. I'm a painting. Rocamadour is a painting. Étienne is a painting, this room is a painting. You think that you're in this room, but you're not. You're looking at the room, you're not in the room."

"This girl could leave Saint Thomas way behind," Oliveira said.

"Why Saint Thomas?" asked La Maga. "That idiot who had to see to believe?"

"Yes, sweet," said Oliveira, thinking that underneath it all La Maga had hit upon the right saint. Happy was she who could believe without seeing, who was at one with the duration and continuity of life. Happy was she who was in the room, who had the freedom of the city in everything that she touched or came in contact with, a fish swimming downstream, a leaf on a tree, a cloud in the sky, an image in a poem. Fish, leaf, cloud, image: that's it precisely, unless . . .

(–84)

4

So they had begun to walk about in a fabulous Paris, letting themselves be guided by the night-time signs, following routes born of a *clochard* phrase, of an attic lit up in the darkness of a street's end, stopping in little confidential squares to kiss on the benches or look at the hopscotch game, those childish rites of a pebble and a hop on one leg to get into Heaven, Home. La Maga spoke about her friends in Montevideo, about her childhood years, about a certain Ledesma, about her father. Oliveira listened without interest, a little sorry that he was not interested; Montevideo was just like Buenos Aires and he had to finish breaking away (what was Traveler up to, that old drifter? What kind of majestic hassles had he got into since he had left? And poor, silly Gekrepten, and the bars downtown). That's why he listened with displeasure and was making sketches in the gravel with a stick while La Maga explained why Chempe and Graciela were good girls and how it had hurt her that Luciana had not come to the ship to see her off. Luciana was a snob, which she couldn't put up with in anybody.

"What does snob mean to you?" asked Oliveira, becoming interested.

"Well," La Maga answered, lowering her head with the air of someone who senses that she is about to say something stupid, "I was travelling third class, but I think that if I had gone second class Luciana would have come to say goodbye."

"That's the best definition I've ever heard," said Oliveira.

"And besides, there was Rocamadour," La Maga said.

That's how Oliveira found out about the existence of Rocamadour, who in Montevideo had been plain Carlos Francisco. La Maga didn't seem disposed to go into very great detail about Rocamadour's origins except that she had not wanted an abortion and was beginning to regret the fact now.

"But I don't really regret it all. My problem now is making ends meet. Madame Irène costs a lot and I have to take singing lessons. All that costs a lot."

La Maga didn't really know why she had come to Paris, and Oliveira was able to deduce that with just a little mixup in tickets, tourist agents, and visas she might just as well have disembarked in Singapore or Cape Town. The main thing was that she had left Montevideo to confront what she modestly called "life". The great advantage of Paris was that she knew quite a bit of French (in the style of the Pitman School of Languages) and that she would be able to see artistic masterpieces, the best films, *Kultur* in its most eminent forms. Oliveira was moved by all this (although Rocamadour had shaken him up a bit, he didn't know why), and he thought of some of the slick girls he had known in Buenos Aires, incapable of getting any farther away than Mar del Plata, in spite of such great metaphysical desires for planetary experience. And this kid, with a child to boot, gets herself a third-class ticket and takes off to study singing in Paris without a penny in her pocket. For what it was worth, she was already giving him lessons in how to look at and see things; lessons she was not aware of, just her way of stopping suddenly in the street to peep into an entranceway where there was nothing, but where a green glow could be seen farther in, then to duck furtively into the courtyard so that the gatekeeper would not get annoyed and sometimes look at an old statue or an ivy-covered curbing, or nothing, just the worn-out paving made of round stones, mould on the walls, a watchmaker's sign, a little old man sitting in the shade in a corner, and the cats, always, inevitably the *minouche morrongos miau-miau kitten kat chat gato gatto*; greys and whites and blacks, sewer cats, masters of time and of the warm pavement, La Maga's invariable friends as she tickled their bellies and spoke to them in a language somewhere between banal and mysterious; making dates with them, giving advice and admonitions. Suddenly Oliveira felt funny walking with La Maga, but it was no use getting annoyed because La Maga almost inevitably would knock over beer glasses or pull her leg out from under the table in just the right way so that the waiter would trip over it and start to curse. He was happy in spite of being exasperated all the time with that business of not doing things the way they ought to be done, of the way she resolutely ignored the larger figures of an account to go into ecstasies over the tail of a modest 3, or would stop short in the middle of the street (a black Renault came to a halt about five feet away and the driver stuck his head out and used his Picardy accent to call her a whore). She would stop as if there was a real view to be seen from the middle of the street, as if the sight of the distant Panthéon was much better from there than from the pavement. Things like that.

Oliveira already knew Perico and Ronald. La Maga introduced him to Étienne and Étienne introduced them both to Gregorovius. The Serpent Club began to take shape at night in Saint-Germain-des-Prés. Everybody accepted La Maga's presence right away as something inevitable and natural, even though they would get annoyed with having to explain to her almost everything they were talking about, or because she would send a helping of fried potatoes flying through the air simply because she didn't know how to use a fork in the proper fashion and the potatoes would almost always land on the heads of the people at the next table, and excuses would have to be made, telling how thoughtless La Maga was. La Maga did not get along very well with them as a group. Oliveira realized that she preferred to be with them individually, to walk along the street with Étienne or with Babs, to bring them into her world, never consciously, but bringing them in all the same because they were people who only wanted to escape the ordinary routine of buses and history, and therefore, in one way or another, all the people in the Club were thankful to La Maga even though they would rain insults on her at the slightest provocation. Étienne, sure of himself as a dog or a postbox, would get furious when La Maga came out with one of her comments concerning his latest painting, and even Perico Romero had to admit that-when-it-came-to-being-a-female-La-Maga-took-the-cake. For weeks or months (keeping track of time was difficult for Oliveira, happy, *ergo* futureless) they walked and walked around Paris looking at things, letting happen whatever had to happen, loving and fighting, and all of this outside the stream of news, family obligations and physical and moral burdens of any sort.

Toc, toc.

"Come on, let's wake up," Oliveira would say from time to time.

"What for?" La Maga would reply, watching the *péniches* sail under the pont Neuf. "Toc, toc, you've got a bird in your head. Toc, toc, he picks at you all the time, he wants you to give him some Argentinian food to eat. Toc, toc."

"OK," grumbled Oliveira. "Don't get me mixed up with Rocamadour. Before we're through we'll be speaking Gliglish to some clerk or doorman and there'll be hell to pay. Look at that guy following the Negro girl."

"I know her. She works in a café on the Rue de Provence. She likes girls. The poor guy has had it."

"Did she try anything with you?"

"Naturally. But we became friends just the same. I gave her my rouge and she gave me a book by somebody called Retef, no . . . wait, Retif . . . "

"I see. So you didn't go to bed with her? It could have been fun for a woman like you."

"Did you ever go to bed with a man, Horacio?"

"Of course. For the experience, you know."

La Maga looked at him out of the corner of her eye, suspecting that he was kidding her, that all of this came from his being furious over the toc-toc bird in his head, the bird that asked him for Argentinian food. Then she threw herself at him to the great surprise of a couple strolling along the Rue Saint-Sulpice, and she mussed up his hair as she laughed. Oliveira had to hold her arms down and they began to laugh. The couple looked at them and although the husband had a hint of a smile, his wife was much too scandalized by such behaviour.

"You're right," Oliveira confessed finally. "I'm incurable. Talking about waking up when, after all, it's so nice to be asleep like this."

They stopped by a shop window to look at book titles. La Maga began to ask questions, using the colours of the covers as her guide. Flaubert had to be put in his period for her, she had to be told that Montesquieu, how Raymond Radiguet, explained to about when Théophile Gautier. La Maga listened, drawing on the window with her finger. "A bird in my head wants me to give him some Argentinian food to eat," Oliveira was thinking as he heard himself talking. "Oh, me. Oh, brother!"

"But don't you see that you can't learn anything this way," he finally told her. "You think you can get an education on the street, love, and you can't. If that's what you want, subscribe to the *Reader's Digest*."

"Oh, no. Not that crap."

A bird in his head, Oliveira was saying to himself. Not her, but him. But what did she have in her head? Air or chick-pea flour, something hard to grasp. The centre was not in the head.

"She closes her eyes and hits the bull's-eye," thought Oliveira. "The Zen method of archery, precisely. But she hits the bull's-eye because she doesn't know that it is the method. But in my case . . . Toc, toc. And that's how it goes."

When La Maga would ask about Zen (such things could happen with the Club, where they were always talking about nostalgic things, wisdom so distant that they came to think of it as fundamental, the obverse of a medal, the far side of the moon, always), Gregorovius would try to explain the rudiments of metaphysics while Oliveira would sip his pernod and watch, enjoying it. It was madness to try to explain anything to La Maga. Fauconnier was right, for people like her the mystery begins precisely with the explanation. La Maga heard the words *immanence* and *transcendence* and she opened up two big beautiful eyes which cut off Gregorovius's metaphysics. Finally she convinced herself that she had understood Zen and sighed with fatigue. Only Oliveira knew that La Maga was always reaching those great timeless plateaus that they were all seeking through dialectics.

"Don't learn any stupid facts," he would advise her. "Why wear glasses if you don't need them?"

La Maga was not quite sure. She was terribly in awe of Oliveira and Étienne, who could keep an argument going for three hours without a break. There was something like a circle of chalk around Étienne and Oliveira and she wanted to get inside, to understand why the principle of indetermination was so important in literature, why Morelli, of whom they spoke so much, whom they admired so much, wanted his book to be a crystal ball in which the micro- and the macrocosm would come together in an annihilating vision.

"It's impossible to explain to you," said Étienne. "This is Meccano number 7 and you're barely in number 2."

La Maga became sad, she picked up a leaf from the edge of the pavement and spoke to it for a while, moved it along the palm of her hand, turned it over and upside down, stroked it, and finally she took off the leafy part and left the veins exposed, a delicate green ghost was reflected against her skin. Étienne snatched it away brusquely and held it against the light.

That's why they admired her, a little ashamed at having been so brutish with her, and La Maga would take advantage by ordering another pint or, if possible, some fried potatoes.

(–71)

5

The first time had been in a hotel on the Rue Valette. They were walking along aimlessly and stopping in the doorways, drizzle after lunch is always bitter and something ought to be done about that frozen dust, against those raincoats smelling of rubber, and suddenly La Maga drew herself close to Oliveira and they looked at each other like fools. HOTEL, the old woman behind the rickety desk greeted them with an understanding air and what else was there to do in this rotten weather. She dragged one foot and it was painful to see her climb the stairs, stopping at each step to drag up her sick leg, which was thicker than the other, and go through the same manoeuvre all the way to the fourth floor. There was a smell of toilet soap, of soup, on the rug in the hallway someone had spilled a blue liquid which had taken the shape of a pair of wings. The room had two windows with red curtains, full of patches. A damp light spread out like an angel over to the bed with a yellow spread.

La Maga had thought to play the innocent, staying by the window, pretending to look at the street while Oliveira checked the bolt on the door. She must have had a system all worked out for this sort of thing, or maybe it just always happened the same way. First she put her purse on the table and looked for her cigarettes, she looked at the street, taking deep drags, she commented on the wallpaper, she waited, obviously she waited, all effort was being made so that the man could best play his role and would have all the time necessary to take the initiative. At one point they had burst out laughing, it was all too silly. Flung into a corner, the yellow bedspread looked like a shapeless doll against the wall.

They had got into the habit of comparing spreads, doors, lamps, curtains. They preferred the hotel rooms of the *cinquième arrondissement* to those of the *sixième*. In the *septième* they had no luck at all, something was always happening: pounding in the room next door or the plumbing made a lugubrious sound, and it was then that Oliveira had told La Maga the story of Troppmann. La Maga listened as she held him tight, and she would have to read the story by Turgenev. It was incredible what she would have to read in those two years (she didn't know why they were two years). Another time it was Petiot, another time Weidmann, another time Christie. It ended up with the hotel always giving them the urge to talk about crimes, but La Maga would also be engulfed by a wave of seriousness and she would ask with her eyes fixed on the flat ceiling whether Sienese painting was really as fantastic as Étienne claimed, whether they shouldn't try to save up to buy a record-player and the works of Hugo Wolf, which she would sometimes hum, breaking off in the middle, forgetful and furious. Oliveira liked to make love to La Maga because there was nothing more important to her and at the same time, in a way hard to understand, she was in a sense dependent on his pleasure, she would reach him for a moment and would therefore cling desperately and prolong it. It was as if she had woken and recognized her real name, and then she would fall back into that always somewhat twilight zone that enchanted Oliveira, fearful of perfection, but La Maga really did suffer when she returned to her memories and to everything that in some obscure way she had to think about but could not. Then he would have to kiss her deeply, incite her to new play, and the other woman, the reconciled one, would grow beneath him and pull him down, and she would surrender then like a frantic animal, her eyes lost, her hands twisted inward, mythical and terrible, like a statue rolling down a mountainside, clutching time with her nails, with a gurgling sound and a moaning growl that lasted interminably. One night she sank her teeth into him, bit him in the shoulder until the blood came, because he had fallen to one side, a little forgetful already, and there was a confused and wordless pact. Oliveira felt that La Maga wanted death from him, something in her which was not her waking self, a dark form demanding annihilation, the slow wound which on its back breaks the stars at night and gives space back to questions and terrors. Only that time, off centre like a mythical matador for whom killing is returning the bull to the sea and the sea to the heavens, he bothered La Maga in a long night which they did not speak much about later. He turned her into Pasiphaë, he bent her over and used her as if she were a young boy, he knew her and he demanded the slavishness of the most abject whore, he magnified her into a constellation, he held her in his arms smelling of blood, he made her drink the semen which ran into her mouth like a challenge to the Logos, he sucked out the shadow from her womb and her rump and raised himself to her face to anoint her with herself in that ultimate work of knowledge that only a man can give to a woman, he wore her out with skin and hair and drool and moans, he drained her completely of her magnificent strength, he threw her against a pillow and sheet and felt her crying with happiness against his face which another cigarette was returning to the night from the room and from the hotel.

Later on Oliveira began to worry that she would think herself jaded, that the play would move on to sacrifice. Above all he feared that most subtle form of gratitude which turns into dog-like love. He did not want freedom, the only suit that fit La Maga, to be lost in any strong femininity. He didn't have to worry, because as soon as La Maga was back on the level of black coffee and a trip to the toilet, it was obvious that she had fallen back into the worst of confusions. Terribly mistreated that night, opened up to an absorbent space that beats and expands, his first words when she was back on this side came like whiplashes, as they had to, and when she came back to the side of the bed she was the image of a progressive consternation which tried to soften itself with smiles and a vague hope, which left Oliveira quite satisfied. Since he did not love her, since desire would stop (because he did not love, desire would stop), he would have to avoid like the devil any kind of sacred ritualizing of their play. For days, for weeks, for some months, every hotel room and every square, every position of love, and every dawn in a marketplace café: a savage circus, subtle operation, and rational balance. That's how it came to be known that La Maga was really waiting for Horacio to kill her and that hers would be a phoenix death, entry into the council of philosophers, that is to say, the discussions of the Serpent Club. La Maga wanted to learn, she wanted to be ed-you-kay-ted. Horacio was the exalted, the chosen one, the one to fill the role of purifying priest, and since they never understood each other because when they were discussing something they would be off on different tracks and different interests (and she knew this and understood it well), therefore the only possibility of coming together would be if Horacio were to kill her while making love, where she could get together with him in the heaven of some hotel room where they would come together equal and naked and there the resurrection of the phoenix could take place after he had strangled her delightfully, dripping a string of saliva into her open mouth, looking at her ecstatically as if he had just begun to recognize her, to make her really his, to take her to his side.

(–81)

6

The technique was to make a vague date in some neighbourhood at a certain hour. They liked to challenge the danger of not meeting, of spending the day alone sulking in a café or on a park bench, reading-another-book. The another-book theory was Oliveira's, and La Maga had accepted it by pure osmosis. For her, in truth, almost all books were one-book-less; she would have liked to be overcome by an immense thirst and for an infinite period of time (calculated as between three and five years) to read the complete works of Goethe, Homer, Dylan Thomas, Mauriac, Faulkner, Baudelaire, Roberto Arlt, Saint Augustine, and other writers whose names would keep coming up in conversation in the Club. Oliveira would answer this with a sour shrug of his shoulders and talk about the distortions of the Río de la Plata, where a breed of full-time readers has developed, where libraries swarm with old maids who have forsaken love and sunshine, where the smell of printer's ink can end the joy of garlic in a home. He wasn't reading much then, too busy looking at trees, pieces of string he found on the ground, the yellowed films he saw in movie clubs, the women in the Latin Quarter. His vague intellectual tendencies had become resolved in aimless meditation, and when La Maga would ask him for help, a date or an explanation, he would only supply it grudgingly, as if it were something useless. "But you already know it," La Maga would say, resentfully. Then he would take the trouble to explain to her the difference between familiarity and knowledge, and he would ask her to try some individual research projects, which La Maga would not finish and which would drive her to her wit's end.

Since they would never normally be in certain places, they would agree to meet there and they almost always found each other. The meetings were so incredible at times that Oliveira once more brought up the problem of probability and examined the case cautiously from all angles. La Maga could not possibly have decided to turn that corner of the Rue de Vaugirard at the precise moment in which he, five blocks down the street, decided not to go along the Rue de Buci and headed for the Rue Monsieur-le-Prince for no apparent reason, letting himself go along until suddenly he saw her stopped in front of a shop window, absorbed in the contemplation of a stuffed monkey. Seated in a café they carefully reconstructed their routes, the quick changes, trying to find some telepathic explanation and always failing, and yet they had met in that labyrinth of streets, they almost always met and they laughed wildly, certain of some enriching power. Oliveira was fascinated by La Maga's store of nonsense, her calm disdain for the simplest calculation. What for him had been analysis of probabilities, choice, or simply faith in himself as a diviner, for her was simple chance. "And what if you hadn't met me?" he would ask her. "I don't know, but you're here, you see . . . " For some reason the answer made the question worthless, it showed the logical basis of ordinary common sense. After that Oliveira would feel better able to resist his bookish prejudices, and paradoxically La Maga would fight off her disdain for scholarly knowledge. Thus they went along, Punch and Judy, attracting each other and repelling, as love must do if it is not to end up as calendar art or a pop tune. But love, that word . . .

(–7)

7

I touch your mouth, I touch the edge of your mouth with my finger, I am drawing it as if it were something my hand was sketching, as if for the first time your mouth opened a little, and all I have to do is close my eyes to erase it and start all over again, every time I can make the mouth I want appear, the mouth which my hand chooses and sketches on your face, and which by some chance that I do not seek to understand coincides exactly with your mouth which smiles beneath the one my hand is sketching on you.

You look at me, from close up you look at me, closer and closer and then we play cyclops, we look closer and closer at one another and our eyes get larger, they come closer, they merge into one and the two cyclopses look at each other, blending as they breathe, our mouths touch and struggle in gentle warmth, biting each other with their lips, barely holding their tongues on their teeth, playing in corners where a heavy air comes and goes with an old perfume and a silence. Then my hands go to sink into your hair, to cherish slowly the depth of your hair while we kiss as if our mouths were filled with flowers or with fish, with lively movements and dark fragrance. And if we bite each other the pain is sweet, and if we smother each other in a brief and terrible sucking in together of our breaths, that momentary death is beautiful. And there is but one saliva and one flavour of ripe fruit, and I feel you tremble against me like a moon on the water.

(–8)

8

In the afternoon we used to go to see the fish on the Quai de la Mégisserie, in March, the leopard month, the crouching month, but now with a yellow sun which took on a little more red each day. From the pavement along the river, paying no attention to the *bouquinistes* who give nothing without pay, we would wait for the moment when we could see the fishbowls (we went along slowly, delaying), all the fishbowls out in the sun, and as if hung in the air hundreds of pink and black fish, motionless birds in their round air. An absurd joy would take us by the waist and you would sing, dragging me across the street to enter the world of fish hanging in the air.

They bring out the bowls, those great pitchers, onto the street and there among tourists and excited children and ladies who collect exotic varieties (*550 fr. pièce*) are the fishbowls underneath the sun, spheres of water which the sun mixes with the air and the pink and black birds dance around softly in a little chunk of air, slow cold birds. We would look at them, trying to bring our eyes up to the glass, touching it with our noses, annoying the old women who sell them as they go about with their nets to hunt aquatic butterflies, and we understood less and less what a fish is. We went along that path of not understanding and getting closer to those creatures that could not understand each other. We walked through the fishbowls and were as close as our friend, the woman in the second shop as you come from the Pont Neuf, who told you: "Cold water kills them, cold water is a sad thing . . . " And I remember the maid in the hotel who told me about a fern: "Don't water it, put a plate of water under the pot, then when it wants to drink it can, and when it doesn't want to, it doesn't . . . " And I thought about that unbelievable thing that we had read, that a single fish will get sad in its bowl and that all one has to do is put a mirror next to it and the fish is happy again . . .

We used to go into the shops where the more delicate species would have special tanks with thermometers and red worms. We would find out along with exclamations which used to infuriate the saleswomen – they were so sure that we were not going to buy anything at *550 fr. pièce* – all about the behaviour, the love, and the shape of the fish. The moment was delicately delicious, something like very thin chocolate or orange paste from Martinique; and we were getting drunk on metaphors and analogies, always trying to get into it. And that perfectly Giotto fish, do you remember, and those two that played about like jade dogs, or a fish which was the exact shadow of a violet cloud . . . We found out how life goes on in shapes without a third dimension, that they disappear when they face you, or at most leave a thin motionless pink line in the water. A flick of a fin and there he is miraculously again with eyes, whiskers, fins, and from his belly sometimes coming out and floating a transparent ribbon of excrement which has not come loose, ballast which suddenly puts them amongst us, which plucks them out from the perfection of their pure imagery, which compromises them, to use one of those fine words we so much liked to use around there in those days.

(–93)

9

They came into the Rue Vaneau from the Rue de Varennes. It was drizzling and La Maga clutched Oliveira's arm even tighter, pressing herself against his raincoat, which smelled like cold soup. Étienne and Perico were arguing over the possibility of explaining the world through painting and words. Oliveira put his arm carelessly around La Maga's waist. That might be an explanation too, an arm squeezing a thin, warm waist. As they walked he could feel the light play of her muscles, a sort of monotonous and persistent speech, an insistent Berlitz, I-love-you, I-love-you. Not an explanation: a pure verb, to-love, to-love. "And always following the verb, the copulative," Oliveira thought grammatically. If La Maga could only have understood how suddenly he was bothered by obedience to desire, "useless solitary obedience", as a poet had once called it, a waist so warm, wet hair against his cheek, the Toulouse-Lautrec way that La Maga used to walk snuggled up to him. In the beginning was the copulative, to rape is to explain, but not always the other way around. To discover the anti-explanatory method, so that this I-love-you, I-love-you would be the hub of the wheel. And Time? Everything begins again, there is no absolute. Then there must be feed or faeces, everything becomes critical again. Desire every so often, never too different and always something else: a trick of time to create illusions. "A love like a fire which burns eternally in the contemplation of Totality. But suddenly one breaks out into wild babble."

"Explain, explain," grumbled Étienne. "If you people can't name something you're incapable of seeing it. And this is called a dog and that's a house, as the guy from Duino used to say. You've got to show, Perico, not explain. I paint, therefore I am."

"Show what?" Perico Romero asked.

"The only reasons for our being alive."

"This creature thinks that the only sense is the sense of sight and all that can come from it," Perico answered.

"Painting is more than just a visual product," Étienne said. "I paint with my whole body. In that sense I'm no different from your Cervantes or your Tirso de What's-his-name. What I can't stand is this mania for explanations, the Logos understood exclusively as a verb."

"And so forth," Oliveira said grumpily. "Speaking of senses, the pair of you sound like a dialogue between two deaf men."

La Maga squeezed him tighter. "Now this one is going to come out with one of her asinine comments," thought Oliveira. "She has to rub first, make an epidermic decision." He felt a sort of hateful tenderness, something so contradictory that it must have been truth itself. "We ought to invent the sweet slap, the bee-kick. But in this world ultimate syntheses are yet to be discovered. Perico is right, the great Logos is watching. What a pity. We would have to have amoricide, for example, the real black light, the antimatter that troubles Gregorovius so much."

"Say, is Gregorovius coming to the recording session?" asked Oliveira.

Perico thought that he was, and Étienne thought that Mondrian.

"Think about Mondrian a minute," Étienne was saying. "Next to him Klee's magic symbols are nothing. Klee played with fate, the gifts of culture. Pure sensibility can be satisfied with Mondrian, but you need a whole bag of other tricks with Klee. A sophisticate for sophisticates. Chinese, really. Mondrian, on the other hand, paints the absolute. Stand naked in front of him and it's one thing or the other: either you see or you don't see. Pleasure, thrills, allusions, fears, delights are completely superfluous."

"Do you understand what he's saying?" La Maga asked. "It seems to me that he's not being fair to Klee."

"Fairness or unfairness has nothing to do with this," said Oliveira. "He's trying to say something else. Don't immediately turn it into something personal."

"But why does he say that such beautiful things are no good for Mondrian?"

"He's trying to say that basically a painting like one of Klee's calls for a degree *ès lettres*, or at least *ès poésies*, while all that Mondrian wants is for a person to mondrianate and that's all."

"That's not it," said Étienne.

"Of course it is," Oliveira said. "According to you a Mondrian canvas is sufficient unto itself. Therefore it calls upon your innocence more than on your experience. I mean Edenic innocence, not stupidity. Even that metaphor you used about standing naked in front of a picture has a pre-Adamite smell about it. Paradoxically, Klee is much more modest since he asks for the co-operation of the viewer and is not sufficient unto himself. The fact of the matter is that Klee is history while Mondrian is atemporality. And you're dying to find the absolute. Do I make myself clear?"

"No," said Étienne. "*C'est vache comme il pleut.*"

"You said it, *coño,*" said Perico, "and that son of a bitch Ronald lives with the devil."

"Let us stiffen our pace," said Oliveira, mimicking his Spanish accent. "Let us sneak our bodies out from under this drizzle."

"There you go. I almost like your rain and your chicken better. It sure knows how to rain in Buenos Aires."

"The absolute," La Maga was saying, kicking a pebble from puddle to puddle. "What is an absolute, Horacio?"

"Look," Oliveira said, "it's just that moment in which something attains its maximum depth, its maximum reach, its maximum sense, and becomes completely uninteresting."

"There comes Wong," Perico observed. "The Chinaman's wetter than a wonton in a soup."

Almost at the same time, they spied Gregorovius coming around the corner of the Rue de Babylone, loaded down as usual with a briefcase bulging with books. Wong and Gregorovius stopped under the lamppost (and looked as if they were taking a shower together) and greeted each other with a certain solemnity. In the doorway of Ronald's building there was an interlude of umbrella-closing, *comment ça va,* who's got a match, the *minuterie* is broken, what a lousy night, *ah oui c'est vache,* and a rather confused ascent, broken at the first landing by a couple sitting on the steps and deeply engaged in the act of kissing.

"*Allez, c'est pas une heure pour faire les cons,*" said Étienne.

"*Ta gueule,*" answered a muffled voice, "*montez, montez, ne vous gênez pas. Ta bouche, mon trésor.*"

"*Salaud, va,*" Étienne said. "That's Guy Monod, an old friend of mine."

Ronald and Babs were waiting on the fifth floor, each holding a candle and smelling of cheap vodka. Wong made a sign and everybody stopped on the stairs and broke into an *a capella* version of the profane anthem of the Serpent Club. Then they ran into the apartment before the neighbours came to their doors.

Ronald was leaning against the door, redheadedly, wearing a checked shirt.

"The place is surrounded by telescopes, damn it. At ten o'clock at night the great god Silence is enthroned and woe to anyone who is irreverent. Yesterday some official came up to bawl us out. What did the gentleman tell us, Babs?"

"He mentioned 'repeated complaints'."

"So what are we going to do?" asked Ronald as he opened the door to let Guy Monod slip in.

"We'll do this," said Babs with a flawless gesture of the arm and a resonant oral fart.

"What about your chick?" Ronald asked.

"I don't know, she got lost," Guy said. "I think she's gone. We were making out fine on the stairs, and all of a sudden. Farther up she just wasn't there. What the hell anyway, she's Swiss."

(–104)

10

At night the clouds were flat and red over the Latin Quarter, the air was still damp as a listless breeze blew a few last drops against the dimly lit window, the panes were dirty, one broken and patched up with a piece of pink adhesive. Up above, under the lead gutters, the pigeons must have been sleeping, also lead, wrapped up in themselves, perfect antigargoyles. Protected by the window was that mossy parallelepiped, smelling of vodka and candles, damp clothing and leftover food, which was a kind of studio for Babs the ceramicist and Ronald the musician, the seat of the Club, wicker chairs, stained pillows, bits of pencil and wire on the floor, a stuffed owl with half his head gone, a poorly played and corny tune on an old record with a deep needle-scratch, an incessant scratch rasp scrape, a terrible saxophone that one night in 1928 or '29 had played as if it were afraid of getting lost, backed up by schoolgirl drums, a mediocre piano. But then an incisive guitar came in which seemed to signal a transition to something else and suddenly (Ronald had alerted them by holding up his finger) a cornet broke loose from the rest of the group and blew the first notes of the melody, landing on them as on a diving board. Bix took off with everything he had, and the clear sketch was inscribed on the silence as if it had been scratched there. Two corpses sparred fraternally, clinching and breaking, Bix and Eddie Lang (whose real name was Salvatore Massaro) played catch with *I'm Coming Virginia*, and I wonder where Bix is buried, thought Oliveira, and Eddie Lang, how many miles apart are their two nothings that one future night in Paris were to fight, guitar against cornet, gin against bad luck, jazz.

"I like it here. It's warm, it's dark."

"That Bix is a crazy son of a bitch. Put on *Jazz Me Blues*."

"The influence of technique on art," said Ronald, digging his hands into a pile of records, looking casually at the labels. "Before

LPs came out those guys had less than three minutes to play in. Nowadays a wild man like Stan Getz can come along in front of a mike and turn himself loose, blow anything he wants to. Poor Bix had to be satisfied with one chorus and as soon as he got warmed up, snap, it was all over. They must have got sore as hell when they cut records."

"I don't know," said Perico. "It's like writing a sonnet instead of an ode, and I don't know a damned thing about this crap. I only came because I was sick of staying in my room reading an endless essay by Julián Marías."

(–65)

11

Gregorovius let his glass be filled with vodka and began to drink with dainty sips. Two candles were burning on the mantelpiece where Babs kept bottles of beer and her dirty stockings. Gregorovius admired the listless burning of the candles through the hyaline glass, it was so foreign to all of them and so out of their time, like Bix's cornet, coming and going from a different time. He was annoyed by the feet of Guy Monod, who was on the couch either sleeping or listening with his eyes closed. La Maga came over and sat on the floor with a cigarette in her mouth. The green candles burned in her eyes. Gregorovius looked at her in ecstasy and remembered a street in Morlaix at dusk, a high aqueduct, clouds.

"This light is so much like you, something that comes and goes, always moving."

"Like Horacio's shadow," La Maga said. "His nose grows and shrinks. It's amazing."

"Babs is a shepherdess of shadows," Gregorovius said, "she works in clay, concrete shadows . . . Here everything breathes, a lost contact is established again; music helps, vodka, friendship . . . Those shadows in the cornice; the room has lungs, it palpitates. Yes, electricity is eleatic, it has turned our shadows to stone. Now they are part of the furniture and the faces. But here, on the other hand . . . Look at that moulding, how its shadow is breathing, that volute that rises and falls. In those days man lived in a soft and porous night, in a continuous dialogue. The terrors, what a luxury for the imagination . . . "

He put his palms together, keeping only his thumbs apart: a dog began to open his mouth and move his ears on the wall. La Maga laughed. Then Gregorovius asked her what it was like in Montevideo, the dog suddenly dissolved, because he wasn't sure that she was Uruguayan; Lester Young and the Kansas City Six. Shh . . . (Ronald, finger to his lips).

"Uruguay always sounded so strange to me. I picture Montevideo with lots of steeples all with bells cast after a battle. And you can't tell me that Montevideo doesn't have giant lizards along the river bank."

"Certainly," said La Maga. "All you have to do is take the bus to Pocitos."

"And do people in Montevideo really know Lautréamont?"

"Lautréamont?" asked La Maga.

Gregorovius sighed and drank more vodka. Lester Young, tenor; Dickie Wells, trombone; Joe Bushkin, piano; Bill Coleman, trumpet; John Simmons, bass; Jo Jones, drums. *Four O'Clock Drag.* Yes, tremendous lizards, trombones on the river bank, blues crawling along, *drag* probably meant a lizard in time, an endless crawling at four o'clock in the morning. Or maybe something completely different. "Oh, Lautréamont," La Maga said, suddenly remembering. "Yes, I think they know him quite well."

"He was from Uruguay, although you wouldn't think so."

"No, you wouldn't," said La Maga, coming to.

"Actually, Lautréamont . . . But Ronald's getting annoyed, he's put on one of his idols. I guess we'll have to shut up. But let's talk very low while you tell me about Montevideo."

"*Ah, merde alors,*" said Étienne, looking at them furiously. The vibes were testing the air, taking wrong steps upstairs, skipping a step, jumping five at once and coming down again on the top one. Lionel Hampton was balancing *Save It Pretty Mama*, letting it go as it fell down and spun around on the tip of his toe among pieces of glass, instant constellations, five stars, three stars, ten stars, he was extinguishing them with the tip of his slipper, he was rocking in a hammock twirling a Japanese parasol wildly in his hand and the whole band came in on the final fall, a hoarse trumpet, earth, down again, floating to a landing, *finibus*, all over. Gregorovius was listening to the whisper of Montevideo according to La Maga, and perhaps he would finally learn more about her, about her childhood, whether her name really was Lucía like Mimi in *La Bohème*; he was at that vodka level where the night began to become magnanimous and everything promised him fidelity and hope. Guy Monod had doubled up his legs and his hard soles no longer dug into Gregorovius's spine. La Maga was leaning on him a bit and he felt the soft warmth of her body, every movement she made to follow the music or the rhythm of her speech. With eyes open a crack Gregorovius managed to make out the corner where Ronald and Wong were selecting and passing records, Oliveira and Babs were on the floor, leaning against an Eskimo pelt on the wall, Horacio keeping cadence with the smoke, Babs lost to vodka, unpaid rent, and dyes that faded at three hundred degrees, a blue which melded into orangey rhombuses, something intolerable. Oliveira's lips were moving in the silence of the smoke, he was talking to himself, backwards, to some other thing that imperceptibly twisted Gregorovius's innards, he didn't know why, probably because that apparent absence of Horacio's was a fraud, which left him for La Maga to play with while he was there moving his lips in silence, speaking to La Maga through himself in the midst of the smoke and the jazz, laughing to himself inwardly at so much Lautréamont, at so much Montevideo.

(–136)

12

Gregorovius had always enjoyed meetings of the Club because it was really not a club at all in the strictest sense. He liked Ronald because of his anarchy, because of Babs, because of the way they were carefully killing themselves without worrying about anything, given over to the reading of Carson McCullers, Miller, Raymond Queneau, to jazz as a quiet exercise in freedom, to the unrestricted knowledge that they both were failures in the arts. He liked, if that's the word for it, Horacio Oliveira, with whom he had a sort of persecutive relationship in that Oliveira's presence always exasperated Gregorovius from the moment they came together, even after he had been out looking for Horacio, although he would not admit it, and Horacio would be amused by the cheap mysteries Gregorovius used to cover up his origins and way of life, by the fact that Gregorovius was in love with La Maga and did not think that Horacio knew, and the two of them would accept and reject each other at the same time in a sort of tight bullfight which in the last analysis was one of the reasons for the Club's get-togethers. They worked hard at being the knowing ones, at arranging a set of allusions to frustrate La Maga and infuriate Babs; all they had to do was mention something in passing, as now when Gregorovius was thinking that there really was a disillusioned persecution between him and Horacio, and immediately one of them would quote the hound of heaven, "I fled him," and so forth, and all the while La Maga would look at them with a kind of humble despair as one of them was in a state of I-flew-so-high-so-high-I-caught-my-prey and they would end up laughing at themselves. But it was too late because Horacio would be appalled at this exhibitionism of associative memory, and Gregorovius would feel himself touched with the annoyance that he had helped bring about, and between them both a certain resentment of accomplices would build up and two minutes later they would be at it again, and that, among other things, is what went on at meetings of the Club.

"This is one of the few times I've had such lousy vodka here," said Gregorovius as he filled his glass. "Lucía, you were about to tell me about your childhood. It's not hard for me to picture you on the river bank, with pigtails and rosy cheeks, like the girls I used to know in Transylvania, before they turned pale under the influence of this damned Lutetian climate."

"Lutetian?" asked La Maga.

Gregorovius sighed. He began to explain and La Maga was listening humbly and in a studious sort of way, just as she always did and with great intensity until rescued by some distraction. Ronald had just put on an old Coleman Hawkins record and La Maga seemed resentful that the explanation was ruining the music, and besides, it wasn't what she usually expected from an explanation, a tingling of the skin, a need to breathe deeply as Hawkins must have breathed just before taking another turn at the melody and as she would breathe when Horacio would deign to explain some really deep line of poetry for her, adding to it that other fabulous depth which could have been now if he instead of Gregorovius had been explaining this business about Lutetians, and how he would have made it blend into Hawkins's music, along with the green candles, a tickle, a deep breath which would be the only thing she could be sure of, something comparable only to Rocamadour or Horacio's lips or sometimes an adagio from Mozart that could barely be heard because the record was in such bad shape.

"Don't be like that," Gregorovius said humbly. "All I wanted was to understand your life a little better, what you are, how you happen to have so many facets."

"My life," said La Maga. "Even if I were drunk I wouldn't tell you about it. And you won't understand me any better after hearing about my childhood. Besides, I didn't have any childhood."

"I didn't either. In Herzegovina."

"Mine in Montevideo. I'll tell you one thing. Sometimes I dream about grammar school, it's so horrible I wake up screaming. And aged fifteen, I don't know whether you were ever fifteen years old."

"I think so," Gregorovius said uncertainly.

"I was, in a house with a courtyard and flowerpots where my

father used to drink *mate* and read dirty magazines. Does your father ever come back to you? His ghost I mean?"

"No, actually my mother is more apt to," Gregorovius said. "Especially the Glasgow one. My Glasgow mother comes back sometimes, but she's not a ghost, just a memory that's a little too wet, that's all. She goes away with an Alka-Seltzer, it's easy. But you . . . ?"

"How should I know," La Maga said impatiently. "It's that music, those green candles, Horacio over there in the corner, like an Indian. Why must I tell how he comes back? But a few nights ago I was at home waiting for Horacio, I was sitting near the bed and outside it was raining a little, the way it does on that record. Yes, it was something like that, I was looking at the bed and waiting for Horacio, I don't remember how the bed was made, and suddenly I saw my father lying with his back towards me and covering his face as he always did when he was drunk and beginning to fall asleep, I saw his legs and could make out his hand on his chest. I felt my hair stand on end, I wanted to scream, everything you feel at times like that, you must have been afraid sometime . . . I wanted to run away, the door was so far off, at the other end of the hallway and more hallways, the door was farther and farther away and I could see the pink bedspread going up and down, I could hear my father snoring, in a moment I would see a hand, then eyes, then his hooked nose, no, I shouldn't be telling you all this, finally I screamed so loud that the woman upstairs came down and made me some tea, and later on Horacio said I was hysterical."

Gregorovius stroked her hair and La Maga lowered her head. "Here it comes," Oliveira was thinking, and he stopped following Dizzy Gillespie's tricks as he swung on the high trapeze without a net, "here it comes, it was bound to. He's crazy about the girl and that's his way of showing it, with his ten fingers. The same game over and over. We keep falling into worn-out moulds, learning every trite role there is like idiots. But just as if I were stroking her hair, while she told me sagas of the Río de la Plata, we feel sorry for her and we have to take her home, all of us a little drunk, and put her to bed, petting her gently as we take off her clothes, slowly, button by button, every zip, and she does want to, wants to, doesn't want to, straightens up, covers her face, cries, hugs us as if suggesting something sublime, wiggles out of her slip, kicks off a shoe with a gesture that connotes protest and gets us as excited as we ever can get, how base, how base. I'm going to have to smash you in the face, Ossip Gregorovius my poor friend. No desire, no pity, exactly what Dizzy is blowing, without pity, without desire, just as absolutely without pity as what Dizzy is blowing."

"What a damned drag," Oliveira said. "Take that crap off the machine. I'm not coming to the Club any more if I have to listen to that clown."

"The gentleman doesn't like bop," Ronald said sarcastically. "Wait a minute, I'll put on something by Paul Whiteman for you."

"Let's compromise," Étienne said. "Common consent, sweet Ronald: let's hear Bessie Smith, the dove in a cage of bronze."

Ronald and Babs began to laugh for some obscure reason and Ronald looked through the pile of old records. The needle made a terrible scratch, something began to move deep down as if there were layers and layers of cotton between voice and ears, Bessie singing with a bandaged face, stuck in a hamper of soiled clothes, and her voice got more and more muffled, it came out stuck to rags and proclaimed with neither anger nor pleading, "I wanna be somebody's baby doll", it fell back to wait, a street-corner voice, one from a houseful of grannies, "to be somebody's baby doll", hotter and more yearning, panting now "I wanna be somebody's baby doll . . ."

Oliveira burned his mouth with a long drink of vodka, put his arm around Babs's shoulders, and rested against her comfortable body. "The intercessors," he thought, sinking softly into the tobacco smoke. Bessie's voice thinned out towards the end of the side, and now Ronald was flipping the Bakelite disc (if it was Bakelite) and from this piece of worn-out material the *Empty Bed Blues* would be born again, a night in the twenties in some corner of the United States. Ronald had closed his eyes, his hands on his knees, faintly keeping time. Wong and Étienne also had their eyes shut, the room was almost dark and the needle scratched on the old record; it was hard for Oliveira to believe that all of this was taking place. Why there, why the Club, those stupid rites, why did those blues come out like that when Bessie sang them? "The intercessors," he thought once more, snuggling up to Babs who was completely drunk and was crying quietly as she listened to Bessie, trembling in time to the rhythm or counterpoint, weeping inside so as not to get far away from the blues about an empty bed, tomorrow morning, shoes in puddles, unpaid rent, fear of old age, the ashen image of dawn in the mirror at the foot of the bed, the blues, life's infinite melancholy. "The intercessors, one unreality showing us another, like painted saints pointing towards Heaven. This cannot exist, we cannot really be here, I cannot be someone whose name is Horacio. That ghost there, that voice of a Negro woman killed in an automobile accident twenty years ago: links in a non-existent chain, how do we support ourselves here, how can we be meeting tonight if it is not a mere play of illusions, of rules that are accepted and agreed upon, a deck of cards in the hands of an inconceivable dealer . . . "

"Don't cry," Oliveira whispered to Babs. "Don't cry, Babs, none of this is true."

"Oh yes, oh yes it is true," Babs said, blowing her nose. "It is true."

"It could be true," said Oliveira, kissing her on the cheek, "but it isn't."

"Like those shadows," Babs said, snuffing and swallowing the mucus and moving her hand from side to side. "And it makes you sad, Horacio, because everything is so beautiful."

But all this, Bessie's singing, Coleman Hawkins's cooing, weren't they illusions, or something even worse, the illusion of other illusions, a dizzy chain going backwards, back to a monkey looking at himself in the water on that first day? But Babs was crying, Babs had said, "Oh yes, oh yes it is true," and Oliveira, a little drunk too, felt that the truth now lay in that Bessie and Hawkins were illusions, because only illusions were capable of moving their adherents, illusions and not truths. And there was more than this, there was intercession, the arrival through illusions to a plane, a zone impossible to think about because all thought destroyed it as soon as it attempted to isolate it. A hand of smoke took his hand, started him downward, if it was downward, showed him a centre, if it was a centre, put it in his stomach, where the vodka was softly making crystal bubbles, some sort of infinitely beautiful and desperate illusion which some time back he had called immortality. Closing his eyes he managed to tell himself that if a simple ritual was able to excentrate him like this the better to show him a centre, to excentrate him towards a centre which was nonetheless inconceivable, perhaps everything was not lost and some day, in different circumstances, after other proofs, arrival would be possible. But arrival where, for what? He was too drunk even to set up a working hypothesis, to form an idea of a possible route. He was not drunk enough to stop thinking consecutively, and this poor power of thought was sufficient for him to feel that it was carrying him away farther and farther from something too distant, too precious to be seen through this stupidly propitious mist, vodka mist, Maga mist, Bessie Smith mist. He began to see green rings spinning wildly about, he opened his eyes. Usually after seeing the rings he would feel like vomiting.

(–106)

13

Wrapped up in smoke Ronald was pulling out record after record, scarcely bothering to find out what the others wanted, and once in a while Babs would get up from the floor and start digging through the piles of old 78s, she would pick out four or five and put them on the table within reach of Ronald, who would lean forward and pet Babs who would twist away laughing and sit on his lap but just for a moment because Ronald wanted to be quiet while he listened to *Don't Play Me Cheap.*

Satchmo was singing:

> So what's the use
> if you're gonna cut off my juice

and Babs wiggled on Ronald's knees, excited by Satchmo's style of singing, the theme was vulgar enough to let her take liberties which Ronald would never condone when Satchmo sang the *Yellow Dog Blues*, and because in the breath that Ronald was blowing on the back of her neck there was a mixture of vodka and sauerkraut that aroused Babs fantastically. From her high outlook, a sort of delicate pyramid of smoke and music and vodka and sauerkraut and Ronald's hands marching up and down, Babs could condescend to look downward through her half-closed eyes and she saw Oliveira on the floor, his back against the Eskimo pelt on the wall, smoking and dead drunk now, with a resentful and bitter South American face whose mouth would smile from time to time between drags, Oliveira's lips which Babs had once desired (not now) were curved a little while the rest of his face looked washed-out and absent. As much as he liked jazz, Oliveira could never get into the spirit of it like Ronald, whether it was good or bad, hot or cool, white or black, old or modern, Chicago or New Orleans, never jazz, never what was now Satchmo, Ronald and Babs, "So what's the use if you're gonna cut off my juice," and then the trumpet's flaming up, the yellow phallus breaking the air and having fun, coming forward and drawing back and towards the end three ascending notes, pure hypnotic gold, a perfect pause where all the swing of the world was beating in an intolerable instant, and then the super-sharp ejaculation slipping and falling like a rocket in the sexual night, Ronald's hand caressing Babs's neck and the scratching of the needle while the record kept on turning and the silence there was in all true music slowly unstuck itself from the walls, slithered out from underneath the couch, and opened up like lips or like cocoons.

"*Ça alors,*" said Étienne.

"Yes, Armstrong's great period," said Ronald, examining the pile of records Babs had picked out. "Like Picasso's giant period, if you like. Nowadays they're both a pair of pigs. To think that doctors have invented ways to be rejuvenated . . . They'll go on screwing us for another twenty years, wait and see."

"Not us," Étienne said. "We've already shot them down and just at the right moment, and all I ask is for someone to do the same for me when my time is up."

"Just at the right moment? You're not asking for much, kiddo," said Oliveira, yawning. "But you're right, we have given them the *coup de grâce* already. With a rose instead of a bullet, if you want to think of it that way. What's left is habit and carbon paper. To think that Armstrong has just now gone to Buenos Aires for the first time and you can imagine the thousands of boobs who will think they're listening to something great while Satchmo, with more tricks than an old fighter, bobbing and weaving, tired and amortized and without giving a damn what he does, strictly routine, while some of my friends whom I respect and who twenty years ago would cover their ears if you put on *Mahogany Hall Stomp* now pay God knows how much for an orchestra seat to listen to that reheated stuff. Of course, my country itself is reheated too, with all my patriotic love I'm forced to admit it."

"Starting with you," said Perico from behind a dictionary. "You've come here in the same mould as all of your countrymen who take off for Paris to get their 'sentimental education'. At least in Spain we learn all about that in brothels and at bullfights, *coño*."

"And from the Countess Pardo Bazán," said Oliveira, yawning

again. "Everything else you say is true, old boy. What I should really be doing is playing cards with Traveler. You didn't know him, did you. You don't know anything about all that. So what's the use of talking about it?"

(–115)

14

He came out of the corner he had been stuck in, he put one foot on a piece of floor after having examined it as if it had been vital to pick out the exact spot on which to place his foot, then he brought out the other one with the same caution, and six feet away from Ronald and Babs he began to shrivel down until he was impeccably installed on the floor.

"It's raining," said Wong, pointing at the skylight.

Wafting the smoke away with his hand, Oliveira looked at Wong with friendly contentment.

"It's best to be at sea-level where all one can see are shoes and knees all around. Where's your glass?"

"Over there," said Wong.

It turned out that it was full and within reach. They began to drink, appreciatively, and Ronald put on a John Coltrane record which made Perico snort. Then a Sidney Bechet from his Paris *merengue* period, something that seemed to be poking a little fun at Spanish prejudices.

"Is it true that you're writing a book about tortures?"

"Not exactly," said Wong.

"What is it, then?"

"In China one has a different conception of art."

"I know, we've all read Mirbeau the Chinese. Is it true that you have photographs of tortures taken in Peking in 1920 or around that time?"

"Oh, no," said Wong smiling. "They're all faded, they're not worth looking at."

"Do you really carry the worst one around in your wallet?"

"Oh, no," Wong said.

"And did you show it to some women in a café?"

"They were so insistent," said Wong. "The worst of it was they didn't understand at all."

"Let me see it," said Oliveira, putting out his hand.

Wong began to look at the hand, smiling. Oliveira was too drunk to insist. He drank some more vodka and shifted his position. A piece of paper folded four times was placed in his hand. Instead of Wong he saw a kind of Cheshire cat smiling, sort of bowing in all the smoke. The post must have been six feet high, but there were eight posts, except that it was the same post repeated eight times in four series of two photos each, which went from left to right and from top to bottom, the post was the same in spite of slight differences in focus, all that was different was the prisoner tied to the post, the faces of the people around (there was a woman on the left) and the position of the executioner, standing to the left out of deference to the photographer, some American or Danish ethnologist who had a firm hand but a bad camera, an ancient Kodak that took bad pictures, so that except for the second picture, where the choice of knives had indicated work on the right ear, and the rest of the naked body could be seen clearly, the other pictures, because of the blood which was beginning to cover the body and the poor quality of the film or the development, were rather disappointing, especially from the fourth one on, in which the prisoner appeared as a blackish mass on which one could make out an open mouth and a very white arm, and the three last pictures were practically the same except for the position of the executioner, in the sixth picture crouching next to his bag of knives, taking out one at random (but he must have been cheating, because if he was going to begin with the deepest cuts . . .), and looking more closely one could see that the victim was alive because one foot was sticking out in spite of the pressure of his bonds, and his head was thrown back, his mouth still open, on the ground Chinese gentility must have spread an abundant amount of sawdust because the pool was no bigger, it made an almost perfect oval around the post. "The seventh is the critical one," Wong's voice came out from behind the vodka and the smoke, and one had to look closely because blood was pouring out around the breasts which had been deeply excised (between the second and third pictures), but one could see in the seventh that a decisive cut had been made because the shape of the thighs which had been turned outward a bit had changed, and if one brought the picture up close one could see that the change was not in the thighs but in the groin, instead of the hazy splotch in the first picture it looked like something pouring out of a hole, something like a little girl who has been raped, with blood flowing down her thighs. And if Wong did not think highly of the eighth picture he must have been right because the victim could not have been alive any more, no one lets his head fall to the side that way. "According to what I have been told the whole operation took an hour and a half," Wong observed with ceremony. The piece of paper was folded in four, a black leather wallet opened its mouth like a crocodile and gobbled it up from amidst the smoke. "Of course, Peking is not what it used to be. I'm sorry I showed you something so primitive, but one cannot carry certain other documents in one's wallet, there have to be explanations, an initiation . . . " His voice came from so far away it seemed to be a prolongation of the images, the gloss of a ceremonious scholar. Above or below, Big Bill Broonzy had begun to chant *See, See, Rider*, and as always everything came together from the unreconcilable forms, a grotesque collage which made its adjustments with vodka and Kantian categories, those tranquillizers against any too sharp coagulation of reality. Or as almost always happened, closing one's eyes and going back, to the cottony world of any other night chosen carefully among the cards of the open deck. "See, see, rider," Big Bill was singing, another corpse, "see what you have done."

(–114)

15

It was so natural for him to remember then that night on the Saint-Martin canal, the proposition they had made him (1,000 francs) to see a film at the home of a Swiss doctor. During the war an Axis surgeon had arranged to film a hanging in all of its details. Two rolls in all, but silent. However, the photography was excellent, they swore. You could pay on the way out.

In the moment necessary to resolve it all and say no and leave the café with the Haitian girl who knew the friend of the Swiss doctor, he had had time to imagine the scene and put himself as always on the side of the victim. There was no reason to waste words on the hanging of whoever-he-was, but if that somebody had known (and the refinement could have been precisely in telling him so) that a camera was going to record every moment of his grimaces and twistings for the pleasure of future dilettantes . . . "No matter how it hurts me, I shall never be indifferent like Étienne," Oliveira thought. "What it amounts to is that I insist on the unheard-of idea that man was meant for something else. Then, of course . . . What poor tools we have to find a way out of this dungeon." The worst was that he had looked at Wong's picture with coldness only because the one they were torturing had not been his father, to say nothing of the forty years that had passed since it all took place in Peking.

"Look," Oliveira told Babs, who had come back to him after having quarrelled with Ronald, who had insisted on listening to Ma Rainey and had put Fats Waller down, "it's incredible how bastardly we can get. What did Christ think about before he fell asleep? Suddenly in the midst of a smile your mouth can turn into a big hairy spider."

"Oh, no," said Babs. "Not delirium tremens at this time of night."

"It's all superficial, baby, everything is epi-der-mic. Look, when I was a kid I used to drag them out for all the old ladies in the family, sisters and all that, the whole genealogical mess, you know why?

Well, all kinds of silly reasons, but among them because for those ladies when anyone passed on, as they would say, any kick-off which took place in their circle was much more important than a war, an earthquake which kills ten thousand people, things like that. We're cretins, but such cretins it's hard to imagine, Babs, because to come to this we've had to read Plato, the Church Fathers, the classics, without overlooking a single one, and beyond that to know everything that can be known about the knowable, and that's the precise moment that one arrives at a cretinism so incredible that he's capable of grabbing his poor illiterate mother by her shawl and blowing his top over the fact that she is upset by the death of the Jew on the corner or the girl on the third floor. And you talk to her about the earthquake in Bab-el-Mandeb or the offensive at Vardar Ingh, and you think the poor devil feels any abstract pity for the liquidation of three divisions of the Iranian army . . . ?"

"Take it easy," Babs said in English. "Have a drink, sonny, and don't be such a murder to me."

"And what it really comes down to is a case of eyes that can't see . . . Why, tell me why we must beat old ladies about the head with our puritan adolescence of shitty little cretins? Oh, brother, I'm stewed. I'm going home."

But it was hard for him to give up the warm Eskimo pelt, the distant and almost indifferent contemplation of Gregorovius as he plied La Maga with his sentimental interview. Breaking away from everything as if he were plucking a cadaverous old rooster who had resisted to the last in the name of the cock he once had been, he let out a sigh of relief on hearing the theme of *Blue Interlude*, a record he had once owned in Buenos Aires. He couldn't remember all of them, but he did know that Benny Cartel was on it and maybe Chu Berry, and hearing the difficult simplicity of Teddy Wilson in his solo, he decided to wait for the end of the record. Wong had said it was raining; it had been raining all day. That must be Chu Berry, unless it was Coleman Hawkins in person, but no, it wasn't Hawk. "It's incredible how we're cheating ourselves," thought Oliveira looking at La Maga who was looking at Gregorovius who was looking at the air. "We'll end up going to the Bibliothèque Mazarine to take notes on mandrakes, Bantu necklaces, or the comparative history of nail clippers." Think of a repertory of insignificant things, the enormous work which goes into studying them and gaining a basic knowledge of them. A history of nail clippers, two thousand volumes to acquire the certain knowledge that until 1675 these small things had never received any mention. Suddenly in Mainz someone does a picture of a woman cutting a nail. It is not exactly a pair of nail clippers, but it looks like it. In the eighteenth century a certain Philip McKinney of Baltimore patents the first nail clippers with a spring attached: the problem is solved, the fingers can squeeze with all their strength to cut toenails, incredibly tough, and the clippers will snap back automatically. Five hundred notes, a year of work. If we were to turn now to the invention of the screw or to the use of the verb *gond* in eighteenth-century Pali literature. Anything would be more interesting than to guess the conversation between La Maga and Gregorovius. To find a barricade, anything, Benny Carter, nail clippers, the verb *gond*, another drink, a ceremonial impalement conducted carefully by an executioner attentive to the smallest details, or Champion Jack Dupree lost in the blues, a better barricade than he because (and the needle was making a horrible noise)

> Say goodbye, goodbye to whiskey
> Lordy, so long to gin,
> Say goodbye, goodbye to whiskey
> Lordy, so long to gin.
> I just want my reefers,
> I just want to feel high again –

So that in all certainty Ronald would come back to Big Bill Broonzy, led by associations Oliveira knew about and respected, and Big Bill would tell them about another barricade with the same voice that La Maga was using to tell Gregorovius about her childhood in Montevideo, Big Bill without bitterness, "matter of fact",

> They said if you white, you all right,
> If you brown, stick aroun',
> But as you black,
> Mm, mm, brother, get back, get back, get back.

"I know already that nothing can come of it," said Gregorovius. "Memories only change the least interesting part of the past."

"Yes, nothing can come of it," La Maga said.

"That's why if I asked you to tell me about Montevideo it was because you're like a queen of hearts to me, all front, no substance. I put it that way so that you'll understand me."

"And Montevideo is the substance . . . Nonsense, nonsense, nonsense. What do you call the past? As far as I'm concerned everything that has happened to me happened yesterday, last night, no earlier."

"So much the better," said Gregorovius. "Now you're a queen only not of hearts."

"It wasn't so long ago for me. It's far away, very far away, but not so long ago. The arcades of the Plaza Independencia, you know them too, Horacio, that sad square with all those restaurants, knowing there had been a killing that afternoon, the newsboys selling their papers in and out of the arcade."

"The lottery and all its prizes," Horacio said.

"The woman carved up in El Salto, politics, soccer . . . "

"The boat to the racetrack, a drink of Ancap brandy. Local colour, eh."

"It must have been quite exotic," said Gregorovius, putting himself in a position so that he would block off Oliveira's view and be more alone with La Maga, who was looking at the candles and keeping time with her foot.

"There was no such thing as time in Montevideo in those days," La Maga said. "We used to live near the river, in a large house with a courtyard. I was always thirteen years old, I remember it so well. A blue sky, thirteen years old, my school teacher was cross-eyed. One day I fell in love with a blond boy who sold newspapers in the square. He had a way of saying 'paypuh' that made me feel empty somewhere here . . . He wore long pants but he couldn't have been more than twelve. My father was not working then and spent the afternoons drinking *mate* in the courtyard. I lost my mother when I was five years old, some aunts brought me up but they went to the country later on. When I was thirteen there were only my father and I at home. It was a kind of tenement, not a home. There was an Italian, two old women, and a Negro and his wife who fought at night but later on would play the guitar and sing. The Negro had red eyes, like a wet mouth. I didn't like them very much and preferred to play in the street. If my father found me playing in the street he made me come in and would spank me. One day while he was spanking me I saw the Negro peeking through his half-opened door. At first I didn't really catch on, I thought he was scratching his leg, something he was doing with his hand . . . Father was too busy hitting me with a belt. It's funny how you can lose your innocence all at once, without even knowing that you've passed into another existence. That night in the kitchen the Negro couple sang until quite late. I was in my room and I had cried so much that I was terribly thirsty, but I didn't want to leave my room. My father was drinking *mate* in the doorway. You can't imagine how hot it was because you're all from cold countries. It was the humidity that was bad there near the river, I think it's worse in Buenos Aires, Horacio has told me it's worse, I don't know. That night my clothes stuck to me, everybody was drinking *mate* that night, two or three times I went out and got a drink from the tap in the courtyard among the geraniums. I had the idea that water from that tap was cooler. There wasn't a star in the sky, the geraniums had a harsh smell about them, they're vulgar plants, very beautiful, you have to stroke a geranium leaf. The lights were out in the other rooms already and father had gone out to the bar run by one-eyed Ramos, and I went into the courtyard and there was the empty *mate* gourd he always left by the door so that the tramps from the lot next door would not steal it. I remember that when I crossed the courtyard the moon came out a little and I stopped to look at it, the moon always made me feel coldish, and I made a face that could be seen from the stars, I believed in such things, I was only thirteen. Then I drank some more from the tap and went back to my room upstairs, climbing up an iron staircase where once I had sprained my ankle when I was nine years old. When I was about to light the candle on my night-table a hot hand grabbed my shoulder, I heard the door close, another hand covered my mouth, and I began to notice Negro smell, the Negro was pawing me all over and whispering things in my ear, slobbering on my face, pulling off my clothes, and there was nothing I could do, not even scream because I knew he would kill me if I screamed and I didn't want him to kill me, anything would have been better than that, to die would have been the worst offence, the most complete stupidity. Why are you looking at me like that, Horacio? I'm telling how the Negro in the tenement raped me, Gregorovius did so want to know how I lived in Uruguay."

"Don't spare us any details," said Oliveira.

"Oh, a general idea is enough," said Gregorovius.

"There's no such thing as a general idea," Oliveira said.

(–120)

16

"When he left my room it was almost dawn and I didn't even know how to cry any more."

"The dirty bastard," Babs said.

"Oh, La Maga richly deserved that homage," said Étienne. "The only funny thing, as always, is the diabolical separation of form and content. Everything you've said is exactly the same as what happens between lovers, except for the slight resistance and the probably stronger aggression."

"Chapter 8, Section 4, Paragraph A," Oliveira said. "*Presses Universitaires Françaises.*"

"*Ta gueule,*" said Étienne.

"Let's cap it off," Ronald said. "It's about time we heard something like *Hot and Bothered.*"

"A proper title for the reminiscences we've just heard," said Oliveira, lifting up his glass. "That Negro was quite a guy."

"It's not a subject for jokes," Gregorovius said.

"You were the one who dragged it out, friend."

"And you're drunk, Horacio."

"Of course. It's the great moment, the lucid moment. You, child, should have got a job in some gerontological clinic. Just look at Ossip, your pleasant recollections have taken twenty years off him."

"He dragged it out," said La Maga resentfully. "Now he'll start saying how he didn't enjoy it. Give me a vodka, Horacio."

But Oliveira didn't seem disposed to get mixed up with La Maga and Gregorovius, who was muttering explanations that she was barely listening to. Wong got more of his attention as he offered to make some coffee. Very hot and very strong, a secret he had learned at the casino in Menton. The Club applauded unanimously. Ronald lovingly kissed the label on one record, started the turntable, put the needle on in a ritualistic sort of way. For a moment the Ellington machine obliterated them with that fabulous sparring between trumpet and Baby Cox, the subtle and easygoing entrance of Johnny Hodges, the crescendo (but the rhythm was already getting to be a little stiff after thirty years, an old tiger who could still ripple) with riffs which were both tense and loose at the same time, a difficult minor miracle: "I swing, therefore I am." Leaning against the Eskimo pelt, looking at the green candles through his glass of vodka (we used to go to look at the fish on the Quai de la Mégisserie) it was almost easy to come to the conclusion that what was called reality deserved that disparaging phrase of the Duke's, "It don't mean a thing if it ain't got that swing," but why had the hand of Gregorovius stopped caressing La Maga's hair, there was poor Ossip, sleeker than a seal, all broken up by that distant deflowering, it was pitiful to look at him, so tense in that atmosphere where the music was breaking down resistance and was weaving everything into a kind of common breathing, the peace of an enormous heart beating for all, drawing them all into itself. And now a cracked voice, making its way out of a worn-out record, suggesting unknowingly that old Renaissance invitation, that old Anacreontic sadness, a *carpe diem* from Chicago, 1922.

> You so beautiful but you gotta die some day,
> You so beautiful but you gotta die some day,
> All I want's a little lovin' before you pass away.

Every so often the words of the dead fit the thoughts of the living (if the one group is living and the other is dead). You so beautiful. *Je ne veux pas mourir sans avoir compris pourquoi j'avais vécu.* A blues song, René Daumal, Horacio Oliveira, but you gotta die some day, you so beautiful but – And that's why Gregorovius insisted on knowing about La Maga's past, so that she would die a little less from that other backward-moving death composed entirely of things dragged along by time, so as to put her in her own time, you so beautiful but you gotta, so as not to love a ghost who lets her hair be stroked under a green light, poor Ossip, and how terrible the night was turning out, everything so incredibly so, Guy Monod's shoes, but you gotta die some day, Ireneo the Negro (later on, when she had more courage, La Maga would tell him about Ledesma, about the men at carnival-time, the saga of Montevideo). And suddenly with cool perfection, Earl Hines was giving his first variation of *I Ain't Got Nobody*, and even Perico, lost in some remote reading, lifted up his head and listened, La Maga had rested her head on Gregorovius's thigh and was looking at the floor, at the piece of Oriental rug, a red strand that disappeared into the socle, an empty glass next to a table-leg. She wanted to smoke but she wasn't going to ask Gregorovius for a cigarette, without knowing why she wasn't going to ask him, and she wasn't going to ask Horacio either, but she knew why she wasn't going to ask him, she didn't want to see his eyes as he laughed and again took revenge for her lying close to Gregorovius and for not having approached him all evening. Helpless, she thought sublime thoughts, quotations from poems which made her feel that she was in the very heart of the artichoke, on one side "I ain't got nobody, and nobody cares for me," which was not entirely true, because at least two people were present who were in a bad mood over her, and at the same time a line from Perse, something like "*Tu es là, mon amour, et je n'ai lieu qu'en toi,*" where La Maga took refuge snuggling up to the sound of *lieu*, of *Tu es là, mon amour*, the bland acceptance of a fate which made her shut her eyes and made her body feel like an offering, something that anybody could have and dirty and exalt like Ireneo, while Hines's music matched the red and blue spots which danced around behind her eyelids, which for some reason were called Volaná and Valené, Volaná on the left ("and nobody cares for me") spinning madly, Valené on top, hanging like a star in a pierodellafrancesca blue, *et je n'ai lieu qu'en toi*, Volaná and Valené, Ronald would never be able to play the piano like Earl Hines, Horacio and she should really own that record to listen to at night in the dark, to learn how to make love to the phrasing, those long, nervous caresses, "I ain't got nobody" on the back, on the shoulders, fingers behind the neck, nails working in and out of the hair, one last whirlwind and Valené merges with Volaná, *tu est là, mon amour* and nobody cares for me, Horacio was there but nobody bothered with her, nobody was petting her head, Valené and Volaná had disappeared and her eyelids hurt from having squeezed them together so tightly, she could hear Ronald talking and then the smell of coffee, ah, a wonderful smell of coffee, dear Wong, Wong Wong Wong.

She got up blinking, glanced at Gregorovius who looked like something spoiled and dirty. Someone passed her a cup.

(–137)

17

"I don't like to talk about him just for the sake of talking," La Maga said.

"That's all right," said Gregorovius. "I was just asking."

"If you just want to hear talking, I can talk about something else."

"Don't get annoyed."

"Horacio is like guava jelly," La Maga said.

"What's guava jelly?"

"Horacio is like a glass of water in a storm."

"Ah," said Gregorovius.

"He must have been born during that period Madame Léonie talks about when she's a little tipsy. A time when nobody was upset, when streetcars were pulled by horses and wars took place in open country. There were no such things as sleeping pills, Madame Léonie says."

"The beautiful golden age," said Gregorovius. "They told me about times like that too, in Odessa. My mother, so romantic, with her hair down . . . They kept pineapple plants on the balconies and at night there was no need for chamber pots, it was extraordinary. But I can't picture Horacio in those royal-jelly days."

"I can't either, but he wouldn't have been so sad. In these times everything hurts him, even aspirin hurts him. Really, last night I made him take an aspirin because he had a toothache. He grabbed it and started to look at it, it was terribly hard for him to decide to swallow it. He said funny things, that it was unhealthy to use things one really knew nothing about, things invented by other people to calm other things that we also know nothing about . . . You know how he is when he goes off on a tangent."

"You repeated the word 'thing' several times," Gregorovius said. "It's rather vulgar, but it does show, on the other hand, what's wrong with Horacio. Obviously a victim of thingness."

"What is thingness?" La Maga asked.

"Thingness is that unpleasant feeling that where our presumption ends our punishment begins. I'm sorry I have to use abstract and almost allegorical language, but I mean that Oliveira is pathologically sensitive to the pressure of what is around him, the world he lives in, his fate, to speak kindly. In a word, he can't stand his surroundings. More briefly, he has a world-ache. You had an inkling of it, Lucía, and with delightful innocence you felt that Oliveira would be happier in any of the pocket-sized Arcadias manufactured by the Madame Léonies of this world, not to mention my mother, the one in Odessa. Because you probably didn't believe that business about the pineapples, I suppose."

"Or the chamber pots either," said La Maga. "It's hard to believe."

Guy Monod decided to wake up when Ronald and Étienne agreed to listen to Jelly Roll Morton; opening one eye he decided that the back outlined in the light of the green candles must belong to Gregorovius. He shuddered, the green candles seen from a bed made a bad impression on him, the rain on the skylight was strangely mixed with the remnants of his dream-images, he had been dreaming about an absurdly sunny place, where Gaby was walking around nude and feeding crumbs to a group of stupid pigeons the size of ducks. "I have a headache," Guy said to himself. He was not in the least interested in Jelly Roll Morton although it was amusing to hear the rain on the skylight as Jelly Roll sang: "Stood on a corner, an' she was soakin' wet . . . " Wong would certainly have come up with a theory about real and poetic time, but was it true that Wong had mentioned making coffee? Gaby feeding the pigeons crumbs and Wong, the voice of Wong going in between Gaby's nude legs in a garden with brightly coloured flowers, saying: "A secret I learned in the casino at Menton." Quite possible, after all, that Wong would appear with a pot full of coffee.

Jelly Roll was at the piano beating the time softly with his foot for lack of a better rhythm section. Jelly Roll could sing *Mamie's Blues* rocking a little, staring up at some decoration on the ceiling, or it was a fly that came and went or a spot that came and went in Jelly Roll's eyes. "Eleven twenty-four took my baby away-ay . . . " That's what life had been, trains bringing people and taking them away while you stood on the corner with wet feet, listening to a pianola and laughter and beating on the yellow windows of the saloon where you didn't always have enough money to go in. "Eleven twenty-four took my baby away-ay . . . " Babs had taken so many trains in her life, she liked to go by train if in the end there was some friend waiting for her, if Ronald softly put his hand on her hip the way he was doing now, sketching out the music on her skin, "Eleven-thirteen'll carry her back one day," obviously some train would bring her back again, but who knows if Jelly Roll was going to be on that platform, at that piano, that time he sang the blues about Mamie Desdume, the rain on a Paris skylight at one o'clock in the morning, wet feet, and a whore who muttered "If you can't hand me a dollar then hand me a rotten dime," Babs had said things like that in Cincinnati, every woman had said things like that somewhere, even in the bed of a king, Babs had a very special idea of what the bed of a king was like but in any case some woman must have said something like, "If you can't give me a million, gimme a lousy grand," a matter of proportions, and why was Jelly Roll's piano so sad, so much that rain that woke Guy up, that was making La Maga cry, and Wong who wasn't coming with the coffee.

"It's too much," Étienne said, sighing. "I don't know why I stand for that rubbish. It's moving, but it's rubbish."

"It's no Pisanello medallion, of course," Oliveira said.

"Or opus whatever-you-want by Schoenberg," said Ronald. "Why did you want to hear it? Besides intelligence you also lack charity. Have you ever stood with your feet in a puddle at midnight? Jelly Roll has, you can tell when he sings, it's something you learn."

"I can paint better if my feet are dry," Étienne said. "And don't come around with any Salvation Army arguments. Why don't you put on something more intelligent, like those Sonny Rollins solos. At least those modern guys make you think of Jackson Pollock or Tobey, it's easy to see that they've left the age of the pianola and the box of watercolours."

"He's capable of believing in progress in art," Oliveira said yawning. "Don't pay any attention to him, Ronald, and with that hand you have free dig out that little record of the *Stack O'Lee Blues*, when all's said and done I think it has a fine piano solo on it."

"That business about progress in art is ancient nonsense," Étienne said, "but in jazz as in any art there's always a flock of fakers. Music that can be translated into emotion is one thing, but emotion which pretends to pass as music is another. Paternal grief in F sharp, sarcastic laughter in yellow, violet and black. No, my boy, it's hard to say where art begins, but it's never that stuff."

No one seemed disposed to contradict him because Wong had quietly appeared with the coffee and Ronald, shrugging his shoulders, had turned loose Fred Waring and his Pennsylvanians and after a terrible scratching they reached the theme that fascinated Oliveira, an anonymous trumpet followed by the piano, all wrapped up in the smoke of an old record-player and a bad recording, of a corny pre-jazz band, all in all like those old records, showboats, Storyville nights, where the old only really universal music of the century had come from, something that brought people closer together and in a better way than Esperanto, UNESCO or airlines, a music which was primitive enough to have gained such universality and good enough to make its own history, with schisms, abdications, and heresies, its Charleston, its Black Bottom, its Shimmy, its Fox Trot, its Stomp, its Blues, to label its forms, this style and the other one, swing, bebop, cool, a counterpoint of romanticism and classicism, hot and intellectual jazz, human music, music with a history in contrast to stupid animal dance music, the polka, the waltz, the *zamba*, a music that could be known and liked in Copenhagen as well as in Mendoza or Cape Town, a music that brings adolescents together, with records under their arms, that gives them names and melodies to use as passwords so they can know each other and become intimate and feel less lonely surrounded by bosses, families, and bitter love affairs, a music that accepts all imaginations and tastes, a collection of instrumental 78s with Freddie Keppard or Bunk Johnson, the reactionary cult of Dixieland, an academic specialization in Bix Beiderbecke, or in the adventures of Thelonious Monk, Horace Silver or Thad Jones, the vulgarities of Erroll Garner or Art Tatum, repentance and rejection, a preference for small groups, mysterious recordings with false names and strange titles and labels made up on the spur of the moment, and that whole freemasonry of Saturday nights in a student's room or in some basement café with girls who would rather dance to *Stardust* or *When Your Man Is Going to Put You Down*, and have a sweet slow smell of perfume and skin and heat, and let themselves be kissed when the hour is late and somebody has put on *The Blues with a Feeling* and hardly anybody is really dancing, just standing up together, swaying back and forth, and everything is hazy and dirty and lowdown and every man is in a mood to tear off those warm girdles as his hands go stroking shoulders and the girls have their mouths half-opened and turn themselves over to delightful fear and the night, while a trumpet comes on to possess them in the name of all men, taking them with a single hot phrase that drops them like a cut flower into the arms of their partners, and there comes a motionless race, a jump up into the night air, over the city, until a miniature piano brings them to again, exhausted, reconciled, and still virgins until next Saturday, all of this from a kind of music that horrifies solid citizens who think that nothing is true unless there are programmes and ushers, and that's the way things are and jazz is like a bird who migrates or emigrates or immigrates or transmigrates, roadblock jumper, smuggler, something that runs and mixes in and tonight in Vienna Ella Fitzgerald is singing while in Paris Kenny Clarke is helping open a new *cave* and in Perpignan Oscar Peterson's fingers are dancing around and Satchmo, everywhere, with that gift of omnipresence given him by the Lord, in Birmingham, in Warsaw, in Milan, in Buenos Aires, in Geneva, in the whole world, is inevitable, is rain and bread and salt, something completely beyond national ritual, sacred traditions, language and folklore: a cloud without frontiers, a spy of air and water, an archetypal form, something from before, from below, that brings Mexicans together with Norwegians and Russians and Spaniards, brings them back into that obscure and forgotten central flame, clumsily and badly and precariously he delivers them back to a betrayed origin, he shows them that perhaps there have been other paths and that the one they took was maybe not the only one or the best one, or that perhaps there have been other paths and that the one they took was the best, but that perhaps there were other paths that made for softer walking and that they had not taken those, or that they only took them in a halfway sort of way, and that a man is always more than a man and always less than a man, more than a man because he has in himself all that jazz suggests and lies in wait for and even anticipates, and less than a man because he has made an aesthetic and sterile game out of this liberty, a chessboard where one must be bishop or knight, a definition of liberty which is taught in schools, in the very schools where the pupils are never taught ragtime rhythm or the first notes of the blues, and so forth and so on.

> I could sit right here and think a thousand miles away,
> I could sit right here and think a thousand miles away,
> Since I had the blues this bad, I can't remember the day.

(–97)

18

There was no use asking himself what he was doing there at that time and with that group, those dear friends strangers still yesterday and tomorrow, people who were but a fleeting episode in place and time. Babs, Ronald, Ossip, Jelly Roll, Akhnaton: what difference did it make? The same shadows from the same green candles. A binge at its highest moment. Doubtful vodka, terribly strong.

If he could have conceived of an extrapolation of all this, understanding the Club, understanding the *Cold Wagon Blues*, understanding La Maga's love, understanding every thread that would become unravelled from the cuff of things and reach down to his fingers, every puppet and every puppeteer, like an epiphany; understanding them, not as symbols of some other unattainable reality perhaps, but as agents of potency (such language, such lack of decorum), just like lines of flight along a track that he ought to follow at this very moment, disentangling himself from the Eskimo pelt which was so delightfully warm and so scented and so Eskimo that it was frightening, getting down to the level of things, down, down in a solo flight, down to the corner, the corner all by itself, Max's café, Max all by himself, the streetlight on the Rue de Bellechase where . . . where alone. And maybe from that moment on.

But all on a level that could be called me-ta-phy-si-cal. Because Horacio, words . . . That is to say that words, for Horacio . . . (a question mulled over many times in moments of insomnia). Taking La Maga's hand, taking it in the rain as if it were cigarette smoke, something that is part of one, in the rain. To make love with her again but a little bit on her side, less easy indifference, a denial that at best is swamped by the uselessness of the effort, the straw man teaching algorithms in some hazy university to grubby swots or colonels' daughters. If all this, the predawn tapioca starting to stick to the skylight, La Maga's so sad face as she looked at Gregorovius looking at La Maga looking at Gregorovius, *Struttin' With Some Barbecue*, Babs who was crying again, hidden from Ronald who was not crying but who hid his face in the sticky smoke, the vodka transformed into a truly saintly halo, Perico the Spanish ghost up on a stool of disdain and Pavlovian stylistics, if everything were able to be extrapolated, if everything just *did not exist*, if he were there just so somebody (anybody, but he at the moment, because he was the one who was doing the thinking, in any case he was the one who knew that he was really thinking, eh, Cartesius, you old fuck), so that somebody could extract from all that was going on by striving and biting and especially by delving, it was hard to say how but by delving down to the very dregs, that out of all this there might pop up some grasshopper of peace, some cricket of contentment, that a person might be able to enter any gate and come into any garden, an allegorical garden as far as the others were concerned, just as mandalas are allegorical for everyone else, and in that garden he would find a flower and that flower would be La Maga, or Babs, or Wong, but described and describing itself, reconstituted outside their appearances among the Club, back to what they were, emerged, dawning, at best this all might be just a nostalgic view of the earthly paradise, an ideal of purity, except that purity had come to be inevitably the product of simplification, the bishop moves, rooks move, the knight jumps, pawns fall away, and in the centre of the board, big as anthracite lions the kings remain flanked by the cleanest and last and purest of their armies, at dawn the deciding lances will be crossed, fate will be served, peace will reign. A pureness as of coitus between crocodiles, not the pureness of oh Mary my mother with dirty feet; a pureness of a slate roof with doves who naturally shit on the heads of ladies wild with rage and radishes, a pureness of . . . Horacio, Horacio, please.

Pureness.

(Enough. Come on. Go home, take a bath, read *Our Lady of Paris* or *The She-Wolves of Machecoul*, finish your binge. Extrapolation, what a word.)

Pureness. Horrible word. Pea-your, then ness. Think about it a bit. Brisset and his plays on words. Why are you crying? Who's crying, huh?

Pea-your, understand it like an epiphany. Damn language. To understand. Not to make sense: to understand. A hint of a paradise that can be won again: it cannot be that we are here in order not to be. Brisset? Man descends from the level of the frogs . . . Blind as a bat, drunk as a butterfly, *foutu, royalement foutu devant les portes que peut-être* . . . (An ice-cube on the back of his neck, go to bed. Problem: Johnny Dodds or Albert Nicholas? Dodds, he was almost sure of it. Note: ask Ronald.) A bad line of poetry floating down from the skylight: "*Antes de caer en la nada con el último diástole* . . . " High as a kite. The doors of perception by Aldley Huxdous. Get yourself a tiny bit of mescaline, brother, the rest is bliss and diarrhoea (all in English). But let's get serious (yes, it was Johnny Dodds, you find the proof by indirection. The drummer had to be Zutty Singleton, ergo the clarinet is Johnny Dodds, jazzology, deductive science, particularly easy after four o'clock in the morning. Hardly advisable for ladies and clerics). Let's get serious, Horacio, before we struggle up in a while and head for the street, let's ask ourselves a question while we have our soul in the palm of our hand (the palm of the hand? In the palm of our tongue, or something like that. Toponymy, anatology, descriptology, two volumes with il-lus-tra-tions), let's ask whether we should attack from above or from below (but, hey now, I'm making sense, the vodka has pinned them like butterflies onto a tray, A is A, a rose is a rose is a rose, April is the cruellest month, everything in its place and a place for every rose is a rose is a rose . . .)

Huf. Beware the Jabberwocky my son.

Horacio slid down a little more and saw very clearly everything he wanted to see. He wasn't sure whether he should attack from above or from below, with a concentration of all his forces or rather as now, dispersed and liquid, full forward to the skylight, against the green candles, or to La Maga's sad, sheeplike face, or against Ma Rainey who was singing *Jelly Bean Blues*. Better this way, spread out and receptive, spongy, the way everything is spongy as long as a person looks a lot and has good eyes. He wasn't so drunk that he didn't have the feeling that his house was a shambles, that inside nothing was in place but at the same time – to be sure, marvellously sure – on the floor or on the ceiling, under the bed or floating in a washbasin there were stars and chunks of eternity, poems like suns and enormous faces of women and cats where the fury of their species was fired up, in the mixture of garbage and jade plaques in their own language where words were woven night and day into furious battles between ants and centipedes, blasphemy existed with the pure mention of essences, the perfect image with the basest slang. Disorder was triumphant and ran through the rooms with its hair entangled in disgusting braids, glass eyes, its hands holding cards that would not meld, letters without heading or signature, and the soup was getting cold upon the table, the floor was covered with cast-off pants, rotten apples, stained bandages. And suddenly from all this there came some horrid music, it was beyond the felted order of homes where untouchable kin put things in order, in the midst of the confusion where the past was incapable of finding a button on a shirt and the present shaved itself with pieces of a broken bottle because it could not find a razor stuck away somewhere in some flowerpot, in the midst of a time which opened up like a weather vane to whatever wind was blowing, a man breathed until he could no longer do so, he felt that he had lived until he reached the delirium of the very act of taking in the confusion which surrounded him and he asked himself if any of this had meaning. All disorder had meaning if it seemed to come out of itself, perhaps through madness one could arrive at that reason which is not the reason whose weakness is madness. "To go from disorder to order," thought Oliveira. "Yes, but what kind of order can there be which does not mimic the basest, most debased, and most unhealthy of disorders? The order of the gods is called cyclone or leukaemia, the poet's order is called antimatter, firm space, flowers of trembling lips, God, I'm drunk, Jesus, I've got to get to bed." And La Maga was crying, Guy had disappeared, Étienne had left after Perico, and Gregorovius, Wong and Ronald were looking at a record that was spinning slowly, thirty-three and a third revolutions per minute, no more no less, and in these revolutions there was *Oscar's Blues*, Oscar himself on piano, of course, a certain Oscar Peterson, a certain pianist half tiger, half felt, a certain sad, fat pianist, a guy on piano and the rain on the skylight, all those things, literature, after all.

(–153)

19

"I think I understand you," La Maga said, running her hand through his hair. "You're looking for something you don't know. I've been doing the same thing and I don't know what it is either. But they're two different things. What you were talking about the other night . . . Yes, you're a Mondrian and I'm a Vieira da Silva."

"So," Oliveira said, "I'm a Mondrian after all."

"Yes, Horacio."

"You meant to say someone of a rigorous nature."

"I said a Mondrian."

"And didn't it occur to you that behind this Mondrian there might lurk a Vieira da Silva reality?"

"Yes, but up till now you haven't come out of the Mondrian reality. You're afraid, you want to be sure of yourself. I don't know . . . You're more like a doctor than a poet."

"Forget about poets," Oliveira said. "And don't try to hurt Mondrian with the comparison."

"Mondrian is wonderful, but he doesn't let you breathe. I always strangle a little bit inside. And when you start talking about the search for unity, then I start to see a lot of beautiful things, but they're all dead, pressed flowers and things like that."

"Let's see, Lucía: are you quite sure what unity is?"

"My name is Lucía but you don't have to call me that," La Maga said. "Unity, of course I know what it is. You're trying to say that everything in your life comes together so that you can see it all at the same time. Is that what you mean?"

"More or less," Oliveira conceded. "It's incredible how hard it is for you to grasp abstract ideas. Unity, plurality . . . Can't you feel them without feeling the need for examples? Can't you? Let's see, now: your life, do you think it is a unity?"

"No, I don't think so. It's pieces, things that happened to me."

"But you in turn went through those things like the string went through those green stones. And speaking of stones, where did you get that necklace?"

"Ossip gave it to me," La Maga said. "It was his mother's, the one from Odessa."

Oliveira sucked slowly on his *mate*. La Maga went over to the cot that Ronald had lent them so that they could have Rocamadour in the apartment. With the cot and Rocamadour and the complaints of the tenants there was barely any living-space left, but nobody could tell La Maga that Rocamadour would have been better off in a children's hospital. It had been necessary to go with her to the country the same day that Madame Irène had sent the telegram, wrap Rocamadour up in a bunch of rags and blankets, put him to bed, stoke up the fire in the stove, tolerate Rocamadour's wailing when the time came for a suppository or a pill or the bottle which was useless in covering up the taste of the medicine he had to take. Oliveira made himself another *mate* and out of the corner of his eye looked at the cover of a *Deutsche Grammophon Gesellschaft* that Ronald had lent him, wondering when he could listen to it without getting Rocamadour wailing and twisting. He was horrified by La Maga's laziness with Rocamadour's nappies, the way she would sing at him to distract him, the smell that emanated from his bed, cotton, wails, the stupid assurance of La Maga that it wasn't anything, that if she did what she should for her son he would be all right in a matter of days. It made no sense, it was all maybe, maybe not. What was he doing there? A month ago they both had had their places still, even after they had decided to live together. La Maga had said that they could save money this way, they only had to buy one paper a day, they wouldn't waste food. She could iron his clothes, and heat, electricity . . . Oliveira had been about to admire that brusque attack on common sense. He finally accepted because old Trouille was having troubles and owed him close to thirty thousand francs, at the time it seemed just as logical to live with La Maga as by himself, he had been walking around thinking about every detail and pondering every little thing that seemed to come upon him like a great crisis. He had come to the conclusion that the continuous presence of La Maga would stop him from speculating so much, but naturally he had not thought about the possibilities of Rocamadour. Even so, he had been able to keep to himself from time to time, until Rocamadour's howls would bring him back to a healthy grouchiness. "I'm going to end up like a character out of Walter Pater," Oliveira would think to himself. "One soliloquy after another, an endless vice. Marius the Epicurean, 'pure vice'. The only salvation left to me is the smell of that brat's piss."

"I always suspected you would end up going to bed with Ossip," Oliveira said.

"Rocamadour has a fever," La Maga said.

Oliveira made himself another *mate*. He had to watch out for his *mate*, in Paris it cost five hundred francs a kilo in chemists and it was terrible stuff, sold in the pharmacy of Saint-Lazare station next to a gaudy sign that said "*maté sauvage, cueilli par les indiens*", diuretic, antibiotic, and emollient. Luckily the lawyer from Rosario, who happened to be his brother, had sent him ten pounds of Cruz de Malta brand, but there wasn't much left. "If my *mate* runs out I've had it," Oliveira thought. "My only real conversation is with this green gourd." He studied the strange behaviour of the *mate*, how the herb would breathe fragrantly as it came up on top of the water and how it would dive as he sucked and would cling to itself, everything fine lost and all smell except for that little bit that would come up in the water like breath and stimulate his Argentinian iron lung, so sad and solitary. It had been some time now that Oliveira had been paying attention to unimportant things, and the little green gourd had the advantage that as he meditated upon it, it never occurred to his perfidious intelligence to endow it with such ideas as one extracts from mountains, the moon, the horizon, an adolescent girl, a bird, or a horse. "This *mate* might show me where the centre is," Oliveira thought (and the idea that La Maga and Ossip were seeing each other became frail and lost its strength, for a moment the green gourd was stronger, it proposed its own little petulant volcano, its smoky crater; an atmosphere which hovered over the other rather cold air of the flat in spite of the stove that had been lit around nine o'clock that night). "And just what is this centre that I don't know what it really is; can it be the coordinates of some unity? I'm walking back and forth in an apartment whose floor is tiled with flat stones and one of these stones is the exact spot where I ought to stop so that everything would come into its proper focus. The exact spot," Oliveira said emphatically, kidding himself a little so as to know that he was not just playing with words. "A shapeless quadrilateral in which we must look for the precise angle (and the importance of this example is that the angel is horribly a cute and won must have his knows right up on to the canvas so that suddenly all the senseless lines will come together to form a portrait of Francis I or the Battle of Sinigaglia, something that deflies descrumption)." But that unity, the sum of all the actions which define a life, seemed to go into hiding in the face of any previous sign that life itself could end like a played-out drink of *mate*, that is to say that only those left behind, the biographers, would recognize the unity, and all that was really not of the least importance as far as Oliveira was concerned. The problem consisted in grasping that unity without becoming a hero, without becoming a saint, or a criminal, or a boxing champ, or a statesman, or a shepherd. To grasp unity in the midst of diversity, so that that unity might be the vortex of a whirlwind and not the sediment in a clean, cold *mate* gourd.

"I'm going to give him a quarter of an aspirin," La Maga said.

"If you can make him take it you'll be better than Ambroise Paré," said Oliveira. "Come and have a *mate*, I just made some."

The idea of unity was worrying him because it seemed so easy to fall into the worst traps. When he had been a student on the Calle Viamonte around 1930, he had found out (first) to his surprise and (later) with irony, that an awful lot of people would set themselves up comfortably in a supposed unity of person which was nothing but a linguistic unity and a premature sclerosis of character. These people would set up a system of principles which had never been fundamentally proven, and which were nothing more than a concession to the word itself, to a verbal idea of strength; rejection and attraction were subjected, displaced, got out of the way, then replaced by their verbal equivalents. And in this way duty, morals, the immoral and the amoral, justice, charity, the European and the American, day and night, wives, sweethearts, and girlfriends, the army and the bar, the flag and Yankee or Moscow gold, abstract art and the Battle of Caseros came to be like teeth and hair, something accepted and inevitably incorporated, something which was not alive or capable of being analysed because *that's the way it is* and it makes us what we are, fulfils and strengthens. Man's rape by word, the masterful vengeance of word upon its progenitor, all this filled Oliveira's thoughts with bitter lack of confidence, forced to seek help from the enemy itself to open a path to the point where he might just be able to be dismissed and follow it – but with what means on what clear night or shady day? – until he could reach a complete reconciliation with himself and with the reality in which he lived. To arrive at the word without words (how far, how improbable), to grasp a deep unity without recourse to reasoning conscience, something that when all was said and done would be like sitting there sipping *mate* and looking at Rocamadour's little bottom up in the air as La Maga's fingers came and went with bits of cotton, and Rocamadour wailed because he could not stand being plucked at.

(–90)

20

"I always suspected you'd end up going to bed with him," Oliveira said.

La Maga put a clean nappy on her son, who was not bleating as much now, and wiped her hands with a piece of cotton wool.

"Please wash your hands like a civilized person," Oliveira said, "and get rid of all that crap."

"Right away," La Maga said. Oliveira was able to stand her look (which was always hard on him) and La Maga got a newspaper, opened it up on the bed, put in the cotton wool, bundled it up, and left the room to go and throw it down the toilet on the landing. When she came back her hands were red and shining; Oliveira handed her the gourd. She sat down on the low easy chair and sucked the *mate* in a deliberate sort of way. She always damaged the gourd, moving the straw around from one side to another as if she were mixing batter.

"After all," Oliveira said, blowing smoke through his nose, "the least you could have done was to tell me. Now it's going to cost me six hundred francs to hire a taxi to move my stuff. And it's not easy finding a room these days, either."

"You don't have to move out," La Maga said. "How long do you plan to go on lying to yourself?"

"Lying to yourself," Oliveira said. "You sound like a bestselling novel from the Río de la Plata. All you have to do now is laugh with all the force of your insides at my unparalleled boorishness, and we can put it all in print."

"He's stopped crying," La Maga said, looking at the bed. "Let's speak quietly, he'll go to sleep quite easily with the aspirin. I never in my life went to bed with Gregorovius."

"Oh yes you did."

"No, Horacio. Why wouldn't I have told you? Ever since I met you I haven't had any other lover but you. I don't care if I sound stupid and you laugh at the way I say it. I speak the best way I can, I don't know how to say what I feel."

"OK, OK," Oliveira said in a tired tone, having another *mate.* "Maybe your son has changed you then. For some time now you've been converted into what they call a mother."

"But Rocamadour is sick."

"All right," Oliveira said, "if that's the way you want it. But I see a different kind of change. Really, it's that we can't stand much of each other any more."

"You're the one who can't stand me. You're the one who can't stand Rocamadour."

"That's true. I hadn't thought about the boy. Three is too many for one room. And to think that with Ossip it will be four is more than I can take."

"Ossip has nothing to do with this."

"Please put the kettle on," Oliveira said.

"He has nothing to do with this," La Maga repeated. "Why do you want to make me suffer, silly? I know you're tired of me and don't love me any more. You never did love me, it was something else, some kind of dream you had. Leave, Horacio, you don't have to stay. The same thing has happened to me so many times . . . "

She looked over at the bed. Rocamadour was asleep.

"So many times," Oliveira said, putting fresh *yerba mate* into his gourd. "You have a remarkable frankness when it comes to amorous autobiography. Just ask Ossip. To meet you and hear the story about the Negro is one and the same thing."

"I have to tell it, you don't understand."

"I don't understand, but it's awful."

"I think I have to tell it even if it is awful. It's only right that a woman tell a man what her life has been like if she wants to. I'm talking about you, not Ossip. You could have told me about your girlfriends or not if you wanted to, but I had to tell everything. You know, it's the only way to get rid of a man before you start to fall in love with someone else, the only way to get them out the door so the two of us can be alone in the room."

"A kind of ceremony of expiation, and maybe propitiatory too. First the Negro."

"Yes," La Maga said, looking at him. "First the Negro. Then Ledesma."

"Then Ledesma, of course."

"And the three up the alley, on carnival night."

"Ahead," said Oliveira, sipping his *mate*, as he remembered an obscene game he played as a boy in Buenos Aires and kept it up to show his exasperation.

"And Monsieur Vincent, the hotel keeper's brother."

"Behind."

"And a soldier who was weeping in a park."

"Ahead."

"And you."

"Behind. But the idea of putting me on the list in my presence just bears out my gloomiest premonitions. You really should have recited the complete list to Gregorovius."

La Maga stirred with the straw. She had lowered her head and her hair fell over her face all at once, covering up the expression that Oliveira had been studying with an indifferent air.

> *Después fuiste la amiguita*
> *de un viejo boticario*
> *y el hijo de un comisario*
> *todo el vento te sacó*

Oliveira was singing the old tango in a low voice. La Maga sucked on the straw and shrugged her shoulders, not looking at him. "Poor thing," Oliveira thought. He reached out his hand and drew her hair back, brutally, as if opening a curtain. The straw made a dry sound between her teeth.

"It's almost as if you had slapped me," La Maga said, putting two fingers to her trembling lips. "I really don't care, but . . ."

"You just do happen to care," Oliveira said. "If you hadn't been looking at me like that I would have despised you. You're a marvel, Rocamadour and everything."

"What good is it for me for you to say that?"

"It's good for me."

"Yes, it's good for you. Everything's good for you if it helps you keep on searching."

"Sweet," Oliveira said softly, "it's a known fact that tears ruin the taste of *mate*."

"Maybe my crying is good for you too."

"Yes, it is as long as you hold me to blame."

"Go away, Horacio, that's the best thing."

"It probably is. But look, anyway, if I leave now I will be committing an act that would be awfully close to heroism, I mean, leaving you alone and with a sick child."

"Yes," La Maga said with a Homeric smile coming out from behind her tears. "Awfully close to heroism, yes."

"And since I'm by no stretch a hero, I think I'd better stay until we find out what we can adjust ourselves to, as my brother says in his elegant style."

"Stay then."

"But you do understand how and why I reject that heroic course?"

"Yes, certainly."

"Come on, explain to me why I'm not leaving."

"You're not leaving because you're just bourgeois enough to think what Ronald and Babs and your other friends would say."

"Precisely. I'm glad you see that you didn't figure in my decision at all. I'm not staying out of friendship or out of pity or because someone has to give Rocamadour his bottle. And much less because you and I still have something in common."

"You're so funny sometimes," La Maga said.

"Sure I am," Oliveira said. "Bob Hope is just a turd next to me."

"When you said that we didn't have anything in common any more, you held your mouth in a certain way."

"Sort of like this, eh?"

"Yes, it's incredible."

They had to take out their handkerchiefs and cover their faces with both hands, they let out such loud guffaws that Rocamadour might wake up, it was something terrible. Although Oliveira tried to hold her, biting his handkerchief and weeping with laughter, La Maga slowly slipped out of the chair which had the front legs shorter than the rear ones and so helped her slide down until she was on the floor caught between Oliveira's legs as he laughed with a sort of jerky hiccup and finally spit out the handkerchief in one last burst.

"Show me the face again, the one I make when I say things like that," Oliveira begged.

"Like this," La Maga said and again they rolled around until Oliveira doubled over holding his stomach, and La Maga saw his face opposite hers, and his eyes shining at her among the tears.

They kissed backwards, she face up and he with his hair hanging down like a fringe, they kissed and bit each other a little because their mouths did not recognize one another, they were kissing different mouths, trying to find each other with their hands in a devilish mess of hanging hair and *mate*, which was dripping onto La Maga's skirt from the gourd which had tipped over on the edge of the table.

"Tell me how Ossip makes love," Oliveira whispered, putting his lips hard against La Maga's. "The blood is rushing to my head, I can't do this much longer, it's frightening."

"He does it very well," La Maga said, biting his lip. "Much better than you and much longer."

"But does he retilate your murt? Don't lie to me. Does he really retilate it?"

"A lot. Everywhere, sometimes too much. It's a wonderful feeling."

"And does he make you put your plinnies in between his argusts?"

"Yes, and then we trewst our porcies until he says he's had enough, and I can't take it any more either, and we have to hurry up, you understand. But you wouldn't understand that, you always stay in the smallest gumphy."

"Me or anybody else," Oliveira grumbled, getting up. "Christ, this *mate* is lousy, I'm going out for a while."

"Don't you want me to keep on talking to you of Ossip?" said La Maga. "In Gliglish."

"I'm getting sick of Gliglish. Besides, you haven't got any imagination, you always say the same things. Gumphy, some invention that is. And you don't say 'talking to you of'."

"I invented Gliglish," La Maga said resentfully. "You come out with anything you want and sound like a million dollars, but that's not real Gliglish."

"Getting back to Ossip . . . "

"Don't be silly, Horacio, I tell you I have not gone to bed with him. Do I have to give you the sacred oath of the Sioux Indians?"

"No, I think I'm finally beginning to believe you."

"And later on," La Maga said, "I'll probably end up sleeping with Ossip, but you'll be the one who wanted it all along."

"But do you really think you could like that guy?"

"No. The fact is I owe money at the chemist's. I don't want a penny from you, and I can't borrow money from Ossip and just leave him with his illusions intact."

"I see now," Oliveira said. "Your good Samaritan side is coming out. You couldn't leave that soldier crying in the park either."

"No I couldn't, Horacio. You can see how different we are."

"Yes, pity was never one of my strong points. But I could have been crying at a time like that too, and then you would have . . ."

"I can't picture you crying," La Maga said. "You'd consider it a waste."

"I've cried in the past."

"Only from rage. You don't know how to cry, Horacio, it's one of those things you don't know how to do."

Oliveira pulled La Maga over and sat her down on his lap. He thought about the Maga smell, the back of the Maga neck, and it made him sad. It was that same smell that once before . . . "To find out what's behind something," he thought confusedly. "Yes, that's one of the things I don't know how to do, that and crying and having pity."

"We were never in love," he said, kissing her hair.

"Speak for yourself," La Maga said, closing her eyes. "You have no way of telling whether I'm in love with you or not. You don't even know how to do that."

"Do you think I'm so blind?"

"On the contrary, I think it might do you some good to be a little blind."

"Ah, yes. Touch replaces definitions, instinct goes beyond intelligence. The magic route, the dark night of the soul."

"It would do you good," La Maga insisted as she always did when she did not understand something and wanted to cover up.

"Look, I know enough to know that everybody can go his own way. I think that I have to be alone, Lucía; in all truth, I don't know what I'm going to do. It's not fair to you or to Rocamadour who I think is waking up for me to treat you so badly and I don't want it to go on that way."

"You don't have to worry about me or about Rocamadour."

"I'm not worried, but the three of us are getting under each other's feet, it's uncomfortable and unaesthetic. I may not be blind enough for you, sweetie, but my optic nerve is good enough to let me see that you are going to get along perfectly well without me. No girlfriend of mine has ever committed suicide, even though my pride bleeds when I admit it."

"Yes, Horacio."

"So if I can summon up enough heroism to run out on you tonight or tomorrow, we can say that nothing happened here."

"Nothing," La Maga said.

"You can take your kid back to Madame Irène's, and you can come back to Paris and pick up where you left off."

"That's right."

"You'll see a lot of movies, keep on reading novels, you'll take walks and risk your life in the worst neighbourhoods at the worst hours."

"Yes, all that."

"You'll pick up a lot of strange things in the street, you'll bring them home, and you'll make something out of them. Wong will teach you sleight-of-hand tricks and Ossip will follow six feet behind you with his hands clasped in an attitude of humble reverence."

"Please, Horacio," La Maga said, hugging him and burying her face.

"Of course we will meet by magic in the strangest places, like that night in the Place de la Bastille, remember?"

"On the Rue Daval."

"I was quite drunk and you came around the corner and we stood looking at one another like idiots."

"Because I thought you were going to a concert that night."

"And you had told me that you had an appointment with Madame Léonie."

"That's why we thought it was so funny meeting on the Rue Daval."

"You were wearing your green sweater and you had stopped to console a pederast."

"They had beaten him up and thrown him out of a café, and he was crying so."

"Another time I remember we met near the Quai de Jemmapes."

"It was hot."

"You never told me what you were looking for along the Quai de Jemmapes."

"Oh, I wasn't looking for anything."

"You had a coin in your hand."

"I found it on the edge of the pavement. It was shining."

"Then we went to the Place de la République where the acrobats were and we won a box of sweets."

"They were awful."

"And another time I was coming out of the movies in Mouton-Duvernet and you were sitting in a pavement café with a Negro and a Filipino."

"And you never told me what you were doing in Mouton-Duvernet."

"I was going to a chiropodist," Oliveira said. "He had a waiting room papered with violet and reddish-purple scenes: gondolas, palm trees, and lovers embracing in the moonlight. Think of it, the same thing repeated five hundred times in six-by-four-inch squares."

"That's why you went, not because of the calluses."

"They weren't calluses, my dear. I had a genuine wart on the sole of my foot. Due to a vitamin deficiency, I think."

"Did it go away?" La Maga asked, raising her head and looking at him with great intensity.

Rocamadour woke up at the first burst of laughter and began to whimper. Oliveira sighed, now they would go through the same thing all over again, for a while he would see La Maga only from behind as she leaned over the bed, her hands moving back and forth. He began to prepare some *mate* and took out a cigarette. He didn't want to think. La Maga went to wash her hands and came back. They both reached for the gourd and scarcely glanced at one another.

"The best thing about all this," said Oliveira, "is that we're not in competition with the soap operas. Don't look at me like that; if you think a little you'll figure out what I mean."

"I've figured it out," La Maga said. "That's not why I'm looking at you like this."

"Oh, you think maybe . . . "

"A little, yes. But let's not talk again."

"You're right. Well, I think I'll take a little walk."

"Don't come back," La Maga said.

"Come on, let's not carry this to extremes," Oliveira said. "Where do you expect me to sleep tonight? Gordian knots are one thing, but the wind in the street is another. It must be minus five out there."

"It would be better if you didn't come back," La Maga said. "It's easy for me to say it right now, understand?"

"Well, anyway," Oliveira said, "I think we ought to be congratulated on our *savoir faire*."

"I feel so sorry for you, Horacio."

"Oh no; hold it right there."

"You know that sometimes I really can see. I see things so clearly. To think that an hour ago I thought the best thing to do would be to go and jump in the river."

"Body of an unidentified woman found in Seine . . . But you swim like a swan."

"I feel sorry for you," La Maga repeated. "I can see now. That night we met behind Notre-Dame I also saw that . . . But I refused to believe it. You were wearing a lovely blue shirt. It was the first time we went to a hotel, wasn't it?"

"No, but that doesn't make any difference. And you taught me to speak Gliglish."

"If I were to tell you that I did it all out of pity."

"Come off it," Oliveira said, looking at her with surprise.

"You were in danger that night. It was obvious, like a siren in the distance . . . I can't explain it."

"The only dangers for me are metaphysical," Oliveira said. "They're not going to haul me out of the water with grappling hooks, believe me. I will explode from an intestinal occlusion, the Asian flu, or a Peugeot 403."

"I don't know," La Maga said. "Sometimes I think about killing myself, but then I can see that I'm not going to do it. Don't think that it's only because of Rocamadour, it was the same before he came. The idea of killing myself always makes me feel good. But you never think about it . . . Why did you say metaphysical dangers? There are also metaphysical rivers, Horacio. You're going to jump into one of those rivers."

"It would have to be the Tao," said Oliveira.

"I thought I could have protected you. Don't tell me. Then right away I saw you didn't need me. We made love like two musicians who got together to work over some sonatas."

"What you're saying is delightful."

"That's how it was, the piano on one side and the violin on the other and out of that the sonata came, but you can see now that underneath it all we never really met. I realized it at once Horacio, but the sonatas were so beautiful."

"Yes, love."

"And Gliglish."

"Sure."

"And everything, the Club, that night on the Quai de Bercy under the trees, when we hunted stars until dawn and told stories about princes, and you were thirsty and we bought a bottle of expensive champagne, and we drank it on the river bank."

"And then a *clochard* came along and we gave him half the bottle."

"And the *clochard* knew a lot of Latin and Oriental things and you were talking to him about something like . . . Averroes, I think."

"Yes, Averroes."

"And the night the soldier patted my behind in the Foire du Trône and you punched him in the face and they arrested all of us."

"Don't let Rocamadour hear," Oliveira said laughing.

"Luckily Rocamadour won't ever remember anything about you, there's still nothing behind his eyes. Like the birds who eat the crumbs you throw them. They look at you, they eat the crumbs, they fly away . . . Nothing left."

"Yes," Oliveira said. "Nothing left."

The woman who lived on the third floor was shouting on the landing, drunk as usual at that hour. Oliveira glanced vaguely at the door, but La Maga drew him to her, and she slipped down to grasp his knees, trembling and weeping.

"Why are you torturing yourself that way?" Oliveira asked. "Metaphysical rivers are flowing everywhere. You don't have to go very far to find one. Look, no one has as much right to drown as I have, dopey. I promise you one thing: I'll remember you in my last moments so that they'll be all the more bitter. A real cheap novel, with a cover in three different colours."

"Don't leave," La Maga murmured, hugging his legs.

"I just want to walk around a little, that's all."

"No, don't leave."

"Let me go. You know very well I'm going to come back, at least for tonight."

"Let's go out together," La Maga said. "Look, Rocamadour is asleep, he'll be quiet until it's time for his bottle. We've got two hours, let's go to that café in the Arab quarter, that sad little café where we feel so good."

But Oliveira wanted to go out alone. Slowly he began to extract his legs from La Maga's embrace. He stroked her head, he ran his fingers around her neck, he kissed the back of it, he kissed her behind an ear, listening to her cry as her hair hung down over her face. "No blackmail," he thought. "Let's cry face to face, but not that cheap sobbing you pick up from the movies." He raised her face up, he made her look at him.

"I'm the bastard," Oliveira said. "Let me take care of paying myself back. Cry over your son, who could be dying for all we know, but don't waste your tears on me. Jesus, I bet there hasn't been a scene like this since Zola's times. Please let me leave."

"Why?" La Maga asked without getting up from the floor, looking at him like a dog.

"Why why?"

"Why?"

"Oh, you mean why all this. You'll find out, I don't think that either you or I is too much to blame. We're not grown up yet, Lucía. It's a virtue, but it costs a lot. Children always end up pulling each other's hair when they've finished playing. That's the way it probably is. Think about it."

(–126)

21

The same thing happens to everybody, the statue of Janus is a useless waste, the *truth* is that after forty years of age we have our real face on the back of our heads, looking desperately backwards. It is what in all truth is called a *commonplace.* You can't do anything about it, that's about the strength of it, with the words that come twisting out from between the bored lips of one-faced adolescents. Surrounded by boys in baggy sweaters and delightfully dirty girls in the smoke of the *cafés-crème* of Saint-Germain-des-Prés who read Durrell, Beauvoir, Duras, Douassot, Queneau, Sarraute, here I am a Frenchified Argentinian (horror of horrors), already beyond the adolescent vogue, the cool, with an *Etes-vous fous?* of René Crevel anachronistically in my hands, with the whole body of surrealism in my memory, with the mark of Antonin Artaud in my pelvis, with the *Ionisations* of Edgard Varèse in my ears, with Picasso in my eyes (but I seem to be a Mondrian, at least that's what I've been told).

"*Tu sèmes des syllabes pour récolter des étoiles,*" Crevel kids me.

"One does what he can," I answer.

"And that female, *n'arrêtera-t-elle donc pas de secouer l'arbre à sanglots*?"

"You're unfair," I tell him. "She's just crying a little bit, it's little more than a complaint."

It's sad to reach the point in life where it's easier to open a book to page ninety-six and converse with the author, from café to grave, from boredom to suicide, while at the tables around people are talking about Algeria, Adenauer, Mijanou, Bardot, Guy Trébert, Sidney Bechet, Michel Butor, Nabokov, Zao-Wu-Ki, Luison Bobet, and in my country the boys do talk, what do the boys talk about in my country? I don't know any more, I'm so far away, but they don't talk about Spilimbergo any more, they don't talk about Justo Suárez, they don't talk about the Shark of Quillà, they don't talk about

Bonini, they don't talk about Leguisamo. *It's all quite natural.* The catch is that nature and reality become enemies for some unknown reason, there is a time when nature sounds horribly false, when the reality of age twenty rubs elbows with that of age forty and on each elbow there is a razor-blade which slashes our jackets. I discover new worlds which are simultaneous and alien, and every time I get the feeling more and more that to agree is the worst of illusions. Why this thirst for universality, why this struggle against time? I also read Sarraute and look at a picture of Guy Trébert in handcuffs, but those are *things that happen to me*, while if I must be the one who decides, it's almost always in a backward direction. My hand pokes around the bookcase, I take down Crevel, I take down Roberto Arlt, I take down Jarry. Today fascinates me, but always from the point of view of yesterday (did I say phascinate?), and that's how at my age the past becomes present and the present is a strange and confused future where boys in baggy sweaters and long-haired girls drink their *cafés-crème* and pet each other with the slow gracefulness of cats or plants.

We must fight against this.

We must establish ourselves in the present once more.

It seems that I am a Mondrian, therefore . . .

But Mondrian painted his present forty years ago.

(A picture of Mondrian looking exactly like a typical orchestra conductor (Julio de Caro, *ecco!*) with glasses and plastered-down hair and stiff collar, with the frightful air of a clerk dancing with a waterfront whore. What kind of present did Mondrian feel while he was dancing? Those canvases of his, that picture of him . . . Ab-bysses.)

You're getting old, Horacio. Quintus Horatius Oliveira, you're getting old, Flaccus. You're getting flaccid and old, Oliveira.

"*Il verse son vitriol entre les cuisses des faubourgs*," Crevel mocks.

What am I going to do? In the midst of this great disorder I still think I'm a weather vane that after every spin must show where north or south lies. It takes little imagination to call someone a weather vane: you see the spins but never the intention, the point of the arrow which tries to huddle down and hide in the river of the wind.

There are metaphysical rivers. Yes, my love, of course. And you are taking care of your son, crying from time to time, and here it is another day with another yellow sun that doesn't warm. *J'habite à Saint-Germain-des-Prés, et chaque soir j'ai rendez-vous avec Verlaine. / Ce gros pierrot n'a pas changé, et pour courir le guilledou* . . . Twenty francs in the slot and Leo Ferré will sing to you of his loves, or Gilbert Bécaud, or Guy Béart. Back in my country: *Si quiere ver la vida color de rosa / Eche veinte centavos en la ranura* . . . Better turn on the radio (the rent falls due next Monday, I thought I'd better tell you) and listen to some chamber music, probably Mozart, or have you put on some record with the volume turned low so as not to wake up Rocamadour. And I don't think you're really aware that Rocamadour is very sick, terribly weak and sick, and that he would get better care in a hospital. But I can't talk about these things with you any more, let's say it's all over and I'm wandering around here, walking up and down trying to find north, south, if I really am looking for them. If I really am looking for them. But if I'm not, what's this all about? Oh, my love, I miss you, I feel the pain of you in my skin, in my throat, every time I breathe it's as if an emptiness came into my chest where you no longer are.

"*Toi*," Crevel says, "*toujours pret à grimper les cinq étages des pythonisses faubouriennes, qui ouvrent grandes les portes du futur* . . ."

And why not, why shouldn't I go looking for La Maga, most of the time it was just a case of putting in an appearance, going along the rue de Seine to the arch leading into the Quai de Conti and I would see her slender form against the olive-ashen light which floats along the river on the Pont des Arts, we used to go along there in search of shadows, to eat fried potatoes in the Faubourg Saint-Denis, to kiss by the barges on the Saint-Martin canal. With her I would feel a new air come over me, the fantastic patterns of the sunset or the way things would put themselves in patterns when we would be together by the bars of the Cour de Rohan and the tramps would ascend into the fearful moonlit world of witnesses and judges . . . Why shouldn't I love La Maga and possess her beneath all those ceilings purchased for six hundred francs, in beds with musty and unravelled spreads, for in that crazy hopscotch, in that race of moneybags I recognized myself and called myself by name, finally and until I would escape from time and all its labelled monkey-cages, where from its show windows Omega Electron Girard Perregaud Vacheron & Constantin marked the hours and the minutes of sacrosanct castrating obligations, into an atmosphere where the last bonds were being loosed and pleasure was a mirror of reconciliation, a mirror for larks but a mirror, something like a sacrament from one being to another, a dance around the altar, a coming on of sleep with mouth to mouth, sometimes without untangling ourselves, our sexes warmly joined, our necks like twining vegetative signposts, our hands determinedly caressing thigh and neck . . .

"*Tu t'accroches à des histoires*," Crevel says. "*Tu étreins des mots* . . ."

"No, old man, that's more like what they do across the ocean, which you know nothing about. It's been a long time since I went to bed with words on. I still wear them, like you or anybody else, but I give them a good brushing before I put them on."

Crevel is distrustful and I understand why. A whole canefield of words has grown up between La Maga and me, we have only been separated by a few hours and a few blocks and my sorrow is already *called* sorrow, and my love is *called* love . . . I shall keep on feeling less and less and remembering more and more, but what is memory if not the language of feeling, a dictionary of faces and days and smells which repeat themselves like the verbs and adjectives in a speech, sneaking in behind the thing itself, into the pure present, making us sad or teaching us vicariously until one's self itself becomes a vicar, the backward-looking face opens its eyes wide, the real face slowly becomes dim as in old pictures and Janus is suddenly any one of us. I'm saying all of this to Crevel but I'm speaking to La Maga, now that we're so far apart. And I don't talk to her with the words that only used to serve to make us misunderstand each other, now that it's too late I begin to choose others, hers, the ones wrapped up in what she understands and which has no name, sparks and emanations which crackle in the air between two bodies or which can fill a room or a line of poetry with gold dust. But isn't this the way we have been living, softly slashing at each other? No, that's not the way; she might have wanted to, but once again I imposed the false order that hides chaos pretending that I was dedicated to a profound existence while all the time it was one that barely dipped its toe into the terrible waters. There are metaphysical rivers, she swims in them like that swallow swimming in the air, spinning madly around a belfry, letting herself drop so that she can rise up all the better with the swoop. I describe and define and desire those rivers, but she swims in them. I look for them, find them, observe them from the bridge, but she swims in them. And she doesn't know it, any more than the swallow. It's not necessary to know things as I do, one can live in disorder without being held back by any sense of order. That disorder is her mysterious order, that bohemia of body and soul which opens its true doors wide for her. Her life is not disorder except for me, buried among the prejudices I despise and respect at the same time. Me, inexorably condemned to be pardoned by La Maga who judges me without knowing it. Oh, let me come in, let me see some day the way your eyes see.

Useless. Condemned to be acquitted. Go home and read Spinoza. La Maga doesn't know who Spinoza is. La Maga reads tedious Russian and German novels and Pérez Galdós and forgets immediately after what she has read. She will never suspect that she has condemned me to read Spinoza. A strange judge, a judge with her hands, with her racing down the street, a judge because she can just look at me and leave me naked, a judge by being silly and unhappy and upset and dull and less than anything. By everything I have known from my bitter knowledge, with my rusty slide rule of a college graduate and enlightened man, by all of that, a judge. Fall down, swallow, with those sharp scissors with which you cut the sky of Saint-Germain-des-Prés, pluck out these eyes that look without seeing, I have quickly been condemned without appeal to those blue gallows to which the hands of the woman caring for her son have raised me, let the execution be quick, quickly back to the false order of being alone and recovering one's self-sufficiency, self-knowledge, self-awareness. And with so much knowledge a useless anxiety to pity something, to have it rain here inside, so that at long last it will start to rain and smell of earth and living things, yes, living things at long last.

(–79)

22

Opinion had it that the old man had slipped, that the car had jumped the red light, that the old man had tried to commit suicide, that things were getting worse than ever in Paris, that traffic was terrible, that it was not the old man's fault, that it was the old man's fault, that the brakes on the car were not working right, that the old man had been frightfully careless, that living was getting more expensive every day, that there were too many foreigners in Paris who didn't understand the traffic laws and were taking work away from Frenchmen.

The old man didn't seem to be hurt too badly. He was smiling weakly and stroking his moustache. An ambulance arrived, they put him on a stretcher, the driver of the car kept gesticulating and explaining the accident to the policeman and to the onlookers.

"He lives at 32 Rue Madame," said a blond boy who had been speaking to Oliveira and others who had stopped. "He's a writer, I know him. He writes books."

"The bumper hit his legs, but the driver already had the brakes on."

"It hit him in the chest," the boy said. "The old man slipped on some shit in the street."

"It hit him on the legs," Oliveira said.

"It all depends on your point of view," said an enormously short man.

"It hit him in the chest," the boy said. "I saw it with my own two eyes."

"In that case . . . Shouldn't someone tell his family?"

"He doesn't have any family, he's a writer."

"Oh," said Oliveira.

"He has a cat and lots of books. Once I delivered a package to him for the concierge and he invited me in. There were books all over the place. Something like this was bound to happen to him, writers are so absent-minded. That'll be the day, when I get hit by a car . . . "

A few drops of rain began to fall and they immediately dissolved the circle of witnesses. Putting up the collar of his lumberjacket, Oliveira turned his nose into the cold wind and began to walk in no direction in particular. He was sure that the old man had not been seriously injured, but he kept on seeing his face, which could almost be described as placid, perplexed maybe, as they carried him in the stretcher and spoke friendly comforting words to him, "*Allez, pépère, c'est rien, ça!*" from the stretcher-bearer, a redhead who must have said the same thing to everybody. "A complete lack of communication," Oliveira thought. "It's not so much that we're alone, that's a well-known fact that any fool can plainly see. Being alone is basically being alone on a certain level in which other lonelinesses could communicate with us if that were the case. But bring on any conflict, an accident in the street or a declaration of war, provoke the brutal crossing of different levels, and a man who is perhaps an outstanding Sanskrit scholar or a quantum physicist becomes a *pépère* in the eyes of the stretcher-bearer who arrives on the scene. Edgar Allan Poe on a stretcher, Verlaine in the hands of a sawbones, Nerval and Artaud facing psychiatrists. What could that Italian Galen have known about Keats as he bled him and helped him die of hunger? If men like them are silent, as is most likely, the others will triumph blindly, without evil intent, of course, without knowing that the consumptive over there, that injured man lying naked on that bed, are doubly alone, surrounded by beings who move about as if behind a glass, from a different place in time . . . "

Stopping in a doorway he lit a cigarette. It was towards the end of the afternoon and groups of girls were coming out of offices, with the need to laugh, to speak in shouts, to push each other, to soak up just this quarter-of-an-hour's worth before falling back into the world of beef and weekly magazines. Oliveira kept on walking. Without having to dramatize, the smallest bit of objectivity would bring out into the open all the absurdity of Paris, the gregarious life. Since he had been thinking about poets, it was easy to remember all of those who had denounced the solitude of man among his fellows, the comedy of greetings, the "excuse me" when people met on the stairs, the seat that is given to women on the underground, the brotherhood observed in politics and sports. Only a biological and sexual optimism is capable of covering up the isolation of some, no matter what John Donne might have felt about it. Contacts made in action in tribes in work in bed on the sports ground were contacts between branches and leaves which reached out and caressed each other from tree to tree while the trunks stood there disdainfully and irreconcilably parallel. "*Underneath it all* we could be what we are on the surface," Oliveira thought, "but we would have to live in a different way. And what does it mean to live in a different way? Maybe to live absurdly in order to do away with the absurd, to dive into one's self with such force that the leap will end up in the arms of someone else. Yes, maybe love, but that *otherness* lasts only as long as a woman lasts, and besides only as everything concerns that woman. Basically there is no such thing as otherness, maybe just that pleasant thing called togetherness. Of course, that is something . . . " Love, an ontologizing ceremony, a giver of being. And that is why he was thinking only now of what he should have thought about in the beginning: without the possession of self, there was no possession of otherness, and who could really possess himself? Who had come back from himself, from that absolute solitude which meant not even being in one's own company, having to go to the movies or to a whorehouse or to friends' houses or to get involved in a time-consuming profession or in marriage so that at least one could be alone-along-with-all-the-others? That's how, paradoxically, solitude would lead to the heights of sociability, to the great illusion of the company of others, to the solitary man in a maze of mirrors and echoes. But people like him and so many others (or those who reject themselves but know themselves close up) got into the worst paradox, the one of reaching the border of otherness perhaps and not being able to cross over. That true otherness made up of delicate contacts, marvellous adjustments with the world, could not be attained from just one point; the outstretched hand had to find response in another hand stretched out from the beyond, from the other part.

(–62)

23

Standing on a corner, fed up with the rarified atmosphere of his musing (and the fact that he kept on thinking, he didn't know why, about the injured old man lying in a hospital bed surrounded by doctors and medical students and nurses, amiably impersonal as they asked him his name, age, occupation, told him it wasn't anything, that they would take care of him right away with shots and dressings), Oliveira had begun to look at what was going on around him and how any street corner in any city was the perfect illustration of what he had been thinking and almost took his work away from him. In the café, protected from the cold (a matter of going in and having a glass of wine), a group of bricklayers were talking with the man behind the bar. Two students were reading and writing at one table and Oliveira saw them look up and look at the bricklayers, go back to their books or notebooks, look up again. From one glass cage to another, look, withdraw, look: that's all there was to it. Up above the pavement section of the café, which was closed, a young woman on the second floor seemed to be sewing or cutting out a dress by the window. Her upswept hair was moving in time to what she was doing and Oliveira tried to picture her thoughts, her shears, her children who would be coming back from school any moment now, her husband finishing work in an office or in a bank. The bricklayers, the students, the woman, and now a tramp turned the corner of the street with a bottle of red wine sticking out of his pocket, pushing a baby carriage filled with old newspapers, tin cans, torn and dirty clothes, a headless doll, a package with a fishtail sticking out. The bricklayers, the students, the woman, the tramp, and in a booth looking like someone condemned to the pillory, LOTERIE NATIONALE, an old woman with unrepatriated bits of straggly hair popping out from underneath a kind of grey bonnet, blue mittens on her hands, TIRAGE MERCREDI, waiting but not in wait for customers, a charcoal brazier by her feet, encased in her vertical coffin, motionless, half-frozen, offering good fortune and thinking God knows what, clots of ideas, senile commonplaces, the teacher who used to give her sweets when she was a girl, a husband killed on the Somme, a travelling-salesman son, at night her garret without running water, a three-day soup, *boeuf bourguignon* which is cheaper than a cut of meat, TIRAGE MERCREDI. The bricklayers, the students, the tramp, the lottery woman, every group, everybody in his glass cage, but let an old man fall under a car and right away there is a general running to the scene of the accident, an animated exchange of opinion, of criticism, disparities and coincidences until it starts to rain again and the bricklayers go back to the bar, the students to their table, the X's to X and the Z's to Z.

"Only by living absurdly is it possible to break out of this infinite absurdity," Oliveira repeated. "But Jesus, I'm going to get soaked, I've got to get under somewhere." He spotted the posters of the Salle de Géographie and took refuge in the doorway. A lecture about Australia, the unknown continent. A meeting of the disciples of the Christ of Monfavet. A piano concert by Madame Berthe Trépat. Open registration for a course on meteors. Win a black belt in judo in five months. A lecture on the urbanization of Lyons. The piano concert was going to start very soon and it didn't cost much. Oliveira looked at the sky, shrugged his shoulders, and went in. He thought vaguely about going to Ronald's or to Étienne's studio, but it was better to leave that for night-time. He didn't know why, but he thought it was funny for an artist to be named Berthe Trépat. He also thought it was amusing that he was taking refuge in a concert to get away from himself for a little while, an ironic illustration of what he had been thinking about while he was wandering about the streets. "We're nothing," he thought, as he passed 120 francs at tooth-level to the old woman caged up in the ticket booth. He got a ticket in the tenth row out of the pure perversity of the old woman, since the concert was about to start and there was nobody else except a few old bald heads, a few old beards, and some others who partook of both qualities, who had an air of being from the neighbourhood or from the family, two women between forty and forty-five with old coats and dripping umbrellas, a few young people, couples mostly and arguing strenuously with shoves and the noise of sweets being chewed and the squeaking of the old Vienna seats. Twenty people in all. It smelled like a rainy afternoon, the big theatre was cold and damp, and one could hear talking backstage behind the backdrop. An old man had lit his pipe and Oliveira was quick to dig out a Gauloise. He didn't feel too well, one of his shoes was full of water, and the musty smell and the smell of wet clothes bothered him a little. He took a deep drag, getting the cigarette hot and making it fall apart. A deaf-mute buzzer sounded outside, and one of the young people began to clap vigorously. The ancient usher, with her beret pulled to one side and make-up on that she surely must have slept in, closed a curtain at the back of the hall. At that point Oliveira remembered that they had given him a programme. It was a sloppy mimeographed sheet on which he could make out with some effort that Madame Berthe Trépat, gold medallist, would play the *Three Discontinuous Movements* of Rose Bob (première), the *Pavan for General Leclerc*, by Alix Alix (first time for a civilian audience) and the *Délibes–Saint-Saëns Synthesis*, by Délibes, Saint-Saëns, and Berthe Trépat.

"Shit," Oliveira thought. "What a fucking programme."

Somehow a double-chinned, white-haired gentleman appeared behind the piano. He was dressed in black and his pink hand fingered a chain that hung across his fancy waistcoat. Oliveira thought he noticed grease spots on the waistcoat. A young lady in a purple raincoat and gold-rimmed glasses started to applaud in a flat tone. With a croaking voice that had an extraordinary resemblance to that of a macaw, the double-chinned old man introduced the concert by explaining that Rose Bob was a former pupil of Madame Berthe Trépat and that the *Pavan* by Alix Alix had been written by a distinguished army officer who concealed himself behind that modest pseudonym, and that both pieces were written in the most rigorous observation of the most modern form of musical composition. As for the *Délibes–Saint-Saëns Synthesis* (and here the old man rolled his eyes on high), it represented for contemporary music one of the most profound innovations to which the composer, Madame Trépat, had given the name "prophetic syncretism". The term was quite precise, since the musical genius of Délibes and Saint-Saëns tended towards osmosis, towards interfusion and the interphonic approach which had become paralyzed by the excessively individualistic interpretation of Western music and thus prevented from surging forth into a higher and more synthetic creation which had been awaiting the genius and intuition of Madame Trépat. In fact, her sensitivity had discovered affinities which most listeners had missed and she had undertaken the noble but arduous task of being the mediumistic bridge by which the meeting of these two noble sons of France was to be consummated. It was pre-eminently the moment to remind everyone that in addition to her activities as a music teacher, Madame Berthe Trépat would soon be celebrating her twenty-fifth anniversary as a composer. The speaker would not take it upon himself in a simple introduction to a concert, much as he would like to, to go on at deserving length with an analysis of Madame Trépat's musical accomplishments, because the audience was growing impatient. In any case, and so that he could give the key to those who would be hearing for the first time the works of Rose Bob and Madame Trépat, he would sum up their art by mentioning antistructural constructions, that is to say, autonomous cells of sound, the result of pure inspiration, held together by the general intent of the work but completely free of classical moulds, dodecaphonic or atonal (he stressed the last two words). Thus, for example, the *Three Discontinuous Movements* by Rose Bob, one of Madame Trépat's favourite students, had their start in the reaction aroused in the spirit of the composer by the sound of a door being slammed shut, and the thirty-two chords which made up the first movement were the resulting repercussions of that sound on the aesthetic plane; the speaker did not think that he would be violating a confidence if he told his cultured audience that the technique employed in the composition of the *Saint-Saëns Synthesis* was based on the most primitive and esoteric forces of creation. He would never forget the rare privilege he had had of being present at one phase of the synthesis as Madame Trépat held a dowsing pendulum over the scores of the two masters in order to choose those passages whose influence upon the pendulum corroborated the astounding intuitions of Madame Trépat. And although he could say much more, the speaker felt that he should retire after saluting in Madame Berthe Trépat one of the beacons of French genius and a pathetic example of how the general public lives in ignorance of misunderstood genius.

His jowls were shaking and the old man, seized by a fit of coughing and emotion, withdrew behind the curtains. Forty hands gave out with a dry applause and several matches lost their heads.

Oliveira slouched in his seat as far as possible and felt better. The old man in the accident must have been feeling better too in his hospital bed, sunk in the sleepiness which follows shock, that happy interregnum in which one abdicates self-government and the bed becomes a ship, with paid vacations, any break at all with daily routine. "I'm almost capable of going to visit him one of these days," Oliveira said to himself. "But at best I would just spoil his desert island and become the footprint in the sand. God, but you're getting sentimental."

The applause made him open his eyes and observe the hard work Madame Berthe Trépat was putting into her bow of thanks. Before he had even taken a good look at her face, her shoes had stopped him in his tracks, men's shoes, incapable of disguise by any skirt. Square and heelless, with useless feminine ribbons. What followed up from them was both stiff and broad, a fat-lady stuck into a merciless corset. But Berthe Trépat was not really fat; the best you could say was that she was robust. She must have had sciatica or lumbago, something which made her move all at once, frontally now, waving with effort, and then from the side, outlined between the stool and the piano and folding herself geometrically until seated. From that position the artist turned her head around brusquely and bowed again, although the applause had stopped. "Somebody up above must be pulling strings," Oliveira thought. He liked marionettes and puppets, and he was expecting miracles of prophetic syncretism. Berthe Trépat looked at the audience once more, all the sins of the moon suddenly seemed concentrated in her face that appeared to be covered with flour, and her cherry-red mouth opened up to assume the shape of an Egyptian barge. Profile once again, her little parrot-beak nose pointed for a moment at the keyboard while her hands perched on the keys from C to B like two dried-up chamois bags. The thirty-two chords of the first discontinuous movement began to sound. There were five seconds between the first and the second, fifteen between the second and third. On arriving at the fifteenth chord, Rose Bob had decided on a pause of twenty-five seconds. Oliveira, who at first had appreciated the good Weberian use of silence that Rose Bob was making use of in her pauses, noticed that overuse was rapidly dissipating the effect. Between chords seven and eight there was coughing, between twelve and thirteen somebody struck a match noisily, between fourteen and fifteen he clearly heard the expression "*Ah, merde alors!*" contributed by a young blonde girl. Around the twentieth chord one of the more ancient ladies, a real virginal pickle, gripped her umbrella and opened her mouth to say something that was mercifully swallowed up by the twenty-first chord. Amused, Oliveira looked at Berthe Trépat, suspecting that the pianist was studying them all with what is called the corner of her eye. Out of that corner of the hook-nosed profile of Berthe Trépat a celestial grey glance seemed to come, and it occurred to Oliveira that probably the poor woman was counting the house. At chord twenty-three a man with a neat, round bald spot got up indignantly and after snorting and huffing left the hall, digging in his heels during the eight-second silence ordained by Rose Bob. After chord twenty-four the pauses began to get smaller, and between twenty-eight and thirty-two there was a rhythm like that of a dirge which could not help but have some effect. Berthe Trépat took her shoes off the pedals, put her left hand in her lap, and started on the second movement. This movement lasted for only four bars, each of three notes of equal value. The third movement consisted mainly in coming from the extreme registers of the keyboard and in approaching the middle chromatically, repeating the operation back out again, all in the midst of triplets and other adornments. At a given moment, which no one could foresee, the pianist stopped playing and stood up quickly, bowing with an air which seemed to bespeak a challenge, but in which Oliveira seemed to discern a note of insecurity or even fear. One couple applauded madly; Oliveira found himself applauding in turn and not knowing why (and when he found out why he got angry and stopped applauding). Berthe Trépat went back to her profile almost at once and ran her finger over the keyboard while she waited for them to quieten down. She began to play the *Pavan for General Leclerc.*

In the two or three minutes that followed, Oliveira had some trouble in dividing his attention between the extraordinary stew that Berthe Trépat was boiling up at full steam and the furtive or forthright way in which young and old were leaving the concert. A mixture of Liszt and Rachmaninoff, the *Pavan* was the tiresome repetition of two or three themes which then got lost in innumerable variations, bits of bravura (rather poorly played, with holes and stitching everywhere) and the solemnities of a catafalque upon a caisson, broken by sudden fireworks which seemed to delight the mysterious Alix Alix. Once or twice Oliveira was worried that the towering Salammbô hairdo of Berthe Trépat would suddenly collapse, but who knows how many hairpins were reinforcing it, amidst the rumble and tumble of the *Pavan*. The orgiastic arpeggios which announced the end came on, and three themes were successively repeated (one of which had been lifted bodily from Strauss's *Don Juan*) and Berthe Trépat let the chords rain down with growing intensity, modified by the hysterical repetition of the first theme and two chords composed of the gravest notes, the last of which came out markedly false for the right hand, but it was something that could happen to anyone and Oliveira applauded warmly; he had really enjoyed it.

The artist turned around to face the audience with one of her rare springlike motions and bowed. Since she seemed to be counting the house with her eyes, she could not have failed to calculate that there were no more than eight or nine people left. With dignity Berthe Trépat went off stage left, and the usher drew the curtain and sold sweets to the audience.

On the one hand he wanted to leave, but all during the concert there had been an atmosphere which had fascinated Oliveira. After all, poor Madame Trépat had been trying to present works in première, which in itself was a great thing in this world of the polonaise, the clair de lune, and the ritual fire dance. There was something moving about that face of a burlap-stuffed doll, of a plush turtle, of an immense nitwit stuck in a rancid world of chipped teapots, old women who had heard Risler play, art and poetry lectures in halls covered with old wallpaper, of budgets of forty thousand francs a month and furtive borrowing from friends to get through the month, the cult of au-then-tic Akademia Raymond Duncan art, and it was easy to imagine what Alix Alix and Rose Bob looked like, the base calculations before renting the hall, the mimeographed programme done by some well-meaning pupil, the fruitless lists of people to invite, the empty feeling backstage when they saw the empty hall and still had to go on, gold medal and all, she still has to go on. It was almost a chapter out of Céline and Oliveira felt himself incapable of thinking beyond the general atmosphere, beyond the useless and defeatist survival of such artistic activities among groups of people equally defeated and useless. "Of course it had to be my fate, getting stuck inside this moth-eaten set-up," Oliveira raged to himself. "An old man underneath a car, and now Madame Trépat. And let's not think about the lousy weather outside or about myself. Above all, let's not talk about myself."

Four people were left in the hall, and he thought it best to go and sit in the first row to provide a bit more company for the pianist. He was amused by this act of solidarity, but as soon as he was seated at the front he lit a cigarette. For some reason a woman decided to leave at the exact moment at which Berthe Trépat had come back on stage, and she took a strong look at her before she drew herself up to make a bow to the empty hall. Oliveira thought that the woman who had left deserved a hard kick in the arse. He suddenly realized that all of his reactions came from a certain sympathy for Berthe Trépat, in spite of the *Pavan* and Rose Bob. "It's been a long time since something like this happened to me," he thought. "I wonder if I'm getting soft with age." So many metaphysical rivers and suddenly he wants to go visit the old man in the hospital, or he is surprised to find himself applauding this madwoman in a corset. Strange. It must be the cold, his wet shoes.

The *Délibes–Saint-Saëns Synthesis* must have been going on for three minutes or so when the couple who had been the mainstay of the audience that remained got up and ostentatiously left. Again Oliveira thought he could make out a sideglance from Berthe Trépat, but now it was as if her hands had gone stiff, she bent over the piano and with tremendous effort, taking advantage of every pause to glance out of the corner of her eye at the seats where Oliveira and a peaceful-looking man were listening with what seemed to be the signs of rapt attention. The prophetic syncretism was not long in revealing its secret, even for a layman like Oliveira: three measures of *Le Rouet d'Omphale* were followed by four more from *Les Filles de Cadix*, then her left hand offered "*Mon coeur s'ouvre à ta voix*", while the right one spasmodically interspersed the theme of the bells from *Lakmé*, together they passed successively into the *Danse Macabre* and *Coppélia*, until other themes which the programme attributed to the *Hymne à Victor Hugo*, *Jean de Nivelle* and *Sur les bords du Nil* alternated showily with the better-known ones, and as far as prophetic was concerned, nothing could have been more successful, as was shown by the soft laughter of the peaceful-looking man while as a person of good breeding he covered his mouth with his glove, and Oliveira had to admit the guy was right, that he shouldn't be asked to be quiet, and Berthe Trépat must have felt the same because she kept making more and more mistakes, it seemed as if her hands had become paralysed, she kept leaning forward shaking her forearms and raising her elbows like a hen settling into her nest. "*Mon coeur s'ouvre à ta voix*," "*Où va la jeune hindoue?*" again two syncretic chords, a stray arpeggio, *Les Filles de Cadix, tra-la-la-la*, like a hiccup, several notes together (surprisingly) in the manner of Pierre Boulez, and the peaceful-looking man let out a sort of bellow and ran out holding his gloves up to his mouth, just as Berthe Trépat lowered her hands and looked fixedly at the keyboard, and a long second passed, an interminable second, something desperately empty between Oliveira and Berthe Trépat alone in the hall.

"Bravo," Oliveira said, understanding that applause would have been out of place. "Bravo, madame."

Without standing up Berthe Trépat turned a little on the stool and put her elbow on middle C. They looked at each other. Oliveira got up and went to the edge of the stage.

"Very interesting," he said. "Really, madame, I listened to your concert with real interest."

What a bastard.

Berthe Trépat looked at the empty hall. One of her eyelids was trembling a little. She seemed to be asking herself something, waiting for something. Oliveira sensed that he should keep on talking.

"An artist like you must be aware of the lack of understanding and the snobbery of the public. Deep down I know that you were playing for yourself."

"For myself," Berthe Trépat repeated in a macaw voice strikingly similar to that of the gentleman who had introduced her.

"For whom, then?" Oliveira asked, climbing onto the stage with the ease of a dreamer. "An artist can only count on the stars, as Nietzsche said."

"Who are you?" Berthe Trépat was startled.

"Oh, someone who is interested in manifestations . . . " He could have run words together the way he always did. All he could say was that he was here, looking for a little companionship without really knowing why.

Berthe Trépat was listening, still a little absent. She got up with difficulty and looked at the hall, the curtains.

"Yes," she said. "It's getting late. I've got to go home." She had said it to herself as if it were a punishment or something.

"Could I have the pleasure of accompanying you for a while?" said Oliveira as he leaned forward. "I mean if no one is waiting for you in your dressing room or at the stage door."

"There's no one. Valentin left after he introduced me. What did you think of the introduction?"

"Interesting," Oliveira said, more and more certain that he was dreaming and that he wanted to keep on dreaming.

"Valentin can do better," Berthe Trépat said. "And I thought it was nasty of him . . . yes, nasty . . . to leave the way he did, as if I were some old rag."

"He spoke of you and your work with great admiration."

"For five hundred francs he would speak about a dead fish with great admiration. Five hundred francs!" Berthe Trépat was lost in her thoughts.

"I'm playing the fool," Oliveira told himself. He bowed and got down off the stage; maybe she had forgotten about his offer. But she was looking at him and Oliveira saw that she was crying.

"Valentin is a swine. All of them . . . there were more than two hundred people, you saw them, more than two hundred. That's remarkable for a première, don't you think? And they all paid, don't think we sent out any complimentary tickets. Over two hundred, and now you're the only one left. Valentin left, I . . . "

"Some absences can mean a real success," Oliveira said in some incredible way.

"But why did they leave? Did you see them go? Over two hundred, I tell you, and prominent people, I'm sure I spotted Madame de Roche, Doctor Lacour, Montellier, the teacher whose pupil got the latest grand prize in violin . . . I don't think they liked the *Pavan* too much and that's why they left, don't you think? Because they left before my *Synthesis*, that's for certain, I saw them myself."

"Of course," Oliveira said. "You have to admit, the *Pavan* . . . "

"It isn't really a pavan at all," Berthe Trépat said. "It's a piece of shit. It's Valentin's fault, they warned me that Valentin was sleeping with Alix Alix. Why do I have to keep a queer, young man? Me, gold medallist, I'll show you my notices, hits, in Grenoble, in Puy . . . "

The tears were running down to her throat and getting lost among the withered pores of her ashen skin. She took Oliveira's hand and shook it. At any moment she was going to become hysterical.

"Why don't you get your coat and we'll get out of here," Oliveira said hurriedly. "The outside air will do you good, we can have something to drink, for me it would be a great . . . "

"Something to drink," Berthe Trépat repeated. "Gold medal."

"Whatever you want," Oliveira said incongruously. He made a motion to free himself, but the pianist gripped his arm and came closer. Oliveira could smell the sweat of the concert mixed with naphthaline and benzoin (as well as piss and cheap perfume). First Rocamadour and now Berthe Trépat, it was unbelievable. "Gold medal," she kept saying, crying and snuffling. Suddenly a great sob shook her as if a chord had burst into the air. "And it's the same old thing . . . " Oliveira finally understood as he fought in vain to get away from personal feelings, to take refuge in some metaphysical river, naturally. Offering no resistance, Berthe Trépat let herself be led back towards the curtains where the usher was looking at them, holding a torch and a feathered hat.

"Doesn't Madame feel well?"

"It's emotion," Oliveira said. "She's getting over it now. Where is her coat?"

Among easels and creaky tables, a harp and a coatrack, there was a chair with a green raincoat on it. Oliveira helped Berthe Trépat, who kept her head down but was not crying any more.

They went out through a little door and along a dark passageway and came out on the boulevard. It was drizzling.

"It'll be hard getting a taxi," said Oliveira, who barely had three hundred francs in his pocket. "Do you live far?"

"No, near the Panthéon, I'd really rather walk."

"Yes, it would be better."

Berthe Trépat moved ahead slowly, swaying her head from side to side. The hood of the raincoat gave her a martial look or something like Ubu Roi. Oliveira huddled into his lumberjacket and pulled the collar up high. The air was crisp, he was beginning to get hungry.

"You're very nice," she said. "You shouldn't bother. What did you think of my *Synthesis*?"

"I'm just an amateur, madame. Music for me, if I can say so . . . "

"You didn't like it," Berthe Trépat said.

"A première . . . "

"We worked for months with Valentin. Night and day, trying to bring the inspirations together."

"Of course you must admit that Délibes – "

"Is a genius," Berthe Trépat said. "Erik Satie admitted it one day in my presence. And no matter what Doctor Lacour says about Satie's pulling my leg . . . what would you say. Of course, you must know what the old man was like . . . But I can read people, young man, and I know full well that Satie was convinced, yes, convinced. What country are you from, young man?"

"From Argentina, madame, and I'm really not a young man, by the way."

"Ah, Argentina. The pampas . . . And do you think they would be interested in my work there?"

"I'm sure of it, madame."

"Maybe you could get me an appointment with the Ambassador. If Thibaud was able to go to Argentina and Montevideo, why not me, I play my own music. You must have noticed that, it's basic: my own music. Almost always premières."

"Do you do much composing?" Oliveira asked and felt like a mouthful of vomit.

"I'm working on my Opus 83 . . . no, let's see . . . Now that I think of it, I should have spoken with Madame Nolet before I left . . . It concerns money, of course. Two hundred people, that means . . . " It was lost in a murmur, and Oliveira asked himself whether it wouldn't really be more merciful to tell the truth outright, but she already knew, of course she knew.

"It's scandalous," Berthe Trépat said. "Two years ago I played in the same hall, Poulenc promised to come . . . Do you understand? Poulenc himself. I was at the pinnacle of inspiration that afternoon, it was too bad that a last-minute commitment stopped him from coming . . . but you know, musicians who are all the rage . . . And that was the time that Madame Nolet charged me half the take," she added angrily. "Exactly half. Of course it came out the same, counting on two hundred people . . . "

"Madame," Oliveira said, taking her softly by the arm and leading her into the Rue de Seine, "the lights were out and maybe you had trouble seeing how many people there were."

"Oh, no," Berthe Trépat said. "I'm sure I'm right, but you've made me lose track. Excuse me, I have to work out . . . " She was lost again in a dedicated whispering, and she kept on moving her lips and fingers, completely unaware of where Oliveira was taking her, and almost even of his presence. Everything she was saying aloud she could have said to herself, Paris is full of people who go along the street talking to themselves, Oliveira himself was no exception, in fact the exception was that he was playing the fool as he walked along beside the old woman seeing this tarnished puppet home, this poor blown-up balloon in which stupidity and madness were dancing the real night-time pavan. "It's repulsive, I ought to fling her down against a step and stamp on her face, squash her like an insect, make her fall apart like a piano dropped from the tenth floor. True charity would be to get her out of her world, stop her from suffering like a dog with all her illusions which even she does not believe, which she builds up so that she will not feel the wetness in her shoes, her empty room, or that dirty, white-haired old man. She repels me and I'm going to disappear at the next corner, and who will know, after all. What a day, my God, what a day."

If they could only get to the Rue Lobineau he would take off like a bat and the old woman could get on home by herself. Oliveira looked behind, he waited for the right moment, shaking his arm as if something were hanging down from it, something that had sneaked up and was hanging from his elbow. But it was Berthe Trépat's hand there, clinging with resolution. Berthe Trépat was hanging on with all her might to Oliveira's arm and he was looking out for the Rue Lobineau as he helped her cross the street and went with her towards the Rue de Tournon.

"They must have lit the stove by now," Berthe Trépat said. "It's not that the weather is so cold, really, but we artists like our warmth. Don't you think so? You must come up and have a drink with Valentin and me."

"Oh, no, madame," Oliveira said. "No indeed, it's been a great pleasure and honour just to have seen you home, besides – "

"Don't be so modest, young man. You are young, you know, isn't that so? I can tell that you're young, your arm for example . . . " Her fingers dug a little into the sleeve of his lumberjacket. "I always look older than I am. You know, an artist's life . . . "

"Of course," Oliveira said. "As for me, I'm over forty, so you've been flattering me."

That's how the words came out of his mouth and he couldn't help it, it was too much, really. Hanging on to his arm Berthe Trépat talked about other times and every so often she would stop in the middle of what she was saying and seem to be putting something back together in her mind. Sometimes she would stick a finger in her nose and look at Oliveira out of the corner of her eye; in order to stick her finger up her nose she would quickly pull off her glove, pretending that she wanted to scratch the palm of her hand (after delicately removing it from Oliveira's arm), and would raise it up with a motion worthy of a pianist to scratch one nostril for a split second. Oliveira pretended to look away, and when he looked back again Berthe Trépat was clinging to his arm again with her glove back on. They went along like that in the rain talking about many things. On passing the Luxembourg they spoke about life in Paris, more difficult every day, the pitiless competition of young people whose inexperience was matched only by their insolence, a public that was incurably snobbish, the price of beef in the Saint-Germain market or on the Rue de Buci, places where the elite go to get a good cut of meat at reasonable prices. Two or three times Berthe Trépat had asked Oliveira in a friendly sort of way what he did for a living, about his ambitions, and especially about his failures, but before he could reply everything suddenly had to do with Valentin's inexplicable disappearance, the mistake of playing Alix Alix's *Pavan* out of consideration for Valentin, but that was the last time that would happen. "A queer," Berthe Trépat muttered, and Oliveira felt her hand tighten on his lumberjacket. "Me, mind you, having to play a shapeless piece of shit for that bastard when I have fifteen pieces of my own that are waiting to be played in public . . ."

Then she would stop in the rain, peaceful inside her raincoat (but Oliveira began to feel water coming in through the collar of his lumberjacket, a collar made from rabbit skin or rat skin, which had begun to stink like a cage in the zoo, it always did that whenever it rained and there was nothing he could do about it), and stand there looking at him as if waiting for an answer. Oliveira smiled in a warm sort of way, tugging at her a little to lead her towards the Rue de Médicis.

"You're too modest, too reserved," Berthe Trépat was saying. "Tell me about yourself, let's see. I'll bet you're a poet, right? So was Valentin when we were young . . . The *Evening Ode*, a hit in the

Mercure de France . . . A card from Thibaudet. I can remember it as if it had been just this morning. Valentin was weeping in bed, whenever he had to cry he would lie face down on the bed, it was very touching."

Oliveira tried to picture Valentin crying face down on the bed but all that came to mind was a little Valentin red as a crab, he was really imagining Rocamadour crying face down on the bed and La Maga trying to give him a suppository while Rocamadour resisted and arched his back, slipping his little bottom out of La Maga's clumsy hands. They must have given the old man who had been in the accident a suppository in the hospital too, it was incredible how popular they had become, he would have to make a philosophical analysis of this surprising vindication of the anus, its elevation to a second mouth, into something that no longer limited itself to excretion but which could swallow and digest those rose green white little anti-aircraft shells. But Berthe Trépat would not let him concentrate and again she wanted to know about his life and held his arm sometimes with one hand, sometimes with two, turning towards him a little bit with a girlish air which made him shiver even in the middle of the night. All right, he was an Argentinian who had been in Paris for some time, trying to . . . Let's see, what was he trying to do? It was hard to explain it all at once like that. What he was looking for was –

"Beauty, exaltation, the golden bough," Berthe Trépat said. "Don't say a word, I can make a perfect guess. I also came to Paris, from Pau, quite a few years ago, looking for the golden bough. But I was weak, young man, I was . . . What's your name?"

"Oliveira," Oliveira said.

"Oliveira . . . *Desolives*, the Mediterranean . . . I'm from the South too, we're panic, young man, we're both panic. Not like Valentin, who is from Lille. Northerners, cold as fish, like quicksilver. Do you believe in the Great Work? Fulcanelli, you understand . . . No need to answer, I can see that you're an initiate. Perhaps you haven't reached the experiences that really count yet, while I . . . Take the *Synthesis*, for example. What Valentin said is right, radiesthesia points out kindred souls to me and I think that shows through in the piece. Or don't you think so?"

"Oh, yes."

"You have a lot of karma, you can spot it in a minute . . . " her hand gripped him strongly; the pianist was ascending to a state of meditation and to do that she had to hold herself tightly against Oliveira who resisted only slightly, just enough to get her to cross the square and go up the Rue Soufflot. "If Étienne or Wong sees me they'll give me a hard time," thought Oliveira. But why should he care what Étienne or Wong might think, as if after the metaphysical rivers mixed with dirty pieces of cotton the future might have some importance. "Now it's just as if I'd never been in Paris and still here I am stupidly attentive to what is happening to me and it bothers me that this poor old woman is starting to come on with the sadness bit, the clutch of a dying man after the pavan and the complete flop of the concert. I'm worse than a kitchen rag, worse than dirty cotton, I really have nothing to do with my own self." Because this idea stayed with him, at that hour of the night and in the rain and stuck to Berthe Trépat, he began to feel like the last light in a huge mansion where all the other lights had gone out one by one, he began to get the notion that all of this was not he, that somewhere he was waiting for himself, that this person walking in the Latin Quarter hauling along an old woman who was hysterical and maybe a nymphomaniac was only a *Doppelgänger*, while the other one, the other . . . "Did you stay there in your Almagro neighbourhood? Or did you drown on the voyage, in whores' beds, in meaningful experiences, in the well-known necessary disorder? Everything seems to console me, it's comfortable to think of one's salvation even though it's just barely, the guy who is going to be hanged must keep on thinking that something will happen at the last minute, an earthquake, a noose that breaks twice so that they have to pardon him, the phone call from the governor, the uprising that will set him free. And now this old girl is just about ready to start grabbing at my fly."

But Berthe Trépat was lost in didascalic convolutions and had begun to tell with enthusiasm of her meeting with Germaine Tailleferre in the Gare de Lyon and how Tailleferre had said that the *Prelude for Orange Rhombuses* was extremely interesting and that she would speak to Marguerite Long about it so she could include it in one of her concerts.

"It would have been a success, Mr Oliveira, a triumph. But you know impresarios, little dictators, even the best artists are victims . . . Valentin thought that perhaps one of the younger pianists, someone who wouldn't worry, could do it . . . But they're just as ruined as the old ones, they're all cut from the same cloth."

"What about yourself, in another concert . . ."

"I never want to play again," Berthe Trépat said, hiding her face although Oliveira was careful about looking at her. "It's a shame that I still have to appear on stage to introduce my music when I should really be a muse, you know, the one who inspires artists; they would all come to me and beg me to let them play my things, beg me, yes, beg me. And I would give them permission, because I think my work is the spark that should ignite the sensibility of the public here and in the United States, in Hungary . . . Yes, I would give them my permission, but first they would have to come to me and ask for the honour of interpreting my music."

She clutched Oliveira's arm, and without knowing why, he had decided to go along the Rue Saint-Jacques and was walking along with the pianist gently in tow. An icy wind was blowing into their faces, filling their eyes and mouths with water, but Berthe Trépat seemed indifferent to any kind of weather, hanging on to Oliveira's arm as she began to sputter something that would be broken every few words by a hiccup or a short cackle that could have been one of spite or mockery. No, she didn't live on the Rue Saint-Jacques. No, but she didn't care where she lived either. She would just as soon keep on walking like that all night long, more than two hundred people for the première of the *Synthesis*.

"Valentin is going to get worried if you don't go home," Oliveira said, mentally grasping for something to say, a rudder to steer this corseted ball who was rolling along like a sea urchin in the wind and the rain. From out of her lengthy and disjointed rambling he was able to piece together the fact that Berthe Trépat lived on the Rue de l'Estrapade. Half-lost, Oliveira wiped the water out of his eyes with his free hand and got his bearings like a Conrad hero standing in the prow of a ship. He suddenly had a terrible urge to laugh (and it hurt his empty stomach, cramped his muscles, it was strange and painful and when he would tell Wong about it he wouldn't begin to believe it). Not at Berthe Trépat, who was going on about the honours she had received in Montpellier and Pau, with an occasional reference to the gold medal. Nor at his having been stupid enough to volunteer his company. He wasn't quite sure where the urge to laugh was coming from, it came from something previous, something farther back, not because of the concert, which should have been the most laughable thing in the world. Joy, something like a physical form of joy. Even though it was hard for him to believe it, joy. He could have laughed with contentment, pure, delightful, inexplicable contentment. "I'm going crazy," he thought. "And with this nut on my arm, it must be contagious." He didn't have the slightest reason to feel happy, water was seeping through the soles of his shoes and down his collar, Berthe Trépat was grasping his arm tighter and tighter and suddenly she began to be racked by a great sob, every time she mentioned Valentin she would shake all over and weep, it was a kind of conditioned reflex which in no way could have produced happiness in anyone, not even a madman. And Oliveira, while he wanted to burst out laughing in the worst way, carefully took hold of Berthe Trépat and was slowly leading her towards the Rue de l'Estrapade, towards Number Four, and there was no reason to think so, and much less understand it, but everything was just fine that way, taking Berthe Trépat to Number Four Rue de l'Estrapade, seeing as much as possible that she didn't step in any puddles or go under the water pouring out of the spouts on the cornices at the corner of the Rue Clotilde. The idle mention of a drink at her place (with Valentin) didn't seem bad at all to Oliveira; he would have to climb five or six floors towing the pianist after him, go into an apartment where Valentin had probably not lit the stove (but there would be a miraculous salamander, a bottle of cognac, they could take off their shoes, put their feet next to the fire, talk about art and about the gold medal). And he might even be able to come back some other night to Berthe Trépat and Valentin's place with a bottle of wine and keep them company, cheer them up. It was something like going to visit the old man in the hospital, going anywhere where until that moment it had not occurred to him to go, to the hospital, to the Rue de l'Estrapade. Before the joy there came the thing that was giving him terrible cramps in the stomach, a hand clasped underneath his skin like a delightful torture (he would have to ask Wong, a hand clasped underneath his skin).

"Number Four, right?"

"Yes, that house with the balcony," Berthe Trépat said. "An eighteenth-century mansion. Valentin said that Ninon de Lenclos had lived on the fourth floor. He's such a liar. Ninon de Lenclos. Oh, yes, Valentin lies all the time. It's almost stopped raining, hasn't it?"

"It's not raining so much," Oliveira conceded. "Let's cross here, all right?"

"The neighbours," Berthe Trépat said, looking at the café on the corner. "Naturally, the old woman from the eighth floor . . . You can't imagine how much she drinks. Do you see her there at the side table? She's looking at us, tomorrow the gossip will start . . . "

"Please, madame," Oliveira said. "Look out for that puddle."

"Oh, I know her, and the landlord too. They hate me because of Valentin. I've got to admit he has done some . . . He can't stand the old woman on the eighth floor, so one night when he came home quite drunk he daubed cat shit all over her door, from top to bottom, he made drawings with it . . . I'll never forget the uproar . . . Valentin in the tub taking the crap off, because in his true artistic enthusiasm he had got it all over himself, while I had to deal with the police, the old woman, the whole neighbourhood . . . You can't imagine what I've gone through, and me, with my standing . . . Valentin is awful, like a child."

Oliveira could see the white-haired man again, his jowls, his gold chain. It was like a path suddenly opening up in the middle of the wall: all you have to do is edge one shoulder in a little bit and enter, open a path through the stones, go through their thickness and come out into something else. The hand was clutching at his stomach so much that he was feeling nauseous. He was inconceivably happy.

"I'd like to have a *fine à leau* before I go up," Berthe Trépat said, stopping at the doorway and looking at him. "This pleasant walk has made me a little cold, and besides, the rain . . . "

"With pleasure," Oliveira said, disappointed. "But maybe it would be better if you went right up and took off your shoes, your feet are soaked."

"There's enough heat in the café," Berthe Trépat said. "I don't know whether Valentin has come home, it's just like him to be wandering around here looking for some friends. On nights like this he falls terribly in love with anyone, he's like a puppy, believe me."

"I'll bet he's home and has the stove going," Oliveira artfully suggested. "A good glass of punch, some wool socks . . . You've got to take care of yourself, madame."

"Oh, I'm like a rock. But I don't have any money to pay for anything in the café. Tomorrow I'll have to go back to the concert hall and pick up my *cachet* . . . It isn't safe to go around at night with so much money in your purse, this neighbourhood, terrible . . . "

"It would be my pleasure to buy you a drink," Oliveira said. He had managed to get her into the doorway and warm, damp air came from the hallway, musty-smelling, like mushroom sauce. His contentment was slowly going away as if it had kept on walking along alone down the street instead of staying with him in the doorway. But he had to fight against that idea, the joy had only lasted a few minutes, but it had been so new, so something else, and that moment when she had described Valentin in the bath all anointed with cat filth, the feeling had come over him that he could take a step forward, a real step, something without feet or legs, a step through a stone wall, and he could go in there and go forward and save himself from the other side, from the rain in his face and the water in his shoes. It was impossible to understand all that, as it always was with something so necessary to be understood. A joy, a hand underneath his skin squeezing his stomach, a hope – if it was possible to think of a word that way, if it was possible that something confused which he could not grasp could materialize under a notion of hope, it was just too idiotic, it was incredibly beautiful and now it was going away, it was going away in the rain because Berthe Trépat had not invited him up, she was sending him back to the corner café, re-enlisting him in the order of the day, in everything that had happened all during the day, Crevel, the docks on the Seine, the desire to go off in any direction, the old man on the stretcher, the mimeographed programme, Rose Bob, the water in his shoes. With a gesture that was slow enough to lift a mountain off his shoulders, Oliveira pointed at the two cafés which broke the darkness on the corner. But Berthe Trépat didn't seem to have any preference; suddenly she forgot her intentions, muttered something without letting go of Oliveira's arm, and was looking furtively into the darkened corridor.

"He's back," she said quickly, fixing her teary eyes on Oliveira. "He's up there, I can feel it. And somebody's with him, that's for sure, every time he introduced me at a concert he would run home to jump into bed with one of his boyfriends."

She was panting, digging her fingers into Oliveira's arm, and turning around every minute to peer into the darkness. From up above they heard a muffled mewing, like someone running along a felt path, the noise of which echoed down along the spiral of the staircase. Oliveira didn't know what to say and he took out a cigarette and lit it with some difficulty.

"I've forgotten my key," Berthe Trépat said so low that it was hard to hear her. "He never leaves a key for me when he's going to go to bed with one of them."

"But you really must get some rest, madame."

"What does he care whether I rest or explode. They've probably lit the fire and they're using up all the coal that Dr Lemoine gave me. And they're probably naked, naked. Yes, in my bed, naked, the bastards. And tomorrow I'll have to put everything in order, and Valentin has probably vomited on the pillow, he always does . . . Tomorrow like always. Me. Tomorrow."

"Don't you have any friends around here, somewhere where you could spend the night?" Oliveira asked.

"No," Berthe Trépat answered out of the corner of her eye. "Believe me, young man, most of my friends live in Neuilly. The only thing I have here are those old women and the Algerians on the eighth floor, a dirty lot."

"If you want me to, I'll go up and tell Valentin to open up," Oliveira said. "Maybe if you wait in the café we can arrange everything."

"Arrange what?" Berthe Trépat said, dragging out her words as if she were drunk. "He won't open up, I know him too well. They'll keep quiet in the dark. Why should they want light, now of all times? They'll turn on the lights later, when Valentin feels sure that I've gone to spend the night in a hotel or a café."

"If I knock on the door it will startle them. I don't think Valentin wants to have a scene."

"Nothing bothers him when he's like this, nothing bothers him at all. It wouldn't be beyond him to get dressed up in my clothes and walk into the police station on the corner singing the *Marseillaise*. He almost did it once. Robert from the warehouse caught him in time and brought him home. Robert was a good boy, he had his quirks too and he understood."

"Let me go up," Oliveira insisted. "You go to the café on the corner and wait for me. I'll fix things, you can't spend the whole night like this."

The hall light went on just as Berthe Trépat was about to give him a stronger answer. She jumped and ran out into the street, making a show of getting away from Oliveira, who stood there not knowing what to do. A couple was coming down the stairs, they passed without looking and went along towards the Rue Thouin. With a nervous glance behind, Berthe Trépat huddled back into the doorway. It was raining hard.

Not feeling like it at all, but asking himself what else he could do, Oliveira went inside looking for the stairway. He could not have taken more than three steps when Berthe Trépat grabbed him by the arm and hauled him back towards the door. She was mumbling all sorts of orders, prayers, everything got mixed up in a kind of cackling counterpoint that alternated between words and interjections and Oliveira let himself be led along, giving up to whatever might come. The light went out but it went on again in a few moments and they heard voices saying goodbye on the second or third floor. Berthe Trépat let go of Oliveira and leaned against the side of the door, pretending that she was buttoning up her raincoat as if she was getting ready to go out. She didn't move until the two men who were coming down went by her, looking at Oliveira in an incurious way and mumbling the *pardon* that goes with all hallway encounters. For a minute Oliveira considered going upstairs without any further ado, but he wasn't sure which floor she lived on. He took a heavy drag on his cigarette, back in the darkness, waiting for something to happen or for nothing to happen. In spite of the rain Berthe Trépat's sobs began to get clearer and clearer. He went over and put his hand on her shoulder. "Please, Madame Trépat, don't carry on like that. Tell me what we can do, there must be some way out of this."

"Leave me alone, leave me alone," the pianist muttered.

"You're worn out, you've got to get to bed. Anyway, let's go to a hotel, I don't have any money either, but I can make a deal with the manager, I'll pay him tomorrow. I know a hotel on the Rue Valette, it's not far."

"A hotel," Berthe Trépat said, turning around and looking at him.

"It's not good, but it is a way for you to get a good night's sleep."

"Do you really mean to take me to a hotel?"

"Madame, I will take you to the hotel, I will speak to the clerk and have him give you a room."

"A hotel, you want to take me to a hotel?"

"I don't want anything," Oliveira said, losing his patience. "I can't offer you my own place for the simple reason that I don't have any. You won't let me go up and make Valentin open the door. Would you rather I left? In that case, I'll say good night to you."

But who can tell whether he really did say all that or whether he was only thinking it. He had never been so far away from those words that at some other moment might have been the ones that came to his mind straight away. This wasn't the way to do things. He didn't know exactly what to do, but this certainly wasn't the way. And Berthe Trépat was looking at him as she huddled against the doorway. No, he hadn't said anything, he had been standing quietly beside her, and strange as it seemed, he still wanted to help, do something for Berthe Trépat who was looking straight at him and raising her hand little by little, and suddenly she let it go full force across Oliveira's face and he drew back confused, avoiding the worst of the slap but feeling the lash of her slender fingers, the instantaneous scratch of her nails.

"A hotel," Berthe Trépat repeated. "Just listen, all of you, just listen to what he said."

She was looking down the darkened hallway, moving her eyes about, her fervent painted lips were twisting around like something independent, given a life of their own, and in his upset state Oliveira thought he saw once more the hands of La Maga trying to shove the suppository into Rocamadour, and Rocamadour was clutching the cheeks of his behind together as he bellowed horribly and Berthe Trépat twisted her mouth from one side to the other, her eyes fixed on an invisible audience in the shadows of the hallway, her absurd hairdo shaking along more and more intensely with the movements of her head.

"Please," Oliveira murmured, stroking the place where she had scratched him and which was bleeding slightly, "how could you think such a thing?"

But she could think it, because (and she shouted it out and the light in the hall went on again) she knew very well what sort of degenerate followed her down the street the way they did with all decent women, but she would not permit it (and the door of the concierge's apartment began to open up and Oliveira saw the face of a monstrous rat peep out, with eyes that looked about avidly) and no monster, no drooling satyr was going to attack her in the doorway of her own home, that's what police are for and the courts – and someone came running down the stairs full speed, a boy with ruffled hair and a gypsy look was leaning on the banister to look and listen at his pleasure – and if her neighbours would not look out for her she was able to look after herself alone, because this wasn't the first time that a degenerate, a dirty exhibitionist had . . .

On the corner of the Rue Tournefort Oliveira realized that he still had the cigarette butt between his fingers, extinguished by the rain and half melted away. Leaning against a lamppost, he lifted up his face and let the rain wet it all over. That was so nobody could tell, with his face all wet in the rain nobody could tell. Then he started to walk slowly, hunched over, with the collar of his lumberjacket buttoned up against his chin; as always, the pelt on the collar stank like something terribly rotten, like a tannery. He wasn't thinking about anything, just letting himself walk along as if he had been looking around, a big, fat-footed dog with his fur hanging down walking in the rain. Once in a while he would lift up his hand and wipe his face, but finally he let it rain, sometimes he would thrust out his lip and drink up some of the salty water running down his cheeks. When much later and near the Jardin des Plantes he picked up again the day's memories, an applied and careful retelling of every minute of that day, he said to himself that he had really not been such an idiot to have felt so happy seeing the old woman home. But that as always he had paid dearly for that foolish happiness. Now he would begin to reproach himself, put himself down little by little until the same old thing was left there, a hole where time was blowing, an imprecise continuum that had no set bounds. "Let's not get literary," he thought while he dug out a cigarette after he had dried his hands a bit with the heat of his trouser pockets. "Let's forget about bringing up those bitchy words, those made-up pimps. That's how it was and too bad. Berthe Trépat . . . It's all been too crazy, but it would have been nice to have gone upstairs and had a drink with her and with Valentin, taken off my shoes next to the fire. Actually that's all I ever wanted to do, the idea of taking off my shoes and drying my socks. I let you down, baby, what you going to do about it. Let's let things lie the way they are, I've got to get to bed. There was no other reason, there couldn't have been any other reason. If I allow myself I might go back to the apartment and spend the night being wet-nurse." From the Rue du Sommerard it would be twenty minutes in the rain; it would be better to pop into the first hotel and go to bed. One after another his matches began to go out. It was enough to make you laugh.

(–124)

24

"I don't know how to explain it," La Maga said as she dried the spoon with a towel that was not too clean. "Other people could probably do a better job of it, but I've always been that way, it's easier to talk about sad things than happy ones."

"It's a law," Gregorovius said. "Perfectly put forth, a profound truth. Raised to the level of literary skill it means that bad writing comes from good feelings, and other things along the same lines. Happiness cannot be explained, Lucía, probably because it is the ultimate moment of the veil of Maya."

La Maga looked at him perplexed and Gregorovius sighed.

"The veil of Maya," he repeated. "But let's not get things confused. You have seen very well that misfortune is, let's say, tangible, perhaps because out of it comes the separation into subject and object. That's why memory is so important, that's why it's so easy to describe catastrophes."

"What happens," said La Maga as she stirred the milk on the stove, "is that happiness belongs to only one person while misfortune seems to belong to everybody."

"A worthy corollary," said Gregorovius. "What's more, I want you to know that I'm not nosy. The other night, at the meeting of the Club . . . Well, Ronald had some vodka that was too much of a tongue-loosener. I don't want you to think that I'm any kind of prier, I just like to know my friends better. You and Horacio . . . What I mean is that there's something about you I can't explain, some kind of mystery in your core. Ronald and Babs say that you're the perfect couple, that you complement each other. I don't see that you complement each other so much."

"What difference does it make?"

"It doesn't make any difference, but you were telling me that Horacio has gone off."

"That has nothing to do with it," La Maga said. "I can't talk about happiness, but that doesn't mean that I haven't been happy. If you want I can go on telling why Horacio left, why it could have been me who left if it hadn't been for Rocamadour." She waved her hand in the direction of the suitcases, the great mess of paper and boxes and records that filled the room. "I've got to take care of all this, I've got to find some place to go . . . I don't want to stay here, it's too sad."

"Étienne could find you a place with good light. When Rocamadour goes back to the country. Something around seven thousand francs a month. In that case, if it's all right with you I'll take this place. I like it, it has an aura. One can think here, it's comfortable."

"Don't you believe it," La Maga said. "Around seven o'clock the girl upstairs begins to sing *Les Amants du Havre*. It's a nice song, but on and on . . . "

Puisque la terre est ronde,
Mon amour t'en fais pas,
Mon amour t'en fais pas.

"That's pretty," Gregorovius said indifferently.

"Yes, it has a great philosophy, that's what Ledesma would have said. No, you didn't know him. It was before Horacio, in Uruguay."

"The Negro?"

"No, the Negro's name was Ireneo."

"Then the story about the Negro was true?"

La Maga looked at him surprised. Gregorovius really was stupid. Except for Horacio (and sometimes . . .) everybody who had ever wanted her always acted like such an idiot. Stirring the milk, she went over to the bed and tried to get Rocamadour to take a few spoonfuls. Rocamadour shrieked and refused, the milk ran down his neck. "Topitopitopi," La Maga kept saying with the voice of a hypnotist giving out prizes. "Topitopitopi," trying to get a spoonful in Rocamadour's mouth as he became flushed and refused to drink, but suddenly he relented for some reason and slid down towards the foot of the bed as he took one spoonful after another to the immense satisfaction of Gregorovius, who was filling his pipe and beginning to feel a little like a father.

"Chin chin," La Maga said, leaving the pot by the side of the bed and tucking in Rocamadour who was rapidly getting drowsy. "He still has a high fever, it must be a hundred and three at least."

"Didn't you use the thermometer?"

"It's hard to get it in, then he'll cry for twenty minutes afterwards, Horacio can't stand it. I can tell by how warm his forehead is. It must be over a hundred and three, I can't understand why it doesn't go down."

"Too much empiricism, I'm afraid," Gregorovius said. "And isn't that milk bad for him when his fever is so high?"

"It's not so high for a child," La Maga said, lighting up a Gauloise. "The best thing would be to turn off the light so he'll fall asleep right away. Over there, next to the door."

A glow was coming from the stove and it seemed to get brighter as they sat opposite each other and smoked for a while without talking. Gregorovius watched La Maga's cigarette go up and down, for a second her strangely placid face would light up like a hot coal, her eyes would glisten as she looked at him, everything was wrapped up in a half-light in which Rocamadour's whimpering and clucking got softer and softer until it stopped altogether, followed by a light hiccup that came periodically. A clock struck eleven.

"He's not coming back," La Maga said. "Of course, he'll have to come for his things, but that's not the same. It's over, kaput."

"I wonder," Gregorovius said cautiously. "Horacio is so sensitive, it's difficult for him to get around in Paris. He thinks that he's doing what he wants to do, that he has a lot of liberty here, but he goes around running into barriers. All you have to do is see him on the street, once I followed him a while, from a distance."

"Spy," La Maga said in a tone that was almost friendly.

"Let's say 'observer'."

"You were really following me, even though I wasn't with him."

"Maybe I was, I didn't stop to think about it at the time. I like to see how people I know act, it's always more exciting than a game of chess. I have discovered that Wong masturbates and that Babs practises a kind of Jansenist charity, her face turned to the wall while she drops a piece of bread with something inside it. There was a time when I used to study my mother. It was in Herzegovina, a long time ago. Adgalle used to fascinate me, she insisted on wearing a blond wig when I knew very well that her hair was black. Nobody in the castle knew this; we had moved in there after Count Rossler died. When I asked her about it (I was barely ten then, it was such a happy time) my mother would laugh and make me swear never to reveal the truth. That truth I had to hide used to make me nervous, it was simpler and more beautiful than the blond wig. The wig was a work of art, my mother could comb her hair quite naturally while the maid was there and no one would suspect anything. But when she was alone, I really don't know why, but I wanted to hide under a sofa or behind the purple curtains. I decided to bore a hole in the wall between the library and my mother's boudoir – I used to work at night when they thought I was asleep. That's how I was able to watch Adgalle take off her blond wig, shake out her black hair which gave her such a different look, so beautiful, and then she took off the other wig and there was the perfect cue-ball, something so disgusting that I vomited most of my goulash on my pillow that night."

"Your childhood sounds like something out of *The Prisoner of Zenda*," La Maga said as she thought about it.

"It was a world of wigs," said Gregorovius. "I wonder what Horacio would have done in my place. We were really going to talk about Horacio, you wanted to tell me something."

"That hiccup is strange," La Maga said, looking at Rocamadour's bed. "It's the first time he's had it."

"Probably his digestion."

"Why do they insist I take him to the hospital? This afternoon again, that ant-faced doctor. I don't want to take him, he wouldn't like it. I can do everything that has to be done. Babs was here this morning and said it wasn't so serious. Horacio didn't think it was serious either."

"Horacio isn't coming back?"

"No. Horacio's gone off out there, looking for things."

"Don't cry, Lucía."

"I'm just blowing my nose. The hiccups have gone."

"Tell me about it, Lucía, if it would help."

"I can't remember anything, it's not worth it. Yes, I remember. Why? Adgalle is a strange name."

"Yes, who knows whether it was her real one. I was told . . . "

"Like the blond wig and the black wig," La Maga said.

"Like everything," said Gregorovius. "You're right, the hiccups have gone away. Now he'll sleep till morning. When did you and Horacio first meet?"

(–134)

25

She would have preferred Gregorovius to be quiet or to talk only about Adgalle, letting her smoke peacefully in the darkness, far removed from the shapes in the room, from the books and records that would have to be packed up so Horacio could take them away when he found a place. But it was no use, he would be still for a moment waiting for her to say something, and then he would ask a question, they all had something to ask her all the time, as if it bothered them that she would rather sing *Mon p'tit voyou* or make sketches with burnt matches or stroke the mangiest cats she could find on the Rue du Sommerard, or give Rocamadour his bottle.

"*Alors, mon p'tit voyou,*" La Maga sang softly, "*la vie, qu'est-ce qu'on s'en fout . . .* "

"I used to adore fishbowls too," said Gregorovius, thinking back. "I lost all interest in them when I was initiated into the duties proper to my sex. In Dubrovnik, a whorehouse where I was taken by a Danish sailor who at the time was my Odessa mother's lover. There was a marvellous aquarium at the foot of the bed, and the bed too had something of an aquarium about it with its pale-blue rippling spread which the fat redhead carefully turned down before she grabbed me by the ears like a rabbit. You can't imagine the fright, Lucía, the terror of all that. We were lying on our backs, next to each other, and she caressed me mechanically, I was cold and she was talking about something or other, about the fight that had just taken place in the bar, of the stormy weather in March . . . The fish went back and forth like her hand on my legs, rising, sinking . . . That's what love-making was, then, a black fish going doggedly back and forth. An image like any other, but quite exact. The infinite repetition of an anxious desire to flee, to go through the glass and go into some other thing."

"Who can tell," La Maga said. "I don't think that fish ever want to get out of their bowls, they almost never touch the glass with their noses."

Gregorovius thought that somewhere Chestov had written about aquariums with a removable glass partition which could be taken out any time and that the fish, who was accustomed to his compartment, would never try to go over to the other side. He would come to a point in the water, turn around and swim back, without discovering that the obstacle was gone, that all he had to do was to keep on going forward . . .

"But that could be love too," Gregorovius said. "How wonderful to be admiring fish in a tank and suddenly to see them pass into the open air, fly away like doves. An idiotic hope, of course. We all draw back for fear of rubbing our noses against something unpleasant. The nose as the limit of the world, a topic for a dissertation. Do you know how they teach cats not to dirty indoors? The technique of an opportune rub. Do you know how they teach pigs not to eat the truffles? A whack on the nose, it's horrible. I think that Pascal was more of an expert on noses than one would gather from his famous Egyptian observation."

"Pascal?" La Maga asked. "What Egyptian observation?"

Gregorovius sighed. They all used to sigh when she asked a question. Horacio and especially Étienne, because Étienne not only used to sigh but would sniff, snort, and call her stupid. "It's so purple to be ignorant," La Maga thought, hurt. Every time somebody was scandalized by one of her questions a purple feeling, a purple mass would envelop her for a moment. She had to take a deep breath so that the purple mass would dissolve, would float about there like the fish, dividing up into a lot of purple rhombuses, kites in the wasteland in the Pocitos quarter, summer at the beach, purple blotches on the sun and the sun was called Ra and was also Egyptian like Pascal. Gregorovius's sigh didn't bother her much now, after Horacio she wouldn't be bothered by anybody's sighs when she asked a question, but in any case, the purple spot always came for a moment, a desire to cry, something which lasted just the time necessary to grind out her cigarette in that irresistible carpet-ruining gesture, supposing that there had been a carpet there.

(–141)

26

"When you come right down to it," Gregorovius said, "Paris is one big metaphor."

He knocked his pipe, tamped the tobacco a bit. La Maga had lit another Gauloise and was singing softly. She was so tired that she didn't even get angry at not understanding what he had said. Since she didn't hasten to ask a question as she would have normally, Gregorovius decided to explain. La Maga was listening from far off, aided by the darkness of the room and the cigarette. She heard bits and pieces, the continual mention of Horacio, Horacio's disorder, the aimless wanderings of almost all of those in the Club, the reasons behind the belief that all of this was leading towards some sense. Sometimes something Gregorovius said would become outlined in the shadows, green or white, sometimes it was an Atlan, at others an Estève, then some sound would whirl around and take shape, grow like a Manessier, like a Wifredo Lam, like a Piaubert, like an Étienne, like a Max Ernst. It was fun, Gregorovius was saying, ". . . and they're all looking out for magical Babylonian pathways, to put it that way, and then . . . ," La Maga saw a resplendent Deyrolles take shape out of the words, a Bissière, but now Gregorovius was talking about the uselessness of an empirical ontology and suddenly it was a Friedländer, a delicate Villon which made a crisscross on the half-light and made it quiver, *empirical ontology*, smoke-blues, pinks, *empirical*, a pale yellow, a hollow where whitish sparks were fluttering.

"Rocamadour has fallen asleep," La Maga said, putting out her cigarette. "I have to sleep for a while too."

"Horacio won't be back tonight, I don't imagine."

"How should I know. Horacio is like a cat, he might be sitting on the floor outside the door, and he might have taken a train to Marseilles."

"I can stay," Gregorovius said. "You go to sleep and I'll watch Rocamadour."

"But I'm not sleepy. I keep seeing things in the air while you're talking. You said 'Paris is one big metaphor', and it was like one of those designs by Sugai, lots of red and black."

"I was thinking of Horacio," Gregorovius said. "It's funny how Horacio has been changing in these months since I first met him. You wouldn't have noticed, I imagine, too close to him and too responsible for the changes."

"Why one big metaphor?"

"He walks around here the way other people look for flight in voodoo or marijuana, Pierre Boulez or Tinguely's painting-machines. He guesses that in some part of Paris, some day or some death or some meeting will show him a key; he's searching for it like a madman. Note that I said like a madman. I mean that he really doesn't know that he's looking for the key, or that the key exists. He has an inkling of its shapes, its disguises; that's why I was talking about a metaphor."

"Why do you say that Horacio has changed?"

"A question to the point, Lucía. When I met Horacio I had him down as an amateur intellectual, I mean an intellectual without rigour. You people are a little like that down there, aren't you? In Mato Grosso, places like that."

"Mato Grosso is in Brazil."

"Along the Paraná, then. Very intelligent and alert, up to date on everything. Much more than us. Italian literature, for example, or English. And the whole Spanish Golden Age, and naturally French literature on the tip of your tongues. Horacio was pretty much like that. It was only too clear. I think it's admirable that he has changed like this in so little time. Now he's turned into a real animal, all you have to do is look at him. Well, he hasn't turned into an animal quite yet, but he's trying his best."

"Don't talk nonsense," La Maga snorted.

"Understand me, what I'm trying to say is that he is looking for the black light, the key, and he's beginning to realize that you don't find those things in libraries. You're the one who really taught him that, and if he's left it's because he's never going to forgive you for it."

"That's not why Horacio left."

"There's a design to that too. He doesn't know why he left and you, the reason for his leaving, are incapable of knowing unless you decide to believe what I'm telling you."

"I don't believe it," La Maga said, sliding off the chair and lying down on the floor. "And besides, I don't understand any of it. And don't bring up Pola. I don't want to talk about Pola."

"Keep on looking at what's being drawn in the darkness," Gregorovius said pleasantly. "We can talk about other things, of course. Did you know that the Chirkin Indians, by always asking missionaries for shears, now have such a collection of them that the number of shears per capita among them far outstrips the figure for any other group of people in the world? I read about that in an article by Alfred Métraux. The world is full of strange things."

"But why is Paris one big metaphor?"

"When I was a boy," Gregorovius said, "the nursemaids used to make love to the Uhlans who were stationed in the Bozsok sector. Since I would get in their way for the performance of those duties, they used to let me play in a huge room full of rugs and tapestries which would have delighted Malte Laurids Brigge. One of the rugs showed the layout of the city of Ophir, according to the legends that have reached the West through storybooks. I used to get on my knees and with my nose or my hands push a yellow ball along, following the course of the Shan-Ten river, crossing walls guarded by black warriors armed with spears, and then after numerous dangers and after bumping my head on the legs of the mahogany table which was in the centre of the rug, I would come to the quarters of the Queen of Sheba and I would curl up like a caterpillar and fall asleep on top of the picture of a triclinium. Yes, Paris is a metaphor. Now that I think about it, you're stretched out on a rug too. What's the picture on it? Ah, lost childhood, closeness, closeness! I've been in this room twenty times and I can't remember the picture on that rug . . . "

"It's so dirty that there isn't much picture left," La Maga said. "I think it shows two peacocks kissing with their bills. It's all rather green."

They were silent, listening to the footsteps of someone coming up the stairs.

(–109)

27

"Oh, Pola," La Maga said. "I know more about her than Horacio does."

"Without ever having seen her, Lucía?"

"But I've seen so much of her," La Maga said impatiently. "Horacio carried her around in his hair, in his overcoat, he shook from her, he washed from her."

"Étienne and Wong told me about the woman," Gregorovius said. "They saw them one day at a street café in Saint-Cloud. Only the stars could tell us what all those people could possibly have been doing in Saint-Cloud, but there they were. Horacio was looking at her the way you would look at an anthill, it seems. Wong used all this later on to work out a complicated theory on sexual saturation; according to him it would be possible to advance in knowledge provided that at a given moment one would reach a certain coefficient in love (they're his words, please excuse the Chinese jargon) which would cause the spirit to crystallize suddenly on another level, become established in a surreality. Do you think that's so, Lucía?"

"I suppose that we're looking for something like that, but we almost always get swindled or do some swindling ourselves. Paris is a great blind love, we are all hopelessly in love, but there is something green, a kind of mist, I don't know. It was the same way in Montevideo, you couldn't really love anybody, strange things would turn up right away, stories of sheets or hairs, and for a woman lots of other things, Ossip, abortions, for example. So."

"Love, sexuality. Are we talking about the same thing?"

"Yes," La Maga said. "If we're talking about love we're talking about sexuality. Not so much the other way around. But sexuality is different from sex, I think."

"No theories," Ossip said unexpectedly. "Dichotomies, like syncretisms . . . Horacio was probably looking for something in Pola that you couldn't give him, I imagine. Getting down to practical matters, that is."

"Horacio is always looking for any number of things," La Maga said. "He was getting tired of me because I don't know how to think, that's all. I have the feeling that Pola thinks all the time."

"Poor love that feeds on thought," Ossip quoted.

"We've got to be fair," La Maga said. "Pola is very beautiful, I know that from the way Horacio's eyes would look at me when he would come back after being with her, he would come back like a match being struck and suddenly his hair would grow, it would only last a second, but it was marvellous, a sort of scratch, a very strong smell of phosphorus and that huge flame that would die down quickly. That's the way he would come home and it was because Pola had filled him with beauty. I used to tell him that, Ossip, and it was only right that I did. We were already a little distant although we were still in love with one another. These things don't happen all of a sudden, Pola was coming up like the sun at the window, I always have to think about things like that to know that I'm telling the truth. She was coming in slowly, breaking up the shadows around me, and Horacio was getting warmed, the same as on shipboard, he was getting tanned, he was happy."

"I never would have believed it. I thought that you . . . Of course, Pola passed on like some of the others. Because we have to talk about Françoise too, for example."

"She didn't matter," La Maga said, flicking her ash on the floor. "It would be the same as if I named people like Ledesma, for example. I'm sure you don't know anything about that any more than you know how the Pola affair finally ended up."

"No."

"Pola is dying," La Maga said. "Not from the pins, that was a joke, even though I was serious when I did it, believe me, I was very serious. She's dying of breast cancer."

"And Horacio . . . "

"Don't be dirty, Ossip. Horacio didn't know anything about it when he left Pola."

"Please, Lucía, I . . . "

"You know very well what you're saying and what you're after here tonight, Ossip. Don't be a swine, I didn't even hint at that."

"But please tell me what?"

"That Horacio knew about it before he left her."

"Please," Gregorovius repeated. "I didn't even . . . "

"Don't be dirty," La Maga said monotonously. "Why should you want to put Horacio down? Don't you know that we've split up, that he's gone away out there in the rain?"

"I'm not after anything," Ossip said, as he seemed to huddle up into the easy chair. "I'm not like that, Lucía, you're always going around misunderstanding me. Do I have to get down on my knees, like the captain of the *Graffin* that time, and beg you to believe me, and to – "

"Leave me alone," La Maga said. "First Pola, then you. All those spots on the wall and this night that never seems to have an end. I wouldn't put it past you to think that I'm killing Pola."

"It never crossed my mind."

"OK, OK. Horacio will never forgive me, even though he's not in love with Pola any more. It's laughable, a worthless little doll, made of wax from a Christmas candle, a delicate green wax, I remember."

"Lucía, it's hard for me to believe that you were capable . . . "

"He'll never forgive me, even though we didn't talk about it. He knows because he saw the doll and he saw the pins. He threw it on the floor, crushed it with his foot. He didn't realize that that made it worse, that it increased the danger. Pola lives on the Rue Dauphine, he used to go to see her almost every afternoon. Do you think he told her about the little green doll, Ossip?"

"Quite probably," Ossip said, hostile and resentful. "All of you are crazy."

"Horacio used to speak about a new order of things, about the possibility of discovering a different life. He always spoke about death when he was talking about life, it was inevitable and we would laugh a lot about it. He told me that he was sleeping with Pola and then I understood that he didn't think it was necessary for me to get upset or make a scene. I wasn't really upset, Ossip, I could go to bed with you right now if I wanted to. It's hard to explain, it's not a matter of being unfaithful and things like that, Horacio used to get furious whenever he would hear the words 'unfaithful' or 'cheating'. I must recognize that from the first time we met he told me that he didn't consider himself obligated in any way. I made the doll because Pola had got into my room, it was too much, I knew that she was capable of stealing my clothes, wearing my stockings, using my make-up, giving Rocamadour his milk."

"But you said you didn't know her."

"She was in Horacio, stupid. Stupid, stupid Ossip. Poor Ossip, so stupid. In his lumberjacket, in the fur collar, you've seen the fur collar on Horacio's lumberjacket. And Pola would be there when he came home, and in the way he would look, and when Horacio would get undressed, there in the corner, and get into that bath – you see it, Ossip? – then Pola would start coming out of his skin, I saw her like ectoplasm and I held back the urge to cry because I knew that I would never get into Pola's flat that way, that Pola would never sense me in Horacio's hair or eyes or body-fuzz. I don't know why; after all, we had been very much in love. I don't know why. Because I don't know how to think and he despises me. For things like that."

(–28)

28

There was walking on the stairway.

"It's probably Horacio," Gregorovius said.

"Probably," said La Maga. "But I rather think it's the watchmaker on the sixth floor, he always comes in late. Would you like to hear some music?"

"At this time of night? We'll wake the baby."

"No, we'll put it on very low, it would be just right to listen to a quartet. We can turn it low enough so that we'll be the only ones who can hear it, let's see."

"It wasn't Horacio," Gregorovius observed.

"I can't say," La Maga said, lighting a match and looking at some records piled in a corner. "He might have sat down outside, he does that sometimes. Sometimes he gets to the door and changes his mind. Turn on the record-player, that white button next to the fireplace."

There was something that looked like a shoebox and La Maga knelt down to put the record on, feeling around in the dark, and the shoebox hummed a little, a distant chord filled the air around her hands. Gregorovius began to fill his pipe, a little scandalized. He didn't like Schoenberg, but it was for a different reason, the time, the sick child, a kind of transgression. That was it, a transgression. An idiot idea. But sometimes he would get spells like that in which a vague sense of order would get back at him for having abandoned it. Stretched out on the floor with her head almost stuck inside the shoebox, La Maga seemed to be sleeping.

Every so often there would be a soft snore from Rocamadour, but Gregorovius was getting lost in the music, he found that he could give in and let himself be carried off without protesting, turn himself over to a dead and buried Viennese. La Maga was smoking stretched out on the floor, her face would light up in the dark, with her eyes closed and her hair over her face, her cheeks shining as if she had been crying, it was stupid to think that she could have been crying, rather she was biting her lips with rage as she listened to the dry sound of a thump from up above, the second one, the third. Gregorovius was startled and was about to shout when he felt a hand holding him by the ankle.

"Pay no attention, it's the old man upstairs."

"But we can barely hear ourselves."

"It's the pipes," La Maga said mysteriously. "Everything gets in there, it's already happened other times."

"The science of acoustics is amazing," Gregorovius said.

"He'll get tired soon," La Maga said. "The fool."

The knocking kept on upstairs. La Maga got up furiously and lowered the volume even more. Eight or nine chords, a pizzicato, and the knocking started again.

"It can't be," Gregorovius said. "It's absolutely impossible that he can hear a thing."

"He has better hearing than we do, that's the worst of it."

"This building is like Dionysus' ear."

"Whose ear? God damn him, right in the adagio. And he keeps on knocking. Rocamadour is going to wake up."

"Maybe it would be better . . ."

"No, I don't want to. Let him break the ceiling down. I'm going to put on a Mario del Monaco record and teach him a lesson, too bad I don't have one. The fool, the dirty bastard."

"Lucía," Gregorovius said softly. "It's past midnight."

"Always the time," La Maga snorted. "I'm going to get out of this place. I couldn't put the volume any lower than it is, we couldn't hear anything. Wait, I'm going to put the last movement on again. Don't worry."

The knocking stopped, for a while the quartet was moving along towards the end without even the rhythmic snoring of Rocamadour. La Maga sighed, with her head practically in the speaker. The knocking started again.

"What a fool," La Maga said. "And that's the way it is all the time."

"Don't be stubborn, Lucía."

"Don't you be a fool. I'm sick of them. I'd love to kick all of them out into the street. Just because I wanted to listen to Schoenberg, just for a while . . ."

She had begun to cry, she reached over and lifted the needle as the last notes were over and since she was next to Gregorovius, leaning over the amplifier to shut it off, it was easy for him to put his arm around her waist and set her down on one of his knees. He began to stroke her hair, clearing it away from her face. La Maga was crying with short sobs, coughing and blowing her tobacco breath in his face.

"Poor thing, poor thing," Gregorovius repeated in rhythm to his caresses. "Nobody loves her, nobody. Everybody is nasty to poor Lucía."

"You stupid arse," La Maga said as she hawked and swallowed in an unctuous sort of way. "I'm crying because I want to cry and especially to avoid anyone consoling me. My God, you've got sharp knees, they cut into me like scissors."

"Sit here a while," Gregorovius begged.

"I don't feel like it," La Maga said. "And why in the world does that idiot keep on pounding like that?"

"Don't pay any attention to him, Lucía. You poor thing . . . "

"He's still knocking, I tell you it's unbelievable."

"Let him knock," Gregorovius advised incongruously.

"You were the one who was worried before," La Maga said, laughing in his face.

"Please, if you knew . . . "

"Oh, I know everything, but be still, Ossip," La Maga said suddenly, catching on. "The guy wasn't knocking because of the record. We can put another one on if we want to."

"Oh Lord, no."

"But can't you still hear him pounding?"

"I'm going up and punch him in the nose," Gregorovius said.

"Right now," La Maga said in encouragement, getting up with a jump so that he could get by. "Tell him that he has no right to wake people up at one o'clock in the morning. Come on, get going, it's the door on the left, there's a shoe nailed to it."

"A shoe nailed to the door?"

"Yes, the old man is completely mad. There's a shoe and a green piece from an accordion. Aren't you going up there?"

"I don't think it's worth it," Gregorovius said wearily. "That all makes it so different, so useless. Lucía, you didn't understand that . . . Well, anyway, the fellow might stop knocking."

La Maga went over to the corner and took down something that in the shadows looked like a feather duster, and Gregorovius heard a tremendous blow on the ceiling. The noise stopped upstairs.

"Now we can listen to what we please," La Maga said.

"I wonder," thought Gregorovius, getting more and more tired.

"For example," La Maga said, "a Brahms sonata. How wonderful, he's got tired of knocking. Wait, I'll find the record, it's around here somewhere. I can't see a thing."

"Horacio is out there," Gregorovius thought. "Sitting on the landing with his back against the door, listening to everything. Like a tarot figure, something that has to resolve itself, a polyhedron in which every edge and every facet keeps its immediate sense, the false one, until the mediating sense is integrated, revelation. And so Brahms, me, the thumps on the ceiling, Horacio: something is slowly heading towards an explanation. But it's all so useless in any case." He wondered what would happen if he tried to embrace La Maga in the dark again. "But he's out there listening. He would be capable of enjoying what he heard, listening to us, he's repulsive sometimes." Besides, he was afraid of Oliveira and it was hard for him to admit it.

"This must be it," La Maga said. "Yes, a half-silver label with two birds on it. Who's talking outside there?"

"A polyhedron, somewhat crystallized, which takes shape little by little in the darkness," Gregorovius thought. "She's going to say this now and outside the other thing will happen and I . . . But I don't know what this is or what the other is."

"It's Horacio," La Maga said.

"Horacio and a woman."

"No, it must be the old man from upstairs."

"The one with the shoe on his door?"

"Yes, he has an old woman's voice, like a magpie. He always goes around wearing an astrakhan hat."

"Better not put the record on," Gregorovius advised. "Let's see what happens."

"So we can't listen to the Brahms sonata after all," La Maga said furiously.

"What a ridiculous subversion of values," Gregorovius thought. "There they are, about to kick each other around on the landing, in pitch dark or whatever you want to call it, and all she can think about is the fact that she won't be able to hear her sonata." But La Maga was right, as always she was the only one who was right. "I'm more prejudiced than I thought," Gregorovius said to himself. "One thinks that just because he is living the life of an *affranchi* and accepts the material and spiritual parasitism of Lutetia, he's managed to get over on the pre-Adamite side. Poor fool, what can you do."

"The rest is silence," Gregorovius said in English as he sighed.

"Silence my foot," answered La Maga, who knew English quite well. "Now watch them start in all over again. The old man will speak first. There he is, '*Mais qu'est-ce que vous foutez?*'" La Maga mimicked with a nasal voice. "Let's see what Horacio answers. I think he's laughing under his breath, when he starts to laugh he can't find the right words, it's incredible. I'm going to see what's going on."

"And we were so comfortable," Gregorovius murmured, as if he had seen the angel of expulsion approaching. Gérard David, Van der Weiden, the Master of Flemalle, at that hour all the angels for some reason seemed to be accursedly Flemish, with chubby, stupid faces, but resplendent with lace and bourgeois admonitions (Daddy-ordered-it, so-you-better-beat-it-you-lousy-sinners). The whole room full of angels, "I looked over Jordan and what did I see / A band of angels comin' after me," always the same finale, police angels, dunning angels, angel angels. Putrefaction of putrefactions, like the blast of cold air that came up the legs of his pants, the angry voices on the landing, the silhouette of La Maga in the doorway.

"*C'est pas des façons, ça,*" the old man was saying. "*Empêcher les gens de dormir à cette heure c'est trop con. J'me plaindrai à la Police, moi, et puis qu'est-ce que vous foutez là, vous planqué par terre contre la porte? J'aurais pu me casser la gueule, merde alors.*"

"Go back to sleep, old man," said Horacio, stretched out comfortably on the floor.

"*Dormir, moi, avec le bordel que fait votre bonne femme? Ça alors comme culot, mais je vous préviens, ça me passera pas comme ça, vous aurez de mes nouvelles.*"

"*Mais de mon frère le Poète on a eu des nouvelles,*" Horacio quoted with a yawn. "Have you been watching this guy?"

"A fool," La Maga said. "You put on a record turned down low and he pounds. You take the record off and he keeps on pounding. What does he want?"

"Well, it's the story of the guy who only drops one shoe."

"I don't know that one," La Maga said.

"It was predictable," said Oliveira. "Old people inspire respect in me, mixed up with other feelings, but as far as this one is concerned, I'd like to buy a bottle of formalin and stick him in it so he'd stop bugging us."

"*Et en plus ça m'insulte dans son charabia de sales métèques,*" the old man said. "*On est en France, ici. Des salauds, quoi. On devrait vous mettre à la porte, c'est une honte. Qu'est-ce que fait le Gouvernement, je me demande. Des Arabes, tous des fripouilles, bande de tueurs.*"

"Come off it with the *sales métèques*, you ought to see that bunch of Frogs pile up the loot in Argentina," Oliveira said. "What were you listening to? I just got here, I'm soaked."

"A Schoenberg quartet. Just now I wanted to listen to a Brahms sonata, turned down very low."

"The best thing would be to let it go till tomorrow," said Oliveira, sizing up the situation and sitting up on one elbow as he lit a Gauloise. "*Rentrez chez vous, monsieur, on vous emmerdera plus pour ce soir.*"

"*Des fainéants,*" the old man said. "*Des tueurs, tous.*"

The astrakhan hat could be seen in the light of the match along with a dirty bathrobe and wrathful little eyes. The hat cast a gigantic shadow on the wall of the stairwell; La Maga was fascinated. Oliveira got up, blew out the match, and went into the apartment, closing the door softly.

"Hello," Oliveira said. "I can't see anything."

"Hello," said Gregorovius. "I'm glad you handled the man upstairs all right."

"*Per modo di dire.* In truth the old man is right, and besides, he's old."

"Being old is no reason," La Maga said.

"It may not be a reason, but it is a safe-conduct pass."

"I remember your saying once that the tragedy of Argentina is in the hands of old men."

"The curtain's already come down on that play," Oliveira said. "It's been just the opposite since Perón, the young ones call the tune and it's almost worse, but what can you do. The idea of age, generation, degrees and class is a great joke. I suppose the reason that we're so uncomfortable whispering like this is because Rocamadour is sleeping his sleep of the just."

"Yes, he fell asleep before we began to listen to some music. You're soaked to the skin, Horacio."

"I went to a piano recital," Oliveira explained.

"Oh," said La Maga. "Well, that's fine. Take off your lumberjacket and I'll fix you a nice hot *mate*."

"And a glass of *caña*, there still must be half a bottle left around here."

"What's *caña*?" Gregorovius asked. "Is it the same as what they call *grappa*?"

"No, more like *barack*. Very good after concerts, especially in the case of first performances and indescribable consequences. Why don't we light a dim and timid little light which won't reach to Rocamadour's eyes?"

La Maga lit a lamp and placed it on the floor, creating a sort of Rembrandt that Oliveira found quite appropriate. The return of the prodigal, the picture of a return, even though it was fleeting and momentary, although he had not really known why he had climbed the stairs slowly to slump by the door and listen to the distant sounds of the end of the quartet and the whispered conversation of Ossip and La Maga. "They must have made love already, like a pair of cats," he thought, looking at them. But no, they must have suspected that he would be back that night, and they had all their clothes on, and Rocamadour was in the bed. If Rocamadour had been lying on a pair of chairs placed together, if Gregorovius had had his shoes and coat off . . . Besides, what the hell difference did it make, since he was the intruder there, his dripping lumberjacket, shot to hell.

"Acoustics," Gregorovius observed. "It's strange how sound gets into things and climbs from floor to floor, passing through a wall to the head of a bed, it's unbelievable. Did you two ever duck underwater in a bathtub?"

"I've thought of it," Oliveira said, tossing his lumberjacket in a corner and sitting down on a stool.

"You can hear everything the people downstairs are saying, all you have to do is put your head underwater and listen. The sounds come through the plumbing, I imagine. Once in Glasgow I discovered that the neighbours were Trotskyites."

"When I think of Glasgow I think of bad weather, a port full of sad people," La Maga said.

"Too many movies," said Oliveira. "But this *mate* is like a pardon, something incredibly conciliatory. Good Lord, look how wet my shoes got. You see, a *mate* is like a full stop and a space. You take one and then you can start a new paragraph."

"I'll never know these delights of the pampas," Gregorovius said. "But you also mentioned a drink, I believe."

"Bring the *caña*," Oliveira ordered. "I think there's over half a bottle left."

"Did you two buy it here?" Gregorovius asked.

"Why the devil does he use the plural," Oliveira thought. "They must have been rolling around here all night, it's an unmistakable sign. But then."

"No, my brother sends it to me. I have a wonderful brother in Rosario. *Caña* and reproaches, an abundance of both."

He passed his empty gourd to La Maga, who had squatted by his feet. He began to feel good. He felt La Maga's fingers on his ankle, on his shoelaces. He let her take off his shoe with a sigh. La Maga took off his wet sock and wrapped his foot in a page of the *Figaro Littéraire*. The *mate* was hot and very bitter.

Gregorovius liked the *caña*, it wasn't just like *barack* but it was similar. He went through a catalogue of Hungarian and Czech drinks, some reminiscences. They could hear the rain falling softly and they felt comfortable, especially Rocamadour, who had been sleeping for more than an hour already without stirring. Gregorovius talked about Transylvania, about some adventures in Salonika. Oliveira remembered that there was a pack of Gauloises on the table and a pair of fleece-lined slippers. Feeling his way, he went over to the table. "In Paris, any mention of something beyond Vienna sounds like literature," Gregorovius was saying, with a voice that seemed to be pleading. Horacio found the cigarettes and opened the drawer of the bedside table to take out the slippers. In the darkness he could make out the figure of Rocamadour lying on his back. Without really knowing why, he stroked his forehead with a finger. "My mother didn't like to talk about Transylvania, she was afraid that people would associate her with stories about vampires and all that . . . And Tokay, you know . . . " Horacio tried to get a better look, kneeling next to the bed. "You can imagine in Montevideo,"

La Maga was saying. "You think that people are all alike, but when you live on the Cerro side of town . . . Is *tokay* a kind of bird?" "Well, in a certain sense." The natural reaction in cases like this. Let's see: first . . . ("What does in a certain sense mean? Is it a bird or isn't it?") But all he had to do was put a finger on the baby's lips, the lack of a response. "I was taking the liberty of using a trite image, Lucía. There is a bird sleeping in all good wines." Forced breathing, idiocy. Another form of idiocy that his hands should be trembling so much, barefoot and wet (his feet would have to be rubbed with alcohol, vigorously if possible). "*Un soir, l'âme du vin chantait dans les bouteilles*," Ossip scanned. "Just like Anacreon, I think . . . " And one could almost touch La Maga's resentful silence, her mental note: Anacreon, a Greek writer no one ever reads. Everybody knows about him except me. And where was that line from, *un soir, l'âme du vin*? Horacio slipped his hand under the sheets, it was a great effort to bring himself to feel Rocamadour's tiny stomach, the cold thighs, there seemed to be a little warmth left farther up, but no, he was so cold. "Fall into the pattern," Horacio thought. "Shout, turn on the light, start the obligatory hustle and bustle. Why?" But maybe, still . . . "Then it means that this instinct is of no use to me, this thing I'm starting to discover from deep down inside of me. If I call out it will be Berthe Trépat all over again, the same stupid attempts, pity. Put the glove on, do what must be done in cases like this. Oh no, that's enough. Why turn on the light and shout if it won't do any good? An actor, a perfect fucking actor. All that can be done is . . . " He heard Gregorovius's glass tinkle against the bottle of *caña*. "Yes, it's quite like *barack*." With a Gauloise in his mouth he struck a match, taking a good look. "You'll wake him up," La Maga said as she put some fresh *yerba mate* in his gourd. Horacio blew the match out brutally. It's a known fact that if the pupils, under a bright light, etc. *Quod erat demonstrandum*. "Like *barack*, but a little less aromatic," Ossip was saying.

"The old man is knocking again," La Maga said.

"It must be a shutter,' said Gregorovius.

"This building doesn't have shutters. He must have gone crazy."

Oliveira put on the slippers and went back to the chair. The *mate* was wonderful, hot and very bitter. There was pounding upstairs, twice, weakly.

"He's killing cockroaches," Gregorovius suggested.

"No, he's got blood in his eye and he doesn't want to let us sleep. Go up and say something to him, Horacio."

"You go up," Oliveira said. "I don't know why, but he's more afraid of you than of me. At least he doesn't come out with xenophobia, apartheid, and other forms of segregation."

"If I go up there I'll tell him so many things that he'll call the police."

"It's raining too hard. Work on his moral side, praise the decorations he has on his door. Talk about your feelings as a mother and things like that. Go ahead."

"I don't feel like it," La Maga said.

"Go ahead, sweetheart," Oliveira said in a low voice.

"But why do you want me to go?"

"To please me. You'll see, he'll stop."

There were two thumps, then one. La Maga got up and went out of the apartment. Horacio followed her, and when he heard her going upstairs he turned on the light and looked at Gregorovius. He pointed to the bed. After a minute he turned out the light while Gregorovius went back to his chair.

"It's incredible," Ossip said as he grabbed the bottle of *caña* in the dark.

"Incredible, of course. Inevitable, all that. No obituaries, old man. All I had to do was leave this flat for one day and the damnedest things happened. Anyway, one thing can be the consolation for the other."

"I don't understand," Gregorovius said.

"You understand beautifully. *Ça va, ça va.* You can't imagine how little I care."

Gregorovius noticed that Oliveira was using the familiar form and this meant that things would be different, if it were still possible . . . He said something about the Red Cross, all-night chemists.

"Do what you want to do, it's all the same to me," Oliveira said. "What a day this has been, brother!"

If he could only flop on the bed and go to sleep for a couple of years. "Chicken," he thought. Gregorovius had caught his contagious immobility and was laboriously lighting his pipe. They could hear talking from far off, La Maga's voice coming through the rain, the old man answering her with his shrill voice. The door of some other apartment slammed, people going out to complain about the noise.

"Basically you're right," Gregorovius admitted. "But isn't there some legal responsibility?"

"With everything that has happened we're in it up to our necks," Oliveira said. "Especially you two, I can always prove that I arrived too late. A mother lets her child die while she takes care of her lover on the floor."

"If you're trying to say . . . "

"It doesn't really matter."

"But it's not true, Horacio."

"It doesn't make any difference to me, consummation is an after-effect. I don't have anything to do with the whole business any more, I only came up because I was soaked and I wanted a *mate.* Hey, people are coming."

"We ought to call an ambulance," Gregorovius said.

"Go ahead then. Doesn't that sound like Ronald's voice?"

"I'm not going to sit here," Gregorovius said. "We've got to do something, I tell you, we've got to do something."

"But I'm quite aware of that. Action, always action. *Die Tätigkeit,* old man. Bang, there weren't many of us left and grandmother gave birth. Keep your voices down, you'll wake the baby."

"Hello," said Ronald.

"Hi," said Babs, struggling to close her umbrella.

"Keep your voices down," said La Maga, who was coming in behind them. "Why didn't you close the umbrella outside?"

"You're right," Babs said. "The same thing always happens to me everywhere I go. Don't make any noise, Ronald. We only stopped by to tell you about Guy, it's unbelievable. Have you blown a fuse?"

"No, it's because of Rocamadour."

"Keep your voice down," Ronald said. "And put that damn umbrella down somewhere."

"It's so hard to close," Babs said. "It opens so easily."

"The old man threatened to call the police," La Maga said, closing the door. "He was ready to hit me, shrieking like a madman. Ossip, you really should see what's in his apartment, you can see a little from the stairway. A table full of empty bottles and in the middle a windmill that's so big it looks lifesize, just like the ones out in the country in Uruguay. And the windmill was turning from the draft, I couldn't help peeping through the crack in the door, the old man was frothing at the mouth he was so angry."

"I can't close it," Babs said. "I'll stick it in this corner."

"It looks like a bat," La Maga said. "Give it to me, I'll close it. See how easy?"

"She's broken two ribs," Babs said to Ronald.

"Stop fussing," Ronald said. "Besides, we'll be leaving right away, we only came to tell you that Guy swallowed a tube of gardenal."

"Poor dear," said Oliveira, who didn't care very much for Guy.

"Étienne found him half-dead, Babs and I had gone to a *vernissage* (I have to tell you about that sometime, it was fabulous), and Guy had gone up to the apartment, got into bed, and poisoned himself."

"He has no manners at all," Oliveira said in English. "*C'est regrettable.*"

"Étienne had come by to look for us, luckily everybody has a key," Babs said. "He heard someone vomiting, went in, and found Guy. He was dying. Étienne ran out to get help. They've taken him to the hospital now and he's in a critical condition. And with all this rain," Babs added, flustered.

"Sit down," La Maga said. "Not there, Ronald, there's a leg missing. It's so dark in here because of Rocamadour. Speak softly."

"Make them some coffee," Oliveira said. "Great weather, eh?"

"I'll have to be going," Gregorovius said. "I wonder where I put my raincoat – no, not there, Lucía . . . "

"Stay and have some coffee," La Maga said. "The Métro has stopped running and it's comfortable here. You can grind some fresh coffee, Horacio."

"It smells stuffy in here," Babs said.

"She always misses the pure outside ozone," Ronald said furiously. "She's like a horse, she only loves pure and unadulterated things. Primary colours, the seven-note scale. I don't think she's human."

"Humanity is an ideal," said Oliveira, feeling around for the coffee grinder. "Air has its story too. Coming from a wet street with lots of ozone, as you said, into an atmosphere whose temperature and make-up have been fifty centuries in the making . . . Babs is a kind of Rip van Winkle of respiration."

"Oh, Rip van Winkle," Babs said delighted. "My grandmother used to read me stories about him."

"In Idaho, we all know," Ronald said. "Well, what happened next was that Étienne called us at the bar on the corner a half-hour ago and told us that it would be best if we stayed away from our place for the night, at least until they know whether Guy is going to die or is going to vomit up the gardenal. It could be bad if the cops came by and found us there, they're pretty good at putting two and two together, and lately all the business with the Club has put them in a bad mood."

"What's wrong with the Club?" La Maga asked, as she dried some cups with a towel.

"Nothing, but that's precisely why we have no defence. The neighbours have complained so much about the noise, the record sessions, the coming and going at all hours . . . And besides, Babs has run-ins with the concierge and all the other women in the building, fifty or sixty of them."

"They're awful," Babs said, chewing a sweet she had taken out of her pocket. "They smell marijuana even if you're only cooking a goulash."

Oliveira was tired of grinding the coffee and passed the grinder to Ronald. Speaking softly, Babs and La Maga were discussing the motives behind Guy's attempted suicide. After fussing so much about his raincoat, Gregorovius had flopped in the easy chair and was very quiet, keeping his unlit pipe in his mouth. The rain was beating on the window. "Schoenberg and Brahms," Oliveira thought, taking out a Gauloise. "It's OK, usually under these circumstances one hears Chopin or the *Todesmusik* for Siegfried. Yesterday's tornado killed between two and three thousand people in Japan. Statistically speaking . . . " But statistics didn't stop his cigarette from tasting oily. He examined it as best he could, lighting another match. It was a perfect Gauloise, very white, with its delicate writing and shreds of its harsh tobacco coming out of the wet end. "I always wet my cigarettes when I'm nervous," he thought. "When I think about things like Rose Bob . . . Yes, it's been a mother of a day, and look what's ahead of us." The best thing would be to tell Ronald so that Ronald could pass it on to Babs in one of those almost telepathic messages that startled Perico Romero so. The theory of communication, one of those fascinating themes that literature had not gone into much until the Huxleys and the Borgeses of the new generation came along. Now Ronald was counting in time to the whispers passing between Babs and La Maga, spinning the grinder vigorously, the coffee wouldn't be ready until doomsday. Oliveira slid off the horrible art nouveau chair and made himself comfortable on the floor, with his head resting on a pile of newspapers. There was a strange glow on the ceiling which must have been more subjective than anything else. When he closed his eyes the glow would last for a moment, then great purple spheres would begin to explode, one after another, *voof, voof, voof,* each sphere evidently corresponded to a systole or a diastole, who could tell. And somewhere in the building, probably on the third floor, a telephone was ringing. An extraordinary thing in Paris at that hour. "Another death," Oliveira thought. "That's the only reason anybody calls up in this city so considerate of sleep." He remembered the time a recently arrived friend from Argentina had thought it quite natural to call him up at ten-thirty in the evening. God knows how, but he had managed to get the number of some telephone in the building from the Bottin guide and he made the call then and there. The face of the gentleman from the fifth floor in his bathrobe, knocking at the door, an icy stare, *quelqu'un vous demande au téléphone,* Oliveira confused, putting on a wrap, going up to the fifth floor, finding a steadfastly annoyed woman, learning that old buddy Hermida was in Paris and when can we get together, man, I've got news from everybody, Traveler, and the boys in the Bidú bar, etc., and the woman hiding her irritation as she waited for Oliveira to start crying when he learned of the death of somebody very close, and Oliveira without knowing why, *vraiment je suis tellement confus, madame, monsieur, c'était un ami qui vient d'arriver, vous comprenez, il n'est pas du tout au courant des habitudes* . . . Oh, Argentina, generous schedules, open house, time to throw away, the whole future in front, all of it, *voof, voof, voof,* but behind the eyes of that one six feet away there was nothing, there couldn't ever be anything, the whole theory of communication ended, no mamma, no dada, no papa, no peepee no *voof voof* no nothing, just *rigor mortis* and people hanging around who didn't even come from Salta or Mexico and so could organize a wake for the *angelito* while they still could listen to music, who couldn't find out like them a way out of the whole death business, people who had never been primitive enough to rise above the distress by means of acceptance or identification, nor yet developed enough to deny all distress and put this "one minor casualty" alongside the three thousand swept away by typhoon Veronica, for example. "But this is all cheap anthropology," Oliveira thought, conscious of a cold feeling in his stomach which was giving him cramps. It was always the solar plexus in the end. "These are the real messages, the warnings beneath the skin. And there is no dictionary for them." Who had turned out the Rembrandt lamp? He couldn't remember, a while back there had been a kind of old-gold dust on the floor, try as he could, he couldn't reconstruct what had happened since Ronald and Babs had come, nothing to do, at some moment La Maga (because it must have been La Maga) or perhaps Gregorovius, someone had turned off the lamp.

"How are you going to make coffee in the dark?"

"I don't know," La Maga said, getting out some cups. "There was some light before."

"Turn it on, Ronald," Oliveira said. "It's underneath your chair there. You have to turn the bulb, it's the classic way."

"This is all quite idiotic," Ronald said, without anyone knowing whether he meant the way the lamp had to be turned on or not. The light made the purple spheres go away, and Oliveira began to like his cigarette better. Now everything was really comfortable, it was warm, there would be coffee.

"Come on over here," Oliveira told Ronald. "You'll be more comfortable than in that chair, it has a kind of point in the middle of it that pricks your bum. Wong would include it in his Peking collection if he knew about it, I'm sure."

"I'm all right here," Ronald said, "at the risk of being misunderstood."

"You're not all right. Come here. And how's that coffee doing, ladies?"

"He's being very masculine tonight," said Babs. "Is he always like that with you?"

"Most of the time," La Maga said without looking at him. "Help me dry this tray."

Oliveira waited for Babs to start the usual comments on the job of making coffee, and when Ronald got off his chair and squatted down near him, he said something in his ear. Listening to them, Gregorovius joined in the conversation about the coffee, and Ronald's answer was lost in the praise of Mocha and how the art of making it had degenerated. Then Ronald got back up on his chair in time to take the cup La Maga was holding out to him. There was a soft pounding on the ceiling, twice, three times. Gregorovius shuddered and drank his coffee down in one gulp. Oliveira was trying not to burst out laughing, which just might have eased his cramp. La Maga looked surprised, in the shadows she looked at everybody in succession and then reached for a cigarette on the table, groping around as if she wanted to get out of something she didn't understand, something like a dream.

"I hear steps," Babs said with a marked Blavatsky tone. "That old man must be crazy, you have to watch out. In Kansas City once . . . No, it's someone coming up the stairs."

"The staircase makes a pattern in your ear," La Maga said. "I feel very sorry for deaf people. It's as if I had my hand on the stairs now and were moving it up the steps one by one. When I was a girl I got an A on a theme I wrote, the story of a little sound. It was a nice little sound, it came and went, things happened to it . . . "

"I, on the other hand . . . " said Babs. "OK, OK, you don't have to pinch me."

"My love," Ronald said, "be still a moment so we can tell whose steps those are. Yes, it's the king of pigments, it's Étienne, it's the great apocalyptic beast."

"He took it calmly," Oliveira thought. "The spoonful of medicine is for two o'clock, I think. We have more than an hour of calm left." He did not understand and he did not want to understand the reason behind the delay, that sort of denial of something already known. Negation, negative . . . "Yes, it's like the negative of reality just-as-it-ought-to-be, that is . . . But don't go getting metaphysical, Horacio. Alas, poor Yorick, *ça suffit.* I can't help it, I think it's better this way than if we turned on the light and released the news like a dove from its cage. A negative. Complete reversal . . . What's most likely is that he's alive and we're all dead. A more modest proposition: he has killed us because we are responsible for his death. Responsible, accomplices in a state of affairs, that is . . . Oh, dear boy, where are you taking yourself, you're the donkey with the carrot hanging down in front of its eyes. And it was Étienne, no less, it was the great painting beast."

"He's out of danger," Étienne said. "Son of a bitch, he's got more lives than Cesare Borgia. And what a job of vomiting . . . "

"Tell us, tell us," Babs said.

"A stomach pump, all kinds of enemas, jabs all over with a needle, a bed with springs, to keep his head down. He threw up the whole menu of the Orestias restaurant, where it seems he had lunch.

What a mess, even stuffed vine leaves. Has anyone noticed that I'm soaked?"

"We've got some hot coffee," Ronald said, "and a foul drink called *caña*."

Étienne snorted, tossed his raincoat in a corner, and went over to the stove.

"How's the baby, Lucía?"

"He's asleep," La Maga said. "He's sleeping quite soundly, fortunately."

"Let's speak quietly," Babs said.

"He regained consciousness around eleven o'clock," Étienne explained in a sort of tender way. "He was a mess, that's for sure. The doctor let me go over to the bed and Guy recognized me. 'You idiot,' I said to him. 'Go fuck yourself,' he answered. The doctor whispered to me that that was a good sign. There were other people in the ward, I got through it pretty well, and you know what hospitals do to me . . ."

"Did you go back to the flat?" Babs asked. "Did you have to go to the police station?"

"No, everything's been taken care of. In any case, it would be wiser if you spent the night here, you should have seen the face on the concierge when they carried Guy out . . . "

"The lousy bastard," Babs said in English.

"I put on a virtuous air and when I passed her I lifted up my hand and said: 'Madame, death is always respectable. This young man has tried to kill himself because he was lovesick over Kreisler.' She just hardened up, believe me, and she kept on looking at me with a pair of eyes that looked like two hardboiled eggs. And just as the stretcher was going out the door, Guy raised up a little, put his hand to his pale cheek, just like a statue on an Etruscan tomb, and puked up some green vomit in the direction of the concierge that landed smack in the middle of the doormat. The stretcher-bearers doubled up laughing, it was fantastic."

"More coffee?" Ronald asked. "And sit down over here on the floor, it's the warmest spot in the room. Give poor Étienne a good cup of coffee."

"I can't see anything," Étienne said. "And why do I have to sit on the floor?"

"To keep Horacio and me company, we're keeping a sort of knight's vigil," Ronald said.

"Come off it, you fool," Oliveira said.

"Pay attention to me, sit down here, and you will learn things that not even Wong knows about. The *Libri Fulgurales*, the writings of the ancient seers. Just this morning I was having so much fun reading the *Bardo*. They're amazing creatures, the Tibetans."

"Who initiated you?" Étienne asked, sliding down between Oliveira and Ronald and drinking his coffee down in one gulp. "A drink," Étienne said, putting his hand out imperiously towards La Maga, who put the bottle of *caña* in it. "Terrible," Étienne said after taking a swig. "Product of Argentina, I suppose. What a country, my God."

"Don't put my country down," Oliveira said. "You're like the old man upstairs."

"Wong put me through several tests," Ronald was explaining. "He says that I have enough intelligence to start destroying it profitably. We agreed that I should read the *Bardo* carefully, and from there we would go on to the fundamental phases of Buddhism. Can there really be a subtle body, Horacio? It seems that when one dies . . . A sort of mental body, you understand."

But Horacio was whispering in Étienne's ear and he was grunting and nodding, smelling of wet streets, hospitals and stuffed cabbage. Babs was telling Gregorovius, who had withdrawn into a kind of indifference, all about the innumerable faults of the concierge. Bursting with erudition, Ronald had to explain the *Bardo* to somebody and he started on La Maga, who was outlined opposite him like a Henry Moore in the darkness, a giantess seen from below, first her knees, about to burst through the black mass of her skirt, then a torso which rose up towards the ceiling, on top of it a pile of hair, darker even than the darkness all around, and on top of all this shadow among the shadows the light of the lamp on the floor which made La Maga's eyes shine as she sat in the easy chair and struggled from time to time against slipping out and falling on the floor because the front legs were shorter than the rear ones.

"Lousy business," Étienne said, taking another drink.

"You can leave if you want," Oliveira said, "but I don't think anything serious will happen, things like this happen every day in this neighbourhood."

"I'll stay," Étienne said. "This drink, what's it called? It's not bad. It smells like fruit."

"Wong says that Jung was all excited about the *Bardo*," Ronald was saying. "It's easy to see why, and the existentialists should give it a careful reading too. Look, at the moment of judgement for a dead person, the King puts a mirror to his face, but this mirror is Karma. The summation of all of the dead person's acts, you see. And the dead person sees all his actions reflected, good and bad, but the reflection doesn't correspond to any reality, it's the projection of mental images . . . Tell me why old Jung shouldn't have been a little amazed. The King of the Dead looks into the mirror, but he is really looking into your memory. Can you think of a better description of psychoanalysis? And what's even more extraordinary, my dear, is that the judgement the King pronounces is not his but your own. You judge yourself without knowing it. Don't you think that Sartre really ought to go to live in Lhasa?"

"It's incredible," La Maga said. "But this book, is it philosophy?"

"It's a book for dead people," Oliveira said.

They were silent, listening to the rain. Gregorovius felt sorry for La Maga, who seemed to be waiting for an explanation and didn't feel like asking any more questions.

"The lamas reveal certain things to dying people," he told her. "To guide them in the beyond, to help them be saved. For example . . . "

Étienne was leaning against Oliveira. Ronald was sitting with his legs crossed and humming *Big Lip Blues*, thinking about Jelly Roll, who was his favourite dead man. Oliveira lit a Gauloise, and as in a painting by La Tour, for a second the flame coloured the faces of his friends, it brought Gregorovius out of the shadows and tied the murmur of his voice to a pair of moving lips, brutally set La Maga in the easy chair, with her face that always became avid at moments of ignorance and explanations, softly bathed placid Babs, and Ronald the musician, lost in his moaning improvisations. Then there was a thump on the ceiling just as the match went out.

"*Il faut tenter de vivre*," Oliveira quoted from his memory. "*Pourquoi?*"

The line had come out of his memory just like the faces in the light of the match, instantaneously and probably gratuitously. Étienne's shoulder was warming him, was transmitting a deceptive presence to him, a nearness that death, that match that went out, was going to erase just as now the faces, the shapes, just as the silence closed in again around the knock from upstairs.

"And that is how," Gregorovius was concluding pedantically, "the *Bardo* brings us back to life, to the necessity of a pure life, precisely at the moment when escape is impossible and we are nailed to a bed with a cancer for a pillow."

"Ah, yes," La Maga said, sighing. She had understood enough, a few pieces of the puzzle were in place, although it would never be as perfect as a kaleidoscope, where each crystal, each stick, each grain of sand arranged itself in a perfect, symmetrical, boring pattern, but with no problems.

"Occidental dichotomies," Oliveira said. "Life and death, this side and that side. That's not what your *Bardo* teaches you, Ossip, although personally I haven't the slightest idea what your *Bardo* does teach you. In any case, it must be something more fluid, less categorized."

"Look," said Étienne, who was feeling remarkably well, even though the news that Oliveira had passed on to him was crawling around his insides like a crab and none of this seemed contradictory. "Look, my ball-beloved Argentine, the Orient is not so different as the Orientalists make it out to be. As soon as you start to give some serious thought to what is written there you begin to feel what you have always felt, the inexplicable attraction of intellectual suicide by means of the intellect itself. The scorpion stabbing itself in the neck, tired of being a scorpion but having to have recourse to its own scorpionness in order to do away with itself as a scorpion. In Madras or in Heidelberg it's basically the same question: there is some sort of indescribable mistake at the very beginning of things, out of which comes this phenomenon which is addressing itself to you at this moment and which you are all listening to. Every attempt at explanation comes to grief for reasons that anyone can understand, and the fact is that in order to define and understand something one would have to be outside of what is being defined and understood. *Ergo*, Madras and Heidelberg console themselves manufacturing positions, some with a rational base, others intuitive, even though the differences between reason and intuition can be far from clear, as anyone who's been to school knows. And for that reason, man only feels secure when he is on grounds that do not touch his deepest part: when he plays, when he conquers, when he puts on his various suits of armour that are products of an ethos, when he hands over the central mystery to some revelation. And on all sides the curious notion that our principal tool, the Logos that madly pulls us up the zoological ladder, is a perfect fraud. And the inevitable corollary, refuge in inspiration and babble, dark night of the soul, aesthetic and metaphysical visions. Madras and Heidelberg are different dosages of the same prescription, sometimes the Yin is in the ascendancy, sometimes the Yang, but at the two points of up and down there remain two examples of Homo sapiens, equally undefined, kicking about madly on the ground as one tries to rise at the expense of the other."

"It's strange," Ronald said. "In any case, it would be stupid to deny a reality even though we might not know what it is. Let's take the up–down axis. How is it that this axis still hasn't been of any use in finding out what goes on at its two extremes? Since Neanderthal man . . ."

"You're just using words," Oliveira said, leaning a little more on Étienne. "We like to take them out of the closet and parade them around the room. Reality, Neanderthal man, see how they play, see how they get into our ears and pull each other along on toboggans."

"That's right," Étienne said harshly. "That's why I prefer my colours: I feel sure."

"Sure of what?"

"Of their effect."

"Of their effect on you, in any case, but not on Ronald's concierge. Your colours are no more certain than my words, old man."

"At least my colours don't try to explain anything."

"And do you accept the idea that there is no explanation?"

"No," said Étienne, "but at the same time I do things that to a small degree take away the bad taste of emptiness. And that basically is the best definition of Homo sapiens."

"It's not a definition, it's a consolation," Gregorovius said, sighing. "Actually, we're like a play that we come in on during the second act. Everything is very pretty but we don't understand a thing. The actors speak and move about no one knows why or for what reason. We project our own ignorance into them and they seem like madmen to us, coming and going in a very decided way. Shakespeare has already said it anyway, and if he didn't say it he should have."

"I think he did say it," La Maga said.

"He did say it," Babs said.

"You see?" said La Maga.

"He also talked about words," Gregorovius said, "and all that Horacio has done is to raise the question in its dialectical form, in a manner of speaking. Like Wittgenstein, whom I admire very much."

"I don't know him," Ronald said, "but you all agree that the problem of reality cannot be faced with sighs."

"Who can tell," Gregorovius said. "Who can tell, Ronald."

"Come on, let's leave poetry out of this. Agreed, that we can't trust words, but actually, words come after this other thing, the fact that a bunch of us are here tonight seated around a lamp."

"Lower your voice," La Maga asked.

"Without any words I feel, I know, that I am here," Ronald insisted. "That's what I call reality. Even if that's all it is."

"Perfect," said Oliveira. "Except that this reality is no guarantee for you or for anybody else unless you transform it into a concept, and then into a convention, a useful scheme. The simple fact that you are on my left and I am on your right makes at least two realities out of this one reality, and realize that I don't want to get abstruse and point out that you and I are two entities that are absolutely out of touch with one another except by means of feelings and words, things that one must mistrust if one is to be serious about it all."

"We're both here," Ronald insisted. "On the right or on the left, it doesn't matter. We're both looking at Babs, everybody hears what I'm saying."

"But those are examples for boys in short pants, my son," Gregorovius moaned. "Horacio is right, you can't just accept like that what you think reality is. The most you can say is that you are; that can't be denied unless you want to start a row. What's wrong is the *ergo*, and what follows the *ergo*, that's well known."

"Don't turn it into a question of schools," Oliveira said. "Let's keep it on the level of a conversation among amateurs, which is what we are. Let's stick with what Ronald has so movingly called reality, and which he thinks is one by itself. Do you still think it's just one, Ronald?"

"Yes. I concede that my way of feeling it or understanding it is different from that of Babs, and that Babs's reality is different from Ossip's, and so on down the line. But it's like the different theories about the Mona Lisa or about endive salad. Reality is there and we're inside it, understanding it each in his own way."

"The only thing that matters is the business of each understanding it in his own way," Oliveira said. "You think that there is a definable reality because you and I are talking in this room and at this time, and because you and I know that within an hour or so something predetermined is going to happen here. All of this gives you a great ontological security, I think; you feel very sure of yourself, firmly planted in yourself and in your surroundings. But if at the same time you could be present in this reality from my position, or from Babs's, if you could be placed, you see, and right now could be in this same room, but from where I am and with everything I am and have been, and with everything that Babs is and has been, you would understand that your cheap egocentrism would not afford you any valid reality. All it would give you would be a belief based on terror, a need to affirm what is around you so that you would not fall into the funnel and come out God knows where."

"We're very different," Ronald said, "I'm very much aware of that. But we find ourselves in certain places outside of ourselves. You and I are looking at that lamp, maybe we don't see the same thing, but neither can we be sure that we don't see the same thing. There is a lamp there, what the hell."

"Don't shout," La Maga said. "I'm going to make more coffee."

"One has the impression," Oliveira said, "that he's following old footprints. We're unimportant little schoolboys warming over arguments that are musty and not at all interesting. And all because, dear Ronald, we've been talking dialectically. We say: you, I, lamp, reality. Take a step back, please. Go ahead, it's not hard. Words disappear. That lamp is a stimulus to the senses, nothing else. Now take another step back. What you call your sight and that stimulus take on an inexplicable relationship, because if we wanted to explain it we would have to take a step forward and everything would go to hell."

"But those steps backward are like unwalking what the species of man has already walked," Gregorovius protested.

"Yes," said Oliveira. "And right there is the great problem, to find out if what you call the species has gone forward or if, as Klages thinks, I believe, at some given point it took the wrong road."

"Without speech there's no such thing as man. Without history man doesn't exist."

"Unless there's a crime there's no such thing as a criminal. There's no proof that man could have been any different."

"We haven't done so badly," Ronald said.

"What means of comparison do you have to think that we've done well? Why have we had to invent Eden, to live submerged in the nostalgia of a lost paradise, to make up utopias, propose a future for ourselves? If a worm could think he would think that he hadn't done too badly. Man has grabbed onto science like an anchor of salvation, as someone said, and I'm not quite sure what he meant. Reason with its use of language has set up a satisfactory architecture, like the delightful, rhythmical composition in Renaissance painting, and it has stuck us in the centre. In spite of all its curiosity and dissatisfaction, science, that is to say reason, begins by calming us down. 'You are in this room, with your friends, opposite that lamp. Don't be frightened, everything's all right. Let's see, now: what is the nature of that luminous phenomenon? Do you know what enriched uranium is? Do you like isotopes, did you know that we have already changed lead into gold?' It's all very exciting, it makes you dizzy, but always from the easy chair in which we are so comfortably seated."

"I'm sitting on the floor," Ronald said, "and to tell the truth, it's not comfortable at all. Listen, Horacio: it makes no sense to deny this reality. It's here, we're part of it. The night is here for both of us, it's raining outside for both of us. How should I know what night is, the weather, the rain, but there they are and they're outside of me, they're things that happen to me, there's nothing I have to do about it."

"But of course," Oliveira said. "No one denies that. What we don't understand is why this has to happen this way, why we are here and it's raining outside. The absurd thing is not things themselves; what is absurd is that the things are there and that we think they are absurd. The relationship between me and what is happening to me escapes me at this moment, but I don't deny that it is happening to me. Of course it's happening to me. And that's what's so absurd."

"It's not very clear," Étienne said.

"It can't be clear, if it were it wouldn't be true; it might be scientifically true, perhaps, but as an absolute it would be false. Clarity is an intellectual requirement, nothing more. If only we could know more clearly, think clearly along the border of science and reason. And when I say 'if only', just try to see that I'm saying something idiotic. Probably the only anchor of salvation is science, uranium 235, things like that. But we have to live, after all."

"Yes," said La Maga, serving coffee. "We have to live, after all."

"Understand, Ronald," Oliveira said, squeezing his knees. "You are much more than your intelligence, it's obvious. Tonight, for example, what's happening to us now, here, it's like one of those paintings by Rembrandt where just a bit of light is shining in a corner, and it's not a physical light, it's not what you calmly call a lamp, with its watts and wicks. The absurd thing is to believe that we can grasp the totality of what constitutes us in this moment or in any moment, and sense it as something coherent, something acceptable, if you want. Every time we enter a crisis the absurdity is total; understand that dialectics can only set our closet in order in moments of calm. You know very well that at the high point of a crisis we always work by impulse, just the opposite of foresight, doing the most unexpected and wildest sort of thing. And at that moment precisely it could be said that there was a sort of saturation of reality, don't you think? Reality comes on fast, it shows itself with all its strength, and precisely at that moment the only way of facing it is to renounce dialectics, it's the moment for shooting somebody, jumping overboard, swallowing a bottle of gardenal like Guy, unleashing the dog, a free hand to do anything. Reason is only good to mummify reality in moments of calm or analyse its future storms, never to resolve a crisis of the moment. But these crises are like metaphysical outbursts, like a state that perhaps, if we hadn't chosen the path of reason, would be the natural and current state of *Pithecanthropus erectus*."

"It's very hot, watch out," La Maga said.

"And these crises that most people think of as terrible, as absurd, I personally think they serve to show us the real absurdity, the absurdity of an ordered and calm world, with a room where different people are drinking coffee at two o'clock in the morning, without any of this having the slightest meaning unless it's hedonistic, how nice it is to be near this stove which does its job so well. Miracles have never seemed absurd to me; the absurdity about them is what comes before and after them."

"And still," said Gregorovius, stretching, "*il faut tenter de vivre.*"

"*Voilà*," Oliveira thought. "Another proof that I won't mention. Of all the millions of possible lines he chooses the one I was thinking about ten minutes ago. What people call chance."

"Well," Étienne said dreamily, "it's not a question of trying to live, since life is something that we have been inevitably presented with. It's been some time now since people have suspected that life and living things are two completely different things. Life lives for itself, whether we like it or not. Guy tried to deny this theory today, but statistically speaking it's incontrovertible. Which torture and concentration camps vouch for. Of all our feelings the only one which really doesn't belong to us is hope. Hope belongs to life, it's life itself defending itself. Etcetera. And with all this I'm going off to bed, because Guy's shenanigans have reduced me to ashes. Ronald, you must come by the studio tomorrow morning, I've just finished a still life that will knock you out."

"Horacio hasn't convinced me," Ronald said. "I agree that a lot of what is around me is absurd, but we probably call it that because that's what we call anything we don't understand yet. Someday we'll know."

"Charming optimist," Oliveira said. "We could also put optimism on the tab of pure life. What gives you strength is that for you there is no future, as is logical in the case of most agnostics. You're always alive, you're always present, everything is in perfect order for you as in a picture by Van Eyck. But if that horrible thing that is not to have faith and at the same time to be heading towards death were to happen to you, to be heading towards the scandal of all scandals, your mirror would fog up pretty fast."

"Come on, Ronald," Babs said. "It's very late, I'm getting sleepy."

"Wait, wait a minute. I was thinking about the death of my father, yes, there's some truth in what you say. I could never fit that piece into the puzzle, it was something that had no explanation. A happy young man, in Alabama. He was walking along the street and a tree fell on him. I was fifteen at the time and they came to get me in school. But there are so many other absurd things, Horacio, so many deaths and mistakes . . . I suppose it's not a question of numbers. It's not a total absurdity as you think."

"The absurdity is that it doesn't look like an absurdity," said Oliveira in an obscure way. "The absurdity is that you go out in the morning and find a bottle of milk on the doorstep and you are at peace because the same thing happened to you yesterday and will happen again tomorrow. It's this stagnation, this so be it, this suspicious lack of exceptions. I don't know, you see, we ought to try some other road."

"By renouncing intelligence?" asked Gregorovius, suspiciously.

"I don't know, maybe. Using it in some other way. Can it be proved beyond doubt that logical principles are part and parcel of our intelligence? There are peoples who are capable of survival within a magical order of things . . . Of course, the unfortunates eat raw worms, but that too is just a question of values."

"Worms, how awful," Babs said. "Ronald, dear, it's getting so late."

"Underneath it all," Ronald said, "what bothers you is legality in all its forms. As soon as a thing begins to function well, you feel trapped. But all of us are a little like that, a band of what they call failures because we don't have professions, degrees, and all that. That's why we're in Paris, man, and your famous absurdity is reduced once and for all to a kind of vague, anarchic ideal that you'll never be able to define in concrete terms."

"You're so very right," Oliveira said. "How nice it would be to go out on the street and put up posters in favour of a free Algeria. And along with everything there is to do in the social struggle."

"Action can give meaning to your life," Ronald said. "You must have read that in Malraux, I suppose."

"*Éditions Nouvelle Revue Française*," Oliveira said.

"But still you keep on masturbating like a monkey, turning false problems round and round, waiting for God knows what. If all of this is absurd you ought to do something to change it."

"Your words sound familiar," Oliveira said. "As soon as you think the discussion is heading towards something you consider more concrete, like your famous bit on action, you get all eloquent. You refuse to see that action, just like inaction, has to be earned. How can one act unless there is a previous central attitude, a sort of acceptance of what we call the good and the true? Your notions about truth and goodness are purely historical, based on an ethic you inherited. But history and ethics are highly dubious as far as I'm concerned."

"Sometime," Étienne said as he stood up, "I'd like to hear more details on what you call the central attitude. Right in the middle of the centre itself there's probably a perfect emptiness."

"Don't think I haven't thought of that," Oliveira said. "But even for aesthetic reasons, which are easy for you to appreciate, you have to admit that between being in a centre and fluttering around its edges there is a qualitative difference that makes you stop and think."

"Horacio," said Gregorovius, "is making great use of those very words he was so emphatically advising us against a while back. He's a man one must not ask for speeches but for other things, foggy and unexplainable things like dreams, coincidences, revelations, and above all, black humour."

"The guy upstairs knocked again," Babs said.

"No, it's the rain," said La Maga. "It's time to give Rocamadour his medicine."

"There's still some time," said Babs, crouching over hurriedly as she held her watch next to the lamp. "Ten to three. Let's go Ronald, it's quite late."

"We'll leave at five past three," Ronald said.

"Why five past three?" La Maga asked.

"Because the first quarter of an hour is always lucky," Gregorovius explained.

"Give me another shot of *caña*," Étienne asked. "*Merde*, it's all gone."

Oliveira put out his cigarette. "The knight's vigil," he thought thankfully. "They're real friends, even Ossip, poor devil. Now we shall have fifteen minutes of chain reactions which no one will be able to avoid, no one, not even by thinking that next year, at this very same hour, the most exact and detailed memory will not be capable of changing the output of adrenalin or saliva, the sweat on the palms of the hands . . . These are the truths that Ronald will always refuse to understand. What have I done tonight? Slightly monstrous, a priori. Perhaps we should have tried an oxygen balloon, something like that. Fool, really; we would only have been prolonging life the way it was in the case of Monsieur Valdemar."

"We ought to prepare her," Ronald whispered in his ear.

"Don't be foolish, please. Can't you sense that she's prepared already, that the smell is floating in the air?"

"Now you begin to speak quietly," La Maga said, "just when there's no reason to any more."

"*Tu parles*," Oliveira thought.

"Smell?" Ronald murmured. "I don't smell anything."

"Well, it'll be three o'clock pretty soon," Étienne said, shivering as if he were cold. "Make an attempt, Ronald; Horacio may not be a genius, but it's easy to sense what he's trying to tell you. All we can do is stay a while longer and go along with whatever happens.

And you, Horacio, now that I think of it, what you said about the Rembrandt painting was rather good. There's metapainting just as there is metamusic, and the old boy was sticking his arms in up to the elbows in what he was doing. Only someone blinded by logic or good manners can stop in front of a Rembrandt and not feel that there is a window there that opens onto something else, a sign. Very dangerous for painting, but on the other hand . . . "

"Painting is an art form like so many others," Oliveira said. "It doesn't need too much protection as far as being a form is concerned. Besides, for every Rembrandt there are a hundred others who are nothing but painters, so painting is quite safe from harm."

"Luckily," Étienne said.

"Luckily," accepted Oliveira. "Luckily everything is going very well in the best of all possible worlds. Turn on the big light, Babs, it's the switch behind your chair."

"I wonder where there's a clean spoon," said La Maga, getting up.

With an effort that seemed repugnant to him, Oliveira avoided looking towards the corner of the room. La Maga was dazzled by the light and was rubbing her eyes, and Babs, Ossip, and the others looked away, looked back, and looked away again. Babs had started to take La Maga by the arm, but something on Ronald's face held her back. Étienne got up slowly, pulling his trousers up since they were still wet. Ossip unfolded himself from the easy chair and was saying something about finding his raincoat. "Now is the time for them to pound on the ceiling," Oliveira thought, closing his eyes. "Several thumps in a row, and then three more, solemnly. But everything is backwards, instead of turning off the lights we turn them on, we're on the stage, there's nothing we can do about it." He got up in turn, and he felt it in his bones, walking all day, the things that had been going on all day long. La Maga had found the spoon on the side, behind a pile of records and books. She began to wipe it with the hem of her skirt, she examined it under the light. "Now she'll put the medicine in the spoon, and then she'll spill half of it before she reaches the bed," Oliveira said to himself, leaning against the wall. They were all so still that La Maga looked at them in wonder, but she was having trouble getting the bottle opened, Babs wanted to help her, hold the spoon for her, and all the while her face was all tightened up as if what La Maga was doing was some indescribable horror, until La Maga poured the liquid into the spoon and put the bottle down carelessly on the table where there was barely room for it between the notebooks and the paper, and holding the spoon like Blondin with a balancing pole, as an angel holds a saint who is about to slide off the edge of a cliff, she began to walk, shuffling her slippers, and started over to the bed with Babs at her side, whose face was twitching and who tried to look and not to look and then to look at Ronald and the others who came up behind her, Oliveira bringing up the rear with his cigarette extinguished in his mouth.

"It always spills on me when . . . " La Maga said, stopping at the edge of the bed.

"Lucía," Babs said, bringing her hands close to her shoulders but not touching them.

The liquid fell on the bedcovers and the spoon fell into it. La Maga shrieked and rolled onto the bed, face down then on her back then on her side as her hands clutched an indifferent ashen little doll who trembled and shook without conviction, uselessly mistreated and cuddled.

"Oh, shit, we should have prepared her for it," Ronald said. "There wasn't any reason, it's a disgrace. Everybody spouting nonsense and this, this . . . "

"Don't get hysterical," Étienne said sharply. "Act like Ossip, at least, he hasn't lost his head. Get some cologne if there's something like it around. I heard the old man upstairs. He's started again."

"He's got good reason," Oliveira said, looking at Babs who was struggling to get La Maga off the bed. "What a night we've been giving him, Jesus."

"He can go fuck himself," Ronald said. "I'd like to go out and smash his face in, the old bastard. If he hasn't got any respect for other people's troubles . . . "

"Take it easy," Oliveira said in English. "There's your cologne, take my handkerchief even if it's not the whitest in the world. Well, we'll have to notify the police."

"I can go," said Gregorovius, who had his raincoat over his arm.

"But of course you're a member of the family," Oliveira said.

"If you could just cry," Babs was saying, stroking La Maga on the forehead as she laid her head on the pillow and was staring at Rocamadour. "Give me a handkerchief with alcohol on it, please, something to bring her round."

Étienne and Ronald began to bustle around the bed. The thumps were coming rhythmically on the ceiling and Ronald looked up each time and once shook his fist hysterically. Oliveira had withdrawn to the stove and was watching and listening from there. He felt that he had been saddled with fatigue and that it was pulling him down, making it hard for him to breathe, to move. He lit another cigarette, the last one in the pack. Things began to get a little better. Babs had rummaged in a corner of the room and after making a sort of cradle out of two chairs and a blanket was conferring with Ronald (it was strange to watch their gestures over La Maga, who was lost in a cold delirium, in a vehement but dry and spasmodic monologue); at one point they covered La Maga's eyes with a handkerchief ("If that's cologne they're going to blind her," Oliveira said to himself), and with extraordinary quickness they helped Étienne lift up Rocamadour and carry him to the improvised cradle while they pulled the bedcover out from under La Maga and put it on top of her, speaking to her softly, caressing her, making her inhale what was on the handkerchief. Gregorovius had gone over to the door and was standing there, not having made up his mind to go out, looking furtively at the bed and then at Oliveira, who had his back turned towards him but sensed that he was looking at him. When he decided to leave, the old man was already on the landing with a stick in his hand, and Ossip jumped back inside. The stick clattered against the door. "That's the way things can keep on piling up," Oliveira said to himself, taking a step towards the door. Ronald, who had guessed what was going on, threw himself furiously towards the door while Babs shouted something at him in English. Gregorovius tried to stop him, but it was too late. Ronald, Ossip and Babs went out followed by Étienne, who glanced at Oliveira as if he were the only one who still had some common sense left.

"Don't let them do anything stupid," Oliveira said to him. "The old man must be eighty and he's crazy."

"*Tous des cons!*" the old man was shouting on the landing. "*Bande de tueurs, si vous croyez que ça va se passer comme ça! Des fripouilles, des fainéants. Tas d'enculés!*"

It was odd that he was not shouting very loudly. Through the half-open door Étienne's voice bounced back like a return shot: "*Ta gueule, pépère.*" Gregorovius had grabbed Ronald by the arm, but in the light that came from the apartment Ronald had been able to see that the old man really was very old and all he did was shake his fist in his face with less conviction each time he did it. Once or twice Oliveira glanced at the bed where La Maga was very still beneath the covers. She was sobbing heavily with her mouth plunged into the pillow, on the exact spot where Rocamadour's head had been. "*Faudrait quand même laisser dormir les gens*," the old man was saying. "*Qu'est-ce que ça me fait, moi, un gosse qu'a claqué? C'est pas une façon d'agir quand même, on est à Paris, pas en Amazonie.*" Étienne's voice became louder and swallowed up the other as he convinced him. Oliveira told himself that it would not be so difficult to go over to the bed, squat down beside it and say a few words in La Maga's ear. "But I would be doing it for myself," he thought. "She's beyond anything. I'm the one who would sleep better afterwards, even if it's just an expression. Me, me, me. I would sleep better after I kissed her and consoled her and repeated everything these people here have already said."

"*Eh bien, moi, messieurs, je respecte la douleur d'une mère*," the old man's voice said. "*Allez, bonsoir messieurs, dames.*"

The rain was slicing down on the window. Paris must be a great grey bubble in which dawn would come up little by little. Oliveira went over to the corner where his lumberjacket was looking like the torso of a quartered criminal, oozing dampness. He put it on slowly, looking all the while towards the bed as if he expected something. He thought of Berthe Trépat's arm on his, the walk in the rain. "*¿De qué te sirvió el verano, oh rui-señor en la nieve?*" he quoted ironically. "Stinking, absolutely stinking. And I'm out of cigarettes, damn it." He would have to go all the way to the Bébert café, but in the end dawn would be just as repugnant there as anywhere else.

"What an old fool," Ronald said, closing the door.

"He went back to his flat," Étienne said. "I think Gregorovius went out to tell the police. Are you staying?"

"No, what for? They won't like it if they find so many people here at this hour. It would be better for Babs to stay, two women are always more convincing in these cases. It's more intimate, understand?"

Étienne looked at him.

"I'd like to know why your mouth is quivering so much," he said.

"Nervous tics," Oliveira said.

"Tics don't go well with the cynical air. I'll go with you, come on."

"Let's go."

He knew that La Maga had sat up in bed and was looking at him. Putting his hands in the pockets of his lumberjacket, he went to the door. Étienne made a sign as if to hold him back and then followed him out. Ronald saw them leave and shrugged his shoulders, furious. "This is all so absurd," he thought. The idea that everything was absurd made him uncomfortable, but he couldn't tell why. He began to help Babs, made himself useful, wetted compresses. The pounding on the ceiling started up again.

(–130)

29

"*Tiens*," said Oliveira.

Gregorovius was huddled by the stove, wrapped up in a black bathrobe, reading. He had hung a lamp on a nail in the wall and with a shade made out of a newspaper was guiding the light just where he needed it.

"I didn't know you had a key."

"Leftover," said Oliveira, tossing his lumberjacket in the usual corner. "I'll let you have it, now that the place is yours."

"Just for a while. It's too cold in here, and besides, I've got that old man upstairs. He pounded on the floor for five minutes this morning. Why, I don't know."

"Habit. Everything has a longer overlap than it should. Take me, for example. I climb the stairs, I take out my key, I open the door . . . It stinks in here."

"Cold as hell," said Gregorovius. "After they finished fumigating I had to keep the window open for forty-eight hours."

"And you were here all the time? *Caritas.* What kind of a guy are you?"

"That wasn't why. I was afraid somebody from the landlady might use that time to get in here and cause trouble. Lucía told me once that the landlady is an old nut and that a lot of tenants have owed her rent for years. When I was in Budapest I was reading law and things like that stick with you."

"You've made a real posh setup for yourself. *Chapeau, mon vieux.* I hope they didn't throw out my *yerba mate*."

"No, it's over there in the bedside table, among the stockings. There's lots of space now."

"So it seems," said Oliveira. "La Maga had an attack of neatness. I don't see any records or books. But now that I think of it . . . "

"She took everything," said Gregorovius.

Oliveira opened the drawer of the bedside table and took out the *yerba mate* and the gourd that went with it. He began to fill the gourd slowly, looking all around. The lyrics of *Mi noche triste* began to run through his head. He counted on his fingers: Thursday, Friday, Saturday. No. Monday, Tuesday, Wednesday. No. Thursday night, Berthe Trépat, *me amuraste / en lo mejor de la vida*, Wednesday (a wild binge; n.b., don't mix vodka and red wine), *dejándome el alma herida / y espina en el corazón.* Thursday, Friday, Ronald and a rented car, a visit to Guy Monod, like an old glove come home, buckets of green vomit, out of danger, *sabiendo que te quería / que vos eras mi alegría / mi esperanza y mi ilusión.* Saturday, where? where? somewhere near Marly-le-Roi, five days in all; no, six, a week more or less, and the room still cold in spite of the stove. Wily old Ossip, king of convenience.

"So she's gone," said Oliveira, plumping down in the easy chair and keeping the little kettle within reach.

Gregorovius nodded. He had his book open on his knees and gave the impression that he would like to keep on reading.

"And she left her place to you."

"She knew I was in delicate shape," said Gregorovius. "My great-aunt stopped sending me my allowance, she's probably dead. Miss Babington hasn't said anything, but with the situation in Cyprus . . . And you know what that can mean to Malta, censorship and all that. Since you had said you were going away, Lucía offered to share the room with me. I wasn't sure, but she insisted."

"It doesn't tie in too well with her leaving."

"But that was before all this happened."

"Before they fumigated?"

"Exactly."

"You've hit the jackpot, Ossip."

"It's all very sad, really," said Gregorovius. "It could have been quite different."

"Don't complain. A room twelve by ten for five thousand francs a month, with running water . . . "

"I want everything to be perfectly clear between us," said Gregorovius. "This room . . . "

"Doesn't belong to me. Take it easy. And La Maga has gone."

"Anyway . . . "

"Where did she go?"

"She said something about Montevideo."

"She hasn't got enough money for that."

"She mentioned Perugia."

"You must mean Lucca. Ever since she read *Sparkenbroke* she's been crazy about those things. Once and for all, tell me where she went."

"I don't have the slightest idea, Horacio. Last Friday she filled a suitcase with books and clothes, bundled a lot of things together, and then two Negroes came and took it all away. She told me I could stay here, but since she was crying all the time you can imagine how hard it was to talk to her."

"I'd like to hit you in the face," said Oliveira, sucking on his *mate.*

"It's not my fault."

"It's not a matter of fault, damn it. You're so damned Dostoevskian, repulsive and pleasant at the same time. A kind of metaphysical arse-kisser. When you put on a smile like that who in hell would ever want to hurt you."

"Oh, I'm one up on you," said Gregorovius. "The mechanics of 'challenge and response' is a bourgeois trait. You're like me, that's why you can't hit me. Don't look at me like that. I don't know what's happened to Lucía. One of the Negroes I mentioned always hangs out in the Café Bonaparte. I've seen him there. He could probably tell you. But why are you looking for her now?"

"What do you mean, 'now'?"

Gregorovius shrugged his shoulders.

"It was a very proper wake," he said. "Especially after we got rid of the police. Socially speaking, people were commenting about the fact that you weren't there. The Club was on your side, but the neighbours and the old man upstairs . . . "

"You mean to tell me that the old man came to the wake?"

"It wasn't really a wake. They let us keep the body until noon, then the authorities came. Efficient and quick, I must admit."

"I can picture the whole thing," said Oliveira. "But there's no reason for La Maga to move without so much as a word."

"She thought you'd been with Pola all the time."

"*Ça alors,*" said Oliveira.

"People do get ideas, you know. It's all your fault that we're using the familiar form and that makes it harder for me to tell you certain things. It's obviously a paradox, but that's the way it is. It must be because it's a false familiarity. You started it the other night."

"I don't see any reason not to be familiar with the man who's been sleeping with my girl."

"I'm getting sick of telling you it wasn't that way. So there's no reason for us to use the familiar form. If La Maga had really drowned, I can see how in the grief of the moment, while we were embracing and consoling each other . . . But that's not how it was. At least I don't think so."

"You saw something in the paper," said Oliveira.

"The description doesn't match at all. We can still use formal address. There it is over there, on the mantel."

The description, in fact, did not match. Oliveira took the newspaper and prepared himself another *mate.* Lucca, Montevideo, *la guitarra en el ropero / para siempre está colgada* . . . And when she puts everything in a suitcase and makes up bundles one might deduce that (take care: all deductions are not necessarily proofs), *nadie en ella toca nada / ni hace sus cuerdas sonar.* Or makes music on its strings.

"Well, I'll find out where she's gone. She couldn't get very far."

"This will always be her home," said Gregorovius, "even though Adgalle is coming to stay with me this spring."

"Your mother?"

"Yes. She sent an emotional telegram in which she mentioned the tetragrammaton. It so happened that I had been reading the *Sefer Yetzirah,* trying to trace its Neoplatonic influences. Adgalle knows her kabala. There'll be some wild arguments."

"Had La Maga said anything that would make you think she'd kill herself?"

"Well, you know women."

"Anything concrete."

"No, I don't think so," said Gregorovius. "She talked a lot about Montevideo."

"She's a fool. She doesn't have a cent."

"About Montevideo and that business of a wax doll."

"Hmm, the doll. And she imagined that . . . "

"She was sure of it. Adgalle will be interested in this; what you called coincidence. Lucía doesn't think it was coincidence. You either, deep inside. Lucía told me that when you found the green doll you threw it on the floor and stepped on it."

"I hate stupidity," said Oliveira virtuously.

"All the pins had been stuck in the breasts, except for one in the organs. Did you know already that Pola was sick when you trampled on the green doll?"

"Yes."

"Adgalle will be fascinated. Do you know anything about poisoned portraits? You mix some poison with the paints and you wait for a favourable moon to paint the portrait. Adgalle tried it on her father, but there were interferences . . . In any case, the old man died of some kind of diphtheria three years later. He was alone in the castle. We had a castle in those days, and when he began to asphyxiate he tried to perform a tracheotomy in front of the mirror by inserting a goose quill or something like that. They found him at the bottom of the stairs. But I don't know why I'm telling you all this."

"Because you don't give a damn, I suppose."

"Yes, maybe," said Gregorovius. "Let's have some coffee. You can feel night coming on at this hour, even though you can't see it."

Oliveira picked up the newspaper. While Ossip put the pot on the fire he began to read the news. "Blonde, about forty-two." How stupid to think that . . . But, of course . . . *Les travaux du grand barrage d'Assouan ont commencé. Avant cinq ans, la vallée moyenne du Nil sera transformée en un immense lac. Des édifices prodigieux, qui comptent parmi les plus admirables de la planète . . .*

(–107)

30

"A misunderstanding, like everything else. But the coffee is up to the occasion. Did you drink all the *caña*?"

"The wake, you understand . . . "

"Of course, the little corpse."

"Ronald was drinking like a beast. He was really upset, nobody could figure out why. Babs was suspicious. Even Lucía was surprised at him. But the watchmaker on the sixth floor brought a bottle of brandy and it was enough for everybody."

"Did many people come?"

"Well, let's see, all the club was there, you weren't there," ("No, I wasn't there") "the watchmaker from the sixth floor, the concierge and her daughter, a woman who looked like a moth, the telegraph man stayed a while, and the police were nosing around for evidence of infanticide, things like that."

"I'm surprised they didn't talk about an autopsy."

"They mentioned it. Babs blew her top, and Lucía . . . A woman came and looked around, touching and feeling . . . There wasn't enough room for all of us on the stairway, everybody outside and it was cold. They did something, but finally they left us alone. I don't know how, but I've got the death certificate here in my wallet if you want to look at it."

"No, tell me more. I'm listening, even if I don't look like it. Come on, keep talking. I'm very upset. It doesn't show, but you can believe me. I'm listening, come on. I can picture the scene perfectly. You're not going to tell me that Ronald helped carry him downstairs?"

"Yes, he and Perico and the watchmaker. I went with Lucía."

"In front."

"And Babs brought up the rear with Étienne."

"Behind."

"Halfway between the fourth and third floors we heard a tremendous thump. Ronald said it was the old man on the fifth floor getting his vengeance. When mother comes I'm going to have her get to know the old man."

"Your mother? Adgalle?"

"She is my mother, after all, the Herzegovina one. She's going to like this place, she's quite receptive and things have happened here . . . I don't just mean the green doll."

"Come on now, let's see, explain to me why your mother is receptive and about this place. Let's talk, eh, we've got to get these pillows all stuffed. Give me the stuffing."

(–57)

31

It had been some time since Gregorovius had given up the illusion of understanding things, but at any rate, he still wanted misunderstandings to have some sort of order, some reason to them. No matter how many times the cards of the deck might be shuffled, laying them out was always a consecutive process, which would take place on the rectangle of a table-top or a bedspread. To get the *mate* drinker from the pampas willing to reveal the order behind his meanderings. In the worst moments to let him improvise for the moment; then it would be difficult for him to extricate himself from his own web. Between one and another *mate* Oliveira condescended to remember some moment from the past or answer questions. He would ask questions in turn with an ironic interest in the burial, in how people acted. He rarely referred directly to La Maga, but it was clear that he suspected some lying was going on. Montevideo, Lucca, some corner of Paris. Gregorovius told himself that Oliveira would have gone running out if he had had any idea where Lucía was staying. He seemed to be a specialist in lost causes. Lose them first, then run after them like a madman.

"Adgalle is going to enjoy her stay in Paris," Oliveira said, changing the *yerba mate* in his gourd. "If she's looking for the gates of assorted hells, all you have to do is show her some of the things that go on here. On a modest level, of course, but hell has been cheapened too. The *nekias* of today: a trip on the Métro at six-thirty, or going to the police to get your *carte de séjour* renewed."

"You would have liked to have found the main gate, eh? A dialogue with Ajax, with Jacques Clément, with Keitel, with Troppmann."

"Yes, but the biggest hole so far is the one in the bathroom. And not even Traveler understands, and that's saying something. Traveler is a friend of mine you don't know."

"You're hiding your cards," said Gregorovius, looking at the floor.

"For example?"

"I don't know, I'm just guessing. All the time I've known you, all you've done is search, but one gets the feeling that what you're looking for is right in your pocket."

"The mystics talked about that, but they didn't mention pockets."

"And in the meantime you mess up the lives of any number of people."

"They're willing, old man, perfectly willing. All I had to do was give a little shove, I walk through, and there I am. No evil intent."

"But what are you after with all that, Horacio?"

"The freedom of the city."

"Here?"

"It's a metaphor. And since Paris is another metaphor (I've heard you say so sometimes) it seems perfectly natural to me that I came here for that reason."

"But Lucía? And Pola?"

"Heterogeneous quantities," Oliveira said. "Just because they're women you think that you can add them up in the same column. Aren't they looking for their happiness too? And you, so puritanical all of a sudden, haven't you slithered in here as a result of meningitis or whatever it was they found the kid had? It's lucky that you and I are not squares because otherwise one of us would be carried out dead and the other one with handcuffs on. Something just right for Sholokov, believe me. But we don't even detest each other, it's so protective in this apartment."

"You're hiding your cards," said Gregorovius, looking at the floor again.

"Elucidate, *mon frère*, do me that small favour."

"You," insisted Gregorovius, "have an imperial notion in the back of your head. Freedom of the city? Rule of the city. Your resentment: a half-cured ambition. You came here to find a statue of yourself waiting for you on the edge of the Place Dauphine. What I don't understand is your method. Ambition, why not? You're outstanding enough in some ways. But up till now all that I've seen you do has been just the opposite of what other ambitious people would have done. Étienne, for example, and we don't even have to mention Perico."

"Ah," said Oliveira. "It seems your eyes are good for something after all."

"Just the opposite," Ossip repeated, "but without denying ambition. And that's what I don't understand."

"Oh, understanding, you know . . . It's all very mixed up. Take the bit that what you call ambition can only be productive if it's denied. Do you like the formula? That's not it, but what I want to say is something that really is unexplainable. You've got to turn round and round like a dog chasing his tail. All of this and what I said about the freedom of the city ought to satisfy you, you fucking Montenegran."

"I understand in an obscure sort of way. Then you . . . It's not a path, like Vedanta or things like that, I hope."

"No, no."

"A lay renunciation, could we call it that?"

"Not that either. I'm not renouncing anything, I simply do what I can so that things renounce me. Didn't you know that if you want to dig a little hole you've got to shovel up the ground and toss it far away?"

"But freedom of the city, well . . . "

"You've put your finger right on it. Remember the dictum: *Nous ne sommes pas au monde.* Now get the gist of it, slowly."

"An ambition to clear the table and start all over again, is that it?"

"A little bit, a touch of that, just a hair, a drop, oh stern Transylvanian, son of three witches."

"You and the others . . . " murmured Gregorovius, looking for his pipe. "What a bunch, my God. Thieves of eternity, atmospheric frauds, hounds of God, cloud-chasers. It's good we've got an education and can define them. Astral swine."

"You do me honour with those definitions," Oliveira said. "It's proof that you're beginning to understand it all fairly well."

"Bah, I prefer breathing oxygen and hydrogen in the dose the Lord prescribes. My alchemy is much less subtle than what all of you practise; all that interests me is the philosopher's stone. A trifle alongside your frauds and your bathrooms and your ontological deductions."

"It's been a long time since we had a metaphysical chat, eh? They're out of favour with our friends, they think you're a snob. Ronald, for example, finds them ghastly. And Étienne never gets out of the solar spectrum. It's nice being here with you."

"We really could have been friends," Gregorovius said, "if you had had something human about you. I suspect that Lucía must have told you that more than once."

"Every five minutes, to be exact. You've got to see what mileage people can get from the word *human*. But why didn't La Maga stay with you since you glow all over with humanity?"

"Because she wasn't in love with me. Humanity takes in all kinds."

"And now she's going back to Montevideo and she'll fall back into a life that . . . "

"She probably went to Lucca. She'll be better off anywhere without you. The same goes for Pola, or me, or the rest of us. Please excuse my frankness."

"But it fits you so well, Ossip Ossipovich. Why fool ourselves? It's impossible to live with a puppeteer who works with shadows, a moth-tamer. Someone who spends his time making pictures out of the iridescent rings the oil makes on the Seine is unacceptable. Me, with my padlocks and keys that I make out of the air, me, writing with smoke. I'll save the answer for you because I see it coming up: there is no substance more deadly than the one that can ooze in anywhere, that breathes without being aware of it, in words or in love or in friendship. It's been a long time now since I should have been left alone to me, myself and I. You've got to admit that I don't go around kissing arse. Get lost, you son of a Bosnian. The next time you run into me on the street you'd better not even know me."

"You're crazy, Horacio. You're stupidly crazy, because it suits you."

Oliveira took a newspaper clipping out of his pocket that he had kept for God knows how long: a list of all-night chemists in Buenos Aires. Ones that were open from eight o'clock on Monday until the same time on Tuesday.

"First district," he read. "446 Reconquista (Tel. 31-5488), 366 Córdoba (Tel. 32-8845), 599 Esmeralda (Tel. 31-1700), 581 Sarmiento (Tel. 32-2021)."

"What's all that?"

"Moments of reality. I'll explain: Reconquista, something we did to the English. Córdoba, a learned city. Esmeralda, a gypsy girl hanged because she was in love with an archdeacon. Sarmiento, he blew a fart and the wind carried it away. Second version: Reconquista, a street of whores and Near Eastern restaurants. Córdoba, wonderful sweetshops. Esmeralda, a river in Colombia. Sarmiento, he never missed school. Third version: Reconquista, a chemist. Esmeralda, another chemist. Sarmiento, another chemist. Fourth version . . . "

"And when I insist you're crazy it's because I don't see any way out of your famous renunciation."

"620 Florida (Tel. 31-2200)."

"You didn't go to the burial because although you renounce many things, you're still not capable of looking your friends in the face."

"749 Hipólito Yrigoyen (Tel. 34-0936)."

"And Lucía is better off at the bottom of the river than in bed with you."

"800 Bolívar. The phone number is hard to make out. If people in the neighbourhood have a sick kid they won't be able to buy him some Terramycin."

"Yes, at the bottom of the river."

"1117 Corrientes (Tel. 35-1468)."

"Or in Lucca, or in Montevideo."

"Or in 1301 Rivadavia (Tel. 38-7841)."

"Keep that list for Pola," Gregorovius said, getting up. "I'm going out, you can do what you feel like. You're not at home, but since nothing has any reality, and we have to start *ex nihil*, etc . . . Help yourself to all these illusions. I'm going out to get a bottle of brandy."

Oliveira caught up with him next to the door and put his hand on his shoulder.

"2099 Lavalle," he said, looking him in the face and smiling. "1501 Cangallo. 53 Pueyrredón."

"You forgot the telephone numbers," Gregorovius said.

"You're beginning to understand," said Oliveira, taking his hand away. "Underneath it all you've got the feeling that I can't say anything to anybody, to you, or to anybody."

The footsteps stopped when they got to the second floor. "He's coming back," Oliveira thought. "He's afraid I'll burn up the bed or cut up the sheets. Poor Ossip." But after a moment the shoes went on their way downstairs. Seated on the bed, he looked at the papers in the drawer of the bedside table. A novel by Pérez Galdós, a bill from the chemist. It was chemist night. Some pieces of paper with scribbling in pencil. La Maga had taken everything, there was a smell left over from before, the paper on the walls, the bed with the striped spread. A novel by Galdós, what an idea. If it wasn't Vicki Baum it was Roger Martin du Gard, and that brought on the strange jump to Tristan L'Hermite, hours on end repeating for any reason at all "*les rêves de l'eau qui songe*", or an artistic edition of *pantungs*, or stories by Schwitters, a kind of ransom, penitence of the most exquisite and sneaky sort, until suddenly one would fall back into John Dos Passos and spend five days swallowing enormous doses of the printed word.

The scribbling was some kind of letter.

(–32)

32

Baby Rocamadour, baby, baby. Rocamadour.

By now I know you're like a mirror, Rocamadour, sleeping or looking at your feet. Here I am holding a mirror and thinking that it's you. But don't you believe it, I'm writing to you because you don't know how to read. If you did know I wouldn't be writing to you or I'd be writing about important things. Some day I'll have to write to you and tell you to behave and keep warm. Someday seems incredible, Rocamadour. Now I can only write to you in the mirror, sometimes I have to dry my finger because it gets wet with tears. Why, Rocamadour? I'm not sad, your mother is a slob, I dropped the borscht I had prepared for Horacio into the fire; you know who Horacio is, Rocamadour, the man who brought you the velvet bunny last Sunday and who got so bored because you and I had so much to say to one another and he wanted to go back to Paris; then you started to cry and he showed you how the rabbit moved its ears; he looked beautiful then, Horacio I mean, some day you'll understand, Rocamadour.

Rocamadour, it's silly to cry like this because I spilled the borscht. The room is full of beetroot-smell, Rocamadour, you'd laugh if you could see the pieces of beetroot and the cream, all over the floor. It's not too bad because I'll have it all cleaned up by the time Horacio comes, but first I have to write to you, it's so foolish to cry like this, the pots have taken on a soft shape, there are things like halos on the windowpanes, and you can't hear the girl upstairs singing, the one who sings *Les Amants du Havre* all day long. When we're together I'll sing it for you, you'll see. *Puisque la terre est ronde, mon amour t'en fais pas, mon amour, t'en fais pas* . . . Horacio whistles it at night when he's writing or sketching. You'd like it, Rocamadour. You'd like it, Horacio gets furious because I like to use the same familiar form Perico does, but it's different in Uruguay. Perico is the man who didn't bring you anything the other day but talked so much about children and their diet. He knows a lot, you'll respect him someday, Rocamadour, and you'll be a fool if you respect him. But there I go with his familiar again.

Rocamadour, Madame Irène is upset because you're so handsome, so happy, so weepy and shouty and pissy. She says that everything is all right and that you're a charming child, but all the time she keeps her hands in the pockets of her apron the way some sneaky animals do, Rocamadour, and that frightens me. When I said so to Horacio he laughed a lot, but he didn't realize what I really meant, I can't explain it. Rocamadour, if only there was some way to read in your eyes what has happened to you in these two weeks, moment by moment. I think I'll try to get a different *nourrice* even though Horacio will get very angry and say, but you're not interested in what he thinks about me. Another *nourrice* who doesn't talk so much, I don't care whether she says you're naughty or cry at night or don't want to eat, I don't care if when she says all that I can feel that she isn't evil, that she's telling me something that won't do you any harm. It's all so strange, Rocamadour, for example, the way I like to say your name and write it down, every time I get the feeling that I'm touching the tip of your nose and that you're laughing, but Madame Irène never uses your name, she says *l'enfant*, just imagine, she doesn't even say *le gosse*, she says *l'enfant*, it's as if she put on rubber gloves every time she spoke, maybe she already has them on and that's why she puts her hands in her pockets and says that you're so good and so handsome.

There's something called time, Rocamadour, it's like a bug that just keeps on walking. I can't explain it to you because you're so small, but what I mean is that Horacio will be back any minute now. Shall I let him read my letter so that he can add something too? No, I wouldn't want anyone to read a letter that was just for me either. A big secret between the two of us, Rocamadour. I'm not crying any more, I'm happy, but it's so hard to understand things, I need so much time to understand just a little of what Horacio and the others understand right away, but they understand everything so well and they can't understand you and me, they don't understand why I can't have you with me, feed you, change your nappies, make you go to sleep or play with me, they don't understand and they really don't care, and I who care so much only know that I can't have you with me, that it would be bad for both of us, that I have to be alone with Horacio, live with Horacio, I don't know for how long, helping him look for what he's looking for and what you'll be looking for too, Rocamadour, because you will be a man and you too will be searching like a big fool.

That's how it is, Rocamadour. In Paris we're like fungus, we grow on the railings of staircases, in dark rooms with greasy smells, where people make love all the time and then fry some eggs and put on Vivaldi records, light cigarettes, and talk like Horacio and Gregorovius and Wong and me, Rocamadour, and like Perico and Ronald and Babs, we all make love and fry eggs and smoke, oh, you can't imagine how we smoke, how we make love, standing up, lying down, on our knees, with our hands, with our mouths, crying or singing, and outside there are all sorts of things, the windows open onto the air and it all begins with a sparrow or a gutter, it rains a lot here, Rocamadour, much more than in the country, and things get rusty, the leaders, the pigeons' feet, the wires Horacio uses to make figures with. We don't have many clothes, we get along with so few, a good overcoat, some shoes to keep the rain out, we're very dirty, everybody is dirty and good-looking in Paris, Rocamadour, the beds smell of night and deep sleep, dust and books underneath, Horacio falls asleep and the book ends up under the bed, we get into terrible fights because we can't find the books and Horacio thinks that Ossip has stolen them, until they show up one day and we laugh, and there just about isn't room for anything, not even another pair of shoes, Rocamadour, to set down a washbasin on the floor we have to move the record-player, but where can we put it because the table is full of books. I couldn't have you here, as small as you are there wouldn't be room for you, you'd bump against the walls. When I think about it I start to cry, Horacio doesn't understand, he thinks I'm wicked, that it's bad of me not bringing you here, even though I know he wouldn't be able to stand you for very long. No one can stand it here for very long, not even you and I, you have to live by fighting each other, it's the law, the only way that things are worth while but it hurts, Rocamadour, and it's dirty and bitter, you wouldn't like it, you see lambs in the fields, or hear the birds perched on the weather vane of the house. Horacio calls me sentimental, he calls me materialist, he calls me everything because I don't bring you or because I want to bring you, because I deny it, because I want to go and see you, because suddenly I understand that I cannot go, because I'm capable of walking for an hour in the rain if in some part of town I don't know they're showing *Potemkin* and I've got to see it even if the world comes to an end, Rocamadour, because the world doesn't matter any more if you don't have the strength to go ahead and choose something that's really true, if you keep yourself neat like a dresser drawer, putting you on one side, Sunday on the other, mother-love, a new toy, the Montparnasse station, the train, the visit you have to make. I don't feel like going, Rocamadour, and you know it's all right and you don't feel bad. Horacio is right, sometimes I don't care about you at all, and I think you'll thank me for that some day when you're able to understand, when you're able to see that the best thing was that I'm the way I am. But just the same I cry, Rocamadour, and I write this letter to you because I don't know, because maybe I'm wrong, because maybe I am wicked or sick or a little stupid, not much, just a little, but that's terrible, it makes me sick to my stomach just thinking about it, I've got my toes curled all the way under and I'm going to split open my shoes if I don't take them off, and I love you so much, Rocamadour, baby Rocamadour, little garlic clove, I love you so much, sugar-nose, sapling, toy pony . . .

(–132)

33

"There's a reason behind his leaving me alone," Oliveira thought as he opened and shut the drawer of the bedside table. "A gracious act or a dirty trick, it's all in the way you look at it. He's probably on the stairs now, listening like a half-baked sadist. He's waiting for the great Karamazov crisis, the Céline attack. Or he's tiptoed off on his Herzegovina toes and after a second glass of kirsch at Bébert's he'll raise mental hell and plan out the ceremonies for the arrival of Adgalle. Torture through waiting: Montevideo, the Seine, or Lucca. Variants: the Marne, Perugia. But then you, really . . . "

Lighting a Gauloise from the butt of the first, he looked into the drawer again, took out the novel, thinking vaguely about pity, a subject for a thesis. Pity for himself: that was more like it. "I never asked for happiness," he thought, thumbing slowly through the novel. "It's not an excuse, it's not a justification. *Nous ne sommes pas au monde. Donc, ergo, dunque* . . . Why should I pity her? Because I found a letter to her son which is really meant for me? Me, author of the complete letters to Rocamadour. No reason for pity. Out there wherever she is her hair is burning like a tower and it singes me from far away, breaks me up into pieces by nothing more than just her absence. And *patati patata.* She's going to get along fine without me and without Rocamadour. A bluebottle fly, delightful, flying towards the sun, runs into a window, bump, a bloody nose, tragedy. Two minutes later so happy, buying a paper doll in a stationery store and running out to put it in an envelope and send it to one of her strange girlfriends with Nordic names scattered about in the weirdest countries. How can you feel pity for a cat, for a lioness? Living-machines, perfect bolts of lightning. My only fault is that I wasn't combustible enough so that she could warm her hands and feet on me at her pleasure. She thought she was getting a burning bush and all she got was a pot of cold water. Poor little darling, shit."

(–67)

34

In September of 1880, a few months after the demise of my And the things she reads, a clumsy novel, in a cheap edition father, I decided to give up my business activities, transferring besides, but you wonder how she can get interested in things them to another house in Jerez whose standing was as solvent like this. To think that she's spent hours on end reading tasteless as that of my own; I liquidated all the credits I could, rented out stuff like this and plenty of other incredible things, *Elle* and the properties, transferred my holdings and inventories, and *France Soir*, those sad magazines Babs lends her. *And moved to* moved to Madrid to take up residence there. My uncle (in truth *Madrid to take up residence there*, I can see how after you swal- my father's first cousin), Don Rafael Bueno de Guzmán y Ataide, low four or five pages you get in the groove and can't stop read- wanted to put me up in his home; but I demurred for fear of ing, a little like the way you can't help sleeping or pissing, losing my independence. I was finally able to effect a compro- slavery or whipping or drooling. *I was finally able to effect a* mise between my comfortable freedom and my uncle's gracious *compromise*, a style that uses prefabricated words to transmit offer; and renting a flat in his building, I arranged matters so superannuated ideas, coins that go from hand to hand, from that I could be alone when I wished or I could enjoy family generation to generation, *te voilà en pleine écholalie. Enjoy* warmth when that became essential. The good gentleman lived, *family warmth*, that's good, shit if that isn't good. Oh, Maga, I should say we lived, in a section that had been built up on a how could you swallow this stuff, and what the hell is the charity site where the charity warehouse had once been. My uncle's flat warehouse, for God's sake. I wonder how much time she spent was the main one, 18,000 *reales* he paid, handsome and happy, reading this stuff, probably convinced that this was life, and even though it was not adequate for such a large family. I took you were right, it is life, that's why we've got to get rid of it. the ground-floor apartment, a little less spacious than the main (The main one, what's that.) And on some afternoons when one, but marvellously extensive for me alone, and I decorated I'd got the bug to cover the whole Egyptian section of the Louvre, it luxuriously and put in all the comforts to which I had become case by case, and I would come home with a taste for *mate* and accustomed. My income, thank God, allowed me to do all of this bread and jam, I'd find you stuck by the window with one of and more.

these fat novels in your hand and sometimes you'd even be

My first impressions of Madrid were surprisingly pleasant, crying, yes, don't deny it, you'd be crying because they'd just since I had not been there since the days of González Brabo. I cut somebody's head off, and you'd hug me as hard as you could was flabbergasted by the beauty and expanse of the newer sec- and want to know where I'd been, but I wouldn't tell you be- tions, the efficient system of communications, the obvious im- cause you're a burden in the Louvre, it's impossible to walk provement in the appearance of the buildings, the streets, and around there with you alongside, your ignorance is the kind that even the people; the pretty little gardens now planted where destroys all pleasure, poor girl, and it's really my fault that you once there had been dusty old squares, the magnificent homes read potboilers because I'm selfish (*dusty old squares*, that's all of the rich, the varied and well-stocked shops, inferior in no right, it reminds me of the squares in provincial towns, or the way, as was evident from the street, to those of Paris or London, streets of La Rioja in 1942, the purple mountains at sunset, that and lastly, the many elegant theatres for all classes, tastes, and feeling of happiness that comes with being alone in a particular incomes. These and other things that I later observed in my spot in the world, and *elegant theatres*. What the hell is the guy social contacts made me understand the rapid advances that talking about? He's just mentioned Paris and London some- our capital had made since 1868, advances more in the manner

where there, he talks about tastes and incomes), you see, Maga,
of whimsical leaps than in that of the solid, progressive move-
you see how these eyes of mine are being pulled along with
ment forward of people who know where they are headed; but
irony through the lines you read with great emotion, convinced
it was no less real because of all this. In a word, my nose had got
of the fact that you were getting all kinds of culture because
the scent of some European culture, of well-being, and even
you were reading a Spanish novelist whose picture is on the
riches and hard work.
fly-leaf, but right now the guy is talking about a scent of Euro-
My uncle is a well-known businessman in Madrid. In years
pean culture, you'd convinced yourself that all this reading
past he had held important positions in the government: he had
would help you understand the micro- and the macrocosm, and
been a consul general; then he had been an attaché in an em-
about all that was ever necessary was for me to come home for
bassy; subsequently his marriage demanded his presence in the
you to take out of the drawer of your desk – because you did
capital; he was with the Treasury for a while, under the protec-
have a desk, you always had to have one around even though I
tion and power of Bravo Murillo, and finally his family responsi-
never found out what kind of work you were doing on it – yes,
bilities made it necessary for him to exchange the vile security
you would take out a folio with poems by Tristan L'Hermite, for
of a salary for the adventures and hopes of work on his own.
example, or a study by Boris de Schloezer, and you would show
He was possessed of a fair amount of ambition, uprightness,
them to me with the uncertain and at the same time proud air of
activity, intelligence, good connections; he began to work as the
someone who has just bought some great things and is going to
agent in diverse commercial matters, and after running about
read them right now. There was no way to make you understand
a bit in pursuit of all this he ended up in command of every-
that you wouldn't ever get anywhere like that, that there were
thing and was able to tuck all of the accounts away in his files.
some things that were too late and others that were too soon, and
He lived off them, however, stirring up those that were dozing
you were always so close to the brink of despair in the very

in his cabinet, moving along those that had come to rest on his centre of joy and relaxation, your baffled heart was always so desk, keeping on the right track, as best he could, a few that full of fog. *Moving along those that had come to rest on his desk,* were in danger of going astray. His friendships with members no, you couldn't count on me for that, your desk was your desk of both parties were helpful to him, as was the high regard in and I didn't put you behind it or take you away from it, I simply which he was held in all branches of the government. No door watched you as you read your novels and looked at the jackets remained closed to him. One might even think that the doormen and the pictures in your folios, and you were hoping that I would of the various ministries owed their existence to him, for they sit down next to you and explain it to you, relieve your mind, do showed deep filial respect and opened doors wide for him as if what every woman hopes a man will do with her, sneak his arm they were the doors of his very own house. I had heard tell that around her waist a little and now he makes her snuggle closer, in certain periods he had made a good deal of money by putting he gives her the urge to drop her tendency to knit sweaters or his active hands on some well-known mining and railway talk, talk, talk on endlessly about everything that doesn't mean stocks; but that in other cases his timid honesty had not been anything. I'm a real beast, what have I got to be proud about, I favourable for him. When I settled in Madrid, his situation, as don't even have you any more because you were so set on losing far as could be seen, must have been comfortable but not yourself (not even losing yourself, because first you would have lavish. He had everything he needed, but he had no savings, had to find yourself), *really not a praiseworthy situation for a* really not a praiseworthy situation for a man who had worked *man who . . .* Praiseworthy, how long has it been since I heard so hard and who was now coming to the end of his days with that word, we're really losing our language in Argentina; when barely enough time in which to recoup his losses.

I was a boy I was aware of a lot more words than I am now, I

He was at that time a man who looked older than he really used to read these same novels, I built up a huge vocabulary that was, always immaculately dressed in the style of the elegant was perfectly useless for anything else, *immaculately, very dis-* young men of the time, and with a very distinguished air. He *tinguished*, yes indeed. I wonder if you really got into the plot was completely clean-shaven, this being a token of loyalty to the of this novel, or whether you used it as a jumping-off point for previous generation to which he belonged. His charm and his those mysterious countries of yours that I used to envy while joviality, always kept in delicate balance, never fell into im- you used to envy me my visits to the Louvre, that you must have pertinent familiarity or petulance. His best would come out in suspected even though you didn't say anything. And there we his conversation, as well as his worst, for knowing how good were getting closer and closer to what had to happen someday he was at speaking, he would let himself be led into the habit of when you would understand fully that I was only going to give describing every detail and his accounts would be lengthened to you part of my time and my life, *and his accounts would be* a tedious degree. Sometimes he would do this right at the very *lengthened to a tedious degree*, that's it exactly, I get boring beginning and would adorn his stories with childish minutiae to even when I reminisce. But how pretty you used to look at the such a degree that one would find it necessary to beg him, for window, with the grey of the sky hovering over your cheek, a heaven's sake, to be brief. When he would be speaking about book in your hands, your mouth always a little intense, doubt something that had happened at home (an exercise he was pas- in your eyes. There was so much lost time in you, you were so sionately fond of), so much time would elapse between the much the shape of what you might have been under different exordium and the firing of the shot, that the listener would have constellations, that taking you in my arms and making love to let his mind wander so far off the subject that the boom would you became a job that was much too tender, that bordered too give him a bit of a start. I am not sure whether I should classify much on charity, and that's where I used to fool myself, let my- as a physical ailment the chronic irritation of his tear-producing self fall into the stupid pride of an intellectual who thinks he's apparatus, which at times, mostly in winter, would make his capable of understanding (*weeping until his nose had begun to*

eyes water so that one would think that he had been weeping *run?*, but that's really too repulsive). Capable of understanding, until his nose had begun to run. I do not know of any other man it makes you want to laugh, Maga. Listen, this is just for you, with a more extensive collection of linen handkerchiefs. Because don't mention it to anyone else. Maga, I was the hollow shape, of that and because of his habit of always holding the white you used to tremble, pure and free as a flame, a stream of quick-fabric in his right hand or in both hands, a friend of mine, an silver, like the first notes of a bird when dawn is breaking, and Andalusian, a wag and a good fellow, of whom I shall speak it's nice to tell you all this in words that used to fascinate you later on, used to call my uncle *la Verónica.*
because you had thought they didn't exist outside poetry, and

He showed me real affection, and during the early days of my that we had every right to use them. Where are you now, where residence in Madrid he was continuously at my side, so that he will we be from today on, two points in an inexplicable universe, could see to it that I was getting installed without difficulties near or far, two points that make a line, two points that drift and so that he could be of help in a hundred little ways. When apart and come close together arbitrarily (*great figures who* we would talk about the family and I would reminisce about my *had made the name of Bueno de Guzmán renowned*, but how childhood or tell anecdotes about my father, a nervous discom-corny can the guy get, Maga, how did you ever get beyond page fort would come over my uncle, a feverish enthusiasm for all five . . .), but I won't explain to you the things they call the great figures who had made the name of Bueno de Guzmán Brownian movements, of course I won't explain them to you renowned, and taking out his handkerchief he would tell me and still both of us, Maga, form a pattern, you a point some-stories that were interminable. He looked upon me as the last where, me another somewhere else, displacing each other, you male representative of a stock rich in great figures, and he would probably now in the Rue de la Huchette, while I'm discovering comfort and spoil me as if I were a child, in spite of my thirty-this novel in your empty apartment, tomorrow you in the Gare de six years. Poor uncle. In these shows of affection, which would

Lyon (if you're going to Lucca, my love) and me on the Rue du cause a considerable increase in the outflow from his eyes, I Chemin Vert, where I've discovered a wonderful little wine, and found a secret and most painful sorrow, a thorn driven deep little by little, Maga, we go along forming an absurd pattern, into the heart of that excellent man. I do not really know exwith our movements we sketch out a pattern just like the ones actly how I came to make that discovery; but I was as certain flies make when they fly around a room, from here to there, that there was a wound he was covering up as if I had seen it suddenly in mid-flight, from there to here, that's what they call with my own two eyes and touched it with my own two hands. Brownian movement, now do you understand? a right angle, an It was a deep grief, overwhelming, the sorrow of not seeing me ascending line, from here to there, from back to front, up, down, married to one of his three daughters; an irremediable annoyspasmodically, slamming on the brakes and starting right up in ance, because his three daughters, alas!, were already married. another direction, and all of this is drawing a picture, a pattern, something non-existent like you and me, like two points lost in Paris that go from here to there, from there to here, drawing their picture, putting on a dance for nobody, not even for themselves, an interminable pattern without any meaning.

(–87)

35

Yes Babs yes. Yes Babs yes. Yes Babs, let's turn out the light, sweetie, see you tomorrow, sleep well, count sheep, it's all over, baby, it's all over. Everybody so nasty with poor Babs, we'll kick them all out of the Club to punish them. Everybody so nasty with poor Babs, nasty Étienne, nasty Perico, nasty Oliveira, Oliveira the worst of the lot, that inquisitor as delightful, delightful Babs had called him so exactly. Yes Babs yes. Rock-a-bye baby. Tura-lura-lura. Yes Babs yes. Something was bound to happen, in any case, there's no living with those people without something happening. Sh, baby, sh. That's the way, go to sleep. The Club's had it, Babs, that's for sure. We'll never see Horacio again, perverse Horacio. Tonight the Club took a jump like a pancake that lands on the ceiling and sticks up there. You can keep holding on to the frying pan, Babs, it won't come down again, don't knock yourself out waiting. Shh, darling, stop crying, the girl is really on a bender, even her soul smells of cognac.

Ronald slipped down a little, steadied himself on Babs, he was falling asleep. Club, Ossip, Perico, let's go back over it: everything had begun because everything had to come to an end, the jealous gods, the fried egg along with Oliveira, the real blame belonged to the god-damned fried egg, according to Étienne there was no need to throw the egg out, a marvel it was with its metallic green tints, and Babs had a kind of Hokusai hairdo: the egg had a smell of carrion that was enough to kill a person, how could the Club hold a session with that egg sitting there a couple of feet away, and suddenly Babs began to cry, the cognac was coming out of her ears, and Ronald realized that while they'd been arguing about timeless things Babs had drunk herself over half a bottle of cognac, the egg business was a way of getting it out and nobody was surprised, Oliveira least of all, that from the egg Babs would little by little get to the business of the burial, preparing herself between hiccups and a sort of fluttering around to bring up the case of the baby, the whole disgusting business. It was no use Wong trying to set up a screen of smiles between Babs and the unaware Oliveira, or making complimentary remarks about the edition of *La Rencontre de la langue d'oïl, de la langue d'oc et du franco-provençal entre Loire et Allier – limites phonetiques et morphologiques*, Wong was very emphatic – by S. Escoffier, a book of great interest, Wong was saying as he pushed Babs along in a greasy sort of way, trying to head her towards the hallway, nothing could have stopped Oliveira from hearing that business about the inquisitor and he raised his eyebrows in a look somewhere between surprised and puzzled, checking with Gregorovius along the way as if the latter could explain the epithet. The Club knew that when Babs got started she was like a catapult, it had happened before; the only solution was a circle around the recording secretary and hostess in charge of food, waiting for time to do its work, no weeping can last for ever, widows remarry. Nothing could be done, Babs was weaving drunkenly among the coats and mufflers of the Club, she came back from the hallway, she wanted to settle accounts with Oliveira, it was just the right moment to tell Oliveira about the inquisitor business, to affirm in her teary way that in all her lousy days she'd never met anyone as low, cold-blooded, bastardly, sadistic, evil, butcher, racist, incapable of the smallest kindness, trash, rotten, piece of shit, slimy, and syphilitic. Items received with infinite delight by Perico and Étienne, and with mixed reactions among the rest, including the recipient.

It was Hurricane Babs, the tornado of the *sixième*: a purée of mashed houses. The Club kept their heads down, sank into their coat collars, dragged on their cigarettes with all their might. When Oliveira managed to say something, there was a great theatrical silence. Oliveira said that he thought the little piece by Nicolas de Staël was very charming and that Wong, now that he was fucking around so much with Escoffier's work, ought to read it, give them a review of it at some other get-together of the Club. Babs called him inquisitor again, and Oliveira must have thought it was a bit funny because he smiled. Babs's hand caught him full across the face. The Club took rapid measures, and Babs went off wailing, lightly held by Wong, who got in between her and a furious Ronald.

The Club closed in around Oliveira so that Babs would be on the outside and she accepted (*a*) the idea of sitting down in an easy chair and (*b*) Perico's handkerchief. It must have been about that time that the facts about the Rue Monge had come up, along with the story of La Maga the Good Samaritan, Ronald seemed to think – he was seeing great green phosphenes in a half-asleep remembrance of the party – that Oliveira had asked Wong if it was true that La Maga was living in a *meublé* on the Rue Monge. And maybe then Wong said that he didn't know, or said that it was true, and somebody, probably Babs from where she was in the chair and with great sobs began to insult Oliveira again, throwing in his face the wonderful abnegation of La Maga the Good Samaritan at the bedside of sick Pola, and it was probably then that Oliveira began to laugh, looking especially at Gregorovius, and asked for more details concerning La Maga the nurse and her abnegation and if it was true that she was living on the Rue Monge, what number, those inevitable cadastral details. Now Ronald was stretching out his hand and putting it between Babs's legs as she grumbled as if she were far away, Ronald liked to sleep with his fingers lost in that vague warm territory, Babs the *agent provocateur* who had brought about the breakup of the Club, he'd have to bawl her out in the morning: things-like-that-are-not-done. But the whole Club had encircled Oliveira in some way or another, as at a shameful trial, and Oliveira had noticed this even before the Club itself, in the centre of the circle he broke out laughing with his cigarette in his mouth and his hands in the pockets of his lumberjacket, and then he had asked (of no one in particular, looking a bit above the heads of those who formed the circle) if the Club was waiting for an *amende honorable* or something like that, and the Club had not understood right off or preferred not to understand, except Babs who from her chair where Ronald was holding her down had started shouting the inquisitor business again, and it sounded almost tomblike at-that-hour-of-the-night. Then Oliveira had stopped laughing, and as if he had suddenly accepted the verdict (although nobody was judging him, because that's not what the Club was for) had thrown his cigarette on the floor, crushed it out with his foot, and after a moment, moving his shoulder a little to avoid the hand of Étienne, who had come forward uncertainly, had spoken in a very low voice, announcing irrevocably that he was withdrawing from the Club and that all the members of the Club, starting with himself and going on down the line, could go fuck the whore that bore them.

Dont acte.

(–121)

36

The Rue Dauphine wasn't far away, maybe it would be worth while going by to check up on what Babs had said. Of course, Gregorovius had known from the very start that La Maga, crazy as ever, would go to see Pola. *Caritas.* La Maga the Good Samaritan. Or better still, *The War Cry*. Did she ever let a day go by without doing her good deed? It was enough to make you laugh. Everything was enough to make you laugh. Or rather, there had been something like a great burst of laughter and that's what they called History. Go to the Rue Dauphine, knock softly on the door of the top-floor apartment and La Maga would appear, Nurse Lucía, to be more exact, no, it was really too much. With a bedpan in her hand or an enema bag. You can't see the patient, it's quite late and she's sleeping. *Vade retro, Asmodeus.* Or they would let him in and serve him coffee, no, worse still, and at some point they would all begin to cry, because it would certainly be contagious, all three of them would cry until they forgave each other, and then anything could happen, dehydrated women are terrible. Or they might put him to count out twenty drops of belladonna, one by one.

"I really ought to go," Oliveira said to a black cat on the Rue Danton. "A certain aesthetic requirement, complete the pattern. Number three, the Clue. But let's not forget about Orpheus. Maybe if I shave my head and cover it with ashes, go there with a tin cup, like a beggar. I am no longer he that ye once knew, oh women. Tragedian. Mime. Night of *empusae* and *lamiae*, evil shadows, the end of the great game. How tiring it gets being the same person all the time. Unpardonably. I will never see them again, it is written. *Qu'as tu fait, toi que violà, de ta jeunesse?* An inquisitor, that girl can really make them up . . . In any case, an autoinquisitor? *et encore* . . . An accurate epitaph: *Too bland.* But a bland inquisition is terrible, semolina tortures, tapioca bonfires, shifting sands, Medusa sucking sneakily. Medusa sneaking suckily. And too much pity underneath it all, me, who thought I was pitiless. It's impossible to want what I want and in the shape I want it, and share life with others besides. I had to know how to be alone and how to let so much wanting do its work, save me or destroy me, but without the Rue Dauphine, without the dead child, without the Club and everything else. Don't you think so, eh?"

The cat did not reply.

It wasn't as cold along the Seine as in the streets, so Oliveira raised the collar of his lumberjacket and went over to look at the water. Since he was not the jumping-off type, he looked for a bridge to get under and do some thinking about that business of the kibbutz, for some time now the idea of the kibbutz had been working on him, a kibbutz of desire. "Strange that all of a sudden an expression should come up like that, one that has no meaning, a kibbutz of desire, until the third time around it begins to take on some meaning little by little and suddenly the expression doesn't seem so absurd any more, like a sentence such as: 'Hope, that lush Palmyra', a completely absurd phrase, a sonorous rumbling of the bowels, while the kibbutz of desire is not absurd at all, it's a way of summing up closed in tight this wandering around from promenade to promenade. Kibbutz; colony, settlement, taking root, the chosen place in which to raise the final tent, where you can walk out into the night and have your face washed by time, and join up with the world, with the Great Madness, with the Grand Stupidity, lay yourself bare to the crystallization of desire, of the meeting. Whatch whout Whoracio," Wholiveira whobserved, sitting down on the rim along the water's edge, listening to the snoring of the *clochards* under their piles of newspapers and burlap bags.

For once in his life it wasn't hard for him to give in to melancholy. Another cigarette that warmed him up, there among the snoring that was coming out of the depths of the earth, he was in a mood to deplore the impossible distance that was separating him from his kibbutz. As long as hope is nothing but a lush Palmyra there was no reason to invent illusions for himself. Quite the opposite, take advantage of the cold of night to get that lucid feeling, with the precision of that astral system up above his head, that his vague search had been a failure and that perhaps victory was to be found in that very fact. First, because it was worthy of him (in his own moments Oliveira thought well of himself as a human specimen), because it was the search for a kibbutz so desperately far away, a citadel that could only be taken with the aid of arms contrived in fantasy, not with the soul of the West or with the spirit, those powers worn away by his own lies as they had so well pointed out in the Club, those alibis used by man the animal as he gets stuck on a road from which there is no turning back. Kibbutz of desire, not of the soul, not of the spirit. And even though desire might also be a rough definition of incomprehensible forces, he could feel it present and at work, present in every mistake and also in every forward leap, that was being a man, not just a body and a soul but that inseparable totality, that ceaseless meeting up with lacks, with everything they had stolen from the poet, the vehement nostalgia for a land where life could be babbled out according to other compasses and other names. Even though death might be waiting at the corner with his broom raised, even though hope was nothing but a lush Palmyra. And a snore, and from time to time a fart.

It was no longer so important, then, to make a mistake as it would have been had the search for his kibbutz been carried out with maps from the Geographical Society, with tested compasses, North pointing north, West west; about all that was needed was to understand, get a quick glimpse that would tell him that in the last analysis his kibbutz was no more impossible at that hour and in that cold and after those last days than if he had been searching after it according to the tribal rites, meritoriously and without earning the showy epithet of inquisitor, without getting his face slapped, without people weeping and a guilty conscience and the urge to chuck everything and go back to his enrolment-card and the protection of a slot in some spiritual or temporal budget. He would die without ever reaching his kibbutz but his kibbutz was there, far away but it was there and he knew that it was there because he was the child of his desire, it was his desire in the same way that he was his own desire and the world or what passed for the world was desire, was his desire or desire itself, it didn't make too much difference at that time of night. And then he was able to cover up his face with his hands, leaving just enough room for his cigarette, and stay there by the river, among the tramps, thinking about his kibbutz.

The *clocharde* woke up out of a dream in which somebody had been telling her repeatedly: "*Ça suffit, conâsse*," and she discovered that Célestin had gone off in the middle of the night taking with him the baby carriage full of some tins of sardines (in bad shape) that had been given to them that afternoon in the Marais ghetto. Toto and Lafleur were sleeping like moles underneath their burlap and the new guy was sitting on a mooring post, smoking. Dawn was breaking.

The *clocharde* daintily removed the successive editions of *France-Soir* covering her, and scratched her head a bit. At six o'clock you could get hot soup on the Rue du Jour. It was practically certain that Célestin would show up to get some soup, and she could get the tins of sardines back if he hadn't already sold them to Pipon or La Vase.

"*Merde*," said the *clocharde*, beginning the complicated task of getting up. And as an encore, "*C'est cul.*"

Wrapping up in a black overcoat that reached down to her ankles, she went over to the newcomer. The newcomer agreed that the cold was almost worse than the police. When she got a cigarette from him and lit it, the *clocharde* got the idea that she knew him from somewhere. The newcomer also said that he knew her from somewhere, and both of them were pleased that they recognized each other at that hour of the morning. Sitting down on the next post, the *clocharde* said that it was still too early to go for soup. They talked about soup for a while, but the newcomer really didn't know too much about soup kitchens, she had to explain to him where the best ones were, he really was green, but he was interested in everything and maybe he would dare take the sardines away from Célestin. They talked about the sardines and the newcomer promised that as soon as he saw Célestin he would ask for them back.

"He'll pull out his hook," the *clocharde* warned. "You'll have to move fast and hit him over the head with something. They had to give Tonio five stitches, he shouted so much they could hear in Pontoise. *C'est cul, Pontoise*," the *clocharde* added, succumbing to nostalgia.

The newcomer was watching dawn break over the point of Vert-Galant, a willow tree was extricating its spider-webs out of the fog. When the *clocharde* asked him why he was shivering so much with such a good lumberjacket, he shrugged and offered her another cigarette. They smoked and smoked, talking and looking at each other sympathetically. The *clocharde* talked about Célestin's habits and the newcomer remembered the afternoons he had seen her hugging Célestin all along the benches and railings of the Pont des Arts, on the corner by the Louvre underneath the tiger-skinned plane trees, in the doorways of Saint-Germain-l'Auxerrois, and one night on the Rue Gît-le-Coeur, kissing and retching alternately, dead drunk, Célestin in a painter's blouse and the *clocharde* wearing as usual four or five dresses and some topcoats and overcoats, carrying a bundle of red material with pieces of sleeves and a broken cornet sticking out, so much in love with Célestin that it was something to see, getting his face all covered with lipstick and greasy stuff, brazenly lost in their public idyll, finally turning down the Rue de Nevers, and then La Maga had said: "She's the one who's in love, he couldn't care less," and she had looked at him for an instant before squatting down to gather up a little piece of green string and wrap it around her finger.

"At this time of the morning it's not so cold any more," the *clocharde* said, as if to encourage him. "I'm going to see if Lafleur has any wine left. Wine makes for a settled night. Célestin took two litres of mine away with him when he took the sardines. No, he hasn't got any left. You're well-dressed, maybe you can buy a litre at Habeb's. And some bread, if you've got enough money." She liked the newcomer very much, although deep down she knew that he wasn't new, that he was just well-dressed and could stand at Habeb's bar and drink one pernod after another without anybody else's complaining about his bad smell and things like that. The newcomer kept on smoking, nodding vaguely, with his head over to one side. A familiar face. Célestin would have known at once because Célestin was good at faces . . . "The cold really starts at nine o'clock. It comes from down there out of the mud. But we can go and get some soup, it's pretty good."

(And when they were almost out of sight down the Rue de Nevers, when they were coming perhaps to the exact spot where Pierre Curie had been run over by a truck ("Pierre Curie?" La Maga asked, baffled and ever ready to learn), they had turned slowly towards the steep river bank, leaning against the stall of a *bouquiniste*, although Oliveira always found that the stalls of the *bouquinistes* took on a funereal tone at night, a string of makeshift coffins lined up along a stone railing, and one snowy night they'd had fun taking a stick and writing RIP on all of the lead boxes, and a policeman had been less amused and had told them so, speaking about things like respect and tourism, they couldn't figure out why he had mentioned the last matter. In those days everything was still kibbutz, or at least the possibility of kibbutz, and walking through the streets writing RIP on the closed-up stalls of the *bouquinistes* and being amazed at the amorous *clocharde* who was a part of a confused series of against-the-grain exercises that had to be performed, approved, left behind. And that's how it was, and it was cold, and there was no kibbutz. Except for the lie of going to Habeb's and buying red wine and inventing a kibbutz like Kubla Khan's, covering the distance between laudanum and old Habeb's cheap wine.)

> In Xanadu did Kubla Khan
> A stately pleasure-dome decree.

"A foreigner," the *clocharde* said with diminishing sympathy for the newcomer. "Spanish, eh. Italian."

"A mixture," Oliveira said, making a manly effort to stand the smell.

"But you have a job, that's obvious," the *clocharde* accused him.

"Well, not exactly. I used to keep books for an old man, but I haven't seen him for quite a while."

"It's nothing to be ashamed of, as long as you don't overdo it. When I was young . . ."

"Emmanuèle," Oliveira said, putting his hand on the place where there must have been a shoulder deep down inside. The *clocharde* was startled at hearing her name; she looked at him suspiciously and then took a hand mirror out of her pocket and examined her mouth. Oliveira wondered what inconceivable chain of circumstances could have caused a *clocharde* to dye her hair. She was intent on the operation of painting her lips with the stub of a lipstick. There was plenty of time to think about himself and what an imbecile he was again. His hand on her shoulder after what had happened with Berthe Trépat. With results that were in the public domain. A self-administered kick in the arse that would flip him around like a glove. *Cretinaccio*, animal, hairy beast. RIP, RIP. *Malgré le tourisme.*

"How did you know my name was Emmanuèle?"

"I don't know. Somebody must have told me."

Emmanuèle took out a pillbox full of pink powder and began to pat it on one cheek. If Célestin had been there, he would have certainly. Surely he would have. Célestin: tireless. Dozens of tins of sardines, *le salaud.* Suddenly she remembered.

"Ah," she said.

"Probably," Oliveira agreed, surrounding himself with smoke as best he could.

"I used to see you there together many times," Emmanuèle said.

"We used to stroll around there."

"But she would only talk to me when she was alone. A nice girl, a little crazy."

"You said it," Oliveira thought. He was listening to Emmanuèle who was remembering more and more, a bundle of odds and ends, a white sweater that still had some wear, a fine girl who didn't work and wasn't wasting her time studying for a degree, a little crazy sometimes, wasting her francs to feed the pigeons on the Ile Saint-Louis, sometimes quite sad, other times breaking up with laughter. Sometimes bad.

"We would argue," Emmanuèle said, "because she told me not to bother Célestin. She never came back, but I liked her a lot."

"Did she talk to you so much?"

"You didn't like it, did you?"

"That's not it," Oliveira said, looking over at the other bank. But that's just what it was, because La Maga hadn't told him more about her dealings with the *clocharde*, and a basic generalization carried him off, etc. Retrospective jealousy, cf. Proust, subtle torture and so on. It was most likely going to rain, the willow began to look as if it was hanging there in the damp air. On the other hand, it wouldn't be so cold, not quite so cold. Perhaps he said something like: "She never spoke about you much to me," because Emmanuèle let out a satisfied and wicked laugh, and kept putting on pink powder with her blackened fingers; from time to time she would lift up her hand and give herself a pat on her matted hair which was wrapped up in a wool scarf with red and green stripes, actually a man's muffler picked up in some dustbin. Finally he had to go, go up into the city, so close by there, twenty feet above, where it began exactly on the other side of the Seine embankment, behind of the lead RIP boxes where the pigeons were talking among themselves and fluffing up as they waited for the first rays of the bland, unforceful sun, the pale eight o'clock pablum that floats down from a mushy sky because it certainly was going to drizzle the way it always did.

When he was already on his way Emmanuèle shouted something at him. He stopped and waited for her, they went up the stairs together. At Habeb's they bought two litres of red wine, they took cover in the arcade along the Rue de l'Hirondelle. Emmanuèle was so kind as to take out a bundle of newspapers from under her coats, and this made a fine cushion to put down in a corner that Oliveira had explored with the help of some timid matches. From the other side of the archway there came some snoring that smelled of garlic and cauliflower and cheap forgetfulness; biting his lip, Oliveira stumbled into the corner and settled himself as comfortably as possible against the wall, close to Emmanuèle who was already sucking on the bottle and snorting with satisfaction after every gulp. Untrain the senses, open your mouth and nose wide and take in the worst of smells, human filth. One minute, two, three, easier and easier, like any apprenticeship. Keeping his nausea under control, Oliveira grabbed the bottle, even though he couldn't see he knew the neck was anointed with spit and lipstick, the darkness sharpened his sense of smell. Closing his eyes to protect himself against something, he wasn't sure what it was, he downed half a pint of wine in one gulp. Then they started to smoke, shoulder to shoulder, satisfied. The nausea went away, not conquered but humiliated, waiting there with its crooked head, and he was able to think about other things. Emmanuèle was talking away, delivering herself of solemn discourses in between hiccups, giving a maternal scolding to a ghostly Célestin, taking inventory of the sardines, her face lighting up at every puff of the cigarette and Oliveira saw the spots of dirt on her forehead, her thick lips stained with wine, the triumphal scarf of the Syrian goddess that had been trampled on by some enemy army, a chryselephantine head rolling around in the dust, with spots of blood and gore but keeping all the while the diadem of red and green stripes, the Great Mother stretched out in the dust and trampled on by drunken soldiers who amused themselves by pissing on her mutilated breasts, until the greatest clown among them knelt down to the acclaim of all the others, his penis standing out erect above the fallen goddess, masturbating onto the marble and letting the sperm trickle into the eye-holes from which officers' hands had already plucked the precious stones, into the half-open mouth which accepted the humiliation as a final offering before rolling off into oblivion. And it was so natural that in the darkness the hand of Emmanuèle should feel along Oliveira's arm and alight there confidently while the other hand sought out the bottle and one could hear the glug-glug and a satisfied snort, so natural that everything ought to be like this with reverse and obverse, the opposite sign as a kind of survival. And even though Wholiveira might mistrust whinebriation, whastute whaccomplice of the Grand Whentrapment, something told him that there was a kibbutz there, that behind it all, always behind, there was hope for a kibbutz. Not a methodical certainty, oh no, dear fellow, never that, much as you might want it that way, nor an *in vino veritas* nor a Fichte-like dialectic or other Spinozan precious stones, only an acceptance of nausea, Heraclitus had got himself buried in a pile of manure to cure himself of dropsy, somebody had told him about it that very night, somebody who already seemed like someone out of another life, someone like Pola or Wong, people he had annoyed only because he had wanted to make contact with the good side, reinvent love as the only way ever to enter his kibbutz. In shit up to his neck, Heraclitus the Obscure, just like the two of them except without wine, and besides, he wanted to cure himself of dropsy. Maybe that's what it was, then, keeping yourself covered with shit up to the neck and also hoping, because Heraclitus certainly must have had to stay under the shit for days on end, and Oliveira was beginning to remember too that Heraclitus had said that if one did not expect he would never find the unexpected, wring the neck of the swan, Heraclitus had said, but no, of course he'd said no such thing, and while he was swallowing another long swig and Emmanuèle was laughing in the shadow as she heard the glug-glug and stroked his arm as if to show him that she was enjoying his company and his promise to take the sardines away from Célestin, there suddenly came up to Oliveira like a winy belch the double Mexican surname of the swan with the twistable neck, and he wanted to laugh so much and tell Emmanuèle, but instead he gave her back the almost empty bottle, and Emmanuèle began to sing in a scrapy sort of way *Les Amants du Havre*, a song that La Maga used to sing when she was sad, but Emmanuèle sang it with a tragic crawl, out of tune and forgetting the words as she petted Oliveira who kept on thinking that only one who expected would be able to find the unexpected, and half-closing his eyes to reject the dim light that was coming in through the entranceway, he thought that far off (across the sea, or was it an access of patriotism?) there was that pure landscape of his kibbutz. It was obvious that he had to twist the swan's neck, even if it hadn't been Heraclitus who had demanded it. He was getting sentimental, *puisque la terre est ronde, mon amour t'en fais pas, mon amour, t'en fais pas* along with the wine and the thick voice that was singing as he was getting sentimental, it would all end in tears and self-commiseration, like Babs, poor little Horacio *anclado en París*, set down in Paris, as the tango says, *cómo habrá cambiado tu calle Corrientes, Suipacha, Esmeralda, y el viejo arrabal.* But even though he put all his anger into the lighting of another Gauloise, very far away in the depth of his eyes he kept on seeing his kibbutz, not across the sea or even most likely across the sea, or there outside in the Rue Galande or in Puteaux or in the Rue de la Tombe Issoire, in any case his kibbutz was always there and it wasn't a mirage.

"It's not a mirage, Emmanuèle."

"*Ta gueule, mon pote,*" said Emmanuèle, feeling down among her innumerable skirts looking for the other bottle.

Then they got onto other things, Emmanuèle told him about a drowned girl that Célestin had seen from up on Grenelle, and Oliveira wanted to know what colour her hair had been but Célestin had only seen her legs sticking up a little bit out of the water, and he had got out of there before the police started up with their damn bit of asking everybody questions. And when they had drunk up almost all of the second bottle and were happier than ever, Emmanuèle recited a passage from *La Mort du loup*, and Oliveira gave her a quick introduction to the sestinas of the *Martín Fierro*. Now and then a truck began to cross the square, they began to hear the sounds that Delius once . . . But it wouldn't do any good to talk to Emmanuèle about Delius in spite of the fact that she was a sensitive woman, that she didn't go along with poetry and expressed herself manually, rubbing up against Oliveira in order to get rid of the cold, stroking his arm, mumbling parts of operas and obscene comments about Célestin. Biting the cigarette with his lips until it seemed to be almost a part of his mouth, Oliveira listened to her, let her rub up against him, kept repeating coldly that he was no better than she was and that if the worst came to the worst he could always cure himself like Heraclitus, it might have been that the Obscure's most penetrating message was the one he had not written down, leaving it up to anecdotes, the voice of his disciples to transmit it so that perhaps some attuned ear might come to understand it one day. He was amused by the friendly and matter-of-fact way in which the hand of Emmanuèle was going to work unbuttoning him, and at the same time he was able to imagine that perhaps the Obscure one had sunk himself up to the neck in shit without even having been sick, without having dropsy at all, simply to sketch out a pattern that his milieu would never have condoned in the shape of a message or lesson, and which he had surreptitiously carried across the border of time until it had arrived, all mixed up with theory, noting nothing but a disagreeable and painful detail, to rest alongside the earth-shaking diamond of *panta rhei*, a barbarian therapy that Hippocrates had already condemned, just as for hygienic reasons he would have condemned the fact that Emmanuèle was little by little leaning more heavily on her drunken friend and with a tongue stained with tannin was humbly licking his prick, helping to maintain its understandable abandon with her fingers and murmuring things in the language one uses when holding cats or nursing babies, completely oblivious of the meditation that was going on up above, bent on a duty that would afford her little profit, following the line of some obscure feeling of pity, so that the newcomer would feel happy on his first night as a *clochard* and maybe he would fall a little in love with her to punish Célestin, would forget about the strange things he had been muttering in his barbarian American language as he slid down a little more against the wall and let himself slide with a sigh, putting his hand on Emmanuèle's hair and imagining for a second (but that must have been hell) that it was Pola's hair, that still once more Pola had thrown herself on top of him among Mexican ponchos and Klee postcards and Durrell's *Quartet*, making him enjoy and enjoy from without, as she was attentive, analytical, and alien, before she demanded her share and stretched out against him trembling, demanding that he take her and injure her, with her painted mouth of a Syrian goddess, like Emmanuèle who was getting up, dragged to her feet by the policeman, sitting down suddenly and saying: *On faisait rien, quoi*, and all of a sudden underneath the grey that in some way was filling up the doorways Oliveira opened his eyes and saw the cop's legs next to where he lay ridiculously unbuttoned, and with an empty bottle rolling away from the gendarme's kick, the second kick on his thigh, the fierce whack right on the top of Emmanuèle's head as she hunched over and moaned, and on his knees for some reason, the only logical position in which he could put the *corpus delicti* back into his trousers as quickly as possible while it shrank prodigiously in a great spirit of co-operation and allowed itself to be closed in and buttoned up, and really now there was nothing wrong but how could you explain that to the policeman who was leading them off to the patrol van parked in the square, how could you explain to Babs that an inquisition was something else, and to Ossip, to Ossip most of all, how could you explain to him that everything still remained to be done and that the only decent thing to do was to take a step back in order to get a better start, let yourself fall down so that maybe you could get up again later on, Emmanuèle so that maybe later on . . .

"Let her go," Oliveira asked the gendarme. "The poor old girl's drunker than I am."

He ducked just in time to miss the swing. Another gendarme grabbed him around the waist, and with one shove pitched him into the patrol van. They tossed Emmanuèle in on top of him and she was singing something that sounded like *Le Temps des cerises.* They left them alone inside the truck, and Oliveira rubbed his thigh which was hurting terribly, and he joined in the singing of *Le Temps des cerises,* if that's what it was. The van started up as if it had been sprung from a catapult.

"*Et tous nos amours,*" Emmanuèle shouted.

"*Et tous nos amours,*" Oliveira said, throwing himself onto the bench and looking for a cigarette. "This bit, old girl, not even Heraclitus."

"*Tu me fais chier,*" Emmanuèle said as she began a weeping that sounded more like howling. "*Et tous nos amours,*" she sang between sobs. Oliveira could hear the cops laughing, looking at them through the grille. "Well, if you wanted tranquillity you're going to get lots of it. Better take advantage of it, forget what you're thinking about," he said to himself. It was OK to call up and tell them all what a funny dream you had had, but that's enough, don't push it. Everybody on his own side, dropsy is cured with patience, with shit, and with solitude. Besides, the Club was all over with, happily *fini,* and all that was left to get rid of would just be a matter of time. The van slammed on its brakes at a corner and when Emmanuèle started to shout *Quand il reviendra, le temps des cerises,* one of the cops opened the window and warned that if they didn't shut up he was going to kick their teeth in. Emmanuèle lay down on the floor of the truck, face down and wailing, and Oliveira put his feet on her behind and settled himself comfortably on the bench. Hopscotch is played with a pebble that you move with the tip of your toe. The things you need: a pavement, a pebble, a toe, and a pretty chalk drawing, preferably in colours. On top is Heaven, on the bottom is Earth, it's very hard to get the pebble up to Heaven, you almost always miscalculate and the stone goes off the drawing. But little by little you start to get the knack of how to jump over the different squares (spiral hopscotch, rectangular hopscotch, fantasy hopscotch, not played very often) and then one day you learn how to leave Earth and make the pebble climb up into Heaven (*Et tous nos amours,* Emmanuèle was sobbing face down), the worst part of it is that precisely at that moment, when practically no one has learned how to make the pebble climb up into Heaven, childhood is over all of a sudden and you're into novels, into the anguish of the senseless divine trajectory, into the speculation about another Heaven that you have to learn to reach too. And since you have come out of childhood (*Je n'oublierai pas le temps des cerises,* Emmanuèle was kicking about on the floor) you forget that in order to get to Heaven you have to have a pebble and a toe. Which is what Heraclitus knew, up to his neck in shit, and probably Emmanuèle too, wiping off the snot with the back of her hand in the midst of the cherry season, or the two fairies who somehow were sitting in the patrol van (but of course, the door had been opened and shut in the midst of shrieks and laughter and the toot of a whistle) and were laughing like mad as they looked at Emmanuèle on the floor and at Oliveira, who wanted a smoke but who didn't have any cigarettes and matches even though he had not remembered the police going through his pockets, *et tous nos amours, et tous nos amours.* A pebble and a toe, what La Maga had known so well and he much less well, and the Club more or less well, and who from a childhood in Burzaco or in the suburbs of Montevideo would show the straight and narrow path to Heaven without need of Vedanta or Zen or collected eschatologies, yes, reach Heaven with kicks, get there with the pebble (carry your cross? Not a very portable object) and with one last kick send the stone up against *l'azur l'azur l'azur l'azur,* crash, a broken pane, the final bed, naughty child, and what difference did it make if behind the broken pane there was the kibbutz, since Heaven was nothing but a childish name for his kibbutz.

"Let's sing and smoke for all of that," Horacio said. "Emmanuèle, get up, you weepy old woman."

"*Et tous nos amours,*" Emmanuèle bellowed.

"*Il est beau,*" one of the fairies said, looking tenderly at Horacio. "*Il a l'air farouche.*"

The other fairy had taken a brass tube out of his pocket and was looking through a hole in the end, smiling and making faces. The younger fairy snatched away the tube and took a look. "You can't see anything, Jo," he said. "Yes you can, doll," said Jo. "No, no, no, no." "Yes you can, yes you can. LOOK THROUGH THE PEEPHOLE AND YOU'LL SEE PATTERNS PRETTY AS CAN BE." "It's nighttime, Jo." Jo took out a box of matches and lit one in front of the kaleidoscope. Squeals of enthusiasm, patterns pretty as can be. *Et tous nos amours*, Emmanuèle declaimed, sitting up on the floor of the van. Everything was so perfect, everything happening right on time, hopscotch and the kaleidoscope, the smaller fairy looking and looking, oh Jo, I can't see anything, more light, more light, Jo. Collapsed on the bench, Horacio greeted the Obscure one, his head of darkness sticking up through the pyramid of manure with two eyes that looked like green stars, patterns pretty as can be, the Obscure one was right, a road to the kibbutz, perhaps the only road to the kibbutz, not the world, people grabbing at the kaleidoscope from the wrong end, then you had to turn it around with the help of Emmanuèle and Pola and Paris and La Maga and Rocamadour, stretch out on the floor like Emmanuèle and from there begin to look out from the mountain of manure, look at the world through the eye of your arsehole and you'll see patterns pretty as can be, the pebble had to pass through the eye of your arsehole, kicked along by the tip of your toe, and from Earth to Heaven the squares would be open, the labyrinth would unfold like the spring of a broken clock as it made workmen's time fly off in a thousand pieces, and through the snot and semen and stink of Emmanuèle and the shit of the Obscure one you would come onto the road leading to the kibbutz of desire, no longer rising up to Heaven (rise up, a hypocritical word, Heaven, *flatus vocis*), but walk along with the pace of a man through a land of men towards the kibbutz far off there but on the same level, just as Heaven was on the same level as Earth on the dirty pavement where you played the game, and one day perhaps you would enter that world where speaking of Heaven did not mean a greasy kitchen rag, and one day someone would see the true outline of the world, patterns pretty as can be, and, perhaps, pushing the stone along, you would end up entering the kibbutz.

(–37)

From this Side

Il faut voyager loin en aimant sa maison

APOLLINAIRE, *Les mamelles de Tirésias*

37

He hated the name Traveler because he had never been outside Argentina except for trips over to Montevideo and once up to Asunción in Paraguay, cities that he remembered with sovereign indifference. At the age of forty he was still stuck on the Calle Cachimayo, and the fact that he was a sort of agent and jack-of-all-trades for a circus called Las Estrellas gave him no hope whatever of travelling around the world Barnum-style; the zone of operations of his circus extended from Santa Fe to Carmen de Patagones, with long runs in the capital, La Plata, and Rosario. When Talita, who was a reader of encyclopedias, would get interested in wandering peoples and cultures, Traveler would grumble and speak with insincere praise about a courtyard with geraniums, an army bunk, and that no place like home bit. As he sucked on one *mate* after another he would dazzle his wife with his wisdom, but it was obvious that he was trying too hard. When he was asleep he would sometimes come out with words that had to do with uprooting, trips abroad, troubles in customs, and inaccurate alidades. If Talita started to tease him when he woke up, he would start to whack her on the behind, and then they would laugh like crazy and it even seemed that Traveler's betrayal of himself did them both some good. One thing had to be recognized and it was that unlike almost all her other friends, Traveler didn't blame life or fate for the fact that he had been unable to travel everywhere he had wanted to. He would just take a stiff drink of gin and call himself an imbecile.

"Of course, I have been his best trip," Talita used to say when the opportunity would present itself, "but he's so silly that he doesn't realize it. I, my dear, have carried him off on the wings of fantasy to the very edge of the horizon."

The lady thus addressed would think that Talita was speaking seriously and would answer along the following lines: "Ah, my dear, men are so incomprehensible" (*sic* for uncomprehending).

Or:

"Believe me, that's just what happens with me and my Juan Antonio. I've always said the same thing to him, but I could just as well be speaking to the wall."

Or:

"How well I can sympathize with you, my dear. Life is such a struggle."

Or:

"Don't worry yourself about it, miss. As long as you have your health and your work."

Then Talita would tell Traveler everything that people had said and the pair of them would laugh and roll around on the kitchen floor until they had dirtied up their clothes. Traveler used to have the most fun hiding in the toilet, with a handkerchief or undershirt crammed into his mouth, and listening while Talita got the ladies from the Pensión Sobrales and some others who lived in the hotel across the street to talk. In moments of optimism, which were never for long, he would work up a soap opera which would make fun of these fat ladies without their realizing it, make them weep copiously and tune in every day. But in any case, he never had travelled, and it was like a black stone in his soul.

"A regular brick," Traveler would explain, feeling his stomach.

"I never saw a black brick," the Manager of the circus, the eventual intimate of so much nostalgia, used to say.

"It got that way from being so sedentary. And to think there have been poets who complained about being *heimatlos*, Ferraguto!"

"Talk so I can understand," the Manager said, always a little upset when he was called by name in such a dramatic sort of way.

"I can't, Boss," Traveler muttered, excusing himself tacitly for having called him by name. "Beautiful foreign words are like an oasis, stopovers. Will we ever go to Costa Rica? To Panama, where long ago royal galleons . . . ? Gardel died in Colombia, Chief, in Colombia!"

"We haven't got the cash," the Manager said, taking out his watch. "I've got to get back to the hotel. Cuca will be starting to kick up a stink."

Traveler was alone in the office and he was wondering what sunsets in Connecticut were like. As consolation he went back over the good things that had happened to him. For example, one of the good things that had happened to him was that one morning in 1940 he had gone into his superior's office in accounts carrying a glass of water. He had come back out without a job as his boss used a piece of tissue to dry off his face. That had been one of the good things that had happened to him, because that very month they had been planning to promote him, just as marrying Talita had been another good thing that had happened to him (even though they both might think otherwise), since Talita had been condemned by her pharmacy degree to grow old dispensing court plasters and Traveler had shown up looking for some suppositories to cure his bronchitis, and out of the explanation he had got from Talita love had foamed up like shampoo in a showerbath. Traveler would even insist that he had fallen in love with Talita at the precise moment when she lowered her eyes and explained how the suppository would be more effective if used after rather than before a good bowel movement.

"You devil," Talita used to say when they would reminisce. "You understood the directions perfectly well, but you played the fool so I would have to explain them to you."

"A pharmacist must serve truth, even when it turns up in the most intimate places. If you only knew my emotions when I inserted the first suppository that afternoon, right after I left you. It was a huge green thing."

"Eucalyptus," Talita said. "You were lucky I didn't sell you one of those that has a garlicky odour and can be smelled fifty feet away."

But sometimes they would turn sad and vaguely understand that once again they had been having fun as a last resort against the melancholy of Buenos Aires and a life that didn't have too much (What else could you say except "too much"? A vague uneasiness at the top of the stomach, the black brick, as always).

Talita explaining Traveler's melancholy moments to Señora Gutusso:

"It gets hold of him around siesta-time, it's like something that comes up out of his pleura."

"He must have something wrong inside," Señora Gutusso says. "It's internal pain, or whatever it is they say."

"It comes out of his soul, señora. My husband is a poet, believe me."

Shut up in the toilet with a towel around his face, Traveler is laughing so hard that his eyes are watering.

"Don't you think it might be some allergy or whatever they call it? My little boy Vítor, you can see him playing in the geraniums out there and he's really a delight, believe me, but when he gets an attack of his celery allergy it's monstrous, his dark little eyes start to close, his mouth puffs up like a toad's, and during it all he can't even bend his toes."

"Bending the toes isn't always too important," Talita says.

Traveler's muffled roars can be heard from the toilet and Talita quickly changes the subject to throw Señora Gutusso off the track. Usually Traveler will leave his hiding place feeling very sad, and Talita understands. Some mention should be made of Talita's understanding. It's an ironic, tender understanding, like something distant. Her love for Traveler is made up of dirty casseroles, long vigils, a gentle acceptance of his nostalgic fantasies and his love for the tango and a game of *truco*. When Traveler gets sad and thinks about the fact that he has never travelled (and Talita knows it's not that that bothers him, that his worries are much deeper), she has to go along with him and not say very much, prepare his *mate*, make sure that he never runs out of tobacco, do her duty as a wife alongside her husband but never casting her shadow on him, and that's what's difficult. Talita is very happy with Traveler, with the circus, grooming the counting cat before it goes on stage, keeping books for the Manager. Sometimes in her modest way she thinks that she is really closer than Traveler to those elemental depths that worry him, but metaphysical contexts upset her somewhat and she ends up convincing herself that he is the only one capable of making a puncture that will release the black and oily flow. It all floats around a little, dresses up in words or patterns, calls itself otherness, calls itself laughing or loving, and it's also the circus and life to call it by its most external and fateful names and who the hell is your aunt anyway.

But since he doesn't have this otherness, Traveler is a man of action. He calls it restricted action because it's not a question of going about knocking yourself out. For the space of four decades he has gone through various phases: football (with the Colegiales, centre forward, not too bad), pedestrianism, politics (a month in the Devoto jail in 1934), cuniculture and apiculture (a farm in Manzanares, bankruptcy within three months, smelly rabbits and ill-tempered bees), auto-racing (relief driver with Marimón, a smash-up in Resistencia, three broken ribs), artistic carpentry (turning out pieces of furniture until they piled up to the ceiling, used only once, a complete failure), marriage and cycling on the Avenida General Paz on Saturdays on a rented bike. Out of all this action he has a mental archive, two languages, a facile hand with the pen, an ironical interest in soteriology and glass balls, the attempt at creating a mandrake by planting a sweet potato in a pot of earth and sperm, the sweet potato flourishing in the wild way sweet potatoes do, invading the furnished room, growing out of the window, the surreptitious intervention of Talita, armed with a pair of scissors, Traveler inspecting the shape of the plant, suspecting something, the humiliating abandonment of the mandrake, gallows plant, *alraune*, leftovers from childhood. Sometimes Traveler talks about a double who is luckier than he, and Talita for some reason doesn't like to hear about it, and she hugs him and kisses him restlessly, does all she can to get those ideas out of his head. Then she takes him out to see Marilyn Monroe, a great favourite of Traveler's, and-slams-on-the-brakes of some purely artistic feelings of jealousy in the darkness of the Presidente Roca movie theatre.

(–98)

38

Talita wasn't so sure that Traveler was very happy about the return of a childhood friend, because the first thing that Traveler did upon learning that a certain Horacio was coming home suddenly to Argentina on the *Andrea C* was to aim a kick at the counting cat of the circus and proclaim that life was a perfect fuckup. In any case, he did go down to the dock to meet him with Talita taking the counting cat along in a basket. Oliveira was coming out of customs carrying a single lightweight suitcase, and when he spotted Traveler he raised his eyebrows in a mixture of surprise and annoyance.

"What's new?"

"Hi," Traveler said, shaking his hand with more feeling than he had expected.

"Hey," Oliveira said, "let's go to a waterfront grill and get some sausages."

"I'd like you to meet my wife," Traveler said.

Oliveira said: "Pleased to meet you," and put out his hand, barely looking at her. Then he asked immediately who the cat was and why they had brought him down to the pier in a basket. Talita, offended by the reception, found him absolutely disagreeable and announced that she was going back to the circus with the cat.

"OK," Traveler said. "Put him by the window on the tram, you know he doesn't like it in the aisle."

In the grill Oliveira began to drink red wine and eat some sausages and *chinchulines.* Since he wasn't being very communicative, Traveler told him all about the circus and how he had got married to Talita. He filled him in on politics and sports, pausing especially to talk about the rise and fall of Pascualito Pérez. Oliveira said that in Paris he had run into Fangio and that old bow-legs had seemed half-asleep. Traveler began to get hungry and ordered some chitterlings. He was pleased that Oliveira accepted his first Argentine cigarette with a smile and smoked it with appreciation. They got into another litre of red wine, and Traveler talked about his work, how he hadn't lost hope of finding something better, that is, something with less work and more cash, waiting all the time for Oliveira to tell him something, he didn't know exactly what, just some direction that could bring them together again after so much time.

"Well, tell me something," he proposed.

"The weather was very changeable," Oliveira said, "but every once in a while there would be good days. Something else: as César Bruto said so well, if you want Paris in October to move 'er, don't forget to see the Louvre. What else? Oh, yes, I went to Vienna once. They have fantastic cafés where fat women bring along their dogs and husbands to eat strudel."

"OK, OK," Traveler said. "You don't have to talk if you don't want to."

"One day I dropped a lump of sugar underneath the table in a restaurant. In Paris, not in Vienna."

"If all you're going to do is talk about cafés, you didn't have to sail across the pond."

"You understand well," Oliveira said, carefully cutting into a string of *chinchulines.* "This is something you can't get in the City of Lights. That's what all the Argentinians used to tell me. They used to weep because they couldn't get good beef, and I even knew a lady who used to think nostalgically about Argentinian wines. She used to say that French wine was no good to mix with soda."

"Jesus," Traveler said.

"And of course the tomatoes and the potatoes here are better than anywhere."

"It's obvious," said Traveler, "that you were hanging out with the upper crust."

"Once in a while. They usually didn't like the way I used to hang, to keep on with your metaphor. Boy, it's muggy."

"That's right," Traveler said. "You're going to have to get yourself acclimatized again."

They kept on along those lines for some twenty-five minutes.

(–39)

39

Of course, Oliveira was not going to tell Traveler anything about his stopover in Montevideo when he had walked through the slums, asking and looking, having a couple of drinks of *caña* to get on the good side of some toughs. And nothing, except that there was a slew of new buildings and that on the waterfront, where he spent the hour before the *Andrea C* sailed, the water was full of dead fish floating belly up, and among the fish here and there a condom softly floating in the murky water. There was nothing else to do but go back on board, thinking that maybe Lucca, that maybe it really had been Lucca or Perugia. And all so much like the divine rocket.

Before disembarking in his mother country, Oliveira had decided that everything that had passed had not been the past and that only a mental error like so many others would have allowed the easy expedient of imagining a future fertilized by games already played. He understood (only on the prow, at dawn, in the yellow fog of the harbour) that nothing would have changed if he had decided to take a stand, reject easy solutions. Maturity, supposing such a thing really did exist, was in the last analysis a kind of hypocrisy. Nothing was mature, nothing could have been more natural than for that woman with a cat in a basket, waiting for him beside Manolo Traveler, to look a little like that other woman who (but what had been the use of wandering through the slums of Montevideo, taking a taxi up to the edge of El Cerro, making use of directions assembled all over again by a restless memory). He had to keep going, either start over again or end it: there was still no bridge as yet. With a suitcase in his hand, he headed for a waterfront grill where one night somebody half-drunk had told him stories about the troubadour Betinoti, and how he used to sing that waltz: *Mi diagnostico es sencillo: / Sé que no tengo remedio.* The idea that a word like "diagnosis" should turn up in a waltz was irresistible to Oliveira, but now he was repeating the lines in a sententious sort of way while Traveler told him about the circus, about K. O. Lausse, and even about Juan Perón.

(–86)

40

He was coming to the realization that his coming back had really been his going away in more than one sense. He was already vegetating with poor, humble Gekrepten in a hotel room across from the Pensión Sobrales where the Travelers were on the rolls. Everything was going well between them, Gekrepten was enchanted, she could prepare magnificent *mates* and even though she made love and *pasta asciutta* rather badly, she had other revealing domestic qualities and she could leave him alone for all the time he needed to ponder the business of coming back and going away, a problem that used to bother him in his free moments as he went from door to door selling bolts of gabardine. At first Traveler had criticized his mania for finding fault with Buenos Aires, for treating the city like a tightly girdled whore, but Oliveira explained to him and Talita that in his criticism there was so much love that only a pair of mental defectives like them would misunderstand his attacks. In the end they realized that he was right, that Oliveira could not make any hypocritical compromise with Buenos Aires, and that at the moment he was much farther away from his own country than when he had been wandering about Europe. Only small things, old things, would make him smile: *mate*, De Caro records, sometimes the waterfront in the afternoon. The three of them used to wander around the city a lot, taking advantage of the fact that Gekrepten was working in a shop, and Traveler could spot that Oliveira was making his peace with the city, fertilizing the soil with enormous quantities of beer. But Talita was more intransigent (a definite characteristic of indifference) and she demanded quick acceptances: Clorindo Testa's painting, for example, or the films of Torre Nilsson. They got into hot arguments over Bioy Casares, David Viñas, Father Castellani, Manauta, and the policies of the YPF. Talita finally came to understand that for Oliveira being in Buenos Aires was exactly the same as if he had been in Bucharest, and that in reality he had not come back but that he had been brought back. Underneath the things they would argue about there was always a layer of pataphysics, the triple coincidence of a histrionic search for lookout points that could excentrate the viewer or the thing being viewed. Because of their battles Talita and Oliveira began to have respect for each other. Traveler would remember when Oliveira was twenty years old and his heart would ache, but it was more likely wind from all the beers.

"The trouble with you is you're not a poet," Traveler would say. "You don't have the same feeling we do for the city, a great big belly heaving slowly underneath the heavens, a huge spider with half his feet in San Vicente, in Burzaco, in Sarandi, in El Palomar, and the rest of them in the water, poor thing, you know how dirty the river is."

"Horacio is a perfectionist," Talita said with pity, for she was already becoming more sure of herself. "A gadfly on a thoroughbred horse. You ought to take a lesson from us, simple inhabitants of Buenos Aires, and still we do know who Pieyre de Mandiargues is."

"And along the streets," Traveler said, rolling his eyes, "girls pass with soft eyes and delicate faces showing the effects of rice and milk and Radio El Mundo in the pleasant foolishness of their face powder."

"Not to mention the emancipated and intellectual women who work in circuses," Talita added modestly.

"And specialists in urban folklore like myself. Remind me when we get back to the room to read you Ivonne Guitry's story of her life, old man, it's fantastic."

"By the way, Señora Gutusso wanted me to tell you that if you don't return her Gardel songbook she'll crown you with a flowerpot," Talita informed him.

"First I've got to read Horacio the life story. Let her wait, the old bitch."

"Is Señora Gutusso that species of gnu who spends her time talking to Gekrepten?" Oliveira asked.

"Yes, it's their turn to be friends this week. You'll see in a few days, that's how things go in this neighbourhood."

"Silver-plated with moonlight," Oliveira said. "It's a lot better than your Saint-Germain-des-Prés," Talita said.

"But of course," said Oliveira, looking at her. Rolling his eyes a little, perhaps . . . And the way she pronounced the French words, the way she had, and if he just squinted a little. (Pharmacist, pity.)

How they loved to play with words, making up games to play those days in the cemetery of the language, turning to page 558 in the Julio Casares dictionary, for example, and playing with *hallulla, hámago, halieto, haloque, hamez, harambel, harbullista, harca,* and *harija.* Underneath it all they were a little sad as they thought about possibilities come to nought and the Argentinian character and time's-inexorable-passage. As for the pharmacist business, Traveler insisted that it was all a matter of barbarian peoples and eminently Merovingian, and he and Oliveira dedicated an epic poem to Talita in which the Pharmaceutical hordes invaded Catalonia, spreading terror, piperine, and hellebore. The whole Pharmaceutical nation, on massive steeds. A meditation on the Pharmaceutical steppes. Oh Empress of the Pharmacists, have pity on the Mushies, the Yokies, the Lazies, and the Stuffies, all of the Runawaydies.

While Traveler was quietly working on the Manager so that Oliveira could get a job with the circus, the object of these manoeuvres was drinking *mate* in his room and catching up on Argentine literature. While he was working at this task the weather suddenly got hot and the sale of gabardine dropped off considerably. They began to get together in Don Crespo's patio. He was a friend of Traveler's and rented rooms to Señora Gutusso and other ladies and gentlemen. With the help of Gekrepten's tenderness (she spoiled him like a child), Oliveira was able to sleep as long as he could bear it and in his lucid intervals he would sometimes look at a book by Crevel that he had found in the bottom of his suitcase, and he was beginning to assume the airs of a hero in a Russian novel. No good could possibly come of this methodical laziness, and that was what he vaguely kept his faith in, in the idea that by half-closing his eyes he would be able to see things outlined more clearly, that by sleeping he would be able to clear up his meninges. Things were not going well with the circus and the Manager didn't even want to think about taking on anybody new. In the early evening, before going to work, the Travelers would go down and have some *mate* with Don Crespo, and Oliveira would come too and they would listen to records on an old phonograph that could still run, which is the way old records ought to be played. Sometimes Talita would sit across from Oliveira and they would play with the cemetery, or challenge each other by balancing questions, another game they had invented with Traveler and which they got a lot of fun out of. Don Crespo thought they were crazy and Señora Gutusso thought they were stupid.

"You never talk very much about all that," Traveler would say sometimes, without looking at Oliveira. He was stronger; when Traveler made up his mind to interrogate him he had to avoid his eyes, and he didn't know why he was never able to mention the capital of France by name, but he always said "that" the way a mother works hard at inventing inoffensive names for her children's pudenda, God's little things.

"It doesn't interest me," Oliveira would answer. "You'll find out."

It was the best way there was to enrage Traveler, a failure as a nomad. Instead of pressing the point he would tune up the horrible guitar he had bought at the Casa América and start playing tangos. Talita would glance at Oliveira, a little resentful. Without making herself obvious. Traveler had convinced her that Oliveira was an oddball, and even though that was plain to see, his oddness must have been something else, must have been off somewhere else. There were nights when everybody seemed to be expecting something. They felt very good together, but it was like the eye of a hurricane. On nights like that, if they opened up the cemetery things would come out like *cisco*, *cisticerco*, *¡cito!*, *cisma*, *cístico*, and *cisión*. Finally they would go to bed with latent ill-humour, and spend the whole night dreaming about happy and funny things, which was probably a contradiction in terms.

(–59)

41

The sun began to hit Oliveira in the face sometime after two in the afternoon. Besides the heat, it made it very hard for him to straighten out nails by hammering them on a tile on the floor (everybody knows how dangerous it is to straighten out a nail with a hammer, there is a moment when the nail is almost upright, but when you hit it with the hammer again it gives half a turn and pinches the fingers you're holding it with; there's a quick perverseness about it all), stubbornly hammering them on a tile (but everybody knows that) stubbornly on a tile (but everybody) stubbornly.

"There isn't a straight one in the lot," Oliveira was thinking as he looked at the nails scattered around on the floor. "And the hardware store is closed now, and they'll throw me out if I pound on the door and ask them to sell me thirty cents' worth of nails. I have to straighten them, there's no other way out."

Each time he managed to get a nail half-straightened, he would lift up his head and whistle in the direction of the open window for Traveler to appear. He could see part of their bedroom quite clearly from his room, and something told him that Traveler was in there, probably in bed with Talita. The Travelers slept a lot in the daytime, not so much because they were tired from working at the circus, but because of a certain principle of laziness that Oliveira respected. It was a shame to wake Traveler up at two-thirty in the afternoon, but the fingers Oliveira was using to hold down the nails were already turning purple, extravasation was setting in from the pounding the blood vessels were taking, giving his fingers the look of underdone meat, which was really repulsive. The more he looked at them, the more he felt like having some *mate* and he was all out of *yerba*: actually there was enough for half a *mate* and Traveler or Talita would have to wrap up what he needed in some paper, using some nails as ballast, and toss it through the window. With some straight nails and some *yerba*, siesta-time would be more tolerable.

"It's fantastic how loud I can whistle," Oliveira thought in amazement. From the floor below where there was a brothel with three women and a girl to run errands, someone was imitating him with a pitiful counter-whistle, something in between a boiling kettle and a toothless hiss. Oliveira was fascinated by the admiration and rivalry aroused by his whistle; he never wasted it, but would save it for important occasions. During his reading hours, which were between one and five o'clock in the morning, but not every morning, he had come to the disconcerting conclusion that whistling was not an important theme in literature. There weren't many authors who made their characters whistle. Practically none of them did. They would condemn them to a rather tiresome repertory of expression (say, answer, sing, shout, babble, mutter, pronounce, whisper, exclaim and declaim), but no hero or heroine had ever crowned the high point of one of their epics with a magnificent whistle of the type that shatters glass. English squires would whistle to call their hounds and some characters in Dickens would whistle for a cab. As far as Argentine literature was concerned, there was very little whistling, and it was a disgrace. That's why, although Oliveira had not read Cambaceres, he considered him a master because he had used "whistle" in one of his titles; sometimes he would think along subsequent lines in which whistling would insinuate itself into Argentina on the surface and underneath, would wrap it up in its glowing twine and offer up to world-wide stupefaction a tight-rolled omelette, that would have little in common with the official version put forth by embassies and what one saw in the well-digested Sunday rotogravure put out by all the Gainza Mitre Pazes, and still less with the ups and downs of the Boca Juniors and the necrophilic cults of the *baguala* and the Boedo section. "Mother-fucker" (to a nail), "they won't even let me think in peace, God damn it." Besides, these ideas were repulsive to him because they were so facile, even though he was convinced that the only way to get a hold on Argentina was to come up on it from the shameful side, find the blush hidden under a century of usurpations of all kinds, as writers had pointed out so well, and therefore the best way was to show it in some way in which it didn't have to take itself so seriously. Who could be the clown who could send such high and mighty national sovereignty off to hell? Who could laugh in its face to see it flush and maybe once in a while smile like someone who has a recognition? But, Jesus, old friend, what a way to piss away a day. Let's see now, maybe this nail won't give me as much of a hard time as the others, it seems to be more tractable.

"God, it's cold," Oliveira said to himself, because he was a great believer in autosuggestion. Sweat was pouring over his eyes out of his hair and it was impossible to hold a nail with the head up because the lightest blow of the hammer would make it slip out of his fingers which were all wet (from the cold) and the nail would pinch him again and he would mash his fingers (from the cold). To make things worse, the sun had begun to shine with full force into the room (it was the moon on snow-covered steppes, and he whistled to goad the horses pulling against their harnesses), by three o'clock the whole place was covered with snow, he would let himself freeze until he got to that sleepy state described so well and maybe even brought about in Slavic stories, and his body would be entombed in the man-killing whiteness of the livid flowers of space. That was pretty good: the livid flowers of space. Right then he hit himself full on the thumb with the hammer. The coldness that had got into him was so intense that he had to roll around on the ground in an attempt to fight off the stiffness that was coming on him from the fact that he was freezing up. When he managed to sit upright waving his hand around, he was wet from head to toe, probably from the melting snow or from that light drizzle that was mingling with the livid flowers of space and refreshed the wolves as it fell on their fur.

Traveler was tying up his pyjama bottoms and from his window he was able to get a clear picture of Oliveira's struggles with the snow and the steppes. He was about to turn around and tell Talita that Oliveira was rolling on the floor shaking his hand, but he realized that the situation was rather serious and that it would be better for him to be a stern and impassive witness.

"It's about time, damn it," Oliveira said. "I've been whistling at you for half an hour. Look what I've done to my hand."

"You didn't get that from selling bolts of gabardine," Traveler said.

"Trying to straighten out nails. I need some straight nails and a little bit of *yerba*."

"That's easy to arrange," Traveler said. "Wait a minute."

"Wrap it up and throw it to me."

"OK," Traveler said. "But now that I think of it, it's going to be hard getting into the kitchen."

"Why?" asked Oliveira. "It's not too far away."

"No, but there's a clothesline with stuff hung up to dry."

"Duck under it," Oliveira suggested. "Cut it down if you have to. The slap of a wet shirt landing on the floor is something unforgettable. If you want, I'll toss you my jackknife. I bet I can stick it right on the window. When I was a kid I could stick a jackknife wherever I wanted to and from thirty feet away."

"The trouble with you," Traveler said, "is that every problem always brings you back to your childhood. I'm sick of telling you to read a little Jung. And look how it all comes back with that jackknife, you make it sound like an interplanetary missile. It's impossible to mention anything to you without your hauling out your jackknife. Just tell me what the devil all this has to do with a little bit of *yerba* and a few nails."

"You didn't follow me," Oliveira said, offended. "First I mentioned my mangled hand, then I mentioned the nails. Then you raised the barrier of a clothesline that was stopping you from going to the kitchen, and it was logical that the clothesline should remind me of my jackknife. You ought to read Edgar Allan Poe. Clothesline and all, you can't follow the thread of anything, that's what's wrong with you."

Traveler leaned on the windowsill and looked out into the street. The little shade that there was had spread out over the pavement, and the sunny part started from the second floor up, a yellow ecstasy grasping out in all directions and literally smacking Oliveira in the face.

"The sun is really screwing you up this afternoon," Traveler said.

"It's not the sun," said Oliveira. "You ought to be able to see that it's the moon and that the cold is just too much. This hand of mine has got all purple from the cold. Gangrene is setting in, and in a few weeks you'll be bringing gladioli to me in the cemetery."

"The moon?" Traveler said, looking up. "I'll be bringing you wet towels in Vieytes, the loony bin."

"What they want most out there are cigarettes," Oliveira said. "You're full of incongruities, Manú."

"I've told you a hundred times not to call me Manú."

"Talita calls you Manú," said Oliveira, shaking his hand as if he wanted to disconnect it from his arm.

"The difference between you and Talita," Traveler said, "is something that is obvious to the touch. I don't understand why you have to pick up her vocabulary. I'm repelled by hermit crabs, symbiosis in all its forms, lichens, and all other parasites."

"My heart really bleeds for your sensitivity," Oliveira said.

"Thank you. So it's *yerba* and nails. What do you want the nails for?"

"I'm not sure yet," Oliveira said, confused. "Actually, I took down the tin of nails and found they were all twisted. I started to straighten them out, but with all this cold, you see . . . It's my idea that as long as I have straight nails I'll know what to use them for."

"Interesting," Traveler said, staring at him. "The strangest things happen to you. First the nails and then their ultimate use. It could be a tremendous lesson, old man."

"You always did understand me," Oliveira said. "And the *yerba*, you should know, I need it to brew up some good old bitter stuff."

"OK," Traveler said. "Hold on. If I take too long you can whistle. Talita likes your whistling."

Shaking his hand, Oliveira went into the bathroom and wet his head and hair. He kept on wetting himself until his undershirt was all soaked, and then he turned to the window to test the theory that if the rays of the sun fall on a wet rag a violent sensation of cold will be produced. "To think that I shall die," Oliveira said to himself, "without having read the headlines: TOWER OF PISA FALLS. It's sad, if you really take a good look at it."

He began to put headlines together, something that always helped to pass the time of day. WOOL CLOGS LOOM AND SUFFOCATES IN WEST LANÚS. He could add up two hundred possible headlines without coming upon any other one that was passable.

"I'm going to have to move," Oliveira muttered. "This room is really too small. I really have to get into Manú's circus and stay with them. *Yerba!*"

Nobody answered.

"*Yerba*," Oliveira said softly. "Yes, *yerba*. Don't come on like that, Manú. To think that we could chat from window to window, you and Talita and maybe Señora Gutusso would join in, or the errand-girl, and we could make up games with the cemetery and other things to play with."

"After all," Oliveira thought, "I can play games with the cemetery all by myself."

He went to get the Dictionary of the Spanish Royal Academy, on the cover of which the word *Royal* stood out like an open wound, having been chipped away by a razor-blade; he opened it at random and worked out the following game from the cemetery for Manú.

"Fed up with the client and her climacteric, they clipped out her clitoris and gave her a clyster, clinically in her cloaca, and as she clucked about the clipping and the clinometric climb to get such clinkers, they sent her off to get some clerical clue to her clingy claim."

"Shit," Oliveira said with admiration. He thought that maybe shit could be a starting point, but he was mistaken because he couldn't find it in the cemetery; but on the other hand the shipworm shirked among the shirts and shivered deep within the shittim wood; the worst of it was that the shifty shingle was shimmying up and down his shin, in some Shinto shire that could be shirred for a shilling.

"It's really the necropolis," he thought. "I can't see how the binding has lasted so long on all this crap."

He began to work out another game, but it didn't come off. He decided to look into the typical dialogues and he looked for the notebook where he had been keeping them after getting inspiration in the subway, cafés, and bars. He had practically finished a typical dialogue between two Spaniards and he put down the finishing touches, but first he poured a pitcher of water over his undershirt.

A TYPICAL DIALOGUE BETWEEN TWO SPANIARDS

LÓPEZ: I had been living in Madrid for a whole year. You know, it was in 1925, and . . .

PÉREZ: In Madrid? Why, just yesterday I was saying to Dr García . . .

LÓPEZ: From 1925 to 1926. I taught literature at the University.

PÉREZ: I was saying to him: "You know, old man, anybody who has lived in Madrid knows what it's all about."

LÓPEZ: A chair was established especially for me so I could give my lectures in Literature.

PÉREZ: Precisely, precisely. Why, just yesterday I was saying to Dr García, who is a very good friend of mine . . .

LÓPEZ: Of course, as you know if you have lived there more than a year, the level of studies leaves much to be desired.

PÉREZ: He's the son of Paco García, the one who was Minister of Trade and raised bulls.

LÓPEZ: A scandal, you can be sure, a real scandal.

PÉREZ: Yes, old man, of course. Well, this Dr García . . .

Oliveira was already a little bored with the dialogue and closed his notebook. "Shiva," he thought suddenly. "Oh, cosmic dancer, how would you shine, infinite bronze, in the light of this sun? Why did I think of Shiva? Buenos Aires. You get along. Funny thing. You end up owning an encyclopedia. *De qué te sirvió el verano, oh ruiseñor.* Of course it could be worse, specializing and spending five years in the study of the behaviour of the Acrididae. But just look at this fantastic list, boy, take a look at this . . . "

It was a slip of yellow paper clipped from some document of vaguely international character. A publication of UNESCO or something of the sort, with a list of names from some Burmese council. Oliveira began to be absorbed in the list and he could not resist the temptation to take out a pencil and compose the following nonsense poem:

U Nu,
U Tin,
Mya Bu,
Thado Thiri Thudama U E Maung,
Sithu U Cho,
Wunna Kyaw Htin U Khin Zaw,
Wunna Kyaw Htin U Thein Han,
Wunna Kyaw Htin U Myo Min,
Thiri Pyanchi U Thant,
Thado Maha Thray Sithu U Chan Htoon.

"The three Wunna Kyaw Htins are a little monotonous," he said to himself as he looked at the lines. "It must mean something like 'His Excellency the Most Exalted'. But the Thiri Pyanchi U Thant is good, that's the one that sounds best. I wonder how you pronounce Htoon."

"Hi," Traveler said.

"Hi," said Oliveira. "Cold enough for you?"

"I'm sorry you had to wait. The nails, you know . . . "

"Of course," said Oliveira. "A nail is a nail, especially if it's straight. Did you wrap them up?"

"No," said Traveler, scratching his breast. "Jesus, what a day. It's like an oven."

"Look," said Oliveira, touching his completely dry undershirt. "You're like the salamander, you live in a world of perpetual pyromania. Did you bring the *yerba*?"

"No," Traveler said. "I completely forgot about the *yerba*. I only brought the nails."

"Well, go and get it, make me up a bundle, and toss it over here."

Traveler looked at his window, then at the street, and finally at Oliveira's window.

"It's going to be a close one," he said. "You know I can never hit anything even six feet away. I've fooled myself twenty times in the circus."

"But it's practically like handing it to me," Oliveira said.

"That's what you say, that's what you say, and the nails will land on top of somebody down in the street and we'll be in trouble."

"Toss me the package and then we can play some games with the cemetery," Oliveira said.

"It would be better if you came over and got it."

"Are you out of your mind? Go down three flights, cross the street through all that ice, climb up three more flights, they don't even do that in *Uncle Tom's Cabin*."

"You're not going to suggest that I undertake that bit of afternoon alpinism, are you?"

"The farthest from my mind," Oliveira said virtuously.

"Or for me to look for a board in the pantry and make a bridge with it?"

"That's not a bad idea at all," Oliveira said, "and it would give us a chance to use the nails, you on your side and me on mine."

"OK, wait a minute," Traveler said and disappeared.

Oliveira stayed there trying to think of a good insult to put Traveler down with the first chance he got. After consulting the cemetery and pouring a pitcher of water over his undershirt, he leaned on the windowsill in the sunlight. Traveler reappeared soon, dragging an enormous plank, which he shoved little by little out of the window. Just then Oliveira noticed that Talita was helping to hold the board, and he greeted her with a whistle. Talita had on a green bathrobe and had it tied so tight that it was easy to see that she didn't have anything else on underneath.

"You're such a drag," Traveler said with a snort. "You get us involved in the damnedest things."

"Shut up, you myriapod from four to five inches in length, with a pair of feet on each of twenty-one rings dividing the body, four eyes, and horny hooked mandibles which on biting exude a very active poison," he said in one breath.

"Mandibles," Traveler commented. "Listen to the words he uses. Hey, if I keep pushing this board out of the window the time will come when the force of gravity will drag Talita and me straight down to hell."

"I can see that," Oliveira said, "but don't forget that the end of the board is too far away for me to grab."

"Stretch out your mandibles a little," Traveler said.

"Don't put me on. Besides you know damned well that I suffer from *horror vacuis*. I'm a real *roseau pensant*, a *caña pensante*."

"The only *caña* I can see in you is the kind that comes from Paraguay," Traveler said furiously. "I really don't know what we can do, this board is beginning to get too heavy, you know of course that weight is a question of relativity. When we carried it out it was quite light, but of course the sun wasn't shining on it the way it is now."

"Pull it back into the room," Oliveira said with a sigh. "This is what we'll do: I have another board, not as long, but it is wider. We'll put a rope around it like a noose and tie the two boards together. I'll tie my end to my bed, you do whatever seems best with yours."

"I think we'd better tie ours onto the handle of a chest of drawers," Talita said. "You go and get yours and we'll get ours ready."

"God, but they can get involved," Oliveira thought as he went to get the board, which was in the hallway between the door of his place and that of a Levantine faith-healer. It was a cedar plank, smoothly planed but missing two or three knots that had fallen out. Oliveira stuck his finger through one of the knotholes to see what it looked like from the other side, and he wondered whether the holes could be used to tie on the rope. The hallway was almost completely dark (it was really the contrast between the sunshine in his room and the shade there) and next to the Levantine's door there was a chair on which he could make out a woman dressed in black. Oliveira nodded to her from behind the board, which he had lifted up and was holding like a huge (and ineffective) shield.

"Hello, mister," the woman in black said. "Hot enough for you?"

"Quite the contrary, madam," Oliveira said. "It's terribly cold."

"Don't be funny," the woman said. "Show some respect for people who are not well."

"But there's nothing wrong with you, madam."

"Nothing wrong? How dare you!"

"All of this is reality," Oliveira thought, grabbing the board and looking at the woman in black. "All of this that I accept as reality every minute and which can't be, can't be."

"It can't be," Oliveira said.

"Go away and don't be cheeky," the woman said. "You ought to be ashamed, coming out in your undershirt at this time of day."

"It's from Masllorens', madam," Oliveira said.

"Disgusting," the woman said.

"All of this stuff I think makes up reality," Oliveira thought, stroking the board, leaning on it. "This display window arranged and lit up by fifty or sixty centuries of hands, imaginations, compromises, pacts, secret liberties."

"Who would think that a man starting to turn grey . . . " the woman in black said.

"To get the idea that you are the centre," Oliveira thought, resting more comfortably on the board. "But it's incalculably stupid. A centre as illusory as it would be to try to find ubiquity. There is no centre, there's a kind of continuous confluence, an undulation of matter. All through the night I'm a motionless body, and on the other side of town a roll of newsprint is being converted into the morning paper, and at eight-forty I will leave the house and at eight twenty the paper will have arrived at the news-stand on the corner, and at eight forty-five my hand and the newspaper will come together and begin to move together through the air, three feet from the ground, heading towards the tram stop . . . "

"Don Bunche is certainly taking his time with that other patient," the woman in black said.

Oliveira lifted up the plank and carried it into his room. Traveler was signalling for him to hurry up, and to calm him down he answered with two shrill whistles. The rope was on top of the wardrobe, he had to bring a chair over and climb up on it.

"Can't you hurry up a little?" Traveler said.

"OK, OK," Oliveira said, going to the window. "Is your board secured?"

"We've tied it to a drawer of the dresser, and Talita has put *Quillet's Self-Teaching Encyclopedia* on top of it."

"Not bad," Oliveira said. "I'm going to put the yearly report of the *Statens Psykologisk-Pedagogiska Institut* on mine. They send it to Gekrepten, God knows why."

"What worries me is how we're going to connect them," Traveler said as he began to move the dresser so that the board started to emerge from the window little by little.

"You look like two Assyrian generals armed with battering-rams and preparing to knock down some walls," said Talita, who was not owner of the encyclopedia in vain. "Is that a German book you mentioned?"

"Swedish, stupid," Oliveira said. "It talks about things like *Mentalhygieniska synpunkter i förskoleundervisning.* Splendid words, worthy of that young man Snorri Sturluson we hear so much about in Argentine literature. Real bronze breastplates, with the talismanic figure of the falcon."

"The wild whirlwinds of Norway," Traveler quoted.

"Are you really a cultured type, or are you just putting it on?" Oliveira asked, a little surprised.

"I won't say the circus doesn't take up a lot of time," Traveler said, "but there's always a little left for me to pin a star on my forehead. This talk of the star on my forehead always comes out when I talk about the circus, pure contamination. I wonder where I got it? Do you have any idea, Talita?"

"No," said Talita, testing the strength of the board. "Probably from some Puerto Rican novel."

"What bothers me is that in my subconscious I know where I read it."

"In some classic?" Oliveira hinted.

"I can't remember what it was about any more," Traveler said, "but it was a book I'll never forget."

"So it seems," Oliveira said.

"Our board is fine," Talita said. "But I don't see how we can fasten it to yours."

Oliveira had finished unwinding the rope; he cut it in two, and with one half he tied the board to the bedsprings. Putting the end of the board on the windowsill, he moved the bed up and the board began to dip down like a lever, with the sill as its fulcrum, until little by little it came to rest on top of Traveler's, while the legs of the bed lifted up about a foot and a half. "The worst part is that it's going to keep on rising as soon as someone tries to cross the bridge," Oliveira thought worriedly. He went over to the wardrobe and began to push it towards the bed.

"Don't you have enough weight?" Talita asked as she sat on the edge of her window and looked over into Oliveira's room.

"We've got to take every precaution," Oliveira said, "so we won't have any avoidable accidents."

He pushed the wardrobe over next to the bed and slowly tipped it over on top of it. Talita marvelled at Oliveira's strength, almost as much as she did at Traveler's astuteness and his inventions. "They're really a pair of glyptodons," she thought, enraptured. The antediluvian ages had always seemed to her to be a refuge of wisdom.

The wardrobe picked up speed as it fell and landed with a thump on the bed, making the whole room shake. There were shouts from down below and Oliveira thought that the Levantine next door must have been putting together some violent shamanistic pressure. He finished placing the wardrobe and then straddled the plank, inside the window, of course.

"Now it can take any weight," he announced. "There won't be any accident to please the girls downstairs who love us so much. None of this will make any sense to them until somebody gets killed down on the street. Life, as they say."

"Aren't you going to tie the boards together with your rope?" Traveler asked.

"Look," Oliveira said. "You know very well that I get dizzy from heights. The very name of Everest makes me feel as if someone had kicked me in the crotch. I hate a lot of people, but no one the way I do Sherpa Tensing, believe me."

"In other words, we are going to have to tie the boards together," Traveler said.

"That's about the strength of it," Oliveira admitted, lighting up a 43.

"See what we've got to do?" Traveler said to Talita. "Try crawling out to the middle of the bridge and tying the rope."

"Me?" Talita said.

"That's what I said."

"Oliveira didn't say I had to crawl out to the middle of the bridge."

"He didn't say so, but he implied it. Besides it would have more style if you were the one who handed him the *yerba*."

"I won't be able to tie the knot," Talita said. "You and Oliveira know how to tie knots, but mine will come undone right away. I won't even be able to get it started."

"We'll tell you how," Traveler condescended.

Talita tightened her bathrobe and picked a thread off her finger. She needed to sigh, but she knew that sighs annoyed Traveler.

"You really want me to be the one who takes the *yerba* over to Oliveira?" she said softly.

"What are you talking about there?" Oliveira asked, leaning halfway out of the window and putting his hands on his plank. The errand-girl had brought a chair out on the pavement and was watching them. Oliveira waved at her with one hand. "A compound fracture in time and space," he thought. "The poor dear thinks we're crazy and she's waiting for a wild flight back to normality. If anyone falls she'll be splattered with blood, that's for sure. And she doesn't know that she'll be splattered with blood, she doesn't know that she put the chair there so that she would be splattered with blood, and she doesn't know that ten minutes ago she had an attack of *tedium vitae* right there in the pantry, just enough to initiate the transference of the chair out onto the pavement. And that the glass of water she drank at two twenty-five is lukewarm and upsetting for her stomach, that centre of afternoon moods, and that it had prepared her for that attack of *tedium vitae* which three tablets of Phillips milk of magnesia would have taken care of perfectly; but she couldn't have known about this last item, certain things that unleash or cut off can only be perceived on an astral plane, if one wishes to use that inane terminology."

"We're not talking about anything," Traveler was saying. "You get the rope ready."

"There it is, a magnificent knot. Come on, Talita, I'll hand it to you from here."

Talita straddled the plank and moved forward a couple of inches, leaning on her hands and picking up her behind and putting it down a little bit farther forward.

"This bathrobe isn't very comfortable," she said. "A pair of your pants or something like that would be better."

"It's too much trouble," Traveler said. "And if you fell off you'd ruin my clothes."

"Take your time," Oliveira said. "Just a little bit more and I can toss you the rope."

"This street is awfully wide," Talita said, looking down. "It's much wider than it looks from the window."

"Windows are the eyes of the city," Traveler said, "and naturally they give the wrong shape to everything they see. Right now you're at a point of great purity, and maybe you can see things the way a pigeon or a horse does, without being aware that they have eyes."

"Save ideas for the *Nouvelle Revue Française* and tie the boards up tight," Oliveira advised.

"It's just like you to blow up if anyone says something you would have loved to have said first. I can hold the board down perfectly well while I think and talk."

"I must be close to the centre," Talita said.

"The centre? You're barely out of the window. You've got at least six feet more to go."

"Not quite so much," Oliveira said by way of encouragement. "I'm going to toss you the rope right now."

"I have the feeling that the board is bending," Talita said.

"It's not bending at all," Traveler said as he straddled the plank, but from inside the window. "It's just shaking a little."

"Besides, the end of it is resting on my board," Oliveira said. "It would be mighty strange if they both broke at the same time."

"Yes, but I weigh a hundred and twenty-five pounds," Talita said. "And when I get to the centre I'll weigh five hundred at least. I can feel the board bending more and more."

"If it was bending, my feet would be off the floor, and I can still feel them firmly planted. All that can happen is that the boards might break, and that would be most unusual."

"The fibres have a lot of resistance lengthwise," Oliveira agreed. "That's the whole story behind a bunch of twigs and other examples. I suppose you've got the *yerba* and the nails."

"I've got them in my pocket," Talita said. "Hurry up and throw me the rope. I'm getting nervous, believe me."

"It's the cold," Oliveira said, twirling the rope like a gaucho. "Watch out that you don't lose your balance. Maybe I'd better rope you, that way we can be more sure that you can tie it on."

"It's funny," he thought, as he watched the lasso go over her head.

"Everything really falls into place piece by piece if you really want it to. The only thing untrue about all this is the analysis of it."

"You're getting there," Traveler announced. "Get into position so you can tie up the boards, they're a little bit apart."

"Look at the good job I did of roping her," Oliveira said. "There you are, Manú, you can't tell me now I couldn't get a job with you people in the circus."

"You hurt my face," Talita complained. "The rope is scratchy."

"I can put on a cowboy hat, come out whistling, and rope anybody or anything," Oliveira proposed with enthusiasm. "The crowd will break out cheering, a show that has few precedents in circus history."

"The sun's starting to get to you," Traveler said, lighting up a cigarette. "And I've told you not to call me Manú."

"I haven't got the strength," Talita said. "The rope is too coarse, it keeps catching on itself."

"The ambivalence of the noose," Oliveira said. "Its natural function sabotaged by a mysterious tendency towards neutralization. I think that's what they call entropy."

"It's pretty tight now," Talita said. "Shall I loop it again? There's still a little left over."

"Yes, tie it around tight," Traveler said. "I hate things that are left over and dangling; it's diabolical."

"A perfectionist," Oliveira said. "Now come on over onto my board and test the bridge."

"I'm afraid," Talita said. "Your board doesn't look as solid as ours."

"What?" said Oliveira, offended. "Can't you see that it's a fine cedar board? Are you comparing it to that piece of pine? Come on, don't worry."

"What do you think, Manú?" Talita asked, looking back.

Traveler, who was about to reply, looked at the spot where the two boards overlapped and at the poorly tied rope. Straddling his board, he could feel it vibrating between his legs in a way that was neither pleasant nor unpleasant. All Talita had to do was put down her hands, pull herself up a little and she would be over on Oliveira's side. The bridge would hold, of course; it was well built.

"Wait a minute," Traveler said doubtfully. "Can't you hand him the package from there?"

"Of course she can't," Oliveira said, surprised. "What are you thinking of? You're ruining everything."

"Like he says, I can't hand it to him from here," Talita admitted. "But I could toss it, the easiest thing in the world from here."

"Toss it?" Oliveira said resentfully. "All this trouble and you're going to end up by tossing me the package?"

"If you stick out your arm you'll only be a foot away from the package," Traveler said. "There's no need for Talita to go all the way over there. She'll toss you the package and that's that."

"She'll miss, the way women always do," Oliveira said, "and the *yerba* will spill all over the street, not to mention the nails."

"Rest assured," Talita said, quickly taking out the package. "Even if it doesn't land in your hand, it will still go through the window."

"Yes, and it'll spill all over the dirty floor and I'll have to drink *mate* that is all full of dust," Oliveira said.

"Don't pay any attention to him," Traveler said. "Go ahead and throw it and come on back."

Talita turned around to look at him, doubting whether he meant what he was saying. Traveler was looking at her in a way that she knew very well, and Talita felt a sort of caress run up over her shoulder. She clutched the package and gauged the distance.

Oliveira had lowered his arms and seemed indifferent to what Talita was or was not going to do. He was looking at Traveler over Talita's head, and Traveler returned his look fixedly. "Those two have got another bridge working between them," Talita thought. "If I were to fall into the street they wouldn't even notice it." She looked down at the cobblestones, she saw the errand-girl looking up at her with her mouth open; two blocks away she saw a woman coming along who must have been Gekrepten. Talita paused with the package resting on the bridge.

"That's the way it is," Oliveira said. "It had to happen, nobody can change you. You come right up to the edge of things and one gets the idea that finally you're going to understand, but it's useless, you see, you start turning them around to read the labels. You always get stuck in the planning stage, man."

"So what?" Traveler said. "Why do I have to play games with you, pal?"

"Games play themselves; you're the one who sticks a pole in the spokes to slow down a wheel."

"A wheel that you invented, if you want to bring that up."

"I don't agree," Oliveira said. "All I did was create the circumstances, as anyone who can understand would see. The game has got to be played clean."

"You sound like a loser, old man."

"It's easy to lose if somebody else is rolling the dice."

"Big shot," Traveler said. "Real gaucho talk."

Talita knew that somehow they were talking about her, and she kept on looking down at the errand-girl, motionless on her chair with her mouth open. "I'd give anything for them to stop arguing," Talita thought. "No matter what they talk about, it's always about me in the end, but that's not what I really mean, still it's almost what I mean." It had occurred to her that it would be very funny to drop the package so that it would fall into the errand-girl's mouth. But she didn't really think it would be funny because she could feel that other bridge stretched out above her, the words that passed back and forth, the laughs, the hot silences.

"It's like a trial," Talita thought. "Like a ritual."

She recognized Gekrepten, who had reached the next corner and was beginning to look up. "Who's judging you?" Oliveira had just said. But it wasn't Traveler they were judging, it was her. A feeling, something sticky, like the sun on the back of her neck and on her legs. She was going to have an attack of sunstroke, that's what the punishment would probably be. "I don't think you're in any position to judge me," Manú had said. Still it wasn't Manú but she who was being judged. And through her God knows what, while stupid Gekrepten was waving her left arm around and making motions as if she was the one who was about to have an attack of sunstroke and fall down into the street, condemned without appeal.

"Why are you wobbling like that?" Traveler said, holding his board with both hands. "Hey, you're making it shake too much. Watch out or we'll all be up the creek."

"I'm not moving," Talita said miserably. "All I wanted to do was toss the package and get back inside again."

"The sun's beating down right on your head, you poor doll," Traveler said. "This is really too much, damn it."

"It's your fault," Oliveira said in a fury. "There's nobody in all Argentina who can fuck things up like you."

"You insist on blaming me," Traveler said objectively. "Hurry up,

Talita. Throw the package in his face so he'll stop screwing around with us once and for all."

"It's a little late for that," Talita said. "I don't know whether I can hit the window now."

"I told you so," Oliveira muttered, and it wasn't often that he muttered and only when he was on the brink of some outrageous thing. "There comes Gekrepten loaded down with bundles. There were only a few of us, and grandmother gave birth."

"Throw him the *yerba* anyway," Traveler said. "Don't worry if you miss."

Talita lowered her head and her hair flowed down over her forehead to her chin. She had to keep on blinking because the sweat was getting into her eyes. Her tongue felt salty and covered with something that could have been sparks, little stars running back and forth and bumping into her gums and the roof of her mouth.

"Wait," Traveler said.

"Are you talking to me?" Oliveira asked.

"No. Wait, Talita. Hang on tight, I'm going to hand you a hat."

"Don't get off the board," Talita pleaded. "I'll fall down into the street."

"The encyclopedia and the dresser will hold it down fine. Don't move, I'll be right back."

The boards dipped a little and Talita hung on desperately. Oliveira whistled with everything he had as if to stop Traveler, but there was nobody in the window any more.

"What a bastard," Oliveira said. "Don't move, don't even breathe. Your life depends on it, believe me."

"I know," Talita said in a wisp of a voice. "That's the way it's always been."

"And to make matters worse, Gekrepten is coming up the stairs. She's going to balls things up, damn it. Don't you move."

"I'm not moving," Talita said. "But I think . . . "

"Yes, but don't even do that," Oliveira said. "Don't move at all, it's the only way."

"They've already passed judgement on me," Talita thought. "Now all I have to do is fall and they can get on with the circus and life."

"What are you crying about?" Oliveira asked with interest.

"I'm not crying," Talita said. "I'm sweating, that's all."

"Look," Oliveira said resentfully, "I may be stupid, but I've never confused tears with perspiration. They're quite different things."

"I'm not crying," Talita said. "I almost never cry, I swear. People like Gekrepten cry and she's coming up the stairs right now, loaded down with bundles. I'm like the swan that sings when it dies," Talita said. "That's from a record of Gardel's."

Oliveira lit a cigarette. The boards had settled together again. He took a satisfying drag.

"Look, until that fool Manú comes back with the hat, what we should do is play seesaw-questions."

"Go ahead," Talita said. "If you want to know, I put a few together yesterday."

"OK. I'll begin and we'll each ask a seesaw-question. The operation which consists of depositing a coat of metal dissolved in a liquid on a solid body by use of electric currents, isn't it an old-fashioned ship, triangular sails, hundred-ton cargo?"

"That's what it is," Talita said, throwing back her hair. "Sailing at random, wandering, missing cannon-shots, civet-scented, collecting payments according to the tithe of first fruits, and isn't it the same as any plant juice used for food, like wine, olive oil, etc.?"

"Very good," Oliveira admitted. "Plant juice, like wine, olive oil . . . It never occurred to me to think of wine as a plant juice. Splendid. But listen to this: To bloom again, turn the fields to bloom, tangle up hair, wool, get tangled in a fight or quarrel, poison water with great mullein or some similar substance to stupefy the fish so they can be taken out, isn't that the ending of a dramatic poem, particularly if it's a tragic one?"

"How beautiful," Talita said enthusiastically, "it's beautiful, Horacio. You really can squeeze the juice out of the cemetery."

"Plant juice," Oliveira said.

The door of the room opened and Gekrepten entered breathing heavily. Gekrepten was a bleached blonde, she could talk quite easily, and she was not in the least surprised to see a wardrobe flung across the bed and a man straddling a board.

"It sure is hot," she said, throwing the bundles on a chair. "It's the worst time of day to go shopping, believe me. What are you doing out there, Talita? I don't know why I always go out at siesta-time."

"Good, good," Oliveira said without looking at her. "Your turn, Talita."

"I can't think of anything else."

"Think a little, you must remember something."

"Yes, the dentist," Gekrepten said. "He always gives me the worst appointments for a filling. Did I tell you I had to go to the dentist today?"

"I remember one now," Talita said.

"And what do you think happened," Gekrepten said. "I get to the dentist's, on the Calle Warnes. I ring the bell, and the receptionist comes to the door. I say: 'Good afternoon.' She says: 'Good afternoon. Please come in.' I come in and she takes me into the waiting room."

"It's like this," Talita said. "One whose cheeks are puffed up, or a row of buckets lashed together and floated like a raft to a place where reeds grow: a storehouse for items of prime necessity, established so that certain persons can acquire them there more economically than in a shop, and everything pertaining to or relative to the eclogue, isn't it like applying the science of galvanism to a living or dead animal?"

"Such beauty," Oliveira said astounded. "It's simply phenomenal."

"She tells me: 'Please sit down for a moment.' And I sit and wait."

"I've still got one left," Oliveira said. "Just a minute, I can't remember it too well."

"There were two women and a man with a child. The minutes dragged on. I tell you I got through three whole issues of *Idilio*. The child was crying, poor thing, and his father was a little nervous . . . I'm not lying when I say that more than two hours passed from the time I had come in at two-thirty. Finally it was my turn, and the dentist says: 'Come in, madam'; I go in, and he says: 'Did the one I put in the other day bother you much?' And I tell him: 'No, doctor, how could it bother me. Besides I only chewed on one side all the time.' He says: 'Good, that's what you have to do. Please sit down.' I sit down and he says: 'Open your mouth, please.' He's very pleasant, that dentist."

"I've got it now," Oliveira said. "Listen carefully, Talita. What are you looking back for?"

"To see if Manú is coming back."

"He'll be back. Listen carefully: the action and effect of passing in opposite directions, or in tournaments and jousts, the movement of a rider to make his mount run his chest against that of his opponent's mount, isn't it a lot like the fastigium, the most critical and serious moment of an illness?"

"It's strange," Talita said thoughtfully. "Is that how they say it in Spanish?"

"Say what?"

"That business about a rider making his mount run his chest against . . . "

"In tournaments, yes," Oliveira said. "It's in the cemetery after all."

"Fastigium is a very pretty word," Talita said. "Too bad it means what it does."

"Hell, the same thing can be said about bologna and lots of other words," Oliveira said. "The Abbé Bremond has already worked on this, but what could he do. Words are like us, they're born with one face and what can you do about it. Think about Kant's face for a moment, tell me what you think. Or Bernardino Rivadavia's, to stay closer to home."

"He put in a plastic filling," Gekrepten said.

"This heat is terrible," Talita said. "Manú said he was going to get me a hat."

"It's hard to tell what that guy will bring back," Oliveira said.

"If it's all right with you, I'll toss you the package and go back inside," Talita said.

Oliveira looked at the bridge, measured the window with a vague motion of his arms, and shook his head.

"You might miss," he said. "Besides, I get a funny feeling having you out there in this freezing cold. Can't you feel icicles forming in your hair and in your nasal passages?"

"No," Talita said. "Are the icicles going to be like fastigiums?"

"In a certain way, yes," Oliveira said. "They're two things that do seem alike from the point of view of their differences, a little like Manú and me, if you think about it a little. You're probably aware that all this trouble with Manú is that we look too much alike."

"The butter has melted," Gekrepten said, spreading some on a piece of dark bread. "The butter, with all this heat, it's a battle."

"The worst difference is in all that," Oliveira said. "The worst of all worst differences. Two guys with dark hair, with the face of a Buenos Aires low-life, with practically the same disdain for the same things, and you . . . "

"Well, I . . . " Talita said.

"There's no reason to hide," Oliveira said. "It's a fact that in some sort of way when you join us the similarity and the difference come out at the same time."

"I don't think I sum up the two of you," Talita said.

"What do you know about it? How could you know? There you are in your room, living and cooking and reading the self-teaching encyclopedia, and at night you go to the circus, and then you think that you're only where you are at that moment. Didn't you ever notice latches on doors, metal buttons, little pieces of glass?"

"Yes, I notice them sometimes," Talita said.

"If you were to take a good look you would see very easily that on all sides, where you least suspect, there are images that copy all your movements. I'm very sensitive to all that foolishness, believe me."

"Come here and drink this milk before it all curdles," Gekrepten said. "Why do you people always talk about such strange things?"

"You're making me too important," Talita said.

"Oh, you can't decide things like that," Oliveira said. "There's a whole order of things you can't decide by yourself, and they're always the most bothersome, even if they're not the most important. I tell you this because it's a great consolation. For example, I was planning to have some *mate*. Now this one comes home and starts to make *café con leche* without anybody asking her. Result: if I don't drink it the milk will curdle. It's not important, but it gets under your skin. Do you know what I'm talking about?"

"Oh, yes," Talita said, looking into his eyes. "It's true that you're like Manú. The pair of you can talk so well about *café con leche* and *mate*, and one ends up realizing that *café con leche* and *mate*, in reality . . ."

"Exactly," Oliveira said. "*In reality*. So let's get back to what I was saying before. The difference between Manú and me is that we're almost exactly alike. At this level, a difference is like an imminent cataclysm. Are we friends? Yes, of course, but I would never be surprised at anything that . . . Notice how ever since we've known each other, I can tell you because you already know that, all we've done is hurt each other. He doesn't like me to be the way I am, all I have to do is try to straighten out some nails and look at the hassle he starts, and he gets you into it along the line. But he doesn't like me to be the way I am because in reality a lot of the things that come to my mind, a lot of the things I do, it's as if I've stolen them out from under his nose. Before he has a chance to think of them, zip, there they are. Bang, bang, he comes to the window and I'm straightening out the nails."

Talita looked backwards and saw the shadow of Traveler, who was listening, hidden between the dresser and the window.

"Well, but you don't have to exaggerate," Talita said. "Some of the things that occur to Manú can't always have occurred to you."

"For example?"

"The milk's getting cold," Gekrepten grumbled. "Shall I put it on the fire a little more, sweet?"

"Make a custard with it tomorrow," Oliveira advised. "Go ahead, Talita."

"No," Talita said with a sigh. "What for? I'm so hot, and I have the feeling I'm going to get sick."

She felt the bridge vibrate as Traveler straddled it by the windowsill. Lying prone and staying on his side of the sill, Traveler put a straw hat on the board. With the aid of a mop handle he began to inch it along the board.

"If it gets the least bit off course it will fall into the street and it will be a terrible drag having to go down and get it."

"I think I'd better come back inside," Talita said, looking at Traveler with a mournful expression.

"But first you've got to give Oliveira his *yerba*," Traveler said.

"It doesn't matter any more," Oliveira said. "In any case, let her throw it, it doesn't make any difference."

Talita looked back and forth at them and remained motionless.

"It's hard to understand you," Traveler said. "All this work and now it turns out that one more *mate*, one less *mate*, it doesn't really matter."

"The minute-hand has made its circle, my son," Oliveira said. "You move in the time-space continuum with the speed of a worm. Think of all that has happened since you decided to go to find that overworked Panama hat. The cycle of the *mate* came to a close without reaching fruition, and in the meantime the ever-faithful Gekrepten made her showy entrance, loaded down with cooking utensils. We are now in the *café con leche* sector, and nothing can be done about it."

"That's some argument," Traveler said.

"That's no argument, it's a proof, arrived at in a perfectly objective way. You tend to move in the continuum, as physicists say, while

I am quite sensitive to the giddy discontinuity of existence. At this very moment the *café con leche* has burst upon the scene, has installed itself, rules, is propagated, and is repeated in hundreds of thousands of homes. The *mate* gourds have been washed, put away, abolished. A temporary *café con leche* mantle now covers this segment of the American continent. Think of all that this presupposes and brings with it. Conscientious mothers lecturing their offspring on the virtues of a lactic diet, children grouped around the pantry table, all smiles on top and all kicks and pinches underneath. To say *café con leche* at this time of day means change, a friendly get-together towards the end of the working day, the recounting of good deeds, deeds to the real estate transitory situations, vague prologues to what six o'clock in the afternoon, that terrible hour of keys in the door and a race to catch the bus, will bring home with brutal concreteness. Practically nobody ever makes love at that hour, they do it either before or after. At that hour people think about a shower (but we'll take one at five o'clock) and people begin to think about something to do in the evening, whether they'll go to see Paulina Singerman or Toco Tarantola (but we're not sure, there's still time). What does all this have to do with *mate* time? I'm not talking about *mate* that's not taken properly, superimposed on the *café con leche,* but the authentic one I wanted, at just the right moment, just when the weather was coldest. And it's all these things that I don't think you understand enough."

"The dressmaker is a crook," Gekrepten said. "Do you have your clothes made by a dressmaker, Talita?"

"No," Talita said. "I know a little bit about cutting and sewing."

"Smart girl. This afternoon after the dentist I run over to the dressmaker's, it's a block away, to inquire about a skirt that should have been ready a week ago. She says to me: 'I'm awfully sorry, miss, but with my mother as sick as she's been I wasn't even able to thread a needle, you might say.' I tell her: 'But I need the skirt.' She says: 'I'm terribly sorry, miss, believe me. A customer like you. But you'll have to forgive me.' I say: 'Forgiving won't get me anything. It would have been better if you'd had it done on time and we'd all be better off.' She says: 'If that's the way you feel, why don't you go to another dressmaker?' And I say: 'Not that I don't feel like it, but since I put in an order with you it would be better if I waited, but I don't think you're very reliable.'"

"Did all that happen?" Oliveira asked.

"Of course," Gekrepten said. "Can't you hear me telling Talita all about it?"

"They're two different matters."

"There you go again."

"There's your example," Oliveira said to Traveler, who looked at him with a furrowed brow. "There's your example of what things are like. Everybody thinks he's talking about something he has in common with everybody else."

"And that's not the way it is, of course," Traveler said. "What a fresh piece of news."

"It's worth repeating, damn it."

"You repeat everything you think is a sanction against somebody."

"God put me here to watch over your city," Oliveira said.

"When you're not judging me you do it to your old lady."

"In order to prod you and keep you both awake," Oliveira said.

"Like a Mosaic mania. It came to you on the way down from Mount Sinai."

"I like things to be as clear as possible," Oliveira said. "It doesn't seem to matter to you that right in the middle of a conversation Gekrepten sticks in a completely fantastic story about a dentist and some damned skirt or other. You don't seem to realize that these outbursts, pardonable when they're beautiful or at least inspired, become repulsive as soon as they start to cut into an order of things, torpedo a structure. How I do go on, old man."

"Horacio is always like this," Gekrepten said. "Don't pay any attention to him, Traveler."

"We're so bland it's unbearable, Manú. We let reality slip through our fingers like any ordinary trickle of water. We had it right there, almost perfect, like a rainbow between our thumb and our little finger. And the work that went into getting it, the time that was required, the way we had to make ourselves deserving of it . . . Boom, the radio says that General Pisotelli has made a declaration . . . *Kaput.* Everything *kaput.* 'Something serious at last,' the errand-girl says, or this one, or maybe even you yourself. And me, because I don't want you to think that I'm infallible. How should I know where truth is? I only know that I liked the feel of that rainbow, like a little toad between my fingers. And this afternoon . . . Look, in spite of the cold I think that we were beginning to hit upon something serious.

Talita, for example, carrying out the amazing feat of not falling off into the street, and you over there, and me . . . One feels certain things, what the hell."

"I'm not sure I understand you," Traveler said. "That business about the rainbow is pretty good anyway. But why are you so intolerant? Live and let live, brother."

"Now that you've had your fun, come and get the wardrobe off the bed," Gekrepten said.

"You see?" Oliveira said.

"I see what you mean," Traveler said, convinced.

"*Quod erat demonstrandum*, old buddy."

"*Quod erat*," Traveler said. "And the worst of it is that we hadn't even got started."

"What do you mean?" Talita said, tossing her hair back and looking to see if Traveler had pushed the hat far enough along.

"Don't get nervous," Traveler advised. "Turn around slowly, put out that hand, that's the way. Wait, I'll push it a little more . . . Didn't I tell you? There it is."

Talita grasped the hat and put it on, all in one motion. Down below there were two boys and a woman who were talking to the errand-girl and looking up at the bridge.

"Now I'll toss the package to Oliveira and that'll be it," Talita said, feeling more sure of herself with the hat on. "Hold the boards tight, it'll be easy."

"Are you going to throw it?" Oliveira asked. "I bet you miss."

"Let her try," Traveler said. "If the package goofs off into the street I hope it hits old lady Gutusso on her nut, repulsive old owl."

"So you don't like her either," Oliveira said. "I'm happy because I can't stand her. What about you, Talita?"

"I'd rather toss the package to you," Talita said.

"OK, OK, but I think you're rushing it too much."

"Oliveira's right," Traveler said. "You don't want to ruin everything right at the end, after all the work that went into it."

"But I'm so hot," Talita said. "I want to come back, Manú."

"You're not so far away that you should be complaining like that. Somebody would think you were writing me a letter from Mato Grosso."

"He's thinking about the *yerba* when he says that," Oliveira explained to Gekrepten, who was looking at the wardrobe.

"Are you going to play much longer?" Gekrepten asked.

"No way," Oliveira said.

"Oh," Gekrepten said. "Just as well."

Talita had taken the package out of her bathrobe and was swinging it back and forth. The bridge began to vibrate, and Traveler and Oliveira held it down with all their strength. Tired of swinging the package, Talita began to wind up with her arm, holding it with her other hand.

"Don't do anything silly," Oliveira said. "Slower, do you hear me? Slower."

"Here it comes," Talita shouted.

"Slower, you're going to fall off."

"I don't care!" Talita shouted, letting the package go. It went full force through the window and broke open as it hit the wardrobe.

"Splendid," Traveler said, looking at Talita as if he were trying to keep the bridge in place with nothing but the strength of his look. "Perfect, my love. You couldn't have made it clearer. That's a *demonstrandum* for you."

The bridge gradually stopped moving. Talita hung on with both hands and lowered her head. Oliveira could only see her hat and her hair hanging down over her shoulders. He raised his eyes and looked at Traveler.

"If you want to know," he said. "I agree, she couldn't have made it clearer."

"At last," Talita thought, looking down at the cobblestones and the pavements. "Anything is better than being out here like this in between the two windows."

"You've got two choices," Traveler said. "Keep going forward, which is easier, and go into Oliveira's, or come back, which is harder, and save yourself going up and down the stairs and crossing the street."

"Come over here, you poor thing," Gekrepten said. "Your face is all covered with perspiration."

"Drunks and little children," Oliveira said.

"Let me rest a minute," Talita said. "I feel a little nauseous."

Oliveira lay prone over the sill and stretched out his hand. All Talita had to do was come forward two feet to touch his hand.

"A perfect gentleman," Traveler said. "It's obvious he's read Professor Maidana's manual of social graces. A real aristo. Don't miss that, Talita."

"It's because of the extreme cold," Oliveira said. "Rest a little, Talita, and then cover the distance in between. Don't pay any attention to him, you know that the snow makes one delirious before the deep sleep sets in."

But Talita had raised herself slowly, and leaning on both arms had worked her behind half a foot backwards. Another grip, another half-foot. Oliveira, still holding out his hand, looked like a passenger on a boat which is slowly pulling away from the pier.

Traveler stretched out his arms and got his hands under Talita's armpits. She didn't move, and then she threw her head back with such a quick movement that the hat went gliding down to the pavement.

"Just like at the bullfight," Oliveira said. "Señora Gutusso is going to try to steal it."

Talita had closed her eyes and was letting herself be held up, hauled off the board and through the window. She felt Traveler's lips on the back of her neck, his quick, hot breath.

"You came back," Traveler murmured. "You came back, you came back."

"Yes," Talita said, going over to the bed. "Didn't you think I would? I threw him his god-damned package and I came back, I threw him the package and I came back, I . . . "

Traveler sat down on the edge of the bed. He was thinking about the rainbow between his fingers, those things that occurred to Oliveira. Talita slipped down beside him and began to cry quietly. "It's her nerves," Traveler thought. "She had a rough time." He wanted to get her a tall glass of water with lemon juice, give her an aspirin, cover her face with a magazine, make her sleep a little. But first he had to pick up the self-teaching encyclopedia, put the dresser back where it belonged, and pull in the board. "This room is such a mess," he thought, kissing Talita. As soon as she stopped crying he would ask her to help him clean up the room. He began to caress her, say things to her.

"At last, at last," Oliveira said.

He left the window and sat down on the edge of the bed, using the space remaining next to the wardrobe. Gekrepten had finished picking up the *yerba* with a spoon.

"It was full of nails," Gekrepten said. "How strange."

"Very strange," Oliveira said.

"I think I'll go down and get Talita's hat. You know how kids are."

"A wise thought," Oliveira said, picking up a nail and twirling it with his fingers.

Gekrepten went down to the street. The children had picked up the hat and were arguing with the errand-girl and Señora Gutusso.

"Give it to me," Gekrepten said with a prim smile. "It belongs to the lady across the way, someone I know."

"Everybody knows her, child," Señora Gutusso said. "What a performance for this time of day, and with children watching."

"There was nothing wrong with it," Gekrepten said without much conviction.

"With her legs out in the air on that board, what an example for the children. You probably couldn't see, but from down here it was quite a sight, I can assure you."

"She had a lot of hair," the smallest child said.

"There you are," said Señora Gutusso. "Children tell what they see, poor things. And what in the world was she doing straddling a board, might I ask? At this hour, when respectable people are having their siesta or are busy at work. Would you straddle a board, madam, if it's not too much to ask?"

"No, I wouldn't," Gekrepten said. "But Talita works in a circus. They're all performers."

"Were they rehearsing?" asked one of the boys. "What circus is that girl with?"

"It wasn't a rehearsal," Gekrepten said. "What happened was that they wanted to give my husband a little *yerba*, and so . . ."

Señora Gutusso looked at the errand-girl. The errand-girl put her finger to her temple and made a circle with it. Gekrepten took the hat in both hands and went back into the building. The boys formed a line and began to sing to the tune of the *Light Cavalry Overture*:

> Oh, they came from behind, oh, they came from behind,
> and they stuck a pole up his aaarse-hole.
> It wouldn't come out, it wouldn't come out,
> the poor man was out of his mind.
>
> (Repeat)

(–148)

42

Il mio supplizio
è quando
non mi credo
in armonia.
UNGARETTI, *I Fiumi*

The job consisted of stopping kids from crawling under the tent, lending a hand with the animals when necessary, helping the man who operated the lights, writing copy for advertisements and the gaudy posters, getting them printed, dealing with the police, keeping the Manager informed of anything wrong that he should know about, helping Señor Manuel Traveler in his administrative work, helping Señora Atalía Donosi de Traveler in the box-office (if necessary), etc.

> Oh, my heart, do not rise up to bear witness against me!
> (*The Book of the Dead*, or inscription on a scarab)

During this time, Dinu Lipatti had died in Europe at the age of thirty-three. They were talking about the job and about Dinu Lipatti all the way to the corner, because Talita thought that it was also good to collect tangible proofs of the non-existence of God or at least of his incurable frivolity. She had suggested that they go out immediately and buy a Lipatti record and go to Don Crespo's to listen to it, but Traveler and Oliveira wanted to have a beer at the corner café and talk about the circus, now that they were colleagues and quite content. Oliveira had-not-failed-to-notice that Traveler had had to make a-heroic-effort to convince the Boss, and that he had convinced him more by chance than for any other reason. They had already decided that Oliveira would give Gekrepten two of the three pieces of cashmere he hadn't sold yet, and that Talita would make herself a tailored suit with the third. A matter of celebrating his appointment. Consequently, Traveler ordered the beers while Talita went to prepare lunch. It was Monday, a day off. On Tuesday there would be a performance at seven and one at nine, with the presentation of 4 BEARS 4, a juggler who had just arrived from Colombo, and, of course, the calculating cat. Oliveira's job would be all gravy at first, until the time came when he would have to pitch in. In the meantime he could watch the performance, which was no worse than any others. Everything was going very well.

Everything was going so well that Traveler lowered his eyes and began to drum on the table. The waiter, who knew them well, came over to argue about the Ferrocarril Oeste team, and Oliveira bet ten pesos on the Chacarita Juniors. As he beat out the rhythm of a *baguala* with his fingers, Traveler was telling himself that everything was perfectly all right this way, and that there was no other way out, while Oliveira was finishing up with the technicalities of his bet and drinking his beer. He had started to think about Egyptian phrases that morning, about Thoth, significantly the god of magic and the inventor of language. They argued for a while whether it wasn't a fallacy to be arguing for a while, since the language they were using, as local and slangy as it might be, was perhaps part of a mantic structure that was by no means tranquillizing. They decided that all things considered, the double ministry of Thoth was a manifest guarantee of coherence in reality or unreality; it made them happy to have left more or less resolved the continuously disagreeable problem of the objective correlative. Magic or the tangible word, there was an Egyptian god who verbally harmonized subjects and objects. Everything was really going very well.

(–75)

43

Everything was perfect in the circus, a spangled fraud with wild music, a calculating cat who reacted to cardboard numbers that had been secretly treated previously with valerian, while ladies were so moved that they made sure that their offspring noticed such an eloquent example of Darwinian evolution. When Oliveira went out onto the still-empty sawdust on the first night and looked up at the opening at the highest point of the red tent, that escape-hatch to a maybe contact, that centre, that eye like a bridge between the earth and liberated space, he stopped laughing and thought that someone else would probably have climbed up the nearest pole to the eye up there as if it were the most natural thing to do, and that that other person was not the one who was smoking and looking up at the high hole there, that other person was not the one who stayed down below smoking in the midst of all the circus shouts.

On one of those early nights he came to understand why Traveler had managed to get him the job. Talita had told him why without beating about the bush while they were counting money in the brick cubicle that served as treasury and office for the circus. Oliveira already knew why in another way, and it was necessary for Talita to tell him from her point of view so that out of the two things there could be born a new time, a present in which he felt himself placed and obligated. He tried to protest, to say that they were things that Traveler had made up, he tried to feel himself once more outside of the others' time (he, dying to agree, mix into things, be) but at the same time he understood that it was certain, that in one way or another he had transgressed the world of Talita and Traveler, without acts, without intentions even, nothing more than giving in to a nostalgic whim. Between one word and another from Talita he saw the shabby line of El Cerro become outlined, he heard the ridiculous Lusitanian phrase that had unconsciously invented a future of cold storage and *caña quemante* rum. It brought out his laugh in Talita's face, just as he had laughed that very morning at the mirror when he was about to brush his teeth.

Talita tied a piece of string around a bundle of ten-peso notes and mechanically began to count the rest.

"What did you expect," Talita said. "I think Manú was right."

"Of course he was," Oliveira said. "But he's an idiot just the same, as you know only too well."

"Not too well. I know it, or rather I knew it when I was straddling the board. You two know it only too well, I'm in the middle like that part of a scale that I never know the name of."

"You're Egeria, our nymph, our bridge, our medium. Now that I think of it, when you're present Manú and I fall into some sort of trance. Even Gekrepten has noticed it, and she told me so, using precisely the same gaudy expression."

"It could be," Talita said, entering the figures. "If you want me to tell you what I think, Manú doesn't know what to do with you. He loves you like a brother, I suppose even you have noticed that, and at the same time he's sorry that you've come back."

"He had no reason to meet me at the dock. I didn't even send him a postcard."

"He found out from Gekrepten, who had filled the balcony with geraniums. Gekrepten found out from the ministry."

"A diabolical process," Oliveira said. "When I discovered that Gekrepten had found out by diplomatic channels, I saw that the only thing left for me to do was let her throw herself into my arms like a crazy calf. Just imagine such abnegation, such extremes of Penelopism."

"If you don't feel like talking about it," Talita said looking at the floor, "we can shut the safe and go and look for Manú."

"I feel like it very much, but the complications your husband raises give me uncomfortable problems of conscience. And that, for me . . . In short, I don't understand why you yourself don't solve the problem."

"Well," Talita said, looking at him in a restful way, "it seems to me that the other afternoon anyone who wasn't stupid would have realized."

"Of course, but there's Manú the next day going to talk to the Boss and getting me this job. Precisely when I was drying my tears with a cloth sample before going out to sell it."

"Manú is a good person," Talita said. "You'll never know how good he is."

"A strange goodness," Oliveira said. "Leaving aside what I will never know, which, when all's said and done, is probably true, allow me to insinuate that Manú probably wants to play with fire. If you look closely, you'll see that it's a circus trick. And you two," Oliveira said, pointing his finger at her, "have accomplices."

"Accomplices?"

"Yes, accomplices. First me, and then someone who's not here. You think you're the pointer on the scales, to use your pretty image, but you don't know that you're leaning your body over to one side. You ought to be aware of it."

"Why don't you go away, Horacio?" Talita asked. "Why don't you leave Manú in peace?"

"I already explained to you, I was on my way out to sell cloth and that beast got me this job. Understand, I'm not going to do the dirty on him, that would be much worse. It's stupid even to think about it."

"And so you're going to hang around here, then, and Manú won't get any sleep."

"Give him some Equanil, girl."

Talita tied up the five-peso notes. When the calculating cat came on they always went out to watch him work because the animal was absolutely fantastic, twice already he had solved a multiplication before the fraud with the valerian had had time to work. Traveler was stunned, and asked his friends to watch. But that night the cat was stupid, he could barely add up to twenty-five, it was tragic. Smoking in one of the entrances to the arena, Traveler and Oliveira decided that the cat probably needed phosphated food, they would have to talk to the Manager. The two clowns, who hated the cat without anyone's really knowing why, were dancing around the platform where the feline was cleaning his whiskers under a mercury lamp. The third time around, while they were singing a Russian song, the cat put out his claws and sprang at the face of the older one. As usual, the public applauded the number madly. In the wagon of the Bonettis, father and son, clowns, the Manager got the cat back and imposed a double fine on them for having provoked the animal.

It was a strange night; looking up as he always found himself doing at that hour, Oliveira could see Sirius in the centre of the black hole and he speculated about the three days when the earth is open, when the manes ascend and there is a bridge between man and the hole on high, a bridge from man to man (because who climbs up to the hole unless it is to wish to come down changed and find one's self again, but in a different way, with one's people?). The twenty-fourth of August was one of the three days on which the earth opened up; of course, what was the use of thinking so much about that since they were only in February. Oliveira could not remember the other two days, it was strange remembering only one date out of three. Why that one precisely? Perhaps because it was an octosyllable, memory plays games like that. But then Truth was probably an Alexandrine or a hendecasyllable; perhaps the rhythms again marking the main stress and scanning the periods of the road. Some more themes for eggheads to write theses about. It was pleasurable watching the juggler, his incredible agility, the milky track on which the tobacco smoke roosted on the heads of hundreds of children from Villa del Parque, a section where luckily there are abundant eucalyptus trees to balance the scales, referring again to that adjudicating instrument, that compartment of the zodiac.

(–125)

44

It was true that Traveler was not getting much sleep, in the middle of the night he would sigh as if he had a weight on his chest and he would embrace Talita who would receive him without saying anything, squeezing herself against him so that he would be able to feel her deeply near him. In the darkness they would kiss each other on the nose, on the mouth, on the eyes, and Traveler would stroke Talita's cheek with a hand that came out from under the sheets and would go back into hiding as if it was cold, although both of them were sweating; then Traveler would murmur four or five numbers, an old habit to go back to sleep again, and Talita would feel his arms loosen, his breathing deepen, and he would settle down. During the day he went about happily and whistled tangos while he prepared *mate* or read, but Talita could not do any cooking without his appearing four or five times with various excuses and talking about something, especially about the lunatic asylum now that the negotiations seemed to be going well and the Manager was speeding up his plans to buy the madhouse. Talita didn't find the idea of the mental hospital very funny, and Traveler knew it. The two of them tried to find the humorous side, promising themselves spectacles worthy of Samuel Beckett, sneering at the poor circus which was winding up its performances in Villa del Parque and getting ready to open in San Isidro. Sometimes Oliveira would pop by to have a *mate*, although he generally stayed in his room taking advantage of the fact that Gekrepten had to go to work and he could read and smoke at his leisure. When Traveler was looking into Talita's somewhat purple eyes while he was helping her pluck a duck, a biweekly luxury that enchanted Talita, a fan of the duck in all of its culinary possibilities, he would tell himself that things were not as bad as they had been, and he even would have preferred for Horacio to come by and join in some *mates*, because they would immediately start to play a number game that they barely understood but which had to be played so that time would pass and the three of them would feel worthy of one another. They also used to read, because from a coincidentally socialist youth, a little theosophical on Traveler's side, the three of them loved reading with commentaries, each in his own way, polemics from the Hispano-Argentine pleasure in wanting to convince and never accepting contrary opinion, and the undeniable possibilities of laughing like crazy and feeling themselves above suffering humanity under the pretext of helping it come out of its shitty contemporary situation.

But it was certain that Traveler was not sleeping well, Talita would repeat it rhetorically while she watched him shave in the light of the morning sun. One stroke, another, Traveler in his undershirt and pyjama bottoms was whistling a drawn-out version of *La gayola* and then he proclaimed with a shout: "Music, moody food of us that trade in love!" and turning around he looked aggressively at Talita who had been plucking the duck that day and was very happy because the quills that came out were a delight and the duck had a benign air not often seen in those rancorous corpses, with their little eyes half open and an imperceptible band like a ray of light between the lids, unfortunate creatures.

"Why do you have such trouble sleeping, Manú?"

"*Music, moo . . . !* Me? Trouble? I don't fall asleep directly, my love, I spend the night meditating on the *Liber penitentialis* in the Macrovius Basca edition that I lifted from Dr Feta the other day when his sister wasn't looking. Of course, I'm going to give it back to him, it must be worth a lot of dough. A *liber penitentialis*, I'll have you know."

"And what might that be?" Talita asked as she now began to understand certain sleight-of-hand tricks and a drawer that had a double lock. "You've been hiding your reading from me, it's the first time that's happened since we've been married."

"There it is, you can look at it as much as you like, but always wash your hands first. I hide it because it's valuable and you're always going around with carrot-scrapings and things like that on your fingers, you're so domestic that you'd ruin any piece of incunabula."

"I don't care about your book," Talita said, offended. "Come here and cut the head off this, I don't like to, even if it is dead."

"I'll use my razor," Traveler proposed. "It'll give the whole business a truculent tone, and besides, it's always good to practise, you never can tell."

"No. Use this knife, it's sharp."

"My razor."

"No. This knife."

Traveler took his razor over to the duck and lopped off its head.

"You've got to learn," he said. "If we take over the asylum it would be good to get experience along the lines of a double murder on the Rue Morgue."

"Is that the way lunatics do their killing?"

"No, my dear, but once in a while they give it a try. Just like sane people, if you will allow me the poor comparison."

"It's cheap," Talita admitted, making the duck into a sort of parallelepiped tied together with white cord.

"As far as my not sleeping well is concerned," Traveler said, cleaning the razor with a piece of toilet paper, "you know perfectly well what's behind it."

"Let's say I do. But you also know that there's no problem involved."

"Problems," Traveler said, "are like Primus heaters, everything is fine until they blow up. I could tell you that there are teleological problems on this earth. They don't seem to exist, like right now, and what happens is that the clock in the bomb is set for twelve o'clock tomorrow. Tick-tock, tick-tock, everything's fine. Tick-tock."

"The worst part," Talita said, "is that you yourself are the one who winds it up."

"My hand, pussycat, is also set for twelve o'clock tomorrow. In the meantime, let's live and let live."

Talita covered the duck with grease, a degrading spectacle.

"Do you have any reason to reproach me?" she asked, as if she were talking to the palmiped.

"Absolutely none at the moment," Traveler said. "We'll see at twelve o'clock tomorrow, if I can prolong the image right up to its climactic outcome."

"You're just like Horacio," Talita said. "It's incredible how much the two of you are alike."

"Tick-tock," Traveler said, looking for his cigarettes. "Tick-tock, tick-tock."

"Yes, you're just like him," Talita insisted, letting go of the duck which fell to the floor with a revolting squashy sound. "He would have said tick-tock, he would have been talking in images all the time too. But are the pair of you ever going to leave me in peace? The reason I'm telling you that you're both alike is so that once and for all we can quit all this absurdity. It can't be possible that everything has changed like this just because Horacio came back. Last night I told him I couldn't take any more, that you two were playing with me, like a tennis ball, you hit me from both sides, it's not right, Manú, it's not right."

Traveler took her in his arms even though Talita was resisting, and after stepping on the duck and slipping so that both of them almost fell down, he managed to control her and kiss her on the tip of her nose.

"Maybe there's no bomb for you, pussycat," he said, smiling with an expression that softened Talita, made her try to get more comfortable in his arms. "Look, I'm not going around looking for lightning to strike me on the head, but I don't feel I should wear a lightning-rod for protection; I think I ought to go out with my head uncovered until it's twelve o'clock on some day. Only after that time, after that day, will I feel the same again. It isn't because of Horacio, love, it isn't only because of Horacio, even though he may have come like some sort of messenger. If he hadn't come, something else like it would have happened to me. I would have read some disillusioning book, or I would have fallen in love with some other woman . . . Those folds of life, you understand, those unexpected evidences of something that a person hadn't suspected and which suddenly turn everything into a crisis. You'll have to learn to understand."

"But do you really think he's after me, and that I . . . ?"

"He's not after you in the least," Traveler said, letting her go. "Horacio doesn't care a damn about you. Don't be offended, I know very well what you're worth and I'll always be jealous of everybody who looks at you or talks to you. But even if Horacio made a pass at you, even in that case, even if you think I'm crazy, I would repeat that he doesn't care a damn about you, and that therefore you've got nothing to worry about. It's something else," Traveler said, raising his voice. "It's something fucking else, God damn it!"

"Oh," Talita said, picking up the duck and wiping off the footprint with a kitchen rag. "You've caved in its ribs. So it's something else. I don't understand at all, but you're probably right."

"And if he were here," Traveler said in a low voice, looking at his cigarette, "he wouldn't understand anything either. But he'd know very well that it's something else. It's incredible, when he's with us it's as if walls collapsed, piles of things all going to hell, and suddenly the sky becomes fantastically beautiful, the stars come out on that baking dish, you can skin them and eat them, that duck is really Lohengrin's swan, and behind, behind . . . "

"Am I disturbing you?" asked Señora Gutusso as she appeared in the hallway door. "You're probably talking about personal matters, I don't want to intrude where I haven't been invited."

"Not at all," Talita said. "Come right in, señora, and look at this beautiful creature."

"Marvellous," Señora Gutusso said. "I always say that duck may be tough, but it has its own special taste."

"Manú stepped on it," Talita said. "I bet it turns out like a ball of fat."

"You said it," Traveler said.

(–102)

45

It was natural to think that he was waiting for him to appear at the window. It was enough waking up at two o'clock on a hot sticky night, with the acrid smell of the flypaper, with two enormous stars planted on the casement of the window, with the window opposite also open.

It was natural because the plank still seemed to be in the casement, and what was a negative in the bright sunlight might be something else perhaps in the middle of the night, turn into a sudden acquiescence, and then he would be there at his window, smoking to drive away the mosquitoes and waiting for sleepwalking Talita to uncouple herself softly from Traveler's body and appear and look at him from darkness to darkness. Perhaps with slow movements of his hand he would sketch signs with the lighted end of his cigarette. Triangles, circumferences, instantaneous coats of arms, symbols of the fatal love potion or of diphenilpropilamine, pharmaceutical abbreviations that she could interpret, or just a luminous back and forth from his mouth to the arm of the chair, from the arm of the chair to his mouth, from his mouth to the arm of the chair, all through the night.

There was nobody at the window. Traveler went over to the hot well, he looked into the street where a defenceless open newspaper let itself be read by a starry sky that seemed almost touchable. The window of the hotel opposite seemed even closer at night, a gymnast could have reached it in one leap. No, he couldn't have. Maybe with death at his heels, but not any other way. There was no sign of the board any more, there was no way across.

Sighing, Traveler went back to bed. He answered a sleepy question of Talita's by stroking her hair and murmuring something. Talita kissed the air, moved her hand around a little, settled down.

If he had been in some part of the black well, stuck back in the depths of the room and from there looking out of the window, he must have seen Traveler, the ectoplasm of his white undershirt. If he had been in some part of the black well waiting for Talita to appear, the indifferent appearance of a white undershirt must have mortified him thoroughly. Now he would be scratching his forearm, his usual gesture of discomfort and resentment, he would squeeze his cigarette between his lips, he would mutter some fitting obscenity, he would probably throw himself onto the bed without the least consideration for Gekrepten, who was in a deep sleep.

But if he had not been in any part of the black well, the act of getting up and going to the window at that time of night was an admission of fear, almost an assent. It was practically the same as taking for granted that neither Horacio nor he had withdrawn the boards. In one way or another there was a way across, it was possible to come and go. Any one of the three, sleepwalking, could go from window to window, walking on the thick air without fear of falling into the street. The bridge would only disappear with the light of day, with the reappearance of the *café con leche* that would bring them back to solid constructions and tear away the cobwebs of the predawn hours with the heavy hand of news bulletins on the radio and a cold shower.

Talita's dreams: She was being taken to an art exhibition in an immense ruined palace, and the pictures were hung at giddy heights, as if someone had turned the prisons of Piranesi into a museum. And so to get to the paintings one had to climb up some archways where one could secure a footing only on the carvings, go through galleries that went to the edge of a stormy sea with waves like lead, climb up spiral staircases to see finally, always poorly, always from below or from one side, the paintings in which the same whitish splotch, the same coagulation of tapioca or milk was repeated to infinity.

Talita's awakening: Sitting up suddenly in bed at nine o'clock in the morning, shaking Traveler who was sleeping face down, slapping him on the behind to wake him up. Traveler stretching out an arm and pinching her on the leg. Talita throwing herself on top of him and pulling his hair. Traveler abusing his strength, twisting her hand until Talita apologized. Kisses, terrible heat.

"I dreamed about a frightful museum. You were taking me there."

"I detest oneiromancy. Make some *mate*, animal."

"Why did you get up last night? It wasn't because you had to pee, when you get up to pee you explain to me first as if I were stupid, you tell me: 'I'm going to get up, I can't hold it any more,' and I feel sorry for you because I can hold it perfectly well all night long, I don't even have to hold it, it's a different metabolism."

"A what?"

"Tell me why you got up. You went over to the window and you sighed."

"Don't bug me."

"Idiot."

"It was hot."

"Tell me why you got up."

"No reason, to see if Horacio wasn't able to sleep either, so we could talk for a while."

"At that hour? The pair of you barely talk during the day."

"It probably would have been different. You never know."

"I dreamt about a horrible museum," Talita says, starting to put on her slip.

"You already told me," Traveler says, looking at the ceiling.

"We don't talk much any more either," Talita says.

"Of course not, it's the humidity."

"But it's as if something is talking, something is using us to talk. Don't you get that feeling? Don't you think we're inhabited in some sort of way? I mean . . . It's hard to explain, really."

"Transhabited would be better. Look, this won't go on for ever. *No te aflijas, Catalina*" – Traveler sings softly – "*ya vendrán tiempos mejores / y te pondré un comedor.*"

"Stupid," Talita says, kissing him on the ear. "This won't go on for ever, this won't go on for ever . . . This shouldn't go on for even one minute more."

"Violent amputations are bad, afterwards the stump hurts for the rest of your life."

"If you want me to tell you the truth," Talita says, "I have the impression that we're raising spiders or centipedes. We take care of them, we attend to them, and they keep on growing, at first they were insignificant little bugs, almost sweet, with so many legs, and suddenly they've grown, they jump at your face. I think I dreamed about spiders too, I remember vaguely."

"Listen to Horacio," Traveler says, pulling on his trousers. "At this hour he whistles like a madman to celebrate Gekrepten's leaving. What a guy."

(–80)

46

"Music, moody food of us that trade in love," Traveler had quoted for the fourth time, tuning up his guitar before offering the tango called *Cotorritu de la suerte.*

Don Crespo was interested in the quotation and Talita went upstairs to get all five acts in Astrana Marín's translation. The Calle Cachimayo was noisy at nightfall, but in Don Crespo's patio, except for the canary Cien Pesos, all that could be heard was Traveler's voice as he came to the part about *la obrerita juguetona y pizpireta / la que diera a su casita la alegría.* Playing the card game *escoba de quince* doesn't call for talking, and Gekrepten kept beating Oliveira time after time as he alternated with Señora Gutusso in the chore of getting rid of twenty-cent pieces. Luck's little parrot (*que augura la vida o muerte*) in the meantime had picked out a pink slip of paper: a boyfriend, long life. Which did not prevent Traveler's voice from assuming a hollow tone as he described the rapid illness of the heroine, *y la tarde en que moría tristemente / preguntando a su mamita: "¿No llegó?"* Trrang.

"Such feeling," Señora Gutusso said. "They say bad things about the tango, but as far as I'm concerned there's no comparison between it and the calypso songs and other trash they play on the radio. Can you pass me some beans, Don Horacio? I need more chips."

Traveler leaned the guitar against a flowerpot, took a deep drag on his *mate,* and got the feeling that the night was going to be a big bore for him. He almost would have preferred having to work or being sick, anything for distraction. He poured himself a shot of *caña* and drank it in one gulp, looking at Don Crespo, who with his glasses on the tip of his nose was moving suspiciously into the preface of the tragedy. Beaten, eighty cents down, Oliveira went over to sit by them and also took a shot.

"It's a fabulous world," Traveler said in a low voice. "The Battle of Actium is going to take place in a little while in there, if the old boy can last that long. And next to him those two madwomen haggling over beans on the strength of their seven-cards."

"They're occupations like any others," Oliveira said. "Do you get the sense of the word? To be occupied, have an occupation. It sends chills up my spine. But look, so we won't get metaphysical I'm going to tell you that my occupation in the circus is pure fraud. I'm earning that money without doing anything."

"Wait till we open in San Isidro, it'll be harder. In Villa del Parque we had all the problems solved already, especially that bribe that had the Boss worried. Now we've got to start all over again with new people and you'll be occupied all right, since you like the expression."

"You don't say. Great, I've really got it made. So I'm really going to have to work?"

"For the first few days, then everything will fall into place. Tell me something, didn't you ever work when you were wandering around Europe?"

"As little as I could manage," Oliveira said. "I was a clandestine bookkeeper. Old man Trouille, a character out of Céline. I'll have to tell you all about it someday if it's worth the trouble, and it isn't."

"I'd like to hear," Traveler said.

"You know, everything's so much up in the air. Anything I told you would be like a piece of the pattern in a rug. It needs a coagulant, to give it some kind of name: plunk, everything falls into its proper place and there taking shape you have a beautiful crystal with all its facets. The bad part," Oliveira said, looking at his fingernails, "is that it's probably coagulated already and I didn't notice, I stayed behind with the old men who listen to people talking about cybernetics and slowly shake their heads thinking that soon it will be time for soup with vermicelli in it."

The canary Cien Pesos gave out a trill that was more of a squeal than anything else.

"All in all," Traveler said, "it occurs to me sometimes that you shouldn't have come back."

"You think about it," Oliveira said. "I live it. Underneath it all it's probably the same thing, but let's not go into a swoon over it. What's killing you and is killing me is modesty, you know. We walk around the house naked, to the great horror of some ladies, but when it comes to talking . . . You understand, sometimes it occurs to me that I might be able to tell you . . . I don't know, perhaps right now words could be good for something, could be useful to us. But since they're not words from everyday life and *mate* in the courtyard, well-oiled conversation, one draws back, from his best friend, no less, who is the one we have most trouble telling such things to. Doesn't it happen to you, that sometimes you confide much more in just anybody?"

"It could be," Traveler said, tuning the guitar. "The worst is that with these ideas one wonders what friends are good for."

"They're good just to be there, and they might just come in handy sometime."

"Whatever you say. So it's going to be hard for us to understand each other the way we used to in the past."

"In the name of the past we carry out the greatest deceits in the present," Oliveira said. "Look, Manolo, you talk about understanding each other, but basically you realize that I also want to come to some sort of understanding with you, and *you* means much more than you yourself. The burden is the fact that real understanding is something else. We're satisfied with too little. When friends understand each other well, when lovers understand each other well, when families understand each other well, then we think that everything is harmonious. Pure illusion, a mirror for larks. Sometimes I feel that there's more understanding between two people punching each other in the face than among those who are there looking on from outside. That's why . . . Hell, I really ought to write for the Sunday supplement of *La Nación*."

"You were doing fine," Traveler said, tuning the first string, "but you finally had one of those attacks of modesty that you were talking about before. You reminded me of Señora Gutusso when she feels obliged to mention her husband's piles."

"This Octavius Caesar says the oddest things," grumbled Don Crespo, looking at them over his glasses. "Here he's talking about Mark Antony's having eaten strange flesh on the Alps. What is he trying to tell me with that expression? Kid, I suppose."

"A featherless biped, more likely," Traveler said.

"It's hard to find anybody in this play who's not crazy," Don Crespo said respectfully. "You should see some of the things Cleopatra does."

"Queens are so complicated," Señora Gutusso said. "That Cleopatra was mixed up in all sorts of things, it was in a movie. Of course times were different then and they didn't have any religion."

"A trick," Talita said, picking up six cards from the deck.

"You're getting lucky . . . "

"I'm still losing really. Manú, I'm running out of change."

"Get some from Don Crespo who has probably reached the age of the pharaohs and will give you pieces of pure gold. Look, Horacio, what you were saying about harmony . . . "

"Well," Oliveira said, "since you insist I turn my pockets inside out and put the lint on the table . . . "

"Something besides turning your pockets inside out. My impression is that you're peacefully watching how everybody else gets all mixed up. You're looking for that thing called harmony, but you're looking for it precisely in the place where you just said it didn't exist, between friends, in the family, in the city. Why are you looking for it in social organisms?"

"I don't know. I'm not even looking for it. It's all just happening to me."

"Why should it happen to you in such a way that the rest of us can't get any sleep because of you?"

"I haven't been sleeping very well either."

"Just to give an example, why did you get together with Gekrepten? Why do you come to see me? Don't you think perhaps that Gekrepten and we are the ones who are destroying your harmony?"

"She wants to drink some mandrake!" Don Crespo shouted, stunned.

"What?" asked Señora Gutusso.

"Mandrake! She tells the slave-girl to pour her some mandrake. She says she wants to sleep. She's completely mad!"

"She ought to take some Bromural," Señora Gutusso said. "Of course in those days . . . "

"You're quite right, old man," Oliveira said, filling the glasses with *caña*. "The only thing wrong is that you're attaching too much importance to Gekrepten."

"What about us?"

"You people, well, you're probably that coagulant we were talking about a while back. It makes me think that our relationship is almost chemical, something outside ourselves. A sort of sketch that is being done. You came to meet me, don't forget."

"And why not? I never thought you would have come back with all that resentment, that they would have changed you so much over there; that you would have given me such an urge to be different . . . That's not what I mean. Hell, you don't live and you don't let live."

A *cielito* was being played on the guitar between them.

"All you have to do is snap your fingers like that," Oliveira said in a very low voice, "and you won't see me again. It wouldn't be fair that just because of me, you and Talita should . . . "

"Leave Talita out of this."

"No," Oliveira said. "I couldn't think of leaving her out. All of us, Talita, you, and I, we form a triangle that is exceedingly trismegistic. I'll tell you again: just give me a signal and I'll break it off. Don't think I haven't noticed how worried you've been."

"You won't fix anything by going away now."

"Why not, man? You don't need me."

Traveler began the prelude to *Malevaje*, stopped. It was already dark, and Don Crespo turned on the light in the courtyard so he could read.

"Look," Traveler said in a low voice. "In any case, some day you're going to beat it and there won't be any need for me to go around giving you signals. I may not be able to sleep at night, as Talita has probably told you, but underneath it all, I'm not sorry you've come back. What's more likely is that I needed you."

"Whatever you say, old man. That's the way things turn out, the best thing is to keep cool. It's not so bad for me either."

"This sounds like a dialogue between two idiots," Traveler said.

"Pure-bred mongoloids," said Oliveira.

"You think you're going to explain something, and it gets worse every time."

"Explanation is a well-dressed mistake," Oliveira said. "Make a note of that."

"Yes, it's much better to talk about other things then, about what's going on in the Radical party. It's just that you . . . But it's like a merry-go-round, it always comes back to the same thing, the white horse, then the red one, the white one again. We're poets, brother."

"Terrific troubadours," Oliveira said, filling up the glasses. "People who don't sleep well and go over to the window to get a breath of fresh air, things like that."

"So you did see me last night."

"Let me think. First Gekrepten got to be a drag and I had to temporize. Just a little, but still . . . Then I slept like a log, trying to forget. Why do you ask?"

"No reason," Traveler said, and slapped his hand across the strings. Jingling her winnings, Señora Gutusso brought a chair over and asked Traveler to sing.

"A man named Enobarbus said in here that night dampness is poisonous," Don Crespo informed them. "They're all crazy in this book, in the middle of a battle they start talking about things that have nothing to do with what's going on."

"Well, then," Traveler said, "let's do the lady's pleasure, if Don Crespo doesn't mind. *Malevaje*, a bona fide tango by Juan de Dios Filiberto. Say, old buddy, remind me to read you Ivonne Guitry's confession, it's something great. Talita, go and get the Gardel anthology. It's on the bedside table, where something like that should be."

"And give it back to me while you're at it," Señora Gutusso said. "I don't need it, but I like to have the books I like close to me. My husband is just the same, I might add."

(–47)

47

I am I, I am he. We are, but I am I, first I am I, I will defend being I until I am unable to fight any longer. I am I, Atalía. *Ego. Yo.* A professional degree, an Argentine, a scarlet fingernail, pretty sometimes, big dark eyes, I. Atalía Donosi, I. *Yo.* Yo-yo, windlass and hawser. Funny.

What a nut, Manú, going to the Casa América and renting this thing just to have some fun. REWIND. What a voice, that's not my voice. False and forced: "I am I, I am he. We are, but I am I, first I am I, I will defend . . ." STOP. Wonderful machine, but it's no good thinking out loud, or maybe you have to get used to it. Manú talks about recording his famous radio script about fine ladies; he won't do anything. The magic eye is really magical, green slits that oscillate, contract, a one-eyed cat staring at me. Maybe I should cover it with a piece of cardboard. REWIND. The tape runs so smoothly, so regularly. VOLUME. Put it on 5 or 5½: "The magic eye is really magical, green slits that osci . . ." But what would really be magic would be for my voice to have said: "The magic eye plays secretly, red slits . . ." Too much echo. I have to put the microphone closer and lower the volume. I am I, I am he. What I really am is a bad parody of Faulkner. Cheap effects. Does he dictate to a magnetic recorder or does he use whiskey for tape? Do you say magnetic recorder or tape recorder? Horacio says magnetic recorder, he was surprised when he saw the machine, he said: "What a fine magnetic recorder, old man!" The manual calls it a tape recorder, they ought to know in the Casa América. Mystery: Why does Manú buy everything, even his shoes, in the Casa América? A fixation, a touch of idiocy. REWIND. This will be funny: " . . . Faulkner. Cheap effects." STOP. It isn't very funny listening to myself again. All this should take time, time, time. All this should take time. REWIND. Let's see if the tone is more natural: " . . . ime, time, time. All this should . . ." The same thing, the voice of a midget with a cold. One thing, though, I do a good job of running it, Manú will be surprised, he doesn't trust me with machines at all. Me, a pharmacist, Horacio doesn't even notice, he looks at a person like mashed potatoes going through a strainer, mush that comes oozing out on the other side, something to sit down to and eat. Rewind? No, let's keep on, let's turn out the lights. Let's try to speak in the third person . . . Then Talita Donosi turns out the lights and there isn't anything except the little magic eye with its red slits (maybe it'll come out green, maybe it'll come out purple) and the glow of her cigarette. Hot, and Manú hasn't come back from San Isidro, eleven-thirty. There's Gekrepten at the window, I don't see her but she's there just the same, she's at the window in her nightgown, and Horacio at his tiny table, with a candle, reading and smoking. Horacio and Gekrepten's room, I don't know why, seems less like a hotel than this one. Stupid, it's enough of a hotel so that even the cockroaches must have the room number written on their backs, and they have to put up with Don Bunche next door and his tubercular patients at twenty pesos a visit, the cripples and the epileptics. And below them the brothel, and the tangos that the errand-girl sings out of tune. REWIND. A good stretch, I should go back half a minute at least. It goes against time, Manú would like to talk about that. Volume 5: " . . . the room number written on their backs . . . " Farther back. REWIND. Now: " . . . Horacio at his tiny table with a green candle . . . " STOP. Tiny, tiny. There's no reason to say tiny when you're a pharmacist. Pure corn. Tiny table! Misapplied tenderness. OK, Talita. Enough of inanities. REWIND. All of it, until the tape is ready to come loose, the trouble with this machine is that you have to judge carefully, if the tape comes loose you lose half a minute putting it back on again. STOP. Just right by an inch. I wonder what I said at the beginning? I can't remember any more but my voice sounded like a frightened little rat, the well-known mike fright. Let's see, volume 5½ so it'll be easier to hear. "I am I, I am he. We are but I am I, fir . . . " And why, why did I say that? I am I, I am he, and then talking about the tiny table, and then getting annoyed. "I am I, I am he. I am I, I am he."

Talita turned off the recorder, shut the cover, looked at it with deep disgust, and poured herself a glass of lemonade. She didn't want to think about the business of the clinic (the Manager called it "the mental clinic", which was idiotic) but if she refused to think about the clinic (besides the fact that this matter of refusing to think was more of a hope than a reality) she immediately got into another equally bothersome sphere. She thought about Manú and Horacio at the same time, in the scales simile that she and Horacio had manipulated in such an ostentatious way in the circus box-office. Then the feeling of being inhabited became stronger, at least the clinic was an idea of fear, of the unknown, a hair-raising vision of raving maniacs in nightshirts chasing her with razors and grabbing stools and bed-legs, vomiting on their temperature charts and masturbating ritually. It was going to be very amusing seeing Manú and Horacio in white lab coats, taking care of the lunatics. "I'll have a certain importance," Talita thought modestly. "The Manager will definitely put me in charge of the clinic's pharmacy. It's probably a little first-aid station. Manú is going to tease me about it as usual." She would have to review certain things, so much gets forgotten, time with its fine sandpaper, the indescribable daily battle that summer, the waterfront and the heat, Horacio coming down the gangplank with a friendless face, the rudeness of sending her off with the cat, you take the streetcar back because we've got to talk. And then a period began that was like waste ground full of twisted cans, hooks that could hurt your feet, dirty puddles, pieces of rag caught on the thistles, the circus at night with Horacio and Manú looking at her or looking at each other, the cat getting stupider every day or really more brilliant, solving problems to the delighted shrieks of the audience, the walks home with stopoffs in bars so Manú and Horacio could drink some beer, talking, talking about nothing, listening to herself talking in this heat and this smoke and the fatigue. *I am I, I am he*, she had said it without thinking, that is, it was beyond being thought, it came from a region where words were like the lunatics in the clinic, menacing or absurd entities living an isolated life of their own, jumping up suddenly without anybody being able to tie them down: *I am I, I am he*, and he wasn't Manú, he was Horacio, the inhabitant, the treacherous attacker, the shadow within the shadow of his room at night, the glow of his cigarette slowly sketching out the shapes of his insomnia.

When Talita was afraid, she would get up and make herself some tea that was half linden, half mint. She did it hoping with great longing that Manú's key would scratch on the door. Manú had said with soaring words: "Horacio doesn't care a damn about you." It was insulting but tranquillizing. Manú had said that even if Horacio had made a pass (and he hadn't, he'd never even hinted)

one of linden

one of mint

the water good and hot, first sign, of boiling, stop

not even then would she have meant anything to him. But then. But if it didn't make any difference to him, why always be there in the corner of the room smoking or reading, *be* (I am I, I am he) there as if he were needing her in some way, yes, just that exactly, needing her, hanging on to her from a distance to reach something, the better to see something, the better to be something. Then it wasn't: I am I, I am he. Then it was the opposite: I am he *because* I am I. Talita sighed, satisfied a little with her good powers of reason and the good taste of the tea.

But that wasn't all there was to it, because then it would have been too easy. It couldn't be (there's a reason for logic) that Horacio was interested and at the same time was not interested. The combination of the two things should have produced a third, something that had nothing to do with love, for example (it was so stupid to think about love when love was only Manú, only Manú until the end of time), something that was close to being a hunt, a search, or rather a terrible expectation, like the cat looking at the canary it cannot reach, a kind of congealing of time and day, a kind of crouching. A lump and a half, the soft smell of the country. A crouching without explanations, the-way-things-look-from-here, or until one day when Horacio would deign to speak, go away, shoot himself, any explanation or material on which one could imagine an explanation. Not that business of being there drinking *mate* and looking at them, making Manú drink *mate* and look at him, making the three of them dance a slow interminable pattern. "I should be a novelist," Talita thought, "marvellous ideas come to me." She was so depressed that she turned on the tape recorder again and sang songs until Traveler came home. They both agreed that Talita's voice did not come out too well, and Traveler showed her how a *baguala* should be sung. They brought the recorder over to the window so Gekrepten could be the impartial judge, and even Horacio if he was in the room, but he wasn't. Gekrepten found everything perfect and they decided to have dinner together at the Travelers', combining a cold roast that Talita had with a tossed salad that Gekrepten would make before coming over. This all seemed perfect to Talita and at the same time there was something like a bedcover about it, or a teapot cover, or some kind of cover, just like the recorder or Traveler's satisfied air, things done or decided, to be put on top, but on top of what, that was the problem and the reason that everything underneath it all was still the way it had been before the half-linden, half-mint tea.

(–110)

48

Next to El Cerro – although you never really do get next to El Cerro, you arrive all at once and never know actually whether you're already there or not, near El Cerro would be better – in a section with low buildings and arguing children, his questions got him nowhere, they would all shatter against pleasant smiles, women who wanted to be helpful but didn't really know anything, people move away, sir, there've been a lot of changes here, maybe if you go to the police they'll be able to tell you. And he didn't stay too long because the ship was going to sail, and though he kept it deep inside himself, everything had been hopeless from the start, his investigations had had their source in his doubts, like playing the numbers or working out a horoscope. Another tram back to the pier to flop down on his bunk until it was time to eat.

That same night, around two o'clock in the morning, was the first time he saw her again. It was hot, and in the steerage where a hundred-odd immigrants were snoring and sweating it was worse than sitting on the coils of a hawser underneath the dull river sky, as all the dampness of the harbour stuck to his skin. Oliveira sat down against a bulkhead to smoke, studying the few stars that were sneaking in and out of the clouds. La Maga came from behind a ventilator funnel, holding something in her hand that was dragging along the deck, and almost immediately she turned her back on him and went towards one of the hatchways. Oliveira made no attempt to follow her; he knew only too well that he was looking at something that would not let itself be followed. He thought that she was probably one of those snobs from first class who like to descend even to the filth of the forecastle, thirsting for something they would call experience or life, things like that. She did look a lot like La Maga, that was certain, but he had supplied the main part of the resemblance, so that once his heart stopped heaving like a mad dog he lit another cigarette and called himself a hopeless idiot.

To have thought that he had seen La Maga was less bitter than the certainty that some uncontrollable desire had brought her up out of the depths of that place defined as the subconscious and had been able to project her onto the silhouette of any one of the women on board. Until that moment he had believed that he could allow himself the luxury of the melancholy memory of certain things, evoke determined stories in a proper time and atmosphere, then put an end to them with the same tranquillity with which he would crush a butt in an ashtray. When Traveler introduced him to Talita on the dock, so ridiculous with that cat in a basket and an air somewhere between pleasant and Alida Valli, he again felt certain remote likenesses condensing quickly into a total false resemblance, as if from out of his apparently so well compartmentalized memory a piece of ectoplasm had suddenly emerged, capable of inhabiting and complementing another body and another face, of looking at him from outside in a way that he had thought for ever restricted to memories.

In the weeks following that were dragged along by Gekrepten's irresistible abnegation and his apprenticeship in the difficult art of selling cashmere samples from door to door, he had more than enough glasses of beer and time spent on park benches in which to dissect episodes. His explorations in El Cerro had seemed on the outside like a discharge of conscience: find, try to explain, say goodbye for ever. That tendency of man to finish cleanly what he does, without leaving any threads hanging. Now he was beginning to realize (a shadow from behind a ventilator, a woman with a cat) that this was not why he had gone to El Cerro. Analytical psychology irritated him, but it was true: this was not why he had gone to El Cerro. Suddenly he was a pit falling infinitely into himself. He scolded himself ironically, right in the middle of the Plaza del Congreso: "And you called that a search? Did you think you were free? What was that business about Heraclitus? Let's see, repeat the steps of liberation, so I can have a little laugh. But you're at the bottom of the funnel, pal." He would have liked to be sure that he had been irreparably debased by his discovery, but he was bothered by a vague satisfaction in the region of his stomach, that feline answer of contentment which the body gives when it laughs at the restless schpells of the schpirit and hunches comfortably into its ribs, its belly, and the flat soles of its feet. The worst of it was that deep down inside he was rather content to feel that way, to feel that he hadn't come back, that he was still going away even though he didn't know where. On top of the contentment he was being burned by a kind of desperation for simple understanding, a cry for something that he would have liked to make into flesh and blood, and which this vegetative contentment was sluggishly rejecting, keeping it at a distance. There were moments when Oliveira would be present like a spectator at this discord, not caring to participate, cynically impartial. That's what happened with the circus, the *mate* sessions in Don Crespo's patio, Traveler's tangos – Oliveira would look at himself out of the corner of his eye in all of those mirrors. He even wrote down some odd thoughts in a notebook that Gekrepten lovingly kept in the dresser drawer, not daring to read it. He was slowly realizing that his visit to El Cerro had been good, precisely because it had been based on other reasons than those he had imagined. To know that he was in love with La Maga was neither a defeat nor any sort of fixation in any outdated order of things; a love that could do without its object, that could find its nourishment in nothingness, that could be totalled up and come out as other strengths, defining them and bringing them together into an impulse that one day would destroy that visceral contentment of a body stuffed with beer and fried potatoes. All the words he used to fill the notebook along with great flourishes in the air and shrill whistles made him laugh like a madman. Traveler would finally come to the window and ask him to quieten down a little. But other times Oliveira would find a certain peace in manual chores, like straightening out nails or unweaving sisal threads, using the fibres to construct a delicate labyrinth which would cling to the lampshade and which Gekrepten would describe as elegant. Maybe love was the highest enrichment, a giver of being; but only by bungling it could one avoid its boomerang effect, let it run off into nothingness, and sustain one's self alone again on this new step of open and porous reality. Killing the beloved object, that ancient fear of man, was the price paid for not stopping on the stairs, just as Faust's plea to the passing moment would not have made sense if he had not abandoned it at the same time, just as one puts down an empty glass on the table. And things like that, and bitter *mate.*

It would have been so easy to organize a coherent scheme, an order of thought and life, a harmony. All that was needed was the usual hypocrisy, elevate the past to the value of experience, derive profit from the wrinkles on one's face, from the knowing look one sees in smiles and silences after forty years. Then one would put on a blue suit, comb one's greying hair, and go to art galleries, to the Sociedad Argentina de Escritores and the Richmond bar, reconciled with the world. A discreet scepticism, an air of having returned, a measured entrance into maturity, into matrimony, into the paternal sermon at carving time or on receipt of an unsatisfactory report card. I am telling you this because I have lived longer than you. I've been around. When I was a boy. They're all alike, *te lo digo yo.* I'm telling you this from my own experience, son. You don't know what life is yet.

And all of it, so ridiculous and gregarious, could have been even worse on other levels, in meditations constantly menaced by *idola fori,* words that falsify institutions, turning things to stone in the name of simplification, moments of fatigue in which one slowly takes the flag of surrender from one's vest pocket. The betrayal could have taken place in perfect solitude, without witnesses or accomplices: hand to hand, believing one's self to be beyond personal compromises and dramas of the senses, beyond the ethical torture of knowing that one is tied to a race or to a people and a language at least. In what is apparently perfect freedom, not having to render accounts to anyone, leaving the game, leaving the crossroads and following any one of the roads put there by circumstance, proclaiming it to be the necessary one or the only one. La Maga was one of those roads, literature was another (burn the notebook at once, even if Gekrepten wu-rr-inggs her hands), laziness was something else, and meditation on the sovereign kicking of the bucket was something else. Stopping in front of a pizzeria at 1300 Corrientes, Oliveira asked himself the great question: "Must one stay at the centre of the crossroads, then, like the hub of a wheel? What good is it to know or to think we know that every road is false if we don't walk with an idea that is not the road itself? We're not Buddha, and there are no trees here to sit under in the lotus position. A cop appears and asks for your identity card."

Walking with an idea that is no longer the road itself. From all that chatter (what a combination, ch, mother of chigger, cheese, and chilli beans) the only thing left was that glimpse. Yes, it was a formula that deserved meditation. In that way his visit to El Cerro would have had to have a meaning after all, in that way La Maga would cease being a lost object and become the image of a possible reunion – no longer with her but on this side of her or on the other side of her, by her, but not her – . And Manú, and the circus, and that incredible idea of the madhouse that they were talking about so much at that time, everything could have meaning just as long as it was extrapolated, the whinevitable whextrapolation at the metaphysical whour, that stately word was always on time. Oliveira took a bite of pizza, burning his gums in his usual gluttonous way, and he felt better. But how many times had he gone through the same cycle on dozens of corners and in cafés in so many cities, how many times had he reached similar conclusions, felt better, thought he could begin to live in a different way; one afternoon, for example, when he had gone in to listen to an idiotic concert, and afterwards . . . Afterwards it had rained so much, why think about it. That's the way it was with Talita, the more he thought about it the worse it was. The woman was beginning to suffer because of him, not for any serious reason, just because he was there and everything seemed to be changing between Talita and Traveler, heaps of little things like that, taken for granted and dismissed, and suddenly they start to get sharp edges and what had started out as a Spanish stew ends up as a Kierkegaardian herring, without going any deeper into the matter. The afternoon with the boards had been a return to order, but Traveler had let the chance of saying what had to be said slip by, so that on that very day when Oliveira would have ordered himself to change neighbourhoods and their lives, he not only had said nothing, but he had got him the job with the circus, proof that . . . In that case pity would have been just as idiotic as the other time: rain, rain. I wonder if Berthe Trépat still plays the piano?

(–111)

49

Talita and Traveler talked at great length about famous madmen and others less well known now that Ferraguto had decided to buy the clinic and turn the circus, cat and all, over to somebody called Suárez Melián. It seemed to them, Talita especially, that the change from circus to clinic was like a step forward, but it was hard for Traveler to see very clearly the reasons for that optimism. In hopes of understanding better they went around in great excitement and were always going over to their windows or down to the street entrance to exchange impressions with Señora Gutusso, Don Bunche, Don Crespo, and even with Gekrepten if she was within range. The worst of it was that in those days there was a lot of talk of a revolt, that the armed forces in Campo de Mayo were about to rise up, and all that seemed much more important to people than the acquisition of a clinic on the Calle Trelles. Finally Talita and Traveler set out to try to find a little normality in a psychiatry text. As usual they got excited over anything, and the day of the duck, it was hard to tell why, their arguments became so violent that Cien Pesos was going crazy in his cage and Don Crespo waited for an acquaintance to go by so he could move his index finger in a circular pattern next to his forehead. On occasions like that thick clouds of duck feathers would come flying out of the kitchen window and there would be a slamming of doors and a hand-to-hand dialectic without quarter which would barely give way to lunchtime, when the duck would disappear right down to the last tegument.

When it was time for coffee and some Mariposa *caña*, a tacit reconciliation brought them together over venerated texts, issues of esoteric reviews, long out of print, cosmological treasures that they felt they had to assimilate as a sort of prelude to their new life. They talked a lot about eccentricities, because Traveler, with Oliveira's approval, had condescended to bring out some old papers and exhibit part of his collection of phenomena, something they had begun together when they were both studying in the long-forgotten university and which they had kept up separately later on. The study of those documents was a fine dessert, and Talita had earned the right to participate thanks to her copies of *Renovigo* (*Periódiko Rebolusionario Bilingue*), a Mexican publication in the Ispamerikan tongue put out by Editorial Lumen, on which a number of madmen had collaborated with exciting results. They only heard from Ferraguto every so often, because the circus was practically in the hands of Suárez Melián already, but it seemed certain that the clinic would be turned over to them around the middle of March. Once or twice Ferraguto had shown up at the circus to watch the calculating cat, from whom he was obviously going to find it difficult to be parted, and both times he spoke about the imminence of the great transaction and the-weighty-responsibilities that would fall on their shoulders (sigh). It seemed practically assured that Talita would be entrusted with the pharmacy, and the poor girl was extremely nervous, reviewing some notes from the time of her anointment. Oliveira and Traveler amused themselves endlessly at her expense, but when they went back to the circus they would both walk around sadly and look at the people and the cat as if a circus were something unappreciably rare.

"They're a lot crazier here," Traveler would say. "There won't be any comparison."

Oliveira would shrug-his-shoulders, incapable of saying that he felt the same way inside, and he would look up at the top of the tent, losing himself stupidly in uncertain ruminations.

"Of course you have changed as you went from place to place," Traveler would grumble. "Me too, but always here, always in this meridian . . ."

He would stretch out his arm and take in the vague geography of Buenos Aires.

"Changes, you know . . ." Oliveira would say.

While they were talking that way they would choke with laughter, and the audience would look at them out of the corner of their eyes because they were distracting their attention.

In moments of confidence, the three of them would admit that they were admirably prepared for their new duties. For example, the arrival of the Sunday edition of *La Nación* would provoke in them a sadness comparable only to people lined up at the movies and reprints from the *Reader's Digest.*

"Contacts are getting cut off more all the time," Traveler would say with a note of prophecy. "You have to give great shouts."

"Colonel Flappa already gave one last night," Talita answered. "Result, a state of siege."

"That's not a shout, girl, just a death-rattle. I'm talking about the things Yrigoyen used to dream about, historic cuspidations, prophetic promissorations, those hopes of mankind that have reached such bad shape in these parts."

"You're talking just like the other one now," Talita said, looking at him worriedly but hiding her characterological glance.

The other one was still at the circus, giving Suárez Melián some last-minute help and being surprised sometimes at the fact that he was becoming so indifferent to everything. He had the feeling that he had turned over the mane he had left to Talita and Traveler, who were getting more and more excited thinking about the clinic; the only thing he really liked doing those days was playing with the calculating cat, who had taken an enormous liking to him and would do additions for his exclusive pleasure. Since Ferraguto had given instructions that the cat was not to be taken into the street except in a basket and with an identification collar like army dog-tags from the Battle of Okinawa, Oliveira understood the cat's feelings and as soon as they were two blocks away from the circus he would leave the basket in a delicatessen he could trust, take the collar off the poor animal, and the two of them would wander around inspecting empty cans in vacant lots or nibbling grass, a delightful occupation. After those hygienic walks it was almost tolerable for Oliveira to become involved in the gatherings in Don Crespo's courtyard, in Gekrepten's tender insistence on knitting him things for winter. The night that Ferraguto telephoned the boarding house to tell Traveler about the imminent date of the great transaction, the three of them were perfecting their notions of the Ispamerikan language, extracted with infinite joy from an issue of *Renovigo.* They became almost sad thinking that in the clinic seriousness, science, abnegation, and all of those things were waiting for them.

"*¿Ké bida no es trajedia?*" Talita read in excellent Ispamerikan. They went on like that until Señora Gutusso arrived with the latest radio news bulletin about Colonel Flappa and his tanks, something real and concrete at last that scattered them immediately, to the surprise of the informant, drunk with patriotic feelings.

(–118)

50

The Calle Trelles was just a step away from the bus stop, a little over three blocks. Ferraguto and Cuca were already there with the superintendent when Talita and Traveler arrived. The great transaction was taking place in a room on the second floor, with two windows that opened onto the courtyard garden where the patients took their walks and a little stream could be seen rising and falling in a concrete fountain. To reach the room Talita and Traveler had to go through several hallways and rooms on the ground floor, where ladies and gentlemen had addressed them in correct Spanish, asking for the kind donation of a pack or two of cigarettes. The male nurse who accompanied them seemed to find this interlude perfectly natural, and the circumstances did not favour any preliminary question in the nature of an orientation. Practically out of cigarettes, they reached the room of the great transaction where Ferraguto pompously introduced them to the superintendent. Halfway through the reading of an unintelligible document Oliveira appeared, and they had to explain to him with whispers and hidden gestures that everything was going along fine and that nobody understood much of anything. When Talita succinctly whispered to him about her complicated arrival shh shh, Oliveira looked at her puzzled because he had come in through an entrance that led right to that door. As for the Boss, he was dressed in black as called for by the occasion.

The heat was the kind that lowered the pitch of the radio announcers' voices as every hour they would first give the weather report and then the official denials of the uprising in Campo de Mayo and Colonel Flappa's grim intentions. The superintendent had interrupted the reading of the document at five minutes to six to turn on his Japanese transistor radio in order to keep up, as he affirmed after begging their pardon, with the news. That expression immediately brought on in Oliveira the classic look of one who has forgotten something in the hallway downstairs (and one that even the superintendent would have to recognize as another form of contact with facts), and in spite of the fierce looks from Traveler and Talita he tore out of the room by the first available door, which was not the one he had come in by.

From a couple of phrases in the document he had surmised that the clinic had five floors and in addition a summerhouse at the rear of the garden. The best thing to do would be to take a turn around the garden, if he could find his way, but he didn't get the chance because no sooner had he gone twenty feet than a young man in shirtsleeves approached smiling, took him by the hand, and led him, swinging his arm the way children do, up to a corridor where there were many doors and something that must have been the opening of a service lift. The idea of getting to know the clinic in the care of a madman was exceedingly agreeable, and the first thing Oliveira did was to offer his companion a cigarette. He was an intelligent-looking young man who accepted the cigarette and whistled with satisfaction. Then it turned out that he was an attendant and that Oliveira was not a patient, the usual misunderstandings in cases like that. The episode was cute and didn't have much to offer, but as they went from one floor to another, Oliveira and Remorino became friendly and the inside topography of the clinic was explained, with anecdotes, jibes at the rest of the personnel, and watch-out-fors between friends. They were in the room where Dr Ovejero kept his guinea pigs and a picture of Monica Vitti when a cross-eyed boy appeared, running over to tell Romorino that if the gentleman with him was Señor Horacio Oliveira, etc. With a sigh, Oliveira went down two flights and returned to the room of the great transaction where the document was dragging along to its conclusions in the midst of Cuca Ferraguto's menopausal rushes and Traveler's rude yawns. Oliveira was still thinking about the figure dressed in pink pyjamas he had glimpsed on turning the corner of the hallway on the fourth floor, a man who was getting old and who was walking along close to the wall stroking a pigeon that seemed to be asleep in his hand. It was exactly at that moment that Cuca Ferraguto let out a kind of bellow.

"What do you mean, they have to okay it?"

"Be quiet, dear," the Boss said. "The gentleman means . . . "

"It's quite clear," said Talita, who had always got along with Cuca and wanted to help her. "The transfer requires the approval of the patients."

"But that's crazy," Cuca said, very *ad hoc.*

"My dear lady," the superintendent said, plucking at his vest with his free hand. "The patients here are very special, and the Méndez Delfino Act is quite clear in this respect. Except for eight or nine who have families that have given their approval, the rest have spent all their lives between one asylum and another, if I may use the term, and no one is responsible for them. In these cases the law allows the superintendent to get from them in lucid moments their approval of the transfer of the clinic to a new owner. Here are their statements, waiting to be signed," he added, showing her a book bound in red with strips cut from the comic section sticking out. "Read them, that's all there is to it."

"If I understand correctly," Ferraguto said, "this negotiation has to be done right now."

"And why do you think I've had you all come here? You as owner and these gentlemen as witnesses: let's start bringing in the patients and we can get it all done this afternoon."

"The point," Traveler said, "is that the ones who sign have to be in what you call their lucid moments."

The superintendent gave him a look of pity and pressed a buzzer. Remorino came in dressed in a smock; he winked at Oliveira and placed the enormous register on a small table. He placed a chair in front of the table, and folded his arms like a Persian executioner. Ferraguto, who had hastened to examine the register with the air of one who understood, asked if the approval should be signed at the bottom of the document, and the superintendent said yes, so now they would call the patients in in alphabetical order and ask them to give their stamp of approval under the influence of a large, round blue fountain pen. In spite of such efficient preparations, Traveler insisted on suggesting that maybe one of the patients would refuse to sign or would throw a sudden scene. Although they didn't dare to back him openly, Cuca and Ferraguto were hanging-on-his-every-word.

(–119)

51

Remorino appeared just then with an old man who seemed rather startled, and who when he recognized the superintendent greeted him with a sort of bow.

"In pyjamas," said Cuca, dumbfounded.

"I noticed when we came in," Ferraguto said.

"They weren't pyjamas. More like . . . "

"Quiet please," the superintendent said. "Come here, Antúnez, and put your signature where Remorino will show you."

The old man examined the register closely while Remorino held the pen out to him. Ferraguto took out his handkerchief and dried his forehead with a few soft dabs.

"This is page eight," Antúnez said, "and I think that I ought to sign on page one."

"Right here," said Remorino, showing him a place in the register. "Come on, your *café con leche* is getting cold."

Antúnez signed with a flourish, bowed to everyone, and went out with little pink steps that delighted Talita. The second pair of pyjamas was much fatter, and after circumnavigating the table he went over and shook hands with the superintendent who took his hand grudgingly and pointed to the register with a curt gesture.

"You know all about it already, so sign the book and then return to your room."

"My room hasn't been swept out," fat pyjamas said.

Cuca made a mental note of the lack of cleanliness. Remorino tried to put the pen in the hand of fat pyjamas, who drew back slowly.

"It'll be cleaned right away," Remorino said. "Sign your name, Don Nicanor."

"Never," said fat pyjamas. "It's a trick."

"Don't talk to me about tricks," the superintendent said. "Dr Ovejero has already explained to you what it's all about. You people sign now and starting tomorrow you get double rations of rice and milk."

"I won't sign unless Don Antúnez agrees," fat pyjamas said.

"It so happens he signed it just before you. Take a look."

"I can't make out the signature. This isn't Don Antúnez's signature. You got him to sign with an electric cattle prod. You killed Don Antúnez."

"Go and bring him back," the superintendent ordered Remorino, who flew out and came back with Antúnez. Fat pyjamas let out an exclamation of joy and went over to shake his hand.

"Tell him you agree and that he doesn't have to worry," the superintendent said. "Let's go, it's getting late."

"Go ahead and sign, son, don't be afraid," Antúnez told fat pyjamas. "After all, it won't change you in the head in any way."

Fat pyjamas dropped the pen. Remorino picked it up with a grumble, and the superintendent got up furiously. Hiding behind Antúnez, fat pyjamas was trembling and clutching at his sleeves. There was a soft knock on the door, and before Remorino could open it there entered without further ado a woman in a pink kimono, who went straight to the register and looked it all over as if it were a pickled sucking-pig. Straightening up satisfied, she put her hand on the register.

"I swear to tell the whole truth," the woman said. "You wouldn't tell me a lie, Don Nicanor."

Fat pyjamas nodded in approval and suddenly accepted the pen that Remorino was offering him and signed just where his hand happened to fall, without taking time for anything.

"Animal," they heard the superintendent mutter. "See if it came out in the right place, Remorino. Not too bad. And now you, Señora Schwitt, now that you're here. Show her the place, Remorino."

"Unless there's some improvement in the social environment I won't sign anything," said Señora Schwitt. "Doors and windows have to be opened to the spirit."

"I want two windows in my room," fat pyjamas said. "And Don Antúnez wants to go to the Franco-Inglesa chemist to buy some cotton wool and lots of other things. This place is so dark."

Turning his head a little, Oliveira saw that Talita was looking at him and he smiled at her. Both of them knew that the other one was thinking that this was all a comedy of idiots, that fat pyjamas and the rest of them were just as crazy as they were. Not very good actors, because they didn't make any effort to appear like decent lunatics in front of people who had done a good job of reading their manual of psychiatry for the layman. For example, over there, gripping her purse in both hands with complete self-assurance and sitting stolidly in her easy chair, Cuca seemed a good deal crazier than the three signatories, who now had begun to complain about something that sounded like the death of a dog, about which Señora Schwitt spread herself around with a luxury of gestures. Nothing was too unforeseeable; the most pedestrian causality continued governing those voluble and loquacious relationships in which the roars of the superintendent served as a continuous bass to the repeated designs of complaints and demands and the Franco-Inglesa. Thus they saw successively how Remorino took away Antúnez and fat pyjamas, how Señora Schwitt disdainfully signed the register, how a skeletal giant entered, a kind of gaunt flame in pink flannel, and behind him a young man with hair gone completely white and malignantly beautiful green eyes. These last two signed without any resistance, but then they decided that they wanted to stay until the end of the ceremony. To avoid any more disputes, the superintendent sent them over to a corner and Remorino went to bring in two more patients, a girl with bulky hips and a frightened man who would not lift his eyes from the floor. More surprising mention was made of the death of a dog. When the patients had signed, the girl curtsied like a ballerina. Cuca Ferraguto replied with a pleasant nod of the head, something that brought on a monstrous laughing attack in Talita and Traveler. There were already ten signatures in the register and Remorino continued bringing people in. There were greetings and a controversy here and there that interrupted things or changed protagonists; every so often a signature. It was already seven-thirty, and Cuca took out a compact and made up her face with the gestures of the wife of the head of a clinic, something in between Madame Curie and Edwige Feuillère. More wiggling on the part of Talita and Traveler, more restlessness on the part of Ferraguto, who alternately consulted the progress in the register and the face of the superintendent. At seven-forty a woman patient declared she would not sign until they killed the dog. Remorino promised her, winking in the direction of Oliveira, who appreciated the confidence. Twenty patients had come through and there were only forty-five left. The superintendent came over to them to let them know that the most difficult cases had already been stamped (that's how he put it) and the best thing to do would be to go into the next room for some beer and news reports. During the break they talked about psychiatry and politics. The revolt had been put down by the government forces, the leaders had surrendered in Luján. Dr Nerio Rojas was at a conference in Amsterdam. The beer, delicious.

At eight-thirty, forty-eight signatures had been obtained. It was getting dark, and the room was heavy with smoke and people in the corners, with the coughing that every so often came from one of those present. Oliveira would have liked to go out into the street, but the superintendent was strict and unyielding. The last three signatories had just demanded changes in the food (Ferraguto signalled Cuca to take notes, that's all they needed, in his clinic meals would be impeccable) and the death of the dog (Cuca put the fingers of her hand together in an Italianate way and showed them to Ferraguto, who shook his head perplexed and looked at the superintendent, who was very tired and shading his eyes with a calendar from a cake-shop). When the old man with the pigeon in the hollow of his hand arrived, slowly petting it as if he wanted to make it sleep, there was a long pause while everyone stopped to contemplate the motionless dove, and it was almost a pity that the patient had to interrupt his rhythmic caresses on the pigeon's back to reach out slowly for the pen that Remorino was holding out to him. After the old man, two sisters entered arm in arm and as soon as they were in the room demanded the death of the dog and other improvements in the establishment. The business of the dog made Remorino laugh, but Oliveira finally felt as if something was getting dammed up in him all the way up to his spleen, and getting up he told Traveler he was going to take a walk and that he would be right back.

"You have to stay," the superintendent said. "You're a witness."

"I'm in the building," Oliveira said. "Check the Méndez Delfino Act, it's all provided for."

"I'll go with you," Traveler said. "We'll be back in five minutes."

"Don't leave the premises," the superintendent said.

"Don't worry," said Traveler. "Come on, old man, I think we can get down to the garden this way. Disappointing, don't you think?"

"Unanimity is boring," Oliveira said. "Not one of them has done anything distinct. Look at the way they are about the dog. Let's sit down by the fountain, the trickle of water has a lustral air about it that will do us good."

"It smells like naphtha," Traveler said. "Really lustral, as a matter of fact."

"What did we expect, really? You can see how they all sign, there's no difference between them and us. No difference at all. We're going to be stupendously comfortable here."

"Well," Traveler said, "there is one difference: they go around in pink."

"Look," Oliveira said, pointing at the upper floors. It was already almost dark, and in the windows of the third and fourth floors lights were going on and off rhythmically. Light in one window and darkness in the one next door. Vice versa. Light on one floor, darkness on the one above, vice versa.

"It's started," Traveler said. "Lots of signatures, but now they're beginning to show their worse side."

They decided to finish their cigarettes next to the lustral trickle, talking about nothing and looking at the lights that were going on and off. That was when Traveler spoke about changes, and then after a silence he could hear Horacio laughing softly in the darkness. He kept on, wanting some certainty but not knowing how to bring up a subject that would slip out of the grasp of words and ideas.

"As if we were vampires, as if a single circulatory system united us – disunited us, that is. Sometimes you and I, sometimes the three of us, let's not fool ourselves. I don't know when it started, that's the way it is and we have to open our eyes to it. I don't think we're here just because we came with the Boss. It would have been easy to have stayed on at the circus with Suárez Melián, we know the work and they appreciate us. But no, we had to come here. The three of us. I'm the first one to blame because I didn't want Talita to think . . . Well, that I was putting you aside in this business of trying to get away from you. A matter of self-respect, you realize."

"Actually," Oliveira said, "I have no reason to take this job. I'm going back to the circus, or better still, away from everything. Buenos Aires is a big place. I already told you all this once."

"Yes, but you'll be leaving after we had this conversation. I mean you'll be doing it for me and that's just what I don't want."

"In any case, explain what you mean by changes."

"How should I know? If I tried to explain, it would get even hazier for me. Look, it's something like this: as long as I'm with you there's no problem, but as soon as I'm alone I get the feeling that you're putting pressure on me, from your room, for example. Remember the other day when you asked me for the nails. Talita feels it too, she looks at me and I get the feeling that the look is meant for you; when the three of us are together, though, she can go for hours without noticing that you're around. You must have spotted that, I suppose."

"Yes. Go on."

"That's all, and that's why I don't think it would be any good for me to help you go off by yourself. It has to be something you decide alone and now since I've been stupid enough to bring the matter up with you, you don't even have the freedom to decide, because you're going to raise the question from the responsibility angle and we'll be done for. The ethical thing in this case would be to pardon the life of a friend, and I can't accept that."

"Oh," said Oliveira. "So you won't allow me to go away, and I can't do it by myself. There's a touch of pink pyjamas about a situation like that, don't you think?"

"There probably is."

"Funny, isn't it?"

"What?"

"All the lights went out at the same time."

"They must have got the last signature. The clinic belongs to the Boss, long live Ferraguto!"

"I guess now we'll have to satisfy them and kill the dog. It's incredible the way they dislike it."

"Not dislike," Traveler said. "For the moment passions don't seem to get very violent here either."

"You have a need for radical solutions, old man. The same thing used to happen to me for a long time, and then . . . "

They began to walk back, carefully, because the garden was very dark and they couldn't remember where the flowerbeds were located. When they stepped on the hopscotch, near the doorway now, Traveler laughed softly and picking up one foot began to hop from square to square. The chalk design glowed weakly in the darkness.

"One of these nights I'm going to tell you about over there," Oliveira said. "I don't want to, but it's probably the only way we can get to kill the dog, to use that image."

Traveler jumped off the hopscotch, and at the same time the lights on the third floor suddenly went on. Oliveira, who was going to say something else, saw Traveler's face come out of the darkness, and in the instant the lights stayed on before going out again, he was surprised by a grimace, a rictus (from the Latin *rictus*, the opening of a mouth: the contraction of the lips, similar to a smile).

"Talking about killing the dog," Traveler said, "did you notice that the head doctor's name is Ovejero? Sheepdog, crazy."

"That's not what you wanted to tell me."

"Look who's complaining about my silences or substitutions," Traveler said. "Of course that's not what I wanted to say, but what the hell's the difference. It's something that can't be expressed. If you want to try to prove it . . . But something tells me it's a little too late already, you know. The pizza's cooled off, you can't turn it over any more. The best thing for us would be to get to work right away, it'll be a good distraction."

Oliveira did not answer, and they went up to the room of the great transaction where the superintendent and Ferraguto were having a double shot of *caña*. Oliveira followed suit immediately, but Traveler went over and sat on the sofa where Talita was reading a novel with a sleepy face. After the last signature, Remorino had removed the register and the patients who had been witnessing the ceremony. Traveler noticed that the superintendent had turned off the ceiling light and was using instead a lamp on the desk; everything was bland and green, they were talking in low and satisfied voices. He heard them making plans to go and have some tripe *genovese* in a restaurant downtown. Talita closed her book and looked at him sleepily, Traveler stroked her hair and he felt better. In any case, the idea of tripe at that hour and in that heat was insane.

(–69)

52

Because he really was unable to *tell* Traveler anything. If he began to pull at the ball of yarn he would get a thread of wool, yards of wool, *lana*, lanadir, lanagnorisis, lanaturner, lannapurna, lanatomy, lannuity, lanativity, lanationality, lanature, *lana ad lanauseam* but never the ball of yarn. He would have had to make Traveler suspect that what he was telling him did not make any direct sense (but what kind of sense did it make?) and that it wasn't any kind of image or allegory either. The unbridgeable difference, a problem of levels that had nothing to do with intelligence or information, it was one thing to play *truco* or discuss John Donne with Traveler, everything took place in a territory of appearances in common; but the other way, to be a kind of monkey among men, to want to be a monkey for reasons that not even the monkey was capable of explaining, beginning with the fact that he had no reasons at all and his strength derived precisely from that, and so on down the line.

The first nights at the clinic were peaceful; the old employees were still doing their work and the new ones limited themselves to observing, gaining experience, and getting together in the pharmacy where Talita, dressed in white, was making the emotional rediscovery of emulsions and barbiturates. The problem was how to get out from under Cuca Ferraguto, who had installed herself in the office, because Cuca seemed to have decided to put her stamp on the clinic, and the Boss himself listened respectfully to the New Deal summarized in such terms as cleanliness, discipline, godcountryand-home, grey pyjamas, and linden tea. Continually stopping by the pharmacy, Cuca kept-her-ears-open to the supposedly professional conversations of the new team. She had some confidence in Talita because the girl had her diploma hung up there, but the husband and his buddy were suspect. Cuca's problem was that in spite of everything she found them terribly charming, which obliged her to debate like Corneille between duty and violent love, while Ferraguto organized the administration and little by little was getting used to the substitution of schizophrenics for sword-swallowers and ampules of insulin for bales of hay. The doctors, three in number, came during the morning and were not much of a bother. The resident, a great poker player, had already become friendly with Oliveira and Traveler; in his office on the fourth floor they worked on possible royal flushes, and pots from ten to a hundred pesos would change hands like-a I wanna should tell you.

The patients much better, thank you.

(–89)

53

And one Thursday, wham-bam, everybody settled at around nine o'clock in the evening. That afternoon the old personnel had left with a great slamming of doors (knowing laughs from Ferraguto and Cuca, firm on the question of severance pay) and a delegation of patients had said goodbye to the people who were leaving with shouts of "The dog is dead, the dog is dead!" which had not prevented them from presenting a petition with five signatures to Ferraguto, demanding chocolate, the afternoon paper, and the death of the dog. The new people were left behind, still a little unsure, and Remorino, who had taken charge of easing the transition, said that everything would run superbly. Radio El Mundo was feeding the sporting spirit of Buenos Aires with reports about the heat wave. A record breaker, you could sweat at your pleasure patriotically, and Remorino had already picked up four or five pairs of pyjamas discarded in the corners. Between him and Oliveira the owners were persuaded to put them back on again, at least the bottoms. Before getting involved in a poker game with Ferraguto and Traveler, Dr Ovejero had told Talita to distribute lemonade without anything to fear at all except to Numbers 6, 18 and 31. This had brought on such an attack of weeping by Number 31 that Talita had to give her a double ration of lemonade. It was already time to proceed *motu proprio*, death to the dog.

How had it been possible that one had begun to live that life so peacefully, without too much strangeness? Perhaps because there had been no previous preparation, because the manual of psychiatry acquired at the Tomás Pardo bookshop had not been exactly propedeutic for Talita and Traveler. Without experience, without any real desires, without anything: man was really the animal who gets accustomed even to not getting accustomed. The morgue, for example: Traveler and Oliveira did not know about it and heretwas Tuesday night and Ovejero sent Remorino up to get them. Number 56 on the third floor had died just as they had expected; they needed help to move him and distract Number 31 who was getting telepalpitations from it all. Remorino explained to them that the outgoing personnel had been very vindictive and had just put in the minimum of work after they found out about the severance business, so there was nothing to do but start working hard, it would get easier as it went along.

How strange that in the inventory read on the day of the great transaction there had been no mention of a morgue. But they've got to keep their cold meat somewhere until the family comes for it or the city sends its wagon. The inventory probably mentioned a storeroom, or a transfer room, or a cold chamber, euphemisms like that, or maybe it simply spoke of the eight freezers. A morgue, after all, was not a pretty thing to mention in a document, Remorino thought. And why eight freezers? Oh, that . . . Some requirement of the federal Department of Health or some arrangement the ex-superintendent had made when he was taking bids, but it hadn't been a bad idea because sometimes there were streaks, like the year San Lorenzo had won the cup (what year was that? Remorino couldn't remember, but it was the year San Lorenzo had ended up in first place), four patients suddenly kicked the bucket, all in one stroke, like nobody's business. Not very usual, of course, with Number 56 you knew in advance, what could you do. Speak low along here so we don't wake them up. What do you want at this time of night, back to bed with you, back to bed. He's a good boy, look how he takes off. He gets the notion to come out in the hall at night, but don't get the idea he's after the women, we've got that business all taken care of. He comes out just because he's crazy, that's all, just like any one of us if you really think about it.

Oliveira and Traveler thought that Remorino was great. A fellow with experience, you could see that right off. They helped the man with the cart, who when he wasn't a stretcher-bearer was simply Number 7, a curable case so that he could help out with easy jobs. They took the cart down on the service lift, a little crowded, and they felt close to Number 56's shape underneath the sheet. His family was coming for him on Monday, they were from Trelew, poor people. They still hadn't come for Number 22, it was too much. People with money, Remorino thought: the worst kind, real vultures, no feelings.

And did the city let Number 22 . . . ? The order was floating around somewhere, one of those things. So the days were going by, two weeks, you can see the advantage of having lots of freezers. For one reason or another there were three of them there now, because Number 2 was there too, she was one of the original patients. That was really something, Number 2 had no family, but the Bureau of Burials had notified them that the truck would come by within forty-eight hours. Remorino added up the hours to amuse himself, and it was three hundred and six already, almost three hundred and seven. He called her an original patient because she was a little old lady left over from the early days, before the time of the doctor who had sold out to Don Ferraguto. Don Ferraguto seems to be a nice guy, doesn't he? To think he used to own a circus, that's really something.

Number 7 opened the door of the lift, pulled out the cart, and went driving wildly down the hallway until Remorino suddenly put on the brakes and took out a key to open the metal door while Traveler and Oliveira took out cigarettes simultaneously, those reflections . . . They really should have brought their overcoats, because there was no heat wave in the morgue, which looked like a barroom with a long table on one side and a refrigerator that reached up to the ceiling on the other wall.

"Go and get a beer," Remorino ordered. "You didn't see anything, eh? Sometimes the rules here are too . . . Better not say anything to Don Ferraguto, we just have some beer once in a while."

Number 7 went to one of the doors of the refrigerator and took out a bottle. While Remorino was opening it with an opener he had on his jackknife, Traveler looked at Oliveira, but Number 7 spoke first.

"Maybe we'd better put him away first, don't you think?"

"You . . . " Remorino began, but he just stood with the open jackknife in his hand. "You're right, boy. Let's go. That one's empty."

"No," said Number 7.

"Are you going to contradict me?"

"I beg your pardon, please," Number 7 said. "But that's the one that's empty."

Remorino stood there looking at him, and Number 7 smiled at him and after a kind of salute went over to the door in dispute and opened it. A bright light came out, something like an aurora borealis or some other hyperborean phenomenon, in the middle of which could be seen the clear outline of two rather large feet.

"Number 22," said Number 7. "Didn't I tell you? I can tell them all by their feet. Number 2's in there. What do you want to bet? Take a look if you don't believe me. Convinced? Well then, let's put him in this empty one. If you would give me a hand, easy, he has to go in head first."

"He's a champion," Remorino said to Traveler in a low voice. "I really can't see why Ovejero keeps him in here. There are no glasses, so we'll have to use what we were born with."

Traveler inhaled smoke all the way down to his knees before taking the bottle. It passed around from hand to hand, and Remorino told the first dirty story.

(–66)

54

From the window of his room on the third floor Oliveira could see the courtyard with its fountain, the trickle of water, Number 8's hopscotch, the three trees shading the geranium beds, and the high wall that hid the houses on the street. Number 8 had been playing hopscotch all afternoon, he was unbeatable, Number 4 and Number 19 had tried to get Heaven away from him, but it was useless, Number 8's foot was a precision instrument, a shot at a square, the stone always stopping in the most favourable position, it was extraordinary. At night the hopscotch had a sort of weak phosphorescence about it and Oliveira liked to look at it from his window. In his bed, giving in to the effects of a cubic centimetre of hypnosis, Number 8 was probably sleeping like a stork, mentally standing on one leg, moving his stone with sharp, infallible strokes towards the conquest of a heaven that seemed to lose its charm once it had been gained. "You're an insufferable romantic," Oliveira thought to himself, preparing a *mate*. "When will you be ready for the pink pyjamas?" He had a letter from the disconsolate Gekrepten on the table, because you can only get out on Saturdays, but what kind of a life is this going to be, my love, I refuse to resign myself to being alone so much of the time, if you could just see our little room. Resting the gourd on the windowsill, Oliveira took a pen out of his pocket and answered the letter. In the first place, there was a telephone (followed by the number); second, they were very busy, but the reorganization shouldn't take more than two weeks and then they would be able to see each other at least on Wednesdays, Saturdays and Sundays. Third, he was running out of *yerba*. "I write as if I were imprisoned," he thought, signing the letter. It was almost eleven o'clock, soon it would be his turn to relieve Traveler who was doing guard duty on the fourth floor. Mixing another *mate*, he read the letter again and licked the envelope. He preferred writing, the telephone was a confusing instrument in Gekrepten's hands, she didn't understand what was being explained to her.

In the left wing the light in the pharmacy went out. Talita came out into the courtyard, locked the door (it was easy to see her in the light of the hot and starry sky) and went indecisively over to the fountain. Oliveira whistled softly, but Talita kept on looking at the jet of water, and even put out an experimental finger and held it in the water for a moment. Then she crossed the courtyard, walking across the hopscotch without any continuity, and disappeared under Oliveira's window. Everything had had something of Leonora Carrington pictures about it, the night with Talita and the hopscotch, a crossing of lines that are unaware of one another, a trickle of water in a fountain. When the figure in pink came out of somewhere and went slowly over to the hopscotch, not daring to step on it, Oliveira knew that everything was coming back into order, that of necessity the pink figure would pick a flat stone out of the several that Number 8 kept piled up next to the flowerbed, and that La Maga, because it was La Maga, would double up her left leg and with the tip of her shoe propel the marker into the first square, would push the marker into the second (and Oliveira trembled a little because the marker had been on the point of going off the hopscotch, the uneven paving had stopped it exactly on the edge of the second square), would enter lightly and remain motionless for a second, like a pink flamingo in the half-light, before bringing her foot slowly up to the marker, calculating the distance to the third square.

Talita raised her head and saw Oliveira in the window. It took her a while to recognize him, and in the meantime she was balancing on one leg, as if holding herself in the air with her hands. Looking at her with an ironical disenchantment, Oliveira recognized his mistake, he saw that the pink was not pink, that Talita was wearing an ash-grey blouse and a skirt that most likely was white. Everything (in a manner of speaking) had an explanation: Talita had come in and had gone out again, attracted by the hopscotch, and that break of a second between her passage and reappearance had been enough to trick him just as on that other night in the prow of the ship, as probably on so many other nights. He scarcely answered the gesture from Talita, who was lowering her head now, concentrating; she calculated and the marker left the second square with force and went into the third, straightened up on end, started rolling along on its edge, left the hopscotch, went one or two paving stones' distance away from the hopscotch.

"You'll need more practice if you want to beat Number 8," Oliveira said.

"What are you doing there?"

"It's hot. Guard duty at eleven-thirty. Letters."

"Oh," Talita said. "What a night."

"Magical," Oliveira said and Talita laughed briefly before disappearing under the entranceway. Oliveira heard her go up the stairs, pass by his door (but she was probably going up in the lift), reach the fourth floor. "I've already admitted that they do look a lot alike," he thought. "That, along with my being an idiot, explains it all, right down to the last detail." But just the same he stayed there looking at the courtyard for a while, the deserted hopscotch, as if to convince himself. At ten past eleven Traveler came down to get him and gave him the report. Number 5 rather restless, notify Ovejero if he got bothersome; the rest were asleep.

The fourth floor was as perfect as a glove, and even Number 5 had calmed down. He accepted a cigarette, smoked it intensely, and explained to Oliveira how the conspiracy of Jewish publishers was holding up the publication of his great work on comets; he promised him an autographed copy. Oliveira left the door half open because he was on to his tricks, and he began to go up and down the hall, looking from time to time through the magic eyes installed thanks to the astuteness of Ovejero, the superintendent, and Liber & Finkel Co.: each room a little Van Eyck, except for that of Number 14 who as always had pasted a stamp over the lens. At twelve o'clock Remorino arrived under the influence of a few glasses of gin; they talked about horses and football, and then Remorino went off to the ground floor to sleep for a while. Number 5 had quietened down completely, and the heat closed in on the silence and half-darkness of the corridor. The idea that someone might try to kill him had not occurred to Oliveira until that moment, but all he needed was an instantaneous picture, a sketch that had more of a shiver than anything else about it, to make him realize that it was not a new idea, that it did not come from the atmosphere of the corridor with its closed doors and the shadow of the service lift in the background. The same thing could have occurred to him in Roque's, or in the subway at five in the afternoon. Or much earlier, in Europe, some night when he was wandering through poor neighbourhoods, wasteland where an old tin can could be used to slit a throat almost as if the two objects were in agreement. Stopping by the shaft of the lift, he looked into the black depths and thought again about the Phlegrean Fields, the way in. In the circus it had been just the opposite, a hole up above, the opening in communication with free space, an image of consummation; now he was at the edge of the pit, the hole of Eleusis, the clinic wrapped in sulphurous vapours, the descent. Turning around he saw the straight line of the hallway to its end, with the faint purple light from the bulbs on the frames of the white doors. He did a foolish thing: picking up his left leg, he took little hops along the hall up to where he was opposite the first door. When he put his left foot down on the green linoleum again he was bathed in sweat. With each hop he had muttered the name of Manú between his teeth. "To think that I had expected a passage," he said to himself leaning against the wall. Impossible to objectivize the first fraction of a thought without finding it grotesque. Passage, for example. To think that he had expected. Expected a passage. Letting himself slide down, he sat on the floor and stared at the linoleum. Passage to what? And why did the clinic have to serve as a passage? What kind of temples did he go around needing, what intercessors, what psychic or moral hormones that could project him outside or inside himself?

When Talita arrived with a glass of lemonade (those ideas of hers, little teacher of the workers' quarter and The Drop of Milk), he brought the matter up right away. Talita wasn't surprised by anything; sitting down opposite him she watched him drink the lemonade in one gulp.

"If Cuca could see us stretched out on the floor she'd have an attack. What a way you have of standing guard. Are they asleep?"

"Yes, I think so. Number 14 covered her peephole, who knows what she's up to. For some reason I don't feel like looking in."

"You're the model of delicacy," Talita said. "But maybe I, as one woman to another . . . "

She returned almost immediately, and this time she sat down next to Oliveira, leaning against the wall.

"Sleeping the sleep of the chaste. Poor Manú had a horrible nightmare. It's always the same, he goes back to sleep but I'm so upset I end up getting out of bed. I thought you might have been warm, you or Remorino, so I made some lemonade. What a summer, and with those walls out there that shut out the breeze. So I look like that other woman."

"A little bit, yes," Oliveira said, "but that's not important. What I would like to know is why I saw you dressed in pink."

"Influence of the environment, you've assimilated her in among the others."

"Yes, that's the easiest explanation if you take everything into account. But you, why did you start to play hopscotch? Have you become assimilated too?"

"You're right," Talita said. "Why did I? I never really did care for hopscotch. But don't you go making up one of your theories about my being possessed, I'm nobody's zombie."

"You don't have to shout it."

"Nobody's," Talita repeated, lowering her voice. "I saw the hopscotch as I was coming in, there was a pebble . . . I played and I went away."

"You lost on the third square. The same thing would have happened to La Maga, she's incapable of keeping things up, she doesn't have the least sense of distance, time falls apart in her hands, she goes around bumping into everyone. Thanks to which, I might say in passing, she is absolutely perfect in her way of denouncing everybody else's perfection. But I was talking about the service lift, I think."

"Yes, you said something and then you drank your lemonade. No, wait, first you drank your lemonade."

"I was probably feeling sorry for myself; when you came I was in the midst of a shamanistic trance, on the point of jumping into the hole to put an end once and for all to conjectures, that svelte word."

"The hole ends in the basement," Talita said. "There are cockroaches, if you want to know, and coloured rags on the floor. Everything is dark and damp, and a little beyond is where the dead people start. Manú told me about it."

"Is Manú asleep?"

"Yes. He had a nightmare, he shouted something about a lost necktie. I already told you."

"It's a great night for confiding," Oliveira said, looking at her slowly.

"Very great," Talita said. "La Maga was just a name, and now she already has a face. The colour of her clothes may still be wrong, though."

"Her clothes are the least important, when I see her again who knows what she'll be wearing. She'll be naked, or she'll be walking with her child in her arms singing him *Les Amants du Havre*, a song you don't know."

"Oh yes I do," Talita said. "They used to play it a lot on Radio Belgrano. La-lá-la, la-lá-la . . . "

Oliveira sketched out a soft slap which turned into a caress. Talita threw her head back and bumped it against the wall of the hallway. She frowned and rubbed the back of her neck, but she kept on humming the tune. She heard a click and then a buzzing that seemed blue in the half-light of the hallway. They heard the service lift coming up, they looked at each other for a second before jumping up. Who could it be at that hour . . . ? Click, it passed the second floor, the blue buzzing. Talita drew back and got behind Oliveira. Click. The pink pyjamas were perfectly visible in the cube of wired glass. Oliveira ran over to the lift and opened the door. An almost cold breath of air came out. The old man looked at him as if he didn't know him and kept on stroking the pigeon; it was easy to see that the pigeon had been white once and that the continuous caressing of the old man's hand had turned it ash-grey. Motionless, with wild eyes, it was resting in the hollow of the hand that held it at chest level, while the fingers kept passing over it from neck to tail, from neck to tail.

"Go to bed, Don López," Oliveira said, breathing heavily.

"It's hot in bed," Don López said. "Look how happy she is when I take her for a walk."

"It's very late, go to your room."

"I'll bring you a cool glass of lemonade," Talita Nightingale promised.

Don López stroked the pigeon and came out of the service lift. They heard him go down the stairs.

"Everybody does what he wants around here," Oliveira muttered, closing the door to the lift. "One of these days there's going to be a general throat-cutting. You can smell it, no matter what they say. That pigeon looked like a revolver."

"We ought to tell Remorino. The old man came up from the basement, it's strange."

"Look, you stay here a while on guard, I'm going down to the basement to have a look; I hope one of the others isn't up to any tricks."

"I'm going down with you."

"OK, the ones up here are fast asleep."

Inside the lift the light was vaguely blue and it went down with a science-fiction buzz. There wasn't a living soul in the basement, but one of the doors of the freezer was ajar and a beam of light was coming out through the opening. Talita stopped in the doorway, with her hand to her mouth, while Oliveira went over. It was Number 56, he remembered very well, the family could come by any time. From Trelew. And in the meantime Number 56 had had a visit from a friend; one could imagine the conversation with the old man with the pigeon, one of those pseudo-dialogues in which the speaker doesn't care whether or not the other party speaks as long as he's there opposite, as long as there's something there opposite, anything, a face, feet sticking out of the ice. The same way as he had just been talking to Talita, telling her what he had seen, telling her that he was afraid, talking all the time about holes and passageways, to Talita or to anybody else, to a pair of feet sticking out of the ice, to any opposite appearance capable of listening and agreeing. But while he was closing the door of the freezer and for some reason holding on to the edge of the table, a vomit of memory began to take hold of him; he told himself that only a day or two before, it had seemed impossible to arrive at the point of telling anything to Traveler, a monkey couldn't tell anything to a man, and suddenly, without knowing why, he had heard himself talking to Talita as if she were La Maga, knowing that she wasn't but talking to her about the hopscotch, his fear in the hallway, the tempting hole. Then (and Talita was there, fifteen feet away, behind him, waiting) it was all like an ending, the appeal to outside pity, the re-entry into the human family, the sponge landing with a repulsive squish in the centre of the ring. He felt as if he had been going away from himself, abandoning himself so he could throw himself – the prodigal son (of a bitch) – into the arms of easy reconciliation, and from there the even easier step into the world, into the possible life, into the time of his years, into the reason that guided the actions of good Argentines, of the human animal in general. He was in his little, comfortable, refrigerated Hades, but there was no Eurydice to look for, apart from the fact that he had come down peacefully in a service lift and now, while he was opening a freezer and taking out a bottle of beer, king of the castle, anything to put an end to that comedy.

"Come and have a drink," he invited. "Much better than lemonade."

Talita took a step and stopped.

"Don't be necrophilic," she said. "Let's get out of here."

"It's the only place that's cool, you've got to admit that. I think I'll bring a bed down here."

"You're pale with the cold," Talita said coming over. "Come on, I don't like your staying here."

"Don't like it? They're not going to come out and eat me, the ones upstairs are much worse."

"Come on, Horacio," Talita repeated. "I don't want you to stay here."

"You . . . " Oliveira said, looking at her angrily, and he stopped to open the beer with a blow of his hand against the edge of a chair. He could see with great clarity a boulevard in the rain, but instead of leading somebody along by the arm, talking to her with pity, he was being led, they had given him a compassionate arm and they were talking to him so that he would be happy, they had so much concern for him that it was absolutely delightful. The past had become turned around, it was changing its sign, it was finally going to happen at last that Pity would not destroy. That woman who played hopscotch had pity on him, it was so obvious that it burned.

"We can talk some more on the third floor," Talita said by way of explanation. "Bring the bottle along and give me a little."

"*Oui madame, bien sûr madame*," Oliveira said.

"You finally said something in French. Manú and I thought that you had taken an oath. Never . . . "

"*Assez*," Oliveira said. "*Tu m'as eu, petite, Céline avait raison, on se croit enculé d'un centimètre et on l'est déjà de plusieurs mètres.*"

Talita looked at him with the look of one who didn't understand, but her hand rose up without her feeling it rise, and she held it for an instant on Oliveira's chest. When she took it away, he started to look at her as if from below, with eyes that looked from somewhere else.

"Who can tell," Oliveira said to someone who was not Talita. "Who can tell if you're the one who spit so much pity out at me tonight. Who can tell if after all the only thing left is to cry over love until you fill four or five buckets. Or let them cry into them for you, the way they're crying into them for you."

Talita turned her back on him and went towards the door. When she stopped to wait for him, upset and at the same time needing to wait for him because to go away at this instant would be like letting him fall into the well (with cockroaches, with coloured rags), she saw that he was smiling and that the smile was not for her either. She had never seen him smile like that, faint-heartedly and at the same time with his whole face open and front-facing, without the usual irony, accepting something that must have come to him from the centre of life, from that other well (with cockroaches, with coloured rags, with a face floating in dirty water?), going up to her in the act of accepting that thing impossible to name that was making him smile. And his kiss was not for her either, it wasn't happening there grotesquely next to a freezer full of corpses, so close to the sleeping Manú. It was as if they were coming together from somewhere else, with some other part of themselves, and it wasn't a question of themselves, as if they were paying or collecting something for others, as if they were the golems of an impossible meeting between their masters. And the Phlegrean Fields, and what Horacio had muttered about the descent, a madness so absolute that Manú and everything that was Manú and was on the level of Manú could not take part in the ceremony, because what was starting there was like the caress on the dove, like the idea of getting up to make some lemonade for the one on guard, like bending a leg and kicking a stone from the first to the second square from the second to the third. In some way they had got into another thing, into that something where one could be dressed in grey and be dressed in pink, where one could have died of drowning in a river (and she was no longer the one who was thinking about that) and appear in a Buenos Aires night to reproduce on the hopscotch the very image of what they had just attained, the last square, the centre of the mandala, the dizzy Ygdrasil through which one came out onto an open beach, an extension without limit, the world beneath the eyelids that the eyes turned inward recognized and obeyed.

(–129)

55

But Traveler was not asleep, after one or two attempts the nightmare kept circling around him and finally he sat up in bed and turned on the light. Talita was not there, somnambulist, sleepless moth, and Traveler drank a glass of *caña* and put on his pyjama top. The wicker easy chair looked cooler than the bed, and it was a good night to stay up reading. Sometimes he heard walking in the entrance hall, and Traveler twice went to the door that opened onto the administrative wing. Nobody was there, not even the wing. Talita must have gone to do some work in the pharmacy, it was incredible how enthusiastic she was about her return to science, scales, antipyretics. Traveler began to read for a while between drinks of *caña*. Still, it was strange that Talita had not come back from the pharmacy. When she did reappear, with a frightening ghostly air, the bottle of *caña* was so low that Traveler didn't much care whether he saw her or didn't see her, and they chatted for a while about many things, while Talita unfolded a nightgown and other diverse theories, almost all of them tolerated by Traveler who tended towards benevolence in the state he was in. Then Talita fell asleep on her back, a restless sleep interrupted by sharp hand movements and moans. It was always the same, it was hard for Traveler to sleep when Talita was restless, but as soon as he was overcome by fatigue she would wake up and at once become fully awake, because he would be complaining or twisting in his dreams, and that's how they would pass the night, as if they were on a seesaw. To make things worse the light had been left on and it was very complicated getting to the switch, that's why they ended up awakening completely, and then Talita turned out the light and squeezed herself a little up against Traveler who was sweating and twisting. "Horacio saw La Maga tonight," Talita said. "He saw her in the courtyard, two hours ago, when you were on guard duty."

"Oh," said Traveler, lifting up his shoulders and looking Braille system for his cigarettes. He added a confused phrase that had come out of what he had just been reading.

"I was La Maga," Talita said, snuggling closer to Traveler. "I don't know if you're aware of that."

"Most likely yes."

"It had to happen some time. What surprises me is that he's become so startled by the mixup."

"Oh, you know, Horacio gets something started and then he looks at it with the same look puppies put on when they've taken a crap and stand there amazed looking at it."

"I think it happened the very day we went to meet him at the dock," Talita said. "It's hard to explain, because he didn't even look at me and between the two of you you treated me like a dog, with the cat under my arm."

Traveler muttered something unintelligible.

"He had me confused with La Maga," Talita insisted.

Traveler listened to her talk, alluding as all women do to fate, to the inevitable concatenation of events, and he would have preferred her to shut up but Talita resisted feverishly, squeezed up against him and insisted on telling things, telling herself, and naturally, telling him. Traveler let himself be carried along.

"First the old man with the pigeon came, and then we went down to the basement. Horacio kept talking all the time we were going down, about those hollows that worry him. He was desperate, Manú, it was frightening to see how peaceful he seemed, and all the time . . . We went down in the service lift, and he went over to shut one of the freezers, it was horrible."

"So you went downstairs," Traveler said. "OK."

"It was different," Talita said. "It wasn't like going down. We were talking, but I felt as if Horacio were somewhere else, talking to someone else, to a drowned woman, for example. It comes back to me now, but he'd never said that La Maga had been drowned in the river."

"She isn't the least bit drowned," Traveler said. "I'm sure of that, although I have to admit I haven't got the slightest idea. Knowing Horacio is enough."

"He thinks she's dead, Manú, and at the same time he feels her close by and tonight it was me. He told me that he'd seen her on the ship too, and under the bridge on the Avenida San Martín . . . He doesn't say it as if he were talking about a hallucination, and he doesn't expect you to believe it either. He says it, that's all, and it's true, it's something that's there. When he closed the freezer and I was afraid and I said something or other, he began to look at me and it was the other one he was looking at. I'm nobody's zombie, Manú, I don't want to be anybody's zombie."

Traveler stroked her hair, but Talita pushed him away impatiently. She had sat down on the bed and he could feel her trembling. Trembling, in that heat. She told him that Horacio had kissed her, and she tried to explain the kiss and since she couldn't find the words she kept touching Traveler in the darkness, her arms fell like cloths over his face, over his arms, slipped down along his chest, rested on his knees, and out of all this came a kind of explanation that Traveler was incapable of rejecting, a contagion that came from farther off, from some place in the depths or on the heights or in some place which was not that night and that room, a contagion that possessed him in turn through Talita, a babbling like an untranslatable announcement, the suspicion that he was facing something that could be an announcement, but the voice that brought it was broken and when it spoke the message it spoke it in some unintelligible language, and yet it was the only necessary thing there within hand's reach, demanding recognition and acceptance, beating itself against a spongy wall of smoke and of cork, unseizable and offering itself naked between the arms but like water pouring down among tears.

"The hard mental crust," Traveler managed to think. Confusedly he heard that fear, that Horacio, that the service lift, that the dove; a communicable system was little by little entering his ear again. So the poor devil was afraid he would kill him, it was laughable.

"Did he really say that? It's hard to believe, you know how proud he is."

"It's something else," Talita said, taking the cigarette away from him and dragging on it with a sort of silent-movie eagerness. "I think the fear he feels is like a last refuge, the crossbar he holds on to before jumping. He's so happy to be afraid tonight, I know he's happy."

"That," said Traveler, breathing like a real yogi, "is something Cuca would not understand, you can be sure. And I must be in an exceedingly intelligent mood tonight, because that business of happy fear is a little hard to take, my love."

Talita slid up on the bed a little and leaned against Traveler. She knew that she was by his side again, that she had not drowned, that he was there holding her up on the surface of the water and that actually there was pity, a marvellous pity. They both felt it at the same moment, and they slid towards each other as if to fall into themselves, into the common earth where words and caresses and mouths enfolded them as a circumference does a circle, those tranquillizing metaphors, that old sadness satisfied with going back to being the same as always, with continuing, keeping afloat against wind and tide, against call and fall.

56

He wondered where he had picked up the habit of always carrying pieces of string in his pockets, of putting coloured threads together and placing them between the pages of books, of constructing all manner of figures with those things and gum tragacanth. As he wound a piece of black string around the doorknob, Oliveira wondered whether the delicateness of the threads didn't give him some kind of perverse satisfaction, and he agreed that maybe *peut-être* and who could say. The only thing certain was that the pieces of string and thread made him happy, that nothing seemed more instructive to him than to construct for example a huge transparent dodecahedron, the work of many hours and much complication, to bring a match close to it later on and watch how a little nothing of a flame would come and go while Gekrepten wr-ung-her-ha-nds and said that it was a shame to burn something so pretty. Difficult to explain to her that the more fragile and perishable the structure, the greater the freedom to make and unmake it. To Oliveira threads seemed to be the only justifiable material for his inventions, and only once in a while, if he found it in the street, did he feel like using a piece of wire or some strap or other. He liked everything he made as full of free space as possible, the air able to enter and leave, especially leave; things like that occurred to him with books, women, obligations, and he did not expect Gekrepten or the cardinal primate to understand those celebrations.

The business of wrapping a black string around the doorknob began almost a couple of hours later, because in the meantime Oliveira made various things in his room and outside it. The idea of the basins was classic and he didn't feel at all proud at having followed it, but in the darkness a basin of water on the floor works out a series of rather subtle defensive values; surprise, terror perhaps, in any case the blind rage that follows the idea of having stuck a Fanacal or Tonsa shoe into the water, and the sock a little bit beyond the shoe, and that all of this drips water while the foot completely perturbed becomes agitated in the sock, and the sock in the shoe, like a drowning rat or one of those poor guys that jealous sultans used to throw into the Bosporus inside a bag that was sewn shut (with string, naturally: everything ended up meeting, it was rather amusing that the basin of water and the threads should come together at the end of his reasoning and not at the beginning, but here Horacio permitted himself the conjecture that the order of reasoning did not have to (*a*) follow physical time, the before and the after, and (*b*) that most likely the reasoning had been unconsciously fulfilled so that it would pass from the notion of thread to that of the watery basin). In short, no sooner was it analysed a bit than it fell into grave suspicions of determinism; it would be best to keep on making barricades without paying too much attention to reasons or preferences. In any case, what came first, the thread or the basin? As execution, the basin, but the thread had been decided first. It wasn't worth the trouble to keep on worrying when life hung in the balance; obtaining basins was much more important, and the first half-hour consisted of a cautious exploration of the third floor and part of the ground floor, from where he returned with five medium-sized basins, three spittoons, and an empty can that had contained a sweet-potato preserve, all brought together under the general denomination of basin. Number 18, who was awake, insisted on keeping him company and Oliveira ended up accepting, having made up his mind to throw him out as soon as the defensive operations reached a certain stage. As far as threads were concerned, Number 18 was very useful, because no sooner was he succinctly informed of the strategic necessities than he rolled his malignantly beautiful green eyes and said that Number 6 had boxes full of coloured thread. The only problem was that Number 6 was on the ground floor, in Remorino's wing, and if Remorino woke up there would be all hell to pay. Number 18 also maintained that Number 6 was crazy, which would complicate the raid on her room. Rolling his malignantly beautiful green eyes, he suggested to Oliveira that he stand guard in the hallway while he took off his shoes and proceeded to seize the threads, but it seemed to Oliveira that this was going too far and he decided that he would assume the personal responsibility of going into Number 6's room at that time of night. It was rather amusing to think about responsibility while he invaded the bedroom of a girl snoring face up, exposed to the worst mischances; with his pockets and his hands full of balls of yarn and coloured threads, Oliveira stood looking at her for a moment, but then he shrugged his shoulders as if to make the monkey of responsibility seem a little lighter. Number 18, who was waiting for him in his room contemplating the basins piled up on the bed, thought that Oliveira had not obtained thread in sufficient quantity. Rolling his malignantly beautiful green eyes, he maintained that to complete the defensive preparations adequately what was needed was a good supply of ball bearings and a Heftpistole. The idea of the ball bearings seemed good to Oliveira, although he didn't have a clear idea of what they might be, but he rejected the Heftpistole completely. Number 18 opened his malignantly beautiful green eyes and said that a Heftpistole was not what the doctor thought it was (he said "doctor" in an obligatory tone so that anybody could see that he was saying it to be annoying) but in view of the negative response he would try to get only the ball bearings. Oliveira let him go, with the faint hope that he would not come back because he felt like being alone. Remorino would get up at two o'clock to relieve him and he had to think of something. If Remorino didn't find him in the hallway he would come looking for him in his room and that wouldn't do, unless the first test of the defences was made at his expense. He rejected the idea because the defences were conceived with a determined attack in mind, and Remorino would enter with a completely different outlook. Now he was beginning to feel more and more fear (and when he felt fear he would look at his wristwatch, and the fear would grow with the hour); he started to smoke, studying the defensive possibilities of the room, and at ten minutes to two he went out to wake up Remorino in person. He handed over a list of instructions that was a gem, with subtle alterations on the temperature entries, the time for tranquillizers, and the syndromatic and eupeptic manifestations of the guests on the second floor, to such a degree that Remorino would have to spend almost all his time with them, while the ones on the third floor, according to the same report, would be sleeping peacefully and the only thing they would need was for no one to come and bother them during the night. Remorino was interested in knowing (without much desire) if those attentions and lack of them came from the high authority of Dr Ovejero, to which Oliveira replied hypocritically with the monosyllabic adverb of affirmation suited to the circumstances. After which they separated in friendly fashion and Remorino went yawning up one flight while Oliveira went trembling up two. But by no means would he accept the help of a Heftpistole, and they ought to be thankful that he agreed to the ball bearings.

He still had a moment of peace, because Number 18 had not returned and it was necessary to go about filling up the basins and the spittoons, placing them in a first line of defence a little bit behind the first barrier of threads (still theoretical but already perfectly planned) and trying the possibilities of advance, the eventual collapse of the first line, and the efficiency of the second. In between two basins Oliveira filled the sink with cold water and put in his face and his hands, soaked his neck and his hair. He was smoking all the time, but he hadn't finished half of any cigarette and he went to the window to throw out the butt and light another one. The butts fell on the hopscotch and Oliveira calculated so that each brilliant eye would burn for a moment in a different square; it was funny. It occurred to him at that hour to fill himself with outside thoughts, *dona nobis pacem, may your patron have pesos that will last for ever*, things like that, and also suddenly strips of mental material came to him, something in between a notion and a feeling, for example, that his digging in was the last of his stupidities, that the only mad thing, and therefore the one worth trying and maybe efficient, would have been to attack instead of defending himself, besiege instead of being there trembling and smoking and waiting for Number 18 to come back with the ball bearings; but it didn't last long, almost like the cigarettes, and his hands trembled and he knew that that was all he had left, and suddenly another memory that was like a hope, a phrase where somebody was saying that the hours of sleep and wakefulness have not been joined into unity yet, and that was followed by a laugh that he heard as if it were not his, and a grimace in which he showed himself once and for all that that unity was too far away and that no part of dreams would be any good to him while he was awake or vice versa. To attack Traveler as the best defence was a possibility, but it meant invading what he felt more and more to be a black mass, a territory where people were sleeping and nobody at all expected to be attacked at that hour of the night and for non-existent causes in terms of the black mass. But while he was feeling that way, it was disagreeable for Oliveira to have formulated it in terms of a black mass, feeling was like a black mass but through his fault and not that of the territory where Traveler was sleeping; that's why it was best not to use words as negative as black mass, and simply call it territory, since one always ended up calling his feelings something. It meant that across from his room the territory began, and to attack the territory was ill-advised since the motives for the attack no longer had intelligibility or the possibility of being sensed by the territory. On the other hand, if he barricaded himself in his room and Traveler came to attack him, no one would be able to maintain that Traveler did not know what he was doing, and the one attacked was perfectly aware and had taken his measures, precautions, and ball bearings, whatever these last might be.

Meanwhile one could stay at a window smoking, studying the disposition of the watery basins and the threads and thinking about the unity so much put to proof by the conflict of territory versus room. It was always going to pain Oliveira that he could not even get a notion of that unity that other times he called centre, and which for lack of more precise dimensions was reduced to images like black shout, kibbutz of desire (so far away now, that kibbutz of dawn and red wine), and even a life worthy of the name because (he felt it while he threw his cigarette on square five) he had been just foolish enough to imagine the possibility of a dignified life coming after diverse minute indignities. Nothing at all that could be thought about, but on the other hand it could be felt in terms of stomach contraction, territory, deep or spasmodic breathing, sweat on the palms of his hands, lighting a cigarette, pulling in his guts, thirst, silent shouts that broke like black masses in his throat (there was always some black mass in that game), desire for sleep, fear of sleeping, anxiety, the image of a dove that had once been white, coloured rags at the bottom of what could have been a passage, Sirius at the top of a tent, and enough, hey, enough please; but it was good to have felt one's self deeply there for an unmeasurable time, without thinking anything, only being that which was there with tongs caught in his stomach. *That* against the territory, waking against sleep. But to say *waking against sleep* was already a return into dialectics, it was to corroborate once more that there wasn't the remotest hope of unity. That's why the arrival of Number 18 with the ball bearings became an excellent pretext to resume the preparations for defence at exactly three-twenty more or less.

Number 18 rolled his malignantly beautiful green eyes and undid a towel in which he had the ball bearings. He said that he had spied on Remorino and that Remorino was so busy with Numbers 31, 7 and 45 that he wouldn't even think of coming up to the third floor. Most probably the patients had resisted with indignation the therapeutic novelties that Remorino was trying to give them, and the distribution of pills and shots would take its own sweet time. In any event, Oliveira thought that it would be well not to lose any more time, and after telling Number 18 that he could use the ball bearings in the way he saw most fitting, he began to test the efficacy of the watery basins, to do which he went out into the hall, overcoming the fear he had of leaving his room and getting into the purple light of the hallway, and he came back in with his eyes closed, imagining himself to be Traveler and walking with his toes turned out a little like Traveler. On his second step (although he knew it) he put his left shoe into a watery spittoon, and when he quickly pulled it out he sent the spittoon flying through the air and luckily it fell on the bed so that it did not make the least noise. Number 18 was under the desk spreading out the ball bearings; he jumped up and rolling his malignantly beautiful green eyes suggested a grouping of bearings between the two rows of basins, in order to complete the surprise of the cold water with the possibility of a magnificent slip. Oliveira did not say anything but he let him do it, and when he had put the watery spittoon back in its place again, he began to wrap a black thread around the doorknob. He stretched this thread to the desk and tied it to the back of the chair; putting the chair on two legs, with the corner resting on the edge of the desk; all that was needed for it to fall on the floor was for someone to try to open the door. Number 18 went out into the hall to try it, and Oliveira held the chair so there would be no noise. He began to be bothered by the friendly presence of Number 18, who from time to time would roll his malignantly beautiful green eyes and try to tell him the story of his arrival at the clinic. Of course all that was needed was to put a finger to one's mouth so that he would be shamefully silent and stay with his back against the wall for five minutes, but at the same time Oliveira gave him a new pack of cigarettes and told him to go to bed without letting himself be seen by Remorino.

"I'll stay with you, doctor," said Number 18.

"No, go ahead. I'll defend myself perfectly well."

"You needed a Heftpistole, I told you so. It puts staples all around, and it's better to hold down the threads."

"I'll fix it myself, old man," Oliveira said. "Go to bed. Thanks just the same."

"Well then, doctor, I hope it all goes fine."

"Good night, have a good sleep."

"Watch the ball bearings, you'll see that they won't let you down. Just leave them the way they are and you'll see."

"OK."

"If it turns out that you need the Heftpistole after all just let me know, Number 16 has one."

"Thanks, see you."

At half-past three Oliveira finished placing the threads. Number 18 had taken speech away, or at least that business of looking at each other from time to time or reaching for a cigarette. Almost in the dark because he had covered the lamp with a green sweater that was slowly getting singed, it was strange to go around like a spider from one side to the other with the threads, from the bed to the door, from the bathroom to the closet, stretching out each time five or six threads and retreating with great care so as not to step on the ball bearings. Finally he was becoming fenced in between the window, one side of the desk (placed against the flat of the wall, on the right), and the bed (up against the wall on the left). Between the door and the last line were strung successively the warning threads (from the doorknob to the leaning chair, from the doorknob to a Martini vermouth ashtray placed on the edge of the sink, and from the doorknob to a dresser drawer, full of books and papers, barely held by the edge), the watery basins in the shape of two irregular defensive lines, but oriented in general from the left wall to the right one, or in other terms from the sink to the closet the first line, and from the legs of the bed to the legs of the desk the second line. There was just about a yard left between the last series of watery basins, over which hung multiple threads, and the wall where the window opened onto the courtyard (two storeys down). Sitting on the edge of the desk, Oliveira lit another cigarette and began to look out of the window;

at a given moment he took off his shirt and put it under the desk. Now he couldn't drink any more even if he was thirsty. He stayed that way, in his undershirt, smoking and looking into the courtyard, but with his attention focused on the door even though from time to time he would become distracted when throwing his cigarette end onto the hopscotch. It wasn't so bad, even if the edge of the desk was hard and the smell of the burned sweater bothered him. He ended up turning off the lamp and little by little he saw a purple beam form under the door, that is to say that when Traveler arrived his rubber-soled slippers would cut the purple band in two places, an involuntary signal that he was about to initiate his attack. When Traveler opened the door several things would happen and many others might happen. The first would be mechanistic and ordained, within the stupid obedience of effect to cause, of chair to string, of doorknob to hand, of hand to will, of will to . . . And that's where one passes to other things that might happen or not, according to whether the blow of the chair on the floor, the breaking into five or six pieces of the Martini ashtray, and the fall of the dresser drawer would have one or another repercussion in Traveler and even in Oliveira himself, because now, while he was lighting another cigarette with the stub of the previous one and threw the butt so that it would fall on the ninth square, and he watched it fall on the eighth and jump to the seventh, motherfucker, now was perhaps the moment to ask himself what he was going to do when the door would open and half the bedroom would go wild and he would hear Traveler's muffled exclamation, if it was an exclamation and if it was muffled. Basically he had been stupid to reject the Heftpistole, because aside from the lamp which didn't weigh anything and the chair, in the corner by the window there wasn't the least kind of defensive arsenal, and with the lamp and the chair he wouldn't get very far if Traveler managed to breach the two lines of watery basins and missed skating on the ball bearings. But it wouldn't happen, the strategy relied on that; defensive arms cannot be of the same nature as offensive arms. The threads, for example, they would produce a terrible effect on Traveler as he advanced in the darkness and felt a sort of subtle resistance grow against his face, on his arms and legs, and he would get that insuperable loathing of a man who runs into a spider-web. Supposing that in two jumps he knocked down all the threads, supposing that he didn't put his shoe in a watery basin and didn't skate on a ball bearing, he would finally reach the sector of the window and in spite of the darkness he would recognize the motionless silhouette on the edge of the desk. It was remotely probable that he would reach there, but if he did, there was no doubt that a Heftpistole would be of absolutely no use to Oliveira, not so much because Number 18 had spoken of staples, but because there was not going to be an encounter as Traveler might imagine it perhaps but something totally different, something that he was incapable of imagining but which he knew with as much certainty as if he were seeing or living it, a slipping of the black mass that came from outside against that which he knew without knowing, an incalculable disengagement between black mass Traveler and what was there smoking on the edge of the desk. Something like waking against sleep (the hours of sleep and wakefulness, someone had said one day, have not been joined into unity yet), but to say wakefulness against sleep was to admit until the end that there existed no hope at all for unity. On the other hand it might happen that Traveler's arrival would be like an extreme point from which to try again the jump of one into the other and at the same time of the other into the one, but that jump would be precisely the opposite of a collision, Oliveira was sure that Traveler territory could not reach him even if he fell on top of him, beat him, tore his undershirt to shreds, spit in his eyes and on his mouth, twisted his arms, and threw him out of the window. But a Heftpistole was of absolutely no use against the territory, since from what he could gather from Number 18 it might turn out to be a buttonhook or something like it, what good was a Traveler knife or a Traveler punch, poor inadequate Heftpistoles to bridge the unbridgeable distance from one body to another in which one body begins by denying the other, or the other denies the one? If in fact Traveler could kill him (and there was some reason for his mouth being dry and for the fact that the palms of his hands were sweating abominably), everything moved to deny that possibility on one plane in which its occurrence in fact would not have any more confirmation than for the murderer. But it was better yet to feel that the murderer was not a murderer, that the territory was not even a territory, to thin and minimize and underestimate the territory so that so much operetta and so much ashtray breaking to pieces on the floor would be nothing more than a noise and contemptible consequences. If he affirmed himself (by fighting against fear) in that total unattachment in relation to the territory, defence was then the best attack, the worst thrust would come from the hilt and not from the blade. Why was he winning himself over with metaphors at that hour of the night when the only sensible senseless thing to do was to leave his eyes alone to watch over the purplish lines at the bottom of the door, that thermometric ray of the territory.

At ten minutes to four Oliveira got up, moving his shoulders to get the stiffness out of them, and went over to sit on the windowsill. It amused him to think that if he had had the good luck to go crazy that night, the liquidation of the Traveler territory would have been absolute. A solution not at all in accord with his pride and his intention of resisting any form of surrender. In any case, to imagine Ferraguto inscribing his name in the register of patients, putting a number on the door and a magic eye to spy on him at night . . . And Talita preparing capsules in the pharmacy, going across the courtyard with great care so as not to step on the hopscotch again. Not to mention Manú, poor fellow, terribly disconsolate over his stupidity and his absurd attempt. Turning his back on the courtyard, reclining dangerously in the windowsill, Oliveira felt fear begin to leave him, and that was bad. He didn't take his eyes off the beam of light, but with every breath a contentment penetrated him finally without words, without anything to do with the territory, and the joy was precisely that, to feel how the territory was giving in. It didn't matter how long; with every breath the warm air of the world was reconciled with him as had already happened one time or another before in his life. He didn't even feel the need to smoke, for a few minutes he had made peace with himself and that was the equivalent of abolishing the territory, of conquering without a battle and of wanting to fall asleep finally in the moment of wakening, on that line where wakefulness and sleep first mixed their waters and discovered that there was no such thing as different waters; but that was bad, naturally, naturally all of that had to see itself interrupted by the brusque interposition of two black sectors halfway across the ray of light and a fussy scratching on the door. "You asked for it," Oliveira thought, slipping down until he was tight against the desk. "The truth is that if I had gone on another minute like that I would have dropped head first onto the hopscotch. Come right in, Manú, it all means you don't exist or I don't exist, or that we're so stupid we believe this and we're going to kill each other, brother, this time it's the payoff, that's all there is to it."

"Come right in," he repeated aloud, but the door didn't open. The soft scratching continued, probably it was a pure coincidence that down below there was someone beside the fountain, a woman with her back turned with long hair and arms hanging by her sides, absorbed in the contemplation of the trickle of water. At that hour and in that darkness it could have just as easily been La Maga as Talita or any one of the madwomen, even Pola if one really thought about it. Nothing stopped him from staring at the woman with her back towards him, since if Traveler decided to come in the defences would function automatically and there would be more than enough time to stop looking at the courtyard and face him. At any rate, it was rather strange that Traveler should keep on scratching at the door as if to ascertain whether he was sleeping (it couldn't be Pola, because Pola's neck was shorter and her hips were more well-defined), unless he too for his part had devised a special system of attack (it could be La Maga or Talita, they looked so much alike and much more so at night and from the third storey) designed to make him lose his mind, knock him off his position on the square (at least from one to eight, because he hadn't been able to get beyond eight, he would never reach Heaven, he would never enter his kibbutz). "What are you waiting for Manú?" Oliveira thought. "What good is all this doing us?" It was Talita of course, who was now looking up and stood motionless again when he stuck his bare arm out of the window and moved it tiredly from side to side.

"Come over here, Maga," Oliveira said. "You look so much alike from here that your name can be changed."

"Close that window," Talita said.

"Impossible, the heat is terrible and your husband is out there scratching on the door in a fearsome way. It's what they call a conjunction of annoying circumstances. But don't you worry, pick up a pebble and try again, who can tell but that with one . . . "

The drawer, the ashtray, and the chair all fell onto the floor at the same time. Crouching down a little, Oliveira looked blinded at the purple rectangle that replaced the door, the black shape moving around, he heard Traveler's curse. The noise must have woken everybody up.

"You simple bastard," Traveler said in the doorway. "Do you want the Boss to throw us all out?"

"He's preaching to me," Oliveira informed Talita. "He always was like a father to me."

"Close the window, please," Talita said.

"There's nothing needed so much as an open window," Oliveira said. "Listen to your husband, one can observe that he's put one foot in the water. He must have a face full of threads, he doesn't know what to do."

"You son of a bitch," Traveler was saying, lashing out in the darkness and pulling threads off himself on all sides. "Turn on the light, God damn it."

"He hasn't fallen on the floor yet," Oliveira informed. "The ball bearings are letting me down."

"Don't lean out like that!" Talita shouted, raising her arms. With his back to the window, with his head turned around to see her and talk to her, Oliveira was leaning farther and farther back. Cuca Ferraguto came running out into the courtyard, and only at that moment did Oliveira realize that it was no longer night-time, Cuca's bathrobe was the same colour as the stones of the courtyard and the walls of the pharmacy. Allowing himself a reconnaissance of the battlefield, he looked into the darkness and observed that in spite of his offensive difficulties, Traveler had decided to close the door. Between two curses he heard the sound of the latch.

"That's the way I like it, hey," Oliveira said. "Alone in the centre of the ring like two men."

"Shit on your soul," Traveler said furiously. "One of my slippers is soaked through, and that's the thing that can upset me worse than anything in the world. Turn on the light at least, you can't see a thing."

"The ambush at Cancha Rayada was something like this," Oliveira said. "You must understand that I'm not going to sacrifice the advantages of my position. Be thankful that I'm answering you, because I don't really have to do that. I had my lessons on the rifle range too, brother."

He heard Traveler breathe heavily. Outside there was a slamming of doors, Ferraguto's voice mixed in with other questions and answers. Traveler's silhouette was becoming more and more visible; everything was drawing a number and fitting into its place, five basins, three spittoons, dozens of ball bearings. They could almost see each other now in that light that was like the dove in the hands of the madman.

"Well," Traveler said, picking up the fallen chair and sitting down on it without much desire. "If you could explain a little of this mess to me."

"It'll be a little hard like. Talking, you know . . . "

"When you want to talk you always find the most unbelievable moments," Traveler said in a rage. "When we're not riding horseback on two planks at ninety degrees in the shade, you catch me with one foot in the water and these damnable threads."

"But always in symmetrical positions," Oliveira said. "Like two twins playing on a seesaw, or more simply like anybody in front of a mirror. Don't you notice it, *Doppelgänger*?"

Without answering Traveler took a cigarette out of his pyjama pocket and lit it while Oliveira took out another and lit it almost at the same time. They looked at each other and began to laugh.

"You're completely off your rocker," Traveler said. "This time there's no way to tell you to turn. To imagine that I . . . "

"Leave the word imagination in peace," Oliveira said. "Limit yourself to the observation that I took my precautions, but that you came. Not someone else. You. At four o'clock in the morning."

"Talita told me, and I thought . . . But do you really believe . . . ?"

"Underneath it all it's probably necessary, Manú. You thought that you got up to come and calm me down, give me assurances. If I had been sleeping you would have come in without any trouble at all, like anybody who goes up to the mirror without any difficulties, of course, one goes quietly up to the mirror with the brush in his hand, and suppose that instead of the brush it was that thing you have there in your pyjamas . . . "

"I always carry it," Traveler said indignantly. "Or do you think we're in some kind of kindergarten here? If you go around unarmed it's because you don't know what's up."

"So finally," Oliveira said, sitting on the edge of the window again and waving his hand at Talita and Cuca, "what I think of all this doesn't matter very much next to what has to be, whether we like it or not. It's been so long that we've been the same dog chasing his tail. It's not that we hate each other; on the contrary. There are other things that use us as playthings, the white pawn and the black pawn, something like that. Let's call it two ways, the necessity that one must be abolished in the other and vice versa."

"I don't hate you," Traveler said. "It's just that you've got me boxed into a place where I don't know what to do any more."

"*Mutatis mutandi*, you met me at the dock with something that looked like an armistice, a white flag, a sad incitement to forget. I don't hate you either, brother, but I denounce you, and that's what you call being boxed in."

"I'm alive," Traveler said looking into his eyes. "Being alive always seems to be the price of something. And you don't want to pay anything. You never wanted to. A kind of existential puritan, a purist. Caesar or nothing, that kind of radical demand. Do you think I'm not surprised at you in my own sort of way? Do you think I'm not surprised that you haven't committed suicide? You're the real *Doppelgänger*, because you're like something disembodied, you're a will in the form of a weather vane, up there. I want this, I want that, I want north and south and everything all at the same time, I want La Maga, I want Talita, and then the gentleman visits the morgue and plants a kiss on his best friend's wife. Everything because realities and memories are mixed up in him to such a non-Euclidean extent."

Oliveira shrugged his shoulders, but he looked at Traveler to make him feel that it was not a gesture of disdain. How could he transmit to him something of that thing that in the territory facing him they called a kiss, a kiss on Talita, a kiss he gave La Maga or Pola, that other game of mirrors like the game of turning his head towards the window and looking at La Maga standing there next to the hopscotch while Cuca and Remorino and Ferraguto, crowding around the door, seemed to be waiting for Traveler to come to the window and announce to them that all was well, and that a capsule of Nembutal or at best a straitjacket for a little while, until the boy got over his fit. The knocks on the door didn't contribute much to understanding either. If at least Manú were capable of feeling that nothing he was thinking made any sense from the window side, that it was only worth something on the basin and ball bearing side, and if the person beating on the door with both his fists would be quiet for just a minute, perhaps then . . . But all he could do was look at La Maga so beautiful beside the hopscotch, and wish that she would move the piece from one square to the other, from earth to Heaven.

" . . . so non-Euclidean."

"I've been waiting for you all this time," Oliveira said tiredly. "You're probably aware that I wasn't going to let myself be disembowelled just like that. Everybody knows what he has to do, Manú. If you want an explanation of what happened down there . . . just that it won't have anything to do with this, and you know that. You know that, *Doppelgänger*, you know that. What difference does the kiss make to you, and what difference does it make to her either? That's between the two of you, after all."

"Open up! Open up immediately!"

"They're taking it rather badly," Traveler said, getting up. "Shall we open up for them? It must be Ovejero."

"As far as I'm concerned . . . "

"He'll want to give you an injection. Talita must have roused up the whole loony-bin."

"Women are too much," Oliveira said. "Look at her there, so well-behaved next to the hopscotch . . . Better not open up, Manú, we're doing fine just the way we are."

Traveler went to the door and put his mouth to the keyhole. Goddamned fools, why don't they stop fucking around with those shouts they pick up in horror movies. He and Oliveira were doing fine and they would open up when it was time. They would be better off making coffee for everybody, there was no living in that clinic.

It was audible enough so that Ferraguto was not convinced, but the voice of Ovejero imposed itself over his like a wise persistent rumble, and finally they left the door alone. For the moment the only sign of upset was the people in the courtyard and the lights on the fourth floor that went on and off continuously, Number 43's happy habit. Shortly afterwards, Ovejero and Ferraguto reappeared in the courtyard, and from there they looked at Oliveira seated on the window and he greeted them, excusing himself for being in his vest. Number 18 had gone over to Ovejero and was telling him something about the Heftpistole, and Ovejero seemed very interested and looked at Oliveira with professional attention, as if he no longer was his best opponent at poker, something which rather amused Oliveira. They had opened almost all the windows on the second floor, and several patients were participating with great vivacity in everything that was going on, which was not very much. La Maga had raised her right arm to attract Oliveira's attention, as if that were necessary, and she was asking him to call Traveler to the window. Oliveira explained to her in the cleverest way he could that it was impossible because the window zone belonged exclusively to the defence, but that perhaps they could arrange a truce. He added that the gesture of calling him by raising her arm made him think of actresses of the past and especially opera singers like Emmy Destinn, Melba, Marjorie Lawrence, Muzio, Bori, and why not Theda Bara and Nita Naldi, he kept spouting names with enormous pleasure and Talita lowered her arm and then raised it again in supplication, Eleonora Duse, naturally, Vilma Banky, Garbo exactly, but of course, and a photograph of Sarah Bernhardt that as a boy he had pasted in a scrapbook, and Karsavina, Baronova, women, those eternal gestures, that perpetuation of destiny although in that case it might not be possible to accede to the pleasant request.

Ferraguto and Cuca were shouting rather contradictory manifestations when Ovejero, who with his sleepy face listened to everything, motioned them to be quiet so that Talita could get through to Oliveira. An operation which was of no avail because Oliveira, after listening for the seventh time to La Maga's plea, turned his back on them and they saw him (although they could not hear him) talking to the invisible Traveler.

"They want you to come over here, you know."

"Look, in any case, just give me a minute. I can go under the threads."

"Nuts," said Oliveira. "It's the last line of defence, if you break it we'll be into hard infighting."

"OK," Traveler said, sitting down on the chair. "Keep on piling up useless words."

"They're not useless," Oliveira said. "If you want to come over here you don't have to ask my permission. I think that's clear."

"You swear you won't jump?"

Oliveira kept looking at him as if Traveler were a giant panda. "At last," he said. "The fat's in the fire. There down below, La Maga is thinking the same thing. And I thought that in spite of everything they might know me a little."

"It's not La Maga," Traveler said. "You know perfectly well it's not La Maga."

"It's not La Maga," Oliveira said. "I know perfectly well it's not La Maga. And you're the standard-bearer, the herald of surrender, of the return to home and order. You're beginning to make me feel sorry, old man."

"Forget about me," Traveler said bitterly. "What I want is for you to give me your word you won't do anything idiotic."

"Take notice that if I jump," Oliveira said, "I'm going to land right on Heaven."

"Come on over here, Horacio, and let me talk to Ovejero. I can fix things up, tomorrow everybody will have forgotten about all this."

"He learned it all in the psychiatry manual," Oliveira said almost startled. "He's a student who has great retentive powers."

"Listen," Traveler said. "If you don't let me come to the window I'm going to have to open the door and that'll be worse."

"It's all the same to me, their coming in is one thing and their getting over here is another."

"You mean that if they try to grab you you'll jump."

"It might mean that from over on your side."

"Please," Traveler said, taking a step forward. "Can't you see it's a bad dream? They're going to think you're really crazy, they're going to think I really did want to kill you."

Oliveira leaned out a little more, and Traveler stopped at the second line of watery basins. Although he had sent the ball bearings flying with a kick, he stopped advancing. Amid the shrieks from Cuca and Talita, Oliveira straightened up and made a pacifying gesture to them. As if defeated, Traveler brought the chair up a little and sat down. They were pounding on the door again, less vigorously than before.

"Don't rack your brains any more," Oliveira said. "Why are you looking for explanations of it, old man? The only real difference between you and me at this moment is that I'm alone. That's why the best thing is for you to go downstairs and rejoin your people, and we'll keep on talking out of the window like good friends. Around eight o'clock I intend to cut out; Gekrepten agreed to wait for me with pancakes and *mate*."

"You're not alone, Horacio. Maybe you wanted to be alone out of pure vanity, play the Buenos Aires Maldoror. You spoke about a *Doppelgänger*, didn't you? Now you can see that someone is following you, that someone is like you even though he's on the other side of your damnable threads."

"It's too bad," Oliveira said, "that you have such a prissy idea of vanity. That's where it lies, making yourself an idea of something, no matter what the cost. Aren't you capable of sensing even for a single second that this might not be like that?"

"Let's say that's what I think. Just the same, there you are leaning next to an open window."

"If you really suspected that this can't be this way, if you really got to the heart of the artichoke . . . Nobody asks you to deny what you're seeing, but if you were only capable of pushing a little, understand, with the tip of your toe . . . "

"If it were only so easy," Traveler said, "if it were only a question of hanging up some idiotic threads . . . I don't say that you haven't given your push, but look at the results."

"What's wrong with them? At least we have the window open and we're breathing in this fabulous dawn, feel the freshness that comes up at this hour. And down below everybody is strolling about in the courtyard, it's extraordinary, they're getting exercise without knowing it. Cuca, take a peek, and the Boss, that type of gentle marmot. And your wife, who is laziness personified. For your part you can't deny that you were never as awake as right now. And when I say awake you understand, right?"

"I wonder if it might not be just the opposite, old man."

"Oh, those are easy solutions, fantastic stories for anthologies. If you were capable of seeing the thing from the other side you probably wouldn't want to move away from there any more. If you were to leave the territory, let's say from square one to square two, or from two to three . . . It's so difficult, *Doppelgänger*, I've spent all night tossing cigarette butts and I can't get beyond square eight. We'd all like to have the millenary kingdom, a kind of Arcadia where it would probably be much more unhappy than here, because it's not a question of happiness, *Doppelgänger*, but where there wouldn't be any more of this dirty game of substitutions that occupies us for fifty or sixty years, and where we could really hold out our hands instead of repeating the gesture of fear and wanting to know if the other person has a knife hidden between his fingers. Speaking of substitutions, it wouldn't seem strange to me at all if you and I were the same, one on each side. Since you called me vain, it appears that I've chosen the more favourable side, but who can tell, Manú. One thing I do know and that's that I can't be on your side any more, everything falls apart in my hands, I get into every kind of mess that can make you go mad, supposing it was that easy. But you're in harmony with the territory and don't want to understand this coming and going, I give a push and something happens to me, then five thousand years of rotten genes draw me back and I fall into the territory again, I splash for two weeks, two years, fifteen years . . . One day I stick my finger into habit and it's incredible how one's finger sinks into habit and comes out the other side, it looks as if I'm finally going to get to the last square and suddenly a woman drowns, let's say, or I get an attack, an attack of useless pity, because that business of pity . . . I mentioned substitutions to you, didn't I? What filth, Manú. Look up that business of substitutions in Dostoevsky. In a word, five thousand years pull me back again and I have to start all over. That's why I feel that you're my *Doppelgänger*, because all the time I'm coming and going from your territory to mine, if I really ever do get to mine, and in those weary passages it seems to me that you're my form staying there looking at me with pity, you're the five thousand years of man piled up into six feet, looking at that clown who wants to get out of his square. Amen."

"Stop fucking around," Traveler shouted at the people pounding on the door again. "Can't anybody talk peacefully in this madhouse?'

"You're wonderful, brother," Oliveira said, moved.

"In any case," Traveler said, moving his chair up a little, "you're not going to deny that you've gone too far this time. Transubstantiations and other plants are all OK but this trick of yours is going to cost us all our jobs, and I'm sorry about it especially for Talita's sake. You can talk all you want about La Maga, but I'm the one who has to feed my wife."

"You're absolutely right," Oliveira said. "One forgets he has a job and things like that. Do you want me to talk to Ferraguto? There he is over by the fountain. I'm sorry, Manú, I didn't want La Maga and you . . . "

"Do you think it's right now to call her La Maga? Don't lie, Horacio."

"I know she's Talita, but a while ago she was La Maga. She's two people, just like us."

"They call that being crazy," Traveler said.

"Everything is called something, you choose and let it go. If you'll excuse me I must attend to the people down below, because they can't take any more of this."

"I'm leaving," Traveler said, getting up.

"That's more like it," said Oliveira. "It's much better for you to leave and not bend your knees the way you are, because I'm going to explain what will happen, you adore explanations just like all the other sons of the five thousand years. As soon as you jump on me, carried away by friendship and your diagnosis, I'll move to one side, because I don't know if you remember the time I used to practise judo with the boys on the Calle Anchorena, and what will happen is that you'll continue your trip through this window and end up as a piece of mucus on square four, and then only if you're lucky because it's more likely that you won't even get beyond two."

Traveler looked at him, and Oliveira saw that his eyes were filling with tears. He made a gesture as if to stroke his hair from a distance.

Traveler waited another second, and then he went to the door and opened it. As soon as Remorino (two other attendants could be seen behind him) tried to enter he grabbed him by the shoulders and shoved him back.

"Leave him alone," he ordered. "He'll be all right in a while. We have to leave him alone, oh fuck it all."

Disregarding the dialogue that had rapidly ascended to tetralogue, hexalogue, and dodecalogue, Oliveira closed his eyes and thought that everything was so good like that, that Traveler really was his brother. He heard the noise of the door as it closed, the voices going away. The door opened again, coinciding with his eyelids which he lifted with great effort.

"Bolt the door," Traveler said. "I don't trust them."

"Thanks," said Oliveira. "Go on down to the courtyard. Talita's very upset."

He went under the few surviving threads and threw the bolt. Before returning to the window he put his face in the water in the sink and drank like an animal, swallowing and licking and snorting. Down below one could hear Remorino's commands as he ordered the patients to their rooms. When he went back, fresh and peaceful, he saw that Traveler was next to Talita and that he had put his arm around her waist. After what Traveler had just done, everything had something like a marvellous feeling of conciliation and that senseless but vivid and present harmony could not be violated, could no longer be falsified, basically Traveler was what he might well have been with a little less cursed imagination, he was the man of the territory, the incurable mistake of the species gone astray, but how much beauty in the mistake and in the five thousand years of false and precarious territory, how much beauty in those eyes that had filled with tears and in that voice that had advised him: "Bolt the door, I don't trust them," how much love in that arm that held the waist of a woman. "Probably," Oliveira thought while he answered the friendly gestures of Dr Ovejero and Ferraguto (a little less friendly), "the only possible way to escape from the territory is to plunge into it over one's head." He was aware that as soon as he got that feeling he would glimpse the image of a man taking an old woman along by the arm through rainy and freezing streets. "Who can tell," he said to himself. "Who can tell if maybe I haven't been staying on the edge, and that there probably was a passage. Manú would have found it, certainly, but the idiot thing is that Manú will never look for it and I, on the other hand . . ."

"Hey, Oliveira, why don't you come on down and have some coffee?" Ferraguto proposed to the visible displeasure of Ovejero. "You've already won the bet, don't you think? Look at Cuca, how upset she is."

"Don't get upset, señora," Oliveira said. "With your experience in the circus you're not going to go soft on me over some nonsense."

"Oh, Oliveira, you and Traveler are awful," Cuca said. "Why don't you do what my husband says? I was just thinking that we all ought to sit down together for some coffee."

"Yes, hey, come on down," Ovejero said, trying to appear casual. "I need your advice on a couple of matters that have to do with some French books."

"I can hear quite well from up here," Oliveira said.

"OK, old man," Ovejero said. "You come on down when you want to, we're going to have some breakfast."

"With nice hot croissants," Cuca said. "Shall we go and make some coffee, Talita?"

"Don't be an arse," Talita said, and in the extraordinary silence that followed her admonition, the meeting of the looks of Traveler and Oliveira was as if two birds had collided in flight and all mixed up together had fallen into square nine, or at least that was how it was enjoyed by those involved. Cuca and Ferraguto were breathing heavily during all this, and finally Cuca opened her mouth to shriek: "Why, what's the meaning of such insolence?" while Ferraguto stuck out his chest and looked Traveler up and down while the latter at the same time was looking at his wife with a mixture of admiration and censure until Ovejero found the appropriate scientific escape and said dryly: "*Hysteria matinensis yugulata*, let's go inside, I have to hand out some pills," at the same time that Number 18, violating Remorino's orders, came out into the courtyard to announce that Number 31 was upset and that there was a telephone call from Mar del Plata. His violent expulsion at the hands of Remorino helped the administrators and Ovejero to evacuate the courtyard without excessive loss of prestige.

"My, my, my," said Oliveira, teetering on the window, "and I thought that pharmacists had such good manners."

"Did you notice?" Traveler said. "She was glorious."

"She sacrificed herself for me," Oliveira said. "The other one is never going to forgive her, not even on her deathbed."

"That really worries me," Talita said. "'With nice hot croissants', get a load of that."

"And what about Ovejero?" Traveler asked. "French books! The only thing missing was for them to tempt you with a banana. I'm surprised you didn't tell them all to go to hell."

That's the way it was, the harmony lasted incredibly long, there were no words that could answer the goodness of those two down there below, looking at him and talking to him from the hopscotch, because Talita had stopped in square three without realizing it, and Traveler had one foot in six, so that the only thing left to do was to move his right hand a little in a timid salute and stay there looking at La Maga, at Manú, telling himself that there was some meeting after all, even though it might only last just for that terribly sweet instant in which the best thing without any doubt at all would be to lean over just a little bit farther out and let himself go, paff the end.

* * *

(–135)

From Diverse Sides

Expendable Chapters

57

"I'm warming up some ideas for when Adgalle arrives. What do you think about my taking her to the Club some night? Étienne and Ronald would be charmed, she's so mad."

"Take her."

"You would have liked her too."

"Why do you talk as if I were dead?"

"I don't know," Ossip said. "I really don't know. You have a look about you."

"This morning I was telling Étienne about some very pretty dreams. Right now I'm getting them all mixed up inside me with some other memories while you go on about the burial with such tender words. It really must have been a moving ceremony, eh. It's so very strange to be able to be in three places at once, but that's just what's happening to me this afternoon, it must be the influence of Morelli. Yes, yes, now I'm going to tell you about it. In four places at once, now that I think about it. I'm getting close to ubiquity, and going crazy is just one step away . . . You're right, I probably won't be able to meet Adgalle, I'll be gone to hell long before."

"Zen has a precise explanation for the possibilities of preubiquity, something similar to the feeling you've just described, if in fact you did have such a feeling."

"That's what it is. I've returned from four simultaneous points: the dream this morning, still alive and wriggling. Some interludes with Pola which I'll spare you, your gaudy description of the kid's burial, and now I realize that all at the same time I've been answering Traveler, a friend in Buenos Aires who never in his fucking life understood a few lines of poetry of mine which began like this, listen to them: 'Between sleep and wakefulness, diving into washbasins.' And it's so easy, if you think about it a little, you ought to understand it. When you wake up, with the remains of a paradise half-seen in dreams hanging down over you like the hair on someone who's been drowned: terrible nausea, anxiety, a feeling of the precarious, the false, especially the useless. You fall inward, while you brush your teeth you really are a diver into washbasins, it's as if the white sink were absorbing you, as if you were slipping down through that hole that carries off tartar, mucus, rheum, dandruff, saliva, and you let yourself go in the hope that maybe you'll return to the other thing, to what you were before you woke up, and it's still floating around, is still inside you, is you yourself, but then it starts to go away . . . Yes, you fall inward for a moment, until the defences of wakefulness, oh pretty words, oh language, take charge and stop you."

"A typical existential experience," Gregorovius said petulantly.

"Naturally, but everything depends on the dosage. In my case the washbasin really sucks me in."

(–70)

58

"You were very wise to come," Gekrepten said as she changed the *yerba.* "You're better off here at home, especially because of the environment over there, what did you expect. You should have taken two or three days off."

"I think you're right," Oliveira said. "And more important than all that, old girl. These fried cakes are sublime."

"How lucky that you like them. Don't eat too many or you'll get indigestion."

"Nothing to worry about," Ovejero said, lighting a cigarette. "Have a good nap now and tonight you'll be in prime condition for drawing a royal flush and lots of aces."

"Don't move," Talita said. "It's incredible how you can't be still."

"My wife is so upset," Ferraguto said.

"Have another fried cake," said Gekrepten.

"Don't give him anything except fruit juice," Ovejero ordered.

"National Corporation of the Learned in Suitable Sciences and their Houses of Science," Oliveira mocked.

"Seriously now, don't eat anything until tomorrow," Ovejero said.

"Here's one with lots of sugar on it," said Gekrepten.

"Try to get some sleep," Traveler said.

"Hey, Remorino, stick around the door and don't let Number 18 bother him," Ovejero said. "He's developed a terrible fixation and all he talks about is some kind of pistol."

"If you want to sleep I'll close the blinds," Gekrepten said, "then you won't hear Don Crespo's radio."

"No, leave them," Oliveira said. "They're playing something by Falú."

"It's already five o'clock," Talita said. "Don't you feel like sleeping?"

"Give him a fresh compress," Traveler said, "that seems to relieve him."

"The *mate* will be ready soon," Gekrepten said. "Do you want me to go out and pick up the *Noticias Gráficas*?"

"Fine," Oliveira said. "And a pack of cigarettes."

"It's hard for him to get to sleep," Traveler said, "but he'll be able to get through the whole night now, Ovejero gave him a double dose."

"Behave yourself, love," Gekrepten said, "I'll be right back. We're going to have steak tonight, how does that suit you?"

"With a tossed salad," Oliveira said.

"He's breathing better," Talita said.

"And I'll make you some rice and milk," Gekrepten said. "I didn't like the look on your face when you arrived."

"The tram was packed," Oliveira said. "You know what the platform is like at eight in the morning and with all this heat."

"Do you really think he'll stay asleep, Manú?"

"As far as I want to believe in something, yes."

"Then let's go up and see the Boss, he's waiting to fire us."

"My wife is so upset," Ferraguto said.

"Why, what's the meaning of such insolence?!" Cuca shouted.

"They were great people," Ovejero said.

"You don't find many like them," said Remorino.

"He refused to believe me when I told him he needed a Heftpistole," said Number 18.

"Beat it back to your room or I'll give you an enema," Ovejero said.

"Death to the dog!" Number 18 said.

(–131)

59

Then, to pass the time, they catch fish they cannot eat; to avoid the rotting of the fishes in the air, notices have been posted all along the beach telling the fishermen to bury them in the sand just as soon as they have been caught.

CLAUDE LÉVI-STRAUSS, *Tristes Tropiques*

(–41)

60

Morelli had been thinking about a list of acknowledgements which he never got around to including in his published works. It had several names: Jelly Roll Morton, Robert Musil, Daisetz Teitaro Suzuki, Raymond Roussel, Kurt Schwitters, Vieira da Silva, Akutagawa, Anton Webern, Greta Garbo, José Lezama Lima, Buñuel, Louis Armstrong, Borges, Michaux, Dino Buzzati, Max Ernst, Pevsner, Gilgamesh (?), Garcilaso, Arcimboldo, René Clair, Piero di Cosimo, Wallace Stevens, Isak Dinesen. The names of Rimbaud, Picasso, Chaplin, Alban Berg and others had a very fine line drawn through them, as though they were too obvious to be mentioned. But in the end he should have done the same to all of them, because Morelli had decided not to include the list in any of his volumes.

(–26)

61

An inconclusive note by Morelli

I will never be able to escape the feeling that there, clinging to my face, intertwined among my fingers, there is something like a dazzling explosion towards the light, an invasion of me in the direction of the other thing or of the other thing towards me, something infinitely crystalline that could coalesce and become total light outside time or space. Like a door of opal and diamond out of which one starts to be the thing one truly is and does not want and does not know and is not able to be.

There is nothing new about that thirst and that suspicion, but there is an ever greater confusion when I face the ersatz things offered me by this day-and-night intelligence, this archive of facts and memories, these passions where I go about leaving pieces of time and skin, these surmises so much underneath and far away from those other surmises there next to me, stuck to my face, prevision already mixed with vision, the denunciation of that feigned freedom with which I move through streets and years.

Since I am no more than this body which has already putrefied in some point of future time, these bones that write anachronically, I feel that the body is demanding itself, demanding from its consciousness the still inconceivable operation that would no longer be putrefaction. This body that I am has the prescience of a state in which as it denies itself as such, and as it simultaneously denies the objective correlative as such, its own consciousness would accede to a state outside the body and outside the world which would be the true accession to being. My body will be, not mine Morelli, not I, the one who in nineteen hundred and fifty has already putrefied in nineteen hundred and eighty, my body will be because behind that door of light (what can we call that besieging certainty stuck to the face) being will be something other than bodies and, than bodies and souls and, than I and the other thing, than yesterday and tomorrow. Everything depends on . . . (a sentence scratched out).

Melancholy finale: A *satori* is instantaneous and resolves everything. But in order to reach it one would have to unwind history, both the one outside and the one inside. *Trop tard pour moi. Crever en italien, voire en occidental, c'est tout ce qui me reste. Mon petit café-crème le matin, si agréable . . .*

(–33)

62

At one time Morelli had been planning a book that never got beyond a few scattered notes. It can be summed up best in this way: "Psychology, a word with the air of an old woman about it. A Swede is working on a chemical theory of thought.* Chemistry, electromagnetism, the secret flow of living matter, everything returns strangely to evoke the idea of mana; in a like manner, on the edge of social behaviour, one might suspect an interaction of a different nature, a billiard game that certain individuals play or are played at, a drama with no Oedipuses, no Rastignacs, no Phaedras, an *impersonal* drama to the extent that the consciences and the passions of the

* *L'Express*, Paris, n.d.

Two months ago a Swedish neurobiologist, Holger Hyden, of the University of Göteborg, presented to the most eminent specialists in the world, gathered in San Francisco, his theories on the chemical nature of mental processes. According to Hyden, the act of thinking, of remembering, of feeling, or of making a decision is manifested by the appearance in the brain, and in the nerves connecting it with other organs, of certain particular molecules which the nerve cells manufacture as a result of the external stimulus. (. . .) The Swedish team was able to effect the delicate separation of the two types of cell in live rabbit tissue, weighed them (in millionths of a millionth of a gram), and determined through analysis the way in which these cells utilized their fuel in various cases.

One of the essential functions of neurons is the transmission of nervous impulses. This transmission operates by means of almost instantaneous electrochemical reactions. It is not easy to surprise a nerve cell at work, but it appears that the Swedes have done so by means of the careful use of certain methods.

It has been proved that the stimulus becomes transformed in the neurons into an increment of certain proteins whose molecules will vary according to the nature of the message. At the same time, the number of proteins in the satellite cells is reduced, as if they were sacrificing their reserves for the sake of the neuron. The information contained in the protein molecule is converted, according to Hyden, into the impulse which the neuron passes on to its neighbours.

The higher functions of the brain – memory and the reasoning faculties – are explained, according to Hyden, by the particular form of the protein molecules characters cannot be seen as having been compromised except a posteriori. As if the subliminal levels were those that wind and unravel the ball of yarn which is the group that has been compromised in the play. Or to please the Swede: as if certain individuals had cut into the deep chemistry of others without having meant to and vice versa, so that the most curious and interesting chain reactions, fissions, and transmutations would result.

"Things being as they are, all that is needed is a pleasant extrapolation in order to postulate a human group that thinks it is reacting psychologically in the classic sense of that tired old word, but which merely represents an instance in that flow of animated matter, in the infinite interactions of what we formerly called desires, sympathies, wills, convictions, and which appear here as something irreducible to all reason and all description: foreign occupying forces, advancing in the quest of their freedom of the city; a quest superior to ourselves as individuals and one which uses us for its own ends, a dark necessity of evading the state of Homo sapiens towards . . . which Homo? Because *sapiens* is another tired old word, one of those that one must scrub clean before attempting to use it with any sort of meaning.

---

which correspond to each type of stimulus. Each neuron in the brain contains millions of different molecules of ribonucleic acid, which are distinguished by the disposition of their basic constituent elements. Each molecule of ribonucleic acid (RNA) corresponds to a well-defined protein, the way a key is perfectly adapted to a lock. The nucleic acids tell the neuron the make-up of the protein molecule it is to form. According to the Swedish researchers, these molecules are the chemical translation of thoughts.

Memory would correspond, therefore, to the ordering in the brain of the nucleic acid molecules, which play the same role as perforated cards in modern computers. For example, the impulse which corresponds to the note mi as it is picked up by the ear, will slide rapidly along from one neuron to another until it has reached all of those containing the molecules of RNA corresponding to that particular stimulus. The cells immediately construct molecules of the corresponding protein which that acid governs, and we have the auditory perception of the note.

The richness and variety of thought is explained by the fact that an average brain contains some ten thousand million neurons, each of which contains in turn several million molecules of various nucleic acids; the number of possible combinations is astronomical. This theory, furthermore, has the advantage of explaining why it has not been possible to discover in the brain clearly defined and special zones for each one of its higher functions; since each neuron has several nucleic acids at hand, it can take part in various mental processes, and evoke diverse thoughts and memories.

"If I were to write this book, standard behaviour (including the most unusual, its deluxe category) would be inexplicable by means of current instrumental psychology. The actors would appear to be unhealthy or complete idiots. Not that they would show themselves incapable of current *challenges and responses*: love, jealousy, pity, and so on down the line, but in them something which Homo sapiens keeps subliminal would laboriously open up a road as if a third eye* were blinking out with effort from under the frontal bone. Everything would be a kind of disquiet, a continuous uprooting, a territory where psychological causality would yield disconcertedly, and those puppets would destroy each other or love each other or recognize each other without suspecting too much that life is trying to change its key in and through and by them, that a barely conceivable attempt is born in man as one other day there were being born the reason-key, the feeling-key, the pragmatism-key. That with each successive defeat there is an approach towards the final mutation, and that man only is in that he searches to be, plans to be, thumbing through words and modes of behaviour and joy sprinkled with blood and other rhetorical pieces like this one."

*Note by Wong (in pencil): "A metaphor chosen with the deliberate intent of suggesting the direction in which he is heading."

(–23)

63

"Don't move," Talita said. "You'd think that instead of a cold compress you were getting oil of vitriol."

"It's like a kind of electricity," Oliveira said.

"Don't talk nonsense."

"I can see all sorts of phosphorescences, it's like something by Norman McLaren."

"Raise your head a minute, the pillow's too low, I'm going to change it for you."

"It would be better if you left the pillow alone and changed my head," Oliveira said. "Surgery is still in its infancy, that you've got to admit."

(–88)

64

One of the times they had met in the Latin Quarter, Pola was looking at the pavement, practically everybody was looking at the pavement. They had to stop and study the profile of Napoleon, alongside it an excellent reproduction of Chartres, and a little farther on, a mare and her foal in a green field. The artists were two blond boys and an Indo-Chinese girl. The chalk box was full of ten- and twenty-franc pieces. From time to time one of the artists would crouch down to perfect some detail, and it was easy to see that at that instant the donations would increase.

"They're using the Penelope system, but without unweaving first," Oliveira said. "That lady, for example, she didn't loosen her purse-strings until little Tsong Tsong got down on the ground to retouch the blond with blue eyes. Work produces sentiment, it's a fact."

"Is her name Tsong Tsong?" Pola asked.

"How should I know. She has nice ankles."

"So much work and tonight the women who sweep the streets will come and it's all over."

"That's precisely why it's so good. Coloured chalk as an eschatological pattern, the theme for a thesis. If the municipal waterwagons didn't put an end to all of it at dawn, Tsong Tsong would come herself with a pail of water. The only thing that really ends is what starts over again in the morning. People throw coins without knowing that they're being cheated, because those pictures are really never erased. They may change pavements or colours, but they're already there in finished form in a hand, a box of chalk, a wise system of movements; if one of those boys were to spend the morning waving his arms around he would deserve ten francs just as much as when he draws Napoleon. But we want proofs. There they are. Give them twenty francs, don't be cheap."

"I already did before you got here."

"Admirable. Fundamentally we're placing those coins in the mouth of the dead, the propitiatory obolus. Homage to the ephemeral, so that cathedral may be a chalk image that a splash of water will carry off in one second. The coin is there, and the cathedral will be reborn tomorrow. We pay for immortality, we pay for things that last. *No money, no cathedral.* Are you made of chalk too?"

But Pola didn't answer him, and he put his arm around her shoulders and they walked Boul' Mich' up and Boul' Mich' down, before wandering slowly towards the Rue Dauphine. A world of coloured chalk was spinning around them and caught them up in its dance, fried potatoes in yellow chalk, red wine in red chalk, a pale soft sky in light blue chalk with a touch of green along the riverside. They tossed another coin in the cigar box to halt the flight of the cathedral, and with that very gesture they condemned it to be erased so it could be again, disappear under the splash of water and return chalk after chalk black and blue and yellow. The Rue Dauphine in grey chalk, the staircase carefully done in tones of brown chalk, the room with its lines of flight astutely drawn in bright green chalk, the curtains in white chalk, the bed with its serape where all the chalks *¡Viva México!*, love, its chalks yearning for the fixative that would keep them in the present, love in perfumed chalk, mouth in orange chalk, sadness and surfeit of colourless chalks spinning around in imperceptible dust, settling on the sleeping faces, on the exhausted chalk of the bodies.

"Everything falls apart when you take hold of it, even if you just look at it," Pola said. "You're like some terrible acid, I'm afraid of you."

"You put too much stock in a few metaphors."

"It isn't just that you say it, it's a way you have . . . I don't know, like a funnel. Sometimes I think I'm going to slip out of your arms and fall into a well. It's worse than dreaming that you're falling in space."

"Maybe you're not entirely lost," Oliveira said.

"Oh, leave me in peace. I know how to live, you know. I live very well the way I live. Here, with my things and my friends."

"Name them, name them. That helps. Give them names then you won't fall. There's the bedside table, the curtain hasn't run away from the window, Claudette is still at the same address, DAN-ton 34 I can't remember the rest, and your mother still writes to you from Aix-en-Provence. Everything's fine."

"You make me afraid, you South American monster," Pola said, squeezing up against him. "We'd agreed that here in my place there wouldn't be any talk about . . . "

"About coloured chalk."

"About all of that."

Oliveira lit a Gauloise and looked at the folded piece of paper on the bedside table.

"Is that the appointment for the tests?"

"Yes, he wants me to have them done immediately. Feel here, it's worse than last week."

It was almost night and Pola looked like a figure out of Bonnard, stretched out on the bed which was being wrapped in a yellowish green by the last light from the window. "The street-sweeper at dawn," Oliveira thought, leaning over to kiss her on the breast, exactly where she had just pointed with a hesitant finger. "But they don't get up to the fifth floor, I've never heard of a street-sweeper or water-wagon getting up to a fifth floor. Apart from the fact that tomorrow the artist would come and do it over exactly the same way, this delicate curve where something . . . " He managed to stop thinking, for just an instant he managed to kiss her without its being anything but his own kiss.

(–155)

65

Sample entry from Club files
Gregorovius, Ossip

Stateless.

Full moon (obverse side, invisible in those yet presputnik days): craters? seas? ashes?

Tends to dress in black, grey, brown. Has never been seen wearing full suit. There are those who affirm that he owns three but will invariably combine jacket of one with trousers of another. This could easily be verified.

Age: says he is forty-eight.

Profession: intellectual. Great-aunt sends modest allowance.

Carte de séjour AC 3456923 (for six months, renewable. It has already been renewed nine times with increasing difficulty each time).

Country of origin: born in Borzok (birth certificate probably false according to declaration by Gregorovius to Paris police. Reasons for his assumption in his dossier).

Country of origin: in the year of his birth Borzok was part of the Austro-Hungarian Empire. Obvious Magyar origin. Likes to imply that he is a Czech.

Country of origin: probably Great Britain. Gregorovius was probably born in Glasgow, the son of a sailor father and landlubber mother, the result of an emergency port of call, a shifting ballast, stout, and excessive xenophilic willingness on the part of Miss Marjorie Babington, 22 Stewart Street.

Gregorovius enjoys creating a picaresque prenatal state for himself and slanders his mothers (has three, depending on type of drunkenness) by attributing licentious habits to them. The Herzogin Magda Razenswill, who appears with whiskey or cognac, was the lesbian author of a pseudo-scientific treatise on *carezza* (translated into four languages). Miss Babington, whose ectoplasm materializes with gin, ended up as a whore on Malta. Third mother is constant problem for Étienne, Ronald and Oliveira, witnesses to her hazy apparition via Beaujolais, Côtes-du-Rhône, or Bourgogne Aligoté. Depending on circumstances her name is Galle, Adgalle or Minti, she lives freely in Herzegovina or Naples, travels to the United States with a vaudeville company, is first woman to smoke in Spain, sells violets outside the Vienna Opera, invents contraceptive devices, dies of typhus, is alive but blind in Huerta, disappears along with the Tsar's chauffeur in Tsarskoie Selo, blackmails her son every leap year, practises hydrotherapy, has suspicious relations with priest from Pontoise, died at the birth of Gregorovius, who is also the son of Santos-Dumont. In some inexplicable way witnesses have noted that these successive (or simultaneous) versions of third mother are always accompanied by references to Gurdjieff, whom Gregorovius admires and despises according to the pendulum.

(–11)

66

Facets of Morelli, his Bouvard et Pécuchet side, his side as the compiler of a literary almanac (sometimes he will give the name of "Almanac" to the body of his work).

He would like to sketch certain ideas, but he is incapable of doing so. The designs which appear in the margins of his notes are terrible. The obsessive repetition of a tremulous spiral, with a rhythm similar to the ones adorning Sanchi's stupa.

He plans one of the many endings to his unfinished book, and he leaves a mockup. The page contains a single sentence: "Underneath it all he knew that one cannot go beyond because there isn't any." The sentence is repeated over and over for the whole length of the page, giving the impression of a wall, of an impediment. There are no periods or commas or margins. A wall, in fact, of words that illustrate the meaning of the sentence, the collision with a wall behind which there is nothing. But towards the bottom and on the right, in one of the sentences the word *any* is missing. A sensitive eye can discover the hole among the bricks, the light that shows through.

(–149)

67

I'm tying my shoes, happy, whistling, and suddenly unhappiness. But this time I caught you, anguish. I sensed you *ahead* of any mental organization, with the first negative judgement. Like a grey colour that might be a pain and might be my stomach. And *almost* at the same time (but afterwards, you won't fool me this time) the way was opened for the intelligible repertory, with an explicatory idea first off: "And now to live another day, etc." From which there follows: "I'm anxious *because* . . . etc."

Ideas under sail, propelled by the primordial wind blowing from underneath (but underneath is only a physical location). All that's needed is a change in the breeze (*but what is it that changes its quadrant?*) and right off, here are the happy little boats, with their coloured sails. "After all, there's no reason to complain, man," like that.

I woke up and I saw the light of dawn through the cracks in the Venetian blinds. It came from so deep in the night that I had a feeling like that of vomiting up myself, the terror of coming into a new day with its same presentation, its mechanical indifference of everytime: consciousness, a sensation of light, opening my eyes, blinds, dawn.

In that second, with that omniscience of half-sleep, I measured the horror of what astounds and enchants religions so much: the eternal perfection of the cosmos, the unending rotation of the globe on its axis. Nausea, the unbearable feeling of coaction. *I am obliged to bear the daily rising of the sun.* It's monstrous. *It's inhuman.*

Before going back to sleep I imagined (I saw) a plastic universe, changeable, full of wondrous chance, an elastic sky, a sun that suddenly is missing or remains fixed or changes its shape.

I was anxious for the dispersal of the fixed constellations, that dirty luminous propaganda put out by the Divine Watchmakers' Trust.

(–83)

68

As soon as he began to amalate the noeme, the clemise began to smother her and they fell into hydromuries, into savage ambonies, into exasperating sustales. Each time that he tried to relamate the hairincops, he became entangled in a whining grimate and had to face up to envulsioning the novalisk, feeling how little by little the arnees would spejune, were becoming peltronated, redoblated, until they were stretched out like the ergomanine trimalciate which drops a few filures of cariaconce. And it was still only the beginning, because right away she tordled her hurgales, allowing him gently to bring up his orfelunes. No sooner had they cofeathered than something like a ulucord encrestored them, extrajuxted them, and paramoved them, suddenly it was the clinon, the sterfurous convulcant of matericks, the slobberdigging raimouth of the orgumion, the sproemes of the merpasm in one superhumitic agopause. Evohé! Evohé! Volposited on the crest of a murelium, they felt themselves being balparammed, perline and marulous. The trock was trembling, the mariplumes were overcome, and everything became resolvirated into a profound pinex, into niolames of argutentic gauzes, into almost cruel cariniers which ordopained them to the limit of their gumphies.

(–9)

69

(*Renovigo*, No. 5: translated from the Ispamerikan)

ANUTHER SUISIDE

It waz a sad surprize to rede in the "Orthografik" the newz ov the demize in San Luis Potosí on march furst last of lootcnant kernel (promoted to kernel on leving the surviss) Adolfo Abila Sanhes. It waz a surprize bekuz we had no newz of hiz having bin il. Furthermor, for sum time now we hav kept a katalog ov owr frends hoo wur suisides, and on won okayzhun "Renovigo" made referens too serten simtums in thoze obzervd. It iz just that Abila Sanhes did not chuze a reevolvr like the anteyklerikl riter Giyermo Delora, nor the nooss like the French esperantist Eujene Lanti.

Abila Sanhes waz a man wurthi of atenshun and apreshiayshun. An onorabl soljer, he brawt onor too hiz profeshun in theeoree and in praktiss. He had a hie ideea ov loyaltee and eevn went onto the feeld ov batl. A man ov kulchur, he tawt seyens to yung peepl and adults. A thinkr, he rote meni thingz for magazeenz and he left a fue unpublishd werks, amung them "Baraks Maxims". A poet, he versifeyed with grate fasilitee in difrent forms. An artist with pen and pensil, he ofen entertaned us with hiz kreayshuns. A lingwist, he likd too tranzlate his own produkshuns in too Inglish, Esperanto, and uther tungs.

Basikly, Abila Sanhes waz a man ov thawt and akshun, ov moralitee and ov kulchur. This is wet made up hiz being.

In the uther colum ther ar sevral entrees, and it iz nachural to hezitate befor lifting the vale on hiz prievt life. But sinse a publik man haz nun and Abila Sanhes waz just that, we wood not be tru too owrselvz if we did not sho the uther side ov the medl. In owr role as biografrz and historiunz we must abandn skruplz.

We met Abila Sanhes pursonalee arownd 1936 in Linares, N.L., and then in Monteray we vizitd him in hiz home, wich seemd prosperus and happee. Yers later wen we vizitd him in Samora the impreshun was compleetlee difrent, we realizd that hiz home waz braking up, and then wekes later, wel, it waz hiz wife hoo dezertd him and hiz childrn skatrd. Finely, in San Luis Potosí, he met a kined yung gerl hoo liked him and she agrede too maree him: that iz how he had a sekund famlee, wich waz mor tolerunt than the ferst won and nevr kame to abandn him.

Wat hapnd ferst with Abila Sanhes, hiz mentl ilness or alkoholism? We doo not no, but both thingz toogethr were the ruinayshun ov hiz life and the kauz ov hiz deth. A sik man in hiz last yers, we had expeld him noing that he waz a suiside heading toards hiz inevitabl end. Won becumz fatalistik wen won obzervz peepl so clerelee heading toards a ner and trajik deth.

The desseessed beleved in a fiucher life. If he fownd that, let him fynd happines ther, even tho with difrent karakteristiks awl ov us, awl hiumans seke it.

(–52)

70

"When I was in my first cause, I did not have God . . . ; I wanted myself and I did not want anything else; I was what I wanted, and I wanted what I was, and I was free of God and of everything . . . That is why we beseech God to free us from God, and to let us conceive the truth and to let us enjoy it eternally, there where the supreme angels, the fly, and the soul are all alike, there where I was and where I wanted that which I was and it was that which I wanted . . . "

MEISTER ECKARDT, sermon: *Beati pauperes spiritu*

(–147)

71

Morelliana

Basically, what is this story about finding a millenary kingdom, an Eden, another world? Everything written these days and worth reading is oriented towards nostalgia. An Arcadia complex, the return to the great uterus, back to Adam, *le bon sauvage* (and so it goes . . .), *Paradise lost, lost because I searched for you in my eternal darkness* . . . And so much for islands (*cf.* Musil) or gurus (if you have the cash for the Paris–Bombay flight) or simply picking up a coffee cup and looking at it all over, not like a coffee cup any more but like evidence of the immense asininity in which we all find ourselves, believing that this object is nothing but a coffee cup while even the most idiot among journalists is assigned to give us a précis of the quanta, Planck and Heisenberg, knocks himself out in three columns explaining that everything vibrates and trembles and is like a cat about to take an enormous hydrogen or cobalt leap which will leave us all with our feet sticking up in the air. An uncouth way of expressing one's self, really.

The coffee cup is white, the noble savage is brown, Planck was a formidable German. Behind all that (it's always behind, convince yourself that this is the key idea of modern thought) Paradise, the other world, trampled innocence which weeping darkly seeks the land of Hurqalyā. In one way or another everyone is looking for it, everyone wants to open the door that leads out to the playground. And not just for Eden, not so much for Eden as such, but just to leave jet planes behind, Nikita's face or Dwight's or Charles's or Francisco's, the waking up to bells, the adjustment to thermometer and weather vane, the retirement from kicks in the arse (forty years of rubbing one's behind so that it won't hurt so much, but it hurts just the same, the tip of the shoe digs in a little deeper every time just the same, and each kick dredges up for just one moment more the poor arse of the cashier or the second lieutenant or the professor of literature or the nurse), and we were saying that Homo sapiens is not seeking the door in order to enter the millenary kingdom (even though it would not be so bad, not really bad at all) but only so he can close it behind his back and wiggle his arse like a contented dog, knowing that the old whore's shoe was left behind, breaking itself against the closed door, and that one can go ahead and unbutton his poor arsehole with a sigh, straighten up, and start walking among the posies in the garden and sit down to look at a cloud for five thousand years, no less, or twenty thousand if that is possible and if nobody gets upset and if he is lucky enough to stay in the garden looking at the posies.

From time to time among the legions of people going about with their arses exposed there is one who not only might want to shut the door for protection against the kicks of the three traditional dimensions, plus the ones supplied by the categories of understanding, by that more than rotten principle of sufficient reason and other infinite drivel, but furthermore, these types believe along with other madmen that we are not in the world, that our venerable parents have set us on a course in the wrong direction and we have to get off it if we do not want to end up as an equestrian statue or transformed into an exemplary grandparent, and that nothing is lost if one maintains as his end the value of proclaiming that everything is lost and that we have to start all over again, like the famous workmen in 1907 who realized one August morning that the tunnel under Monte Brasco was off course and that they would end up by coming out more than twenty yards away from the tunnel being dug by Yugoslav workmen coming from Dublivna. What did the famous workmen do? The famous workmen left their tunnel the way it was, came out on the surface, and after several days and nights of deliberation in various Piedmont bars, began to dig on their own and at their own risk in a different part of Monte Brasco, and they kept on going without worrying about the Yugoslav workmen, and after four months and five days they came out in the southern part of Dublivna, with no small surprise for a retired schoolteacher who saw them appear in his house at bathroom level. A praiseworthy example which the Dublivna workmen should have followed (although one must recognize that the famous workmen had not communicated their intentions) instead of obstinately connecting with a non-existent tunnel, as is the case with so many poets leaning halfway out of the living-room window late at night.

And so one can laugh, and think that it is not serious, but it is serious, laughter has dug more useful tunnels all by itself than all the tears on earth, even though it may barely be known to stiff-necked people, stubborn in their belief that Melpomene is more fruitful than Queen Mab. Once and for all it would be good to arrive at a disagreement in this matter. Perhaps there is one way out, but that exit ought to be an entrance. Perhaps there is a millenary kingdom, but you don't storm a fortress by running away from an enemy charge. Until now this century has been running away from all sorts of things, it has been looking for doorways and sometimes it gets to the bottom of them. What happens afterwards no one knows; some may have managed to see and have perished, instantly erased by great black forgetfulness, others will have conformed to the small escape, the little house in the suburbs, literary or scientific specialization, travel. Escapes are planned, they become technologized, they are furnished with the Modulor or with the Nylon Law. There are imbeciles who still believe that drunkenness is a way, or mescaline, or homosexuality, anything magnificent and inane per se but stupidly elevated into a system, into a key to the kingdom. Maybe there is another world inside this one, but we will not find it cutting out its silhouette from the fabulous tumult of days and lives, we will not find it in either atrophy or hypertrophy. That world does not exist, one has to create it like the phoenix. That world exists in this one, but the way water exists in oxygen and hydrogen, or how pages 78, 457, 3, 271, 688, 75 and 456 of the dictionary of the Spanish Academy have all that is needed for the writing of a hendecasyllable by Garcilaso. Let us say that the world is a figure, it has to be read. By read let us understand generated. Who cares about a dictionary as dictionary? If from delicate alchemies, osmoses and mixtures of simples there finally does arise a Beatrice on the riverbank, why not have a marvellous hint of what could be born of her in turn? What a useless task is man's, his own barber, repeating *ad nauseam* the biweekly trim, opening the same desk, doing the same thing over again, buying the same newspaper, applying the same principles to the same happenings. Maybe there is a millenary kingdom, but if we ever reach it, if we are it, it probably will not be called that any more. Until we take away from time its whip of history, until we prick the blister made of so many *untils*, we shall go on seeing beauty as an end, peace as a desideratum, always from this side of the door where it really is not always so bad, where many people find satisfactory lives, pleasant perfumes, good salaries, fine literature, stereophonic sound, and why then worry one's self about whether the world most likely is finite, whether history is coming to its optimum, whether the human race is emerging from the Middle Ages and entering the era of cybernetics. *Tout va très bien, madame la Marquise, tout va très bien, tout va très bien.*

As far as everything else is concerned, one must be an imbecile, one must be a poet, one must have a harvest moon in order to spend more than five minutes on those nostalgias that can be handled so perfectly in just a moment. Every meeting of international tycoons, of men-of-science, each new artificial satellite, hormone or atomic reactor crushes these false hopes a little more. The kingdom will be made out of plastic material, that is a fact. And the world will not have to be converted into an Orwellian or Huxleyan nightmare; it will be much worse, it will be a delightful world, to the measure of its inhabitants, no mosquitoes, no illiterates, with enormous eighteen-footed hens most likely, each foot a thing of beauty, with remote controlled bathrooms, a different-coloured water according to the days of the week, a nicety of the national hygiene service, with television in every room, great tropical landscapes, for example, for the inhabitants of Reykjavik, scenes of igloos for people in Havana, subtle compensations that will reduce all rebellions to conformity,

and so forth.

That is to say, a satisfactory world for reasonable people.

And will any single person remain in it who is not reasonable?

In some corner, a vestige of the forgotten kingdom. In some violent death, the punishment for having remembered the kingdom. In some laugh, in some tear, the survival of the kingdom. Beneath it all, one does not feel that man will end up killing man. He will escape from it, he will grasp the rudder of the electronic machine, the astral rocket, he will trip up and then they can set a dog on him. Everything can be killed except nostalgia for the kingdom, we carry it in the colour of our eyes, in every love affair, in everything that deeply torments and unties and tricks. *Wishful thinking*, perhaps; but that is just another possible definition of the featherless biped.

(–5)

72

"It was wise of you to come home, love, if you were so tired."

"There's no place like home," Oliveira said.

"Have another little *mate*, it's fresh."

"When you have your eyes closed it tastes even more bitter, amazing. Why don't you let me sleep a little and read a magazine."

"All right, love," Gekrepten said, drying her tears and out of sheer obedience looking for *Idilio*, even though she was in no shape for reading.

"Gekrepten."

"Yes, love."

"Don't worry about all this, old girl."

"Of course not, sweet. Wait and I'll put on another cold compress."

"I'll get up in a while and we'll take a walk along Almagro. They may be showing some technicolor musical."

"Tomorrow, love, it's better for you to get some rest now. The look on your face when you came in . . . "

"It's part of the profession, what can you do about it. No need for you to worry. Listen to Cien Pesos singing down there."

"They must be cleaning out his cage, little dear," Gekrepten said. "He's showing his gratitude . . . "

"Gratitude," Oliveira repeated. "It's nice to show gratitude to the people who keep you caged up."

"Animals don't understand any of that."

"Animals," Oliveira repeated.

(–77)

73

Yes, but who will cure us of the dull fire, the colourless fire that at nightfall runs along the Rue de la Huchette, emerging from the crumbling doorways, from the little entranceways, of the imageless fire that licks the stones and lies in wait in doorways, how shall we cleanse ourselves of the sweet burning that comes after, that nests in us forever allied with time and memory, with sticky things that hold us here on this side, and which will burn sweetly in us until we have been left in ashes. How much better, then, to make a pact with cats and mosses, strike up friendship right away with hoarse-voiced concierges, with the pale and suffering creatures who wait in windows and toy with a dry branch. To burn like this without surcease, to bear the inner burning coming on like fruit's quick ripening, to be the pulse of a bonfire in this thicket of endless stone, walking through the nights of our life, obedient as our blood in its blind circuit.

How often I wonder whether this is only writing, in an age in which we run towards deception through infallible equations and conformity machines. But to ask one's self if we will know how to find the other side of habit or if it is better to let one's self be borne along by its happy cybernetics, is that not literature again? Rebellion, conformity, anguish, earthly sustenance, all the dichotomies: the Yin and the Yang, contemplation or the *Tätigkeit*, oatmeal or partridge *faisandée*, Lascaux or Mathieu, what a hammock of words, what purse-size dialectics with pyjama storms and living-room cataclysms. The very fact that one asks one's self about the possible choice vitiates and muddies up what can be chosen. *Que sí, que no, que en ésta está* . . . It would seem that a choice cannot be dialectical, that the fact of bringing it up impoverishes it, that is to say, falsifies it, that is to say, transforms it into something else. How many eons between the Yin and the Yang? How many, perhaps, between yes and no? Everything is writing, that is to say, a fable. But what good can we get from the truth that pacifies an honest property owner? Our possible truth must be an *invention*, that is to say, scripture, literature, picture, sculpture, agriculture, pisciculture, all the tures in this world. Values, tures, sainthood, a sure, society, a sure, love, pure sure, beauty, a ture of tures. In one of his books Morelli talks about a Neapolitan who spent years sitting in the doorway of his house looking at a screw on the ground. At night he would pick it up and put it under his mattress. The screw was at first a laugh, a jest, communal irritation, a neighbourhood council, a mark of civic duties unfulfilled, finally a shrugging of shoulders, peace, the screw was peace, no one could go along the street without looking out of the corner of his eye at the screw and feeling that it was peace. The fellow dropped dead of a stroke and the screw disappeared as soon as the neighbours got there. One of them has it; perhaps he takes it out secretly and looks at it, puts it away again and goes off to the factory feeling something that he does not understand, an obscure reproval. He only calms down when he takes out the screw and looks at it, stays looking at it until he hears footsteps and has to put it away quickly. Morelli thought that the screw must have been something else, a god or something like that. Too easy a solution. Perhaps the error was in accepting the fact that the object was a screw simply because it was shaped like a screw. Picasso takes a toy car and turns it into the chin of a baboon. The Neapolitan was most likely an idiot, but he also might have been the inventor of a world. From the screw to an eye, from an eye to a star . . . Why surrender to Great Habit? One can choose one's sure, one's invention, that is to say, the screw or the toy car. That is how Paris destroys us slowly, delightfully, tearing us apart among old flowers and paper tablecloths stained with wine, with its colourless fire that comes running out of crumbling doorways at nightfall. An invented fire burns in us, an incandescent sure, a whatsis of the race, a city that is the Great Screw, the horrible needle with its night eye through which the Seine thread runs, a torture machine like a board of nails, agony in a cage crowded with infuriated swallows. We burn within our work, fabulous mortal honour, high challenge of the phoenix. No one will cure us of the dull fire, the colourless fire that at nightfall runs along the Rue de la Huchette. Incurable, perfectly incurable, we select the Great Screw as a sure, we lean towards it, we enter it, we invent it again every day, with every wine-stain on the tablecloth, with every kiss of mould in the dawns of the Cour de Rohan, we invent our conflagration, we burn outwardly from within, maybe that is the choice, maybe words envelop it the way a napkin does a loaf of bread and maybe the fragrance is inside, the flour puffing up, the yes without the no, or the no without the yes, the day without manes, without Ormuz or Ariman, once and for all and in peace and enough.

(–1)

74

The nonconformist as seen by Morelli, a note clipped to a laundry bill with a safety pin: "Acceptance of the pebble and of Beta Centauri, from the pure-as-anodyne to the pure-as-excess. This man moves within the lowest and the highest of frequencies, deliberately disdaining those in between, that is to say, the current band of the human spiritual mass. Incapable of liquidating circumstances, he tries to turn his back on them; too inept to join those who struggle for their liquidation, he thinks therefore that this liquidation is probably a mere substitute for something else equally partial and intolerable, he moves off shrugging his shoulders. To his friends, the fact that he finds his happiness in the trivial, in the puerile, in a piece of string or in a Stan Getz solo indicates a lamentable impoverishment; they do not know that he is also at the other extreme, the approach towards a *summa* that denies itself and goes threading off and hiding, or that the hunt has no end and that it will not even end with the man's death, because his death will not be a death as in the intermediate band, in frequencies that are picked up by ears that listen to Siegfried's funeral march."

Perhaps to correct the exalted tone of the note, a piece of yellow paper scribbled on in pencil: "Pebble and star: absurd images. But the intimate commerce with stones that have been rolled leads one to a passage; between the hand and the stone there vibrates a chord outside time. Fulgurant . . . [an unreadable word] . . . of which Beta Centauri also partakes; names and magnitudes give way, dissolve, stop being what science thinks they are. And then one is into something that purely is (what? what?): a trembling hand that wraps up a transparent stone that also trembles." (Further down, in ink: "It is not a question of pantheism, delightful illusion, fall upward into a heaven set afire at the edge of the sea.")

In another place, this clarification: "To speak of high and low frequencies is to give way again to the *idola fori* and to scientific language, an illusion of the Western world. For my nonconformist, the happy building of a kite and its raising for the joy of children present is not a lowly occupation (low in respect to high, little in respect to much, etc.), but rather a coming together of pure elements, and out of that a momentary harmony, a satisfaction which helps him raise up the rest. In like manner the moments of estrangement, of happy alienation which hurl him into very brief touches of something that could be his paradise, do not represent for him a higher experience than the making of the kite; it is like an end, but not on top or beyond. Nor is it an end that can be understood in time, an accession in which there culminates a process of enriching despoilment; it can come to him while he is sitting on the toilet, and it especially comes between a woman's thighs, between clouds of smoke, and in the midst of reading things rarely treasured by the cultured Sunday rotogravure.

"On the level of day-to-day acts, the attitude of my nonconformist is translated into his refusal of everything that smells like an accepted idea, tradition, a gregarious structure based on fear and falsely reciprocal advantages. It would not be hard for him to be Robinson Crusoe. He is not a misanthrope, but merely accepts from men and women that part which has not been plasticized by the social superstructure; he himself is afraid of his body's getting stuck in the mould and he knows it, but this knowledge is active and not that resignation that keeps time to the rhythm. With his free hand he slaps his own face for most of the day, and in spare moments he slaps the faces of others, and they pay him back in triplicate. He spends his time, therefore, in monstrous rows brought on by lovers, friends, creditors and officials, and in the few moments he has left he makes use of his freedom in a way that startles everyone else and which always ends up in small ridiculous catastrophes, measured against himself and his attainable ambitions; another more secret and evasive freedom works on him but only he (and then just barely) is conscious of its movements."

(–6)

75

It had been so handsome, in days gone by, to feel himself installed in an imperial style of life that authorized sonnets, dialogues with the stars, meditations on Buenos Aires nights, a Goethean serenity at gatherings in the Colón, or at lectures by foreign professors. He was still surrounded by a world that lived that way, that wanted to be that way; deliberately handsome and spruced up, architectural. To sense the distance that now isolated him from that columbarium, all that Oliveira had to do was put on a wry smile and imitate the exaggerated phrases and the luxurious rhythms of yesterday, the aulic ways of speaking and keeping still. In Buenos Aires, the capital of fear, he felt himself surrounded once again by that discreet smoothing off of edges that likes to go by the name of good sense and, on top of it all, that affirmation of sufficiency which lumps together the voices of young and old, its acceptance of the immediate as the true, of the vicarious as the, as the (in front of the mirror, with the tube of toothpaste in his closing fist, Oliveira again let a laugh escape from his face and instead of putting the brush into his mouth he applied it to his reflection and carefully anointed the false face with pink toothpaste, drew a heart right over its mouth, drew hands, feet, letters, obscenities, he ran up and down the mirror with the brush and with the tube, doubling up with laughter, until desolate Gekrepten came in with a sponge, and so forth).

(–43)

76

The Pola affair was hands, as usual. There is dusk, there is the fatigue that comes from having wasted time in cafés, reading newspapers that are always the same newspaper, there is something like the top of a beer bottle that softly squeezes you at stomach level. You're ready for anything, you're capable of falling into the worst traps of inertia and abandon, and all of a sudden a woman opens her purse to pay for a *café-crème*, her fingers play for an instant with the always imperfect clasp on the purse. You get the feeling that the clasp is guarding against an entry into a sign of the zodiac, that when that woman's fingers find a way to slide down the slender golden stem and with an imperceptible half-turn the catch loosens, some outflow will dazzle the customers absorbed in their pernod and Tour de France, or maybe they'll be swallowed up, a purple velvet funnel will pull the world off its hinges, all of the Luxembourg, the Rue Soufflot, the Rue Gay-Lussac, the Café Capoulade, the Fontaine de Médicis, the Rue Monsieur-le-Prince, it will swallow up everything in one last gulp that will leave nothing but an empty table, the open purse, the woman's hands which take out a hundred-franc note and hand it to Père Ragon, while Horacio Oliveira, naturally, the gaudy survivor of the catastrophe, prepares to say what you say at moments of great catastrophe.

"Oh, you know," Pola answered. "Fear is not my forte."

She said: *Oh, vous savez*, a little like the way the sphinx must have spoken before presenting the enigma, almost excusing herself, refusing a prestige that she knew was grand. She spoke like the women in so many novels where the novelist does not wish to waste time and therefore puts the better part of the description into the dialogue, unifying in that way the useful and the pleasant.

"When I say fear," Oliveira observed, sitting on the sphinx's left on the same red plush seat, "I'm thinking especially of reverse sides. You moved that hand as if you were touching a limit and after that a world against the grain began in which, for example, I could be your purse and you Père Ragon."

He was waiting for Pola to laugh and for things to deny that they were so sophisticated, but Pola (he found out later on her name was Pola) did not find the possibility too absurd. When she smiled she showed a set of small and regular teeth against which she drew her lips a little, lips painted a vivid orange, but Oliveira was still on her hands, he was always affected by women's hands, he felt the need to touch them, pass his fingers over each joint, explore with a movement like that of a Japanese kinesiologist the imperceptible route of the veins, discover the condition of the nails, have a chiromantic suspicion of ominous lines and propitious mounds, hear the din of the moon resting against his ear the palm of a small hand a little damp from love or from a cup of tea.

(–101)

77

"You probably realize that after all this . . ."

"*Res non verba*," Oliveira said. "It's one week at about seventy pesos a day, let's call it five hundred and fifty and you can buy the patients a coke with the other ten."

"Please remove your personal effects at once."

"Yes, sometime between today and tomorrow, more likely tomorrow than today."

"Here's your money. Please sign the receipt."

"No pleases. I'll just sign. *Ecco.*"

"My wife is so upset," Ferraguto said, turning his back and taking the cigar out from between his teeth.

"It's feminine sensitivity, menopause, things like that."

"It's dignity, sir."

"Exactly what I was thinking. Speaking of dignity, thanks for the job in the circus. It was fun and there wasn't much to do."

"My wife still can't understand," Ferraguto said, but Oliveira was already at the door. One of the two opened his eyes or closed them. There was also something about the door that was like an eye opening or closing. Ferraguto relit his cigar and put his hands in his pockets. He was thinking about what he was going to say to that unconscious lunatic as soon as he came round. Oliveira let them put the compress on his forehead (or rather it was he who had closed his eyes) and he thought about what he was going to say to Ferraguto when he was sent for.

(–131)

78

The intimacy of the Travelers. When I say goodbye to them in the doorway or in the café on the corner, suddenly it's like a desire to stay near them, watching them live, a voyeur without appetites, friendly, a little sad. Intimacy, what a word, it makes you want to stick the fateful wh in front of it. But what other word could *intimate* (in its first acceptance) the very skin of acquaintance, the epithelial reason for Talita's, Manolo's and my being friends. People think they're friends because they coincide for a few hours a week on a sofa, in the movies, sometimes in a bed, or because they happen to do the same work in an office. When we were young, in a café, how many times did the illusion of identity with our companions make us happy. Identity with men and women of whom we scarcely knew one shape of being, a shape of giving in, a profile. I remember with a timeless clarity the cafés in Buenos Aires where for several hours we would succeed in getting away from family and obligations, where we would enter a territory of smoke and confidence in ourselves and in our friends, where we would accede to something that comforted us in our precarious state which promised us a kind of immortality. And there, twenty years old, we spoke our most lucid words, we knew all about our deepest emotions, we were like gods of pint glasses and dry Cuban rum. The café a little heaven, *cielito lindo*. Afterwards the street was like an expulsion, always, the angel with the flaming sword directing traffic on Corrientes and San Martín. Homeward bound, it's late, back to lawsuits, to the marriage bed, to linden tea for the old lady, to the exam the day after tomorrow, to the ridiculous fiancée who reads Vicki Baum and whom we will marry, there's no way out.

(A strange woman, Talita. She gives the impression of going around with a lighted candle in her hand, showing a path. And the thing that is modesty itself, a rare thing in an Argentine woman with a degree, here where all one needs is the title of land surveyor to be taken seriously. To think that she used to work in a pharmacy, it's cyclopean, it's positively agglutinating. And she combs her hair in such a pretty way.)

I've just now discovered that Manolo is called Manú in moments of intimacy. It seems so natural to Talita, that business of calling Manolo Manú, she doesn't realize that for his friends it's a secret scandal, a bleeding wound. But I, what right have I . . . That of the prodigal son, in any case. Let it be said in passing, the prodigal son will have to look for work, the last digging into the coffers was absolutely speleological. If I accept the advances of poor Gekrepten, who would do anything to go to bed with me, I will have room and shirts assured, and so forth. The idea of going out to sell lengths of cloth is no more idiotic than any other, a question of trying it, but the most fun would be joining the circus with Manolo and Talita. Joining the circus, a beautiful formula. In the beginning was a circus, and that poem of Cummings where it says that at the creation the Old Man drew a circus tent of air into his lungs. You can't say it in Spanish. Yes you can, but you would have to say: *juntó una carpa de circo de aire.* We will accept Gekrepten's offer, a fine girl, and that will allow us to live closer to Manolo and Talita, since topographically we will only be separated by two walls and a thin slice of air. With a brothel close at hand, the store near by, the market just around the corner. To think that Gekrepten *has been waiting for me.* It's incredible how things like that occur to other people. All heroic acts ought to stay at least within one's family, and ere-we-ave that girl at the Travelers' keeping up to date on all my overseas itineraries, and meanwhile she weaves and unweaves the purple sweater waiting for her Odysseus and working in a store on the Calle Maipú. It would be ignoble not to accept Gekrepten's proposals, deny her her full cup of unhappiness. And from one cynicism to another / you're looking like yourself and not your brother. Whodious Whodysseus.

No, but thinking about it frankly, the most absurd thing about these lives we pretend to lead is the false contact in them. Isolated orbits, from time to time two hands will shake, a five-minute chat, a day at the races, a night at the opera, a wake where everybody feels a little more united (and it's true, but then it's all over just when it's time for linking up). And all the same one lives convinced his friends are there, that contact does exist, that agreements or disagreements are profound and lasting. How we all hate each other, without being aware that endearment is the current form of that hatred, and how the reason behind profound hatred is this excentration, the unbridgeable space between me and you, between this and that. All endearment is an ontological clawing, yes, an attempt to seize the unseizable, and I would like to enter into the intimacy of the Travelers under the pretext of knowing them better, of really getting to be the friend, although what I really want is to seize Manú's manna, Talita's elf, their ways of seeing things, their presents and their futures, different from mine. And why this mania for spiritual possession, Horacio? Why this nostalgia for annexations, you, who have just broken your moorings, just sown confusion and despair (perhaps I should have spent a little more time in Montevideo and done a better job of searching) in the illustrious capital of the Latin spirit? The fact is that on one side you've deliberately disconnected yourself from a gaudy chapter in your life, and that you won't even allow yourself the right to speak in the soft language that you liked to babble in so much a few months ago; and at the same time, oh contradictory whidiot, you're literally breaking yourself up in order to enter into the whintimacy of the Travelers, be the Travelers, whinstall yourself in the Travelers, circus whincluded (but the Manager won't give me any work, so I'll have to think seriously about dressing up as a seaman and selling gabardine samples to ladies). You fuckup. Let's see if you can sow confusion in the ranks once more, if you've put in an appearance just to ruin the lives of peaceful people. That time they told me about the guy who thought he was Judas, and how because of that led a dog's life among the best social circles of Buenos Aires. Let's not be vain. At most a loving inquisitor, as I was told one night. Look, madam, what a fine piece. Sixty-five pesos a yard, just because it's for you. Your ma . . . your husband, I beg your pardon, will be very happy when he comes back from wor . . . from business, I beg your pardon. He'll climb up the walls, believe me, on my word as a sailor off the *Río Belén*. Sure, a little smuggling to make something on the side, my kid has got rickets, my wo . . . my wife does sewing in a dress shop, I have to help out a little, you know what I mean.

(–40)

79

An exceedingly pedantic note by Morelli: "To attempt the *roman comique* in the sense in which a text manages to hint at other values and thus collaborates in that anthropophany that we still consider possible. It would seem that the usual novel misses its mark because it limits the reader to its own ambit; the better defined it is, the better the novelist is thought to be. An unavoidable detention in the varying degrees of the dramatic, the psychological, the tragic, the satirical, or the political. To attempt on the other hand a text that would not clutch the reader but which would oblige him to become an accomplice as it whispers to him underneath the conventional exposition other more esoteric directions. Demotic writing for the female-reader (who otherwise will not get beyond the first few pages, rudely lost and scandalized, cursing at what he paid for the book), with a vague reverse side of hieratic writing.

"To provoke, assume a text that is out of line, untied, incongruous, minutely antinovelistic (although not antinovelish). Without prohibiting the genre's great effects if the situation should require it, but keeping in mind the Gidean advice, *ne jamais profiter de l'élan acquis.* Like all creatures of choice in the Western world, the novel is content in a closed order. Resolutely opposed to this, we should search here for an opening and therefore cut the roots of all systematic construction of characters and situations. Method: irony, ceaseless self-criticism, incongruity, imagination in the service of no one.

"An attempt of this type comes from a rejection of literature; a partial rejection since it does depend on words, but one which must oversee every operation undertaken by author and reader. To use the novel in that way, just as one uses a revolver to keep the peace, changing its symbol. To take from literature that part which is a living bridge from man to man, and which the treatise or the essay will permit only among specialists. A narrative that will not be a pretext for the transmission of a 'message' (there is no message, only messengers, and that is the message, just as love is the one who loves); a narrative that will act as a coagulant of experiences, as a catalyst of confused and badly understood notions, which first off will cut into the one who is writing it, for which reason it will have to be written as an antinovel, because every closed order will systematically leave outside those announcements that can make messengers out of us, bring us to our own limits from which we are so far removed, while being face to face with them.

"The strange self-creation of the author through his work. If out of that magma that is a day, the submersion in existence, we wish to raise the power of values that announce anthropophany as their end, what can be done then with pure understanding, with haughty reasoning reason? From the time of the Eleatics until today dialectical thought has had more than enough time to give us its fruits. We are eating them, they are delicious, they are seething with radioactivity. And when the feast is over, why are we so sad, brothers of nineteen hundred and fifty something?"

Another apparently complementary note:

"Situation of the reader. In general every novelist hopes his reader will understand him, by participating in his own experience, or that he will pick up a determined message and incorporate it. The romantic novelist wants to be understood for his own sake or for that of his heroes; the classical novelist wants to teach, leave his trace on the path of history.

"A third possibility: that of making an accomplice of the reader, a travelling companion. Simultaneanize him, provided that the reading will abolish reader's time and substitute author's time. Thus the reader would be able to become a coparticipant and cosufferer of the experience through which the novelist is passing, *at the same moment and in the same form.* All artistic tricks are of no use in obtaining it: the only thing worth anything is the material in gestation, the experiential immediacy (transmitted through words, of course, but the least aesthetic words possible; this is where we get the 'comic' novel, anticlimaxes, irony, so many other directional arrows pointing towards the other thing).

"For that reader, *mon semblable, mon frère,* the comic novel (and what is *Ulysses*?) will have to take place like those dreams where in the margin of some trivial happening we have a presentiment of a more serious anxiety that we do not always manage to decipher. In this sense the comic novel must have an exemplary sense of decorum; not deceive the reader, not mount him astride any emotion or intention at all, but give him rather something like meaningful clay, the beginning of a prototype, with traces of something that may be collective perhaps, human and not individual. Better yet, give him something like a façade, with doors and windows behind which there operates a mystery which the reader-accomplice will have to look for (therefore the complicity) and perhaps will not find (therefore the cosuffering). What the author of this novel might have succeeded in for himself, will be repeated (becoming gigantic, perhaps, and that would be marvellous) in the reader-accomplice. As for the female-reader, he will remain with the façade and we already know that there are very pretty ones among them, very much *trompe l'oeil*, and that in front of them one can keep putting on in a satisfactory way the comedies and the tragedies of the *honnête homme*. With which everything turns out happily, and as for those who protest, they can go and boil their heads."

(–22)

80

When I have just finished cutting my nails or washing my hair, or simply now, while I'm writing, I can hear a gurgling in my stomach,

the feeling that I've left my body behind comes back (I don't retreat into dualisms but I can distinguish between myself and my nails)

and that our bodies are starting to go bad on us, that they need us or they have too much of us (it depends).

Otherwise: at this stage we ought to deserve a better machine. Psychoanalysis shows how the contemplation of the body can bring on early complexes. (And Sartre, who sees in the fact that woman has been "perforated" existentialist implications that can compromise her all her life.) It's painful to think that we're travelling ahead of this body, but that what goes before is error and obstacle and probable uselessness, because these nails, this navel,

I mean something else, almost impossible to grasp: that the "soul" (my me-not-nails) is the soul of a body that does not exist. The soul gave man a push in his corporeal evolution, perhaps, but it's tired of shoving and goes on ahead by itself. It barely takes two steps

the soul breaks up oh because its real body does not exist and lets it fall down plop.

The poor thing goes back home, etc., but that's not what I. After all.

A long talk with Traveler about madness. Talking about dreams, we realized almost at the same time that certain structures we dream could be current forms of madness if they could just continue for a while when we're awake. When we dream we give free rein to our aptitude for madness. At the same time we suspect that all madness is a dream that has taken root.

Popular wisdom: "The poor guy's crazy, a dreamer . . ."

(–46)

81

The business of the sophist, according to Aristophanes, is to invent new reasons.

Let us try to invent new passions, or to reproduce the old ones with a like intensity.

I shall analyse this conclusion once more, from a Pascalian point of view: true belief is somewhere in between superstition and libertinism.

JOSÉ LEZAMA LIMA, *Tratados en La Habana*

(–74)

82

Morelliana

Why am I writing this? I have no clear ideas, I do not even have ideas. There are tugs, impulses, blocks, and everything is looking for a form, then rhythm comes into play and I write within that rhythm, I write by it, moved by it and not by that thing they call thought and which turns out prose, literature, or what have you. First there is a confused situation, which can only be defined by words; I start out from this half-shadow and if what I mean (if what is *meant*) has sufficient strength, the *swing* begins at once, a rhythmic swaying that draws me to the surface, lights everything up, conjugates this confused material and the one who suffers it into a clear third somehow fateful level: sentence, paragraph, page, chapter, book. This swaying, this *swing* in which confused material goes about taking shape, is for me the only certainty of its necessity, because no sooner does it stop than I understand that I no longer have anything to say. And it is also the only reward for my work: to feel that what I have written is like the back of a cat as it is being petted, with sparks and an arching in cadence. In that way by writing I go down into the volcano, I approach the Mothers, I connect with the Centre – whatever it may be. Writing is sketching my mandala and at the same time going through it, inventing purification by purifying one's self; the task of a poor white shaman in nylon socks.

(–99)

83

The invention of the soul by man is hinted at every time the feeling appears that the body is a parasite, something like a worm adhering to the ego. It's enough to feel that one lives (and not only life as an acceptance, as something-that-is-good-that-it-happened) for what is even closest and most loved by the body, the right hand, for example, suddenly to be an object that participates with repugnance in the double condition of not being me and of clinging to me.

I swallow my soup. Then in the midst of what I am reading, I think: "The soup is *in me*, I have it in this pouch which I will never see, my stomach." I feel with two fingers and I touch the mass, the motion of the food there inside. And I am this, a bag with food inside of it.

Then the soul is born: "No, I am not that."

Now that (let's be honest for once)

yes, I am that. With a very pretty means of escape for the use of the finicky: "I am *also that*." Or just a step up: "I am *in* that."

I am reading *The Waves*, that cinerary piece of lace, a fable of froth. A foot below my eyes some soup is slowly moving about in my stomachic pouch, a hair is growing on my thigh, an imperceptible sebaceous cyst is coming out on my shoulder.

At the end of what Balzac might have called an orgy, a certain individual who was not at all metaphysical said to me, thinking he was making a joke, that defecation gave him an impression of unreality. I remember his words: "You get up, you turn around and look, and then you say: *But did I do that?*"

(Like the line from Lorca: "*Sin remedio, hijo mío, ¡vomita! No hay remedio.*" And crazy Swift too, I think: "But Celia, Celia, Celia shits."

On top of physical pain like a metaphysical pinprick, writing abounds. All pain attacks me with a double-edged sword: it makes me aware as never before of the divorce between my ego and my body (and its falseness, its consoling invention) and at the same time it brings my body close to me, *dresses me in it* as pain. I feel it to be more mine than pleasure or mere coenaesthesis. It is really a bond. If I could sketch I would gladly show pain chasing the soul out of the body, but at the same time I would give the impression that it's all untrue: mere characteristics of a complex whose unity lies in not having any.

(–142)

84

Wandering along the Quai des Célestins I step on some dry leaves and when I pick one up and look at it closely I see that it is full of old-gold dust, and underneath some earth profound as musty perfume that sticks to my hand. For all those reasons I bring the dry leaves back to my flat and paste them on a lampshade. Ossip comes, he stays two hours and doesn't even look at the lamp. Another day Étienne comes by, and with his beret still in his hand, *Dis donc, c'est épatant, ça!* and he picks up the lamp, studies the leaves, becomes enthusiastic. Dürer, the veins, and so forth.

A single situation and two versions . . . I keep on thinking about all the leaves I will not see, the gatherer of dry leaves, about so many things that there must be in the air and which these eyes will not see, poor bats out of novels and movies and dried flowers. There must be lamps everywhere, there must be leaves that I will never see.

And so, *de feuille en aiguille*, I think about those exceptional states in which for one instant leaves and invisible lamps are imagined, are felt in an air outside of space. It's very simple, every exaltation or depression pushes me towards a state suitable for

I will call them paravisions

that is to say (that's the worst of it, saying it)

an instantaneous aptitude for going out, so that suddenly I can grasp myself from outside, or from inside but on a different plane,

as if I were somebody who was looking at me

(better still – because in reality I cannot see myself – : like someone who is living me).

It doesn't last, two steps along the street, the time needed for

taking a deep breath (sometimes when I wake up it lasts a little longer, and then it's fabulous) and in that instant I know *what I am* because I know exactly *what I am not* (what I thereupon ignore astutely). But there are no words for a material in between word and pure vision, like a block of evidence. Impossible to objectivize, make precise that defectiveness that I caught during the instant and which was *clear absence* or clear error or clear insufficiency, but

without knowing of *what, what.*

Another way of trying to say it: When it's that, I'm no longer looking towards the world, from me towards the other thing, but for a second I am the world, the outside plane, *the rest looking at me.* I see myself as the others can see me. It's so good it can't be sensed: that's why it scarcely lasts. I measure my defectiveness, I notice everything which through absence or defect we never see in ourselves. I see what I am not. For example (I'm picking this up on the rebound, but it comes from over there): there are enormous regions where I have never been, and what one has not known is what one has not been. An anxiety to start running, go into a house, into that store, jump on a train, devour all of Jouhandeau, know German, know Aurangabad . . . Localized and lamentable examples but ones which can give an idea (an *idea*?).

Another way of wanting to say it: What is defective is felt more as an intuitive poverty than as a mere lack of experience. It really doesn't afflict me not having read all of Jouhandeau, at most the melancholy feeling of too short a life for so many libraries, etc. The lack of experience is inevitable, if I read Joyce I am automatically sacrificing another book and vice versa, etc. The feeling of lack is sharper in

It's a little like this: there are lines in the air next to your head, next to your glance

zones for the detention of your eyes, your smell, your taste,

that is to say you're going around with your limits outside

and you can't get beyond that limit when you think you've caught anything fully, just like an iceberg the thing has a small piece outside and shows it to you, and the enormous rest of it is beyond your limits and that's why the *Titanic* went down. Wholiveira whith whis whexamples.

Let's be serious. Ossip did not see the dry leaves on the lamp simply because his limits are this side of what the lamp meant.

Étienne saw them perfectly, but on the other hand his limits would not let him see that I was bitter and did know what to do about Pola. Ossip realized it at once, and made me see it. That's the way we all go.

I think of man as an amoeba who sticks out pseudopods to catch and envelop his food. There are long and short pseudopods, movements, turnings. One day this all becomes *fixed* (what we call maturity, a full-grown man). On the one side he can go farther, on the other he can't see a lamp two steps away. In this way a guy goes on living fairly well convinced that nothing interesting will escape him, until an instantaneous landslide shows him for a second, unfortunately without giving him time *to know what*,

shows him his divided being, his irregular pseudopods
the suspicion that farther on, where now I can see clear air
or in this indecision, at the crossroads of choice
I myself, in the rest of reality that I don't know,
I'm waiting uselessly for myself.

(*Suite*)

Individuals like Goethe must not have abounded in experiences of this kind. By aptitude or decision (genius lies in choosing to be a genius and *in being right*) they have their pseudopods stuck out as far as they will go in all directions. They encircle with a uniform diameter, their limit is their skin projected spiritually to great distances. It does not seem that they have need to desire what begins (or continues) beyond their enormous spheres. That's why they're classics, hey.

The unknown approaches the amoeba *uso nostro* from all sides. I can know a lot or live a lot in a given sense, but then *the other* thing moves up on the side where I have my lacks and scratches my head with its cold nail. The worst is that it scratches me when there is no itching, while just when it does itch – when I ought to want to know – everything surrounding me is so set, so located, so complete and solid and labelled, that I begin to think that I was dreaming, that I'm fine this way, that I can take care of myself all right and that I shouldn't let myself be carried away by my imagination.

(*Final suite*)

Imagination has been praised to excess. The poor thing cannot move an inch away from the limits of its pseudopods. In this direction, great variety and vivacity. But in the other space, where the cosmic wind that Rilke felt pass over his head blows, Dame Imagination does not go. *Ho detto.*

(–4)

85

Lives which end like literary articles in newspapers and magazines, so pompous on page one and ending up in a skinny tail, back there on page thirty-two, among advertisements for secondhand articles and tubes of toothpaste.

(–150)

86

The people in the Club, with two exceptions, maintained that it was easier to understand Morelli from the quotes he used than from his personal meanderings. Wong insisted until his departure from France (the police refused to renew his *carte de séjour*) that it wasn't worth the trouble champollionizing the old man's rosettes, once you found the two following quotations, both from Pauwels and Bergier:

> Perhaps there is a place in man from where the whole of reality can be perceived. This hypothesis seems delirious. Auguste Comte declared that the chemical composition of a star would never be known. The following year Bunsen invented the spectroscope.
>
> . . . .
>
> Language, just like thought, proceeds from the binary arithmetical functioning of our brain. We classify by yes and no, by positive and negative. (. . .) The only thing that my language proves is the slowness of a world vision limited to the binary. This insufficiency of language is obvious, and is strongly deplored. But what about the insufficiency of binary intelligence itself? Internal existence, the essence of things, escapes it. It can discover that light is continuous and discontinuous at the same time, that a molecule of benzine establishes between its six atoms dual relationships which are nevertheless mutually exclusive; it accepts it, but it cannot understand it, it cannot incorporate into its own structure the reality of the profound structures it examines. In order to do that, it would have to change its state, machines other than the usual ones would have to start functioning in the brain, so that binary reasoning might be replaced with an

analogical consciousness which would assume the shapes and assimilate the inconceivable rhythms of those profound structures . . .

Le Matin des magiciens

(–78)

87

In 1932, Ellington recorded *Baby When You Ain't There*, one of his least praised numbers and one to which the faithful Barry Ulanov does not give any special mention. With a curiously dry voice Cootie Williams sings the lyrics.

Why is it so necessary at certain times to say: "I loved that"? I loved some blues, an image in the street, a poor dry river in the north. Giving testimony, fighting against the nothingness that will sweep us all away. That's how in the air of the soul little things like that will linger; a sparrow that belonged to Lesbia, some blues that in the memory will fill the small space saved for perfumes, stamps and paperweights.

(–105)

88

"Hey, if you move your leg like that I'm going to stick this needle in your ribs," Traveler said.

"Keep on telling me about that business of coloured in yellow," Oliveira said. "With my eyes bandaged it's like a kaleidoscope."

"Coloured in yellow," Traveler said, rubbing the thigh with a piece of cotton, "is under the jurisdiction of the national corporation of commission agents for the corresponding species."

"Animals with yellow fur, vegetables with yellow flowers, and minerals with a yellow look," Oliveira recited obediently. "Why not? After all, Thursday is the fashionable day here, one doesn't work on Sunday, the metamorphoses between Saturday morning and afternoon are extraordinary, people so easy-going. You're hurting something awful. Is that some metal with a yellow look, or what?"

"Distilled water," Traveler said. "So you'll think it's morphine. You're quite right, Ceferino's world only appears strange to guys who believe in their own institutions to the exclusion of those outside. If you thought about everything that changes as soon as you leave the edge of the pavement and take three steps into the street . . . "

"Like going from coloured in yellow to coloured in pampa," Oliveira said. "This thing is making me a little sleepy."

"Water is a soporific. If I had my way I'd shoot you up with nebiole and you'd be more wide awake."

"Explain something to me before I fall asleep."

"I don't think you're going to fall asleep, but go ahead."

(–72)

89

There were two letters from Juan Cuevas, attorney, but the order in which they should be read was material for a polemic. The first was the poetical exposition of what he called "world sovereignty"; the second one, also dictated to a stenographer at the Santo Domingo gate, took its vengeance on the required modesty of the first:

> Make as many copies of this letter as you wish, especially for members of the UN and world officials, who are the lowest kind of swine and international jackals. If on the one hand the Santo Domingo gate is a tragedy of noise, I like it on the other because I can come here and toss the largest stones in history.

The following figured among the stones:

> The Pope in Rome is the greatest swine in history, and not by the slightest chance the vicar of God; Roman clericalism is the pure shit of Satan; every Roman clerical church should be completely razed, so that Christ's light may shine, not only in the depths of human hearts, but also shining on through God's universal light, and I say all of this because I dictated the previous letter to a most charming young lady, who looked at me with such a very languid face that I could not state certain strong items.

Oh chivalrous lawyer! The fierce enemy of Kant, he insisted on "humanizing the current philosophy of the world", to which purpose he decreed:

> And let the novel be more psychopsychiatric, by that I mean let the truly spiritual elements of the soul be set forth as scientific elements of the true universal psychiatry . . .

Abandoning for a few minutes a considerable dialectical arsenal, he peeped into the kingdom of world religion:

> But just so long as humanity follows the path of both universal commandments; and until the hard stones of the world become silken wax under the illuminating light . . .

A poet, and a good one.

> The voices of all the stones in the world will resound from out of all the cataracts and canyons in the world, with little silver threads of voices, an occasion for the endless love of women and of God . . .

Suddenly the archetypal vision invades and spreads out:

> The Cosmos of the Earth, interior just like the universal mental image of God, which would later become condensed matter, is symbolized in the Old Testament by the archangel who turns his head and sees a faint world of lights, of course, I cannot remember passages from the Old Testament word for word, but that is more or less the direction which it takes: it is as if the face of the Universe became the very light of Earth, and remained as an orbit of universal energy around the sun . . . In a like way all Humanity and its peoples must turn their bodies, their souls, and their heads . . . It is the universe and the whole Earth turning towards Christ, laying all the laws of the Earth at his feet . . .

And then,

> . . . all that remains is a sort of universal light that comes from equal lamps, lighting up the innermost heart of peoples . . .

The worst was that suddenly,

> Ladies and gentlemen: I am writing this letter in the midst of frightful noise. And, nevertheless, we shall keep right on offering what we have here to you; the fact is that you still do not realize that in order to write (?) WORLD SOVEREIGNTY in a more perfect way and for it really to arrive at universal understanding, I should at least deserve from you

> some broad help so that each line and each letter will find its proper place, and not this disorder of the sons of the sons of the son of the *chingada* mother of all mothers; fuck the mother of all noises.

But did it make any difference? Ecstasy again in the following line:

> What an excellence of universes! May they flourish like the spiritual light of delightful roses in the hearts of all peoples . . .

And the letter went on to its close in a flowery way, although with some curious last-minute grafts:

> . . . It seems that the whole universe is being brightened with the light of the universal Christ in every human flower, with infinite petals to illuminate eternally all earthly paths; and so it will remain brightened in the light of WORLD SOVEREIGNTY, they say that you no longer love me because you have other lovers. – Very truly yours. Mexico City, September 20, 1956 – . 32 Avenida 5 de Mayo, Room III. – Paris Bldg. JUAN CUEVAS, ATTORNEY.

(–53)

90

He went around thinking in those days, and the bad habit of ruminating about everything at length inevitably made things hard for him. He had been revolving about the great affair, and the inconvenience in which he was living because of La Maga and Rocamadour made him analyse with increasing violence the intersection where he felt he was stuck. In cases like that Oliveira would grab a sheet of paper and write down the grand words over which he went slipping along in his ruminations. He wrote, for example: "The great whaffair", or "the whintersection". It was enough to make him laugh and feel more up to preparing another *mate*. "Whunity," whrote Wholiveira. "The whego and the whother." He used this *wh* the way other people used penicillin. Then he would get back to the matter more slowly and feel better. "The whimportant thing is not to become whinflated," Wholiveira would say to whimself. After moments like this he would feel able to think without having the words play dirty tricks on him. Little more than methodological progress, because the great affair was still invulnerable. "Who would have told you, kid, that you'd end up as a metaphysician?" Oliveira would ask himself. "You have to resist the wardrobe with three bodies, conform to the bedside table of every day's insomnia." Ronald had come by to suggest to him that he accompany him in some vaguely political activities, and all night long (La Maga had not yet brought Rocamadour from the country) they had argued like Arjuna and the Charioteer, about action and passivity, the reasons for risking the present for the sake of the future, the blackmail side of every action that has a social end, the degree to which the risk taken serves at least to palliate an individual guilty conscience, the swinish personal behaviour of everyday life. Ronald had ended up leaving with his head bowed down, not having been able to convince Oliveira that action was needed in support of the Algerian rebels.

Oliveira had had a bad taste in his mouth all day because it had been easier to say no to Ronald than to himself. He was fairly certain of only one thing, and it was that he could not give in without betraying the passive hope by which he had lived since coming to Paris. Giving way to facile generosity and going out to paste up clandestine posters on the street seemed like a mundane explanation to him, a settling of accounts with friends who would appreciate his boldness, more than a real reply to great questions. Measuring the thing from the temporal and the absolute, he felt that he was wrong in the first case and right in the second. He was wrong in not fighting for Algerian independence, or against anti-Semitism or racism. He was right in rejecting the simple stupefaction of collective action and remaining alone once more next to his bitter *mate*, thinking about the great affair, turning it around like a ball of yarn in which you cannot see the end or where there are four or five ends.

It was all right, yes, but one also had to recognize that his character was like a foot that trampled all dialectics of action in the manner of the *Bhagavad-Gita*. Between preparing *mate* and having La Maga prepare it there was no possible doubt. But everything was fissionable and would immediately allow an opposite interpretation: to passive character there corresponded a maximum of freedom and availability, the lazy absence of principles and convictions made him more sensitive to the axial condition of life (what one calls a weather-vane type), capable of rejecting through laziness but at the same time of filling the hollow left by the rejection with a content freely chosen by conscience or by an instinct that is more open, more ecumenical, as it were.

"More whecumenical," Oliveira wisely jotted down.

Besides, what was the true morality of action? A social action like that of the syndicalists was more than justified in the field of history. Happy were those who lived and slept in history. An abnegation was almost always justified as an attitude of religious origin. Happy were those who loved their neighbour as themselves. In every case Oliveira rejected that sally of the ego, that magnanimous invasion of somebody else's corral, an ontological boomerang destined to enrich in the last instance the one who threw it, to give him more humanity, more sainthood. One is always a saint at the expense of somebody else, etc. There was no objection to that action as such, but he pushed it aside with doubts about his personal conduct. He would suspect a betrayal the moment he gave in to posters on the street or activities of a social nature; a betrayal disguised as satisfactory work, daily happiness, satisfied conscience, fulfilled duty. He was too well acquainted with certain communists in Buenos Aires and in Paris, capable of the worst villainy but redeemable in their own minds by "the struggle", by having to leave in the middle of dinner to run to a meeting or finish a job. Social action in those people seemed too much like an alibi, the way children are usually the alibi for mothers' not having to do anything worth while in this life, the way learning with its blinkers is useful in not learning that in the jail down the street they are still guillotining guys who should not be guillotined. False action is almost always the most spectacular, the kind that tears down respect, prestige and whequestrian wheffigies. It's as easy as putting on a pair of slippers, it can even become meritorious ("After all, it would be so nice if the Algerians got independence and we all ought to help a little," Oliveira said to himself); the betrayal was something else, as always it was a denial of the centre, one's installation on the periphery, the marvellous joy of brotherhood with other men who were embarked on the same action. There where a certain human type could reach fulfilment as a hero, Oliveira knew that he was condemned to the worst of comedies. So it was better to sin through omission than through commission. Being an actor meant renouncing the orchestra seats, and he seemed born to be a spectator in the first row. "The worst of it," Oliveira said to himself, "is that I always want to be an active onlooker and that's where the trouble starts."

Whactive whonlooker. He had to whanalyse the whaffair carefully. At that moment certain pictures, certain women, certain poems gave him hopes of someday reaching a position from which he could accept himself with less loathing and less doubt than at that moment. It was no mean advantage for him that his worst defects tended to be useful in that matter which was not a path but rather the search for a halt that comes at the beginning of every path. "My strength is in my weakness," Oliveira thought. "The great decisions I have always made were masks for flight." Most of his undertakings (of his whundertakings) ended not with a bang but a whimper; the great breaks, the bangs without return were the nips of a cornered rat and nothing else. Otherness was rotating ceremoniously, dissolving into time or into space or into behaviour, without violence, from fatigue – like the ending of his sentimental adventures – or from a slow retreat as when one begins to visit a friend less and less, read a poet less and less, go to a café less and less, taking mild doses of nothingness so as not to hurt one's self.

"Nothing ever really happens to me," Oliveira thought. "A flowerpot is never going to fall on my noggin." Why the unrest, then, if it was not the stale attraction of the opposites, the nostalgia for vocation and action? An analysis of this unrest, as far as is possible, would always allude to a dislocation, to an excentration in regard to a kind of order that Oliveira was incapable of defining. He knew that he was a spectator on the edge of the spectacle, like being blindfolded in a theatre: sometimes the secondary meaning of some word would come to him, or of some piece of music, filling him with anxiety because he was capable of sensing that it was the primary meaning. In moments like that he knew he was closer to the centre than many people who lived convinced that they were the axle of the wheel, but his was a useless nearness, a tantalizing instant which did not even take on the quality of torture. Once he had believed in love as an enrichment, an exaltation of interceding forces. One day he realized that his loves were impure because they presupposed that expectation, while the true lover loved without expecting anything but love, blindly accepting that the day would become bluer and the night softer and the tram less uncomfortable. "I can make a dialectical operation even out of soup," Oliveira thought. He ended up by making friends out of the women he had loved, accomplices in a special contemplation of the world around. The women started out by adoring him (they really whadored him), admiring him (a whunlimited whadmiration), then something would make them suspect the void, they would jump back, and he would make their flight easy for them, he would open the door so that they could go and play on the other side. On two occasions he had been at the point of feeling pity and letting them keep the illusion that they understood him, but something told him that his pity was not genuine, it was more a cheap trick of his selfishness and his laziness and his habits. "Pity is being auctioned off," Oliveira would say to himself and let them go; he quickly forgot about them.

(–20)

91

Papers scattered on the table. A hand (Wong's). A voice reads slowly, making mistakes, the *l*'s like hooks, the *e*'s indefinable. Notes, cards with words on them, a line of poetry in some language, the writer's kitchen. Another hand (Ronald's). A resonant voice that knows how to read. Greetings in a low voice to Ossip and to Oliveira who arrive contritely (Babs has gone to let them in, has received them with a knife in each hand). Cognac, golden light, the legend of the profanation of the Eucharist, a small De Staël. The topcoats can be left in the bedroom. A piece of sculpture by (perhaps) Brancusi. In the back of the bedroom, lost between a dressmaker's dummy rigged out as a hussar and a pile of boxes with pieces of wire and cardboard in them. There are not enough chairs, but Oliveira brings over two stools. One of those silences is produced which is comparable, according to Genet, to those observed by refined people when they suddenly perceive in a living room the smell of a silent fart. Soon thereafter Étienne opens up the briefcase and takes out the papers.

"We thought it best to wait for you before we classified them," he says. "In the meantime we've been looking over some odd pages. This bitch threw a beautiful egg into the rubbish bin."

"It was rotten," said Babs.

Gregorovius places a visibly trembling hand on one of the folders. It must be very cold outside, a double cognac then. They are warmed by the colour of the light, and the green folder, the Club. Oliveira looks at the centre of the table, the ash from his cigarette starts to join the ones that fill the ashtray.

(–82)

92

Now he realised that in his highest moments of desire he had not known how to stick his head into the crest of the wave and pass through the fabulous crash of his blood. Loving La Maga had been a sort of rite from which one no longer expected illumination; words and acts had succeeded one another with an inventive monotony, a dance of tarantulas on a moonlit floor, a viscous and prolonged manipulation of echoes. And all the time he had been waiting for a kind of awakening to come from out of that happy drunkenness, a clearer view of what was around him, whether the coloured wall-paper in hotels or the reasons behind any one of his acts, without wanting to understand that by limiting himself to waiting he had abolished all real possibility, as if he had condemned himself in advance to a narrow and trivial present. He had gone from La Maga to Pola in one fell swoop, without offending La Maga or offending himself, without getting annoyed at caressing Pola's pink ear with La Maga's arousing name. Failure with Pola was the repetition of innumerable failures, a game that ultimately is lost but was beautiful to play, while with La Maga he had begun to come out resentful, with a taste of tartar and a cigarette butt that smelled of dawn in the corner of his mouth. That's why he took Pola to the same hotel on the Rue Valette, they found the same old woman who greeted them understandingly, what else was there to do in that lousy weather. It still smelled of toilet soap, of soup, but they had cleaned the blue stain on the rug and there was room for new stains.

"Why here?" Pola asked surprised. She looked at the yellow bedspread, the dull and musty room, the pink-spotted lampshade hanging from the ceiling.

"Here or somewhere else . . . "

"If it's because of money, all you had to do was say so, love."

"If it's a question of revulsion, all we have to do is cut out, sweet."

"It doesn't revolt me. It's ugly, that's all. Probably . . ."

She had smiled at him, as if she were trying to understand. Probably . . . probable . . . Her hand found Oliveira's as they both bent over to remove the cover. All that afternoon he had again been present, another time, one of so many times, the ironical witness sorry for his own body, at the surprises, the enchantments and the deceptions of the ceremony. Habituated without being aware of it to La Maga's rhythms, suddenly a new ocean, a different set of waves shook him in his reflexes, confronted him, seemed to denounce in a vague way his solitude enmeshed in phantoms. The enchantment and the disenchantment of going from one mouth to another, of searching with his eyes closed for a neck where his hand had chastely slept, and feeling that the curve is different, a thicker base, a tendon that tightens briefly with the effort of getting up to kiss or bite. Every instant of his body was opposite a delightful lack of meeting, having to stretch out a little more, or lower his head to find the mouth that formerly was so close up there, to stroke a thinner hip, incite a reply and not get it, insist, confusedly, until he realised that everything had to be invented all over again, that the code has not been formulated, that the keys and the clues will take shape again, will be different, will respond to other things. Weight, smell, the tone in which she laughed and begged, time and precipitation, nothing coincides even if the same, everything is born again even if immortal, love plays at being invented, it flees from itself to return in its surprising spiral, the breasts tilt a different way, the mouth kisses more deeply or as if from far away, and in one moment where before there had been anger and anguish now there is pure play, an incredible frolic, or vice versa, at the moment when before one fell into dreaming, the babbling of sweet foolish things, now there is a tension, something that cannot be communicated but is present and which demands incorporation, something like an insatiable rage. Only the pleasure in his final wingbeat is the same; before and after, the world has broken into pieces and it will be necessary to rename it, finger by finger, lip by lip, shadow by shadow.

The second time was in Pola's apartment, on the Rue Dauphine. If a few phrases had succeeded in giving him an idea of what he was going to find, reality was way beyond the imaginable. Everything was in its place and there was a place for everything. The history of contemporary art was modestly inscribed on postcards: a Klee, a

Poliakoff, a Picasso (with a certain kindly condescension already), a Manessier, and a Fautrier. Hung artistically with a good sense of distance. A small signoria David did not intrude either. A bottle of pernod and one of cognac. On the bed, a Mexican serape. Pola played the guitar sometimes, the memory of a love of high plateaus. In her flat she looked like Michèle Morgan, but she was resolutely dark. Two bookshelves included Durrell's *Alexandria Quartet*, well-read and annotated, translations from Dylan Thomas stained with lipstick, copies of *Two Cities*, Christiane Rochefort, Blondin, Sarraute (uncut), and a few *Nouvelles Revues Françaises*. The rest gravitated about the bed, where Pola wept a little while she recalled a girlfriend who had committed suicide (photos, a page torn out of an intimate diary, a pressed flower). It did not seem strange to Oliveira afterwards that Pola had seemed perverse, that she had been the first to open the door to different kinds of loveplay, that night found them like two people stretched out on a beach where the sand slowly yields to the algae-laden water. It was the first time that he called her Pola Paris, as a joke, and she liked it and repeated it, and bit him on the lip whispering Pola Paris, as if she had assumed the name and wanted to be worthy of it, pole of Paris, Paris of Pola, the greenish light of a neon sign going on and off against the yellow raffia curtain, Pola Paris, Pola Paris, the naked city with its sex in tune to the palpitation of the curtain. Pola Paris, Pola Paris, every time more his, breasts without surprise, the curve of the stomach traced exactly by his caress, without the slightest fear of reaching the limits before or after, a mouth found now and defined, a smaller and more pointed tongue, less saliva, teeth less sharp, lips which opened so that he could touch her gums, enter and run over every warm ripple where it smelled a little of cognac and tobacco.

(–103)

93

But love, that word . . . Horacio the moralist fearful of passions born without some deep-water reason, disconcerted and surly in the city where love is called by all the names of all the streets, all the buildings, all the flats, all the rooms, all the beds, all the dreams, all the things forgotten or remembered. My love, I do not love you for you or for me or for the two of us together, I do not love you because my blood tells me to love you, I love you because you are not mine, because you are from the other side, from there where you invite me to jump and I cannot make the jump, because in the deepest moment of possession you are not in me, I cannot reach you, I cannot act beyond your body, your laugh, there are times when it torments me that you love me (how you like to use the verb to love, with what vulgarity you toss it around among plates and sheets and buses), I'm tormented by your love because I cannot use it as a bridge because a bridge can't be supported by just one side, Wright or Le Corbusier will never make a bridge that is supported by just one side, and don't look at me with those bird's eyes, for you the operation of love is so simple, you'll be cured before me even if you love me as I do not love you. Of course you'll be cured, because you're living in health, after me it'll be someone else, you can change things the way you do a blouse. So sad to listen to Horacio the cynic who wants a passport-love, a mountain pass-love, a key-love, a revolver-love, a love that will give him the thousand eyes of Argos, ubiquity, the silence out of which music is possible, the root out of which a language can be woven. And it's foolish because all that is sleeping a little in you, all you would have to do is submerge yourself in a glass of water like a Japanese flower and little by little coloured petals would begin to bloom, the bent forms would puff up, beauty would grow. Infinite giver, I do not know how to take, forgive me. You're offering me an apple and I have left my teeth on the bedside table. Stop, it's fine that way. I can also be rude, take note of that. But take good note, because it's not gratuitous.

Why stop? For fear of starting fabrications, they're so easy. You get an idea from there, a feeling from the other shelf, you tie them together with the help of words, black bitches, and it turns out that I want you. Partial total: I want you. General total: I love you. That's the way a lot of my friends live, not to mention an uncle and two cousins convinced of the love-they-feel-for-their-wives. From words to deeds; in general without the *verba* there isn't any *res*. What a lot of people call loving consists of picking out a woman and marrying her. They pick her out, I swear, I've seen them. As if you could pick in love, as if it were not a lightning bolt that splits your bones and leaves you staked out in the middle of the courtyard. You'll probably say that they pick her out because-they-love-her, I think it's just the siteoppo. Beatrice wasn't picked out, Juliet wasn't picked out. You don't pick out the rain that soaks you to the skin when you come out of a concert. But I'm alone in my room, I'm falling into tricks of writing, the black bitches get their vengeance any way they can, they're biting me from underneath the table. Do you say underneath or under? They bite you just the same. Why, why, *pourquoi, por qué, warum, perchè* this horror of black bitches? Look at them there in that poem by Nashe, transformed into bees. And there in two lines from Octavio Paz, thighs of the sun, corners of summer. But the same body of a woman belongs to Mary and to La Brinvilliers, eyes that cloud up looking at a beautiful sunset are the same optical instrument that gets pleasure from the twisting of a man being hanged. I'm afraid of that pimping, of ink and of voices, a sea of tongues licking the arse of the world. There's milk and honey underneath your tongue . . . Yes, but it's also been said that dead flies make the perfumer's perfume stink. At war with words, at war, keep everything that might be necessary even though intelligence must be renounced, stick with the simple act of ordering some fried potatoes, and Reuters dispatches, in letters from my noble brother and movie dialogues. Curious, very curious that Puttenham should have had a feeling for words as if they were objects, and even creatures with a life of their own. I too sometimes think that I'm engendering streams of ferocious ants that will devour the world. Oh but that the Roc could breed in silence . . . *Logos, faute éclatante!* To conceive a race that could express itself in drawings, the dance, the macramé, or abstract mimicry. Could they avoid connotations, the root of deception? *Honneur des hommes*, etc. Yes, but an honour that dishonours itself in every phrase, like a brothel of virgins, if such a thing were possible.

From love to philology, you're brilliant, Horacio. It's Morelli's fault, he's like an obsession with you, his crazy experiment makes you catch a glimpse of the lost paradise, poor preAdamite, in a cellophane-wrapped golden age. *This is the age of plastics, man, the age of plastics.* Forget about the bitches. Beat it, the pack of you, we have to think, what's called thinking, that is to say, feeling, locating yourself, and confronting yourself before you let pass the minutest main or subordinate clause. Paris is a centre, you understand, a mandala through which one must pass without dialectics, a labyrinth where pragmatic formulas are of no use except to get lost in. Then a *cogito* which may be a kind of breathing Paris in, getting into it by letting it get in you, *pneuma* and not *logos*. Argentine big buddy, disembarking with the sufficiency of a three-by-five culture, wise in everything, up to date in everything, with acceptable good taste, good knowledge of the history of the human race, the periods of art, the Romanesque and the Gothic, philosophical currents, political tensions, Shell Mex, action and reflection, compromise and liberty, Piero della Francesca and Anton Webern, well-catalogued technology, Lettera 22, Fiat 1600, John XXIII. Wonderful, wonderful. It was a little bookstore on the Rue du Cherche-Midi, it was a soft sense of spinning slowly, it was the afternoon and the hour, it was the flowering season of the year, it was the *Verbum* (in the beginning), it was a man who thought he was a man. What an infinite piece of stupidity, my God. And she came out of the bookstore (I just now realize that it was like a metaphor, her coming out of a bookstore, no less) and we exchanged a couple of words and we went to have a glass of *pelure d'oignon* at a café in Sèvres-Babylone (speaking of metaphors, I a delicate piece of porcelain just arrived, HANDLE WITH CARE, and she Babylonia, root of time, something previous, *primeval being*, terror and delight of beginnings, the romanticism of Atala but with a real tiger waiting behind the tree). And so Sèvres went with Babylonia to have a glass of *pelure d'oignon*, we looked at each other and I think we began to desire each other (but that was later on, on the Rue Réamur) and a memorable dialogue resulted, clothed from head to toe in misunderstandings, maladjustments that dissolved into vague moments of silence, until our hands began to chat, it was sweet stroking hands while we looked at each other and smiled, we lit Gauloises, each in the other's mouth, we rubbed each other with our eyes, we were so much in agreement on everything that it was shameful, Paris was dancing there outside waiting for us, we'd barely disembarked, we were barely alive, everything was there without a name and without a history (especially Babylonia, and poor Sèvres made an enormous effort, fascinated by that Babylonia way of looking at the Gothic without putting labels on it, of walking along the banks of the river without seeing the Norman ducks take flight). When we said goodbye we were like two children who have suddenly become friends at a birthday party and keep looking at one another while their parents take them by the hand and lead them off, and it's a sweet pain and a hope, and you know the name of one is Tony and the other one Lulu, and that's all that's needed for the heart to become a little piece of fruit, and . . .

Horacio, Horacio.

Merde, alors. Why not? I'm talking about then, about Sèvres-Babylone, not about these elegiac scorecards where we know that the game has been played already.

(–68)

94

Morelliana

A piece of prose can turn rotten like a side of beef. For some years now I have been witness to the signs of rot in my writing. Just like me, it has its angina, its jaundice, its appendicitis, but it is ahead of me on its way to final dissolution. After all, rotting means the end of the impurities in the component parts and the return of rights to chemically pure sodium, magnesium, carbon. My prose is rotting syntactically and is heading – with so much work – towards simplicity. I think that is why I no longer know how to write "coherent"; the bucking of a verbal bronco leaves me on foot after a few steps. *Fixer les vertiges*, how good. But I get the feeling that I should establish elements. Poems are waiting for that, and certain kinds of novel or short story or theatre. The rest is the job of stuffing and it does not work out well for me.

"Yes, but elements, are they the essential thing? Establishing carbon is not worth as much as establishing the Guermantes family."

"I think in a vague sort of way that the elements I am aiming for are a result of *composition*. The schoolbook chemistry point of view has been turned inside out. When composition has reached its extreme limit, the territory of the elemental opens up. Establish them and if it is possible, be them."

(–91)

95

In some note or other, Morelli had shown himself to be curiously explicit about his intentions. Giving evidence of a strange anachronism, he became interested in studies or nonstudies such as Zen Buddhism, which in those years was the rash of the beat generation. The anachronism did not lie in that, but in the fact that Morelli seemed much more radical and younger in his spiritual exigencies than those California youngsters getting drunk on Sanskrit words and canned beer. One of the notes referred Suzukianly to language as a kind of exclamation or shout that rises directly out of an inner experience. There followed several examples of dialogues between teachers and pupils, completely unintelligible for a rational ear and for all dualistic and binary logic, just like the answers that teachers give their pupils, consisting in the main of whacking them over the head with a ruler, throwing a pitcher of water in their faces, throwing them out of the room or, in the best cases, throwing the question back at them. Morelli seemed to move about at will in that apparently demented universe, and took it for granted that this pedagogical behaviour constituted the real lesson, the only *manner* in which one could open the pupil's spiritual eye and reveal the truth to him. This violent unnaturalness seemed *natural* to him, in the sense that it abolished the structures which made up the specialty of the Western world, the axes on which man's historical understanding rotated and which in discursive thought (including aesthetic and even poetic feeling) find their instrument of choice.

The tone of the notes (jottings with a view to mnemotechny or an end not too well explained) seemed to indicate that Morelli had gone off into an adventure analogous to the work that he had been painfully writing and publishing over the years. For some of his readers (and for himself) it was laughable to try to write the kind of novel that would do away with the logical articulations of discourse.

One ended up by divining a kind of transaction, a proceeding (even though the absurdity of choosing a narration for ends that did not seem to be narrative might remain standing).*

* Why not? Morelli himself put the question on a sheet of graph paper in the margin of which there was a list of vegetables, probably a *memento buffandi.* Prophets, mystics, dark night of the soul: the frequent use of a story in the form of an apology or a vision. Of course a novel . . . But that scandal was born more from the generic and classificatory mania of the Western monkey than from a real internal contradiction.**

** Without saying that the more violent the internal contradiction, the more efficiently it would be able to supply a technique, as it were, in the Zen manner. Instead of a whack on the head, an absolutely antinovelish novel, with the subsequent scandal and shock, and perhaps with an opening for those best alerted.***

*** As if a hope for this last item, another scrap of paper continued the Suzukian quotation in the sense that the comprehension of the strange language used by the teachers means the comprehension of one's self on the part of the pupil and not that of the sense of the language. Just the reverse of what an astute European philosopher might deduce, the language of the Zen teacher transmits ideas and not feelings or intuitions. That is why it is of no use as far as language as such is concerned, but since the choice of phrases comes from the teacher, the mystery comes to a head in the region best suited for it and the pupil opens himself up, understands himself, and the pedestrian phrase becomes a key.****

**** That is why Étienne, who had made an analytical study of Morelli's tricks (something which had seemed a guarantee of failure to Oliveira), thought he recognized in certain passages of the book, including entire chapters, a kind of gigantic amplification *ad usum homo sapiens* of certain Zen slaps on the face. Those sections of the book Morelli called "archapters" and "chaptypes", verbal nonsense in which one could deduce a mixture that was not in the least Joycean. As for what archetypes had to do with it, it was a theme of restlessness for Wong and Gregorovius.*****

***** An observation by Étienne: In no way did Morelli appear to climb the *bodhi* tree or Sinai or up to any other platform of revelation. No pedagogical attitudes were set forth by which the reader might be guided towards new and green meadows. Without servility (the old man was of Italian origin and he was quick to pick up on what came from the heart, it must be said) he wrote as if he himself, in a desperate and moving attempt, had pictured the teacher who was to enlighten him. He turned loose his Zen phrase, and one kept on listening to it – sometimes for fifty pages, the old monster – , and it would have been absurd and of little faith to suspect that those pages were directed at a reader. If Morelli published them it was partly because of his Italian side ("*Ritorna vincitor!*") and partly because he was enchanted at how gaudy they had turned out.******

****** Étienne saw in Morelli the perfect Western man, the colonizer. When his crop of Buddhist poppies had been harvested, he would return with the seeds to the *Quartier Latin.* If the last revelation was perhaps the one that he had been hoping for most, one would have to recognize that his book was before anything else a literary undertaking, precisely because it was set forth as the destruction of literary forms (formulas).*******

******* Also Western, although it should be said as praise, from the Christian conviction that there is no individual salvation possible, and that one's faults stain everyone else and vice versa. Perhaps that is why (Oliveira had a hunch) he chose the novel form for his meanderings, and published in addition what he kept on finding or unfinding.

(–146)

96

The newsspreadlikewildfire, and practically the whole Club was there at ten o'clock that night. Étienne had the key, Wong bowed down to the ground to counteract the furious reception they got from the concierge, *mais qu'est-ce qu'ils viennent ficher, non mais vraiment ces étrangers, écoutez, je veux bien vous laisser monter puisque vous dites que vous êtes des amis du vi . . . de monsieur Morelli, mais quand même il aurait fallu prévenir, quoi, une bande qui s'amène à dix heures du soir, non, vraiment, Gustave, tu devrais parler au syndic, ça devient trop con,* etc. Babs armed with what Ronald called the alligator's smile, Ronald excited and slapping Étienne on the back, pushing him so he would hurry up, Perico Romero cursing out literature, second floor RODEAU, FOURRURES, third floor DOCTEUR, fourth floor HUSSENOT, it was all too fantastic, Ronald nudging Étienne in the ribs and putting Oliveira down, the bloody bastard, just another of his practical jokes, I suppose, *dis donc, tu vas me foutre la paix, toi,* this is all that Paris is, *coño,* one fucking staircase after another, you get fed up to the fifth shit with all of them. *Si tous les gars du monde . . .* Wong bringing up the rear, Wong has a smile for Gustave, a smile for the concierge, *bloody bastard, coño, ta gueule, salaud.* On the fifth floor the door on the right opened a few inches and Perico saw a gigantic rat in a white nightgown peeking out with one eye and all of her nose. Before she could close the door again, he stuck his shoe in and recited for her that thing that among serpents, the basilisk had an organ so poisonous for all the others and so overwhelming that he frightened them just by hissing and they scattered and fled at his coming, he could kill them with his glance. Madame René Lavalette, née Francillon, did not understand much but she answered with a snort and a shove. Perico pulled out his shoe with an eighth of a second to spare, SLAM. On the sixth they stopped to watch the solemnity with which Étienne inserted the key.

"It can't be," Ronald repeated for the last time. "We're dreaming, as the princesses of Tour et Taxis say. Did you bring the drinks, Babsie? An obolus for Charon, you know. Now the door will open and the magic will begin, I expect to get something out of tonight, there's an end of the world atmosphere."

"The god-damned witch almost broke my toe," Perico said, looking at his shoe. "Open up, god damn it, man, I've had enough of staircases to last me a lifetime."

But the key wouldn't work, even though Wong hinted that in ceremonies of the initiate the simplest movements are overcome by Forces that one must conquer through Patience and Slyness. The lights went out. Who's got a lighter, *coño? Tu pourrais*

Babs	*quand même parler français, non? Ton co-*
	pain l'argencul n'est pas là pour piger ton
Ronald	*charabia.* Give me a match, Ronald. God-
Étienne	damned key, it's all rusted, the old man kept
	it in a glass of water. *Mon copain, mon co-*
Étienne	*pain, c'est pas mon copain.* I don't think he's
Wong	coming. You don't know him. Maybe you
	ought. What the hell. Wanna bet something?
PERICO	*Ah merde, mais c'est la tour de Babel, ma*
Ronald	*parole. Amène ton briquet, Fleuve Jaune de*
PERICO	*mon cul, la poisse, quoi.* On Yin days we've
	got to be patient. Two litres, but good stuff.
Wong	My God, don't fall down the stairwell. I re-
Babs	member one night, in Alabama. The stars
ÉTIENNE	were out, my love. How funny, you ought to
ÉTIENNE	be on radio. There, it's starting to move now,
Babs Ronald	it was stuck, the Yin, of course, stars fell on
Babs Babs	Alabama, my foot's all fucked up, another
Ronald	match, I can't see a thing, *où qu'elle est,*
	la minuterie? It's not working. Somebody's
Ronald	touching me on the arse, my love . . . Shh
	. . . Shh . . . Let Wong go in first to exor-
ÉTIENNE	cise the demons. Oh, by no means. Give a
& chorus	shove, Perico, he's just a Chinaman.

"Shut up, everybody," Ronald said. "We're in other territory, I really mean it. If somebody has come here to have a good time, he can get his arse out of here. Give me the bottles, sweetie. You always drop them when you get overcome with emotion."

"I don't like people who go around pawing me in the dark," Babs said looking at Perico and Wong.

Étienne ran his fingers slowly over the moulding of the door. They waited in silence for him to find the light switch. The apartment was small and dusty, the soft and domesticated lights enveloped it in a golden air in which the Club breathed with relief for the first time and went about looking over the rest of the place, exchanging impressions in low voices: the reproduction of the tablet of Ur, the legend of the profanation of the Eucharist (Paolo Uccello *pinxit*), the photographs of Pound and of Musil, the little picture by De Staël, the enormous quantity of books along the walls, on the floor, on the tables, in the bathroom, in the tiny kitchen, where there was a fried egg halfway between rotten and petrified, most beautiful for Étienne, garbage pail for Babs, *ergo* a sibilant argument while Wong respectfully opened the *Dissertatio de morbis a fascino et fascino contra morbos* by Zwinger, Perico up on a stool as was his speciality, running through a row of Spanish poets of the Golden Age, examining a small astrolabe of tin and ivory, and Ronald standing motionless in front of Morelli's table, a bottle of cognac under each arm, looking at the green velvet notebook, exactly the spot where Balzac would have sat down to write but not Morelli. Then it was true, the old man had been living there, a stone's throw away from the Club, and his damned publisher had declared that he was in Austria or on the Costa Brava every time they asked for his address over the phone. Notebooks to the right and to the left, between twenty and forty, all colours, empty or full, and in the middle an ashtray that was like another one of Morelli's archives, a Pompeiian pile of ashes and burned-out matches.

"She threw the still life into the bin," Étienne said furiously. "If La Maga comes she won't leave a hair on her head. But you, her husband . . ."

"Look at this," Ronald said, showing him the table to calm him down. "And besides, Babs said it was rotten, there's no reason for you to carry on. The meeting has come to order. Étienne is presiding, but how can we continue? What about the Argentinian?"

"The Argentinian and the Transylvanian are missing, Guy is in the country, and La Maga's wandering around God knows where. In any case, we have a quorum. Wong, recording secretary."

"Let's wait a while for Oliveira and Ossip. Babs, treasurer."

"Ronald, secretary. In charge of the bar. Sweet, get some glasses, will you?"

"We stand recessed," Étienne said, sitting down alongside the table. "The Club is meeting tonight to fulfil a desire of Morelli's. While we're waiting for Oliveira, if he's coming, let's drink to the old man's sitting here again one of these days. Good lord, what a ghastly spectacle. We look like a nightmare that Morelli is probably dreaming right now in the hospital. Horrible. The meeting is open for business."

"But let's talk about him in the meantime," said Ronald, whose eyes were filled with natural tears and who was struggling with the cork in the cognac bottle. "There'll never be another session like this, all these years now I've been a novitiate and I didn't know it. And you, Wong, and Perico. All of us. Damn it, I could cry. This is the way a person must feel when he gets to the top of a mountain or breaks a record, things like that. Sorry."

Étienne put a hand on his shoulder. They sat down around the table. Wong turned out the lamps, except the one that was lighting up the green notebook. It was almost a scene for Eusapia Paladino, thought Étienne, who respected spiritualism. They began to talk about Morelli's books and drink cognac.

(–94)

97

Gregorovius, an agent of heteroclite forces, had been interested in a note of Morelli's: "To plunge one's self into a reality or into a possible mode of a reality, and to feel how that which at first sight seemed to be the wildest absurdity comes to have some value, to articulate itself with other forms, absurd or otherwise, until the divergent weave (in relation to the stereotyped sketch of everyday life) appears and is defined in a coherent sketch which only by timid comparison with the former will appear mad or delirious or incomprehensible. Nevertheless, am I not sinning in the direction of an excess of confidence? To refuse to make *psychologies* and at the same time to place a reader – a certain reader, that is true – in contact with a *personal* world, with a personal existence and meditation . . . That reader will be without any bridge, any intermediate link, any casual articulation. Raw things: behaviour, results, ruptures, catastrophes, derision. There where there should be a leave-taking there is a sketch on the wall; instead of a shout, a fishing-pole; a death is resolved in a trio for mandolins. And all of that is leave-taking, shout, and death, but who is prepared to displace himself, remove himself, decentre himself, uncover himself? The outer forms of the novel have changed, but their heroes are still the avatars of Tristram, Jane Eyre, Lafcadio, Leopold Bloom, people from the street, from the home, from the bedroom, *characters.* For every hero like Ulrich (*more* Musil) or Molloy (*more* Beckett), there are five hundred Darleys (*more* Durrell). For my part, I wonder whether one day I will ever succeed in making it felt that the true character and the only one that interests me is the reader, to the degree in which something of what I write ought to contribute to his mutation, displacement, alienation, transportation." In spite of the tacit confession of defeat in the last sentence, Ronald found a presumption in the note that displeased him.

(–18)

98

And that's how blind people are the ones who light our paths. That's how someone, without knowing it, comes to show you irrefutably that you are on a path which he for his part would be incapable of following. La Maga will never know how her finger pointed towards the thin line that shatters the mirror, up to what point certain silences, certain absurd attentions, a certain scurrying of a dazzled centipede were the password for the firm establishment of my being in myself, which meant being in no place. By the way, that metaphor of the thin line . . . If you want happiness the way you say / Poetry away, Horacio, away.

Seen objectively: She was incapable of showing me anything inside my terrain, even in hers she whirled around disconcerted, touching, handling. A frantic bat, the sketch a fly makes in the air of the room. Suddenly, for me seated there looking at her, an indication, a hint. Without her knowing it, the reason for her tears or the order of her shopping list or her way of frying potatoes were *signs.* Morelli spoke of something like that when he wrote: "Reading Heisenberg until noon, notes, cards. The concierge's boy brings me my mail and we talk about a model aeroplane he is building in the kitchen of his apartment. While he tells me about it, he gives two little hops on his left foot, three on his right, two on his left. I ask him why two and three, and not two and two or three and three. He looks at me surprised, he does not understand. Feeling that Heisenberg and I are from the other side of a territory, while the boy is still straddling with one foot in each without knowing it, and that soon he will be only on our side and all communication will have been lost. Communication with what, for what? Well, let us continue reading; Heisenberg probably . . . "

(–38)

99

"It isn't the first time that he's referred to the erosion of language," Étienne said. "I could mention several places where characters lose confidence in themselves to the degree in which they feel they've been drawn through their thought and speech, and they're afraid the sketch may be deceptive. *Honneur des hommes, Saint Langage* . . . We're far away from that."

"Not so very far," Ronald said. "What Morelli is trying to do is give language back its rights. He talks about expurgating it, punishing it, changing 'descend' into 'go down' as a hygienic measure; but what he's really looking for is to give back all its glow to the verb 'descend', so that it can be used the way I use matches and not like a decorative fragment, a piece of the commonplace."

"Yes, but that battle is taking place on several planes," said Oliveira, coming out of a long silence. "In what you've just read to us, it's quite clear that Morelli is condemning in language the reflection of a false or incomplete optic and *Organum* that mask reality and humanity for us. Basically, he didn't really care too much about language, except on the aesthetic plane. But that reference to the *ethos* is unmistakable. Morelli understands that the mere writing of aesthetic is a fraud and a lie and ends up arousing the female-reader, the type that doesn't want any problems but rather solutions, or false and alien problems that will allow him to suffer comfortably seated in his chair, without compromising himself in the drama that should also be his. In Argentina, if the Club will give me permission to fall back on localisms, that kind of fraud has kept us quite content and peaceful for a whole century."

"Happy is he who finds his peers, the active readers," Wong recited. "It's on this little piece of blue paper, in notebook twenty-one. When I first read Morelli (in Meudon, a clandestine movie, Cuban friends) it seemed to me that the whole book was the Great

Tortoise turned on its back. Difficult to understand. Morelli is an extraordinary philosopher, but exceedingly stupid at times."

"Like you," said Perico, getting off his stool and elbowing his way into the group at the table. "All those fantasies about correcting language are jobs for academicians, boy, not to mention grammarians. Descend or go down, the fact is that the character beats it downstairs, and that's that."

"Perico," Étienne said, "is rescuing us from excessive confinement, from getting up into abstractions that Morelli sometimes likes too much."

"I'll tell you something," Perico said threateningly. "As far as I'm concerned, this whole business of abstractions . . ."

The cognac burned Oliveira's throat and he slid thankfully into the argument, where he could still lose himself for a while. In a certain passage (he didn't know exactly which, he would have to hunt for it) Morelli had given some keys to a method of composition. His problem to start with was always a drying up, a Mallarmean horror of facing a blank page, coincident with the necessity of opening himself up at all cost. Inevitable that a part of his work should be a reflection on the problem of writing it. He kept getting farther and farther away from the professional utilization of literature, from that type of short story or poem on which his initial prestige had been based. In some passage or other Morelli said he had reread with nostalgia and even surprise certain texts he had written years before. How could those inventions have flourished, that marvellous and yet so comfortable and simplifying unfolding of a narrator and his narration? In those days it had been as if what he was writing were already laid out in front of him, writing was running a Lettera 22 over words invisible but present, like the diamond in the groove of the record. Now he could write only with effort, examining at every turn a possible opposite, the hidden fallacy (he would have to reread, Oliveira thought, a curious passage that had delighted Étienne), suspicious that every clear idea was inevitably a mistake or half-truth, mistrusting the words that tended to organize themselves euphonically, rhythmically, with the happy murmur that hypnotizes the reader after he has found his first victim in the writer himself. ("Yes, but poetry . . ." "Yes, but that note in which he talks about the 'swing' that puts discourse on the march . . .") Sometimes Morelli was in favour of a bitterly simple conclusion: he no longer had anything to say, the conditioned reflexes of the profession confused necessity with routine, a typical case among writers beyond the age of fifty and the important prizes. But at the same time he felt that he had never been so desirous, so urged to write. Could the delightful anxiety of doing battle with himself line by line be a mere reflection, a routine? Why then immediately a counterblow, the descending stroke of the piston, gasping doubt, dryness, renunciation?

"Hey," Oliveira said, "where's that passage about the single word you liked so much?"

"I know it by heart," Étienne said. "It's the conjunction *if* followed by a footnote, which in turn is followed by a footnote which in turn is followed by another footnote. I was telling Perico that Morelli's theories are not entirely original. It's his way of saying them that makes him intimate, the strength with which he tries to describe, as he says, to earn the right (and earn it for everybody) to enter the house of man once more with his best foot forward. I'm using his very words, or ones that are very much like them."

"We've had enough of surrealists for a while," Perico said.

"It's not a question of the job of verbal liberation," said Étienne. "The surrealists thought that true language and true reality were censored and relegated by the rationalist and bourgeois structure of the Western world. They were right, as any poet knows, but that was just a moment in the complicated peeling of the banana. Result, more than one of them ate it with the skin still on. The surrealists hung from words instead of brutally disengaging themselves from them, as Morelli would like to do from the word itself. Fanatics of the *verbum* in a pure state, frantic wizards, they accepted anything as long as it didn't seem excessively grammatical. They didn't suspect enough that the creation of a whole language, even though it might end up betraying its sense, irrefutably shows human structure, whether that of a Chinese or a redskin. Language means residence in a reality, living in a reality. Even if it's true that the language we use betrays us (and Morelli isn't the only one who shouts it to the four winds), wanting to free it from its taboos isn't enough. We have to relive it, not reanimate it."

"It all sounds most solemn," Perico said.

"It's in any good philosophical work," Gregorovius said timidly. He had been thumbing entomologically through the notebooks and seemed half-asleep. "It's impossible to relive language if one doesn't start by intuiting in a different way almost everything that makes up our reality."

"Intuit," said Oliveira, "is one of those words that can be applied to sweeping just as easily as to scrubbing. Let's not attribute to Morelli the problems of Dilthey, Husserl, or Wittgenstein. The only thing clear in everything the old man has written is that we still utilize language in its current key, with its current finalities, we shall die without ever knowing the real name of the day. It's almost stupid to repeat that life is sold to us, as Malcolm Lowry said, that it's given to us prefabricated. Morelli is also a little stupid when he insists on that, but Étienne has hit the nail on the head: the old man shows himself by the way he does it and he shows us the way out. What good is a writer if he can't destroy literature? And us, we don't want to be female-readers, what good are we if we don't help as much as we can in that destruction?"

"But afterwards, what do we do afterwards?" Babs asked.

"I wonder," said Oliveira. "Until about twenty years ago there was the great answer: Poetry, silly, Poetry. They would gag you with the great word. Poetical vision of the world, conquest of a poetical reality. But then after the last war, you must have noticed that it was all over. We still have poets, nobody can deny that, but no one ever reads them."

"Don't talk nonsense," said Perico. "I read tons of poetry."

"Of course, so do I. But it's not a question of poetry, you know, it's a question of what the surrealists were announcing and what every poet wants and searches for, that well-known poetical reality. Believe me, my dear boy, since nineteen-fifty we've been right in the middle of a technological reality, statistically speaking, at least. Very bad, a pity, it makes you want to tear your hair, but that's how it is."

"I don't give a hoot for technology," Perico said. "Fray Luis, for example . . . "

"We're in the year nineteen-fifty something."

"I'm aware of that, *coño*."

"It doesn't look like it."

"But do you think I'm about to put myself in the position of a meat-beating historicist?"

"No, but you ought to read the newspapers. I don't like technology any more than you, it's just that I feel the world has changed in the last twenty years. Any guy who's past forty has to realize it, and that's why Babs's questions back Morelli and the rest of us up against the wall. It's OK to declare war on language turned whore, literature, as it were, in the name of a reality we think is true, that we think we can reach, that we think is there somewhere in the spirit, if you'll pardon the expression. But Morelli himself sees only the negative side of his battle. He feels he has to wage it, like you and like all of us. So?"

"Let's be methodical," Étienne said. "Let's leave your 'so?' out of it. Morelli's lesson is enough as a first stage."

"You can't talk about stages without presupposing a goal."

"Call it a working hypothesis, anything you like along those lines. What Morelli is looking for is to break the reader's mental habits. Something very modest, as can be seen, nothing comparable to Hannibal crossing the Alps. Up till now, at least, there isn't much metaphysics in Morelli, except that you, Horacio Curiacio, are capable of finding metaphysics in a tin of tomatoes. Morelli is an artist who has a special idea of art, consisting more than anything in knocking over the usual forms, something all good artists have in common. For example, the Chinese-scroll novel makes him explode. The book read from beginning to end like a good child. You've probably noticed already that he gets less and less worried about joining the parts together, that business of one word leading to another . . . When I read Morelli I have the impression he's looking for a less mechanical interaction, one less caused by the elements he works with; he feels that what has already been written just barely conditions what is being written, especially since the old man, after hundreds of pages, doesn't even have a clear memory of what he's done."

"According to which," Perico said, "it turns out that a midget on page twenty is six feet tall on page one hundred. I've noticed that more than once. There are scenes that begin at six in the afternoon and end at five-thirty. A bore."

"And haven't you ever wanted to be a midget or a giant according to the state of your mind?" Ronald asked.

"I'm talking about the soma," Perico said.

"He believes in the soma," Oliveira said. "The soma in time. He believes in time, in the before and in the after. The poor fellow hasn't found some letter of his written twenty years ago in a drawer, he hasn't reread it, he hasn't noticed that nothing is sustained unless we prop it up with a crumb of time, unless we invent time so we don't go crazy."

"That's all part of a trade," Ronald said. "But behind it, behind . . ."

"A poet," Oliveira said, sincerely moved. "Your name ought to be Behind or Beyond, my dear American. Or Yonder, that's such a pretty English word."

"None of it would make any sense if there weren't a behind," Ronald said. "Any author of best-sellers writes better than Morelli. The reason we read him, the reason we're here tonight, is that Morelli has what Bird had, what all of a sudden Cummings or Jackson Pollock have, anyway, so much for examples. And why so much for examples?" Ronald shouted furiously, while Babs looked on admiringly and drinkingineveryoneofhiswordsinonegulp. "I'll quote anything I goddam please. It's easy to see that Morelli doesn't complicate life just because he likes to, and besides, his book is a shameless provocation, just like anything else that's worth something. In this technological world you were talking about, Morelli wants to save something that's dying, but in order to save it, first it has to be killed or at least given such a blood transfusion that the whole thing will be like a resurrection. The mistake of futurist poetry," Ronald said, to the immense admiration of Babs, "was wanting to comment on mechanism, believing that they'd be saved from leukaemia that way. But we won't understand reality any better by talking in a literary way of what's going on at Cape Canaveral, it seems to me."

"And it seems right," Oliveira said. "Let's keep on looking for the Yonder, there are plenty of Yonders that keep opening up one after the other. I'd start by saying that this technological reality that men of science and the readers of *France-Soir* accept today, this world of cortisone, gamma rays, and the elution of plutonium, has as little to do with reality as the world of the *Roman de la Rose*. If I mentioned it a while back to our friend Perico, it was in order to make him take note that his aesthetic criteria and his scale of values are pretty well liquidated and that man, after having expected everything from intelligence and the spirit, feels that he's been betrayed, is vaguely aware that his weapons have been turned against him, that culture, *civiltà*, have misled him into this blind alley where scientific barbarism is nothing but a very understandable reaction. Please excuse my vocabulary."

"Klages has already said all that," said Gregorovius.

"I don't pretend to hold any copyright on it," Oliveira said. "The idea is that reality, whether you accept the version of the Holy See, or of René Char, or of Oppenheimer, is always a conventional reality, incomplete and divided. The surprise some guys show in front of an electron microscope doesn't seem to be any more fruitful to me than the one concierges show at the miracles of Lourdes. Believing in what they call matter, believing in what they call spirit, living in the Emmanuel or taking courses in Zen, considering human destiny as an economic problem or as a complete absurdity, the list is long, the choice is multiple. But the very fact that there can be a choice and that the list is long is enough to show that we're still in prehistory and in prehumanity. I'm not an optimist, I doubt very much whether some day we'll find the real history of real humanity. It's going to be hard going to get to Ronald's famous Yonder because nobody will deny that the problem of reality has to be established in collective terms, not just in the salvation of a few of the elect. Accomplished men, men who have taken the leap outside time and have become integrated in a *summa,* as it were . . . Yes, I suppose they have existed and still do. But that's not enough; I feel that my salvation, supposing I can reach it, must also be the salvation of all, right down to the last man. And that, old man . . . We're no longer in the fields of Assisi, we can no longer hope that the example of a saint will sow the seeds of sainthood, that every guru will be the salvation of all of his disciples."

"Come on back from Benares," Étienne advised. "We were talking about Morelli, I think. And to connect with what you were saying, it occurs to me that this famous Yonder cannot be imagined as a future in time or in space. If we continue holding to Kantian categories, Morelli seems to say, we will never get out of this blind alley. What we call reality, the true reality that we also call Yonder (sometimes it helps to give a lot of names to a partial vision, at least it prevents the notion from becoming closed and rigid), that true reality, I repeat, is not something that is going to happen, a goal, the last step, the end of an evolution. No, it's something that's already here, in us. You can feel it, all you need is the courage to stick your hand into the darkness. I feel it when I'm painting."

"It might be the Evil One," Oliveira said. "It might be a mere aesthetic exaltation. But it might be the other too. Yes, it might be the other too."

"It's here," Babs said, touching her forehead. "I feel it when I'm a little drunk, or when . . ."

She let out a raucous laugh and covered her face. Ronald gave her a tender shove.

"Not it's here," said Wong very seriously. "It is."

"We won't get very far on this road," Oliveira said. "What does poetry give us except that partial-vision? You, me, Babs . . . The kingdom of man was not born out of a few isolated sparks. Everybody has had his moment of vision, but the worst part is falling back into the *hinc* and the *nunc*."

"Bah, you don't understand anything unless it's in absolute terms," Étienne said. "Let me finish what I wanted to say. Morelli thinks that if the lyricists, as our Perico has said, did open the way through petrified and unstable forms, whether a modal adverb, a sense of theme, or whatever you want to make it, they must have had something useful for the first time in their lives. Doing away with the female-reader, or at least severely damaging him, would help all of those who in some way are working to reach the Yonder. The narrative technique of types like that is simply an urge to get out of the rut."

"Yes, only to fall into the mud up to his neck," said Perico, who at eleven o'clock at night was against anything.

"Heraclitus," Gregorovius said, "buried himself in shit up to his neck and cured himself of dropsy."

"Leave Heraclitus in peace," Étienne said. "I'm already beginning to feel foolishly sleepy, but in any case I'm going to say the following, two points: Morelli seems convinced that if a writer keeps on being dominated by the language they have sold him along with the clothes he's wearing and his name and nationality, his work won't have any other value except the aesthetic, a value which the old man seems to despise more and more. He's rather explicit in one place or other: according to him, nothing can be denounced if the denouncing is done within the system that belongs to the thing denounced. Writing against capitalism with the mental baggage and the vocabulary that comes out of capitalism is a waste of time. Historical results like Marxism and what have you will be produced, but the Yonder is not precisely history, the Yonder is like fingertips sticking out of the surface of history, looking for something to cling to."

"Bullshit," said Perico.

"And that's why the writer has to set language on fire, put an end to its coagulated forms and even go beyond it, place in doubt the possibility that language is still in touch with what it pretends to name. Not words as such any more, because that's less important, but rather the total structure of language, of discourse."

"For all of which he uses an exceedingly clear language," Perico said.

"Of course, Morelli doesn't believe in onomatopoeic systems or in lyrics. It's not a question of substituting automatic writing or any other current fraud for syntax. What he wants to do is transgress the total literary deed, the book, if you will. Sometimes the word, sometimes what the word transmits. He works like a guerrilla fighter, he blows up what he can, the rest follows in its path. Don't get the idea that he's a man of letters."

"We should think about leaving," said Babs, who was sleepy.

"Say whatever you want," Perico insisted, "but no real revolution has ever been made against form. What counts is content, man, content."

"We've already had dozens of centuries of literature with content," Oliveira said, "and look at the results. By literature, you understand, I mean everything that can be said or thought."

"Without realizing that the distinction between form and content is false," said Étienne. "Everybody's known that for years. Let's distinguish, rather, between the expressive element, or language as such, and the thing expressed, or reality becoming awareness."

"Whatever you want," Perico said. "What I would like to know is whether the break that Morelli is trying for, I mean the breaking of what you call the expressive element the better to reach the expressible thing, really has any value at this time."

"It probably wouldn't be good for anything," Oliveira said, "but it does make us feel a little less lonely in this blind alley at the service of the Great-Idealist-Realist-Spiritualist-Materialist-Infatuation of the West, Inc."

"Do you think somebody else might have been able to open a way through language until he came to touch it at its roots?" Ronald asked.

"Maybe. Morelli doesn't have the required genius or patience. He points out a path, he takes a few digs with a pickaxe . . . He leaves a book behind. It's not much."

"Let's go," said Babs. "It's getting late and the cognac's all gone."

"And there's something else," said Oliveira. "What he's pursuing is absurd to the degree that nobody knows anything except what he knows, that is to say, an anthropological circumscription. Wittgensteinly speaking, problems link themselves together in a *backward* direction, that is to say that what a man knows can be the knowledge of a man, but he no longer knows what he ought to know about the man himself, so that his notion of reality would be acceptable. The gnoseologists brought up this problem and even thought that they had found solid ground from which they could continue the race forward, towards metaphysics. But the hygienic retreat of a Descartes appears partial and even insignificant to us today, because at this very moment there is a Mr Wilcox in Cleveland who with electrodes and other apparatus is proving that thought and an electromagnetic circuit are the same thing (things that he in turn thinks he knows very well because he knows very well the language that defines them, etc.). Add to that the fact that a Swede has just put forth a very impressive theory on cerebral chemistry. Thinking is the result of the interaction of certain acids, the name of which I do not care to recall. *Acido, ergo sum.* Put a drop on your meninges and there you are, maybe Oppenheimer or Dr Petiot, the eminent murderer. You can see then, how the *cogito*, that Human Operation *par excellence*, is nowadays located in a rather vague region, somewhere between electromagnetism and chemistry, and probably not as different as we used to think from things like an aurora borealis or a picture taken with infrared rays. There goes your *cogito*, a link in the dizzy flow of forces whose steps are called in 1950, *inter alia*, electrical impulses, molecules, atoms, neutrons, protons, positrons, microbitons, radioactive isotopes, grains of cinnabar, cosmic rays: Words, words, words, *Hamlet*, Act Two, I think. Without considering," Oliveira added with a sigh, "that it's probably just the opposite, and the result is that the aurora borealis is a *spiritual* phenomenon, and then we really are what we want to be . . . "

"Along with some similar nihilism, hara-kiri," Étienne said.

"Well of course," Oliveira said. "But getting back to the old man, if what he's after is absurd, because it's like hitting Sugar Ray Robinson with a banana, because it's an insignificant offensive in the midst of the crisis and complete breakup of the classic idea of Homo sapiens, we mustn't forget that you are you and I am I, or at least so it seems to us, and that even if we don't have the slightest certainty about everything our gigantic parents accepted as irrefutable, we still have the pleasant possibility of living and acting *as if*, choosing working hypotheses, attacking like Morelli what seems false to us, in the name of some obscure feeling of certainty, which is probably just as uncertain as the rest, but which makes us lift up our heads and count the little goats or look for the Pleiades again, those childhood animals, those bottomless fireflies. Cognac."

"It's all gone," Babs said. "Let's go, I'm falling asleep."

"In the end, as always, an act of faith," said Étienne, laughing. "It's still the best definition of man. Now, getting back to the subject of the fried egg . . . "

(–35)

100

He put the slug in the slot, slowly dialled the number. At that hour Étienne was probably painting and he hated people to call him in the middle of his work, but he had to call him just the same. The telephone began to ring at the other end, in a studio near the Place d'Italie, three miles from the post office on the Rue Danton. An old woman with the look of a rat had stationed herself in front of the glass booth; she looked furtively at Oliveira who was sitting on the little bench with his face up against the apparatus, and Oliveira felt the old woman looking at him, implacably counting the minutes. The glass in the booth was strangely clean: people were coming and going in the post office, one could hear the dull (and funereal, it was hard to say why) cancelling of stamps. Étienne said something on the other end, and Oliveira pushed the nickel button that established contact and definitively swallowed up the twenty-franc slug.

"Why do you always fuck things up," complained Étienne, who appeared to have recognized him immediately. "You know I'm always working like crazy at this hour."

"Me too," said Oliveira. "I called you because just when I was working I had a dream."

"What do you mean when you were working?"

"Yes, around three in the morning. I dreamed I was going into the kitchen, I was looking for some bread, and I cut off a slice. The bread was different from what we have around here, French bread like the bread in Buenos Aires, you know there's nothing French about it but they call it French bread. You must realize it's a much thicker loaf, light in colour, with lots of soft centre. A loaf made to be spread with butter and jam, you understand."

"I know what you mean," Étienne said. "I've eaten it in Italy."

"You're crazy. It's not like that at all. Someday I'll have to draw you a picture so you can see. Look, it's shaped like a short, fat fish, barely six inches long but quite fat in the middle. That's Buenos Aires French bread."

"Buenos Aires French bread," Étienne repeated.

"Yes, but this happened on the Rue de la Tombe Issoire, before I moved in with La Maga. I was hungry and I took out the loaf to cut off a slice. Then I heard the bread crying. Yes, of course it was a dream, but the bread started to cry when I put the knife to it. An ordinary loaf of French bread and it was crying. I woke up without knowing what was going to happen, I think I still had the knife stuck in the bread when I woke up."

"*Tiens*," said Étienne.

"Now you can see, you wake up from a dream like that, go out into the hall and stick your head under the tap, go back to bed, spend the whole night smoking . . . What could I do, the best thing was to call you, apart from the fact that we could make a date to go and see the old man in the accident I told you about."

"You did the right thing," Étienne said. "It sounds like a child's dream. Children can still dream things like that, or imagine them. My nephew told me once that he had been on the moon. I asked him what he had seen. He answered: 'There was a loaf of bread and a heart.' You realize that after bakery experiences like this you can't look at a child any more without being frightened."

"A loaf of bread and a heart," Oliveira repeated. "Yes, but I only saw a loaf of bread. So. There's an old woman out there who's starting to give me dirty looks. How long do they let you talk in these booths?"

"Six minutes. Then she'll start rapping on the glass. Is there only one old woman?"

"An old woman, a cross-eyed woman with a kid, and a travelling-salesman type. He must be a travelling salesman because besides the notebook he's thumbing through like mad, I can see the points of three pencils sticking out of his breast pocket."

"He could also be a bill collector."

"Now there are two more, a kid of fourteen who's picking his nose, and an old woman with a wild hat, like out of a painting by Cranach."

"You're feeling better," Étienne said.

"Yes, this booth isn't bad. It's a shame so many people are waiting. Do you think we've been talking six minutes?"

"Nowhere near," Étienne said. "Barely three, and not even that."

"Then the old woman has no right to rap on the glass, eh?"

"Let her go to hell. Of course she has no right. You can use your six minutes to tell me about as many dreams as you want to."

"It was just that one," Oliveira said, "but the worst is not the dream. The worst is what they call waking up . . . Don't you think that actually it's now that I'm dreaming?"

"Who can tell? But it's an overworked theme, old man, the philosopher and the butterfly, they're things that everybody knows."

"Yes, but please excuse me for insisting a little. I wanted you to imagine a world where you can cut a loaf of bread without its complaining."

"It's difficult to believe, really," Étienne said.

"No, seriously. Hasn't it ever happened to you that you've woken up sometimes with the exact feeling that at that moment a terrible mistake is beginning?"

"In the midst of that mistake," Étienne said, "I paint magnificent pictures and it doesn't matter to me very much whether I'm a butterfly or Fu Manchu."

"That has nothing to do with it. It seems that thanks to various mistakes Columbus reached Guanahani or whatever the name of the island is. Why that Greek criterion of truth and error?"

"But it wasn't me," Étienne said resentfully. "You're the one who spoke of an incredible mistake."

"That was a figure of speech too," Oliveira said. "The same as calling it a dream. It can't be catalogued, the mistake is precisely the fact that you can't even say whether or not it is a mistake."

"The old woman's going to break the glass," Étienne said. "You can hear her from here."

"Let her go to hell," Oliveira said. "The six minutes can't be up."

"Just about. But then, you have that South American courtesy one hears praised so much."

"It's not six minutes. I'm glad I told you about the dream, and when we get together . . . "

"Come by whenever you want to," Étienne said. "I'm not going to paint any more this morning, you've done me in."

"Can you hear her beating on the window?" Oliveira asked. "Not just the old rat-faced woman, but the kid and the crosseyed woman too. An attendant'll be here any minute."

"Of course you're going to punch them all in the eye."

"No reason to. My great technique is to pretend I don't understand a single word of French."

"You really don't understand very much," Étienne said.

"No. The sad thing is that this is a big joke for you, and really it's not a joke at all. The truth is I don't want to understand anything, if by understanding one must accept what we used to call mistakes. Hey, they've opened the door and there's a guy here tapping me on the shoulder. *Ciao*, thanks for listening to me."

"*Ciao*," said Étienne.

Straightening his jacket, Oliveira left the booth. The attendant was shouting the repertory of the rules in his ear. "If I only had the knife in my hand now," Oliveira thought, taking out his cigarettes, "this guy would probably start to cackle or turn into a bouquet of flowers." But things had become petrified, they were lasting a terribly long time, it was necessary to light his cigarette, being careful not to burn himself because his hand was shaking very much, and he could still hear the shouts of the guy, who was going away, turning around after every two steps to look at him and gesture, and the cross-eyed woman and the travelling salesman were looking at him out of one eye while with the other one they began to keep watch over the old woman so she wouldn't go over six minutes; the old woman in the booth looked exactly like a Quechua mummy in the Museum of Man, one of those that lights up if you push a button. But it was just the opposite as in so many dreams, the old woman was pushing a button on the inside and began to talk with some other old woman stuck away in some attic in the immense dream.

(–76)

101

Barely lifting her head Pola saw the calendar of the Postes Télégraphes Téléphones, a pink cow in a green field with a background of purple mountains underneath a blue sky, Thursday 1, Friday 2, Saturday 3, Sunday 4, Monday 5, Tuesday 6, *Saint Mamert, Sainte Solange, Saint Achille, Saint Servais, Saint Boniface, lever 4 h.12, coucher 19 h.23, lever 4 h.10, coucher 19 h.24, lever coucher, lever coucher, lever coucher, coucher, coucher, coucher.*

Putting her face to Oliveira's shoulder she kissed perspiring skin, tobacco and sleep. With a very distant and free hand she caressed his stomach, came and went along his thighs, played with the hair on his body, wrapping it around her fingers a little and tugging softly so that Oliveira got a little annoyed and bit her in play. A pair of slippers was dragging along the stairway, *Saint Ferdinand, Sainte Pétronille, Saint Fortuné, Sainte Blandine, un, deux, un, deux,* right, left, right, left, good, bad, good, bad, forward, back, forward, back. A hand went along her shoulder, playing spider, one finger, another, another, *Saint Fortuné, Sainte Blandine,* a finger here, another farther on, another on top, another below. The caresses slowly penetrated her, from a different plane. The hour of luxury, surplus, slowly biting, looking for contact with delicate exploration, with feigned hesitancy, putting the tip of the tongue against a skin, slowly digging in a nail, murmuring *coucher 19 h.24, Saint Ferdinand.* Pola raised her head a little and looked at Horacio who had his eyes closed. She wondered whether he did that with his girlfriend too, the mother of the kid. He didn't like to talk about the other girl, he required as a sort of respect that he would not refer to her except when obliged to. When she would ask him, opening one of his eyes with two fingers and kissing him wildly on the mouth that refused to answer, the only consolation then was silence, remaining there one against the other, listening to themselves breathe, with a foot or a hand travelling over to the other body, undertaking soft itineraries without consequence, leftovers of caresses lost in the bed, in the air, ghosts of kisses, little larva worms of perfumes or of habit. No, he didn't like to do that with his girlfriend, only Pola could understand, could fit so well into his whims. So well that it was extraordinary. Even when she moaned, because once she had moaned, she had wanted to free herself, but it was too late, the loop had closed and her rebellion had only served to deepen the pleasure and the pain, the double misunderstanding that they had to overcome because it was false, it could not be that in an embrace, unless yes, unless it had to be that way.

(–144)

102

Exploring like an ant, Wong turned up in Morelli's library an inscribed copy of *Die Verwirrungen des Zöglings Törless*, by Musil, with the following passage firmly underlined:

> What are the things that seem strange to me? The most trivial. Especially inanimate objects. What is there that seems strange about them? Something that I do not know. But it is precisely that! Where in the world do I get this notion of "something" from? I feel that it is there, that it exists. It produces an effect in me as if it were trying to speak. I become exasperated, as one who makes an effort to read the twisted lips of a paralytic, without managing to do so. It is as if he had an additional sense, one more than other people, but one which has not been developed completely, a sense that is there and can be perceived, but which does not function. The world for me is full of silent voices. Does that mean that I am a seer, or that I am having hallucinations?

Ronald found this quotation from *Lord Chandos's Letter*, by Hofmannsthal:

> Just as I had looked at the skin on my little finger in a magnifying glass one day, something like a field with furrows and hollows, so I looked at men and their actions now. I could no longer perceive them with the simplifying look of habit. Everything was breaking down into fragments which in turn were becoming fragmented; I was unable to grasp anything by means of a defined notion.

(–45)

103

Nor would Pola have understood why at night he held back his breath to listen to her sleep, spying on the sounds of her body. Face-up, satisfied, she was breathing heavily, and hardly if ever, out of some uncertain dream, did she move a hand or exhale by raising her lower lip and blowing the air up towards her nose. Horacio remained still, his head a little raised or leaning on his fist, his cigarette hanging down. At three o'clock in the morning the Rue Dauphine was quiet, Pola's breathing came and went, then there was something like a soft running, a minute instantaneous whirlwind, an interior agitation like a second life. Oliveira got up slowly and moved his ear close to the naked skin, rested it on the tense and warm curved drum, listened. Sounds, drops and falls, Cartesian devils and murmurs, a walking of crabs and slugs, a black and muffled world sliding out over plush, running into things here and there and covering up again (Pola breathed heavily, moved a little). A liquid cosmos, fluid, in nocturnal gestation, plasmas rising and falling, the opaque and slow mechanism moving around grudgingly, and suddenly a rumbling, a mad race almost against the skin, a flight and a gurgling of contention or leaking, Pola's stomach a black sky with fat and slow stars, glowing comets, a tumbling of immense vociferant planets, the sea like whispering plankton, its Medusa murmurings, Pola the microcosm, Pola the summing up of universal night in her small fermented night where yoghurt and white wine were mixed with meat and vegetables, centre of a chemistry infinitely rich and mysterious and remote and so near.

(–108)

104

Life as a *commentary* of something else we cannot reach, which is there within reach of the leap we will not take.

Life, a ballet based upon a historical theme, a story based upon a deed that once had been alive, a deed that had lived based upon a real deed.

Life, a photograph of the noumenon, a possession in the shadows (woman, monster?), life, pimp of death, splendid deck of cards, ring of forgotten keys that a pair of palsied hands degrade into a sad game of solitaire.

(–10)

105

Morelliana

I think about forgotten gestures, the multiple signals and words of grandparents, lost little by little, not inherited, fallen one after the other off the tree of time. Tonight I found a candle on a table, and as a game I lit it and walked along the corridor with it. The breeze stirred up by my motion was about to put it out, then I saw my right hand come up all by itself, cup itself, protect the flame with a living lampshade that kept the breeze away. While the flame climbed up again alert, I thought that the gesture had belonged to all of us (I thought *us* and I thought well, or I felt well) for thousands of years, during the Age of Fire, until they changed us over to electric lights. I imagined other gestures, the one that women make when they lift the hem of their skirts, the one that men make looking for the hilt of their swords. Like words lost in childhood, heard for the last time by old people who are heading towards death. In my home no one talks about the "camphor closet" any more, no one talks about "the triv" – the trivet – any more. Like music of the moment, 1920 waltzes, polkas that warmed grandparents' hearts.

I think about those objects, those boxes, those utensils that sometimes would turn up in storerooms, kitchens, or hidden spots, *and whose use no one can explain any more.* The vanity of believing that we understand the works of time: it buries its dead and keeps the keys. Only in dreams, in poetry, in play – lighting a candle, walking with it along the corridor – do we sometimes arrive at what we were before we were this thing that, who knows, we are.

(–96)

106

Between now and tomorrow, babe, morning, we'll have to part,
midnight to morning, babe, tomorrow we'll have to part.
Please remember just one thing about it, I've always been in your heart.

* * *

Cold feet on the kitchen floor, cold feet on the ground,
cold feet everywhere since my man left town.
Cold feet in the butcher shop, cold feet in the store
since nobody comes around to grind my meat no more.
Cold feet on the motor and cold feet on the stones
and cold feet in my bed, 'cause I'm sleeping all alone.

(–13)

107

Written by Morelli in the hospital

The best trait my ancestors have is that of being dead; I am waiting modestly and proudly for the moment when I come into my inheritance from them. I have friends who would not fail to erect a statue of me in which they would represent me face down in the act of peeping into a puddleful of authentic little frogs. By putting a coin in the slot they will see me spit in the water and the frogs will get all stirred up and croak for a minute and a half, just enough time for people to lose all interest in the statue.

(–113)

108

"*La cloche, le clochard, la clocharde, clocharder.* There's even a thesis that was presented at the Sorbonne on the subject of the psychology of the *clochard*."

"Could be," Oliveira said. "But they don't have a Juan Filloy to write *Caterva* for them. What ever happened to Filloy?"

Naturally, La Maga was in no position to know, in the first place because she never knew he had existed. He had to explain to her why Filloy, why *Caterva*. La Maga liked the plot of the book very much, the idea that South American *linyeras* were in a class with *clochards*. She remained firmly convinced that it was an insult to confuse a *linyera* with a beggar, and her liking for the *clocharde* of the Pont des Arts had its roots in reasons that now seemed scientific. Especially in those days when she had discovered, walking along the river bank, that the *clocharde* was in love, sympathy and the desire for everything to turn out well were for La Maga something like the arch of the bridges, which always brought out her feelings, or like those pieces of tin or wire that Oliveira would pick up as they walked along.

"Filloy, shit," Oliveira said looking at the towers of the City Hall and thinking about Cartouche. "My country's so far away, damn it, it's incredible there could be so much salt water in this mad world."

"On the other hand there's not so much air," La Maga answered. "Thirty-two hours' worth, no more, no less."

"That's right. But where do you get the dough for the flight?"

"And the wish to go back, because I really don't."

"Me neither. But let's just suppose. There's no way back. Irrefutable."

"You never talked about going back," La Maga said.

"No one talks about it, wuthering heights, nobody talks about it. It's only the feeling that everything is cool for the guy without bread."

"Paris is free," La Maga quoted. "You said so the day we met.

Going to visit the *clocharde* is free, making love is free, telling you that you're evil is free, not loving you . . . Why did you go to bed with Pola?"

"A matter of perfume," Oliveira said, sitting down on the strip alongside the water's edge. "I thought that she would smell like the Songs of Songs, cinnamon, myrrh, things like that. It was a sure thing, besides."

"The *clocharde* won't be along tonight. She would have been here already, she almost never fails."

"Sometimes they arrest them," Oliveira said. "To fumigate them, I suppose, or so the city can go to sleep peacefully alongside its impassive river. A *clochard* is a worse disgrace than a thief, that's a well-known fact; basically, there's nothing that can be done about them, they have to leave them in peace."

"Tell me about Pola. We may see the *clocharde* in the meantime."

"Night's coming on, the American tourists are thinking about their hotels, their feet hurt, they bought a lot of crap, they've got their Sade, their Miller, their *Onze mille verges*, artistic pictures, pornographic snapshots, Sagans and Buffets. Look how they break up the sky on the bridge side. And leave Pola alone, that doesn't matter. So, the painter folds up his stool, there's no one to watch him any more. It's incredible how clean everything gets, the air is washed like the skin of that girl running over there, look at her, dressed in red."

"Tell me about Pola," La Maga repeated, patting him on the shoulder with the back of her hand.

"Pure pornography," Oliveira said. "You won't like it."

"But you must have told her something about us."

"No. Just generally. What could I tell her? Pola doesn't exist, you know. Where is she? Show her to me."

"Pure sophistry," La Maga said. She had learned the term in arguments with Ronald and Étienne. "She may not be here, but she's on the Rue Dauphine, that's for sure."

"And where is the Rue Dauphine?" asked Oliveira. "*Tiens, la clocharde qui s'amène.* But look, hey, she's wild."

Coming down the steps, staggering under the weight of an enormous bundle, out of which were sticking pieces of unravelled overcoats, red scarves, pairs of trousers picked out of dustbins, pieces of cloth, and even a blackened roll of wire, the *clocharde* reached dock-level below and let out an exclamation somewhere between a grunt and a sigh. On top of an indecipherable base where there probably had been accumulated skin-tight blouses and a brassière capable of holding up a pair of ominous breasts, were being added two, three, maybe four dresses, a complete wardrobe, and on top of it a man's jacket with one sleeve almost torn off, a scarf held together with a tin brooch that had one green and one red stone, and on her incredibly dyed blonde hair a kind of gauzy green clasp hanging to one side.

"She's marvellous," Oliveira said. "She's just seduced the people on the bridge."

"It's obvious that she's in love," La Maga said. "And the way she's made up, look at her lips. And the rouge, she's put on every bit she's got."

"She looks like Grock in one of his worst moments. Or some of Ensor's figures. She's sublime. How can they make love, the pair of them? Because you're not going to tell me they do it by remote control."

"I know a corner near the Hotel Sens where the *clochards* get together for that. The police leave them alone. Madame Léonie told me there's always some police informer among them, secrets come out at times like that. It seems that the *clochards* know a lot about gangsters."

"Gangsters, what a word," Oliveira said. "Yes, of course they'd know. They're on the edge of society, on the rim of fraud. They must know a lot about property owners and priests too. A scrutinizing look into dustbins . . . "

"Here comes the *clochard.* He's drunker than ever. Poor thing, the way she waits for him, see how she left the package on the ground as a signal, she's so sentimental."

"You can say all you want about the Hotel Sens, but I still wonder how they make it," Oliveira muttered. "Look at all those clothes. Because she probably only takes off one or two things when it's not so cold, but underneath she has on five or six more, not counting her underwear. Can you imagine what it must be like, and on wasteland? It's easier for the guy, pants are more manageable."

"They don't get undressed, maybe," La Maga conjectured. "The police wouldn't allow it. And the rain, give a thought to that. They hide in corners, in that bit of wasteland there are some ditches about a foot deep, with rubbish around the edges, where workmen throw rubbish and bottles. I have the feeling they make love standing up."

"With all those clothes? But that's inconceivable. You mean the guy has never seen her naked? That's a hell of a drag."

"Look how they love each other," La Maga said. "The way they look at each other."

"The guy's got wine coming out of his eyes. Eleven per cent tenderness with lots of tannin."

"They love each other, Horacio, they love each other. Her name is Emmanuèle, she used to be a whore in the provinces. She arrived on a *péniche* and stayed on the docks. We talked one night when I was feeling sad. She smells to high heaven, I had to leave after a little while. You know what I asked her? I asked her when she changed her clothes. That's a silly thing to ask. She's very good, she's quite mad, that night she thought she saw wildflowers among the cobblestones, she was naming them for me."

"Like Ophelia," Horacio said. "Nature imitates art."

"Ophelia?"

"I'm sorry, I'm being pedantic. And what did she say when you asked her about her clothes?"

"She started to laugh and drank a pint down in one swallow. She said that the last time she had taken something off she had pulled it over her legs, over her knees. It all fell apart. They get very cold in winter, they grab anything they can find."

"I wouldn't want to be a hospital orderly and have them brought in on a stretcher some night. A prejudice like any other. Pillars of society. I'm thirsty, Maga."

"Go over to Pola's," said La Maga, looking at the *clocharde* who was caressing her lover under the bridge. "Watch, they're going to dance now, they always dance a little at this time."

"He looks like a bear."

"He's so happy," La Maga said, picking up a little white stone and looking it all over.

Horacio took the stone away from her and licked it. It tasted like salt and stone.

"It's mine," La Maga said, trying to get it back.

"Yes, but look at the colour it has when it's with me. It lights up when it's with me."

"It's happier with me. Give it back. It's mine."

They looked at one another. Pola.

"So OK," Horacio said. "It means the same now as any other time. You're being silly, girl, if you only knew how peacefully you can sleep."

"Sleeping alone, that's swell. You see, don't you, I'm not crying. You can keep on talking, I'm not going to cry. I'm like her, watch her dance, she's like the moon, she weighs a ton and she's dancing, she's full of crud and she's dancing. It's an example. Give me my stone."

"Take it. You know, it's hard to say to you: I love you. It's so hard right now."

"Yes, you'd think you were giving me a carbon copy."

"We're talking like a pair of eagles," Horacio said.

"It's enough to make you laugh," La Maga said. "I'll lend it to you if you want, while the *clocharde* is dancing."

"OK," said Horacio, accepting the stone and licking it again. "Why talk about Pola? She's sick and lonely, I'm going to see her, we still make love, but that's all, I don't want to turn her into words, not even with you."

"Emmanuèle's going to fall into the water," said La Maga. "She's drunker than the guy."

"No, it'll all end up with the usual sordidness," Oliveira said, getting up from the edge. "Do you see the noble representative of authority coming this way? Let's go, it's too sad. Just because the poor girl wanted to dance . . . "

"Some old puritan dame must have raised hell up there. If we find her you can kick her in the behind."

"OK. And you can make excuses for me, saying that my leg got away from me, mortar shell, defending Stalingrad, you know."

"Then you come to attention and snap a salute."

"That I can do very well, you know, I learned it in Palermo. Come on, let's get something to drink. I don't want to look back any more, listen to the cop bawling her out. That's where the whole problem lies. Shouldn't I go back and give him a swift kick? Oh, Arjuna, counsel me. And beneath the uniform the smell of civilian ignominy. *Ho detto.* Come on, let's split once and for all. I'm dirtier than Emmanuèle, it's a crud that started collecting centuries ago, *Persil lave plus blanc*, it calls for an almighty detergent, girl, a cosmic soap. You like pretty words? *Salut, Gaston.*"

"*Salut messieurs dames,*" Gaston said. "*Alors, deux petits blancs secs comme d'habitude, hein?*"

"*Comme d'habitude, mon vieux, comme d'habitude. Avec du Persil dedans.*"

Gaston looked at him and went off shaking his head. Oliveira took La Maga's hand and counted her fingers attentively. Then he put the stone in her palm, closed the fingers over it, one by one, and to top it off gave her a kiss. La Maga saw that he had closed his eyes and seemed to be far off. "Actor," she thought tenderly.

(–64)

109

Somewhere Morelli tried to justify his narrative incoherencies, maintaining that the life of others, such as it comes to us in so-called reality, is not a movie but still photography, that is to say, that we cannot grasp the action, only a few of its eleatically recorded fragments. There are only the moments in which we are present with this other one whose life we think we understand, either when they talk about him, or when he tells us what has happened to him or projects in front of us what he intends to do. In the end there is a photograph album, with fixed instants; never the future coming about before us, the step from yesterday to today, the first prick of forgetfulness in the memory. For that reason there was nothing strange about his speaking of characters in the most spasmodic way possible; giving coherence to the series of pictures so they could become a movie (which would have been so very pleasing to the reader he called the female-reader) meant filling in with literature, presumptions, hypotheses and inventions the gaps between one and another photograph. Sometimes the pictures showed a back, a hand resting on a door, the end of a stroll through the countryside, a mouth opening to shout, some shoes in the cupboard, people walking along the Champs de Mars, a postmarked stamp, the smell of Ma Griffe, things like that. Morelli thought that the existence of those pictures, which tried to present all that with the most acuity possible, must have placed the reader in conditions ripe for taking a chance, for participating, almost, in the destiny of the characters. What he would learn from them through his imagination would immediately become hardened into action, with no trick destined to integrate them into what had already been written or was to be written. The bridges between one and another instant in those lives which were so vague and so little characterized would have to be presumed or invented by the reader, everything from the manner in which they combed their hair, even if Morelli did not mention it, to the reasons behind a behaviour or a nonbehaviour, if it seemed unusual and eccentric. The book would have to be something like those sketches proposed by Gestalt psychologists, and therefore certain lines would induce the observer to trace imaginatively the ones that would complete the figure. But sometimes the missing lines were the most important ones, the only ones that really counted. Morelli's coquetry and petulance in this field had no limits.

Reading the book, one had the impression for a while that Morelli had hoped that the accumulation of fragments would quickly crystallize into a total reality. Without having to invent bridges, or sew up different pieces of the tapestry, behold suddenly a city, or a tapestry, or men and women in the absolute perspective of their future, and Morelli, the author, would be the first spectator to marvel at that world that was taking on coherence.

But there was no cause for confidence, because coherence meant basically assimilation in space and time, an ordering to the taste of the female-reader. Morelli would not have agreed to that; rather, it seems, he would have sought a crystallization which, without altering the disorder in which the bodies of his little planetary system circulated, would permit a ubiquitous and total comprehension of all of its reasons for being, whether they were disorder itself, inanity, or gratuity. A crystallization in which nothing would remain subsumed, but where a lucid eye might peep into the kaleidoscope and understand the great polychromatic rose, understand it as a figure, an *imago mundi* that outside the kaleidoscope would be dissolved into a provincial living room, or a concert of aunts having tea and Bagley biscuits.

(–27)

110

The dream was composed like a tower of layers without end rising upward and losing themselves in the infinite, or layers coiling downward, losing themselves in the bowels of the earth. When it swooped me in its undulations, the spiralling began, and this spiral was a labyrinth. There was no vault and no bottom, no walls and no return. But there were themes repeating themselves with exactitude.

ANAÏS NIN, *Winter of Artifice*

(–48)

111

This narration was written by its protagonist, Ivonne Guitry, to Nicolás Díaz, a friend of Gardel's in Bogotá.

My family belonged to the Hungarian intellectual class. My mother was headmistress of a girls' seminary where the elite of a famous city, whose name I do not wish to mention, were educated. With the arrival of the stormy postwar period and the overthrow of thrones, social classes and fortunes, I did not know which way to head in my life. My family lost its fortune, victim of the Trianon [*sic*] borders like thousands and thousands of others. My beauty, my youth, and my upbringing would not permit me to become a humble stenographer. Then the Prince Charming of my life arrived, an aristocrat of cosmopolitan upper circles, frequenters of European resorts. I married him with all of my youthful illusion, in spite of the opposition of my family, because I was young and he was a foreigner.

Honeymoon. Paris, Nice, Capri. Then the shattering of an illusion. I did not know where to turn and I did not dare tell my family of the failure of my marriage. A husband who would never be able to make me a mother. I am already sixteen years old and I am travelling like a pilgrim without a goal, trying to make my troubles disappear. Egypt, Java, Japan, the Celestial Empire, all of the Far East, in a carnival of champagne and false happiness, with my soul in pieces.

The years pass. In 1927 we settled finally on the Côte d'Azur. I am a woman of high society, and cosmopolitan circles, casinos, balls, race tracks all render me homage.

One fine day in summer I took a definitive resolution:

separation. Nature was all in flower: the sea, the fields were opening up in a song of love and enjoyment of youth.

The mimosa festival in Cannes, the carnival of flowers in Nice, springtime in Paris. So I abandoned home, comforts, and wealth, and alone I faced the world . . .

I was eighteen at the time and living alone in Paris, without any definite direction. Paris in 1928. The Paris of orgies and the outpouring of champagne. The Paris of worthless francs. Paris, paradise of the foreigner. Full of Americans and South Americans, little kings of gold. Paris in 1928, where every day a new cabaret was born, a new sensation to make the foreigner loosen his purse.

Eighteen years old, blonde, blue eyes. Alone in Paris.

In order to soften my misfortune I turned myself completely over to pleasure. I always attracted attention in the cabarets because I was alone, squandering champagne on the chorus and tips on the waiters. I had no idea of the value of money.

Sometimes, somebody out of that element that always lives off the cosmopolitan environment discovers my secret sorrow and recommends a remedy for forgetfulness to me . . . Cocaine, morphine, drugs. Then I began to look for exotic places, strange-looking dancers, dark-hued South Americans with their long hair.

In those days a recent arrival, a cabaret singer, was collecting success and applause. He opened in the Florida and sang strange songs in a strange language.

He sang in exotic garb never seen before in those places, Argentine tangos, *rancheras* and *zambas*. He was a rather thin young man, a little dark, with white teeth that captured the attention of all the pretty women in Paris. It was Carlos Gardel. His weepy tangos that he sang with all his soul captivated the audience without anyone's knowing why. His songs at that time – *Caminito, La chacarera, Aquel tapado de armiño, Queja indiana, Entre sueños* – were not modern tangos but songs of old Argentina, the pure soul of the gaucho of the pampas. Gardel was in vogue. There was no elegant dinner party or reception to which he was not invited. His dark face, his white teeth, his fresh and luminous smile, shone everywhere. Cabarets, theatres, music halls, race tracks. He was a permanent guest at Auteuil and Longchamps.

But Gardel preferred to have a good time in his own way, among his own friends, in the circle of his intimates.

At that time there was in Paris a cabaret called Palermo, on the Rue Clichy, frequented almost exclusively by South Americans . . . That's where I met him. Gardel was interested in all women, but all I was interested in was cocaine . . . and champagne. Of course it pleased my feminine vanity to be seen in Paris with the man of the hour, with the idol of womanhood, but it did not tell my heart anything.

That friendship became established on other nights, other walks, other confidences, under the pale Parisian moon, through flowering fields. Many days of romantic interest went by. The man was getting into my soul. His words were silken, his phrases were digging at the rock of my indifference. I went crazy. My luxurious but sad little flat was now full of light. I did not go back to the cabarets. In my beautiful grey living room, by the light of electric lamps, a blonde little head became united to a firm, dark-featured face. My blue bedroom, which had known all the nostalgias of a soul without direction, was now a real love nest. It was my first love.

Time flew fast and fleeting. I can't say how much time went by. The exotic blonde who had dazzled Paris with her extravagances, with her *toiletts dernière cri* [*sic*], with her garden parties in which Russian caviar and champagne were the daily main course, had disappeared.

Months later the eternal habitués of the Palermo, the Florida, the Garon, learned in the press that a blonde ballerina with blue eyes who was now twenty years old was driving the *señoritos* of the River Plate capital mad with her ethereal dances, with her startling brazenness, with all the voluptuousness of her youth in flower.

It was IVONNE GUITRY.

(Etc.)

La escuela gardeleana, Editorial Cisplatina, Montevideo

(–49)

112

Morelliana

I am revising a story that I wanted to be the least literary possible. A despairing job from the word go, in the revision intolerable phrases start to pop up right away. A character comes to some stairs: "Raymond commenced his descent . . . " I scratch it out and write: "Raymond began to go down . . . " I turn away from the revision to ask myself again the real reasons behind this rejection of "literary" language. *Commence his descent* has nothing bad about it unless maybe it is too easy; but *begin to go down* is exactly the same except cruder, more prosaic (that is, a mere vehicle of information), while the other form seems to combine what is useful with what is pleasant to hear. In short, what repels me in "commenced his descent" is the decorative use of a verb and a noun that we almost never use in everyday speech, in short, literary language repels me (in my work, let it be understood). Why?

By persisting in this attitude that has rapidly impoverished almost everything I have written in the last few years, it will not be long before I feel incapable of setting forth the slightest idea, of undertaking the simplest description. If my reasons were those of Hofmannsthal's Lord Chandos, there would be no motive for complaint, but if this rejection of rhetoric (because basically that is what it is) is due only to a verbal withering, correlative and parallel to another one which is vital, then it would be preferable to renounce all writing completely. Rereading the results of what I have written these days bores me. But at the same time, behind that deliberate poverty, behind that "begin to go down" substituted for "commence his descent", I get a glimpse of something that encourages me. I write very badly, but something is happening through it all. The previous "style" was a mirror for lark-readers: they looked at each other, they consoled each other, they recognized each other, like those audiences that wait for, recognize and enjoy the answers of the characters of a Salacrou or an Anouilh. It is much easier to write like that than to write (to "unwrite", almost) as I would want to do now, because there is no longer any dialogue or meeting with the reader, there is only the hope of a certain dialogue with a certain and remote reader. Of course, the problem is located on a moral plane. Perhaps arteriosclerosis, the advance of age accentuates this tendency – a little misanthropic, I fear – to exalt the *ethos* and discover (in my own case it is a rather tardy discovery) that aesthetic orders are more a mirror than a passage for metaphysical anxiety.

I still thirst for the absolute as much as when I was twenty years old, but the delicate twitching, the acid and biting delight of the creative act or of the simple contemplation of beauty, no longer seem to me to be a prize, an access to absolute and satisfactory reality. There is only one beauty which can still give me that access: the one that is an end and not a means, and which is so because its creator has identified in himself his sense of the human condition with his sense of the artist's condition. On the other hand, the merely aesthetic plane seems just that to me: merely. That is the best way I can explain it.

(–154)

113

Nodules of a trip from the end of the Rue de la Glacière to the Rue du Sommerard:

"How long are we still going to date things 'AD'?"

"Literary documents seen two hundred years from now: coprolites."

"Klages was right."

"Morelli and his lesson. Sometimes repulsive, horrible, pitiful. So many words in order to cleanse himself of other words, so much filth so that Piver, Caron, Carven, AD will no longer smell. Maybe he has to go through all of that in order to recover a lost right, the original use of words."

"The original use of words (?). Probably an empty phrase."

"Small coffin, pack of cigarettes, Charon puffs a little and you cross the puddle rocking like a cradle. The boat is for adults only. Women and children free, a push and soon the other side. A Mexican death, a sugar skull, *Kindertotenlieder* . . . "

"Morelli will look at Charon. One myth facing another. An unforeseeable trip on the black waters."

"A hopscotch on the pavement: red chalk, green chalk. CIEL. The pavement, back there in Burzaco, the pebble selected with such tender care, the quick push with the tip of the shoe, slowly, slowly, even if Heaven is close by, all life in front of one."

"An infinite game of chess, so easy to imagine. But cold enters through an opening in the sole, in the window of that hotel a face like a clown's grimaces behind the glass. The shadow of a dove rubs up against the excrement a dog has left behind: Paris."

"Pola Paris. Pola? Go see her, *faire l'amour. Carezza.* Like lazy larva worms. But *larva* also means mask, Morelli wrote about it somewhere."

(–30)

114

May 4, 195 . . . (AP) In spite of the efforts by his lawyers and a final attempt at appeal on May 2, Lou Vincent was executed this morning in the gas chamber at San Quentin prison in the state of California.

. . . his hands and legs tied to the chair. The warden ordered the four jailers to leave the chamber, and after patting Vincent on the back, left in turn. The condemned man was alone in the room as 53 witnesses watched through small windows.

. . . he threw back his head and took a deep breath.

. . . two minutes later his face was bathed in perspiration and his fingers moved as if to free himself from the straps . . .

. . . six minutes, the convulsions were repeated, and Vincent pitched his head backward and forward. He began to froth at the mouth a little.

. . . eight minutes, his head fell forward on his chest after one final convulsion.

. . . At 10.12 Dr Reynolds pronounced the condemned man dead. The witnesses, who included three reporters from . . .

(→117)

115

Morelliana

Using as a basis a series of notes that were often contradictory, the Club deduced that Morelli saw in the contemporary narrative an advance towards what has been poorly termed abstraction. "Music is losing its melody, painting is losing its anecdotal side, the novel is losing its description." Wong, a master at dialectical collages, summed up this passage here: "The novel that interests us is not one that places characters in a situation, but rather one that puts the situation in the characters. By means of this the latter cease to be characters and become people. There is a kind of extrapolation through which they jump out at us, or we at them. Kafka's K. has the same name as his reader, or vice versa." And to this must be added a rather confused note in which Morelli was working up an episode in which he would leave the names of his characters blank, so that in each case the supposed abstraction would have to be resolved in a hypothetical attribution.

(–14)

116

In a passage from Morelli, this epigraph from *L'Abbé C*, by Georges Bataille: "*Il souffrait d'avoir introduit des figures décharnées, qui se déplaçaient dans un monde dément, qui jamais ne pourraient convaincre.*"

A pencilled note, almost illegible: "Yes, he suffers once in a while, but it is the only decent way out. Enough of hedonistic and premasticated novels, with *psychologies*. One must aim at the maximum, be a *voyant* as Rimbaud wanted to be. The hedonistic novelist is nothing but a *voyeur*. On the other hand, enough of purely descriptive techniques, of 'behaviourist' novels, mere movie scripts without the saving grace of images."

Relating it to another passage: "How can one *tell* a story without cooking, without make-up, without winks at the reader? Perhaps by rejecting the supposition that a narrative is a work of art. To feel it the way we would feel the plaster we put on our face to make a mask of it. But the face should be ours."

And maybe also in this odd note: "Lionello Venturi, speaking of Manet and his *Olympia*, points out that Manet did not need nature, beauty, action and moral intent in order to concentrate on the plastic image. Thus, without his knowing it, he is working as if modern art were going back to the Middle Ages. The latter understood art as a series of images, replaced during the Renaissance and the modern period by the representation of reality. The same Venturi (or is it Giulio Carlo Argan?) adds: 'The irony of history has decreed that in the very moment in which the representation of reality was becoming objective, and ultimately photographic and mechanical, a brilliant Parisian who wanted to be realistic should be moved by his formidable genius to return art to its function as the creator of images . . .'"

Morelli adds: "To accustom one's self to use the expression *figure* instead of *image*, to avoid confusions. Yes, everything coincides. But it is not a question of a return to the Middle Ages or anything like it. The mistake of postulating an absolute historical time: there are different times *even though* they may be parallel. In this sense, one of the times of the so-called Middle Ages can coincide with one of the times of the Modern Ages. And that time is what has been perceived and inhabited by painters and writers who refuse to seek support in what surrounds them, to be 'modern' in the sense that their contemporaries understand them, which does not mean that they choose to be anachronistic; they are simply on the margin of the superficial time of their period, and from that other time where everything conforms to the condition of *figure*, where everything has value as a sign and not as a theme of description, they attempt a work which may seem alien or antagonistic to the time and history surrounding them, and which nonetheless includes it, explains it, and in the last analysis orients it towards a transcendence within whose limits man is waiting."

(–3)

117

I have seen a court urged almost to the point of threat to hang two boys, in the face of science, in the face of philosophy, in the face of humanity, in the face of experience, in the face of all the better and more humane thoughts of the age.

Why did not my friend, Mr Marshall, who dug up from the relics of the buried past these precedents that would bring a blush of shame to the face of a savage, read this from Blackstone:

"Under fourteen, though an infant shall be judged to be incapable of guile prima facie, yet if it appeared to the court and the jury that he was capable of guile, and could discern between good and evil, he may be convinced and suffer death."

Thus a girl of thirteen has been burned for killing her mistress.

. . . .

One boy of ten, and another of nine years of age, who had killed their companions were sentenced to death; and the one of ten actually hanged.

Why?

He knew the difference between right and wrong. He had learned that in Sunday School.

CLARENCE DARROW, *Defence of Leopold and Loeb*, 1924

(–15)

118

How shall the murdered man convince his assassin he will not haunt him?

MALCOLM LOWRY, *Under the Volcano*

(–50)

119

Australian love-bird unable to spread wings

An inspector of the RSPCA entered a house and found the bird in a cage barely 8 inches wide. The owner of the bird was required to pay a fine of 2 pounds. In order to protect defenceless creatures we need more than just your moral support. The RSPCA needs your financial support. Contact the Offices, etc.

The Observer, London

(–51)

120

at siesta-time everybody was asleep, it was easy to get out of bed without waking up his mother, creep up to the door, go out slowly, smelling the warm earth floor avidly, escape through the door over to the grazing pen at the back; the willows were full of basket bugs, Ireneo chose a rather large one, sat down beside an anthill, and began to squeeze the bottom of the cocoon little by little until the grub popped its head out through the silky collar, then he had to take it delicately by the scruff of the neck like a cat, pull it gently so as not to hurt it, and there was the grub, naked now, twisting comically in the air; Ireneo set it next to the anthill and lay down in the shade on his stomach, waiting; at that moment the black ants were working furiously, cutting grass and hauling back living and dead insects from everywhere, a scout spotted the grub, his bulk twisting grotesquely, she touched him with her antennae as if she had to be convinced of such good luck, she ran back and forth rubbing antennae with the other ants, a minute later the grub was surrounded, climbed on, he twisted uselessly trying to free himself from the pincers that dug into his flesh while the ants pulled him in the direction of the anthill, dragging him along, Ireneo particularly enjoyed the puzzlement of the ants when they could not get the grub through the mouth of the anthill, the trick was to pick a grub that was thicker than the entrance to the anthill, ants were stupid and did not understand, they pulled on all sides trying to get the grub in but he was twisting furiously, what he was feeling must have been horrible, the ants with their feet and pincers all over his body, on his eyes and skin, he was struggling to free himself and it was worse because more ants came, some really fierce, who stuck their pincers into him and would not let go until they got the head of the grub so that it began to go into the pit of the anthill, and others who came up from down below must have been pulling from inside with all their might to drag him in, Ireneo might have wanted to be inside the anthill also, to see how the ants pulled on the grub sticking their pincers in his eyes and mouth and pulling with every ounce of strength until they got him all inside, until they took him down into the depths and killed him and ate him

(–16)

121

With red ink and manifest complacency, Morelli had copied in one of his notebooks the ending of a poem by Ferlinghetti:

> Yet I have slept with beauty
> in my own weird way
> and I have made a hungry scene or two
> with beauty in my bed
> and so spilled out another poem or two
> and so spilled out another poem or two
> upon the Bosch-like world

(–36)

122

The nurses came and went speaking of Hippocrates. With just a small effort any piece of reality could attach itself to a famous line of poetry. But why bring up enigmas for Étienne, who had taken out his notebook and was happily sketching a flight of white doors, stretchers piled up along the walls and up to the windows where a grey and silky material was coming in, the skeleton of a tree with two doves with bourgeois crops. He would have liked to tell him about the other dream, it was so strange that all morning he had been obsessed by the bread dream, and boom, on the corner of Raspail and Montparnasse the other dream had fallen on him like a wall, or rather, as if all through the morning he had been pushed up against the wall of bread complaining and suddenly, like a movie being run backwards, the wall had come away from him, straightening up in one jump to leave him facing the memory of the other dream.

"Whenever you want," Étienne said, holding on to the sketchbook. "Whenever you feel like it, there's no rush. I still plan to live another forty years, so . . . "

"'Time present and time past,'" Oliveira recited, "'are both perhaps present in time future.' It has been written that today everything is going to end up in lines by T. S. Eliot thinking about a dream, sorry. Let's go right now."

"Yes, because it's all right about the dream. You can take that, take it, but after all . . . "

"It's really about a different dream."

"*Misère!*" said Étienne.

"I didn't tell you about it on the phone because I'd forgot."

"And the bit about the six minutes," Étienne said. "Basically, the authorities are very wise. We always shit on them, but we've got to admit they know what they're doing. Six minutes . . . "

"If I'd thought of it, all I had to do was get out of that booth and go to the next one."

"It's all right," Étienne said. "You tell me about the dream, and then we'll go down those stairs and have a little wine at Montparno. I'll swap your famous old man for a dream. Both things are too much together."

"You hit the nail on the head," Oliveira said, looking at him with interest. "The problem is knowing if those two things can be swapped. What you were telling me just today: butterfly or Chiang Kai-shek? Probably when you swap the old man with me for a dream, what you'll be swapping will be a dream for the old man."

"To tell you the truth, I don't give a damn."

"Painter," said Oliveira.

"Metaphysician," said Étienne. "And now that we're here, there's a nurse over there who's beginning to wonder whether we're a dream or a couple of tramps. What's going to happen? If she comes over to throw us out, is it a nurse who is throwing us out or a dream that throws out two philosophers who are dreaming about a hospital where among other things there is an old man and an enraged butterfly?"

"It was much more simple," Oliveira said, slipping down on the bench a little and closing his eyes. "Look, it was just my childhood house and La Maga's flat, both things together in the same dream. I don't remember when I dreamed it, I'd forgotten it completely and this morning while I was thinking about that business with the loaf of bread . . . "

"You already told me about the loaf of bread."

"Suddenly it's the other thing again and the bread can go to the devil, because they can't be compared. Maybe that's what inspired my dream about the bread . . . Inspired, that's a fine word."

"Don't be ashamed to use it, if it means what I think it does."

"You were thinking about the kid, of course. A required association. But I don't have any feelings of guilt. I didn't kill him."

"Things are not so easy," Étienne said uncomfortably. "Let's go and see the old man, we've had enough of idiot dreams for a while."

"It's really impossible for me to tell you about it," Oliveira said with resignation. "Imagine that when you get to Mars a guy asks you to describe ashes to him. Something like that, more or less."

"Shall we go and see the old man or not?"

"It doesn't make the slightest difference to me. Since we're already here . . . Bed number ten, I think. We should have brought him something, it's stupid coming here like this. In any case, give him a drawing."

"My drawings are for sale," Étienne said.

(–112)

123

The real dream was located in an imprecise zone, next to waking but without his really being awake; he would have had to make use of other references to speak about it, eliminate rotund terms like *dreaming* and *awake* that didn't mean a thing, locate himself rather in that zone where once more his childhood house would be suggested, the living room and the garden in a clear present time, with the colours as they were seen at the age of ten, reds so red, blues of tinted glass shades, green of leaves, green of fragrance, smell, and colour, a single presence at the level of nose and eyes and mouth. But in the dream, the room with its two windows that opened on the garden was at the same time La Maga's room; the forgotten province of Buenos Aires town and the Rue du Sommerard were brought together without any clash, not juxtaposed or overlapped but merged, and in the effortless removal of contradiction there was the sensation of being where one should be, in the essential place, as when one is a child and has no doubts that the living room will be there for a whole lifetime: an inalienable belonging. So that the house in Burzaco and the flat on the Rue du Sommerard were *the place*, and in the dream it was necessary to choose the most peaceful spot in the place, the reason behind the dream seemed to be just that, choosing a peaceful place. There was another person in the place, his sister, who was silently helping him choose the peaceful spot, the way a person participates in some dreams without even being there, and we take it for granted that the person or thing is there and participates; a force with no visible manifestations, something that is or does through a presence that can do without appearances. So he and his sister chose the living room as the most peaceful spot in the place, and it was a good choice because in La Maga's flat one could not play the piano or listen to the radio after ten o'clock at night, the old man upstairs would immediately start pounding on the floor or the people on the fifth floor would delegate a cross-eyed midget girl to go up and complain. Without a single word, since they didn't even seem to be there, he and his sister chose the living room that opened on the garden, rejecting La Maga's flat. In that moment of the dream Oliveira had woken up, perhaps because La Maga had put a leg between his. In the darkness the only thing he felt was that until that instant he had been in his childhood living room with his sister and also a terrible urge to urinate. Pushing La Maga's leg away unceremoniously, he got up and went out to the landing, feeling around for the dim light in the toilet, and without bothering to close the door began to piss, leaning against the wall with one hand, struggling against going to sleep and falling over in that lousy toilet, completely absorbed in the aura of the dream, watching without seeing the stream that was coming out from between his fingers and disappearing down the hole or drifting vaguely around the edges of the dirty porcelain. Maybe the real dream appeared to him at that moment when he felt he was awake and pissing at four o'clock in the morning on a sixth floor on the Rue du Sommerard and knew that the living room that opened on the garden in Burzaco was reality, knew it as only a few undeniable things are known, as one knows that he is himself, that no one but one's self is thinking that, he knew without any surprise or shock that his life as a man awake was a fantasy next to the solidity and permanence of the living room, although after going back to bed there might not be any living room and only the flat on the Rue du Sommerard, he knew that the place was the living room in Burzaco with the smell of Cape jasmine coming through the windows, the room with the old Bluthner piano, with its pink carpet and its little covered chairs, and his sister also with a cover on. He made a violent effort to get out of the aura, reject the place that was tricking him, wide awake enough to let the notion of trickery enter the notion of dream and wakefulness, but while he shook off the last drops and turned out the light, and rubbing his eyes crossed the landing to go back into the flat, everything was less, it was less signal, less landing, less door, less light, less bed, less Maga. Breathing with effort he murmured, "Maga", he murmured, "Paris", perhaps he murmured, "Today". It still sounded far away, hollow, not really alive. He went back to sleep like a person who is looking for his place and his house after a long road in the rain and the cold.

(–145)

124

It was necessary to propose, according to Morelli, a movement on the margin of all *grace*. In what he had done so far about that movement, it was easy to note the swift impoverishment of his novelistic world, not only evident in the almost simian poverty of his characters but also in the simple course of their actions and especially their inactions. He ended by not having anything happen to them, they whirled about in a sarcastic commentary on their inanity, they pretended to adore ridiculous idols which they thought they had discovered. This must have seemed important to Morelli because he had piled up notes on a supposed exigency, a final and desperate recourse to drag himself out of the rut of the immanent and transcendental ethic in search of a nakedness that he called axial and sometimes called *the threshold*. Threshold of what, to what? One could deduce the incitement to something like turning one's self inside out like a glove, as a way of receiving a brazen contact with some reality without the interposition of myths, religions, systems and reticula. It was curious that Morelli enthusiastically embraced the most recent working hypotheses of the physical and biological sciences, he presented himself as convinced that the old dualism had become cracked in the face of the evidence of a common reduction of matter and spirit to notions of energy. As a consequence, his wise monkeys seemed more and more to desire a retreat into themselves, nullifying on one hand the chimeras of a controlled reality, betrayed by the supposed instruments of cognition, and nullifying in turn their own mythopoetic force, their "soul", ending up in a kind of meeting *ab ovo* with a maximum shrinking into that point in which the last spark of (false) humanity will be lost. He seemed to propose – although he never got around to formulating it – a path that would begin with that external and internal liquidation. But he had ended up without words, without people, without things, and potentially, of course, without readers. The Club would sigh, somewhere between depression and exasperation and it was always the same thing or almost.

(–128)

125

The notion of being like a dog among men: material for an indifferent reflection that went on through two drinks of *caña* and a walk through the suburbs, the growing suspicion that only the alpha can yield the omega, that all insistence upon an intermediate period – epsilon, lambda – is the same thing as spinning around with one foot fastened to the ground. The arrow goes from the hand to the target: there's no midway in the journey, there's no century numbered XX between X and XXX. A man should be able to isolate himself from the species within the species itself, and choose the dog or the original fish as a starting point for the march towards himself. There's no passage for the Doctor of Philosophy, there's no opening for the eminent allergist. Inlaid in the species, they will be what they should be and if not they will be nothing. Very worthy men, no doubt about it, but always epsilon, lambda or pi, never alpha and never omega. The man in question doesn't accept those pseudo-fulfilments, the great decaying mask of the Western world. The guy who has wandered as far as the bridge on the Avenida San Martín and stands smoking on a corner watching a woman adjust her stocking, has a completely brainless idea of what he calls fulfilment, and he's not sorry about it because something tells him that the seed lies in brainlessness, that the bark of a dog is closer to the omega than a thesis on the gerund in Tirso de Molina. Such stupid metaphors. But he goes on doggedly, his way of putting words together. What is he searching for? Is he searching for himself? He would not be searching for himself if he had not already found himself. It means that he has found himself (but that's not brainless any more, *ergo* it cannot be trusted. As soon as you turn it loose, Reason supplies you with a special bulletin, arms you with the first syllogism in a chain that leads you nowhere except to a diploma or a ranchstyle bungalow and kids playing on the carpet to the enormous delight of mother). Let's see, let's take it slowly: What is that guy searching for? Is he searching for himself? Is he searching for himself as an individual? As a supposedly timeless individual, or as a historical entity? If it's the latter, a waste of time. If, on the other hand, he's searching for himself along the margin of all contingencies, the business of the dog is probably not so bad. But let's take it slowly (he loves to talk to himself that way, like a father to his son, so that later on he can give himself the great pleasure of all children and kick the old man in the balls), let's take it *piano piano*, let's see what this business of the search is all about. Well, search is just what it is *not*. Subtle, eh. It's not a search because he's already found himself. Just that the finding has not taken any shape. The meat, potatoes and shallots are there, but there isn't any pot. Or let's say that we're no longer with the others, that we've already stopped being a citizen (there's some reason for their weeding me out of everywhere, let Lutetia tell about it), but we still haven't learned how to get out of the dog to reach the thing that doesn't have a name, that conciliation, let's say that reconciliation.

It's a terrible job, splashing around in a circle whose centre is everywhere and whose circumference is nowhere, to use the language of scholasticism. What is being searched for? What is being searched for? Repeat it fifteen thousand times, like hammer-blows on the wall. What is being searched for? What is that conciliation without which life doesn't go beyond being an obscure joke? Not the conciliation of a saint, because if in the notion of going back to the dog, of starting over again from the dog or from the fish or from the ooze and the ugliness and the misery and any other disvaluation, there's always something like a nostalgia for sainthood, it would seem that one yearns for a non-religious sainthood (and here comes brainlessness), a state *without differentiation*, without saints (because a saint is always in some way a saint *and* those who are not saints, and that scandalizes a poor guy like the one admiring the calf of the girl absorbed in adjusting her twisted stocking), that is to say that if there is conciliation it must be something besides a state of sainthood, an exclusive state from the word go. It has to be something immanent, with no sacrifice of lead for gold, cellophane for glass, the least for the most; on the contrary, brainlessness calls for lead to be worth as much as gold, for the most to be contained in the least. An alchemy, a non-Euclidian geometry, an up-to-date indetermination for the operations of the spirit and its benefits. It's not a question of *rising*, an old mental image disproved by history, the old carrot that no longer fools the donkey. It's not a question of perfecting, of decanting, of redeeming, of choosing, of free-willing, of going from the alpha to the omega. *One is already there.* Anybody is already there. The shot is in the pistol; but a trigger has to be squeezed, and it so happens that the finger is making motions to stop a bus, or something similar.

How he talks, how he does go on, this smoking suburban tramp. The girl has already fixed her stocking, all set. You see? Forms of conciliation. *Il mio supplizio* . . . Everything is probably so simple, a pull on the mesh, a finger wet with saliva passing over the continuous part. It would probably be enough to grab one's nose and put it where one's ear is, upset circumstance a little. But no, that wouldn't do it either. Nothing easier than putting the blame on what's outside, as if one were sure that outside and inside are the two main beams of the house. But the fact is that everything is in bad shape, history tells you that, and the very fact that you're thinking about it instead of living it proves to you that it's bad, that we've stuck ourselves into a total disharmony that the sum of our resources disguises with social structure, with history, with Ionic style, with the joy of the Renaissance, with the superficial sadness of romanticism, and that's the way we go and they can turn the dogs on us.

(–44)

126

"Why, with your infernal enchantments, have you torn from me the tranquillity of my early life . . . The sun and the moon shone for me without artifice; I awoke with gentle thoughts, and at dawn I folded my leaves to say my prayers. I saw nothing evil, for I had no eyes; I heard nothing evil, for I had no ears; but I shall have my vengeance!"

Discourse of the Mandrake, in *Elizabeth of Egypt*,
by ACHIM VON ARNIM

(–21)

127

That's how the monsters would pester Cuca so she'd get out of the pharmacy and leave them in peace. Along the way and much more seriously they would discuss Ceferino Piriz's system and the ideas of Morelli. Since Morelli was little known in Argentina, Oliveira lent them his books and told them about some scattered notes he had seen at another time. They found out that Remorino, who was to stay on as an attendant and who would show up at *mate* and *caña* time, was a great initiate in Roberto Arlt, and that produced a considerable impression, so that for a whole week they spoke only of Arlt and how nobody had the right to step on his poncho in a country where carpets were preferred. But mostly they talked with great seriousness about Ceferino, and every once in a while it would occur to them to look at each other in a special way, raising their eyes at the same time, for example, and realizing that all three of them were doing it, that is to say, looking at each other in a special and inexplicable way, like certain looks in a game of *truco* or when a man who is desperately in love has to bear up under tea and pastries with several ladies and even a retired colonel who is explaining the reasons why everything is going badly in the country, and stuck in his chair the man looks at everyone the same way, the colonel, the woman he loves, and the woman's aunts, he looks at them affably because in fact it is a shame the way the country is in the hands of a band of crypto-communists, then from the cream puff, the third one on the left in the tray, and the spoon lying face up on the tablecloth embroidered by the aunts, the affable look is raised for an instant and over the crypto-communists it joins in mid-air the other look that has risen from the Nile-green plastic sugar bowl, and there's no longer anything else, a consummation outside time becomes a soft, sweet secret, and if the men of today were real men and not a bunch of god-damned fairies ("Why,

Ricardo!" "It's all right, Carmen, I just get so riled, I get so riled at what's going on in this country"), *mutatis mutandi* it was a little like the look the monsters gave when it occurred to them from time to time to look at each other with a look that was both furtive and total at the same time, secret and much clearer than when they would look at each other for a long time, but a person isn't a monster without good reason, as Cuca would say to her husband, and the three of them would let out a laugh and feel enormously ashamed at having looked at each other that way when they weren't playing *truco* and weren't illicitly in love. Unless.

(–56)

128

Nous sommes quelques-uns à cette époque à avoir voulu attenter aux choses, créer en nous des espaces à la vie, des espaces qui n'étaient pas et ne semblaient pas devoir trouver place dans l'espace.

ARTAUD, *Le Pèse-nerfs*

(–24)

129

But Traveler was not sleeping, after one or two attempts the nightmare kept circling around him and finally he sat up in bed and turned on the light. Talita was not there, somnambulist, moth of sleeplessness, and Traveler drank a glass of *caña* and put on his pyjama top. The wicker easy chair looked cooler than the bed, and it was a good night to continue his studies of Ceferino Piriz.

Dans cet annonce ou carte – Ceferino said textually – *ye reponds devant ou sur votre demande de suggérer idées pour UNESCO et écrit en el journal "El Diario" de Montevideo.*

A gallicized Ceferino! But there was no danger, *The Light of World Peace*, of which Traveler had some precious extracts, was written in admirable Spanish, the introduction, for example:

> In this announcement I wish to present some extracts from a recently written work of mine entitled *The Light of World Peace.* The aforesaid work has been or is being entered in an international contest . . . but it so happens that I cannot give you the entire work, as the Journal in which it appears will not permit for a certain length of time the aforesaid work to be supplied in its complete formation to anyone who is not in connection with said Journal . . .
>
> Therefore I limit myself in this announcement to the transmission of only some extracts from said work, which, the ones that follow, should not be published yet at this time.

Much more clear than an equivalent text by Julían Marías, for example. With two glasses of *caña* contact was established, and we're off. Traveler began to feel pleased that he had got up and that Talita was out there somewhere feeding her romanticism. For the tenth time he slowly got into Ceferino's text.

> In this book presentation is made of what we might call "the great formula on behalf of world peace". It is so much so that in this great formula there will be a Society of Nations or a UN, whereof this Society is a tendency towards values (precious, etc.) and human races; and lastly, as an undenied example of what is international, there will be a country that is truly exemplary, since it will be composed of 45 NATIONAL CORPORATIONS or ministries of the simple, and of 4 national Powers.

So-so: a ministry of the simple. Oh, Ceferino, natural philosopher, herbalist of Uruguayan paradises, nephelibate . . .

> On the other hand, this formula, great in its dimensions, is not alien, respectively, to the world of seers; to the nature of CHILD principles; from the natural measures that a formula is given entire of itself, it will not allow any alteration in the aforesaid formula given entire of itself; etc.

As always, the wise man seemed to feel a nostalgia for prophecy and intuition, but right away the mania for classification of *Homo occidentalis* raided Ceferino's little ranch and between *mates* it organized civilization into three periods:

> *First period of civilization*
>
> A first period of civilization can be conceived that goes from time immemorial in the past to the year 1940. A period which consisted in that everything was inclining towards the world war around the year 1940.
>
> *Second period of civilization*
>
> A second period of civilization can also be conceived, starting with the year 1940 up to the year 1953. A period that has consisted in everything inclining towards world peace or world reconstruction.
>
> (World reconstruction: acting so that in the world each will have what is his; reconstruct efficiently everything already undone before: buildings, human rights, universal balance of prices; etc., etc.)

Third period of civilization

> A third period of civilization can also be conceived today or during the present, starting in the year 1953 until the future year 2000. A period that consists in everything marching firmly towards the efficient arrangement of things.

For Toynbee, obviously . . . But criticism turns mute in sight of Ceferino's anthropological scheme: Now then, here are human beings facing the aforementioned periods:

> (A) Humans living in the second period as such, in those same days, did not manage to think very much about the first period.
> (B) Humans living, or we who live in this third period of today, in these same times do not think, or we do not think very much about the second period.
> (C) In the tomorrow that is to come later, or is to begin in the year 2000, the humans of those days, and in those days, they will not think very much about the third period: the one of today.

The business of not thinking very much was rather certain, *beati pauperes spiritu*, and now Ceferino went on in the manner of Paul Rivet, running down a classification that had been the high point of afternoons in Don Crespo's courtyard, to wit:

> In the world one can count up to six human races: the white, the yellow, the brown, the black, the red, and the pampa.
> WHITE RACE: of such race are all inhabitants of white skin, such as those of Baltic, Nordic, European, American, etc. countries.
> YELLOW RACE: of such race are all inhabitants of yellow skin, such as Chinese, Japanese, Mongols, Hindus in their majority, etc.
> BROWN RACE: of such race are all inhabitants of naturally brown skin, brown-skinned Russians, brown-skinned Turks, brown-skinned Arabs, Gypsies, etc.
> BLACK RACE: of such race are all inhabitants of black skin, such as inhabitants of West Africa in their great majority, etc.

RED RACE: of such race are all inhabitants of red skin, such as a large part of Ethiopians of dark reddish skin, and of whom the NEGUS or king of Ethiopia is a red example; a large part of Hindus of dark reddish or "coffee-coloured" skin; a large part of Egyptians of dark reddish skin; etc.

PAMPA RACE: of such race are all inhabitants of varied or pampa-coloured skin, such as all Indians of the three Americas.

"Horacio should be here," Traveler said to himself. "He could make some good comments on this part. After all, why not? Cefe has tripped over the classic difficulties of the Gummed Label, and he does what he can, like Linnaeus or the synoptic charts in encyclopedias. The business of the brown race is a solution worthy of genius, you've got to admit."

Walking was heard in the hallway, and Traveler went to the door that opened onto the administrative wing. As Ceferino might have said, the first door, the second door, and the third door were closed. Talita must have gone back to the pharmacy, it was incredible how enthusiastic she was about her return to science, scales and antipyretic adhesives.

Alien to those trifles, Ceferino went on to explain his model Society of Nations:

> A society that might be founded in any part of the world, even if the best is in Europe. A Society that would function permanently, and therefore on all working days. A society where its main building or palace would have at least seven (7) chambers or halls that would be fairly large. Etc.
>
> Now then; of the seven mentioned chambers of the palace of the aforesaid Society a first chamber would be occupied by Delegates from countries of the white race, and its President would be of the same colour; a second chamber would be occupied by Delegates from countries of the yellow race, and its President would be of the same colour; a thir . . .

And so on all the races, or maybe one could skip over the enumeration, but it was not the same after four glasses of *caña*

(Mariposa and not Ancap, unfortunately, because patriotic homage would have been fitting); it was not at all the same, because Ceferino's thought was crystallographic, ruled by symmetry and *horror vacui*, or in other words

> . . . a third chamber would be occupied by Delegates from countries of the brown race, and its President would be of the same colour; a fourth chamber would be occupied by Delegates from countries of the black race, and its President would be of the same colour; a fifth chamber would be occupied by Delegates from countries of the red race, and its President would be of the same colour; a sixth chamber would be occupied by Delegates from countries of the pampa race, and its President would be of the same colour; and one – the – seventh chamber would be occupied by the "General Staff" of all the aforementioned Society of Nations.

Traveler had always been fascinated by that " – the – " which interrupted the rigorous crystallization of the system, like the mysterious garden in a sapphire, that mysterious spot in the gem that determines perhaps the coalescence of the system and which in sapphires irradiates its transparent celestial cross like a congealed energy in the heart of the stone. (And why was it called *garden*, unless because of the influence of gardens of precious stones that appear in Oriental fables?)

Cefe, much less deliquescent, immediately explained the importance of the question:

> More details on the aforementioned seventh chamber: in said seventh chamber of the palace of the Society of Nations will be the Secretary General of all of said Society, and the President General, also of all of said society, but such Secretary General at the same time will be the private secretary of the aforementioned President General.
>
> Still more details: well; in the first chamber will be its corresponding President, who will always preside over the aforesaid first chamber; if we speak with respect to the second chamber, *idem*; if we speak with respect to the third chamber, *idem*; if we speak with respect to the fourth chamber, *idem*;

if we speak with respect to the fifth chamber, *idem*; and if we speak with respect to the sixth chamber, *idem*.

It warmed Traveler's heart to think that this *idem* must have cost Ceferino quite a bit. It was an extraordinary acquiescence towards the reader. But now he was into the heart of the matter, and he proceeded to enumerate what he called "the skilful assignment of the model Society of Nations", *viz.*:

(1) To look after (not to say to fix) the or those values of money in its international circulation; (2) to designate the wages of workers, the salaries of employees, etc.; (3) to designate values on behalf of what is international (give or fix the price of every article for sale, and give value or merit to other things: how many weapons of war a country may possess; how many children may be born, by international convention, to a woman, etc.); (4) to designate how much monetary return as retirement pay is to be received by a retired person, a pensioner, etc.; (5) of up to how many children all respective women in the world are to bear; (6) of equitable distributions in the international sphere; etc.

Why, Traveler wisely wondered, this repetition in matters concerning freedom of the womb and demography? Under (3) it appeared as a value, and under (5) as a concrete matter of the Society's competence. Curious infractions of symmetry, of the implacable rigour of the consecutive and orderly enumeration, which meant perhaps a worry, the suspicion that the classic order was, as always, a sacrifice of truth to beauty. But Ceferino recovered from that romanticism that Traveler suspected in him, and proceeded to an exemplary distribution:

Distribution of the weapons of war:

It is already well known that each respective country in the world has its corresponding square miles of territory.

Well, then, here is an example:

(A) The country that theoretically has 1,000 square miles, will have 1,000 cannons; the country that theoretically has 5,000 square miles, will have 5,000 cannons; etc.

(By this it will be understood, 1 cannon for each square mile);

(B) The country that theoretically has 1,000 square miles, will have 2,000 rifles; the country that theoretically has 5,000 square miles, will have 10,000 rifles; etc.

(By this it will be understood 2 rifles for each square mile); etc.

This example will include all respective countries that exist: France has 2 rifles for each of its square miles; Spain, *idem*; Belgium, *idem*; Russia, *idem*; United States, *idem*; Uruguay, *idem*; China, *idem*; etc., and this will also include all types of weapons of war that exist (a) tanks; (b) machine-guns; (c) terror bombs; rifles; etc.

(–139)

130

Perils of the Zip

The British Medical Journal speaks of a new type of accident that can befall boys. This accident is caused by the use of a zip in place of buttons in trouser flies (our medical correspondent informs us).

The danger lies in the prepuce's being caught in the fastener. Two cases have already been reported. In both of them circumcision had to be resorted to in order to free the child.

The accident is more likely to occur when the child goes to the bathroom unaccompanied. In an attempt to help him, parents can make matters worse by pulling on the zip in the wrong direction, as the child will be in no condition to tell whether the accident happened when he was pulling the zip up or when he was pulling it down. If the child has already been circumcised, the damage can be much more severe.

The doctor advises that by cutting the bottom part of the zip with pliers or shears the two halves can easily be separated. But a local anaesthetic will have to be administered for the extraction of the part imbedded in the skin.

The Observer, London

(–151)

131

"What do you think about our getting into the national corporation of monks of the prayer of the sign of the cross?"

"Either that or getting into the national budget . . . "

"We'd have a heavy time of it," Traveler said, watching Oliveira's breathing. "I remember perfectly, our obligations would be those of praying for or blessing people, objects, and those very mysterious regions that Ceferino calls sites of places."

"This must be one," Oliveira said as if from far away. "It's the site of a definite place, old buddy."

"And we would also have to bless planted fields, and boyfriends badly affected by a rival."

"Call Cefe about it," said the voice of Oliveira from some site of a place. "I'd like that . . . Hey, now that I think of it, Cefe comes from Uruguay."

Traveler didn't say anything, and he looked at Ovejero who came in and took the pulse of the *hysteria matinensis yugulata.*

"Monks who are always to combat all spiritual ills," Oliveira said distinctly.

"Aha," said Ovejero by way of encouragement.

(–58)

132

And while somebody explains something as always, I don't know why I am in this café, in all cafés, in the Elephant & Castle, in the Dupont Barbès, in the Sacher, in the Pedrocchi, in the Gijón, in the Greco, in the Café de la Paix, in the Café Mozart, in the Florian, in the Capoulade, in Les Deux Magots, in the bar that puts its chairs out on the Colleone square, in the Café Dante fifty yards away from the tomb of the Scaligers and that face on a pink sarcophagus that looks as if it had been burned by the tears of Saint Mary of Egypt, in the café across from the Giudecca, with aged and impoverished marchionesses drinking scrupulous tea and getting expansive with dusty ambassadors, in the Jandilla, in the Floccos, in the Cluny, in the Richmond in Suipacha, in El Olmo, in the Closerie des Lilas, in the Stéphane (which is on the Rue Mallarmé), in the Tokio (which is in Chivilcoy), in the Chien Qui Fume, in the Opern Café, in the Dôme, in the Café du Vieux Port, in cafés anywhere where

> We make our meek adjustments,
> Contented with such random consolations
> As the wind deposits
> In slithered and too ample pockets.

Hart Crane *dixit.* But they're more than that, they are the neutral territory for the stateless of the soul, the motionless centre of the wheel from where one can reach himself in full career, see himself enter and leave like a maniac, wrapped up in women or I O U's or epistemological theses, and while the coffee swirls around the little cup that goes from mouth to mouth along the edge of days, can loosely attempt revision and balance, equally removed from the ego that came into the café an hour ago and from the ego that will leave within another hour. Self-witness and self-judge, an ironical autobiography between two cigarettes.

In cafés I remember dreams, one no man's land revives another, now I remember one, but no, I only remember that I must have dreamed something marvellous and that in the end I felt as if expelled (or leaving, but forcibly) from the dream that remained irremediably behind me. I don't know if I even closed a door behind me, I think I did; in fact a separation was established between what had already been dreamed (perfect, spherical, finished) and the present. But I kept on sleeping, that business of expulsion and the door closing I also dreamed. A single and terrible certainty dominated that instant of transition within the dream; to know that irremediably that expulsion brought with it the complete forgetting of the previous marvel. I suppose that the feeling of a door closing was just that, fateful and instantaneous forgetting. The most startling is remembering also having dreamed that I was forgetting the previous dream, and that that dream *had to be* forgotten (my expulsion from its finished sphere).

All this must have, I imagine, an Edenic root. Perhaps Eden, as some would like to see it, is the mythopoetic projection of good old foetal times that persist in the unconscious. I suddenly understand better the frightening gesture of Masaccio's Adam. He covers his face to protect his vision, what had been his; he preserves in that small manual night the last landscape of his paradise. And he cries (because the gesture is also one that accompanies weeping) when he realizes that it is useless, that the real punishment is the one about to begin: the forgetting of Eden, that is to say, bovine conformity, the cheap and dirty joy of work and sweat of the brow and paid vacations.

(–61)

133

Of course, as Traveler thought right away, what counted were results. Still, why so much pragmatism? He was doing Ceferino an injustice, since his geopolitical system had not been tested out as so many others that were equally brainless (and just as promising, one had to recognize that). Cefe intrepidly stuck to his theoretical terrain and almost immediately launched another crushing demonstration:

> Wages of workers of the world:
>
> In accordance with the Society of Nations it will be or is to be that if, for example, a French worker, let us say a steelworker, for example, earns a definite daily wage between a *minimum* base of 8 pesos and a *maximum* base of 10 pesos, then it will have to be that an Italian steelworker will also have to earn the same amount, between 8 pesos and 10 pesos a day; in addition: if an Italian steelworker earns the same aforesaid, between 8 pesos and 10 pesos a day, then a Spanish steelworker will also have to earn between 8 pesos and 10 pesos a day; in addition: if a Spanish steelworker earns between 8 pesos and 10 pesos a day, then a Russian steelworker will also have to earn between 8 pesos and 10 pesos a day; in addition: if a Russian steelworker earns between 8 pesos and 10 pesos a day, then an American steelworker will also have to earn between 8 pesos and 10 pesos a day; etc.

"What's the reason for that 'etc.,'" Traveler thought, "for the fact that at a given moment Ceferino stops and chooses that et cetera that is so painful to him? It can't just be the weariness of repetition, because it's obvious that he loves it, or the feeling of monotony, because it's obvious that he loves it (his style is rubbing off on you)." The fact was that the "etc." left Ceferino a little nostalgic, a cosmologist obliged to give in to an irritating reader's digest. The poor fellow recovered his loss at the end of his list of steelworkers:

> (For the rest, in this thesis, if we kept on speaking, there will or there should be room for all countries respectively, or rather for all steelworkers of all respective countries.)

"But," Traveler thought, pouring himself another *caña* and cutting it with soda, "it's strange that Talita hasn't come back." He should go and take a look. He was sorry to leave Ceferino's world in full process of development just when Cefe was about to enumerate the 45 National Corporations which would make up the exemplary country:

> (1) NATIONAL CORPORATION OF THE MINISTRY OF THE INTERIOR (all branches and employees in general of the Ministry of the Interior). (The ministration of all stability for every establishment, etc.); (2) NATIONAL CORPORATION OF THE MINISTRY OF THE TREASURY (all branches and employees in general of the Ministry of the Treasury). (The ministration as patronage of all goods (all property) within the national territory, etc.); (3)

And that's the way the corporations went, 45 in number, among which 5, 10, 11 and 12 stood out in their own way:

> (5) NATIONAL CORPORATION OF THE MINISTRY OF CIVIL FAVOUR (all branches and employees in general of said Ministry). (Education, Enlightenment, Love of one neighbour for another, Control, Registry (books of), Health, Sexual Education, etc.). (The ministration or Control and Registry (lawyer . . .) which will furnish "Courts of Instruction", "Civil Courts", "Council of the Child", "Judge of Minors", "Registries": births, deceases, etc.) (The Ministration which will include everything that may be part of Civil Favour: MATRIMONY, FATHER, SON, NEIGHBOUR, DOMICILE, INDIVIDUAL, INDIVIDUAL OF GOOD OR BAD BEHAVIOUR, INDIVIDUAL OF PUBLIC IMMORALITY, INDIVIDUAL WITH BAD ILLNESSES, HOME (FAMILY AND), UNDESIRABLE PERSON, HEAD OF FAMILY, CHILD, MINOR, FIANCÉ, CONCUBINAGE, etc.).

. . . .

(10) NATIONAL CORPORATION OF ESTATES (all rural establishments for the Major Breeding of animals and all employees in general of said establishments). (Major Breeding or the breeding of corpulent animals: oxen, horses, ostriches, elephants, camels, giraffes, whales, etc.);

(11) NATIONAL CORPORATION OF FARMS (all agricultural farms or large farms, and all employees in general of said establishments). (Cultivations of every respective type of plant, except vegetables and fruit trees);

(12) NATIONAL CORPORATION OF ANIMAL BREEDING HOUSES (all establishments for the Minor Breeding of animals, and all employees in general of said establishments). (Minor breeding or the breeding of noncorpulent animals: pigs, sheep, goats, dogs, tigers, lions, cats, hares, hens, ducks, wasps, fish, butterflies, mice, insects, microbes, etc.)

Touched, Traveler forgot all about the hour and how the level of the *caña* was going down. The problems came to him like caresses: Why exempt vegetables and fruit trees? Why did the word wasp have something diabolical about it? And that almost Edenic vision of a farm where goats were raised alongside tigers, mice, butterflies, lions and microbes . . . Choking with laughter he went out into the hall. The almost tangible aspect of an estate where the employees-of-said-establishment were arguing as they tried to breed a whale became superimposed on the austere vision of the night-time hallway. It was a hallucination worthy of the place and the time, it seemed perfectly foolish to wonder what Talita was doing in the pharmacy or in the courtyard, when the order of Corporations continued to offer itself as a guiding light.

(25) NATIONAL CORPORATION OF HOSPITALS AND RELATED HOUSES (all hospitals of all types, workshops for repairs and adjustments, houses for the curing of hides, stables for the curing of horses, dental clinics, barber shops, houses for the pruning of plants, houses for the arrangement of intricate legal forms, etc., and also all employees in general of said establishments).

"There it is," Traveler said. "A break that proves Ceferino's perfect central healthiness. Horacio is right, there's no reason to accept the order of things the way daddy hands them to us. Cefe thinks that the fact that something is being repaired unites a dentist and intricate legal forms; accidents are just as valuable as essences . . . But it's pure poetry, boy. Cefe is breaking the hard mental crust, as somebody or other said, and he's beginning to see the world from a different angle. Of course this is what they call being batty."

When Talita came in he was on the twenty-eighth Corporation:

> (28) NATIONAL CORPORATION OF SCIENTIFIC DETECTIVES-ERRANT AND THEIR HOUSES OF SCIENCE (all places for detectives and/or investigation police, all places for explorers (travellers) and all places for scientific explorers, and all employees in general of said same establishments). (All of the above-mentioned employees must belong to a class that is to be called "ERRANT".)

Talita and Traveler liked this part less, it was as if Ceferino were abandoning himself too soon to a persecutory worry. But perhaps the scientific detectives-errant were not mere investigators; the "errant" business invested them with a quixotic air that Cefe, probably taking it as understood, had not bothered to emphasize.

> (29) NATIONAL CORPORATION OF SCIENTIFIC DETECTIVES HAVING TO DO WITH PLEAS AND THEIR HOUSES OF SCIENCE (all places for detectives and/or Investigation police, and all places for explorers, and all employees in general of said same establishments). (All of the above-mentioned employees are to belong to a class that is to be called "PLEAS", and the places and employees of this class are to be separate from those of other classes such as the already mentioned "ERRANT".
>
> (30) NATIONAL CORPORATION OF SCIENTIFIC DETECTIVES HAVING TO DO WITH FINAL BOUNDARIES AND THEIR HOUSES OF SCIENCE (all places for detectives and/or Investigation police, and all places for explorers, and all employees in general of said same establishments). (All of the above-mentioned employees are to belong to a class that is to be called "BOUNDARIES", and the places and employees of this class are to be separate from those of other classes such as the already mentioned "ERRANT" and "PLEAS".)

"It's as if he were talking about orders of chivalry," Talita said convinced. "But the strange thing is that in these three corporations of detectives, the only thing he mentions is the places."

"That's one thing, and the other is the meaning of 'final boundaries'."

"He must be deriving *final* from *fine.* But that doesn't solve anything. What's the difference."

"What's the difference," Traveler repeated. "You're so right. The beautiful part is that there exists the possibility of a world where there will be detectives-errant, plea detectives, and final-boundary detectives. That's why it seems quite natural to me that Cefe turns now from chivalry to religious orders, with an interlude that looks like a concession to the scientifical (you've got to call it something) spirit of the times. I'll read it to you:"

> (31) NATIONAL CORPORATION OF THE LEARNED IN SUITABLE SCIENCES AND THEIR HOUSES OF SCIENCE (all houses or communal places for the learned in suitable sciences and all of the aforementioned learned men). (Learned men in suitable sciences: physicians, homoeopaths, healers (all surgeons), midwives, technicians, mechanics (all types of technicians), engineers of the second grade or architects of every branch (all executors of plans already drawn beforehand, such as would be an engineer of the second grade), classifiers in general, astronomers, astrologers, spiritualists, full doctors in every branch of the law or laws (all experts), classifiers of generic species, accountants, translators, primary school teachers (all composers), trackers – men – of murderers, pathfinders or guides, plant grafters, barbers, etc.)

"Look at this," Traveler said, taking a drink of *caña* at one gulp. "He's an absolute genius!"

"It'll be a great country for barbers," Talita said, flopping on the bed and closing her eyes. "They come pretty high on the scale. What I don't understand is why the tracers of murderers have to be men."

"I've never heard of a female tracker," Traveler said, "and probably Cefe didn't find it very appropriate. You must have noticed that he's a terrible puritan in sexual matters, it comes out all the time."

"It's hot, too damned hot," Talita said. "Did you notice how he likes to include classifiers, and even repeats the name? So let's have the mystical leap you were going to read me."

"Get ready to catalogue," Traveler said.

(32) NATIONAL CORPORATION OF MONKS OF THE PRAYER OF THE SIGN OF THE CROSS AND THEIR HOUSES OF SCIENCE (all communal houses of monks, and all monks). (Monks or men who bless, who are to remain outside all extraneous cults, uniquely and only for the world of the word and the curative mysteries of the "conquest" of the latter.) (Monks who are always to combat all spiritual ills, all harm earned or put into goods or bodies, etc.) (Penitent and anchorite monks who are to pray for and bless sometimes people, sometimes objects, sometimes sites of places, sometimes planted fields, sometimes a boyfriend badly affected by a rival, etc.)

(33) NATIONAL CORPORATION OF CHURCHGOING GUARDIANS OF COLLECTIONS AND THEIR HOUSES OF COLLECTION (all houses of collection, and *idem*, houses – deposits, warehouses, archives, museums, cemeteries, jails, asylums, homes for the blind, etc., and also all employees in general of said establishments). (Collections: example: an archive keeps files in a collection; a cemetery keeps corpses in a collection; a jail keeps prisoners in a collection, etc.)

"Even Espronceda didn't think of the cemetery bit," Traveler said. "You can't deny the analogy between the Chacarita cemetery and an archive . . . Ceferino has an intuition for relationships, and that, basically, is true intelligence, don't you think? After introductions like these, his final classification isn't strange at all, quite the contrary. A world like this should be tried."

Talita didn't say anything, but she lifted her upper lip like a festoon and let out a sigh that had its origins in what is called the first signs of sleep. Traveler took another drink of *caña* and got into the final and definitive Corporations:

(40) NATIONAL CORPORATION OF COMMISSION AGENTS FOR COLOURED SPECIES COLOURED IN RED AND HOUSES OF ACTIVE LABOUR FOR THE BENEFIT OF SPECIES COLOURED IN RED (all communal houses of

commission agents for generic species coloured in red, or the main Offices of said agents, and also all said agents). (Generic species coloured in red: animals with fur coloured in red; plants with flowers coloured in red, and minerals with the look of coloured in red.)

(41) NATIONAL CORPORATION OF COMMISSION AGENTS FOR SPECIES COLOURED IN BLACK AND HOUSES OF ACTIVE LABOUR FOR THE BENEFIT OF SPECIES COLOURED BLACK (all communal houses of commission agents for generic species in black, or the main Offices of said agents, and also all said agents). (Generic species coloured in black or simply black animals with black fur, plants with black flowers, and minerals with a black look.)

(42) NATIONAL CORPORATION OF COMMISSION AGENTS FOR SPECIES COLOURED IN BROWN AND HOUSES OF ACTIVE LABOUR FOR THE BENEFIT OF BROWN SPECIES (all communal houses of commission agents for generic species coloured in brown, or the main Offices of said agents, and also all said agents). (Generic species coloured in brown or simply brown: animals with brown fur, plants with brown flowers, and minerals with a brown look.)

(43) NATIONAL CORPORATION OF COMMISSION AGENTS FOR SPECIES COLOURED IN YELLOW AND HOUSES OF ACTIVE LABOUR FOR THE BENEFIT OF SPECIES COLOURED IN YELLOW (all communal houses of commission agents for generic species coloured in yellow, or the main Offices of said agents, and also all said agents). (Generic species coloured in yellow or simply yellow: animals with yellow fur, plants with yellow flowers, and minerals with a yellow look.)

(44) NATIONAL CORPORATION OF COMMISSION AGENTS FOR SPECIES IN WHITE AND HOUSES OF ACTIVE LABOUR FOR THE BENEFIT OF SPECIES COLOURED IN WHITE (all communal houses of commission agents for generic species coloured in white, or the main Offices of said agents, and also all said agents.) (Generic species coloured in white: animals with white fur, plants with white flowers, and minerals with a white look.)

(45) NATIONAL CORPORATION OF COMMISSION AGENTS FOR SPECIES IN PAMPA AND HOUSES OF ACTIVE LABOUR FOR THE BENEFIT OF SPECIES COLOURED IN PAMPA (all communal houses of commission agents for generic species coloured in pampa, or the main Offices of said agents, and also all said agents). (Generic species coloured in pampa or simply pampa: animals with pampa fur, vegetables with pampa flowers, and minerals with a pampa look.)

Break the hard mental crust . . . How did Ceferino visualize what he had written? What dazzling reality (or not) showing him scenes in which polar bears moved about in a vast marble backdrop, among Cape jasmines? Or crows nesting in a pile of coal with black tulips in their beaks . . . And why "coloured in black", "coloured in white"? Shouldn't it be "in colour"? But then, why: "coloured in yellow or simply yellow"? What colours were they that couldn't be translated by Michaux's or Huxley's marijuana? Ceferino's notes, useful to lose one's self a little more (if that was useful), didn't go very far. In any case:

Concerning the aforementioned pampa colour: pampa colour is all of that colour which is varied, or which is formed by two or more kinds of paint.

And a highly necessary clarification:

Concerning the aforementioned or alluded agents for generic species: said agents are to be Governors, for through them none of the generic species shall disappear from the earth; the generic types, within their class, shall not cross, either one class with another, or one type with another, or one race with another, or one generic colour with another generic colour, etc.

Ceferino Piriz, a purist, a racist! A cosmos of pure colours, Mondrianesque to an intolerable degree! Dangerous Ceferino Piriz, always a possible candidate for Deputy, perhaps for President! On guard, Uruguay! And another *caña* before going to sleep while Cefe, drunk with colours, allows himself a last poem in which, as in a huge canvas by Ensor, everything explosive explodes into material for masks and antimasks. Militarism suddenly erupts in his system, and the treatment, somewhere between macaronic and trismegistical, that the Uruguayan philosopher reserved for it, had to be seen. Or in other words:

> As for the announced work *The Light of World Peace*, the question is that it includes a rather detailed explanation of militarism, but now, in a brief summary, we shall give the following version(s) dealing with militarism:
>
> *Police* ("Metropolitan" type) *for military men born under the zodiacal sign of Aries; Unions of fundamental antigovernment for military men born under the zodiacal sign of Taurus; the Direction and sponsorship of public festivities and social gatherings (dances, soirées, arrangement of betrothals: bringing fiancés together, etc.) for military men born under the zodiacal sign of Gemini; Aviation (military) for military men born under the zodiacal sign of Cancer; the Pen in support of fundamental government (military journalism, and political wizardry for the benefit of all fundamental and national Government) for military men born under the zodiacal sign of Leo; Artillery (heavy weapons in general and bombs) for military men born under the zodiacal sign of Virgo; Sponsorship and practical production of public and/or national celebrations (the use of adequate disguises on the part of military men in moments for the incorporation of either a military parade, or a festival like those called "harvest", etc.) for military men born under the zodiacal sign of Scorpio; Cavalry (regular cavalry and motorized cavalry, with their respective participation, either of fusileers, or lancers, or machete bearers: typical example: "Republican Guard", or of swordsmen, etc.) for military men born under the zodiacal sign of Capricorn; and practical military Service (couriers, orderlies, firemen, practical missionaries, servants of the practical, etc.) for military men born under the zodiacal sign of Aquarius.*

Shaking Talita, who woke up indignantly, Traveler read her the part on militarism and the two of them had to cover their heads with the pillow so they wouldn't wake up the whole clinic. But first they came to agree that the majority of Argentine military men were born under the zodiacal sign of Taurus. Traveler was so drunk, born under the zodiacal sign of Scorpio, that he declared himself ready to appeal immediately in his status as second lieutenant in the reserves for permission to make use of adequate disguises on the part of military men.

"We will organize tremendous festivals of the type called harvest," Traveler said, taking his head out from under the pillow and sticking it back again as soon as he finished the sentence. "You shall see along with all your fellows of the pampa race, because there isn't the least doubt that you're a pampa, or that you're formed by two or more kinds of paint."

"I'm white," Talita said. "And it's too bad you weren't born under the zodiacal sign of Capricorn, because I'd love you to be a swordsman. Or at least a courier or an orderly."

"Couriers are Aquarius. Horacio is Cancer, isn't he?"

"If he isn't, he deserves to be," Talita said, closing her eyes.

"Aviation touches him a bit. All you have to do is imagine him piloting one of those Bang-Bangs and there you have him crashing his plane into the Confitería del Aguila at tea and crumpet time. It would be inevitable."

Talita turned out the light and snuggled a little closer to Traveler, who was sweating and twisting, wrapped up in diverse signs of the zodiac, national corporations of commission agents who had a yellow look.

"Horacio saw La Maga tonight," Talita said. "He saw her in the courtyard, two hours ago, when you were on guard duty."

"Oh," said Traveler lifting up his shoulders and looking for his cigarettes by Braille. "We would have to place him among the churchgoing guardians of collections."

"I was La Maga," Talita said, snuggling closer to Traveler. "I don't know if you're aware of that."

"Most likely yes."

"It had to happen some time. What surprises me is that he's become so startled by the mixup."

"Oh you know, Horacio gets something started and then he looks at it with the same look puppies put on when they've taken a crap and stand there amazed looking at it."

"I think it happened the very day we went to meet him at the dock," Talita said. "It's hard to explain, because he didn't even look at me and between the two of you you treated me like a dog, with the cat under my arm."

"Breeding of noncorpulent animals," Traveler said.

"He had me confused with La Maga," Talita insisted. "Everything else had to follow as if Ceferino had enumerated it, one thing after another."

"La Maga," Traveler said, dragging on his cigarette until his face was lit up in the darkness, "is also from Uruguay. So you see there's a certain order."

"Let me talk, Manú."

"Better not. What for?"

"First the old man with the pigeon came, and then we went down to the basement. Horacio kept talking all the time we were going down, about those hollows that worry him. He was desperate, Manú, it was frightening to see how peaceful he seemed, and all the time . . . We went down in the service lift, and he went over to shut one of the freezers, it was horrible."

"So you went downstairs," Traveler said. "OK."

"It was different," Talita said. "It wasn't like going down. We were talking, but I felt as if Horacio were somewhere else, talking to someone else, to a drowned woman, for example. It comes back to me now, but he'd never said that La Maga had been drowned in the river."

"She isn't the least bit drowned," Traveler said. "I'm sure of that, although I have to admit I haven't got the slightest idea. Knowing Horacio is enough."

"He thinks she's dead, Manú, and at the same time he feels her close by and tonight it was me. He told me that he's seen her on the ship too, and under the bridge on the Avenida San Martín . . . He doesn't say it as if he were talking about a hallucination, and he doesn't expect you to believe it either. He says it, that's all, and it's true, it's something that's there. When he closed the freezer and I was afraid and I said something or other, he began to look at me and it was the other one he was looking at. I'm nobody's zombie, Manú, I don't want to be anybody's zombie."

Traveler stroked her hair, but Talita pushed him away impatiently. She had sat down on the bed and he could feel her trembling. Trembling, in that heat. She told him that Horacio had kissed her and she tried to explain the kiss, and since she couldn't find the words she kept touching Traveler in the darkness, her arms fell like cloths over his face, over his arms, slipped down along his chest, rested on his knees, and out of all this came a kind of explanation that Traveler was incapable of rejecting, a contagion that came from farther off, from some place in the depths or on the heights or in some place which was not that night and that room, a contagion that possessed him in turn through Talita, a babbling like an untranslatable announcement, the suspicion that he was facing something that could be an announcement, but the voice that brought it was broken and when it spoke the message it spoke it in some unintelligible language, and yet it was the only necessary thing there within hand's reach, demanding recognition and acceptance, beating itself against a spongy wall of smoke and cork, unseizable and offering itself naked between the arms but like water pouring down among tears.

"The hard mental crust," Traveler managed to think. Confusedly he heard that fear, that Horacio, that the service lift, that the dove; a communicable system was little by little entering his ear again. So the poor devil was afraid he would kill him, it was laughable.

"Did he really say that? It's hard to believe, you know how proud he is."

"It's something else," Talita said, taking the cigarette away from him and dragging on it with a sort of silent-movie eagerness. "I think the fear he feels is like a last refuge, the crossbar he holds onto before jumping. He's so happy to be afraid tonight, I know he's happy."

"That," said Traveler, breathing like a real yogi, "is something Cuca would not understand, you can be sure. And I must be in an exceedingly intelligent mood tonight, because that business of happy fear is a little hard to take, my love."

Talita slid up on the bed a little and leaned against Traveler. She knew that she was by his side again, that she had not drowned, that he was there holding her up on the surface of the water and that actually there was pity, a marvellous pity. They both felt it at the same moment, and they slid towards each other as if to fall into themselves, into the common earth where words and caresses and mouths enfolded them as a circumference does a circle, those tranquillizing metaphors, that old sadness satisfied with going back to being the same as always, with continuing, keeping afloat against wind and tide, against call and fall.

(–140)

134

The Flower Garden

One must be aware of the fact that a garden that is very strictly planned, in the style of "French parks", consisting of flower-beds, stone pots and trellises arranged geometrically, calls for great competence and much care.

On the other hand, in a garden of "English" type, the mistakes of the amateur are more easily disguised. A few bushes, a bed of grass, and a single flowerbed with mixed flowers that stands out neatly, in the shelter of a well-located wall or fence, are the essential elements of a very decorative and very practical combination.

If some varieties unfortunately do not yield the desired results, it will be easy to replace them by means of transplants; imperfection or lack of care in the combination will not be visible because the other flowers, arranged in patches that differ as to surface, height and colour, will always form a grouping that will be pleasant to the eye.

This type of planting, very popular in England and the United States, is called a "mixed border". Flowers set out this way, mixed in together and showing each other off as if they had grown naturally, will give your garden a rural and natural aspect, while planting done in rows, squares and circles always has an artificial character about it and requires absolute perfection.

Therefore, for practical as well as aesthetic reasons, it is proper to advise a mixed-border arrangement for the amateur gardener.

Almanach Hachette

(–25)

135

"They're delicious," Gekrepten said. "I already ate two while I was frying them, they're a real delicacy, believe me."

"Make me another bitter *mate*, old girl," Oliveira said.

"Right away, love. Wait till I change your cold compress first."

"Thanks. It's very strange eating fried cakes with your eyes bandaged. That's how they should train the guys who are going to discover the cosmos for us."

"The ones who fly to the moon in those machines? They put them in a capsule or something like that, right?"

"Yes, and they give them fried cakes and *mate*."

(–63)

136

Morelli's mania for quotations:

"It would be difficult for me to explain the publication in one single book of poems and a denial of poetry, of the diary of a dead man and the notes of a prelate friend of mine . . ."

GEORGES BATAILLE, *Haine de la poésie*

(–12)

137

Morelliana

If the volume or the tone of the work can lead one to believe that the author is attempting a sum, hasten to point out to him that he is face to face with the opposite attempt, that of an implacable *subtraction.*

(–17)

138

Sometimes La Maga and I feel like profaning our memories. It all depends on so little, an afternoon's bad mood, the anguish over what can happen if we start looking at each other straight in the eye. Little by little, along the meandering of a dialogue that's like a piece of shredded rag, we begin to remember. Two different worlds, alien, almost always irreconcilable, come into our words, and as if by common consent the joke comes into being. I usually start scornfully, remembering my old blind cult of friendship, misunderstood loyalties that gave little in return, the humble obstinacy of banners carried to political rallies, to intellectual lectures, to fervent love affairs. I laugh at a suspicious honesty that so many times caused its own or someone else's misfortune, while underneath betrayals and moments of dishonesty were spinning their webs and I could not prevent them, I could only allow others to betray or be dishonest to my face and doubly to blame could not do anything to prevent them. I make fun of my uncles and their decanted decency, stuck in shit up to their necks where the immaculate stiff collar still glows. They would fall over on their backs if they knew that they were wallowing in manure, convinced, the one in Tucuman and the other in Nueve de Julio, that they are the model of decanted Argentinity (those are the words they use). And yet I have fond memories of them. And yet I will trample on those memories on days when La Maga and I get fed up with Paris and want to do ourselves some harm.

When La Maga stops laughing and asks me why I say such things about my uncles, I wish they could be there listening behind the door like the old man on the sixth floor. I prepare a careful explanation, because I do not want to be unjust or to exaggerate. I also want it to be helpful for La Maga, because she has never been able to understand moral questions (just like Étienne, but less selfishly; just because the only responsibility she believes in is of the present, the very moment when one must be good or noble; underneath it all, for reasons just as hedonistic and selfish as Étienne's).

Then I explain that my two most honourable uncles are a pair of perfect Argentines as the expression was understood in 1915, a period in the high point of their lives that varied between ranching and business. When one talks about "Latin Americans of yesteryear", he means anti-Semites, xenophobes, bourgeoisie rooted in a nostalgia for the small ranch where Indian girls prepared *mate* for ten pesos a month, all with the bluest and whitest of patriotic sentiments, a respect for everything military and for expeditions into the frontier, with dozens of starched shirts, even though his salary isn't big enough for monthly payments to that abject being the whole family calls the "Russian", dealt with by shouts, threats, and at best with bullying phrases. When La Maga starts to share this vision (of which she personally hasn't the slightest experience) I hasten to show her that within this general panorama of my two uncles and their respective families there are people with excellent qualities. Self-sacrificing parents and their children, citizens who go to the polls and read serious newspapers, hard-working officials well thought of by their superiors and colleagues, people capable of staying up nights on end at the bedside of a person who is ill, or of doing some magnificent gauchesque sort of thing. La Maga looks at me perplexed, afraid I'm making fun of her. I have to insist, explain why I love my uncles so much, why only when we get fed up with streets and the weather it occurs to me to haul their remains out of the shadows and trample on the memories I still have of them. Then La Maga perks up a bit and starts talking about her mother, whom she loves and detests in proportions that vary with the moment. Sometimes she terrifies me with the way in which she can refer to a childhood episode that other times she has mentioned with laughter, as if it were amusing, and suddenly it becomes a sinister knot, a kind of swamp with leeches and ticks that pursue and suck. At moments like that La Maga's face looks like a fox's, her nostrils narrow, she turns pale, she speaks in jerks and starts, twisting her hands and panting and, like a huge, obscene piece of chewing-gum, her mother's pasty face begins to appear, her mother's poorly dressed body, the suburban street her mother lives on like an old spittoon on a wasteland, the misery in which her mother is a hand that scrubs a pot with a greasy rag. The worst of it is that La Maga can't go on for very long; soon she starts to cry, hiding her face against me, huddling down to an incredible degree, we have to prepare tea, forget about everything, go off somewhere or make love, make love without any uncles or mother, almost always that or going to sleep, but almost always that.

(–127)

139

The notes of the piano (la, re, mi flat, do, ti, ti flat, mi, so), those of the violin (la, mi, ti flat, mi), those of the horn (la, ti flat, la, ti flat, mi, so), represent the musical equivalent of the names of ArnoLD SCHoenberg, Anton WEBErn, and ALBAn BErG (according to the German system in which H represents ti, B ti flat, and S (ES) mi flat). There is nothing new about this kind of musical anagram. It must be recalled that Bach used his own name in a similar way and that the same procedure was common property among polyphonic composers of the 16th century (. . .) Another significant analogy with the Violin Concerto consists in the strict symmetry of the whole. In the Violin Concerto the key number is two: two separate movements, each divided into two parts, as well as the violin-orchestra division in the instrumental grouping. In the *Kammerkonzert*, on the other hand, the number three stands out: the dedication represents the Maestro and his two disciples; the instruments are grouped in three categories: piano, violin, and a combination of wind instruments; its architecture is the building up of three linked movements, each of which reveals to a greater or lesser degree a tripartite composition.

From the anonymous commentary on the Chamber Concerto
for violin, piano, and thirteen wind instruments
by ALBAN BERG (Pathé Vox recording PL 8660)

(–133)

140

In hopes of something more exciting, exercises in profanation and the far-out, in the pharmacy between midnight and two in the morning, once Cuca had gone off to get-a-good-night's-sleep (or before, so she would go: Cuca sticks it out, but she gets terribly tired from the effort of resisting with a bounteous smile and a sort of turning her back on the monsters' verbal assaults. Every time she leaves a little earlier to get some sleep, and the monsters smile pleasantly as they wish her good night. Talita, with her greater neutrality, is pasting on labels or consulting the *Index Pharmacorum Gottinga*).

The sort of thing they do: translating with Manichaean inversion a famous sonnet:

> The deflowered, dead, and fearful past,
> Can it but bring us back with sombre flap of wing?

Reading a page from Traveler's notebook: "Waiting my turn in the barber shop, spotting a UNESCO publication, and picking up on the following names: Opintotoveri/Työläusopiskelija/Työväenopisto. It seems that these are the names of some pedagogical journals from Finland. Complete unreality for the reader. Does it all really exist? For millions of blond-headed people, Opinotoveri means the Supervisor of General Education. For me . . . (Wrath). But they don't know what *cafisho* means (Buenos Aires satisfaction). Irreality multiplies. To think that specialists can foretell from the fact that one can reach Helsinki in a few hours in a Boeing 707 . . . The results of personal extrapolation. Give me a crew-cut, Pedro."

Linguistic forms of alienation. Pensive Talita, face to face with Genshiryoku Kokunai Jijo, that in no way seems to resemble the development of nuclear activity in Japan. She is just becoming convinced by superposition and differentiation when her husband, that malignant provider of material picked up in barber shops, shows her the variant Genshiryoku Kaigai Jijo, evidently the development of nuclear activities abroad. Talita's enthusiasm, convinced analytically that Kokunai = Japan and Kaigai = abroad. The confusion on the part of Matsui, the drycleaner on the Calle Lascano, when he is confronted with a polyglot exhibition by Talita, who turns away, poor thing, with her tail between her legs.

Profanations: starting with such suppositions as the famous line: "Christ's visible homosexuality," and building up to a coherent and satisfactory system. Postulating that Beethoven was a coprofage, etc. Defending the undeniable sainthood of Sir Roger Casement, as it is evident in *The Black Diaries.* The bewilderment of Cuca, confirmed and practising.

Basically it's a question of alienating one's self out of purely professional abnegation. They still laugh too much (impossible for Attila to be a stamp collector) but that business about *Arbeit macht Frei* will still have results, believe me, Cuca. For example, the rape of the Bishop of Fano must be a case of . . .

(–138)

141

It didn't take many pages to see that Morelli was aiming at something else. His allusions to the profound blanket of the *Zeitgeist*, the passages where lo(co)gic ended up by hanging itself by its own shoelaces, unable to deny the incongruity that has become a law, were evidence of the work's speleological intent. Morelli advanced and retreated in such an open violation of equilibrium and principles of space that should really be called *moral*, that it well might have happened (although, in fact, it did not happen, but nobody could be sure) that the happenings he spoke about might have all happened in five minutes that were capable of linking the Battle of Actium with the *Anschluss* of Austria (the three A's may have had something to do with his choice or, more probably, the acceptance of those historic moments), or the fact that a person who rang the doorbell of a house on the Calle Cochabamba, at number twelve hundred, would be able to open the door into a courtyard of Menander's house in Pompeii. That was all rather trivial and Buñuel, and its value as a mere incitement or as a parabola open to a deeper and more scabrous sense was not lost on those in the Club. Thanks to those exercises in flying around, so like the ones that get so showy in the Gospels, the Upanishads, and other matter loaded with shamanistic trinitrotoluene, Morelli allowed himself the pleasure of continuing to pretend a literature that he would mine, undermine and ridicule at its very inner base. Suddenly the words, a whole language, the superstructure of a style, a semantic, a psychology, and a factitiousness rushed towards hair-raising hara-kiris. *Banzai!* Even towards a new order, or no guarantee whatsoever: finally, there would always be a thread stretched out to the beyond, coming out of the book, pointing towards a perhaps, a maybe, a who knows, which would leave any petrifying aspect of the work in abeyance. And the thing that distressed Perico Romero, a man in need of certainties, made Oliveira tremble with delight, heightened the imagination of Étienne, Wong, and Ronald, and obliged La Maga to dance barefoot with an artichoke in each hand.

Along the route of arguments stained with Calvados and tobacco, Étienne and Oliveira had wondered why Morelli hated literature, and why he hated it from the standpoint of literature itself, instead of repeating Rimbaud's *exeunt* or exercising on his left temple the notorious effectiveness of a Colt ·32. Oliveira was inclined to believe that Morelli had been suspicious of the demoniacal nature of all re-creative writing (and what literature wasn't like that, even if it was something like the excipient that would make a person swallow a gnosis, a praxis, or an ethos out of all the ones that were wandering around or that could be invented?). After hefting the most inciting passages, he had ended by becoming sensitive to a special tone of Morelli's writing. The first possible description of that tone was one of disenchantment, but underneath one could sense that the disenchantment did not refer to the circumstances and happenings narrated in the book, but rather to the way they were narrated, that – Morelli had disguised it as much as possible – he was reverting definitively to what was being told. The elimination of the pseudo-conflict between content and form came up again to the degree that the old man was denouncing formal material and using it in his own way; when he doubted his tools he was at the same time disqualifying the work he did with them. What the book told about had no use whatsoever, because it was poorly told, simply because it was told, it was literature. Again one turned to the irritation of the author with his writing and with writing in general. The apparent paradox lay in that Morelli was accumulating episodes that were imagined and foe-used in the most diverse forms; trying to attack them and resolve them with every skill of a writer worthy of the name. He didn't seem to be proposing a theory, it offered no difficulty for intellectual reflection, but from everything he had written there would appear with an efficiency infinitely greater than that of any statement or analysis, the profound corrosion of a world denounced as false, the attack by accumulation and not by destruction, an almost diabolical irony that might be suspicious of the success of great passages of bravado, episodes rigorously constructed, the apparent feeling of literary happiness that for years had been building up his fame among readers of short stories and novels.

For those with a delicate sense of smell, a world sumptuously orchestrated was being resolved into nothingness; but right there the mystery began, because at the same time one was presented with the total nihilism of the work, a more careful intuition might suspect that this was not Morelli's intent, that the virtual self-destruction found in every fragment of his work was a kind of search for the noble metal among the slag. One had to pause here, for fear of mixing up the doors and going out on a limb. The fiercest arguments between Oliveira and Étienne would occur at this level of their hopes, because they feared they were making mistakes, that they were a pair of perfect cretins insisting on the belief that the Tower of Babel could not be built if in the end it was meaningless. Occidental morality at this point seemed like a pimp to them, as one by one it insinuated all the illusions of thirty centuries that had been inevitably inherited, assimilated, and digested. It was hard to deny belief in the fact that a flower could be beautiful to no end; it was bitter to accept the fact that one could dance in darkness. Morelli's allusions to an inversion of signs, to a world seen with other and from other dimensions, as an inevitable preparation for a purer vision (and all of this in a resplendently written passage, and at the same time suspicious of the farce, of icy irony before the mirror) exasperated them as it offered them the roost of an almost hope, of a justification but at the same time denied them total security, keeping them in an unbearable ambiguity. If there was any consolation left it was the thought that Morelli too moved about in that same ambiguity, orchestrating a work whose legitimate first hearing could well have been the most absolute of silences. That's how they went along through the pages, cursing and fascinated, and La Maga would always end up curling herself up like a cat in an easy chair, tired of uncertainties, looking at how dawn was breaking over the slate roofs, through all the smoke that fills in among a pair of eyes and a closed window and an ardently useless night.

(–60)

142

1. "I can't tell what she was like," Ronald said. "We'll never know. All we know about her is the effect she had on other people. We were something like her mirrors, or she was our mirror. I can't explain it."

2. "She used to be so silly," Étienne said. "Blessed be the silly, et cetera. I swear to you that I'm speaking seriously, I'm quoting seriously. Her silliness used to irritate me. Horacio insisted it was just a lack of information, but he was wrong. There's a well-known difference between ignorance and silliness, and everybody knows that, except somebody who's silly, luckily for him. She thought that by studying, her famous studying, she could get to be intelligent. She confused knowledge with understanding. The poor girl had a good understanding of so many things that we don't sense because we know so much about them."

3. "Don't fall into echolalia," Ronald said. "That whole deck of antinomies, polarizations. For me, her silliness was the price she paid for being so vegetative, so much of a snail, so stuck onto the most mysterious of things. That's it, think about it: she wasn't capable of believing in names, she had to put her finger on something and only then would she admit that it was. You don't get very far that way. It's like turning your back on the whole Western world, all of the Schools. It's no good for living in a city, having to earn your keep. That's what was gnawing at her."

4. "Yes, yes, but on the other hand she was capable of infinite moments of happiness, I used to watch her with envy. The shape of a glass, for example. What else am I looking for in painting, tell me. Killing myself, driving myself along such frightening paths, all I do is come out with a fork and two olives. Salt and the centre of the world have to be there, in that spot on the tablecloth. She'd arrive and sense it. One night she came over to my studio, I found her in

front of a painting I'd finished that morning. She was crying the way she used to cry, with her whole face, horrible and marvellous. She was looking at my painting and crying. I wasn't enough of a man to tell her I had cried that morning too. To think that it could have given her so much tranquillity, you know how much she doubted, how small she felt, surrounded by our clever brilliance."

5. "One cries for many reasons," Ronald said. "That doesn't prove anything."

6. "At least it proves a contact. How many others looking at that painting had shown their appreciation with polished phrases, a list of influences, all the possible commentaries *round about*. You see, you had to reach a level where it would be possible to join both things together. I think I'm already there, but I'm one of the few."

7. "You're probably king of the few," Ronald said. "Anything at all is enough to make you take off."

6. "I know that's how it is," Étienne said. "I know that. But it's taken me a lifetime to get my two hands to work together, the left one to its heart, the right one to its brush and canvas. At first I was someone who would look at Raphael and think about Perugino, pounce like a lobster on Leo Battista Alberti, connect, link, Pico here, Lorenzo Valla there, but look, Burckhardt says, Berenson denies, Argan thinks, those blues are Sienese, those blurs are from Masaccio. I don't remember when, it was in Rome, in the Barberini gallery, I was analysing an Andrea del Sarto, what they call analysing, and all of a sudden I saw. Don't ask me to explain anything. I saw it (and not the whole painting, just a detail in the background, a small figure on a road). Tears came to my eyes, I mean it."

5. "That doesn't prove anything," Ronald said. "One cries for many reasons."

4. "It's no good answering you. She probably would have understood much better. We're all really on the same road, except that some people start on the lefthand side and some on the right. Sometimes, right in the middle, somebody sees the piece of tablecloth with the glass on it, the fork, the olives."

3. "You're talking figures," Ronald said. "It's always the same thing."

2. "There's no other way to get back what's been lost, what's strayed away. She was closer to it and she sensed it. Her only mistake was in wanting a proof that the closeness was worth all our rhetoric.

Nobody could give her that proof, first because we're incapable of conceiving of it, and second because in one way or another we're comfortably installed and satisfied in our collective science. It's common knowledge that Fowler lets us sleep peacefully, there he is within reach, with all the answers. And it's true, but only because we're no longer capable of asking the questions that would liquidate him. When La Maga would ask why trees covered themselves in summer . . . but it's useless, man, it's better to shut up."

1. "Yes, we can't really explain any of that at all," Ronald said.

(–34)

143

In the morning, still persisting in the dozing that the hair-raising shriek of the alarm could not change into sharp wakefulness, they would dutifully tell each other about the dreams they had had that night. Head to head, caressing each other, mingling hands and feet, they tried to put into words the world they had been living in during darkness. Traveler, a friend from Oliveira's youth, was fascinated by Talita's dreams, her mouth, tight or smiling according to the telling, the gestures and exclamations with which she would accentuate it, her ingenuous conjectures about the reason and meaning of her dreams. Then it would be his turn to tell about his, and sometimes in the middle of a telling his hands would begin to caress and they would go from dreams to love, fall asleep again, be late everywhere they were going.

Listening to Talita, her voice a little sticky from sleep, looking at her hair spread out on the pillow, Traveler was startled that everything could be like that. He stuck out a finger, touched Talita on the temple, the forehead. ("And then my sister became my Aunt Irene, but I'm not sure"), he would test the barrier so few inches away from his own head ("And I was a boy naked in a pile of straw and I was looking at the raging river as it rose, a gigantic wave . . . "). They had fallen asleep with their heads touching and there, in that physical immediacy, in that almost total coincidence of attitudes, positions, breathing, the same tick-tock, the same stimuli of street and city, the same magnetic radiations, the same brand of coffee, the same stellar conjunction, the same night for both of them, tightly embraced there, they had dreamed different dreams, they had lived unlike adventures, one had smiled while the other had fled frightened by herself, one had taken an exam in algebra again while the other was coming to a city built of white stone. Talita would put pleasure or doubt into the morning retelling, but Traveler would secretly insist on looking for correspondences. How was it possible that his daytime companion would inevitably turn off into that divorce, that inadmissible solitude of the dreamer? Sometimes his image would become part of Talita's dreams, or the image of Talita would share the horror of one of Traveler's nightmares. But they did not know it, it was necessary for one to tell the other on awakening: "Then you grabbed me by the hand and told me . . ." And Traveler discovered that while in Talita's dream he had grabbed her hand and talked to her, in his own dream he had been in bed with Talita's best friend or had been talking with the manager of the Las Estrellas circus, or swimming in Mar del Plata. The presence of his ghost in an alien dream had reduced him to the status of a tool, with no precedence whatsoever over manikins, unknown cities, railway stations, stairways, all the paraphernalia of night-time reproductions. Next to Talita, wrapping up her face and head with his lips and fingers, Traveler could feel the impassable barrier, the dizzy distance that not even love could leap. For a long time he waited for a miracle, that the dream Talita was about to tell him in the morning would also be the one he had dreamed. He waited for it, incited it, provoked it, calling upon all possible analogies, looking for similarities that suddenly would bring him to a recognition. Only once, without Talita's assigning it the least importance, did they dream analogous dreams. Talita spoke about a hotel that she and her mother had gone to where everybody had to bring his own chair. Then Traveler remembered his dream: a hotel without bathrooms, which obliged everyone to take a towel and go through a railway station to take a bath in some imprecise place. He told her: "We almost dreamed the same dream, we were in hotels without chairs and without bathrooms." Talita was amused and laughed, it was already time to get up, they were shamefully lazy.

Traveler kept on hoping and waiting less and less. The dreams came back, each one on its own side. Their heads would fall asleep touching each other and in each one the curtain would rise on a different stage. Traveler thought ironically that they were like those two cinemas side by side on the Calle Lavalle, and he lost his hopes completely. He lost his faith that what he wanted could happen, and he knew that without faith it would not happen. He knew that without faith nothing that should happen would happen, and with faith almost never either.

(–100)

144

Perfumes, Orphic hymns, civets in the first and second meanings . . . Here you smell of sardonyx. Here of chrysoprase. Here, wait a minute, here it's like parsley but just a hint, a small piece lost in a chamois skin. Here your own smell starts. How strange, really, that a woman cannot smell herself the way a man can smell her. Here exactly. Don't move, let me. You smell of royal jelly, of honey in a tobacco pouch, of seaweed even though the place might make it topical. There are so many kinds of seaweed, La Maga smelled of fresh seaweed, pulled up by the sea's last surf. Of the wave itself. On some days the smell of seaweed would become mixed up with a thicker cadence, then I would have to have recourse to perversion – but it was a Palatine perversion, you understand, a Bulgaroctonous luxury, that of a seneschal surrounded by nocturnal obedience – , to bring my lips up to hers, touch with my tongue that light pink flame that fluttered surrounded by shadow, and then, as now I do with you, I would slowly separate her thighs, hold her a little to one side and breathe into her interminably, feeling how her hand, without my asking, would begin to break me up the way a flame begins to pluck its topazes out of a wrinkled newspaper. Then the perfumes would stop miraculously and everything was taste, biting, essential juices running about the mouth, the fall into that shadow, the primeval darkness, the hub of the wheel of origins. Yes, in that instant of the most crouching animality, closest to excretion and its unspeakable apparatus, there the initial and final figures are sketched, there in the viscous cavern of your daily relaxation stands the trembling Aldebaran, genes and constellations jump, everything becomes alpha and omega, *coquille, cunt, concha, con, coño*, millennium, Armageddon, Terramycin, oh shut up, don't come on with your despicable show, your easy mirrors. The silence of your skin, its abysses with the roll of emerald dice, gadflies and phoenixes and craters . . .

(–92)

145

Morelliana

A quotation:

These, then, are the fundamental, capital and philosophical reasons that have induced me to construct my work on the basis of individual parts – conceiving the work as a particle of the work – and treating man as a fusion of parts of the body and parts of the soul – while I treat all Humanity as a mixture of parts. But if someone were to make this sort of objection to me: that this partial conception of mine is not, in truth, any conception at all, but a mockery, joke, raillery and trick, and that I, instead of subjecting myself to the severe rules and canons of Art, am trying to make fun of them by means of irresponsible jests, romps and leers, I would answer yes, that it's true, that my aims are precisely that. And God knows – I do not hesitate to confess it – I want to turn away a little, gentlemen, from your Art, just as from you yourselves, because I cannot stand alongside that Art, with your conceptions, your artistic attitude, and all of your artistic milieu!

GOMBROWICZ, *Ferdydurke*, Chapter IV. Preface to the Honer lined with child

(–222)

146

LETTER to *The Observer*

Dear Sir:

Has there been any indication from your readers of the scarcity of butterflies this year? In this area which is usually quite prolific, I have seen practically none with the exception of a few flights of Fritillaries. Since March I have seen but one example of an Apantesis virgo, no Catocala cares at all, very few Swallowtails, one Quelonia, no Peacock's Eyes, no Hipposcatics, and not even a single Red Admiral in my garden, which last summer was teeming with butterflies.

I wonder if this scarcity is widespread, and if so, what is the cause of it?

M. WASHBOURN

PITCHCOMBE, GLOS.

(–29)

147

Why so far from the gods? Perhaps simply by asking.

And so what? Man is the animal who asks. The day when we will really learn how to ask there will be a dialogue. Right now questions sweep us away from the answers. What *epiphany* can we expect if we are drowning in the falsest of freedoms, the Judeo-Christian dialectic? We need a real *Novam Organum*, we have to open our windows up wide and throw everything out into the street, but above all we also have to throw out the window and ourselves along with it. It is either a case of death or a continuing flight. We have to do it, in some way or another we have to do it. To have the strength to plunge into the midst of parties and crown the head of the dazzling lady of the house with a beautiful green frog, a gift of night, and suffer without horror the vengeance of her lackeys.

(–31)

148

Concerning the etymology offered by Gabio Basso for the word person.

A wise and ingenious explanation, by my lights, that of Gabio Basso, in his treatise *On the Origin of Words*, of the word *person*, mask. He thinks that this word has its origin in the verb *personare*, to retain. This is how he explains his opinion: "Since the mask covers the face completely except for an opening where the mouth is, the voice, instead of scattering in all directions, narrows down to escape through one single opening and therefore acquires a stronger and more penetrating sound. Thus, since the mask makes the human voice more sonorous and firm, it has been given the name *person*, and as a consequence of the formation of this word, the letter *o* as it appears in it is long."

AUEIO GELIO, *Attic Nights*

(–42)

149

Mis pasos en esta calle
Resuenan
En otra calle
Donde
Oigo mis pasos
Pasar en esta calle
Donde
Sólo es real la niebla

(My steps along this street
Resound
Along another street
Where
I hear my steps
Resound along this street
Where
Only the fog is real.)

OCTAVIO PAZ

(–54)

150

Hospital Items

The York County Hospital informs us that the Dowager Duchess of Grafton, who last Sunday fractured a leg, had a restful day yesterday.

The Sunday Times, London

(–95)

151

Morelliana

It is enough to take a momentary look with everyday eyes at the behaviour of a cat or a fly to feel that the new vision towards which science seems to be heading, that disanthropomorphization urgently proposed by biologists and physicists as the only possible conjoinment with phenomena such as instinct or vegetative life, is nothing but the remote, isolated, insistent voice by which certain lines of Buddhism, Vedanta, Sufism, Western mysticism urge us to renounce mortality once and for all.

(–152)

152

The Abuse of Consciousness

This house I am living in resembles my own in every way: the disposition of the rooms, the smell of the entrance hall, the furniture, the light that slants in the morning, becomes attenuated at noon, overlaps in the afternoon; everything is the same, even the paths and the trees in the garden, and that old tumbledown gate and the paving stones in the courtyard.

The hours and minutes of the time that passes also resemble the hours and minutes of my own life. In the moment in which they spin me around, I tell myself: "They seem real. How much they resemble the real hours I am living at this moment!"

For my part, if indeed I have done away with every reflective surface in my house, in spite of it all, the inevitable windowpane insists on returning my reflection, I see someone there who looks like me. Yes, he looks very much like me, I recognize him!

But no one must think that it is I! After all! Everything is false here. When they give me back *my* house and *my* life, then I shall find my own true face.

JEAN TARDIEU

(–143)

153

"Even though you're from Buenos Aires and all that, they'll stick you with a sorrel horse if you don't watch out."

"I'll try to watch out."

"That would be wise."

CAMBACERES, *Música sentimental*

(–19)

154

In any case, their shoes were walking on linoleum-like material, their noses smelled a bittersweet aseptic powder, the old man was installed in his bed up against two pillows, his nose like a hook caught in the air holding him upright. Livid, with mortuary rings underneath his eyes. The extraordinary zigzag of his temperature chart. And why had they gone to all that trouble?

They said it was nothing, the Argentine friend had happened to be a witness to the accident, the French friend was a dauber, all hospitals, the same infinite filth. Morelli, yes, the writer.

"It's impossible," Étienne said.

Why not, stone-in-the-water-editions: plop, nothing more is known about him. Morelli took the trouble to tell them that some four hundred copies had been sold (and given away). And then this fact, two in New Zealand, a tender statistic.

Oliveira took out a cigarette with a trembling hand, and he looked at the nurse who gave him an affirmative signal and went away, leaving them hedged in between the two yellowish screens. They sat down on the foot of the bed after pushing aside some notebooks and piles of paper.

"If we had only seen it in the newspapers . . . " Étienne said.

"It came out in the *Figaro*," Morelli said. "Underneath an item about the abominable snowman."

"You know about it," Oliveira managed to murmur. "But all in all I guess it's better that way. Every fat-arsed woman would have shown up with her autograph book and a jar of homemade jam."

"Rhubarb jam," Morelli said. "That's the nicest kind. But it's better if they don't come."

"As for us," Oliveira put in, really worried, "if we're bothering you, all you have to do is say so. There'll be other times, and all that. You know what I mean?"

"You came without knowing who I was. Personally, I think you should stay a while. This ward is peaceful, and the person who was shouting the most stopped last night at two o'clock. The screens are perfect, the courtesy of a doctor who had seen me writing. On the one hand he prohibited me from continuing, but then the nurses put up the screens and nobody bothers me.

"When will you be able to go home?"

"Never," Morelli said. "My bones are going to end up here, my dear boys."

"Nonsense," Étienne said respectfully.

"Just a question of time. But I feel all right, my problems with the concierge are ended. Nobody brings me my mail, not even the letters from New Zealand, with their pretty stamps. When a stillborn book is published, the only result is a small but faithful correspondence. The lady in New Zealand, the young man in Sheffield. A sensitive freemasonry, the voluptuous feeling of being one of so few partaking of an adventure. But right now, really . . . "

"I never thought about writing to you," Oliveira said. "Some friends of mine and I are familiar with your work, we think it's so . . . But God protect me from words like that, I think I make myself understood just the same. The fact is that we've spent whole nights discussing and still we never realized that you were here in Paris."

"Up till a year ago I was living in Vierzon. I came to Paris because I wanted to do a little exploration in some libraries. Vierzon, to be sure . . . My publisher had orders not to give out my address. Who knows how those few admirers found out. My back hurts me a lot, boys."

"You'd rather we left," Étienne said. "We'll come back tomorrow in any case."

"It would hurt just as much even if you weren't here," Morelli said. "Let's have a smoke, and take advantage of the fact that they ordered me not to."

It was a question of finding a non-literary way of speaking.

When the nurse went by, Morelli drew the butt into his mouth with a diabolical deftness and glanced at Oliveira with the air of a child who was disguised as an old man that was a real delight.

* * *

. . . starting off a little from Ezra Pound's central ideas, but without his pedantry and the confusion of peripheral symbols and primordial meanings.

Thirty-eight point two. Thirty-seven point five. Thirty-eight point three. X-ray (an incomprehensible symbol).

. . . knowing that a few people can approach those attempts without thinking that they're some new literary game. *Benissimo.* Worst of all, there is so much missing and he would die without having finished the game.

"The twenty-fifth move, black resigns," Morelli said, throwing his head back. Suddenly he seemed much older. "It's too bad, the game is just getting interesting. Is it true that there is an Indian chess game with sixty pieces on each side?"

"It's possible," Oliveira said. "The infinite game."

"The one who conquers the centre wins. From that point he dominates all possibilities, and it's senseless for his adversary to insist on continuing the play. But the centre might be in some side square, or even off the board."

"Or in a vest pocket."

"Figures," Morelli said. "It's so difficult to escape from them, beautiful as they are. Mental women, really. I would have liked to have understood Mallarmé better, his sense of absence and silence was much more than just an extreme recourse, a metaphysical impasse. One day in Jeréz de la Frontera I heard a cannon-shot twenty-five yards away and I discovered another meaning of silence. And dogs that can hear a whistle inaudible to us . . . You're a painter, I believe."

His hands worked down along his sides, picking up his notebooks one by one, smoothing out some wrinkled pages. From time to time, still talking, Morelli would glance at one of the pages and slip it into the notebooks held together by paper clips. Once or twice he would take a pencil out of his pyjama pocket and number a page.

"You write, I suppose."

"No," Oliveira said. "What could I write about? In order to do that you have to have some certainty that you've lived."

"Existence precedes essence," Morelli said with a smile.

"If you want to put it that way. My case isn't exactly like that."

"You're getting tired," Étienne said. "Let's go, Horacio, you're all set to keep on talking . . . I know him, sir, he's terrible."

Morelli kept on smiling and putting pages together, as he looked at them he seemed to be identifying and comparing them. He slid down a bit, looking for a better place to rest his head. Oliveira got up.

"It's the key to my apartment," Morelli said. "I would really be very happy."

"It really will be quite a job," Oliveira said.

"No, it's not as difficult as it seems. The notebooks will help you, there's a system of colours, numbers and letters. You'll work it out at once. For example, this goes in the blue notebook, a place I call the sea, but that's marginal, a game so I can understand myself better. Number 52: all you have to do is put it in its place between 51 and 53. Arabic numerals, the easiest thing in the world."

"But you can do it for yourself in a few days," Étienne said.

"I haven't been sleeping well. I'm outside of the notebook too. Do it for me, since you came to see me. Put all of this in its place and I'll feel much better here. This is really a fine hospital."

Étienne looked at Oliveira, and Oliveira, et cetera. The imaginable surprise. A real honour, so undeserved.

"Then make a package of it all and send it on to Paku. Publisher of avant-garde books, Rue de l'Arbre Sec. Did you know that Paku is the Akkadian name for Hermes? I always thought . . . But we'll talk about that another day."

"But what if we should make a mistake," Oliveira said, "and get things all mixed up. There was a terrible complication in the first volume, this guy here and I argued hours on end as to whether there hadn't been some mistake in the printing of the texts."

"Who cares," Morelli said. "You can read my book any way you want to. *Liber Fulguralis*, mantic pages, and that's how it goes. The most I do is set it up the way I would like to reread it. And in the worst of cases, if they do make a mistake, it might just turn out perfect. A trick on the part of Hermes Paku, the winged fabricator of subterfuges and lures. Do you like those words?"

"No," Oliveira said. "Neither subterfuge nor lure. They both seem rather decayed to me."

"You've got to be careful," Morelli said, closing his eyes. "We're all chasing after purity, breaking old daubed blisters. One day José Bergamin almost fell down dead when I took the liberty of deflating two pages of his, proving that . . . But watch out, my friends, what we call purity is probably . . . "

"Malevich's perfect square," Étienne said.

"*Ecco.* We were saying that we have to think about Hermes, let him have his fun. Take all of this, put it in order, since you've come to see me. Maybe I'll be able to drop over and take a look."

"We'll come back tomorrow if you want us to."

"Fine, I'll have some more things written by then. I'm going to drive you crazy. Bring me some Gauloises."

Étienne gave him his packet. With the key in his hand Oliveira didn't know what to say. Everything was wrong, none of it should have taken place that day, it was a lousy move in a sixty-piece chess game, a useless joy in the midst of the worst sadness, having to drive it off the way one does a fly, prefer sadness when the only thing that had come into his hands was that key to happiness, a step towards something he needed and admired, a key to open Morelli's door, Morelli's world, and in the midst of happiness to feel himself sad and dirty, with his tired skin and bleary eyes, smelling like a sleepless night, like a guilty absence, like a lack of the distance necessary to understand whether he had done well all of what he had been doing and not doing during those days, listening to La Maga's gasps, the knocking on the ceiling, bearing up under the icy rain in his face, dawn on the Pont Marie, the sour belches that came from wine mixed up with *caña* and with vodka and with more wine, the sensation of carrying in his pocket a hand that was not his, a hand of Rocamadour, a piece of drooling night; wetting his thighs, joy so late or maybe too soon (a consolation: probably too soon, still undeserved, but then, perhaps, *vielleicht, tal vez, forse, peut-être*, oh, shit, shit, see you tomorrow maestro, shit shit infinite shit, yes, at visiting time, the interminable obstinacy of shit around the face and around the world, a world of shit, we'll bring him some fruit, archeshit of countershit, supershit of infrashit, shit among shits, *dans cet hôpital Laennec découvrit l'auscultation*: maybe still . . . A key, an ineffable figure. A key. Still, maybe, he could go out into the street and keep on walking, with a key in his pocket. Maybe still, a Morelli key, a turn of the key and entering into something else, maybe still.

* * *

"When you come right down to it, it was a posthumous meeting, a question of days," Étienne said in the café.

"Get going," Oliveira said. "I'm sorry if I'm letting you down, but you'd better get going on it. Tell Ronald and Perico, we'll meet at the old man's place at ten o'clock."

"The time's no good," Étienne said. "The concierge won't let us in."

Oliveira took out the key, spun it around in a sunbeam, handed it over as if he were surrendering a city.

(–85)

155

It's incredible how all sorts of things can come out of a pair of trousers, fuzz, watches, clippings, crumbly aspirins, you stick your hand in to pull out your handkerchief and you pull a dead rat out by the tail, things like that are perfectly possible. While he was on his way to pick up Étienne, still affected by the dream about bread and that other memory of a dream that had suddenly appeared like an accident in the streets, suddenly boom, nothing he could do about it, Oliveira had stuck his hand in the pocket of his brown trousers, right on the corner of Raspail and Montparnasse, all the time half-looking at the gigantic twisted toad in his dressing-gown, Balzac Rodin or Rodin Balzac, and the inextricable mixture of two lightning flashes in his wrathful helicoid, and his hand had pulled out a clipping with a schedule of all-night chemists in Buenos Aires and another one that turned out to be a list of advertisements for soothsayers and fortunetellers. It was amusing to discover that Madame Colomier, a Hungarian soothsayer (who most likely was one of Gregorovius's mothers) lived on the Rue des Abbesses and possessed *secrets des bohèmes pour retour d'affections perdues.* From there one could go on to the great promise: *Désenvoûtements,* after which the reference to a *voyance sur photo* seemed slightly laughable. It would have been of interest to Étienne, an amateur Orientalist, to find out that Professor Mihn *vs offre le vérit. Talisman de l'Arbre Sacré de l'Inde. Broch. c. 1 NF timb. B.P. 27, Cannes.* How could anyone fail to be surprised at the existence of Mme Sanson, *Medium-Tarots, prédict. étonnantes, 23 Rue Hermel* (especially since Hermel, who was probably a zoologist, had an alchemist's name), and discover with South American pride the rotund proclamation of Anita, *cartes, dates précises,* of Joana-Jopez (*sic*), *secrets indiens, tarots espagnols,* and Mme Juanita, *voyante par domino, coquillage, fleur.* He would certainly have to take La Maga to visit Mme Juanita. *Coquillage, fleur!* But not La Maga, not any more. La Maga would have liked to have discovered her fate by means of flowers. *Seule* MARZAK *prouve retour affection.* But why the need to prove anything? That you can tell right off. The scientific tone of Jane de Nys was better, *reprend ses* VISIONS *exactes sur photogr. cheveux, écrit. Tour magnétiste intégral.* When he came alongside the Montparnasse cemetery, after crumpling it into a ball, Oliveira took careful aim and sent the soothsayers off to join up with Baudelaire on the other side of the wall, with Devéria, with Aloysius Bertrand, with people worthy of having their hands examined by fortunetellers, the likes of Mme Frédérika, *la voyante de l'élite parisienne et internationale, célèbre par ses prédictions dans la presse et la radio mondiales, de retour de Cannes.* Yeah, and with Barbey d'Aurevilly, who would have had them all burned at the stake if he could have, and also of course, Maupassant too, I hope the piece of paper landed on Maupassant's grave or Aloysius Bertrand's, but those were things that one had no way of knowing from outside.

It seemed stupid to Étienne that Oliveira had come to bother him at that hour of the morning, even though he was waiting there with three paintings he wanted to show him, but Oliveira said right away that the best thing would be to take advantage of the fabulous sun hanging over the Boulevard Montparnasse, and go over to the Necker Hospital and visit the old man. Étienne gave a curse under his breath and closed up his studio. The concierge, who liked them very much, told them that their faces looked like two recently disinterred corpses, men from outer space, and from that last bit they discovered that Madame Bobet was a reader of science fiction and they thought that was great. When they got to the Chien Qui Fume they had two glasses of white wine, arguing about dreams and painting as possible answers to NATO and other nuisances of the moment. It didn't seem excessively strange to Étienne that Oliveira wanted to go and visit a guy he didn't know, they agreed it would be easier, et cetera. At the bar a woman was giving a vehement description of a sunset in Nantes, where according to what she said her daughter lived. Étienne and Oliveira listened attentively to words like sun, breeze, lawn, moon, blackbirds, peace, the lame girl, God, six thousand five hundred francs, fog, rhododendrons, old age, your aunt, celestial, I hope they don't forget, flowerpots.

Then they admired the impressive plaque: DANS CET HÔPITAL, LAENNEC DECOUVRIT L'AUSCULTATION, and both of them thought (and said so) that auscultation must have been some kind of snake or salamander hiding away in the Necker Hospital, and chased, God knows why, through strange corridors and cellars it finally surrendered panting to the young savant. Oliveira made inquiries and they sent him to the Chauffard ward, third floor on the right.

"Probably no one has come to see him," Oliveira said. "And what a coincidence that his name should be Morelli."

"He's most likely dead already," Étienne said, looking at the fountain with goldfish in the open courtyard.

"They would have told me. The guy just looked at me, that's all. I didn't want to ask him if he'd had any visitors before."

"We could have visited him just the same without going by the main desk."

Et cetera. There are moments when because of displeasure, or fear, or because one has to climb two flights of stairs and smell phenol, conversation becomes abundant, the way it does when one has to console a person whose child has died and you invent the stupidest kind of talk sitting next to the mother and buttoning up her half-open bathrobe saying: "There, now, you mustn't catch cold." The mother sighs: "Thank you." You say: "You wouldn't think so, but at this time of year it gets cool very early." The mother says: "Yes, that's true." You say: "Wouldn't you like a wrap?" No. The outer-shelter chapter over. You attack the inner-shelter chapter: "I'll make you a cup of tea." But no, she doesn't feel like one. "But you ought to have something. You can't just sit there so long without something in your stomach." She doesn't know what time it is. "A little after eight. You haven't had anything since four-thirty. And this morning you barely touched your food. You have to eat something, even if it's just some toast and jam." She doesn't feel like it. "Take some, just to please me, just try some." A sigh, neither yes or no. "Look, of course you want something. I'm going to make some tea right now." If that doesn't work there's always the business with the chairs. "These chairs are so uncomfortable, you'll get cramp." No, it's fine. "No, your back must be all stiff, you've been sitting in that hard chair all afternoon. Why don't you lie down for a while." Oh no, I couldn't do that. In some mysterious way the bed is like a betrayal. "Come on, maybe you ought to take a quick nap." A double betrayal. "You need one, it'll be a good rest for you. I'll stay with you." No, she's fine just the way she is. "All right, but I'll get you a pillow for your back." All right. "Your legs are going to get stiff, I'll bring you a footstool so you can raise them up a bit." Thank you. "And after a while you'll go and lie down. Promise me." A sigh. "All right, all right, I'm not trying to pamper you. If the doctor had said so you'd have to obey him." In short. "You have to get some sleep, love." Variations *ad libitum*.

"Perchance to dream," Étienne murmured, thinking about the variations with every step.

"We should have bought a bottle of cognac," Oliveira said. "You've got some cash."

"But we don't even know him. And he's probably dead, really. Look at that redhead, I'd like her to give me a massage. Sometimes I get fantasies about nursing and nurses. Don't you ever?"

"When I was fifteen. Something awful. Eros armed with an intramuscular hypodermic that was like an arrow, wonderful girls who would wash me from top to bottom, I used to expire in their arms."

"In short, a masturbator."

"So what? Why be ashamed of masturbating? A lesser art next to the other one, but in any case it does have its divine proportions, its unities in time, action and place, and any other rhetoric you might want to apply. When I was nine I used to masturbate under an *ombú* tree, it was really patriotic."

"An *ombú* tree?"

"It's a kind of baobab," Oliveira said, "but I'll let you in on a secret if you swear never to tell any other Frenchman. An *ombú* isn't really a tree: it's a weed."

"Well, so it wasn't so serious after all."

"How do French boys masturbate then?"

"I don't remember."

"You remember only too well. We had our own wild systems down there. Hammer-style, umbrella-style . . . You get it? I can't listen to certain tangos without remembering how my aunt used to play them."

"I don't get the relationship," Étienne said.

"That's because you can't see the piano. There was a space between the piano and the wall and I used to hide in there to jerk off. My aunt would be playing *Milonguita* or *Flores negras*, something sad like that, it used to help me with my dreams of death and sacrifice. The first time I came on the parquet it was horrible, I thought the stain wouldn't come out. I didn't even have a handkerchief. I whipped off one of my socks and rubbed like crazy. My aunt was playing *La payanca*, I'll whistle it for you if you want me to, it's quite sad . . . "

"Whistling is not allowed in the hospital. But one feels the sadness just the same. You're all screwed up, Horacio."

"I'm on the lookout for them, pal. The king is dead, long live the king. If you think that because of a woman . . . *Ombú*, woman, they're all weeds when you come right down to it."

"Cheap," Étienne said. "Much too cheap. B-movies, dialogue you can buy by the foot, you know what I mean. Third floor, stop. Madame . . . "

"Par là," the nurse said.

"We still haven't run into the auscultation," Oliveira informed her.

"Knock it off," the nurse said.

"Take a lesson," Étienne said. "A lot of dreaming about a complaining loaf of bread, a lot of screwing everybody up, and then your jokes don't even come off. Why don't you go to the country for a while? You've really got an expression that Soutine could use, old man."

"Basically," Oliveira said, "what bugs you is that I've pulled you away from your chromatic jerking off, your filthy daily daubs, and solidarity makes you drift along with me through Paris the day after the funeral. My sad old pal, he's got to have some fun. Friend calls, you have to adjust. Friend mentions hospital, OK, let's go."

"To tell the truth," Étienne said, "I worry less and less about you. I should have been out walking with poor Lucía. She's the one who needs it."

"Wrong," Oliveira said, sitting down on a bench. "La Maga has Ossip, she has distractions, Hugo Wolf, things like that. Basically La Maga has a personal life, even though it's taken me a long time to realize it. On the other hand I'm empty, an enormous freedom in which to dream and wander around, the toys have all been broken, no problem. Give me a light."

"You can't smoke in a hospital."

"We are the makers of manners, eh. It's good for auscultation."

"The Chauffard ward is over there," Étienne said. "We can't sit on this bench all day."

"Wait till I finish my cigarette."

(–123)

ALSO AVAILABLE IN HARVILL PANTHERS

Giuseppe Tomasi di Lampedusa

THE LEOPARD

Translated from the Italian by Archibald Colquhoun

"The poetry of Lampedusa's novel flows into the Sicilian countryside . . . a work of great artistry"

PETER ACKROYD

"Every once in a while, like certain golden moments of happiness, infinitely memorable, one stumbles on a book or writer, and the impact is like an indelible mark. Lampedusa's *The Leopard*, his only novel, and a masterpiece, is such a work" **BRUCE ARNOLD**, ***Independent***

Boris Pasternak

DOCTOR ZHIVAGO

Translated from the Russian
by Manya Harari and Max Hayward

"The first work of genius to come out of Russia since the Revolution" **V. S. PRITCHETT**

"A book that made a most profound impression upon me and the memory of which still does . . . not since Shakespeare has love been so fully, vividly, scrupulously and directly communicated . . . The novel is a total experience, not parts or aspects: of what other twentieth-century work of the imagination could this be said?"

ISAIAH BERLIN, *Sunday Times*

Peter Heøg

MISS SMILLA'S FEELING FOR SNOW

Translated from the Danish by F. David

"A subtle novel, yet direct, clever, wistful, unforgettable"
RUTH RENDELL

"Smilla Jaspersen is a wonderfully unique creation of snow and warmth and irony. She shimmers with intelligence"
MARTIN CRUZ SMITH

Peter Heøg

BORDERLINERS

Translated from the Danish by Barbara Haveland

"It exerts the same chill grip on the imagination as its predecessor *Miss Smilla's Feeling for Snow*, posing questions and withholding answers with the same disconcerting skill . . . The power of the novel lies in the awesome truthfulness of the child's voice" SALLY LAIRD, *Observer*

"The sustained intensity and brilliance with which the lives of these 'dark and dubious children' are captured is overpowering" JOHN MELMOTH, *Sunday Times*

Georges Perec

LIFE, A USER'S MANUAL

Translated from the French by David Bellos

"A dazzling, crazy-quilt monument to the imagination"
PAUL AUSTER, *New York Times*

"One of the great novels of the century"
GABRIEL JOSIPOVICI, *Times Literary Supplement*

Theodore Zeldin

THE FRENCH

"He opens up before us a marvellously varied landscape, not of fields and cathedrals, but of anger and passion, of love and ridicule, a subtle mosaic, patiently constructed out of the daily experiences of French people . . . Like a talented film director, he makes the masks fall" ***Quotidien de Paris***

"Highly intelligent, observant, perceptive, humorous and sympathetic" ***Spectator***

Jan Wiese

THE NAKED MADONNA

Translated from the Norwegian by Tom Geddes

"Certainly one of the finest pieces of fiction to have emerged from Norway in the last decade. Beautifully translated . . . it carves a curious niche somewhere between Umberto Eco and Hans Christian Andersen, crossing complex historical mystery with moral fable" PAUL SUSSMAN, *Spectator*

Eduardo Mendoza

THE YEAR OF THE FLOOD

Translated from the Spanish by Nick Caistor

"A magnificent short novel . . . a rural elegy and political fable and an adventure story all in one"

MICHAEL EAUDE, *Times Literary Supplement*

"All the characters and relationships are sharply and subtly drawn" JOHN SPURLING, *Sunday Times*

To join the mailing list and for a full list of titles please write to

THE HARVILL PRESS
2 AZTEC ROW • BERNERS ROAD
LONDON N1 0PW • UK

enclosing a stamped-addressed envelope

www.harvill-press.com